"After decades of rhetorical criticism of the Gospel of John, here is a serious study of the origins of the Johannine writings, including the three Letters. The author, a recognized Johannine scholar, presents a hypothesis of three literary layers in the Gospel of John which he attributes to three successive authors. Von Wahlde's contribution differs from earlier literary analyses of the Johannine writings by refining the criteria for the distinction of layers. His work can be recommended to all readers interested in the history of Johannine Christianity."

— JOHANNES BEUTLER, SJ
Hochschule St. Georgen,
Frankfurt am Main, Germany

"No one has analysed the composition history of the Gospel and Letters of John with such consistency and thoroughness as von Wahlde. The clarity of his exposition, as he lays bare the criteria that must be used to identify the traditions, his respectful use of other scholarship, and his lucid commentary on each of the strata make this work a milestone in Johannine scholarship."

— FRANCIS J. MOLONEY, SDB
Australian Catholic University

The Eerdmans Critical Commentary

†David Noel Freedman, *General Editor*
Astrid B. Beck, *Associate Editor*

THE EERDMANS CRITICAL COMMENTARY offers the best of contemporary Old and New Testament scholarship, seeking to give modern readers clear insight into the biblical text, including its background, its interpretation, and its application.

Contributors to the ECC series are among the foremost authorities in biblical scholarship worldwide. Representing a broad range of confessional backgrounds, authors are charged to remain sensitive to the original meaning of the text and to bring alive its relevance for today. Each volume includes the author's own translation, critical notes, and commentary on literary, historical, cultural, and theological aspects of the text.

Accessible to serious general readers and scholars alike, these commentaries reflect the contributions of recent textual, philological, literary, historical, and archaeological inquiry, benefiting as well from newer methodological approaches. ECC volumes are "critical" in terms of their detailed, systematic explanation of the biblical text. Although exposition is based on the original and cognate languages, English translations provide complete access to the discussion and interpretation of these primary sources.

THE GOSPEL AND LETTERS OF JOHN

VOLUME 1

Introduction, Analysis, and Reference

Urban C. von Wahlde

WILLIAM B. EERDMANS PUBLISHING COMPANY
GRAND RAPIDS, MICHIGAN / CAMBRIDGE, U.K.

© 2010 Urban C. von Wahlde
All rights reserved

Published 2010 by
Wm. B. Eerdmans Publishing Co.
2140 Oak Industrial Drive N.E., Grand Rapids, Michigan 49505 /
P.O. Box 163, Cambridge CB3 9PU U.K.

Library of Congress Cataloging-in-Publication Data

Von Wahlde, Urban C.
The Gospel and Letters of John / Urban C. von Wahlde.
   p.   cm.   — (The Eerdmans critical commentary)
Includes bibliographical references and index.
ISBN 978-0-8028-0991-9 (Introduction) (pbk: alk. paper)
ISBN 978-0-8028-2217-8 (Gospel) (pbk: alk. paper)
ISBN 978-0-8028-2218-5 (Epistles) (pbk: alk. paper)
1. Bible. N.T. John — Commentaries.
2. Bible. N.T. Epistles of John — Commentaries.
I. Title.

BS2601.V66   2010
226.5′07 — dc22

2008044624

www.eerdmans.com

*For Carol,
Michael, and Lisa*

Contents

Preface	xl
Abbreviations	xlii
INTRODUCTION	**1**
A. General Introduction	1
1. The Complexity of the Johannine Tradition and the Task of the Commentator	1
2. The Value of Such Work for the Interpretation of the Gospel	2
3. General Issues regarding the Gospel of John: Its Historicity, Background, Relation to the Synoptics, and the Like	5
4. The Authorship of the Johannine Literature	6
B. The Greek Text of the Gospel and Letters	7
1. Light on Textual Criticism as a Result of the View Presented in This Commentary	8
2. General Notes on the Translation of the Gospel and the Letters	9
C. The Features That Suggest That the Present Gospel Has Undergone Editing: The Aporias	10
D. Past Attempts to Deal with the Aporias	12

Contents

E.	The Criteria Used in Earlier Analyses	16
	1. The Aporias Themselves	17
	2. Changes in Terminology	17
	3. Doublets	18
	4. *Wiederaufnahme*	18
	5. Style	19
	6. Synoptic Comparison	21
	7. Differences in Theology	22
F.	The Approach Employed in This Analysis	22
	1. Overview	22
	2. Determining Literary Seams	23
	a. Aporias	23
	b. *Wiederaufnahme*	24
	c. Other Resumptive Devices	25
	3. Determining the Identity of the Material of the First Two Editions	25
	a. The Starting Point: Two Editions of the Gospel Identified First by the Presence of Two Sets of Terms for Religious Authorities	27
	b. Other Features Occurring Consistently within These Two Bodies of Material	28
	c. Consistency and Contrast in Usage	29
	d. Extending the Process to Other Material of the First and Second Editions	30
	4. Determining the Identity of the Material of the Third Edition	30
	a. Continuity and Discontinuity of Features in the Third Edition	31
	b. Mixing of Terms from Various Strata	33
G.	Some Questions and Concerns about Such an Analysis	34
	1. What Sort of "Coherence" Is to Be Expected in First-Century Texts?	34
	2. Imitation of the Style of a Previous Author?	36
	3. Variations in Style by the Same Author?	36

Contents

4. The Order of the Editions	37
5. An Oral Prehistory to the Material of the First Edition?	38
6. Some Interpretive Principles Implied in Reading Such a Text	39
7. A Parallel Instance	41
8. Circularity of Argument?	42
9. Ambiguity of Features	42

H. The Organization of This Volume and the Process of Acquainting Oneself with the Three Editions and with the Role of 1 John ... 43

1. The Translation, the Typeface, and the Summaries ... 44
2. A Synthetic and a Contextual Approach and Some Suggestions for Beginning ... 45
   a. Synthetic Analysis ... 45
   b. Contextual Analysis ... 46
   c. How to Begin? ... 46
3. 1 John and the Third Edition ... 47
4. A Note on the Relation between the Third Edition and 1 John ... 49
5. Some Final Comments on the Analysis of the Composition in Volume 2 ... 49

I. An Overview of the History of the Johannine Community together with an Overview of the Documents It Produced ... 50

1. The First Edition of the Gospel (A.D. 55-65?) ... 50
2. Johannine Theology Develops; Conflict with the Synagogue Becomes Critical; and the Second Edition Is Written (A.D. 60-65?) ... 51
3. An Internal Crisis and the Writing of the Johannine Letters (A.D. 65-70?) ... 52
4. The Death of the Elder (A.D. 80-90?) ... 53
5. The Third Edition of the Gospel (A.D. 90-95?) ... 53

Contents

PART 1: THE FIRST EDITION OF THE GOSPEL — 57

Introduction — 57

Section 1. An Overview of the First Edition — 58

Section 2. The Criteria Used for the Identification of the Material of the First Edition — 63

1. Characteristic Terminology — 63

    1E-1. In the first edition, the religious authorities are referred to as "Pharisees" (Pharisaioi), "chief priests" (archiereis), and "rulers" (archontes). This contrasts with the usage of the second edition where the expression "the Jews" (Ioudaioi) is used in the more generalized (and uniquely Johannine) sense to refer to religious authorities (2E-1). — 63

    1E-2. In the first edition, Jesus' miracles are referred to as "signs" (sēmeia). In the second edition, they are referred to as "works" (erga) (2E-2). In the third edition, the term is "signs and wonders" (sēmeia kai terata) (3E-56F). — 68

    1E-3. In the first edition, the term Ioudaioi refers to "Judeans," that is, to the inhabitants of Judea. This usage is limited to, and is distinctive of, the first edition. In the second edition, Ioudaioi is used in a distinctive way as a blanket term to refer to religious authorities (2E-1). — 70

    1E-4. In the first edition, there is a consistent pattern of translation of religious and geographical terms. This is not found in the later editions. — 74

2. Characteristics of Narrative Orientation — 76

    1E-5. In the first edition, there is a consistent use of stereotyped formulas of belief. There is nothing comparable to this in the other editions. — 76

    1E-6. In the first edition, there is a pattern of portraying belief as occurring in "tandem" or "chain reaction" sequence. This pattern is not found in either of the later editions. — 79

    1E-7. In the first edition, attention is repeatedly called to the quantity and quality of Jesus' signs. This is not found in the later editions. — 80

Contents

1E-8. In the first edition, there is an emphasis on the variety of groups that come to belief in Jesus. There is nothing comparable to this in either the second or third editions. — 82

1E-9. In the first edition, there are repeated reports of division of opinion among the religious authorities regarding Jesus. In the second edition, there is no division among the authorities and the authorities' hostility is presented as unified, formalized, and solidified (2E-9). — 83

1E-10. In the first edition, the hostility of the Pharisees increases throughout the ministry, coming to a climax in the decision to arrest Jesus. In the second edition, the level of hostility of the authorities is present in an essentially steady state from the beginning and does not significantly change thereafter except to manifest itself repeatedly in attempts to kill Jesus (2E-5). — 84

1E-11. In the first edition, there are repeated reports of the reaction of the Pharisees following on reports of belief among the common people. This is not found in the later editions. — 85

1E-12. In the first edition, the religious authorities' ("Pharisees," "chief priests," and "rulers") reaction to Jesus and to the belief of the crowds is almost exclusively on the basis of his signs. In the second edition, the authorities virtually ignore the miracles and focus on the claims of Jesus regarding his relation with the Father (2E-7). — 86

1E-13. In the first edition, the common people show no fear for the authorities and at times debate with them and react to them with disdain. In the second edition, the people (and disciples) are consistently said to react to the authorities ("the Jews") with abject fear, expressed particularly in the phrase "for fear of the Jews" (2E-6). — 87

1E-14. In the first edition, it is the religious authorities ("Pharisees," "chief priests," and "rulers") who regularly react with fear and apprehension to the belief of the common people. In the second edition, the reverse is true: there is no hint of such attitudes in the monolithic posture of "the Jews," and the people fear the authorities (2E-6, 2E-8). — 88

1E-15. In the first edition, the supernatural knowledge of Jesus affects individuals within the narrative and is seen as a miracle, leading to belief. In the second edition, supernatural knowledge is reported only in the asides of the narrator and functions, for

Contents

      the reader, not as a miracle but as a demonstration of Jesus' superiority to, and independence of, human affairs (2E-10).   89

  1E-16. *In the first edition, there are numerous explanations of terms and customs as being "of the Jews." Such explanations are not found in the later editions, which, while they show little interest in details of history, geography, or terminology, exhibit and presume detailed knowledge of the Jewish Scriptures, customs, and methods of argument.*   91

  1E-17. *In the first edition, the religious authorities as a group (identified as "Pharisees," "chief priests," or "rulers") never dialogue with Jesus. This is also true of the Ioudaioi (in the sense of "Judeans"), who do not engage in conversation with Jesus. In the second edition, the religious authorities, now identified by the term "the Jews," are presented as almost always in dialogue with Jesus (2E-11).*   92

3. Theological Characteristics   93

  1E-18. *In the first edition, belief is based almost exclusively on the miracles of Jesus; in the second edition, belief is based on a variety of "witnesses" to Jesus (2E-14).*   94

  1E-19. *In the first edition, there is a marked focus on details that demonstrate the greatness of the miracles. This does not appear in the later editions.*   96

  1E-20. *In the first edition, belief is presented as an easy affair, something that occurs readily. In the second edition, belief is something that only the disciples attain, and then fully only after the Resurrection.*   97

  1E-21. *Both the Christology of the first edition and the accusations leveled at Jesus occur within the realm of traditional expectations. That is, the Christology is a traditional one, making no divine claims. The accusations also do not contain a refutation of any claims that could be said to be divine. However, the later editions are marked by a radically higher Christology that constantly affirms the divinity of Jesus. This is particularly evident in the material of the second edition (2E-15; 2E-26, 27, 28, 29, 30).*   98

  1E-22. *In the first edition, the authorities condemn Jesus to death because of his miracles and because of fear of the Roman authorities. In the second edition, he is condemned because of blasphemy (2E-25).*   101

Contents

4. Features of the First Edition ... 102

   1E-23F. The first edition contains the primary narrative of the Gospel. The chronology, narrative sequence, and geographical distribution of the ministry stem from the first edition. ... 102

   1E-24F. In the first edition, there is a special focus on Mosaic motifs. In the second edition, references to Moses are part of a larger plan in which Jesus is shown to be greater than all the major figures of Israel (greater than Jacob, 4:12; greater than Moses, 6:30-32; greater than Abraham, 8:53). ... 102

   1E-25F. The first edition contains twenty topographical references that either are not mentioned in the Synoptics or that contain details not mentioned in the Synoptics. ... 102

   1E-26F. In addition to these topographical references, there is other information in the first edition that reveals specific and precise knowledge of Judaism in the first century. ... 103

   1E-27F. In the first edition, there are numerous elements that have no function in the present form of the Gospel. These were referred to as "small, undigested scraps" by Dodd. All, or almost all, of these appear in the first edition. ... 103

   1E-28F. In the first edition, questions are posed that are not answered and statements are made that are responded to in ways that do not fully address the original statement. Rather, the narrative sequence is broken and the answer given is of an entirely different type and from a different author (see also 2E-33F). ... 103

5. Concluding Comments on the Characteristics of the First Edition ... 104

Section 3. Synthesis of the First Edition ... 104

1. The Structure of the First Edition ... 105
2. The Theology of the First Edition ... 108
   a. The Purpose of the First Edition ... 109
   b. The Chronology, Sequence, and Geography of the Ministry in the First Edition ... 109
   c. The Narrative Focus on the Magnitude of Jesus' Signs, the Belief of the People, and the Hostility of the Authorities ... 111
   d. Elements of a Mosaic Christology? ... 112
   e. Are the Signs of the First Edition "Symbolic"? ... 113

Contents

f. A Low Christology Throughout		114
3. The Genre of the First Edition		114
a. The Narrative Role of Geography in the First Edition		114
4. The Worldview of the First Edition		115
5. The Identity and Social Location of the Community at the Time of the First Edition		116
a. Jewish Christian		116
b. Sectarian Leanings?		117
c. An Independent Tradition		117
d. Translations and Explanations of Jewish Feasts and Customs		118
e. Relationships with Followers of John the Baptist		119
f. Conclusions		120
6. The Historicity of Material in the First Edition		120
a. Overarching Issues of the Ministry of Jesus		121
b. Jesus and John the Baptist		123
c. The Accuracy and Detail of Geographical and Topographical Information		124
d. Other Features Exhibiting Accurate and Detailed Knowledge of Jewish Affairs		126
e. The Historicity of Individual Miracles		128
f. Unhistorical Elements in the First Edition?		128
7. The Relation of Material in the First Edition to the Synoptics		130
8. The Author of the First Edition		131
9. The Date of Composition of the First Edition		133
10. The Place of Composition of the First Edition		134

PART 2: THE SECOND EDITION OF THE GOSPEL — 137

Introduction	137
Section 1. An Overview of the Second Edition	138
Section 2. The Criteria Used for the Identification of Material of the Second Edition	144
1. Characteristic Terminology	144

Contents

2E-1. *In the second edition of the Gospel, those who represent the authoritative religious position of the Jewish religion are referred to exclusively by the term* Ioudaioi. *This contrasts with the use of "Pharisees" (Pharisaioi), "chief priests" (archiereis), and "rulers" (archontes) for religious authorities in the first edition (1E-1). It also contrasts with the use of* Ioudaioi, *referring to "Judeans," in the first edition (1E-3).*   145

2E-2. *In the second edition, the term "works" (erga) is used to designate Jesus' miracles rather than "signs" (sēmeia), which was the term characteristic of the first edition (1E-2). In the third edition, the expression "signs and wonders" appears (3E-55F).*   150

2E-3. *In the second edition, "sign" (sēmeion) is used in a pejorative sense as a proof demanded by the religious authorities rather than in a positive sense as it was used in the first edition (1E-2).*   153

2E-4. *In the second edition,* ergon *("work") is used as an overall theological conception to describe the ministry given to Jesus by the Father. This contrasts with the use of* entolē *("commandment") to describe the ministry in the third edition (3E-6).*   155

2. Characteristics of Narrative Orientation   156

2E-5. *In the second edition, the religious authorities exhibit an intense level of hostility toward Jesus throughout his ministry, rather than the increasing hostility found in the first edition (1E-10).*   156

2E-6. *In the second edition, the common people fear the religious authorities and never dare to debate with them, in contrast to the first edition where the common people (and temple police) regularly assert themselves over against the authorities and even enter into debate with them (1E-13).*   158

2E-7. *In the second edition, almost no concern is expressed regarding the quantity or magnitude of Jesus' miracles, in contrast to the first edition where this was a preoccupation of the authorities (1E-12). Moreover, when the miracles are discussed in the second edition, they are discussed in a different way, as we shall see below.*   159

2E-8. *In the second edition, "the Jews" do not react in fear or apprehension to the belief of the masses. In the first edition, the authorities regularly are concerned about and even fearful of the belief of the common people (1E-14).*   161

Contents

- **2E-9.** *In the second edition, the religious authorities show no division of opinion about Jesus but represent a solid and unified hostility, in contrast with the first edition where the religious authorities (and the common people) are regularly divided in their opinion about Jesus (1E-9).* — 162

- **2E-10.** *In the second edition, the supernatural knowledge of Jesus functions to demonstrate his superiority in relation to human events. In the first edition, such supernatural knowledge functions within the narrative to lead to belief (1E-15).* — 163

- **2E-11.** *"The Jews" in the second edition are almost always in dialogue, and almost always in dialogue with Jesus. The "Pharisees," "chief priests," and "rulers" of the first edition, as a group, never enter into dialogue with Jesus. In the third edition, the author at times takes over the term "the Jews," and they appear in dialogue in that edition (cf. 6:52) (1E-17).* — 164

- **2E-12.** *The second edition is framed in the worldview typical of the canonical Jewish Scriptures. This worldview is not dualistic but contains a number of contrasts that must be distinguished from dualism. However, the worldview of the third edition is clearly marked by the modified (ethical) dualism typical of apocalyptic (cf. 3E-8 to 3E-19).* — 165

3. Literary Characteristics — 169

- **2E-13.** *The author of the second edition introduces the device of "misunderstanding." This consists of a statement by Jesus that is understood on a "material" (or "physical") level, whereas it was intended to be understood on the "spiritual" level. Where this device is taken over by the author of the third edition, it is accompanied by features distinctive of the third edition.* — 169

4. Theological Characteristics — 172

- **2E-14.** *In the second edition, belief is conceived of as having a wider basis than just the miracles of Jesus (1E-18). In the third edition, the list of witnesses is extended to include that of the Paraclete and of the disciples. In addition, the focus will be on the proper content of belief and of proper "confession" of Jesus (3E-26).* — 173

- **2E-15.** *The second edition is marked by a consistent high Christology in contrast to the consistent low Christology of the first edition (1E-21). In the third edition, the Christology continues to affirm the divinity of Jesus but takes this a step further by* *identifying Jesus even more closely with attributes of God the Father (3E-26).* ... 174

2E-16. *In the second edition, the Spirit is conceived of in an unqualified sense, whereas in the third edition, the Spirit is conceptualized in terms of a dualism where there is a multiplicity of spirits (3E-12). As a result, in the third edition the Spirit is identified as "the Holy Spirit" or "the Spirit of Truth" and implicitly contrasted with the Spirit of Deception, a contrast that is explicit in 1 John.* ... 176

2E-17. *In the second edition, the believer is said to be born "of the Spirit" or "from above." In the third edition, the believer is said to be born "of God" (3E-39). (There is no discussion of such birth in the first edition.)* ... 176

2E-18. *In the second edition, there are repeated statements that deny the importance of the physical, "fleshly" aspects of existence and stress only the spiritual elements. In the third edition, there is a noticeable emphasis on the value of the material and physical as part of the spiritual reality (3E-41).* ... 177

2E-19. *In the second edition, the death of Jesus is seen as a "departure" to the Father. This contrasts with two elements of the third edition. First, in the third edition, the death of Jesus is seen as having an expiatory effect, a sacrificial, salvific death "for his own" and "for the world," a death that takes away sin (3E-33). Second, in the third edition, the "departure" of Jesus is conceived of as part of a larger schema of "descent and return," a schema that presumes the preexistence of Jesus (3E-34, 3E-53F). (There is no discussion of the theological purpose of the death of Jesus remaining in the first edition.)* ... 177

2E-20. *In the second edition, the removal of sin is associated with the power of the Holy Spirit; in the third edition, sin is removed through the sacrificial, atoning death of Jesus (3E-33). (There is no discussion of this in the remaining material of the first edition.)* ... 179

2E-21. *In the second edition, "judgment" (i.e., declaration of guilt) is an event that takes place in the present time and is not conducted by an external agent (i.e., God) but occurs in the event of unbelief itself. In the third edition, there is a conviction that there will be a universal "judgment" (i.e., a rendering of accountability) at the end of time (3E-17). (There is no discussion of judgment remaining in the first edition.)* ... 181

2E-22. *In the second and third editions of the Gospel, there are references to the "hour" of Jesus. Both of these designations serve to indicate that Jesus is not subject to human planning or human intentions. Rather, he responds to the time determined for him by the Father. However, the framework within which this "hour" is conceived and presented is different in the second and third editions (3E-24).*   182

2E-23. *In the second edition, the notion of immanence (or "indwelling") is introduced. Such immanence is predicated of the relationship between Jesus and the Father, thus establishing the intimacy of their relationship. However, in the third edition, the notion of immanence between the Father and Son is extended to include, and to be a model for, the relationship of both the Father and the Son with the believer and applied to the relationship between believers (3E-42).*   184

2E-24. *In the second edition, the notion of "joy" is described as "irremovable" and is the joy in the Resurrection that will follow on the sorrow associated with the Passion and Death. In the third edition, "joy" is described as "complete" and is the eschatological joy associated with the realization of the future hopes associated with the coming of Jesus (3E-36).*   186

2E-25. *In the second edition, the reasons for putting Jesus to death are based on the charge that "he makes himself Son of God" (19:7). In the first edition, when Caiaphas convened the Sanhedrin, the decision to put Jesus to death was based on the fear that if Jesus were allowed to continue as he was, the Romans would come and destroy the Temple and the nation (11:48) (1E-22).*   187

5. Some Aspects of Theology Introduced in the Second Edition but Taken Over by the Author of the Third Edition   187

2E-26X. *The second edition introduces the presentation of Jesus as referring to God as his "Father." This does not appear in the first edition. Where it is taken over by the author of the third edition (3E-46X), it is accompanied by other features that are unique to the third edition.*   189

2E-27X. *The second edition introduces the presentation of Jesus as referring to himself as "Son" in relation to God. This does not occur in the first edition, and where it is taken over by the author of the third edition (3E-47X), it appears together with features unique to that edition.*   189

2E-28X. In conjunction with the conception of Jesus as "Son" in relation to the "Father," the author of the second edition also introduced the conception of Jesus as "sent" by the Father. This does not appear in the first edition, and where it appears in the third edition, it appears with features distinctive of that edition (3E-48X). 190

2E-29X. The notion of "eternal life" is introduced by the author of the second edition and is a major motif. It is also taken over by the author of the third edition, although various aspects of its presentation are modified in connection with the issues in focus at the time of the community crisis (3E-49X). 191

2E-30X. The author of the second edition introduces theological terminology not found in the first edition. This terminology is central to his theological presentation but is also taken over by the author of the third edition (3E-50X). 192

6. Features of the Second Edition That Become Apparent Once the Analysis Is Complete   193

2E-31F. In the second edition, there are a number of features that are anachronistic to the ministry of Jesus but that accurately reflect the circumstances of the community at the end of the first century. This contrasts with the presentation in the first edition, where there is considerable accuracy and detail with regard to the specific elements of the historical ministry of Jesus (1E-25F, 26F, 27F). 193

2E-32F. In the second edition, quotations from Scripture are typically introduced by some variation of the formula "as it is written [in the Scripture]," while quotations in the third edition are typically introduced by some variation of the formula "in order that the Scripture may be fulfilled" (3E-51F). 195

2E-33F. The second edition manifests an awareness, and use, of sophisticated rabbinic argument that is not found in the first or third editions. 195

2E-34F. Questions that are posed in the first edition are regularly answered by material of the second edition (see 1E-28F). 196

Section 3. Synthesis of the Second Edition   197
1. The Structure of the Second Edition   197
2. The Theology of the Second Edition   203
   a. Christology   205

b. Belief	205
c. Pneumatology	206
d. Eternal Life	206
e. Eschatology	207
f. Knowledge of God	207
g. Soteriology	208
h. Ethics	209
i. Anthropology	209
j. Ecclesiology	210
k. The Religious Significance of Material Reality	210
3. The Genre of the Second Edition	211
a. The Arrangement of the Material and the Question of Narrative Sequence	211
b. The Narrative Role of Geography in the Second Edition	213
4. The Identity and Social Location of the Community at the Time of the Second Edition	214
a. "The Jews" and the Synagogue	214
b. Polemic against the Followers of John the Baptist?	216
5. The Background of the Second Edition	217
6. The Value of the Material Found in the Second Edition for the Study of the Historical Jesus	218
a. Historical Sequence	219
b. Time Frame	219
c. The Words of Jesus	219
d. Terminology	220
e. The Hostility of "the Jews"	220
f. Christology	221
g. John the Baptist	221
h. The Cleansing of the Temple	221
i. The Unnamed Feast	221
j. Summary	222
7. The Value of the Material Found in the Second Edition as a Reflection of Circumstances in the Later First Century	222

- a. Jewish Thought and Argument Reflected in the Second Edition — 223
- b. Historical Circumstances of the Contemporary Johannine Community — 223
8. The Relation of Material in the Second Edition to the Synoptics — 224
9. The Author of the Second Edition — 224
10. The Date of the Second Edition — 225
11. The Place of Composition of the Second Edition — 227

PART 3: THE THIRD EDITION OF THE GOSPEL — 229

Introduction: The Next Stage in the Development of the Tradition and a Choice of Ways for the Reader to Proceed — 229

Section 1. An Overview of the Third Edition — 231

Section 2. The Criteria Used for the Identification of the Third Edition — 236

1. Characteristic Terminology — 237

3E-1. In the third edition, kyrios ("Lord") is used in the religious sense to refer to Jesus as the (divine) Lord. This is not found in the earlier editions. — 237

3E-2. In the third edition, the title "Jesus Christ" appears and is applied to Jesus. This title does not appear in either of the earlier editions. — 241

3E-3. In the third edition, the term erga ("works") appears always in the plural and always in the phrase erga poiein or erga ergazesthai with the meaning "to do the will" (of someone). This usage contrasts with the use of erga in the second edition to refer to the miracles of Jesus and to his ministry (2E-2). — 242

3E-4. In the third edition, adelphos ("brother") is used in a religious sense to refer to fellow community members. This is not found in the earlier editions. — 244

3E-5. In the third edition, teknon/teknion ("child"/"little child") is used as a designation for members of the community in their relation with Jesus and/or God. This is not found in the earlier editions. — 245

Contents

- **3E-6.** *In the third edition,* entolē *("commandment") is used as a theological conceptualization of the ministry given to Jesus by the Father. This contrasts with the use of* ergon *("work"), which is used to describe the ministry in the second edition (2E-4).* — 246

- **3E-7.** *In the third edition, reference is made to a distinct group of disciples within the larger group. This group is known as "the Twelve." The other editions make no reference to this group.* — 249

2. Characteristics of Narrative Orientation: An Apocalyptic Worldview — 250

- **3E-8.** *In the third edition, the imagery of "light" and "darkness" is used to describe opposing realms of good and evil. This is not present in prior editions.* — 256

- **3E-9.** *In the third edition, the term "works" is used in the idiomatic expression "to do the works of . . ." as a way of describing allegiance of persons to either good or evil within a context of apocalyptic dualism. In the second edition, "works" designates the miracles performed by Jesus (2E-2).* — 260

- **3E-10.** *In the third edition, the phrase "son(s) of . . ." is used to describe allegiance to either good or evil and is characteristic of apocalyptic dualism. This is not present in the earlier editions.* — 263

- **3E-11.** *In the third edition, the expression "being of . . ." (the truth, the earth, the world, etc.) is used to identify the allegiance of individuals. This does not appear in the other editions.* — 265

- **3E-12.** *In the third edition, there is a duality of Spirits in which the Spirit is described as the Spirit of Truth (and implicitly opposed to the Spirit of Deception). This view contrasts with the presentation of the Spirit in the second edition, where the issue was the presence or the absence of the Spirit of God (2E-6).* — 268

- **3E-13.** *In the third edition, there are two dualistic titles typical of apocalyptic by which the devil is identified. The first is "Ruler of This World," and the second is "The Evil One." These are not present in either of the other editions.* — 272

- **3E-14.** *In the third edition, the title "Son of Man" is regularly used to describe Jesus as the agent of God. This title is typical of apocalyptic and does not appear in the earlier editions.* — 274

- **3E-15.** *In the third edition, the obligation to love is understood in a sectarian sense as love to be focused on the members of one's*

Contents

community. *This conception is typical of apocalyptic and is not found in the earlier editions of the Gospel.*   277

3E-16. *In the third edition, there is belief in a final apocalyptic eschatology that involves the notions of "a last day" and the return of Jesus. This is not found in the earlier editions (but see 2E-21).*   282

3E-17. *In the third edition, there is a conviction of a universal accountability (i.e., "judgment," in the neutral sense of the word) at the end of time. This is typical of apocalyptic thought. In the second edition, there was the conviction that judgment (in the negative sense) took place in the present and that the believer would not undergo judgment (2E-21). There is no discussion of judgment remaining in the first edition.*   286

3E-18. *In the third edition, there are two instances of the term "Kingdom of God." This terminology, so prominent in the Synoptics, appears in the Gospel of John only twice and is due to the apocalyptic worldview of the author of the third edition.*   288

3E-19. *Finally, there are other apocalyptic elements that appear in the gospel but appear so infrequently that they do not merit separate listing. Nevertheless, they are helpful in recognizing the apocalyptic orientation of the material where they appear. The terms are listed here and commented on briefly.*   290

3. Literary Characteristics   294

3E-20. *In the third edition, there are a number of instances where, without explanation, the plural of the first- and second-person pronouns is introduced in contexts where the singular had been previously used and where the singular would be expected.*   294

3E-21. *In the third edition, there are a number of instances where terminology characteristic of the first and second editions is mixed with features of the third edition.*   297

3E-22. *A distinctive pattern of mixing terminology appears in the case of the terms for religious authorities. In the third edition, the author, who does not have a distinctive term for religious authorities, uses whichever term has been used most recently. This contrasts with the use in the second edition, where the author substitutes his own term ("the Jews") for the terminology of the first edition.*   300

3E-23. *In the third edition, there are a number of topics or terms that are developed only minimally but which are developed in* *greater detail in 1 John. Not only does the recognition of this fact help to confirm that 1 John was written prior to the third edition of the Gospel, but at times it provides valuable background for the meaning of a term.*   301

4. Theological Characteristics   305

    3E-24. In the third edition, the ministry of Jesus is conceptualized as being composed of "day" (the public ministry) and "night" (the Passion). This enables the author of the third edition to take up the theme of the "hour" of Jesus from the second edition and to integrate it with the concepts of "light" and "darkness" typical of his apocalyptic viewpoint.   305

    3E-25. In the third edition, the overarching structure echoes that of 1 John, where the first part of the letter focuses on the proclamation of God as light and the second focuses on the proclamation to love one another. Thus, in the first half of the (third edition of the) Gospel (i.e., the public ministry), Jesus is presented as the light of the world. In the second half of the Gospel (i.e., the Passion and Resurrection), Jesus is presented as loving his own even to death.   306

    3E-26. In the third edition, the distinctive Christology is presented in a variety of ways. There are six primary ways, and these are discussed in the following characteristics. There are also a number of ways in which this is presented that appear relatively infrequently. These are grouped and discussed here. All of these are advances over the theology of the second edition and seek to identify Jesus ever more closely with God the Father. None of these features appear in earlier editions.   307

    3E-27. In the third edition, the sonship of Jesus is specified as being "unique" (monogenēs). In the second edition, Jesus is identified as "Son" but without specification of the uniqueness of his sonship (cf. 2E-27X).   308

    3E-28. In the third edition, the author affirms the preexistence of Jesus. Affirmation of preexistence is not present in earlier editions.   309

    3E-29. In the third edition, Jesus identifies himself as "I AM" (Egō eimi), the LXX rendition of the divine name. This does not appear in other editions.   310

Contents

3E-30. In the third edition, Jesus is said to have been given the Spirit "without measure." This specifies his possession of the Spirit in a way not found in the second edition.   311

3E-31. In the third edition, there is an emphasis on the permanence and abiding importance of the words of Jesus spoken in his historical ministry. While the second edition stresses the words of Jesus as one of the essential witnesses to him, the third edition emphasizes the permanent validity of those words.   311

3E-32. In the third edition, particular emphasis is placed on the role of Jesus as essential for gaining access to eternal life. This was not present in the earlier editions.   313

3E-33. In the third edition, the death of Jesus is understood as having an essential, salvific importance to it. This contrasts with the view of the second edition (2E-19), which presented the death of Jesus in terms of a departure to the Father, preparatory to the sending of the Spirit.   315

3E-34. In the third edition, the ministry of Jesus is conceived of as beginning with a "descent" from heaven and ending with a "return" to the Father. In the second edition, there is only the conception of the "departure" of Jesus to the Father, which is not yet conceived of in relation to a belief in preexistence (2E-19).   318

3E-35. In the third edition, the function of the Spirit (in the Paraclete passages) is defined in such a way as to make it clear that the Spirit does not speak on his own but reminds the listeners of what Jesus has said. In the second edition, the emphasis is on the necessity of receiving the Spirit, and the role of the Spirit is not qualified in any way.   320

3E-36. In the third edition, "joy" is understood as complete in that the future ("eschatological") hopes of the people have been fulfilled in the ministry of Jesus. In the second edition, joy was conceived of as "irremovable" in the Resurrection of Jesus that followed the pain and sorrow of the Passion (2E-24).   322

3E-37. In the second edition, "eternal life" had been conceived of as beginning in the present and continuing after physical death but without mention of the resurrection of the body. In the third edition, this belief is complemented by the introduction of explicit statements of belief in bodily resurrection.   324

Contents

3E-38. In the third edition, there is an emphasis on the importance of proper ethical behavior. This is not found in the earlier editions. ... 326

3E-39. In the third edition, the birth that the believer is said to experience is said to be "from God." In the second edition, it is said to be "from the Spirit" (2E-17). ... 328

3E-40. In the third edition, the figure of the Beloved Disciple appears. He does not appear in the earlier editions. ... 328

3E-41. In the third edition, the importance of the material and physical is affirmed, whereas this was downplayed in the second edition (2E-18). This value is expressed both in the importance of the fact that the Word became "flesh" and also by the value attributed to ritual sacraments, including the rite of initiation (Baptism) and the sacred meal (the Eucharist). ... 331

3E-42. In the third edition, the relationship of mutual indwelling between the Father and the Son is extended to include a relationship with believers. In the second edition, the focus was on the indwelling of the Son in the Father (2E-23). ... 335

3E-43. In the third edition, there are four references to Jesus "choosing" the disciples. This contrasts with the second edition, where there is frequent mention of the Father "giving" believers/disciples to Jesus. ... 337

3E-44. In the third edition, there are repeated statements expressing the need, and the hope, for unity among believers. This does not appear in the other editions. ... 337

3E-45. In the third edition, the basis for belief continues to be the "witnesses" to Jesus as it was in the second edition (cf. 2E-14). However, in the third edition, the list of witnesses is extended from four to six. In the first edition, the basis of belief had only been the "signs" performed by Jesus (1E-18). ... 337

5. Some Theological Features Introduced in the Second Edition and Taken Over by the Author of the Third ... 338

3E-46X. In the third edition, the author continues the use of the title "Father" for God as it was introduced by the author of the second edition (2E-26). However, the material in which it appears is marked by other features distinctive of the third edition. As we have seen, the title does not appear in the first edition. ... 338

3E-47X. The notion of Jesus as "Son" is introduced by the author of the second edition (2E-27X) and is taken over by the author of the third. ... 339

3E-48X. The notion of Jesus as "sent" by the Father, which was introduced into the Gospel by the author of the second edition (2E-28X), is taken over by the author of the third. ... 339

3E-49X. The author of the third edition takes over the conception of eternal life of the second edition, where it was first introduced, but in the third edition this conception is qualified by conditions or requirements that are not evident in the texts of the second edition and which are elements in the author's response to the opponents at the time of 1 John. ... 339

3E-50X. Among the words of the second edition taken over by the third author are "glory/glorify" and "witness." Although the terms are taken over from the second edition, they have different meanings when used by the author of the third. ... 341

6. Features of the Third Edition That Become Apparent Once the Analysis Is Complete ... 342

3E-51F. One of the most widespread features of the second and third editions is the type of formula used to introduce quotations from, and references to, Scripture. In the third edition, quotations and references are introduced by the formula "in order that the Scripture may be fulfilled . . ." (hina plērōthē hē graphē . . .) or some variation of it. In the second edition, quotations and references are introduced by the formula "as it is written . . ." (kathōs estin gegrammenon . . .) or a minor variation of it (2E-32F). ... 342

3E-52F. In the second edition, there is frequent mention of "the world" in both a positive and a negative sense. The same is true of the third edition. The precise meaning of this term is difficult to determine in all cases. However, one particular formulation using this term, namely, the expression "of this world," used as an indication of allegiance and identity, is dualistic and appears only in the third edition and in 1 John. ... 343

3E-53F. In the third edition, the verbs "descend" (katabainō) and "ascend" (anabainō) have a theological meaning not found in the other editions of the Gospel. ... 345

3E-54F. In the third edition, the verb hypsoō *("to lift up") is used to refer to the Crucifixion of Jesus. This does not appear in the other editions.*   347

3E-55F. In the third edition, it is said that Jesus has "seen" God and tells of what he has "seen." This is not present in earlier editions of the Gospel.   347

3E-56F. In the third edition, a number of passages and terms have been introduced into the Gospel because of their similarity to the Synoptic accounts. This does not appear in the other editions.   349

3E-57F. In the third edition, the author frequently makes brief modifications to the text and does so by "bundling" (grouping) his additions together into a relatively brief context and then addressing the issue seldom or not at all again. This is not evident in the other editions.   351

Section 3. Synthesis of the Third Edition   353

1. The Structure of the Third Edition   353
   a. The Overarching Structure of the Third Edition   353
      (1) The Prologue (1:1-18)   354
      (2) Jesus as the Light of the World (1:19–12:50)   354
      (3) Jesus as the Embodiment of Love (13:1–20:31)   355
      (4) Epilogue (21:1-25)   356
   b. Other Elements of the Structure of the Third Edition   357
      (1) "Glossing"   357
      (2) Addition by Grouping   357
2. The Literary Genre of the Material of the Third Edition   357
3. The Theology of the Third Edition   358
   a. Elements of Theology Related to the Crisis at the Time of 1 John   359
      (1) Christology   359
      (2) Belief   360
      (3) Pneumatology   360
      (4) Eternal Life   360
      (5) Eschatology   361
      (6) Knowledge of God   361
      (7) Soteriology   361

Contents

(8) Ethics	361
(9) Anthropology	361
(10) Ecclesiology	362
(11) Religious Significance of Material Reality	362
b. Elements of the Theology of the Third Edition Not Paralleled in 1 John	362
(1) Ecclesiology	362
(2) Ritual Concerns	363
(3) Bodily Resurrection	363
(4) Correlation with the Synoptic Gospels	363
(5) The Role of the Beloved Disciple	363
4. The Theology of the Third Edition and That of 1 John	364
a. Similarities between the Third Edition and 1 John	365
(1) The Worldview of the Third Edition and That of 1 John	365
(2) The Structure of 1 John and That of the Third Edition	365
(3) Similarities in Terminology	365
b. Terminology in 1 John but Not in the Third Edition	365
c. Terminology in the Third Edition but Not in 1 John	366
5. The Identity and Social Location of the Community at the Time of the Third Edition	367
6. Background of the Material in the Third Edition	367
7. The Historical Value of Material Found in the Third Edition	369
8. The Relation of Material in the Third Edition to the Synoptics	369
9. The Author of the Third Edition	374
a. Is the Author of the Third Edition the Author of 1 John?	375
b. Is the Author of the Third Edition the Beloved Disciple?	375
c. Who, Then, Is the Author of the Third Edition?	375
10. The Date of the Third Edition	376
a. Dating Relative to the Composition of 1 John	376
b. Assigning a Specific Date to the Third Edition	385
(1) External Evidence	385
(a) The Earliest Manuscript Evidence	385
(b) The Earliest Citation	386

(2) Internal Evidence	389
c. Conclusions regarding the Dating of the Third Edition	390
11. The Place of Composition	390
a. External Evidence	391
b. Internal Evidence	392

PART 4: A HISTORY OF THE DEVELOPMENT OF JOHANNINE THEOLOGY — 395

Section 1. The Development of Johannine Theology: Christology	397
1. The Christology of the First Edition	399
a. A Low Christology in the Affirmations about Jesus	399
b. Low Christology in Accusations Brought against Jesus by the Jewish Authorities	399
c. A Moses Christology	400
d. Other Elements of the Christology of the First Edition	401
2. The Christology of the Second Edition	402
a. Jesus' Exalted Claims	402
(1) Jesus as the "Son" in Relation to "the Father"	402
(2) Jesus as "Son"	403
(3) God as "Father"	403
(4) Jesus as "Sent" by the Father	404
(5) The Son Does the Same Work as the Father	405
b. Jesus' Dependency on, and Orientation toward, the Father	406
(1) The Priority of the Father	406
(2) Jesus Does Only What He Hears from the Father	406
(3) Jesus Seeks the Glory of the Father	407
(4) Jesus' Success and His Glory as Given to Him by the Father	407
(5) Jesus' Relationship with the Father	407
c. Jesus as Preexistent in the Second Edition?	408
d. Traditional Titles in the Second Edition	409
(1) Son of God	409

(2) Christ		409
(3) King		410
e. Conclusions		410
3. The Background of the Christology of the Second Edition		411
a. Sending		411
b. Apprenticeship		412
c. Agency		412
d. The Figure of Wisdom		413
e. Jesus as Possessing the Life of the Father		417
f. Conclusion		418
4. The Christology of 1 John		419
a. The View of the Opponents		419
b. The View of the Author of 1 John		420
(1) The Unique Identity of Jesus		420
(2) The Abiding Importance of Jesus		421
5. The Christology of the Third Edition		422
a. Jesus as Son		423
b. Jesus' Possession of the Spirit		423
c. Jesus as Preexistent		423
d. Jesus as Son of Man		424
e. The Relationship between Jesus and the Father in the Third Edition		425
(1) Jesus as *Egō Eimi*		425
(2) Jesus Is to Be Honored Just as the Father Is		426
(3) Jesus Is Addressed as "My Lord and My God"		426
(4) Jesus' Continuing Dependence upon, and Subordination to, the Father		426
(5) The Abiding Importance of Jesus		427
(6) Jesus Has Been Given What He Has by the Father		428
(7) Conclusion		428
6. The Background of the Christology in the Third Edition		429
a. The Apocalyptic Son of Man		429
b. Wisdom Motifs		429

Contents

    c. The Son with the Full Authority of the Father   430

Section 2. The Development of Johannine Theology: Belief   431

1. Belief in the First Edition   431
   a. Belief Based on Signs   431
   b. The Content of Belief   432
2. Belief in the Second Edition   432
   a. Response to the Four Witnesses   432
   b. The Second Edition and a Critique of Faith Based on Signs?   433
   c. The Object of Belief   433
   d. Belief, Eternal Life, and the Reception of the Spirit   434
   e. The Content of Belief   435
   f. Belief and Being "Given" by the Father   435
3. The Background of Belief in the Second Edition   436
4. Belief in 1 John   436
   a. The View of the Opponents   436
   b. The View of the Author   437
      (1) The Abiding Importance of the Words of Jesus   437
      (2) The Correct Understanding of Jesus   438
5. Belief in the Third Edition   439
   a. The Further Witnesses to Jesus   439
   b. The Content of True Belief   440
   c. The Permanent Importance of the Word of Jesus   440
   d. The Spirit-Paraclete and the Words of Jesus   440
   e. Critique of Miracle-Faith   441
6. The Background of Belief in 1 John and in the Third Edition   442

Section 3. The Development of Johannine Theology: Pneumatology   442

1. The Spirit in the First Edition   443
2. The Spirit in the Second Edition   443
   a. The Central Role of Pneumatology in the Second Edition   443
   b. The Spirit and Jesus   445
   c. The Spirit and the Believer   446

Contents

d. Is the Spirit Presented as a Personal Being in the Second Edition?	447
3. The Background of the Presentation of the Spirit in the Second Edition	448
4. The Spirit in 1 John	449
a. The View of the Opponents	449
b. The View of the Author	449
c. Is the Conception of the Spirit in 1 John Less Developed?	451
5. The Spirit in the Third Edition	452
a. The Spirit as Paraclete	454
b. The Holy Spirit in 1:33	455
c. Conclusion	456
6. The Background of the Presentation of the Spirit in 1 John and the Third Edition	457
Section 4. The Development of Johannine Theology: Eternal Life	**459**
1. Eternal Life in the First Edition	459
2. Eternal Life in the Second Edition	459
a. The Present Possession of Eternal Life	461
b. Conclusion	462
3. The Background of Eternal Life in the Second Edition	463
a. Natural Life and Spirit	463
b. Eternal Life and the Spirit in the Old Testament	465
c. The Nature of Eternal Life in Pre-Christian Judaism	467
4. Eternal Life in 1 John	469
a. The View of the Opponents and the View of the Author of 1 John	469
(1) The Role of Jesus in Relation to Eternal Life	469
(2) Eternal Life and Mutual Love	470
(3) The Future Dimension of Eternal Life	470
(4) Eternal Life and Sin unto Death	471
(5) Bodily Resurrection in 1 John?	471
5. Eternal Life in the Third Edition	472
a. Jesus' Possession of Eternal Life	472

b. Obedience and Eternal Life	472
c. The Role of Jesus in the Bestowal of Eternal Life	473
d. Eternal Life and the Eucharist	473
6. The Background of the Presentation of Eternal Life in 1 John and in the Third Edition	474
a. The Spirit and Natural Life	474
b. The Spirit and Eternal Life	475
c. The Present Possession of Eternal Life in the Sectarian Documents of Qumran and the *Testaments of the Twelve Patriarchs*	476
d. "Having Life in Oneself"	476
e. Eternal Life with Future Bodily Resurrection in the Sectarian Documents of Qumran and the *Testaments of the Twelve Patriarchs*	477
f. Disputes over Immortality/Resurrection Elsewhere in Early Christianity	481
Section 5. The Development of Johannine Theology: Eschatology	**482**
1. Eschatology in the First Edition	482
2. Eschatology in the Second Edition	483
a. Eternal Life in the Present	484
b. References to Judgment	484
3. The Background of the Eschatology in the Second Edition	485
4. Eschatology in 1 John	486
a. The View of the Opponents	486
b. The View of the Author	486
(1) The "Last Day" or the "Last Hour"	487
(2) A Future Coming of Jesus	487
(3) A Final Judgment	487
(4) A Future State of Eternal Life Different from the Present	487
5. The Background of Eschatology in 1 John	488
a. In the Sectarian Documents of Qumran	489
b. In the *Testaments of the Twelve Patriarchs*	489
c. Elsewhere in Apocalyptic Judaism	490
6. Eschatology in the Third Edition	490

a. Passages with a Present Eschatology	491
b. Passages with a Future Eschatology	492
c. Passages of the Third Edition Where the Time Aspect of Judgment Is Less Clear	492
7. The Background of Eschatology in the Third Edition	493
Section 6. The Development of Johannine Theology: Knowing God	**494**
1. Knowing God in the First Edition	494
2. Knowing God in the Second Edition	494
a. Knowing Persons, Not Doctrine	496
b. Teacher and Teaching	496
c. The Language of the Gospel	496
d. Direct Knowledge of God and "Tradition"	496
3. The Background of the Concept of Knowing God in the Second Edition	497
4. Knowing God in 1 John	499
a. The View of the Opponents and the View of the Author of 1 John	499
b. The Opponents Do Not "Know"	499
c. The Believer "Knows"	499
d. The Expressions Used by the Author	499
e. The Believer Knows Persons	500
f. The Nature of This Knowing and Its Source	500
g. Tests for Determining True Knowing	501
(1) "Knowing" and the First Johannine Commandment	501
(2) Stress on What Was "from the Beginning"	502
(3) "Progressives" and the Teaching of the Christ	502
(4) Conclusions	502
5. Knowing God in the Third Edition	503
a. The First Commandment in the Third Edition	504
b. The Additional Witnesses	504
c. The Paraclete and the Words of Jesus	505
d. Direct Knowledge in the Third Edition	506

Contents

6. The Background of the Concept of "Knowing" God
   in 1 John and in the Third Edition ... 506
7. Conclusion ... 507

Section 7. The Development of Johannine Theology: Soteriology ... 508

1. Soteriology in the First Edition ... 508
2. Soteriology in the Second Edition ... 508
3. The Background of Soteriology in the Second Edition ... 511
   a. In the Old Testament ... 511
   b. In the Sectarian Documents of Qumran ... 511
   c. Elsewhere in Apocalyptic Judaism ... 512
4. Soteriology in 1 John ... 513
   a. The View of the Opponents ... 513
   b. The View of the Author ... 513
      (1) Jesus' Death Was a Death for His Own ... 513
      (2) The Death of Jesus Takes Away Sin ... 514
      (3) The Death of Jesus Involved the Giving of His "Flesh" and "Blood," "for the Life of the World" ... 514
5. Soteriology in the Third Edition ... 515
   a. Jesus' Death as a Death for His Own ... 516
   b. The Death of Jesus Takes Away Sin ... 517
   c. The Death of Jesus Involved the Giving of His "Flesh" and "Blood," "for the Life of the World" ... 518
   d. The Death of Jesus Interpreted against the Model of Abraham's Sacrifice of Isaac ... 518
   e. Jesus as "Saving" and as "Savior" ... 519
6. The Background of Soteriology in 1 John and in the Third Edition ... 519
   a. The Concept of Vicarious Atonement in Judaism ... 520
   b. The Absence of an Atoning Eschatological Figure in Judaism ... 521
   c. The Concept of Vicarious Atonement Elsewhere in Early Christianity ... 521

Section 8. The Development of Johannine Theology: Ethics ... 522

1. Ethics in the First Edition ... 522

2. Ethics in the Second Edition	522
3. The Background of Ethical Perfectionism in the Second Edition	524
4. Ethics in 1 John	525
a. The View of the Opponents	525
b. The View of the Author	526
5. Ethics in the Third Edition	527
a. Ethics and References to Sinful Actions	527
b. Ethics and Final Judgment	527
c. The Love Commandment	528
d. Conclusion	529
6. The Background of the Attitude toward Ethics in 1 John and in the Third Edition	529
a. Ethical Perfectionism and Sin in the Sectarian Documents of Qumran and in the *Testaments of the Twelve Patriarchs*	529
b. Ethical Perfectionism and Sin Elsewhere in Jewish Apocalyptic	531
c. Sectarian Love in the Sectarian Documents of Qumran and the *Testaments of the Twelve Patriarchs*	532
Section 9. The Development of Johannine Theology: Anthropology	**532**
1. Anthropology in the First Edition	532
2. Anthropology in the Second Edition	532
3. The Background of the Anthropology of the Second Edition	535
4. Anthropology in 1 John	535
a. The View of the Opponents and That of the Author	535
b. Believers as "Children of God"	535
c. Believers as "Anointed"	536
5. Anthropology in the Third Edition	538
6. The Background of the Anthropology of 1 John and of the Third Edition	539
a. The Anthropology of 1 John and the Third Edition and That of Apocalyptic	539
b. Similarities between the Anthropology of 1 John and the Third Edition and That of the Sectarian Documents of Qumran	539

Contents

c. Parallels to the Anthropology of 1 John and of the Third Author Elsewhere in Early Christianity	540

Section 10. The Development of Johannine Theology: Ecclesiology — 540

1. Ecclesiology in the First Edition — 540
2. Ecclesiology in the Second Edition — 541
3. A Background for the View of Ecclesiology in the Second Edition? — 542
4. Ecclesiology in 1 John — and in 3 John — 543
   a. Ecclesiology in 1 John — 543
   b. Ecclesiology in 3 John — 545
5. Ecclesiology in the Third Edition — 545
6. A Background of the Ecclesiology of the Johannine Letters and the Third Edition — 547
   a. In the Sectarian Documents of Qumran — 547
   b. Elsewhere in Earliest Christianity — 548

Section 11. The Development of Johannine Theology: The Religious Significance of Material Reality — 548

1. The Religious Significance of Material Reality in the First Edition — 550
2. The Religious Significance of Material Reality in the Second Edition — 550
3. The Background of the Attitude toward Material Reality in the Second Edition — 552
4. The Religious Significance of Material Reality in 1 John — 552
   a. The View of the Opponents — 552
   b. The View of the Author — 553
5. The Religious Significance of Material Reality in the Third Edition — 555
   a. The Importance of Material Reality in General — 555
   b. The Importance of Ritual Actions — 555
   c. The Role of Human Mediators — 556
   d. Bodily Resurrection — 557
   e. The Resurrection of Jesus — 558

Contents

  f. A Final Observation on the Significance
   of the Physical and Material in the Third Edition   558
 6. The Background of These Various Attitudes
  toward the Religious Significance of Material Reality   559
  a. In the Old Testament   559
  b. In the Sectarian Documents of Qumran   559

PART 5: REFERENCE   561

The Text of the Gospel   561

The Text of the Johannine Letters   610

Bibliography   626

 1. General Reference   626
 2. Texts   626
 3. Commentaries on the Gospel of John   627
 4. Articles and Monographs on the Gospel of John   629
 5. Commentaries on the Johannine Letters   680
 6. Articles and Monographs on the Johannine Letters   681

INDEXES

Authors   685

Subjects   691

Scripture and Other Ancient Literature   699

Preface

Writing this commentary is the result of many years of study and reflection on the Johannine tradition. Becoming intimately acquainted with the thought of this Gospel has been a particularly fascinating journey. Not only has it been a privilege to attempt to explain the meaning of a foundational document of Christianity, but it has been an adventure to sense the ideals and the struggles of this community as it came to articulate its understanding of Jesus of Nazareth. It was not only a community that underwent the trauma of expulsion from the synagogue in which its members had grown up and within whose traditions they sought to understand the importance of Jesus but also one that underwent yet another, internal struggle about the meaning and importance of Jesus. It is a sector of early Christianity about which there is much to learn and yet one that has left us many clues in its literature from which to learn. It is hoped that this commentary has been sensitive to many of those clues.

Work on this commentary was made possible by the support of individuals throughout my career too many to mention. I apologize to all those who names I have forgotten and whose assistance I fail to recognize here. But some do stand out. The first and greatest encouragement was from my *Doktorvater*, Noel Lazure, who critiqued all of my early work with a thoroughness and an openness that taught me to be careful in my reading and to be open to where the evidence led. At the University of Scranton, then-dean William Parente showed constant interest in, and support for, my work. At Loyola University, where I have taught for the past twenty-six years, my deans have been very supportive in giving me leaves of absence and travel grants for research and for attending international meetings. They are Fr. Lawrence Biondi, S.J., Dr. James Wiser, Dr. Francis Catania, Dr. Kathleen McCourt, Dr. John Smarelli, and Dr. Isaiah Crawford. My chairpersons — Dr. Patout Burns, Dr. Jon Nilson, Dr. John McCarthy, Fr. David Stagaman, S.J., and Dr. Patricia Jung — were also the first

Preface

line of support. I owe particular gratitude to Dr. Ron Walker, Senior Vice-President at Loyola, who gave special assistance and assigned me a teaching load that allowed me to continue research during the period of my own chairmanship of the Department of Theology.

Michael Glazier first suggested that "I had a commentary in me" and invited me to write for the Sacra Pagina series. Special gratitude for these volumes themselves is due to David Noel Freedman, the editor of the Eerdmans Critical Commentary, who, along with his co-editor, Dr. Astrid Beck, accepted the volumes for the series. His death in April 2008 was an enormous loss to the field of biblical studies. At Eerdmans, Allen Myers, Milton Essenburg, and Linda Bieze have been very patient and supportive of the project.

Among colleagues, Robert Fortna first instilled in me the interest in discovering the history of the composition of the Gospel of John. Raymond Brown's erudition and example were a constant help. In a review of my first book, Alan Culpepper suggested that the thesis first put forward there might well lead to a "major commentary." That also gave me much encouragement at a time when I needed it. I am also grateful for the support and friendship of my colleagues in the Department of Theology at Loyola as well as for the collegiality of the members of the Catholic Biblical Association of America and the Johannine Literature Section of the Society of Biblical Literature and the Johannine Seminar of the Society for New Testament Studies, who have provided a forum for ideas and are themselves models of scholarship. It is a privilege to have persons of such intelligence and character as friends.

I also must thank my graduate assistants at Loyola over the years, especially Thomas Boone, Joseph Latham, Alec Lucas, Teresa Calpino, Brian Dennert, and Lauren O'Connell. They have put in hour on hour of proofreading the work in these pages.

Finally, I am thankful for the support of my family. Michael and Lisa, both now married, heard about this project all too often — and now their spouses do too! But I am most grateful for the support-beyond-support of my wife Carol through the years of our marriage. When we were dating, she gave me a paperweight lettered "Love Costs." Carol has paid a great price! And my gratitude is beyond words.

URBAN C. VON WAHLDE
Loyola University of Chicago
Summer 2010

Abbreviations

I. MISCELLANEOUS

Part	Volume 1 (excluding the Introduction) is divided into five "Parts" (The First Edition, the Second Edition, the Third Edition, the History of the Development of Johannine Theology, and Reference)
Section	Parts One, Two, and Three of Volume 1 each have three "Sections": Overview, Characteristics, and Synthesis.
1E	First Edition (texts of the first edition are printed in regular type)
2E	Second Edition (texts of the second edition are printed in italic)
3E	Third Edition (texts of the third edition are printed in bold)
(1E-1), (2E-1), (3E-1), etc.	A reference to a particular criterion of a given edition An "F" following the number indicates that it is a "feature," a common element that appears only after the analysis is complete but signals the resulting consistency of the material. An "X" following the number of the criterion indicates that the characteristic is common to both the second and third editions.
Author of the first edition, etc.	To avoid the confusion caused by the designations "first author," "first editor," "second editor," I will not use the term "editor" and simply refer to "first author," "second author," and "third author" as the ones responsible for each edition.

Abbreviations

Evangelist, Redactor	To avoid confusion, I will not use these terms except when quoting the work of others.
Characteristics	These are traits of the Gospel that are used in the identification of material from the various editions.
Features	These are traits of the Gospel that emerge from the analysis and can be seen to appear consistently in a given edition. However, this consistency appears only later and so is distinguished from the "Characteristics."

II. BIBLICAL BOOKS (INCLUDING THE DEUTEROCANONICAL)

A. Hebrew Bible/Old Testament

Gen	Genesis	Song	Song of Songs
Exod	Exodus	Isa	Isaiah
Lev	Leviticus	Jer	Jeremiah
Num	Numbers	Lam	Lamentations
Deut	Deuteronomy	Ezek	Ezekiel
Josh	Joshua	Dan	Daniel
Judg	Judges	Hos	Hosea
Ruth	Ruth	Joel	Joel
1-2 Sam	1-2 Samuel	Amos	Amos
1-2 Kings	1-2 Kings	Obad	Obadiah
1-2 Chr	1-2 Chronicles	Jonah	Jonah
Ezra	Ezra	Mic	Micah
Neh	Nehemiah	Nah	Nahum
Esth	Esther	Hab	Habakkuk
Job	Job	Zeph	Zephaniah
Ps/Pss	Psalms	Hag	Haggai
Prov	Proverbs	Zech	Zechariah
Eccl	Ecclesiastes	Mal	Malachi

B. Apocrypha and Septuagint

Bar	Baruch	Add Esth	Additions to Esther
Add Dan	Additions to Daniel	Ep Jer	Epistle of Jeremiah
1-2 Esd	1-2 Esdras	Jdt	Judith

Abbreviations

1-2 Macc	1-2 Maccabees	Sir	Sirach/
3-4 Macc	3-4 Maccabees		Ecclesiasticus
Pr Man	Prayer of	Tob	Tobit
	Manasseh	Wis	Wisdom of
Ps 151	Psalm 151		Solomon

C. Old Testament Pseudepigrapha

Apoc. Ab.	*Apocalypse of Abraham*	*TDan*	*Testament of Dan*
Apoc. Adam	*Apocalypse of Adam*	*TGad*	*Testament of Gad*
		TIss	*Testament of Issachar*
Apoc. Mos.	*Apocalypse of Moses*	*TJos*	*Testament of Joseph*
		TJud	*Testament of Judah*
2 Bar.	*2 Baruch*	*TLev*	*Testament of Levi*
1 Enoch	*1 Enoch (Ethiopic Apocalypse)*	*TNaph*	*Testament of Naphtali*
Jos. Asen.	*Joseph and Aseneth*	*TReu*	*Testament of Reuben*
Jub.	*Jubilees*		
Pss Sol	*Psalms of Solomon*	*TSim*	*Testament of Simeon*
TAsh	*Testament of Asher*		
TBenj	*Testament of Benjamin*	*TZeb*	*Testament of Zebulum*

D. New Testament

Matt	Matthew	1-2 Thess	1-2 Thessalonians
Mark	Mark	1-2 Tim	1-2 Timothy
Luke	Luke	Titus	Titus
John	John	Phlm	Philemon
Acts	Acts	Heb	Hebrews
Rom	Romans	Jas	James
1-2 Cor	1-2 Corinthians	1-2 Pet	1-2 Peter
Gal	Galatians	1-2-3 John	1-2-3 John
Eph	Ephesians	Jude	Jude
Phil	Philippians	Rev	Revelation
Col	Colossians		

Abbreviations

III. OTHER LITERATURE

A. Ignatius of Antioch
Eph.	*Letter to the Ephesians*
Mag.	*Letter to the Magnesians*
Phil.	*Letter to the Philadelphians*
Smyrn.	*Letter to the Smyrneans*
Trall.	*Letter to the Trallians*

B. Polycarp
Phil.   *Letter to the Philippians*

C. *Did.*   *Didache*

D. Irenaeus
Adv. Haer.   *Against All Heresies*

E. Justin
Apol.	*Apology*
Dial.	*Dialogue with Trypho*

F. Eusebius
Chron.	*Chronicon*
Hist.	*Ecclesiastical History*
Onom.	*Onomasticon*

G. Josephus
Ant.	*Antiquities of the Jews*
Life	*Life*
J.W.	*Jewish War*

H. Philo
Cher.	*De cherubim*
Conf.	*De confusione linguarum*
Det.	*Quod deterius potiori insidari soleat*
Ebr.	*De ebrietate*
Flacc.	*In Flaccum*
Fug.	*De fuga et inventione*
Her.	*Quis rerum divinarum heres sit?*
Hypoth.	*Hypothetica*
Leg.	*Legum allegoriae*

Legat.   *Legatio ad Gaium*
Mos.   *De vita Mosis*
Post.   *De posteritate Caini*
Somn.   *De somniis*
Spec.   *De specialibus legibus*

I. Polybius
Hist.   *Histories*

J. Tacitus
Ann.   *Annals*

IV. DOCUMENTS FROM QUMRAN (SECTARIAN AND OTHER)

Scrolls are identified, first, by the number of the cave where they were found, next by "Q" for "Qumran," and then by the number assigned to the work by the scrolls team.

V. RABBINIC WORKS

Mishnah   Tractates from the Mishnah are identified by the prefix *m*. All translations are from H. Danby, *The Mishnah*.
Talmud   References to the Babylonian Talmud will be prefixed with *b*; references to the Jerusalem Talmud will be prefixed with a *j*.
Tosefta   References to the Tosefta will be indicated by the prefix "*t*."

VI. PERIODICALS, REFERENCE WORKS, AND SERIALS

AB	Anchor Bible
ABD	*Anchor Bible Dictionary* (D. N. Freedman, ed.; 6 vols.; New York: Doubleday, 1992)
ABRL	Anchor Bible Reference Library
AGJU	Arbeiten zur Geschichte des antiken Judentums und des Urchristentums
AJBI	*Annual of the Japanese Biblical Institute*
AnBib	Analecta biblica
ANRW	*Aufstieg und Niedergang der römischen Welt: Geschichte und*

Abbreviations

	Kultur Roms im Spiegel der neueren Forschung (H. Temporini and W. Haase, eds.; Berlin: W. de Gruyter, 1972-)
APF	*Archiv für Papyrusforschung*
AsSeign	*Assemblées du Seigneur*
ATANT	Abhandlungen zur Theologie des Alten und Neuen Testaments
AThR	*Anglican Theological Review*
AThRSup	Anglican Theological Review Supplementary Series
BAR	*Biblical Archaeology Review*
BBET	Beiträge zur biblischen Exegese und Theologie
BCFT	Beiträge zur Förderung christlicher Theologie
BD	Beloved Disciple ("the disciple whom Jesus loved")
BDAG	W. Bauer, F. Danker, W. F. Arndt, and F. W. Gingrich, *A Greek-English Lexicon of the New Testament and Other Early Christian Literature* (3d ed.; Chicago: University of Chicago Press, 1999)
BETL	*Bibliotheca ephemeridum theologicarum lovaniensium*
BEvT	*Beiträge zur evangelischen Theologie*
BGU	*Aegyptische Urkunden aus den königlichen Museen zu Berlin: Griechische Urkunden* (15 vols.; Berlin: Weidmann, 1895-1983)
BHT	Beiträge zur historischen Theologie
Bib	*Biblica*
BibLeb	*Bibel und Leben*
BJRL	*Bulletin of the John Rylands University Library of Manchester*
BK	*Bibel und Kirche*
BLit	*Bibliothèque liturgique*
BN	*Biblische Notizen*
BSac	*Bibliotheca sacra*
BT	*The Bible Translator*
BTB	*Biblical Theology Bulletin*
BTS	*Bible et terre sainte*
BU	Biblische Untersuchungen
BulETS	*Bulletin of the Evangelical Theology Society*
BVC	*Bible et vie chrétienne*
BWANT	Beiträge zur Wissenschaft vom Alten und Neuen Testament
BZ	*Biblische Zeitschrift*
BZNW	Beihefte zur Zeitschrift für die neutestamentliche Wissenschaft
CahRB	Cahiers de la Revue biblique

Abbreviations

CBQ	*Catholic Biblical Quarterly*
CBQMS	Catholic Biblical Quarterly Monograph Series
CDSSE	*The Complete Dead Sea Scrolls in English* (G. Vermes, trans.; New York: Penguin, 1997)
CIJ	*Corpus inscriptionum judaicorum*
ConBNT	Coniectanea neotestamentica or Coniectanea biblica: New Testament Series
DACL	*Dictionnaire d'archéologie chrétienne et de liturgie* (F. Cabrol, O.S.B., and H. Leclercq, O.S.B., eds.; 15 vols.; Paris: Letouzey and Ané, 1907-53)
DBSup	*Dictionaire de la Bible Supplément* (L. Pirot, ed.; Paris: Letouzey and Ané, 1928-66)
DJD	Discoveries in the Judaean Desert
DRev	*Downside Review*
DSSE	*The Dead Sea Scrolls in English* (G. Vermes, trans. and ed.; 4th ed.; Baltimore: Penguin, 1995)
DSST	*The Dead Sea Scrolls in Translation* (F. García Martínez, ed.; 2d ed.; Leiden: Brill; Grand Rapids: Eerdmans, 1996)
EB	Echter Bibel
EBib	*Études bibliques*
EKKNT	Evangelisch-katholischer Kommentar zum Neuen Testament
EPRO	Études préliminaires aux religions orientales dans l'empire romain
ErbAuf	*Erbe und Aufbau*
ET	English translation
ETL	*Ephemerides theologicae lovanienses*
EvQ	*Evangelical Quarterly*
ExpTim	*Expository Times*
FB	Forschung zur Bibel
FRLANT	Forschungen zur Religion und Literatur des Alten und Neuen Testaments
GNT[4]	*Greek New Testament* (B. Aland, K. Aland, J. Karavidopoulos, C. M. Martini, and B. M. Metzger, eds.; 4th ed. rev.; Stuttgart: Biblia-Druck, 1993)
HDB	Herder's Dictionary of the Bible
HeyJ	*Heythrop Journal*
HibJ	*Hibbert Journal*
HNT	Handbuch zum Neuen Testament
HTR	*Harvard Theological Review*
HTS	Harvard Theological Studies

Abbreviations

HUT	*Hermeneutische Untersuchungen zur Theologie*
IBS	*Irish Biblical Studies*
ICC	International Critical Commentary
IEJ	*Israel Exploration Journal*
IndTheolStud	*Indian Theological Studies*
Int	*Interpretation*
ISPCK	International Society for the Propagation of Christian Knowledge
JAAR	*Journal of the American Academy of Religion*
JAC	*Jahrbuch für Antike und Christentum*
JAMA	*Journal of the American Medical Association*
JBL	*Journal of Biblical Literature*
JES	*Journal of Ecumenical Studies*
JETS	*Journal of the Evangelical Theological Society*
JJS	*Journal of Jewish Studies*
JNES	*Journal of Near Eastern Studies*
JQR	*Jewish Quarterly Review*
JSNT	*Journal for the Study of the New Testament*
JSNTSup	Journal for the Study of the New Testament: Supplement Series
JSOT	*Journal for the Study of the Old Testament*
JSOTSup	Journal for the Study of the Old Testament: Supplement Series
JSP	*Journal for the Study of the Pseudepigrapha*
JTSA	*Journal of Theology for Southern Africa*
JTS	*Journal of Theological Studies*
KD	*Kerygma und Dogma*
LS	*Louvain Studies*
LTP	*Laval théologique et philosophique*
LumVie	*Lumière et vie*
LXX	The Septuagint
LXX-S	The Sinaiticus manuscript of the Septuagint
MNTC	Moffatt New Testament Commentary
MScRel	*Mélanges de science religieuse*
MT	Masoretic Text
MTZ	*Münchener theologische Zeitschrift*
NCBC	New Century Bible Commentary
NIBCNT	New International Bible Commentary on the New Testament
NJBC	*New Jerome Biblical Commentary* (R. E. Brown et al., eds.; Englewood Cliffs, NJ: Prentice Hall, 1990)

Abbreviations

NICNT	New International Commentary on the New Testament
NovT	*Novum Testamentum*
NovTSup	Novum Testamentum Supplements
NRTh	*La nouvelle revue théologique*
NT	New Testament
NTAbh	Neutestamentliche Abhandlungen
NTB	*New Testament Background*
NTD	Das Neue Testament Deutsch
NTOA	Novum Testamentum et orbis antiquus
NTS	*New Testament Studies*
NTSMS	New Testament Studies Monograph Series
OT	Old Testament
OTP	*Old Testament Pseudepigrapha* (J. Charlesworth, ed.; 2 vols.; Garden City, NY: Doubleday, 1983)
PEQ	*Palestine Exploration Quarterly*
QD	Quaestiones disputatae
RB	*Revue biblique*
RevistB	*Revista bíblica*
RevExp	*Review and Expositor*
RevQ	*Revue de Qumran*
RevScRel	*Revue des sciences religieuses*
RHPR	*Revue d'histoire et de philosophie religieuses*
RQ	*Römische Quartalschrift für christliche Altertumskunde und Kirchengeschichte*
RSPT	*Revue des sciences philosophiques et théologiques*
RSR	*Recherches de science religieuse*
RTL	*Revue théologique de Louvain*
SA	Studia anselmiana
SANT	Studien zum Alten und Neuen Testament
SBAB	Stuttgarter biblische Aufsatzbände
SBB	Stuttgarter biblische Beiträge
SBL	Society of Biblical Literature
SBLDS	SBL Dissertation Series
SBLMS	SBL Monograph Series
SBLSBS	Society of Biblical Literature Sources for Biblical Study
SBLSP	*Society of Biblical Literature Seminar Papers*
SBLSS	Society of Biblical Literature Symposium Series
SBLTT	Society of Biblical Literature Texts and Translations
SBS	Stuttgarter Bibelstudien
SBT	Studies in Biblical Theology
ScEs	*Science et esprit*

SDQ	Sectarian Documents from Qumran (the documents composed by the members of the Qumran community and therefore excluding the biblical, apocryphal, and pseudepigraphical works found there). The SDQ will be understood to include the following: 1QS (the *Community Rule*), 1QH (the *Thanksgiving Hymns*), 1QM (the *War Scroll*), 1QSa (the *Messianic Rule*), CD (the *Damascus Document*), 4Q180-81, 4Q280, 4Q286-87, 11QMelch, 4QMidEsch, and the Pesharim
SE	*Studia evangelica*
Sem	*Semitica*
SJLA	Studies in Judaism in Late Antiquity
SJT	*Scottish Journal of Theology*
SNTSMS	Society for New Testament Studies Monograph Series
SPCK	Society for the Propagation of Christian Knowledge
SR	*Studies in Religion*
ST	*Studia theologica*
STDJ	*Studies on the Texts of the Desert of Judah*
Str-B	Strack, H., and Billerbeck, P. *Kommentar zum Neuen Testament aus Talmud und Midrasch* (6 vols.; 3d ed.; München: C. H. Beck'sche Verlagsbuchhandlung, 1961)
StudNeot	Studia neotestamentica
SUNT	Studien zur Umwelt des Neuen Testaments
SUNY	State University of New York
SVTP	Studia in Veteris Testamenti pseudepigraphica
TalBab	Babylonian Talmud
TDNT	Kittel, G., and Friedrich, G. (eds.), *Theological Dictionary of the New Testament*
TGl	*Theologie und Glaube*
THKNT	Theologischer Handkommentar zum Neuen Testament
TLZ	*Theologische Literaturzeitung*
TRu	*Theologische Rundschau*
TS	*Theological Studies*
T12P	*Testaments of the Twelve Patriarchs*
TU	Texte und Untersuchungen
TZ	*Theologische Zeitschrift*
VD	*Verbum Domini*
VigChri	*Vigiliae christianae*
VT	*Vetus Testamentum*
WBC	Word Biblical Commentary

Abbreviations

WMANT	*Wissenschaftliche Monographien zum Alten und Neuen Testament*
WUNT	*Wissenschaftliche Untersuchungen zum Neuen Testament*
ZEE	*Zeitschrift für evangelische Ethik*
ZKT	*Zeitschrift für katholische Theologie*
ZNW	*Zeitschrift für die neutestamentliche Wissenschaft*
ZPE	*Zeitschrift für Papyrologie und Epigraphik*
ZTK	*Zeitschrift für Theologie und Kirche (ZThK)*

* * *

All bibliographical references are given in short form and can be found in full form in the Bibliography.

Introduction

A. GENERAL INTRODUCTION

1. The Complexity of the Johannine Tradition and the Task of the Commentator

The Johannine Gospel contains an account of the words and deeds of Jesus as preserved in, and understood by, the Johannine community, a first-century Christian community founded on the testimony of a person it referred to as "the disciple whom Jesus loved," a disciple whom it claimed to be an eyewitness to the ministry of Jesus. The Letters, in turn, attempt to set forth the correct understanding of those words and the correct application of them to the lives of believers.

This Commentary attempts to explain the present text of that Gospel and those three Letters of John for readers who seek to understand the religious meaning of those texts. However, a detailed explanation of these texts asks more of the reader than does a commentary on many other works of the New Testament. The Gospel and Letters of John are generally recognized to be a uniquely profound contribution to the theology of the New Testament. At the same time, they are generally recognized to have had a particularly complex origin. The Gospel in its present form is not the work of a single individual but has gone through a series of three editions at the hands of three different individuals. The identification of which material belongs to which edition has been a perennial problem for interpreters and has inevitably impeded the fullest understanding of the Gospel. The situation is complicated by the need to understand the First Letter of John in relation to the Gospel and to determine the nature of the conflict that divided the community at the time 1 John was written.

Anyone familiar with Johannine scholarship will recognize that past commentaries have attempted to deal with these problems in various ways with greater or lesser success. The present Commentary puts forward a new understanding of these issues. In what follows, I will argue that it is possible to understand the composition of the Gospel and the relation of the Letters to this composition with a clarity that has not been previously achieved. However, to establish which material belongs to each of the editions, to establish the nature of the crisis that divided the community at the time of 1 John, and to determine the relation of that crisis to the writing of the Gospel necessarily involve some detailed argumentation. Such argumentation will be unappealing to those readers who would like to pick up this Commentary and simply find out "what the Gospel means."[1]

Yet the fact remains that, if we are able to identify the material of the various editions with some certainty, we will have made considerable progress toward understanding the Gospel and the Letters in all their richness. To be able to distinguish the material of one edition from that of another means that we must first work to identify the most prominent features of each edition. Scholars in the past have attempted to do this, but it must be said that their attempts have not achieved widespread acceptance. Yet the identification of such features is crucial to the identification of the material. Without these criteria we are faced only with unfounded proposals and subjectivism.

2. The Value of Such Work for the Interpretation of the Gospel

In the past some have questioned the value of attempting to discover the genesis of the Gospel. Some have argued that it simply cannot be done. Others would argue that such an approach breaks up the text and makes reading it too complicated. Still others would say that such an endeavor has no value for preaching the Gospel. In spite of such concerns, it is essential to pursue an understanding of the origin of the Gospel for a variety of reasons.

First, the identification of the three editions of the Gospel is not an arcane academic pursuit. If the Gospel is a result of multiple authorship, interpretation will not be complete until the process of composition has been discovered. It is one of the most basic convictions of biblical scholarship that one cannot approach multilayered texts naively, as if they are the work of a single individual. This is as true of the work of Pauline scholars, who readily recognize that some Letters in their present form represent compilations of previously independent

---

1. While it is impossible to avoid the complexity of the Johannine tradition completely, suggestions will be made later in this Introduction for using the Commentary without engaging all of the details.

material, as it is for experts in the study of the Dead Sea Scrolls who regularly warn against reading documents such as the *Rule of the Community* as if they are single, unified compositions. Yet frustration with identifying the process by which the Gospel of John was composed has led to a considerable neglect of the enterprise in favor of reading the Gospel from the point of view of narrative criticism, a method that can provide helpful insights but that inevitably ignores some central questions regarding the thought of the Gospel.

The fact that the Gospel is a composite cries out for an explanation that takes this development into account. As a composite document, the present Gospel lacks the unity, coherence, and emphasis characteristic of the work of a single author.[2] To pretend that the inconsistencies and contradictions do not exist is to close one's eyes to the nature of the text before us.[3] The human mind seeks order and meaning, and, in the face of a text such as the Gospel of John, there is the inevitable tendency to interpret one text in the light of another so that it will all make sense. However, to do this without recognizing the variety (and hierarchy) of voices within the text is to "harmonize" these viewpoints and results in a view of Johannine theology that is not true to the text itself.

To admit the problems, while acknowledging the inability to explain them, results inevitably in an interpretation in which the voices remain to some extent a cacophony. Identifying the material of the various editions enables the reader to determine the theological orientation of each of the editions with considerable precision. By identifying these various "voices" within the text

---

2. To use such criteria as "unity, coherence, and emphasis" is not to import modern criteria into the discussion of ancient texts anachronistically. Within the Gospel of John one can notice the obvious unity, coherence, and emphasis in a text such as that of 9:6-34. This is an example of an extended text that clearly has unity, coherence, and emphasis, with the sole exception of some details caused by the later insertion of vv. 18-23. Texts such as this show us what an original reader could have expected from the Gospel.

Nevertheless, audiences in the ancient world found acceptable texts that had been edited and reedited, as was the Gospel of John. Just how an ancient audience would approach such composite texts is not certain. It is true that such unevenness is evident in modern texts where the final form of the document, often an official statement, is the result of considerable debate involving various viewpoints. Such complexity sometimes results in the juxtaposition of viewpoints that are not in complete harmony with one another. Knowing the process enables one to understand the text itself better and to know what can and cannot be expected from the text.

3. Even scholars who are reluctant to discuss the Gospel in terms of an editing process are forced to conclude that *some* editing has taken place. For example, R. E. Brown, who became increasingly wary of the ability to determine pre-Gospel traditions with any precision (*Death* 22-23), was forced to conclude that the view of a hierarchical organization in John 21 could be understood only as an addition later than any other part of the Gospel or the Epistles (*Epistles* 111-12). Also, Culpepper, who in many ways set the agenda for a synchronic reading of the Gospel, points out in *Legend*, esp. 72, 84, that all of the passages involving "the disciple whom Jesus loved" are secondary additions to their context.

Introduction

and the sequence of their appearance, we will be able to relate them to one another in such a way that they become a symphony rather than a cacophony.

Second, by being able to understand the composition process, we will be better able to understand Johannine theology. The aspects of Johannine theology that remain unexplained, or not fully explained, are numerous. Why is it that at times the Gospel gives the impression that belief is easy and attained by many, while at other times it gives the impression that this belief is insufficient? How are the titles "Son of God" and "Christ" intended to be understood? Do they represent "high" or "low" Christology? What is the relation between the Christology of the Gospel and that of the First Letter? If the First Letter is written after the Gospel, why is its Christology so much less sophisticated than that of the Gospel? The same could be said of the various presentations of the Spirit within the Gospel. What is the relation between the complex and personal presentation of the Spirit as "Paraclete" in the Farewell Discourses to that of the remainder of the Gospel — and to that of 1 John?

Too often commentators have harmonized texts that, in fact, come from different authors. Assuming that one expression is simply a stylistic variant of another, they read the one in the light of the other. However, if we understand the editing of the Gospel as well as the circumstances that led to that editing, we will be able to recognize more fully the importance of such statements and the fact that, in many cases, these variations in expression are important attempts to specify elements of the tradition that had not been clarified previously. For example, when we understand the circumstances that led to the composition of 1 John and then understand the relation of the third edition of the Gospel to those same circumstances, we can see that references to the Son as "unique" (*monogenēs*) are not casual descriptive epithets but meant to affirm in a precise way the distinctiveness of Jesus ("the Son") over against other "children" (sons/daughters) of God.

Does the Gospel value the role of what could be called sacramental actions? Or is the "flesh" truly "useless," as 6:63 says, and is only the Spirit of importance? What of the fact that the Gospel contains details of narrative, geography, and chronology that are remarkably accurate as well as other details that are unconcerned with a truly historical presentation and anachronistic to the ministry? Because some have read the Gospel without being aware of such problems, they may find a discussion of them irrelevant at first. But for those readers the present Commentary will also serve as an introduction to a clearer understanding of the actual nature of the text of the Gospel and Letters. Ignorance of such problems does not contribute to one's religious faith but hinders an intelligent appropriation of it.

Third, when the material of each of the editions is identified with some certainty, it will be possible to learn many more details about the social history of the

General Introduction

Johannine community. Even now it is apparent that this community underwent crises in its relationships with three distinct sectors of its social world. The community first underwent the trauma of separation from its parent Judaism, a separation brought on by its understanding of Jesus. Later it experienced the pain of a schism within its own ranks over the understanding of its own tradition. Finally, there is evidence that the Johannine community was also concerned, at yet another point in its history, to relate its own existence as well as its traditions to other sectors of early Christianity, notably that segment represented by what is commonly called the Petrine tradition. If we are able to explain in some detail the process of composition of the Gospel and its relation to the Johannine Letters, we will be able to see in greater detail the growth and development of this remarkable community in a variety of contexts in both first-century Judaism and Christianity as well as the theological issues involved in each of these crises.

Fourth, not only does understanding the genesis of the present text make it possible to give a more precise interpretation of the text, but it also makes it possible to distinguish individual stages in the development of Johannine theology in a way that was never before possible.[4] As a result of such increased knowledge, we are able to begin to write a history of the development of that theology. In the course of this Commentary, it will become clear that the Johannine community wrestled in a uniquely profound way with many of the most fundamental and most central issues of Christian theology: the identity of Jesus as divine and as human; his relation to the Father; his relation to the Spirit; the identity and the prerogatives of the believer, and even the identity of the believer in relation to Jesus. At issue in the Johannine history was the question of how salvation is achieved.

3. General Issues regarding the Gospel of John: Its Historicity, Background, Relation to the Synoptics, and the Like

It is standard practice, in commentaries on the Gospel and Letters of John, to discuss in the Introduction a number of overarching features of importance for

---

4. Speaking of attempts to analyze the editorial history of the Gospel, Moloney (*Gospel* 13) has commented: "... the narrative of the Gospel of John must ... not be dissected into its constituent parts to be left, in pieces, on the scholar's table." In the end, I think the reader will agree, the present analysis hardly results in a lifeless dismemberment but rather reveals the remarkable strength, vigor, and growth of the Johannine tradition. The analysis reveals a series of social and theological crises that have produced one of the most (if not the most) profound series of reflections on the meaning of Jesus Christ to emerge within early Christianity.

Note: All commentaries on the Gospel will be referred to simply as *Gospel* in the footnotes. The exact titles are given in the Bibliography.

Introduction

understanding the Gospel and Letters. Because the Gospel is a composite of three editions, these features are best discussed, not with respect to the Gospel as a whole, but in relation to the individual strata of the Gospel. Consequently, such topics as literary genre, religious background, worldview, and the relation of the material to that of the Synoptics will not be discussed until after the analysis of the various editions is complete. Then these questions will be posed and answered in the light of the individual editions of the Gospel and a series of answers will be proposed that will be much more nuanced than would otherwise be possible.

4. The Authorship of the Johannine Literature

The authorship of the Johannine literature is particularly complex. Because it is so complex, I have divided the discussion into more manageable units. In order to guide the reader through these various discussions, and to make as clear as possible where a given topic is presented, I will indicate here where each element of the discussion can be found.

There are three editions of the Gospel, each by a different person. What can be known of these individuals is given in Section 3 of the Analysis of each of the editions in Volume 1.

Because there has been such a constant tradition of attributing the authorship of the Gospel to John the son of Zebedee, a separate discussion needs to be given to both the external and internal evidence for this tradition. This is done in Volume 3, Appendix 7 (John the Son of Zebedee).

Because there are three "Letters" in the Johannine tradition, we must ask the question whether the same individual is the author of all three Letters, and we must also ask about the relation of this author to those of the various editions of the Gospel. This is done in the General Introduction to the Letters. There the discussion centers on internal evidence for authorship.

Because the author of 2 and 3 John identifies himself as "the Elder," we must ask about the use of this title in early Christianity and whether the usage as known elsewhere can be said to apply also to the author of 2 and 3 John. In connection with this, we must examine the statement of Papias about "John the Elder" and whether this figure could be the Elder of 2 and 3 John. These issues are discussed in Volume 3, Appendix 8 (The Elder and the Elders).

Finally, we must ask about the figure of the "disciple whom Jesus loved" (the Beloved Disciple; henceforth BD) as he appears in the third edition of the Gospel. Again, we must learn what can be determined from internal evidence and then ask about the possible relationship of this figure to any of the other figures associated with the authorship: Is the BD John the son of Zebedee? Is he

Papias's John the Elder? Is he the author of the third edition? These issues are discussed in Volume 3, Appendix 9 (The Beloved Disciple).

The authors of the first and second editions are distinct individuals about whom we can know very little and what we do know is gained from an examination of their compositions. There is a single author of the three Johannine Letters. He is the figure identified as "the Elder," a figure who was an eyewitness to the ministry and who lived a long life but did not die as a martyr. While there are some indications that "the Elder" may be "John the Elder" as described by Papias, there are too many uncertainties to reach a firm conclusion on the matter. The Elder of the Letters is the figure identified in the third edition of the Gospel as "the disciple whom Jesus loved." But the Elder (i.e., the Beloved Disciple) is not the author of the third edition, although he is the source of the tradition enshrined in it.

B. THE GREEK TEXT OF THE GOSPEL AND LETTERS

This Commentary is based on an analysis of the critical Greek text of the Gospel and the three Letters.[5] Of all New Testament books, the Gospel of John is the most widely attested and the one attested by the earliest manuscripts. At the present time, in addition to P^{52}, the so-called "Rylands Fragment," which is generally considered the earliest of all New Testament manuscripts,[6] there are twenty-two papyrus manuscripts of the Gospel ranging from the second to the seventh century.[7] Of these, eleven date from the third century or earlier.[8] These papyrus manuscripts represent the earliest witnesses to the text of the Gospel,

---

5. Comments regarding the Greek text of the Letters will be found in the Introduction to that Commentary.

6. Three Johannine papyrus manuscripts are among the oldest of all extant NT manuscripts. P^{52} (also known as "the Rylands Fragment" for the library in Manchester, England, where it is preserved) holds pride of place among all NT manuscripts as the earliest positively identified part of any book of the NT. The fragment, which is written on both sides (and therefore from a codex rather than a scroll), measures about 3.5 × 2.5 inches and contains parts of John 18:31-33, 37-38. It was found in Egypt in 1920 and is generally dated to about A.D. 125. See Roberts, *Fragment*; Aland, *Text*. However, some scholars have questioned this dating and suggest that it comes from the second half of the second century; see, for example, Strecker, *Epistles* xli n. 78. Although less well known, P^{90} (containing John 18:36–19:7) is the second oldest NT manuscript, dating before 200 A.D. See Skeat, *Oxyrhyncus Papyri L*. The extensive and important P^{66} is arguably the third oldest NT manuscript and dates from about A.D. 200 (from about the same time as the two other oldest ([non-Johannine] papyri [$P^{32, 46}$]). For the contents of P^{66} see below. See Martin and Barns, *Papyrus Bodmer II: Supplement*; Aland, "Papyri III."

7. $P^{2, 5, 6, 22, 28, 36, 39, 44, 45, 52, 55, 59, 60, 63, 66, 75, 76, 80, 84, 90, 93, 95}$. See Aland, *Text* 96-102.

8. $P^{5, 22, 28, 45, 52, 66, 75, 80, 90, 95}$. See Aland, *Text* 96-102.

Introduction

and the papyrus testimony to the Gospel is so extensive that, as pointed out by Comfort, "when all the [papyrus] MSS [of the Gospel of John] are compiled together, they cover nearly the entire book, with a great deal of overlap."[9] This is a remarkable state of affairs considering that all of this evidence antedates the great uncials (Sinaiticus, Vaticanus, and Alexandrinus) of the fourth and fifth centuries. Together these papyri and the uncials afford textual critics unique resources for the establishment of the text of the Johannine Gospel.

Even this rich array of early manuscripts does not excuse the scholar from a critical analysis of the relevant manuscripts. Such textual criticism is a fully developed and highly refined science. The most recent fruit of this science is the production of the critical edition of the Greek New Testament represented in Nestle-Aland's *Novum Testamentum Graece* (27th ed.) and in the United Bible Societies' *The Greek New Testament* (4th ed.). This common text (in fact, the N-A and the UBS are in agreement with one another and simply represent separate editions) is the culmination of the most careful scholarship and the best judgment of specialists in the area of textual criticism. In order to avoid excessive repetition, the Nestle^{27} and UBS^4 text will be presumed throughout this Commentary unless stated otherwise.[10]

1. Light on Textual Criticism as a Result of the View Presented in This Commentary

Several well-attested variants that are regarded with suspicion by critics take on new meaning in the light of the editorial process uncovered in this analysis. Although I will call special attention to these texts in the Notes to the Commentary, it will also be helpful to mention them here.

For example, in 4:1 *kyrios* appears in two very early papyrus witnesses (P^{66}, P^{75}), yet is discounted by the UBS committee on the grounds that it is more likely that a scribe would change *Iēsous* to *kyrios* than the reverse. Yet as

---

9. Comfort, "Greek Text." According to the listing given by Comfort, the verses not preserved in the papyri include 14:31; 15:1; 16:5, 8-10; 21:10-11, 14, 16, 21-22. As a result of an independent checking against the listing of contents of the papyri in Aland, *Text* 96-102, I would correct Comfort's list to exclude 16:10 (two letters of which are found in P^{66}) and to include in the list (i.e., no papyrus fragment exists) 20:21 and 21:24-25. There are also lacunae in many verses, esp. in chapters 14–21, as Comfort points out.

The majority of the text is covered by two quite extensive manuscripts, P^{66} and P^{75}. P^{66} contains 1:1–6:11; 6:35–14:26, 29-30; 15:2-26; 16:2-4, 6-7; 16:10–20:20, 22-23; 20:25–21:9. P^{75} contains 1:1–11:45, 48-57; 12:3–13:1, 8-9; 14:8-30; 15:7-8. See Aland, *Text* 100-101.

10. The reader is referred to the extensive list of variants in the Nestle-Aland text, to the evaluative listing in *GNT*^{4}, and to Metzger et al., *Commentary*, for further discussion.

the analysis below will show, *kyrios* as an original reading is quite understandable in light of the editorial process the text has undergone at that point.

In addition, several other well-attested (but otherwise difficult) variants now appear to be not errors, but accurate (albeit awkward) readings created by the editing process. The variants and the places where they occur are: (1) *prōton* in 1:41; (2) *kyrios* in 4:1 (already mentioned); (3) the phrase *eucharistēsantos tou kyriou* in 6:23; (4) the reading Son of "Man" rather than Son of "God" in 9:35; (5) the plural relative pronoun in 11:45 (now accepted by Nestle[27]); (6) the reading *hote* rather than *hoti* in 12:17; and (7) the tense of the subjunctive in 20:31. Of particular significance is (8) the inclusion of the words *ei mē tous podas* in 13:10, a problem that is regularly treated as a manuscript problem but that now can be shown to be, not a manuscript problem at all, but a particularly disruptive instance of editing. All of these will be discussed in more detail in the appropriate Notes.

When these readings are viewed in the light of the Gospel's editorial history, their presence (and the strength of the manuscript evidence) is immediately explainable. This happens with sufficient regularity that it serves as an unexpected confirmation of the theory being put forward.

There is also one prominent text in 1 John where new light is shed on textual matters by the Commentary. That is at 1 John 4:3. This text will be discussed in the Commentary on the Letters in Volume 3.

2. General Notes on the Translation of the Gospel and the Letters

Every translation involves a complex series of choices. It is perhaps appropriate to say something regarding the choices I have made. First, the translation is not intended for public reading. Consequently, "readability" has not been a primary goal. Nor is the translation intended for private reading by someone not generally familiar with the thought and world of the New Testament. Consequently, it will not use periphrastic constructions that make the English more readable but which stray considerably from a literal translation of the Greek. Rather, the translation has been done first with the hope of making the Greek of the Gospel available to the reader who does not know Greek. It is, in this sense, a working translation designed to complement the Commentary.

The Greek of the Johannine Gospel is not elegant. At times fidelity to the original would demand an awkwardness and infelicity that readers would be inclined to attribute to the translator rather than to the original. Nevertheless, some of these infelicities have been deliberately retained. At other times sentences are overly long and involved. In order to be faithful to the text, therefore, it has been necessary to duplicate these less than perfect features.

Introduction

Particularly difficult is the fact that the Gospel makes considerable use of the particles *oun* ("therefore," "then"), *de* ("but," "then"), and *kai* ("and"). Often they do not carry the full force of their literal meaning; many times they are almost untranslatable. To have translated every occurrence would have made the translation hopelessly wooden. As a result they have often been omitted.

The Gospel also makes frequent use of the historical present. I have chosen to translate such instances by the tense appropriate to the context. Finally, the translation is that of a document not written in gender-neutral language. Fidelity to the grammar and thought of the original document requires that the original, gender-specific language be retained. However, where gender-neutral language can be introduced without detriment to the thought of the original and to the wording of the sentence, it will be done.

C. THE FEATURES THAT SUGGEST THAT THE PRESENT GOSPEL HAS UNDERGONE EDITING: THE APORIAS

We must now turn briefly to the datum that, more than any other single feature, reveals the literary character of the Gospel: the so-called "aporias."

The Gospel of John was composed in the second half of the first century of the Christian era. It belongs to a culture and a literary tradition in which multiple layers of authorship in a single document were common. For the readers of the final form of the Gospel, this could not have been unusual. Both the canonical and noncanonical Jewish Scriptures contain many books that indicate multiple layers of editing. The most famous example of this is the Pentateuch with its multiple layers of traditions. Documents with such editing are also evident elsewhere in the New Testament. For example, we know that Matthew and Luke have used and "reedited" Mark as well as using other sources. Even Paul's Letters, in their canonical form, give evidence of being edited combinations of two or more Letters.

The indications that such editing has occurred in the Gospel of John are both numerous and compelling. There are frequent instances of awkward sequence, contrasts in theology, alternations in language, contradictions, and varieties of viewpoint. Together these literary problems are called "aporiai," the plural of a Greek word meaning "blocks" or "obstructions."[11] That is, these are features that prevent a smooth, consistent reading of the material.

One of the most striking examples occurs in the interpretation of the parable of the shepherd in John 10:7-13. Six of the verses are reproduced below

---

11. The Greek singular is *aporia,* and the Greek plural is *aporiai.* The term is often used in the plural Anglicized form as "aporias."

The Aporias

with two typefaces in order to demonstrate the awkwardness of the present text.

> 7 *So Jesus said again, "Amen, amen, I say to you,* **I am the gate for the sheep.** 8 *All who came [before me] were thieves and bandits, but the sheep did not listen to them.*
>
> 9 **"I am the gate. If someone enters through me, that person will be saved and will go in and come out and will find pasture.** 10 *The thief does not come except to steal, slay, and destroy. I came so that they might have life, and have it abundantly.*
>
> 11 *"I am the good shepherd.* **The good shepherd lays down his life for his sheep.** 12 **Someone hired, who is not the shepherd, for whom the sheep are not his own, seeing the wolf coming, leaves the sheep and flees — and the wolf grabs them and scatters them —** 13 **because he is hired and does not have a concern for the sheep.**

In this passage, two images from the parable are developed: Jesus as the gate and Jesus as the shepherd. Yet when this is read in the context of the parable itself, one is struck by the fact that the image of the gate hardly plays a role at all. In the original parable the major element is the contrast between the shepherd who knows the sheep and the thieves who do not. Second, and even more striking, is the relationship between v. 8 and v. 7. After describing himself as the gate in v. 7, Jesus says that all who came before him were thieves and robbers. In the context "all" would logically refer to "gates," but that would be nonsense. Verse 8 pertains to the development of the image of the shepherd, not to that of the gate — yet the mention of Jesus as the shepherd does not appear until v. 11!

Further problems arise in v. 9. This verse ignores the content of v. 8 and returns to and develops the image of the gate. But then v. 10 returns to the notion of thieves and contrasts Jesus as the good shepherd with the thieves. Then, for the first time, v. 11 actually introduces the primary image of Jesus as the shepherd. But the problems are not over, for the shepherd now is interpreted not as calling his sheep but as laying down his life for them. Moreover, the image of the "hireling," who does not care for the sheep and who will run away when the wolf comes, is now introduced, although there was no mention of a such a figure in the original parable.

It is apparent from the way the original parable is developed that the image of the sheep and the shepherd was so meaningful to the Johannine community that it was developed in several ways, each of which had its own valuable lesson. But only one of these was truly the "original" interpretation of the parable! The other interpretations either developed features that were secondary in the original parable (but inconsistent on a literary level with the original interpretation)

Introduction

or added features not present in the original. The theological purpose of each is readily understandable. The literary technique is evident: the text consists of an original interpretation together with two later reinterpretations.

It is passages such as this — and such passages are ubiquitous — which reveal the complexity of the present text of the Gospel. But at the same time such passages demonstrate that it is unrealistic to attempt to treat the text of the Gospel as a simple, unified, and coherent composition emerging from the work of a single hand.

At the same time, not all aporias are equally evident. They range from the obvious to the subtle, from the patent to the ambiguous. The most obvious are those that break the narrative or logical sequence (as we saw above). Nevertheless, at times the text is such that it is difficult to determine whether a given phrase, clause, sentence, or even paragraph is the work of a single author or has been edited.[12] This should not be surprising. We must allow for the possibility that there will be times when the editing has not left *any* immediately discernible traces of awkwardness. The aporias are accidental markers of editing; they are not a code that is to be "broken" or a set of signals to be translated woodenly.

For many modern readers, even more so since the advent of narrative criticism, there has been a tendency to focus on the text as a whole and not to pay significant attention to such features. This is understandable. But the more familiar one is with the text of the Gospel and the more willing one is to hold the overall meaning of a text in suspension (without harmonizing it awkwardly with other parts of the Gospel), the more likely one is to appreciate the full range of evidence that editing has taken place.

D. PAST ATTEMPTS TO DEAL WITH THE APORIAS

In the past, commentators have sought to deal with this unevenness in various ways. Some have commented on the text as if it were unified, either unaware of the various literary disjunctures and inconsistencies or explaining them away as variations that are insignificant. At times this seems to be a result of a naive view of the text. At other times, it is a result of careful scholarly argument for unity. Perhaps the most extensive example of such argument in this regard is that of E. Ruckstuhl.[13]

There are also those who have sought to account for the present text by

---

12. A sufficient number of seams are evident to make an analysis of the Gospel possible and to provide a more focused, specific, and clear interpretation of the Gospel. But in the last analysis we cannot expect mechanical rigidity or consistency in the text that will make all interpretation facile.

13. Ruckstuhl, *Einheit*; also, together with Dschulnigg, *Stilkritik*.

arguing that the original text has been accidentally disarranged. The British scholar J. H. Bernard put forward such a theory early in the twentieth century.[14] The most famous and most extensive theory of this kind was that put forward by Bultmann.[15] It is not uncommon even today for some German scholars to rearrange the order of sections of the Gospel for the purposes of comment, although their proposals are much less extensive than Bultmann's.[16] In general, these proposals have not enjoyed wide acceptance. Perhaps the chief obstacle is the fact that, if such dislocation occurred, it occurred so early that not even the earliest papyri show evidence of a different original order. As will be seen in this Commentary, there appears to be an explanation for such features which, while recognizing the problem, also accounts for the present order of the text.[17]

Other scholars have attempted to deal with the issue by explaining the text in terms of the variety of "traditions" (rather than "sources") which the Gospel enshrines. This approach recognizes the problems put forward by the text but deals with only the more obvious discrepancies. This is the approach taken by, among others, R. E. Brown, Lindars, and Beasley-Murray. This approach recognizes the problem but deals with it only partially in that the issue is not pursued with sufficient specificity or detail.

Still others have recognized the unevenness and inconsistencies and have sought to account for them either through theories of "sources" used by a single Evangelist or as a document which has gone through successive editings.[18] These scholars then comment on the text either in its final form or on each of

14. Bernard (*Gospel* 1:xvi-xxx) discusses the issue and proposes his own view of dislocations.

15. Bultmann, *Gospel*. Bultmann's theory of accidental disarrangement is explained by Smith (*Composition* 116-212), who also provides a copy of the entire text as rearranged.

16. Schnackenburg (*Gospel* 2:1-9) also rearranges the text somewhat, although not as extensively as Bultmann. For example, Schnackenburg reverses the order of chapters 5 and 6 and places 7:15-24 at the end of chapter 5. So also J. Becker, *Evangelium* 1:188, 227.

17. The most famous of the transpositions proposed by scholars is that of chapters 5 and 6, already referred to. However, there is considerable evidence that, in the first edition, the order of the miracles in chapters 5 and 6 was indeed other than that of the present Gospel but that the present order is the deliberate work of the second author — for reasons of "theological" order. Such willingness to transpose material and "violate" the narrative order also becomes a significant indicator that for the second author there was little concern for narrative sequence.

18. The number and complexity of the theories proposed is so extensive that detailed comment on each is not possible. For critique, the reader is referred to the following more extensive discussions of source criticism: Mendner, "Literarkritik" 418-32; Lindars, *Behind* 27-42; Kysar, *Evangelist* 13-54; Richter, "Sogenannten" 280-87; Teeple, *Origin* 30-52; Schmithals, *Johannesevangelium und Johannesbriefe* 100-196; Sloyan, *Saying* 28-49; Smith, *Johannine* 39-61; van Belle, *Signs (passim)*. It is a common observation of reviewers that past works have provided individual insights that are valuable but the overall theories have not been successful (see, e.g., R. E. Brown's review of the theory of Boismard-Lamouille in *CBQ* 40 [1978] 624-28).

Introduction

the sources that have been uncovered. The articles and monographs dealing with this issue are numerous, but here I will call attention to only a few of the most well known.[19]

The first modern scholar to propose that the Gospel had been subjected to successive editings was Wellhausen (1908).[20] He was soon followed by Wendt (1911).[21] In 1936, Hirsch sought to explain the editing in a monograph on the topic.[22] As part of his influential commentary, Bultmann constructed perhaps the most widely known and discussed theory of the century.[23] A German scholar who did not live to complete a study of the entire Gospel but whose insights were often particularly valuable was Richter.[24] In the United States, Fortna put forward a theory regarding the "signs gospel" at the base of the present Gospel[25] and later sought to explain the redactional alterations of that material.[26] The French Do-

---

19. I have focused here on scholars who have provided monographs on the issue. Many commentators (e.g., J. Becker, R. E. Brown, and Schnackenburg) have also provided discussions of the topic as part of their work, but they will not be treated here. See also the surveys referred to in the previous note.

20. Wellhausen, *Evangelium*. Wellhausen provided a very short analysis of the Gospel but was the first to comment on the two sets of terms for religious authorities.

21. Wendt, *Gospel*; idem, *Schichten*. Wendt was the first to notice the shift between "signs" and "works" as terms for miracles. Wendt's goal was to separate out the theological work of the evangelist in order to return to the true historical account of Jesus' ministry.

22. Hirsch, *Evangelium*; idem, *Studien*. Hirsch concluded that the Gospel had gone through two editions and that a redactor was responsible for altering the arrangement set forth by the Evangelist. In his second book, Hirsch helpfully provides the full Greek text of the Gospel, marked to show precisely the material of the Evangelist (E) and the Ecclesiastical Redactor (R).

23. Bultmann, *Gospel*. Bultmann proposed that the Gospel was chiefly the work of an Evangelist, who brought together miracle accounts ("signs source") and discourse material ("discourse source") and joined it with an account of the Passion ("passion source"). However, the primary work was that of the Evangelist himself. After the time of the Evangelist, the Gospel somehow became disarranged and was eventually rearranged by an Ecclesiastical Redactor who also made a number of additions that disrupted the original thought of the Evangelist. The Ecclesiastical Redactor introduced an apocalyptic viewpoint and attempted to make the Gospel more acceptable to the other streams of early Christianity.

24. His work in this regard consisted primarily of a series of articles now collected in Richter, *Studien*. Like Bultmann, Richter saw three strata in the Gospel. In his view, the final editor had an antidocetic purpose rather than an "ecclesiastical" one as proposed by Bultmann.

25. Fortna, *Signs*. Fortna differed from Bultmann in seeing the miracles as part of a narrative including the Passion rather than simply as a compilation of miracles.

26. Fortna, *Predecessor*. In his first work Fortna sought to identify the "Signs Gospel," and in his second he studied the Evangelist's additions to, and modifications of, the Signs Gospel. Thus, Fortna sees the Gospel as consisting of two strata: the Signs Gospel and the work of the Evangelist, with additional, but infrequent, interpolations. Fortna (*Predecessor* 3) concluded that the remainder of the Gospel could not yet be studied since sufficient criteria for the task had not been developed.

Past Attempts to Deal with the Aporias

minican priest, M.-É. Boismard,[27] has produced a massive study of the entire Gospel. Boismard has been particularly helpful in his discussion of criteria for the analysis as well as in his identification of editorial techniques. As is the case with the work of Fortna, in spite of numerous valuable insights Boismard's proposal has not gained widespread recognition as a basis for further development.[28]

Others have acknowledged the presence of the various disjunctures and recognize that these features may represent various editions but have despaired of being able to assign material to various editions in a way that would solve the problem.[29] These persons will then choose to comment on the text in its present form in the belief that the final form of the text "made sense to somebody," and so this form of the text is the proper object for commentary.[30]

As a result of this skepticism with respect to fully understanding the gene-

---

27. Boismard-Lamouille (*Jean* 11) see the Gospel as developing in four stages. The first stage, which Boismard-Lamouille call "Jean 1," was a complete narrative but consisted of only five miracles and did not contain the major discourses of the present Gospel. This document was known to both Luke and Mark (and so within his larger study of the relations of all four Gospels is also called "Document C" [i.e., "Commun"]). This was edited and expanded by "Jean 2-A," who added two miracles known to the Synoptics and the discourses. Later, this same person moved from Palestine to Asia Minor and, confronted by problems there, produced his second edition ("Jean 2-B"). At this time he introduced the schema of the feasts and made Passover the primary focus. He also changed the order of some of the material of his earlier edition. At this stage, the Gospel was influenced by Paul, by Luke (both Gospel and Acts), as well as by the Qumran documents. The similarities of the Qumran documents to the Johannine Letters become evident at this stage also. A third author (Jean 3) then introduced a number of passages that were doublets of material found in earlier editions. He also shifted the order of chapters 5–6 and introduced a future eschatology. He also softened the anti-Jewish tendencies of Jean 2.

28. The complexity of the Boismard-Lamouille theory attempts to account for not only the Gospel's development in itself but in relation to the Synoptic tradition. Yet, in my opinion, the process envisaged by Boismard-Lamouille is needlessly complex and, at the same time, does not recognize many of the consistencies of language and worldview that indicate similarity of origin. I find his analysis of 6:22-59 to be a particularly striking example of these problems.

29. For example, M. de Jonge (*Stranger* viii) comments: "The present author is very skeptical about the possibility of delineating the literary sources in the Fourth Gospel and does not share the optimism displayed by some of his colleagues when they try to distinguish between sources and redaction." Painter (*Quest* 102) comments: "Identifying clues leads to the recognition of the process of composition, but this does not mean that sources and layers of composition can be identified with precision.... We may have to be content with a general hypothesis that cannot be worked out in fine detail." See also Carson, "Source Criticism" 411-29; idem, *Gospel* 41-45.

30. This is the approach taken by Barrett, Carson, Lindars, Beasley-Murray, and others. It is also the approach taken in the main by R. E. Brown, although at times he calls attention to elements whose presence appears to be the result of editing. Even more optimistic is Schnelle (*Evangelium* 26), who sees the present Gospel, not as the result of a more or less accidental work of editing and joining of materials but the direct expression of an imposing literary and theological will.

sis of the present Gospel text, scholars have sought other means of dealing with the aporias. One of the most popular alternatives to the traditional approach is that of narrative criticism. Narrative criticism has been applied not only to the Gospels in general, but to the Gospel of John in particular. This method attempts to read the text from the point of view of the final editor, thus seeking to view the text as a whole as well as avoiding the seemingly fruitless attempt to discover the actual process by which the Gospel was composed. The first to apply such methods in a comprehensive way was Culpepper.[31] In recent years, narrative criticism has flourished as a basis for commentaries on the Gospel as well as for more specialized studies.[32] Although narrative criticism is often spoken of as a single method, in fact it comprises a series of approaches.

A lingering question that is often posed to narrative critics is whether such a method, which was developed from the analysis of modern literature, is fully adequate for the study of texts that are the result of multiple authorship. In addition, as narrative critics would themselves admit, there is the potential danger of giving in to the tendency to harmonize the text, that is, to interpret one instance in the light of the other without respecting sufficiently the distinctions present in the text. Yet the careful reader of the Gospel must be aware that even the best narrative commentary does not fully account for the present state of the text, although it may remain a meaningful interpretation of it.[33]

E. THE CRITERIA USED IN EARLIER ANALYSES

If earlier attempts at understanding the origin and development of the text have failed, this failure does not mean that such understanding cannot be achieved. The major problem has been the development of the proper criteria for identifying the material of the various editions. Scholars who have sought to identify the editing of the Gospels have suggested a variety of ways of determining the nature and extent of the editing. A review of these methods will be helpful both

---

31. Culpepper, *Anatomy*.

32. Among these are the commentaries of Talbert, *Gospel*; Stibbe, *Gospel*. The most extensive to date is the three-volume work of Moloney, *Belief; Signs; Glory*, and also his *Gospel*.

33. For example, attempts to identify the implied reader (i.e., the reader that is mirrored in the text) give conflicting results. The reader is said to be aware of "Jewish traditions, feasts, liturgies" (cf. Moloney, *Belief* 21). The implied reader is also shown to be someone who does not know the meaning of such elementary terms as "Rabbi" (1:38) or "Messiah" (1:41), both of which are translated for the reader. The implied reader is presumed to understand the complicated rabbinic argument of 5:17 and the homiletic format of 6:30-50 but needs to hear that the stone jars at the home in Cana are for "the purification of the Jews" (2:6) and that Passover is a "feast of the Jews" (6:4).

in terms of appreciating the work of past scholars and of demonstrating the way in which the method of the present study both agrees with and differs from these earlier attempts.

1. The Aporias Themselves

While almost all scholars have paid attention to aporias as markers of editing, Fortna has taken this as his fundamental operating principle. This is coupled with Fortna's conviction that the Gospel is composed of only two editions. Because of this, the aporias themselves can be used to indicate changes in authorship; then, in Fortna's words, the two editions "come apart in our hands."[34] One then only needs to determine which of the two bodies of material is the earlier and which the later.[35]

However, there are significant problems with Fortna's approach. First, the presumption that there are only two strata in the Gospel is just that — a presumption. So many scholars have presented arguments and/or intuitive judgments for the existence of three editions that one needs to justify the conviction that there are only two editions. Such a simple division of the material runs the risk of harmonizing material that should be attributed to separate authors. The second problem is more limiting. Fortna himself recognizes that the method he employs cannot be applied beyond the "signs material." As a result, he confines his analysis to the relatively minor additions and modifications of the signs material, recognizing that it is not possible, within the framework of his approach, to analyze the remainder of the Gospel.

2. Changes in Terminology

At the beginning of the twentieth century, two German scholars, Wellhausen and Wendt, called attention to what they saw as indicators of multiple authorship in changes in terminology within the Gospel. Wellhausen called attention to what he saw as two terms for religious authorities. At times the authorities were referred to as "Pharisees," "chief priests," and "rulers," and at other times as "the Jews." However, this observation did not gain wide acceptance. The chief problem with Wellhausen's observation was that it did not take into account

---

34. Fortna discusses his method in *Predecessor* 1-11. The quote is taken from p. 6.

35. This approach is substantially different from that taken by Fortna in his first book, *Signs*, where he laid out three kinds of criteria for identifying material (see *Signs* 15-22). The present author finds that approach much more satisfying and traces much of his interest and inspiration for understanding the literary genesis of John to Fortna's first book.

Introduction

that not all instances of "the Jews" had the same meaning. It is only later, when we recognize the variety of usages of the term, that Wellhausen's insight can be modified and used profitably.

In 1912, Wendt argued for two editions of the Gospel based on the differing terminology for miracles. One author used "signs," while the other used "works." As was the case with Wellhausen, acceptance was not widespread because unless distinctions were made in the various ways these terms were used, they were not helpful as criteria.

3. Doublets

In his commentary of 1966, R. E. Brown, who is generally quite cautious, if not skeptical, about the possibility of identifying editorial work, proposed a generalized theory of the origin of the Gospel. This has been discussed above. At times Brown did attempt to suggest specific groups of material that were the work of later editors. One of the indicators used by Brown was the existence of passages that seem to resemble each other so much that they could be seen as duplicate versions of the same material. He sees the second ("variant") version of the material as the work of the Evangelist but incorporated into the Gospel by a later redactor. These passages do not differ from the remainder of the Gospel in style or vocabulary. Yet they are awkward in their present context and were added by a redactor. Brown lists the following: 6:51-58, parallel to 6:35-50; 3:31-36, parallel to what precedes it; 12:44-50, parallel to what precedes those verses. But the most extensive doublet occurs within the Farewell Discourses, where 16:4-33 duplicates 14:1-31.[36]

Boismard also spoke of "doublets" of material but in a somewhat different sense than Brown.[37] Boismard saw doublets in 6:35-50 and 6:51-58; 7:28-36 and 8:19-22; 11:19-21 and 11:29, 31-32, and called them one of the most important criteria for the study of the composition of the Gospel.

4. *Wiederaufnahme*

In past analyses of the Gospel, scholars have called attention to instances of awkward repetition that seems to frame material inserted by an editor.[38] Boismard, more than any other scholar, has brought this into prominence as a tool

---

36. R. E. Brown, *Gospel* 1:xxxvi-xxxvii.
37. Boismard-Lamouille, *Jean* 13-14.
38. Fortna, *Signs* 78; Robinson/Koester, *Trajectories* 244-45.

for editorial analysis.[39] I have also attempted to draw attention to it in two articles.[40] More will be said about this in the discussion of my own theory in the section that follows.

5. Style

The most controversial of the proposed criteria is that of style. Many scholars would agree that there is a certain distinctiveness to the "style" of the Gospel, yet it has been difficult to describe this style with any precision. Consequently, this argument has been used for and against multiple authorship. Extensive arguments from style intended to demonstrate the literary unity of the Gospel were developed first by Schweizer,[41] then by Ruckstuhl,[42] and then in a revised form by the combined efforts of Ruckstuhl and Dschulnigg.[43] Even more extensive arguments have been developed on the basis of style to prove multiple authorship, most notably those of Boismard.[44] Such indicators of style have ranged in number from thirty-three (Schweizer) to over four hundred (Boismard).

Such arguments have not convinced significant numbers of scholars.[45] First, the definition of style itself is still much disputed. Features that appear in the Johannine literature but not elsewhere in the New Testament may be those of a given person's "style" (idiolect), may be part of the common language of the community (sociolect), or in some cases may simply be called for by the subject matter and therefore not a matter of style at all. Moreover, at times analyses of Johannine "style" include features that have to do with content rather than style strictly so called and are more properly considered "theology."

Second, as Boismard has pointed out, the possibilities of accounting for

---

39. Boismard, "Procédé" 235-42; idem, *Jean* 12-13; idem, *Vie* 16-18.
40. von Wahlde, "Technique" 520-33; idem, *"Wiederaufnahme"* 542-49.
41. Schweizer, *Egō Eimi*.
42. Ruckstuhl, *Einheit*; idem, "Language" 125-48.
43. Ruckstuhl and Dschulnigg, *Stilkritik*.
44. Boismard-Lamouille, *Jean*. Earlier, Teeple (*Origin*) had attempted another theory based on style, focusing on the appearance of arthrous and anarthrous nouns as indicators of that style.
45. Even a more conservative scholar such as Carson, who argues for the unity of the Gospel text and who admittedly is in sympathy with the conclusion proposed by Ruckstuhl/ Dschulnigg, wonders "if questions of source criticism and the uniformity of the style can be adequately handled on so narrow a basis (as that proposed by Ruckstuhl/Dschulnigg)" (review, *JBL* 113, 1 [1994] 152). See also Botha, *Samaritan Woman* 22-25. The analysis of Boismard-Lamouille has been the object of very extensive review, most notably by Neirynck, "Examen Critique" 363-478. See also the extensive comments of Heekerens (*Zeichen-Quelle* 27-32), who also touches on many of the issues raised here.

Introduction

features of style are so complex as to practically defy the possibility of analysis. One could argue that, if two editions are by the same person, the style may be similar or perhaps identical, in spite of the fact that the work contains two editorial levels. If one author modifies another author's work, the resulting passage may contain features of both (which could be identified with relative ease), or it is possible that the second author has retouched the material so thoroughly that he has removed most or all distinctive features of the original author. It is also possible that a later author may imitate the style of an earlier author. In that case, similar or identical features should in actuality be attributed to separate authors.[46]

It is very likely that no scholar will have identified all features of a given author's style, and so a passage written by him may not appear to be so. Among the possibilities of accounting for a given style characteristic as it appears in the final edition of a work that has gone through four editions (as in Boismard's theory) could be that it is (1) a characteristic of the first author; (2) a characteristic of the second author (either a characteristic of his [3] first or [4] second edition or perhaps [5] both); (6) a characteristic of the third author; or (7) the imitation of features of either of the earlier authors (8) (9) (10) by the third author. Nor does any of these possibilities address the common phenomenon of (11) simple variations in language that are a normal part of human speech and writing to avoid monotony and which do not reflect editorial activity at all.[47] Finally, some elements of "style" are so superficial that they could well be introduced into larger bodies of traditional material without altering the character of the original.[48]

---

46. An example of this is the common observation that Luke tends to imitate the style of the Septuagint.

47. For example, in the Gospel an important theological aspect of Jesus' ministry is his repeated reference to his departure. At least three verbs are used for this: *hypagō, aperchomai,* and *poreuomai*. These occur in various texts, particularly in the Farewell Discourses. I would attribute no distinction to the differences in usage other than the desire to introduce variety to prevent a wooden or boring composition.

This alteration, however, is clearly different from the distinctions that are present in the usage of "sign" for miracle in some passages and "work" in others. Each of these is a quasi-technical term and reflects a distinct theological framework. Such differences in usage should not be confused with the prior example. Harmonizing the distinctive terms for "miracle" results in a blurring of the theological perspectives representative of each term as well as of the original context of each.

48. One example of this might well be the ubiquitous *oun* ("therefore"), which appears throughout the Johannine Gospel. While it is distinctive of the Fourth Gospel and seemingly explainable as a characteristic of "style" (and certainly without any theological purpose), it could well have been simply overlaid by the final author.

The same could be true of the expression "Amen, amen, I say to you . . . ," which is also unique to the Gospel of John. It appears twenty-five times (see the Commentary at 1:51) and in material of both the second and third editions.

Part of the difficulty is precisely the need to be as objective as possible in the analysis. Because of the myriad difficulties in both definition and application, a convincing identification of the style of the Johannine Gospel has so far proved elusive. It is apparent from the analysis conducted here that the author of the third edition took over a number of the terms and concepts of earlier editions yet gave them his own theological stamp. Such a process of editing would render useless most of the criteria of style as defined currently by scholars. As a result, there will be no attempt to deal with individual features of style in the course of this Commentary.[49]

6. Synoptic Comparison

Several scholars (e.g., J. Becker, Boismard, and Fortna) have made considerable use of Synoptic comparison as a means of determining editing within the Johannine Gospel.[50] There is considerable danger in this since this presupposes: (1) that the author(s) knew one or another of the Synoptics, and (2) that somehow the writing of the Gospel was affected by that knowledge or by the content of the other Gospels. Yet the fact is that the Gospel of John shows considerable evidence of going its own way.[51] This in itself calls for caution with respect to any use of Synoptic comparison. Secondly, since we are not sure of the attitude of the Johannine authors toward the Synoptics, we cannot presume that they would react in one way rather than another. Finally, we would be better to specify features intrinsic to the Gospel itself for identifying the material of the various strata. By referring only to criteria within the Gospel itself, one works within the document itself and avoids all presuppositions about external relations.

Nevertheless, there seem to be two situations in which some comparison with the Synoptics is useful and methodologically sound. The first is that in the scene of the Crucifixion, there are a few elements that are similar to elements in

---

49. The recent study of the style of the "Signs Source" (Felton and Thatcher, "Stylometry") provides a helpful discussion of the myriad problems confronting style analysis. Style analysis presumes that the blocks selected for analysis are themselves homogeneous, something that cannot be taken for granted. Consequently, the analysis conducted by Felton/Thatcher, which is based on selected one-hundred-word blocks of material, will be valid only if it can be proved that such blocks of material are indeed homogeneous. Of course, this is precisely what they are attempting to determine.

50. In addition, the Catholic University at Leuven holds Synoptic comparison as a basic principle for its study of the sources of the Gospel. See esp. van Belle, "Tradition."

51. For example, J. Becker (*Evangelium* 2:547-48) argues that the original edition of the Gospel could not have had a reference to a hearing before Annas since such a hearing was unknown to the Synoptics. This presupposes that the Synoptics are more historical and seems to presuppose that the three of them constitute three independent sources, which they do not.

the Crucifixion scene in Mark. In Mark, the pattern is extensive enough to indicate that the elements are a theological rewriting of the scene in the light of Psalm 22. The fact that elements with parallels in Psalm 22 also appear in John indicates at least that these parallels go back not to simple memory of the Crucifixion events themselves but to a tradition about the Crucifixion in which the scene was already interpreted in the light of Psalm 22.

The second is that a small number of verses are so intrusive within their context and yet so similar to Synoptic sayings that the conclusion seems unavoidable that at a late stage in the Gospel's composition these verses were added in a deliberate (but uneven) attempt to reflect the Synoptic tradition.[52]

7. Differences in Theology

Numerous studies have pointed to theological motifs as distinguishing various editions of the Gospel. According to Westermann, the Old Testament provides "unequivocal criteria that make it possible to differentiate between biblical and gnostic motifs in the controversy dialogues. At the same time, it becomes clear that the earlier layer of the controversy dialogues agrees in all essentials with the remainder of the Gospel and that the gnostic influence is almost entirely confined to the later layer of the controversy dialogues."[53] Nevertheless, as is frequently pointed out, theological criteria alone are also the most ambiguous (in spite of Westermann's claim) since how one determines what does and does not belong to a particular theological viewpoint is in danger of being simply the subjective judgment of the interpreter.[54]

F. THE APPROACH EMPLOYED IN THIS ANALYSIS

1. Overview

Because the analysis of the Gospel depends so much on the way the analysis is conducted and on the criteria involved, I will provide some extended comments on the method in general and the overall process by which the analysis is

---

52. This phenomenon will be discussed as a criterion in Part 3, Section 3.7 below.
53. Westermann, *Gospel* 69.
54. One example can be given. Westermann sees the "later," gnostic stratum of the Gospel as devaluing the OT (*Gospel* 69). But what Westermann sees as devaluation (cf. the children of Abraham in chapter 8 and the manna of chapter 6) is seen by R. E. Brown as "replacement." Yet for Brown the replacement of these OT figures is not at all a devaluation but a coming to fulfillment in Jesus.

conducted. This discussion will conclude with additional comments on a number of the problematic issues often associated with such an undertaking.

The analysis contained in this study begins, as do almost all other studies, from the presence of aporias in the text. These are used to determine the literary "seams" between the various layers of material within the Gospel. However, the identity of the material is determined by numerous features characteristic of each edition. The features used in the identification of each edition are basically of three types: terminology (linguistic features), narrative orientation (ideological features), and theology (theological features).

We will now turn to a more detailed discussion of the methods and criteria used.

2. Determining Literary Seams

a. Aporias

As was mentioned above, the starting point for this analysis is recognition of the aporias. These various inconsistencies, disjunctures, and breaks in sequence are used to identify the literary seams. These seams indicate where the material from one author ends and another begins. Such aporias are a hallmark of the Gospel of John.[55]

It is the presence of these aporias that first indicated to scholars that the text of the Gospel had been edited, and these aporias remain, in general, the clearest indication of where material of a given edition begins and ends.[56]

It was said above that editing can be identified "in most cases" by the presence of these seams. Such seams are an accidental by-product of editing; they are not deliberate. *But at the same time, it should not be supposed that in all cases editing left such seams.* There are undoubtedly some instances where the editing was generally not disruptive — at least in terms of not interrupting the narrative sequence. The only hint may be that theological concepts appear to be inconsistent with one another — where the pattern present elsewhere would

---

55. Yet at the same time such aporias are hardly unique to John. Reediting of material was a common practice in the ancient world, and although we recognize the fact, we do not fully understand the principles that guided it. It is clear that what was traditional was revered, and although it could be modified, it seems that there was a strong aversion to simply reject what had gone before. How the authors/editors of the Gospel of John actually understood their constraints and their liberties is something that we will begin to understand only when we are able to actually identify the extent and purpose of their work.

56. The earliest, and one of the most thorough, discussions of the aporias was that of Schwartz, "Aporien."

Introduction

lead us not to expect them. In these instances, the danger of being subjective in the analysis increases considerably. Nevertheless, there seem to be few instances where this is indeed the case.

The work is complicated by the fact that there will inevitably be disagreement among scholars about what constitutes an aporia. Some are predisposed to see the entire text as a unity and therefore explain away such problematic features as not really problems at all. In the opinion of many scholars, such a position simply harmonizes the text and does not do it justice. But even among the more critical scholars, there will be disagreement about some features. Awareness of the full extent of the aporias in the Gospel requires not only considerable *sensitivity to the text* but considerable *knowledge of it*. The only means by which we can judge the accuracy of claims of editing in such cases is by first gaining a sense of the consistency of the theological features in the remainder of the Gospel and then comparing the given instance with the "pattern."[57]

Although the presence of aporias is the most common indicator of editing in the Gospel, it is not the only one. Two other indicators of such seams should be mentioned here.

b. Wiederaufnahme

The editorial device known as the "repetitive resumptive" *(Wiederaufnahme)* was referred to above.[58] It is also a valuable tool to identify breaks in sequence caused by editing. After making an insertion, the editor repeats some of the material from before the insertion as a way of attempting to resume the original sequence. This technique was a common one in ancient literature, and numerous instances of it appear throughout the Old and New Testaments. In the Gospel of John it appears in both narrative and discourse. When the technique appears in narrative, the resumption is frequently marked by some variation of "When therefore . . ." *(hōs oun* or *hote oun)*.[59] When it appears in discourse, it frequently takes the form of a simple repetition of the material from before the

---

57. See, for example, at 2:11; 8:26b; 20:23, 31.

58. This technique has been the object of considerable study. See, for example, Hirsch, "Stilkritik" 128-43; Fortna, *Signs*, 31, 41, 53 n. 4, 78, 120; von Wahlde, "Technique" 520-33; idem, *"Wiederaufnahme"* 542-49; Boismard-Lamouille, *Jean* 13a, and specific texts as noted in Boismard's index under "reprise rédactionelle"; Boismard, "Procédé" 235-42; van Dyke Parunak, "Typesetting" 153-68. Neirynck has surveyed the scholarly study of the technique and provided bibliography in "L'Epanalepsis," 303-33. See, most recently, Person, "Reassessment" 239-48.

59. Examples of the repetitive resumptive in narrative include 4:30-40, 43-45, 47bc-49; 6:22-24.

insertion.⁶⁰ However, repetition alone is not an infallible marker of editing; repetition as a mark of literary style is also possible. Nevertheless, when such repetition serves no stylistic function and when it appears together with incongruity (aporias) in the intervening material, its function as an editorial marker becomes clear.

c. Other Resumptive Devices

The phrase *Tauta eipōn*... ("Having said these things...") (along with its number and gender variants *touto* and *eipousa*) appears eleven times in the Gospel: 7:9; 9:6; 11:28, 43; 13:21; 18:1, 38; 20:14, 20, 22; 21:19. Nothing in this brief phrase itself would suggest that it is a redactional marker. It can be used simply for what it appears to be — a participial phrase indicating relationship between actions. However, it often appears in contexts where it creates an abrupt transition between unrelated ideas and as such is almost surely an indicator that an author is either adding material or resuming the sequence of an earlier edition.⁶¹ Wherever it occurs, it calls for scrutiny; but at the same time it will be apparent that not every use in fact functions as an editorial device.⁶² We will discuss these as they appear.

3. Determining the Identity of the Material of the First Two Editions

While the above techniques are the best indicators of literary seams — that is, indicators of where the material of a given edition begins or ends — they do not identify the material itself as belonging to one edition rather than another. The *identification* of the material is accomplished primarily by means of features that can be shown to be characteristic of a given edition. These are of three basic types: characteristic terminology, features of narrative orientation ("ideology"), and differences in theological outlook.⁶³

The first criterion is the recognition that, within the Gospel, there are dif-

---

60. For examples of the "simple" (i.e., without any characteristic markers) repetitive resumptive in discourse, see 6:49-50, 59; 13:10-18.

61. It appears to function as an editorial marker in 7:9; 9:6; 11:28; 13:21; 18:38; 20:14, 22.

62. For example, there is no evidence that it functions as an editorial device in 11:43; 18:1; 20:14; 21:19.

63. Occasionally, other features that aid in the identification of material will be introduced in the analysis of an individual passage. These will be noted in the discussion of the Composition of those passages.

Introduction

ferences in terminology for the same object or concept. These terms are consistent within an edition, but also distinctive of that edition. Thus, as we shall see, the term for religious authorities in the first edition is consistent and distinctive of that edition, but in the second edition another term is used that is consistent within that edition and distinctive of it. The same is true of the terms for miracle, and, as we shall see, for a number of other terms. Although at times the same word will appear in different editions with different meanings, within the same edition the meaning remains the same. Consequently, in order to make use of the terminology as a criterion, one must critically determine the meaning of a term in a given context. Nevertheless, in a majority of cases, this can be done with considerable certainty. As a result the differences in terminology are probably as close to objective criteria as it is possible to get.[64]

The second criterion consists of differences in narrative orientation within the Gospel. Narrative orientation (also referred to at times as "ideology") reflects attitudes, minor elements of narrative presentation, and presuppositions reflected in the writing of a given author.[65] These features differ considerably from edition to edition. For example, in the first edition, the common people feel free to debate and disagree with the religious authorities. Yet in the second edition, the people fear "the Jews" and avoid them and do not dare to disagree with them. These ideological features are elements of the thought that are distinctive of a given edition but not directly theological and therefore not as likely to be the focus of attention of the author.

The third criterion, theological criteria, focuses on differences in the presentation of the religious message of the Gospel. Presumably, in a religious document these features will form the focus of the author's intention. While in the Gospel the theological viewpoint of a given edition necessarily shares much of

---

64. "Objectivity" here is not used in the scientific sense. I have argued that it is necessary to recognize that all of the primary linguistic markers are in fact used with various meanings and that one meaning is characteristic of a given edition, another characteristic of another, and so on. This inevitably calls upon the reader to affirm that such differences in meaning do in fact exist. Inevitably, in human literature some changes in meaning are less clear than others. However, as will be seen in what follows, the basic meaning of each of the terms is clear enough to make firm judgments about the material. Ambiguities may remain regarding some instances. That will provide subject matter for further study.

65. Throughout this Commentary, particularly in those sections where we are speaking of the person responsible for one or other of the three editions of the Gospel, the term "author" will be used rather than "editor," even though the term "editor" would in some ways be more precise. Such a precise use would be liable to create confusion, for then we would have to speak of the *author* of the first edition and the *editors* of the second and third editions. But the *first* editor is then responsible for the *second* edition. The meaning is clearer and the danger of confusion averted if we speak throughout of "the author of the first edition, the author of the second edition, etc."

the theological viewpoint(s) that preceded it, nevertheless it will become clear that there are elements that are distinctive of a given edition and distinguish it from the work of the other authors. It has always been a concern among scholars that the use of theological criteria is likely to be a subjective exercise. However, the fact that the theological features identified here correlate so closely and so consistently with the ideological and the linguistic features makes them less likely to be simply a subjective reading of the text.

In the past the difficulty in establishing proper criteria for analysis of the history of the composition of the Gospel has been the major factor stymieing progress. It is in the discovery and clarification of proper features of each edition that the present study hopes to make one of its primary contributions.

In order to assist the reader to understand and evaluate these criteria more thoroughly, something should be said about the process by which these criteria are determined as well as about the expectations placed upon the results.

a. The Starting Point: Two Editions of the Gospel Identified First by the Presence of Two Sets of Terms for Religious Authorities

The most striking and most extensive set of contrasting features in the Gospel of John is the existence of two distinct sets of terms for religious authorities in the Gospel. The first set is composed of three terms, terms that are specific and historically accurate: *Pharisaioi* ("Pharisees"), *archiereis* ("chief priests"), and *archontes* ("rulers"). These terms are characteristic of what will later be shown to be the first edition of the Gospel.

The second set of terms is the historically anachronistic use of the word *hoi Ioudaioi* ("the Jews") to refer to Jewish religious authorities. As will become clear later, this term for religious authorities is characteristic of the second edition of the Gospel.

While this is not the first study to recognize the presence of distinct sets of terms for religious authorities,[66] it is the first to be able to make them the foundation for the analysis of the complete Gospel. One of the advances of the present study is the recognition that the word *Ioudaioi* has a variety of meanings in the Gospel and that not *all* instances refer to religious authorities. Consequently, it is necessary to identify critically which uses of the term in the Gos-

---

66. The first to make this distinction was Wellhausen, *Evangelium*. Since that time a number of scholars have recognized the presence of the differing terms but have not sufficiently distinguished between the various meanings of the terms. A detailed listing of such scholars will be given in the discussion of these terms in the Analysis of the first edition (Part 1, Section 2.1, 1E-1).

pel refer to the religious authorities because it is only these instances that are characteristic of the second edition of the Gospel.

When these two sets of terms for religious authorities are critically identified, we discover that we are in the presence of features that are distributed so extensively throughout the Gospel that, when coupled with the presence of aporias and other markers of literary seams, they provide a suitable starting point for identifying a core of each of the first two editions.

b. Other Features Occurring Consistently within These Two Bodies of Material

Once initial blocks of material are identified on the basis of the terms for religious authorities, it immediately becomes evident that other features occur consistently within each of these sets of material. For example, within passages where the religious authorities are identified as "Pharisees," chief priests, and rulers, the term for miracle is consistently *sēmeion* ("sign"). On the other hand, in passages where the authorities are identified as "Jews," the word for miracle is *erga* ("works").

As was the case with the terms for religious authorities, this is not the first study to notice these differences in the terminology for miracles.[67] Yet earlier studies tended simply to take all instances of a term together as indicators of a given literary stratum. This study recognizes that, because these terms also do not always have the same meaning within the Gospel, it is important to distinguish critically the various meanings before associating the terms with the various editions. Thus, as we shall see in detail below, the term "work" *(ergon)* has three meanings in the Gospel. However, only one of these is a designation for miracle. Once such distinctions have been made, the consistency of usage within a given edition becomes clear. These distinctions and the grounds for making them will be discussed in detail in the listing of the characteristics in the Analysis of each of the editions.

This process then continues, and other features of the two bodies of material first identified by means of the distinct terms for religious authorities are identified. These features, as was mentioned before, are of three types: other characteristic terminology, ideological traits, and theological traits.

The first edition has a narrative orientation that distinguishes it from that of the second edition. For example, in the first edition the hostility of the "Pharisees, chief priests, and rulers" increases throughout the Gospel, while in the

---

67. Remarkably, Wendt *(Gospel; Schichten)* made this observation both before and after the work of Wellhausen, but neither noticed the correlation between the two sets of terms.

second edition "the Jews" exhibit the same level of intense hostility throughout.[68] Also in the first edition, the common people regularly resist the will or actions of the authorities. Thus, in 7:45-49 the temple police do not arrest Jesus at Tabernacles as they were commanded by "the Pharisees and chief priests"; in 9:24-34 the man born blind debates the identity of Jesus with "the Pharisees." However, in the second edition the opposite is the case. There the people are regularly said to "fear the Jews"; they do not speak openly because of "fear of 'the Jews.'" In the first edition, there are repeated references to the quantity and quality of Jesus' signs; there is none of this in the second edition. While not properly theological, these features of each edition are both consistent within the given edition and also contrast with the presentation in the other edition.

Theological features are easier to recognize. For example, in the first edition there are repeated statements that suggest that there was widespread belief among various segments of society, that this belief was based entirely on signs and that this belief was not difficult to achieve but a ready and regular reaction to the signs. However, in the second edition belief is presented in a more sophisticated and complex manner. Belief is now said to be the result of response to "witnesses." In addition to belief based on the witness of the miracles (now termed "works"), belief was also based on the witness of John, on the witness of the word of Jesus, and on the witness of Scripture. These are radically different approaches to belief, but it is clear how the one could build upon the other.

Another example of theological differences between the two bodies of material is the presentation of Christology. In the first edition, the Christology is entirely within the framework of traditional categories of Jewish expectation. So we hear of a discussion whether Jesus is the Christ, Elijah, or the Prophet, whether he is "from God," and so on. In the second edition, the discussion takes place on an entirely different level and the issue is consistently focused on the claims of Jesus to have God as his own Father and to be making himself equal with God. In the second edition, Jesus is regularly accused of blasphemy, but the issue does not arise in the first edition.

c. Consistency and Contrast in Usage

Thus, when the two sets of material first identified by the distinctive terms for religious authorities are analyzed further, the result is an extensive list of ideo-

---

68. The features listed above are precisely those that contrast with features of other editions. This listing does not address at all the features that the editions hold in common. It is recognized that the second and third editions built on the prior edition(s). There were numerous features that each edition held in common with the one before it. See also below, F.4.a, "Continuity and Discontinuity of Features."

Introduction

logical and theological features that appear consistently within one body of material and not in the other. This *consistency of portrayal in language, ideology, and theology* becomes an important argument for the accuracy of the analysis. But from the point of view of establishing the accuracy of the criteria, it is even more significant that often the features of the first edition *contrast* with parallel features in the second edition.[69] As we saw above, in the first edition the people do not show the same fear of the authorities ("Pharisees," chief priests," and "rulers") as they do in the second edition where the people are regularly said to "fear the Jews."

The fact that the features arrived at by the above process are *consistent* within a given edition and often *contrast* with those of the other edition is a strong indication that the features identified are truly those of different editions.

d. Extending the Process to Other Material of the First and Second Editions

The most basic characteristics (i.e., differences in terminology, especially the terms for religious authorities and for miracles) will not appear in every passage of the Gospel, nor would it be realistic to expect them to do so. However, once additional (i.e., ideological and theological) traits have been identified as characteristic of a given edition, they are able to serve as criteria for extending the analysis to material where the primary linguistic characteristics do not appear. Thus, it is possible to analyze the remainder of the Gospel.[70]

4. Determining the Identity of the Material of the Third Edition

To this point we have spoken of distinguishing two groups of material. Once the characteristics of these two editions are established, it becomes clear that the problem of the genesis of the Gospel has not been completely solved. There remain aporias and distinct theological views, particularly within the body of

---

69. The same will be true of the relation between the second and third edition, and at times between the third and the first.

70. It should also be noted that while the various characteristics and features of the three editions listed in Parts 1, 2, and 3 are the major criteria used for determining the identity of the material, these are not the *only* criteria. A variety of other factors specific to a particular context can be useful in identifying material also. For example, in a passage in which the primary sequence comes from the second edition, the fact that material interrupts that sequence indicates that the secondary material comes from the third edition. These other criteria are not listed, but their value will be evident in the analysis.

The Approach Employed in This Analysis

material identified as belonging to the second edition, but also at times within the material of the earliest version. These are the surest indicators *that* editing has taken place and also *where* the seams of such editing occur.

We also notice, once again, that there are distinctive linguistic, ideological, and theological characteristics in the material set off by these aporias. For example, in the third edition *kyrios* ("Lord") is used in the religious sense to refer to Jesus in spite of the fact that elsewhere in the Gospel it is used in the secular sense to mean "Sir" or "Master," a common, respectful form of address to males. Another example of linguistic characteristics of this edition is the use of "brother" *(adelphos)* to refer to one's coreligionist rather than to one's sibling. However, in the third edition the linguistic markers are not so extensive as to serve as the best foundation for the analysis. Rather, in the third edition it is an ideological characteristic, namely, the introduction of the apocalyptic worldview, that becomes the most extensive feature and therefore the foundational element for the analysis. This viewpoint is able to be defined and identified by the presence of specific features that, once again, appear consistently within a given body of material.

Thus, as was the case with the identification of the other editions, in addition to the linguistic and ideological markers there are extensive theological features that appear consistently within the third edition but are absent from the previous editions. Likewise, these groups of features occur so frequently and overlap with one another so consistently that their use as reliable criteria is assured and allows for extending the analysis to the entire Gospel.[71]

a. Continuity and Discontinuity of Features in the Third Edition

It will be noted that the second edition contrasts first of all with the first edition. This is understandable since the second edition would necessarily have arisen out of the community's need to expand the perspective first expressed within the prior edition of the Gospel. At the same time the community's "new" perspective would have been developed to some extent in dialogue with the theology of the prior version of the community's Gospel.[72] Thus, it would be

---

71. Any theory is best tested against the entire corpus of the literature, and the theory of the origin and development of the Johannine material will be spelled out here for the entire Gospel, and then the Letters will be related to the development in the Gospel. One will then able to judge: (1) whether the criteria do occur consistently; (2) whether the resulting bodies of material can be said to have a consistent theological orientation; and (3) whether these bodies of material make sense as developments of one another and so provide a theory of growth and development that is plausible and consistent with what is known of other sectors of early Christianity.

72. While this is still apparent in the present Gospel, it must be stressed constantly that

Introduction

wrong to think that there is no continuity between the two editions. Rather, there is both continuity and discontinuity. Thus, the second edition takes up the notion of belief that is brought about by "signs" and that was characteristic of the first edition ("continuity"). But at the same time there is discontinuity in the sense that the second edition takes up the beliefs of the first edition of the Gospel but puts them into a larger framework in which belief is understood to come about through the four "witnesses" mentioned above. Moreover, the second edition introduces an overall theological viewpoint that vastly expands the theological horizon of the first edition.

Consequently, from the point of view of methodology, it is particularly important to allow for the inevitable discontinuity but also for continuity when studying the relationship between the various editions. This is particularly true with respect to the relationship between the second and third editions of the Gospel. Many of the features introduced by the second author are taken over by the author of the third edition (e.g., the notion of God as "Father" and Jesus as "Son," much of the distinctive vocabulary of the Gospel such as the notion of the "Spirit," of "eternal life," of "witness," of "glory," etc.).[73] This would be so precisely because there was a continuity of theological tradition in the community between the time of the second and third editions but at the same time disagreement that first led to the composition of 1 John and eventually to the theological clarification contained in the third edition.[74] Consequently, when speaking of features of the second edition, I will generally refer to them as having been *introduced* by the second author rather than as *unique* to his writing. Such features will contrast (sometimes radically) with those of the first edition but will not always contrast in the same way and to the same extent with the third edition.

Contrasts between the second and third editions will be evident where there are changes in terminology, narrative orientation, and/or theology.[75]

To say this another way: in spite of the fact that the third edition takes

---

we do not have the entire text of the first edition and so probably do not know the entire literary/theological context against which the theology of the second edition was developed.

73. This is less evident in the case of the relation between the first and the second editions simply because the first edition is so concerned with a narrative of the ministry and the second is so concerned with theological interpretation.

74. The same type of process is also evident in 1 John, where the author is able to affirm many aspects of the opponents' views but at the same time to say that those views need to be qualified in order to be adequate.

75. But, as was indicated above, the author of the third edition agreed with, and took over, much of the theology of the second edition and sought only to correct or to nuance it in ways that he thought necessary. Thus, the changes by the third author were of two basic types. At times he would add to the material of the second edition, and at other times he would seek to correct or nuance the material of the second edition.

The Approach Employed in This Analysis

over many of the features of the second edition, the third author has a distinct "agenda." This is revealed by the considerable variety of terminology and also by ideological and theological features that distinguish his edition from the first and the second. Just how these are distinct from the presentation in the second edition will be made clear in the Analysis of the Third Edition. In the Analysis of the Second and Third Editions, those features introduced by the author of the second edition and taken over by the author of the third will be distinguished from those features that are unique to a given stratum.

b. Mixing of Terms from Various Strata

It is important to notice that I am calling attention to a *consistency* of usage rather than an *exclusivity* of usage. While in some cases, all instances of a feature are identified with a given edition, it is apparent that in a number of cases, the mixing of characteristics is an actual feature of the third edition. Suggesting that this technique is distinctive of the third edition is not a *deus ex machina* intended to account for a failure of the criteria I have proposed. Rather, such mixing is a consistent feature of the third edition, particularly within the literary seams that mark transitions between bodies of material.

One instance of such mixing is especially striking. As one becomes familiar with the usage in the Gospel, it becomes evident that the third author adopted no distinctive terminology for religious authorities and simply took over the terminology that had appeared in the text most recently. These instances will be pointed out in the analysis of the Composition of individual passages.[76]

As will be seen in what follows, I have proposed a total of twenty-eight "characteristics" and "features" for identifying the material of the first edition, thirty-five characteristics and features for identifying the second edition,[77] and fifty-seven criteria and features for identifying the third.[78] This is an extensive list.

Because the criteria are the building blocks for the identification of the material, it is important that their accuracy and validity be well established. It is

---

76. This is a "feature" of the third edition and is discussed in 3E-22. Among the notable examples is the use of *Ioudaioi* by the third author in John 6:51-58 and the use of *Pharisaioi*, also by the third author, in 8:12. See also the discussion of the Composition of 7:19-20, 25; 12:42.

77. They include features that distinguish the second from the first but that are taken over by the author of the third and also consistent features that appear once the analysis is complete but that are not technically "criteria." The value of these secondary elements will be discussed where they are introduced in the analysis of the second edition (see Part 2, Section 2.5 and 2.6).

78. This includes five elements that distinguish the third edition from the first but that are held in common with the second edition.

Introduction

for this reason that this study is arranged as it is. As will be explained in more detail below, in Volume 1 the criteria are laid out and all instances of each characteristic are gathered together so that the reader is able to examine them and the consistency of their usage. Such an overview is not possible when the features are studied only individually within their context in the Gospel.[79]

In the Commentary in Volume 2, the reader will be able to see how these features appear *in their context within the Gospel* and how they overlap with one another, thus confirming the analysis by the redundancy of the features. At the same time, by means of the "genetic" commentary, the reader is able to see how one edition builds upon and complements the other.

G. SOME QUESTIONS AND CONCERNS ABOUT SUCH AN ANALYSIS

Before moving to a detailed discussion of the features of the three editions, it may be helpful to address several possible questions about editorial analysis in general and this analysis in particular.

1. What Sort of "Coherence" Is to Be Expected in First-Century Texts?

Some might well argue that the analysis proposed here seeks to impose a logical unity and a consistency of thought on the Gospel that should not be expected of first-century texts. Two observations should be made in response to this concern.

First, it is clear that the present order of the Gospel was acceptable to the original community whose Gospel it was and who considered it as normative (and eventually canonical) Scripture. Redacted (or "reedited," or "glossed") documents were not at all uncommon in the first century. Such documents were obviously acceptable to the community.

Secondly, not all documents manifest such a difficult sequence as does the Gospel of John. There is abundant evidence that ancient readers, no less than modern ones, expected and were able to recognize logically coherent sequence as easily as we do. Perhaps the most forceful argument for such a statement is the Gospel itself, where the removal of secondary (or tertiary) material yields a sequence that is "cleaner" and "crisper" — a sequence that is coherent and logical by any modern standard.

---

79. More will be said of this below in the discussion of the organization of the Commentary (see section H below).

Some Questions and Concerns

Although there are many examples, for the present the reader is directed to two passages in the Farewell Discourses where a much more coherent text is achieved by the removal of later editorial additions. The first is 13:33-37. When vv. 34-35 are removed, the resulting sequence is much clearer than with the two verses dealing with the love commandment present.

In v. 33 Jesus announces his departure:

"... yet a little time I am with you. You will seek me, and as I told the Jews, 'Where I am going you are not able to come,' I also tell you now. 34 **A new commandment I give you, that you love one another; as I loved you, you also should love one another.** 35 **By this all will know that you are my disciples, if you have love for one another.**"

36 *Simon Peter said to him, "Master, where are you going?" Jesus responded [to him], "Where I am going, you are not able to follow me now, but you will follow later."*

The present text of the passage is quite awkward when examined closely. Jesus' comment about his departure is followed by his giving the disciples a new commandment, and that is developed in some detail over the course of two verses. But then, without explanation, Simon Peter responds not to the giving of the new commandment (in fact, the material of the new commandment does not come in for any comment at all on the part of Simon Peter and no further on the part of Jesus for the remainder of the chapter) but to Jesus' words about his departure. When the verses about the new commandment are removed, a clear and consistent sequence emerges.

The second passage (14:18-22) is near the first and involves another question by one of the disciples to Jesus. Again the sequence becomes much clearer when the editorial addition (v. 21) is removed.

But we can also observe a passage such as 7:40-52, a passage consisting of twelve verses all of which come from the first edition. The unity and coherence of the text is evident. One could look also at 9:13-17 and 9:24-34 to see other examples of such unified and coherent texts. From examples such as these, it is clear that our expectations of narrative coherence are no different from theirs.

From these two facts, it is appropriate to conclude that we must recognize different sorts of unity in the Gospel. There is what might be called "logical" unity (or "coherence"), that is, the unity and coherence normally expected of narrative. There are instances of this evident in the Gospel even in its present form. There is also the "editorial unity" in which the unity is based on something other than simple narrative sequence. This unity exists on the level of theological intention. At this level, the focus was on the fact that a particular theological view was represented in the text in spite of any narratological awkwardness that might result. The Gospel of John was essentially a theological document. It enshrined what the community understood to be the truth about Jesus and his purpose. It was this unity that overshadowed any mere narrative consistency. To recognize this is not to impose some modern, anachronistic standard on first-century materials.

2. Imitation of the Style of a Previous Author?

In the past scholars were concerned that later editors imitated the style of previous authors and thus made identification of distinctive features impossible. In fact, what we experience in the Gospel is a dialogue with (and sometimes correction of) an earlier viewpoint by a later editor, but it is done within a single tradition. This is hardly "imitation." Given the consistent way such different (and at times contrasting) features appear, it is hard to believe that there was a desire on the part of any of the authors to conceal their point of view or to imitate the features of a prior edition.

The reader should be cautioned that, while the analysis presented here may be successful in identifying much of the material belonging to each edition, it should not be thought that it is therefore possible to isolate and identify all the material of a given edition with equal clarity or certainty. Human language is complex, and characteristics of a given composition do not necessarily occur in every section of a given composition. The characteristics described in the following pages occur throughout a considerable range of material in the Gospel. Where the primary characteristics do not occur, the secondary features often do. At times only a few, more ambiguous features may be evident. Inevitably this will mean that the analysis there may be less certain.

Moreover, it should be obvious (although it has often been overlooked in such studies of the Gospel) that each edition is not totally distinct from the other as if they held nothing in common with one another. The crucial point is to be able to distinguish what is being introduced anew from what is being carried over from the previous edition. This can be, and is, done in the following analysis.

3. Variations in Style by the Same Author?

Much of the theory presented here begins from the conviction that the authors of the three editions used different terms to refer to the same reality. It could well be objected that authors who are at all accomplished will regularly alternate words and phrases simply for variety of expression and to bring a certain richness to their presentation. It could be argued that the approach taken here is therefore too wooden and attempts to make distinctions where the author did not intend them and where differences of wording were simply stylistic.

I would agree that variations in style do exist and should be recognized as such. Yet almost all scholars recognize that "Pharisees, chief priests, and rulers," on the one hand, and "the Jews," on the other, refer to the same group: they both are terms for religious authorities.[80] These differing sets of terms are hardly due to simple variation; they are too radically different. It is difficult to imagine literature in which alternation between such strikingly different terms would be considered "stylistic."

But the strongest argument against the view that these changes are stylistic is the consistency of the association of these terms with *other terms and features* attributed to a given edition coupled with the fact that these terms and features do not appear intermixed with the other set of features.[81] Stylistic variation would, by its very nature, require that they be intermingled "for variety's sake."[82]

4. The Order of the Editions

I have proposed that there were three editions of the Gospel of John. Ultimately the validity of the sequence proposed here will be evident from the full analysis itself. However, it can be said in general that, given the form and extent of the material of each edition, the order proposed is the only reasonable one. The material identified here as coming from the first edition is mainly narrative and gives no indication of being dependent upon or a development of any other material in the Gospel.[83] Likewise, the material of the second edition is under-

---

80. I have pointed out elsewhere (von Wahlde, "'Jews'" 33-60) that from a review of those scholars who in the past have argued that "the Jews" in the Gospel referred to both authorities and common people, these scholars did not present actual evidence for this position but in all cases simply asserted it. The only passages where there is possible evidence that "the Jews" refers to common people is in 6:41, 52, and even those are at best ambiguous. From the analysis presented in the Commentary, the purpose and the nature of the usage in these texts will also become clear.

81. Where such mixture does occur, it is an indication of editing.

82. The reader will note that the features of the edition do not appear primarily within the narrative of the individual miracles (since the content is inherently different for each miracle) but in what is commonly known as the "third element" of the miracle form (i.e., the reaction of the onlookers) — and the other material of that edition.

83. For example, within John 4:1-42, the only reasonable view of the development of the material is that vv. 10-15, 19-24, 31-38 (all 2E) are a development of a basic narrative found in vv. 1-9, 16-18, 25-30, 39 (1E). Moreover, vv. 40-42 are clearly "secondary" to the original narrative

standable only as a modification of other material; its shape and extent indicate that it could not constitute the foundational material of the Gospel. The same is true for the relationship between the material of the third and the second.[84]

The features of the first edition permeate the material to such an extent that it is not possible to separate the body of the miracles from their surrounding narrative structure. For example, the third element of the miracle form, the attestation, is exemplified by stereotyped expressions of belief. That this is so is particularly evident in chapter 5, where the statement of belief has been removed and replaced by material from the second edition. Moreover, other features typical of the first edition occur within the miracle material itself, thus indicating that the author had not simply taken over the texts of the miracles from another source.

5. An Oral Prehistory to the Material of the First Edition?

It will be noticed that the history of the Gospel presented here does not attempt to trace the origin of the material back beyond the first written version to the form of the material in the oral tradition. This was the project of Bultmann and, to a certain extent, Fortna. J. P. Meier also does so in his analysis of the historicity of the material. Meier in fact attempts to discover, where possible, how much of the material goes back to the narrative of the original event.

For a number of reasons, I have not attempted this. First, as is commonly recognized, the "miracle form" consists of three essential elements: (1) a description of the need requiring a miracle; (2) a narrative of the miraculous action; (3) some form of attestation or amazement by the onlookers. Within the Gospel there are a number of instances where this third element is expressed in terms of the stereotyped form of belief characteristic of the first edition.[85] This

---

but identified with the third edition by their particular theological orientation, which both contrasts with the orientation of the second edition and at the same time is consistent with other material of the third edition.

84. The examples of this are so numerous that they would defy summary. However, one particularly clear example may be pointed out here. John 5:26-30 cannot be reasonably conceived of as the base upon which 5:19-25 are built. Likewise, 6:51-58 can only be understood as a development of 6:30-50. Given the nature of the material, it is not reasonable to conceive of the reverse.

85. Fortna (*Predecessor* 58) would attribute this to redactional work on a pre-Johannine level and would not count it as part of the "form" of the miracle. This relies too much on Synoptic form-criticism, which did not contend with a belief subsequent to the performance of the miracle. In the Johannine tradition, the attestation of belief that follows the miracle is a consistent part of the form of the miracle. It is this fact that makes the absence of any statement of belief following 5:1-9 so striking.

indicates that the miracle material in its present form is due to the author of the first edition. In addition, features that I have identified as characteristic of the first edition regularly appear within the material of the miracles themselves. While it could be argued that the characteristics of the first edition within the individual miracles have been added, it is not possible to say that about the stereotyped expression of belief that is part of the miracle form itself. Therefore, it is clear that the miracles *in their present form* cannot be separated from the narrative of the first edition so as to confirm that the miracles came from a separate *written* source as Bultmann claimed. On the basis of our general knowledge of the Gospel and their prehistories, it could be reasonably argued that the material circulated in an *oral* form before being put into writing, but so did much (if not all) of the other traditions found in the Gospels.

In short, there is no evidence that the miracle accounts were written down as isolated narratives and then incorporated by another author into a sequential narrative. Therefore, it seems that we can say with confidence that the first edition is truly the bedrock *of the written tradition* of the Johannine community.

6. Some Interpretive Principles Implied in Reading Such a Text

How did a contemporary reader approach the reading and interpretation of a text that is multilayered in the way the Gospel of John is? We have no contemporary accounts that deal with such issues. But what we do have is evidence that the contemporary reader always considered the written text a derived form of the oral word that, in turn, was always considered primary. Thus, in contrast to modern readers, who assign a primacy to the written word and in cases of dispute have the written word take precedence over the spoken word, the ancient reader did just the reverse. Thus, in the case of the Gospel of John, the author of the third edition (and the community that stood behind him) would have been the one to explain the "real" meaning, for he was the one who put the Gospel in its final form.

But beyond this, there are other principles that are important for interpreting the Gospel.

(1) The "real" Gospel is the Gospel in its canonical form.

There is sometimes talk among scholars about uncovering the "real" Gospel of John, implying that the work of the "final redactor" has interfered with the true meaning of the Gospel. I strongly reject that notion. The only genuine Gospel of John is the one we have now in its canonical form. The first, or the second, edition is not the "real" Gospel. This conviction is based on another, which follows.

(2) The Gospel is primarily a theological document rather than a historical or literary one. While we may use the Gospel as a means of getting back to

Introduction

the events and words of the life of Jesus, the primary purpose of the Gospel was not simply to record those events. Nor was the primary purpose of the Gospel to construct a document intended to be known for its literary merits.[86] The primary purpose of the Gospel was to communicate the community's understanding of Jesus and to lead the reader to belief (cf. 20:30-31).[87]

(3) But once we are ready to understand the Gospel in its final form as a theological document, there remain a number of questions about how the original readers must have interpreted the text. Did the second and third authors simply "allow" the material of the previous edition to remain or does the presence of such material indicate that they affirm its meaning and implications strongly? There are no general answers to this. For example, in the case of references to the baptizing activity of Jesus, it would seem that the later author "allowed" the previous notices to remain but then also "denied" them.

In many cases, the relation between the editions becomes clear from the context. For example, in terms of what gives rise to belief, the miracles (signs) of the first edition are not denied but are located within a wider scheme of belief that includes the witness of John the Baptist, the words of Jesus, and the Scripture in addition to the miracles. Thus, the limited understanding of belief of the first edition is affirmed but taken up into a larger and more sophisticated schema of the bases for belief.

In cases where different views are juxtaposed, both views are intended to be seen as complementary. For example, although the second edition expressed views only of a realized eschatology, the final text of the Gospel affirms a view in which one's possession of eternal life has both a present *and* a future dimension.

In still other places, it seems that the voice of the third edition has final sway. For example, the second edition does not have an apocalyptic worldview. The third edition introduces this along with its other material. This suggests that the community affirms that the apocalyptic worldview is an important part of the community's way of looking at reality.

---

86. This does not mean to deny *a priori* that the author could use various literary devices in order to communicate his theological message. However, the primary focus is on theology, not on creating a work of literature for its own sake. Thus, many of the insights of narrative criticism are valuable and need to be taken seriously where they can be shown to apply. In addition, the Gospel exhibits a number of features that can be understood as dramatic techniques. See Schenke, *Johannesevangelium*, esp. 202-23.

87. There was a conflict within the Johannine tradition over the interpretation of the tradition. We know that some members departed from the community because of their differing interpretation. While their interpretation may have been founded on the second edition of the Gospel, that part of the Johannine community that remained faithful and that was accepted by the larger circle of Christianity had a different interpretation of the material than was preserved in the second edition. It is the view of this second group that is preserved in canonical John. This final version of the Gospel is the version we ultimately seek to understand.

(4) We also have an important external clue about how the tradition was to be interpreted: the First Letter of John. Within the First Epistle, many of the issues that are important to the second and third editions are treated but in a different genre.[88] From the First Epistle, it is clear that the author agrees with many elements of the opponents' interpretation, an interpretation based on the second edition of the Gospel. Yet he argues that his opponents' view alone is not enough but should be complemented by, and at times corrected by, another perspective that he would argue was present "from the beginning." We can also learn something from his way of arguing. In many cases, he does not attempt to explain the nuances between the view of the opponents and the additional perspective he would supply. He simply affirms both! Thus, by such juxtaposition and dual affirmation, he leads his reader to find the "nuanced" truth within these two poles.[89]

7. A Parallel Instance

For some, the difficulties for interpretation presented by a multilayered text may seem sufficient to reject the enterprise altogether and to return to a "simpler age." But the problem here is no different from those problems involved in attempting to do a "theology" of the New Testament. It has long been recognized that the New Testament, as a whole, does not speak with a single voice. This raises questions for the interpreter. Is there a canon within the canon? Is there a voice that is louder than the others? For the New Testament as a whole, this is not an easy question to answer, and attempts have given rise to a variety of theories. However, with respect to the Gospel of John, we have a ready answer: the sequence of the voices is clear within the Gospel and the final voice is the controlling voice.

---

88. In the Gospel, theology is presented within the context of historical events and the nuancing and correcting of ideas is more subtle. In 1 John, these issues are treated in a more analytical form where comparison is more explicit than in the Gospel. Consequently, the differences between the author of 1 John and his opponents often appear in a clearer light in 1 John than they do in the Gospel itself.

89. Thus, for example, those texts that speak of the relation between the Son and the Father in a "subordinationist" way, when seen in the context of the third edition, are complemented by a view that not only sees Jesus' sonship as unique over against that of the believer but also "raises" Jesus' status to that of equality with the Father. This is done through various explanatory expressions as well as by attributing to him the titles "I AM" and "Lord."

Introduction

8. Circularity of Argument?

There is the danger in any analysis such as this that one has, in the end, created a circular argument. By wishing the results, the investigator separates the material according to the theology he superimposes upon the text and so creates what he wishes for. As a guard against this, the present analysis seeks to demonstrate the consistent presence of features that are *not theological* in each of the passages. Every attempt has been made to proceed in as objective a way as possible, beginning from linguistic features and proceeding to ideological and then to theological characteristics. Seldom, if ever, does the identification of a passage rest on the presence of a single feature. The fact that multiple features appear in a given passage (redundancy) is valuable because not only does it confirm the correctness of the analysis of the given passage but at the same time it confirms the general observation that certain features are consistent within a given edition. Such analysis shows that each edition is a web of interrelated linguistic, ideological, and theological features.[90] Where linguistic features are unclear or absent, frequently ideological and/or theological features are more evident.[91]

9. Ambiguity of Features

The shifts in terminology, ideology, and theology in the Johannine literature were not designed as a code. They were not intended as clues by which the "secret" of the Gospel of John could be unlocked. They are simply the terms and viewpoints used by the individual authors to articulate their understanding of what took place in the ministry of Jesus of Nazareth. The inevitable result is that at times texts are unclear; the precise meaning of terms, viewpoint, and theology is ambiguous. This is not a fault of method; it is a fact of the text as a complex, multilayered entity. Because of this, it would be wrong to point to an individual instance of ambiguity as disproving the validity of a given feature. The argument here is first for *patterns* of usage. It is inevitable that at times the pattern is not as clear as it is at others.

It is equally important to remember, as was said above, that not every in-

---

90. From the viewpoint of the finished analysis, each edition can be described as a web of interrelated and intermixed features. However, the generation of the list of characteristic features took place by another process, which is described below. This method was used to ensure that the analysis was sufficiently rigorous from a methodological point of view.

91. Within the discussion of Composition in the Commentary proper, the reference number of the criterion will be given in parentheses in order to facilitate consultation with the discussion of that characteristic in Volume 1.

stance of editing will be marked by an obvious break in narrative sequence. There are instances where it seems that in terms of the overall orientation of an edition, some particular material may be secondary, yet no aporias may be evident, at least in the sense of aporias that interrupt the flow of narrative or discourse. In such instances, the only suggestion of editing may be the inconsistency of thought. Such instances will be perhaps the most ambiguous of all.[92]

Often the presence of other features helps resolve ambiguity that may exist regarding one feature of a given text. But this is not always the case. There are some instances where ambiguity is thoroughgoing. This is a problem for that text, not for the method. It would be wrong to conclude that any anomaly regarding a single text, or even more than one, could be seen to refute the existence of a pattern established by a much larger number of instances.

One of the chief goals of this Commentary is to provide a set of criteria for identifying the various editions of John's Gospel. These criteria are observable and testable phenomena. I argue that each of the three groups of material identified by these criteria exhibits a consistent ideological and theological orientation and that the material of each edition can be explained as a reasonable development of and reaction to the prior editions. If these criteria are not valid, then ultimately the other conclusions will not stand — or if they do, they will do so by accident.

While the view of the Gospel presented here is in many respects new, those familiar with Johannine studies will recognize that many individual features of the Gospel discussed in this Commentary have been noticed by other scholars. The present study is deeply indebted to the insights of those who have written on the Gospel before and seeks to incorporate these observations (often in only a slightly altered form) into a larger framework that is consistent not only theologically but also linguistically and ideologically. Hopefully this deep indebtedness is adequately acknowledged in the notes throughout.

H. THE ORGANIZATION OF THIS VOLUME AND THE PROCESS OF ACQUAINTING ONESELF WITH THE THREE EDITIONS AND WITH THE ROLE OF 1 JOHN

It is possible to take up this Commentary and to study a single passage or chapter without studying the structure of the Gospel as a whole. The Notes will be particularly helpful in understanding the details of the background of individ-

---

92. While many of the features of each edition are readily recognized, the identification of *all* the material of a given edition is considerably more difficult, particularly in those sections where there are fewer features or the features are more ambiguous.

Introduction

ual words, phrases, customs, and history. It is possible to read the Interpretation of the individual passages and learn from the viewpoint presented there.

Yet it must be borne in mind that a casual reading of the Johannine Gospel itself does not readily yield a full appreciation of the Gospel. Without some sense of the overall development of the tradition, it would be difficult to read the interpretation of a single episode or chapter and to fully understand it. The Commentary makes no pretense to be a "handy reference work." The goal here has been to account for the full literary and theological development of the Johannine literature. That development is complex. Consequently, a full understanding will necessarily require some time and effort on the part of the reader.

1. The Translation, the Typeface, and the Summaries

Although all of the commentator's analysis has been done on the critical Greek text, almost all characteristic elements of the editions are identifiable within the English translation that accompanies the Commentary. This is the commentator's original translation and is designed to reflect those features of the Gospel that are characteristic of the individual editions of the Gospel but that are sometimes overlooked or minimized in other translations. The text is given in three typefaces, reflecting which material belongs to which edition. This should help in understanding the analysis as well as the process of growth within the tradition.

More importantly perhaps, the attempt has been made to provide Summaries and Overviews throughout so that the reader will not lose the way through the pages of the Gospel and through the history of this remarkable community. The first of these Summaries is presented below at the end of this Introduction. There the reader will find a summary overview of the history of the Johannine community as it is revealed in its writings. This Summary also contains a first and most general sense of the orientation of each of the editions of the Gospel.

In order to locate the remainder of the Summaries with ease, something should be said of the organization of this first volume. Volume 1 is divided into five "Parts." The first three of these "Parts" discuss the three editions of the Gospel in detail. Part 4 is different from the first three. It discusses the history of the development of Johannine theology as it is evident in eleven areas of the community's thought. Part 5 contains a reference copy of the Gospel with the various editions indicated and a copy of the Letters arranged in sense lines. It also contains the Bibliography.

The first three "Parts" each consist of three "Sections." Section 1 of each Part contains a summary of that edition. These summaries provide a sense of

The Organization of This Volume

the features used as criteria in the Analysis of that edition.[93] For many, this summary will be a sufficient introduction to the criteria.

Section 2 lists and discusses the characteristics of the edition in detail.

Section 3 presents a synthetic view of the edition as it is revealed by the Analysis. This will discuss such issues as the structure of that edition, the major theological emphases, the religious and cultural background of the material in that edition, matters of historical accuracy, relation to the Synoptics, and so on.

2. A Synthetic and a Contextual Approach and Some Suggestions for Beginning

It should be apparent that identifying the characteristics of each of the three editions of the Gospel is not a simple task. That is why a solution has eluded scholars for over a hundred years. In order to assist in clarifying the characteristics and the actual analysis, this Commentary has provided both a synthetic and a contextual discussion of the material.

a. Synthetic Analysis

The synthetic analysis is presented in Volume 1. In this volume, the criteria for the identification of each of the editions are gathered together and each of the texts where these features appear is discussed briefly. The first volume of this Commentary has been lengthened considerably by this discussion. However, such a discussion has an essential role in the overall understanding of the history of the composition of the Gospel. As was discussed above, if a given edition of the Gospel has features that appear consistently within that edition, those features cannot be expected to be equally clear or equally obvious in all cases. However, when the instances are gathered together and examined as a group, the consistencies are able to be observed more closely than would be the case otherwise. Moreover, by studying the texts together, the ambiguities are able to be understood against the background of those instances where the matter is clearer. The end result is that one is able to judge more closely whether a particular feature can indeed be said to be "characteristic" of a given author. This does not remove all ambiguity, but it does provide a context within which a good deal of the ambiguity can be dealt with and resolved.

---

93. All of the pertinent statements in this summary are cross-referenced to the particular criterion where the more detailed discussion is given. Thus, 1E-1 refers to the first criterion for the first edition. In like manner, 2E-2 would refer to the second criterion for the second edition, and so on.

b. Contextual Analysis

The contextual study of the features is done in the Commentary itself. There each feature appears in the actual text of the Gospel. When one examines the actual passages, it becomes clear that often several features appear in the same passage. This redundancy also helps in the confirmation of the analysis. At times, when the presence of one feature is not so clear, the presence of others establishes the primary identification and so aids in determining those that are less clear.

c. How to Begin?

Perhaps *the worst* way of attempting to understand the composition of the Johannine tradition would be simply to begin with the Prologue of the Gospel (1:1-18) and to attempt to work from there through the remainder of the Gospel. The Prologue is based on a hymn in use within the community and was probably affixed to the Gospel near the end of the history of the Gospel's composition. It is hardly typical of the remainder of the Gospel. Nor is 1:19 necessarily the best starting point. The editing at the beginning of the Gospel is complex, and the features are not as clearly present or as neatly distinguished from one another as they are elsewhere.

Although each person must necessarily determine his or her own way into the material, I would suggest that the reader begin by becoming familiar with the development of the tradition in its most general lines. This can be done by reading the Summaries of each of the editions. These are presented in Section 1 of the Analysis of each edition (in Parts 1, 2, and 3 of this volume).

Once the reader has a sense of the character and orientation of the first edition as a whole, it may be useful to turn to some of the passages where characteristics of the first edition are the most obvious. By reading examples of the actual material, one can readily get a sense of how these characteristics actually occur in the first edition.

With a sense of the features and orientation of the first edition, the reader will be able to study the characteristics of the second edition more profitably and will be able to see how these features differ from those of the first edition. Moreover, the theological purpose of the second edition and the way it dialogues with the previous edition will become evident. The reader should then review the material of the second edition throughout, becoming aware of its own characteristic literary and theological features but also its theological unity and the cumulative effect of the considerable changes that are introduced in this edition.

The Organization of This Volume

With this in mind, I would suggest that there are passages in each edition that illustrate certain (but not all) the features of a given edition with particular clarity. Looking at those texts may help the reader to see many of the distinctive features of a given edition with a clarity that would not otherwise be possible. Some particularly distinctive passages from each of the editions are listed below.

In the first edition, the association of the distinctive terms for miracle as well as the easy belief and the stereotyped structure of belief is particularly clear in 2:23. When this is viewed in connection with 3:1-3 (without 2:24-25), the typical reaction of authorities ("Pharisees," "ruler of the Jews") to the "signs" as well as the decidedly low Christology are also evident. A similar pattern appears in 7:31-32. Other passages where the features of the first edition are particularly clear are 7:45-52; 9:13-18, 24-34. The narration of miracles ("signs") in the first edition, together with the stereotyped statement of belief on the part of various groups, is particularly apparent in 4:1-40 (without the verses noted in the discussion of the Composition) and 11:1-45 (again without the verses noted). That the aftermath of the Lazarus miracle (11:47-53) comes from the first edition, except for vv. 51-52, is also particularly evident.

When passages such as these are compared with passages from the second edition such as 2:18-22; 5:9b-18; 10:22-39, the differences in terminology, narrative orientation, and Christology should be immediately apparent. Because the theological outlook of the second edition came into conflict with that of the author of 1 John and that of the third author, there is understandably more editorial retouching within the material of the second edition (by the author of the third edition), and so there tend to be fewer blocks of material from the second edition that remain free of internal editing. Yet, if the reader seeks to compare the outlook of the second/third edition with that of the first, there are numerous other passages where the theological outlook of the second/third editions contrasts strikingly with that of the first. Most apparent among these are the major discourses of 5:19-47; 6:30-58; 8:12-59.

3. 1 John and the Third Edition

After gaining some familiarity with the major features of the first two editions, the reader has a choice. If the reader would like to understand the remaining text of the Gospel (i.e., the third edition), then he/she should proceed to a study of the features of the third edition.

However, an alternate approach might be better. After studying the characteristics of the second edition, the reader might turn to the discussion of the crisis that divided the community at the time of 1 John. In doing this, the reader

Introduction

will notice that the internal community crisis concerns the interpretation of the Gospel precisely as it stood in its second edition. The purpose of 1 John is to argue that the opponents hold to a one-sided understanding of the community's theology and that this view needs to be corrected and nuanced in several ways. This correcting and nuancing is done in the pages of 1 John.

At this point, the reader should return to the Gospel to gain the same sort of overall perspective of the third edition as had been gained earlier regarding the first and second editions. The reader will then be in a position to see firsthand how the material of the third edition attempts to refute the views of the opponents by incorporating material that corrects and nuances the theology of the second edition. Finally, in order to sharpen the understanding of the relation between the third edition and 1 John, the reader should study Volume 1, Section 3:4, 5, 6, and 7, which compare the thought of 1 John with that of the third edition. This will reveal the ways in which the third edition both echoes 1 John and goes beyond it in its theological understanding of Jesus.

The material of the third edition is more difficult to recognize in a brief overview. This is so for two reasons. First, the third author tends to work by "glossing" the earlier texts rather than by composing large blocks of material. Second, the third author does not introduce striking changes in terminology such as were used by the first and second authors. Yet, on closer analysis, it becomes clear that, even though the Gospel as a whole is not apocalyptic, there is much material within the Gospel that is decidedly apocalyptic in orientation (recall that 1 John is obviously and entirely apocalyptic). For example, a review of 3:11-21 reveals numerous apocalyptic elements. The introduction of the apocalyptic view of final judgment and bodily resurrection are also apparent in the addition in 5:26-29. The consistent appearance of the title "Son of Man" in these passages is also an indication of the material's origin. The contrast between the portrayal of the Spirit in the second edition and that in the third (where it is portrayed in dualistic language and where its function is oriented to countering the excesses of the opponents) should also be clear. Several of the secondary interpretations of the parable of the shepherd, while not manifesting apocalyptic categories, reflect the theological interests of the third author. Moreover, the awkwardness of their relation to the original context is readily recognized. A large block of material dealing with the central role of Jesus and with the need for ethics is apparent in 15:4-17.

These are just a few of the features that appear in the third edition. But, hopefully, they can give the reader a sense of the material. *Above all, it should be emphasized that while the characteristics of any given edition are quite clear in some instances, in others they are inevitably less so. This is not necessarily a fault of the analysis but only the reality of the text.*

The Organization of This Volume

4. A Note on the Relation between the Third Edition and 1 John

When one studies the views of the opponents in the First Letter, it becomes clear that those opinions echo the theology of the second edition. Moreover, the views of the author of 1 John are similar in many ways to those of the author of the third edition. Yet it is clear from a detailed comparison of the material of the third edition of the Gospel with that of 1 John that 1 John comes from a period in the history of the community *after* the composition of the second edition of the Gospel but *before* the composition of the third. This fact complicates considerably the analysis of both the Gospel and 1 John. This conclusion has not been arrived at lightly, and I have proposed it only after repeated review of the evidence because this is the only conclusion that makes full sense of the (extensive) evidence.[94]

At the same time, it should be pointed out that the distinctions between the second and third editions of the Gospel have been arrived at *on the basis of features within the Gospel itself and not on the basis of some presumed similarity with 1 John.*

5. Some Final Comments on the Analysis of the Composition in Volume 2

In the Commentary proper, in Volume 2, there will be a discussion of the Composition of each of the passages of the Gospel. Each discussion will point out the aporias in the passage that suggest editing and then point out the characteristics that identify the material as coming from a given edition. In this discussion, I have attempted to cross-reference the particular characteristic being talked about. However, in the discussion of a given passage, occasionally other criteria will be used in addition to those listed in Volume 1. These will be criteria that are simply contextual. For example, it is reasonable to suppose that material that interrupts the sequence of material of the second edition must necessarily come from the later (third) edition rather than the earlier one. Various editorial devices, particularly the "repetitive resumptive" *(Wiederaufnahme),* are also identified by contextual features and cannot be cross-referenced.

Finally, there are some features of the individual editions that are quite striking when viewed in retrospect but which, if constantly cross-referenced, would be cumbersome. For example, as is pointed out in 2E-7, in the second edition almost no concern is expressed regarding the miracles of Jesus. To point

---

94. The features of 1 John and of the third edition of the Gospel that demonstrate this fact are discussed in detail in the Commentary on 1 John in the discussion of the dating of 1 John relative to the third edition of the Gospel (Introduction, E.2).

Introduction

out in each passage from the second edition that there was no attention in that passage to the miracles of Jesus would be very laborious. The same is true of references to God as "Father" (3E-46X), to Jesus as "Son" (3E-47X), and to Jesus as being "sent" (3E-47X). These concepts are introduced in the second edition and taken over by the author of the third. Consequently, they cannot be used in distinguishing between the second and third edition, but they can be very helpful in distinguishing these editions from the first. However, to list every time such terms appear would burden the analysis excessively. As a result, these features, and other like them, will be mentioned only when they are of particular significance in the discussion of the Composition. However, a review of the Summary (Section 1 of Parts 1, 2, and 3 of Vol. 1) and/or the Synthesis (Section 3 of Parts 1, 2, and 3 of Vol. 1) of each edition should enable the reader to appreciate their significance.

I. AN OVERVIEW OF THE HISTORY OF THE JOHANNINE COMMUNITY TOGETHER WITH AN OVERVIEW OF THE DOCUMENTS IT PRODUCED

This Introduction will end with a sketch of the general contours of each of the documents of the Johannine tradition within its historical context. It is intended as an overall guide to the various stages of the literary, theological, and social history of the community as this is reflected in the various editions of the Gospel as well as in the three Letters. It is provided to guide the reader through the detailed analysis that follows. Greater detail and evidence justifying the positions presented here will be found in the Analysis of each edition as well as in the pages of the Commentaries.[95] The references to Papias, Polycarp, and Ignatius are provided in order to situate the events of the Johannine community in relation to their lives and their references to the Johannine literature.

1. The First Edition of the Gospel (A.D. 55-65?)

The first edition of the Gospel was a complete narrative of the ministry of Jesus (including his Passion, Death, and Resurrection) and including all the miracles of the present Gospel. It was structured around the increasing magnitude of the miracles together with the increasing belief of the people but tempered by the increasing hostility of the religious authorities. It was typified linguistically by

---

95. A somewhat longer summary of each edition is also presented in Section 1of, the Analysis of each of the editions in Volume 1.

the use of "Pharisees," "chief priests," and "rulers" as the terms for religious authorities and "signs" as the characteristic term for miracles.

Its Christology was a traditional Jewish one focusing on an identification of Jesus as greater than Moses. Its description of events is generally considered to be historically accurate and to preserve many traditions not found elsewhere in the Gospels.

Its theology was traditionally Jewish, and its community was Jewish Christian. It exhibits a remarkably detailed knowledge of the locale of Jesus' ministry and was probably produced in Judea before the destruction of the Temple in A.D. 70. It focused on the ministry of Jesus in Judea, and probably came from there. No substantial information is available about the identity of its author, although some general features can be deduced from the text. The dating is speculative.[96]

2. Johannine Theology Develops; Conflict with the Synagogue Becomes Critical; and the Second Edition Is Written (A.D. 60-65?)

During the period following the composition of the first edition of the Gospel, the community, by means of continued reflection upon the meaning of Jesus' ministry, developed a much more profound theological understanding of it in the light of the Jewish tradition but an understanding that set the community critically at odds with its parent Judaism. While a major reason for this conflict is undoubtedly the simple failure of the majority of Jews to believe that Jesus was the Messiah, a particularly critical issue was the community's "high" Christology. The result was eventual exclusion from the synagogue and possibly the death of some members.

The second edition is shaped by conflict with fellow Jews in the synagogue. A major feature of its presentation was debate with "official Judaism" (in whatever form the Johannine community experienced this, either as the leaders of the local synagogue or as some more broadly based authority). This official Judaism is designated in the Gospel as "the Jews." These debates concern the claims of Jesus regarding himself. Jesus claims that he is sent by the Father, that he does the work of the Father, and that he is the "Son" of God. "The Jews" regularly accuse Jesus of blasphemy because he calls God his own Father and claims to be equal with God.

A chief element of the theology of this edition is the conviction that Jesus

---

96. The reasons for the dating are given in the discussions of each edition of the Gospel but it must be said that *in all cases the dating is speculative at best!* However, as I indicated above, I would argue that there is strong evidence for the *relative* dating of the stages both in the history of the community and in history of the composition of the Gospel and of 1 John.

heralds the eschatological outpouring of God's Spirit and that those who believe in Jesus would receive this Spirit after his glorification. The prerogatives of the reception of the Spirit (as presented in the Old Testament) mean that the believer would be radically transformed and would now have eternal life in the present, would not undergo judgment, would have direct knowledge of God, and would have no need of ethical directives or religious rituals.

As a result, the acceptance of the claims of Jesus is of central importance because reception of the Spirit depends on this belief. Yet belief is presented as being more broadly based than it was at the time of the first edition. Now such belief comes about not just because of "signs" but because of the various "witnesses" to Jesus: the witness of John the Baptist, the witness of the "works" (the characteristic term for miracles in the second edition), the witness of the Father (through the words of Jesus), and the witness of the Scriptures.

The second author makes use of much material from the first edition but provides a more complex and theologically profound structure around the conception of the basic "witnesses" to Jesus. At the beginning of the Gospel, the disciples are shown to respond positively to these witnesses. However, when these witnesses are presented to "the Jews" in the major discourses of chapters 6–10, "the Jews" do not believe.

The second edition blends the horizon of the ministry with the horizon of the later Johannine community. For example, "the Jews" and others within the public ministry, who regularly misunderstand what Jesus is saying, are considered guilty because, even though the Spirit was not given until after the glorification of Jesus, *within the horizon of the community* the Spirit had already been given and so unbelief was sinful. Likewise, people who, within the ministry, believe in Jesus are cast out of the synagogue because within the horizon of the community such expulsion was already happening.

While the first edition of the Gospel was remarkably accurate historically and reflected detailed knowledge of Jerusalem, Palestine, and Jewish customs, the material of this edition contains a number of elements that are anachronistic to the ministry but that reflect accurately the theology and historical circumstances of the community in the latter third of the first century.

The community is Jewish-Christian and is probably located in Judea. The dating is speculative.

3. An Internal Crisis and the Writing of the Johannine Letters (A.D. 65-70?)

After its traumatic separation from the parent synagogue, the Johannine community experiences yet another crisis. This time the crisis is caused by an internal division over the understanding of its own tradition. The author of 1 John represents one interpretation of the tradition, while his opponents represent another. The opponents base their position on a literal reading of the second edition of the Gospel as it would be understood against the background of the promises regarding the eschatological outpouring of the Spirit and its prerogatives. The result of the conflict is the departure of the opponents from the community, something which has apparently taken place before the writing of 1 John.

In response to this crisis, "the Elder" (an eyewitness to the ministry of Jesus and a founding witness of the Johannine tradition as it is enshrined in the canonical Gospel) writes 1 John as a means of clarifying the tradition. In his tract, he corrects his opponents by presenting an understanding of the tradition that balances the role of Jesus with that of the Spirit, showing the importance and the permanence of both their roles.

The Elder also introduces an apocalyptic worldview as the framework for understanding the events that have transpired and will transpire. Whereas the second edition had found its closest conceptual background and worldview in the canonical Jewish Scriptures, the conceptual background of 1 John is apocalyptic and its language and conceptual framework has particular affinities with the background of the SDQ (Sectarian Documents from Qumran) and the *T12P (Testaments of the Twelve Patriarchs)*.

The author's "tract" on Johannine theology is loosely structured around the themes of "light" and "love," themes that dominate the first and second halves of 1 John respectively.

Sometime later the author, now of sufficiently advanced age that he refers to himself as "the Elder," writes 2 and 3 John to outlying communities dealing with problems arising there. Again, dating is speculative.

4. The Death of the Elder (A.D. 80-90?)

Between the time of the Third Epistle and the third edition of the Gospel, the Elder dies. During this period the Johannine community experiences the need to articulate its relation to the Great Church both in terms of its Gospel tradition and of leadership roles associated with Peter.

5. The Third Edition of the Gospel (A.D. 90-95?)

Soon after the death of the Elder, a final edition of the Gospel is composed. This edition has two purposes. First, it enshrines the understanding of the tradition

Introduction

as put forward in 1 John by the Elder (whom the community now refers to as "the Beloved Disciple"). By incorporating this understanding within the Gospel tradition, the author demonstrates his conviction that this understanding is what they received from Jesus.

Second, the final edition also addresses new issues and makes explicit other beliefs of the community. Among these issues are belief in bodily resurrection of the dead, and the importance of ritual actions such as Baptism, the Eucharist, and forgiveness of sins. The third edition also seeks to clarify the relation between the Johannine Gospel tradition and that of the Synoptics. In addition, it clarifies the relation between the authority and insight of the Johannine community enshrined in the witness of the BD and the leadership of the Great Church symbolized by the person of Peter.

As in 1 John, the worldview of the third edition of the Gospel is apocalyptic, with particular affinities with the language and concepts of the SDQ and the T12P.

The third edition of the Gospel does not destroy the structure of the second edition but rather superimposes a loose thematic arrangement that echoes the structure of 1 John. Thus, the themes of Jesus as "light" and of Jesus as "loving" dominate the accounts of the public ministry and the Passion respectively.

The makeup of the community is not as clear now, and there is evidence that the community may be located in Asia Minor, perhaps Ephesus. Dating of the final edition is speculative, but all three editions are in evidence on the Rylands' Fragment.

An Overview of the History of the Johannine Community

Johannine Literary History	Year	Community and Related History
	50	
1st Edition		
	60	– Birth of Papias – Community expelled from synagogue
2nd Edition		– Death of Peter
	70	– Schism within Johannine Community – Disciple later known as "the Elder" writes 1 John
1 John		
2 and 3 John	80	– 2 and 3 John written by author, who refers to self as "the Elder" – Papias speaks with "John, the Elder" – Death of "the Elder"
	90	
3rd Edition		– Community bestows title of "Beloved Disciple" upon Elder
	100	– *Letter of Polycarp* knows 1 John and 2 John
	110	– Ignatius, who knew the Gospel, dies
	120	
		– P^{32} (Rylands Fragment)
	130	– Papias, who spoke with John the Elder, dies

PART 1

The First Edition of the Gospel

INTRODUCTION

As was pointed out in the Introduction, Parts 1, 2, and 3 of this volume will each consist of three sections.

Section 1 of this Part will consist of an overview of the first edition. This is provided as an orientation to what follows and more particularly will provide a simplified listing of the various features by which the material of the first edition can be identified within the Gospel. Some readers, at least at the outset, will not wish to pursue a detailed analysis of the individual features of the edition. For these persons, this summary will be sufficient. When this Overview is compared with those of the second and third editions, it will be apparent how distinctive the material of each edition is. The extent to which these features can be said to be truly distinct from other similar features in the Gospel and the extent to which these features are truly distributed in the way that is proposed will ultimately establish their appropriateness for identifying the material of the various editions.

Section 2 presents a detailed Analysis of each of the characteristics used in the identification of the material of the first edition. In this detailed discussion, the characteristics will be divided into three categories: terminology, narrative orientation, and theology. Here all instances in the Gospel where the given characteristic appears are gathered together and discussed individually. By doing this, the interested reader is able to pursue the study to the extent and depth desired.

Section 3 describes in a comprehensive way various aspects of the first edition as they are revealed by the Analysis. This will include a discussion of the structure of the first edition, its genre, a survey of its theology, a discussion of the circumstances of the community at the time of the first edition, the historical value of the material, the religious and conceptual background, the relation of the material to the Synoptics, the author, the date of composition, and the locale.

SECTION 1. AN OVERVIEW OF THE FIRST EDITION

The first edition of the Gospel was a narrative of the complete ministry of Jesus, ranging from his encounter with John the Baptist at Bethany beyond the Jordan to his encounter with disciples after his Resurrection (1E-23F). This first Gospel focused on the miracles of Jesus (1E-18) and recounted them in all their power as "signs" that Jesus was truly "from God," that he was the "Messiah" and the "Son of God" — and that he should be believed. In all of this, the categories are those of traditional Jewish expectation (1E-21).

Throughout his ministry Jesus' miracles increase in magnitude, culminating in the raising of Lazarus from the dead (1E-19). This final miracle, performed shortly before the third Passover since the beginning of the ministry, impels the Pharisees and chief priests, who had previously been suspicious and who had even attempted without success to bring Jesus in for questioning, to join with the chief priests to call together a Sanhedrin and to formally condemn Jesus to death. The reason given is that, if Jesus were allowed to continue, the Romans might well come and destroy the Temple and the people (1E-22).

We can identify the material of this edition of the Gospel, first, by the terms it uses for religious authorities ("Pharisees," "chief priests," and "rulers") (1E-1) and, second, by the use of "signs" as the characteristic term for miracles (1E-2). The use of the word "sign" for miracle is significant, for it is the same term that was used in the Jewish Scriptures to describe the miracles of Moses at the Exodus (1E-24F). Also, as was the case with the Mosaic signs, the miracles of Jesus in the first edition are presented as *leading to* belief rather than as actions that *presuppose* belief, as in the Synoptics. Another significant indication of the parallels drawn between Jesus and Moses is the fact that, within the first edition, there is considerable speculation whether Jesus was "the Prophet." This title, which appears only within the first edition and nowhere else in the New Testament, reflects the Jewish hope based on Deut 18:15-18 for a future prophet like Moses who would appear in the last days.

In this edition, the Greek word *Ioudaioi* (which itself has a variety of meanings) is used with the meaning "Judeans," that is, inhabitants of the region of Judea (1E-3). Just as is the case with the terms for religious authorities and the term for miracle, this usage does not appear in the other editions. The first edition is also marked by a consistent but curious pattern of translation of terms between Greek and Hebrew (1E-4). Often, religious terms appear first in Hebrew and then are translated into Greek. At the same time there are a number of

Section 1. An Overview of the First Edition

geographical references that appear first in Greek and then are translated into Hebrew. In this edition, we also notice repeated explanations of Jewish feasts and customs (1E-16). Such explanations are not present in the later editions. What is curious about this process of translating and explaining is that, while they are so prominent in the first edition, not all places or terms are translated and, even more significantly, in the later editions, concepts and terms that are much more complex and specifically Jewish are not explained or translated. This would give the impression that this first edition was composed for an audience significantly different from that of the later editions.

The first edition is also marked by stereotyped formulas of belief in which it is said that "many [of a particular group] came to believe in Jesus because of his signs" (1E-5). Not only is the statement of this belief formulaic in its expression, but it always involves the term "signs" and seems intent to demonstrate that such belief occurred in widely diverse groups of people (i.e., the people of Jerusalem, the Samaritans, the people of Judea, etc.) (1E-8). Also characteristic of belief in the first edition is the way this is often portrayed as occurring in a chain-reaction sequence (1E-6). Thus, one disciple believes in Jesus and gets another who in turn also believes; the Samaritan woman believes and gets others to do the same; the royal official comes to believe along with his entire household; so also the crowd witnesses the raising of Lazarus and then tells others who also believe. None of this appears in later editions.

The first edition focused almost exclusively on the "signs" of Jesus. Because of this, it is not surprising to find that in the first edition there is also repeated reference to the *quantity* and *quality* of Jesus' signs (1E-7). Remarks about the signs constantly use adjectives such as "many" *(polla)*, "so many" *(tosauta)*, "so great" *(toiauta)*, and the like. There are other statements that create the same effect, statements such as that of the crowd in chapter 7 wondering whether the Christ could be expected to perform "more signs" than this man. And in chapter 10 John is contrasted with Jesus in that John performed "no signs." There is nothing like this in the other editions.

We spoke above of the religious authorities. In the first edition, there is a division of opinion about Jesus among the religious authorities (1E-9). This is evident as late as chapter 9, where "the Pharisees" debate among themselves regarding the meaning of Jesus' signs. Yet, as we shall see below, there is not a hint of division regarding Jesus among the authorities of the second edition. In the first edition, there are clear indications that the hostility of the authorities increases throughout his ministry, beginning with the skepticism of 2:24 and culminating in the decision of the Sanhedrin to put Jesus to death (1E-10). But when we compare this with the presentation in the second edition, we see that the hostility toward Jesus is intense from the beginning and that there are repeated attempts to put Jesus to death beginning as early as chapter 5. Thus, the

The First Edition of the Gospel

first edition presents a more historically plausible account of the ministry (1E-23F) with a true narrative development, while the second edition seeks to represent typical resistance to Jesus on the part of official Judaism.

We can also see that the portrayal of the authorities in the two editions is different in other important respects. In the first edition, there is first a narrative report of belief among the people, usually on the basis of signs. This is followed immediately by some reaction on the part of the "Pharisees, chief priests, and/or rulers" (1E-11). It is also evident that people such as the temple police of chapter 7 and the blind man of chapter 9 resist the urgings of the religious authorities, fail to obey their orders, and, in the case of the man born blind of chapter 9, talk back to and even debate with them (1E-13). By the scene of the triumphal entry into Jerusalem, in chapter 12, the Pharisees are actually fearing the reaction of the people and express their own inadequacy in dealing with Jesus (1E-14). In the second edition, there is no such debate. "The Jews" in these texts are monolithic and so intensely hostile throughout that the only reaction on the part of the common people is abject fear of them. So we see the statements that people did not speak "for fear of the Jews"; that people hid "because they were fearing the Jews." Such expressions as these are never associated with the authorities, described as "Pharisees," "chief priests," and "rulers." Related to this is the fact that, in the first edition, the religious authorities fear the Romans. Yet in the second edition, there is no evidence that "the Jews" fear the Romans. Indeed, during the trial of Jesus they seem to intimidate even Pilate.

When the "Pharisees," "chief priests," and "rulers" react to Jesus, they do so almost exclusively on the basis of his signs (1E-12). In the second edition, "the Jews" almost ignore the miracles of Jesus and focus on his claims to equality with the Father, charging him with blasphemy.

In the first edition, the religious authorities as a group are never in dialogue with Jesus (1E-17) but rather talk among themselves and with others. In the second edition, "the Jews" are almost always in dialogue and debate with Jesus. This is their primary narrative role!

There are a number of instances of supernatural knowledge on the part of Jesus in the Gospel as a whole. In the first edition, this supernatural knowledge of Jesus functions as a "sign" to bring about belief (1E-15). But in the second edition, such supernatural knowledge functions only for the reader, to indicate Jesus' superiority to all human plans and intentions.

Theologically, the first edition focuses almost entirely on the miracles of Jesus, as we have seen (1E-18). There is marked attention to details that demonstrate the greatness of the miracles and why they should be a cause of belief (1E-19). Such belief is also presented as an easy affair (1E-20) and something that occurs in various groups within the nation and even among the Samaritans. It is only the "Pharisees," "chief priests," and "rulers" who do not believe! But in the

Section 1. An Overview of the First Edition

second edition, belief is a much more complex affair. In that edition, belief on the basis of miracles continues to be seen as a valid form of belief, but the entire context shifts. Now (1) they are termed "works" (not "signs"), (2) they are described as a "witness" to the identity of Jesus, and (3) the works are one of four "witnesses" to Jesus (alongside the witness of John, the witness of the words of Jesus, and the witness of the Scriptures).

When we look at the Christology of the first edition, it is immediately apparent that the discussion of Jesus' identity is always on the level of "low" Christology (1E-21). We have seen the references to him as "the Prophet." There is also the general discussion whether Jesus is "from God," whether he is Elijah returned, whether he is "the Christ," "the one who is to come," "the Son of God." But even with such titles as "Son of God" it is clear from the context that the title is being used in a traditional sense rather than in the later "Christian" sense. In short, there is not a hint of the "high" Christology that marks the second and third editions.

The structure of the first edition is built around the constantly increasing magnitude of the signs of Jesus, together with the increasingly widespread belief of the people and the increasing hostility of the religious authorities. This structure is still evident from what remains in the Gospel even though the original order of the multiplication and the healing at the Pool of Bethesda has been reversed by the second author. This edition was a true narrative (1E-23F). The narrative moved toward a true climax in the decision of the Sanhedrin and then to arrest, trial, death, and resurrection. We will see that the second edition, unlike the first, regularly ignores all elements of narratology in order to pursue its theological purposes.

When we examine the material of the first edition, we find that it is this material that preserves the numerous traditions unique to the Gospel (1E-25F; 26F). It is, for example, in the first edition that we find the twenty geographical references that are either unique to this Gospel or that contain details mentioned nowhere else in the New Testament. At the same time, scholars now know that all of these details preserve accurate information and reflect a remarkably detailed knowledge of first-century Palestine.

It is in the material of this edition that we find the other information that presents a chronology of the ministry different from that of the Synoptics. It is here that we read of multiple trips to Jerusalem and of the chronology of the Passion that places both the Last Supper and the death of Jesus before the occurrence of Passover. And it is also this chronology that is increasingly being judged to be more accurate than that of the Synoptics.

When the first edition is compared with the second in this respect, it becomes clear once again how different the first is from the second. In the second, we see no concern for historical sequence, almost no concern for locating events with particular geographical locations. Instead we see disruptions of narrative time, we see anachronistic elements such as synagogue exclusion and a general level of theological reflection too advanced to have been articulated during the historical ministry. In the first edition, there is none of the symbolism so typical of the second edition. There is no reference to Jesus as "living bread," or "the good shepherd," or "the gate," or "the true vine," let alone statements by Jesus referring to himself as "the Resurrection and the Life" or "the Way, the Truth, and the Light."

In spite of all that we can know about the first edition, it is also clear that a considerable amount of the first edition has not been preserved. This is evident both from the fact that questions posed in the first edition are regularly answered by material of later editions and also from the fact that many topics central to a full presentation of Jesus are absent. Just how much material was removed is impossible to say. Yet, the theological *lacunae* are striking. There is no mention of the Spirit, no mention of eschatology, no significant teaching of Jesus, no ethical instruction, no significant soteriology. Whether the absence of these topics is due to editing or whether they were never part of the first edition is impossible to say. It is clear from the material of the first edition present in chapter 9 that the first edition did contain extended discussions regarding Jesus. Thus, the first edition may have been considerably longer than would appear from what remains. Although some of the material bears a similarity to the Synoptics, there was no concern at this stage of the tradition to imitate (or to avoid) the material (or the sequence) of the Synoptic Gospels.

We know very little of when the first edition was composed. We do not know the identity of the author or where it was composed. But we do know that the author must have been a Jew with considerable familiarity regarding the ministry of Jesus and with Palestine.

In all, the first edition emerges as document with a very clear identity and profile. Once we become familiar with the features that mark this material, it becomes quite easy to recognize it and to get a clear sense of its overall purpose and orientation. The orientation (and the limits) of this material becomes clearer when the material of this edition is studied in detail, as it will be in Section 2 below. It becomes even more clear when the material of this edition is compared with that of the second and third editions, as will be done in Parts 2 and 3 below.

SECTION 2. THE CRITERIA USED FOR THE IDENTIFICATION OF THE MATERIAL OF THE FIRST EDITION

Section 1 contained an overview of the first edition. That overview attempted to provide a summary of both the features and the theology of that edition. But none of the statements made there was actually argued. Without detailed justification for this view of the material, there will be no genuine foundation for the analysis conducted in the Commentary. As a result, Section 2 will contain a detailed discussion of each of these characteristic features.[1] These are the features that will be used in the Commentary as criteria in identifying the material of the first edition. These will be divided, as was said before, into various categories: (1) characteristic terminology, (2) characteristics of narrative orientation, and (3) theological characteristics. In a large number of cases, several of these features appear in the same passage, thus confirming the Analysis by this redundancy. In addition, many of these features contrast with similar features in the later editions of the Gospel, particularly the second.

In addition to these characteristics, several "features" of the first edition become evident after the primary analysis has been conducted. These are listed with an "F" after them to identify them as such features.

1. Characteristic Terminology

The first category of features deals with the terminology characteristic of the first edition. While the terms themselves are easy to identify, at times the same term can be used with multiple meanings; therefore, it is important to determine which of the meanings is present in a given text.

1E-1. In the first edition, the religious authorities are referred to as "Pharisees" *(Pharisaioi)*, "chief priests" *(archiereis)*, and "rulers" *(archontes)*. This contrasts with the usage of the second edition, where the expression "the Jews" *(Ioudaioi)* is used in the more generalized (and uniquely Johannine) sense to refer to religious authorities (2E-1).[2]

---

1. Many of the characteristics listed here are those first developed in my *Earliest Version*. However, the number of criteria has been increased and the analysis extended considerably.

2. In the past, scholars have called attention to various aspects of this alternation in terms. Wellhausen *(Evangelium)* was the first to propose that the two sets of terms were from different authors. He was followed by Spitta, *Johannes-Evangelium* 202-3; White, *Identity*; von

The First Edition of the Gospel

The term "Pharisees" *(Pharisaioi)* occurs nineteen times in the Gospel excluding its appearance in the pericope of the woman taken in adultery: 1:24; 3:1; 4:1; 7:32 (twice), 45, 47, 48; 8:13; 9:13, 15, 16, 40; 11:46, 47, 57; 12:19, 42; 18:3. The term "chief priests" *(archiereis)* (in the plural rather than the singular)[3] occurs ten times: 7:32, 45; 11:47, 57; 12:10; 18:3, 35; 19:6, 15, 21. The term "rulers" *(archontes)* occurs four times in the sense of religious authorities: 3:1; 7:26, 48; 12:42.[4]

These three terms are often intermixed with one another. For example, "Pharisees" occurs with "rulers" three times (3:1; 7:48; and 12:42) and with "chief priests" five times (7:32, 45; 11:47, 57; and 18:3). The intermixing of these terms indicates that they constitute *one interrelated set* of terms to refer to Jewish religious authorities.

In the Gospel as a whole, another term is also used to refer to religious authorities: "the Jews" *(hoi Ioudaioi).*[5] These two sets of terms constitute distinct frames of reference with respect to religious authorities and are not integrated with one another. This can be confirmed by three features in the distribution of the terms within the Gospel.

First, the terms for religious authorities typical of the first edition never appear intermixed with the term "the Jews" in the sense of religious authorities. There are three passages that would seem to be exceptions to this and should be addressed more closely. For example, in 1:19-28, we see "Jews from Jerusalem" and "priests and Levites" in 1:19 and "Pharisees" in 1:24. Certainly "Jews" in 1:19 does not refer to a group of religious authorities (the authorities are referred to

---

Wahlde, "Terms"; idem, *Earliest Version* 31-36; J. Becker, *Evangelium;* Ashton, "Identity" 40-75, cf. esp. 62 ("There is the general thesis that in the great majority of instances commonly accepted as 'typical' the term *Ioudaioi* occurs in passages that suggest that the rift between Christians and Jews is either imminent or has already taken place.... The Pharisees passages, or at any rate the most important of them, reflect an earlier stage in the history of the Johannine community, when real debate with the leaders of the parent community was still possible and still in fact going on").

On the other hand, Hirsch *(Studien* 68-69, passim) attributes "Pharisees" and "chief priests" sometimes to the first edition and sometimes to the second (final) edition. Bultmann *(Gospel* 279 n. 1 and elsewhere) says that the "opponents are referred to indifferently as *Ioudaioi* . . . or *Pharisaioi."* Fortna *(Predecessor)* also attributes both sets of terms to the Evangelist. J. Becker *(Evangelium* 2:561) struggles with the alternation and concludes that the second author uses both sets of terms. Boismard-Lamouille *(Jean)* attributes both to the same author.

3. In the analysis, only the plural is significant since it refers to a *group*, and it is the terms for groups of authorities that are being contrasted.

4. This does not include the use of "ruler" in the phrase "ruler of this world" (e.g., 14:30; 16:11) since it does not refer to religious authorities and since it refers to a specific individual (Satan). In fact, this latter phrase is typical of the apocalyptic worldview and characteristic of the third edition (see 3E-14).

5. Although the use of this term will be discussed in detail in 1E-3 and 2E-1, the conclusions of those discussions are presumed here.

Section 2. The Criteria Used for the First Edition

as "priests and Levites" in 1:19 and "Pharisees" in 1:24). But the usage is still difficult because nowhere else in the Gospel do we hear of Judeans sending authorities. The closest parallel is in 11:45, where some Judeans report to the Pharisees. But this is hardly a perfect parallel. Nevertheless, the most likely meaning for the term here is "Judeans" since the group is certainly not a group of authorities.[6] A second instance appears in 3:1, where the phrase "ruler of the Jews" (*archōn tōn Ioudaiōn*) appears. But in this case, the word "Jews" is not used in the hostile sense, typical of the second edition, referring to religious authorities, but to the nationality of the "rulers." It thus exemplifies the third of the meanings associated with "the Jews."

Second, there are instances where blocks of material containing the two sets of terms are juxtaposed and at first appear to be the work of the same author. In every case, we find aporias of various sorts indicating the presence of literary seams between the two bodies of material. In 7:31-36, the term "Pharisees" appears (7:32), and also "the Jews" (7:35). However, when they are examined closely, it becomes evident that vv. 33-36 represent material from the second edition that has been used to develop and comment on vv. 31-32, which come from the first edition.[7] A second example is found in 8:12-59, where "Pharisees" occurs in 8:12 and "the Jews" occurs in the remainder of the chapter. Again there are aporias that distinguish 8:12 from the material that follows. A third instance of juxtaposition is 9:13-41, where "Pharisees" appears in 9:13, 15, and 16 and "the Jews" appears in 9:18, 22 (twice).[8] But once again several striking aporias appear, which indicate that 9:18-22 come from the second edition and have been inserted into the surrounding material that comes from the first edition.

The third (and the most remarkable) indication that the two sets of terms are the work of different authors is found in two passages where material originally narrated in the first edition is referred to by the author of the second edition. In his references to the first edition, the author of the second edition *substitutes his own terminology* for authorities (i.e., "the Jews") for the terminology of the first edition ("Pharisees," "chief priests"), thus showing his consistency in the use of such terminology. The remarkable consistency demonstrated by this phenomenon indicates beyond a doubt that the two sets of terms are intended to be distinct and separate.

---

6. Throughout the Analysis of the three editions, the reader will be alerted to texts that require particular discussion. At times, the synthetic view presented here may be of more help; at other times, the perspective of the specific context may be of greater help.

7. There will be further discussion of the passage in the Composition section of the Commentary.

8. Although the term "Pharisees" appears in v. 40, it is involved in a "mixing" of features typical of the third edition. See the further discussion in 3E-21.

The First Edition of the Gospel

11:47-50; 18:3//18:12-14

In 18:12-14, the author of the second edition says:

> So together the cohort and the tribune and the attendants **of the Jews** arrested Jesus, bound him, and led him to Annas first. For he was the father-in-law of Caiaphas, who was the high priest that year. It was Caiaphas who counseled **the Jews** that it was beneficial that one person die for the people.

This passage refers to two earlier passages originally narrated in the first edition. The first of these texts is 18:3:

> So Judas, taking the cohort and the attendants **of the Pharisees and chief priests**, came there with lanterns, torches, and weapons.

The second of the original texts is 11:47-50, where Caiaphas addresses the Sanhedrin convened by "the chief priests and Pharisees":

> So **the chief priests and the Pharisees** convened the Sanhedrin and said, "What are we to do because this man performs many signs? If we allow him thus, everyone will believe in him, and the Romans will come and will destroy our Temple and our people. One of them, **Caiaphas, the chief priest for that year, said to them**, 'You know nothing! Nor do you realize that it is beneficial for us that one person die for the people lest the entire people be destroyed.'"

This substitution of terminology by the author of the second edition is quite consistent and provides a third type of confirmation that the various terms do not constitute a single integrated frame of reference for religious authorities.

4:1-3//7:1

There is another set of instances in which we see the authors of the first and second editions describe *different but similar* actions, again using their own distinctive terminology. In each case the authors describe Jesus' avoidance of Judea and his retreat to Galilee because of the hostility of the religious authorities. The fact that the actions are almost identical shows all the more clearly the distinctive terminology in each.

In 4:1, we read:

Section 2. The Criteria Used for the First Edition

"When therefore the Lord learned that **the Pharisees** had heard that he was baptizing and making more disciples than John, . . . he departed from Judean territory and returned again to Galilee."[9]

In 7:1, we read:

And later Jesus moved about in Galilee. He did not want to move about in Judea because **the Jews** *were seeking to kill him.*

In both instances we hear of Jesus retreating to Galilee because of the hostility of the religious authorities. In the first passage, which comes from the earliest version of the Gospel, the religious authorities are referred to as "Pharisees." In 7:1, which comes from the second edition, the authorities are referred to as "the Jews."

Thus, in all, we find three types of *intrinsic* evidence that these two sets of terms constitute separate frames of reference. Moreover, we will notice two other features of these terms that confirm the foregoing conclusions. First, the terms ("Pharisees," "chief priests," and "rulers") are concrete and represent the ordinary terms in use during the first century, terms that are found regularly in contemporary literature.[10] The more generalized use of "the Jews" in the second edition is not the ordinary terminology for referring to religious authorities but groups all parties together and appears to be a monolithic group opposed to the claims of Jesus (and the Johannine community).[11]

Finally, there is important additional evidence that confirms that these two sets of terms come from separate authors. When material associated with either of these two sets of terms is examined more closely, many other features are discovered that are not only *consistently associated* with the same set of terms but that *regularly contrast* with similar features in the other body of material.[12] The combination of the consistency and contrast of these sets of terms

---

9. The first four words of v. 1 are a later modification, as is v. 2 (which is omitted from the text above). Details are given in the discussion of Composition in the Commentary.

10. It was once thought that the combination of the term "Pharisees" with "chief priests" was inaccurate historically. However this is not the case. See the detailed discussion below in the Synthesis of the First Edition (Part 1, Section 3.6.d).

11. At the same time, this distinctive usage can be explained within the historical context of the second edition, as we shall see later.

12. In the past, scholars have noticed differences in the use of these terms for religious authorities. However, the use of them as criteria for determining the origin of the Gospel failed because scholars had not recognized that one cannot simply attribute all instances of the *word* to the same author but only *those instances that have the same meaning*. As we will see below, scholars have gradually come to recognize the need for such distinctions, not only in the use of *Ioudaioi* but also in the use of terms such as *sēmeion* and *ergon*. When those distinctions in

The First Edition of the Gospel

with so many other features provides an amount of evidence that indicates conclusively the existence of two distinct bodies of material in the Gospel that are the work of separate authors.[13] It is to these other features, features that appear *consistently* within the first edition and that in many cases *contrast* with features in later editions, that we now turn.

1E-2. In the first edition, Jesus' miracles are referred to as "signs" *(sēmeia)*. **In the second edition, they are referred to as "works"** *(erga)* **(2E-2). In the third edition, the term is "signs and wonders"** *(sēmeia kai terata)* **(3E-56F).**

The word "sign(s)" *(sēmeia)* appears seventeen times in the Gospel: 2:11, 18, 23; 3:2; 4:48, 54; 6:2, 14, 26, 30; 7:31; 9:16; 10:41; 11:47; 12:18, 37; 20:30. It is one of the most distinctive elements of the Johannine vocabulary. It has been the subject of immense study, yet some disagreement remains regarding its meaning.[14] This analysis will help clarify that meaning.

The first observation regarding the use of "signs" in the Gospel is that it is one of two terms used for miracle. The other term is "works" *(erga)*, which, as we shall see below, is characteristic of the second edition. Secondly, it is clear that "signs" consistently appears in material where the religious authorities are referred to as "Pharisees," "chief priests," and "rulers" *(Pharisaioi, archiereis, archontes)*.[15] Thus, in 2:23[16] and 3:2, the term "signs" appears; in 3:1-2, Nicodemus is described

---

meaning are combined with the differences in terminology, the consistency of usage of terms *with the same meaning* emerges quite clearly.

This would argue against the critique of Painter (*Quest* 108-10), who, in his discussion of my earlier book *The Earliest Version*, comments: "To maintain his position von Wahlde interprets 'Jews' in different senses." See also his comments on the various uses of "signs" and "works" (108-9). This is not a fault but a virtue. Not only are these distinctions supported by the evidence of the Gospel but also by the conclusions of other scholars who do so without any desire to attribute them to different authors.

13. The same will be true *mutatis mutandis* for the material of the third edition.

14. Wendt (*Gospel* and *Schichten*) made this a primary criterion of his analysis of the strata in the Gospel. However, Wendt did not distinguish which uses of the term were typical of a given author. Boismard-Lamouille, on the other hand, finds the term "signs" in three of his strata (*Jean* 505). Perhaps the only modern scholar not to attribute the term "signs" to the earliest stratum of the Gospel is Schnelle (*Antidocetic* 148), who takes a view exactly opposite of the usual one, arguing that all instances except 2:18; 6:30 are redactional (144-48, 162-63). For extensive bibliography on "signs" and "works," see van Belle, *Signs Source* 379-404.

15. I have deliberately used the word "consistently" rather than "exclusively." It will be argued in the presentation of the characteristics of the third edition that at times the author of that edition took over terminology from earlier editions and in so doing destroyed some of the consistency of the earlier usage. Yet, as will be shown, these instances of "mixing" are themselves consistent with respect to the contexts in which they appear. For a fuller discussion, see 3E-21.

16. Verse 23 was originally followed by 3:1, and was later separated by the addition of

Section 2. The Criteria Used for the First Edition

as "Pharisee" and a "ruler."[17] In 7:31, the term "signs" appears, followed in 7:32 by "Pharisees" (twice) and "chief priests." In 9:16, the term "signs" appears and the authorities are referred to as "Pharisees" (vv. 13, 15, 16). In 11:47, "signs" appears together with references to "Pharisees" (v. 47) and "chief priests" (v. 47). In 12:18, the term "sign" appears again, and it is associated with "Pharisees" in v. 19. Thirdly, this association of "sign" with "Pharisees," "chief priests," and "rulers" contrasts with the usage in the second edition, where the characteristic term for miracle is "works" *(erga)* and the characteristic term for religious authorities is "the Jews" *(hoi Ioudaioi)*. See, for example, 5:36 (and the verb "work" in 5:18) (cf. "the Jews" in 5:10, 15, 16, 18); 10:25, 32, 33, 37 (cf. "the Jews" in 10:24, 31, 33).

Texts Requiring Further Discussion

Although the pattern of usage of "signs" is consistent in the first edition, there are some instances that require more discussion. Here we will discuss further only these elements of the term "sign(s)," leaving further discussion of the term "work(s)" for the Analysis of the second edition.

It is clear from the list above that not all instances of "sign" appear in passages where there is mention of religious authorities. This should not be surprising. Nevertheless, the meaning of the term in these cases is the same as in the other instances, and there is no reason to think that they belong to another edition. Nevertheless, four instances of the term "sign" are more complicated and require further discussion. First, there are two instances where it occurs with "the Jews" (2:18; 6:30). There are also two instances where it appears in material that, upon further analysis, would seem to come from the third edition (4:48; 6:26).

2:18 and 6:30

Two of the exceptional instances mentioned above (2:18 and 6:30) have several characteristics that indicate a different (yet internally consistent) usage. First, in contrast to the usage in the first edition, in 2:18 and 6:30 a sign is *demanded* as a christological proof; in the first edition, signs are requested, but not as proof regarding Jesus but simply because the person is in need. Recognizing this, Schnackenburg comments: "There is no continuity between this very negative

---

vv. 24-25 at the time of the second edition. For details, see the discussion of those verses in the Composition section.

17. Several other features characteristic of the first edition are found in this passage, but for the present only the linguistic terms will be noted.

concept of sign and the positive understanding of it in the Fourth Gospel."[18] Second, in 2:18 and 6:30 the notion of what constitutes a sign is different. In the first edition, a "sign" is simply a miracle; in 2:18 and 6:30, Jesus proposes something of an entirely different order. In 2:18, he speaks enigmatically of his Resurrection, arguing that this will be the sign they need. In 6:30, he presents himself symbolically as the bread of life. In neither case does Jesus' response involve a miracle. Third, in both cases Jesus' verbal response leads to a *misunderstanding* of the real meaning of Jesus' words, something, as we shall see in 2E-12, that is typical of the second edition. Fourth, the persons who demand the "sign" are labeled "Jews" rather than "Pharisees," "chief priests," or "rulers." Together these features indicate, not only that the meaning associated with "signs" is different in 2:18 and in 6:30, but also that all of the features associated with its use in 2:18 and 6:30 are characteristic of material in the second edition rather than in the first.[19] This is the use of another author.

4:48; 6:26

Two additional instances are distinct and require comment. In 4:48, the word "sign" appears in the phrase "signs and wonders" *(sēmeia kai terata).* Here the term refers to miracles. Moreover, in some other works of the New Testament and in the Septuagint this phrase is almost a technical phrase for miracles.[20] Yet the phrase occurs only here in the Johannine literature. This distinctiveness, together with other features of 4:48, suggests that the use is neither that of the first nor of the second edition. Because of the complexity of the material, the reader is referred to the discussion of the Composition for details.

The last instance requiring comment is 6:26. Here the word "signs" is used in a context where the remainder of the features suggest that the material comes from the third edition. Again, because of the complexity of the material, detailed analysis is given in the discussion of the Composition of 6:26.

1E-3. In the first edition, the term *Ioudaioi* refers to "Judeans," that is, to the inhabitants of Judea. This usage is limited to, and is distinctive of, the first edition.

---

18. Schnackenburg, *Gospel* 1:517. The difference in usage in 2:18 and 6:30 is widely recognized. See, for example, Barrett, *Gospel* 77; R. E. Brown, *Gospel* 1:115, 265, 527-29; Leon-Dufour, "Miracles" 269-86, esp. 277-78; Schnelle, *Antidocetic* 145-46; Welch, *Zeichen* 52-53. Almost all of the above are not concerned with editorial analysis; *nevertheless,* they recognize a difference in meaning.

19. Details are given in the discussion of Composition in the Commentary.

20. In the NT, see particularly Acts 2:19, 22, 43; 4:30; 5:12; 6:8; 7:36; 14:3; 15:12, but also Mark 13:22; Matt 24:24; Rom 15:19; 2 Cor 12:12; 2 Thess 2:9; Heb 2:4.

Section 2. The Criteria Used for the First Edition

In the second edition, *Ioudaioi* is used in a distinctive way as a blanket term to refer to religious authorities (2E-1).

It was noted above that the Greek word *Ioudaioi* (singular *Ioudaios*) appears in the second edition as a term referring to religious authorities. The discussion of the various meanings of the word was postponed until this point since the focus above was on "Pharisees" and related terms.

"The Jews" appears seventy-one times in the Fourth Gospel — more often than in any other work of the New Testament.[21] It is one of the most distinctive terms of the Gospel and has been the object of considerable study.[22] As is recognized by scholars, it is used with several meanings in the Gospel.[23]

The first meaning of *Ioudaioi* is one that is perhaps most common in ancient literature. In this use, the term *Ioudaioi* refers to the Jews as a political, ethnic, or religious grouping. This usage is found throughout ancient literature, perhaps most notably in Josephus. There it appears commonly in contexts where Jews are speaking of their fellow Jews to non-Jews. This will be discussed in detail below in 1E-16.

The second meaning of the term refers specifically to the region and the inhabitants of Judea as contrasted with the other regions of Palestine (and their inhabitants).[24] With this meaning, *Ioudaioi* would be translated "Judean" in English. This usage was also common in the ancient world but, within the Gospel, appears only in the first edition. We will discuss the evidence for this meaning in detail momentarily.

The third distinct usage of *Ioudaioi* is unique to the Gospel of John. In these instances, it is used in an absolute sense, not in association with or modifying another noun. In all cases, this refers not to the nation as a whole nor to

---

21. A full listing of appearances will be given in 2E-1. It always appears in the plural, except in 3:25.

22. For a bibliography prior to 1982, see von Wahlde, "'Jews'" 54 n. 1. For a bibliography and comment from 1983 to 1998, see von Wahlde, "Fifteen." Among the works to be added to this list are Culpepper, *Gospel* 291-95; Reinhartz, *Befriending*; Rensberger, "Anti-Judaism."

23. See, for example, R. E. Brown, *Gospel* 1:xxxvii, lxxi-lxxiii, 427-28; Schnackenburg, *Gospel* 1:286-87; Meier, *Marginal* 2:808, 864 n. 125; von Wahlde, "Jews" 33-60. See also the scholars surveyed by von Wahlde, "Fifteen."

24. Although there are many possible instances of this in Josephus, the clearest are those where the Judeans are contrasted with inhabitants of other regions. See, for example, Josephus (*Ant.* 17.10.2 §254), where he refers to the inhabitants of various regions and then to "the Judeans themselves." Moreover, later in the same context Josephus refers to the inhabitants of all of these regions being attacked by the Romans (§257) and then refers to them in their commonality as "Jews," thus switching to the national sense. See also *War* 2.12.8 §247; 3.3.4 §48). Lowe ("*Ioudaioi*" 111-15) gives some helpful examples of such usage, but his attempt to see this as the primary usage in the Gospel is not convincing.

The First Edition of the Gospel

"Judeans" but to the religious authorities, and connotes hostility to Jesus. This usage will be treated in detail in section 2E-1.

Of these various usages of the term *Ioudaioi*, the second is distinctive of the first edition.[25] As is evident from what was said above, the word *Ioudaioi* carries with it the same potential for confusion as the name "New York." That is, when one hears the name, one must decide from context whether "New York" refers to the state or the city. So it is with the Gospel of John. On the basis of contextual evidence, it is clear that *Ioudaios* appears with the meaning "Judean(s)" thirteen times (1:19; 3:25; 10:19; 11:19, 31, 33, 36, 45, 54; 12:9, 11; 19:20, 31). Three times it refers to the land of Judea (3:22; 4:3; 7:3).

The identification of *Ioudaioi* in these instances as "Judeans" rather than simply as "Jews" is confirmed first by the association of this group with Judea and particularly with the city of Jerusalem.[26] Moreover, this group is primarily neutral in its assessment of Jesus. They exhibit suspicion (1:19) and division (11:45-46) but never the undivided hostility typical of the "hostile" use of the term. Finally, they are not religious authorities but are distinguished from them.

This use first appears in 1:19. These persons are in Judea at the time and are associated with the city of Jerusalem (cf. 1:19). They are not religious authorities but are distinguished from the authorities identified here as "priests and Levites," terms that are more specific and concrete than any used in the second edition. Moreover, the authorities are later identified further in 1:24 as "Pharisees." Finally, these common people impel the authorities to action in a way similar to that described in 11:45-50, where the common people, again identified as "Judeans," impel the authorities to convene the Sanhedrin.

In 3:22, it is said that Jesus and his disciples went *eis tēn Ioudaian gēn* (literally, "into the Jewish/Judean countryside"). Since Jesus has been in Judea throughout the previous part of the chapter, it is obvious that this does not mean that he enters the country as a whole, but rather that he goes out into the *Judean* countryside.

In 3:25, there is a report of an inquiry on the part of a "Jew" (this is the only instance in the Gospel of the singular of the word applied to a person).

---

25. Among the scholars who have pointed out this "regional" meaning are R. E. Brown, *Gospel* 1:xxxvii, 427-28; Meier, *Marginal* 2:808, 864 n. 125; von Wahlde, "Jews"; G. Harvey, *True*, esp. 84-86; Rissi, "'Juden,'" esp. 2100-2103. Lowe *("Ioudaioi")* and Malina/Rohrbaugh *(Social Science)* would also see this meaning, although they see *only* this meaning. This is an extreme position, as most scholars have recognized. More recently, Tomson ("Names" 120-40, 266-89) studied the term in the extant literature, coins, and epigrapha and rejected the notion that *any* instances refer to Judeans ("Names" 282). This is an equally extreme position and difficult to reconcile with instances such as 3:22, 26; 4:3.

26. For a similar opinion see Rissi, "'Juden,'" esp. 2102. However, 7:1 constitutes a special case. See the discussion in 1E-1 above and of Composition in the Commentary.

Section 2. The Criteria Used for the First Edition

This is somewhat ambiguous. While it could refer to a single "Jew" in the national sense, more likely it refers to a Judean since it has just been stated that Jesus is in the Judean countryside. Finally, it occurs within material that can almost certainly be identified as from the first edition on other grounds.

The notice in 4:3 indicates that Jesus departs from *Ioudaia* and heads for *Galilaia*. Here also the region of Judea is contrasted with that of Galilee and the context makes it clear that the region of Judea, not the country, is referred to. In 7:3, Jesus' brothers urge him to go *eis tēn Ioudaian*. Since he is said to be in Galilee in 7:1, the contrast of regions indicates that Judea is the intended meaning here. In 10:19, *Ioudaioi* probably means "Judean." Although the identification cannot be said to be certain and although the text contains features of both the first and the third edition, the features linking it to the first edition appear to be the most convincing.[27]

The regional use next appears several times in the Lazarus passage (11:19, 31, 33, 36, 45) as well as in the 11:54; 12:9, 11; 19:20. In the instances of chapter 11, this group is again associated with Jerusalem (cf. 11:18, 19). This association is also evident in the instances of 12:9-11 where the "Jews" "come out" (from the city) to see Lazarus. It is explicit in 19:20, where it is said that the group read the title on the cross of Jesus because the cross was near the city of Jerusalem. Moreover, these people are not the authorities but are distinguished from them in 11:45 and in 12:9-11. Finally, they do not show unanimity of hostility to Jesus but rather are divided in their assessment, some believing (11:45; 12:11) and some not (11:46).

We have seen contextual features that indicate instances where *Ioudaioi* refers to Judeans. This is confirmed by the fact that *Ioudaioi* in the sense of Judeans appears regularly (a total of ten times) with the other terms characteristic of the first edition. It appears with the term "Pharisees" in 1:19 (cf. v. 24), 4:3 (cf. v. 1), and 11:45 (cf. v. 46). The usage in 11:45 is the same as that earlier in chapter 11 (vv. 19, 31, 33, 36). In 12:9, 11 and in 19:20 it is associated with "chief priests" (cf. 12:10; 19:21). In addition to these associations with the primary terms, it appears with a considerable number of other features of the first edition, and together these features mark it as unmistakably from the first edition.[28] Only the instance of 19:31 remains. This instance is ambiguous, and discussion of the text will be postponed to the discussion of the verse in the commentary proper in Volume 2.

---

27. Further detail is given in the discussion of Composition in the Commentary.
28. For further detail, consult the discussion of Composition in the Commentary.
29. The consistent pattern of these translations is noticed by J. Becker (*Evangelium* 2:585), but they are attributed to what Becker would see as the second edition.

The First Edition of the Gospel

1E-4. In the first edition, there is a consistent pattern of translation of religious and geographical terms. This is not found in the later editions.[29]

Nine times in the first edition there are instances in which terms are given both in Hebrew (Aramaic) and in Greek. There is a consistency in the way these are handled. Religious terms are given first in Hebrew (Aramaic) and then translated into Greek; geographical references are given first in Greek and then in Hebrew (Aramaic).

The following texts contain translations of religious terms: 1:38 ("'Rabbi' [which, translated, means Teacher]"), 1:41 ("'We have found the Messiah' [which is translated Christ]"); 1:42 ("'You will be called Cephas' [which, translated, means Peter]"); 4:25 ("'I know the Messiah is coming, the one called Christ'"); 20:16 ("... she said to him in Hebrew, 'Rabbouni' [which is translated Teacher]").[30]

Geographical terms appear first in Greek and then are translated into Hebrew. In 5:2, the place is identified with its Greek name ("the Sheep Gate") and then the pool is identified by its Hebrew name, using the same expression as elsewhere ("called in Hebrew Bethzatha"). In 9:7, the name of the pool is given as "Siloam," the Greek form of the Hebrew "Shiloah." In the "translation" the Hebrew form is not given, presumably because it was so similar to the Greek form; rather, the *meaning* of the name is given.[31]

In 19:13, we read that Pilate "sat in the official's chair in the place called Lithostrotos (but in Hebrew, Gabbatha)." Here the pattern is consistent: first the Greek, then the Hebrew. However, here the Hebrew is not a *translation* of Lithostrotos (which means "stone pavement") but rather the Hebrew name for the place (Gabbatha means "raised place"). This variation is truly remarkable because it indicates that the process is not simply a slavish translation but a genuine attempt to provide the Hebrew equivalent.

In 19:17, Jesus is described as carrying his cross "to what is called the Place

---

30. Three times in the Gospel (11:16; 20:24; 21:2) Thomas is identified as "the one called Twin" *(ho legomenos Didymos)*. The Greek form does not appear in the Synoptics, where Thomas is mentioned only once in each Gospel: Matt 10:3; Mark 3:18; Luke 6:15.

In spite of the verbal similarity of this expression to the translation of terms in the first edition, this is not the same phenomenon. Even though the Greek form is in fact a translation of the Aramaic *Thōmas*, it is not *presented* as such. This can be seen from a comparison of this form with the form given in the translation of *Cephas* in 1:42. There the purpose of the translation is to give the meaning of *Cephas*, namely, that it means *Petros* ("rock"), and it is said to be a translation. However, in the use of the phrase in relation to Thomas, the emphasis is not on the Greek as a translation of the name but simply on the presentation of the Greek form of his name, which was evidently the more common form of his name within the Johannine community.

31. Among those who resist seeing a symbolic meaning in "sent" is Bernard (*Gospel* 2:329), who rightly points to its exact verbal parallel with the translation of Peter's name in 1:38.

Section 2. The Criteria Used for the First Edition

of the Skull (which is called in Hebrew Golgotha)." Again, first the Greek and then the Hebrew.

The purpose of these translations is often thought to be to explain the terms for Gentile readers. But that is only half of the story, for *the place-names are generally given first in their Greek form and then translated to the Hebrew.* This would suggest a document coming from a Jewish religious group (which used its own Hebrew [Aramaic] language for religious terms) existing in a Greco/Roman environment where place-names appeared primarily in their Hellenistic form. The author then regularly translated these names to make them more readily recognizable to Jewish readers who would be more familiar with their Hebrew (Aramaic) form.[32]

In addition to the instances mentioned above, a similar (but not identical) phenomenon appears in 2:23, 6:1, and 6:4. In the first and third instances (2:23 and 6:4), the Hebrew religious term *Pascha* is given and immediately followed either by "the feast" (2:23) or "the feast of the Jews." In 6:1, a place is identified two ways: "the Sea of Galilee, of Tiberias." That is, the "traditional" name is given first and then its more modern, secular (Roman) name.[33] None of these is specifically a translation, but the technique is so similar that they are grouped together with the explicit translations.

In intention, this translation and this duplication of terms are identical to the explanations of Jewish customs, feasts, and names for authorities as well as the explanation of the term "King of the Jews." They indicate that the author was aware that some of his audience may well have needed such explanations.[34]

---

32. Fortna (*Predecessor* 45) addresses this phenomenon in conjunction with 1:38b, 41b, and 42b and attributes them to his second stratum on the grounds that they "obviously" reflect a post-Jewish situation. Fortna does not comment on the parallel (but reverse) phenomenon of the translation of Greek place-names into Hebrew. These translations are similar in function to the use of the phrase "of the Jews" to identify feasts and customs.

While it is curious that such translations would be part of the earliest stratum of the Gospel (which demonstrates such familiarity with Palestine and with Jewish customs), it is undeniable that they appear consistently and exclusively within the material of the first edition; thus they are listed here as objective markers of that first edition. It is nevertheless possible that they were all neatly inserted by a later author without creating aporias. At the same time, it is difficult to imagine that they reflect the second or third editions, given both the intensely Jewish character of the second edition and the fact that the interests of the second and third editions are so focused within rather than out toward, for example, Gentiles, who would lack this knowledge.

33. The order of the names is also reversed, with the traditional name first and the Roman name second. On the names of the Sea of Galilee, see the Note at 6:2 in the Commentary. The true Hebrew name here would be Gennesaret (cf. Luke 5:1), but the common name in the Gospels is "Sea of Galilee." "Sea of Tiberias" appears alone in 21:1, suggesting that for the author of the third edition (from which 21:1 comes) the Roman name had supplanted the more traditional one.

34. This also reflects what were probably, in varying degrees, the circumstances in Palestine in the first century. Although we cannot speak with certainty about the entire country, it can

2. Characteristics of Narrative Orientation

We now turn to a second type of characteristic evident in the first edition. These features are characteristics within the material that has been isolated by means of the criteria based on characteristic terminology. I have called these "characteristics of narrative orientation" because they are features within the narrative that reveal various attitudes on the part of the author to elements of the narrative development. They might also be referred to as "ideological" in the sense that they reflect certain underlying attitudes presupposed by the author and not directly concerned with theology.

Not only do the features listed here appear *consistently* within passages identified by the characteristic terminology, but they also *consistently contrast with ideological features in the second edition*. This consistency again indicates that they are genuinely distinctive of a given edition. Not only are these features useful for what they reveal about the differences in narrative orientation in the various editions, but they also confirm the identity of the material first identified by characteristic terminology. Finally, they are useful for extending the analysis to material where the characteristic terms themselves do not appear.

1E-5. In the first edition, there is a consistent use of stereotyped formulas of belief. There is nothing comparable to this in the other editions.

In the Gospel of John, it is typical for belief to follow rather than to precede the working of a miracle. In the first edition, this belief appears in expressions that are so similar that they can be said to be "stereotyped" or "formulaic": (1) the statements contain the expression of belief; (2) this belief is said to be a result of "signs" (rather than "works" or "words"); and (3) it appears in either of two formulas: (a) "... many of the [with the specific name of the group inserted] believed in him," or (b) "and 'they' [with or without the name of the group] believed in him."

---

be shown that in cities such as Jerusalem, there was an identifiable layer of Greek influence and beneath this a very strong and vibrant Jewish base. Josephus (*Ant.* 1.5 §121) speaks of the practice of the Greeks, who, when they came to power, were responsible for changing the names of nations to make them more intelligible to themselves. What Josephus refers to regarding the names of nations would undoubtedly have taken place with respect to other names also. This was only one element of the overall effect of Hellenization. In Jerusalem, this influence was also seen in architecture, social institutions such as the theater and the hippodrome, forms of government, etc. At the same time, the predominant language of a place like Jerusalem continued to be Aramaic rather than Greek, and existing alongside the Hellenistic institutions was the equally clear evidence of Jerusalem as a "thoroughly Jewish city." See the discussion in Levine, *Judaism and Hellenism* 29, 33-95 and the bibliography there; on the language of Jerusalem, see 72-84.

Section 2. The Criteria Used for the First Edition

These formulas of belief always occur in conjunction with other features typical of the earliest version. This confirms their origin and identity.[35] We will look first at the instances where primary characteristics accompany the formulas and then at the others where the features are not primary ones.

In 2:11, we read: "Jesus did this, the beginning of his signs, in Cana of Galilee, and he revealed his glory, **and his disciples believed in him**." Here the word "signs" appears, clearly linking it with the first edition.

In 2:23, it is stated: "When he was in Jerusalem at the Passover — at the feast — , **many believed in his name, seeing his signs that he was performing**." Here again the word "signs" is used for miracles.

In 4:39, it is said: "**From that town many of the Samaritans believed in him** because of the word of the woman who witnessed, 'He told me everything I have done.'" In this case, although there is no mention of "signs" in the immediate context, two features indicate that it is intended as one. First, the belief is on the basis of a miracle: "He told me everything I have done." Second, in the report of 4:54, the healing of the official's son is referred to as the "second sign" that Jesus performed coming from Judea into Galilee, thus indicating that the Samaritan episode was also considered a "sign."

In 4:53, we find a miracle closely related by context to the story of the Samaritan woman. The belief is expressed as: "The father remembered that was the very hour when Jesus said, 'Your son lives' — and **he himself believed, and his entire household**." The miracle is referred to as a "sign" in 4:54.

Yet another appears in 7:31: "**From among the common people, however, many believed in him;** and they said, 'When the Christ comes, will he perform more signs than this man?'" Again the term "signs" appears. In addition, in the following verse (7:32) we read: "'The Pharisees' heard the common people murmuring these things about him, and the chief priests and the Pharisees sent temple police to seize him." In this verse the authorities are three times identified in terms characteristic of the first edition.

The case of 10:41-42 is particularly striking. In basic content, it is a comparison of John the Baptist with Jesus: "And many came to him and said, 'On the one hand, John performed no sign; and, on the other, everything John said about this man was true.' **And many believed in him there**." While not a reac-

---

35. This is one of the significant ways in which the present analysis would differ from that of Bultmann. Bultmann (*Gospel* 130 n. 3) calls attention to these formulas of belief and observes that "... the constantly recurring observation that many believed (7.31; 8.30; 10.42; 11.45; 12:42) is typical of the Evangelist, as is the general reference to Jesus' *sēmeia* (3.2; 6.2; 7.31; 11.47; 12.37; indirectly 10.41)." This fails to notice the consistency of terminology for miracles and for religious authorities, and the conception of "easy belief" that contrasts with that in the material marked by the terminology of the second edition. Nevertheless, it is to Bultmann's credit that he noticed the consistency in the stereotyped pattern as well as in terminology.

The First Edition of the Gospel

tion to a specific miracle, the point of comparison is precisely the miracles of Jesus identified as "signs" — and the fact that John did not perform them. The second verse, then, contains the stereotyped formula of belief in Jesus, echoing once again the belief based on signs.

In 11:45, we see the reaction of the people to the raising of Lazarus. In this case the formula again functions as part of the miracle form, providing the attestation of the raising: "So **many of the Judeans, those who had come to Mary and who had seen the things he had done, believed in him**." We can see that it appears in the "long form" of the formula, in which "many of" and the group are identified. The actual word "sign" does not appear, but the phrase "what he had done" refers to the miracle as the basis of their belief, and in v. 47 we will see that the "signs" are explicitly referred to.

The stereotyped formula appears again in 12:11: ". . . because of him **many of the Judeans were going off and believing in Jesus**." The primary linguistic feature present here is the reference to "Judeans."

After such an extended series of passages exhibiting the consistent usage of this formula, 12:42 provides a puzzling instance. On the one hand, the verse ("Nevertheless, indeed even **many of the rulers believed in him**, but because of the Pharisees . . .") is marked as coming from the first edition by the presence of the characteristic term for religious authorities. On the other hand, it leads into material that almost certainly does not come from the first edition. In the light of the consistent usage elsewhere, this can only be seen as an instance where later editing has obscured the original sequence. As will be seen in detail in the discussion of Composition within the Commentary, this is precisely the case.

Finally, in 8:30 there is what appears to be another instance of the formula. This verse has traditionally been recognized as a major problem for all interpreters. The verse in full reads: "When Jesus said these things, many believed in him." Although this appears to be an instance of the formula, several features suggest that it is not — or, if it is, that it has been heavily edited. First, the belief is said to be on the part of "the Jews," who, in the surrounding context, exhibit nothing but hostility. Second, this is the only instance in which the belief is not founded on a miracle or hearing the report of one. Third, the following verses give no hint of belief. Consequently, it seems likely that this verse either is a minor fragment of the first edition or that it comes from a later author. More will be said about this verse in the Commentary. It will then be apparent that it is only when its full context and the surrounding features are understood that its true identity and function can be grasped.

In all, we have seen nine certain instances and one additional possible instance of this stereotyped formula of belief. The formula appears so frequently, is spread throughout so much of the ministry, and is so regularly linked with the signs that it becomes one of the salient ideological features of the first edi-

Section 2. The Criteria Used for the First Edition

tion. Together these expressions demonstrate the extent to which belief in the earliest version of the Gospel was portrayed as being based on the miracles of Jesus, and together they embody the widely recognized and typical Johannine feature that belief occurs after the working of a miracle. It is also noteworthy to recall here that in no case is such belief associated with or based on "works" (the term for "miracle" in the second edition)!

Finally, the appearance of this formulaic expression tells us much about the nature of the material in the first edition. The study of form criticism has shown that the typical miracle consists of three elements: (1) the description of an affliction, (2) the working of the miracle by Jesus to cure that affliction, and (3) the attestation of, or reaction to, the miracle by the onlookers. The fact that the formulaic statements function in many cases as the third element of the miracle form shows that these statements were an integral part of the miracle narratives. The fact that features of the first edition appear within the miracle form itself and not simply in the surrounding material demonstrates that the miracle narratives are, in their written form, the work of the first author and do not constitute a "source" taken over by him. Moreover, the fact that *not all of the formulas* appear as constituent parts of the miracle form is a clear indication that the first edition consisted of more than a simple collection of miracle reports; it was an extended narrative of the ministry.[36]

1E-6. In the first edition, there is a pattern of portraying belief as occurring in "tandem" or "chain reaction" sequence. This pattern is not found in either of the later editions.[37]

Often in the Gospel, first an individual or group comes to belief and then, on the basis of the report of that person or group, another person or group comes to belief. This "tandem" (or "chain reaction") belief occurs six times in the Gospel and always in material of the first edition.

The first three instances appear at the beginning of the public ministry. Two instances of such chain-reaction belief are clear. In 1:40, we read that An-

---

36. That the first edition consisted of a complete narrative account is also confirmed by the various other features of the first edition that occur within the narrative material itself rather than simply within "transitions."

37. Aspects of this are regularly commented on by scholars. John 1:35-49 is the longest and most easily recognized "chain." That the chain may have been broken by editing is also frequently pointed out. See, for example, Boismard, "Traditions" 40; Bultmann, *Gospel* 98; R. E. Brown, *Gospel* 1:85-86; Martyn, *Christian History* 35-36; Fortna, *Predecessor* 39-40, 46. However, no scholar that I am aware of has recognized that all instances of such tandem or chain-reaction belief should be grouped together.

The First Edition of the Gospel

drew, one of the first disciples to meet Jesus, goes to get his brother Simon Peter. Secondly, we read in 1:45 that Philip, after he comes to belief in Jesus, gets Nathanael. A third instance is also probable. Although in the present form of the text Jesus is the one who is said to get Philip, it is likely that in the first edition Andrew had also been the one to get Philip. This is indicated by the fact that in v. 41 Andrew is said to get Peter "first," thus suggesting that he also caused a second person to believe in Jesus. But in the present Gospel, that second person is not named. Second, the structure of v. 43a in its present form is quite awkward and suggests that the original sequence has been interrupted by an editor's insertion of the statement that Jesus wanted to go to Galilee. With this insertion, the subject of the verb "found" becomes (somewhat awkwardly) Jesus. Together these factors suggest that in the first edition, there was a third instance of tandem belief. These instances are not immediately associated with the notion of "sign." On the basis of the numerous other criteria (e.g., the translation of terms) the identity of these instances can be determined with certainty.[38]

The next instance of tandem belief is in the story of the Samaritan woman, where the woman herself first comes to belief and then reports her belief to the townspeople (4:28-29), who also come to belief (4:39). The fifth instance is that of the official in Cana, about whom it is said in 4:53: "He himself believed, and his entire household." This is identified as a "sign" in the same verse. The sixth instance follows the raising of Lazarus. In 11:45, we read that many of the Judeans came to belief in Jesus. Then in 12:9-11 and 17-18 we hear that a second crowd comes to Bethany not only to see Jesus but also to see Lazarus himself. And on the basis of this, many more come to belief.[39]

We have pointed out six instances of this feature, a number that is substantial enough to suggest that this form of belief was important for the author and his community. While it may indicate a missionary interest in which others are led to the faith, it may also be simply a way of portraying the ease with which Jesus attracted others from various groups to himself.

1E-7. In the first edition, attention is repeatedly called to the quantity and quality of Jesus' signs. This is not found in the later editions.

In the material of the first edition, there is a repeated emphasis on, and recognition of, the quantity and quality of Jesus' signs. This recognition occurs both

---

38. This will be evident from the discussion of the Composition in the Commentary.
39. As was the case with the episode of the Samaritan woman, the number of crowds is raised to an awkward three by the later addition in 12:12-16.

Section 2. The Criteria Used for the First Edition

among those who believe and among those who do not. What is striking is not just that there is an emphasis on the quantity and quality of the signs, but that various types of adjectives are used to express the conviction.

In 3:2, Nicodemus is attracted to Jesus by his miracles and says, "Rabbi, we know that you have come as a teacher from God. For no one is able to perform these signs that you perform unless God is with him." The word order of the Greek is striking: *oudeis gar dynatai **tauta ta sēmeia** poiein ha sy poieis. . . .*

In 4:45, it is said that the Galileans had seen "all that he had done in Jerusalem at the feast *(**panta** heōrakotes **hosa** epoiēsen en Hierosolymois en tē heortē)."* Again both the word order and the correlation of "all" and "as many as" call attention to the number of his miracles.

In 7:31, the crowd asks, "When the Christ comes, will he perform more signs *(**mē pleiona sēmeia** poiēsei)* than this man?" Here the number of the signs is so great that the crowd cannot conceive of even the Messiah doing more!

In 9:16, when the Pharisees discuss the healing of the blind man, some point out that the person who did it must be a sinner since he does not keep the Sabbath, but others comment, "How is a sinful person able to perform such signs *(**toiauta sēmeia poiein**)?"*

In 10:40-42, a text we have examined above, what is remarkable is the contrast between John the Baptist and Jesus and the statement that "John performed no sign." Again the word order of the Greek is emphatic and stresses the (lack of) quantity of John's signs: *Iōannēs men **sēmeion epoiēsen ouden**.*

In 11:47, when some of the people of Judea report the raising of Lazarus and the Pharisees and chief priests convene a Sanhedrin, they focus on his miracles: "What are we to do, because this man performs many signs? *(hoti houtos ho anthrōpos **polla poiei sēmeia**)."*

In 12:37, the narrator *of the first edition* sums up the public ministry by saying, "But even though he did so many signs before the . . . *(**Tosauta de autou sēmeia pepoiēkotos** emprosthen autōn . . .)."*

Finally, in 20:30 Jesus' ministry is again summed up: "On the one hand, Jesus performed many and varied signs *(**Polla men oun kai alla sēmeia epoiēsen** . . .)* before [his] disciples that are not written in this book."

This means that of the fourteen times the word "sign" appears in the first edition, eight instances are explicitly qualified by adjectives pointing to the number and magnitude of those signs.

In addition to this specific use of adjectives to show the greatness of the signs, a more generalized emphasis is evident in each of the signs themselves. Although each of these will be discussed below, the emphasis can be seen briefly in 2:1-11, where attention is called to the quantity and the quality of the wine produced; in 4:4-42, in the emphasis on the fact that Jesus told the woman "all I have ever done"; in 4:46-54, from the fact that the boy was at the point of

The First Edition of the Gospel

death; in 5:1-9, from the fact that the man had been crippled for thirty-eight years; in 6:3-14, from the contrast between the few loaves and fishes, the great size of the crowd, and the larger amount of food left over after all had eaten; in 6:16-21, from the magnitude of the storm and the suddenness of the arrival of Jesus and the disciples; in 9:1-41, from the fact that the man who was healed was *born* blind; in 11:1-45, from the fact that Lazarus was now dead three days and was giving forth a stench; and, finally, in the aftermath of the raising of Lazarus, from the fact that still more people came to Bethany to see Lazarus and to believe in Jesus.

In the second edition, there is no such emphasis on the magnitude of the miracles, and where attention is called to them, the adjective, the attitudes, and the theological conceptions associated with the term are of a totally different order.

1E-8. In the first edition, there is an emphasis on the variety of groups that come to belief in Jesus. There is nothing comparable to this in either the second or third editions.

The first edition is clearly interested to show that belief in Jesus was not confined to a single group or a single sector of society. This is evident in two ways. First, in the stereotyped formulas of belief, there is a noticeable emphasis on the variety of groups who come to belief, but apart from this there are numerous general remarks indicating such interest.

We will look first at those instances that show connections to the primary features of the first edition. In 2:11, we hear of the disciples coming to belief *(kai episteusan . . . hoi mathētai autou)* (cf. "signs," v. 11). In 2:23, "many people" in Jerusalem for the feast believe *(polloi episteusan)* (cf. "signs," v. 23). In 4:39, "many of the Samaritans from that city *(ek de tēs poleōs ekeinēs polloi episteusan . . .)*" are said to come to belief (termed as "sign" implicitly in 4:54). In 7:31, "many of the common people" of Jerusalem believe *(ek tou ochlou de polloi episteusan . . .)* (cf. "signs," v. 32). In 10:42, we hear that "many people there," that is, beyond the Jordan, where John was baptizing, came to belief *(kai polloi episteusan . . . ekei)* (cf. "sign," v. 41). In 11:45, "many of the Judeans" believe in him *(Polloi oun ek tōn Ioudaiōn hoi elthontes pros tēn Mariam kai theasamenoi ha epoiēsen, episteusan . . .)* (cf. "chief priests," "Pharisees," and "signs" in v. 47); in 12:9, "the large crowd of Judeans" in Jerusalem who knew that Jesus and Lazarus were in Bethany (cf. "Judeans," "chief priests") came. In 12:19, the "Pharisees" comment, "Behold, the whole world is going after him." In 12:42, we read that "even many of the rulers" believed in him (cf. "rulers," "Pharisees," v. 42).

Section 2. The Criteria Used for the First Edition

There are also more general comments of widespread belief.[40] In 4:1, we hear that Jesus is making more disciples than John (cf. "Pharisees," v. 1). The royal official who believes, along with his entire household (4:46-54), represents another sector of society (cf. "sign," v. 54). Finally, in 20:30-31 the author expresses the hope that "the signs" will be a source of belief for the one who is reading the text of the Gospel.

The instances that can be identified with the first edition through secondary characteristics include the following:[41]

In 1:35-49, it is notable that the first disciples are said to have been disciples of John the Baptist before coming to belief. Thus, one can conclude that believers also have come from that group. In 3:26, when Jesus goes into the Judean countryside, we are told through the mouths of the disciples of John that Jesus is baptizing and "everyone is going to him." Thus, the people of the countryside also believe. In 4:45, we read of belief at the feast of Passover in Jerusalem, but the verse also tells us that some of those were Galileans and that they were now welcoming him into Galilee. At the end of the public ministry (12:20), we hear of "some Greeks" (probably symbolic of the first of the Gentiles) who want to "see Jesus."

In all we have seen sixteen texts that speak of belief in various sectors of society. The fact that much of it is so stereotyped lends further support to the deliberateness of the reporting and to the fact that the first edition intended to stress the fact that so many and such varied individuals and groups came to believe in Jesus.

In the second and third editions, there is nothing comparable to this.

1E-9. In the first edition, there are repeated reports of division of opinion among the religious authorities regarding Jesus. In the second edition, there is no division among the authorities and the authorities' hostility is presented as unified, formalized, and solidified (2E-9).

We now come to a number of features of the first edition that concern the portrayal of the authorities where they are identified as "Pharisees," "chief priests," and "rulers." These will concern both the portrayal of the religious authorities themselves and their relationship with other people within the narrative as well as their narrative function in general. In all cases there is a

---

40. These are less stereotyped than the previous and are more evident in retrospect. Thus while they confirm the analysis, they are not used in the Analysis of the Composition.

41. The reader is directed to the discussion of Composition within the Commentary proper for the evidence in each case that the material is from the first edition.

The First Edition of the Gospel

clear contrast between the portrayal in the first edition and that in the second and third editions.[42]

In the material of the first edition, there are four references to division among the religious authorities about Jesus. In 7:45-48, there is division of opinion about Jesus, with the Pharisees on one side and the temple police on the other. Later in the same passage (7:48-52), there is division of opinion between the majority of the Pharisees and Nicodemus, who was also a Pharisee, about the possibility of Jesus being "the Prophet." In the discussion of the implications of the healing of the man born blind, again there is a division among the Pharisees (9:16) whether Jesus could be from God. Even at this relatively late period in the ministry, there was still a variety of opinion among the Pharisees with respect to Jesus. Finally, in 12:42 we hear, at the end of the ministry, that "many" of the Pharisees believed in Jesus![43]

These four references to division among the authorities all involve the Pharisees, and the mention of such division does not stand out in any sense as artificial or contrived; it is simply part of the narrative. Yet there is no such division among the authorities when they are identified as "the Jews." In the material of the second edition, the unanimity of "the Jews'" judgment and its finality regarding Jesus are striking and clear. In 9:18-23, the finality of "the Jews'" position is particularly striking when contrasted with the attitude of "the Pharisees' in the surrounding context.

1E-10. In the first edition, the hostility of the Pharisees increases throughout the ministry, coming to a climax in the decision to arrest Jesus. In the second edition, the level of hostility of the authorities is present in an essentially steady state from the beginning and does not significantly change thereafter except to manifest itself repeatedly in attempts to kill Jesus (2E-5).

In the first edition, the hostility to Jesus on the part of the "Pharisees," "chief priests," and "rulers" begins with the curiosity of Nicodemus (3:1-2), and increases to hostility when the Pharisees learn about the baptizing and the number of disciples Jesus is making (4:1).[44] It becomes more intense at the Feast of

---

42. I will continue to make reference to possible parallels in the third edition, although in fact there is little focused concern on the portrayal of the religious authorities in that edition.

43. We have indicated earlier that this verse presents problems in its larger context but that the identity of the first half of the verse is certain given the clarity of the features involved. In fact, the portrayal of the continued division among the Pharisees and the fact that some of them believed is consistent with the portrayal of the Pharisees elsewhere in the first edition and is another indication that the first half of the verse is indeed from the first edition.

44. Fortna ("Locale" 90-91) noted with curiosity that, in some texts, hostility toward Je-

Section 2. The Criteria Used for the First Edition

Tabernacles, where an attempt is made to arrest Jesus for questioning (7:32, 45-52) and where he is said not to be the Prophet like Moses since the Prophet does not come from Galilee (v. 52). In the discussion regarding the healing of the blind man (9:13-17, 24-34), the majority of the Pharisees are convinced that "this man is not from God because he does not keep the Sabbath" (v. 25), and they do not know "where this one is from" (v. 29). However, a marked change occurs after the raising of Lazarus. It is then that the Pharisees and chief priests conclude that, if they allow him to continue, the Romans will come and destroy their Temple and take away their freedom. Their hostility has increased to the point that they convene the Sanhedrin and condemn him to death (11:47-50). This is further evidenced by their desire to have others inform on him (11:57). This portrayal of the authorities' hostility could be described as typical of a narrative portrayal and typical of what one would expect from such a confrontation.

In the second edition, "the Jews" exhibit an intense and level state of hostility throughout the Gospel. The portrayal in this edition is not concerned with narrative development but with a static portrayal of various aspects of the hostility of official Judaism. We will discuss this in detail in 2E-9. In the third edition, there is no significant concern with the role of the authorities.[45]

1E-11. In the first edition, there are repeated reports of the reaction of the Pharisees following on reports of belief among the common people. This is not found in the later editions.

In the first edition, the belief in Jesus on the part of various groups is regularly followed by a reaction on the part of the religious authorities. It is true that (at least from the viewpoint of the Gospel writers), during his ministry, belief in Jesus on the part of various groups would lead to a reaction on the part of the religious authorities, but here we are focusing on the literary expression of this fact and the way this is presented in such a consistent pattern. In the first edition, there are a number of instances where such reactions are expressed immediately after such belief. Other times the reaction is less immediate, but still striking.

First, we will look at the examples that contain primary characteristics

---

sus seemed to increase throughout the Gospel while, in others, it seemed to be of equal intensity throughout. When the texts listed by Fortna are examined, they correspond remarkably with texts I have attributed to the first and second editions respectively.

45. Although the third edition refers to "the Jews" (e.g., 6:52), it is not concerned with the overall attitude of the authorities but with the theological issues pertinent to the circumstances of the third edition. See also 3E-21.

and where the reaction is most immediate and stereotyped. In 2:23-25,[46] the belief of the crowds is followed by the reaction of Nicodemus in 3:1-2. (Nicodemus is identified as a "Pharisee" and a "ruler," and there is mention of "signs" in 2:23 and 3:2.) Here, in the first reaction, there is curiosity rather than hostility. In 7:31, the common people are said to believe in Jesus and to be convinced that the Messiah could not work more signs than Jesus. Immediately (in 7:32) the Pharisees are said to react by sending attendants to arrest Jesus.

When the crowd reports the raising of Lazarus to the Pharisees, they, together with the chief priests, react by convening the Sanhedrin (11:47-50). Yet another reaction occurs in 11:57, where, when "the Pharisees" hear the crowds speculating about whether Jesus will come to the feast, they react once more by giving notice that if anyone knows where he is, they should inform the authorities so they may arrest him.

In 12:9-11, we hear that a large crowd of people of Judea come from Jerusalem to Bethany because of Jesus and to see Lazarus who has been raised from the dead. Immediately we are informed that "the chief priests" react by planning to kill Lazarus also. In 12:18, we hear that a third crowd welcomes Jesus "because he had done this sign." Immediately we hear the reaction of the "Pharisees" that they are getting nowhere and that "the whole world" is going after him.

Other reactions of the "Pharisees" and "chief priests" that are less immediate include the discussion in 7:45-52 when the attendants return without arresting Jesus and the long discussion following the healing of the man born blind (9:13-17, 24-34).

In the second edition, the authorities (presented as "the Jews") nowhere react to the actions of the people either in fear of them or concern for the impact of their reactions to Jesus.

1E-12. In the first edition, the religious authorities' ("Pharisees," "chief priests," and "rulers") reaction to Jesus and to the belief of the crowds is almost exclusively on the basis of his signs. In the second edition, the authorities virtually ignore the miracles and focus on the claims of Jesus regarding his relation with the Father (2E-7).

In the section immediately above, we noted the pattern in which there is almost immediate reaction to the belief of the crowds by the religious authorities

---

46. As will be explained in the Commentary, there is considerable evidence that 2:24-25 were not part of the first edition but added later. If this is true, the reaction of Nicodemus is all the more striking and clear.

Section 2. The Criteria Used for the First Edition

(identified as "Pharisees," "chief priests," and "rulers"). In this section, we are calling attention to the fact that their reaction is almost always to his "signs." This is true in the cases discussed immediately above, 3:1 (". . . we know, . . . [f]or no one is able to perform these signs"); 7:32 (cf. "signs" in v. 31); in 9:13-17, 24-34, the entire discussion centers on the meaning of the signs (vv. 16, 25-26, 31-34); in 11:47-50 (". . . the chief priests and the Pharisees convened the Sanhedrin and said, '. . . this man performs many signs . . .'"); in 12:10 the desire of the religious authorities to kill Lazarus contains an all-but-explicit concern for the sign of his being raised from the dead; and in 12:18, when the third crowd welcomes Jesus because of the "sign," the Pharisees once again react.

One instance that does not explicitly deal with signs is the indirect reference in 4:1. This should be construed simply as a general concern about his popularity. The only other passage in which signs are not the source of concern is 7:45-52, where again the discussion is generally vague but expresses concern about the scriptural basis for the Prophet like Moses coming from Galilee.

In the second edition, the concern of the religious authorities (now identified as "the Jews") is focused on the claims of Jesus rather than on his miracles. Strikingly, "the Jews" even dismiss concern with the miracles themselves and say that they seek to stone him "not for a good work but for blasphemy, and because you who are a human being make yourself God" (10:33). We will see this in detail in 2E-7.

In the third edition, no significant attention is given to this issue.

1E-13. In the first edition, the common people show no fear for the authorities and at times debate with them and react to them with disdain. In the second edition, the people (and disciples) are consistently said to react to the authorities ("the Jews") with abject fear, expressed particularly in the phrase "for fear of the Jews" (2E-6).

In the first edition, there are several situations in which the common people show no fear of the authorities and in fact talk back to or ignore them. In 7:45, the temple police who had been sent by the "Pharisees" and "chief priests" return without arresting Jesus. When asked by the "Pharisees," they imply by their response that they have been so impressed by the way he spoke that they did not arrest him. The Pharisees then actually "lower" themselves to enter into theological debate with the temple police!

In chapter 9, the man born blind engages in extended debate with the "Pharisees" (vv. 15-17, 24-34).[47] Far from being fearful, he argues the meaning

---

47. The list of adjectives used by commentators captures this well. Bernard (*Gospel* 2:335)

The First Edition of the Gospel

of the miracles and says to the authorities: "I told you already, and you did not listen." Later he says: "This is what is surprising, that you do not know where he is from." And later he says: "Unless this man was from God, he would not be able to do anything." In chapters 11–12, the chief priests have given orders for people to inform the authorities about Jesus (11:57), yet the people appear to ignore this order and continue to come to Bethany to see both Jesus and Lazarus.

In the second edition, the situation is radically different. In that edition, the people are said "to fear the Jews." These comments are striking and commonly noticed because they present a picture of the authorities as such fear-inspiring individuals that no one will dare to resist or confront them.

1E-14. In the first edition, it is the religious authorities ("Pharisees," "chief priests," and "rulers") who regularly react with fear and apprehension to the belief of the common people. In the second edition, the reverse is true: there is no hint of such attitudes in the monolithic posture of "the Jews," and the people fear the authorities (2E-6, 2E-8).

Earlier (1E-11) attention was called to the *pattern* of reaction of the Pharisees, chief priests, and rulers to the people, a pattern in which a response immediately follows an expression of belief by a group of the common people. That pattern does not appear in the second edition. In 1E-12 attention was called to the fact that this was a reaction *to Jesus' signs*. Here, attention is being called not to the pattern but to the *nature* of that reaction. In the first edition, the authorities exhibit a variety of reactions ranging from concern to fear, frustration, anxiety, and exasperation. These reactions are typical of narrative. In the second edition, there is not a hint of fear among the religious authorities who are now identified as "the Jews," but only unanimous, unswerving hostility that inspires fear in others.

There are four places in the first edition where these typical reactions are evident. In all cases the authorities are described as "Pharisees" (rather than "the Jews").[48] Two of these instances are particularly striking, and are discussed first.

---

refers to the man's response in v. 27 as "irritable," and to his question whether they want to become disciples of Jesus as an "ironical gibe"; by v. 30 he is "thoroughly angry" and "mocking." Carson (*Gospel* 366) calls the man "sharp, quick-witted, and eventually quite sardonic." Certainly, no one in the Gospel relates to "the Jews" with anything in any way approximating these reactions.

48. All of the passages discussed contain primary markers of the first edition, and so no special discussion of the features is necessary.

Section 2. The Criteria Used for the First Edition

In 11:45-50, after the raising of Lazarus, the Pharisees and chief priests convene the Sanhedrin and express their common fears: if they allow Jesus to continue, the Romans will come and destroy the Temple and their nation. Here their fear is quite evident, and it is directed at what will happen if the Romans become involved. In 11:57, the Pharisees and chief priests give orders that, if anyone should know where Jesus was, the person should provide information "so they might seize him." But instead of informing on him, the people have gone out to Bethany to see both Jesus and Lazarus, and more have come to believe in him.

In 12:19, the reaction of the "Pharisees" to the belief of the masses reaches a high point of frustration and anxiety, and they say: "You see that your efforts are useless. Behold, the whole world is going after him!" This is a totally different reaction from that of "the Jews" anywhere in the Gospel!

But there are other instances of concern and fear, although less striking. In 4:1-4, "the Pharisees" express concern at the fact that Jesus is baptizing and making more disciples than John. This is not precisely fear, but it is a concern that seems to connote an inability to deal with the popularity Jesus is gaining.

In 7:32, the "Pharisees" decide to arrest Jesus to bring him in for questioning. Their decision is based precisely on the fact that they have heard the common people speculating that this man is the Messiah. This alarms the Pharisees, who decide to send the attendants to arrest Jesus; but it is to no avail since Jesus impresses them also. In exasperation, the Pharisees claim that the attendants are also deceived and that the common people cannot be right, for they do not know the Law. But the Pharisees sense and express their lack of success in dealing with popular reaction to Jesus.

When this series of reactions is compared with the reactions of the authorities identified as "the Jews," a remarkable difference is evident. As we shall see in detail in the Analysis of the second edition, "the Jews" show no concern at all with the reaction of the people. There is no evidence of uncertainty, fear, or apprehension. These authorities are concerned only with Jesus and not with the reaction of the people. They are angry and hostile, not fearful. Rather, as we have seen, the people fear them! Indeed, in the second edition even Pilate seems to fear "the Jews" (e.g., 19:7-8).

In the third edition, there is no significant concern with this topic.[49]

1E-15. In the first edition, the supernatural knowledge of Jesus affects individuals within the narrative and functions as a miracle, leading to belief. In the second edition, supernatural knowledge is reported only in the asides of the narrator

---

49. But see the Note on 6:52 in the Commentary.

The First Edition of the Gospel

and functions, for the reader, not as a miracle but as a demonstration of Jesus' superiority to, and independence of, human affairs (2E-10).[50]

All of the Gospels attribute foreknowledge to Jesus, and it is not the intention here to notice its presence or absence in a given edition of the Gospel of John. Rather, what is distinctive is the particular theological purpose this foreknowledge is put to by the authors of the first and second editions. Their view of its importance is consistent and yet different for each.

In the first edition, the supernatural knowledge of Jesus functions as a miracle that leads to belief. There are two clear cases of this, and three other instances that may reflect the same intention. In Jesus' encounter with the Samaritan woman (4:1-7, 16-18, 25-30, 39), it is his knowledge of her marital history that leads her to see him as the Messiah ("Come, see a person who told me everything I have done"). This episode is implicitly identified as a "sign" in 4:54.

In 1:47-49, Jesus' knowledge of Nathanael's whereabouts before they meet leads Nathanael to believe in Jesus.[51] This is quite clear, and in the first edition it was probably thought of as a "sign" even though it was not a public one and in spite of the statement in 2:11 that the Cana miracle was the "first" of Jesus' signs. It is also possible that Jesus' statement that Peter was the "son of John" (1:42) was intended by the author of the first edition as a demonstration of supernatural knowledge on the part of Jesus. In fact, it is a knowledge of Peter's ancestry, but there is no statement of belief on the basis of this knowledge as there was in the case of both the Samaritan woman and Nathanael.

In 11:11-14, after being informed that Lazarus is ill, Jesus remained where he was for two days. Then he tells the disciples that Lazarus has died. This is not an exhibition of supernatural knowledge intended to demonstrate for the reader that Jesus is above all things human (as in the second edition) since it functions within the narrative. Yet this knowledge does not function precisely to bring about belief either. Since it is similar to the knowledge of Peter's father and of Nathanael's whereabouts and since the manifestation of this knowledge is intended for the disciples, it seems correct to include it here.

---

50. The distinction between these two functions of Jesus' foreknowledge is hardly noticed within the literature on John. One partial exception is Dauer (*Passionsgeschichte* 37-38), who discusses various forms of the "knowledge" of Jesus. However, he lists 2:24-25 among the instances of what he calls *Wissenwunder* (along with the instances from the Nathanael and Samaritan episodes). This is clearly incorrect. Moreover, he fails to discuss the instances in 6:4, 15. Dauer lists other instances that imply a supernatural knowledge on the part of Jesus (e.g., the prediction of his Resurrection in 2:19, references to the "lifting up" of the Son of Man, etc.). While those other instances are useful to observe, in them the focus is not on a particular use to which the foreknowledge is put.

51. As will be seen in the Commentary, this material is not identified by primary linguistic criteria but by a substantial number of ideological and theological features.

Section 2. The Criteria Used for the First Edition

In the second edition, matters are quite different. Although there are repeated references to the supernatural knowledge of Jesus there, such references are not directed to the characters within the narrative as examples of his "signs," but are directed to the reader, and their purpose is not to bring about belief to confirm for the reader the superiority of Jesus to all things human. We shall see this in detail in 2E-10.

1E-16. **In the first edition, there are numerous explanations of terms and customs as being "of the Jews." Such explanations are not found in the later editions, which, while they show little interest in details of history, geography, or terminology, exhibit and presume detailed knowledge of the Jewish Scriptures, customs, and methods of argument.**

It was mentioned earlier[52] that the term "the Jews" has three distinct meanings in the Gospel. Of these one (with the meaning "Judean") is found only in the first edition, as we have seen. A second use (in the hostile sense referring to "religious authorities") is typical of the second edition. That will be discussed in 2E-1.

The third use of the term is one that refers to the Jewish people as a whole. It was the most common use of the term in the ancient world. In the Gospel of John, this usage appears twenty-one times (2:6, 13; 3:1; 4:9a, 9b, 22; 5:1; 6:4; 7:2; 11:55; 18:20, 33, 35, 39; 19:3, 19, 21a, 21b, 21c, 40, 42). In this sense, it is used to identify individuals as "Jews" in a context that distinguishes them from non-Jews. At times this is explicit; other times it is implicit.[53]

Here we point out, first, that in the genitive plural *(tōn Ioudaiōn)* ("of the Jews") this term occurs sixteen times, always in explanations of various sorts. It is used to refer to Jewish religious or ethnic customs (2:6; 19:40, 42), to Jewish feasts (2:13; 5:1; 6:4; 7:2; 11:55), to Jewish religious authorities (3:1; 19:21a),[54] and

---

52. See 1E-3 above.

53. For example, in the Gospel "Jews" are distinguished from Samaritans (John 4:9a, 9b, 22) and Romans (John 18:20, 35). It is clear from Josephus that, although *Ioudaia* and *Ioudaioi* could be used to refer to the region of Judea, this need not always be the case. The entirety of Palestine could be referred to as *Ioudaia* (e.g., Josephus, *War* 3.1.1 §1), and the inhabitants of the country as a whole could be referred to as *Ioudaioi*. But in Josephus, *War* 2.12.3 §232, people who are previously referred to as Galileans *(Galilaioi)* are referred to more generally as Jews *(Ioudaioi)*.

54. This usage appears, for example, in Josephus, *War* 2.16.2 §336, where he refers to *Ioudaiōn hoi te archiereis hama tois dynatois kai hē boulē*... ("the chief priests of the Jews, together with the powerful men and the Council...").

A parallel use can also be found in the *Letter of Soumaios,* where an adjutant to Simon bar-Kokhba refers to the *kriteiabolē Ioudaiōn* ("the citron-waving of the Jews") in connection with the Feast of Tabernacles. See Devillers, "Lettre" 556-81.

The First Edition of the Gospel

in the phrase "King of the Jews" (18:33, 39; 19:3, 19, 21b, 21c). In all of these instances, the term is used to describe something that would ordinarily be known to other Jews. In this sense it functions in a way very similar to the translations discussed in 1E-4.

Where this plural form appears in the phrase "King of the Jews" (18:33, 39; 19:3, 21b, 21c), the term is intended in the national sense but is not an explanation in precisely the same way as the others. The remaining instances (4:9a, 9b, 22; 18:20, 35) do not occur in explanations but are references to "the Jews" in the simple national sense. Thus, all instances of the national sense of the term listed so far appear in the first edition. Only one instance is problematic: 7:2. This text is more difficult to determine. In light of the consistent association of the other texts with the first edition and, given the lack of clear association of the phrase with any other edition, it is likely that 7:2 also is from the first edition and that the ambiguity results from the disturbance of the context by editing. This instance will also be analyzed in greater detail in the discussion of Composition in the Commentary itself.

Some scholars have argued that this use is intended to distance the writer from "the Jews," thus indicating a hostility similar to that which is typical of the second edition.[55] This is almost certainly not the case. Rather, this perception is due to the fact that because there is such hostility in the "Johannine" usage of *Ioudaioi* (yet to be discussed in detail), there is a tendency to read this hostility into other uses of the word in the Gospel. If the Gospel did not contain the instances that are commonly labeled "Johannine" and that exhibit such hostility, there would be no reason to treat these other instances as hostile since they are paralleled frequently in ancient literature where no such distancing or hostility is intended. Even now, when they are read independently of the larger context, it is clear that there is no hostility or distancing inherent in the expression.

1E-17. In the first edition, the religious authorities *as a group* (identified as "Pharisees," "chief priests," or "rulers") never dialogue with Jesus.[56] This is also true of the *Ioudaioi* (in the sense of "Judeans"), who do not engage in conversation with Jesus. In the second edition, the religious authorities, now identified by the term "the Jews," are presented as almost always in dialogue with Jesus (2E-11).

---

55. For example, R. E. Brown, *Community* 49.
56. It will be seen in what follows that this refers only to the religious authorities as a group. Nicodemus speaks as an individual with Jesus in 3:1-2.

Section 2. The Criteria Used for the First Edition

This feature of the narrative orientation of the first edition is quite pronounced but is also somewhat complex in its detail, and so it has been left to this point. It will be described as a feature that emerges from the analysis rather than strictly a criterion for the analysis. Yet it is so striking that it should be noticed.

Throughout the first edition, the Pharisees and chief priests (as a group) are regularly presented as in dialogue with various groups, but only in 3:1-2, where Nicodemus (a single individual) speaks with Jesus, is that dialogue with Jesus himself. Nowhere do the Pharisees as a group enter into such dialogue with Jesus. For example, the Pharisees appear in dialogue with the temple police (7:45, 47, 48), among themselves (7:50-52; 11:47; 12:19), and with the man born blind (9:15, 16). The "chief priests" appear in dialogue with the temple police in 7:45.[57]

In the second edition, the reverse is true: "the Jews" are constantly engaged in dialogue with Jesus. This is true, for example, of their appearance in 2:18-22; in 5:10-18; in 6:41; in 7:14-18, 33-36;[58] and in 8:22-27. They also engage in dialogue among themselves (7:11) and with other persons (e.g., 9:18-22), but the chief characteristic is their dialogue with Jesus himself, a feature that contrasts starkly with the narrative role of the Pharisees and chief priests in the first edition.

There are two apparent exceptions to the pattern in the first edition. The first is in 8:12, and the second in 9:40. In both instances the Pharisees speak with Jesus. Analysis of both passages shows that the verses have been edited and contain the "mixing" of features characteristic of the third edition (3E-21). A full discussion of these passages can be found in the Commentary.

Finally, it should be pointed out that, while dialogue between the religious authorities (as a group) and Jesus is not present in the first edition, such dialogue is a primary feature of the second edition. Moreover, it continues to be a (minor) feature of the third edition.

3. Theological Characteristics

Our intention here is to point to some of the more obvious theological differences between the first and subsequent editions of the Gospel. These are so different that they can be used to identify the material in which they occur. However, the features pointed out below are by no means intended to be an

---

57. The term "ruler(s)" appears in conjunction with other terms in 3:1-2 and in 7:48, but the term is never used as the primary designation of a group in dialogue with Jesus.

58. Although this could be construed as "the Jews" speaking among themselves, I am inclined to understand it as a response to the words of Jesus in 7:33-34.

The First Edition of the Gospel

adequate summary of the theological orientation of the first edition but only to represent certain more obvious elements typical of the first edition *that contrast with features of the other editions.*

We will treat the theology of the first edition more completely in two other places. First, following the Analysis of the characteristics of the first edition, we will turn to a description of the overall orientation of the first edition. More importantly, after the Analysis of the three editions is complete, we will turn to a more detailed study of eleven central elements of Johannine theology and will describe each as it changes and develops throughout the four stages of the community's theology evident in the Gospel and the Letters.

The theological characteristics listed here are derived from the material that was identified on the basis of distinctive terms and ideological criteria. These features are helpful because there are a number of instances in which these features not only are consistent within the first edition but also contrast with theological features of the second (and the third) editions. Such contrast, together with the consistency of appearance, indicates that the Analysis has uncovered genuine characteristics of the various editions. In addition, by using theological criteria we are able to extend the Analysis to passages that do not contain the other criteria. It must be recognized, however, that the identification of passages that contain only theological features is necessarily less certain than passages that contain other types of features and particularly passages that contain a *variety* of other types of features.

As was the case with the literary criteria discussed in the previous section, there are some theological differences between the first and the second edition that are quite obvious but cannot be used as criteria. These will be discussed in the section "The Development of Johannine Theology," but some can be mentioned here. For example, in the first edition there is no mention of the Spirit, no soteriology is evident, and no eschatology is evident. Whether this conspicuous absence of such basic theological features is due to later editorial work or is simply the nature of the original document is impossible to say, but the fact itself is obvious and indisputable.

1E-18. In the first edition, belief is based almost exclusively on the miracles of Jesus; in the second edition, belief is based on a variety of "witnesses" to Jesus (2E-14).

In the material of the first edition, there is an overwhelming concentration on the "signs" of Jesus. We have investigated this from the point of view of narrative orientation in 1E-5, 1E-7 above. Here we point to the fact that belief is almost exclusively concerned with such miracles. In 2:11, the disciples believed

Section 2. The Criteria Used for the First Edition

because of the sign at Cana; in 2:23, the crowds in Jerusalem at Passover believe because of signs; in 3:1-2, Nicodemus questions Jesus on the basis of signs. In 4:1-39, the Samaritan woman and the townspeople come to belief because of signs; in 4:46-54, the official and his household believe because of a sign. In 6:2, the crowds follow Jesus because of his signs; in 6:3-14, the crowds see the sign of the multiplication and believe; in Jerusalem in 7:31, the crowds see the signs and proclaim Jesus "Messiah." The discussion following the healing of the blind man in 9:1-34 centers on the meaning of Jesus' signs; in 10:40-41, John the Baptist is said to have performed "no sign." In the aftermath of the raising of Lazarus, some of the crowd believe because of the sign (11:45) and the Pharisees are alarmed because of the signs (11:47). In 12:18, the crowd goes out to meet Jesus because of the sign. Finally, in 20:30 the narrator explains that the signs are recorded so that the reader might believe. Such a review can only be seen as a testimonial to the overwhelming concentration of the first edition on the miracles of Jesus.

Even though there is discussion of the origin of the Messiah and the Prophet like Moses and the scriptural basis for this, it is finally the signs that are the basis for belief. There are some instances in which persons believe on the report of another (1:35-49; 4:39; 4:53; 10:42; 12:9-11), yet it is always a report of signs that leads to this belief. Even the "conclusion" in 20:30-31 proposes only the signs as the basis for belief.

There is one possible exception to this that should be discussed — 1:35-49, where the coming of the first disciples to Jesus is narrated. The first two, Andrew and the unnamed disciple, are said to follow Jesus because of the words of John the Baptist (cf. vv. 36-37). Andrew then gets Peter, his brother; and, in the first edition, it seems that he later gets Philip. Philip in turn brings Nathanael to Jesus, and he confesses Jesus as the Son of God and the King of Israel. A number of comments should be made about the passage. The belief of Nathanael can be said to be the result of a "sign" since it is the demonstration of Jesus' miraculous knowledge of Nathanael's whereabouts that leads to Nathanael's belief. But what of the other three? Peter's and Philip's coming to belief is a result of a "chain reaction" report from Andrew, and the basis for the belief is not stated. It could be argued, then, that only Andrew and the unnamed disciple definitely come to Jesus on the basis of something other than belief in miracles.

Yet there are factors that may make us wary of taking even this at face value. First, as will be explained in detail in the Commentary, v. 36 (or at least part of it) probably comes from the third edition. Second, within the structure of the second edition, the coming of the disciples to Jesus as the result of the words of the Baptist illustrates one of the four important means of belief (i.e., what will be called the four "witnesses" to belief). If this is so, then the entire notion of the belief of the first disciples being the result of the words of the Baptist may be the work of the author of the second edition rather than of the author of the first. While I am not convinced that any completely satisfactory solution is possible, it does not seem appropriate to consider these verses an instance that disproves the observation about a faith based on signs that accounts for all other belief in the first edition.

It will be seen in the Analysis of the second and third editions that the conception of belief in those editions is much more complex and more broadly based than it is in the first edition, involving not only his "works" but also his "words" and the Scripture (cf. 5:31-40). Moreover, where the "works" are spoken of in connection with belief, they are said to "witness" about Jesus (5:36; 10:25) and to excite "wonder" (5:20, 7:21). But in the second and third editions the miracles are not said to bring about *belief* even though Jesus, in the second edition, regularly urges his listeners to believe because of his "works" (10:25-26; 14:11). There is none of this urging on the part of Jesus in the first edition, where his miracles are designated as "signs."

1E-19. In the first edition, there is a marked focus on details that demonstrate the greatness of the miracles. This does not appear in the later editions.

In 1E-7, we called attention to the various adjectives that are regularly used to mark the greatness of the signs of Jesus in the first edition. Here we call attention to features of the miracles themselves which tend to "heighten" the miraculous.[59] If there is an exception to this, it is that when Jesus meets Nathanael, he tells him of Nathanael's whereabouts before they met. Of itself, this is miraculous but not "heightened." In the other miracles, the greatness is explicitly stated. In the Cana miracle, the six jars used for purification hold 120 gallons (2:6) and so produce 120 gallons of wine, an enormous quantity of wine that is said to be *better* than all the other wine (2:10). Jesus reveals to the Samaritan woman not only that her current husband is not a true husband but her entire marital history, which she describes as "everything I have done" (4:29). The official's son who is sick at Capernaum is healed by the word of Jesus at a distance.

The paralytic at Bethesda has been ill for thirty-eight years (5:5). The multiplication (6:1-14) feeds five thousand people with only five loaves and two fish, yet there are twelve baskets of leftovers.[60] The blind man who was healed had been blind from birth. This sort of healing is described by onlookers in the

---

59. See also, for example, Lindars, *Behind* 35; Meier, *Marginal* 2:698, 718; Nicol, *Semeia* 42-43.

60. These figures are found in the Synoptic accounts also, and so we cannot say that the Johannine author has created them. Nevertheless, the numbers themselves are great.

Section 2. The Criteria Used for the First Edition

text itself as something that had never happened before (9:32). Lazarus had been in the tomb for four days already (11:17), and there was a stench (11:39), yet he is called forth simply by the word of Jesus.

This concentration on specific numbers that exemplify the magnitude of Jesus' miracles does not appear in the later editions. In a sense, the absence of this feature is of little significance since, with the possible exception of the miracle narrated in chapter 21, all of the miracles occur in the material of the first edition.[61] Yet the concentration on the specifics is significant, for it indicates that the intention of the author is to stress in this way also the magnitude of Jesus' signs.

1E-20. In the first edition, belief is presented as an easy affair, something that occurs readily. In the second edition, belief is something that only the disciples attain, and then fully only after the Resurrection.

In the first edition, belief in general is presented as an easy affair. We have seen earlier that the miracles of Jesus consistently lead to belief of "many" in widely diverse sectors of society.[62] The ease with which the belief is reported is surprising, and the impression of its ease is reinforced by the stereotyped expression of such belief. In 1E-5, we saw nine such expressions, from chapters 2, 4, 7, 10, 11, and 12. Never was there a qualification of the belief or a suggestion (except by later editors) that such belief could be less than adequate.[63] It is only among the authorities that belief is not so easy, yet it is reported that even among the Pharisees "many believed" (12:42). Such belief is also apparent in 1:35-49; 3:26; 4:1-3; 5:1-9a; 6:1-4, 5-15; 12:17-19, although it does not appear in stereotyped form in these instances.

As we will see in more detail in the Analysis of the second edition, in that edition belief is not portrayed as being nearly as easy as it was in the first edition. This is true not only of the religious authorities but also of the common people and even of the disciples. Not only is belief more complex and based on more than just miracles, but true belief is presented as also requiring a depth of perception (e.g., seeing the "glory" of Jesus, responding to the witnesses) not found in the first edition. Most importantly, the insight necessary for proper belief also requires the reception of the Holy Spirit, and so such belief will not be adequate until after the departure of Jesus to the Father.

61. One could well argue that the mention of 153 fish (21:11) is an example of such interest in specific numbers. However, as will be shown in the Commentary, most commentators see this number as being symbolic rather than intended to stress the magnitude of the catch.

62. See 1E-5, 1E-6, and 1E-9.

63. Some examples of the qualification of such belief by later editors are evident in 2:24-25; 4:40-42, 48.

The First Edition of the Gospel

In the third edition, belief is nuanced even further. For example, the third edition will shift the concern from one of belief versus nonbelief (as is the case in the first two editions) to a concern for correct versus incorrect belief. The conception of each edition is clear from the material of each still present in the Gospel, but the contrast (and complementarity) of each is also evident.

1E-21. Both the Christology of the first edition and the accusations leveled at Jesus occur within the realm of traditional expectations. That is, the Christology is a traditional one, making no divine claims. The accusations also do not contain a refutation of any claims that could be said to be divine. However, the later editions are marked by a radically higher Christology that constantly affirms the divinity of Jesus. This is particularly evident in the material of the second edition (2E-15; 2E-26, 27, 28, 29, 30).

As used here, "low" Christology refers to any titles applied to Jesus that can be said to stem from and to be compatible with the traditional hopes of the Jews regarding the hoped-for agent for the fulfillment of God's promises to the nation. Nowhere in that series of hopes, as they are expressed in the Jewish canon, the deuterocanonical books, the Apocrypha or Pseudepigrapha, is the agent of God said to be divine.

As scholars have attempted to discover how particular titles were understood within early Christianity, it has become clear that some of the most common titles applied to Jesus are ambiguous. Most notable among these are the titles "Son of God" and "Messiah." These titles are used both among Jews and among Christians in ways that did not intend to confer divinity. Yet at the same time, they are also used in contexts that would indicate that at least for that author they did imply the attribution of divine claims to Jesus.[64] This also seems to be true of the use of these titles in the Johannine literature. Consequently, in what follows we will treat the titles "Messiah" and "Son of God" as capable of both a low and a high christological meaning and will not consider them as distinctive of any edition.

In the Gospel as a whole, as it is understood through the application of these criteria, the first-edition Christology was a "low" Christology. The second (and third) editions attributed a "high" Christology to Jesus, and this is a major, and readily recognizable, theological difference between the first and subsequent editions. But beyond the positive titles used for Jesus, it is also important

---

64. The title "Son of Man" seems to have been understood in both a divine and a non-divine sense. However, "Son of Man" does not appear in either the first or second edition and will be treated separately below (3E-14).

Section 2. The Criteria Used for the First Edition

to see that even the *accusations* leveled at Jesus in the first edition do not concern blasphemy or claims relating either to divinity or preexistence as they do in later editions.

In the first edition, then, we find a Christology that is in keeping with the traditional future hopes of the Jews.[65] In 1:38, Jesus is greeted with the title "Rabbi" (teacher). While this is a title, it is so general that it is debatable whether it can be truly called "christological" at all. In v. 41, Andrew proclaims Jesus "the Messiah." In v. 45, Philip describes Jesus as "the one that Moses (in the Law) and the Prophets wrote about." Nathanael describes Jesus as "the Son of God and the King of Israel." Allowing for the ambiguity of the title "Son of God," all are traditional titles. In 3:2, Nicodemus says that "We know that you have come as a teacher from God." Nicodemus concludes that God is "with" Jesus, for otherwise no one could perform such signs. Clearly, this is a low Christology.

The next to apply a "messianic" title to Jesus is the Samaritan woman. In 4:25, she speaks of the Messiah as coming, "the one called Christ." Jesus in turn identifies himself as that Messiah. Then in v. 29, the woman identifies (albeit somewhat tentatively) Jesus as the Messiah to her townspeople.[66] The next instance of a messianic title is in 6:14, where the crowd that has witnessed the multiplication of the loaves proclaims Jesus "the Prophet who is coming into the world." This is the Prophet like Moses, promised by Moses in Deut 18:15-18. The Gospel of John is the only canonical Gospel to mention this eschatological prophet, and it is only within the first edition of John that the figure appears.[67]

In 7:26, there is speculation that the "rulers" know that Jesus is the Christ; in 7:31 there is further speculation about the nature of the Christ, and in 7:41 some call Jesus "the Christ." In 7:52, the Pharisees conclude the discussion of Jesus' identity by denying that he is a ("the"?) prophet. Although the discussion includes a number of titles, nowhere do they go beyond traditional titles or categories.

In the aftermath of the healing of the man born blind, the discussion continues within the confines of traditional categories. The Pharisees (9:16) say

---

65. It is perhaps more accurate to speak of "future hopes" than of "eschatological" or "messianic" hopes since by definition those narrow the scope of such expectations and promises. However, the three terms are often used interchangeably.

66. The woman also addresses Jesus with the Greek word *kyrios*, as do numerous other individuals in the Gospel. This too is ambiguous but for a different reason than are "Son of God," "Messiah," and "Son of Man." *Kyrios* has a secular meaning translated "Sir" as well as a religious meaning in which it would be translated "Lord." The meaning can only be determined by context. The religious use of *kyrios* is distinctive of the third edition, as we will see in 3E-1. The secular use is not characteristic of any given edition.

67. "The Prophet" is also mentioned in 1:21, 25; 7:40; and possibly at 7:52. See the Note on 7:52 in the Commentary.

The First Edition of the Gospel

that he cannot be "from God" because he violates the Sabbath. Others speculate that a sinful person would not be able to perform such signs. The man himself calls Jesus "a prophet" in v. 17. In v. 24, the Pharisees call Jesus "a sinner." In v. 29 Moses is identified as one to whom God spoke, but the Pharisees do not know where Jesus is "from." The man then affirms (v. 31) that Jesus is "God fearing" and "does his [God's] will" and that "unless this man was from God, he would not be able to do anything." Throughout there is a considerable variety of possible categories applied to Jesus and either rejected or accepted. Yet in none of them does the discussion ever reach above the level of the traditional.[68]

The identity of Jesus is again discussed in 10:19-21, and some think that Jesus is possessed while others deny it. While no specific title is applied, it is significant that the accusation is not one of blasphemy or of making himself equal to God, as is the case in the second edition. Within the first edition not only the titles but the entire discussion takes place within the realm of traditional (nondivine) categories. When he comes to the house of Martha and Mary after the death of Lazarus, Jesus is identified as "Sir" and "Master," but no other title (within the material of the first edition) is applied to him.

Low Christology is also apparent in 11:17-22, 39, where Martha refers to Jesus as "Sir/Master" in contrast with her claim that he is "the Christ, the Son of God, the one who is coming into the world" in vv. 23-27, material of the third edition.

During the Passion, there is repeated discussion of Jesus' identity and his actions. The discussion is about his teaching (18:20), but there is nothing more specific in the hearing before Annas. Before Pilate, Jesus is accused of being "King of the Jews" (18:34), he is mocked under the pretense of the same title (19:3), and his kingship is rejected by the chief priests (19:15). The title on the cross is the same (19:19-22). In the account of the Resurrection appearances remaining from the first edition the only title we hear from Mary is "Rabbouni" (Teacher) (20:16).

Finally, in the conclusion to the first edition, the narrator proposes what to all appearances is the most complete confession of Jesus as he envisions it: ". . . these have been written so that you may believe that Jesus is the Christ, the Son of God. . . ." In the context of the remainder of the first edition, there is no reason to think that these concluding titles are meant to affirm anything of Jesus other than what had been traditionally understood by these titles and what was understood throughout the remainder of that first edition.

We will treat the Christology of the second edition in the introduction to that edition. However, for the present it may be helpful to recall how in the sec-

---

68. As we will see in the discussion of the Composition, 9:35-41 do not belong to the first edition.

Section 2. The Criteria Used for the First Edition

ond edition, in passages associated with authorities identified as "the Jews," the complaint is regularly that Jesus makes God his own Father (5:18) and that he makes himself equal with God (5:18; 10:33; 19:7). The change in Christology from the first to the second editions could not be more striking. Furthermore, as we will see in the Analysis of the third edition, the author of that edition will begin to articulate a belief that not only is Jesus divine but he is also preexistent — yet he continues to use the titles "Christ" and "Son of God" as the anchor points of his confession.

1E-22. In the first edition, the authorities condemn Jesus to death because of his miracles and because of fear of the Roman authorities. In the second edition, he is condemned because of blasphemy (2E-25).

This is a relatively minor element in the Gospel as a whole, but it is useful in the discussion of the Passion and helps to clarify the considerable differences apparent there.

In the first edition, the cause given for putting Jesus to death (and the first time death itself is mentioned as a possible punishment) is stated quite clearly in 11:46-50. There the reason for the decision to put Jesus to death is his signs. The Pharisees and chief priests fear that, if Jesus is allowed to continue working these signs and to continue to gain in popularity among the people, the Romans will come and destroy the Temple and the nation itself. Their concern at this point is political rather than religious.

It is true that in the hearing before Annas, Jesus is asked about his disciples and his teaching (18:19), but the meaning of this is ambiguous at best. Jesus says that he has not taught in secret. Throughout the Roman trial, the accusation is that Jesus claims to be "King of the Jews" (18:33, 39). He is mocked as a king (19:5-6) and is crucified as a king (19:15-16).[69]

In the second edition, where "the Jews" propose charges against Jesus, it is first because he "does evil" (18:30); then later, in 19:7, "the Jews" say that he ought to die "because he made himself Son of God." Thus, not only the portrayal within the ministry but also the reason for condemnation is consistent with the larger theological focus of each edition.

---

69. This element of the tradition is common to all the Gospels and indeed continues as a theme into the second edition. It is, nevertheless, quite consistent with the presentation in the remainder of the first edition.

4. Features of the First Edition

The use of the term "features" here is intended in something of a technical sense. After the analysis of the material has been conducted by means of the criteria listed above, the overall contours of the thought of the first edition emerge in considerable detail. These contours are valuable because, in retrospect, they show the consistency of the portrayal in the first edition. These "features" were not used in the identification of the material, but once the material has been identified, they are useful in that they serve to confirm the analysis conducted previously. However, I would not claim that these features have the same weight as the criteria, and so the listing of the features is followed by an "F" to distinguish them.

1E-23F. The first edition contains the primary narrative of the Gospel. The chronology, narrative sequence, and geographical distribution of the ministry stem from the first edition.

This narrative is outlined in Section 3.2.b below and will not be repeated here. It will be noted, however, that the material of the second edition seldom carries the narrative of the Gospel but is intent on articulation of the theological viewpoint of the author or the unbelief of "the Jews" and the response of Jesus to that. Attention will be called to this feature of the first edition only occasionally, where it contrasts with the surrounding material.

1E-24F. In the first edition, there is a special focus on Mosaic motifs. In the second edition, references to Moses are part of a larger plan in which Jesus is shown to be greater than all the major figures of Israel (greater than Jacob, 4:12; greater than Moses, 6:30-32; greater than Abraham, 8:53).

The focus on Moses Christology is evident from such elements as the use of "sign" to refer to miracles, the attribution of the title "the Prophet (like Moses)" to Jesus. This feature is discussed in detail in Section 3.2.d below, and that discussion will not be repeated here. It is listed here separately as a feature to facilitate cross-referencing.

1E-25F. The first edition contains twenty topographical references that either are not mentioned in the Synoptics or that contain details not mentioned in the Synoptics.

Section 2. The Criteria Used for the First Edition

These topographical references are listed and discussed below in Section 3.6.c, and that discussion will not be repeated here.

1E-26F. In addition to these topographical references, there is other information in the first edition that reveals specific and precise knowledge of Judaism in the first century.

These are discussed in Section 3.6.d, and that discussion will not be repeated here.

1E-27F. In the first edition, there are numerous elements that have no function in the present form of the Gospel. These were referred to as "small, undigested scraps" by Dodd. All, or almost all, of these appear in the first edition.

The purpose of this observation is not to account for every detail of the Gospel that is not followed up in some manner in the remainder of the Gospel, but rather to call attention to more obvious elements of narrative that appear but have no role in the present narrative sequence. Examples of this are the mention of "priests and Levites" in 1:19; the mention of "first" in the sequence of Andrew getting Peter "first" in 1:41; the mention of the brothers of Jesus and the trip to Capernaum in 2:12; the mention of Jesus himself baptizing in 3:22 and 4:1; the reference to the question of "the Judean" "about purification" in 3:25; the reference to the "many" miracles upon the sick in 6:2; the reference to the "Jerusalemites" in 7:25; the statement about "the Greeks" coming to Jerusalem for Passover in 12:20-22; finally, the interrogation before the high priest (18:19-23) brings up issues that have not been significant during Jesus' ministry as it is portrayed in the present Gospel.

All of these features reflect a state of the Gospel that, at one time, contained elements of narrative that have been truncated or ignored by later authors.

1E-28F. In the first edition, questions are posed that are not answered and statements are made that are responded to in ways that do not fully address the original statement. Rather, the narrative sequence is broken and the answer given is of an entirely different type and from a different author (see also 2E-33F).

This technique is the work of the second author, and the instances will be discussed at greater length in 2E-34F. However, because this affects the relation of that material to the first edition, the instances are also listed here.

The First Edition of the Gospel

In 3:2, Nicodemus asks about the meaning of Jesus' "signs," but Jesus responds in terms of birth from the Spirit. In 3:26, the disciples of John ask about the popularity of Jesus, but John responds in the lofty language of the second and third editions. In 7:27, the common people are discussing the origin of the Christ in quite straightforward terms, but Jesus (who is not even said to be present) responds in the language and concepts of the second edition. The same process occurs in 7:32 where, in language of the first edition, the temple police are sent to arrest Jesus, but Jesus responds (again without reference to even being present in the same place) in the language and thought of the second edition. A particularly striking example appears in 12:22, where the response of Jesus is in the language of the second edition.[70] Finally, in 18:33-35, the question about Jesus' kingship, which is posed in the first edition, is answered on an entirely different level than was intended by the original question.

5. Concluding Comments on the Characteristics of the First Edition

We have now reviewed all of the characteristics and features of the first edition. It is the presence of these features that is used to identify the material of the first edition of the Gospel. That process will be conducted in detail in the Commentary itself. It will also be in the Commentary that we will be able to see how multiple characteristics appear in the same passages. This redundancy will be of considerable value for confirming the identity of the material.

SECTION 3. SYNTHESIS OF THE FIRST EDITION

Once the material of the first edition has been identified and isolated within the Gospel text, it is possible to describe the overall character of the first edition as it emerges from this analysis. The overall contours of the first edition are quite distinctive. When they are fully appreciated and when they are compared with the contours of the second edition, it becomes overwhelmingly clear that we are dealing with distinct layers of tradition within the Gospel.

It was mentioned in the Introduction to this volume that, once it is possible to identify the various editions of the Gospel, questions regarding the structure of the Gospel, the history-of-religions background, the relation of the material to the Synoptics, and the like. are best answered not for the Gospel as a whole but in relation to each edition. That this is true will become evident once

---

70. Here the third author has also inserted a response between the original context of the first edition and the response of the second edition.

Section 3. Synthesis of the First Edition

the overall contours of the three editions are grasped. We turn now to a description of the character of the first edition.

1. The Structure of the First Edition[71]

As will be seen from the outline that follows, the first edition was a complete narrative of the public ministry, beginning with the encounter of Jesus with John the Baptist and continuing through to appearances of the risen Jesus to his followers.[72]

Yet not all of the first edition is preserved in the present canonical Gospel. There are a number of places where the text of the first edition has been replaced by material from the second edition. For example, the fragmentary exchange between Nicodemus and Jesus in 3:1-3 was certainly the beginning of an extended discussion although, in the current text, all but the first few verses have now been replaced by material from the second edition. There are a number of other instances where a question is posed or an event occurs in the first edition and is answered or reflected on in the second (e.g., 3:22-26/27-30; 7:26b-27/28-30; 7:31-32/33-36; 12:20-22/23-30).

At the same time there are enough instances where extended sequences from the first edition remain to give us a clear sense of the type of material the Gospel did contain, beyond the narrative of the signs themselves. The discussion between the man born blind and the Pharisees following the miracle in 9:1-34 is a prime example of how the original Gospel was capable of such extended debate.[73] Another fragment of extended discussion appears in 7:40-52. Thus, it is likely that many of the now-truncated exchanges were much longer in the first edition. However, the conclusion of the first edition in 20:30-31 is

---

71. Whenever mention is made of the first edition as a whole, it should be understood that this is a reference to the first edition *as evident from the material remaining in the canonical form of the Gospel*. Unless stated otherwise, verse citations are inclusive and do not attempt to exclude intervening additions from other editions.

72. That the earliest literary stratum of the Gospel was such a connected narrative is generally recognized. For a very brief but helpful listing of scholars (mainly German) who have seen a *Grundschrift* or *Grundevangelium* at the basis of the Gospel see Richter, "Vater und Gott," esp. 267-68; idem, "Sogenannten" 280-87; and, at greater length, the book of van Belle, *Signs*.

Perhaps the most famous view that the earliest material was not a connected narrative was that of Bultmann, who thought of the miracles alone as constituting a source. Recently, Meier (*Marginal* 2:863) has also expressed skepticism whether there was a single narrative source containing the miracles.

73. 9:18-22, 35-41 are excluded from this since they come from later editions. The reasons for this will be treated in detail in the discussion of the Composition of those verses.

The First Edition of the Gospel

probably intact except for minor (but theologically significant) editing. Those verses are very consistent with the orientation of the first edition and suggest that the character of the first edition was probably much as it is described here.

All of this makes it clear that, although much of the first edition remains, there is much we do not have. Knowing this necessarily makes us more cautious about claiming to know the full contours of the first edition. This is particularly true with respect to comments regarding what is lacking to the first edition. We simply cannot tell whether there was no mention of a topic or whether such mention has been omitted by a later author. At the same time, as we shall see in the discussion of the first edition's theology, many of the theological contours of the first edition can be established with considerable certainty.

OUTLINE OF THE STRUCTURE OF THE FIRST EDITION

I. The Wondrous Signs of Jesus: The Belief of the People and the Unbelief of the Pharisees, Chief Priests, and Rulers (1:19–12:20)

1:19-49: John's report about Jesus and the "chain reaction" belief of the disciples. Jesus' sign demonstrating his miraculous knowledge of the whereabouts of Nathanael.

2:1-11: The sign of Jesus at the wedding at Cana and the belief of the disciples.

2:23–3:3: The signs of Jesus at the Passover in Jerusalem and the belief of the crowds, followed by the reaction of Nicodemus, one of the rulers.

3:22-26: The disciples of John the Baptist discuss with their master Jesus' baptizing and the fact of his success.

4:1-4: Jesus moves from Judea to Galilee because of the Pharisees.

4:5-39: The sign in which Jesus demonstrates his knowledge of the Samaritan woman's marital history. The belief of the woman and the "chain reaction" belief of the townspeople.

4:43-45: The Galileans welcome Jesus on the basis of his Jerusalem signs.

4:46-54: The second sign after leaving Judea: the official's son is healed at a distance by the word of Jesus. The belief of the official and the "chain reaction" belief of the official's household.

6:1-2: A report of Jesus' signs over the sick.

6:3-14: The sign of the miraculous feeding of a crowd of 5,000 men and the belief of the crowds.

Section 3. Synthesis of the First Edition

6:16-25: The sign of Jesus walking on the water.

5:1-9: The sign of Jesus' healing of a man crippled for thirty-eight years in Jerusalem at Passover.

7:25-52: Jesus at Tabernacles:
  a. belief of the crowds on the basis of his signs and reaction of the Pharisees and the chief priests, who send attendants to arrest Jesus (7:26-27, 31-32)
  b. discussion of Jesus' messianic status among the people (7:40-44)
  c. failure of the attendants to arrest Jesus and discussion regarding Jesus by the Pharisees and other rulers (7:45-52)

9:1-34: The sign of Jesus healing a man born blind and the reaction of the Pharisees.

10:19-21: Divided opinion about Jesus among the people.

10:40-41: Final comparison of Jesus with John the Baptist on the basis of signs.

11:1-53: The sign of Jesus' raising Lazarus from the dead and the aftermath:
  a. the raising itself (11:1-44)
  b. some of the people believe (11:45)
  c. some report him to the Pharisees (11:46)
  d. the Pharisees and chief priests convene the Sanhedrin and decree the death of Jesus (11:47-50, 53)

11:54: Jesus departs for Ephraim (11:54).

11:55-57: The crowds come to Jerusalem for Passover and discuss Jesus; the Pharisees and chief priests give orders to inform on Jesus.

12:1-8: Jesus comes to dinner at Lazarus's house in Bethany.

12:9-11: The crowds hear reports of the raising of Lazarus and come to see both Jesus and Lazarus: their "chain reaction" belief. The chief priests react by decreeing the death of Lazarus.

12:17-19: The final entry of Jesus into Jerusalem and the reaction of the Pharisees.

12:20-22: Some Greek Jews want to see Jesus.

II. The Passion and Resurrection of Jesus (18:1–20:30)

18:1-11: The arrest of Jesus.

18:19-24: The chief priest interrogates Jesus about his teaching and his disciples.

18:28: Jesus is led from Caiaphas to Pilate.

The First Edition of the Gospel

18:29: Pilate inquires about the charges against Jesus.

18:33-35: Pilate interrogates Jesus.

18:38b: Pilate reports to the authorities that he finds no guilt in Jesus and offers to release Jesus or Barabbas.

19:1-3: Pilate scourges Jesus, and the soldiers crown him with thorns and mock him.

19:5-6: Pilate leads Jesus out, and the chief priests and attendants cry for his Crucifixion.

19:13-16a: Pilate takes his seat on the *bema* and turns Jesus over to be crucified.

19:16b-22: Jesus is led out to Golgotha and is crucified.

19:23-25: The soldiers divide the garments of Jesus; his mother and other women stand near the cross.

19:39-42: Nicodemus removes the body of Jesus and buries it.

20:1, 11, 14-16: Mary Magdalene comes to the tomb on the first day of the week, sees the tomb opened, and begins to cry. She turns and sees a person she thinks is the gardener but discovers it is Jesus.

20:30-31a: The concluding summary of the Gospel

2. The Theology of the First Edition

In Part 4 of this volume, we will provide a history of the development of Johannine theology as it is evident in each of the four stages of the community's history and literature. There we will examine eleven central theological categories: Christology, belief, pneumatology, eternal life, eschatology, knowledge of God, soteriology, ethics, anthropology, ecclesiology, and attitude toward material reality. The theology of the first edition will also be treated there. As will be clear from an examination of Part 4, aside from the category of Christology there is relatively little discussion of those other aspects of theology in *what remains of* the first edition. Moreover, the first edition is rich in other aspects of theology, and so one needs to consult both what follows and what is discussed in Part 4 in order to have a fully adequate overview of the first edition's theology.

As we begin this survey of the theology of the first edition, two observations are important. First, it is important to remember once again that we are able to discuss only the theology *as it appears in the material that is still extant within the present Gospel.* We cannot be certain that what we are describing here

Section 3. Synthesis of the First Edition

is in fact an accurate representation of the entire theology of the community at the first stage of its existence.

Second, the account of the theology of the first edition given here can only be described as a "sketch." Much more detailed work needs to be done in order to provide a complete analysis of almost any aspect of what is discussed below. What follows is intended to point out some of the main lines of the theology that appears in the text as it is identified by the analysis.[74]

a. The Purpose of the First Edition

The first edition is essentially a narrative account of the marvelous deeds of Jesus. In the present Gospel, there is almost no theological elaboration in this narrative, other than to show that his signs demonstrated that he was the fulfillment of the nation's future hopes.[75] It may be that the repeated mention of tandem belief indicates a missionary interest where one person or group brings another to belief. But even here it is equally likely that this was intended to reinforce the sense of the overwhelming public support that Jesus enjoyed rather than missionary interest.[76] The overall orientation seems intended to bring people to belief rather than to strengthen or clarify belief.

b. The Chronology, Sequence, and Geography of the Ministry in the First Edition

The first edition contains the primary narrative of the Gospel. Except for a relatively few modifications made by later authors, the overall chronology of the ministry, the sequence of events, and the geographical distribution of the ministry stem from the first edition.

The first edition begins with the witness of John the Baptist in Judea and the resultant coming of the first disciples to Jesus. Although Jesus then (somewhat awkwardly)[77] goes to Galilee for the wedding feast (2:1-12, 13) and a brief

---

74. There will be additional discussion of theology in Part 4 of this volume, where the development of the eleven central topics of Johannine theology will be traced throughout the stages evident in the Johannine literature.

75. However, the expansion of the story of the man born blind within the first edition suggests that the first edition was originally considerably longer than is apparent in the present Gospel.

76. Thus I would disagree with Bultmann (*Gospel* 208-9), who points to a missionary theme in the tandem belief following the healing of the official's son.

77. See the comment on 1:43 in the discussion of Composition in the Commentary. It may be that 1:43 is the work of an editor tying these verses to the material that follows in 2:1-11.

The First Edition of the Gospel

stay in Capernaum, soon afterward he goes to Judea (Jerusalem) for Passover (2:13, 23), and he remains in Jerusalem (3:1-2) and the Judean countryside (3:22-26) until he is forced to retreat to Galilee because of the religious authorities (4:1-4).[78]

Along the way from Judea, he stays briefly among the Samaritans (4:4-39) and converts a significant number of them. His subsequent return to Galilee is also greeted positively (4:45), as is his healing of the official's son in Cana (4:46-54). If we are correct about the original sequence of material of the first edition, shortly before Passover Jesus (still in Galilee because of Pharisaic hostility) crosses to the far shore of the Sea of Galilee (6:1-4), multiplies bread and fish for a group of five thousand (6:5-14), and appears to his disciples that night walking on the sea (6:15-21).

Jesus goes to Jerusalem for Passover (5:1).[79] There he heals a man paralyzed for thirty-eight years (5:2-9). What occurred between that point and the Feast of Tabernacles is unclear from the present state of the Gospel, but Jesus is later presented as going up to Jerusalem for Tabernacles (7:1). From that time on, Jesus remains in Judea except for a brief journey across the Jordan (10:40-42). Not long before Passover, he goes to Bethany, where he raises Lazarus from the dead (11:1-45). This is followed by a retreat to Ephraim (11:54), with an eventual return to Bethany (12:1-2) before his final entry into Jerusalem (12:17).[80] After his final entry into Jerusalem and the meal with his disciples, he is arrested, crucified, and buried. After his Resurrection, he appears to Mary in the garden near the tomb (20:1, 11c-16).[81]

From this review of the ministry in the first edition, we see that the ministry includes three Passovers (2:23; 5:1; 11:55), indicating a ministry of more than two years.[82] The sequence also indicates three trips to Jerusalem (2:23; 5:1; 7:2).[83]

---

78. See also the studies of Meeks, "Galilee" and Fortna, "Locale."

79. It will be recalled that in the first edition chapter 6 preceded chapter 5 and what is now called simply "the feast" in 5:1 was almost surely the Passover, said (in what is now 6:4) to be "near."

80. This is the first mention of his appearance in Jerusalem for this third Passover in material of the first edition. Presumably, the first edition had an account of the entry that has now been supplanted by that of the second edition.

81. Again we must realize that this is all that remains. We do not know whether the first edition had accounts of appearances to the disciples themselves in Jerusalem. The fact that the second edition presents the next two appearances as in Jerusalem suggests that this was the case.

82. More specifically, they indicate a ministry of two years plus the undetermined amount of time from the public witness of John the Baptist to the first Passover. More will be said about this below in the discussion of the historical value of the material in the first edition.

83. This presumes a return to Galilee not narrated in the material still extant but presupposed by the notice in 7:2.

Section 3. Synthesis of the First Edition

c. The Narrative Focus on the Magnitude of Jesus' Signs, the Belief of the People, and the Hostility of the Authorities

The first edition consists mainly of narrative punctuated by exchanges among those who have witnessed Jesus' actions. The miracles of Jesus are presented in such a way as to show that throughout his ministry his miracles increased in power and magnitude, culminating in the raising of Lazarus, a miracle that led to the decision on the part of the religious authorities to put Jesus to death.

This magnitude is emphasized by a consistent focus on the "quantitative" aspects of the miracles. Thus, the first ("private") sign shows Jesus demonstrating knowledge of Nathanael's character before he meets him (1:47-48). Next, the Cana miracle (2:1-11) involves *six* jars, each holding *two or three* measures, providing over 160 gallons of wine! Jesus knows that the Samaritan woman (4:4-39) has had *five* husbands, and the woman says that Jesus told her *all* she had done. The official's son (4:46-54) is *at the point of death,* and Jesus heals him *with a word* and *at a distance* of about twenty miles.[84] The cripple at the Pool of Bethesda (5:1-9) has been paralyzed *for thirty-eight years.* The crowd near the Sea of Tiberias (6:5-14) numbers *five thousand men,* and they are fed with *five* loaves and *two* fish. Jesus comes to the disciples walking *on the water in the midst of a storm* (6:16-21). The blind man (9:12) is of a special type; he has been *blind from birth* (9:1; cf. 9:32). Finally, Lazarus (11:1-45) is not only dead and buried but has been in the tomb *four days already.* From the relatively "trivial" miracles of providing wine for a wedding and demonstrating knowledge of the woman's marital past, the miracles progress to healings of a child at the point of death. Later a huge crowd is fed with almost nothing, and a man crippled for thirty-eight years is healed. A man blind from birth is healed (it had never been heard that one blind from birth could be healed!), and finally a man dead for four days is raised from the dead! The increasing magnitude is evident throughout.

In the discussion of the ideological criteria it was pointed out that there is a massive focus in the first edition on the belief of the common people because of the miracles of Jesus. This focus is achieved through individual reports, but most clearly by means of several stereotyped expressions that specifically mention that large numbers of people from various sectors of society and in various geographical regions came to belief in Jesus because of his miracles.

The first edition of the Gospel also appears to be oriented, at least in part, to debate with religious authorities. Although there are references to some oth-

---

84. Because of this focus on Judea as the intended locale for his ministry, it is undoubtedly significant that he finds ready acceptance elsewhere — in Galilee and even among the heretical Samaritans!

ers not believing,[85] the unbelief is centered on the Pharisees and chief priests. But even some of them are inclined to belief (12:42).

The reasons for this rejection are varied. It has to do with his place of origin (7:52), the fact that he violates the Sabbath (9:16), and the dangers that his ministry posed for "national security" (11:48-50). There is also mention, during the Passion, of Jesus being questioned by the religious authorities about "his disciples and his teaching" (18:19), but this is too vague to be helpful about their precise concerns. Before Pilate he is accused of claiming to be "King of the Jews." This charge is consistent with the concerns expressed by the Pharisees and chief priests in 11:48-50.

While there are a variety of charges against Jesus, it would seem that debate over the meaning of his miracles occupied a primary role in the first edition. So, for example, we see that both Jesus' discussion with Nicodemus in chapter 3 and the extended discussion between the Pharisees and the man born blind in chapter 9 concern the theological implications of Jesus' signs.

d. Elements of a Mosaic Christology?

In the past scholars have called attention to what seems to be a special interest on the part of the Gospel of John in Moses and Moses motifs.[86] Prominent among the Johannine motifs associated with Moses is the title of "the Prophet," a title that is found only in John within the New Testament. John the Baptist denies that he is the Prophet; the crowd that witnessed the multiplication associates Jesus with the Prophet (6:14); some among the crowd at Tabernacles argue that Jesus is the Prophet (7:40); the Pharisees argue that the Prophet could not come from Galilee (7:52). The prominence given to this title suggests a "northern" (Mosaic) orientation. Meeks suggested that the desire of the crowd in 6:14 to make Jesus king and to declare him "the Prophet" in the light of his bread/manna miracle, derived from traditions that associated Moses not only with the bread but also with kingship.[87]

While not all allusions to Moses come from the first edition, the title of "the Prophet" does appear only in the first edition. But even in the first edition, this title appears alongside other titles, and in the end the author confesses Jesus not as "the Prophet" but as "the Christ, the Son of God" (20:31).

---

85. See, for example, the references to divisions in the crowds in 7:31, 40-41 and the statement in 11:45 that some of the Judeans did not believe in Jesus and so reported the raising of Lazarus to the authorities.
86. See, for example, Teeple, *Mosaic*; Glasson, *Moses*; Pancaro, *Law*; Boismard, *Moses or Jesus*. See also the work by Meeks referred to below.
87. Meeks, *Prophet-King*.

Section 3. Synthesis of the First Edition

When we turn to the second edition, we will see a radically different orientation, in which the discussion transcends all geographical location and all traditional titles.

e. Are the Signs of the First Edition "Symbolic"?

The Gospel of John, as a whole, is the most symbolic of Gospels. Jesus speaks of "water" but actually means the Holy Spirit; he speaks of Bread from Heaven but refers to himself. He is also the shepherd, the gate, the vine, and so on. With such symbolism evident in the Gospel as a whole, it is natural to ask whether miracles such as the feeding of the five thousand are really meant to refer to spiritual feeding, whether the healing of the blind man is meant to refer to spiritual healing, whether the giving of life to Lazarus illustrates Jesus' ability to give eternal life, and the like.

Once we have achieved greater clarity with respect to the genesis of the Gospel, it is possible to provide a more adequate perspective on this issue. It seems clear that, *within the first edition,* the signs were not intended to be symbolic. The symbolism so evident in the present Gospel results from the use made of certain miracles by the author of the second edition. Thus, in the second edition, the healing of the official's son and the healing of the thirty-eight-year paralytic both function as symbols of Jesus' power to give life and to judge, as they are explained in 5:19-30. This is not their function within the first edition of the Gospel. Within the first edition, they function as proofs of Jesus' identity. However, they are taken over by the author of the second edition, and it is this incorporation into the second edition that results in a symbolic meaning being drawn out of them.

While a miracle such as the multiplication of the loaves (first edition) has been joined to a discourse that looks at the provision of bread from a symbolic perspective (second edition), the symbolic perspective is the result of later editing; it is not present in the narrative of the miracle itself. The raising of Lazarus, which comes from the first edition, is the greatest demonstration of Jesus' power. As such it prompts the religious authorities to put him to death. At the same time, the miracle has been developed into a symbol of Jesus' ability to give life, *but this is the work of later authors.*

This means also that we need to understand the term "sign" in a critical way. Does it mean "sign" in the sense of a symbol that points to a spiritual reality beyond itself? The *word* can have this meaning, and, given the extensive way in which the miracles (and other elements of the narrative) have been developed symbolically, it is fair to say that someone reading the final edition of the Gospel could take it to mean that. But as it functions in the earliest version of the Gospel, "sign" does *not* mean symbol; rather, it means legitimation of claims by demonstration of a power that can only be given by God.

f. A Low Christology Throughout

Although the Christology of the first edition will be discussed in detail in Part 4, it should be pointed out briefly here that there is no evidence of a "high" Christology in the first edition. The titles and the discussion throughout are those of traditional Jewish expectation. Jesus is said to be "the Prophet," "the one of whom Moses and the prophets wrote," "the Messiah," and "King of Israel." When the Pharisees debate whether he is "from God," it is clear from the way this is associated with Jesus' signs that their question is nothing other than whether Jesus is "from God" the way Moses was attested by signs as being "from God." We will see this in greater detail in Part 4.

3. The Genre of the First Edition

It should be clear that the genre of the first edition is true narrative. In his account, the author attempts to present in a literary way significant events from the public ministry of Jesus beginning with his meeting with John the Baptist and extending through to his Resurrection. The author of the first edition sought to demonstrate in a literary way the increasing magnitude of the miracles of Jesus together with the increasing faith of the people and the increasing hostility of the religious authorities, leading to a death that ultimately resulted in Jesus' Resurrection. It is the material of the first edition that can be best and most appropriately studied by the methods of modern narrative criticism.

a. The Narrative Role of Geography in the First Edition

Much has been made of the geographical orientation of John's Gospel.[88] From the analysis conducted here, it becomes evident that this focus on the theological significance of Galilee and Judea comes from the first edition. Jesus is a Galilean who is active primarily in Judea but meets resistance and hostility from the religious authorities there. They despise him partly because he comes from Galilee (7:52). As a result, he must retreat to Galilee as a place of safety and of

---

88. See, for example, Bassler, "Galileans" 243-57; Fortna, "Locale" 58-94; Meeks, "Breaking" 93-115, esp. 96-103; Scobie, "Geography" 77-84.

Section 3. Synthesis of the First Edition

positive reception. Judea is the place of hostility. When we turn to the second edition, we see that there is no interest in geography as a *theologoumenon*.

4. The Worldview of the First Edition

For one who comes to the Gospel of John from the study of the Synoptics, one of the most striking elements of the background and worldview of the first edition is the lack of apocalyptic features. As we shall see, such an absence of apocalyptic is also characteristic of the second edition, although, within the third edition, the worldview is clearly and strikingly apocalyptic. Naturally this is of considerable interest for the identification and study of the Gospel's strata. But it is also of considerable interest for the understanding of the background of the earliest stages of the Johannine community. When this lack of apocalyptic orientation in the first two stages of the community's existence is compared with what we know of the worldview of the rest of early Christianity, the fact is all the more striking, for the earliest Christian thinking (represented in Paul) is apocalyptic through and through. The same is true of the other canonical Gospels. If apocalyptic was considered marginal to the thought of traditional Judaism of the day, there is no marginality to the conceptual world of the first edition. There are no references to the Son of Man nor to the Kingdom of God; there are no exorcisms, no dualism.

But this lack of apocalyptic orientation does not make the Gospel less Jewish. In fact, it makes it more Jewish at least in the sense that the Jewishness is more the traditional Judaism found in the canonical Scriptures rather than the more sectarian views of apocalyptic. The expectations regarding an agent for the accomplishment of the promises made to Israel are quite traditional. The portrayal of Jesus is wholly in keeping with the understanding of expectations regarding Moses and David, with some possible allusions to the Elijah-Elisha cycles.[89]

---

89. These miracles would include primarily the provision of food in the scene of the multiplication that is seen as a parallel to the provision of barley by Elisha in 2 Kings 4:42-44. There are distant parallels between the cure of the official's son and the cure by Elisha of the son of the Shunammite woman in 2 Kings 4:25-37. But the distinctiveness of these parallels is weakened by the fact that the first of these miracles is common to all the Gospels and so hardly characteristic of the Fourth Gospel and by the fact that the parallels in the second instance are quite general.

Moreover, the Elijah motifs could well be intended not to portray northern sensitivities but to show a similarity between Jesus and Elijah as one of the two figures (Moses being the other) who were said by Scripture to come in the future. Schneiders also sees an emphasis on northern interests in the Samaritan episode in "A Case Study."

The First Edition of the Gospel

5. The Identity and Social Location of the Community at the Time of the First Edition

The Johannine Gospel as a whole is the most "autobiographical" of the Gospels.[90] Yet the first edition is relatively free of this autobiographical character, which appears prominently in the Gospel's second and third editions. Nevertheless, some aspects of the community's identity can be gathered from the text.

a. Jewish Christian

In 1 Cor 1:22, Paul seeks to characterize what would appeal most to Jews and to Greeks in their search for the Messiah. With regard to Jews, Paul says, ". . . the Jews seek signs. . . ." In many respects, the first edition of John's Gospel functions in just this way, as a proof from signs that Jesus was indeed the Messiah. We may also say that this is true of the concentration on figures of traditional Jewish expectation. In every case where the implications of Jesus' miracles are discussed, they are discussed in terms of titles such as "the messiah," "the prophet," "a prophet," or "the son of God," as we have seen above. All of this suggests that the intended audience of the first edition was a Jewish one. Almost certainly this was an audience of fellow Jews *within the synagogue*. That is, the document that served as the "first edition" of the Johannine Gospel had been composed as a way to propose evidence that would be attractive to fellow Jews. It contained nothing that would be intrinsically offensive to fellow Jews.

---

90. Thus, I would disagree with the thesis of Bauckham ("For Whom") and others, who argue that the Gospels were not written for a particular community but were intended, from the start, for all Christians everywhere. Bauckham claims that this is an "unargued assumption" (11). While he makes his argument for all the Gospels, I speak only about the issue in relation to the Gospel of John. The issues that the Johannine authors confront are those particular to his group of communities. This is, in my mind, absolutely clear from the Second and Third Letters of John, which deal with the same sort of specific errors that are confronted in 1 John and which are reflected in both the second and third editions of the Gospel. This view will be argued in detail in my Commentary on those Letters.

Yet there is a value to what Bauckham proposes if it is qualified. It is important to distinguish between the purpose for which the Gospels were *written* and the purpose for which they were *circulated*. We know that a number of other "Gospels" were written in the first century (cf. Luke 1:1-4). But these did not survive — certainly they did not survive as part of the collection the Christian community as a whole considered authoritative (i.e., the canon). By the year 200, there was general agreement about a collection of four Gospels that expressed what the community as a whole thought was essential. These gained wide circulation, just as Paul's letters, which were originally written for individual communities, were later collected and circulated far beyond the communities for which they were originally intended.

Section 3. Synthesis of the First Edition

Other Jews might not accept the argument of the first edition that Jesus was "from God," but, unlike what is asserted in the second edition, the intrinsic claims made for Jesus would not be such as to appear to contradict the basic Jewish belief in one God.

b. Sectarian Leanings?

Yet there are indications that the Johannine community is one with sectarian leanings, although this is not the sectarianism often associated with the Essenes and Qumran. Some of Jesus' closest followers had been disciples of John the Baptist (1:35-49), and John's followers were looked upon with suspicion by the Jerusalem officials (cf. 1:19-24). At least for a time the Johannine movement was itself a baptizing movement (3:22-23). The community also exhibited an interest in Samaritans (cf. 4:1-40), and some Samaritans had become believers. These were also outside the pale of Jerusalem Judaism.

As was the case with the Essenes and the group associated with John, there seems to have been a marked consciousness of purity issues in the Johannine community at this time. For example, at the wedding feast there are said to be six stone jars for purification (2:6). The interest in the purification rituals of John and Jesus is sufficient to extend beyond the context of Jesus' being baptized by John (3:22-23; 4:1). Reference is made to a concern on the part of John's disciples regarding "cleansing" (3:25). People with special impurities are said to come up to Jerusalem from the countryside early in order to purify themselves (11:55) before Passover. In the Passion, it is said that Jesus' accusers did not enter the Praetorium lest they be defiled and not be able to eat the Passover (18:28). Did the community at the time of the first edition observe such purity laws? We do not know. There is no explicit debate about their validity in the first edition, but again we must be careful not to argue from the absence of such material.

c. An Independent Tradition

In terms of its contents, the first edition demonstrates a marked independence from the traditions known from other sectors of early Christianity. This Gospel contains much information about the ministry of Jesus that is unique within the New Testament. The first edition includes miracles with little or no similarity to Synoptic miracles (e.g., the Wine Miracle, the Healing of the Cripple at the Pool, and the Raising of Lazarus). It includes discussion of christological titles that appear nowhere else in the tradition. For example, the title "the

The First Edition of the Gospel

Prophet (like Moses)" as appropriate for Jesus appears here but nowhere else in the New Testament. It has a conception of the character and length of the public ministry that is quite different from that of the other Gospels. Its overall portrayal of the Passion, including chronology, is distinctive.[91]

It is true that there is minimal similarity to the Synoptics in the healing of the official's son, in the cure of the man born blind, and particularly in the multiplication story. But, although these have general parallels in the Synoptics, one gets the impression that the Johannine accounts are independent traditions. It is impossible to imagine that there would not be some similarity since all Gospels recount the deeds of the same person.

d. Translations and Explanations of Jewish Feasts and Customs

Another feature of the first edition is the frequency with which there are explanations and translations of various names and terms. Such explanations do not appear in the later editions. Since these may tell us something about the nature of the community being addressed by the first edition, it is important to pause and reflect on those explanations.

Some of these references are explanations of Jewish customs. Thus, in 2:6 we hear of water jugs used "for the purification ritual of the Jews." In 19:40, we hear of Nicodemus binding the body of Jesus with burial cloths together with spices, "as is the burial custom of the Jews." A large number of references identify feasts as being "of the Jews": 2:13 ("the Passover of the Jews"); 5:1 ("a feast of the Jews"); 6:4 ("Passover, the feast of the Jews"); 7:2 ("Tabernacles, the feast of the Jews"); 11:55 ("the Passover of the Jews"); 19:42 ("the Preparation Day of the Jews"). Twice this expression is used to identify religious authorities as being *Jewish*. In 3:1, Nicodemus is identified as a ruler "of the Jews"; in 19:21a, the chief priests are identified as "of the Jews."[92]

It could well be asked whether these explanations are truly a part of the first edition or whether in fact they have been inserted into the first edition by a later author. While it seems that the most likely explanation is that they have all come from the first edition, it is curious that a document that is so Jewish would explain such basic issues while taking more complex ones for granted.

---

91. R. E. Brown (*Death* 2:909) lists twenty elements just in the scenes of the Crucifixion and burial that are present in one or more of the Synoptics but absent from John.

92. It is in one sense puzzling that the chief priests are so identified here since they have been mentioned repeatedly since chapter 7 without any such explanation. But perhaps all we can say is that this should not be surprising in a Gospel where Jesus is said three times to baptize before it is said that he did *not* baptize! It is perhaps equally puzzling to the modern mind why these terms — and others — were explained and other more obscure ones were not.

Section 3. Synthesis of the First Edition

From one point of view, what is significant for our purposes is that all of these translations and explanations do in fact appear in the material of the first edition as we have defined it. Whatever the reason, the features are a consistent element of the first edition. Second, such notices are not incompatible with a document that otherwise shows considerable familiarity with Palestine and with Jewish customs, since at least the translations of place-names seem intended precisely for Jewish readers.

Third, nevertheless, it must be admitted that we cannot completely rule out editing. It is at least theoretically possible that all such additions could be made without introducing any aporias. But then who would be responsible? As we shall see in detail later, the author of the second edition is intent on a debate that is occurring between the Johannine community and its Jewish matrix. The specific religious/social issue is exclusion from the synagogue. This is a *very* Jewish debate and is not the kind of context that is interested in explaining terms for "outsiders." If we look at the third edition, a similar situation seems to hold, for in that edition the issue is an internal one, namely, the community has divided over the understanding and interpretation of its own traditions and there is no evident interest in a context that would call forth such features. Therefore, it seems most likely that what the literary phenomena themselves suggest is true: these explanations are in every case relics of the first edition and betray a period in the community's history when the "Gospel" had a somewhat wider audience than is apparent in the later editions.

Therefore, it seems that while the author was quite familiar with Jewish customs and with Palestine (and especially Judea and Jerusalem itself), it may be that his audience was not so familiar and that the first author sought to explain elements of this knowledge for those individuals. Given the relative simplicity of the first edition, it would seem fair to say that the explanations, while not exhaustive, are fairly extensive and so could prove genuinely helpful to a reader of that edition. If the readership of the first edition needed such explanations, there is no indication that later authors saw any need for them. It is true that the authors were not as concerned with geography as was the first author, but the tenor of the argument in all editions is so fully Jewish that it is difficult to believe that a significant part of the community was non-Jewish.

e. Relationships with Followers of John the Baptist

Below we will ask about the historicity of the material dealing with John the Baptist. Here we ask about the theological role of John. In the first edition, there are four scenes that involve John directly or indirectly. These give him a prominence that he does not have in any other canonical document. In 1:35-39, we see that the first followers of Jesus had been followers of John the Baptist but have now gone over to Jesus because of John's witness. In 3:22-26, we learn first that Jesus and John were engaged in parallel baptizing ministries. Second, we learn that Jesus is baptizing and making more disciples than John (cf. also 4:1). We also learn that this is causing concern among the followers of John. Finally, in 10:40-42 the author returns to a comparison of Jesus and John and has the crowd observe that John "performed no sign" but that Jesus performed many.

From these four scenes, a clear direction emerges in which, by every criterion, Jesus is superior to John. First, John himself witnesses to Jesus as the one John was preparing for. Second, the people themselves demonstrate the superiority of Jesus by their popular acclamation. Third, Jesus performs signs. This would suggest strongly that at the time of the first edition the community was composed of more than just two former disciples of John and that the two groups continued to be in enough contact to make a record of the superiority of Jesus something that continued to be useful.

f. Conclusions

From the above, the following features of the community emerge. The community at the time of the first edition was nonapocalyptic, but possibly sectarian, composed primarily of Jews but perhaps containing some non-Jews. It was in close contact with followers of John the Baptist and had drawn some of its members from the circle of his followers.

6. The Historicity of Material in the First Edition

There are widely divergent views regarding the historical value of the material in the Gospel of John. It is not possible in this study to enter into this discussion in any detail. Yet it is possible to indicate briefly that many of the elements of the first edition, when judged by the canons of historical science, appear to be historical and to represent an independent source of information that is at times more reliable than that of the Synoptics.[93] This is interesting in itself, but it is doubly curious and indeed significant when it is compared with the second edition of the Gospel, which contains so many elements that are anachronistic in relation to Jesus' ministry.

---

93. For an extended discussion of the following topics, see Dodd, *Tradition*; Meier, *Marginal* 1:167-95. See also, but more briefly, R. E. Brown, *Death* 1:17-19. Moloney ("Jesus of History," 42-48) also treats some of this material, agreeing to a considerable extent with Dodd and Meier.

Section 3. Synthesis of the First Edition

Here I will call attention to the remarkably consistent way in which various aspects of the material from the Gospel that have been considered historical, derive from the first edition of the Gospel. Because the treatment must necessarily be brief, I will dialogue particularly with the recent, monumental work of Meier[94] but will also draw on other historical and archaeological studies as appropriate.

In the Analysis of the second edition, I will discuss in some detail which elements of the second edition can be said to be historical and which are manifestly anachronistic. At that time the way the two editions contrast in this regard will become apparent.

a. Overarching Issues of the Ministry of Jesus

Three issues that pertain to the ministry of Jesus as a whole and to his Passion are those of the length of the public ministry of Jesus, the number of trips taken to Jerusalem, and the chronology of the Passion.

As is well known, in the Synoptics the ministry of Jesus appears to last less than a year, yet in the Gospel of John it is more than two years in length.[95] Meier, after a thorough investigation of the length of Jesus' ministry on grounds other than that of the Johannine chronology itself, concludes that the ministry of Jesus probably began in A.D. 28 and ended with his death on Friday, April 7, A.D. 30. He then goes on to comment that, if we accept these findings, "we have a 'snug fit' with the Johannine outline: two years plus a month or two."[96]

The first edition refers to three trips by Jesus to Jerusalem (2:13; 5:1; 7:26b[97]). This is a relatively minor point within the overall concern for historicity, but it is in sharp contrast with the view of the Synoptics. Once again Meier accepts as accurate the Johannine report of these repeated visits to Jerusalem: "He [Jesus] regularly alternated his activity between his home area of Galilee

---

94. See the prior footnote. On his recognition of the special problems involved in determining the historicity of the events in the Johannine Gospel, see Meier, *Marginal* 2:118.

95. As Meier (*Marginal* 1:403, 405) points out, there are indications in the Synoptics that would not by themselves suggest a ministry of more than a year but that, if allowed some credence, could *fit with* a theory of a longer ministry. That is, the Synoptic chronology does not rule out a longer ministry even though it does not portray it.

96. Meier, *Marginal* 1:406. He goes on to say: "On the other hand, the close correlation between the minimum time demanded by John's presentation and the span of A.D. 28 to 30 that I established on other grounds counsels reserve rather than expansive speculation" (p. 406). See also his overall summary on p. 407.

97. The beginning of the narrative of the trip to Jerusalem for Tabernacles has been heavily edited, and so it is not clear from the material of the first edition that the trip took place at Tabernacles, but Jesus comes to Jerusalem again, and so this would constitute a third trip.

The First Edition of the Gospel

and Jerusalem (including the surrounding area of Judea), going up to the holy city for the great feasts. . . ."[98]

The chronology of the Passion in the Gospel of John differs from that of the Synoptics in that, in John, Jesus dies on the day before Passover rather than on Passover itself as in the Synoptics. Within the Gospel this chronology is established in the material of the first edition.[99] While admitting that the issue is a complicated one, Meier, after an extensive discussion, concludes: "In the end, a number of considerations lead me to favor the basic outline of the Johannine chronology as the most likely."[100]

---

98. Meier, *Marginal* 1:407. Meier bases his judgment here on coherence of the Johannine material with passing comments and details in the Synoptic material that could be read as implying several trips to Jerusalem (pp. 403-4, 405). As was the case with the overall chronology of the ministry, the Synoptic sayings of themselves would not be sufficient to establish the likelihood of repeated trips; but, when aligned with the explicit Johannine accounts, they do not contradict but rather tend to confirm it. Meier, in his discussion of Jesus' status as a layman (*Marginal* 1:349), warns against seeing his repeated criticism of the Jerusalem authorities as a "stereotype of Galileans as obstreperous rebels who were unconcerned about worship in the Jerusalem temple." He points to Sean Freyne's conclusion that Galileans in general were faithful to their duty of pilgrimage to the Temple in Jerusalem (Freyne, *Galilee* 259-97). Meier concludes: "We should think of Jesus as belonging to a pious Jewish laity that regularly went up to Jerusalem to worship even as it bewailed the failings of at least the upper-level priests who officiated there" (*Marginal* 1:349).

99. There are four references in the Gospel to the fact that the trial, death, and burial took place on the Day of Preparation for Passover: 18:28; 19:14, 31, 42. Of these, three instances (18:28; 19:14, 42) come from the first edition; this chronology, which had been establshed in the first edition, is taken over by the author of the third edition in 19:31. For details, see the discussion of the Composition of the individual passages.

100. Meier, *Marginal* 1:386-401, quote on 395. Meier proposes (1) that Jeremias, a primary proponent of the Synoptic dating, has not allowed the Gospel accounts to speak on their own terms and his use of OT, Qumran, and Philonic material is not sufficiently critical; (2) that the Synoptic portrayal of the trials is by and large unlikely — especially on a Passover, when the authorities would normally be celebrating the solemn feast at home; (3) that one could argue that the underlying narrative of the Synoptic accounts does not say that the last meal took place on Passover either; (4) therefore, it is conceivable that the last meal in the Synoptics is not intended to be a Passover meal either; (5) the amnesty granted to Barabbas is more easily explainable by the Johannine chronology; (6) the Marcan and Matthean Passover scenes imply that the owner of the house and Jesus' group were celebrating the Passover at the same time in the same house, something that would be unlikely.

R. E. Brown also dedicates Appendix II in his *Death* to a discussion of the chronology of the Passion and death (*Death* 2: Appendix II, 1350-78). His conclusions, which agree with those of Meier, appear on pp. 1369-73.

Section 3. Synthesis of the First Edition

b. Jesus and John the Baptist

As we have seen above, John the Baptist figures prominently in the material of the first edition. There we see a picture of baptizing activity under the leadership of John. Some of John's own disciples become the first followers of Jesus (1:35-40). Meier concludes that the indications for the first disciples coming from the circle of John's disciples "generate only a certain degree of probability — and scholars differ on the degree of probability involved."[101] He goes on to comment:

> ... it is difficult to imagine him [the author of the Gospel] making up the story that some of the most important disciples of Jesus had first chosen the Baptist as their master.... When all the Johannine theology is stripped away, an embarrassing and surprising fact remains ... : some of the most important disciples of Jesus first gave their allegiance to the Baptist, and only after a while transferred it to Jesus, whom they first met in the Baptist's circle.[102]

The first edition also gives evidence of an early baptizing ministry on the part of Jesus himself (3:22, 26; 4:1). Regarding this question, Meier says:

> [In 4:2, the final redactor] apparently found the idea of Jesus baptizing objectionable, and ... he issues a "clarification" correcting any false impression the narrative might give. Thus, the final redactor supplies us with perhaps the best NT example of how the criterion of embarrassment works.
>
> For it is precisely the criterion of embarrassment that ... comes into play here. If the historical Jesus did baptize, the entire Synoptic tradition was so embarrassed by the fact that it simply suppressed this aspect of Jesus' public life.... The main reason why the picture of Jesus baptizing is included in the Gospel may be that it was too deeply rooted in the Johannine tradition and too widely known to friend and foe alike to be simply omitted.[103]

Meier also concludes that the statement that John did not work signs (10:40-42) is probably historical. He comments: "This statement, however polemical in context, may be based on historical tradition. Not only all the various Gospel sources but also Josephus indicate that Jesus was known as a miracle-worker among his contemporaries, while John apparently was not."[104]

Thus, Meier judges all of this information regarding John the Baptist and

---

101. Meier, *Marginal* 2:123.
102. Meier, *Marginal* 2:120.
103. Meier, *Marginal* 2:121-23.
104. Meier, *Marginal* 2:170-71.

the baptizing activity of Jesus, most of which serves no significant theological agenda within the Gospel, as very likely to be historical. As such it gives us unique evidence of the wider context of such eschatological movements in the first century but also provides a unique perspective on the early history of the Johannine community itself.

c. The Accuracy and Detail of Geographical and Topographical Information

There are approximately forty-five topographical references in the Gospel of John as a whole. Of these references, a number are to places that are well known and need no corroboration.[105] However, there are twenty references that are unique to John within the New Testament or that contain details unique to John. All of these occur in material of the first edition of the Gospel.[106]

Of these, the authenticity and accuracy of nine sites have been identified with certainty through archaeology, pilgrim reports, and/or other references in literature roughly contemporary with the New Testament: Cana of Galilee (2:1, 11; 4:46-54; 21:2); Jacob's Well (4:4-6); Mt. Gerizim (4:20); the Sheep Gate in Jerusalem (5:2); the Pool of Bethesda (5:2);[107] the Sea of Tiberias (6:1; 21:1); the city of Tiberias (6:23); the Pool of Siloam (9:1-12);[108] and Ephraim in the region near the desert (11:54).

---

105. For example, the references to Nazareth, Bethlehem, Jerusalem, and the Temple.

106. Further details on aspects of this section (together with extensive bibliography) can be found in von Wahlde, "Archaeology."

107. The Pool of Bethesda (5:2), "which has five porticoes," was long thought to be symbolic and fictional. However, archaeology proved decades ago that the Johannine account provides accurate information not only about the pool but about its location near the Sheep Gate. For the early history of the excavations, see Jeremias, *Rediscovery*. In the 1970s and 1980s two revisionist studies (Duprez, *Jésus* and Pierre/Rousée, "Sainte-Marie") were written that rejected a number of earlier conclusions, most notably that the healing had taken place at the larger pools to the west. These studies argued that in fact the healing could have taken place only at the much smaller eastern pools. However, this contradicts all of the information given in the Gospel as well as misunderstanding the nature of the larger pools. For a detailed discussion of the issue, see my "Pool(s)." For a detailed discussion of the southern pool as a *miqveh*, see Gibson, "Pool." See also the discussion in the Note to 5:2 in the Commentary.

108. Because the name of the pool means "sent," some scholars thought this was purely symbolic. However, the pool is mentioned in both Josephus and in the *Copper Scroll* from Qumran. Meier (*Marginal* 2:696) comments: "The miracle in John 9:1 + 6-7, like other Johannine stories set in and around Jerusalem, shows knowledge of — and, more importantly, takes for granted — the topography of pre-A.D. 70 Jerusalem."

In the summer of 2004, Reich and Shukron began excavating the area immediately to the south of the pool at the mouth of Hezekiah's Tunnel. This area, formerly known to have been a

Section 3. Synthesis of the First Edition

Secondly, there are six sites not unique to the Gospel but about which John gives incidental details not mentioned elsewhere, thus supplying further evidence of the accuracy, the detail, and the independence of the author's knowledge: Bethsaida, which is identified as the town of Peter and Andrew (1:44); the presence of sheep and oxen at the location where the cleansing of the Temple took place (2:13-16);[109] the description of Bethany as located fifteen *stadia* from Jerusalem (11:1, 18; 12:1); the mention of the Kidron as "winter-flowing" (18:1);[110] the mention of Golgotha as outside the walls (19:20), and the location of the tomb in which Jesus is placed as nearby the site of the Crucifixion (19:41) and in a garden (20:15).[111]

Finally, there are four additional sites that this Gospel alone mentions that have not been definitively located: Bethany beyond the Jordan (1:28; 10:40), Aenon-near-Salim (3:23), Sychar (4:5), and the Lithostrotos (19:13). Nevertheless, substantial hypotheses have been advanced regarding each of these,[112] and there are no reasonable grounds today for arguing that they are anything but accurate also, even if still not definitively located.

In all these instances, the material of the first edition is quite accurate

---

reservoir from pre-Israelite times, is now shown to have been converted to a public *miqveh*, for ritual purification, sometime in the second century B.C. It may be that the smaller pool at the mouth of the Tunnel served as an *'otzer* for the larger pool. If so, Jesus would have sent the blind man to the southern pool rather than to the more northerly (traditional) site. For a first discussion of the pool, see Shanks, "Siloam," and Reich/Shukron, "Pool."

109. The problem here is that such animals would not be allowed in the Temple Mount proper; as a result, some have suggested that the Johannine information is inaccurate. However, if Jesus is reacting to an *abuse*, it could well be that they were precisely in a location that was not normally acceptable. On the other hand, it is also possible that the animals were kept in chambers connected to the corridors extending from the Huldah gates. We cannot be certain about its location, but there is no reason to rule out the Johannine account as impossible. See Charlesworth, *Jesus within Judaism* 109, 111.

110. The Kidron valley is mentioned only in the Gospel of John. As it appears in 18:1, it is defined as "the winter-flowing" Kidron. Two features of it are noteworthy. First, the fact that the Kidron, the valley east of Jerusalem, is "winter-flowing" is corroborated even by present-day experience that the valley runs with water only in the winter (i.e., rainy) season and so is shown to reflect accurate knowledge of the region. Second, the mention itself is significant inasmuch as this is the only mention of the place in the NT and precludes the possibility of borrowing.

111. The Johannine account differs from that of the Synoptics in several ways and gives a more detailed description of the location. Only John gives the Hebrew name for the site, and only John mentions that it was in a garden and that the tomb was near the site of Crucifixion. From Josephus, we know that the locations now preserved in the Church of the Holy Sepulcher as the places of Crucifixion and burial were outside the walls as they existed at the time of Jesus and also that the site was located outside the so-called Garden Gate. Thus, the Johannine account proves to be the most detailed and accurate account of the locations we have.

112. Indeed, many scholars would assert more confidently than I have here that these, too, have been identified with certainty. See the discussion in my article referred to above.

and detailed even where such accuracy is only incidental to the narrative. In this way, the material of the first edition consistently demonstrates the author's precise knowledge of pre–A.D. 70 Palestine in general and of Jerusalem in particular.

d. Other Features Exhibiting Accurate and Detailed Knowledge of Jewish Affairs

In addition to these larger issues of historicity in the first edition of the Gospel, there are a number of other details, often incidental, that reveal specific and precise knowledge of Judaism in the first century. Among these are the following:

The Stone Jars in 2:6

In John 2:6, in the account of the changing of water into wine at Cana of Galilee, there is mention of "six stone jars" for the purposes of purification, each containing two or three measures. Such stone jars were important for purification rites because they could not be contaminated by impure substances, in contrast to pottery jars, which, if they came in contact with impure liquids, were permanently contaminated and had to be destroyed.[113]

The 'Am ha'aretz

In 7:49, the Pharisees refer to "this crowd that does not know the Law." This is certainly a reference to the group that is identified in the rabbinic literature as the 'am ha'aretz.[114] Although some scholars would identify *all* "sinners" as 'am ha'aretz, E. P. Sanders (probably rightly) argues that this is incorrect.[115] Later rabbinic literature identifies the 'am ha'aretz as disregarding proper purity concerns and as being ignorant of the Law.[116] This latter charge is the one evident

---

113. *m. Kelim* 2:1. See also *m. Betzah* 2:3, 9; *t. Shabbat* 17:1. Recently, the archaeological work of Magen ("Stone Vessel") has enabled us to learn considerably more about such jars. Stone jars have been discovered in various places throughout Israel. A factory was found in the Hizma caves north of Jerusalem. Some stone jars were carved from blocks of stone weighing almost 700 pounds and had a capacity approximating that of the jars mentioned in John 2:6. Magen ("Stone Vessel" 256) suggests that the use of stoneware for eating and drinking began about the year 170 B.C. and ended with the destruction of Jerusalem.

114. See, for example, the valuable study of Oppenheimer, *'Am Ha'aretz*.

115. E. P. Sanders, *Judaism* 174-211, esp. 177-82.

116. On purity concerns, see *b. Hagigah* 24b; on ignorance of the Law, see *b. Erubin* 53a/b; *b. Megillah* 24b.

Section 3. Synthesis of the First Edition

in the comment of the Pharisees in John 7:49. As such, the incidental information about the crowd reflects historically accurate knowledge of the Pharisaic designation of this group.

The Portrayal of "Chief Priests and Pharisees" Acting Together as a Group

In his book *History and Theology in the Fourth Gospel,* Martyn argued that the Johannine picture of chief priests associating with and combining with Pharisees was historically inaccurate.[117] Martyn used this as a major part of his argument that the Gospel was simultaneously constructed on two levels. However, as I have argued in detail elsewhere,[118] the fact that the combination appears not only in John but also in Matthew and in Josephus clearly indicates that the combination is neither a Johannine invention (since it occurs in Matthew and Josephus), nor a Christian one (since it occurs in Josephus), but simply an accurate reflection of a somewhat unusual coalition between these groups when mutual convenience required it.[119] Again the fact that the author was aware of such uncommon but nevertheless factual alliances indicates the extent of the author's knowledge of first-century Judaism.

Purification from Corpse Impurity for Passover

It was necessary for Jews who had contracted corpse impurity to arrive in Jerusalem seven days before Passover in order to undergo proper purification at the Temple.[120] This practice is alluded to in John 11:55 and is mentioned only in John among the Gospels. As was the case in the other instances above, this information is not required by the theology but introduced only to explain why people would be coming to Jerusalem so early. Once again the accuracy in minor details is striking.

---

117. Martyn, *History* 84-85. Martyn called it "a very strange combination" (84).
118. von Wahlde, "Relationships" 506-22.
119. This view is now accepted by, for example, Tomson, "'Jews'" 323-24.

120. Two issues are involved here: first, the necessity of purity for the one bringing the lamb to the Temple for sacrifice and for the eating of the Passover meal. The eating of the meal was also thought to take place in the Temple (although for practical purposes the home was considered an extension of the Temple). So E. P. Sanders, *Judaism* 133-35.

Second, the ritual of purification from corpse impurity extended over seven days and is described in Num 19:11-22. On the third and seventh days, the person was sprinkled with a mixture of water and ashes from a ritually sacrificed and cremated red heifer. See E. P. Sanders, *Judaism* 215-16.

The First Edition of the Gospel

e. The Historicity of Individual Miracles

One could also ask about the historicity of the individual miracles in the Gospel of John. How do the canons of secular history evaluate them as historical events? This issue is even more complex because of issues of form, tradition, and redaction as well as the complexities associated with the very notion of miracle, which do not admit of the same sort of historical inquiry as the other elements to which we have called attention.[121] Such a discussion is beyond the scope of the present study.[122]

Moreover, it could be pointed out that the issue of historicity with respect to the miracles is not the same as the issue of historicity regarding other elements of the Gospel. If individual miracles give indications of being theological constructs rather than reports of actual events, we are not faced with the same issue as the lack of historicity in matters such as chronology, geography, and archaeology, for the lack of historicity regarding miracles (if indeed there is such) would normally be attributed to deliberate choice rather than to sheer ignorance.

f. Unhistorical Elements in the First Edition?

In spite of the considerable evidence of historical accuracy in the first edition, there are other features that require comment. Again taking our cue from Meier's study, we must ask about the absence of any account of John baptizing Jesus. Meier is convinced that the baptism of Jesus by John is one of the most certainly established facts about the historical ministry of Jesus.[123] As curious as this fact is, it is impossible to make a judgment about the absence of material since it could have been deliberately omitted by a later author.[124] When we look at the second edition later and inquire about the historical value of that material, we will have reason to raise the question again.

The accuracy of 7:52 depends on which manuscript variant is adopted. According to the more commonly attested reading, the Pharisees claim that "no prophet comes from Galilee." If this reading is correct, the statement is factually

---

121. Among the uniquely Johannine miracles, the historicity of both the changing of water to wine at Cana and the episode with the Samaritan woman are often called into question. See, for example, Meier, *Marginal* 2:934-39, on the first Cana miracle, and Schneiders, "A Case Study" 186.

122. Meier (*Marginal* 2:509-645) has an extended and very helpful discussion of the nature of miracles as understood by both the modern and the ancient mind.

123. Meier, *Marginal* 2:100-105, esp. 105.

124. Meier, *Marginal* 2:100-105.

Section 3. Synthesis of the First Edition

inaccurate since 2 Kings 14:25 says that Jonah, son of Amittai, is from Gath-Hepher in Galilee.

However, many scholars are now inclined to think that the original reading of 7:52 included the definite article, thus stating: "*The Prophet* does not come from Galilee." If this is so, then there is no problem of historical inaccuracy.

Another passage often said to be historically incorrect is the description of the arresting party in 18:3. There the party is composed of a Roman cohort together with the temple police. There are three proposed problems here: (1) According to the description, there was a *speira* of Roman troops. The *speira* was equivalent to a cohort, which would normally be made up of 600 soldiers and commanded by a *chiliarchos*, who was the equivalent of the Roman *tribunus militum*. Is this an excessively large number of troops for the arrest of Jesus? (2) Would it be likely that the Romans would choose to band together with the temple police? (3) Moreover, would it be likely that Roman soldiers would deliver a prisoner to the high priest rather than directly to the Roman procurator?

These are difficult questions, and full discussion is beyond the scope of this study. Nevertheless, some comments can be made. Regarding the first point: If the number is exaggerated, such a distortion could be understood in relation to the practice of Josephus, who regularly exaggerates numbers in his accounts.[125] It may be exaggerated without indicating total ignorance. Secondly, we can ask whether the circumstances can be imagined when such a number would seem reasonable. Four days[126] before Passover, Jesus had been in Bethany and a large crowd of people had come out of Jerusalem to see Jesus and Lazarus. On the day after that,[127] Jesus had entered the city accompanied by a large crowd that was giving him a public acclamation. According to the first edition, the Pharisees' reaction was that "the whole world" was going after him (12:19). Moreover, according to the first edition, both the Sanhedrin (11:48) and the Romans (18:33, 39; 19:2-5, 15-16, 19-22) perceived him as a threat to national security; in other words, the Pharisees and chief priests feared that the Romans would see him as a political threat and the Romans themselves judge

---

125. Scholars regularly call attention to the remarkable numbers of pilgrims proposed by Josephus as coming to Passover. While this may be inaccurate, it is not the kind of inaccuracy that reflects lack of knowledge of the reality. It is most likely a literary convention, although one not necessarily shared by all authors. See the discussion of the population of Jerusalem and of the numbers of pilgrims thought to come to Jerusalem for festivals in E. P. Sanders, *Judaism* 125-28.

126. According to 12:1, it was six days before Passover. Since by Jewish reckoning the count includes the first and last days, and since it was now the day before Passover, Jesus' arrival in Bethany would have been four days earlier.

127. According to 12:12, the popular demonstration for Jesus upon his entry into the city was "the next day."

The First Edition of the Gospel

him in terms of supposed kingship. Because Jesus was being perceived in political terms, because he had already caused two popular demonstrations in the last four days, and because this had happened at Passover, it would seem plausible to think that the Romans, who regularly showed enormous force in Jerusalem at Passover,[128] could have sent a large body of troops to arrest Jesus, not knowing what to expect at the time of the arrest.[129]

Regarding the second problem, R. E. Brown, in his extensive study of the Passion accounts in the Gospels, reviews evidence for Roman participation with Jewish troops and concludes that this aspect of the scene is fully plausible.[130] I will not repeat that here.

Regarding the third problem, Brown also concedes that it was possible for Roman troops to hand over a Jewish prisoner to the highest Jewish authorities — for example, in order to find out their opinion of Jesus. Brown concludes: "No matter how fascinating the historical implications of the Johannine scene, we have no way of confirming or denying it."[131]

Thus, while there are undoubtedly elements of the first edition whose historicity we are not able to positively confirm, there is no doubt about the remarkable accuracy demonstrated in a wide variety of elements throughout the edition.

7. The Relation of Material in the First Edition to the Synoptics

Although there are some general similarities between John and the Synoptics, it is the differences from the Synoptics that are most substantial. As we have seen above, the chronology, sequence, and geography of the ministry in the first edition are markedly different from that of the Synoptics. Whereas Jesus' ministry in the Synoptics is less than one year, in the first edition it is more than two years. Whereas in the Synoptics there is a report of only one trip to Jerusalem, in the first edition there are reports of three. Whereas the focus of Jesus' ministry in the Synoptics is on Galilee, the focus in the first edition of John is on Judea.

As we saw in the discussion of the date of Jesus' final meal and his Crucifixion, the first edition differs markedly from the Synoptics and the Johannine account was more likely to be the historically accurate one. There are Synoptic disciples that are absent from the first edition; there are Johannine disciples not

---

128. See the references to Josephus in the Note to 18:3 in Volume 2.

129. R. E. Brown (*Death* 1:692) suggests that the Romans probably did not find Jesus to be a threat. I am inclined to think otherwise. Even at the arrest, the tradition portrays an initial attempt at armed resistance on the part of Peter. If this was so close to being a reality, the Romans could well have had grounds to conclude that Jesus was a threat.

130. R. E. Brown, *Death* 1:250-51.

131. R. E. Brown, *Death* 1:251.

Section 3. Synthesis of the First Edition

mentioned in the Synoptics. The majority of the miracles narrated in the first edition are absent from the Synoptics: the miraculous knowledge of Nathanael's whereabouts, the wedding miracle at Cana, the miraculous knowledge of the Samaritan woman's past, the healing of the paralytic in Jerusalem, and the raising of Lazarus.

Four other miracles require more discussion than is possible here. Although there is a rough parallel to the healing of the official's son in the Synoptics (i.e., Matt 8:5-13; 15:21-28; Luke 7:1-10), in my opinion the similarity is so general that no borrowing can be proved. The same is true of the healing of the man born blind, an account that also has rough Synoptic parallels (Mark 8:22-26; 10:46-52; Matt 9:27-31; 21:29-34; Luke 18:35-43). I am also inclined to the same judgment about those Johannine miracles (the multiplication and the walking on the water) that are closest to the Synoptics. Debate also continues regarding the Passion narrative, in spite of obvious differences.

While it is not possible to settle these details here, it is significant to point out that the Johannine tradition evident in the first edition varies so considerably in other respects from the Synoptics that it is impossible to believe that any form of imitation was intended.

At the same time, as we shall see later, there is considerable evidence that the author of the third edition *did know the Synoptics and made a substantial number of attempts to bring elements of the Johannine Gospel into accord with the Synoptics.* In my opinion, it is there, in the third edition, rather than at the earlier stages of the tradition, that evidence of the knowledge and use of the Synoptics is most fruitfully sought.

8. The Author of the First Edition[132]

Our discussion here will focus on what can be learned about the author of the first edition from information internal to the Gospel.

---

132. The topic of the authorship of the Johannine literature is a particularly complex one. Because it is so complex, I have divided the discussion into what are hopefully more manageable units. In order to guide the reader through these various discussions, and to make as clear as possible where a given topic is presented, the following summary is provided.

There are three editions of the Gospel, each by a different person. What can be known of these individuals is given in the Analysis of each of the editions in this volume.

Because there has been such a constant tradition of attributing the authorship of the Gospel to John the son of Zebedee, a separate discussion needs to be given to both the external and internal evidence for this tradition. This is done in Vol. 3, Appendix 7 (John the Son of Zebedee).

Because there are three "Letters" in the Johannine tradition, we must question whether the same individual is author of all three Letters, and we must ask about the relation of this au-

The First Edition of the Gospel

The author of the first edition was someone with detailed, accurate knowledge of Judea and Palestine. The nature and tenor of the arguments adduced suggest that the author was probably a Christian Jew. He spoke in terms of traditional Jewish expectations. The titles he used were Jewish ("Messiah," "Son of God," "King of Israel," "the one of whom Moses and the prophets spoke"), and in fact he introduces a Jewish title not known elsewhere in the Gospels, "the Prophet" (like Moses). He is inclined to use the Hebrew (Aramaic) forms of terms, although he translates them to Greek. Place-names are often translated also, but the process is the reverse, with the Greek name given first and then the Hebrew (or at least traditional) name given second.[133] The arguments for and against the claims of Jesus operate on a traditional level and involve issues of origin for the Messiah, whether the/a prophet comes from Galilee, whether Jesus is "from God," and the meaning of the signs. This also suggests that the author was a Christian Jew.

The notion of repeated trips to Judea comes from the first edition. And in the first edition there is a decided focus on a ministry in Judea. This suggests that the author was living in Judea. This may be all we can say of the author of the first edition: he was probably a Christian Jew residing in Judea.

---

thor to those of the various editions of the Gospel. The question of the authorship of the Letters is discussed in the General Introduction to the Letters (Vol. 3). There, the discussion centers on internal evidence for authorship.

Because the author of 2 and 3 John identifies himself as "the Elder," we must ask about the use of this title in early Christianity and whether the author of 2 and 3 John can be identified as belonging to any of these categories known elsewhere. In connection with this, we must examine the statement of Papias about "John the Elder" and whether this figure could be the Elder of 2 and 3 John. These issues are discussed in Vol. 3, Appendix 8 (The Elder and the Elders).

Finally, we must ask about the figure of the "Beloved Disciple" as he appears in the third edition of the Gospel. Again, we must learn what can be determined from internal evidence, and then we must ask about the possible relationship of this figure to any of the other figures associated with the authorship (i.e., is the BD John the son of Zebedee? Is he John the Elder? Is he the author of the third edition? These issues are discussed in Vol. 3, Appendix 9 (The Beloved Disciple).

As a further guide to the discussion, I provide a brief summary of my views here. The authors of the first and second editions are distinct individuals about whom we can know very little. What we do know is gained from an examination of their compositions. There is a single author of the three Johannine Letters. He is the figure identified as "the Elder" in 2 and 3 John. He was an eyewitness to the ministry and lived a long life but did not die as a martyr. While there are some indications that "the Elder" may be "John the Elder" as described by Papias, we cannot be certain of this. The Elder is the same figure as that identified in the third edition of the Gospel as "the disciple whom Jesus loved." The Elder (i.e., the Beloved Disciple) is not the author of the third edition although he is source of the tradition enshrined in it.

133. See 1E-4.

Section 3. Synthesis of the First Edition

9. The Date of Composition of the First Edition[134]

There are no external data to indicate the date of composition of the first edition. Consequently, we must rely on information in the first edition itself.

Some scholars[135] attempt to date the Gospel relatively by comparing the theological "development" within the Gospel with that of Paul's correspondence. For example, it is common to compare the attention given in John to such concerns as food laws, the Gentile mission, the imminence of the Parousia, and future versus realized eschatology with the discussion of these issues in Paul.

Such theological criteria are ambiguous at best since they presume a systematic and synchronic theological development throughout all sectors of Christianity. For example, preexistence as found in John's Gospel (which many would judge to be "late" by these criteria) is also found in the Pauline hymns. Many interpreters would suggest that the apocalyptic eschatology of the third edition is "early," yet it *postdates* the realized eschatology of the second edition. For these reasons, theological development cannot be used as a criterion.

In the material of the earliest version *as it remains in the present Gospel,* there is no trace of many of the features that are often used to date New Testament documents. The Christology of the first edition is consistently traditional and "low." But this is of relatively little help except when comparing the first with the second edition. We do not see references that might be able to be associated with external events, particularly the events of A.D. 70. There is no trace of eschatology, either present or future, in the first edition.

As we have seen, the first edition preserves a good amount of information that is not found in the Synoptics and that has proven to be accurate recollection. In many cases, the Johannine accounts appear to preserve earlier traditions than those preserved in the Synoptics.[136] For example, the comment in 3:22-26 and 4:1 that Jesus himself conducted a baptizing ministry is probably earlier than that of the Synoptics. The date of the death of Jesus on the day *before* Passover is probably the correct one. This is not a later theological development but a recollection more accurate than that of the Synoptics. This suggests that this stratum of the Johannine account is quite early.

---

134. Among those who argue for an early date of the Gospel as a whole are the following. J. A. T. Robinson *(Priority)* argues for a date before A.D. 70. Berger *(Im Anfang)* also contends that the Gospel was written before A.D. 70. Thyen ("Johannesevangelium" 200-225, esp. 215) proposes that John knew Luke and so argues that the Gospel must date from after A.D. 85.

135. For example, Berger, *Im Anfang.*

136. It is not true that because a document preserves early traditions it is early. However, given the lack of better information, the best judgment we can make is that the first edition of John was as early as the earliest of the Synoptics.

Together these features could well suggest that the first edition is as old as, or older than, the Gospel of Mark.[137] The best that we can do, it seems, is to date the first edition in relation to the second edition of the Gospel; and we shall see evidence in the discussion of that edition that the second edition was composed before the beginning of the Jewish Revolt in A.D. 66. Because of that, a date in the fifties for the first edition would not seem unreasonable.[138] Although there is internal evidence that the first edition is quite early, it must be recognized that determining a specific date is entirely speculative.

10. The Place of Composition of the First Edition

The only evidence we have for identifying the place where the first edition was written is internal to the first edition. Yet the evidence is both consistent and considerable that at least the author and possibly the community came from Judea.

In the first edition the focus of the ministry is Judea. The mention of repeated trips to Judea comes from the first edition, as does the description of an extended ministry in Judea. This is evident from Jesus' presence at Passover in Jerusalem in 2:13, 23; 3:1-2 and then in a ministry in the Judean countryside in 3:22-26. After that the only time spent outside Judea is a relatively short period in Samaria and Galilee (4:1-54; 6:1-15).[139] In 5:1, Jesus returns to Judea (Jerusalem) for a feast. In 7:1, he goes up to Jerusalem for Tabernacles, and he does not return to Galilee thereafter.[140] Moreover, the only post-Resurrection appearance in the first edition is in Judea (20:1, 11-16). All of this not only focuses on the importance of Judea but also contrasts with the Synoptics, which focus on the ministry in Galilee.

But the first edition's portrayal of Judea is not a favorable one. It seems that the first author presents the ministry in Galilee, and specifically the reac-

---

137. In 5:2, there is the comment that "In Jerusalem, near the Sheep Gate, there *is* a pool...." Robinson (*Priority* 70) argues from the present tense here that in the writer's time, the Temple was still in existence. This is uncertain as proof since it seems that the two pools still functioned during the reign of Hadrian.

138. This represents a change from my view in the *Earliest Version* (173-74), where I proposed a date between 70-80. The essential change is that I am now inclined to posit the composition of the first edition (and perhaps the second) before the fall of Jerusalem on the basis of the admittedly tenuous indications discussed above.

139. This assumes that the original order of the first edition was as discussed above.

140. It is possible that the location at Tabernacles is the work of a later author. If, in the first edition, the multiplication miracle now in chapter 6 *preceded* the trip to Jerusalem now in chapter 5, then it could well have been that the scenes in Jerusalem were a continuation of the trip referred to in what is now 5:1. We simply have no way of knowing for sure.

Section 3. Synthesis of the First Edition

tion of the Galileans to Jesus, as a foil to the ministry in Judea and the reaction of the authorities there. Jesus is given a positive reaction in Galilee, and, according to 4:1, he retreats there when the Pharisees become hostile. When he gets there in 4:43, 45, the narrator speaks of a positive reception. In 7:52, the religious authorities berate Nicodemus, calling him a Galilean as if one who was positively oriented to Jesus would most likely be a Galilean.

But the ministry that does take place in Galilee seems presented, not so much as a deliberate intention, but as a *retreat* from the Judean ministry because of hostility (cf. 4:1, 3). Thus, even this returns the focus to Judea. The first edition also contains an overall geographical emphasis on Judea and a substantial focus on Judeans, designating them as such in 1:19; 3:25; 11:19, 31, 33, 36, 45, 54; 12:9, 11; 19:20. Moreover, the first edition shows considerable detailed knowledge of Jerusalem (5:2; 9:7; 11:18; 18:1; 19:41, etc.). All of these features strongly suggest that the first edition was written in Judea and was addressed to a Jewish-Christian community centered there.

PART 2

The Second Edition of the Gospel

INTRODUCTION

The second edition of the Johannine Gospel brings about a remarkable transformation of the tradition as it had been expressed in the first edition. The transformation is profound, but at the same time it builds on and incorporates the material of the first edition into its more developed theological viewpoint.

In the discussion of the criteria of the first edition, it was pointed out that the features of the first two editions were identified not only by the presence of literary seams that showed the presence of editing but also by positive features of each edition. It is quite helpful for the analysis that many of the features of the two editions also contrast with one another. These contrasts exist in the distinctive terms used for religious authorities and for miracles but also, surprisingly, in many of the characteristics of narrative orientation.

It should also be recognized at the outset that the second author introduces a number of features that do not appear in the first edition but which are taken over by the author of the third edition. This is not "imitation" but simply indicates a continuity between the theological viewpoint of the second and third editions. For example, terminology such as "glory," the designation of Jesus as "the Son," references to Jesus' "being sent," and the like are introduced in the second edition and so contrast with the first, but at the same time these features are taken over by the third author and appear regularly in the third edition. It is most accurate to speak of these features as being *introduced* in the second edition rather than their being *exclusive* to it.

That this should occur should not be surprising. As we shall see, the theology of the third edition is, in many ways, quite similar to that of the second edition and, in many other ways, seeks to clarify and nuance it. Consequently, it

The Second Edition of the Gospel

should be no surprise that there would be both continuity and discontinuity in the theology of the second and third editions.[1]

The characteristics listed in Section 2 below are distinctive of that edition and do not appear in either the first or the third edition. Consequently, they can be used as criteria for identifying the material of the second edition.

There are also a few characteristics common to both the second and third editions that contrast so sharply with the material of the first edition that they are useful for distinguishing the material of the first edition from the latter two editions. In the listing below, these are designated with an "X" to indicate that they are common to the second and third editions.

Finally, once the analysis of the second edition has been completed by means of the "characteristics," it becomes apparent that there are "features" that can be recognized to occur consistently within the material of the second edition but which could not be predicted or expected to occur exclusively within a given edition. Yet, once the analysis is complete, such consistency emerges. In some instances, this consistency is quite striking and serves to confirm that the analysis (conducted on the basis of the distinctive characteristics) is accurate. These are listed last.

The discussion of the second edition will follow the same general arrangement as that of the first edition. In Section 1, I will give an overview of the entire edition.[2] In Section 2, there will be a detailed discussion of the individual features distinctive of the second edition. In Section 3, there will be a more detailed synthesis of the second edition as this emerges from the analysis.

SECTION 1. AN OVERVIEW OF THE SECOND EDITION

As was done in the analysis of the first edition, a summary overview of the entire second edition is presented here. This will serve as an orientation to the second edition and will provide a summary of the features used to identify the material of the edition. Then the reader may return to the analysis in Section 2 for a detailed discussion of the features.

In the first edition of the Gospel, the characteristic terms for religious authorities were "Pharisees," "chief priests," and "rulers." Now in the second edition, the characteristic term for those who represent the official position of Ju-

---

1. This taking over of features from the second edition into the third is not to be confused with the process of "mixing" that has been referred to above. "Mixing" involves the use of *terminology* (rather than *theology*) from the earlier editions. Moreover, "mixing" involves terminology from the first edition as well as the second.

2. As was the case before, the specific characteristic being referred to in the overview will be cross-referenced to the specific characteristics as described in Section 2.

Section 1. An Overview of the Second Edition

daism is the single term "the Jews" *(hoi Ioudaioi)* (2E-1).[3] However, as we saw in the discussion of the word *Ioudaioi* in the first edition, the various meanings of this term must be distinguished. Although this word can also be used to designate the inhabitants of Judea (1E-3) and the entire nation as a religious and ethnic group (1E-16), in a number of instances in the Gospel this term is used to refer to a group of persons who are distinguished from other Jews and who exercise functions and present opinions typical of the Jewish tradition over against the views of Jesus and the Johannine community. It is these that are of importance for the present discussion, for they contrast with the terms for authorities in the first edition. The specific instances of the term that function in this way will be listed in the detailed discussion that follows in Section 2.

As "sign" was used for miracle in the first edition, so "work" is the characteristic term for miracle in the second edition (2E-2). This shift in terminology is not intended for its own sake but in fact reflects a change in perspective within the second edition. Thus, the individual "works" of Jesus are seen by the second author to be individual aspects of the larger "work" of "the Father" (2E-26X) that Jesus, "the Son" (2E-27X), has been "sent" (2E-28X) to bring to completion (2E-4). Moreover, in the second edition, the word "sign" appears twice, but the use of "sign" here is conceived of much differently than in the first. In the second edition, the term is used in a pejorative sense as a proof that is demanded by "the Jews" (and rejected by Jesus) rather than being used in the positive sense typical of the first edition (2E-3).

The narrative perspective of the second edition is also quite different from that of the first. In the second, the author presents the hostility of the religious authorities as having essentially the same level of intensity from the beginning (2E-5). This contrasts with the presentation in the first edition where the hostility of the authorities grows throughout the Gospel. In this sense, it is apparent that the second author is not concerned about matters of narrative realism but rather about simply presenting representative objections of "the Jews" regarding Jesus, objections more at home in the community at the end of the first century than in the actual historical ministry of Jesus.

Moreover, in the second edition there is no indication of division among the religious authorities. They constitute a monolithic group united in their opposition to Jesus and devoid of features that would individuate them (2E-9). In this way the authorities simply represent "those opposed to Jesus" and illustrate the objections to Jesus typical of later first-century Judaism. These authorities are in almost constant dialogue with Jesus (2E-11) in contrast with the religious authorities of the first edition, who, as we have seen, are never in dialogue with

---

3. As was the case in Part 1, the notations in parentheses are cross-referenced to the more detailed discussion of the individual topics in Section 2.

Jesus. In the second edition, the common people are in deathly fear of the authorities, and this is expressed in the stereotyped expression "for fear of the Jews" or "because they were fearing the Jews" (2E-6). In this edition, in contrast to the presentation in the first, "the Jews" exhibit no fear of, or concern for, the actions of the common people but rather inspire fear in them and even in Pilate (2E-8).

In the second edition, almost no interest is expressed in the miracles of Jesus themselves (2E-7). Instead, the focus is on the christological claims of Jesus — and these are always matters of high Christology (2E-15) rather than the low Christology of the first edition. In chapter 5, where the issue begins as one of Sabbath violation, the debate quickly moves to matters of Christology and the objection that Jesus makes God his own Father. In chapter 10, "the Jews" say to Jesus, "We do not stone you for a good work [i.e., because of your miracles] but for blasphemy. . . ." In the trial before Pilate, "the Jews" again say that their chief objection is that Jesus "makes himself God." As part of the Christology of this edition, Jesus is portrayed as in a state of indwelling with the Father as a result of which he can say that he and the Father are "one" (2E-23). In short, the obsessive focus of the second edition is high Christology as the focus of the first edition had been the miracles.

As part of this high Christology, the second edition portrays Jesus as superior to all human events. In contrast to the first edition, his supernatural knowledge functions to show this superiority (2E-10). Jesus has an "hour" set by the Father (2E-22), and before that hour human efforts against him are of no avail. He cannot be arrested; he cannot be stoned; he cannot be seized.

The worldview of the second edition is, like that of the first, simply the traditional view of the Jewish Scriptures (2E-12). One of the most prominent literary features of the second edition is the introduction of the notion of "misunderstanding," the technique by which a person takes the words of Jesus to refer to a material reality rather than the spiritual reality intended by Jesus (2E-13). This technique occurs frequently in the Gospel and always in the second edition.

The second edition introduces what can only be called a radical new theology as well as a number of topics not found in the first edition.[4] In its barest

---

4. It should be noted that this is one of three treatments of the theology of the second edition in this Analysis. This treatment (the first to appear) is the most general and is intended to help the reader understand the basic orientation of the second edition. Another, more detailed summary will be given below in Part 2, Section 3. Finally, the third discussion of the second edition's theology is given in Part 4, where all of the topics addressed in summary fashion earlier are taken up in considerably more detail along with elements of the religious worldview within which they have been cast. In each case, the discussion is structured according to the same eleven theological topics. These eleven topics will also serve as a framework within which to understand the theology of 1 John and of the third edition. Giving three such treatments necessar-

Section 1. An Overview of the Second Edition

outlines, the theology of the second edition presents Jesus as one who possesses the Spirit and who is "Son" (2E-27X) in relation to God as "Father" (2E-26X) But Jesus' understanding of God as Father, as presented by the Evangelist, is quite different from the traditional Jewish understanding of God as Father. Jesus is "sent" (2E-28X) by the Father to bring the Father's "work" to "completion." Jesus' "works" (miracles) are conceived of as elements that contribute to the completion of this overall "work." In doing the "work" of the Father Jesus seeks only the "glory" (2E-30X) of the Father, but at the same time his actions reveal both his own "glory" and that of the Father (#1 Christology[5]).

Belief in Jesus is primarily acceptance of his claims about himself and is based on four "witnesses" (John the Baptist, the works of Jesus, the words of Jesus, and the Scriptures) (2E-30X) (#2 Belief). Jesus promises the gift of the eschatological Spirit to those who believe in him (#3 Pneumatology). This gift of the Spirit, typically described symbolically under the rubric of "living water," will result in believers possessing all of the prerogatives associated with the eschatological outpouring of the Spirit in the Jewish Scriptures. The first and most important of these is that the Spirit that is the principle of eternal life will bring believers to a new level of existence so that they will possess eternal life and live with the life of God himself (2E-29X) (#4 Eternal Life). This life comes to believers in the present ("realized eschatology"), and at death they pass beyond death and continue in eternal life (2E-21) (#5 Eschatology). The gift of the Spirit also makes full and complete knowledge of God and of his will a reality. As a result, believers have no need of specific teaching from Jesus since the eschatological Spirit will give all who receive it an internal knowledge of God and of his will (#6 Knowledge of God).[6] Yet, in contrast with the presentation in the third edition, the Spirit is presented here more as a power than as a person, and in an absolute sense, without qualification and without the context in which there was a "Spirit of Deceit" opposed to this "Spirit of Truth."

It is clear that, in the second edition, the death of Jesus is not thought of as an atonement for sin. Rather, it is understood as his departure to the Father (2E-19) and the prerequisite for his giving of the Spirit. Thus, the focus is on the

---

ily involves repetition. However, it is hoped that this repetition may be helpful for the reader both in gaining an overall sense of the edition and in dealing with the analysis in a more manageable way.

5. The numbered topics in parentheses refer to the eleven major theological topics that form the core of the discussion of the theology of the second and third editions of the Gospel and of 1 John. These categories will be discussed in detail in Part 4 and referred to throughout the Commentary.

6. The Gospel, even in its present form, gives little attention to the content of the teaching of Jesus apart from his words about himself.

The Second Edition of the Gospel

giving of the Spirit. This cleansing from sin in the second edition was thought to be accomplished by the action of the Spirit (2E-20).

Not only are believers cleansed of past sin but, because they are so radically transformed by the Spirit and now have inward knowledge of God and live with the life of God, they are also cleansed of any evil inclination that would lead to future sin. As a result, they have no need of ethics (#8 Ethics).

Because believers are transformed by the gift of the Spirit, they can be said to be "born again" of the Spirit, and since they live now with the life of God, they can be truly said to be "children" of God. It is evident that the status of believers is seen as so exalted that it begins to blur with that of Jesus, who was also born of human parents, given the Spirit, and embodied in himself all of the prerogatives of the Spirit (#9 Anthropology).[7] This can challenge any sense of a unique role for Jesus from the perspective of anthropology just as forgiveness of sin through the Spirit challenged a role for Jesus in soteriology.

At the time of the second edition, the Johannine community gives no indication of having any hierarchical organization. The believer's relationship is with the Spirit, with Jesus, and with the Father. It is the common beliefs of the community that bind them together — and these are responsible for their expulsion from the synagogue. In everything, it is the Spirit that matters, and all material prerogatives such as one's physical birth, where one worships, or human leadership, are insignificant since it is the Spirit that gives life (2E-18). There is no talk of what will later be identified as ritual actions such as the Eucharist or Baptism. There is no belief in bodily resurrection. What matters is only the Spirit and the eternal life in immortality that comes through the Spirit (#11 Religious Significance of Material Reality).

The focus of this second edition was on theological issues, and the author sought to portray the conflict between his community and the synagogue against the backdrop of the ministry of Jesus. As a result, the material of the second edition contains a number of features that are anachronistic with regard to his ministry, but which reflect accurately the situation of the community at the time of the second edition (2E-31F). Rather than the historical reality of a variety of groups with religious authority, there are only "the Jews." Rather than discussing traditional titles, the second edition centers on a level of advanced Christology appropriate to the later first century rather than Jesus' ministry. And there is the portrayal of formal synagogue exclusion, a pro-

---

7. From the perspective of the present Gospel, it is impossible to hold such a view. However, as the analysis will show, it is only at the time of the third edition that the Gospel expresses those elements of Christology that definitively distinguish the status of Jesus from that of the believer. It is only in 1 John and in the third edition that Jesus is designated the "unique" Son, and it is only in these later stages of the tradition that Jesus is explicitly said to be preexistent and to be "I AM."

Section 1. An Overview of the Second Edition

cess that took place much later in the first century than the actual ministry of Jesus.

Rather than using the simple narrative sequence of the first edition, the second author imposes an artificial theological arrangement upon the material, accompanied by the inevitable disruption of the earlier narrative sequence. This artificial arrangement focuses primarily on illustrating the various "witnesses" to Jesus and the responses to them (2E-14). Taking up material from the first edition and modifying it only slightly, the second author begins his presentation by showing that the disciples were models of proper response to Jesus. Their belief is based on a proper response to all four of the witnesses to Jesus. In the narrative and discourse units of chapters 6–10, the author shows how Jesus provided ample evidence of each of these witnesses also to "the Jews," but they rejected them.

Another of the second author's foci is Jesus' promise of the Spirit. He portrays this by means of a series of passages in which Jesus offers the Spirit to those he meets. Here again the second author takes up material from the first edition and modifies it, introducing themes dealing with the Spirit (especially in the discussion with Nicodemus and with the Samaritan woman). Not only does the second edition disrupt the sequence of the narrative, but it also disregards the time sequence of true narrative by presuming the availability during Jesus' ministry of realities that were present only after his death (e.g., the gift of the Spirit offered to the Samaritan woman).

The material of this second edition proceeds primarily through discourse and debate, rather than by narrative (2E-11). Where there is narrative, it serves the purposes of the debate that follows, and that debate is the ultimate focus. The second edition is Jewish throughout and reflects various forms of sophisticated rabbinic thought and argument not evident in the first edition (2E-33F). We see, for example, that, in chapter 5, Jesus' justification for his work on the Sabbath is based on the rabbinic argument that God himself worked on the Sabbath. The discourse of chapter 6 is cast in the stereotyped format of Jewish exegetical homilies on Scripture. In chapter 7, Jesus makes use of the rabbinic argument of *qal wāḥōmer*. In chapter 8, Jesus justifies his witness on the basis of rabbinic laws regarding what constitutes such valid witness.

In contrast to the material of the first edition, the second edition has no desire to record Jesus' ministry but focuses almost exclusively on theological issues. As a result, the material of the second edition is of little use for discussions of the historical ministry. Nevertheless, the material reflects quite accurately the history and theology of the later community as it confronted opposition within the synagogue!

As was the case with the first edition, what we know of the author, the community, the date, and the locale of composition is slight and can only be gleaned from the material itself. The author was a Jew, knowledgeable in later Jewish thought. The second edition was undoubtedly composed some years after the first edition, but the locale of its composition is difficult to determine. The fact that it is cast in the traditional Jewish worldview rather than the more radical and more Hellenized worldview of apocalyptic tells us that it represents what was probably a truly faithful picture of the response of traditional Jewish believers to Jesus.

SECTION 2. THE CRITERIA USED FOR THE IDENTIFICATION OF MATERIAL OF THE SECOND EDITION

As we turn to the detailed discussion of the characteristics of the second edition, the method employed will again be that described in the section "Methodology" in the Introduction. Again, three types of criteria will be identified: (1) characteristic terminology, (2) narrative orientation (ideological features), and (3) theological features. What was said about the relative merits of these three types of criteria as well as about the value of the appearance of multiple features in the same passage remains valid. In addition to these characteristics, there are other elements that are introduced by the author of the second edition but that will also be taken over by the third author. In order to distinguish these from "characteristics," they will be listed with an "X" after the number.

Finally, there are the "features" of the second edition. These are elements of the second edition that appear to be distinctive only in retrospect, after the primary analysis is complete. Yet, while there would be no reason to suspect that they would be distinctive of a given edition, in retrospect they appear to be so. These are identified by an "F" after the number.[8]

1. Characteristic Terminology

There are four characteristic terms that, with their distinctive meanings, can be used to identify the material of the second edition.

---

8. One particularly striking example of a feature is the formula used by the second author to introduce quotations of Scripture. While there would be no reason to expect this, and while they do not appear solely in passages where they could be identified by primary characteristics, once the analysis is complete, it is quite apparent that the formula "as it is written in Scripture" appears in the second edition but not in the third. This will, of course, be discussed in more detail below (cf. 2E-32F).

Section 2. The Criteria Used for the Second Edition

2E-1. In the second edition of the Gospel, those who represent the authoritative religious position of the Jewish religion are referred to exclusively by the term *Ioudaioi*. This contrasts with the use of "Pharisees" *(Pharisaioi)*, "chief priests" *(archiereis)*, and "rulers" *(archontes)* for religious authorities in the first edition (1E-1).[9] It also contrasts with the use of *Ioudaioi*, referring to "Judeans," in the first edition (1E-3).

As we saw previously,[10] the use of *Ioudaioi* in the Gospel is complex. We discussed the use of the term to designate regional origin ("Judean") in 1E-3 and to designate national origin ("Jews") in 1E-16. Here we will take up the third of these uses, the "hostile" sense, the use in which the term designates the religious authorities opposed to Jesus. This use is characteristic of the second edition. When found with this meaning, the term will always be written "the Jews" (i.e., in quotation marks).

Although this is the third of the uses to be discussed, it is the one that is most distinctive of the Gospel and the one to which most attention must be paid. It is a term and a usage that has been much misunderstood and that has given rise to an immensely unfortunate history of interpretation. It is hoped that the analysis here will provide some clarity regarding the origin and the original intention of that usage.

This usage of the term *Ioudaioi* to refer to religious authorities will be referred to as the "hostile" use (since this is a characteristic of all instances).[11] This use occurs thirty-seven times in the Gospel: 2:18, 20; 5:10, 15, 16, 18; 6:41, 52; 7:1*,[12] 11, 13, 15*, 35*; 8:22, 31*, 48*, 52*, 57*; 9:18, 22a, 22b; 10:24, 31, 33; 11:8; 13:33; 18:12, 14, 31, 36, 38; 19:7, 12, 14, 31, 38; 20:19. There are two prominent features of all these texts: (1) they refer to a single unified group, as can be seen by several overlapping characteristics; (2) the texts where they appear consistently present the authoritative religious view of the Jewish religion as it was understood by the author of the second edition.

---

9. The argument here is a development of that presented in my article, "Survey."

10. See 1E-3.

11. No exact parallel to the usage in the Gospel of John has been found. One Pauline text (1 Thess 2:14) is close in meaning and is often referred to as the "Johannine interpolation." Another parallel is found in Josephus' *Life* 23 §113. Josephus describes the defection of two nobles from Trachonitis and their arrival as Secessionists. He comments that "the Jews would have forced them to be circumcised if they desired to reside among them." Josephus is himself a Jew, but he speaks of "the Jews" as a quasi-authoritative group within the nation and representative of a particular religious viewpoint.

12. Texts marked with an asterisk require extended discussion. This is given below and in the discussion of Composition in the Commentary.

The Second Edition of the Gospel

Distinctive Features

That these texts represent a single group is clear from their several distinctive, overlapping features. The first characteristic is that, in these instances, *Ioudaioi* does not have either its nationalistic or its regional meaning since these *Ioudaioi* are regularly distinguished from other persons who by nationality or regional origin are also Jews. For example, the common people, who are Jews, are afraid to act "for fear of the Jews" (7:13). The parents of the man born blind, who are themselves Jewish, are afraid of "the Jews" (9:18-22), as are the disciples (20:19), who are also Jews.

Second, this group exhibits a single, undifferentiated reaction to Jesus. These *Ioudaioi* exhibit a constant, mortal hostility to Jesus, and this hostility is without a sense of development. From their second appearance it is explicit that they seek to kill him (5:18; 7:1), or to stone him (10:31; 11:8). They accuse him of making himself equal with God and of blasphemy in doing so (5:18; 10:33; 19:7). While there are instances where the hostility is less overtly intense (2:18, 20), the group in these instances nevertheless manifests skepticism, unbelief, and hostility. There is no openness, nor even neutrality, on their part to his claims.

Third, there is never any division or disagreement about Jesus among this group. This circumstance contrasts with the portrayal in the first edition where there was regular evidence of division among the authorities when they were identified as "Pharisees," "chief priests," and "rulers."[13]

Fourth, there are several types of evidence that indicate that the term, when used this way, is intended to refer to religious authorities rather than to common people.[14]

(a) The term appears in contexts where it alternates with other terms for religious authorities. For example, in 7:32 the authorities are referred to as "Pharisees," and in 7:35 they are referred to as "the Jews."[15] In 9:13, 15, 16, the reli-

---

13. See 1E-9.
14. I studied these features in a preliminary way in "Terms" 231-53 and *Earliest* 31-36.
15. R. E. Brown, in his posthumously published *Introduction/John* (165 n. 39), has criticized the present author's work on "the Jews" on two counts: (1) that "von Wahlde's own position ... is overstated (he has to admit that 6:41, 52 constitutes an exception) ... ," and that, (2) with respect to 7:35, "von Wahlde ... resort(s) to the theory that the sequence of texts is artificial." In fact, I had argued specifically that *almost* all texts reflected such alternation, and I had readily admitted that 6:41, 52 did not fit the pattern. If thirty-five of thirty-seven instances of the term form a pattern, then it seems difficult to say there is no pattern, especially since the two "exceptions" could well have been created by later editorial activity.

With regard to the second criticism, in the original edition of his commentary, Brown (1:lxxi) indicated that "the term has various shades of meaning in the Gospel." First, it has a religious, nationalistic designation. Second, "... there is one stratum of Johannine material, partic-

Section 2. The Criteria Used for the Second Edition

gious authorities are referred to as "Pharisees"; in 9:18, 22a, 22b they are called "the Jews."[16]

(b) There are also instances where the author of the second edition refers back to events originally narrated in the first edition but refers to them as "the Jews," thus substituting his own characteristic terminology for the earlier terms. Examples of this appear in 18:12-14, where the term "the Jews" is used to refer back to 11:45-52, and in 18:3, where the term "chief priests and Pharisees" is used. This was discussed in detail in 1E-1.

(c) Moreover, people who are ethnically Jews are said to fear "the Jews." These "Jews," then, are an authoritative subgroup within the nation. The people report to them (5:15) as to people in authority.

(d) Still further, "the Jews" perform functions characteristic of religious authorities. In 5:10, they conduct an interrogation of the man who had been healed. "The Jews" are concerned that the man has violated the Sabbath. These are concerns of religious officials. In 9:22, we hear that these "Jews" have passed an edict of excommunication against those who would confess Jesus to be the Christ. Again, this action is typical of religious officials.

(e) A final indication that "the Jews" refers to religious authorities occurs in 7:15-20, where the common people are said not to be aware of the intention of "the Jews" to kill Jesus. Therefore, it is clear that "the Jews" are not the common people but a group distinguished from them. In this context, the fact that "the Jews" want to kill Jesus indicates that they are an authoritative group.

---

ularly evident in xi-xii, where the term 'the Jews' simply refers to Judeans and thus covers both Jesus' enemies and those who believe in him." But then Brown continues: "Leaving aside these exceptions, some of which are obvious, others of which are explicable in terms of literary criticism, the Fourth Gospel uses 'the Jews' as an almost technical term for *the religious authorities, particularly those in Jerusalem, who are hostile to Jesus*" (italics original).

From this it is clear that Brown originally held that, aside from instances of the nationalistic use and those where the term refers to Judeans (i.e., in chapters 11–12), "the Jews" always refers to religious authorities. My analysis of his view was correct, and I would stand by it. However, in his revised *Introduction,* Brown reveals an increasing inclination toward a narrative reading of the Gospel, and this undoubtedly led to his criticism of my view as ". . . resort[ing] to the theory that the sequence of texts [i.e., in 7:35] is artificial. I contend that the primary issue is what John means to hearers/readers in the present sequence, the only one given to us." (Material in brackets is mine.) Whether this inconsistency between Brown's own earlier and later views would have been recognized and eventually dealt with if he had lived to complete his *Introduction* is impossible to say. (It should also be said that Moloney, the editor of the volume, puts Brown's comments in perspective by calling positive attention to the position I espouse in my article "Fifteen" [*Introduction/Gospel* 165 n. 39].)

16. Although the term "Pharisees" appears in 9:40, it requires special discussion. Details are given in the Commentary.

The Second Edition of the Gospel

In all of the thirty-seven texts, hostility is evident; there is no neutrality or belief.[17] In all thirty-seven texts, this hostility is undivided, showing no indication of hesitation or uncertainty on the part of any member of the group.[18] In all the texts, the hostility does not grow or develop throughout the Gospel but exhibits the same level of intensity throughout. These three characteristics mark all of these texts as a unit.

That the expression "the Jews" in these texts is intended to refer to religious authorities is patently clear in fourteen cases (5:10, 15, 16, 18; 7:13, 15; 8:18, 22a, 22b; 18:12, 14, 36; 19:38; 20:19). While in the other cases indications that the group is authoritative are not explicit,[19] their actions and attitudes are fully consistent with the actions of those identified explicitly as authorities and exhibit the same undivided and intense hostility as the other cases.[20] Moreover, as past surveys have indicated, there is no substantial evidence to suggest that the group is ever thought to be composed of common people except for 6:41, 52.[21] Here the term *Ioudaioi* alternates with *ochlos* ("crowd," 6:22, 24) and would seem to be identified with this common people.

But even here the usage is more consistent than would first appear. First, while the alternation with *ochlos* in chapter 6 is significant and needs to be addressed, it is equally if not more significant that of the thirty-seven instances of the term, only these two give any indication of referring to the common people. As will be apparent from the discussion of the Composition, these are anomalies rather than instances that disprove the rule. Furthermore, when 6:41, 52 are examined in their context, a considerable number of features emerge that indicate that these two instances are in fact intended to refer to the same (authoritative) group as the remaining thirty-five. Full discussion of these texts is reserved for the Commentary. In the light of that discussion, it becomes evident that 6:41, 52 are examples of the inevitable ambiguity that re-

---

17. Some would point to 8:30-31 as a possible exception. Editing there, however, has obscured the text. For details, see the discussion of Composition in the Commentary.

18. The only instance that could be said to diverge is 6:52, where "the Jews" are said to fight among themselves. However, the notion there is not one of division (there is no hint of opposing views) but simply anger expressed within the group. Moreover, this passage as a whole is an instance where the author of the third edition has taken over terminology from the second edition and "mixed" it with his own. Complete treatment is given in the discussion of Composition in the Commentary.

19. For the author to have made some explicit reference in each instance would, in fact, have been quite artificial.

20. For an extended discussion of the overlapping features, together with a discussion of individual texts, see von Wahlde, "Survey" 47-49.

21. It is particularly revealing that of scholars who think the term refers to both authorities and common people, the only texts they agree on unanimously are 6:41, 52; a majority could not agree on any other text as referring to common people. See "Survey," 34-41.

Section 2. The Criteria Used for the Second Edition

sults from human language but texts that can be explained by an examination of the wider context.[22]

In his posthumously edited and published *Introduction to the Gospel of John*, R. E. Brown states that "one must ask why John would use the designation 'the Jews,' which in itself has no implication of 'authorities,' if he was thinking only of the authorities." I would respond that they are called "the Jews" because this group represents the authoritative religious position of the Jewish tradition. They represent a unified and hostile religious viewpoint different from that of Jesus and of the Johannine author. I think the use is identical to a modern instance in which one would describe what "the Presbyterians" or "the Catholics" would think. The problem is complicated by the fact that, in the ancient world, "Jew" could have a political, ethnic, social, and/or religious meaning. Throughout the Gospel it is patently clear that it is only the religious meaning that is in view in these texts.[23]

Some comment should also be made about 7:1. The use in this verse presents the strongest evidence for understanding the hostile Jews (who seek to kill Jesus!) as referring to "Judeans" since in this instance the term would appear to have a geographical meaning. However, in the remainder of the first edition, there is an obvious interest in showing Galilee as a region of safety and Judea as a region of danger. This interest is confined to the first edition.[24] However, when we look at the second edition and all of the other instances of the "Johannine" use of "the Jews," there is no interest in establishing or retaining an association of hostility with a particular geographical region. As a result, I am convinced that, in 7:1, *Ioudaioi* does not mean "Judean" but is used in the hostile sense and represents a kind of *Wiederaufnahme*, a repetition of the statement first found in 4:1, to explain why Jesus was in Galilee (again).

---

22. It should be noted that, from a methodological point of view, all of the instances listed here are treated as coming from the second edition. In this, they contrast sharply with the usage in the first edition. However, as I have mentioned, the third author has occasionally taken over "the Jews" and used ("mixed") it in the material of the third edition. This is discussed in detail in 3E-21 and has its own consistency, as we shall see.

23. R. E. Brown, *Introduction/Gospel* 164. This usage does not negate the history of misinterpretation of the term, but it should make it clear that the author was hardly anti-Semitic or even "anti-Jewish." Clearly the author(s) of the Gospel held a position that disagreed with the official Judaism of his day, but the author(s) would have considered themselves the true heirs to Judaism and so would not have thought that there was something wrong with Judaism *as they understood it*. They used the language and worldview of that time, although it would hardly be appropriate to use those terms and that worldview today. But true historical criticism demands that we distinguish how it would have been understood then from the way the same language is (all too readily) understood today.

24. For further discussion of the role of geography in the second edition, see Part 2, Section 3.3.b.

The Second Edition of the Gospel

2E-2. In the second edition, the term "works" (*erga*) is used to designate Jesus' miracles rather than "signs" (*sēmeia*), which was the term characteristic of the first edition (1E-2). In the third edition, the expression "signs and wonders" appears (3E-55F).

The noun *ergon* occurs twenty-seven times in the Gospel: 3:19, 20, 21; 4:34; 5:20, 36 (twice); 6:28, 29; 7:3, 7, 21; 8:39, 41; 9:3, 4; 10:25, 32 (twice), 33, 37, 38; 14:10, 11, 12; 15:24; 17:4. In addition, the verb *ergazomai* occurs seven times: 3:21; 5:17; 6:27, 28, 30; 9:4 (twice).

There are three distinct usages of this term.[25] Recognizing this helps considerably in understanding the usage of the term throughout the Gospel. In the first set of texts, the noun and verb are used to refer to the miracles of Jesus, and these are the instances that will concern us here. In a second set of texts, the noun and verb are used as a theological conceptualization of the ministry of Jesus as a whole. This use is distinct from but closely related to the first. This second use will be studied below (2E-4). Finally, there is a third use that appears in the idiomatic expression *erga ergazesthai* meaning "to do the works of" someone (in the sense of "doing the will" of someone). This third use is verbally related to the others but very different in meaning. This usage appears regularly in apocalyptic literature and reflects the dualistic worldview of apocalyptic. In the Gospel this usage appears regularly in contexts marked by other apocalyptic elements and is a distinguishing feature of the third edition. It will be studied in the Analysis of that edition (3E-9).

Ergon *as a Term for Miracle*

Ergon ("work"), as a term for miracle, appears fifteen times in the Gospel: 5:20, 36 (twice); 7:3,[26] 21; 9:3; 10:25, 32 (twice), 33, 37, 38; 14:10, 11; 15:24.

In the first instance (5:20), the plural appears in a promise that the listeners will see "greater works" than those already performed. In 5:36, the "works" of Jesus are said to witness to him. It will also be noted that throughout the chapter, the religious authorities are referred to as "the Jews," showing the consistency of the appearance of these sets of terms together.

In 7:3, the brothers of Jesus want him to demonstrate his "works" in Judea. There can be no doubt that this refers to Jesus' miracles. In 7:21, "work" is

---

25. This is discussed in more detail in von Wahlde, *Commandments* 39-45. The dualistic use of *ergon* is also studied in my "Faith" 304-15.

26. The use here appears in a passage that may well come from the third edition. See the discussion in the Commentary.

Section 2. The Criteria Used for the Second Edition

a synonym for miracle: "I have performed only one work, and you all marvel." In 9:3, when speaking of the reason for the man being born blind, Jesus says that it is not because of sin but so that "the works of God might be manifest in him." These are the miracles of Jesus.

Throughout chapter 10 (vv. 25, 32 [twice], 33, 37, 38) there are repeated references to the miracles of Jesus identified as "works." In v. 25, Jesus says that his works witness to him. This is a reference to the usage in 5:36 where the witness value of the works of Jesus was aligned with that of the other witnesses (cf. the remainder of 5:31-40). In v. 32, he describes his miracles as *polla erga kala* ("many striking works") and then asks which of them was the grounds for their wanting to stone him. "The Jews" respond that it is not for his miracles that they stone him *(peri kalou ergou ou lithazomen se)* but for blasphemy. Jesus then in v. 37 reasserts the importance of the fact that he performs the works of the Father, and in v. 38 he urges his listeners to believe, if not himself, at least the works. All cases refer to miracles. In chapter 10, the religious authorities appear again and are referred to as "the Jews," showing once again the consistency of usage of both terms.

In 14:10, 11, Jesus once again refers to his miracles as works and urges the disciples to see that they demonstrate that the Father abides in him. He urges them to believe it on his authority, but if not, then to believe on the basis of the works themselves. In 15:24, Jesus refers one final time to his works in the context of the three major witnesses to him (as had been spelled out first in 5:31-40).[27]

Throughout, the background of *ergon* as miracle is consistent with the canonical Old Testament background of the activity of God both in creation and in history (e.g., Exod 34:10; Num 16:28; Ps 8:3; Isa 5:12-13).

"Works" as the Term for Miracles on the Lips of Jesus

Some scholars have pointed out (not entirely correctly) that the term "works" appears exclusively on the lips of Jesus in John.[28] On the basis of this alleged feature, some would argue that the term is not the work of a distinct author but simply represents Jesus' more profound characterization of his miracles.

This is almost certainly incorrect for several reasons. First, while it is generally true that it is Jesus who employs the term "works" for miracles, it is not

---

27. Although the word "witness" itself is not used in v. 24, the same three de facto witnesses appear in vv. 22-25 and are then augmented by the additional witnesses of the Paraclete and the disciples themselves (vv. 26-27) — and these are explicitly identified as "witnesses." This is discussed in detail at the appropriate places in the Commentary. As we shall see, the addition of the final two witnesses is the work of the author of the third edition.

28. For example, Painter, *Quest* 109; Welch, *Zeichen* 55-57.

universally true. In 7:3, "his brothers" urge Jesus to go to Judea so that "his disciples" may see "the works" that he performs. In 10:33, "the Jews" use the term in their response. A theory such as the above must deal with these exceptions. Moreover, it is incorrect to say that "works" is Jesus' designation for his own wondrous deeds, because Jesus promises his disciples that they, too, will do them (14:12).

Second, the Gospel's narrator uses the term "signs" (e.g., 20:30-31) as a positive evaluation of Jesus' ministry and urges them as the foundation of belief. However, if we suppose that both *ergon* and *sēmeion* come from the same author, we are faced with the difficulty of the narrator using a less profound term than does the Jesus he writes about. Yet nowhere do we get the impression that the narrator's description of faith is less than adequate.

Third, it should be noted that almost all discourse material of the Gospel occurs in the second edition. Since this is so, it should not be surprising that its characteristic term ("works") appears mainly in dialogue and discourse.

Fourth, and perhaps most importantly, while the terms for miracle are different in the first and second editions and while adjectives associated with the terms are different, what is most striking is the entire cluster of ideas and attitudes associated with each. This can be described fully only in the Commentary, but some brief examples may help to illustrate this fact.

Comparing the Theology of Signs and Works

While the circle of discourse of the "signs" is quite simple, focusing primarily on the performance of many and varied signs, in various geographical regions and among various groups of people, and widespread belief among these groups and a reaction of fear and disbelief on the part of the Pharisees and chief priests, the theological context of the "works" is considerably different.

The "works" in 5:20 transcend simple miracles and involve the basic prerogatives of God the Father that he shares with Jesus. Moreover, the "works" are consistently associated with the concept of "witness" so that when the second author describes the witnesses to Jesus, he uses his own terminology ("works"). In 5:36, the "works" are spoken of as "witnesses" to Jesus and are ranged alongside the witness of John the Baptist, the witness of the Father in the words of Jesus, and the Scriptures as other witnesses. This association of works and witness appears again in 10:25, where an even more detailed exposition of the witness value of the works is given (also vv. 32, 33, 37, 38). Finally, the witnesses to Jesus are listed a third time (15:20-25), and again the "works" appear (15:24).

In addition to the association of works with witness, it is clear from its use in chapters 5 and 10 that the "works" are consistently associated with the (high

Section 2. The Criteria Used for the Second Edition

christological) claims of Jesus regarding equality with God. We saw this above with respect to 5:20. In 10:33, it is again explicit: "We do not stone you for a good work but for blasphemy, and because you who are a human make yourself God." In addition, both in chapters 5 and 10, the works appear in contexts that associate them with the concept of (eternal) life, yet another feature typical of the second edition and not associated with the "signs."

In 9:3, the miracles are called the works "of God," a designation that never appears in conjunction with the signs.[29] In 14:10, 11, it is the Father abiding in Jesus who performs the works. In the next verse, the listener is urged to believe that Jesus is in the Father and that the Father is in Jesus. These references to both the high Christology and to indwelling are totally foreign to the "signs" material, as is any promise regarding the disciples performing "greater works" than Jesus.

In the first edition, the constant question was whether the signs showed sufficiently that Jesus was "from God." The implication of the "works" is radically different. The "works" are sharing in the overall work given to Jesus; they show that he is the Son and has been sent by the Father (5:36). From this basic insight, others flow. The works point to the fact that the Father has sent the Son and has given him the power to give life and to judge (5:21-23). They point to the fact that there is justification for his "making himself God" (10:33) and for his claim that the Father is "in" him and he "in" the Father (10:38).

In other words, in the second edition, the works are intended to reveal that Jesus stands in relation to God as Son to Father as well as the nature and the depth of that relationship. This insight is considerably different in type, detail, and depth from the much simpler insight demonstrated in the first edition.

Thus, there can be no doubt that the two terms for miracles are distinct not only with respect to the terms employed but also with respect to the whole range of theological conceptions associated with each.

2E-3. In the second edition, "sign" (*sēmeion*) is used in a pejorative sense as a proof demanded by the religious authorities rather than in a positive sense as it was used in the first edition (1E-2).

In the Introduction to the first edition, we saw that *sēmeion* was the characteristic word for miracle in that edition. However, there are two instances of the term that differ from that usage and that appear exclusively with material coming from the second edition. These are 2:18 and 6:30.

---

29. The signs are described as being evidence that God is "with" him (3:2) or that God hears him (9:31).

Scholars regularly point out that the use of the term has a different meaning here than elsewhere in the Gospel.[30] This usage is distinctive in five respects:

(1) The signs in 2:18 and 6:30 are demanded rather than freely given. This happens nowhere else in the Gospel.

(2) In the first edition, the signs are presented as being numerous. Statements such as 2:23; 3:2; 4:45; and 6:2 describe an abundance of signs in addition to those others that are narrated in detail (2:1-11; 4:4-39, 46-54, etc.). Moreover, the authorities (identified as "Pharisees," "chief priests," and "rulers") regularly are shown to be well aware of the signs and take note of the number and magnitude of them and comment on them (e.g., 3:2; 9:16; 11:47). In addition, they are said to fear (12:18-19, also implicit in 7:31-32) or deny (9:30-31) the implications and the impact of the signs. The demands for a sign in 2:18; 6:30 are incompatible with such a conception.

(3) Aside from the overall incongruity of the two conceptions, the demand for a sign in 2:18 is incongruous in the immediate context of Nicodemus's reaction as well as the notice of multiple signs in 2:23. The demand for a sign in 6:30 is incongruous in the light of the multiplication of the loaves, which took place immediately before it.

(4) In 2:18 and 6:30, a response is given to the request but the "sign" given is not of the same sort as is given in all texts dealing with signs. In 2:18 and 6:30, the sign promised by Jesus is a christological event in which the "sign" is neither a miracle nor a legitimating sign but rather a reflection (or "symbol") of his deeper christological identity. In 2:13-22, "the Jews" demand a sign to show Jesus' authority for cleansing the Temple. Jesus does not refuse to give a sign but gives "the Jews" one of a different order. What Jesus offers legitimates him, but not through a demonstration of power like the signs in the first edition.

(5) In 2:18, and 6:30 "sign" appears in conjunction with the term "the Jews" rather than with "Pharisees," "chief priests," and "rulers." This happens nowhere else in the Gospel.

In 6:30, again a sign is demanded, but the sign is not a miracle but the giving of Jesus as "bread from heaven." When "the Jews" (mentioned specifically in 6:41) demand a sign, they remind Jesus that their fathers had eaten bread in the desert, implying that God through Moses had given them this bread. In effect, they demand a sign from Jesus similar to the miraculous giving of bread in the desert. Jesus does not perform a miracle but promises, by reinterpreting the Scriptures, to give the "true bread."

(6) Finally, in both instances it is significant that Jesus' response is followed by misunderstanding on the part of "the Jews." This technique of misun-

---

30. For literature on this issue, see the discussion of these texts in 1E-2.

Section 2. The Criteria Used for the Second Edition

derstanding is elsewhere characteristic of the second edition rather than the first.

Thus, we see that the use of "sign" in the second edition, although at first glance seeming to be similar to the use of the first edition, is in fact radically different from it.

The Relation between "Sign" and "Work" in the Second Edition

Although both "sign" and "work" appear in the second edition, they are used with different meanings. "Work" is the term that characterizes the activity of Jesus throughout; it carries rich connotations not only of the creative activity of God in the Old Testament but also of the interrelationship of the Son and the Father.[31] When looking at "sign" as used in 2:18 and 6:30 from this point of view, it becomes evident that the author of the second edition looks upon the attitude that *demands* a response from Jesus as one that will not be honored. The Jesus of the second edition is above being controlled or commanded to do anything. It is in this sense that "work" is a term that is proper to and describes well Jesus' own understanding of his miraculous activity. As such, it is related to the conception of his ministry as a whole as a "work," as we will see immediately below.

2E-4. In the second edition, *ergon* ("work") is used as an overall theological conception to describe the ministry given to Jesus by the Father. This contrasts with the use of *entolē* ("commandment") to describe the ministry in the third edition (3E-6).

In the second edition of the Gospel, the term "work" is also used, in addition to its restricted use to refer to miracles, as a theological conception for the overall ministry of Jesus as given to him by the Father. These two uses are closely related. What is significant, however, is that this aspect of the term used to refer to his entire ministry contrasts with the use of "commandment" as a conceptualization of his ministry in the third edition.[32]

The conception of the ministry as a "work" given by the Father to complete appears first in 4:34, where Jesus, when offered food by the disciples, replies that he has food that they are not aware of: "My food is to do the will of the

---

31. The background of *ergon/ergazomai* is discussed in my *Commandments* 43-45.

32. The use of "commandment" as a conception of the ministry in the third edition will be studied in 3E-6.

155

The Second Edition of the Gospel

one who sent me and to bring his work to completion *(teleiōsō autou to ergon)."* The same conception appears in 5:17, where Jesus compares his activity on the Sabbath to that of the Father: "My Father works *(ergazetai)* until now, and I work also *(kagō ergazomai)."* A third time, in 17:4, in his high-priestly prayer, Jesus asserts that he has glorified the Father on earth, "having brought to completion the work that you gave me to perform" *(to ergon teleiōsas ho dedōkas moi)*. Thus, the individual "works" (miracles) of Jesus are seen as elements of the overall "work" (ministry) that Jesus will bring to completion. This conception is also alluded to in 5:17 and in 19:30. In the first, it is said that Jesus is "working" just as the Father "works." In the second, Jesus declares, "It is finished." Here the "it" is the "work" given to Jesus to be completed.

2. Characteristics of Narrative Orientation

The characteristics of narrative orientation are features present within the material that have been isolated by means of the linguistic criteria. As was indicated in the Introduction to the first edition, not only do the features listed here appear *consistently* within passages identified by the characteristic terminology, but they also *consistently contrast with similar ideological features in the first edition*. This indicates that they are genuinely characteristics of the second edition. As has been said above, these features are useful not only for confirming the analysis of material where characteristic terms appear (through redundancy) but also for extending the analysis to material where the linguistic criteria do not appear.

2E-5. In the second edition, the religious authorities exhibit an intense level of hostility toward Jesus throughout his ministry, rather than the increasing hostility found in the first edition (1E-10).

In the second edition, the hostility of "the Jews" does not exhibit the normal narrative development as does the authorities' hostility as portrayed in the first edition.[33] When they first appear (2:18-22), "the Jews" exhibit hostility. Their

---

33. Scholars such as Kysar ("Anti-Semitism" 113-27; cf. 115), Fortna ("Locale" 58-94), and Porsch ("Teufel" 50-57) see the hostility of "the Jews" as constant throughout. See also Smith (*Gospel* 134) on the awkwardness of 5:17-19. However, Culpepper (*Anatomy* 126-28) holds that the hostility increases. In doing so, Culpepper downplays the references about "seeking to kill him" (5:18; 7:1; 8:37) and the attempts to stone him (8:59; 10:31). In my view, these texts indicate that an attitude of mortal hostility exists explicitly from chapter 5 on. "The Jews" have appeared only one other time (2:18, 22) in the Gospel to this point; although there is no mention of a de-

Section 2. The Criteria Used for the Second Edition

demand for a sign does not at all reflect the curiosity of Nicodemus who appears later (3:1-3), nor can it be correlated with the description of the hostility of the Pharisees in 4:1 who are said to be motivated by the fact that Jesus makes more disciples than John.

"The Jews" next appear in 5:10-20. Here there is a sense not just that the reaction of "the Jews" is to this miracle but that the miracle is chosen as one example among many such occasions for hostility. Verse 16 ("Because of this 'the Jews' were persecuting [*ediōkon*] Jesus") uses the imperfect to show typical, repeated behavior rather than a single occurrence.

In the material of the second edition we hear as early as 5:18 that they were seeking to kill Jesus. There is no buildup of hostility, culminating in a decision of the Sanhedrin, as there is in the first edition.[34] This specific mention of seeking to kill occurs again in 7:1; 8:36 and 11:8.[35] In 8:59 and 10:31-33, we see "the Jews" actually taking up stones to kill Jesus. It is only through a miraculous disappearance that he is able to escape.[36]

Even "the Jews'" hostility to the people who would confess Jesus as the Christ (9:18-23) has *already been decided* prior to the time of the interrogation of the man and his parents; it is not something that develops in the narrative action itself.

As we have seen already, in the first edition the narrative presents a more historically plausible view of the authorities' hostility. In 11:47-53, the chief priests and Pharisees convened the Sanhedrin and took counsel to kill him. The last verse, 11:53, makes it quite clear that this is a new decision ("So *from that day*, they took counsel to kill him"). Moreover, in the days following this decision, the authorities spread word that people should inform the authorities of his whereabouts. In all of this presentation, there was clearly a sense of climax.

Finally, it should be noted that, on a simple linguistic basis, the authorities described as "Pharisees," "chief priests," and "rulers" are never said to "seek to kill" Jesus, nor do they attempt to stone him. Those who do so are "the Jews," and, as we have seen, they are repeatedly said to do so.

---

sire to kill, already they are hostile; and there is no indication of anything other than this hostility in the remainder of the passages where they appear.

34. Smith (*Gospel* 337) comments regarding "the Jews" in the Passion: "Officially, condemnation by 'the Jews' has occurred more than once (beginning in 5:18) and will continue into the trial before Pilate (18:28–19:16)."

35. John 7:19 puts the issue of "the Jews'" attempts to kill Jesus on Jesus' own lips. However, there are particular problems associated with this verse. See the discussion of Composition in the Commentary for full details.

36. At first, 18:31 ("We are not allowed to kill anyone") would seem to be inconsistent with this view, but it is probably intended to refer specifically to the process of crucifixion. Clearly, "the Jews" had the ability to kill by stoning (cf. Acts 7:58), and they had repeatedly sought to do so elsewhere in the Gospel (8:59; 10:31).

The Second Edition of the Gospel

As we shall see later in more detail, from the perspective of the second edition, the presentation of hostility toward Jesus as existing in a steady state from the beginning has as its purpose to present and summarize the common Jewish objections to the Johannine believers at the time of the later community (the time of the second edition) rather than during the ministry of Jesus itself.[37]

2E-6. In the second edition, the common people fear the religious authorities and never dare to debate with them, in contrast to the first edition where the common people (and temple police) regularly assert themselves over against the authorities and even enter into debate with them (1E-13).

In the second edition, the common people are repeatedly and *by means of a stereotyped expression* said to "fear the Jews." In 7:13, we hear that the people do not speak openly of Jesus "for fear of the Jews." In 9:18-23, the parents of the man born blind do not answer the authorities "because they were fearing the Jews." In 19:38, Joseph of Arimathea is said to be a disciple of Jesus but in secret, "for fear of the Jews." After the crucifixion, the disciples are hidden in the upper room "for fear of the Jews" (20:19).

Fear of religious authorities is also a consistent reaction in the second edition in a more general way. There are two instances of this. In chapter 5, the man who had been healed is questioned about the name of the man who healed him. He later finds out and reports it to them in an almost subservient way. In 19:7-8, we hear that even Pilate "feared." This fear is partly if not entirely directed at "the Jews." In 19:12, Pilate, who is said now to be seeking a way to free Jesus, is threatened by "the Jews" with the possible charge of disloyalty to Caesar if he frees him. There is not a hint of any other reaction than intimidation on the part of "the Jews" and fear on the part of others.

It should also be noted that in the second edition this fear of the authorities is always expressed with the stereotyped expression "fear of the Jews" (in either its nominal or verbal form). We never find anything similar to "for fear of the *Pharisees*" (or "chief priests" or "rulers") in the Gospel. This alone is a clear indication of two independent "systems" of referring to the religious authorities!

Second, not only is the phrase consistent linguistically but the attitude expressed contrasts sharply with the presentation of this relationship in the first edition. In the first edition, as we saw earlier in detail, the people entered into

---

37. The existence of this steady-state hostility is the first indication we have seen that, at the time of the second edition, the author was not concerned to present a true narrative of the ministry, in the sense that "narrative" is understood among literary critics today.

Section 2. The Criteria Used for the Second Edition

debate and spoke back to the authorities, and the authorities seemed to fear the reaction of the people. This is a radically different portrayal![38]

2E-7. In the second edition, almost no concern is expressed regarding the quantity or magnitude of Jesus' miracles, in contrast to the first edition where this was a preoccupation of the authorities (1E-12). Moreover, when the miracles are discussed in the second edition, they are discussed in a different way, as we shall see below.

There are two related elements here. First, the language associated with the miracles is considerably different in each of the editions. Second, the overall attitude toward the miracles is considerably different.

It will be recalled that in the first edition there was an overwhelming preoccupation with the "signs" of Jesus. In the second edition, there is less concern with the miracles than in the first edition. However, where the reaction to the miracles appears, it is both distinctive and consistent.

In the first edition, the term for miracle was "sign" *(sēmeion)*, and it was regularly modified by adjectives such as "many" *(polla)*, "such" *(toiauta)*, "so great" *(tosauta)*, and "more" *(pleiona)*. These adjectives are never associated with the *erga*.

The reaction to the *erga* is expressed with the verb "wonder" *(thaumazō)* (5:20; 7:21), and the word *erga* is qualified with the adjectives "good" *(kalon)* (10:32-33) and "greater" *(meizona)* (1:50; 5:20; 14:12). These terms are never associated with *sēmeion*. Only the adjective "many" *(polla)* (10:32) is used in both.

"Good" *(kalon)* is used to describe a miracle only once (10:32-33). There it is joined with "many" *(polla)* in 10:32, where Jesus says to "the Jews": "I have shown you many good works *(polla erga kala)* from the Father." "The Jews" minimize the role of the miracles themselves and show little concern for them. They focus rather on the claims of Jesus: "We do not stone you for a good work but for blasphemy, and because you who are a human make yourself God" (10:33).

When Jesus speaks, he acknowledges that the works that he performs cause people to "marvel" *(thaumazein)*, but he tells his listeners that they will see even "greater than these" *(meizona toutōn)*.

Thus, in 1:50, in the addition (by the author of the second edition) to the narrative of Jesus' supernatural knowledge of Nathanael's whereabouts, Jesus

---

38. It could be argued that the "rulers" fear "the Pharisees" in 12:42. However, as will be apparent in the discussion of the composition of 12:42, the original content of the verse is impossible to determine, given the amount of editing and the considerable mixing of features that have resulted.

The Second Edition of the Gospel

tells him: "You will see greater things than these." In the Greek, there is only a nominalized adjective, and it would literally read "... greater than these." Several elements indicate that the word *erga* is to be understood with *meizona* here. First, the context of 1:47-49 (which has described an instance of Jesus' miraculous knowledge) naturally suggests that "greater than these" would refer to greater miracles.

Secondly, the form of *meizona* is neuter plural and would agree grammatically with *erga*. Thirdly, the fact that *meizōn* is used with *erga* in the second edition (cf. 5:20; 14:12) (and never with *sēmeion*) would suggest that *erga* is the term to be understood here. Finally, we find an expression in 5:20 that is identical to that of 1:50 except for the fact that *erga* is expressed. Moreover, in 5:20 the promised works are those of giving life and judging. These conceptions are of a totally different order than the miracles identified as signs and so eminently qualify as "greater."[39]

In 7:21, Jesus speaks of performing only "one work," and the listeners respond in wonder *(hen ergon epoiēsa kai pantes thaumazete)*. As was the case in 5:20, it is difficult to tell whether the "wonder" spoken of has a positive or negative tone.

In 10:24-38, we come as close to an emphasis on Jesus' actual miracles as anywhere in the second edition. Jesus attempts to call the attention of "the Jews" to his "works," but they deny a concern for the works and speak instead of a concern for blasphemy. Verses 32-33 state: "Jesus responded to them, 'I have shown you many good works from the Father. For what kind of work among them do you stone me?' The Jews responded to him, 'We do not stone you for a good work but for blasphemy, and because you who are a human make yourself God.'" This is a different attitude from that of the first edition.

Not only is the overall attitude different from that of the first edition, but the language and tone are different as well. In 10:32, Jesus says: "I have shown you many good works from the Father *(polla erga kala edeixa hymin ek tou patros)*." First, as was pointed out above, *kalon* is never used to describe a *sēmeion*. In addition, the first edition never speaks of the "signs" being "from the Father," as is done here. In 10:25, Jesus had spoken of his works "witnessing" to him; there is no mention of the "signs" "witnessing" to Jesus.[40] Nor are the signs ever linked to a discussion of blasphemy, of high Christology, or of indwelling, as is the case here. The circle of theological discourse surrounding the "works" is of an entirely different order than that surrounding the *sēmeia*.

---

39. The raising of Lazarus is an example of giving physical life, but the life spoken of in 5:20 is spiritual life, of which the giving of physical life is only a symbol.

40. The Samaritan woman "witnesses" about a "sign," but in this case "witness" simply means "report."

Section 2. The Criteria Used for the Second Edition

In 14:12, as part of his departure address(es), Jesus says: "Amen, amen, I say to you, the one believing in me will perform the works that I perform and will do greater than these, because I am going to the Father (... *ho pisteuōn eis eme ta erga ha egō poiō kakeinos poiēsei, kai meizona toutōn poiēsei ...*)." Here the disciples are promised that they will be able to do what Jesus had done: both to do the works that Jesus had performed and also to do the greater works that Jesus did (giving life and judging). Again, the circle of discourse surrounding this discussion is of a totally different order from that surrounding the signs, which are always the individual acts of Jesus performed within his historical ministry and concerning which there is no promise that the disciples will perform similar miracles.

In 15:24, there is a reference to the greatness of the "works" ("If I had not performed works among them that no one else performed ... [*ei ta erga mē epoiēsa en autois ha oudeis allos epoiēsen*...]"), but again the context is very different from that of the first edition. The "works" here are associated with the other "witnesses" to Jesus (the words of Jesus, and the Scriptures) and the people spoken about are equated with the "world." Moreover, here in material of the second edition, it is Jesus himself who calls attention to the magnitude of his miracles, and he claims that people[41] have not responded to the greatness of his works; in the first edition exactly the opposite had been true.

In the third edition, there is no significant discussion of the miracles. But the author uses the terms "signs and wonders" in 4:48 and takes over the term "works" in 7:4.[42]

2E-8. In the second edition, "the Jews" do not react in fear or apprehension to the belief of the masses. In the first edition, the authorities regularly are concerned about and even fearful of the belief of the common people (1E-14).

As we have seen (1E-14), in the first edition the "Pharisees," "chief priests," and "rulers" regularly react to the belief of the masses. There are no instances in the Gospel where this can be said to be the case with the authorities identified as "the Jews." Rather, the religious authorities identified as "the Jews" inspire fear in others. Possible exceptions can be looked at.

In 5:10, 16, "the Jews" say to the man who had been healed that it is not permissible for him to carry his pallet on the Sabbath. This is not the same sort

---

41. Just who these people are is difficult to determine from the context. In its present context the audience is "the world," but this material (15:18-21) is from the third edition. In the second edition, the witnesses had been presented to "the Jews" in chapters 6, 8, and 10.

42. This represents the "mixing" of terms from earlier strata typical of the third edition. See 3E-21.

of reaction that we find in the first edition. The concern here is with an infraction of the law by the man himself. More importantly, the questioning of the man becomes simply the springboard for debate with, and persecution of, Jesus, which becomes evident in vv. 16-18 and in Jesus' response in vv. 19-47. In 7:11-13, "the Jews" seek out Jesus, but there is no expression of fear or apprehension on their part. Rather, their action inspires fear in the people and is evidently to be understood as an instance of "the Jews'" desire to kill him (cf. 7:1). In 7:15, 35, "the Jews" react to Jesus but question his teaching. In the first case, it is about the source of his "education"; in the second it is a failure to understand the content of his teaching. In neither case is there apprehension but only hostility. In 9:18-23, "the Jews" express doubt whether the blind man had in fact been blind. This is not apprehension but skepticism. Indeed, the verses indicate fear *of* "the Jews" rather than fear *by* "the Jews." In these verses from the second edition, the focus again is on the fear *of* "the Jews" by others (i.e., the parents).

Thus, a consistent pattern appears in this aspect of the narrative orientation of the second edition. In the first edition, as we have seen, there are repeated examples of a reaction on the part of the "Pharisees," "chief priests," and "rulers" to the "signs." In the third edition, there is no evidence of such reactions.[43]

2E-9. In the second edition, the religious authorities show no division of opinion about Jesus, but represent a solid and unified hostility, in contrast with the first edition where the religious authorities (and the common people) are regularly divided in their opinion about Jesus (1E-9).

In the second edition, opposition to Jesus on the part of "the Jews" is not only intense from the beginning but there is never an indication of division. This is true of their reaction to Jesus' cleansing of the Temple (2:18-22), of their reaction to his healing of the man at the Pool of Bethesda (5:9b-18),[44] and of their reaction to the Bread-of-Life discourse (6:30-50) and to the discourse of 8:31-59.[45] In the brief insertion of material into the interrogation of the man born

---

43. One could possibly look at the reaction of "the Jews" in 6:51-58, where (in material from the third edition) they (mixing of terms) are said to fight among themselves. The meaning of this is not clear since there is no evidence of disagreement or division among this group itself. The ambiguity here is due to the fact that it is not the work of the second author.

44. Regarding 5:17-19, Smith *(Gospel* 134) comments: ". . . hostility to Jesus suddenly emerges without what would seem a natural, or even requisite, development in the narrative." See also the comments of Fortna, "Locale," referred to in the discussion of 1E-9.

45. This is true of the portrayal of "the Jews" in the material of the second edition within 8:12-59. It will be argued that 8:31-32a, along with several other sections of chapter 8, in their present form come from the third edition. See 3E-21.

Section 2. The Criteria Used for the Second Edition

blind (9:18-23), it is particularly striking. Whereas in the surrounding material (where the authorities are described as "Pharisees") there is division among the authorities (v. 16) about whether "this man is from God," in vv. 18-23 we are told that "the Jews" were so unified, and had been so unified, in their hostility that they had already reached a formal decision that anyone who confessed Jesus as the Christ should be put out of the synagogue! The contrast here is unmistakable. In 10:22-39, once again the opposition of "the Jews" is unified without any hint of division. The same is true of all the instances where they appear again in the Passion (18:14, 36, 38; 19:7, 12, 14, 38).

In the first edition, there is repeated mention of division among the authorities, as we have seen (1E-9).

2E-10. In the second edition, the supernatural knowledge of Jesus functions to demonstrate his superiority in relation to human events. In the first edition, such supernatural knowledge functions within the narrative to lead to belief (1E-15).

In the second edition, Jesus' supernatural knowledge functions not within the story-line, having an effect on the characters, but only for the reader, demonstrating Jesus' supreme foreknowledge and his superiority to all human planning and events. For example, in 2:24-25, the narrator tells the reader that Jesus "did not entrust himself to them because he knew all things, and because he had no need of anyone to bear witness about human nature." This is an aside to the reader rather than something that has an effect on the plot.

In 6:6, the reader is told that Jesus' inquiry about where to get loaves to feed the crowd is said to be a test of Philip, "for [Jesus] himself knew what he was about to do." The narrator wants to make sure that the reader does not think this was actual ignorance on the part of Jesus.

After the multiplication (6:15), "Jesus, knowing that they [the crowd] were about to come and to take him by force so they might make him king, again went up the mountain alone, by himself." Here only the reader is informed of the reason for Jesus' retreat up the mountain.

When many of his disciples cease to believe in him after the teaching in the synagogue in Capernaum, the reader is told that Jesus knew "from the beginning" those who did not believe in him as well as the identity of his betrayer (6:64b). It is significant that the author of the second edition rules out the possibility that this is experiential knowledge, gained from his dealing with Judas and other unbelievers, for he says specifically that Jesus knew this "from the beginning." He wants to make clear that this is knowledge that sets Jesus above any contingency of human affairs.

The Second Edition of the Gospel

Finally, at the time of his arrest (18:4-9), the author of the second edition makes it clear that this arrest is not a surprise for Jesus, because he knew "all things that were to befall him."

When this presentation of the supernatural knowledge of Jesus is compared with that in the first edition, both the differences between the two sets and the purposes of the two become clear. In the first edition, the supernatural knowledge of Jesus functions as one of his signs. It is further evidence of his miraculous abilities, and its demonstration leads to belief. In the second edition, it is solely for the benefit of the reader so that the latter becomes aware of the divinity of Jesus manifest in his supreme superiority to, and independence of, human plans and affairs.[46]

2E-11. "The Jews" in the second edition are almost always in dialogue, and almost always in dialogue *with Jesus*. The "Pharisees," "chief priests," and "rulers" of the first edition, as a group, never enter into dialogue with Jesus (1E-17). In the third edition, the author at times takes over the term "the Jews," and they appear in dialogue in that edition (cf. 6:52).

Within the public ministry, "the Jews" appear in dialogue or discourse nineteen times; only five times do they appear in narrative or comments by the narrator. In 2:18, 20, "the Jews" appear in the dialogue with Jesus about the Temple. In 5:10, 15, 16, 18, they appear in the dialogue with Jesus concerning the healing of the thirty-eight-year paralytic. In 6:41, 52*,[47] they appear in the discourse of Jesus on the Bread of Life. In 7:15, 35, they appear in dialogue material (with Jesus) inserted into the narrative at Tabernacles. In 8:22, 48*, 52*, 57*, they appear in extended dialogue with Jesus. In 9:18, they appear in a dialogue inserted into the debate following the healing of the man born blind. Here, they are in dialogue with the parents of the man born blind, and this is the only instance of "the Jews" in dialogue with someone other than Jesus throughout his public ministry. In 10:24, 31, 33, once again they appear in dialogue with Jesus at Dedication. In 11:8, they appear in a brief reference by Thomas as part of the Lazarus episode. Within the public ministry, only 7:1, 11, 13; 8:31; 9:22 constitute references to "the Jews" by the narrator and so appear in narrative.

---

46. There is mention of the foreknowledge of Jesus also in the third edition (cf. 6:71; 12:33). In 6:71, the motif is carried over from the use of the technique in the second edition immediately above (v. 64). In 12:33, there is no sense that the author is trying to establish or confirm that by this foreknowledge Jesus could be shown to be superior to any human plans for him. In the third edition, such statements are expressed in the more general manner common to the Synoptics.

47. An asterisk indicates its appearance in material of the third edition.

Section 2. The Criteria Used for the Second Edition

Within the Passion, "the Jews" appear in 18:12, 14, 31*, 36,[48] 38; 19:7, 12, 14, 31, 38. Of these, none is in dialogue directly with Jesus, as is understandable. However, 18:12, 14, 36, 38; 19:14, 31, 38 introduce "the Jews" to the narrative, and in 18:31*, 36; 19:7, 12 "the Jews" appear in dialogue with Pilate. In 20:19, there is a final narrative reference to the disciples' "fear of the Jews."

Yet, the "Pharisees," "chief priests," and "rulers," as a group, never appear in dialogue with Jesus, and a single Pharisee (Nicodemus) dialogues with Jesus only once.[49] This is a stark contrast and indicates that the primary function of "the Jews" in the second edition is to present objections to Jesus.

As is true of all features listed in this section, this is not so much a criterion for determining authorship as a feature that confirms the correctness of the distinctions made on other grounds. Nevertheless, recognizing this difference in orientation helps us recognize how central to the second edition is the discussion of the claims of Jesus with "the Jews" rather than such things as the narration of miracles or other events in the life of Jesus. The second edition is concerned not so much with the events as with the meaning of the events and the claims that arise from them.[50]

Narrative Orientation: Worldview

2E-12. **The second edition is framed in the worldview typical of the canonical Jewish Scriptures. This worldview is not dualistic but contains a number of contrasts that must be distinguished from dualism. However, the worldview of the third edition is clearly marked by the modified (ethical) dualism typical of apocalyptic (cf. 3E-8 to 3E-19).**[51]

---

48. This is a reference to "the Jews" by Jesus, but it appears in dialogue as did 11:8.

49. The instance of dialogue with the Pharisees in 9:40 is due to mixing of characteristics. For a discussion, see the Commentary and 3E-21.

50. When this is extended to include all material identified with the two editions, the emphasis on narrative in the first edition and dialogue/discourse in the second becomes all the clearer.

51. One of the most insightful presentations of Johannine dualism is that by J. Becker, *Evangelium* 1:Exkurs 3, 147-51; idem, "Beobachtungen" 71-87. Becker rightly points out that there are sections of the Gospel that contain no dualism whatsoever (he would include the Signs Source here) but would see a variety of dualisms elsewhere in the Gospel. He attributes two of them to the Evangelist and claims that the KR (ecclesiastical redactor) had several dualistic conceptions. Becker would hold that the earliest form of "dualism" is represented by 3:19-21 and that in the later stages of the development of the Gospel this dualism remains evident but is modified in various ways and combined with other features. He recognizes the contrasts between spirit and flesh, between life and death, and between truth and falsehood (*Evangelium* 149) but sees them as part of this later modification. While many of Becker's insights are helpful, attributing

The Second Edition of the Gospel

The distinction described in this characteristic is extremely important for the proper understanding of the Gospel. Here we will discuss the worldview of the second edition and especially some of the features of that edition that appear to be dualistic but are not. In the Analysis of the third edition, we will discuss the characteristics of the apocalyptic worldview that mark the third edition.

The worldview of the Old Testament is not dualistic. The world is composed of heaven and earth. Under the earth are the ocean and the netherworld (Sheol). All is created by God. Although elements of older mythological conceptions are evident occasionally, those are not dominant. In the Scriptures that were normative at the time of the Gospel's composition, there is no hint of a "second" power in heaven that is in any way equal to God or contending with him. In other words, the traditional Old Testament worldview contains none of the cosmological or anthropological dualism typical of the *T12P*, the SDQ, or various parts of the New Testament.[52]

From time to time various Old Testament writers propose stark alternatives to their readers, and do so in terms that may appear at first to be dualistic, for example, Jer 21:8 ("See, I put before you the way of Life and the way of Death"); Ps 1:6 ("The LORD oversees the way of the righteous, but the way of the wicked will disappear").[53] Light and darkness are also contrasted in Mic 7:8 ("When I rest in darkness, the LORD will be a light to me"). But in all of these there is a simple comparison of two alternatives. There is no evidence of a dualistic worldview. The same is true for Isa 42:6-7, where Israel will be a "light to the nations ... to bring out ... those who sit in darkness." In all of this there is no overriding conception of beings or forces that bring about this opposition.

This is the worldview of the second edition of the Gospel. And in it, as in the Old Testament, there is a series of repeated and emphatic contrasts compatible with this worldview. In the second edition, these contrasts are centered on the question of whether or not one has received the promised gift of the eschatological Spirit. As we will see in detail in the discussion of the theology of the Gospel,[54] "salvation" in the Fourth Gospel consists primarily in having eternal

---

the apocalyptic dualism to an early stage of the community is incorrect and creates problems for the understanding of the community's later development.

By first identifying the material of the editions on the basis of other criteria (i.e., linguistic, ideological, and theological), one is able to get a clearer picture of which worldview is the earlier. This enables one to see that for the third author, the worldview of apocalyptic was an important part of what he wanted to "correct" in the earlier edition. This also avoids the awkwardness of attributing the same dualism to various authors, as Becker suggests.

52. This has been demonstrated in detail by Böcher, *Dualismus*, esp. 23-25, 72-76. A number of the observations here are based on his analysis.

53. See also Pss 25:10; 119:30; 139:24.

54. See "The Development of Johannine Theology: Eternal Life" in Part 4 of this volume.

Section 2. The Criteria Used for the Second Edition

life. This eternal life is gained through the possession of the Spirit of God. It is this Spirit of God, given in its eschatological fullness as promised in the Old Testament, that is promised by Jesus to those who believe in him.[55] As a result, the basic option for those who meet Jesus is to believe or not and, as a result, to receive the Spirit or not. This series of contrasts derives from a totally distinct frame of reference from those so-called "contrasts" that, in fact, are dualistic opposites.

If, in the Gospel as it now stands, some of these contrasts appear to be dualistic, it is because, in the present Gospel, there *is* a dualism and the elements of the Gospel that are in fact *contrasts* are easily interpreted within the context of that dualism. However, as the analysis of the editing shows, some parts of the Gospel are not dualistic and others are. The introduction of dualism is the result of the work of the author of the third edition of the Gospel. By understanding the editing of the gospel, we are able to better distinguish those elements that are simple contrasts from those that are genuinely dualistic.

The Contrast of Spirit and Flesh in the Second Edition

One of the major contrasts in the (second edition of the) Gospel is the contrast between the Spirit and the flesh. We will discuss the role of the Spirit in detail in Part 4, Section 3 ("The Development of Johannine Theology: Pneumatology"), but for the present it is important to notice that this basic contrast between having the Spirit and not is also expressed by a number of images involving other contrasts that are not dualistic. In the dialogue with Nicodemus, Jesus contrasts "natural" birth with birth "from above." In that dialogue, Jesus also contrasts "that which is born of the flesh" with "that which is born of the Spirit" (3:3-10). In the dialogue with the Samaritan woman, "living" water is contrasted with "well" water, and worship "in the Temple" with worship "in the Spirit." In 5:24-25, it is explained that the one who has the Spirit has life; the one who does not remains in the realm of death. In 6:63, there is a contrast between "the Spirit" as the source of life and "the flesh," which is useless. In every case, the distinctions are a matter of contrasts. They contrast having the Spirit with not having the Spirit. Such contrasts are to be distinguished from opposed pairs that are a result of influence by supernatural beings that are dualistically opposed and where there is a multiplicity of opposed spirits.[56]

---

55. To be sure, this takes place in a conflict of time frameworks, in that although Jesus offers the Spirit during his ministry and the effects of not accepting it are clear, it is equally clear that the Spirit will not actually be given until after the glorification of Jesus (cf. 7:37-39). Thus, the portrayal of the rejection of Jesus and the rejection of the Spirit is in fact an anachronistic imposition of the post-Resurrection situation onto the period of the public ministry.

56. It should perhaps be noted that this contrast is also communicated by the Johannine

However, some texts are ambiguous; and it is more difficult, if not impossible, to always determine whether they represent contrasts or dualism. For example, 3:12 mentions heavenly realities and earthly realities. While this could appear to be a simple contrast, the fact that the verse is part of a larger unit (3:11-21) that is so thoroughly marked by apocalyptic features makes it difficult to think that these were intended to be contrasts. And if they can be conceived of as simple contrasts, they are contrasts that are built on the fact that Jesus speaks of heavenly realities because he has "seen" these realities, and so the ultimate distinction is between Jesus and everyone else.

A similar case occurs in 3:31-36, where Jesus speaks of his descent from preexistence in heaven and so claims to be "above all." Likewise, the one who is not from heaven is said to be "of the earth." Whether this is dualistic in itself is not totally clear, yet within the context of the remainder of 3:31-36, which is thoroughly marked as being apocalyptic, the judgment must be that it is intended to reflect the dualism of the remainder of that passage.[57]

The Contrast of the Spirit of Truth and the Spirit of Deception in the Third Edition

We shall see the apocalyptic dualism of the third edition in more detail in the Analysis of that edition. For the present, an indication of the differences can be given by pointing out the considerably different conception of the Spirit in both 1 John[58] and in the third edition from that of the second edition. In the second edition, the issue was whether one had the Spirit or not; in the third edition (and in 1 John), the issue is not whether one has the Spirit or not, but *which* Spirit one has.

---

technique of misunderstanding. It is precisely the fact that a person takes the words of Jesus to refer to a reality that is only material rather than one that is based on the Spirit that causes these misunderstandings.

Ashton (*Understanding* 207) makes the same point: "We must conclude that without further specification the contrast between heaven and earth or above and below is not, properly speaking, dualistic at all. . . . Contrasted with this there is a horizontal opposition, which is played out on earth. This is genuinely dualistic." Ashton is rightly sensitive to the differences within the Gospel. The contribution of the present study is to identify the material of the Gospel with various editions on the grounds of literary criteria and then to notice that these worldviews are characteristic of distinct editions.

57. Bauckham ("Qumran") has attempted to investigate what he describes as two dualisms in the Gospel. He points out that the dualism of light and darkness is different from that of above and below and that the two dualisms never combine or overlap ("Qumran" 106-7). While I would applaud his attempt to distinguish these categories, I would argue that a more adequate division is between the features that are dualistic and the ones that are not.

58. As we shall see further below, 1 John is also apocalyptic in its worldview.

Section 2. The Criteria Used for the Second Edition

It is characteristic of the apocalyptic worldview that there are a multitude of spirits (both good and evil) and that these influence people (through "possession") and so affect their actions and attitudes. Thus, in 1 John, alongside of references to the Spirit in an unqualified way, we also read of this Spirit as "the Spirit of Truth," which is contrasted (implicitly in the third edition and explicitly in 1 John) with "the Spirit of Deception." The full paradigm of this dualistic conception is evident most clearly in 1 John 4:1-4. In the third edition of the Gospel, this conception is less fully expressed, but we find clear evidence of this view in the Paraclete passages, which refer to the Spirit as the "Spirit of Truth."

Although there is a basic difference in the worldview of the two editions, the two worldviews are not totally incompatible. It is a relatively short step theologically for the author of the third edition to see those who (in the second edition) reject the Spirit ("of Truth") as being under the influence of the Spirit of Deception. Thus, the groups that had been contrasted in the second edition are now viewed within a genuinely dualistic worldview. The introduction of the apocalyptic worldview implied more than just a simple reconfiguration of categories. In fact, it introduced a considerable number of convictions that considerably modified the theology of the Gospel (e.g., a Second Coming of Jesus and a final judgment). But these will be discussed more fully in the Introduction to the third edition.[59]

3. Literary Characteristics

2E-13. The author of the second edition introduces the device of "misunderstanding." This consists of a statement by Jesus that is understood on a "material" (or "physical") level, whereas it was intended to be understood on the "spiritual" level. Where this device is taken over by the author of the third edition, it is accompanied by features distinctive of the third edition.

In the second edition, the author introduces a large number of dialogues in which Jesus' listeners "misunderstand" the meaning of his words. Such misunderstandings have a special literary/theological function within the Gospel. Nevertheless, while all scholars have recognized the presence of such misunderstandings, there is some dispute about just what constitutes a "true" misunderstanding.[60] Bultmann argued that a misunderstanding always included a

---

59. It would be very cumbersome to call attention to every passage that is *not* apocalyptic. As a result, I will not make reference to this trait of the second edition except where it is particularly significant.

60. Culpepper (*Anatomy* 152-65) provides a useful overview of some of the major studies.

contrast between a material (or "earthly") and a spiritual understanding of a given term or topic.[61] For example, when Jesus speaks to Nicodemus about the necessity of being "born again," Nicodemus thinks of another physical birth rather than of a spiritual birth.

Others have argued that this is too restrictive and excludes instances where the similarity is great enough to suggest that the intention is the same. For example, Culpepper provides the following broader definition of misunderstanding: "(1) Jesus makes a statement that is ambiguous, metaphorical, or contains a double entendre; (2) his dialogue partner responds either in terms of the literal meaning of Jesus' statement or by a question or protest that shows that he or she has missed the 'higher' meaning of Jesus' words; (3) in most instances an explanation is then offered by Jesus or (less frequently) the narrator."[62]

But there are problems with this definition also. One immediate problem is that Culpepper's definition may not be all that different from Bultmann's since Culpepper's term "higher" is little different from the distinction pointed out by Bultmann. The third element of Culpepper's definition is difficult to assess since according to his view the third element need not be present and is therefore not essential.

However, my chief concern with Culpepper's list is that it does not distinguish between texts in which a person *fails* to understand and those in which the person *mis*-understands. While this distinction may seem artificial, I think it is not. "True" misunderstandings have a distinct literary/theological function: to show a mind that is fixed on the level of the earthly and incapable of perceiving the spiritual. Theologically, this serves to show the need for the Spirit in order to have proper understanding. Failure to understand is a different matter and is cleared up by further explanation.

The following list of misunderstandings is based on that of Culpepper with some modifications.[63] Some of the texts listed by Culpepper are excluded because they are not true cases of "misunderstanding" or because they do not have a theological function. These texts will be listed in the notes together with the reasons for excluding them. Second, the list will include four instances of misunderstanding not listed by Culpepper together with the reasons for including them. These are marked with an asterisk in the list that follows.

There are sixteen examples of misunderstanding in the Gospel. Of these, all appear in the second edition except the two listed in boldface, which come from the third edition. None appears in material of the first edition. Thus, we

---

61. Bultmann, *Gospel* 127 n. 1. However, Bultmann, followed by Dodd, would see this technique against the background of Hellenistic literature.
62. Culpepper, *Anatomy* 152.
63. Culpepper, *Anatomy* 161-62.

Section 2. The Criteria Used for the Second Edition

see 2:19-21 (in which "the Jews" misunderstand the meaning of Jesus' words about rebuilding the Temple); 3:3-10 (in which Nicodemus misunderstands the meaning of Jesus' words about a second birth); 4:10-15 (in which the Samaritan woman misunderstands the meaning of Jesus' words about living water); 4:19-24* (in which the Samaritan woman misunderstands the meaning of true worship); 4:32-34 (in which the disciples misunderstand the meaning of Jesus' words about the food he has to eat); 6:32-40 (in which "the Jews" misunderstand the meaning of Jesus' words about his origin); **6:51-53** (in which "the Jews" misunderstand how he can give his flesh to eat and his blood to drink); 7:15-20* (in which "the Jews" misunderstand the meaning of Jesus' words about the origin of his teaching); 7:25-29 (in which Jesus' listeners misunderstand the meaning of his words about his origin); 7:33-36* (in which "the Jews" misunderstand the meaning of Jesus' words about where he is going); 8:21-22 (in which "the Jews" misunderstand the meaning of Jesus' words about where he is going); 8:31-35 (in which "the Jews" misunderstand the meaning of Jesus' words about slavery); **8:51-53** (in which "the Jews" misunderstand his words about his death); 13:36 (in which Peter misunderstands); 14:4-7 (in which Thomas misunderstands); 14:8 (in which Philip misunderstands); 14:22 (in which Judas misunderstands).[64]

As was said above, all but two instances of this device appear in the second edition. The two instances that appear in the third edition do so in material that is an extension of material from the second edition and that seems intended to mimic the prior literary form. In these cases, the content of the mis-

---

64. I have excluded three texts listed by Culpepper. I would argue that 13:36-38 is not a true misunderstanding. Here Peter "misunderstands" the meaning of Jesus' words about departure. The original *lack of understanding* (from the second edition) about where Jesus is going (as expressed in 13:36ab, and answered by Jesus in 14:4) is turned into a *misunderstanding* of the word "follow," which is meant to refer not to a promise that Peter will now go along with Jesus but to "following" in the sense of a martyr's death, as is discussed more fully in chapter 21. The misunderstanding here, however, has a totally different function and is not related to a contrast of the material and spiritual understanding of existence but rather to a double meaning of "follow" which involves what might be called the "commonsense" meaning and a "technical" meaning of the term. This is really not the same literary device, and it does not have the same function. Further, 14:7-9 (in which Philip does not understand the meaning of Jesus' words about seeing the Father) should not be included as a true misunderstanding since it is a *failure* to understand rather than a *mis*understanding. In 16:16-19, Jesus speaks of seeing the disciples "in a little while." Although one could understand this as referring (1) to "a little while" without reference to a resurrection or even his death, there are two other meanings each of which could be considered "reasonable"; (2) that the disciples will see him in three days when he has risen; or (3) that they will see him "on the last day," which will occur soon. There is no evidence that the disciples understand Jesus in the sense of (1). Therefore they must adopt either (2) or (3). This means that one can hold to a "reasonable" meaning and still misunderstand. The answer given by Jesus is debated even by modern scholars.

understanding involves a topic associated with either the crisis of 1 John or other theological features of the third edition. These will be discussed in detail in the Analysis of the third edition.

Finally, it should be noticed that the technique of misunderstanding is also an example of the use of anachronisms typical of the second edition (2E-30F). These misunderstandings are the result of a failure to respond to the Spirit, but from the point of view of the actual ministry of Jesus, the Spirit had not yet been given; consequently, from that perspective, those who misunderstand would not be guilty for this failure. However, from the perspective and time frame of the community at the time it was expelled from the synagogue, the author would see those who misunderstood as being fully guilty of not believing in Jesus.

4. Theological Characteristics

The theological characteristics listed here are derived from the material that was identified on the basis of linguistic and ideological criteria. These are characteristics that can be used as criteria in the identification of material.

As we begin this section, it will be noticed that the number of theological characteristics listed here is relatively small compared to those of the first edition. This may be surprising, given the radical shift in theology evident in the second edition. There are two reasons for this.

First, many of the features of the second edition were *introduced* by the author of the second edition (and therefore contrast with features in the first edition) but are *taken over* by the author of the third edition; therefore, *in these features,* the material of the second edition does not contrast with that of the third. Consequently, this section focuses on those features that are unique to the second edition. It is these that are used as criteria for the Analysis. A few of the more dominant features that appear in both the second and third editions are provided in a separate listing below. The reasons for this will be given there.

However, the description of the overall theology of the second edition in Part 2 will be based on conclusions arrived at by the separation of the material of the third edition from that of the second. Thus, the theological overview presented in Section 3 below is based not just on a contrast between the first and second edition but also on a contrast of the second and third editions.

A second reason why the listing of characteristics here is shorter is that several of the salient theological characteristics of the second edition are actually the *absence* of a characteristic. For example, it is crucial to the understanding of the second edition to note that in that edition there are no statements regarding matters of ethics nor is there any significant mention of the content of

Section 2. The Criteria Used for the Second Edition

the teaching of Jesus other than that which pertains to his person and to belief in him. Although these are major features of the second edition, they are not useful as criteria in the analysis since not every instance of material without reference to the content of Jesus' teaching or to ethics could be considered therefore to be from the second edition. Rather, this is a major feature that is noticeable in the material *once it has been identified on other grounds*. While it is a "feature," it cannot be used as a "criterion."

As a result of these two factors, *some of the features which are most characteristic of the theology of the second edition are not listed here. Because of this, it would be wrong to think of the listing that follows as an outline of the theology of the second edition. It is not.* Such an outline will be available only in the overview of the theology in Section 3 and in the more extensive treatment in "The Development of Johannine Theology" in Part 4 of this volume. The treatment in each of these places will be different. In Section 3 below, we will give an overview of the theology of the second edition. That section will attempt to provide a synthesis and an overview of the major theological aspects of the third edition. In Part 4 of this volume, the focus will be on the development of Johannine theology throughout the four stages of its history evident in the Gospel and Letters. There the treatment will be chronological in format rather than synthetic. It will also be more detailed, but at the same time it will be restricted to eleven major areas of Johannine theology: Christology, belief, pneumatology, eternal life, eschatology, knowledge of God, ecclesiology, soteriology, ethics, anthropology, and attitude toward the material aspects of reality. Thus, by its arrangement and detail, Part 4 will both explain and contrast the understanding of a given topic throughout the four stages of the community's history.

2E-14. In the second edition, belief is conceived of as having a wider basis than just the miracles of Jesus (1E-18). In the third edition, the list of witnesses is extended to include that of the Paraclete and of the disciples. In addition, the focus will be on the proper *content* of belief and of proper "confession" of Jesus (3E-26).

It will be recalled that, in the first edition, belief was associated almost exclusively with the "signs" of Jesus. Throughout the edition, individual signs are narrated and more general references are made to the numerous signs that Jesus performed. These signs eventually are said to be the primary reason for condemning him to death.

In the second edition, not only is belief discussed in terms of response to the "works" of Jesus, but one of the major theological assertions is that belief in Jesus has a wider basis than just his miracles. The paradigmatic presentation of the basis for belief takes place in 5:31-40. There Jesus explains that he does not witness to himself but that there are other witnesses. He then lists the witness of John, his works, his word (which is the word of the Father), and the Scriptures.

For the present, it is valuable to see how the author of the second edition has taken the emphasis on "signs" from the first edition and integrated it into a larger theological framework. Thus, the author demonstrates that belief is a multifaceted phenomenon and that its proximate roots are more complex than was evident within the first edition. The author of the second edition then uses this paradigm of belief to demonstrate the fullness of the belief of the disciples (1:19–2:22), and he uses the three "essential" witnesses to structure his dialogue with "the Jews" in chapters 6–10.[65]

In the third edition, there is little concern for the basis of belief. Rather, the primary concern will be to explain the proper content of belief and the proper confession of Jesus.

2E-15. The second edition is marked by a consistent high Christology in contrast to the consistent low Christology of the first edition (1E-21). In the third edition, the Christology continues to affirm the divinity of Jesus but takes this a step further by identifying Jesus even more closely with attributes of God the Father (3E-26).

As we have seen, in the first edition the christological discussion is extensive but does not rise above the level of traditional titles and expectations. In the second edition, the discussion of the identity of Jesus focuses almost exclusively on claims to divinity.

Our purpose here is to indicate briefly the vast shift in the understanding of who Jesus is in the second edition by listing some general aspects of it. Later, in 2E-27X, 2E-28X, and 2E-29X, we will discuss the second author's introduction of three major elements of this Christology that are more immediately evident and that become so central to Johannine theology that they are taken over by the author of the third edition. These three elements are (1) the use of "Father" for God in a way that transcends any traditional understanding; (2) the use of "Son" for Jesus, also in a way that transcends the traditional use of the term; (3) the reference to Jesus as "sent." As was said above, these three elements of theology and Christology are *introduced* by the second author and *taken over* by the third. Because they are taken over by the third author, they cannot be used to distinguish material of the second author from that of the third, but

---

65. For a full treatment, see the discussion of the structure of the second edition and the overview of the theology in Section 3 below.

Section 2. The Criteria Used for the Second Edition

they are very useful in distinguishing material of the second and third editions from that of the first.[66] These concepts and their background are discussed in detail in the appropriate section of "The Development of Johannine Theology" in Part 4, and that will not be repeated here.

In addition to the use of these terms, there are various statements of Jesus that indicate his equality with God. These are generally presented in material where the authorities are identified as "the Jews." Thus, in Jesus' discussion with "the Jews" in 5:16-18, the debate moves rapidly from the issue of Sabbath violation to the justification that Jesus makes for that activity. He appropriates for himself the divine exclusion from the Sabbath law by explaining, "My Father works until now, and I work also." "The Jews" then seek to kill him not only because of the Sabbath violation but because of his claims (1) that he makes God his own Father, (2) and that, implicitly, he makes himself equal with God. The exalted nature of Jesus' claims is quite clear and indeed is recognized as such and rejected by "the Jews."

A similar instance of reaction by "the Jews" to divine claims appears in Jesus' sermon at Dedication (10:22-39). When Jesus speaks of his works, "the Jews" explain that they do not stone him for his works "but for blasphemy, and because you who are a human make yourself God."

A third example of "the Jews" recognizing Jesus' divine claims occurs in the Passion (19:7), where they explain that their purpose in putting Jesus to death is that he has committed blasphemy, "because he made himself Son of God."

But the high Christology is hardly limited to these types of statements. In 5:21-25, Jesus claims to possess powers reserved for God: the power to judge and the power to give life. He makes such statements as: "I and the Father are one" (10:30); "the Father is in me and I in the Father" (10:38; 14:10, 11, 20). Finally, Jesus explains that his testimony is based on personal experience. He speaks "what he has heard" (8:26bc, 28cd).

In addition to this discussion of the more general statements about high Christology, immediately following we will discuss the second edition's use (1) of "Father" as it was understood in relation to Jesus, (2) of "Son" as a title for Jesus, and (3) of "sent" as applying to Jesus.

Many aspects of this high Christology are shared with the third edition, but the third edition has distinctive features of its own. As a brief indication of the shift that will take place there, we can point to the affirmation of Jesus' preexistence as well as his appropriation of the title "I AM" in the third edition. We will see this in detail in the Analysis of that edition.

---

66. Because of the frequency with which the terms "Father," "Son," and "sent" are used in the Gospel, they will not be pointed out in the Commentary except in places where the use is particularly striking.

The Second Edition of the Gospel

2E-16. In the second edition, the Spirit is conceived of in an unqualified sense, whereas in the third edition, the Spirit is conceptualized in terms of a dualism where there is a multiplicity of spirits (3E-12). As a result, in the third edition the Spirit is identified as "the Holy Spirit" or "the Spirit of Truth" and implicitly contrasted with the Spirit of Deception, a contrast that is explicit in 1 John.

Within the canonical Old Testament, the references to the Spirit of God are always in what might be termed an "absolute" (unqualified) expression. That is, the only contrast intended is between having the Spirit or not having it. Or, to put it another way, it is a contrast between having a natural spirit and having the Spirit of God. Having a natural spirit resulted in ordinary human life (with concomitant death).[67] Having the Spirit of God would result in one not dying but living forever as God did. In the second edition, *pneuma* is used only in the absolute form. It appears this way thirteen times (1:32; 3:5, 6, 8 [twice]; 4:23, 24 [twice]; 6:63 [twice]; 7:39 [twice]; 19:30). The one exception to this pattern is 20:22, where the term "holy" Spirit appears in material of the second edition. That verse certainly comes from the second edition, and so the appearance of "holy" before "spirit" in this instance is puzzling. The usage here does not fit what is otherwise an extensive and consistent pattern. This suggests that the adjective has been added by the third author. But there is no evidence of editing other than this inconsistency.

As we will see in the Analysis of the third edition, where references to the Spirit occur in that edition, there is some indication that the author is speaking from within an apocalyptic viewpoint in which there was a plurality of spirits, some good and some evil. The point of the distinction is that the one the believer would receive was the Spirit that God would give (rather than that which came from the devil). In the third edition, this good spirit is variously referred to as the "Holy" Spirit or "the Spirit of Truth," an expression that does not appear in the second edition.[68]

2E-17. In the second edition, the believer is said to be born "of the Spirit" or "from above." In the third edition, the believer is said to be born "of God" (3E-39). There is no discussion of such birth in the first edition.

In the second edition, the notion of being "born" is used to describe the process by which one gains eternal life through the gift of the Spirit. This is discussed in

---

67. For a detailed discussion of the OT background of this usage, see the discussion of the pneumatology of the second edition below (Part 4, Section 3.2.a).

68. It will be noted that in the third edition there is no explicit reference to the "Spirit of Deceit" or the "Spirit of Deception," although the existence of such are implied by the reference to the Spirit of Truth. However, in 1 John, the contrast is explicit — most extensively in 4:1-6.

Section 2. The Criteria Used for the Second Edition

detail in 3:5, 6, and 8. However, in the Prologue (third edition), this birth is said to be "of God" (1:13). While the single occurrence of this terminology would not ordinarily seem significant and could be looked upon as stylistic variation, when we look at the usage in 1 John, we see that birth "of God" is used exclusively there and appears nine times: 1 John 2:29; 3:9 (twice); 4:7; 5:1 (twice), 4, 18 (twice). In the light of this consistency, the appearance of that terminology in a section marked otherwise by features of the third edition confirms that this shift is not accidental.

2E-18. In the second edition, there are repeated statements that deny the importance of the physical, "fleshly" aspects of existence and stress only the spiritual elements. In the third edition, there is a noticeable emphasis on the value of the material and physical as part of the spiritual reality (3E-41).[69]

The second edition focused on the bestowal of the eschatological Spirit. This spirit was far superior to the natural spirit with which humanity was endowed. The importance of the Spirit results in a denial of any value to things on the natural, physical level. For example, in the second edition, Jesus tells Nicodemus (3:6), "That which is born of the flesh is flesh, and that which is born of the Spirit is Spirit." In 4:19-24, Jesus explains to the Samaritan woman that in the future the proper place of worship will be neither Gerizim nor Jerusalem but "in Spirit and truth." In 6:63, Jesus states that "The Spirit is what gives life; the flesh is useless." In addition, we notice the lack of religious ritual in the second edition (e.g., the omission of the institution of the Eucharist at the Last Supper) and the lack of any reference to bodily resurrection.

At the same time, as we will see in the discussion of the third edition (3E-41), there is emphasis on religious ritual in the author's insistence on rebirth from water as well as from the Spirit (3:5), on the importance of the Eucharist (6:51-58), and on human intermediaries in the forgiveness of sin (20:23). In addition, the third author affirms in the clearest way the importance of the physical death of Jesus as an act with intrinsic value (3E-33) as well as the reality of bodily resurrection (3E-37).[70]

2E-19. In the second edition, the death of Jesus is seen as a "departure" to the Father. This contrasts with two elements of the third edition. First, in the third edi-

---

69. This topic is also discussed in Part 4 ("The Development of Johannine Theology"), Section 11.

70. This aspect of the theology of the second and third editions of the Gospel is discussed further in Part 4, Section 11.2 and 11.4.

The Second Edition of the Gospel

tion, the death of Jesus is seen as having an expiatory effect, a sacrificial, salvific death "for his own" and "for the world," a death that takes away sin (3E-33). Second, in the third edition, the "departure" of Jesus is conceived of as part of a larger schema of "descent and return," a schema that presumes the preexistence of Jesus (3E-34, 3E-53F). (There is no discussion of the theological purpose of the death of Jesus remaining in the first edition.)[71]

Here we will treat the passages that speak of the death of Jesus as departure. While it is common to discuss the "coming" of Jesus along with his "departure" (often spoken of as "descent" and "return"), this combination is not found in the second edition, but only in the third, where the "descent" is understood to imply preexistence. In the second edition, Jesus is "sent" by the Father (much as a prophet is "sent"), but this sending does not imply his preexistence in a heavenly state but only the fact he has been given a mission by the Father. This distinction will become clearer as we progress.

Statements that reflect the departure schema are numerous. In chapter 7, we see a discussion of both his coming and his departure. In 7:28, Jesus discusses first his origin when he says: "And you know me, and you know where I am from. And I have not come of myself. . . ." But there is no indication that this "coming" implies preexistence. When he speaks of "coming," Jesus refers to his mission from the Father. This is clarified in 7:28b and 7:29a, where it is a matter of being "from God" or "coming of oneself." The issue is who has determined the mission of Jesus: the Father sent him. In 7:33-36, Jesus speaks of his departure: "I am with you for only a little time, and I go to the one who sent me."[72] This is not a return, but simply a departure. Again the notion of "sending" cannot be confused with the notion of descent. In 8:21, Jesus says, "I am going away, and you will seek me. . . ."

As is understandable, references to the departure of Jesus are more numerous in the material of the Last Supper and the Farewell Discourses. In 13:1, the narrator explains: ". . . Jesus, knowing that his hour had come when he was to depart from this world to the Father. . . ." In 13:33: ". . . as I told the Jews, 'Where I go, you are not able to come,' I also tell you now." In 13:36, Simon Peter asks, "Master, where are you going?" In 14:4, Jesus says: "And where I go, you know the way." In 14:12, we see ". . . because I am going to the Father." In 14:28, "If you loved me, you would rejoice because I go to the Father. . . ."[73] In 16:4b-5a

---

71. Among the scholars who recognize this distinctive view of Jesus' death are: Richter, "Deutung" 21-36; Forestell, *Word;* Müller, "Bedeutung" 49-51; Nicholson, *Death;* and Thyen, *Studien,* esp. 243-51.

72. 8:14c-16b also speaks of "coming" and "going," but it does so only in reference to Jesus' self-knowledge in this regard. This text comes from the third edition.

73. Although the words "If I had not come and spoken to them . . ." could be thought to

Section 2. The Criteria Used for the Second Edition

Jesus says, "I did not say these things to you from the beginning because I was with you. But now I go to the one who sent me...."

Elsewhere in this Commentary, I have stated that it is dangerous to argue from the absence of a feature because one cannot always tell whether the absence is deliberate or accidental. The same might be said about statements that speak only of departure. However, while there is no way to prove that every instance where only departure is spoken of is deliberate, there is one instance where it can be shown that there the earlier view is modified by the later. In the Commentary on 13:1-4, attention is called to the way in which the initial sentences of chapter 13 are overloaded, repetitious, and cumbersome. In those verses, the authors make two references to what Jesus knew about the coming events. In 13:1bc, we hear from the second author: ". . . knowing that his hour had come when he was to depart from this world to the Father. . . ." Then, in a parallel statement from the third author in v. 3, we read: ". . . knowing that the Father had put all things into his hands, and that he had come forth from God and was going to God. . . ."[74] In the first statement, the notion is of simple departure; the second statement is about the complete schema typical of the third edition. Thus, we see an example of each side by side, and contextual features confirm that the two are not simply accidental variations of each other. At the same time, the departure schema of the second edition could easily be taken up by the author of the third edition and incorporated into his more comprehensive and more profoundly significant descent-return schema.

2E-20. In the second edition, the removal of sin is associated with the power of the Holy Spirit; in the third edition, sin is removed through the sacrificial, atoning death of Jesus (3E-33). (There is no discussion of this in the remaining material of the first edition.)

In the second edition, there is no explicit reference to the removal of sin. This in itself is strange, but perhaps to be expected. At the time of the second edition, the removal of sin was thought to have taken place through washing by the ("living") water of the Spirit. But this was corrected by the author of 1 John and the author of the third edition.[75]

Nevertheless, as will be argued in detail in the Commentary, there are sig-

---

refer to "descent," this is not the case. Not only is "coming" ambiguous and able to refer to the "coming" of a prophet-like figure, the statement occurs in the introduction to the last review of the three witnesses to Jesus, material that comes from the second edition.

74. As will be seen in the discussion of Composition, other factors in both of these participial phrases identify them as coming from the second and third editions respectively.

75. See also von Wahlde, "Death" 579-90.

nificant indications that the footwashing (13:4-11) was originally intended to symbolize that the disciples must be washed free of sin by the water (i.e., the Spirit) which Jesus would give. This washing was necessary if the disciples were to have an "inheritance" *(meros)* with Jesus!

However, beyond this, there are six other indications that suggest that in the second edition sin was washed away by the Spirit rather than by the atoning blood of Jesus. First, there is the fact that in the second edition there are no references to the forgiveness of sin, as I have indicated. Second, in 1 John and in the third edition, there are numerous statements that insist that the death of Jesus was an atonement for sin. This indicates that there was a conflict over the issue of the forgiveness of sin and particularly regarding who was responsible for its removal. Third, we have ample evidence that, in both the Old Testament and in the SDQ, the bestowal of the eschatological Spirit was to result in a cleansing from sin.[76] Because the role of the eschatological Spirit was so dominant in other aspects of the second author's thinking, it is difficult to imagine that this was not also true of his understanding of the forgiveness of sin. Fourth, although we do not have texts dealing with the forgiveness of sin through the Spirit, we do have clear evidence that the community at the time of the second edition held to a theory of perfectionism that obviated the need for ethical directives. This belief is so closely connected to the belief in the forgiveness of sins and radical transformation to a state of impeccability through the Spirit that it becomes difficult not to believe that the second edition held that the eschatological Spirit cleansed from sin.

Fifth, there is yet another hint that this was the view of the second author. In 20:23, there is a single text that speaks of the forgiveness of sin. In it, the power to forgive and retain others' sins is given to the disciples. It will be argued in the Commentary that this statement comes from the third edition. The fact that the verse is placed immediately after the scene of the bestowal of the Spirit from the text of the second edition may well be an indication that even at the time of the third edition there was a recognition of some association of forgiveness of sin with the Spirit.

But perhaps the most striking of all is the statement in 1 John 5:6 (cf. 1 John 5:7-8) that Jesus did not come in water only but in water and blood. This statement is echoed in John 19:32-35, where we read that both water and blood poured forth from the pierced side of Jesus. As is explained in detail in the Commentary on the various texts, at the time of the second edition it was predicted that ("living") water would flow from the side of Jesus at his glorification (7:37-39). But in 1 John this is corrected (5:6, 7-8) to say that Jesus came not only

---

76. We will see the background for this in the discussion of the pneumatology of the second edition (Part 4, Section 3.2.a).

Section 2. The Criteria Used for the Second Edition

in water (i.e., to give the Spirit) but "in water and blood" (i.e., Jesus gave the Spirit, but his death was also an atonement in blood). This is then repeated in the third edition's account of blood and water flowing from the side of Jesus. Although scholars never comment on the matter, it is certainly a curious discrepancy that 7:37-39 predicts the giving of water and that at the death of Jesus both blood and water flow from his belly. The fact that the later tradition (i.e., 1 John and the third edition of the Gospel) emphasizes an element of soteriology that is completely absent from the earlier stages (i.e., the first and second editions) of the tradition confirms that at the time of the second edition the removal of sin was associated only with the Spirit and that the references to the atoning blood of Jesus were later additions.

2E-21. **In the second edition, "judgment" (i.e., declaration of guilt) is an event that takes place in the present time and is not conducted by an external agent (i.e., God) but occurs in the event of unbelief itself. In the third edition, there is a conviction that there will be a universal "judgment" (i.e., a rendering of accountability) at the end of time (3E-17). (There is no discussion of judgment remaining in the first edition.)**

The nouns *krisis* and *krima* ("judgment") and the verb *krinō* ("to judge") appear twenty-four times in the Gospel (3:17,[77] **18**, 19; 5:22, **22**, 24, **27**, 29, **30** [twice]; 8:**15**, **16**, 16, **26**, **50**; 9:39; 12:31, 47 [twice], 48 [twice]; 16:8, 11, **11**). Of these, the notion of judgment appears in only one passage in the second edition (5:24-25, 30). That passage makes it clear that, for the believer, eternal life begins in the present (v. 24). And the believer has crossed over from (spiritual) death to (eternal) life. That means that once the person has received eternal life, that individual will undergo physical death but will continue to live because he/she possesses the life of God and will exist in a state of spiritual immortality. Because the believer "has crossed over from death to life," he/she will *not* undergo judgment (i.e., condemnation).

In the third edition, the notion of judgment is more complex and will be treated in detail in 3E-17. However, we can point to one important difference in the third edition: according to the third author, "on the last day" there will be a resurrection in which some will rise to life and some will rise to condemnation (i.e., judgment). In this conception, all persons, believers and unbelievers alike, will undergo scrutiny at the end of time, and some will be rewarded with eternal life while others will be judged guilty.

The conception that is introduced by the author of the third edition is best

---

77. Boldface indicates a verb form.

The Second Edition of the Gospel

expressed in two verses (5:28-29) which follow closely on the passage just quoted: "Do not marvel at this, that an hour is coming in which all those in the tombs will hear his voice and will come forth, those who have done good to a resurrection of life, those who have practiced evil to a resurrection of judgment."

In these verses, there is a decisive time "on the last day" when there will be a physical resurrection (3E-37) and a universal scrutiny (3E-17). This universal scrutiny will evaluate the deeds of the individual and bestow the appropriate recompense for such deeds. This apocalyptic concept will be discussed in detail in 3E-17 and in the treatment of eschatology of the third edition in Part 4, Section 5.

2E-22. In the second and third editions of the Gospel, there are references to the "hour" of Jesus. Both of these designations serve to indicate that Jesus is not subject to human planning or human intentions. Rather, he responds to the time determined for him by the Father. However, the framework within which this "hour" is conceived and presented is different in the second and third editions.

In the second edition, the "hour" refers to the general advent of the period of salvation or of the Passion, Death, and Resurrection. In the third edition, the notion of the "hour" is subsumed into a larger framework in which there are twelve "hours" in the "day" and Jesus is able to work during the "day." However, the "night" will come, and no one will be able to work during the "darkness" (3E-24).

"Hour" occurs twenty-three times in the Gospel and in a variety of senses. First, it is used as a simple time reference (1:39; 4:6, 52, 53; 19:14, 27). Second, it is used in a general sense to refer to some undetermined future time (5:28; 16:2, 4, 25, 32). Third, it is used as a reference to the "hour" of Jesus' Passion and Resurrection (e.g., 7:30; 8:20; 12:23, 27; 13:1; 17:1; cf. also 7:6[78]). Fourth, it is used as a reference to the hour in which salvation is made present to the believer (e.g., 4:21, 23; 5:25). Fifth, and finally, it is used as a reference to segments of the public ministry that together comprised twelve hours and made up the "day" of the public ministry (e.g., 2:4; 9:4; 11:9). The day contrasts with the "night," which is the time of the Passion (9:4; 11:10; 13:30; cf. 12:35, 46).

> 78. When his "brothers" ask him to go up to the Feast of Tabernacles (7:3-10), Jesus tells them that the time is not right for him but the time is always right for them *(ho kairos ho emos oupō parestin, ho de kairos ho hymeteros pantote estin hetoimos)*. The "brothers" go up, and then in fact Jesus goes up "in secret." What is different here is that the term *kairos* is used in place of the customary *hōra* (hour). This hapax legomenon is introduced by the author of the third edition as a synonym for "hour."

Section 2. The Criteria Used for the Second Edition

Leaving aside the simple references to time in category one and the general references to future time in category two, we are able to see that the instances in the third and fourth categories all come from the second author except for 12:23. However, an examination of 12:23 in its literary context suggests that the use of "hour" in 12:23 was done in imitation of "hour" as it appears in 12:27, which originally followed 12:22 in the second edition but which has now been pushed back to 12:27 by the insertion of 12:23-26. If this explanation of 12:23 is correct, then its appearance is accounted for and is not a true exception to the pattern.[79] As a result, we may say that all of the instances of the third and fourth categories come from the second edition. Thus, the second author uses "hour" to refer to the advent of the larger period of salvation and of the hour of Jesus' Passion, Death, and Resurrection.

Finally, the instances in the fifth category, composed of uses of "hour" in relation to "day" and "night," all come from the third edition. This is compatible with the idea, introduced by the third author, of the public ministry as a time of light for the world and the Passion as a time of darkness.

In summary, then, we see that there is no theological use of the term "hour" in the first edition of the Gospel. In the second edition, the "hour" is part of the conception that no one is able to alter the appointed course of Jesus' public ministry. The authorities cannot arrest him before his hour (7:20; 8:20). Yet when it arrives, Jesus recognizes the hour in which his (second) glorification will take place (13:1) and does not seek to be saved from it (12:27). All of these are characteristic of the second edition.[80]

The notion of "hour" is also employed by the author of the third edition (e.g., 2:4; 11:9; 12:23; cf. 9:4-5). But he does so to incorporate it into a larger framework that speaks of "day"/"night" and "light"/"darkness." The public ministry is conceived of as "day," while the time of the Passion is the "night." Thus, in 11:9 we read that there are twelve "hours" in the "day" and that Jesus works during the "day" because he is the "light" of the world while he is in it. But the beginning of the ministry is also determined by the Father, and there is an "hour" for that also (2:4). When "night" comes (13:30), no one is able to work. This is described further in 3E-24.

---

79. In effect, it would be another instance of the mixing of terms occurring with some frequency in the third edition.

80. The notion of the "hour" of Jesus appears once in material of the third edition, where it is said that "the hour has come for the Son of Man to be glorified." Given the fact that "hour" appears twice in the following verses from the second edition, it is likely that the third author simply made use of the notion but inserted his material prior to that of the second edition. As such, it represents a case of the mixing of terms by the author of the third edition (see 3E-21).

The Second Edition of the Gospel

2E-23. In the second edition, the notion of immanence (or "indwelling") is introduced. Such immanence is predicated of the relationship between Jesus and the Father, thus establishing the intimacy of their relationship. However, in the third edition, the notion of immanence between the Father and Son is extended to include, and to be a model for, the relationship of both the Father and the Son with the believer and applied to the relationship between believers (3E-42).[81]

The concept of immanence in the Gospel is a complex topic, and although a complete treatment is not possible here, some of the major lines may be sketched out.[82]

In the Gospel as a whole, four prominent expressions are used to describe the mutual relationships involving Jesus, the Father, the Paraclete, and the believer.[83] In this section we will list the four expressions together with the texts where they appear; then we will draw conclusions regarding their use in the second edition. In the Introduction to the third edition, we will discuss the expressions of immanence appearing in that edition (3E-43).[84]

References Involving the Notion of Being "One"

In the second edition, it is said once that "the Father and I are one" (10:30).

In the third edition, the expression appears in two verses. In 17:21, 22, Jesus and the Father are said to be one; and believers are urged to be one with one another and also "in" Jesus and the Father. ("... so that all may be one, just as you, Father, are in me and I am in you, so that they also may be in us ..." [17:21]; "... so that they may be one as we are one. I in them and you in me, so they may be brought to perfect unity" [17:22].)

---

81. Treatments of the notion of immanence include Borig, Weinstock 199-236; R. E. Brown, Gospel 1:510-12; Epistles 259-61, 283-84; Hauck, "Menō" 574-76; Malatesta, Interiority; Mealand, "Language" 19-34; Schnackenburg, Epistles 99-103; Strecker, Epistles 44-45; Scholtissek, In Ihm sein.

82. The verb menō alone appears thirty-eight times in the Gospel (1:32, 33, 38, 39 [twice]; 2:12; 3:36; 4:40; 5:38; 6:27, 56; 7:9; 8:31, 35 [twice]; 9:41; 10:40; 11:6, 54; 12:24, 34, 46; 14:10, 17, 25; 15:4 [three times], 5, 6, 7 [twice], 9, 10, 16; 19:31; 21:22, 23), but many of these occurrences do not intend the notion of immanence being discussed here.

83. R. E. Brown (Epistles 283) would limit the discussion only to einai en and menein en. But the other expressions are sufficiently related to be considered together with them.

84. R. E. Brown (Epistles 259-60) gives a very helpful chart showing the variety of usage associated with immanence and indwelling. However, the analysis presented here will show, I think, how much greater consistency (and development) of usage is evident when the same list of instances is viewed within a theory of the development of the tradition.

Section 2. The Criteria Used for the Second Edition

References Involving the Use of menein *("remain," "abide")*

The usage of *menein* in the Gospel is complex, and we include here only those instances where a theological meaning is intended.[85]

In the second edition, it appears once: "But the Father abiding in me *(en emoi menōn)* performs his works" (14:10).

In the third edition, a variety of relationships are described by this verb. Jesus remains in the believer (15:4, 5). The believer remains in Jesus (6:56; 15:4 [twice], 5, 6, 7). The Father and Jesus will make their abode with the believer *(monēn poiein)* (14:23). The Paraclete remains among the disciples and is in them (14:17).[86]

References to Being "in" the Father and the Reverse

In the second edition, the expression to be "in" appears five times for the relationship between Jesus and the Father (10:38; 14:10 [twice], 11, 20). It always expresses both a unity and an intimacy, and implies a constancy for this relationship. He urges his listeners to come to realize "that the Father is in me and I am in the Father" (10:38).

In the third edition, similar expressions occur twice. Once (17:21-22) the full set of relationships is expressed — in conjunction with the expression to be "one": ". . . so that all may be one, just as you, Father, are in me and I am in you so that they also may be in us . . . so that they may be one as we are one. I in them and you in me, so they may be brought to perfect unity."

References to "Not Being Alone"

In the second edition, there are three references to Jesus "not being alone." In the discourse of chapter 8, it appears twice: "I am not alone, but I am together with the Father who sent me" (8:16); "the one who sent me is with me. He did

---

85. In this connection it should be noted that such references involve the use of the preposition *en* rather than *para*. Among the uses that are excluded are those that speak simply of continued physical presence in a place; also instances such as "the word of God remaining in you" (5:38); "you remain in my word" (8:31); "the bread that remains to eternal life" (6:27); "the son remains in the house forever" (8:35); "your sin remains" (9:41); and "the Christ remains forever" (12:34). Finally, the references to the Spirit descending and "remaining" on Jesus (1:32, 33) are sufficiently distinct from this other notion that they are also excluded.

86. There is no reference in the third edition to Jesus remaining in the Father, although it is said that Jesus keeps the commandments of the Father and remains in his love.

not leave me alone because I always do that which is pleasing to him" (8:29). In the Passion, the disciples will leave Jesus "alone," but he will not be truly alone because the Father is with him ("And I am not alone because the Father is with me" [16:32]).[87]

This expression does not appear in the third edition.

General Comments on the Notion of Immanence in the Second Edition

From the texts above, a clear pattern emerges. In the second edition, the first of the immanence expressions, that of being "one" with one another appears only once and is applied to the relationship between Jesus and the Father.

The second expression (the verb *menein*) is not used in the second edition, although the analogous *monēn poiein* is used once (14:10). There it appears together with the third of the expressions (to be "in") (cf. 14:10-11) and is synonymous with it. The fourth expression (not being "alone") appears three times to describe the relationship of intimacy between Father and Son (8:16, 29; 16:32).

The most notable conclusion from this is that in the second edition immanence functions solely to describe the relation between Jesus and the Father. It affirms the unity and intimacy of Jesus and the Father and so serves the edition's Christology.

As we shall see in the Analysis of the third edition, although there is still reference to the immanence of the Father and Son, the third author extends this to affirm that it is possible for the believer to have this same kind of intimate relationship with the Father and Son and Spirit.

2E-24. In the second edition, the notion of "joy" is described as "irremovable" and is the joy in the Resurrection that will follow on the sorrow associated with the Passion and Death. In the third edition, "joy" is described as "complete" and is the eschatological joy associated with the realization of the future hopes associated with the coming of Jesus (3E-36).[88]

The concept of joy does not play a major role in the development of Johannine theology, but it must be said that it is a constituent part and appears throughout the Johannine literature. It is one of the relatively few concepts that appears in

---

87. Here the expression "to be with me" also appears, but it is synonymous with "not being alone."

88. This feature of the Gospel was pointed out to me by my former doctoral student, Michaelsami Arockiam. It is discussed in his book, *Joy* 1-85, esp. 83-85.

Section 2. The Criteria Used for the Second Edition

every document — and in every edition of the Gospel except the first. Here we will treat the notions of irremovable joy and complete joy in 3E-36.

The notion of irremovable joy is found in the second edition in 16:22 ("now you are sad, but again I will see you, and your hearts will rejoice, and no one will take your joy from you"). This conception appears only once in the Johannine literature and is associated with the joy of childbirth. Jesus has just explained to the disciples that in a little time they will not see him and again in a little time they will see Jesus. He compares the sorrow of the disciples with the sorrow and pain of a woman in childbirth; there is pain and sorrow before the birth, but when the child is born there is great joy. Jesus explains that while the disciples are sorrowful now, Jesus will see them again, and their hearts will rejoice, and "no one will take your joy from you." Thus, the joy at the Resurrection will be a joy that is truly irremovable, because the Resurrection will signal an event that can never be denied or reversed.

2E-25. In the second edition, the reasons for putting Jesus to death are based on the charge that "he makes himself Son of God" (19:7). In the first edition, when Caiaphas convened the Sanhedrin, the decision to put Jesus to death was based on the fear that if Jesus were allowed to continue as he was, the Romans would come and destroy the Temple and the nation (11:48) (1E-22).

The charge that is brought against Jesus in the trial before Pilate (19:7) is consistent with the charges against Jesus throughout the ministry. Jesus is accused of blasphemy based on his claims regarding his relationship with the Father. These claims are of a high Christology throughout (cf. esp. 5:17-19; 10:33).

In the first edition, the discussion by all persons (not just the authorities) had been on the level of low Christology (i.e., traditional titles). As the ministry progresses, the Pharisees and chief priests increasingly fear the reaction of the people and finally, several days before Passover, the chief priests and Pharisees convene the Sanhedrin and declare that if nothing is done to stop the influence of Jesus, the Romans will destroy the Temple and take away their independence. This is a major difference in orientation.

5. Some Aspects of Theology Introduced in the Second Edition but Taken Over by the Author of the Third Edition

The theology of the second edition brings about a radical transformation in the theology of the Gospel as a whole. However, many of the features that contrast most with those of the first edition are also taken over by the author of the third. This should not be surprising. The need for a third edition was brought about by a dispute over the interpretation of the tradition as it was expressed in the second edition. As a result, only those features that the third author thought should be nuanced or complemented are changed. That this is so is also confirmed by the way the author of 1 John agrees with the substance of many of the opinions of his opponents but at the same time modifies or nuances them in some way.

Two aspects of this will be evident in what follows. First, the features that are taken over by the third author are almost exclusively theological features, and these are features of the second edition. This is understandable because the theology of the document is what is most in focus. At the same time, where he wishes to modify or complement *the theology* of the second edition, the third author's changes are clear from close analysis.

Where the third author takes over *other* material typical of an earlier edition (i.e., material that is not directly theological), he tends to do it indiscriminately, thus mixing it with his own or that of another edition. As a result, he takes over the terms "the Jews" (6:52) and "the Pharisees" (12:42); he also borrows the term "works" (7:3), but the theology is distinctive. This process should not be surprising and is in accord with what would generally be considered to be the normal process of "editing."

Because features found in both the second and the third edition cannot be said to be distinctive of, or "unique" to, the second edition, they cannot be used to distinguish the material of the second from that of the third edition. However, they can be used to distinguish the material of the second and third from that of the first edition. In the listing given below, the number of such features is quite restricted. A complete listing would make the analysis impossibly cumbersome. When they are used as criteria, their special character will be noted by an "X" following the number.[89]

---

89. To presume that each edition was marked only by "distinctive" criteria would give results like those that can stem from the use of the criterion of dissimilarity in "historical Jesus" research. According to this criterion, only those elements of the teaching of Jesus can be labeled authentic which cannot be explained as coming either from contemporary Judaism or from the later church. Although such a process would seem to provide a sense of what is distinctive in the teaching of Jesus, in fact it is liable to give a *caricature* of Jesus' teaching since by its very definition it presumes that Jesus held nothing in common with the Judaism of his time. If we take as typical of the second edition only those features of the Gospel that do not also appear in the third edition, we identify material that is unique to the third edition, but at the same time it produces a caricature of the edition as a whole since it would not include all of those features introduced by the second author but held in common with the third. On the limits of the criterion of dissimilarity, see, for example, Meier, *Marginal* 1:171-74. See also Harvey, *Constraints* 1-10.

Section 2. The Criteria Used for the Second Edition

2E-26X. The second edition introduces the presentation of Jesus as referring to God as his "Father." This does not appear in the first edition. Where it is taken over by the author of the third edition, it is accompanied by other features that are unique to the third edition (3E-46X).

Throughout the Old Testament, there are references to God as "Father." In the Gospel of John, "Father" is also used of God in this traditional way (cf. 4:21, 23). In this usage, the title is not a matter of contention between Jesus and his opponents. The opponents of Jesus use it themselves about themselves when in 8:41 they claim, "God is our Father."

But in the second edition Jesus regularly refers to God as "Father" in a way that transcends this ordinary meaning. That Jesus intends this title in a special sense is recognized by "the Jews" in 5:18, where they treat such a claim as blasphemy and seek to kill him because of it.

That it is used by the author of the second edition is evident first of all from the twenty-two times where it appears in passages in the public ministry in which the authorities are identified as "the Jews" (2:16; 5:17, 18; 6:32, 37, 40, 44, 45, 46 [twice]; 8:27, 29, 30, 32, 36, 37, 38 [twice]; 15:1, 8, 23, 24). It appears another forty times in passages that do not contain the term "the Jews" but are identified as coming from the second edition on other grounds (5:19, 20, 21, 22, 23 [twice], 26, 36 [twice], 37, 43, 45; 8:16, 18, 19 [twice]; 11:41; 12:27, 28; 13:1, 3; 14:7, 8, 9, 10 [twice], 11, 12, 20; 16:3, 17, 25, 28 [twice], 32; 17:1, 24, 25; 18:11; 20:21).

It is almost always associated with the discourse and dialogue material of the Gospel. It appears primarily on the lips of Jesus but at times on the lips of others who talk with Jesus. It is also used by the narrator. Because of the large number of instances, the individual texts will not be discussed here. Details on the Composition are available in the Commentary, and the theological significance of the title will be discussed in Part 4 of this volume, which deals with the development of Johannine theology.

The great majority of the instances appear in the material of the second edition. It was also taken over by the author of the third edition, and appears forty-four times in that edition. In the third edition, the title is accompanied by features that are distinctive of the third edition. This usage will be discussed in detail in the Analysis of the third edition.

2E-27X. The second edition introduces the presentation of Jesus as referring to himself as "Son" in relation to God. This does not occur in the first edition, and where it is taken over by the author of the third edition (3E-47X), it appears together with features unique to that edition.

The Second Edition of the Gospel

The word "Son," introduced by the author of the second edition, is, as Schnackenburg says, "the privileged Christological title and Jesus' own preferred way of referring to himself."[90] When Jesus speaks of himself as "the Son," it is always (either implicitly or explicitly) in relation to God as "the Father": 5:19 (twice), 20, 21, 22, 23 (twice); 6:40; 14:13; 17:1 (twice). In these instances the Son is understood as divine in the narrow sense.

While the number of instances of the term in this sense is relatively small, this is to be explained by the fact that, in most instances, it is Jesus who is speaking, and therefore he refers to himself as "me" rather than as "the Son."[91]

The title does not appear in the first edition, and where it appears in the third edition, it either appears with other features distinctive of the third edition or the title itself is modified in various ways (e.g., by the addition of the adjective *monogenēs*). We will see this in greater detail in the Analysis of the third edition.

2E-28X. In conjunction with the conception of Jesus as "Son" in relation to the "Father," the author of the second edition also introduced the conception of Jesus as "sent" by the Father. This does not appear in the first edition, and where it appears in the third edition, it appears with features distinctive of that edition (3E-48X).[92]

This notion of sending is communicated by the use of two Greek verbs, *pempō* and *apostellō*, although it appears that the author intends no difference in meaning in the use of these two verbs. In the Gospel the participial phrase *ho pempsas me* is often used to modify "the Father." It appears in the second edi-

---

90. Schnackenburg (*Gospel* 2:102). It is important to study the Father-Son relationship apart from the title "Son of God." The title "Son of God" has a long history of usage within Judaism (cf. the treatment of that title elsewhere in this Commentary). Moreover, within the early Christian community and particularly within the Johannine community, "Son of God" functioned as a confessional formula while the "Son" title does not.

91. This is is also complemented by the use of "son" in the titles "Son of God" and "Son of Man." These titles, however, cannot be used as criteria since "Son of God" appears with varying connotations in all three editions and "Son of Man" appears only in the third.

92. It will be noticed that the notion of being "sent by the Father" is not unlike the notion in the first edition that Jesus is "from God." But there is an important distinction between the two. In the second edition, it is not simply "God" who is "with" Jesus but the "Father." This term is introduced in the second edition as the special designation of the relation between Jesus and God. No longer is Jesus' relation conceived of in terms of the prophetic stamp of approval, but as the relation of Father and Son. This "Father/Son" relationship is intended by Jesus (and understood by "the Jews") as the designation of a relationship that far transcends the relationship spoken of in OT Judaism.

Section 2. The Criteria Used for the Second Edition

tion with *pempō* (5:23, 37; 6:44; 8:16, 18) and with *apostellō* (5:36; 10:36; 11:42; 17:8, 18, 21, 23, 25).[93] At other times it appears alone as a nominalized phrase (with the verb *pempō* in 4:34; 5:24, 30; 6:38, 39; 7:16, 18, 28, 33; 8:26, 29; 12:44, 45; 13:20; 15:21; 16:5); but the use of *apostellō* in this form does not appear in the Gospel.[94]

2E-29X. **The notion of "eternal life" is introduced by the author of the second edition and is a major motif. It is also taken over by the author of the third edition, although various aspects of its presentation are modified in connection with the issues in focus at the time of the community crisis (3E-49X).**

The notion of eternal life is introduced by the author of the second edition. It is the central soteriological concept of the second edition. The development of this concept within the Johannine tradition will be discussed in detail in Part 4 of this volume. Here we will point only to the main lines of its use.

In the second edition, the noun appears sixteen times and the verb *zaō* (apart from those instances where it refers to normal physical life) appears five times (4:10,[95] **11**, 14, 36; 5:24 [twice], **25**, 39, 40; 6:33, 35, 40, 47, 48, 63; **7:38**; 10:10, 28; **14:19**; 17:2; 20:31). The cognate *zōopoieō* occurs in 5:21 and 6:63. In all of these instances, the terms refer to the life that God gives and which comes from the possession of the Spirit. The texts involve the offer of "living water" (the Spirit) (4:10, 11, 14; 7:38), eternal life as a contrast with death (5:21, 24 [twice], 25), and general statements about obtaining life (5:39, 40; 6:33, 35, 40, 47, 48, 63; 10:10, 28; 14:19; 17:2; 20:31). In all these cases, the texts speak of life in what might be called a "simple" sense. That is, it has none of the development evident in those instances that come from the third edition.

In the third edition, although the author speaks of eternal life with the same general meaning, its possession is regularly qualified by conditions or requirements that are not present in the texts of the second edition. In all cases, these qualifications can be shown to be related to issues the author of 1 John

---

93. In addition to the use of *apostellō* with "Father," this verb appears with *theos* (God) as subject (3:17, 34; 17:3) and with *ekeinos* ("that one") as subject (5:38; 6:29; 7:29; 8:42). (*Pempō* does not appear in these combinations.)

94. This "sending" does not imply any sense of preexistence on the part of Jesus. Although it is common to read "sending" in the context of the more profound "descent-return" schema of the third edition, a close reading indicates that this need not be the case. When Jesus says that he has not come "of himself," he is indicating that he has not come of his own intention but is responding to the will of the Father. He was "sent" by the Father. This is also the basis of his knowing the Father. This is the language of a mission rather than of preexistence.

95. Boldface indicates texts where the verb appears.

thought to be crucial to his own position in confrontation with the view of the opponents. We will see this in detail in the discussion of "The Development of Johannine Theology" in Part 4, Section 4.

2E-30X. The author of the second edition introduces theological terminology not found in the first edition. This terminology is central to his theological presentation but is also taken over by the author of the third edition (3E-50X).

The two most prominent examples of this vocabulary are "glory/glorify" and "witness."

Glory/Glorify

"Glory" (noun) and "glorify" (verb) appear a total of thirty-five times in the Gospel.[96] Of these, none appears in the first edition. Nineteen examples appear in the second edition (2:11; 5:41, 44; 7:18, **39**;[97] **8:54** [three times]; 11:4 [twice]; 12:**16**, **28** [twice], 43 [twice]; 15:8; 17:1, 4, 22). It appears sixteen times in the third edition (1:14; 8:50; 11:40; 12:**23**, 41; 13:**31** [twice], **32** [twice]; 14:13; 16:14; 17:5, 10, 24; 21:**19**). As we shall see, the notion of the two ways in which Jesus is glorified is one of the primary organizational principles of the second edition. Here we note only its distribution among the editions. Its meaning will be discussed in more detail in the Commentary at the time of its first appearance (1:14).

Witness

Although this verb is used in the more general sense of "stating emphatically" (4:44; 13:21) or "reporting" (4:39; 12:17), the predominant use is in its narrower sense of "bearing testimony about," with Jesus (or "the light") as its object. In this sense it appears twenty-two times. It is almost totally absent from the first edition (only 3:26). In the second edition the term appears fourteen times (1:19, 32, 34; 5:31, 32, 33, 36, 37, 39; 8:13, 14, 18 [twice]; 10:25). As will be explained in detail below, in the second edition the notion of "witness" is an important structuring element, and in all instances it is used precisely in reference to this structure. It also appears six times in the third edition (1:7, 8, 15; 3:11; 15:26, 27; 19:35;

---

96. Of these, all are theologically significant except 9:24 (where it appears in an idiomatic expression).
97. Boldface indicates a text where the verb form appears.

Section 2. The Criteria Used for the Second Edition

21:24). It will be noted that, in the third edition, it appears first in the Prologue and primarily in passages where the disciples (cf. "we," 3:11) are witnessing or where the Beloved Disciple is said to witness. These are also theologically significant since, as we shall see, the third author extends the list of "witnesses" to Jesus to include the disciples.

As a result, the distribution of this term between the editions confirms well the theological observations about the importance of "witness" for the structure of the second edition and for the theological elaboration of this in the third.

6. Features of the Second Edition That Become Apparent Once the Analysis Is Complete

2E-31F. In the second edition, there are a number of features that are anachronistic to the ministry of Jesus but that accurately reflect the circumstances of the community at the end of the first century. This contrasts with the presentation in the first edition, where there is considerable accuracy and detail with regard to the specific elements of the historical ministry of Jesus (1E-25F, 26F, 27F).

The second edition of the Gospel attempted to understand the ministry of Jesus in ways that would enable the community to confront the problems it experienced in its relation to the synagogue. In formulating the Gospel in this way, the author introduced a number of features that were anachronistic to the ministry of Jesus. Examples of this anachronism would include the christological debates that reflect a much fuller and deeper understanding of the identity of Jesus than either the first edition of the Johannine Gospel or any of the Synoptics.

A fuller list of the features that are anachronistic to the ministry is given in Section 3.6. However, some of the more striking ones are listed here to provide a sense of the extent to which such anachronisms pervade the second edition.

The first and most extensive example is the use of "the Jews" for religious authorities in the second edition. As is commonly pointed out, this term ignores the specific terms for the various parties and officials of first-century Judaism, titles such as were found in the first edition. The second author simply groups all such authorities together under the general rubric "the Jews." This undoubtedly reflects a time in the history of the community when the specific distinctions were no longer of importance since the essential distinction was between the authoritative position of Judaism contemporary with the community and the beliefs of the community itself.

The second example of such anachronism is the use of the expression *aposynagōgos poiein* (to expel from the synagogue). This expression is much

The Second Edition of the Gospel

less frequent, but is even clearer. The way this expression is used (e.g., 9:22; 12:42;[98] 16:3) reflects a stage in relations between "the Jews" and the Johannine Christians that is more developed than would be possible during the actual ministry of Jesus. Rather, this exclusion reflects a position that is presented as not simply a spontaneous reaction but an official position arrived at deliberately. Such a formal declaration could hardly be said to reflect the conditions within Jesus' ministry itself.[99]

A third anachronism is the high Christology of the second edition. It is commonly pointed out that the Christology of the Gospel in general is the highest in the New Testament. The highest level of christological affirmation attributed to the disciples in the Synoptics has already been achieved by the "Johannine" disciples in the first chapter. Yet at the end of that chapter in John, the promise is made that the disciples will see "more." This "more" is fulfilled in the various statements of the second edition that take the understanding of Jesus to a much higher level. This higher level is evident throughout in the affirmations of the equality of Jesus with God as well as in the recognition by "the Jews" that Jesus "makes himself equal to God." None of this is as explicit in the Synoptic Gospels as it is in John. Such a Christology reflects a longer period of reflection under the influence of the Spirit than is represented in the Synoptics.[100]

A fourth anachronism would include the attribution of a degree of guilt to various individuals and groups for their "misunderstanding" of Jesus that is inappropriate for the period of his historical ministry. This guilt is due to their failure to respond to the Spirit and, during the historical ministry of Jesus, the Spirit "was not yet" because Jesus had not yet been glorified. Yet, these misunderstandings reflected quite well the failure of the contemporaries of the community to respond properly to Jesus in the postministry period.

These anachronisms should not be taken as an argument against the thoroughly Jewish character of the second edition. Rather, the Judaism and the circumstances evident in the second edition are just as accurate as those details of the first edition, except that, in the second edition, the details accurately reflect

---

98. The use in 12:42 is complicated by the editing performed by the author of the third edition. See the discussion in the Commentary.

99. The references to exclusion from the synagogue are generally thought to reflect the conditions in Judaism about the year A.D. 90. However, some literature now questions the accuracy of this dating. Nevertheless, the action envisaged in the Johannine texts is not paralleled in any other Gospel or in the Acts, and so the general estimation of their anachronicity must remain. For a minority view to the contrary, see Carson, *Gospel* 369-72.

100. It could also be pointed out that the Gospel as a whole lacks a concern with the issues of fasting, eating with sinners, purity in food preparation, and the like, issues that are of concern in the Synoptics. However, as true as this is, it is difficult to tell whether this was never an issue for the community at the time of either the first or second editions or whether it was omitted by the later authors. Consequently, it is not included here.

Section 2. The Criteria Used for the Second Edition

the historical circumstances and theological issues of the community *at the time of the second edition,* not at the time of the historical ministry.[101]

2E-32F. In the second edition, quotations from Scripture are typically introduced by some variation of the formula "as it is written [in the Scripture]" while quotations in the third edition are typically introduced by some variation of the formula "in order that the Scripture may be fulfilled" (3E-51F).

This is listed here for completeness but is discussed in detail in Appendix 1 of Volume 3 (Quotations of the Old Testament).

2E-33F. The second edition manifests an awareness, and use, of sophisticated rabbinic argument that is not found in the first or third editions.

The second edition exhibits repeated examples of sophisticated rabbinic argument and debate that are not present in the first edition. For example, the debate between Jesus and "the Jews" in 5:17-18 reflects an important debate among Jews whether God himself was bound by the Sabbath Law since, according to Gen 2:3, God rested on the seventh day.[102]

The question was discussed by Philo (*Cher.* 86–90; *Leg.* 1.5-6). It was also regularly addressed by the rabbis. *Exodus Rabbah* 30.9 recounts a challenge put to rabbis Gamaliel II, Joshua ben Chananiah, Eliezer ben Azariah, and Aqiba whether God rested. In both cases the answer is that in essence God does continue to work on the Sabbath since without such work creation would fall out of existence. This is the same position taken by Jesus and is used as the background that Jesus uses to justify his action on the Sabbath, thus not only claiming that God is his Father but also asserting the exclusive prerogative of God for his activity.[103] What is important for our purposes here is the way this statement reflects knowledge of sophisticated Jewish argument.

---

101. This view of the second edition revises in a substantial way the approach taken by Martyn *(History),* who saw the entire Gospel written on two levels that mixed a narrative perspective of the historical ministry with the perspective of the community itself. While Martyn thought that the two levels were the work of a single individual, the evidence suggests that this was not the case. The work of the first author was focused on a more historical presentation, while the author of the second edition incorporated material enshrining the perspective and issues of the later community.

102. See, for example, the extended discussion of the parallels in Dodd, *Interpretation* 320-22.

103. Moloney *(Signs* 2:8) also cites *Mekilta Sabbata* 2:25; *Genesis Rabbah* 11:5, 10, 12; and *Ta'anit* 2a and refers to Bernard, "Guérison" 13-34.

The Second Edition of the Gospel

Another particularly striking example of Jewish "argument" in the second edition is found in the structure of the Bread-of-Life discourse in 6:30-59. As Borgen has shown, the structure of this discourse bears a remarkable resemblance to the typical structure of first-century Jewish exegetical homilies.[104] The parallels will be explained in detail in the Commentary itself and so will not be given here. However, the parallels are remarkable especially when allowances are made for the shift from monologue to the dialogue form of the discourse in the Gospel.

A third example of rabbinic argument appears in 7:22-24. Among the rabbis it was argued that circumcision was allowed even on the Sabbath (*m. Shabbat* 18:3; 19:2; *m. Nedarim* 3:11). Jesus, basing himself on this rabbinic decision, argues for another case by *qal wahōmer* ("from the lesser to the greater") that if circumcision is allowed on the Sabbath, how much more so the healing of the entire person.[105]

Yet another example is the use of the rabbinic principle that testimony cannot be validated by only one witness. In 8:16b-18, Jesus invokes this principle in support of his own testimony.

2E-34F. Questions that are posed in the first edition are regularly answered by material of the second edition (see 1E-28F).

There exist, in various places in the Gospel, instances in which a question is asked and a response is given that does not deal directly with the question. Such responses either take the question in a different sense or do not answer it at all but simply introduce another topic. These can be seen simply as examples of aporias, but they are so regular that they appear to be intended as a particular technique.

This pattern in which a question or topic posed by the one edition is addressed by material from the later edition occurs six times in the Gospel. In each case, the response takes the discussion to a higher level than that proposed in the previous material. In 3:1-2 (1E), Nicodemus speculates on the meaning of Jesus' signs, but in 3:3-10 (2E) Jesus does not discuss the signs but the need for the Spirit. In 3:22-26, the disciples of John the Baptist discuss purification with "a Jew" and then ask John about the popularity of Jesus in 3:27-30. The answer given by John speaks of this success being given "from heaven," that is, from God. Thus, like the

---

104. P. Borgen, *Bread, passim*.

105. For example, see the discussion in R. E. Brown, *Gospel* 1:312-13; Schnackenburg, *Gospel* 2:134. Brown points out that it was elsewhere recognized by rabbis (*Yoma* 85b) that healing on the Sabbath was allowed if a person's life was in danger. However, in the case of the man who had been at the pool for thirty-eight years (if this is indeed the miracle referred to), there was no immediate threat to life and the healing could have been postponed.

other such instances, this provides an answer of a different order from that expected by the question, and that answer comes from the second edition.

In 7:26b-27 (1E), the crowd is discussing the origin of Jesus. Without an indication that he is even present, in 7:28-30 (2E) Jesus speaks out in the Temple and responds to the question but on a radically different level, a level typical of the second edition. The same technique is used later in the chapter. After the crowd professes belief on the basis of Jesus' signs, the Pharisees send temple police to arrest him. Again without any indication of place or time, Jesus is presented as speaking and as addressing the attempts of the Pharisees even though the earlier narrative gives no indication that Jesus has even heard them (7:33-36). He speaks of his going away and of their attempts to seek him and not find him, in a way that addresses their attempt to arrest him, but on a different level. Again the shift is identified by the presence of "the Jews" in v. 35 as coming from the second edition.

In chapter 12, we have a final instance of the technique. In 12:20-22, after Jesus has entered the city of Jerusalem in triumph, "some Greeks" wish to see Jesus. Philip and Andrew approach Jesus with the request, but in his response Jesus makes no reference to their coming nor to their request, but speaks of the advent of his "hour." In the present text, the following material is that of the third edition rather than that of the second. Consequently, this could be an instance of the technique being taken over by the author of the third edition or, as is more likely, vv. 23-26 are a later insertion by the author of the third edition and interrupt the original sequence, which had begun with v. 27 and which is from the second edition.[106]

SECTION 3. SYNTHESIS OF THE SECOND EDITION

Having finished listing the criteria used in the Analysis, we now turn to summarize a number of the elements of the second edition as they emerge from this Analysis.

1. The Structure of the Second Edition[107]

The theological framework of the second edition is at the same time simple and complex. The ministry is composed of two parts each of which will bring glory

---

106. See the full discussion of this in the Commentary.
107. The structure is reproduced as it is evident from the material present in the canonical form of the Gospel. The italic text represents the material of the second edition, while the text in normal typeface represents material from the first edition as it has been taken over and incorporated into the second edition by the author of that edition. The division into typefaces

to the Father. Jesus conceives of his ministry as a "work" given to him by the Father (4:34; 5:17; 9:3; 17:4). This work is related to the work of God in creation, and Jesus is sent by the Father to bring his (i.e., the Father's) work to completion (4:34; 17:4; 19:30b). Jesus' miracles are called "works" and are part of this larger "work." The length of the public ministry is determined by the Father. When Jesus' "hour" comes (cf. 7:30; 8:20; 12:27), he will depart to the Father (13:1, 33, 36; 14:4-5, 28; 16:5) — through his Passion and Death. His Passion and Death are also identified as Jesus' second "glorification" (11:4; 12:28).

In his public ministry (1:19–12:50), Jesus offers the Spirit, the principle of eternal life, to those who believe in him (3:3-10; 4:10-15; 7:37-39), and speaks of its necessity (4:19-24). Jesus explains to his listeners (esp. 5:31-40) that there are four witnesses that show that he speaks the truth and is to be believed. These four are: (1) the witness of John the Baptist, (2) the witness of the works of Jesus, (3) the witness of his words, and (4) the witness of Scripture. At the beginning of Jesus' public ministry, the disciples experience, and respond positively to, these witnesses (1:19-2:22) and are shown as models of belief. During his public ministry, Jesus also presents this witness to "the Jews" primarily through the three essential witnesses (cf. 5:32-35), that of Scripture (6:1-50), that of his words (8:13-59), and that of his works (9:1–10:38), but "the Jews" do not respond positively (15:2-25) and do not believe (cf. 12:37-50).

To respond positively to the witnesses to Jesus is to see his glory. The disciples saw Jesus' glory (2:11), but "the Jews" and "the world" did not see it (12:43). Jesus did not seek his own glory but that of the Father (5:41-44).[108]

With this as an outline, we may trace the work of the second author throughout the public ministry as follows.

The first presentation of the witnesses appears in 1:19-2:22, where the author presents the disciples as responding properly to the four witnesses to Jesus.[109] In doing so, the author of the second edition has made use of material from the first edition but has arranged it according to his own purposes and also composed material of his own to fill out the presentation. Thus, the disci-

---

necessarily represents a simplification. A definitive listing of the material of the second edition can be found in the Commentary.

108. Once one understands the literary and theological development of the Gospel, it becomes evident that the division of the Gospel into "the Book of Signs" and "the Book of Glory" calls attention to a mix of features from different editions. In the first edition, the entire Gospel was a "Book of Signs." In the second edition, one might refer to the twofold division as "two books of glory," and the third edition might well refer to this twofold division as the demonstration of "Jesus as light and Jesus as loving," as the third author overlaid his own theological conceptualization that he adapted from 1 John.

109. In many cases, the verses given in parentheses will include material from the other editions. However, the reader's attention is directed only to the material of the second edition within the overall range of verses.

Section 3. Synthesis of the Second Edition

ples are shown to respond positively to the witness of John the Baptist (using material largely from the first edition in 1:19-51, particularly 1:29-51). In Cana (2:1-11), they believe on the basis of the first of his public signs.[110] Then, in the incidents in Jerusalem at Passover (2:13-22 — in material of his own composition), they are said to respond (after the Resurrection) to the word of Jesus and to the Scriptures (cf. 2:22).[111]

The *placement* of the material now in 1:19-49 is due to the second author. This is evident particularly in 1:43, which is not only awkward in its present location but which clearly prepares for the Galilean miracle at the wedding feast. Thus, the second author *took over* both the material dealing with advent of the first disciples on the basis of a report from John (1:19-49) and the report of the Cana miracle (2:1-11) from the first edition but *arranged it* according to the pattern of the "witnesses" (which he would later articulate paradigmatically in 5:31-40) and then added his own material in 2:18-22 as examples of how the disciples responded to the word of Jesus and the Scriptures (the third and fourth witnesses as listed in 5:31-40).

In the material that runs from 2:23 to 4:42, the author takes over several incidents from the continuing narrative of the first edition but develops them with material explaining the role and the necessity of the Spirit. This is evident from the way material that is presented in the basic framework of the first edition is modified by the incorporation of material from the second edition. There are four of these additions, and all deal with the nature and necessity of the Spirit. Thus, Jesus speaks of the Spirit in the author's modification (3:3-10) of the Nicodemus episode as well as his additions to the episode of John the Baptist and his disciples (cf. 3:27-28), and the additions to the Samaritan episode (4:10-15 and 19-24).

The author then continues with material from the first edition (the second Cana miracle [4:46-54] and the Healing at the Pool of Bethsaida [5:1-9])[112]

---

110. The term "sign" is used and is evidence that the author has taken over this material from the first edition.

111. After the intense focus on the disciples in these first four incidents of the ministry, the disciples recede into the background, and although they appear in minor roles throughout the ministry, they do not become the true focus again until the Farewell Discourses, where they are given instructions for the future in keeping with the testamentary form of the discourses. The only other time in the ministry where they could be said to be the center of attention is in 6:60-71. See the discussion of these verses in the Commentary.

For another view of the witnesses that takes in 1:19–2:11, see Talbert, *Gospel* 86 and "Artistry." Talbert's view of the witnesses does not take into account those of 2:13-22, nor does his view account for the explicit statements of belief on the part of the disciples, nor does it see the use of those witnesses in the major discourses of chapters 6, 8, and 10.

112. In the first edition, this miracle had occurred after the multiplication, but the author transposed it with the narrative of the multiplication because not only did the healing miracle

The Second Edition of the Gospel

and uses them as the narrative foundation illustrating Jesus' ability to give life and to judge. The second author then explains and develops these two powers in the architectonic discourse of 5:9b-47.

In the Commentary, we will call attention to the various features of the healing of the official's son that emphasize Jesus' ability to give life. We will also note how the healing of the man at the pool is the only miracle of the Gospel that does not result in belief on the part of the healed person and, moreover, results in the somewhat ominous statement of Jesus, "Sin no more, lest something worse befall you." Thus, in a statement (which is part of his addition to the original miracle) the second author makes the miracle a hint of the judgment that Jesus will be shown to have the power to perform.

In chapters 6-10, the major structure is created by the author's presentation of three complexes of narrative followed by discourse in which he illustrates how "the Jews" were given the opportunity to respond to the witness of the Scripture (6:1-50), the witness of his word (7:1-8:59), and the witness of his works (9:1-10:39). In each of these there is a combination of narrative and discourse, and in each the discourse illustrates one of the witnesses. Thus, in 6:1-50, there is the "multiplication complex" (the multiplication and the walking on the sea, from the first edition) amplified by the Bread-of-Life discourse (6:30-50), which illustrates, by means of the homiletic exegesis, how Scripture witnesses to Jesus. In 7:1-8:59, the narrative of the events at Tabernacles (7:1-52) is amplified by the discourse of 8:12-59, which focuses on the "word" of Jesus and illustrates how Jesus' word witnesses to him (cf. the explicit statement regarding the witness of Jesus' words in 8:14-16 [without vv. 14c-16a]).[113] Then in 9:1-10:39, the author takes over the healing of the blind man as the narrative base for his discourse (10:1-10, 22-39)[114] in which he illustrates the witness value of the works of Jesus (see the explicit statement regarding witness of the works in 10:25).

In the concluding section of the public ministry, the author returns to the theme of glory and sees the approach of the hour as the approach of his second glorification and his departure to the Father. In 11:4-5, we see Jesus and the disciples speak of the danger that awaits them in Judea. Jesus refers to the miracle

---

provide a more suitable narrative to illustrate "judgment" but the multiplication provided a more appropriate foundation for his homily on Jesus as the true bread from heaven.

113. Although the narrative is punctuated by brief elements of dialogue, the basic material is narrative. Moreover, the dialogue and debate are examples of Jesus speaking his word and "the Jews" responding to it. Chapter 8 then reflects on this.

114. The composition of chapter 10 is complex, but the overriding relationship of the narrative in chapter 9 to the discourse in 10:22-39 is clear. However, the placement of the parable of the shepherd as it was in the second edition is now obscured by the editing in 9:35-41. This is discussed at greater length in the Commentary.

Section 3. Synthesis of the Second Edition

as the means through which he will be "glorified." In this instance, "glory" begins to take on the second of its connotations, the glory that will be demonstrated during his Passion and Death. This theme returns again in 12:27-30, where Jesus speaks of the arrival of his "hour" and the fact that the Father will glorify Jesus "again."

In preparation for the full enactment of the hour, Jesus holds his last meal with the disciples on the eve of Passover. During the meal he washes the feet of the disciples as a symbol of the washing that will take place in the giving of the Spirit (13:1-11). After the meal, he prepares the disciples for the coming events. He predicts his departure (13:31–14:7), but promises that the disciples will do greater works than he has done (14:8-12). He tells them that he is going away but that they will see him again shortly (after his death) (14:18-22), and speaks again of his departure (14:27-29). He speaks of the failure of "the Jews" to believe (15:22-25) and of the persecution the disciples will undergo (16:1-4), and again of his permanent departure (16:4b-25). He promises them that a time is coming when he will no longer speak in parables but openly (i.e., through the Spirit) (16:25-32). Then in chapter 17, he prays to the Father to glorify him so that he may glorify the Father again (17:1-4), and he prays that the disciples may be protected from the world (17:7-19).

The modifications by the second author in the Passion itself occur mainly in the charge of blasphemy brought against Jesus (19:7-12) and in Jesus' cry at his death that the work he was given to do was complete (19:30b), and so he gives forth the Spirit (19:30c). In the time after the death of Jesus, he appears to his disciples as he had promised and confers the Spirit upon them (20:19-22).

*   *   *

This view of the ministry can be outlined as follows:[115]

I. Jesus' First Glorification, the Time before the Hour (1:1–12:50)

   A. 1:19–2:22: *The Disciples Respond to the Witnesses of Jesus*

      1:19-51: The Witness of John

      2:1-11: The Witness of the Miracles

      2:12-17: *The Witness of Scripture*

      2:18-22: *The Witness of the Word of Jesus*

   B. 2:23–4:42: *Jesus and the Spirit*

      2:23–3:10: Nicodemus *and the Necessity of the Spirit*

---

115. Plain type in the outline gives a rough approximation of material from the first edition. Italic type gives an approximation of material from the second edition.

The Second Edition of the Gospel

      3:22-30: John the Baptist and Jesus *and the Success of Jesus as Given by God*

      4:1-42: The Samaritan Woman *and the Offer of the Spirit and Worship in the Spirit and the Spiritual Harvest*

  C. 4:43–5:47: *Narrative and Discourse: Two Narratives Which Illustrate the Powers of God Given to Jesus together with an Architectonic Discourse in Which Jesus Presents (1) His Claim to the Two Powers of God, (2) the Four Witnesses to Him, (3) the Nature of His Glory*

    1. Two Narratives That Illustrate the Two Powers Given to Jesus
       4:43-54: Narrative of the Official's Son: Jesus Restores Life
       5:1-19: Narrative of a Healing on the Sabbath: Jesus Heals a Paralytic *and Follows This with a Word of Possible Judgment*

    2. A Discourse on Relation of Jesus to the Father
       5:20-30 *The Father Has Given the Son His Two Powers*
       5:31-40 *There Are Four Witnesses to Jesus*
       5:41-47 *The Father Is to Receive Glory through the Son*

  D. 6:1-71: *Narrative and Discourse: The Scripture as Witness to Jesus*

    1. 6:1-21: Narrative of a Miraculous Feeding near Passover and Jesus' Crossing the Sea of Galilee

    2. 6:22-59: *Discourse on Scripture as Witness*

    3. 6:60-71: *The Disciples and the Aftermath of the Multiplication*

  E. 7:1–8:59: *Narrative and Discourse: The Word of Jesus as Witness*

    1. 7:1-52: Narrative of Jesus' Preaching at Tabernacles

    2. 8:12-59: *Discourse on the Word of Jesus as Witness*

  F. 9:1–10:41: Narrative and Discourse: The Works of Jesus as Witness

    1. 9:1–10:21: Narrative of the Healing of a Blind Man and Jesus as Shepherd

    2. 10:22-41: *Discourse on the Works of Jesus as Witness*

  G. 11:1–12:50: *The Climactic Demonstration of Jesus' Two Powers:* Giving Life and Bringing Judgment

    1. 11:1-57: *Narrative with Dialogue:* Jesus Gives Life to Lazarus

    2. 12:1-50: *Narrative with Dialogue:* Jesus Speaks of Judgment at the End of His Ministry

II. The Arrival of the Hour and Jesus' Second Glorification (13:1–20:31).

  A. 13:1–17:26: *Farewell Discourses with the Disciples*

    1. 13:38–14:25: *The Departure of Jesus*

    2. 15:18–16:4a: *Persecution and Witnesses to Jesus*

Section 3. Synthesis of the Second Edition

   3. 16:4b-33: *The Coming Departure of Jesus and the Scattering of the Disciples*
   4. 17:1-19: *The Prayer of Jesus*
 B. 18:1–19:42: The Departure of Jesus
   1. 18:1-11: The Arrest
   2. 18:12-27: The Trial before Annas
   3. 18:28–19:16a: The Trial before Pilate
   4. 19:16b-30: The Crucifixion and Death
   5. 19:31-42: The Burial
 C. 20:1-31: His Appearances and Bestowal of the Spirit
   1. 20:1-18: The First Appearance
   2. 20:19-31: The Second Appearance

2. The Theology of the Second Edition

The theology that will be outlined below is based solely on the material identified by the criteria established earlier in this section. Nevertheless, the full theological importance of some elements of the second edition are not evident until they are read in the light of the crisis in 1 John. Thus, 1 John is of considerable help in fully understanding the implications of several aspects of the second edition. Two examples may help.

It is often said that the Gospel of John is remarkably lacking in specific ethical instruction. In those few instances where it does speak of ethics, the Gospel does so exclusively under the rubric of the love commandment. Moreover, it is commonly proposed that a variety of features of those texts indicate that all the references to the love commandment stem from the later (third) edition. If this is true (and it will be shown to be such on the basis of the analysis of the third edition), this means that the second edition evidently had *no* references to ethics of any sort.

While it is possible to speculate on the reasons for this, such a theory would seem by itself to be unusual and perhaps unlikely. Yet, when we read in 1 John that the one group within the community held to a theory of ethical perfectionism and so *rejected* the need for ethics, it becomes clear that the "ethical vacuum" of the Gospel is not accidental. The conflict that is implicit at one stage and in one document of the tradition is made explicit at another stage and in another document.

Moreover, this evidence from 1 John that the value of ethical directives was an issue for the community at the time of 1 John helps confirm the literary analysis of the third edition. Once we see that perfectionism was an issue for the community at the time of 1 John, it becomes clear that the sense of an overriding *unconcern* for ethics in the second edition — and the proposal that ethical texts in the Gospel are the result of the third author — are not simply the illusion of an overzealous interpreter.[116]

A second example. Scholars often point out the extraordinary emphasis on "knowing" God. Yet within the Gospel there is no explicit indication that the claim to know God is understood as a derivative of possession of the eschatological Spirit or that such a position could be interpreted as meaning that the Spirit is the sufficient source of true knowing and that the words of Jesus would be thought of as having no permanent value. Yet, when we turn to 1 John, we can tell that the knowledge the author is speaking of is understood to come from one's possession of the Spirit. Thus, 1 John 2:20 ("You have an anointing from the Holy One, and you know all") and 2:27 ("... the anointing that you received from him [God] abides in you, and you do not have need that anyone teach you; but as his anointing teaches you about all things ...").

And while it may be unconvincing at first to suggest that those passages of the third edition that speak of "keeping the word" of Jesus were intended to emphasize the importance of the historical words of Jesus vis-à-vis the claims of personal inspiration, when we read in 1 John and 2 John about the importance of "keeping his word" (1 John 2:5, 7; 2 John 4) and of remaining "in the teaching of the Christ" (2:9-10), it becomes clear that the conflict that was implicitly present in the second edition of the Gospel is made explicit in 1 John. Thus, by the judicious use of 1 John, issues and contrasts that would otherwise remain possible but unproved are able to be clarified and explained with a good deal of certainty.[117]

Consequently, reference will be made regularly to 1 John in what follows. The value of 1 John will become even more fully evident when each of these elements of the theology is discussed in greater detail in Part 4.

In what follows immediately below, I will give only a summary sketch of the basic theological convictions of the second author. Full discussion will be postponed to Part 4. In that treatment, there will be a detailed description of the view of the given author together with the citation of the texts where it is found in the second edition. In the case of the material from the second edition, there will also be a detailed discussion of these convictions in relation to the Old Testament convictions about the prerogatives of the eschatological Spirit.

The brief discussion here will be done by means of a series of numbered

---

116. The fact that this fits well with the belief that such perfectionism will be a gift of the eschatological Spirit confirms this view and reveals the basis for the second author's interpretation.

117. This provides additional confirmation of proposals that see the Paraclete texts of the Gospel (texts in which the Paraclete is said "not to speak on his own") as the work of a later author.

Section 3. Synthesis of the Second Edition

statements, each of which focuses on a central conviction of the author of the second edition or a topic which becomes important in the later editions. These numbered statements correspond to the section number in Part 4, where a detailed discussion of each of these topics will be given.

Arranging the material in this way will enable the reader to get an overview of the theology of the second edition here. The same numbering will be used when discussing the views of the author and of his opponents in 1 John and also in the third edition. This will facilitate comparison of the convictions of one author with another. At the same time, by postponing complete discussion of each topic until Part 4, we will be able to gather the views of all four stages of the tradition in one place and so observe more clearly how Johannine theology developed throughout the period witnessed in the writings of the tradition.

a. Christology

In the second edition, there is a massive interest in Christology. The primary reason for this is that unless a person accepts the claims of Jesus and believes "in his name," that individual will not receive the Spirit that Jesus offers. In this edition, the dominant understanding of Jesus is of him as the Son sent by the Father. This complex of ideas is introduced at the time of the second edition, but, as we shall see, it is also taken over in 1 John and in the third edition, although the ideas are modified, nuanced, and clarified in these later stages of the tradition.

In all such cases, the understandings of both "Son" and "Father" are distinct from the traditional Jewish understanding in which any devout Jew could be referred to as "son" or could refer to God as "Father." That this is so is evident from the reaction created among "the Jews" by Jesus' claims. Yet Jesus seeks only to do the will of the Father and to seek the Father's glory. He is sent to complete the work of the Father.

Nevertheless, in addition to this primary focus of the second edition's Christology, there is a continued articulation of the identity of Jesus in terms of traditional titles, for example, "Son of God," "Christ," and "king." Of these, he shows most interest in "Son of God" and some minor interest in "Christ," and he rejects the application of "king" to Jesus at least when it is applied by the common people.

b. Belief

In the second edition, the theology of belief was not based just on the working of miracles (which the first edition had termed "signs"). Rather, there were a variety of witnesses to Jesus. This conviction structures much of the presentation of the second edition and is given in detail in the discussion of the structure of the second edition.

The full range of these witnesses is given in 5:31-40 and includes (1) John the Baptist, (2) the works of Jesus, (3) the word of Jesus (which is the word of the Father), and (4) the Scriptures. In his presentation of the Gospel, the second author shows that the disciples were models of belief and responded to all four of the witnesses (1:19–2:22). In 6:1–10:39, the second author shows "the Jews" rejecting the witness of Scripture, the witness of the word of Jesus, and the witness of Jesus' works, and so failing to believe. He also makes a final reference to the rejection of these witnesses in 15:22-25.

c. Pneumatology

The single overriding goal of the ministry of Jesus is to offer the eschatological Spirit to those who believe in him. This offer is made in various ways, sometimes directly (7:37-39), sometimes figuratively (4:10-15), but it is a constant theme. Moreover, it is sometimes said that Jesus offers the believer eternal life, which comes through the possession of the Spirit (5:25; 6:33, 40, 47-50). As he had promised, on the evening of the first day of his Resurrection, Jesus bestows his Spirit upon the disciples (20:22). This offer of the eschatological Spirit would have been understood well by Jewish listeners against the considerable Old Testament background of such expectation.

Although there is no specific mention of this in the second edition, we are to recognize that the reception of this Spirit was generally understood as constituting an "anointing." Thus, Jesus, who himself possesses the Spirit, is the "Christ." That first-century Jews would have readily associated the possession of the Spirit with anointing is clear from the Old Testament.

Later in the tradition (at the time of 1 John) the use of anointing in connection with the Spirit does become explicit and it is clear that the possession of an anointing was also predicated of the believer. The conviction that the believer has an anointing just as Jesus did presents an area of potential challenge to the unique role of Jesus. This will be discussed further in the section "Anthropology" below.

d. Eternal Life

In the second edition, the reception of the Spirit results in the transformation of the individual from the realm of natural life that ends in death to the realm of

Section 3. Synthesis of the Second Edition

the life of God that is eternal life. Because of this rebirth, the person was now looked upon as "divinized" and so could properly be called a "child of God." Thus, there could be said to be a parallel between the status of Jesus as "son" and the believer as "child" of God.

This conception also would have been understood against the background of the "spirit" as the principle of life, and therefore the possession of God's Spirit would result in living with the very life of God. Because it makes no reference to bodily resurrection, this view of eternal life is properly called "spiritual immortality," a view common among some Jews of the first century.

e. Eschatology

In the second edition, the possession of the Spirit gives eternal life in the present. The transformation occurs in the present and not in some future period at the end of time. Although the Old Testament background for when the attainment of eternal life took place is not clear, it is evident from the SDQ that the Jewish community at Qumran saw itself as living in eschatological times and believing that it already possessed various eschatological gifts.

In this view, the one who believes receives eternal life in the present time and so passes over from spiritual death to spiritual life and will not undergo judgment.

f. Knowledge of God

It is clear in the Old Testament that possession of this Spirit will bring about direct knowledge of God. But in the second edition, there are no explicit statements about the possibility of direct knowledge of God. What is clear in the second edition is the massive concentration on "knowing" God (and not knowing him) as well as "knowing" other things related to God, Jesus, and eternal life. This feature, which is generally recognized as one of the characteristics of the Gospel as a whole, and which at one time led scholars to see Gnosticism as the background of the Gospel, is now seen against this Old Testament background as a prerogative of the eschatological Spirit.

A second element of the second edition that is of significance here is the obvious lack of didactic material in the second edition except insofar as such "teaching" relates to understanding the true identity of Jesus. This notable absence is explained well when it is recognized that such teaching would not be necessary once direct knowledge is granted through the possession of the Spirit.

g. Soteriology

Although it is not immediately evident and certainly not explicit in the text of the second edition as we have it today, within the larger context of the Johannine tradition it seems almost certain that the author of the second edition held the conviction that sin was forgiven through the cleansing activity of the eschatological Spirit.

First, there is nothing that could be called clear evidence (at least within the material that remains within the present Gospel) of a conviction on the part of the author of the second edition that the Spirit was the agent that cleansed the individual from sin. There may have been such a conviction, but, if so, it has been removed by the author of the third edition. *At the same time,* it should also be pointed out that in the second edition of the Gospel there is no indication that the death of Jesus resulted in the forgiveness of sin either. In fact, it is fair to say that there is a great soteriological silence in the present text of the second edition!

Yet, if we look to first-century Judaism, we find abundant evidence that the Spirit cleanses from sin. These texts are so abundant as to leave no room for doubt about this matter. It is also true that there was no evidence in first-century Judaism of a conviction that a being (either human or divine) would die in order to attain eschatological salvation for others.

When we turn to 1 John, we gain a new perspective on the understanding of the community at the time of the second edition. At the time of 1 John, the author's opponents deny that the death of Jesus was soteriologically significant, and the author of 1 John makes it abundantly clear that Jesus' death was an atonement for sin and that we are freed from sin by his blood.

There are two other indications that this is the correct view of the second edition's position. It will be noted that in the second edition the Spirit is bestowed upon the disciples on Easter night. It is striking that immediately following this *the author of the third edition* chose to position his comment about the role of the disciples in the forgiveness of sin. As we will see below, the author of the third edition was intent on affirming the importance of a ritual element in various aspects of the community's life. Thus, he chooses to emphasize the ritual element of forgiveness of sin immediately after the scene of the bestowal of the Spirit. This does not prove the matter, but the juxtaposition of matters dealing with the forgiveness of sin with the bestowal of the Spirit would seem to indicate an awareness of such a relation.

There is also a text in 1 John 5:6 which may have some relevance for this issue. As will be explained in detail in the Commentary, this verse argues that Jesus did not come only to give the Spirit but also to remove sin by his death. Again the forgiveness of sin through the death of Jesus is juxtaposed to the giv-

Section 3. Synthesis of the Second Edition

ing of the Spirit. Thus Jesus did not come only to give the Spirit; his (atoning) death was also essential to his purposes.

h. Ethics

In the second edition, there is no direct evidence of any belief in perfectionism on the part of the author. Yet what is abundantly clear is that in the second edition there is no mention of ethical directives. The only sin is the failure to believe in Jesus. The author of the second edition saw no need to present ethical directives as did the Synoptic writers and Paul. Why is this so?

Again there is abundant evidence that in first-century Judaism, people would have believed that reception of the eschatological Spirit so transformed a person that they would no longer sin but would be fully faithful to God.

When we come to 1 John, the issue becomes clear: perfectionism is an issue within the community. While the opponents hold an opinion of perfectionism that the author of 1 John finds inappropriate, he himself recognizes a kind of perfectionism that could properly be called "inchoate" perfectionism. The author believes that the believer is radically sinless, but this inchoate perfectionism does not do away with the possibility of sin. Consequently, the believer is in need of ethical directives for all of his relationships and obligations on the human level. These are summarized in the love commandment.

In the third edition of the Gospel, the author incorporates ethical directives in the form of the love commandment and continues the tradition made clear by the author of 1 John.

i. Anthropology

The theology of the second edition also led to the development of a distinctive anthropology. We have seen above that the reception of the eschatological Spirit brings about a radical transformation in the believer. By receiving the Spirit, the believer receives eternal life. This reception of eternal life is thought of as a new birth, a birth to a new form of life that is literally the life of God himself. Thus, the reception of the Spirit raises the believer to a uniquely exalted status, making him or her a "child" of God. Although it is not explicit within the second edition, the numerous ways in which the status of the believer parallels the status of Jesus is understood by some in such a way as to become a threat to the unique status of Jesus.

Although the implications of this theology are not apparent in the second edition itself, when we look at the tradition as it was understood at the time of

1 John, it becomes clear that this has become the case. Because they were members of the same community, the author and his opponents had held the same tradition in common but now understood it differently. At the time of the third edition, the opponents "do away" with Jesus. They are said not to "have" the Son, and so on.

What was present in the second edition that could be the basis of such a view? It must be remembered that, in the Christology of the second edition, there is no mention of the preexistence of Jesus. Rather, he is presented as one upon whom the Spirit descended and who exhibited all of the traits of one transformed by the Spirit. Throughout the second edition Jesus is identified as having earthly roots (father and mother), a homeland (Galilee), brothers (in the physical sense), but at the same time as being now a "Son" of the "Father" sent by him to announce the outpouring of the Spirit on all who believed. He was also *christos,* anointed by this Spirit.

When this understanding of Jesus is compared with the extraordinarily exalted status of the believer, it could well be seen that some who understood their possession of the Spirit to be absolute would now argue that their possession of the Spirit meant that Jesus no longer occupied a unique role vis-à-vis salvation or vis-à-vis the believer. As a result, the author of 1 John will make numerous distinctions between the status of Jesus and the status of the believer. He will do this first of all by making clear that Jesus was a "unique" *(monogenēs)* Son, that he was preexistent, and that he is completely equal with the Father. The author of 1 John also says that the believer has received "of the Spirit" rather than receiving the Spirit completely (a view that comes to expression in the third edition when the author says that the Father gave Jesus the Spirit "without measure").

j. Ecclesiology

In the second edition, there is no indication of a concern for a community dimension to the religious experience of the believer. Nor is there a hint of an authoritative structure or of rituals of a social nature. That there was some sort of association between believers is certain since it would have been as a group that they would have been expelled from the synagogue. But the only explicit relationship is the one between the believer and Jesus, the Spirit, and the Father.

k. The Religious Significance of Material Reality

Finally, in the second edition there is a conviction that the realm of the physical and material is not of significance for attaining eternal life. This is evident in

Section 3. Synthesis of the Second Edition

the constant contrast of the material and the spiritual and is expressed in the clearest of terms in 6:63, where the author says, "The Spirit is what gives life; the flesh is useless."

The Judaism of Jesus' time was deeply committed to an extensive system of ritual actions, but the question is whether these were seen as to be done away with in the eschatological age. The Old Testament does not address this issue.

3. The Genre of the Second Edition

It was clear in our Analysis of the first edition that the author presented his material in a true narrative of Jesus' public ministry. However, a number of features of the second edition indicate that the second author has considerably different concerns. Some of these are discussed below. We will conclude with specific remarks on the genre of the second edition.

a. The Arrangement of the Material and the Question of Narrative Sequence

In general, the author of the second edition takes over the narrative base of the first edition and builds on it, although he has excised considerable portions of it. At the same time, the second author has little concern for narrative sequence or for proper chronology. His interest is theological, and his order is artificial and theological, as we have seen in the discussion of the structure of the Gospel. Some examples will help account for notable (and heretofore puzzling) features of the Gospel.

For example, the author of the second edition is responsible for the present arrangement of the material in 1:19–2:22. In his arrangement, he is primarily concerned to present the disciples as responding properly to the witnesses of Jesus. In this view, the material of 1:19-51 represents the original response of the disciples to the witness of John the Baptist. In order to connect this with the account of the wine miracle in Cana, the second author must create a narrative progression toward Galilee. He does so by the insertion of 1:43, which, although it points to the coming trip to Galilee, interrupts the sequence of the disciples attracting other disciples in a "chain reaction."[118] The insertion is awkward at best and shows the artificiality of the present sequence.

Also connected with the arrangement of 1:19–2:22 is the location of "The

---

118. It is very likely that in the first edition of the Gospel, it was Peter rather than Jesus who attracted Philip, as we have seen.

The Second Edition of the Gospel

Cleansing of the Temple" in 2:13-22. This material, as is explained in the discussion of the Composition, is from the second edition. Moreover, its location is due to theological reasons (i.e., examples of the third and fourth witnesses to Jesus). Although this does not *prove* that the incident is not in historical order, it does provide a strong argument for its location being artificial rather than historical.

Another example concerns the traditional problem regarding the order of chapters 5 and 6. It seems certain, given the literary evidence still present in the Gospel, that in the first edition, the multiplication of the loaves took place immediately after the healing of the official's son, that the healing of the man at the pool took place after the multiplication, and that the Passover described as "near" at the time of the multiplication was in fact the (now unnamed) feast mentioned in 5:1 for which Jesus came to Jerusalem.

Yet the theological value of the present arrangement is also apparent. The healing of the cripple at the Pool of Bethesda (5:1-9) has been made to serve well as an illustration of the theme of "judgment," just as the healing of the official's son serves as an illustration of the theme of "giving life." At the same time, the feeding of the multitude, now moved to a point *after* 5:19-47, provides an ideal narrative foundation for the discourse on the Bread of Life and the concomitant "witness" of Scripture (6:30-51). By reversing the order of the two miracles, the author of the second edition was able to achieve both goals admirably.

Nor does the second author exhibit a concern for a consistent time perspective that is typical of true narrative. There are numerous examples of this. In some instances, he jumps from the perspective of Jesus' ministry to the perspective of the period after the Resurrection. Just above, we saw that the author used first-edition material to show the response of the disciples to the witness of John the Baptist. In the Wine Miracle (also from the first edition), he showed their response to the witness of the miracles of Jesus. Then, in his own (second edition) material (2:14-22), he shows the response of the disciples to the final two witnesses, the Word and the Scriptures. But in his presentation, he adopts a time perspective from after the Resurrection in order to show the disciples understanding the Scripture (about his zeal for the Temple) and the word of Jesus (with respect to his prediction of raising up the temple of his body in three days). Although quite awkward from a narrative perspective, the placement makes sense theologically as evidence of a proper response to the "witnesses" to Jesus.

At other times, the second author imposes expectations that are appropriate only in a post-Resurrection perspective onto figures within the narrative time frame of the historical ministry. Thus, the time perspective *of the narrative* is that of the ministry of Jesus and therefore appropriate to the time *before* the bestowal of the Spirit, yet *the belief and insights expected* of the characters are

Section 3. Synthesis of the Second Edition

possible only in the period after the bestowal of the Spirit. This is patently clear in 7:37-39, where the second author presents Jesus as inviting the crowds at Tabernacles to come to him and receive living water. Yet the narrator immediately identifies this living water with the Spirit and explains that the Spirit would not be given until after Jesus was glorified. Thus, the offer of Jesus shows a clear disregard for time sequence. The same is true of Jesus' offer of living water to the Samaritan woman in 4:10-15.

This collapse of narrative time is also evident in the author's use of "misunderstanding." In the second edition, characters such as Nicodemus, the Samaritan woman, "the Jews," and others regularly misunderstand Jesus. Yet the understanding that Jesus expects of persons is one that is possible only if one has the Spirit. Nevertheless, as we have seen (7:39), the Spirit has not yet been given.

The lack of concern for narrative realism is also evident in the portrayal of the hostility of "the Jews" as unified and intense from the beginning, without the development or division that would be typical of a historical portrayal. Finally, such lack of concern for a consistent time perspective is evident in the various anachronisms of the second edition already discussed.[119]

b. The Narrative Role of Geography in the Second Edition

In the first edition, there was a repeated emphasis on Judea as a place of unbelief and hostility and Galilee as a place of belief and safety. Judea as a place of danger continues to be a motif in the second edition, as is evident from 7:1 and 11:8. Yet, the author is not consistent in his portrayal. Two instances are striking and shed light on this issue. In 6:41,[120] "the Jews" appear in Galilee in the synagogue at Capernaum. This is the only time they appear outside of Judea in the Gospel. In 7:1, "the Jews" are associated with, but also restricted to, Judea, so that Galilee can be considered a safe haven from them. This is inconsistent with their appearance in Galilee in 6:41.

As was pointed out, the only appearance of "the Jews" in Galilee is in 6:41. From the larger structure of the narrative, it would seem that the second author's desire to use the narrative of the multiplication in Galilee as the basis for the exegetical homily of Jesus as the Bread of Life (as his presentation of the "witness" of Scripture) reveals the author's basic lack of concern for narrative consistency in favor of his theological interests.

---

119. In Section 3.6 below, I will discuss the issue of the historicity of the material in detail. That also has a bearing on the current topic but is treated separately.

120. Because the instance of "the Jews" in 6:52 appears to be the reuse of this term by the author of the third edition, it is not included here.

The Second Edition of the Gospel

The second instance (7:1) indicates that "the Jews" are to be identified with and restricted to Judea and (together with 11:8) would seem to indicate his view of Judea as a place of danger. While this is true, the motif of escape to Galilee to avoid danger is a motif of the first edition (cf. 4:1-4), whereas in the second edition Jesus is unaffected by danger not because he is able to escape to Galilee but because his "hour" has not yet come. This is true in 11:8 and elsewhere (e.g., 8:20). Rather, 7:1 is *best* explained as a *reprise* of the theme of hostility in Judea from the first edition. In the first edition (4:1-4), Judea was a place of hostility and Galilee a place of safety. In the interval between 4:1-4 (where Jesus escaped to Galilee to avoid "the Pharisees") and 7:1, Jesus has returned to Judea. In 7:1, Jesus is again back in Galilee, and the reason for that return is once again the hostility of the religious officials, but now given in the language of the second edition.[121] For the author of the second edition, the geographical motif is incidental. But his chief intent is to show the objections of "official Judaism," and that can take place in Judea (as in 7:1) or in a synagogue in Galilee (as in 6:41).

Thus, we see that the author's purposes and literary strategies are not only distinct but also radically different from those of the first author. Although such differences reveal a Gospel that is more complex than was previously thought, identifying the literary strata of the Gospel results in considerable gain since we are now able to demonstrate a consistency that was not evident before but that is present within individual strata rather than in the Gospel as a whole.

4. The Identity and Social Location of the Community at the Time of the Second Edition

a. "The Jews" and the Synagogue

At the time of the second edition, the Johannine community was a Jewish-Christian group, in the midst of, or having just emerged from, a thoroughgoing conflict with its parent Jewish matrix, resulting in expulsion from the synagogue. The community included among its members common people (9:18-23) but also individuals from the class of religious authorities (12:42). Being a member of the community involved not only hostility and expulsion from the synagogue (9:22; 12:42; 16:2) but also the real possibility of being put to death (16:2).

Particularly indicative of the historical circumstances of the community at the time of the second edition is the presentation of "the Jews." "The Jews" are

---

121. Note the use of *Ioudaioi* in the hostile sense, particularly the reference to the attempts to kill him.

Section 3. Synthesis of the Second Edition

the primary interlocutors with Jesus in the second edition, especially within chapters 5-10. This group is to be identified (everywhere except 6:41-52), on the basis of the contextual clues, with the religious authorities rather than with the entire nation. Since in 6:41, 52, "the Jews" alternates with a group identified in 6:22, 24 as "the crowd," on purely contextual grounds it would seem that they were intended to refer to a larger circle. However, I am convinced that even here "the Jews" are intended to represent the official position of Judaism over against those who believe in Jesus. Thus, in my view, it is correct to say that "the Jews" in the Gospel represent the official *religious* opposition to Jesus by Jewish officials exercising authority over the synagogue of which the Johannine community had been a part. This group speaks forth the objections brought against Christianity by the synagogue and the objections that led to the expulsion of the Johannine community from the synagogue. This group was "official" from the point of view of the Johannine community, that is, it was able to exercise exclusion. Whether this opposition was a result of a generalized decree or the decision of a local authority cannot be determined precisely.

The fact that people who were ethnically Jews (i.e., the Johannine community) could refer to the opposition as "the Jews" suggests that such a separation has already taken place, at least on the level of understanding represented in the second edition. The fact that the Johannine community was *expelled* from the synagogue indicates, however, that they thought of themselves as genuine Jews and as standing within the tradition of Judaism rather than as breaking with their parent tradition. That the community at the time of the second edition was Jewish-Christian is clear from the fact that its members are being excluded from the synagogue and from the nature of the arguments presented, which presume an intra-Jewish debate (e.g., use of Old Testament Scripture, Jewish homiletic techniques, appeal to the rabbinic law of witnesses, etc.).

That the community is now coming to understand itself as distinct from the Jewish community is clear from the fact that they, like many of the characters in the narrative, are Jews by birth and by religion but yet label the hostile authorities "the Jews." Some members of the ruling elite had been believers when they were members of the synagogue but did not confess openly lest they be put out of the synagogue. Others like Joseph of Arimathea had been secret believers but came to make their confession public, as did Joseph by his request for permission to remove the body of Jesus for burial. That all of these elements stem from the second edition is quite clear from the text of the second edition as it is identified by the criteria listed above in Section 2.

The Gospel of John as a whole has often been said to be cast in the form of a trial, with "witnesses" and "judgment" and "interrogations."[122] There is an

---

122. See esp. A. E. Harvey, *Trial*.

"interrogation" of John the Baptist by officials in the beginning. There is speech about "accusation" (5:45-46). There is an attempt at a preliminary arrest and trial in 7:32-52 with a discussion of one of the basic rules of procedure. There is a formal meeting of a Sanhedrin in 11:47-53. The term "paraclete," which can mean "advocate," is a term often associated with legal proceedings. The (P)araclete will "witness" (15:26); he will "convict" the world (16:8-11). The form of the trials (both before Annas and before Pilate) in the Passion is seen by some to be specifically structured in this regard. Some speak of Pilate himself being on trial during the Passion, and some indeed see the "world" as on trial throughout the Gospel. This overall cast is true.

If we attempted to associate this trial imagery with a single edition we would be unsuccessful. Because Jesus was historically put on trial, it is inevitable that a trial will be part of any Gospel. However, the emphasis on claims, testing of claims, witnesses, and judgment seems to be most explicit in the material of the second edition, and this is almost certainly due to the desire to establish as just the claims of the community over against official Judaism as the community faced expulsion from the synagogue and so ultimately faced being branded as "heretics."

b. Polemic against the Followers of John the Baptist?

As we have seen, in the *first* edition John the Baptist figured more prominently than in the other Gospels. However, the portrayal of Jesus and John the Baptist in the *second* edition contrasts sharply with the presentation in the first. In the scenes associating Jesus with John, the fact that John does not baptize Jesus is itself striking, given the considerable evidence for this in the remainder of the Christian tradition.[123] Along with a number of other scholars, I am inclined to suggest that the author of the second edition has removed any notice of the baptism of Jesus in order to avoid any appearance of making John the Baptist responsible for the beginning of Jesus' ministry.[124] Also in 1:20-21, 25, John denies any eschatological role independent of his witness to Jesus. Whether the first edition had a baptism scene cannot be determined.

In 3:27-30 the author of the second edition provides a "new" answer to the

---

123. Meier (*Marginal* 2:105) describes the baptism of Jesus by John as one of the most firmly established historical events of Jesus' ministry. Meier would contend, on the basis of 1 John 5:6, that the Johannine community knew of Jesus' baptism. However, as will be explained in the Commentary on that verse, the reference to coming "in water" almost surely does not refer to Jesus' baptism by John.

124. There are dangers inherent in any argument from silence, especially since this argument is also based on Synoptic comparison, another criterion that can be unreliable.

Section 3. Synthesis of the Second Edition

question of John the Baptist's followers about the popularity of Jesus. Again, radical subordination to Jesus is evident. In the language of the second edition, John makes it perfectly clear that he does not seek to compete with Jesus but rather seeks to recede in importance now that Jesus has come. But more importantly he says that this has been given "from above." This statement shows John recognizing the success of Jesus as having been ordained by God. Although there is a polemic against John, it is really a polemic against all things of a purely human character. The same is true of 5:32-36a.

In 5:32-36a, after indicating that John is a witness to Jesus (and nothing more), Jesus also shows that John is not even an essential witness; Jesus has other witnesses "greater than John." Even John's positive role as witness is diminished in comparison with those of the other witnesses.

Thus, in the second edition, the polemic against John the Baptist is not against him in particular. Rather, he becomes another example of the "human," and so his baptism is not important and his witness to Jesus is not essential. Throughout the second edition, as we have seen, Jesus is above responding to human prompting of any sort. His mother does not determine his hour; "the Jews" do not determine the time of his death. Consequently, in the second edition the relativization of John is at least in part due simply to the fact that he is human, and all human designs and endeavors are insignificant when compared with the divine.

5. The Background of the Second Edition

Throughout the first two-thirds of the twentieth century the nature of the background of the Gospel of John was hotly debated. The debate focused on three major proposals: (1) that the Gospel should be understood against a background of Hellenistic religion; (2) that it should be understood against a background of Gnosticism; and (3) that it should be understood against the background of Judaism, both canonical and sectarian.

In the latter third of the twentieth century, there began a groundswell of agreement that the third of these options provides the clearest parallels to the thought and worldview of the Gospel.[125] While recognizing the value of this proposal, I would propose that the Gospel's background can be clarified with more precision than previously when we ask the question separately about each edition. The closest parallels to the thought *of the second edition* are found in

---

125. Nevertheless, attempts to view the Gospel against the background of Gnosticism continue. For recent examples, see Schmithals, *Johannesevangelium und Johannesbriefe* and Westermann, *Gospel*. Westermann sees a gnostic addition in the later strata of the discourses.

The Second Edition of the Gospel

what might be termed "pre-Rabbinic" Judaism, that is, canonical, nonapocalyptic, nondualistic Jewish thought, while the closest parallels to the third edition, as we shall see later, are found in the equally Jewish but noncanonical, apocalyptic Jewish literature as evidenced in the SDQ and in the *T12P*.

Due mainly to the impetus of Bultmann, who saw the background of the Gospel as gnostic, scholars have often identified the dualism of the Gospel as gnostic, particularly on the basis of statements about Jesus or others being "from above/below" or "from this world/not of this world." After the discovery of the Qumran Scrolls, the close similarities between the apocalyptic worldview of the Scrolls and some aspects of the Gospel became evident. When the material reflecting this apocalyptic dualism was identified and bracketed, it became possible to study the remaining "dualism" more closely.

It would now appear that one of the clearest "opposed pairs" in the Gospel is not dualism at all but a *contrast* between the world imbued with the eschatological Spirit and the world without this Spirit. So, for example, there is the contrast between "birth from the flesh" and "birth from the Spirit" (3:3-10). The appearance of this contrast elsewhere in the Gospel (e.g., 6:63), especially when coupled with the repeated promises of eternal life from the Spirit, showed that having or not having the Spirit became the basis for the quasi-gnostic contrasts as well as for the frequent misunderstandings in the Gospel. It would now appear that there is no substantial evidence for Gnosticism in the Gospel. Rather, this and other aspects of the second edition are Jewish and are presented against the background of the canonical Scriptures, in a type of what might be called "pre-Rabbinic Judaism."

Finally, as is pointed out in detail in the Part 4, Section 1.3.d, the parallels between the Johannine Jesus and revealed Wisdom in the Jewish Scriptures indicate that Wisdom literature played a significant role in the portrayal of Johannine Christology.

6. The Value of the Material Found in the Second Edition for the Study of the Historical Jesus

In our study of the first edition, it was clear that a number of aspects of the presentation of Jesus' ministry there had a good chance of being historically accurate. When we come to the material of the second edition, we find a situation that is more complex. Asking the question about the historical value of this material is in fact to implicitly ask two questions: (1) what is the value of the material of the second edition for the study of the historical Jesus; and (2) what is the value of the material of the second edition for the study of Christianity at the time of the composition of the second edition? The second author has a very

Section 3. Synthesis of the Second Edition

clear literary and theological agenda, but this results in the second edition being more directly useful for understanding the social and theological circumstances of a particular Christian community in the later part of the first century than as a portrayal of the ministry itself. We will take a detailed look at these two aspects of the material respectively in this and the following sections.

a. Historical Sequence

As we have seen, the author of the second edition had no concern to preserve the narrative sequence of the first edition but freely rearranged and added to the material of the first edition to suit his theological purposes. This indicates that *a fortiori* he had no interest in presenting the ministry in its precise historical sequence.

b. Time Frame

We have already seen that the perspective of the second edition is theological rather than historical.[126] The author regularly reads post-Resurrection expectations (such as the insight expected) back into the pre-Resurrection period. Moreover, he reads historical circumstances (such as formal synagogue exclusion) from the period of the later community back into Jesus' ministry. Finally, he does the same with the christological insights typical of the later community. All of this indicates that the author is focused on portraying matters of theology and the conflicts of his own community against the backdrop of Jesus' ministry rather than attempting to simply portray the ministry itself.

c. The Words of Jesus

Determining the historicity of the words of Jesus is a particularly complex task, and its results are often quite speculative. In fact, it is also a task that can be conducted apart from the analysis of the various editions of the Gospel.

Yet something can be said of the overall issue. While there is no doubt that the words of Jesus in the Synoptics have undergone modification in the oral tradition and in the redaction of the Evangelists, studies indicate that within the Synoptics there are accurate historical recollections of the words of Jesus. Although it may also be the case that in the Gospel of John Synoptic-like

---

126. See Part 2, Section 3.2 and 3.3.a above.

sayings underlie some of the Johannine discourses, it is evident from a cursory survey of the form that the words of Jesus in the second edition bear little resemblance to the words of Jesus in the Synoptics.[127]

It is widely proposed that the particular formulation of the words of Jesus in the Gospel is due to the author's (and the community's) convictions regarding the role of the Paraclete in transmitting the message of Jesus.[128] The authors of both 1 John and of the third edition, while chastising the opponents for a conception of the Spirit that was completely unbridled and unrelated to the words of Jesus, nevertheless held to an understanding of the Spirit that "will teach you all things." This is an understanding of the Spirit that is more "independent" than that of almost any other sector of early Christianity.

d. Terminology

Still other features suggest that the author had little interest in presenting Jesus' ministry with historical precision. For example, rather than the historically accurate terms for religious authorities such as "Pharisees," "chief priests," and "rulers," as were used in the first edition, the second author uses the blanket term "the Jews."

e. The Hostility of "the Jews"

Not only is the terminology for religious authorities in the second edition anachronistic, but the hostility of "the Jews" toward Jesus in the second edition is portrayed as equally intense throughout the ministry rather than, as is more likely, increasing throughout the ministry and reaching a climax in the arrest. Thus, it too is not historically accurate.

---

127. Over fifty years ago, Dodd studied the form of the dialogues and sayings of Jesus. Although scholars would now disagree with some of Dodd's conclusions, his comparison of both the Johannine dialogues and the sayings with their Synoptic counterparts indicates just how different they are (*Tradition* 315-420). See also his earlier article, "'Herrenworte'" 75-86.

128. Smith (*Johannine* 15-16) comments: ". . . it may be of considerable significance that the Paraclete of the Fourth Gospel is said to recall (14:25-26) and expand upon (16:12-15) what Jesus taught in his earthly ministry. From this observation to the conjecture that the words of Jesus in the Fourth Gospel, so obviously spoken from the standpoint of a spirit-inspired post-Resurrection community (cf. John 7:39; 20:22), are to be regarded as the fulfillment of the promise of the Paraclete rather than words of the historical Jesus is but a short step." See also the article by Boring ("Influence," 113-123), which argues much the same thing and which provides extensive bibliography.

Section 3. Synthesis of the Second Edition

f. Christology

Yet another anachronistic aspect of the presentation of Jesus in the second edition is its Christology. The debate about the identity of Jesus in the second edition centers on the nature of his sonship and his relation to the Father. The issue whether and in what sense he can be said to be "equal with the Father" was not debated within the ministry itself. The same is true of the repeated statements of Jesus in which he claims the title "I AM" for himself. Finally, the acclamation of Thomas, "My Lord and my God!" almost surely reflects the insight of the later community rather than the historical events of the week after the Resurrection.

g. John the Baptist

It was mentioned above that the baptism of Jesus by John the Baptist is thought to be one of the most certainly established facts of the ministry of Jesus. Yet although there are a number of references to John in the second edition, the presentation seems more theological than historical. The most striking example of this is that there is no mention of an actual baptism of Jesus in the second edition. The absence of something is not in itself significant. However, given the focus on John the Baptist in both the first and second editions, it is curious that there is no mention of Jesus' baptism.

h. The Cleansing of the Temple

It is also certain that the second author is the one responsible for locating the cleansing of the Temple within Jesus' first trip to Jerusalem. This placement does not represent historical reminiscence but an artificial arrangement for theological purposes.[129]

i. The Unnamed Feast

After the reversal of chapters 5 and 6, the feast of chapter 5 goes unnamed, showing the author's unconcern for its exact identity. In the first edition, there

---

129. See above on the structure of 1:19–2:22. This is corroborated by Meier (*Marginal* 1:380-82, quote on 381), who comments that "... most critics hold that John or his tradition has purposely moved the cleansing back to the beginning of the ministry for theological and literary purposes...."

was evidence of occasional division among the authorities and uncertainty about how to handle Jesus, while in the second edition there was no hint of division. This also confirms that the second author was not concerned with a portrayal that reflected the vicissitudes of the actual ministry but rather the "essential" qualities of the theological confrontation between belief in Jesus and Jewish unbelief.

j. Summary

In all these ways, the presentation by the second author differs radically from that of the first edition.[130] While the presentation of the second author rests upon historical facts and historical events, historical verisimilitude and historical details fade into relative oblivion. The author abstracts from the concrete and seeks to describe what is essential to belief and what is at the heart of the conflict that has led to Jewish unbelief and to expulsion of the community from the synagogue.[131] In this respect it is correct to say that the second edition contains many features anachronistic to the ministry. While it may be that there are details in the second edition that are useful for the historical quest, their presentation is incidental to the author's intention.

7. The Value of the Material Found in the Second Edition as a Reflection of Circumstances in the Later First Century

Although the author of the second edition shows little or no concern for preserving the chronology or concrete details of the ministry of Jesus, the material of the second edition reflects a detailed knowledge, and use, of sophisticated Jewish argument. *But this is a Judaism and a historical context of the later third of the first century rather than of the ministry of Jesus itself.*

---

130. The one exception to this seems to be found at the beginning of the discourse in 10:22-39. There the time is given as the Feast of Dedication and the location as being in the Portico of Solomon. Given the utter consistency of the second author's unconcern for such detail elsewhere, it could well be proposed that this material was taken over from the first edition. If so, there are no marks of editing that would indicate it other than precisely this atypical concern for time and place.

131. If what I have described here is correct, this phenomenon would seem to cause particular difficulty for attempts to read the entire Gospel from a narratological perspective. Such readings presume an authorial interest in narrative flow, in plot, character, and setting, and this does not seem to be the concern of the author of the second edition.

Section 3. Synthesis of the Second Edition

We have touched on aspects of this topic throughout Section 3. Here we will only summarize.

a. Jewish Thought and Argument Reflected in the Second Edition

The second edition reflects aspects of the Jewish tradition as well as forms of sophisticated argument not evident in the first (or third) edition. From the point of view of the overall understanding of the second edition, the authenticity of argument in the second edition affirms its true "Jewishness" in spite of its evident lack of concern for the historical details of Jesus' ministry.

The Jewishness of the community is evident in a variety of ways. It is evident first of all in the type of issues that are debated. Thus, the argument of 5:16-18, whether the Sabbath was so sacred that even God rested on the Sabbath, is paralleled in later rabbinic materials. The second edition, in its portrayal of the homily of Jesus in the synagogue at Capernaum, employs the complex and stylized techniques of Jewish exegetical homilies as known from the Midrashim. The portrayal of Jewish hopes regarding the eschatological outpouring of the Spirit demonstrates a more detailed knowledge of this dimension of Jewish expectations about the future than any other New Testament work.

The portrayal of Jesus as both a prophet like Moses and a king (6:15) has been shown to reflect postbiblical traditions (current in the first century) which join the titles of prophet and king and apply them to Moses.[132] D. M. Smith has commented: "... the fit between 'the Jews'' rejection of Jesus and Judaism's historical positions is recognizable, so that the view that 'the Jews' represent historical Judaism and unbelief seems a reasonable one."[133] I would agree while affirming that this is a reflection of a community under siege from its parent Judaism rather than a reflection of the plight of the disciples during Jesus' ministry.

b. Historical Circumstances of the Contemporary Johannine Community

We have discussed the circumstances of the community above. Here we need recall only that, unlike the first edition of the Gospel, the second focuses on and reflects to a remarkable degree the circumstances of the community. Later first-century Christology and later situations of debate and of formal synagogue exclusion are all mirrored in the text of the second edition. In this sense, the text

---

132. See the Commentary on 6:15. See also Meeks, *Prophet-King* (passim); idem, "Moses."
133. Smith, "Learned" 217-35, here 221.

of the second edition is very useful for providing certain types of information about later first-century Jewish Christianity.[134]

8. The Relation of Material in the Second Edition to the Synoptics

The question of the relation of the second edition to the Synoptics is a simple one: there is no significant evidence of knowledge of the Synoptics by the second author. As in the first edition, there are some similarities to the Synoptics, but these are so distant that there is no real evidence that the author either knew or used the Synoptics. The most that can be said is that there is the possibility that both the Synoptics and the second edition of John reflect traditions about the same events. But there are no verbal similarities.

9. The Author of the Second Edition

What little we are able to know of the author of the second edition comes from indications within the material of the second edition. First, we may be reasonably certain that the author was a Christian of Jewish ethnic and religious background. He belonged to a community that was Jewish in origin but had come to believe in Jesus as the Christ and the Son of God. He had experienced expulsion from that Jewish community because of that belief.

He knew the Jewish Scriptures well, although he seems to have known them primarily through the LXX version. He presents his theology within the compass of traditional Jewish thinking, although his conclusions are far from traditional. He is capable of sophisticated rabbinic argument, as is evidenced by his awareness of the dispute regarding whether God could work on the Sabbath (5:17) and by his use of the format of synagogue Scripture homilies (6:30-50).

His distinctive formulation of the words of Jesus suggests that he wrote in the conviction that the Spirit was the source of his (and the community's) deeper understanding of the tradition.

One of the most puzzling questions is the relationship of the author of the second edition to the BD. In the Analysis of the third edition, it will be proposed and evidence will be given that the person who is identified as the Elder in 2 and 3 John is also the author of 1 John. Moreover, it will be proposed that the person referred to in the third edition of the Gospel as "the disciple whom Jesus loved" was the same as the person known as the Elder in the other documents.

Could this person have been the author of the second edition? That is a

---

134. See also the list of anachronisms given in 2E-31F.

Section 3. Synthesis of the Second Edition

trying question. On the one hand, it is difficult to imagine that the community would have joined the material about the BD to a tradition with which he had no real relation before his nuancing of it. On the other hand, given the clarity and force with which the author of 1 John addresses the misunderstanding of the opponents, it seems difficult to believe that he would have written a document as ambiguous as the second edition. R. E. Brown has taken another approach and argued that because the Gospel was written during a time of intense polemic against the synagogue, the tradition was distorted in the sense that those elements useful for the debate were emphasized and those that were less useful were downplayed, with the result that when the Gospel was read in a later social situation it was easy to misinterpret the sections that were distorted.[135] This is possible. The other possibility is that the second edition was genuinely deficient and was "corrected" by the author of 1 John in his own tract and then later corrected in the Gospel itself by the author of the third edition. On purely historical grounds, I see no way of deciding among these possibilities.

10. The Date of the Second Edition

For the last thirty years, the dating of the Gospel as a whole has relied to a considerable extent on the dating of the references to expulsion from the synagogue in the Gospel. Formal excommunication from the synagogue is generally associated with the insertion of the "blessing" on the heretics *(Birkat ha'minim)* at the Council of Jamnia. However, scholars have recently raised an increasing number of questions about this proposal.[136] There are at least six issues that now call into question this previous certitude. (1) It is difficult if not impossible to know whether the wording of the benediction as reported in the medieval *genizah* manuscript is the same as was in use in first-century Palestine. (2) It is not clear who was included in the curse (blessing): was it intended primarily against Christians or mainly against other heretics but including Christians? (3) Was the benediction aimed at the *presence* of persons who held errant views in the synagogue, or was it intended to prevent such persons from *presiding* at the services in the synagogue? (4) Was the curse actually instituted earlier and the action at Jamnia simply a revision of it? (5) How formal and universal was the curse? (6) What was the purpose of the ban: primarily to exclude or primarily to chastise and then call back?

---

135. R. E. Brown, *Epistles* 71-73, 97-100.

136. See particularly Segal, "Ruler"; Horbury, "Benediction." Wilson *(Strangers* 179-83) provides a good summary discussion of the problems involved with equating the Johannine expulsion with the *Birkat ha'minim.* See also Setzer *(Responses* 87-93).

The Second Edition of the Gospel

To discuss all of these possibilities here is not possible. In my mind, the most significant objection to associating the synagogue exclusion referred to in the Gospel with that referred to in the Eighteen Benedictions is the fact that we have no way of knowing whether the action described in the Gospel was the result of a universal edict (i.e., from the Council of Jamnia) or the result of a decision by the local synagogue. This makes it less likely that we can use the *Birkat ha'minim* to date the Gospel.

But other possible ways have been suggested for dating the Gospel. Lack of concern for the issues that preoccupy the authors of the Synoptic Gospels and are so apparent in the Letters of Paul (issues such as ritual washing, attitudes to circumcision, admission of Gentiles, etc.) suggests to some that the Gospel is "late" and therefore to be dated toward the end of the first century. This is the traditional date, and it is consistent with a traditional dating of synagogue exclusion to about the year 90. However, given the emphasis on the radical transformation brought about by the gift of the Spirit and the consequent insignificance of rituals *of any sort*, it would be dangerous to use the lack of reference to them in this Gospel as a sign that the Gospel was composed late in the century.

Another feature often used in dating the various Gospels is the presence of references to the destruction of the Temple. These are often thought to reflect the fact that the author knew of the Temple's destruction. Two references to the Temple in the second edition may be of help.[137] In 2:18-22 (2E), Jesus makes a prediction that is understood by his listeners to refer to the destruction of the Temple. But the author explains that he was *not* referring to the destruction of the Temple but to the destruction of his body. This statement can be interpreted in either of two ways. It could mean that the Temple had been destroyed and Jesus did not rebuild it in three days. But it could also mean that the destruction of the Temple had *not* taken place as Jesus had predicted (and the author explains that Jesus was talking about his body and the Resurrection).

Another more significant text is 4:19-24 (2E). This is part of the exchange between Jesus and the Samaritan woman. Here the Samaritan woman asks about the proper place of worship: Gerizim or Jerusalem. From this straightforward question, it would appear fairly clear that worshiping at the Temple in Jerusalem was still a possibility.[138] After the destruction of Jerusalem and the

---

137. There is also a reference to the possible destruction of the Temple in the first edition (11:48), but the verse does not indicate one way or the other whether the Temple has indeed been destroyed.

138. One might argue that the Temple on Gerizim had been destroyed over a hundred years earlier and Samaritans continued to worship there. But I think this is to "overinterpret" the statement. For Jews, worshiping in Jerusalem necessarily meant the offering of sacrifice in the Temple. After the destruction of the Temple by the Romans, the question would not be posed as it is in 4:19-24.

Section 3. Synthesis of the Second Edition

Temple by the Romans, there was no possibility of Jewish presence in Jerusalem, let alone worship in the area formerly occupied by the Temple. This suggests that the second edition was written prior to A.D. 66.

If we also attempt to determine the date of the second edition in reference to the later events of the community, we find ourselves leaning toward an earlier rather than a later date. As is argued in the discussion of the dating of 1 John and of the dating of the third edition, the references to the BD as an eyewitness, as the one who referred to himself as "Elder" as well as to his death, all suggest that the BD died in the mid-eighties A.D. Allowing for the schism which developed after the writing of the second edition as well as for the writing of 1 John and later 2 and 3 John would mean that the second edition was written a considerable time before the mid-eighties.

Given the internal indications that the second edition was written before A.D. 66 and allowing for these later events it appears that the most reasonable date for the second edition is before A.D. 66.

11. The Place of Composition of the Second Edition

There is no evidence internal to the Gospel that is useful for identifying a specific location for the composition of the second edition.

PART 3

The Third Edition of the Gospel

INTRODUCTION: THE NEXT STAGE IN THE DEVELOPMENT OF THE TRADITION AND A CHOICE OF WAYS FOR THE READER TO PROCEED

At this point in the study of the Johannine tradition, the reader is faced with a choice. It is a choice forced by the complexity of the Johannine tradition. If the primary intention of the reader is to understand the Gospel, then he/she should continue on to study the characteristics of the third edition of the Gospel. This is a suitable way to proceed and, in fact, it is by means of a contrast between the features of the third edition and those of the second that the character of the third is ultimately defined.

However, if the reader would like to pursue the entirety of Johannine theology in the order in which it developed, then he/she should turn to the study of 1 John. The reason for this is that *1 John represents a stage in the development of the tradition later than the second edition but prior to the third edition of the Gospel.* It is clear from the pages of 1 John that a crisis had developed within the community. Although there have been many theories about the nature of this crisis, the most likely theory is, in my opinion, a version of that proposed by R. E. Brown and others that the crisis arose over the interpretation of the Johannine tradition. I would modify this only to say that the conflict at the time of 1 John was a conflict over the tradition *as it appeared in written form in the second edition of the Gospel.*[1] The "opponents" of 1 John hold to an interpreta-

---

1. R. E. Brown (*Epistles* 72-73) argued that the dispute was over the Gospel in its final form and that the opponents simply neglected or interpreted in their own way those elements that would seem to contradict their own. I would argue that this is not the way texts are interpreted at a time of dispute — or at any other time. If a motif is present, attention would be called

tion of the tradition similar to that of the second edition of the Gospel, while the author of 1 John argues that their understanding is insufficient. The author of 1 John then goes on to articulate the various ways in which their understanding needs to be corrected, and he provides the nuances necessary for a proper understanding of the tradition.

If the reader proceeds by attending first to 1 John and the issues there, and then continues on, the final step would be to appropriate the thought of the third edition in relation to that of 1 John that preceded it and also in relation to the second edition of the Gospel, the interpretation of which caused such a conflict within the community.

It is argued here that the third edition of the Gospel not only presumes the existence of 1 John but also goes beyond it in several respects. Such a theory complicates the interpretation of the Gospel because it involves the interruption of the reading of the Gospel's development by attention to another document that is, in some ways, equally complicated. It cannot be stressed too much that I have reached this conclusion regarding the order of composition of the documents only because I feel forced to do so by the evidence. For many who read the Gospel, such a proposal will be dismissed out of hand simply because it renders the full understanding of the tradition so complex. Nevertheless, I think that the evidence shows persuasively that the third edition of the Gospel genuinely represents a stage beyond that of 1 John and therefore in itself represents the most fully developed theological material, not only of the Gospel, but also of the Johannine tradition. But the third edition cannot be fully understood by itself but only in relation to what has gone before.

However, if the reader chooses to read the third edition immediately, he/she should at least be somewhat familiar with the general nature of the crisis that divided the community at the time of 1 John. He/she should expect to find it more difficult to identify the precise purpose of the third author's additions since the detailed elements of this crisis are first spelled out in the pages of 1 John. The reader should also be ready to meet some issues in the third edition that do not directly deal with the internal crisis.

Whichever approach is taken, it should be remembered that although *the theological nature of the crisis* is clearest in 1 John, *the literary analysis* by which the material of the third edition is distinguished from that of the second edition is done *solely on the basis of features within the Gospel itself*.[2]

---

to it. Rather, these "minor elements" referred to by Brown are by and large motifs that are of considerable importance *in 1 John*. *In the Gospel,* these motifs are the work of the third author, who sought to make this understanding of the tradition explicit within the Gospel text.

2. In the discussion of the theology of the second edition, I made reference to the fact that some features of the Gospel, which would perhaps be considered only "curious" in the con-

Section 1. An Overview of the Third Edition

SECTION 1. AN OVERVIEW OF THE THIRD EDITION

As was the case in the discussion of the features of the first and second editions, this first section will present an overview of the analysis of the third edition. Its purpose is to give the reader a first view of the nature of the third edition. In the second section, we will give a detailed discussion of the features that serve as criteria for identifying the material of the third edition. Then, in the third section, we will summarize the theology of the third edition as it emerges from the analysis along with the issues of date, author, location, and so on.

Like the authors before him, the third author uses distinctive terminology and has distinctive literary techniques and a distinctive theology. However, unlike the previous two editions, the third edition has no distinctive features of narrative orientation since the third author focuses almost entirely on theology rather than on narrative. The third author introduces a number of new terms or terms with new meanings. In the earlier editions, *kyrios* was used in the secular sense as a form of respectful address or to refer to the "master," for example, in a slave relationship. Now it is used in the religious sense, meaning "Lord" (3E-1). *Adelphos* is now used in the religious sense of one's coreligionist (3E-4; 3E-23: 2). The disciples are at times referred to as "the Twelve" (3E-7). Believers are referred to as "children" or as "little children" (3E-5). The title "Jesus Christ" appears for the first time (3E-2). In addition, a more substantive change is the use of "commandment" as a conceptualization of the ministry of Jesus (in contrast to the use of "work" for this in the second edition) (3E-6). Yet in a remarkable contrast to these distinctive terms used by the third author, there is no distinctive terminology for religious authorities. Rather, the third author simply adopts the terminology that had been employed most recently and uses it to communicate his own distinctive theology (3E-22).

However, the most far-reaching aspect of the third edition is its introduction of the apocalyptic worldview. This represents a major change within the world of the Gospel, but one that had been introduced to the Johannine tradition as a whole by the author of 1 John. This dualism finds its closest parallels in the SDQ and the *T12P*. In the identification of this material within the Gospel, I have focused on using what might be called "micro-features" of apocalyptic rather than "macro-features" because these more detailed elements are more likely to be apparent where larger elements of apocalyptic thought may not be

---

text of the Gospel, take on new meaning when the context is extended to include that of 1 John. For example, the absence of any significant attention to the teaching of Jesus and a lack of attention to ethics within the second edition is curious, but when we see that at the time of 1 John such issues were disputed and in fact corrected by the author of 1 John, then we are able to understand more clearly the significance of the "silence" of the second edition on these matters. Thus, 1 John helps in *understanding the theological crisis* as it is echoed in the Gospel.

The Third Edition of the Gospel

as evident. Among the elements of apocalyptic with parallels in the Synoptic Gospels is the use of the title "Son of Man," which is associated with apocalyptic and appears only in the third edition (3E-14). So also are the two references to the "Kingdom of God" (3E-18).

This edition also introduces a fundamental symbolic expression of apocalyptic dualism: the images of light and darkness (3E-8). In the third edition, we read of "the Spirit of Truth" (which had been explicitly contrasted with "the Spirit of Deception" in 1 John) (3E-12). There is also the dualism implicit in such expressions as "knowing the truth" (3E-19). There are several expressions that show a person's relation to one's spiritual "father" (generally expressed as a pair of dualistically opposed possibilities of such fathers). Along with this, there is the expression "sons of . . ." (especially the distinctive expression "sons of light"), used to describe spiritual relationship to a father (3E-10); the expression "being of . . . (this or that 'father')" also appears (3E-11). The term "works" is used in the idiomatic expression "to do the works of," meaning to do the will of someone, that is, one's "father," again conceived of dualistically (3E-3; 3E-9). The obligation to love is not expressed in a universal way such that love of one's enemies is encouraged; rather, the love is sectarian, directed only to the members of one's community (3E-15). There are the convictions (typical of apocalyptic) of a Second Coming of Jesus (3E-16); of a future judgment at the end of time (3E-17);[3] and of the coming wrath of God (3E-19:3)[4] (#5 "Eschatology").

If the first author had presented a straightforward narrative of the miracles of Jesus, and if the second author had chosen to arrange the material of the Gospel artificially to demonstrate the "witnesses" to Jesus, the third author also superimposes his own distinctive structure, one that echoes the overriding structure of 1 John (3E-25). He symbolizes Jesus as the light of the world.[5] Thus, by building on the theme of the "hour" of Jesus from the second edition, the third author presents the public ministry as a "day" of twelve "hours" in which

---

3. In Johannine theology, "judging" and "judgment" have meanings that are different from the common one. In Johannine theology, these terms always have a negative connotation and are better represented in English by the words "condemning" and "condemnation." Thus, in Johannine theology, on the last day all people will arise either to a resurrection of life or a resurrection of judgment (cf. John 5:29). Consequently, the future eschatology associated with the apocalyptic worldview is best and most accurately described as a time of "final accountability." However, the intermixing of these two meanings is so common that some confusion cannot be avoided and it seems too awkward to constantly substitute the term "final accountability." As a result, the distinction in meaning will be made explicit only where it is thought to be essential.

4. The number after the colon indicates the subdivision of 3E-19 being referred to.

5. The word "light" is often used as a descriptive title for Jesus in the Johannine Gospel, and for God in the Johannine Letters. However, its use is often meant to carry both a physical and a theological meaning. To capitalize the word makes a choice which limits this meaning; as a result, the word will not be capitalized except where it appears in a quotation of others.

Section 1. An Overview of the Third Edition

"the light" shines. The Passion is "the night," a time when Jesus demonstrates his love to the utmost (3E-24).

In addition to the imposition of this overarching perspective, the third author comments on the text of the Gospel by means of extensive glossing. That is, he makes additions of considerably varying length but primarily in relation to material that already existed rather than by creating new narrative. Theologically, these glosses have two specific intentions. First, the third author seeks to clarify the thought of the Gospel in accord with the views put forward by the author of 1 John. Second, the author seeks to address a number of other topics that go beyond the issues of 1 John but which he considers important for the later community.

In the discussion of the theology of the second edition, we saw eleven theological categories that contained distinctive elements of that author's theology. In his editing of the Gospel, the third author presents his own distinct perspective on each of these eleven topics.[6] Thus, in matters of Christology, the author provides an even more exalted understanding of Jesus than the second author had done (3E-26). Jesus is now said to be preexistent (3E-28), to have descended from heaven and to have returned there after his death (3E-34), to have a unique sonship (3E-27), to have the Spirit without measure (3E-30), and ultimately to be "I AM" (3E-29) (#1 "Christology"). Thus, not only does the author exalt the person of Jesus but he also distinguishes his status more clearly from that of the believer (#9 "Anthropology").

In matters of belief, the third author preserves the second author's view of the "witnesses" to Jesus but includes two additional witnesses (the Spirit of Truth and the disciples) appropriate for the time after Jesus' ministry. In addition, the third author focuses on the proper *content* of that belief. A correct belief is essential (as we have seen in the discussion of Christology), and that belief must be based on the historical words of Jesus (3E-31). No one can attain eternal life except through Jesus (3E-32) (#2 "Belief"). The third author now views the Spirit within the context of apocalyptic; whereas for the second author the issue was the contrast between Spirit and flesh (i.e., whether one had the Spirit or not), the issue for the third author is essentially whether one has "the Spirit of Truth" (as opposed to "the Spirit of Deception") (3E-12). And so the third author is careful to point out that the Spirit of Truth will remind the

---

6. This is the first of three summary treatments of the theology of the third edition. Each treatment has a distinct purpose and varies in detail. This first summary is intended to provide an overview of the theology so that the reader can begin to understand the orientation of the third edition. Evidence for these conclusions is not presented here. The second and somewhat more detailed summary of the theology of the third edition will occur in Section 3 below. Finally, in Part 4, each of these topics will be discussed in detail together with remarks on the background of these concepts where appropriate.

The Third Edition of the Gospel

disciples of what Jesus had told them. The Spirit of Truth will not speak on his own but only what he hears (3E-35). Thus, the Spirit will not diverge from the message of Jesus. The third author emphasizes this in order to refute the opponents' view that the specific teaching of Jesus was not important and that there was no need to record it except insofar as it pertained to his promise of the Spirit (#3 Pneumatology).

The third author shares with the second author the conviction that Jesus came to give eternal life through the imparting of the Spirit. However, in the second edition of the Gospel, there had been no discussion of ethics (i.e., the behavior expected of the believer), and the result is the so-called "ethical vacuum" of the Gospel. From a reading of 1 John, it becomes apparent that this lack of ethics is due to the fact that the opponents claimed to have a "perfectionism" based on their possession of the eschatological Spirit that guaranteed freedom from future sin. The third author agrees with the author of 1 John that the believer's possession of eternal life is inchoative (#4 "Eternal Life") but that the believer is still capable of sin and so needs the commandment of mutual love, modeled on the love that Jesus exhibited to his own (3E-38) (#8 "Ethics").

In keeping with the apocalyptic viewpoint, all believers are accountable for their actions and will undergo a final judgment and possible condemnation. For those whose actions are good, the possession of eternal life will become final in physical resurrection from the dead (3E-37) (#5 "Eschatology").

The third author agrees with the author of the second edition that the believer is given the prerogative of "knowing" God, but the historical word of Jesus has a priority over, and is the measure of, any direct knowledge the believer may claim to have (cf. 3E-6; 3E-31) (#6 "Knowledge of God"). In matters of "Soteriology" (#7), the view of the third edition differs radically from that expressed in the second edition. In various ways, the third author affirms that Jesus' death was not just a departure to the Father, but a death that took away the sin of the world (3E-32; 3E-33). This issue was addressed repeatedly in 1 John, and the third author now makes it clear also within the Gospel itself.

In matters of ecclesiology, the third author shows a remarkable departure from the perspective of earlier stages of the tradition. In keeping with his view that the realm of the physical and the material has a continuing importance, we see that a human person, the Beloved Disciple, has a special role as witness to the tradition (3E-40). At the same time, the community recognizes a role for human leadership in the person of Peter (3E-41). By repeated comparison of the roles of these two individuals, it becomes clear that the community now accepts the importance of human leadership and that this leadership is embodied in Peter rather than in the Beloved Disciple. Although this is a very minimal ecclesiology, when viewed within the history and theology of the Johannine tradition, it represents a major change from earlier periods in the community (#10 "Ecclesiology").

Section 1. An Overview of the Third Edition

Finally, the third author holds a radically different appraisal of the role of material reality in religious affairs (3E-41). He would not say, with the second author, that "the flesh is useless." Rather, he would affirm, along with the author of 1 John, that the physical death of Jesus ("in blood") was essential for gaining eternal life. Moreover, physical resurrection was an essential element in the future life, and participation in "physical" rituals such as the Eucharist was also essential for obtaining eternal life. Moreover, the human authority of Peter becomes significant in addition to the role of the Spirit, as we have seen (#11 "The Religious Significance of Material Reality").

Beyond these theological features, it becomes clear from the analysis of the material of the third edition that in some cases the third author intended to introduce elements into his Gospel that would correlate the Johannine tradition with that of the Synoptics (3E-56F). These comments are loosely tied to their context and at times introduce confusion in relation to earlier elements of the Gospel. Yet the actual content is so similar to that found in the Synoptics that it would appear that the primary purpose of their inclusion was precisely to reflect that similarity.

At the time of the third edition, the social location of the community manifests yet another (fourth) distinctive configuration. The community is one that is in continuity with the tradition as manifest at the time of the second edition, but like the community at the time of 1 John, it now exists apart from the synagogue. Unlike the community at the time of 1 John, the community now manifests contact with other areas of early Christianity as well as a desire to be seen as existing in harmony with the Petrine tradition and the Great Church.

When we attempt to determine the date of the third edition, we address both the actual date of the third edition and the date of the third edition relative to that of 1 John. I would propose that, on the basis of external evidence involving the first citation of the Gospel, the final edition was probably composed as early as A.D. 95 and likely before A.D. 117. However, perhaps more importantly, there is considerable evidence that the third edition was written *after the composition of 1 John.*

The discussion of the author necessarily involves the figure of the Beloved Disciple. In my view the BD was a historical figure, probably the person who identifies himself as the Elder in 2 and 3 John. By the time of the third edition, this disciple has died and the community has assigned to him the honorific title "the disciple whom Jesus loved." This is a title that he surely would not have given to himself. Thus, while the Elder may be the author of 1 John, he is not the author of the third edition, even though the third edition has as one of its goals to enshrine his views within the Gospel tradition. Beyond the general characteristics known from the third edition itself, we do not know the identity of the author of the third edition.

The Third Edition of the Gospel

The place where the third edition was written cannot be determined with certainty, but a number of indications suggest that the Gospel may have reached its final form in or near Ephesus.

SECTION 2. THE CRITERIA USED FOR THE IDENTIFICATION OF THE THIRD EDITION

In the identification of the first and second editions of the Gospel, the primary features were the differences in terminology, first for religious authorities and then for miracles. It was on the basis of the appearance of each of these sets of terms themselves that the first sorting of material was made. On the basis of that sorting, the other features of each edition emerged.

However, once the identification of the (first) two editions was complete, it became clear that not all of the material of the Gospel had been accounted for. There were still numerous aporias directly related to sequence as well as differences of linguistic usage, ideology, theology, and literary usage. Thus, a theory of two editions could not explain fully the Gospel in its present form.

At that point, it was possible to identify a third set of features (linguistic, ideological, theological, and literary) distinct from those of the previous two editions, characteristics which were internally coherent and which revealed the existence of a third literary stratum within the Gospel.

Aside from the specific characteristics of the third edition (which will be listed below), several other overarching elements of this third edition become evident from the identification of the third stratum. First, although the linguistic differences are roughly as numerous as in the first two editions, they are not as extensive. Second, the most pervasive feature of the third edition turns out to be an ideological feature: the adoption of a worldview of apocalyptic (modified) dualism. Third, it is also soon clear that particularly the theological and ideological features of this third edition are in dialogue primarily (but not exclusively) with the material of the second edition.[7] At the same time, the third edition did not reject the thought of the second edition outright but accepted much of it while nevertheless attempting to modify other aspects. As a result, concepts introduced in the second edition will appear in the third edition, but they will be able to be identified as due to the third author first by the literary

---

7. Some scholars (e.g., Painter, *Quest* 306-7) would argue that, although there are secondary additions to some Gospel material, this need not indicate that another person was responsible for the addition but that the Evangelist himself could have done it. The differences between the material of the second and third editions are so significant that the author would have had to have undergone a radical transformation of worldview in order to have written the material. I judge this to be highly unlikely.

seams that mark the material off from surrounding material, but also by the presence of features that are distinctive of the third edition. Fourth, it also becomes apparent that as a whole the features of the third edition (particularly the theological features) are very similar to (but not identical with) the language, ideology, theology, and literary features of the First Epistle of John.[8]

With this as a background, we may now discuss the individual features of the third edition. A total of forty-five features are characteristic of this edition. This number is greater than was the case previously and is due primarily to the considerable number of individual elements of the apocalyptic worldview manifest in the third edition.

1. Characteristic Terminology

3E-1. In the third edition, *kyrios* ("Lord") is used in the religious sense to refer to Jesus as the (divine) Lord. This is not found in the earlier editions.

In the third edition, the word *kyrios* appears several times in the religious sense of the word to refer to Jesus as "Lord." However, while the religious use is characteristic of the third edition, it is not true that the "secular" use is characteristic of one or other of the remaining editions. The secular use seems to appear in all three editions.

It is important to review all the instances of the term in the Gospel and to distinguish the various meanings. While the meaning in some instances is quite clear, some occurrences are inevitably ambiguous.[9] First, *kyrios* appears in direct address as a common but respectful form of address, connoting recogni-

---

8. A considerable number of scholars recognize some similarity between elements of the Gospel thought to be "late" and elements in 1 John (see, e.g., J. Becker, Thyen, and Richter).

9. Meier (*Marginal* 2:863 n. 124) is an example of a recent scholar who has attempted to sort out the various meanings of *kyrios* in the Gospel. He proposes three usages: (1) The vocative *kyrie* is used of Jesus by others. This is equivalent in many ways to the first meaning I have distinguished but which I define in terms of its *meaning* as "master," a common but respectful form of address. (2) Meier defines the second type as occurring in sayings material in which Jesus refers to himself as viewed by others. Meier cites 13:13-14. I would argue that the meaning intended in 13:13-14 is no different from Meier's first category, but that the usage in 13:16 *is* a different meaning, the literal meaning "master" as opposed to "slave." Meier's third category is "the Evangelist's use of *ho kyrios* of the risen Jesus in chapter 20." He notices the extraneous uses in 4:1 and 6:23 but dismisses them on textual grounds. He then assigns 11:2 to the hand of the redactor but feels that he cannot be sure since we have so little of the redactor's work outside of chapter 21. As I argue below and in detail in the Notes on 4:1 and 6:23, the textual evidence for *kyrios* in those verses is quite strong and should be preferred on the grounds that it is, in fact, the more difficult reading.

The Third Edition of the Gospel

tion of some degree of superiority in the addressee. This is its "secular" use and appears most frequently in the Gospel: 4:11, 15, 19, 49; 5:7; 6:34, 68; 9:36; 11:3, 12, 21, 32, 34, 39; 12:21; 13:6, 9, 25, 36, 37; 14:5, 8, 22; 20:13b,[10] 15.

A second but related use is found in those cases where the term in the sense of "master" is contrasted with that of "servant" or "slave." This usage occurs in John 13:13, 14, 16; 15:15, 20. These two meanings of the term appear within both the first and second editions of the Gospel, and possibly the third edition.

The fourth usage, and the one in focus here, is the distinctly Christian use in which Jesus is referred to as "Lord." The exalted nature of this title can be seen from the fact that in the LXX it is the title used to translate YHWH. Within the Gospel, this religious use appears only in the third edition. The religious sense can often be distinguished by the presence of the article *(ho)* before the word (i.e., "the" Lord). This religious use appears eighteen times in the Gospel: 4:1; 6:23; 9:38; 11:2, 27; 20:2, 18, 20, 25, 28; 21:7 (twice), 12, 15, 16, 17, 20, 21. These are reviewed below, where the evidence for seeing the meaning as the "religious" one is discussed.

In 4:1, the term "Lord" appears in a comment by the Evangelist and is his insertion into material the remainder of which comes from the first edition. This text is complicated somewhat by variant readings, but the evidence for *kyrios* is strong — and it is the *lectio difficilior*. Full details are given in the Commentary.[11] In 6:23, the term appears again in a comment by the Evangelist and the religious sense is intended.[12]

The use in 9:38 is problematic, but it may well be intended to have the religious sense. The term appears only two times in chapter 9: in v. 36 and v. 38. There is no reason to think that the use in v. 36 has the religious meaning. The most logical meaning would be the deferential, "Sir." However, in v. 38 the man uses it in his expression of belief, and this expression of belief is one of divinity since the verse continues by saying that the man "prostrated himself before" Jesus.

In 11:2, we find another instance in which the religious sense of the term is intended. In 11:27, however, the usage is somewhat ambiguous. Two elements are pertinent. First, the term is used in direct address and parallels several other

---

10. That the title has its secular sense here is evident from the use of "my" with the title.

11. Bultmann (*Gospel* 1:176 n. 2) calls the instances prior to chapter 20 "clumsy glosses" but finds the usage in chapters 20 and 21 appropriate. While it is now possible to see that the usage throughout comes from the same author, Bultmann's comments on the individual instances are very useful in sorting out the religious from the secular sense. R. E. Brown (*Gospel* 1:164) dismisses the reading in 4:1 on the grounds of his assessment of the textual evidence. The assessment of the early papyri has changed since the appearance of Brown's commentary.

12. R. E. Brown (*Gospel* 1:258) recognizes the religious sense here and calls it "non-Johannine."

Section 2. The Criteria Used for the Third Edition

uses in the first-edition narrative where the word is used in its normal secular sense (cf. 11:12, 21, 32, 34, 39). However, in 11:23-27 it is used as a form of address for Jesus in the context of other titles such as "the Christ," "the Son of God," and "the one coming into the world," and so it is possible that the religious meaning is intended here. Second, in 11:28 (1E) *didaskalos* is used when referring to Jesus, not *kyrios*. This would suggest that in the original stratum *didaskalos* would be the normal term when referring to Jesus in the third person, even if *kyrios* would be the appropriate term in direct address.[13] In any event, the evidence tilts in the direction of concluding that the religious sense is intended here.

Although the frequency of use increases in chapters 20 and 21, this is not simply a reflection of post-Resurrection faith on the part of the disciples since it has been used three times previous to the Resurrection (4:1; 6:23; 11:2).[14]

In chapter 20, the term appears with diverse meanings. It is used in the secular sense to address "the gardener" (20:15); the secular use is probably also intended in v. 13. However, the first occurrence (20:2) is somewhat less certain, although I would conclude that it comes from the third edition. Some scholars argue that its use in v. 2 is the secular sense since this fits well with a theory of a progression in profundity of titles throughout the chapter.[15] I am inclined to think that the third author did not intend a neat progression and that he simply used it in the religious sense even though it would be somewhat strange to a modern reader for Mary to use such a title at this point in the narrative, before she had come to belief in the Resurrection.[16] More compelling, however, is the fact that here the term is used as a reference to Jesus in the third person. Nowhere is the secular sense used in that way. The fact that the surrounding material is identified on other grounds as coming from the third edition is also consistent with this view.

---

13. This is R. E. Brown's position (*Gospel* 1:425). It is possible, but it is nevertheless true that "teacher" appears in material associated with the first edition of the Gospel; therefore, the real issue may be greater than the change in forms of reference, particularly given the proximity of three other christological titles.

14. Hartmann ("Vorlage") thinks that the instances in vv. 2, 18, 20, and 25 are from a source used by the Evangelist. What is useful in this is the recognition (a) that the usage here is the same as in 4:1; 6:23; 11:2, and (b) that it reflects the religious use of the term.

15. Bultmann (*Gospel* 683 n. 11) calls the formulation "remarkable" and notices the contrast with Mary's title for Jesus in v. 16. Observing the problem that Mary refers to Jesus as Lord in v. 2 but has not yet reached full faith, R. E. Brown (*Gospel* 2:984) points out that a similar problem would arise regarding v. 13 — but does not attempt to deal with the problem there either.

16. This goes counter to the views of many who would see such progressions throughout. Rather, I would say that there is a clear progression in the profundity of the insights from edition to edition (from traditional to high Christology, to the application of the divine titles to Jesus) and that thus de facto such a progression appears in many places, but I am less inclined to see a deliberate narrative suspense created by the various authors.

The Third Edition of the Gospel

In v. 18, the term is used in the religious sense,[17] as also in v. 20 and v. 25.[18] The use of "Lord" in Thomas's confession of Jesus in v. 28 is also the religious sense.

In chapter 21 "Lord" appears several times. In v. 7a, it is first used by the Beloved Disciple to refer to Jesus in a recognition scene and is clearly used in the religious sense.[19] In v. 7c it is also patently used in the religious sense in a comment by the narrator. In v. 12 it appears in another comment by the Evangelist and is once again used in the religious sense. In vv. 15, 16, 17, 20, 21, the religious sense also appears, always in instances where Peter is addressing Jesus.

The texts that I have attributed to the author of the third edition have attracted attention in the past, and there is considerable agreement that they constitute a distinct usage within the Gospel. In addition, there is considerable speculation that at least some of them may well represent the work of a later hand.

Bernard considered the verses that we have identified as "the religious use" to indeed have a special meaning. He states in his Commentary that 4:1; 6:23; and 11:2 are "all explanatory glosses, not from the hand of John, but written after the first draft of the story had been completed." The post-Resurrection instances he sees as evidence of special reverence "exhibited in writing of Him who had risen."[20]

Bultmann thought the uses in 4:1; 6:23; 11:2 were "clumsy glosses," but at the same time he considered them original and as corrected by later texts that substituted "Jesus" "to bring the text in line with Johannine usage."[21] His explanation for the post-Resurrection usage is uncertain and speaks of it as "probably to be explained on the supposition that the Evangelist chooses the term in adherence to the section of the source in v. 13."[22]

R. E. Brown would agree that all of the instances I have referred to as having the "religious sense" do, in fact, have this meaning.[23] However, Brown refers to it as the "post-Resurrection" use. There are two problems with the designation of this use simply as "post-Resurrection." First, it appears before the Resur-

---

17. Bultmann (*Gospel* 689 n. 2) comments: "Here, for the first time in Jn, the *kyrios*-title has its genuine pathos. It is wholly suitable for the Risen One."

18. Bultmann (*Gospel* 694) signals his understanding by using the capitalized form in his comment. R. E. Brown (*Gospel* 2:1022) comments on v. 20: "Now the Johannine writer himself begins to use 'the Lord,' the post-Resurrectional title of Jesus." This does not account for the narrator's use in 4:1; 6:23; 11:2.

19. Bultmann (*Gospel* 708) considers it the religious use. If there is any preliminary ambiguity about the use here, it should be taken away by the use of the same term by the narrator later in the verse (v. 7b). The juxtaposition makes both instances clear.

20. Bernard, *Gospel* 1:132-33.

21. Bultmann, *Gospel* 176 n. 3.

22. Bultmann, *Gospel* 683 n. 11.

23. R. E. Brown, *Gospel* 2:984.

Section 2. The Criteria Used for the Third Edition

rection (e.g., 6:23; 11:2; Brown does not accept it as original at 4:1), and, second, it is not a term that appears only within the narrative itself but also in the comments of the narrator. While it is true that the disciples use it as a designation of Jesus only after the Resurrection, the usage as a whole is characteristic of the third edition in a variety of locations.[24]

Although it has been argued that "Lord" was not used as a title for God by Jews and would not have been a part of the early Christian kerygma, we now know, on the basis of a fragmentary Aramaic translation of Job found at Qumran, as well as from 4QEn^{b}1 iv 5, that "Lord" was used as a title for God among first-century Jews.[25] That the evidence for this comes from Qumran is also significant for identifying the background of thought for the third edition.

3E-2. In the third edition, the title "Jesus Christ" appears and is applied to Jesus. This title does not appear in either of the earlier editions.

The use of this title is listed here as a *linguistic* indication of the third edition rather than a theological feature because it is viewed here as a linguistic combination not present in earlier editions of the Gospel. It is precisely the *combination* that is of interest here; what the combination means will be discussed later.

In the Gospel, the title "Jesus Christ" appears in the Prologue at 1:17 ("grace and truth came through Jesus Christ") and in 17:3 ("whom you have sent, Jesus Christ"). The fact that the combination appears so seldom in the Gospel and that the first time is in the Prologue (which is marked through and through as coming from the third edition)[26] suggests that the term may be characteristic of the third edition. The appearance of the term in 17:3 also appears to be due to the author of the third edition.[27] The fact that Jesus speaks of himself here as "Jesus Christ" is indeed awkward. Moreover, the fact that the

---

24. Schnackenburg (*Gospel* 1:422 n. 4) also agrees that all of the instances listed here constitute a distinct usage. He suggests that the instances in 4:1, 6:23, and 11:2 may be due to the redactor. He also points to the instances of chapters 20 and 21 as a special perception of the risen Jesus. Beasley-Murray (*Gospel* 187) suggests that 4:2, 6:22-23, and 11:2 may be glosses by a redactor but does not specifically address the peculiar use of "Lord" elsewhere in the Gospel. J. Becker (*Evangelium* 1:203) attributes it to his Redactor. Haenchen (*Gospel* 2:211a) attributes all the religious uses to the redactor. See also the discussion in Vermes, *Jesus the Jew* 103-28; Fitzmyer, "*Kyrios*-Title" in *Wandering* 115-42.

25. On the Targum of Job, see van der Ploeg and van der Woude, *Targum de Job* 58. On 4QEn^b 1 iv 5, see Milik, *Books of Enoch* 175. Fitzmyer ("*Kyrios*-Title" in *Wandering* 115-42) also points to similar usage in the Hebrew form of Psalm 151 (11QPs^a 28:7-8) and in 4Q403 1 i 28.

26. For the evidence for this assertion, see the analysis of the Composition of the Prologue in the Commentary.

27. See the discussion of the Composition of the verse in the Commentary.

object of belief in 17:3 is God *and* Jesus Christ suggests a similarity to the issues of 1 John, where the opponents believe in God but not in Jesus as the Christ.

If this evidence (at least in the case of 17:3) is less than overwhelming, it is significant that when we turn to the Letters, we see that the title is much more common. In 1 John, the title appears seven times (1:3; 2:1; 3:23; 4:2; 5:6, 20). In 2 John, it appears twice (vv. 3, 7). This is impressive, but the significance of this emerges more clearly when we observe that *Christos* is *never* used without *Iēsous* in 1 John (except in 2:22 and 5:1) or in 2 John. In these instances, both titles appear but are separated so that the precise affirmation can be made that Jesus *is* the Christ.[28]

In the light of this pattern of usage, it seems clear that the combination can be said to be typical of the Letters rather than of the Gospel. This, together with the previous indications that it was from the third edition, builds a substantial case for concluding that the presence of the title in the Gospel is due to the author of the third edition.

3E-3. In the third edition, the term *erga* ("works") appears always in the plural and always in the phrase *erga poiein* or *erga ergazesthai* with the meaning "to do the will" (of someone). This usage contrasts with the use of *erga* in the second edition to refer to the miracles of Jesus and to his ministry (2E-2).[29]

In the third edition, "to do the works of someone" has the meaning of "to do the will of someone." In this sense, the usage has two characteristics: it refers to "doing the will of" someone, and it always occurs in a dualistic context.

The first instance of this use in the Gospel occurs in 6:28-29. Also, this is one of the more complicated instances, since linguistically it shifts from the plural to the singular for grammatical purposes. Thus, Jesus had told the crowd, "Do not work for the bread that perishes but for the bread that remains unto eternal life." The crowd asks (v. 28), "What should we do, to do the works of God?" Jesus responds, "This is the work of God, that you believe in the one whom he sent." Often this has been taken as the Johannine solution to the problem of faith and works. However, when the idiomatic expression is understood, it becomes clear that what is at stake is the question, "What should we do, to do the will of God?" Jesus then responds: "This is the will of God, that you believe in the one whom he sent." Not only does this explanation avoid the awkward-

---

28. In 2 John, the only instance where the title appears without *Iēsous* is in v. 9 ("[the one] who does not remain in the teaching of the Christ"). The use of "the Christ" alone as a designation of Jesus is distinctive in itself rather than an exception to the pattern discussed here.

29. This contrast in usage is listed here insofar as it is a difference in terminology. It will be referred to below insofar as it reflects a dualistic worldview.

Section 2. The Criteria Used for the Third Edition

ness of a single instance of the topic of faith and works, but it also fits linguistically with several other instances in the Gospel as well as several parallel instances in the Dead Sea Scrolls.[30]

The same usage appears in 8:39, 41, and the context makes the meaning much clearer. In 8:39, Jesus says to his interlocutors, "If you were children of Abraham, you would do the works of Abraham." He then explains that they seek to kill him (v. 40) and that doing this should be classified as "doing the works of [their] father." This is paralleled explicitly in v. 44, where Jesus says, "You are of your father the devil, and you want to do his wishes." Thus, here doing the works of another certainly does not mean performing miracles but rather acting in a way typical of another or doing the will of another. Because they are "children of" a person, they "do [that person's] works" (vv. 39, 41, 42). These people are also described as being "of" your father (vv. 44, 47 [twice]). Throughout, this is an instance of ethical (apocalyptic) dualism. This dualism is expressed by referring to a person's actions as the works either of Abraham, or of God, or of the devil. Likewise, people are referred to as being "of" Abraham, and the like or "of" the devil.

This usage has close parallels in the *Damascus Document* from Qumran and the *T12P.*

In the *Damascus Document* we read:

"Hear now, my sons, and I will uncover your eyes that you may see and understand the works of God, that you choose that which pleases Him and reject that which He hates, that you may walk perfectly in all His ways and not follow after thoughts of the guilty inclination and after eyes of lust." (CD 2:14-16; DSSE[4] 98)

Here "the works of God" are those actions that could be said to be his will, to be characteristic of, or pleasing to, God. In this dualistic use in CD and in John, the phrase has an ethical dimension. Their actions are good or bad as they reflect their father. This use is not found in the canonical Old Testament.

In the *T12P,* this same dualistic worldview gives birth to the same and similar expressions. For example, *TNaph* 2:10 says, ". . . you are unable to perform the works of light while you are in darkness *(houtōs oude en skotei dynēsesthe poiēsai erga phōtos)."* A similar example appears in *TLev* 19:1, where the dualistic framework is again clear: "And now, My Children, listen to all things. Choose for yourselves either the darkness or the light, either the law of the Lord or the works of Beliar *(ē nomon kyriou ē erga Beliar)."*

---

30. For further discussion see Bergmeier, "Glaube"; von Wahlde, "Faith"; idem, *Commandments* 42-43.

The Third Edition of the Gospel

3E-4. In the third edition, *adelphos* ("brother") is used in a religious sense to refer to fellow community members. This is not found in the earlier editions.

The common meaning of the term *adelphos* is "brother" in the sense of sibling. It is used in this sense in both the first and second editions (1:40, 41; 2:12; 6:8; 7:3, 5, 10; 11:19, 32; *adelphē* appears in 11:1, 3, 5, 28, 39) as well as in the third edition (11:2, 21, 23).

However, in the third edition the author introduces the term twice after the Resurrection with a different meaning (20:17; 21:23). Here the term assumes its "religious" meaning and connotes a new relationship between Jesus and the disciples.

In 20:17, Jesus instructs Mary Magdalene to go to "my brothers." Some have thought that "my" here refers to Jesus' blood brothers mentioned in 2:12. However, this is unlikely, given the proximity of the statement to the statement later in the same verse about Jesus' return to "my Father and to your Father, and my God and your God." This is the first time in the Gospel that God is referred to as the Father of the disciples also. It is surely on the basis of this changed relationship that the disciples are now referred to as the "brothers" of Jesus. Yet the use is unusual since it is the only time in the Johannine literature that the disciples are referred to as "brothers" of Jesus rather than of one another.

In 21:23, the Evangelist comments that "the word went out to the brothers" that the Beloved Disciple would not die. Once again the term is used to refer to the members of the community in their spiritual relation to one another, but there is no mention of a relationship with Jesus himself in this case.

The use of "brother" in the religious sense appears only minimally in the Gospel (two times), and so its usefulness as a criterion is limited. While it might be argued that the term is intended to reflect a changed relationship after the Resurrection, we see that this "religious" usage of *adelphos* had appeared in the Johannine Letters (1 John and 3 John) and can be said to be a common theological term there (1 John 2:9, 10, 11; 3:10, 13, 14, 15, 16, 17; 4:20, 21; 5:16; 3 John 3, 5, 10).[31] In the Letters, the term never has the meaning "blood brother" but always "brother in religion." This distribution of the term (infrequent in the Gospel but frequent in the Letters) strongly suggests that the term is a more integral part of the theological vocabulary of the Letters and that the appearance of the term in the Gospel is very likely a result of editorial insertion.[32]

---

31. The use of "brother" to refer to other Christians and even to Jesus as a brother through the Spirit is not unique to the Johannine literature. See, for example, Rom 8:29 and Heb 2:9-10. However, in the Johannine literature, the complex of ideas associated with "brotherhood" is more developed and includes the references to "birth," "life," and "Fatherhood," and the designation of believers as "children."

32. As we shall see in the sections that follow, this is true of a number of other elements in

Section 2. The Criteria Used for the Third Edition

3E-5. In the third edition, *teknon/teknion* ("child"/"little child") is used as a designation for members of the community in their relation with Jesus and/or God. This is not found in the earlier editions.[33]

As was the case with the term "brother" used in the religious sense, *teknon/teknion* ("child"/"little child") appears only seldom in the Gospel but relatively more frequently in the Letters. We will treat the usage in the Letters first because it is more extensive and clearer.

In 1 John, the term *teknon* appears five times (1 John 2:12; 3:1, 2, 10; 5:2). It appears always in the phrase "children of God" (except in the second instance of 3:10, where it refers to "children of the devil"), but never in direct address. In 1 John, *teknion* appears seven times (1 John 2:1, 12, 28; 3:7, 18; 4:4; 5:21). It always appears in direct address and never in the phrase "children of God." From this we see that *teknon* is used as a designation of the believer's status before God, but the similar *teknion* is used by the author as a term of endearment for his fellow community members.[34]

In 2 and 3 John, *teknon* appears four times (2 John 1, 4, 13; 3 John 4). In 2 John, the usage is somewhat different. Believers are referred to as children *(tekna)* of "the Elect Lady" (1, 4) and "of your Elect Sister" (13). In 3 John 4, the author speaks of "my children" *(tekna)*. This usage is derivative of the first.

Teknon and *teknia* do not occur often in the Gospel, but where they do, they have a meaning and form a pattern of usage that is consistent with the usage in 1 John. *Teknon* is used to refer specifically to "children of God." Theologically the first of these usages is important since the believer is called a "child of God" because of his/her rebirth through the reception of the Holy Spirit. This rebirth results in the possession of eternal life and a raising of the person to the status of child of God. Believers are referred to explicitly as "children of God" (always using *teknon*, never *teknia*) in the Gospel in 1:12 and 11:52.

Teknia, on the other hand, is used in direct address, but *teknon* is not. In

---

the vocabulary and theology of 1 John; that is, many terms that appear regularly and frequently in 1 John also appear but much less frequently in the material of the third edition of the Gospel. (See, e.g., the use of "other Paraclete," which is unintelligible without 1 John 2:1; "commandment"; the specification of the commandments; "light" and "darkness"; the apocalyptic framework; etc.)

33. "Children" also appears in the *T12P* (e.g., *TReu* 1:3; *TSim* 3:1; *TZeb* 8:5) as a form of address, but its use there is in relation to the address of the "fathers" (i.e., the patriarchs). See Böcher, *Dualismus* 53. Böcher rightly sees the Johannine use as related to the notion of "brothers."

34. Lieu (*Epistles* 68) proposes that in the Gospel and in 1 John *teknon* is used to describe one's spiritual origin but *teknia* is used in direct address to members of the community. According to Lieu, in 2 John and 3 John *teknon* is used for direct address. However, in 2 John and 3 John the term is never used in true direct address but only in reference. Rather, *teknion* and *paidion* are diminutive, to express the intimacy of the relationship between the speaker and the readers.

The Third Edition of the Gospel

John 13:33 the disciples are described as "little children" by Jesus, referring to their relation to God the Father rather than to Jesus.

From this usage we may conclude the following: first, we may separate the use of *teknon* from that of *teknia*. The first term is intended to refer to believers in their role as children of God. Second, the meaning of *teknia* is more ambiguous. Since it is used in direct address, it may mean either "my" children, a term of familiarity, or it may have the more specific meaning, "children" (of God). I think the second possibility is less likely.

Third, whatever the precise purpose of *teknia*, the use of this term and that of *teknon* in the Gospel are consistent with its use in 1 John. This, together with the fact that the two terms occur more frequently in 1 John, forms yet another consistent pattern of usage between the third edition and 1 John.[35]

3E-6. In the third edition, *entolē* ("commandment") is used as a theological conceptualization of the ministry given to Jesus by the Father. This contrasts with the use of *ergon* ("work"), which is used to describe the ministry in the second edition (2E-4).[36]

In the discussion of the characteristics of the second edition, we saw how "work" is the central term in a complex of ideas that articulated a particular understanding not only of the miracles of Jesus, but of the ministry of Jesus as a whole. In addition, within the same complex is the theological understanding of the power to work miracles given to the disciples.

In the third edition, there appears another conception of the ministry with its own distinctive orientation, that of "commandment."[37] The noun "commandment" *(entolē)*, in a religious context,[38] appears ten times in the Gospel (10:18; 12:49, 50; 13:34; 14:15, 21, 31; 15:10 [twice], 12); the verb "command" *(entellomai)* occurs three times (14:31; 15:14, 17). From the usage in the Gospel we see that two commandments are given to Jesus by the Father. The first of these commandments is described in 10:17-18: Jesus lays down his life for his sheep, and he takes it up again. "I received this commandment from the Father"

---

35. Once in the Gospel (21:5), "young men" *(paidia)* is used to address the disciples. This term, however, appears as a term for members of the community in 1 John 2:14, 18, and provides another parallel in language use between the third edition and 1 John. In 1 John, however, *paidia* is distinguished from *teknia* and *pateres*. In John 21:5, no such distinction is implied.

36. I have discussed the commandments of the Johannine tradition in detail in *Commandments* and in Vol. 3, Appendix 5.

37. So also Schnackenburg (*Gospel* 2:175), who states: "There is a special formulation, *entolēn didonai*, used in John for the entire mission and task...."

38. Its use in 11:57 is not relevant.

Section 2. The Criteria Used for the Third Edition

(10:18b). Again in 14:30-31 Jesus speaks of the coming of the "ruler of the world" and his own coming Passion. He then adds: "But in order that the world may know that I love the Father, I do just as the Father has commanded me." This also would seem to be a general reference to his willingness to suffer and to lay down his life for his sheep out of love for the sheep — and for the Father.

The second commandment given to Jesus is spoken of in 12:49-50: ". . . I do not speak of myself, but the Father who sent me has himself given me a commandment what to say and what to speak. And I know that his commandment is eternal life. Therefore, those things that I say, I say just as the Father told me." Here the commandment is directed at what Jesus is to say and to speak. Consequently, we are correct to say that Jesus has been given two commandments by the Father.

However, just as the Father has given Jesus two commandments, so Jesus in turn gives the disciples two commandments. The first of these is spoken of in 13:34: "A new commandment I give you, that, as I loved you, you also should love one another." In 15:10, Jesus makes a general exhortation to the disciples. If they keep his commandments they will remain in his love. He then goes on to parallel this with his own relation to the Father: ". . . just as I have kept the commandments of my Father and I remain in his love." In 15:12, he repeats the first commandment: "This is my commandment, that you love one another as I have loved you." And again in 15:17: "These things I command you: love one another." Not only does Jesus say that their general obedience to the commandments will be rewarded with continuing love just as his own obedience to the Father is rewarded, but he commands them to love one another. Further, 15:12 explicitly gives Jesus as the model of the love the disciples are to have for one another.

Then, in 14:15, 21, Jesus says again that if the disciple loves Jesus, the disciple will keep Jesus' commandments. Then, in a parallel statement, Jesus specifies the second commandment, saying (v. 23) that the one who loves him keeps Jesus' word. Jesus then says the reverse (v. 24): "The one who does not love me does not keep my words." Jesus then concludes by affirming that ". . . the word that you hear is not mine but of the Father who sent me." Thus we see a second commandment given by Jesus to the disciples: that the disciples show love by keeping the commandments given by Jesus, and this is the commandment to keep his word.

Thus, in the Gospel two commandments are given to Jesus, and the correlates of these two commandments are the two commandments given by Jesus to the disciples. Just as the Father gives Jesus the commandment to *speak* the word of the Father, so Jesus gives the disciples the commandment to *keep* the word of Jesus (received from the Father). Just as Jesus was given a commandment what to do (to lay down his life out of love for his friends), so he gives the disciples a commandment to love one another as he has loved them.

While it is important to point out that this conception of "commandment" speaks of obligations of both Jesus and of the disciples, here it is the commandment given to Jesus (and which contrasts with the concept of "work" that is used for his ministry in the second edition) that is the focus.

Just as the concept of "work" derives from the Old Testament portrayal of the creative activity of God, so the concept of "commandment" derives from the Old Testament portrayal of the covenant obligations of Israel and the conditional blessings attendant upon them.[39]

It could be argued that, rather than being from different authors, the variation in terminology could be the work of a single author and intended simply to be stylistically (or even theologically) alternative expressions for the same basic content, but several features suggest that this is not the case.

First, there is the fact of the close correlation between the elements of each complex of ideas. The theology associated with "work" is consistent throughout, and the various elements form a harmonious and integrated whole consistent with the same Old Testament background. The complex of ideas associated with "commandment" is similar: this complex is developed against a distinct background, but the relation between the commandments given to Jesus and those given to the disciples is also consistent. In short, they form unified but distinct complexes of ideas.

Second, as is the case with other features of the third edition, the concept of commandment plays a minor role in the Gospel but a major role in 1 John, forming in fact an important structural feature of 1 John. It also plays a major role in the theological argument of 2 John.

In 1 John the commandments are developed once in the first half in 2:3-11; near the middle in 3:21-24; and in the second half in 4:21–5:5.[40] These will be discussed in greater detail in the Commentary on the Letters, but an outline of their use follows. In 1 John 2:3-6, the Elder identifies the commandment in terms of keeping the word and then discusses whether this is a "new" or "old" commandment. "And by this we are certain that we know him [God]: if we keep his commandments. The one claiming, 'I have come to know him,' but not keeping his [God's] commandments is a liar, and the truth is not present in him. But the one who keeps his [God's] word — in this person the love of God is truly brought to perfection. . . . I am not writing to you about a 'new' commandment. . . . This 'old' commandment is the word that you have heard."

---

39. For detailed discussion of the Deuteronomic background of "commandment," see von Wahlde, *Commandments* 226-44.

40. In the Letters, the commandments are described as being "of God" rather than "of Jesus." This difference in attribution is one of several such instances in 1 John and the third edition. It is due to the fact that while the role of Jesus is in dispute in 1 John, the author and his opponents have a common belief in "the Father" and so it is to the Father that the author appeals. (See von Wahlde, *Commandments* 49-70, 204-5.)

Section 2. The Criteria Used for the Third Edition

In 1 John 3:23, the two commandments are described together in a neat chiastic arrangement. Here the commandment to keep the word of Jesus is paraphrased as a commandment "that we believe in the name of his Son Jesus Christ": "And this is his [God's] commandment, that we believe in the name of his Son Jesus Christ and that we love one another as he has given us a commandment." In 1 John 4:21: "And we have this commandment from him, that the one loving God should also love his brother."

In 2 John the commandment to keep the word of Jesus is presented in a complicated staircase parallelism in vv. 4-6. One element of it, however, is expressed in v. 4: "I rejoiced greatly to find some of your children walking in truth, just as we received a commandment from the Father."[41]

Third, each emphasizes distinct theological themes. These themes are distinctive of the second and third editions respectively and are able to be identified with other theological elements of each edition and elements that are of direct relevance for the situation of the community in each stage of its history.

Finally, as will be seen in the discussion of the Composition of these passages, there is considerable evidence that the commandment material has been added to the context in which it presently appears. All of this indicates that the notion of "commandment" is distinct from the notion of "work" and is characteristic of the third edition of the Gospel.

3E-7. **In the third edition, reference is made to a distinct group of disciples within the larger group. This group is known as "the Twelve." The other editions make no reference to this group.**[42]

In the Gospel, the ordinary term for the followers of Jesus is "disciple." This appears over seventy times, in all three editions. However, in addition to this term there is also the term "the Twelve." This group is referred to only four times, distributed in two passages: 6:67, 70, 71; 20:24.

The calling of disciples is narrated only in 1:35-51, and there only Andrew, Peter, Philip, and Nathanael are mentioned by name, although another unnamed disciple is said to be with Andrew when they first meet Jesus. Thomas is mentioned for the first time in 11:16, and again in 14:5; 20:24, 26, 27, 28; 21:2. We hear of the "sons of Zebedee" in 21:2, although they are not named. Finally,

---

41. The ambiguity of "it" in v. 6 has caused much confusion about the meaning of the verse. However, once the chaining technique throughout vv. 5-6 is noticed, the identification of the antecedent becomes clear. This is discussed in the Commentary on 2 John. It is examined in more detail in von Wahlde, "Foundation."

42. Among scholars who consider the mention of the Twelve to be redactional is Thyen, "Entwicklungen" 278.

there is the Beloved Disciple, mentioned but not named seven times certainly (13:21-27; 19:26-27, 32-37; 20:2-10; 21:7, 20-23, 24), and two others for which the evidence is ambiguous (1:35-40; 18:15-18).

If we suppose that neither of the unnamed disciples is the Beloved Disciple, then the total number of disciples mentioned in the Gospel is ten. If the unnamed disciples are equated with the BD, then we have a total of eight. In any event, nowhere in the Gospel are twelve disciples mentioned by name. Nor is there any reference to the choosing of a distinct group of twelve from a larger group, as there is, for example, in Mark 3:13-19. Consequently, it is correct to say that a reader who was familiar only with the literary world of the Johannine Gospel would not even know what was being referred to by a group of disciples known as "the Twelve." It is only with knowledge of other (Synoptic) traditions outside of the Gospel that the reader is able to divine a special significance in this term. We also notice that the term does not have a specific function within the Johannine text other than to define an inner circle of disciples who remained faithful to Jesus. Yet this is awkward over against the portrayal of other disciples in the Gospel who remained faithful, for example, Nathanael, and, especially, the Beloved Disciple.

We will see below that the third edition exhibits knowledge of traditions with a distinct relation to the Synoptics and a desire to incorporate them within the Johannine Gospel tradition.[43] This designation of a group of "the Twelve" reflects that tendency.

2. Characteristics of Narrative Orientation: An Apocalyptic Worldview[44]

In the previous two editions, there were a considerable number of ideological features typical of each edition. The same is true of the third edition. However, in the third edition these features lead to a more extensive restructuring of the worldview than was the case in the first two editions. While the first and second editions presumed the worldview typical of the Old Testament, the third edition contains extensive features typical of the worldview found in the various Jewish apocalypses, other intertestamental literature such as the *T12P*, the SDQ, and indeed other works of the New Testament.

Apocalyptic is a multifaceted phenomenon exhibiting a number of fea-

---

43. On the appearance of Synoptic features in the third edition, see the discussion of "The Relation of the Third Edition to the Synoptics" in Section 3 below.

44. Bibliography includes: J. Becker, "Beobachtungen"; Böcher, *Dualismus*; Boismard, "First Epistle of John" 156-65; R. E. Brown, "Scrolls"; Price, "Light"; Charlesworth, "Critical."

Section 2. The Criteria Used for the Third Edition

tures which *together* form "apocalyptic" as a genre.[45] The worldview of apocalyptic is one of modified dualism, a view in which the world is engaged in a struggle between opposing forces of good and evil but with the recognition that ultimately God is the source of all creation and the (temporary) sway of evil has been mysteriously allowed by him. The two principles of good and evil influence human life and action through the medium of spirits, both good and evil. Persons are said to be "possessed" particularly by the evil spirits; exorcisms are necessary to free the individual from such domination. Less extreme forms of human allegiance to one or other principle are also seen as determined by one's own ethical behavior.

The world of apocalyptic also includes a conviction that at some point God will intervene either alone or through an agent (often described as "the Son of Man") to bring about a final victory over the power of evil in the world. This final victory is regularly thought to include a universal judgment at the end of time, a judgment in which persons are evaluated according to their good or evil deeds. The good are brought to their reward, which is often conceived of as eternal life with God. The evil are judged and brought either to the realm of death or to a realm of eternal punishment. At times the reward of eternal life also includes a resurrection of the body.

Symbolism plays a large role in the literary portrayal of such dualism. The opposing spiritual forces are often described as forces of "light" and "darkness," of "truth" and "falsehood." The source of good or evil as it is manifested in the individual is described as one's "father." Good or evil persons are correspondingly described as "sons of. . . ." Allegiance and actions are described in images such as "doing the works of one's father" (in the sense of doing the will of) their "father." In the passive voice, the works are described as done "in" (God, Satan, Belial, etc.).

---

45. This description of features characteristic of apocalyptic is based both on several of the articles found in J. J. Collins, *Morphology*, and in J. J. Collins, *Imagination*. Ashton (*Understanding* 383-406) also attempts to provide a definition incorporating a number of these features in relation to the Johannine literature. Ashton's definition includes (1) a narrative (2) composed in a time of social unrest (3) in which an angelic being makes revelations (4) to a human seer (5) by dreams or visions (6) in which case the seer may believe that he has been transported to heaven (p. 386). This is perhaps more a definition of an apocalypse than of the apocalyptic worldview.

J. J. Collins (*Imagination* 9) comments: "The genre is not constituted by one or more distinctive themes but by a distinctive combination of elements, all of which are also found elsewhere." Collins rightly distinguishes "apocalypse" as a literary genre from "apocalyptic" as a worldview. The expression of this worldview is not restricted to actual apocalypses. Even though many of the Qumran sect's documents are pervasively apocalyptic in worldview and in structure, none of its major documents was an apocalypse. This is also the view of Nickelsburg, *Resurrection*, 146, and Cross, *Ancient* 76-78, 198-206. See also J. J. Collins, *Apocalypticism* 7-11. For a contrary view see Stegemann, "Bedeutung."

Other human actions of allegiance to God or to evil, expressed symbolically, include (with the image of fatherhood and of light) being a "son of the light" or (with the image of truth) "doing" the truth (falsehood); "walking in" truth (falsehood); "walking in" the light (darkness).

Another characteristic that appears commonly with this view of (apocalyptic) modified dualism is a view of the obligation to love that is not universal in scope, not extended to the enemy or the stranger, but focused on and limited to the fellow members of one's community. This is often referred to as "sectarian love."

Among the apocalyptic writings with the greatest similarity to the material of the third edition are the sectarian documents among the Dead Sea Scrolls (SDQ) and the *Testaments of the Twelve Patriarchs (T12P)*.[46] In what follows, reference will regularly be made to parallels in these sets of documents, although, as the occasion suggests, reference will also be made to other Jewish and Christian apocalyptic documents.[47]

Dualistic Elements in the Dead Sea Scrolls

The SDQ provide a clear illustration of the variety and shades of thought that coexist within the apocalyptic framework.[48] The SDQ also provide some more

---

46. Apocalyptic features of the Dead Sea Scrolls and the *T12P* and similarities in the Johannine literature have been widely documented. The most thorough treatment is that of Böcher, *Dualismus*. Many of Böcher's observations continue to be valid, although the view of dualism advocated by Böcher differs somewhat from that employed here. Among the others who have noticed the close parallels among the (apocalyptic) Johannine dualism, the SDQ, and the *T12P* are R. E. Brown, "Scrolls"; J. Becker, "Beobachtungen" 71-87, cf. esp. 80; idem, *Evangelium* 1:147-51; H. Braun, *Qumran* 1:112-13, 123-24; 2: §6; Charlesworth, "Critical" 76-106; Pilgaard, "Scrolls."

47. Both the *T12P* and the SDQ are complex collections, from various time periods and from various authors. This is particularly true of the SDQ, but it is also true, although to a somewhat lesser extent, of the *T12P*. These collections contain a variety of views on a given topic (including dualism) from document to document. Moreover, some documents among the *T12P* and the SDQ have undergone editing, and this has at times introduced more than one perspective within a single document. However, our purpose here is to show the presence of a given type of dualism, not to argue that it is the only type found in the documents. It is true that, in the NT, the Johannine documents exhibit the greatest similarities to the SDQ and the *T12P*. It is also true that the apocalyptic language of the Johannine documents finds its closest parallels in the SDQ. But neither statement claims that the apocalyptic worldview of the Johannine literature has been derived directly from the SDQ or the *T12P*.

48. The question of what constitutes a sectarian document is a complicated one and is not addressed here (see the discussion in Newsom, "Sectually Explicit" 172-79). A listing of the texts considered "sectarian" in this discussion can be found in the List of Abbreviations at the

Section 2. The Criteria Used for the Third Edition

general benefits for our consideration of apocalyptic. First, although the Qumran community is regularly considered by scholars to be an apocalyptic community with an apocalyptic worldview, there is no evidence that the community produced a complete apocalypse of its own. Copies of apocalypses found there were not written by that community. However, there is no doubt that the community possessed an apocalyptic worldview.[49] This is significant for adjudicating the apocalyptic worldview within 1 John and within the third edition.

Second, in the SDQ, the dualism of spirits and the cosmic struggle appear in different forms in the various documents and not every document contains the entire apocalyptic schema.[50] For example, in 1QM the description of the war between the sons of light and the sons of darkness led by Michael and Belial is explicit and detailed.[51] In 1QS, there is detailed discussion of the influences exerted upon the sons of light and sons of darkness by the two spirits. In addition, there is a description of their origin, the plan of the end of their domination, and the rewards given to the good and evil. But there is little or no explicit reference to the war.

In a third document (CD 5:19), we hear that "... in ancient times, Moses and Aaron arose by the hand of the Prince of Lights, and Satan in his cunning raised up Jannes . . ." *(CDSSE)*. This is yet another facet of the overall schema. As J. J. Collins says, "... although CD does not undertake to expound the dualism of Belial and the Prince of Lights, it presupposes that doctrine."[52] Hence we can see how literature composed by the same community can possess the same basic worldview but emphasize now one aspect and now another in various documents.

---

beginning of this volume under "SDQ." The texts listed are the same as those established by Puech (*Croyance* 772). Newsom ("'Sectually Explicit'" 169-71) would agree with Puech's listing except that she does not discuss some of the fragmentary works listed by Puech. See also the listing by J. J. Collins, *Apocalypticism* 8. The "new" numbering of 1QH, as proposed by Puech, is used throughout.

The focus here is on dualism as found in the sectarian writings. The terminology in some of the dualistic texts at Qumran has parallels in the NT *only* within the Gospel of John.

49. For a description of how the apocalyptic worldview could provide the backdrop for the development of Qumran documents even without producing an apocalypse, see the analysis of 1QS in Newsom, "Apocalyptic" 135-44. See also J. J. Collins, *Apocalypticism* 8.

50. So J. J. Collins, *Imagination* 130, 132.

51. Ashton (*Understanding* 387) would also say that the *War Scroll* at Qumran is "not apocalyptic because there is no hint of any heavenly intermediary." This is overly demanding as a criterion. In a library of documents that incorporate the apocalyptic viewpoint not every document need be a full apocalypse; clearly the *War Scroll* reflects the apocalyptic worldview of ethical dualism!

52. J. J. Collins, *Imagination* 132.

The Third Edition of the Gospel

This is important also for the study of Johannine apocalyptic. While we find the same worldview expressed in both 1 John and the third edition, each has its own emphasis, each has its own features, and neither contains all of the features of the apocalyptic schema, but both presuppose it.

Dualistic Elements in the Testaments of the Twelve Patriarchs

In addition to the SDQ, the documents exhibiting the closest parallels to the worldview and language of the apocalyptic elements of the Gospel are those known as the *Testaments of the Twelve Patriarchs (T12P)*.[53] These twelve doc-

---

53. The complete *Testaments* exist today only in Greek, but Aramaic fragments related to some of the *Testaments* have been found in the Qumran caves (see below). The critical text of the *T12P* is edited by M. de Jonge.

The usefulness of the *T12P* for the present study is potentially affected by two factors: the uncertain date of their composition and questions regarding Christian interpolations. These two questions are related to one another, for the Christian interpolations are generally dated to about A.D. 200. If one were to argue that the *T12P* in their entirety (or their majority) came from that period, they would be useless for the comparisons suggested here.

There is no question that the *T12P* have a number of passages that are Christian in origin. The question, however, is whether the documents themselves are essentially Christian in origin or fundamentally Jewish with later Christian reediting. Philonenko *(Interpolations)* argued that the Christian interpolations were relatively few and could be readily isolated. However, M. de Jonge, the editor of the critical text and author (together with Hollander) of the major commentary on the *T12P*, argued that the *T12P* should be viewed simply as a Christian composition from about A.D. 200. De Jonge has since moderated that view and would now recognize the existence of a Jewish substratum, although he would argue that it is not possible to identify the extent of this substratum, with any confidence (cf. "Main Issues" 508-24).

Kee, in his Introduction to the translation appearing in *OTP*, proposes that the *T12P* are a Jewish work composed about 200 B.C. with perhaps ten Christian interpolations. Recently J. VanderKam *(Early Judaism* 101) has argued, "... it seems more likely that the *Testaments of the Twelve Patriarchs* is a Jewish work with some Christian additions." This is based at least partially on his view that the Aramaic Levi text from Qumran (4Q213) "has a large amount of material" that appears in *Testament of Levi* and that an Aramaic *Testament of Naphtali* (4Q215) is related to the *Testament of Judah*. The Aramaic Levi from Qumran (4Q213) has been dated to at least the middle of the second century B.C.

The result of this scholarship is a fairly clear consensus that the *T12P* are, in the main, Jewish and pre-Christian. (See the survey by J. J. Collins, "Testamentary Literature" 268-76.) Indicative of the attempts to distinguish the original Jewish substratum from the later interpolations is the work of Ulrichsen *(Grundschrift* 71-206).

It is also likely that the *T12P* are not the work of a single author or probably even a single period but are a collection of documents, the earliest of which may be pre-Maccabean. As a result, the collection as a whole does not always represent a single view on a given subject, for example, resurrection of the body. An effort will be made to reflect an awareness of this variety in discussing the *Testaments*. In any event, my purpose here is to show the existence of parallels

Section 2. The Criteria Used for the Third Edition

uments are written in testamentary form and claim to be the last words of the twelve sons of Jacob to their sons before their death. Although both provenance and dating are uncertain, dating them to the early first century B.C. is not unreasonable, but their provenance is more uncertain. Copies of some of the *Testaments* have been found at Qumran. The *T12P* are apocalyptic and at times messianic. Theologically they bear some similarity to the SDQ in that both express a hope for two messiahs.[54] Yet they are quite different in their attitude toward obedience to the Law. Thus, they are best understood, not in relation to the SDQ, but as an independent witness to the variety of late Second Temple apocalyptic thought. While their overall theology is considerably different from that of the SDQ, the Gospel of John, and the Letters of John, they exhibit a worldview and a terminology that are remarkably similar to all of these.

Because of the variety of elements that make up apocalyptic literature and because the overlapping occurrence of a number of these features strengthens the argument that a given passage of the third edition is apocalyptic, the various apocalyptic elements will be listed and discussed individually rather than as a single feature.

Many of these apocalyptic features have a theological dimension to them and could well be listed among the theological features of the third edition. However, because they are more generally defined as elements of the apocalyptic worldview, they are listed here in the discussion of characteristics even though they may be discussed from the perspective of their theology in Part 4.

Since apocalyptic elements are found *only* in the third edition within the Gospel, there will generally be no comparison and contrast between these and features of the other two editions.[55] Rather, we will focus on demonstrating parallels between the apocalyptic sections of the Gospel and similar features elsewhere in apocalyptic literature. In addition, we will list similar apocalyptic elements as they are found in the Johannine Letters, thus confirming the relationship between the third edition of the Gospel and the Johannine Letters.[56]

---

between the language and worldview present within the collection rather than to argue that these features are characteristic of every part of the collection.

54. For *T12P* texts, see Kee, *OTP,* 779.

55. There are some exceptions to this, for example, "judgment," which appears in a "realized" form in the second edition and is complemented by a "future" form in the third.

56. A number of scholars have proposed that the final level of material in the Gospel is dualistic (e.g., Bultmann and J. Becker). J. Becker (*Evangelium* 2:421) wrongly sees the "above/below" contrast as part of the apocalyptic worldview.

3E-8. In the third edition, the imagery of "light" and "darkness" is used to describe opposing realms of good and evil. This is not present in prior editions.[57]

While the images of light and darkness do not occur only in dualism, their appearance as opposed pairs and in other characteristic ways marks their use in the third edition as dualistic.[58]

---

57. J. Becker (*Evangelium* 1:148) considers 3:19-21 the clearest example of this dualism, which he calls deterministic. He sees (as I would) the closest history-of-religions parallels to this dualism in the SDQ and the *T12P*. However, in my opinion, he puts too much emphasis on the deterministic elements.

58. This is not to deny the presence of the terms in nonapocalyptic literature. For example, light and darkness appear in the canonical Jewish Scriptures (e.g., Isa 9:2; Amos 5:18), elsewhere in the NT (e.g., Matt 6:13; Luke 12:3; 1 Pet 2:9), and in the Nag Hammadi materials (e.g., *Gospel of Thomas* 24). However, the dualistic use of these terms is an entirely different conceptualization of the terms, particularly in the way these two terms form part of a larger worldview. This is readily recognized by scholars. For example, VanderKam (*Today* 183-184) comments, in discussing the dualism of light and darkness at Qumran: "The Johannine literature in the New Testament has long been considered the most productive source of comparative material. . . ." See also the extensive discussion in J. J. Collins, *Imagination* 126-33.

Recently, Bauckham ("Qumran" 10-115) has argued that the usage in the Gospel is not dualistic and that the dissimilarities between the usage in the Scrolls and in the Gospel of John outweigh the similarities. One of Bauckham's goals is to refute the claim that the Johannine imagery is "derived" from the Scrolls. I would agree that attempts to make this extreme claim are unwarranted and this aspect of his argument is justified. However, most scholars would argue simply that there are similarities between the two bodies of literature rather than dependence of one on the other. Bauckham also argues that the imagery employed in the Gospel of John is not dualistic. Here he seems to raise the standard of proof too high. He is correct when he says that in the Gospel of John "light/darkness" do not appear in the same passage with terms such as "Spirit of Truth/Spirit of Deceit." But there is no reason to demand that they do so. For example, 1 John, which Bauckham does not treat and which is generally recognized to be apocalyptic throughout, has both sets of terms but never in the same passage. But what requires the author to do so? Finally, Bauckham argues that in the Gospel of John the imagery of light/darkness is expanded to include the imagery of "day/night," something not found in the Scrolls. However, in 1 Thess 5:1-5 the image of light/darkness appears within an apocalyptic worldview and is expanded to include the image of "day" as in the Gospel of John. The same appears in the *T12P* (see especially the parallelism in *TNaph* 2:6-7 and in 2:10, where the contrast is clear). Both sets of documents are apocalyptic even if not precisely the same as those used in 1QS 3:13–4:26.

Aune ("Dualism") has also argued that the Johannine writings do not reflect the type of dualism found in the SDQ but have much in common with conversion language in Judaism and in early Christianity. However, a basic flaw in Aune's argument, as I would see it, is that he fails to distinguish between "contrasting categories" (above/below; spirit/flesh) and those categories that are truly dualistic. Aune's identification of references to "above" and "below" as elements of "the basic structure of Johannine dualism" seems to contradict his own definition of dualism as involving "causal principles" ("Dualism" 284-85). As Aune rightly recognizes elsewhere ("Dualism" 286), the categories of "above" and "below" reflect the traditional categories of "flesh" and "spirit" and so cannot be said to be truly "dualistic." To merge these categories with those that in-

Section 2. The Criteria Used for the Third Edition

In the Gospel, "light" appears throughout the Prologue (1:4, 5, 7, 8 [twice], 9). However, the instances in vv. 4 and 5 belong to the hymn itself and so should not be attributed directly to the author of the third edition. The term also appears periodically throughout the rest of the Gospel: 3:19 (twice), 20 (twice), 21; 5:35; 8:12; 9:5; 11:9, 10; 12:35 (twice), 36 (three times), 46. All of these are used dualistically except 5:35. In the Gospel, "darkness" *(skotia)* appears twice in the Prologue in 1:5 and elsewhere in 3:19 *(skotos)*; 6:17; 8:12; 12:35 (twice), 46; 20:1. All of these are dualistic except 6:17; 20:1.

The hymn's portrayal of the dualistic struggle between light and darkness in 1:4-5 is evident in the description of light shining in the darkness and the darkness not "overcoming" it. This echoes the cosmic battle of apocalyptic. So also the instances inserted by the third author in vv. 7, 8, and 9.

The next group of verses where the image appears is 3:19-21 (v. 21: "light" [twice]; "darkness"; v. 20: "light" [twice]; v. 21: "light"). Here again there is a struggle between light and darkness and an expressed preference for the darkness by those whose deeds are sinful and a preference for the light by those who "do the truth." The third appearance of "light" as a dualistic symbol is in 8:12, where Jesus again is described as the "light of the world" (cf. 1:9, where he is described as the "light... coming into the world"), is contrasted with "darkness," and is again described as the "light of life." The dualistic worldview is clear, as is reference to the Prologue. Equally remarkable is the fact that the themes of "light" and "darkness," although they form the core of this programmatic statement at the beginning of the discourse of 8:12-59, do not appear again anywhere in the discourse.

The fourth appearance of "light" is in 9:4-5, verses that contextualize the healing of the blind man. In 9:4-5, Jesus again describes himself as the "light of the world" and then describes his public ministry as the "day" (when the "light" shines) and contrasts it with the "night," which is coming and during which no one is able to work. The fifth time the image of "light" appears is in 11:9-10. In response to the fear of the disciples that if Jesus returns to Bethany, he will be in danger, Jesus responds as he did in chapter 9, by speaking about the day, that there are twelve hours in the day and, if a person walks during the day, the person will not stumble because "the light of this world" is shining. This is then contrasted with walking in the night. Again Jesus' ministry is described as "day," the time when the "light" is shining.

The sixth instance is in 12:35-36. Again Jesus warns his listeners that the

---

volve true dualism is inevitably to create a model that does not have a parallel at Qumran. In addition, while Aune recognizes that comparisons based simply on the theology of the documents is not appropriate, he does not recognize that *the worldview* of the SDQ and the *T12P* and (elements of) the Johannine Gospel are functionally identical even though they may be independent of one another literarily.

"light" will be among them only a short time and that they should make use of the light lest they be overcome by the darkness. He then urges them to "believe" in the light so that they may become "sons of light." The seventh time the imagery is used is in 12:46, where Jesus identifies himself as light coming into the world lest those who believe remain in darkness. Finally, in 13:31 the imagery of "night" brings the time of "light" to a close. After Judas goes out, the author of the third edition makes use of the imagery one final time to declare, "It was night."

When viewed within their contexts, it becomes obvious that the author of the third edition has used these two symbols to depict the effect of Jesus on the world. The world was in darkness before Jesus came. While he is in the world, he is the light of the world — until his Passion, which is a time of darkness. Throughout the remainder, we can easily see (1) that the imagery of light is regularly associated with that of darkness; (2) the usage of these pairs is dualistic throughout; and (3) the passages where these appear are distributed in a meaningful pattern throughout the Gospel so as to structure the presentation of Jesus' ministry.

In the Letters

In the Johannine Letters, the images of light (1 John 1:5, 7 [twice]; 2:8, 9, 10) and darkness (1:5; 2:8, 9, 11 [three times]) also appear regularly.[59] The images are so prominent in 1 John that Feuillet[60] and, following him, R. E. Brown[61] have considered the image of "light"/"darkness" as one of the major structuring elements of the First Epistle.[62] Whether the author of the third edition took over these symbols from 1 John or from the community's hymn now found in the Prologue, or whether he simply employed them independently is difficult to say. However, the similarity of the structure of the third edition to that of 1 John suggests that the author of the third edition was influenced either by the structure of 1 John or by that of the hymn. As we shall see below, the imagery of light and darkness was also a significant one for the Qumran Community and for the community that produced the T12P. Consequently, it is good to realize that these symbols were so powerful that they spoke strongly but independently to various communities with such dualistic worldviews.[63]

---

59. Neither image appears in 2 or 3 John.
60. Feuillet, "Structure."
61. Brown, *Epistles* 123-29.
62. Both speak of the author of 1 John "patterning" the structure of 1 John on that of the Gospel. I would argue that the process was actually the reverse of this. The author of the third edition took over these symbols from 1 John where they were used to structure it. Thus, the third author provided a final, overarching, symbolic structure to the Gospel.
63. The dualistic usage of light/darkness also appears elsewhere in the NT, most notably in Eph 5:8 (twice), 9, 13 (twice). See also 2 Cor 4:6; 6:14; 1 Thess 5:5.

Section 2. The Criteria Used for the Third Edition

Parallels to This Usage in Other Apocalyptic Literature

In the Dead Sea Scrolls

Soon after the discovery of the Dead Sea Scrolls, it was recognized that one of their striking features was the repeated use of the imagery of contrast between "light" and "darkness."[64] Early on, James Charlesworth commented, "Perhaps the most conspicuous characteristic of the dualism in this document [1QS] is the predominance of the light-*versus*-darkness *motif*" (italics original).[65] Among the scrolls of the Qumran community, the dualism of light and darkness appears most pervasively in the *War Scroll* (1QM) and in 1QS.

In the *War Scroll*, the opposition between the "sons of light" and the "sons of darkness" appears at the beginning (cf. 1QM 1:1-10) but also at 13:6, "Truly they are the company of Darkness, but the company of God is one of [eternal] Light." 13:16 adds: "[For Thou hast appointed] the day of battle from ancient times . . . [to come to the aid] of truth and to destroy iniquity, to bring Darkness low and to magnify Light . . . to stand for ever, and to destroy all the sons of Darkness."[66]

In 1QS, the members of the community are urged to "love all the sons of light . . . and hate all the sons of darkness . . ." (1:10). Also: "All the children of righteousness are ruled by the Prince of Light and walk in the ways of light, but all the children of injustice are ruled by the Angel of Darkness and walk in the ways of darkness" (3:21) *(CDSSE).*[67]

In the Testaments of the Twelve Patriarchs

A clear example of the dualistic use of light and darkness appears in *TLev* 19:1 ("And now, my children, you heard all things. Therefore, choose for yourselves either the darkness [*to skotos*] or the light [*to phōs*]"). The apocalyptic dualism is implicit in *TZeb* 9:8, where the Lord is described as the "light of righteousness" who will "set free the captive sons of men from Beliar[68] and trample every spirit of deception." *TNaph* 2:10 says, "Thus neither are you able, while you are in darkness, to perform the works of light." *TJos* 20:2 has, "The Lord will be with you in light, and Beliar will be with the Egyptians in darkness." *TBenj* 5:3

---

64. See, for example, R. E. Brown, "Scrolls" 146-49; Price, "Light" 15, 18-19.
65. Charlesworth, "Critical" 78. This continues to be recognized as fundamental. See, for example, VanderKam, *Today* 110-11; Vermes, *Perspective* 182-83.
66. See also 1QM 14:7; 15:10; 16:10.
67. Among the other texts that reflect this are 1QS 2:17; 3:25; and 4:5.
68. Beliar as a designation of Satan is uncommon in the NT. It appears only in 2 Cor 6:15, in a passage that has much in common with the dualism of the SDQ.

says, "Where there is light of good works for understanding, the darkness shrinks away from that person."

As was said earlier, in the third edition these two symbols become the overriding ones for the public ministry in the Gospel. It is easy to see that the very positioning of the passages has been designed to bring the symbolism to attention at the beginning of Jesus' ministry in the Nicodemus complex and later in the Gospel at the beginning of important scenes: the discourse of chapter 8, with the healing of the blind man and the raising of Lazarus, and then of chapter 12 where the final public offering of the light takes place.

As we read the other characteristics of apocalyptic in the sections that follow and compare them with the texts of the Gospel, we will notice how consistently those other apocalyptic aspects occur in conjunction with passages marked by the terminology of "light" and "darkness."

3E-9. In the third edition, the term "works" is used in the idiomatic expression "to do the works of . . ." as a way of describing allegiance of persons to either good or evil within a context of apocalyptic dualism. In the second edition, "works" designates the miracles performed by Jesus (2E-2).[69]

The distribution of the word "work" *(ergon)* has been described under the discussion of the term as a characteristic of the second edition. Here attention will be called to those instances of the term that refer, not to "miracles" as in the second edition, but to those instances that are used in the idiomatic expression "to do the works of" *(erga ergazesthai, erga poiein)*. This expression occurs only in apocalyptic dualism and means "to do the will of someone."[70] The expression in this sense appears three times in the Gospel: 3:21; 6:28-29; 8:39, 41. With this meaning, the expression is characteristic of apocalyptic and is found both at Qumran (CD 2:14-16) and in the *T12P* (*TLev* 19:1; *TNaph* 2:9-3:1).

In CD 2:14-16, we read:

"Hear now, my sons, and I will uncover your eyes that you may see and understand the works of God, that you choose that which pleases Him and reject that which He hates, that you may walk perfectly in all His ways and

---

69. This contrast was treated previously (3E-3) insofar as it represents a difference in terminology. Here the apocalyptic background of the usage is being discussed. For bibliography, see 3E-3.

70. Note that "to do the will of" occurs often in the first and second editions with the same meaning (4:34; 5:30 [twice]; 6:38 [twice], 39, 40; 7:17 [all 2E]; 9:31 [1E]), but this dualistic expression is not used there.

Section 2. The Criteria Used for the Third Edition

not follow after thoughts of the guilty inclination and after eyes of lust." *(CDSSE)*

In this passage the term does not apply to works of the Law in a legalistic sense nor to any sort of miraculous act but is in parallel with "that which pleases Him." They are the actions that are typical of, or appropriate to, God. Moreover, the dualistic context of the choices that confront persons is clear: "to choose . . . to reject."

In *TLev* 19:1, which speaks of choosing "the Law of the Lord or the works of Beliar" *(ē nomon kyriou ē erga Beliar)*, the meaning and the dualistic context are just as clear.

Both the images of light and darkness and the choice of "that which pleases the Lord" and the "works of Beliar" are also contrasted. "Works" of Beliar does not have a legalistic sense but refers to actions that would be considered typical of or desired by Beliar.

Finally, we see in *TNaph* 2:6–3:1 a passage that reflects the conviction that one cannot perform good deeds unless one's inner convictions correspond with those deeds. Yet this is expressed throughout in the context of the alternative choices of the dualistic thought-world:

> As is his planning, so also is his action; as is his heart, so is his speech; as is his eye, so also is his sleep; as is his soul, so also is his thought, either on the Law of the Lord or on the law of Beliar *(ē en tō nomō kyriou ē en nomō Beliar)*. . . . If you tell the eye to hear, it cannot; so you are unable to perform the works of the light while you are in darkness *(oude en skotei dynēsesthe poiēsai erga phōtos)*. Do not be eager to corrupt your actions through avarice or to beguile your souls by empty phrases, because being silent in cleanness of heart you will be able to hold fast to the will of God and to cast aside the will of the devil.

Here we see first the phrase "the law of the Lord" contrasted with "the law of Beliar," confirming the terminology we had seen before in *TLev* 19:1. Second, we see not only the dualistic use of light and darkness but also the use of "works," in the sense of deeds typical of a given mentality, contrasted with being in darkness. It is not used in a "legalistic" sense. Finally, the dualism is expressed by contrasting "hold[ing] fast God's will" with "shunt[ing] aside the will of Beliar." Throughout there is a fluidity and an interchangeability in the use of "Law," "works," and "will" to mean that which is characteristic of, or desired by someone, actions that are typical of a given allegiance. This is the dualistic use.

In the Gospel, the first appearance of this expression is in 6:28-29: "They said to him, 'What should we do, to do the works of God?' Jesus responded and said to them, 'This is the work of God, that you believe in the one whom he sent.'" The interpretation of these verses has varied. A common approach has been to see this as referring to the issue of faith and works. The crowd asks about "works of the Law," and Jesus responds in terms of faith. However, that this is the meaning is unlikely since the question of "faith and works" is not an issue as such elsewhere in the Gospel. Moreover, it is unlikely that the topic is really an issue here either since the surrounding context really focuses on the single issue of the crowd's believing acceptance of Jesus. Part of the difficulty in grasping this meaning is the fact that "works" shifts to the singular in v. 28 because it is to be equated with the single action of believing in Jesus.[71]

In fact, the issue is what is pleasing to God. In 6:26, Jesus reproves the crowd for not really understanding the sign that he had performed. He urges them to "work for the bread that remains unto eternal life." In the light of this, the crowd responds, using the same verb, but now in the dualistic sense. Literally the verse reads: "What do we work for to work the works of God." Paraphrasing this we would get: "What do we do to do what pleases God." Then Jesus answers, "This is what pleases God, that you believe in the one whom he has sent."

The other two appearances of this idiom are in 8:39, 41. Here the context is somewhat clearer since it is dualistic. The issue is the father of Jesus and the father of "the Jews." Jesus speaks what he heard from his father, and they do what they heard from their father. When "the Jews" respond that Abraham is their father, Jesus says, "If you were children of Abraham, you would do the works of Abraham *(ta erga tou Abraam epoieite)*." Jesus then goes on to say (v. 41): "You do the works of your father *(hymeis poieite ta erga tou patros hymōn)*." Here Jesus means that the devil is their father. "The Jews" then reply that God is their father, and Jesus responds that if he were their father, they would perform actions that were typical of him. He then uses another common dualistic expression "to be of" to explain that they are "of" their father the devil.[72] In v. 47 he describes the one who is "of" God and denies that they are truly "of" God.

As we have seen throughout, the expression "to do the works of" occurs consistently (and exclusively) in dualistic contexts both within and without the Gospel and is a reliable marker of dualism in the Gospel.

---

71. The use of the singular in this sense is also found in the *T12P*. In *TBenj* 6:7, the patriarch speaks of the "good person" who should not be governed by the spirit of deceit. The good person is not two-faced (*diplos;* lit. "double"), that is, the good person acts without duplicity, without hypocrisy. But on the other hand, ". . . every work of Beliar is two-faced and does not have integrity" *(tou Beliar de pan ergon diploun esti kai ouk echei aplotēta)*." Here also the singular "work" is used to describe that which is "characteristic of" or "typical of" Beliar.

72. This expression will be discussed below.

Section 2. The Criteria Used for the Third Edition

3E-10. In the third edition, the phrase "son(s) of . . ." is used to describe allegiance to either good or evil and is characteristic of apocalyptic dualism. This is not present in the earlier editions.

There are two instances in the Gospel where the expression "son/sons of" appears: 12:36 and 17:12. The expression does not appear in the Letters. As a result, it cannot be said to be a major indicator of authorship within the third edition. Yet it is listed here because, in spite of infrequent appearance, it is a feature that reflects the worldview typical of modified dualism and occurs frequently in the sectarian documents from Qumran, always in a dualistic context.

The first instance of the phrase in the Gospel is dualistic (12:36: "While you have the light, believe in the light, so that you may become sons of light"). The second (17:12: "and none of them was destroyed except the son of destruction so that the Scripture might be fulfilled") is less clear and will require further discussion below.

The use of "sons of . . ." to refer to one's allegiance (either to good or to evil) is common in and, according to Fitzmyer, exclusive to the Qumran documents apart from the New Testament.[73] It is so frequent in the Qumran scrolls that it becomes a major means of characterizing the two opposed groups. In 1QM (the *War Scroll*) from Qumran the great battle against the forces of evil is described. At the very beginning "the exiled sons of light" (1:1) are said to join the battle. "(W)hen the Kittim fall, . . . that shall be the day appointed from ancient times for the battle of destruction of the sons of darkness" (1:10). Throughout the scroll there are repeated references to the opposition between "the Sons of Light" (also 1QM 1:13) and "the Sons of Darkness" (1QM 1:10; 13:16; 14:16; 16:10).

At the beginning of the *Rule of the Community* (1QS), the dualistic framework is clearly established. The Master of the community is to "admit into the Covenant of Grace all those who have freely devoted themselves to the observance of God's precepts, . . . that they may love all the sons of light, each according to his lot in God's design, and hate all the sons of darkness, each according to his guilt in God's vengeance" (1:10) (DSSE⁴ 70).[74]

The phrase also appears elsewhere in the New Testament, for example, in Luke 16:8, where the "children *(huioi)* of this age" are contrasted with "the children *(huioi)* of light."[75] In 1 Thess 5:5, speaking of the coming of the Day of the

---

73. Fitzmyer, who studies the expression extensively in relation to its appearance in Luke 16:8, says (*Luke* 1108) that the "division of humanity into two groups by the expressions 'sons of light' and 'sons of darkness' is found nowhere else outside the Qumran literature — and by implication also in the NT."

74. See also 1QS 2:17; 3:14, 23, 24.

75. On the dualistic background of the expression in Luke 16:8, see Fitzmyer, *Luke* 1,108.

Lord, Paul describes his listeners as "sons of the light" and denies that they are "of the night." Eph 5:8 uses a similar expression when the author urges his listeners to "walk as children *(tekna)* of the light."

However, as one reads the Sectarian Documents of Qumran, it becomes clear that, in addition to the common appearance of the expressions "sons of light/sons of darkness," there are other analogous expressions for describing good and evil that do not use only "light" and "darkness." For example, in 1QS 2:25, we hear of "sons of the everlasting Company." In 4:6, 7, we hear of the "sons of truth." If we note the relation between the terms used for the guiding spirits of good and evil and those whom they influence, the way is left open for the use of the term "son of destruction" at Qumran also. For example, the guiding powers are described in similar terms: the "Prince of Light" (1QS 3:20) and the "Angel of Darkness" (1QS 3:21, 22). There are also "Spirits of Light and Darkness" (1QS 3:25). The good spirit is variously described as "the spirit of holiness" (1QS 4:21); "the spirit of truth" (1QS 4:22, 24); the evil spirit is described as "the spirit of injustice" (1QS 4:21, 24). In 1QH 13:12 we hear of the "Angels of Destruction" who "walk according to the precepts of Darkness" (*DSSE*[4] 139). Thus, if there is a Prince of Light, one can be a son of light. If there is a Spirit of Truth, one can be a son of truth. If there is an Angel of Darkness, one can be a son of darkness.

Similar to this expression is the use of "son of destruction" in John 17:12. It is commonly recognized that this term reflects the apocalyptic worldview.[76] Commentators at least since the time of Bernard have noted the appearance of the same phrase in 2 Thess 2:3, where the author is speaking of signs of the Parousia and refers to the revelation of the "one of iniquity, the son of destruction" *(ho anthrōpos tēs anomias, ho huios tēs apōleias)*.[77] As Lindars says of the passage in 2 Thessalonians: ". . . he is not the Devil himself, but a sort of incarnation of evil, one in whom the Devil has absolute sway. . . ." Bernard also had pointed to its appearance in *Jub.* 10:3, where, in a dualistic context, it refers to those sons of Noah who died in the flood as "children of perdition" led astray by demons.[78]

The apocalyptic background of this expression is also confirmed by the overall context of John 17:11d-16, which is apocalyptic. Consequently, it is appropriate to conclude that "son(s) of" in both 12:36 and 17:12 reflect the worldview of modified dualism and that these expressions were readily recognized as dualistic expressions. In the Gospel, this dualism is found only in the third edition.

---

76. See, for example, R. E. Brown, *Gospel* 2:760; Reim, *Hintergrund* 45-46.
77. Bernard, *Gospel* 2:571. More recently R. E. Brown, *Gospel* 2:760; Lindars, *Gospel* 526.
78. Bernard, *Gospel* 2:571.

Section 2. The Criteria Used for the Third Edition

1 John

In 1 John, this duality of classes is developed extensively in 2:28–3:10. Throughout, the contrast is between the one who acts "justly" and the one who does not and between the one who sins and the one who does not. In each case one's actions are said to reveal one's parentage. As a result, individuals are said to be either "born of God" (2:29) or not; they are said to be "from the devil" or not (3:8); and they are said to be either "children of God" or "children of the devil." Thus, the author describes in detail the two ("dualistic") alternatives of parentage, just as he will describe in detail the two (dualistically opposed) spirits in 4:1-6. The only difference from the terminology of 3E is that in 3E the terminology in the two cases mentioned is "sons" *(huioi)* rather than "children" *(tekna)*.[79]

3E-11. In the third edition, the expression "being of . . ." (the truth, the earth, the world, etc.) is used to identify the allegiance of individuals. This does not appear in the other editions.

In the Gospel the Greek phrase *einai ek* appears thirty-six times: 1:24, 35, 44, 46; 3:1, 31 (four times); 6:71; 7:17, 22 (twice), 42, 50, 52; 8:23 (four times), 44, 47 (twice); 10:16, 26, 32; 12:2, 20; 15:19 (twice); 17:14 (twice); 18:17, 25, 36, 37.

The Greek phrase *einai ek* has a variety of meanings in the Gospel and so of itself cannot be used in an unqualified way as a characteristic of dualism.[80] First, it is used as a partitive genitive indicating that an individual is a member of a particular group (e.g., at 1:24, where it is said that along with John the Bap-

---

79. Although the author of the third edition uses the terminology "sons of light" in a stereotyped way, he never refers to individuals as "sons of God." That terminology is reserved for Jesus. Instead, he uses "child" *(teknon)* throughout (see above, 3E-5).

80. The failure to distinguish the various meanings of *einai ek* weakens the recent studies of Trumbower *(Born)* and Keck, "Derivation." Keck is correct in rejecting the predestination that Trumbower sees, but distinguishing the various uses of the term would enable scholars to arrive at a clearer reading of the texts and would distinguish those that are dualistic from those in which "ordinary" derivation or relatedness is intended.

R. E. Brown *(Epistles* 513-14) would agree with many of the occurrences in the above listing but is somewhat more generous in identifying texts as dualistic. For example, he would include John 6:32 (". . . but my Father gives you the true bread from heaven"). He would also include 10:16, 26 (where believers are spoken of as being "of my sheep") and 18:17, 25 (where Peter is identified as being "one of his disciples"). These do not reflect the same dualistic context as the others but simply identify the believer's allegiance. Not all statements of allegiance are cast in dualistic terms. However, apart from these instances, the texts cited by Brown agree with those I have listed above.

tist were "two of his disciples"). Other instances of this use are 1:35; 3:1; 6:71; 7:50; 10:26; 12:2, 20; 18:17, 25). Second, it can be used to indicate geographical origin (e.g., in 1:44, where Philip is said to be "of the city" of Andrew and Peter). This use also appears in 1:46 and 7:52. Third, *einai ek* can be used to indicate more general origin in passages such as 7:17, where Jesus speaks of his teaching being "of God" ("of Moses," 7:22 [twice]; "of the seed of David," 7:42; "from this sheepfold," 10:16; "from the Father," 10:32). In 3:31, the phrase is used three times, contrasting origin from describing how the one who is "of the earth" acts. In 8:23, it is used four times but in two different senses. In v. 23a, it is used of origin ("you are of the things below; I am of the things above"). In v. 23b, its use is more ambiguous and seems to combine the notion of origin with that of allegiance (see below).

However, in a fourth set of instances the phrase appears in contexts where the alternative is presented of belonging to one or the other group. In some instances this meaning is quite clear. For example, in 8:44, the opponents are described as being "of their father the devil" as contrasted with being "of God" or "of Abraham." In 8:47, the expression refers to the one who is "of God" and to the one who is not "of God." In 18:37, Jesus speaks of everyone who is "of the truth." Yet in other instances, the meaning is not as clear and it is difficult to tell whether the usage refers primarily to one's place of origin or to the object of one's allegiance. In fact, these two are at times closely related in the Gospel. For example, in 3:31, Jesus speaks of the one who "comes from above" and the one who is "of the earth." While the statement reflects "origin," there is also the implication of the allegiance or orientation which is characteristic of that origin. In 8:23, Jesus contrasts his listeners' being "of the things below" with his own being "of the things above." Again there is a matter of origin but also the matter of orientation that follows from that origin. 15:19 speaks twice of being (and not being) "of the world," as does 17:14 (twice). In 18:36, Jesus denies (twice) that his kingdom is "of this world." In these cases, it is a matter of origin and less a matter of allegiance, although the latter cannot be completely excluded. Nevertheless, all cases where there is an expressed comparison between two dualistically opposed groups appear in the third edition.

The use of the phrase in both its ordinary and its dualistic uses has been studied most extensively by de la Potterie.[81] De la Potterie, as the title of his book indicates, focuses on the use of the phrase with "truth" (together they appear three times in the Johannine writings) but also surveys all of the other uses of the phrase "to be of."

De la Potterie is able to find no appearances of the expression elsewhere either in pre-Christian literature or in the New Testament and claims that it is a

---

81. De la Potterie, *Vérité* 1:593-693.

Section 2. The Criteria Used for the Third Edition

Johannine creation. Nevertheless, de la Potterie recognizes the dualistic background of its use with "truth" and with other such terminology. He finds its closest parallels in terminology in the apocalyptic *1 Enoch*[82] and 1QS[83] and suggests that the phrase is derived from the somewhat longer "you are [a son] of...."[84] He sees a parallel between this phrase and "to be of God" and suggests an analogy between the two: they are both expressions used to designate believers in the context of eschatological dualism.[85] While both expressions are dualistic, "to be of" refers to the *present actual state* of the individual rather than the individual's *origin*.

1 John

In 1 John, the phrase "to be of" appears nineteen times. The majority of the instances denote dualistic allegiance: 2:19 (the second, third, and fourth instances, meaning "of us"), 21 ("of the truth"); 3:8 ("of the devil"), 10 ("of God"), 12 ("of the Evil One"), 19 ("of the truth"); 4:4 ("of God"), 5 ("of the world"), 6 (twice), 19 ("of God"). Other instances (the first one in 2:19; 4:1, 2, 3, 7 ["of God"]) do not denote allegiance but rather the source of something and are grouped separately. The instances in 2:16 denote two possible origins, but the two possible origins are elsewhere dualistically opposed.

Schnackenburg describes the phrase as meaning "to belong to a certain realm..., group or category."[86] R. E. Brown does not discuss the expression in his commentary on the Gospel, but in his commentary on the Letters he gives substantial space to the topic.[87] Brown also has no doubts about the dualistic background of the expression: "The main theological usage of *einai ek* is in the Johannine dualistic world-view to indicate origin from and/or adherence to one side or the other."[88]

This dualistic use of *einai ek* is another instance of language that appears relatively infrequently in the Gospel but with greater frequency in 1 John. As was said above, although there are many close parallels to this dualistic use elsewhere in intertestamental Judaism, no precise parallels have been found.

---

82. Particularly *1 Enoch* 105:2 (cf. 95:2; 104:9, 13).
83. De la Potterie (*Vérité* 1:600) quotes numerous texts from 1QS (2:14, 24, 26; 3:19; 4:5-6; 8:6, etc.), 1QM (1:1, 7; 17:8), and 1QH (2:14; 6:29; 7:30; 9:35; 10:27; 11:11). All of these reflect a dualistic worldview and divide persons or groups into opposed groups.
84. De la Potterie, *Vérité* 1:601.
85. De la Potterie, *Vérité* 1:602, 613.
86. Schnackenburg, *Epistles* 203.
87. R. E. Brown, *Epistles* 312-13.
88. R. E. Brown, *Epistles* 313.

The Third Edition of the Gospel

3E-12. In the third edition, there is a duality of Spirits in which the Spirit is described as the Spirit of Truth (and implicitly opposed to the Spirit of Deception). This view contrasts with the presentation of the Spirit in the second edition, where the issue was the presence or the absence of the Spirit of God (2E-6).[89]

In the second edition, the issue was that the Spirit[90] is necessary for adequate belief and the distinction was made between those who possess the Spirit and those who do not. In the third edition (and in 1 John), the issue is not *whether* one has the Spirit but *which* Spirit one has: the Spirit of God (the Spirit of Truth) or the evil spirit, the Spirit of Deception.

The third edition (and 1 John), which adopts the worldview of apocalyptic, presents the world as under the influence of opposing spirits. In apocalyptic generally, these opposing spirits are known by a variety of titles. But characteristic of them all is the fact that one is a good spirit and the other is an evil spirit. The one has its origin in God; the other in Satan (Beliar/Belial[91]).

The presence of this apocalyptic view is most fully developed in 1 John, and the use of this terminology in the Johannine writings will be clearer if we begin by looking at 1 John.[92]

In the Letters

In 1 John, this dualism of spirits is expressed in a variety of ways.

First, at times the opposing spirits are referred to simply as "the spirits" (4:1, 2). The evil spirit is known as "the Spirit of the Antichrist" (1 John 2:18

---

89. Böcher (*Dualismus* 34-39, 77-78) discusses this feature of the T12P, the SDQ, and the Johannine literature. Böcher points out that the SDQ see a plural number of "spirits" of good and evil in contrast to the single spirit of good and single spirit of evil in John. While this is true, it is not significant since they all function within the same type of dualistic framework. De la Potterie (*Vérité* 1:282-86) also recognizes its close parallels in the Scrolls and the T12P.

90. The capitalization of spirit is often taken to indicate that the word refers to the Spirit of God. In apocalyptic literature, where both good and evil spirits are being referred to, it is difficult to know whether to capitalize the word or not. Moreover, in this apocalyptic literature generally one can sense a kind of ambivalence about whether the spirit is a true being or a force or simply a metaphor for attitudes. This reflects what was probably a spectrum of concepts about these "spirits." It is appropriate to consider all of the texts as essentially related rather than as distinct conceptualizations.

91. These are the terms commonly used in the Dead Sea Scrolls and in the T12P.

92. Bauckham ("Qumran" 113-14) argues that there is no reason to think that "Spirit of Truth" in the Gospel is dualistic since it does not appear with an opposed Spirit. Yet to say this is not to say it all. For this is not the case in 1 John (4:1-6). And the Gospel presumes knowledge of 1 John both here and in the reference to the Paraclete as "another" (which implies knowledge of 1 John 2:1).

Section 2. The Criteria Used for the Third Edition

[twice], 22; 4:3; 2 John 7).[93] The evil spirit is also known as "the Spirit of Deception" (1 John 4:6).

The good spirit is known as "the Spirit of Truth" (4:6) and as "the Spirit of God" (4:2).[94]

This dualistic contrast is so important to the understanding of the Epistle and so clear in 1 John 4:1-6 that the most pertinent parts deserve to be quoted:

> Beloved, *do not believe every spirit, but test the spirits* to see if they are from God, because many false prophets have gone out into the world. In this you know *the Spirit of God*. . . . And this is *the (spirit) of the Antichrist,* which you have heard is coming and is now already in the world. You are of God, Dear Children, and you have conquered them, because *he who is in you is greater than he who is in the world*. . . . They are of the world. . . . We are of God. . . . From this we know *the Spirit of Truth and the Spirit of Deception.* (1 John 4:1-2a, 3b, 5a, 6a, 6de)

The contrast between opposing spirits is clear: the reader is being asked not just to accept the Spirit, but to test the Spirits.

Yet another instance of a dualistic title for Satan is his description as "the Evil One." This title appears five times in 1 John (2:13, 14; 3:12; 5:18, 19). In each case it refers to a personal source of evil opposed to God. According to 1 John, the believer is said to conquer the Evil One (2:13, 14). The believer is said not to belong to the Evil One and not to be touched by him (5:18), while the world lies in his grasp (5:19). The picture is of apocalyptic dualism mirrored in the opposition to God and by the desire of the Evil One to dominate persons in this world.

In all of the above cases, the view is consistent: now it is not a matter of whether one has the Spirit or not, but which spirit one has. Throughout, the view of 1 John is dualistic. However, in the Gospel there are a number of places where hints of this dualistic view of the Spirit is in evidence — always in the material from the third edition.

---

93. As a title, this is unique to the Johannine literature.

94. It is also known simply as "the Spirit" (3:24; 4:13; 5:6 [twice], 8). This term, which is not dualistic in itself, is the common term in the Gospel. In the Letters, it is always clear from the context that it functions as a kind of abbreviated reference for "the Spirit of Truth" (e.g., 3:24, where the Spirit is identified as "that he gave us"; 4:1, where the reader is cautioned not to believe "every" spirit and where in ensuing verses the contrast between the good and evil spirits becomes explicit; and 5:6, where the Spirit is equated with the truth).

The Third Edition of the Gospel

Duality of Spirits in the Gospel

In spite of the fact that the common term in the Gospel is simply "the Spirit," two types of titles are used to describe the dualistically opposed spirits of good and evil in the Gospel. Each appears in material of the third edition.

The first set is evident in the Paraclete passages. When we examine the Paraclete passages within the Gospel, we find terminology the implications of which are much clearer in the light of the dualistic, apocalyptic framework of 1 John as it is quoted above.

Thus, in 14:16-17, the Paraclete is identified as "the Spirit of Truth"; in 14:26 the Paraclete is identified as "the Holy Spirit"; in 15:26, the Paraclete is again identified as "the Spirit of Truth"; in 16:7-15, again the Paraclete is identified as "the Spirit of Truth" (v. 13). Thus, every time the Paraclete is mentioned it is further identified by one of these dualistic titles.

The Spirit is mentioned one other time (3:34) in what would appear to be the unqualified sense in material of the third edition.[95] This would appear to be the only "exception" to the pattern apparent elsewhere. But there is almost surely an explanation for the lack of a modifier in 3:34. Because 3:34 spoke of *God* giving the Spirit to Jesus — and giving it without measure — it was probably not thought necessary by the author of the third edition to qualify the term as he did, and was to do, elsewhere, where it was more helpful to make the distinction between spirits clear. It is clear that the Spirit spoken of here is the Spirit of God!

As will be seen in detail in the Commentary, the evidence for seeing the Paraclete passages as coming from the third edition of the Gospel is somewhat complex but in the end very persuasive.[96] Here I will summarize briefly the types of arguments that support this view.

First, there are the literary features themselves, the aporias and the evidence of literary seams. These are of varying degrees of clarity and are discussed in the analysis of the composition of the individual passages. Alone they

---

95. The instances in 11:33; 13:21 are not relevant to this usage.

96. The question of the secondary or tertiary character of the Paraclete passages is one that has been suggested and discussed repeatedly by scholars. See, for example, Wellhausen, *Erweiterungen*; Bultmann, *Gospel* 566-72; Bornkamm, "Paraklet" *(TDNT)*; Windisch, *Spirit-Paraclete*; Schneider, "Abschiedsreden"; Beasley-Murray (*Gospel* 256, 270). More recently, Kysar (*Gospel* 227) has seen all of the Paraclete passages as loosely related to their context, "which suggests that they may have been insertions in the process of the evolution of the Farewell Discourses."

For a summary of opposing views, see de la Potterie, *Vérité* 1:339-341. De la Potterie is reluctant to talk of a written source but recognizes that they have "a certain independence from their immediate context," that they form a conceptual whole within themselves, that they manifest traces of previous tradition, and that "they are not the simple composition of the evangelist" (341). This is as far as one can go without actually saying they are editorial additions!

Section 2. The Criteria Used for the Third Edition

are not completely persuasive. Second, there is the apocalyptic viewpoint present in each. Third, there are the differences in the presentation of the "Spirit" and the "Paraclete" as outlined above. Fourth, as will be seen in the discussion of 15:22-25, the author of the second edition summarized his theology of witness by indications of how Jesus was hated in spite of the witness of his words and works and that this fulfilled the Scripture: "They have hated me freely." In the present state of the Gospel, the list of witnesses is extended to include now two additional witnesses in the time after Jesus' public ministry: the Paraclete and the disciples. In the light of the pervasive use of the three witnesses as a structuring element in the second edition, the mention here of the Paraclete and the disciples as witnesses gives a clear indication that they are extensions by the third author.

Fifth, there are two elements of the portrayal of the Paraclete that make full sense only in the light of 1 John. The fact that in the Gospel the Paraclete is referred to as "another" Paraclete finds no explanation within the Gospel itself but is clarified by the statement of 1 John 2:1 that describes Jesus as a Paraclete — and therefore the first one. In addition, the description of the Paraclete as the "Spirit of Truth" can be fully understood only when it is seen that this title is one half of a pair and is intended to be contrasted with the "Spirit of Deception." Together they constitute a description of the world as dominated by a dualistically opposed pair of spirits. Sixth, the Paraclete theology is more intelligible as a response to the issues of the community at the time of the third edition than any other. Given the number and variety of the features above, it seems only reasonable to conclude that the Paraclete passages are indeed secondary.[97]

The second "set" of terms that would appear to come from a dualistic background is more ambiguous: references to the "holy" Spirit. The term "Holy" Spirit appears within the Old Testament (e.g., Ps 51:11; Isa 63:10, 11; Wis 1:5; 9:17) where the context is *not* dualistic; nevertheless, the usage of Spirit in the simple, absolute form is so constant within the second edition that it seems likely that "holy" Spirit was intended to contrast implicitly this Spirit with an "unclean" or "evil" spirit and so to echo the apocalyptic conception of spirit. The designation "holy Spirit" appears in 1:33, 14:26, and 20:22. Of these, the first two occur in material of the third edition and would suggest that it was intended to be dualistic. The third appears in the scene of the actual conferral of the Spirit in 20:22. That material is from the second edition. Although there are no overt markers of editing, it is very possible that, after the discussion of the importance of distinguishing the good Spirit from the evil spirit, the third author felt it important to make the specification here.

---

97. The background of this conception will be treated in conjunction with the background of the next characteristic (below).

The Third Edition of the Gospel

3E-13. In the third edition, there are two dualistic titles typical of apocalyptic by which the devil is identified. The first is "Ruler of This World," and the second is "The Evil One." These are not present in either of the other editions.

We have already seen that, in the third edition, the conception of the Spirit is modified so as to be seen as one of two possible spirits within humanity — and that this contrasts with the presentation in the second edition. There are also dualistic titles given to the devil: Ruler of This World and The Evil One.

In the Gospel, Satan is described by the title "ruler of this world" three times (12:31; 14:30; 16:11).[98] In 12:31, the notion of the "ruler of this world" being "thrown out" echoes the cosmic battle of apocalyptic. In 14:30, the advent of Jesus' Passion is described by saying that the ruler of this world is "coming." This portrays the coming Passion as ultimately an earthly reflection and manifestation of the cosmic power of Satan. The Passion is part of the cosmic battle between God and Satan. Finally, in 16:11, the ruler of this world is said to be "already judged" in the action of Jesus undergoing his Passion, a battle that Jesus will ultimately win. And once again the title reflects the cosmic battle and the way events of this world are portrayed as reflections of that battle.

The second title is "the Evil One" *(ho ponēros)*. This title appears only once, in 17:15. Yet from the way the term is used with the definite article, it is clear that "the Evil One," the personal source of evil, is referred to. This is one of the terms that appears in the third edition of the Gospel but that cannot be fully appreciated without knowing the background of its development in 1 John.

The personification of evil as "the Evil One" *(ho ponēros)* is common in 1 John. In 1 John 2:13, 14, the believer is said to have conquered the Evil One. In 1 John 3:12, Cain was said to belong to (or be under the influence of) the Evil One. On the other hand, in 1 John 5:18 we read that the one who is born of God is not seized by the Evil One but (5:19) that the entire world lies in the grip of the Evil One.[99]

In the Dead Sea Scrolls[100]

In the Dead Sea Scrolls the term "Spirit(s) of Truth" appears in a description of the basic pattern of dualism: "He [God] has appointed for him two spirits in

---

98. Pointed out also by R. E. Brown, "Qumran" 148. Kovacs ("Ruler") recognizes the relationship between this title and other elements of (modified) dualism in the Gospel, as does Segal, "Ruler." This title does not appear in 1 John.
99. This term is also discussed in 3E-19 below.
100. The notion of "spirit" at Qumran has been studied in detail by Sekki, *Ruah*. Sekki (and others before him) have warned against seeing the dualism of Spirits as expressed in 1QS 3:13–4:26 as the only or even the primary conception of the Spirit in the sectarian documents

Section 2. The Criteria Used for the Third Edition

which to walk until the time of His visitation: the spirits of truth and injustice" (1QS 3:19 — *DSSE*⁴ 73). Again in 1QS 4:21: ". . . He [God] will shed upon him the spirit of truth . . ." (*DSSE*⁴ 75). Yet again: "Until now the spirits of truth and injustice struggle in the hearts of men" (1QS 4:23 — *DSSE*⁴ 75). The same expression appears in 1QM 13:11: ". . . and all the spirits of truth are under his dominion" (*DSSE*⁴ 139). Besides "Spirit of Injustice" in the Qumran documents, the evil spirits are called "the Spirits of his [Satan's] company" and "the Angels of Destruction" (1QM 13:12-13 — *DSSE*⁴ 139); "spirits of destruction" (1QM 14:10 — *DSSE*⁴ 140); "the spirits of wickedness" (1QM 15:14 — *DSSE*⁴ 141).[101]

In all three documents there is a clear resemblance in the dualistic portrayal of these opposed Spirits. At the same time, there are differences. While in the *T12P* (e.g., *TSim* 4:4) and in the Johannine literature the Spirit is the Spirit of God, at Qumran (e.g., 1QS 3:25) the opposed spirits are said to be created by God. In spite of the theological significance of this distinction, for the purposes of presenting the worldview of these documents this difference is not crucial, and it is clear that all three sets of documents reflect a similar view of opposed spirits.

It is important to note, however, that the OT uses "spirit of understanding," "spirit of deception," and the like in a way that is meant to denote the particular effect of the Spirit (e.g., Sir 39:6; Isa 4:4; 11:2; 28:6). This is *not* a dualistic usage.

In the Testaments of the Twelve Patriarchs[102]

This description of opposed spirits of good and evil was common in apocalyptic thought. *TJud* 20:1-5 is remarkably close to the section of 1 John quoted above:

> Therefore, understand, My Children, that two spirits *(duo pneumata)* await humanity: the spirit of truth and the spirit of error *(to tēs alētheias kai to tēs planēs)*. And in the middle is the mind that chooses which to incline to, if it wishes. The deeds *of truth and the things of error* are written in the breast of

---

from Qumran. It is important, however, to assess the use and understanding of Spirit in the sectarian scrolls in conjunction with the presence or absence of other features of the apocalyptic worldview. Sekki's study confirms the presence and importance of the OT view of the eschatological outpouring of the Spirit as a major element of their future hopes.

See also de la Potterie ("Parole" 178) and Böcher (*Dualismus* 36-37), both of whom point to the Qumran background of the phrase "Spirit of Truth."

101. Similar terms also appear in the *Martyrdom and Ascension of Isaiah* 2:4, where Beliar is described as "ruling this world." In 2 Cor 4:4, there is a reference to "the god of this world."

102. See the discussion in Böcher, *Dualismus* 34-35, with additional citations.

humans. And the Lord knows each one. There is no moment in which the works of humanity can escape notice, because they are written in the marrow of the bones before the Lord. And *the spirit of truth* witnesses to all things and brings all accusations. He who has sinned is on fire in his heart and cannot raise his head to the judge.

The title "Spirit of Truth" appears twice in this passage. This term appears less frequently than the term "spirit of deception" (see below), but synonyms such as "spirit of grace" (*TJud* 24:3) regularly occur. At times the opposite of the spirit of deception is portrayed as an angel (e.g., *TBenj* 6:1). At times both the good and the evil spirits are referred to as angels (*TAsh* 6:4). In *TBenj* 8:3 the spirit of good is identified as "the spirit of God."

In the *T12P*, "Spirit of Deception" appears frequently (*TReu* 3:2; *TSim* 3:1; *TLev* 3:3; *TZeb* 9:7, 8; *TDan* 5:5; *TAsh* 6:2; *TBenj* 6:1), although other terms also appear.

There are close parallels to the Johannine "ruler of this world" in the *T12P*. In *TSim* 2:7 and *TJud* 19:4,[103] the evil spirit is called "Ruler of Deceit" *(ho archōn tēs planēs)*. *TDan* 5:6 says, ". . . your ruler is Satan" *(ho archōn hymōn estin ho Satanas)*. *TSim* 6:6-7, in a kind of cosmic judgment scene, states that "all the spirits of deception will be handed over for trampling" *(dothēsontai panta ta pneumata tēs planēs eis katapatēsin)* and that "humans will rule evil spirits" *(anthrōpoi basileusousin tōn ponērōn pneumatōn)*.[104]

Although at times the spirits are said to dominate and control humanity, this is not total determinism since persons are also said to cooperate with the evil spirits (e.g., by "imitating" the evil spirits, *TAsh* 6:2).

3E-14. In the third edition, the title "Son of Man" is regularly used to describe Jesus as the agent of God. This title is typical of apocalyptic and does not appear in the earlier editions.[105]

The christological title "Son of Man" appears thirteen times in the Gospel: 1:51; 3:13, 14; 5:27; 6:27, 53, 62; 8:28; 9:35; 12:23, 34 (twice); 13:31. The title itself and various topics associated with it have been the object of continued debate and the subject of innumerable articles and monographs. While it is true that, outside

---

103. Many of the dualistic terms discussed here appear throughout *TJud* 19:1–20:5.

104. This passage is likely to be a Christian interpolation, but the author employs the categories of apocalyptic and the two spirits.

105. Recent bibliography includes Ashton, *Understanding* 383-406; Burkett, *Son of Man*; J. J. Collins, "Son of Man" 448-66; Coppens, "Fils de l'homme"; idem, "Logia"; Moloney, *Son of Man*; Painter, *Quest* 319-41; Rhea, *Son of Man*; Slater, "One."

Section 2. The Criteria Used for the Third Edition

the Gospel of John, the title appears in material that is certainly apocalyptic, among scholars it is debated whether it originated in apocalyptic circles and whether it appears only there.[106]

For the purposes of our analysis here, it can be noted, first, that the analysis of the composition of the Gospel of John indicates that this title appears exclusively in the material of the third edition. Second, it can be noted that this material consistently contains other features that identify the passages with apocalyptic. This confluence of features confirms that, at least in Johannine circles, the title was seen as an element of the apocalyptic worldview.

The term occurs for the first time in 1:51, in the "second addition" to the confession of Nathanael. In the Commentary it will be seen that v. 51 has several features that indicate that it has been added to the context as an appendix to 1:50, which itself had been added to the material of the first edition that ended in v. 49. In 3:13, 14 the title appears twice in the extended section of material from the third edition stretching from 3:11-21. This is the first of the so-called "lifting up" passages in the Gospel, in which the Son of Man's death on the cross is seen as life-giving. Apocalyptic, as well as other, features of the third edition abound. In 5:27, the title appears in association with the notions of future judgment and bodily resurrection, in one of the passages most commonly thought to come from the third edition.

In 6:27, the title appears in connection with dualistic language of "doing the works of" and speaks of the bread that Jesus will *give* rather than that which he *is*, thus pointing forward to vv. 51-58. In 6:53, "Son of Man" appears again in the appendix to the original Bread-of-Life discourse. In this appendix (as had been hinted in 6:27) the bread is Eucharistic and the Son-of-Man title appears again. In 6:62, the title appears for a final time in chapter 6. Here it interrupts the discussion of the scandal of the words of Jesus by speaking of the scandal of the cross.

In 8:28, the second "lifting up" passage occurs, again Jesus is referred to as the Son of Man, and he identifies himself as "I AM." In 9:35, the Son of Man appears again and is said to be "worshipped" by the man who had been blind. Je-

---

106. Recently J. J. Collins ("Son of Man") has argued that both the *Similitudes of Enoch* and *4 Ezra* 13 can be shown to have known and developed the figure of the Son of Man in Daniel 7 in the direction of a preexistent, heavenly savior figure and that such a figure was therefore known to at least some sectors of first-century Judaism. Given the apocalyptic nature of both *Enoch* and *4 Ezra*, this has much to say about an *apocalyptic* use of the title in first-century Judaism. Collins's view has recently been adopted by Slater, "One."

Not every scholar thinks that the term is to be understood against the background of apocalyptic. See, for example, the survey in Burkett, *Son of Man*, esp. 17-20, 38-39. Burkett himself sees the title as derived from the use of the phrase in Prov 30:1-4. Rhea (*Son of Man*) attempts to understand it against a prophetic background of the term in Psalms, Ezekiel, and *Testament of Abraham*.

sus in turn speaks of himself as "judge" — a function of the apocalyptic Son of Man as described in 5:26-30, especially v. 27.

In 12:23, Jesus announces the arrival of the time for his glorification. While doing so, he identifies himself as the Son of Man. Apart from this title, the material is difficult to identify since it is immediately followed by what appear to be later Synoptic-like interpolations.

In 12:34, the context is again patently clear. What is particularly interesting here is the appearance of the third (and final) "lifting up" statement by Jesus. Here it appears without explicit reference to the Son of Man, but the crowd makes the title explicit even though it is mentioned nowhere previously in the context. This confirms that the author of the third edition regularly and exclusively associated the title with the notion of being "lifted up." Apocalyptic and other features of the third edition abound in this section that stretches from 12:31 to 12:36b.

In 13:31, in what appears at first to be almost a doublet of 12:23, Jesus identifies himself as the Son of Man and summarizes his public ministry as the time when he was glorified but then affirms that his coming Passion will also glorify him. The context here at the beginning of the Farewell Discourses is difficult to define, but as the discussion of the Composition will show, it is likely that the material comes from the third edition, especially in the light of the consistency of the title's use previously.

In a departure from the pattern noticed before, the title "Son of Man" does not appear in the Letters. This is probably because the title throughout the Gospel is used primarily as a self-designation by Jesus.[107] The fact that the title was such a prominent one for Jesus in the Synoptics may also help account for its presence in the Gospel (3E-55F). "Son of Man" does not appear as a title for a messianic figure in the SDQ or the T12P.[108]

It should also be noted that, in first-century Judaism, the figure of the Son of Man was considered preexistent in at least some circles. For example, in 1 Enoch 48:3, the Son of Man is described as given a name before the sun and the stars were created. In 1 Enoch 70:1, he is described as already present in heaven in the antediluvian period before Enoch was exalted. Also, 4 Ezra 13:26 refers to the Son of Man as "the one whom the Most High has kept for many ages."[109] The preexistence of the Johannine Son of Man is evident in texts such as 3:13 and 6:62.

---

107. The crowd uses the title twice (12:34) in discussion with Jesus, but it is never used by them independently of such a context.

108. The title appears with some frequency in the T12P but with the nontitular meaning of "human being." See, for example, TLev 3:10 and TJos 2:5.

109. For a detailed discussion leading to this conclusion, see J. J. Collins, "Son of Man" 448-66, esp. 455, 462, 465.

Section 2. The Criteria Used for the Third Edition

3E-15. In the third edition, the obligation to love is understood in a sectarian sense as love to be focused on the members of one's community.[110] This conception is typical of apocalyptic and is not found in the earlier editions of the Gospel.[111]

The Johannine obligation "to love one another" is treated here as an ideological feature of the third edition because such sectarian love is characteristic of apocalyptic literature. The love commandment appears in the third edition in 13:34-35; 15:12, 17. This conception of mutual love also appears in the Johannine Letters and has its closest parallels in the sectarian documents from Qumran and the *T12P*.[112]

In the Johannine Letters

This notion of intracommunity love first appears in the first two Letters of John. Although there are many indications that the love-commandment passages are an editorial addition within the Gospel, the obligation of mutual love is integral to the thought and structure of 1 and 2 John. It is expressed both as loving "one another" (1 John 3:11, 23; 4:7, 11, 12; 2 John 5) and as loving "one's brother" (1 John 2:10; 3:10, 14; 4:20, 21) (see also 5:1, 2).[113]

In the Gospel of John

The Johannine form of the love commandment appears four times in the Gospel. It appears for the first time in 13:34, where it is designated a "new" commandment: "A new commandment I give you, that, as I love you, you also should love one another." The injunction is then repeated in the following verse: "In this all will know that you are disciples of mine, if you have love for one another." It appears again in 15:12, where once again it is designated a commandment and the love of Jesus for his own is presented as the model for the

---

110. Bibliography includes R. F. Collins, "Commandment"; Fensham, "Love"; Fuller, *Essays*; Perkins, *Love*; Segovia, *Relationships*; Spicq, *Agapē*; von Wahlde, *Commandments* 242-43, 268-74.

111. As I have indicated above (3E-6) and in more detail in Vol. 3, Appendix 5, the love commandment is part of a larger complex of the Johannine commandments. The notion of commandment as a conceptualization of the ministry of Jesus is discussed in 3E-6, and the overall theology of the Johannine commandments is taken up in Vol. 3, Appendix 5.

112. Here the focus is on the "love commandment" itself, although the Johannine conception of love in general merits its own discussion. See particularly Spicq, *Agapē*, and Segovia, *Relationships*.

113. Segovia (*Relationships* 121, 123, 125) regularly suggests that texts dealing with the love commandment appear to deal more closely with the *Sitz im Leben* of 1 John than with that of the Gospel.

believers' love of each other. Finally, in 15:17 Jesus says: "These things I command you: love one another."

This understanding of Christian love is different from the Synoptic version in three respects. First, love of others is developed more fully in the Johannine writings and plays a larger role within the community. Second, in the Gospel of John, Christian love is to be modeled on the love that Jesus has shown the Christian rather than on what one would expect to be done to oneself. Third, in the Johannine understanding, Christian love is focused on the members of the community and not extended outward to those who are seen as evil.[114]

As will be seen in detail in the Commentary, contrary to its appearance in the Letters, the love commandment in the Gospel is always awkward in its literary context. This is a clear indication of the fact that it is a later addition to the context.

In the Dead Sea Scrolls

The possibility of parallels between the Johannine and Qumran conceptions of love has been noticed with some regularity. A close parallel to the "Johannine" conception of intracommunity love is found in 1QS 1:1-4:

> [The Master shall teach the sai]nts to live [according to] the Book of the Community Rule, that they may seek God with a whole heart and soul, and do what is good and right before Him as He commanded by the hand of Moses and all His servants the Prophets; that they may love all that He has chosen and hate all that he has rejected.... (*DSSE*[4] 70)

An even closer parallel is found in 1QS 1:10. According to 1QS 1:10, those admitted to the community are commanded

> ... that they may love all the sons of light ... and hate all the sons of darkness.... (*DSSE*[4] 70)

1QS 4:5 speaks of the need to exercise "great charity towards all the sons of truth" (*DSSE*[4] 73). CD 6:14 (*DSSE*[4] 101) urges them to "separate from the sons of the Pit," and 6:21 says, "They shall love each man his brother as himself...."

---

114. The sectarian character of the love commandment in John and its similarity to the Qumran commandment are recognized by many scholars. See, for example, F. M. Braun, "L'arrière-fond"; R. E. Brown, "Scrolls," esp. 163-67; R. F. Collins, "Commandment," esp. 252-56. Among those who reject this view is Schnackenburg, *Epistles* 112-13.

Section 2. The Criteria Used for the Third Edition

It is clear from the larger context of these statements at Qumran that the purpose of this intracommunity love is not only to give mutual support but to avoid contamination by association with those the community considered to be doing the work of Satan. In this dualistic worldview, to give love to those who do evil would seem to be partaking in their evil (cf. 2 John 10-11).

Nevertheless, some would see indications of another view that would seem to extend love also to one's enemies. R. E. Brown, referring to Grossouw, points out that this is not the only picture at Qumran.[115] For example, 1QS 10:18 says: "I will pay to no man the reward of evil; I will pursue him with goodness. For judgment of all the living is with God." Brown comments: "These two trends are puzzling." Yet the key to the relation between the two attitudes is expressed well further on where the author of 1QS (10:19-21) clarifies that, *in spite of his forgiveness of moral transgression, he will not forgive false teaching and doctrinal evil:*

> ". . . my wrath shall not turn from the men of falsehood, and I will not rejoice until judgment is made. I will bear no rancour against them that turn from transgression, but will have no pity on all who depart from the way. I will offer no comfort to the smitten until their way becomes perfect." (CDSSE)

Thus, the community distinguishes between two types of evil: one moral and one doctrinal. The former can be forgiven; the latter cannot. I would suggest that this is precisely the attitude of the Johannine community!

(4) In the Testaments of the Twelve Patriarchs

When we turn to the *T12P*, we find a number of passages that use terminology identical with the Johannine "loving one another."[116] For example, in *TZeb* 8:5-6:

> For when we went down into Egypt, Joseph did not hold a grudge against us. When he saw me, he was moved with compassion. Whomever you see, do not harbor resentment, my children; love one another *(agapate allēlous)*, and do not calculate the wrong done by each to his brothers. This shatters unity, and scatters all kinship, and stirs up the soul. He who recalls evil receives neither compassion nor mercy. *(OTP)*

---

115. Grossouw, "Scrolls," quoted by R. E. Brown, "Scrolls" 164.
116. It is generally recognized that the passages dealing with the love commandment in the *T12P* do not belong to the Christian interpolations. See, for example, Konradt, "Bruderliebe" 297 n. 2.

The context here seems to imply that the love is meant to be extended within a blood-related group — brothers in the sense of siblings. This notion is found in a number of other texts from the *T12P*: *TDan* 5:3 ("Love the Lord all your life and love one another with a true heart"); *TGad* 6:1 ("And now, My Children, may each love his brother and keep hatred from your hearts, loving one another in work and in word and in understanding of the soul"); 6:3 ("Love one another from the heart, and if someone sins against you, tell him in peace . . ."); 7:7 ("Keep hatred from your soul and love one another in straightness of heart").

As in the SDQ, forgiveness and mercy are encouraged and hatred seems always to be the enemy of love and the enemy of God. *TGad* 4:1–6:1 has a long exhortation against hatred culminating in the section quoted above (*TGad* 6:1) where, after the urging to love, the readers are also urged to "keep hatred from your hearts." Yet here too the avoidance of hatred speaks to the type of moral evil that 1QS also seeks to forgive. In this sense love is to be extended to everyone: in *TIss* 7:6 Issachar says, "I loved the Lord with all my strength, and likewise I loved every person as my children." Thus, the *T12P* exhibits the same terminology of restricted love as both the SDQ and the Johannine writings and also exhibits the forgiveness of moral failings and love extended beyond just the "brothers" or his "children."[117]

However, in the *T12P*, the focus throughout is on moral failure rather than doctrinal. Even though expressions such as "the Spirit of Deceit" are used, the manifestations of such deceit are seen as moral. Perhaps the closest we can come is the statement in *TAsh* 4:5 that describes good persons:

> For they live in zeal for God, staying away from those things which God also hates and renounces through his commandments, keeping back evil from good.

Here God is said to "hate" that which is evil. Thus, while we do not find instances of "hating" persons, such "hatred" would be implicit in such statements as the one from *TAsh*.

Thus, in spite of the verbal parallels, the overall conception of sectarian love in the *T12P* is not as clear as that found in the Johannine writings and in the SDQ. Nevertheless, there are some conceptions in the *T12P* that are related to this conception of sectarian love.[118]

At Qumran, while love for the sons of light is encouraged, hatred of those in darkness is also encouraged. Some would say that the second half of this di-

---

117. See also the extended examples of such love in *TZeb* 5:1–8:6.
118. See also Konradt, "Bruderliebe."

Section 2. The Criteria Used for the Third Edition

chotomy is not found in the Johannine writings.[119] The Johannine community is never encouraged to "hate" those who have gone out. Yet it must be remembered first of all that 1 John exhorts the members of the community about conduct primarily in relation to its own members. It does not focus on how others are to be treated.[120] The principal reason for this may well be that the love command serves as the primary ethical directive for the community, a kind of "umbrella" that comprehends all ethical obligations. The author of 1 John is exhorting his own followers about the importance of putting love into action, not about their attitude toward outsiders.

Nevertheless, in spite of this focus within, there are clear indications of the "hatred" of the opponents the author and his community considered evil. Long ago, F. M. Braun[121] suggested that 1 John 2:15 was an example of such "hatred" (although the word is not used):

> Do not love the world, or the things in the world. If a person loves the world, the love of the Father is not in that person.

This certainly expresses the kind of abhorrence of evil and the avoidance of evil that we see paralleled in the Qumran literature. Moreover, in 2 John 10-11, the author exhorts his listeners to refuse love and welcome to certain people. This too would seem to qualify as the kind of "hatred" of evil that Qumran speaks of:

> If someone approaches you and does not bring this teaching, do not receive him into your house and do not greet him. For the one who gives him a greeting also takes part in his evil deeds.

Here the Greek for "taking part in" is *koinōnein*, a cognate of *koinōnia*, the word used to describe the fellowship of believers. *Koinonia* was the word used at the beginning of 1 John to describe the fellowship that results from accepting all that the author and his followers proclaim. From 2 John 10-11, we see that those who do not profess the correct teaching are to be excluded from the community. This is certainly the intention of the exhortation to "hate" that we see at Qumran.

A third example of this exclusionary "hatred" is also evident in 3 John, where the author praises Gaius for acting "faithfully in whatever you do for the

---

119. Augenstein, *Liebesgebot* 178.

120. An exception to this may be 1 John 5:16-17, if the "sin unto death" about which the community is not to pray is understood as the sin of separating oneself from the community (as the opponents have done).

121. F. M. Braun, "Arrière-fond" 17-18.

brothers" (v. 5). The Elder explains that "we ought to receive such as these, so that we may become co-workers with the truth" (v. 8). However, the Elder then complains that Diotrephes has in fact excluded these missionaries from the community on the same grounds — that he felt that they were not witnessing to the truth. Consequently, we can be sure that the community practiced such "hatred" although it is not explicitly described as it was at Qumran.

A fourth example is in fact the example of Jesus himself, who in the High-Priestly Prayer of chapter 17 says, "I pray on their behalf. I do not pray on behalf of the world, but on behalf of those whom you have given me."[122] While not speaking of "hate," the prayer of Jesus does exclude "the world." Thus, the exclusion ("hatred" in the sectarian sense) is directed to those who have shown themselves evil by their rejection of God.

3E-16. In the third edition, there is belief in a final apocalyptic eschatology that involves the notions of "a last day" and the return of Jesus. This is not found in the earlier editions (but see 2E-21).[123]

Apocalyptic eschatology typically involves three elements: (1) a final, accountability (2) for all people, and (3) bodily resurrection. In this section (3E-16), we will treat the notion of the "last day" and the return of Jesus. In section 3E-17, we will treat the notion of universal accountability, and in section 3E-37, we will treat the notion of bodily resurrection. None of these features is found in the first or second editions.

The Last Day

In the second edition, there is no notion of an end of time involving a "last day." However, in the third edition, this notion appears with some frequency.

In the Gospel

In the third edition of the Gospel, the notion of "the last day" appears first in chapter 6 (vv. 39, 40, 44, 54) in repeated references to resurrection "on the last day." The notion of a resurrection on the last day also appears in 11:24. Finally,

---

122. Pointed out by R. F. Collins, "Commandment" 252 n. 151.
123. Dodd ("First Epistle" 142-44) saw this as one of the ways in which the First Epistle diverges from the Gospel. While the emphasis is certainly greater and much clearer in the First Epistle, the conception does underlie at least one text in the Gospel.

Section 2. The Criteria Used for the Third Edition

in 12:48 we learn that there will be a judgment on that day. Thus we see that in the third edition, the apocalyptic notion of "last day," resurrection, and judgment all appear in association with one another.

In the Letters

In the Letters, the notion of a "last day" does not appear. However, the notions of "the world passing away" and the related "last hour" appear in 1 John 2:17-18 and the notion of a "day of judgment" in 4:17. In addition, the author speaks of the appearance of "the Antichrist" (2:18; 4:3) and "the Liar" (2:22), figures commonly associated with the great trial which preceded the last day. Finally, the reappearance of Jesus at that time (1 John 2:28; 3:2) to conduct judgment also confirms the underlying notion of a "last day" at the end of time.

The Background of the Notion of "the Last Day"

Because the notion of "the last day" is closely associated with the return of God's intermediary at the end of time, these will be treated together below.

The Return of Jesus

In the Second Edition

In the second edition of the Gospel, the departure of Jesus is spoken of as being permanent. He departs, and when he does, he sends the Spirit. Since judgment occurs in the present moment of decision for or against Jesus, there is no talk of a final or future judgment, nor is there mention of any future return of Jesus.

In the Letters

However, in the Letters, a belief in a return of Jesus is evident. In 1 John 2:28 we find the actual term *parousia:* "And now, Dear Children, abide in him [Jesus], so that when he [Jesus] is revealed, we may have confidence and not shrink from him [Jesus] at his coming *(parousia)*."

The notion of a return is also evident in 1 John 3:2 (". . . it has not yet been revealed what we will be. We know that when he [Jesus] is revealed, we will be like him [Jesus], and that we will see him [Jesus] as he is").[124] This future revela-

---

124. The text then goes on to urge: "And everyone having this hope in him makes himself holy, as that one is holy." Thus, we see yet another aspect of the apocalyptic scenario in which

tion of Jesus, although not specifically identified as his *parousia*, certainly refers to it implicitly. Also, in 2 John 8, we see an implicit reference to a future time of reward. This too implies the return of Jesus to conduct judgment and to provide reward. This apocalyptic framework so dominates the Letters that the entire context can be said to support these explicit and implicit references to a future coming of Jesus at the time of future reward and punishment. However, it should be noted that at the time of 1 John there is no mention of bodily resurrection.

In the Third Edition

In the third edition, the notion of a return at the end of time is also evident. As was the case in 1 John, this concept is closely connected with the notions of the last day and a final accountability. But in the third edition, there are also frequent explicit references to bodily resurrection.[125]

In John 14:2-3, Jesus says, "In the house of my Father there are many rooms. If not, would I have told you that I go to prepare a place for you? And if I go and prepare a place for you, I will come again and will take you up to myself, so that where I am, you also may be." This mention of departure to prepare a place for the disciples and a return to take them with him presumes the apocalyptic framework of a Second Coming *(parousia)* even though it does not use the term *parousia* itself.[126]

The Background of the Notion of the "Return" of God or His Intermediary

The notion of the return of God's intermediary at the time of final "judgment" is not unique to the New Testament. In the earliest of apocalyptic texts (Daniel 7), the figure of the Son of Man will be present at the final eschatological judgment and so provides a precedent and model for such a "coming" of Jesus.

In the SDQ, the judgment of evil is envisaged in a variety of ways. In some texts, the eschatological judgment will be a transcendent one at the end of time. In CD 8:3, we read that the faithful and the unfaithful will be saved and destroyed respectively in the future by God himself, and the time is described as "That shall be the day when God will visit." This is close to the notion of the "coming" *(parousia)*.

---

the goodness or evil of one's actions will affect one's status before Jesus at his coming. This is discussed as a separate aspect below.

125. The notion of bodily resurrection is also addressed in 3E-37. Here it is treated from the perspective of the apocalyptic framework within which it appears.

126. See the close parallel in 1 Thess 4:14-17.

Section 2. The Criteria Used for the Third Edition

In still other texts, we see evidence of an agent of God who conducts judgment. For example, 11QMelch 18 describes Melchizedek himself as this agent of God in judging all peoples: "[And h]e will, by his strength, judge the holy ones of God, executing judgment as it is written concerning him in the Songs of David . . ." (*DSSE* 361). The notion of a *parousia* is not explicit here but is implied by the fact that Melchizedek is "present" to conduct judgment.

In the *T12P*, the conclusions are ambiguous if we base our investigation only on the use of the word *parousia*. The term *parousia* appears only twice in the *T12P* (*TLev* 8:15; *TJud* 22:2). Of those only the latter can be said to have any kind of eschatological reference. It describes a period in which evil will predominate and the faithful of Israel will suffer ". . . until the savior of Israel comes, until the appearance *(parousia)* of the God of righteousness." However, from the context it is not clear that the time period spoken of is the eschatological one.

However, a clearer sense emerges in *TSim* 6:1-7, which paints a picture of the fulfillment of eschatological hopes in which there will be victory and great peace. *TSim* 6:5 speaks of the appearance of "the Great One of Israel on the earth." This appears in a scene that involves bodily resurrection of the patriarch Simeon (v. 7) and a time when "all the spirits of deception will be given over to be trampled and humans will rule the evil spirits" (v. 6) (cf. 1 John 4:6). The appearance of the Great One of Israel on earth seems intended to be an integral part of the period of peace as well as of the victory over evil spirits. A similar scene appears in *TAsh* 7:1-7, where there is again mention of the time when "the Most High will visit the earth." Although it is likely that these passages contain Christian interpolations, the notion of *parousia* as depicted in these passages differs from the Christian conception, which sees the *parousia* as a "return" of Jesus who had previously been present. Yet, even so, the notion of *parousia* in itself does not connote "return."

Whereas many of the elements of the apocalyptic background of the third edition have their clearest parallels in the SDQ and in the *T12P*, we find no explicit and unambiguous parallels to the use of the term *parousia* itself. However, there are numerous parallels to the use of the term elsewhere in the apocalyptic sections of the New Testament. Matthew speaks of the *parousia* of Jesus in his eschatological discourse, describing it as the "coming" of the Son of Man three times (24:27, 37, 39). In Matt 24:3 it is directly associated with the end of the age; in other texts it is implied (1 Thess 2:19; 3:13; 4:15; 5:23). Paul's First Letter to the Corinthians (15:23) speaks of the resurrection of those who are "of Christ" at his coming.[127] His Second Letter to the Thessalonians (2:1-8) speaks of the coming of the Lord and the destruction of the Lawless One, who is revealed now for a

---

127. The synonymous "Day of the Lord" appears in 1 Thess 5:2; 2 Thess 2:2. 2 Thess 1:10 refers to it simply as "that day."

time.[128] It may be, then, that the term *parousia* was used primarily in Christian circles to refer to the return of Christ to conduct judgment. In any event, its use in this context is widely attested in the New Testament and is always in an apocalyptic context.

3E-17. In the third edition, there is a conviction of a universal accountability (i.e., "judgment," in the neutral sense of the word) at the end of time. This is typical of apocalyptic thought. In the second edition, there was the conviction that judgment (in the negative sense) took place in the present and that the believer would not undergo judgment (2E-21). There is no discussion of judgment in the first edition.[129]

In 2E-21, we saw the conception of judgment found in the second edition. In that conception, the believer receives eternal life and so does not undergo judgment. Moreover, we saw briefly that the third edition contains a conception of a universal judgment (in the neutral sense) on the last day. All believers will undergo this scrutiny and will receive appropriate recompense depending on their deeds. For the third author, these two conceptions of "judgment" could be integrated with one another. Thus, for the third author, the one who believes in the name of Jesus receives life "in the present" and so avoids judgment (i.e., condemnation) that would result from unbelief. However, unlike the second author, the third author held the conviction that it was possible for the believer to continue to sin even after receiving eternal life. Because of this, at the end of time, at the coming of Jesus, when those in the tombs were resurrected, there was to be a final "judgment" (i.e., accounting). In this accounting, those whose deeds were good would have a resurrection of life and those whose deeds were evil would have a resurrection to judgment (i.e., condemnation).

The roots of this notion of "judgment" appear first in 1 John. In 1 John, the author speaks of already being children of God (3:1), of having gone over from death into life (3:14), but at the same time he repeatedly speaks of the idea of a universal accounting at the end of time. For example, there are repeated

---

128. The figure of the Lawless One is parallel to that of the Antichrist of 1 John 2:18, 22; 4:3; 2 John 7.

129. This is not listed as a "characteristic" of the second edition since such present judgment also appears in the third edition. However, future final judgment appears only in the third edition and so is listed as a criterion. On the notion of a development in the presentation of eschatology in the Gospel see particularly Boismard, "L'évolution" 514-18. Boismard treats three themes: judgment, resurrection, and the final return of Christ and shows a development in each. While I would agree that such development exists, I would not agree that it takes the same shape as that proposed by Boismard.

Section 2. The Criteria Used for the Third Edition

references to the "(second) coming" of Jesus (1 John 2:28; implicit in 3:2 and 2 John 8) (3E-16). Implicit in these texts is the notion that the Second Coming is a time of accountability. However, the author of 1 John speaks of that time of accountability in positive terms and encourages the believer to remain faithful so as to be able to have confidence and not shrink from him "in his coming" (2:28). This surely is an implicit reference to the future day of accounting. Other references to Jesus' coming and to his future "revelation" also hint at such an accounting but also teach that the believer should have confidence on that day (cf. 3:2). Only once is a reference to "judgment" explicit, and that is in 1 John 4:17. Yet even here the author is positive in his message and wants the believer to "have confidence on the day of judgment."[130]

The Second Letter of John holds these same convictions and in v. 8 urges the believer to be vigilant so that he/she will "not lose those things which you have worked for, but that you receive a full recompense."

In the third edition of the Gospel, the author holds the same views regarding accountability as the author of 1 John. However, in the third edition there is more talk of judgment as impending condemnation because of guilt. In 3:17, the author says that Jesus was not sent to judge but to save. But he acknowledges that the one who does not believe does not receive eternal life and is "judged" (found guilty) in the very act of unbelief.

In 5:22, we read that the Father has given the power to judge (i.e., to find guilty) to the Son. This is repeated in v. 27 and is attributed to Jesus as the "Son of Man." In v. 29, we read that those who have "practiced evil" will rise from the tombs to a resurrection of judgment." In chapter 6, the third author makes several references to the believer being "raised up on the last day." All of these statements also implicitly refer to accountability on the day when they are raised from the tombs.

In chapter 8, there is a series of remarks about judgment.[131] In v. 16, Jesus speaks of his ability to declare judgment (of guilt) and explains that this ability comes from his oneness with the Father: ". . . if I do judge, my judgment is true because I am not alone." As a result, it can also be said that the Father judges (cf. 8:50) even though, from another perspective, the Father has given all judgment to the Son (5:22). Again in v. 26, Jesus asserts that he has the power to "judge," that is, to declare guilt.

In his conclusion to the story of the man born blind, the third author presents Jesus as the Son of Man, and Jesus declares that he has come for judg-

---

130. Although the *concept* of the final judgment and the last day is the same in the third edition and in the Letters, the *terminology* varies somewhat.

131. In v. 15, the word appears but is used to refer to decisions based on "the flesh" (i.e, on human standards) rather than God's. This is not the characteristic sense of "judgment."

The Third Edition of the Gospel

ment (condemnation) upon those who claim to see but do not. It is as the Son of Man that Jesus had been appointed judge in 5:27, and here he is presented as exercising that function.

The next discussion of "judgment" occurs in 12:31, where the judgment (condemnation) of the world is said to take place. This does not refer to individual judgment but to the apocalyptic overthrow of cosmic evil ("the ruler of this world") that is spoken of in the Synoptics.

In 12:46-50, we see another series of statements about judgment. Again Jesus declares that he has not come to judge but to save (as he had previously in 3:16, 17). But he also declares that the person who does not keep Jesus' words has a judge, and that the words of Jesus will be the judge of the person "on the last day" because his words are not his own but those of the Father. Thus, in a third variation on the theme of Jesus as judge, the third author explains that Jesus' unity with the Father is the reason that Jesus' words are not his own but those of the Father. As a result of this unity of Jesus' words with those of the Father, the words themselves can be said to declare guilty the one who hears the words of Jesus and does not keep them.

Jesus speaks of judgment a final time in 16:8-11. Here the notion of judgment is connected with the cosmic apocalyptic judgment of the ruler of the world, and Jesus promises that the Paraclete will show the world its error with regard to judgment.[132]

3E-18. In the third edition, there are two instances of the term "Kingdom of God." This terminology, so prominent in the Synoptics, appears in the Gospel of John only twice and is due to the apocalyptic worldview of the author of the third edition.

The phrase "Kingdom of God" plays a central role in the Synoptics and is said to be *the* central concept in the teaching of Jesus.[133] The background of the concept is primarily, if not exclusively, apocalyptic. Given the apocalyptic background of the Synoptic Gospels as well as the dominance of this term in them, one must necessarily ask whether its appearance in John is due to editing.

As we will see in the discussion of the Composition of 3:3-10, the relation of the two appearances of the term to their surrounding context is such that they would not immediately appear to be additions. While not every in-

---

132. The apocalyptic background of this conception will be discussed in detail in Part 4, Section 5.

133. Meier (*Marginal* 2:237-506) has studied this concept exhaustively and what follows is based on his work.

Section 2. The Criteria Used for the Third Edition

stance of editing will necessarily leave obvious evidence, the presence of the terms in chapter 3 is quite awkward from an ideological point of view, and this by itself is significant evidence that the terms have been added. Another factor suggesting that they have been added by the author of the third edition is the fact that these occurrences are the only two in the entire Gospel, and both instances are so close together. Elsewhere in the Gospel the third author has a habit of introducing "glosses" into a text repeatedly within a short span of text but then not introducing them again elsewhere (cf. 3E-57F). Other examples include the introduction of ". . . and I will raise that person up on the last day" four times within 6:30-59 but nowhere else. In 8:12-59, he introduces the use of I AM (in the "divine" sense) three times (although the author does use this again in 13:19 and in 18:6). This pattern, together with the term's awkwardness in the context, is reason enough to conclude that it is an addition to the text.

In the Letters

In spite of the apocalyptic orientation of the Letters, the term does not appear there. This is also significant and indicates that it is only the third author who has a concern for the term and may well have introduced it in order to have the Gospel echo the Synoptics.

At Qumran

The importance of the concept in apocalyptic is demonstrated in the scrolls from Qumran. In 1QS there is repeated mention of the "dominion of Satan" in such a way as to indicate that it is conceived of as a period of time, for example, 1:23. In 1QS 2:19, the reference is even more explicit: "Thus shall they do, year by year, for as long as the dominion of Satan endures." Moreover, 1QS 3:23 speaks of "the children of injustice" as "ruled" by the Angel of Darkness. The notions of both "dominion" and "ruling" parallel with other terms the notion of "kingship." Meier suggests that there is no mention of God as exercising kingship here in order to preserve his transcendence.[134] Whether or not this is true, even if the term is not used, the *notion* that people live under the "dominion" of opposing forces is certainly present.

In 1QM, the document that describes the eschatological battle, God is referred to as king several times (1QM 12:8, 19). The kingship of God is referred to in 6:6; 12:7. The notion of "dominion" by good or evil is referred to regularly (1:1; 10:12; 13:11; 14:9; 17:5; 18:1, 11). In short, the notion of such dominion/ruling/

---

134. Meier, *Marginal* 1:266.

The Third Edition of the Gospel

kingdom becomes an important one in the apocalyptic depiction of the opposing "companies" in the eschatological battle.[135]

In the Testaments of the Twelve Patriarchs

Finally, it is not insignificant that the concept also appears in the *T12P*, the other body of literature with so many details in common both with the SDQ and parts of the Gospel and the Letters.

In *TDan* 5:13–6:4, we find a description first of the Holy One of Israel "ruling" *(basileuōn)* over them in humility and poverty. This is contrasted with the enemy, who is Satan and his spirits. The children of Dan are urged to draw near to God and his angel, who will stand in opposition to the kingdom of the enemy *(katenanti tēs basileias tou echthrou)*. This is the dualistic opposition expressed in terms of dominion that we have seen at Qumran.

TBenj 9:1-2 speaks of the "kingdom of the Lord" not being among Benjamin's children because of their sinfulness. But later (10:6-10) Benjamin says that, in the last days, they (his children) will all prostrate themselves before the king (the Lord), who will conduct judgment over all of Israel.

From his survey of the pre–New Testament usage, Meier concludes that "the symbol [of the kingdom of God] was especially prominent in eschatological or apocalyptic contexts, conjuring up hopes of Israel's definitive salvation in the future."[136] The fact that it appears in an apocalyptic sense in the *T12P* and in the SDQ is all the more significant since it is precisely in these (apocalyptic) documents that we find the greatest number of similarities to the usage in the third edition of the Gospel.

3E-19. **Finally, there are other apocalyptic elements that appear in the Gospel, but appear so infrequently that they do not merit separate listing. Nevertheless, they are helpful in recognizing the apocalyptic orientation of the material where they appear. The terms are listed here and commented on briefly.**

"Knowing the Truth"

In the third edition, Jesus speaks of "knowing the truth," an expression implicitly contrasted with "knowing deceit" and characteristic of apocalyptic. This phrase does not appear in the earlier editions.

The phrase appears once in the Gospel and once in 2 John. In 2 John 1, the

---

135. Meier, *Marginal* 1:268-69.
136. Meier, *Marginal* 1:269.

Section 2. The Criteria Used for the Third Edition

phrase "and all those who know the truth" is used to describe the other members of the author's community, who are said to love the Elect Lady and the members of her community. In John 8:32, the term is complexive of the entire message of Jesus and is addressed to those who "remain in his word."

Both de la Potterie[137] and Charlesworth[138] argue that the background of this phrase is to be found in apocalyptic. The earliest appearance is in Tob 5:14 (LXX-S). As de la Potterie points out, while 5:14 may appear to have the simple meaning of knowing the identity of his angelic visitor, when this is read in the context of 12:11, it becomes evident that the meaning is more complex and refers to an apocalyptic revelation. De la Potterie also points out that all the significant vocabulary in 12:11 (the verse that gives the fuller understanding of 5:14) is apocalyptic.

1 Enoch 106:7-13 also provides parallels of the apocalyptic usage where the knowledge to be gained is given in a revelatory experience.

In the SDQ, the theme of knowing the truth occurs frequently (1QH 10:6; 14:12; 15:26; 17:35; 18:20, 29; 19:9-10; 1QS 9:17, 18). In 1QH 14:12, the exact phrase appears: the clause, "All the nations will know your truth . . . ," appears in synonymous parallelism with "all the peoples, your glory" and is used as a general reference to revelation.[139]

Doing the Truth (Gk. poiein tēn alētheian)

As it is used in the Johannine literature, this phrase is used exclusively in a dualistic context characteristic of apocalyptic.[140] It appears in John 3:21, and in a related expression in 8:44 and in 1 John 1:6. In each of these texts, it is used dualistically to contrast with doing evil deeds (3:21) or with lying (8:44; 1 John 1:6).

The "Wrath" of God

It was common in apocalyptic to speak of the "wrath of God" as a feature of the final judgment by God. God's wrath was not thought of as being revealed *only* at the final judgment. It was capable of present manifestation also.

---

137. De la Potterie, *Vérité* 1:541-45.

138. Charlesworth, "Scrolls/Jesus" 75. Charlesworth cites 1QH 6:12; 9:35; 10:20, 29 as significant parallels.

139. This section of 1QH has a number of parallels to the dualistic language of John, including reference to atonement, "deeds done in truth," "knowing truth," and "knowing glory."

140. The qualification here is a significant one. I do not claim that the term is used exclusively in apocalyptic circles. A very similar expression appears in the OT. See de la Potterie, *Vérité* 2:480-82.

The Third Edition of the Gospel

Only once in the Gospel is there mention of the "wrath" of God, and this appears in conjunction with other features that identify it with the scene of future apocalyptic judgment. John 3:36 speaks of life and of judgment. It begins by affirming that the believer has eternal life (in the present) but then also states that the one who does not obey the Son *will not* see life (in a future sense), thus affirming a future dimension that is distinct from the present. It then goes on to say that the "wrath of God" awaits that person *(menei ep' auton)*. As is explained in the Note on 3:36, the use of the accusative with the preposition here also indicates a future dimension to this wrath, thus linking the entire verse with the apocalyptic notion of God's wrath revealed in final judgment. This image of wrath does not appear in the Johannine Letters.

Elsewhere in the New Testament, the conception of the "wrath" of God confirms this picture. Although the anger of God can be manifested in the present (e.g., Rom 1:18; 1 Thess 2:16; Heb 3:8, quoting Ps 95:9), in the New Testament it is more commonly associated with the day of eschatological judgment (e.g., Matt 3:7; Luke 3:7; 21:23; Rom 2:5, 8; 3:5; 5:9; Eph 2:3; 1 Thess 1:10; 5:9). It also is common in contexts where the rewards of the just and the punishment of the unjust are described (e.g., Matt 3:7-10; Rom 3:5-8; Eph 2:3-6).[141]

Eph 5:6 speaks of the wrath of God coming upon the disobedient (... *erchetai hē orgē tou theou epi tous huious tēs apeitheias*) in a way very similar to the present instance.[142]

This eschatological wrath is also evident in the SDQ. In 1QS 4:11-12, it is said that the lot of those who walk in darkness will be to experience "everlasting damnation by the avenging wrath of the fury of God . . ." (*DSSE*⁴ 74). CD 2:7 speaks of the patience and forgiveness of God to those who turn from sin but "power, might, and great flaming wrath at the hand of all the Angels of Destruction" (*DSSE*⁴ 98) to those who do not obey the covenant.[143] The wrath of God is also manifested within history, as when it was unleashed against the idols of Egypt (1QM 14:1). The notion of eschatological wrath does not play a role in the T12P.

---

141. Barrett, *Gospel* 227. MacGregor ("Wrath" 101-9) points out that of the thirteen Pauline passages where wrath appears, eight use the term in connection with the judgment of the last day (Rom 2:5; 3:5; 5:9; 12:19; 1 Thess 1:10; 5:9; Col 3:6, and Eph 5:6). In two others, the reference is probable but not certain (Rom 4:15; Eph 2:3), and in only two does it seem to also have a component directed to the present time, although even there the eschatological aspect is present (Rom 1:18; 1 Thess 2:16). In a final text, the wrath is spoken of as "postponed" (Rom 9:22 [103-4]).

142. There is in fact considerable similarity between a number of aspects of the language and thought of Eph 5:6-14 and those of John 3:19-21, 36, indicating their common dualistic/apocalyptic worldview.

143. See also CD 8:15.

Section 2. The Criteria Used for the Third Edition

"Walking"

In the third edition, the verb *peripateō* has a meaning that does not appear in the earlier editions.

In the Gospel, the verb *peripateō* appears seventeen times. It has two meanings: (1) a general one meaning simply "to walk, or walk about," without a particular connotation; (2) a more restricted meaning in which it is associated with words symbolic of Jesus' ministry. The general meaning appears in all three editions (the first [1:36; 5:8, 9; 6:19; 11:54], second [5:11, 12; 10:23], and third [7:1 {twice}; 21:18]) editions. However, the special meaning appears only in the third edition (i.e., walking "in the darkness" [8:12; 12:35], "in the day" [11:9], "in the night" [11:10], and "in the light" [12:35]). The instance in 6:66, where it is a synonym for being a disciple ("[many of the disciples] no longer walked with him"), should probably be grouped with this also.

This usage also appears frequently in the Letters. There it is used in the expressions to walk "in darkness" (1 John 1:6; 2:11), "in the light" (1 John 1:7), and "in truth" (2 John 4, 6; 3 John 3, 4 ["in *the* truth"]) and also as a description of how one is to act ("it is necessary to walk as he walked," 1 John 2:6; "in order that we may walk according to the commandments," 2 John 6).

While there is no specific theological meaning associated with the word itself in this usage, its usage is significant in that it is associated (in the third edition and in the Letters) with a dualistic worldview. Again, the consistency of usage in the Gospel helps confirm in retrospect the accuracy of the analysis.

References to Demonic Possession

Another of the apocalyptic features of the third edition is the mention of demon possession. The notion of such possession played a central role in the apocalyptic presentation of the Synoptics (and elsewhere). This is not found in the first two editions of the Gospel of John.

Even in the third edition, there are no accounts of demon possession or of exorcisms in the Gospel. However, there are several references to it. In 7:20, there is a brief allusion to it in the crowd's statement that Jesus is possessed by a demon. In 8:48-49, "the Jews" claim that Jesus is a Samaritan and possessed. This sentiment is expressed again in 8:52. In 10:20-21, there is a division among the people of Judea, and they exclaim that Jesus is possessed, but others deny it. This instance presents particular problems that suggest there is a mixing of material from the first and third editions. This is discussed in more detail in the analysis of the Composition of the verses in the Commentary. In 13:27, it is said that Satan entered into Judas, a final reference to demonic possession.

3. Literary Characteristics

In material of the third edition, two features seem to be described best as "literary characteristics." They have to do neither with terminology nor with narrative orientation, nor are they theological. But they are consistently associated with material of the third edition.

3E-20. In the third edition, there are a number of instances where, without explanation, the plural of the first- and second-person pronouns is introduced in contexts where the singular had been previously used and where the singular would be expected.

In the third edition, in contexts where the singular of pronouns had been used previously, the author frequently and unexpectedly introduces the plural of the first-person pronoun (from "I" to "we") and the second-person pronoun (from singular "you" to plural "you") without explanation. This sudden shift suggests that the speaker is no longer a single individual (typically Jesus) but a group (the Johannine community), and the addressee is no longer the single individual previously addressed but now a group (the community?). What makes the situation more complex is the fact that this does not happen every time there is direct address in the third edition, yet it does happen frequently enough that it emerges as a distinctive feature of the Gospel's third edition.

In 1:50-51, there are two additions to the end of the scene in which the first disciples come to Jesus. In v. 50, Jesus addresses Nathanael using the second-person singular four times. But in v. 51, without explanation, the second-person plural is introduced and appears twice — after the verse begins with the singular: "Amen, amen, I say to you [sing.], you [pl.] will see the sky opened up...." Other features mark the verse as coming from the last edition; yet the purpose of the change is not clear.[144]

In 3:7, Jesus begins by speaking in the singular ("I") to a singular "you," but when quoting himself he unexplainably shifts to the plural of the addressee: "Do not be surprised [sing. imperative] that I said to you [sing.], 'It is necessary for you (plural) to be born again.'" A further peculiarity is that the

---

144. Bultmann (*Gospel* 105), Barrett (*Gospel* 186), and Schnackenburg (*Gospel* 1:318) are among those who think that the saying is addressed to all the disciples. But this is unlikely since there is no indication that anyone other than Nathanael is present. Fortna (*Predecessor* 44) rightly notes the presence of the plural here and in 4:48 and attributes it to the Evangelist. When all such instances are viewed together and in conjunction with other features that appear consistently with it, this explanation becomes more difficult to sustain.

Section 2. The Criteria Used for the Third Edition

singular returns in the next verse (v. 8) but then the use of the plural returns soon after, in v. 11.[145]

John 3:11 begins "Amen, amen, I [sing.] say to you [sing.], that we [pl.] say what we [pl.] know, and we [pl.] bear witness to what we [pl.]) have seen, and (all of) you [pl.] do not accept our [pl.] witness." R. E. Brown reviews various attempts to explain the plural here (plural of majesty, joining of words of Jesus and the Father).[146] I am inclined to think that Jesus is (as Brown puts it) "slipping into a dialogue between the church ('we') and the Synagogue ('you')." However, I would modify this to say that it is a dialogue between the community and the former members of the community who are the opponents in 1 John. This is an admittedly imperfect solution since the speaker returns to the singular in the following verse.[147] However, it has the benefit of being both reasonable and consistent even if it does not fully account for the later return to the singular.[148]

John 3:12 then complicates the matter even more. It returns to the singular of the speaker but continues the plural of the addressee: "If I [sing.] have spoken to you [pl.] about earthly realities and you [pl.] do not believe, how will you [pl.] believe if I [sing.] speak to you [pl.] about heavenly realities?"

Together the two plurals occur a total of ten times! The larger section of which these verses are a part extends from v. 11 to v. 21 and is marked by several other features of the third edition, notably the title "Son of Man" (vv. 13, 14), various theological features ("unique" as a designation for the son, the son sent to "save") plus the characteristic dualism of light and darkness used in an ethical sense, "works" used in the sense of ethical actions, and the dualistic phrase "works done in God." These will be discussed in detail in the Commentary.

---

145. The plural *oidamen* is used by Nicodemus in 3:2, but here it *is* reasonable to conclude that Nicodemus is speaking as a representative of a group of religious authorities; he is stating the common opinion of the religious authorities. R. E. Brown (*Gospel* 1:131) suggests that the plural in v. 7 returns to this plural audience, but that does not explain the awkwardness of the shift within the verse from the singular to the plural — and the return to the singular in the surrounding verses.

146. R. E. Brown, *Gospel* 1:132.

147. R. E. Brown (*Gospel* 1:132) suggests that v. 11 is a continuation of the rebuttal of Nicodemus from v. 10 and that, as v. 10 took over the term "teacher" from v. 2 and now applied it to Nicodemus, so in v. 11 the Evangelist takes over the "we know" of Nicodemus and turns it around, now with "we" as the speaker. There are two problems with this explanation. First, the problem of who "we" now refers to remains; second, that there is such a switch here in v. 11 would not carry much meaning. Further, it is difficult to see this as a "parody" of Nicodemus's arrogance, as Brown proposes.

148. This is also the solution adopted by Bernard (*Gospel* 1:110). Barrett (*Gospel* 211) says, "The community of those who have been born of water and Spirit addresses the synagogue."

The Third Edition of the Gospel

In 4:48, Jesus uses the plural when he addresses the official whose son is ill: "Unless you [pl.] see signs and wonders, you [pl.] do not believe." Again the appearance of the plural is sudden and without explanation. The verse also contains the unique phrase "signs and wonders" as a designation for miracles. We must suppose that the verse has been added by the author of the third edition and was intended to relativize faith based simply on the miraculous.[149]

In 9:4, there is a mixture of singular and plural for the speaker. Jesus speaks of himself but first uses the first-person plural and then later the first-person singular: "It is necessary for us [pl.] to work the works of the one who sent me [sing.]."[150] This usage is quite similar to that of 3:7, including beginning the sentence with *dei* ("It is necessary . . .") and then following with *hēmas* (you, pl.) followed by the infinitive. Once again the fact that the verse comes from the last edition is confirmed by other features from the third edition, as explained in the Commentary.[151]

These six instances are the clearest and most striking in that there is no apparent reason (intrinsic to the context) for the shift.[152] But in addition to these, there are other instances of the plural that deserve attention. The first of these is in the Prologue. "We" is used there (1:14 [twice], 16), although its introduction is not disruptive as it is in the instances mentioned above. Since there had been no speaker before, there is no problem with the Prologue beginning with the plural. Yet this occurrence is so similar to the ones discussed above

---

149. R. E. Brown (*Gospel* 1:131), Schnackenburg (*Gospel* 1:466), Barrett (*Gospel* 247), and others suggest that it addresses all the Galileans mentioned in 4:45. The envisioning of a larger audience is more plausible here than in the case of either 1:51 or 3:7, 11, 12. But this explanation is still awkward, given the fact that the man is not portrayed elsewhere as a symbol of a group — except by those who think that he is a Gentile and represents a Gentile faith. But there is really no evidence in the Gospel that he is intended as such a symbol (see Commentary).

150. Bernard (*Gospel* 2:326) adopts the singular reading throughout, although this can no longer be substantiated on textual grounds. See Metzger, *Commentary* ad locum.

151. Bultmann (*Gospel* 331, n. 7) thinks that originally the verse contained the singular in both places but that it was altered by the Evangelist to fashion a more universal principle and thus avoid what he sees as the scandal caused by the possibility of Jesus being limited by the "night." Barrett (*Gospel* 357) again sees it as the voice of the community.

152. There are three other possible candidates for such a shift in grammatical number, but on closer inspection they are not of the same type. John 4:22 contains the plural, but in this case it seems clear that Jesus is speaking in the plural by associating himself with the remainder of observant Jews. In 14:11-14, there is also a shift from the singular to the plural. However, the Farewell Discourses are regularly addressed to the listeners in the plural, and when a single disciple asks a question, the response begins in the singular and then returns to the plural.

In 20:2, when Mary Magdalene speaks to Peter, she says that "we" do not know where they have taken Jesus' body. The change here seems unlikely to be an echo of the "voice of the community." While it may simply be a random and unmeaningful shift, it could be seen as a relic of a source in which Mary Magdalene had come to the tomb with others.

Section 2. The Criteria Used for the Third Edition

that it seems to provide a possible explanation for the more puzzling ones: it seems to function as the "voice of the community."[153]

Finally, toward the close of chapter 21, the plural again appears (21:24). Here it is (as it was in the Prologue) the voice of the community that seems to be represented. It is not the author or the witness to the tradition himself since the verse testifies about the veracity of the BD.

Throughout the discussion of the features of the third edition, attention has been called to parallels between the third edition and 1 John. Such similarity exists even here. The First Letter of John is dominated by the use of "we" by the author. Examples are too numerous to list. But throughout the first chapter the author speaks in the first-person plural, and it is not until 2:1 that the first-person singular appears. After that, the two alternate, but the singular is used almost entirely in expressions dealing with the writing of the Epistle and the plural is consistently used to refer to the witness being borne about the various convictions of the author's community. Yet even here the meaning of the "we" is disputed.[154] It refers, however, to a group within the author's community who have authority and who are able to address the "you" (pl.) of the addressees through the voice of the Elder. Although the nature of the evidence is such that one cannot prove conclusively that the same motive lies behind the use of the plural in 1 John, in the Prologue and Epilogue of the Gospel, and in the anomalous occurrences in material of the third edition, this seems to be the most reasonable and the most consistent conclusion.

3E-21. In the third edition, there are a number of instances where terminology characteristic of the first and second editions is mixed with features of the third edition.

There are a limited number of places in the Gospel where terminology that is otherwise used consistently within a given edition is mixed with terminology from another edition. Here we must distinguish the terminology that pertains to narrative from that which pertains to theology.

We have already seen that the author of the third edition shared many views with the author of the second edition and so adopted much of his theological terminology. This should not be considered "mixing" — this is simply an indication of the numerous ways in which the third edition built upon the work of

---

153. Schnackenburg (*Gospel* 1:270) identifies them as "those who saw the glory of the incarnate Logos — the witnesses, in fact, of his work on earth. . . ."

154. There are a variety of understandings of "we" in the First Epistle. R. E. Brown (*Epistles* 158-61) summarizes the approaches. Brown himself favors the view that it refers to the members of the author's community.

the second edition. These were, after all, members of the same community and the same tradition. Yet, in passages from the third edition, even if much of the theological background is that of the second edition, the third author will nuance the views of the second edition by means of his own distinctive additions.

However, there are several instances where this mixing uses terminology in ways that indicate a true inconsistency. These passages are the work of the third author throughout. A listing of the instances follows with a brief description. Full details are given in the Commentary.[155] This technique was mentioned in the Introduction (Section F.4.b, above). There it was pointed out that this is not simply a *deus ex machina* intended to solve the unsolvable. This is a "consistent inconsistency" that follows a pattern and gives every indication of being a true feature of the third author's work.

In 4:1, *kyrios* (typical of the third edition) appears in the initial temporal clause, but elsewhere in vv. 1-4 the characteristics are those of the first edition. This verse presents a clear example of the kind of startling mixture typical of the third author — and his use of the theologically distinctive use of "Lord." Notice also the resulting awkwardness of sentence structure.

After meeting the crowd that has crossed the lake to Capernaum, Jesus speaks (6:26-29) of their "not seeing signs." This term, which is characteristic of the first edition, appears here in association with several features of the third edition (e.g., the "Son of Man" as title; Jesus "giving" rather than "being" the bread; the dualistic use of "works").

In the so-called "Eucharistic addition" to the Bread-of-Life discourse (6:51-58), the interlocutors are identified as "the Jews." Yet the theological and ideological content of the verses is that of the third edition.

In 7:19, there is what might be called an "ideological aporia." In this verse, the crowd manifests ignorance of attempts to kill Jesus. Yet the chapter had begun with just such a general notice (cf. 7:1 — 2E). Moreover, the crowd had expressed fear of speaking openly about Jesus in 7:13 (also 2E). This verse, however, expresses ignorance of such attempts. Moreover, it introduces the notion of demonic possession, something typical of apocalyptic and the third edition. This suggests that the verse is somehow a bridge between the material of the second edition before and after it.

John 7:25 employs the unique expression "Jerusalemites" *(Ierosolymitōn)* and a reference to the attempts to kill Jesus (elsewhere by "the Jews" this early in the Gospel) but mixes them with the description of the authorities as "rulers"

---

155. I have included here all instances where terminology is mixed in material of the third edition. The next criterion in the list distinguishes a particular form of mixing that deals with the use of terms for religious authorities. Those instances are also included here as a form of the more general mixing.

Section 2. The Criteria Used for the Third Edition

(typical of the first edition) in v. 27 and also describes Jesus as speaking openly without response from the religious authorities. This also is inconsistent with the surrounding context and is probably from the author of the third edition. It is likely that those verses, together with v. 19 (described immediately above), are literary sutures by the author of the third edition, attempting to attach vv. 19-24 to the context both before and after it.

John 8:12-13 are an insertion at the beginning of the discourse on the witness value of the word of Jesus. In these two verses there is a mixture of the terms "light," "darkness," and "light of life" (characteristic of the third edition) with a response using "the Pharisees" (characteristic of the first edition) and "witness" (characteristic, in this usage, of the second). However, beginning in v. 14 the material exhibits a consistent pattern of language and thought from the second edition. It is likely that the author of the third edition has chosen to insert this proclamation on the part of Jesus at the beginning of the discourse in order to present it as the cause of the debate about the witness value of Jesus' words.

In 8:30-31 there appears to be a formulaic statement of belief ("many believed in him," a phrase typical of the first edition), but what follows is not from the first edition. First, the belief is based on the word of Jesus rather than on his signs, as is the case elsewhere in the first edition. Second, in v. 31, Jesus is said to speak with those who believed in him, who are identified as "the Jews." Third, in the remainder of the chapter "the Jews" are the most hostile of opponents, and within five verses they are said to be seeking to kill him. The author of the third edition has probably created this awkward combination in order to address specific problems of belief at the time of the community's internal crisis.

In 8:38-52, 55d-58, the editing is complex. However, it becomes evident that the author of the third edition has introduced the apocalyptic viewpoint here and made substantive additions. Because of the extent of the material, it is not possible to discuss the passage in detail, but the editing is particularly evident in 8:38-47, where the author introduces an extended discussion of "parentage" according to a stereotyped apocalyptic pattern. Moreover, he focuses on the theme of "keeping the word" of Jesus, a theological theme of the third author. Yet, at the same time, the third author uses the term "the Jews," otherwise characteristic of the third edition. Details are given in the Commentary.

The verses that make up 9:35-41 come from the third edition and are appended to the previous material of the first edition. Here the third author again takes up "the Pharisees," terminology typical of the first edition, but uses it in a context where the remainder of the material is typical of the third edition.[156]

In 12:23, the third author employs the term "hour" from the second edition as the designation of the divinely appointed time for the glorification of

---

156. The detailed justification for this attribution is given in the Commentary.

The Third Edition of the Gospel

the Son of Man. In the second edition material which follows the insertion of 12:23-26 (3E), the author had used the notion of "hour" twice as the specification of the end of the public ministry, and it is very likely that, given his acquaintance with the notion, the third author chooses to use this term to designate the appointed end of Jesus' ministry as a kind of proleptic reference to vv. 27-30. This would not be a significant irregularity since, as we have seen, the third author had regularly made use of the notion of "hour" as part of his larger conception (e.g., 11:9; cf. 9:4-5).

John 12:42-43 are a particularly difficult case. In v. 42, the authorities are identified as "rulers" and appear in a stereotyped expression of belief. Another group of religious authorities is identified as "Pharisees." All of these are characteristics of the first edition. But then the verse takes a sudden turn and these authorities are said not to "confess" lest "they be expelled from the synagogue" (both of these features are characteristic of the second edition). The resulting sentence structure is awkward. In the second edition, the verses probably had another form, and they have been blended together by the author of the third edition in order to serve as a transition to vv. 44-50, verses that have been inserted by the author of the third edition.

Finally, there is 18:36-38. As will be pointed out in more detail in the discussion of the Composition of these verses, the majority of the material reflects the third edition, yet the term "the Jews" is used to refer to the religious authorities.

It was suggested at the beginning of this analysis that the usage of language, concepts, and ideology was very consistent in each of the three editions. These twelve passages appear to be the only passages in the Gospel where the terms associated with narrative from various strata are mixed. But even here the occurrence of these inconsistencies seems to be somewhat consistent and to indicate that rather than being indications that the criteria are incorrect, the criteria are so consistent that such mixing becomes obvious and is itself a feature of the editorial work of the author of the third edition.

3E-22. A distinctive pattern of mixing terminology appears in the case of the terms for religious authorities. In the third edition, the author, who does not have a distinctive term for religious authorities, uses whichever term has been used most recently. This contrasts with the use in the second edition, where the author substitutes his own term ("the Jews") for the terminology of the first edition.

The author does not always adopt the terminology of the same edition, for example, that of the second edition, as we might expect, but rather adopts whatever terminology had been used most recently. Thus, while the third author is directly concerned with providing his distinctive theological perspective, he

Section 2. The Criteria Used for the Third Edition

was apparently content to take over the terminology of earlier editions for the narrative. This occurs eight times in the Gospel.

In 6:52, the third author uses "the Jews" in a passage appended to material of the second edition in 6:30-50. In 8:13, he employs the term "Pharisees," which follows material of the first edition from 7:52. Yet in the remainder of chapter 8 (8:31, 48, 52, 57), where he is modifying material from the second edition, he uses the term "the Jews," which is taken over from the surrounding material of the second edition. In 9:35-41, which is appended to material of the first edition, he uses the term "Pharisees." In 12:42 the context is obscured by editing, but it appears that the original material had been from the first edition.

3E-23. In the third edition, there are a number of topics or terms that are developed only minimally but which are developed in greater detail in 1 John. Not only does the recognition of this fact help to confirm that 1 John was written prior to the third edition of the Gospel, but at times it provides valuable background for the meaning of a term.

The fact that a number of terms and topics are developed more fully in 1 John than in the Gospel is an indication that the third author presumed knowledge of the thought of 1 John. In the first group of instances below, our understanding of the use of the term in the Gospel is aided by an examination of its use in 1 John because the context is more developed there. In the second group, our understanding is not necessarily improved by a review of the usage in 1 John, but it becomes clear that the use of the term is more widespread there.

Group 1

A "New" Commandment

In John 13:34-35, Jesus speaks of the "new" commandment of mutual love. In what sense this is intended to be "new" is not clear from the context of the brief insertion in the Gospel. However, in 1 John 2:8, the discussion of the "new" commandment is part of a larger discussion in which the author explains that the commandment is *not* new, but an *old* one that they had had "from the beginning." But then the author went on to explain that the commandment was also "new" in the sense that, from the point of view of 1 John, it had only recently been realized in the ministry of Jesus and had begun to be realized in the lives of believers. Thus once again the notion as expressed in the third edition depends on 1 John for a presentation of the full paradigm within which the concept is cast.

The Third Edition of the Gospel

Spirit of Truth

In the third edition, the title "Spirit of Truth" is used three times as a description of the Paraclete/Spirit (14:17; 15:26; 16:13). While the title itself suggests that it is one half of the dualistic pair, the other of which is the "Spirit of Deception," the use of it alone in the Gospel is an incomplete paradigm. However, in 1 John 4:1-6, we find the complete paradigm, involving both the Spirit of Truth and the Spirit of Deception.

The notion of "Paraclete" as applied to the Spirit is new in the third edition, but here we are focusing on the title "Spirit of Truth," which did appear first in 1 John. In the third edition, this title appears more frequently and in a more developed way than it had in 1 John, but the paradigm of contrasting spirits appears only in 1 John and so provides the foundation for the usage in the third edition.

Righteousness

In the third edition of the Gospel, the notion of "righteousness" appears only in 16:8 and in the explanation in 16:10.[157] Yet the noun appears three times in 1 John (2:29; 3:7, 10), always in reference to the believer who "does righteousness" and who is then said to be born of God (2:29) and to be "righteous" as God is righteous (3:7). In 3:10, the one not "doing righteousness" is said not to be "of God," and this person is also said to be the one who does not love his brother. The adjective *dikaios* appears five times, twice as a description of Jesus (1:9; 2:1), twice as a description of God (2:29; 3:7), and once as a description of the believer (3:7).

Given the more extensive development of the notion in 1 John, we are better able to understand what it means when the author of the third edition says that the Paraclete will prove the world wrong about righteousness (see the Note to 16:8 and the Interpretation of the relevant verses in the Commentary).

Conquest/Conquer

In the third edition of the Gospel, the notion of "conquering"/"conquest" appears only in 16:33, where it is said that Jesus has conquered the world. In 1 John, the concept occurs more frequently (2:13, 14; 4:4; 5:4 [twice], 5). The key to understanding the concept in 1 John is to be found in 4:4c, which says,

---

157. The adjective "righteous" *(dikaios)* is attributed to God in 17:25 (in material of the third edition). It also appears in 5:30 and in 7:24, where it is used as a description of a judgment that is "just." These latter two instances, which are not attributes of a person, do not belong to the same usage.

Section 2. The Criteria Used for the Third Edition

"You have conquered them because he who is in you is greater than he who is in the world." He who is in the "world" is "the Evil One" (cf. 2:13, 14). Consequently, since believers have conquered "them" (4:4) and since "they" have gone out into the world (4:1d) and are "of the world" (4:5), believers can be said to have also conquered "the world" and "the Evil One." This, then, presents the paradigm of what is conquered and how one conquers. It is an apocalyptic concept.

In the Gospel, this paradigm is reflected in the single statement in 16:33, where Jesus says that he has conquered the world.

Liar/Lying

In the Gospel (8:44), there are three references to the devil as the one who "speaks the Lie," as "a liar," and as "the Father of Lying"; these — and the related instance in 8:55 — are the only references to lying in the Gospel. Yet, in 1 John, the topic of "the Liar" who opposes the truth was a significant, and dualistically oriented, theme and appears in 1:10; 2:4, 22; 4:20; 5:10. In addition, the verb "to lie" appears in 1:6 and the etymologically related "lying prophet" (Gk. *pseudoprophētēs*, usually translated "false prophet") appears in 4:1.

In 1 John 1:6, lying is contrasted with "doing the truth." In 1:10, the opponents who claim they have not sinned are said to make God a liar! In 2:4, the one who does not keep the commandments is said to be a liar and not to have the truth in him. In 2:22, "the Liar" is the one who denies that Jesus is the Christ. In 4:1, the "lying prophets" do not have the Spirit of God. In 4:20, the one who claims to love God but hates his brother is a liar. Finally, the one who does not accept the witness of the Son makes God a liar.

When we realize the extent to which the notion of "lying" permeates 1 John, we are in a better position to recognize the reason for its incorporation into the work of the third author in chapter 8.

Evil (Gk. ponēros)

The word *ponēros* occurs only three times in the Gospel — 3:19; 7:7; and 17:15 — although it appears five times in 1 John and once each in 2 John and 3 John. While these absolute numbers may not appear to be substantially greater in 1, 2, and 3 John, when we consider the relative size of the documents involved, it becomes clear that the usage in the Letters is considerably greater relative to the size of the Gospel.

In the third edition, the word *ponēros* ("evil") appears three times. Each time it is in the context of apocalyptic dualism.

While a term appearing only three times in the Gospel is not of major im-

The Third Edition of the Gospel

portance, what makes the use of *ponēros* in the third edition significant is the fact that its use echoes the more extensive usage in 1 John and reflects one of that author's basic paradigms for articulating his dualistic view of humanity.

In John 3:19 (3E), the third author speaks of *erga ponēra* ("evil works") as preventing a person from coming to the light. In 7:7 (3E), Jesus witnesses against the world that its deeds *(erga)* are evil *(ponēra)*. In 17:15 (3E), Jesus prays that the Father may keep the disciples from the Evil One *(ek tou ponērou)*. Thus, both deeds are seen as evil and, implicitly, they are derived from domination by the Evil One.[158]

However, the paradigm for this usage appears in the Letters, in 1 John 3:12, where it is said that Cain was "of the Evil One" *(tou ponērou)*, and killed his brother "because his [Cain's] works were evil" *(hoti ta erga autou ponēra ēn)*. This is another version of the stereotyped paradigm, common in 1 John, where one's actions reveal one's allegiance.

Elsewhere in 1 John, *ho ponēros* is used as a term for the embodiment of evil (i.e., the Evil One). In 1 John 2:13, 14, the Elder had written to the young people of the community that they had conquered the Evil One. In 3:12, Cain was said to be "of" the Evil One *(ek tou ponērou)*, and his deeds *(erga)* were evil *(ponēra)*. In 5:18-19, it is said that evil *(ponēros)* will not take hold of the believer but that the whole world lies in the grip of the Evil One *(ponēros)*.

In 2 John 11, anyone who gave a greeting to or accepted an opponent took part in his evil deeds *(ergois ponērois)*. In 3 John 8, Diotrephes slanders the Elder with evil words *(logois ponērois)*.

This usage does not appear in either of the other editions, where the term *kakos* is used both in the first (18:23) and in the second (18:30).

Group 2

Jesus Christ

This title has been treated as a linguistic marker in 3E-2. There it was pointed out that the combination appears much more frequently in 1 John than in the Gospel — and that where it appears in the Gospel it is in the third edition. Further details are given in the discussion of 3E-2.

---

158. It is not claimed here that the word *ponēros* is intrinsically associated with the apocalyptic worldview, but only that it appears exclusively in an apocalyptic context in the Johannine literature.

Section 2. The Criteria Used for the Third Edition

Brother (adelphos)

The use of "brother" (in the religious sense) has been discussed in detail in 3E-4 as a linguistic characteristic of the third edition. It is noted here as an instance of a term used frequently in 1 John and incorporated into the Gospel at the time of the third edition.

Child/Little Child (teknon/teknion)

The use of "child" and "little child" (always in the plural) has been discussed in detail in 3E-5 as a linguistic characteristic of the third edition. It is noted here as an instance of a term used frequently in 1 John and incorporated into the Gospel at the time of the third edition.

4. Theological Characteristics

It is evident that the theological characteristics of each edition echo the central purpose of the author's work. They contain his views on a number of issues and aspects of the life and message of Jesus that he considered integral to a full understanding of the Christian life.

Here we will treat first those theological features that are distinctive of the third edition and that do not appear in any of the earlier editions. After that we will treat a limited number of theological features introduced by the author of the second edition but taken over by the author of the third. Although the features treated first are sufficiently distinctive to be able to be used as criteria, this listing should not be thought of as a complete description of the theology of the third edition. That will be given in the general survey of the theology of the third edition, which will appear in Section 2 below.

3E-24. In the third edition, the ministry of Jesus is conceptualized as being composed of "day" (the public ministry) and "night" (the Passion). This enables the author of the third edition to take up the theme of the "hour" of Jesus from the second edition and to integrate it with the concepts of "light" and "darkness" typical of his apocalyptic viewpoint.

The author of the third edition takes over the notion of the "hour" as an indication of the divinely ordained time of his Passion and Death from the second edition and incorporates it into a remarkably complex symbolic framework. First, the author introduces the dualistic contrast between "light" and "darkness."¹⁵⁹ This imagery of light and darkness together with "hour" then leads to a secondary framework of the "day" *(hēmera)* (9:4; 11:9 [twice]) and "night" *(nyx)* (9:4; 11:10; 13:30). Thus, the "day" is the period in which Jesus will work (9:4) and is composed of "twelve hours" (11:9). But when the "night" comes, Jesus will not work (9:4). Just as the Father has determined the coming of the "night," so the Father has determined the first "hour" of the "day" — and so Jesus cannot respond to the wishes of his mother at the wedding in Cana, but to the coming of his "hour." In relation to the day, Jesus describes himself as "the light of the world" *(to phōs tou kosmou)* (8:12; 9:5), a play on words echoing a common expression for the sun.

Second, in 11:5, Jesus speaks of there being twelve hours in the day, when the "light of this world shines," but he also says that night is coming when no one is able to work — a reference to his coming Passion (cf. 9:4; cf. 11:10). The arrival of the Passion after the departure of Judas is then symbolically announced by the author's statement in 13:30: "It was night."

It is important to notice that, in the second edition, there is only one "hour" appointed for Jesus by the Father: the hour of the Passion. But when the notion of the "hour" is taken up by the author of the third edition, he modifies it to refer to the twelve "hours" in the day. Thus for the third author there are several "hours" as opposed to the single hour of the Passion for the second author (cf. also 12:23).

The complex of associations made up of light, darkness; day, night; twelve hours; and light of the world are built up of symbols taken from apocalyptic and related to the theme of the "hour" of Jesus from the second edition. Together they provide one dimension of the overarching (and fully developed) structural framework of the Gospel in the third edition.¹⁶⁰ As will be seen in the analysis of the individual passages, all of these terms appear consistently and exclusively in the material of the third edition.

3E-25. **In the third edition, the overarching structure echoes that of 1 John, where the first part of the letter focuses on the proclamation of God as light and the second focuses on the proclamation to love one another. Thus, in the first half of the (third edition of the) Gospel (i.e., the public ministry), Jesus is presented as**

---

159. This contrast of "light" and "darkness" is discussed in 3E-8.

160. It will be noted that the image of Jesus as "light" (with its correlative "darkness") is only one element of the overarching structure of the third edition, one that structures the public ministry. The other element is Jesus as the embodiment of love, an element that structures the second half of the Gospel. For a discussion of the structure of the third edition, see Part 3, Section 3.1 below.

Section 2. The Criteria Used for the Third Edition

the light of the world. In the second half of the Gospel (i.e., the Passion and Resurrection), Jesus is presented as loving his own even to death.

This is discussed in Part 3, Section 3.1 ("The Structure of the Third Edition") and Section 3.4.a.(2) ("The Structure of 1 John and That of the Third Edition"). The verses involved are (1) Jesus as the Light: 3:19-21; 8:12; 9:4-5; 11:9-10; 12:35-36, 46; 13:30; (2) Jesus' demonstration of love: 10:15-17; 13:1, 12-17; 15:9, 13. That discussion will not be repeated here.

3E-26. In the third edition, the distinctive Christology is presented in a variety of ways. There are six primary ways, and these are discussed in the following characteristics. There are also a number of ways in which this is presented that appear relatively infrequently. These are grouped and discussed here. All of these are advances over the theology of the second edition and seek to identify Jesus ever more closely with God the Father. None of these features appear in earlier editions.

The third author expresses his distinctive Christology in six primary ways: (1) by the attribution of the title "Lord" (in the religious sense as it is applied to God the Father) to Jesus; (2) by the description of his sonship as "unique" *(monogenēs)*; (3) by the attribution of preexistence to Jesus; (4) by the adoption of the title "I AM" *(Ego Eimi)* by Jesus; (5) by the use of the confessional title "My Lord and My God" for Jesus; and (6) by the attribution of the apocalyptic title "Son of Man" to Jesus, which focuses on the apocalyptic worldview but also reflects the high Christology of the third author.[161] Because these aspects of the third edition are so distinctive, I have chosen to treat these features individually rather than as a single "characteristic."[162]

However, there are still other means by which the third author presents his distinctively high Christology. These are used less frequently and so are listed and discussed here as a group. But they are important in the way they speak so clearly of the equality of the Son with the Father.

1. In the third edition, Jesus is described as having "life in himself." As is explained in the Note to John 5:26 in the Commentary, in the case of mortal humans, life was "lent" to the person, whereas God had "life in himself." Based on

---

[161]. The Son of Man in the Gospel is said to be preexistent (3:13; 6:62), and in 9:35-38 the man born blind "worships" the Son of Man.

[162]. The first has already been treated in 3E-1 above. The fourth is treated in 3E-29 and in Vol. 3, Appendix 2. The fifth does not require special discussion since it is a combination of (2) with the unambiguous term "God." The sixth is treated in 3E-14.

The Third Edition of the Gospel

this same principle, Jesus declares, "I have the power to lay it [my life] down, and the power to take it up again" (10:18).

2. There are a variety of statements that declare that the Son "has everything the Father has." Thus, there is no distinction in terms of qualities or powers. This appears in the form: "[The Father] does not bestow the Spirit in a limited way" (3:34); "The Father ... has given all things into his hands" (3:35); "the Father ... shows him all things that he himself does" (5:20); "the Father ... has given all judgment to the Son" (5:22). In addition, Jesus himself (exercising a power reserved to God) will raise people from the dead on the last day (6:39, 40d, 44c, 54). In the Farewell Discourses, Jesus in the third edition affirms, "Everything the Father has is mine" (16:15).[163]

3. There is the striking statement: "... so that all may honor the Son just as they honor the Father" (5:23).

4. In 9:38, when Jesus identifies himself as the Son of Man to the man born blind, the man confesses his belief and "worships" Jesus.[164]

3E-27. In the third edition, the sonship of Jesus is specified as being "unique" (*monogenēs*). In the second edition, Jesus is identified as "Son" but without specification of the uniqueness of his sonship (cf. 2E-27X).

In the third edition, Jesus is declared to be the "unique" Son of God. This assertion is achieved by the use of the Greek term *monogenēs*, a term that has become famous in the development of Christology in the Christian churches. While this term was at one time thought to mean "only begotten" (from *mono*, meaning "only," and *gennaō*, meaning "to give birth"), Moody argued strongly that the word is actually from *mono* (meaning "only") and *genos* (meaning "type" or "kind").[165]

---

163. Although verbally similar, 13:3 has a considerably different meaning.

164. There are also other statements that could be conceived of as expressing divinity, for example, the declarations of Jesus, "I am the Resurrection and the Life" (11:25) and "I am the way, the truth, and the life" (14:6). However, I believe that these are intended as functional rather than ontological statements and so have not included them in this listing. However, it is clear on other grounds that they come from the third edition.

165. Moody, "Only Son." Recently Pendrick ("*MONOGENĒS*") has argued again and extensively for the position espoused by Moody, but on the grounds of usage rather than etymology. Pendrick ("*MONOGENĒS*" 587) argues that the interpretation of the adjective as meaning "only begotten" "originates in, and is the result of, developments in Christology that do not antedate the second century AD." I would disagree with Pendrick only insofar as he does not distinguish between the meanings "only" and "unique." In the sense he describes, the meaning "unique" is more appropriate. Certainly it is the meaning intended in the Johannine context, where there are other "children of God."

Section 2. The Criteria Used for the Third Edition

This affirmation, while seemingly insignificant in itself and in its context in the Gospel, becomes important in the light of the crisis the community faced in the third period of its history. Some of the community were evidently claiming that their birth from the Spirit in its eschatological form (which gave them the life of God and which furthermore made them "children of God") made them equal to Jesus, the man from Nazareth, who also had the eschatological outpouring of the Spirit and who was "Son of God." In order to counter this, the author of the third edition argued that while the status of the Christian was that of a true "child of God," the sonship of Jesus was unique.

Dahms has pointed out that, in both instances where "unique" appears in the Gospel, it occurs in a context in which the spiritual birth of the Christian had previously been the topic (cf. John 1:13-18; 3:3-18).[166] Dahms would see this as an argument for connecting *monogenēs* with "begetting" (rather than with the stem of "type"), but there is another explanation, namely, that the term *monogenēs* is used in these contexts precisely to distinguish the nature of Jesus' relationship to the Father from the relationship of Christians, who, although they are able to call God Father, are never themselves given the title "sons" ("daughters") but only "children." This was not a pedantic use of language but a careful one that carried with it significant theological implications.[167]

In the Gospel, the term appears four times (1:14, 18; 3:16, 18), always in the third edition.[168] In the Letters, the term appears once, at 1 John 4:9. If by this term the author affirmed the uniqueness of Jesus, as we shall see shortly, the community also specified in several ways just what constituted the uniqueness of his sonship.

3E-28. In the third edition, the author affirms the preexistence of Jesus. Affirmation of preexistence is not present in earlier editions.

When we look at 1 John, we see several statements that connote preexistence.[169] It is a consistent perspective of 1 John that Jesus' appearance or "coming" into the world is described as his being "revealed" (1:2 [twice]; 2:28; 3:2, 5, 8). Thus,

---

166. Dahms, *"Monogenēs"* 230-31. The same relationship between the mention of the spiritual birth of Christians and the uniqueness of the sonship of Jesus occurs in 1 John 4:7-9.

167. See also de Boer, "Death" 326-46, esp. 328.

168. Thus, the introduction of the term is what is distinctive. However, the third author does not use it *every* time he refers to the Son. Whether its presence in the original hymn that lies at the base of 1:1-18 is due to the third author is impossible to say.

169. "Preexistence" refers to the conviction that the person Jesus existed before he came into the world and into human history.

Jesus' coming into the world was not understood to be the beginning of his existence but only the revelation of it through his presence in the world.

When we turn to the Gospel, we see that the articulation of Jesus' preexistence is clearer and more direct than in 1 John, indicating development in the notion since the time of that writing. From the first line of the Prologue, the preexistence of Jesus is affirmed. In 1:1, the Word is spoken of as being in existence "in the beginning"; in v. 2 it is said that he was with God "in the beginning." This is not the beginning of creation since it is said in v. 3 that all things were made *through* the Word. Finally, in v. 10, there is a reaffirmation of the fact that the world had its existence through the Word. Therefore, the only possible conclusion is that the Word was in existence with God before creation.

John the Baptist also testifies to the preexistence of Jesus twice. In 1:15, he states: "The one coming after me ranks above me because he existed before me." In 1:30, he writes: "After me comes a man who ranks above me because he existed before me."

The preexistence of Jesus is also attested in passages where Jesus is said to have come down from heaven, for example, 3:13; 6:38. It is also evident in 6:62, which speaks of the Son of Man ascending "to where he was before."

The preexistence of Jesus is also affirmed in 8:58, where Jesus says, "Before Abraham was, I AM."

In 13:3, there is a statement of what must be considered the "parabola" Christology that affirms the descent of Jesus and his subsequent return to the Father.

In 17:5 ("And now glorify me, Father, in your presence with the glory that I had with you before the world existed"), Jesus' preexistence is again affirmed and explained in the most explicit of terms in this request to be endowed once again with preexistent glory.

Also, given the clear statement of preexistence in 17:5, this certainly must be the context intended for 17:24 (". . . so they may see the glory that you have given me, because you loved me before the beginning of the world").

Preexistence is also implicit in those passages where Jesus is said to have "seen" the Father. These are treated separately below (3E-54F).

3E-29. In the third edition, Jesus identifies himself as "I AM" *(Egō Eimi)*, **the LXX rendition of the divine name. This does not appear in other editions.**

This feature is discussed in Volume 3, Appendix 2. Its relation to the third edition is discussed in Section C of that appendix. Instances appear in 8:24, 28, 58; 13:19; 18:5-9. Included in this category are the references to the Father giving his own name to Jesus in 17:6, 11, 26.

Section 2. The Criteria Used for the Third Edition

3E-30. **In the third edition, Jesus is said to have been given the Spirit "without measure." This specifies his possession of the Spirit in a way not found in the second edition.**

In the second edition, there had been an emphasis on Jesus' promise of the eschatological Spirit to all who believed in him. As has been seen, the possession of the Spirit gave the believer prerogatives that, in the eyes of some, challenged the unique status of Jesus. In 3:34, the author of the third edition presents his understanding that Jesus, "the one God sent," speaks the words of God because the Father bestowed the Spirit "not in a limited way" *(ou gar ek metrou)*. This curious statement applies only to Jesus, as is clear from the context, and is given as the basis for the fact that Jesus speaks the very words of God. In this sense, this possession of the Spirit would be distinguished from that of believers.

Since the statement appears only once in the Gospel, it cannot be said to be a feature which assists in the identification of material, but it does emerge as a significant element of Christology, which distinguishes the status and nature of Jesus from that of the believer. That the statement comes from the third author is evident from the numerous features of 3:31-36 typical of the third edition. These are described in detail in the Commentary. It should also be noted that 1 John had said explicitly that the believer has received "of" the Spirit (1 John 3:24; 4:13). Thus, the two documents express a clear difference between the ways Jesus and the believer relate to the Spirit.

3E-31. **In the third edition, there is an emphasis on the permanence and abiding importance of the words of Jesus spoken in his historical ministry. While the second edition stresses the words of Jesus as one of the essential witnesses to him, the third edition emphasizes the permanent validity of those words.**

One of the major theological concerns of both 1 John and of the last edition of the Gospel is the importance of the words of the "historical" Jesus, that is, the validity of the "tradition" ("what was from the beginning") over against any claimed inspiration by the Spirit that diverged from this tradition.[170] This need to remain faithful to the historical words of Jesus is communicated first by means of the injunction to "keep my word" *(tērein ton logon ton emon)* but also by synonyms, as we shall see.

The notion of commandment was introduced into the Johannine tradi-

---

170. For the role this had in confronting the crisis of 1 John, see Vol. 3, Appendix 4 (The Crisis That Divided the Johannine Community).

The Third Edition of the Gospel

tion at the time of 1 John. As we saw earlier, the author of the third edition took over the notion of "commandment" from 1 John and developed it so that, in the third edition, not only did "commandment" describe the two essential obligations of the believer but it correlated these with two essential obligations given to Jesus by the Father (cf. 3E-6). Here attention is called to the fact that, within the Gospel, this first commandment is specified as such in the extended discussion of 14:15-24.[171] Jesus begins (14:15) by reminding the disciples that if they love him they will keep his commandments. After introducing the Paraclete and the promise of his return, he takes up the question of commandments in 14:21, and repeats the general exhortation of v. 15: "The one possessing my commandments and keeping them is the one loving me." Then Jesus specifies this love: "If a person loves me, *the person will keep my word*, and the Father will love the person, and we will come to the person and will make our abode with the person. The one who does not love me *does not keep my words. And the word that you hear is not mine, but of the Father who sent me.*" It is here that we receive the definition of the first commandment: it is to "keep the word of Jesus." Although the "commandment" to keep the word of Jesus is specified only once (in 14:15-24), the exhortation to "keep the word" of Jesus appears also in 8:51, 52, 55; 15:20 (twice); 17:6.

As we have seen, at the time of the second edition of the Gospel, the discourse of chapter 8 was formulated to develop the notion of the word of Jesus as a witness to him.[172] We also saw how the entire discourse is marked by references to "the word" (both *logos* and *lalia*) of Jesus. But twice toward the end of the chapter (vv. 51-52, 55c-58), in additions by the third author, Jesus urges his listeners to "keep his word" just as he keeps the word of the Father. Those who "keep the word" of Jesus will not see death forever. Here there can be no doubt that what is being referred to is the message of Jesus conceived of as a whole. Moreover, the presence of other features of the third edition confirms that these verses are the work of the author of the third edition in the light of the crisis facing the community.

In 15:20, the phrase appears again in a passing comment. Jesus is speaking of the hatred the world has against both him and the disciples and in a reference to the saying "a slave is not greater than his master," he comments that if "they"

---

171. The discussion of the individual commandments given to the disciples (where "commandment" is in the singular) always begins with a statement of general exhortation to keep the commandments (in the plural). This is true, for example, in 14:15a and 14:21, before the discussion of the commandment to keep Jesus' word. The plural of general exhortation also appears in 15:9b-10a, where it precedes the commandment (now in the singular) to love one another. For further discussion, see Vol. 3, Appendix 5 (The Johannine Commandments).

172. See the discussion of the structure of the second edition in Part 2, Section 3.1 above. See also the discussion of 5:31-40, as well as the overview of chapters 7–8 in the Commentary.

Section 2. The Criteria Used for the Third Edition

keep his word, they will also keep the word of the disciples.[173] Finally, in 17:6 Jesus speaks of "true" disciples and says that they have "kept your word."[174] In all instances there are other features in the context that suggest that this material has come from the third edition.

It should also be noted that the importance of the "historical" words of Jesus is attested by the third author's words concerning the Paraclete. When the author of the third edition speaks of the Paraclete, he will make the point (in 16:13d-e) that the Paraclete will not speak "on his own authority" (Gk. *aph' heautou*) but will speak what he hears. In v. 14 the Paraclete is said to glorify Jesus because "he will take from what is mine [i.e., Jesus'] and announce it to you." In both cases it is quite clear that the Paraclete will not go beyond the words of Jesus in his inspiration. This is in contrast to those who are described in 2 John 9 as "continuing on and not remaining in the teaching of the Christ." The Paraclete is not a Spirit that will teach things other than those taught previously by Jesus. Hence, as we shall see, the permanent value of the words of Jesus is attested to both from the point of view of the words themselves and from that of the particular role of the Spirit/Paraclete.[175]

3E-32. In the third edition, a particular emphasis is placed on the role of Jesus as essential for gaining access to eternal life. This was not present in the earlier editions.

We have already seen several of the ways in which the uniqueness of Jesus is stressed in the third edition. Another of these is the conviction that Jesus is the sole point of access to eternal life. This is expressed primarily through secondary interpretations of both the parable of the shepherd and the parable of the vine. Each of these interpretations is the work of the author of the third edition.

In the Letters, the essential role of Jesus was expressed in statements such as 1 John 2:23, where those denying the Son are said not to have the Father; and in statements such as 5:12, where it is said that one cannot have life without having the Son ("the one who has the Son has life; the one not having the Son of God does not have life"). However, in the third edition of the Gospel, various images are used that make this point even more forcefully.

---

173. In 15:7, there is what appears to be an alternate formula for this same idea: "If you remain in me, and my words remain in you...."

174. That these passages belong to the third edition can be seen in the discussion of the Composition of the verses.

175. Another more ambiguous instance appears in 6:68, where, in material of the third edition, Peter proclaims that Jesus has "the words of eternal life." Given its appearance in material of the third edition, the phrase probably is intended to refer once more to the permanent importance of the words of Jesus, but the context and the phrasing make this less certain.

The Third Edition of the Gospel

The Parable of the Shepherd

As will be seen in the Commentary on 10:7-18, the identification of Jesus as "the gate for the sheep" (vv. 7c, 9a) is not a primary development of the theme of the parable of the sheep and the shepherd since in the parable itself the contrast is between the shepherd and the thief, two persons and how they enter the sheepfold. However, in vv. 7c, 9, Jesus is identified not as a shepherd but as "the gate." Here the point is that the sheep (the believers) must enter through the gate (Jesus). If they do, they will (1) be saved, (2) will go in and come out, and (3) find pasture. Thus, this part of the parable is, as is commonly recognized by commentators, a presentation of Jesus as the sole means by which one is able to find "life."[176]

The Parable of the Vine

When we turn to the parable of the vine, we find a similar situation of a parable with two interpretations. Again, the fact that the material comes from the third edition is readily recognizable but requires some attention to the details of the scene before the differences become clear. These features are treated in detail in the Commentary. However, in the first part of the parable of the vine (vv. 1-3), the image is that of the relation between the vine, the branches, and the vinedresser. The vinedresser cuts off branches that are not bearing fruit and prunes those that do. This image is concluded by a statement that the disciples are "pruned" (in Greek the same word is used for "prune" and for "cleanse") by the word that Jesus has spoken.

In vv. 4-6, the author of the third edition introduces another image: the need of the branch to remain attached to the vine. Now the issue is the desire or lack of desire on the part of the branch (the believers) to remain attached to the vine (Jesus). It is not a question of the vinedresser doing the cutting but of the branches being willing to remain attached. This image is not part of the original parable. As can be seen, in this second interpretation the issue is also the fact that Jesus is the sole source of life for the believer. "Without me you are not able to do anything" (v. 5); without Jesus there is no life.

While the meaning of each interpretation is clear, the purpose of adding such comments is less clear until we read 1 John and find that there is a dispute about the role of Jesus in salvation. If the opponents claim that they have the

---

176. For example, Schnackenburg (*Gospel* 2:289): "There is but one entrance to the sheep.... There is but one bringer of salvation, one way to the Father ... one and absolute way to salvation...." Lindars (*Gospel* 489) says: "A disciple who breaks fellowship with him is useless." Bultmann (*Gospel* 377) sees the image of the door as indicative of "the exclusiveness and absoluteness of the revelation [of Jesus]."

Section 2. The Criteria Used for the Third Edition

Spirit, and if they see the Spirit as the sole effective source of eternal life, then the role of Jesus is not permanent and his life on earth has not accomplished anything other than to embody and to prophesy the eschatological outpouring of the Spirit. However, by placing these interpretations on the lips of Jesus, the author of the third edition asserts the critical role of Jesus as the source of life and prevents such a one-sided interpretation.

3E-33. In the third edition, the death of Jesus is understood as having an essential, salvific importance to it. This contrasts with the view of the second edition (2E-19), which presented the death of Jesus in terms of a departure to the Father, preparatory to the sending of the Spirit.[177]

In the third edition of the Gospel, the author inserts a variety of (generally) short statements that are designed to make present within the Gospel the author's convictions about the essential role of Jesus in salvation. While the categories in which these convictions are expressed are similar in a number of respects to those used in 1 John, they are not identical. We will move from the more specific to the more general.

First, the death of Jesus takes away sin. This group of statements speaks of the role of Jesus' death in the process of removal of sin. In the Letters, this is a dominant view, for example, in 1 John 2:2, which says, "he [Jesus] is an atonement for our sins, and not only for ours but also for those of the entire world. . . ." (See also 1 John 3:8.)

In the Gospel, he is described as the "Lamb of God" (1:29, 36), a figure associated with the Passover lamb, which was killed and whose blood freed the Israelites. This Lamb of God is also said explicitly to take away the sin of the world (1:29). This is fulfilled in 19:32-37, where Jesus' death is shown to be similar to that of the Passover lamb both as to the time of his death (while the lambs are being sacrificed for Passover) and to the fact that his legs were not broken (intended to indicate the fulfillment of Exod 12:10, 46; Num 9:12 about the Passover lamb).[178]

---

177. On atonement in the Gospel, see Grigsby, "Cross" 69-94; Hengel, *Atonement*; idem, *Johannine Question* 64-67. See also R. E. Brown, *Epistles*, referred to below. On atonement in the Letters: Bogart, *Perfectionism*, esp. 35-37; R. E. Brown, *Epistles* 201-3, 218; de Boer, "Death," 326-46; Dodd, *Epistles* 25; idem, "First Epistle" 144-46.

A number of scholars have noted the tension between the view of the death of Jesus in the Gospel and in 1 John. For example, U. B. Müller, *Geschichte;* Nicholson, *Departure;* Forestell, *Word;* de Boer, *Perspectives*. But see also Knöppler *(Theologia crucis)*, who would see this theology as implicitly pervading the Gospel.

178. It is possible, although less likely, that the verse alludes to Ps 33:21 (LXX). See the discussion in Grigsby, "Cross" 84-85.

The Third Edition of the Gospel

The second group of statements speaks in general terms of Jesus' death "for" *(hyper)* (his own, his sheep, us, etc.).[179] Again, this view is quite evident in the Letters. In 1 John 3:16 we read "that one has laid down his life for us *(hyper hēmōn)*" (see also 1 John 1:7 and 5:6).

In the third edition, examples include 6:51 ("The bread that I will give is my flesh for the life of the world [*hyper tēs tou kosmou zōēs*]");[180] 10:15b ("I lay down my life for the sheep [*hyper tōn probatōn*]");[181] 11:51 ("Jesus was about to die for the nation [*hyper tou ethnous*]");[182] 15:13 ("No one has greater love than this, that a person lay down his life for his friends [*hyper tōn philōn*]").[183]

Another statement from the third edition with a similar intention appears in the brief insertion of 8:36: "So, if the Son frees you, you will be genuinely free." This statement, which interrupts the context of the second edition surrounding it, speaks by means of allusion to the fact that the Son will free them from their enslavement to sin. In this statement the action of the Son is described as central to freeing them, but the nature of that action is not made clear.

The third type of statement speaks of the death of Jesus as involving the giving of his "flesh" and/or "blood." In these statements there is an explicit mention of the "flesh" and/or "blood" of Jesus. 1 John 1:7 states: "the blood of Jesus his Son cleanses us from all sin." In 1 John 5:6, the author speaks of Jesus as "the one coming through . . . blood."

In the Gospel, 6:51 says, "The bread that I will give is my flesh for the life of the world" *(hē sarx mou estin hyper tēs tou kosmou zōēs)*.[184] Here the empha-

---

179. Barrett (*Gospel* 375) lists 6:51; 10:11, 15; 11:50-52; 18:14 as examples of the use of *hyper* in this sense, and comments, "The word, however, though certainly suggesting a sacrificial (in no technical sense) death for the benefit of others, conveys no more precise shade of meaning."

M. Thompson (*Humanity* 92) comments: "When used with any verb meaning 'to die,' *hyper* suggests that such a death is 'for the benefit of others.'" Nicholson (*Departure* 2) speaks of these *hyper*-sayings as expressing the notion of sacrifice and atonement.

180. So also, for example, Barrett, *Gospel* 298; Bultmann, *Gospel* 234-35; Beasley-Murray, *Gospel* 94; Haenchen, *Gospel* 1:294; Moloney, *Gospel* 138.

181. See also 10:11b, where the similar expression appears in the parable itself. On this as referring to Jesus' sacrificial death, see, for example, Barrett, *Gospel* 376; Beasley-Murray, *Gospel* 171; R. E. Brown, *Gospel* 1:395; Bultmann, *Gospel* 384; Ridderbos, *Gospel* 362.

182. The essential element here is that it is through the death of Jesus that this saving event takes place, and that the death itself results in a benefit for others. So also, for example, Barrett, *Gospel* 406; Bultmann, *Gospel* 411-12; Dodd, *Interpretation* 233; Ridderbos, *Gospel* 409; Moloney, *Signs* 175.

183. Although 17:19 is a verbal parallel, the meaning is different. 18:14 is a repetition of 11:50 and probably did not have the sacrificial meaning, which was introduced only in the interpretation of those verses in 11:51-52. For further detail, see the discussion of the Composition of those verses.

184. Dodd (*Interpretation* 360) speaks of the "hint" of his death as vicarious.

Section 2. The Criteria Used for the Third Edition

sis is on his flesh and its role in gaining life.[185] Even though the references to the "blood" of Jesus in 6:53-56 should be understood as sacramental, the statements are important because the sacrament is linked specifically to his flesh and blood as being "for the life of the world." Also in 19:34, when the side of Jesus is pierced by the lance, the author observes that the lancing brings forth "blood and water," a comment intended to confess the importance of *both* the Spirit (living water) and the death (blood) of Jesus for salvation.[186]

Fourth, there are expressions that speak of Jesus "saving" (the world, us, etc.). These expressions attribute, in a general way, an efficacy to the actions of Jesus in themselves (as opposed to actions that prepare for the giving of the Spirit). Although these do not refer explicitly to the death of Jesus, they focus on the actions of Jesus as being themselves salvific, and so they should be considered here.

In 1 John this is found explicitly in 4:14, which states that "the Father has sent the Son as Savior of the world."

In the third edition, this view is expressed in various ways. For example, we see in 3:17, "God did not send his Son . . . to judge, but so that the world may be saved through him"; in 4:42, ". . . we know that this is truly the Savior of the world"; in 10:9, "If someone enters through me, he will be saved . . ."; and 12:47, ". . . I did not come to judge the world, but to save the world."[187]

Finally, it would seem that the giving of the Son by the Father was conceived by the author against the model of Abraham's willingness to sacrifice Isaac. This view, one quite different from the earlier ones and found only in the third edition, is expressed in John 3:16. Several scholars have argued that, in the first century, in the so-called Akedah tradition, Isaac was seen as the prime example of sacrifice, as one who was willing to give himself in death as an offering.[188] These scholars see a parallel between this and the description in 3:16 of

---

185. Menken ("John 6,51c-58" 10, nn. 26, 27) lists John 10:11, 15; 11:50-52; 15:13; 17:19; 18:14 as examples of this usage. He sees the expression elsewhere in Mark 14:24 and parallels; Rom 5:6-8; 1 Cor 5:14-15; 11:24; 15:3; Heb 6:20; 1 Pet 2:21; 1 John 3:16. With *didōmi*, the expression occurs in Luke 22:19; Gal 1:4; 2:20; Eph 5:2, 25; 1 Tim 2:6; Tit 2:14. De Jonge ("Death," 142-51, esp. 145) also lists a number of these so-called "surrender" texts.

186. See the Note on 19:35.

187. This includes all religious uses of the verb, the abstract noun ("salvation"), and the personal noun ("savior"). Three other instances (5:34; 11:12; 12:27) do not refer to the same sort of activity. Of these, only 5:34 requires some comment. As is explained in more detail in the Commentary, the exact meaning of "save" in 5:34 is not clear. However, it is clear (1) that it does not refer to the saving act of the death of Jesus, and (2) that the witness of John is not considered a true source of salvation in any sense comparable to that of Jesus. Therefore, it is unlikely that the verb should be taken in the same sense as intended in the third edition and equally unlikely that it comes from the third edition.

188. For the background of this conception, see Part 4, Section 7.4.

The Third Edition of the Gospel

God giving his unique son that the world may be saved through him. F. M. Braun has called attention to three parallels with the Isaac story: (1) the only son is delivered to death by his father; (2) this son is the one upon whom depends the fulfillment of the covenant; (3) from the sacrifice of the only son, the fruit of the promises extends to all peoples.[189]

Thus, in all of these instances, the death of Jesus is seen (either explicitly or implicitly) to be the action that achieves salvific effects for the believer. This view is distinct from the view, in the second edition, of his death as "departure."[190]

3E-34. In the third edition, the ministry of Jesus is conceived of as beginning with a "descent" from heaven and ending with a "return" to the Father. In the second edition, there is only the conception of the "departure" of Jesus to the Father, which is not yet conceived of in relation to a belief in preexistence (2E-19).

In the third edition, Jesus is understood to have existed prior to the time he spent on earth. Consequently, the ministry itself is not the absolute "beginning." Rather, the ministry begins with a descent from heaven. In this view, Jesus' death is not a "departure" (as it was in the second edition) but a "return" to where he was before. This pattern constitutes what R. E. Brown has called a "parabola" Christology. It appears again and again in the material of the third edition, taking up the conception of the departure of Jesus from the second edition and incorporating it into a greater and more profound theological framework.

Apart from the Prologue, which will be discussed below, the first example of this schema appears in 3:13 ("No one has ascended into heaven except the one come down from heaven, the Son of Man").[191] It is also implicit in 3:19 ("This is the judgment, that the Light has come into the world . . ."). It is evident in 3:31 ("The one who comes from above is above all"). In 6:62, we see another reference to return. This time it is the return of the Son of Man "to where he was be-

---

189. F. M. Braun, *Jean* 157. Grigsby ("Cross" 88-89), who adopts Braun's view, sees a possible parallel between Jesus, who carries the wood of the cross, and Isaac, who carries the wood for the sacrifice. While there is a certain parallelism, it is difficult to know whether it was intentional.

190. There are other passages that may hint at an understanding of the death as atonement, but they are not so clear. For example, 3:14 says that "the Son of Man must be lifted up, so that everyone believing in him may have everlasting life." This expression occurs in material that is associated otherwise with that of the third edition. In addition, a very similar expression occurs in 1 John 4:9 ("He has sent his unique Son into the world so that we may live through him").

191. Typically, the material in which this schema appears also contains other features of the third edition. Here the descent-return schema appears together with the title "Son of Man." In order to see these passages in context, the reader is referred to the discussion of the Composition of each of these passages (in the Commentary proper in Vol. 2).

Section 2. The Criteria Used for the Third Edition

fore." In 8:14b-16, we again see a reference to descent and return. Here the fact that Jesus knows "where he came from and where he is going" is the basis for his ability to witness to himself. What makes it particularly clear that these verses are intended to have this meaning and that they come from the third edition is that they are a *secondary* basis for Jesus' ability to witness to himself and that they interrupt the sequence of v. 14a with v. 17a. In the second edition (found here in vv. 13bc, 14a, and then in vv. 17-18), the basis of Jesus' ability to witness to himself had been the fact that the Law accepts the witness of two persons and that Jesus conceived of himself as the first witness and of his Father as the second.

It is also likely that Jesus' statement that "I came from God and am now present" in 8:42 reflects a belief in preexistence. Here the Greek verb for "come" is not the usual *erchomai* but *exerchomai* ("to come 'out'"). The second verb, *hēkō*, has a perfect tense meaning even though the verb form is grammatically the present tense. Moreover, the verb combines the meaning of "to come and so to be present." This combination of verbs seems intended to allude to Jesus' preexistence prior to his appearance on earth.

At the beginning of the so-called "Book of Glory" (which is, for the third author, the "beginning of the greatest demonstration of Jesus as 'loving'") (13:3), the narrator places the actions of Jesus within the context of his self-knowledge and says: ". . . knowing . . . that he had come forth from God and that he was going to God. . . ."

The most succinct expression of this pattern appears in 16:28, where Jesus says: "I came from the Father, and I have come into the world. Again I leave the world, and I go to the Father."[192]

In our discussion so far, I have not discussed two sets of texts, those of the Prologue and those of chapter 6.

I have not included the Prologue in this discussion because its origin as a hymn within the community and its use of terminology found nowhere else in the Gospel could be seen to compromise its relevance as a characteristic of the third author. Nevertheless, it speaks of the coming (in the sense of descent) of the eternal Word into the world. Although it does not speak explicitly of the departure of the Word, its departure is implicit in the fact that its presence in the world is described as a "pitching of a tent," "tabernacling," that is, a temporary presence within the world. This certainly implies the eventual return of the Word to where it was before. Thus, while the Prologue is consistent with the schema of descent and return, it is treated separately because of its origin.

The second set of texts, those in chapter 6, which speak of the bread com-

---

192. On the question whether such statements indicate a belief in the preexistence of Jesus, see the discussion in Part 4, Section 1.1.

ing down from heaven, are of a different sort and require some comment. In the original quotation posed by Jesus' listeners, the speakers quote Ps 77:24: "he gave them bread from heaven to eat." Jesus then reinterprets "he" as referring to the Father, not Moses, and reinterprets himself as the "bread from heaven." Does the author understand the references to "bread from heaven," as they are applied to Jesus, simply as an echo of the same phrase as it had appeared in the Scripture quotation,[193] or does he intend them to be taken as referring to a descent of Jesus from heaven in a way that would imply preexistence?

In order to avoid repetition, I have chosen to address all the instances in chapter 6 together in the Addendum to 6:25-50 in the Commentary. There I will propose that only the instance in v. 38 is intended to refer to actual descent from heaven in a way that implies preexistence. The others are modeled on the phrase as it appears in the Old Testament and are simply intended to reflect that usage.

3E-35. In the third edition, the function of the Spirit (in the Paraclete passages) is defined in such a way as to make it clear that the Spirit does not speak on his own but reminds his listeners of what Jesus has said. In the second edition, the emphasis is on the necessity of receiving the Spirit, and the role of the Spirit is not qualified in any way.

We have seen previously that in the third edition, the notion of the Spirit is conceived of in a dualistic way typical of apocalyptic. We further saw that this Spirit was given the titles "Spirit of Truth," "Paraclete," and the like. When we look at the content of those passages where the Spirit is defined as the Paraclete, we see that the function of the Spirit is closely related to the activity of Jesus and indeed is limited by it.

Although the purpose of this specification of the relationship between the Spirit and Jesus is not fully clear in the context of the Gospel alone, when the material of the third edition is related to the message and the problems of the community at the time of 1 John, its importance is clear. While the opponents had understood the outpouring of the Spirit against the backdrop of Old Testament eschatological hopes, they believed that the Spirit would be their sole source of inspiration. Even though Jesus may have possessed the Spirit, they felt that their own possession of the Spirit in its eschatological fullness would make any reliance on his words unnecessary. However, the author of the third edition counteracts this by two features of his own clarifying the identity

---

193. In addition to its appearance in Ps 77:24, it also appears in Exod 16:4; Ps 104:40; Wis 16:20; Neh 19:15 with minor variations in wording.

Section 2. The Criteria Used for the Third Edition

and role of the Spirit. First, he explains that it is not just an issue of whether one has the Spirit or not, but (in his apocalyptic view) it is a question of *which* spirit one has. The believer needs to test the Spirit. Thus, by the titles he has given the Spirit ("Holy Spirit," "Spirit of Truth") he makes this clear. In addition, he stresses that the Spirit will be tied directly to the words of Jesus; the Spirit will not speak on his own. Thus, he articulates the relation and the function of both Jesus and the Spirit in a way different from that proposed by the opponents. As we review each of the Paraclete passages, we will see both the titles and the function of the Spirit-Paraclete as the author of the third edition understood it.

In the first passage (14:16-17) the Paraclete is related to Jesus by identifying it as "another" Paraclete. In this the relation to Jesus is described only minimally (as "another" Paraclete). The remainder of the saying focuses on the facts that (1) it will be with the disciples forever, (2) it is the Spirit of Truth, (3) the world is not able to accept it, and (4) the disciples now possess it and it remains with them and is in them.

In the second passage (14:26), the Paraclete is identified as "the Holy Spirit," sent in Jesus' name, who will "teach you all things, and will remind you of all things that I have told you." The function of the Paraclete is related to the action of Jesus. The Paraclete will remind the disciples of what Jesus has said — and in so doing will teach them about all that he has said. Although less explicit here, the intention is to relate the action of the Paraclete to the words of Jesus.

The third Paraclete passage (15:26) is perhaps the shortest. Its function is again an extension of the activity of Jesus. In vv. 22-25, the author of the second edition has summarized a final time the three witnesses to Jesus (his words, his works, and Scripture). But now, in v. 26, the author of the third edition extends the list of witnesses to include the two witnesses that will function in the time after the departure of Jesus. The first additional witness is the Paraclete (v. 26), which is the focus of our attention at present. The second and final of the additional witnesses is the disciples (v. 27). In function, the Paraclete will witness to Jesus; it will not speak on its own or without regard to Jesus.

The fourth of the Paraclete passages (16:7-11) is the most difficult to understand. However, as we shall see in detail in the Notes to 16:7-11, the function of the Paraclete is to convict the world of three things: sin, righteousness, and judgment. In each case, however, Jesus figures either directly or indirectly. The "sin" of which the Paraclete convicts the world is the failure to believe in Jesus; the "righteousness" is the verdict passed on Jesus, who, because he is righteous, goes to the Father, and the "judgment" is the verdict passed on the "ruler of this world," the Evil One, who has been cast out through the death of Jesus.

In the fifth passage (16:12-15), the Paraclete serves as the one who brings insight to the disciples and who illumines them regarding the meaning of Jesus' words. In v. 12, it is said that the Paraclete will follow Jesus and make understandable what the disciples cannot bear at present. But the Paraclete "will not speak on his own, but will speak whatever he hears." Thus, the Spirit-Paraclete is not able to speak on his own and will not give the disciples new revelations, but will only speak what he hears. It is said again, from another perspective, that the Paraclete will glorify Jesus. Contrary to the understanding of the Spirit held by the opponents of 1 John, the Spirit will be closely tied to the words and person of Jesus. "He will take from what is mine and will proclaim it to you" (16:15). Thus, the role of the Spirit is qualified and in a sense redefined in these passages in a way that does not occur in the other Spirit passages in the Gospel.

But throughout, the role of the Paraclete is related to the activity of Jesus and is described by titles and in connection with other concepts typical of apocalyptic (as we shall see in the Commentary).

3E-36. In the third edition, "joy" is understood as complete in that the future ("eschatological") hopes of the people have been fulfilled in the ministry of Jesus. In the second edition, joy was conceived of as "irremovable" in the Resurrection of Jesus that followed the pain and sorrow of the Passion (2E-24).

We have seen that in the second edition the notion of joy appears only once, at least in those parts of the second edition that remain in the final Gospel. There it was a minor motif but nevertheless significant. When we turn to the concept of joy in the later tradition, we find a significant shift. The notion of joy that is found in 1 John, 2 John, and 3 John is of joy "that is brought to fulfillment." The Greek verb here is *pleroō* ("to fulfill"). This joy is brought about in the fulfillment of the eschatological hopes of the community. Jesus has come; he is the Messiah and the Son of God; he is the one they had hoped for; and the appropriate response is eschatological joy.

Although we must move ahead to texts from the third edition for a moment, we are able to get a good sense of this eschatological joy from two elements of the third edition. First, the author tells us that joy is the appropriate response to the arrival of Jesus, the nation's eschatological hope. This is confirmed by 8:56, where the third author speaks of Abraham and says that "Abraham, your father, rejoiced to see my day, and he did see it and rejoiced." This is precisely the joy that the third author speaks of as the possession of the disciples. The disciples are to rejoice because the eschaton has arrived in Jesus! In 20:20, we see the fulfillment of this joy when the third author describes the disciples' first meeting with the risen Jesus and says: "So the disciples rejoiced, seeing the Lord."

Secondly, it is helpful to note that the eschatological dimension of this joy is also echoed in the third author's belief that the Scriptures are being brought

Section 2. The Criteria Used for the Third Edition

to eschatological fulfillment in Jesus. As we will see in 3E-51F, the third author's characteristic way of introducing Scripture is to say that it has been "fulfilled" (*pleroō*) by Jesus. That is, there is a sense of the "filling out" of the meaning of Scripture in the events and words of Jesus' ministry.

With this in mind, we may turn to an examination of joy in the Letters. As has been the case regularly, the particular conception that is found in the third edition is found first in 1 John. This is also the case with the third author's notion of joy. In 1 John 1:4, the author explains that he is writing his words "so that our joy may be brought to fulfillment." The writing of 1 John will result in fullness of joy for the author in that, by writing his tract, he will explain "the Truth" that they had experienced "from the beginning" and erase any possibility of doubt about the correct meaning of the tradition. It will also be a source of joy for the recipients in that they will be strengthened in their belief by the witness of the author. The author's tract will put to rest their doubts and restore the fullness of joy that should be theirs in the possession of "the Truth." This joy is a joy that has been "brought to fulfillment." It is the fullness of joy that is typical of the eschatological age. And it is this eschatological dimension of joy that will continue to mark joy for the author of 1 John and for the author of the third edition.

In 2 John 12, the author explains, at the end of his letter, that he hopes to speak with the community face to face and that such a meeting will result in their joy, the joy of both the community and the author, being brought to fulfillment. Again, the author had just finished saying that he had much to share with them and hoped to do it face to face. This complete sharing would again be a confirmation that both the community and the author possessed "the Truth" and "what was from the beginning" — and that should be the cause of perfectly fulfilled joy.[194]

In the third edition, the notion of joy always occurs in the framework of eschatological fulfillment, as it had in the Letters. It is a joy that is appropriate for the coming of the age of fulfillment of Israel's hope, and it is a complete joy.

In 3:29, John the Baptist describes himself as the friend of the bridegroom. And he is happy when he sees the bridegroom coming. The joy the groomsman experiences at the arrival of the bridegroom is similar to the joy that is brought to fulfillment in the arrival of Jesus because John recognizes that Jesus' arrival is the arrival of the fullness of the eschatological hour. Like Abraham (8:56), John has "seen the day" of Jesus and his joy is brought to fulfillment.

The remainder of the third author's references to joy appear in the Fare-

---

194. It should be noted that references to "joy" appear two other times in the Letters (2 John 4 and 3 John 4), but these are part of the standard introduction to a letter and so are not treated here.

The Third Edition of the Gospel

well Discourses. This is not surprising since the Passion is imminent and the disciples need to be exhorted to find joy in what is to come. In 15:11, Jesus expresses his hope that the disciples will obey his commandments, just as Jesus obeys the commandments given him by the Father and, as a result, remains in the love of the Father. If the disciples obey Jesus' commandments, they will remain in Jesus' love, and his joy will be in them, and the joy of the disciples will be brought to eschatological completion.

In 16:24, Jesus urges his disciples to make petitions to the Father in his name. Up to this point, petitions to the Father would be only in the name of the Father, but now they may ask in the name of Jesus. When they do this they are guaranteed to receive what they ask for, and, in this granting of their requests, their joy will be brought to completion in the recognition of the eschatological reality that has come to be in Jesus.

Finally, in 17:13, in the second part of his prayer to the Father, Jesus prays for the disciples. He recalls that they will not be "lost," so that Scripture might be fulfilled. He says this to his disciples so that the disciples might know this fully and so that they might have confidence and might experience Jesus' own joy, the joy that is in him as he does will of the Father.

3E-37. In the second edition, "eternal life" had been conceived of as beginning in the present and continuing after physical death but without mention of the resurrection of the body.[195] In the third edition, this belief is complemented by the introduction of explicit statements of belief in bodily resurrection.[196]

In the second edition of the Gospel, eternal life is conceived of as beginning in this life and extending beyond death. This is the so-called "realized eschatology" of the Gospel. In this view there is no mention of bodily resurrection as a component of eternal life. A belief in immortality (rather than in physical resurrection of the dead) played a role in some sectors of Judaism, and so it is not surprising that at one stage in its development this Jewish-Christian commu-

---

195. As was the case with judgment, the notion of eternal life realized in the present is not listed as a criterion of the second edition since it appears in both the second and the third. However, the introduction of eternal life with bodily resurrection is distinctive of the third edition.

196. Here we will treat of eternal life insofar as it appears in a present or future manifestation. Below (3E-49X) we will address the topic of "eternal life" itself.

The most exhaustive study is that of Puech, *Croyance*. Puech studies all such references in the Qumran documents against a thorough review of all references to resurrection and future life in the OT, NT, Apocrypha, Pseudepigrapha (including the *T12P*), and earliest postapostolic writings. See also Nickelsburg, *Resurrection*; Perkins, *Resurrection*, esp. 37-69; Wright, *Resurrection* 85-206.

Section 2. The Criteria Used for the Third Edition

nity held to such a belief.[197] A belief in immortality also seems evident in some other sectors of early Christianity but was considered erroneous teaching.[198]

However, the third edition also contains a belief in a universal judgment at the end of time. It is important to realize that this does not negate the view of eternal life in the present but complements it with the apocalyptic viewpoint. As a result, it is not possible to argue that the presence of eternal life "in the present" is characteristic of the second edition.[199] What we can say is that the only view of eternal life in the second edition is that of life in the present, and only in the third edition is the future dimension of life evident.

In some instances it is difficult if not impossible to be sure which dimension of life is being spoken of. For example, 3:36a would seem to speak of present possession of eternal life (and this is certainly its literal meaning). However, given its presence in a text marked by a number of apocalyptic features and given the future dimension of life described in the final part of the verse, it may be that v. 18 simply means that the believer has eternal life "in store" for him/herself.

The two views of eternal life are most clearly contrasted in 5:21-30, where the realized view of life and judgment is expressed in vv. 21-25 and the future (apocalyptic) view is expressed in vv. 26-30. Elsewhere in the third edition, the view of life in its future dimension is evidenced in texts that speak of life in a future way (e.g., 3:36b). The belief in resurrection characteristic of the third edition is also evident in 6:39, 40d, 44c, and 54b.[200]

---

197. In earlier scholarship, immortality (as opposed to resurrection of the body) was thought of as reflecting a Hellenistic influence upon the tradition. However, it is now recognized that immortality was a component of Jewish religious belief during the two centuries before Jesus. Perhaps the most famous example is from the deuterocanonical Wisdom of Solomon (e.g., 3:1-4; 5:14-15). See also *Jos. Asen.* 8:5; 15:5, 6; 16:16; 19:5. Among Jews of the first century such belief in immortality is also found in Philo and Josephus.

For a discussion, see Bacon, "Immortality" 259-94; Nickelsburg, *Resurrection;* J. Becker, *Auferstehung*, esp. 117-48; Perkins, *Resurrection* 37-69, esp. 51-56; Wright, *Resurrection* 129-200; Segal, *Life* 248-396.

198. See, for example, 2 Tim 2:18 ("Those who say the resurrection has already taken place"). See also Justin (*Dialogue* 80:4), who speaks of people who call themselves Christians and who "say that there is no resurrection of the dead but upon their death their souls are taken up into heaven."

199. It is appropriate to say, however, that the denial of a future judgment was particular to the second edition and is corrected by the conviction in a future, universal judgment in the third edition.

200. *Zōē* (the Greek word for "life") appears thirty-seven times in the Gospel (* denotes the phrase "eternal life"): 1:4; 3:15*, 16*, 36* (twice); 4:14*, 36*; 5:24* (twice), 26 (twice), 29, 39*, 40; 6:27*, 33, 35, 40*, 47*, 48, 51 (twice), 53, 54*, 63, 68*; 8:12; 10:10, 28*; 11:25; 12:25*, 50*; 14:6; 17:2*, 3*; 20:31. It appears thirteen times in 1 John (1:1, 2 [twice*]; 2:25*; 3:14, 15*; 5:11* [twice], 12 [twice], 13*, 16, 20*) but not in either 2 or 3 John. In all cases, even when it does not

The Third Edition of the Gospel

It will be noticed, however, that in 1 John there is no mention of bodily resurrection. This is one of the ways in which the author of the third edition represents a development over the theology of 1 John.

3E-38. In the third edition, there is an emphasis on the importance of proper ethical behavior. This is not found in the earlier editions.

In his commentary on the Epistles, R. E. Brown made reference to the Gospel's "strange silence on ethical matters."[201] Meeks comments that "[The Fourth Gospel] offers no explicit moral instruction."[202] Observations of this type are common about the Johannine Gospel. They indicate, if not the *total* absence of ethical instruction, certainly the *relative* absence of ethics when the Gospel of John is compared to the Synoptic Gospels.

Brown has observed that the major sin in the Gospel is the sin of unbelief.[203] While I would agree with that, I would qualify it in two ways. First, while unbelief is the major sin, the reason why belief is so essential is that it leads to the reception of the Spirit. Lack of belief in Jesus meant that one would not receive either the promised Spirit or the eternal life that came about as a result of rebirth as a child of God from that Spirit. Secondly, the greater clarity gained through the analysis of the literary history of the Gospel enables us to qualify Brown's statement in another way. We can now see that the failure to believe is the major sin *in the second edition*. However, *in the third edition*, there is an emphasis on ethics in various, often subtle, ways. As is the case with many of the features of the third edition, the passages that address or allude to the ethical dimension are often so subtle that their role is difficult to understand. However, when these features are viewed in the light of the crisis confronted by 1 John, their full importance becomes apparent.

I would agree with J. Becker, who comments that a shift from emphasis on faith as the guarantee of salvation to emphasis on brotherly love is observable between the work of the Evangelist of the Gospel and the final redactor and is also observable in 1 John.[204]

Among the topics addressed by the author of 1 John is that of sinfulness. In an almost paradoxical way, the author speaks both of the believer's sinfulness

---

appear with the adjective "eternal," the term "life" refers to "eternal life," the life that comes from birth from the Spirit and that makes one a child of God.

201. R. E. Brown, *Epistles* 54-55, 79-86, 98; quotation on 80.
202. Meeks, "Ethics" 317-26, quotation on 317.
203. R. E. Brown, *Epistles* 81; also R. E. Brown, *Community* 123-35. Also Barrett, "Lamb" 210-18, esp. 210. This position is also adopted by Bogart, *Perfectionism* 55.
204. J. Becker, *Evangelium* 2:483.

Section 2. The Criteria Used for the Third Edition

(1:8–2:2; 2:12) and his/her sinlessness. It is clear from the claims that are countered in 1 John (cf. esp. 2:8-10) that the author's opponents claim to be sinless, perhaps in the past but certainly in the present, in the sense that they are no longer capable of committing sin. In short, they claim a perfectionism.

However, the author of 1 John, in his refutation of them, walks a tightrope, as he does in so many aspects of his refutation of the opponents. He both claims an *incipient* sinlessness for the believer (3:6-10) and emphasizes that the believer is still capable of sin and must work to make him/herself holy for the time of the Second Coming of Jesus (3:3). In addition, he exhorts his readers to move beyond words to action: "Children, let us not love in word nor with the tongue, but in work and in truth" (3:18). At the time of the Second Coming, there will be a universal judgment, and although the believer has received eternal life through the Spirit and although he/she has the potential for being sinless, he/she is capable of sin. But if the believer loves (i.e., performs the proper actions), then he/she will have confidence on the day of judgment (4:17-18).

As we have seen above, at the time of the second edition, the great sin was unbelief since, if one believed, one would receive the Spirit, be freed from sin through the Spirit (as could be seen in the Old Testament description of the effects of the eschatological Spirit), come to "know" God fully, and be incapable of sin in the future.

In order to modify and correct this one-sided view, the author of the third edition subtly calls attention to the ethical dimension of human life. His comments are of two types. First, there are references to the importance of one's works for example, 3:19, where he speaks of the works of those who love darkness as "sinful." In addition, v. 20 speaks of the one who "does evil" not wanting to come to the light "lest his works be condemned." And in v. 21 he says that the one who "does the truth comes to the light, so that his works may be manifest that they have been done in God." In v. 36, we may see another subtle allusion to moral action when the author speaks of "obeying" the Son.

In 5:29, the author speaks of those "who have done good" and those "who have done evil," and again the moral dimension of these actions seems to be what is in focus.[205]

In 8:24, the third author inserts a statement declaring that unless Jesus' listeners believe that I AM, they will die in their sins. Jesus repeats this twice, and the plural contrasts with the similar statement in v. 21, where the singular "sin" appears in the second edition and refers to the sin of unbelief. Thus the third author makes it clear that ethical transgressions are also at issue.

Secondly, there is the commandment given by Jesus to his disciples: love

---

205. As we have seen, however, "doing the works" of God in 6:28-29 and 9:4 is an idiom and is not a reference to ethical behavior.

one another (13:34-35; 15:12, 17). This commandment becomes the overarching moral directive of the community.[206] It is commanded in the texts given above, and it is exemplified in Jesus' washing of the feet of the disciples (in its second interpretation) in 13:12-17. In this commandment the author sums up all possible ethical directives of a more specific type. As a result, even when the ethical concerns of the third edition are taken into account, it is proper to say that the Johannine tradition remains vague and imprecise about specific ethical directives found in the other Gospel traditions.[207] Yet now at least the roots of such traditions are incorporated within the Gospel, and though the exhortation is quite general by most standards, the importance and the basic thrust of such ethics are clearly attested.

3E-39. In the third edition, the birth that the believer is said to experience is said to be "from God." In the second edition, it is said to be "from the Spirit" or "from above" (2E-17).

As was indicated in the analysis of the second edition, (re-)birth from the Spirit was the means of gaining eternal life. However, in the Prologue to the Gospel, the believer is said to be born "of God" (1:13). However, it will be recalled from the discussion there that, in spite of the fact that this usage appears only once in the third edition, in 1 John the concept of "birth" is more widespread and is consistently attributed to God (1 John 3:9 [twice]; 4:7; 5:1 [twice], 4, 18 [twice]). In the light of this consistency of usage, it becomes clear that the usage is not accidental. Within the overall context of 1 John, it will be clear that this is another instance of attributing to God the Father what is attributed to Jesus or the Spirit in the Gospel.

3E-40. In the third edition, the figure of the Beloved Disciple appears. He does not appear in the earlier editions.[208]

---

206. There is another commandment ("to keep the word of Jesus"), but, while this could be looked upon as a moral directive, it is focused on the content of belief and should be viewed as dealing with Christology rather than with ethics. See Vol. 3, Appendix 5 (The Johannine Commandments).

207. The closest that 1 John comes to mentioning specific sins is in 2:16, where the author says that "everything in the world — the desire of the flesh, the desire of the eyes, and the lust of life — is not from the Father but from the world."

208. See, for example, Bauckham, "Beloved"; R. E. Brown, *Community*; de Jonge, "Beloved"; Kügler, *Jünger*; Lorenzen, *Lieblingjünger*; Schnackenburg (*Gospel* 3:375-88); Thyen, "Entwicklungen." An extensive bibliography is given in the recent book-length treatment by Charles-

Section 2. The Criteria Used for the Third Edition

The figure of the Beloved Disciple ("the disciple whom Jesus loved") is unique to the Johannine Gospel in the New Testament. He appears for the first time at the Last Supper but then appears regularly until the very end of the Gospel in 21:24. In all there are seven passages where the BD certainly appears (13:21-27; 19:26-27, 32-37; 20:2-10; 21:7, 20-23, 24) and two others in which the evidence is ambiguous (1:35-40; 18:15-18).

As is evident from the analysis of the Composition, the passages dealing with the BD consistently appear to be secondary additions within the context in which they appear.[209]

It will be argued in the Commentary that the passages dealing with the BD attempt to describe the authority figure who lies behind the material of the third edition. While I would state his role as the authority figure for the material of the third edition, undoubtedly the followers of the BD would argue that he is the source of the entire tradition (as the followers of the author of the third edition understand it).

When we begin to address the role of the BD, it would seem proper at first to attempt to associate him with the material of the earlier or perhaps earliest edition of the Gospel since he is referred to again and again as an eyewitness. However, two features argue against such a position. First, the literary evidence suggests that the BD passages belong to the last literary layer within the Gospel. Secondly, it seems reasonable to suppose that it was at the time of the greatest controversy within the community, when the correctness of the recorded tradition was being questioned from within, that it would have been most necessary to appeal to an eyewitness as the source of the interpretation that was being advanced in the third edition.

The Relation of the Beloved Disciple Passages to the Third Edition

The material of the BD passages consistently shows clear signs of being secondary additions to the context in which they appear. This identifies them as additions to the Gospel. However, the passages display remarkably little *internal* relationship to the third edition. Consequently, it is important to review the passages themselves to determine whether it is correct to identify them as part of the third edition.

---

worth *(Beloved)*. Charlesworth focuses on the question of the person represented by the title and concludes that it is the disciple Thomas.

209. Many scholars, among them Culpepper (*Legend* 72, 84); de Jonge ("Beloved" 105-8); Lorenzen (*Lieblingsjünger* 76-77, 108-9); and Thyen ("Entwicklungen" 267), see the BD passages as additions to the Gospel at a "later" stage of its development. Schnackenburg (*Gospel* 3:377 n. 9a) also cites earlier critics with this view. Bultmann at times attributes the BD to the Evangelist and at times to the Ecclesiastical Redactor. See Smith, *Composition* 220-22.

The Third Edition of the Gospel

In 1:35, 37, 40, there is mention of two disciples, of whom one is Andrew. The other of the two does not figure in the narrative action. If the other of these two disciples is the BD, we learn nothing about him other than that he was originally a disciple of John the Baptist and that he was a follower of Jesus from the beginning. These are not inconsequential features. If he was a follower of a baptist movement, it would provide a possible source for familiarity with the apocalyptic worldview associated with the baptizing Essene movement. Moreover, the fact that he was present from the beginning of Jesus' ministry would strengthen the credibility of his role as a witness.

John 13:21-27 reveals much about the identity of the BD and shows his closeness to Jesus and his superiority to Peter, but it does not seem to address other issues of the third edition. The meaning of 19:26-27 is the object of much discussion, but it is certainly intended to indicate the faithfulness of the BD in that he is with Jesus even to the foot of the cross. He is again contrasted with Peter, who by this time had denied Jesus and had run away during the Passion. It also focuses on the intimacy of the relationship between the mother of Jesus and the BD. But beyond this there is no evidence of the other issues of the third edition.

In 18:15-18, we encounter the second of the references to "another" disciple. If this is the BD, then we have another implicit example of the superiority of the BD to Peter. In this case, both Peter and the BD are in the courtyard, but only Peter denies that he is a disciple of Jesus; the BD remains faithful. The fact that it is the BD who gains entrance for Peter seems insignificant, much like the comment that the BD ran faster than Peter to the tomb of Jesus.

In 19:32-37, we have the clearest involvement of the BD in the larger theological issues of the third edition — and yet the BD is not even mentioned by name. But the witness here is understood to be the BD since he was the only disciple present at the cross. The BD witnesses to the fact that Jesus dies as the Paschal Lamb (the Lamb who takes away the sin of the world, according to 1:29). Moreover, he witnesses that both blood and water came from the side of Jesus. And so he affirms both that the living water of the Spirit has emerged and that the blood of Jesus will take away sin.

In 20:2-10, the BD is again contrasted with Peter. The fact that the BD runs faster is probably inconsequential, but the fact that he stands aside to allow Peter to enter the tomb first is not. The BD recognizes a certain primacy for Peter. Yet the BD immediately is shown to be superior to Peter in that the BD sees the empty tomb and comes to belief in the resurrection while (implicitly) Peter does not. No other themes appear.

In 21:7, we have an almost identical interplay of themes. When the BD recognizes that it is the Lord speaking to them from shore, he again emerges as superior to Peter, particularly in the realm of spiritual insight.

Section 2. The Criteria Used for the Third Edition

In 21:20-23, the issue is the death of the BD. The community had just experienced the death of the BD, and many had believed that he would not die before the return of Jesus.

Finally, in 21:24, the narrator affirms that it has been the BD who has borne witness about "these things," and he affirms that his witness is true.

Conclusion

What we see then from this review of the BD passages is that his main function within the Gospel is as witness. The BD grounds the fact that this community has a superior understanding of Jesus because of his own spiritual insight. Yet the passages also confirm that the community recognizes Peter as the one to whom authority over the communities was given. At the same time, this review confirms that they exhibit only a minimal amount of concern for themes of the third edition (19:35 is an exception). This must be acknowledged. However, two other factors need to be considered. First, there is evidence (discussed in detail in the analysis of the Composition) that the passages have been added to the Gospel after the composition of the second edition (cf. especially the relation of 13:21-27 to what surrounds it and the relation of 19:31-37 to 19:38). While this does not prove that they come from the third edition, it increases the probability of it. Secondly, the BD passages do have some ties to the third edition in 19:35 and at the same time do not exhibit features that would separate them from the concerns of that edition. As a result, it seems best to consider them as part of the third edition, and intended specifically to ground the truth of the witness of the third edition in order to confirm it against the challenge of the opponents who were interpreting the tradition in a way different from the BD's followers.

3E-41. **In the third edition, the importance of the material and physical is affirmed, whereas this was downplayed in the second edition (2E-18). This value is expressed both in the importance of the fact that the Word became "flesh" and by the value attributed to ritual sacraments, including the rite of initiation (Baptism) and the sacred meal (the Eucharist).**[210]

In the second edition, the material world was denigrated in the attempt to point to the importance of the Spirit, because the author of the second edition strove to impress on his readers the importance of the eschatological outpouring of the Spirit.

---

210. For bibliography related to this topic, see literature referred to in Part 4, Section 11.

The Third Edition of the Gospel

In the third edition, the audience is now one that agrees that the eschatological outpouring has taken place but that the realm of the material is important and should be reaffirmed, not in place of the Spirit but as a dimension of the communication of the Spirit. Consequently, "flesh" now has a positive connotation. It is this dimension of the presentation of the Gospel that is often referred to as the Gospel's "sacramental interest."[211]

Scholars have differed considerably in their estimation of a sacramental dimension in the Gospel of John. This has ranged from those who see no allusions at all, to views that see allusions to actions that were later considered "sacraments," to passages where actual rituals of the community seem to be referred to. For the purposes of the present discussion, a sacrament will be defined as an external ("material") action understood to be a vehicle for the communication of a spiritual reality. In this sense, it will be harmonious with the view of the third edition, which reasserts the value of the "material" in relation to the spiritual.

It should also be pointed out that in the second edition of the Gospel it is a common practice to speak of material, physical images such as birth, water, bread, origin, and departure in such a way as to point to the spiritual. Thus, when Jesus offers the Samaritan woman "living water," the actual physical water is not important except as a symbol. However, in passages with a sacramental interest, the actual physical object or action takes on an importance in the communication of the spiritual. In this sense, texts that speak of Jesus as "the bread come down from heaven" will not be viewed as sacramental since, even though they may be seen to have a sacramental "overtone," they are intended primarily as *symbols* of spiritual realities rather than as *vehicles* of the spiritual.

The revaluation of the material and physical spheres is seen first of all in the affirmation by the author of the third edition of the material dimension of the existence of Jesus. In 1:14, Jesus himself is spoken of in both the most exalted and the most material of terms, when the author says: "The Word became flesh."[212] The physical existence of Jesus is important as the manifestation of God within the world. But the fact that he became flesh within the

---

211. In what follows, I will speak only about the role of the material as a vehicle for the holy. Others have sought to find references to the sacramental in various symbols of the Gospel. For example, some have seen references to Baptism in many of the passages that mention water. Many have associated the Eucharist with passages that speak of meals, food, bread, the vine, wine, and the flesh and blood of the Son of Man. Some have even found references to matrimony at Cana and the anointing of the sick in the washing of the feet of Jesus in 12:1-8.

212. One need think only of 6:63 ("The Spirit is what gives life; the flesh is useless") to see just how sharp the contrast is between these two estimations of the value of the physical/material aspects of reality.

Section 2. The Criteria Used for the Third Edition

world, like other human beings, is precisely what is emphasized and seen to be important.

When we look at the possible allusion to Baptism in 3:5, the role of the material is more difficult to determine. Many commentators recognize at least the possibility that, when Jesus speaks in 3:5 of the necessity of being reborn of "water" and the Spirit, he is affirming the importance of the water of Baptism as a vehicle of the transmission of the Spirit.

The meaning of this verse is complicated by the fact that the image of water is used by the author of the second edition to symbolize the gift of the Spirit (e.g., 4:10-15; 7:37-39). In favor of a sacramental understanding of the reference to water in 3:5 is the fact that the image of water here is not an inherent part of the overall symbolism of the passage since water is not an inherent element of the notion of birth as used in the discourse. In the instances where water is a symbol of the Spirit, the image of water is the focus of the symbolism. For example, in chapter 4, where Jesus offers the Samaritan woman living water, water *is* the symbol of the Spirit.[213] In 7:37-39, it is said that water will flow from the side of Christ. It is then explained that water refers to the Spirit. Again water is the image that symbolizes the Spirit. In chapter 3, however, the symbol is (re)birth, not water. And so the introduction of water here is very likely to be secondary and so a symbol of the initiation rite by which the community saw the Spirit to be conferred.

Nor can the combination "water and Spirit" in 3:5 be seen as an example of hendiadys, as is the phrase "Spirit and truth" in 4:23-24. Therefore, it seems that, after excluding these other possibilities, the sacramental interpretation of water in the verse is the most likely.

The question whether there is a sacramental dimension in 6:30-59 has also resulted in a considerable variety of opinion. While some scholars would deny any sacramental interest in the chapter, most would seem to find some degree of reference to the Eucharist. What is debated is where this begins.

I will not enter into a discussion here of whether the general references to Jesus as "bread come down from heaven" have a Eucharistic overtone. In the second edition of the Gospel, a number of material images are used as pointers to spiritual realities. These instances are symbolic but not sacramental. Some scholars argue that allusions to the Eucharist begin in the way the scene of the multiplication itself is portrayed. The evidence commonly proposed is the reference to "having given thanks," which comes from the Greek verb *eucharisteō*, which later became the technical term for the ritual reenactment of the Lord's

---

213. There is a variety of opinions about what is being symbolized by the water in chapter 4. The interpretation offered here is based on the explanation in 7:37-39, where living water is explicitly said to be a symbol of the Spirit.

The Third Edition of the Gospel

Supper. However, three points need to be made. First, that this is an allusion to the Christian ritual is doubtful at best since "giving thanks" was part of the normal procedure of blessing before eating food.[214] Second, the possibility that the use of the word itself in the Gospel of John carries with itself a sacramental sense is lessened by the fact that the Gospel uses the same word for Jesus' action in the prayer before the raising of Lazarus where no sacramental meaning is intended. It is more likely that in 6:11 the word is being used interchangeably with *eulogeō*, the equally common verb for "blessing."

It is more likely that the first reference to the Eucharistic ritual is in 6:23.[215] Here the verb appears with *kyrios* in the genitive absolute: "the Lord having given thanks." The fact that the author has chosen this term to characterize the events of the day before suggests strongly that the meaning of the verb has changed from the more general one of "giving thanks" to an almost technical reference to the ritual.

The other verses most commonly seen as having a Eucharistic meaning are 6:51-58. Yet even here there is considerable disagreement. What is important for our purposes here is the introduction of the emphasis on flesh. For the first time the bread that Jesus will give is his "flesh" (v. 51). "Eating the flesh" (vv. 52, 53) and "feeding on"[216] the flesh (vv. 54, 55, 56), as well as "drinking the blood" (vv. 53, 54, 55, 56), become dominant concepts in these verses. The emphasis on the "material" here is obvious. Moreover, it contrasts sharply with the statement in v. 63 about the flesh being useless. That the references are to the Eucharist is confirmed by the use of flesh and blood to refer to the Eucharist elsewhere in the New Testament (e.g., 1 Cor 10:16). Consequently, the sacramental dimension (as it is defined above) of these verses seems well established.

In 19:34, a verse that comes from the third edition, it is said that blood and water poured out from the pierced side of Jesus. It will be argued below in the Commentary that these words probably refer to the fact that Jesus came not

---

214. Audet ("Esquisse" 371-99) argues that *eucharisteō* parallels the use of *barak* in Hebrew. Barrett (*Gospel* 276) points to separate blessings for both the bread and the wine: "Blessed art thou, O Lord our God, King of the universe, who bringest forth bread from the earth"; "Blessed art thou . . . who gives us the fruit of the vine." Barrett continues, "It follows that there is nothing in the acts here ascribed to Jesus that would be out of place or even unusual in any Jewish meal. . . ." The later tradition saw in the act of feeding as well as in the term used a "type" of the later Eucharist, but there is nothing in the wording or the act itself that is sacramental.

215. So also Schnackenburg (*Gospel* 2:16), who would agree with this view in almost all aspects, namely, that the use of *eucharisteō* in v. 11 is not sacramental but that the use in v. 23 may well be both sacramental and the work of an editor.

216. The author introduces the more graphic word *trōgein* in place of *phagein* here. The verbs are discussed in the Notes in the Commentary.

Section 2. The Criteria Used for the Third Edition

only in water (i.e., by giving the Spirit) but also by blood (i.e., by giving his life for our sins). If this is the case, the reference to the blood of Jesus again affirms the importance of the role of the physical death of Jesus.

In many discussions of the sacramental dimension of the Gospel, the bestowal of the power to forgive sins is singled out as a clear example of a sacrament. The bestowal of this power is an example of the bestowal of a spiritual power that the disciples will exercise in the future. But the verse seems to presume some communication of the nature of the sins that would allow the disciple to decide whether to forgive or not, and so it would seem that this was intended by the community as a "sacramental" action.

Up to this point we have noted the contrast in the approaches of the second and third editions. It should also be noted that a reevaluation of the role of the physical begins in 1 John. In 1 John, there are repeated affirmations that the message the author preaches is based on what "we have heard, . . . looked at with our eyes, . . . we have seen and our hands have touched" (1:1); the death of Jesus was an atoning death (2:2; 4:10); his blood cleanses the believer (1:7, 9; 5:6-7) and takes away sins (1:7, 9; 2:2, 12).[217]

The importance of the material is also evident in the emphasis on the fact that the word is what they heard (2:7) and the need for demonstrating their righteousness within the physical world through love of one another (esp. 2:9), through the sharing of material goods (3:17), through deeds in addition to words (3:18), and through other actions aimed at increasing holiness (3:3). It is also in this sense that the author stresses the importance of the confession that Jesus came "in the flesh" (4:2; 2 John 7). Nevertheless, in 1 John there is little of the expressed interest in sacramental ritual that is found in the third edition.[218] The perspective of 1 John will be discussed in detail in Part 4.

3E-42. In the third edition, the relationship of mutual indwelling between the Father and the Son is extended to include a relationship with believers. In the second edition, the focus was on the indwelling of the Son in the Father (2E-23).[219]

The variety of expressions for this concept as well as a detailed listing of where such expressions occur in the Gospel has been laid out in the discussion of im-

---

217. This is not contradicted, however, by the references to the transitoriness of "everything in the world" (2:16-17) since that simply speaks of the ultimate superiority of the spiritual, not whether it has a role in salvation.

218. Many scholars would see indications of and references to an initiation ritual behind various elements of 1 John. However, if this is correct, it is the only ritual mentioned in 1 John. See further the discussion "Material Aspects of Religion" (Part 4, Section 11).

219. For bibliography, see the discussion of immanence in the second edition (2E-23).

manence in the second edition. Here we will draw conclusions for the usage only as it appears in the third edition.

In the third edition, all of the expressions for immanence appear except for that of not being "alone." However, it is notable that in the third edition the notion does not focus primarily on the relationship between Jesus and the Father (as in the second edition) but on the relationship between Jesus and the believer; or among Jesus, the Father, and the believer; or on the relationship among believers. In each case, the intimacy of the relationship between Father and Son (i.e., immanence) is used as a model for these further relationships.

The first of the expressions, the notion of "oneness," present in the second edition, appears again in the third edition. Here it is focused primarily on the hoped-for oneness (unity) among believers (17:21, 22). The oneness of Jesus and the Father are used as the perfect example of this relationship. However, in these expressions the unity seems not to refer to an ontological relationship but a unity of conviction and belief.

The second expression (the notion of "remaining") appears first in the third author's expansion of the Bread-of-Life discourse, where the one who eats Jesus' flesh "remains" in Jesus (6:56). This is further explained by the statement that as Jesus is sent by the Father and lives through him, so the one feeding on Jesus will live through Jesus. Here the "remaining" seems to refer to an ontological relationship: the essence of life is not possible without remaining in Jesus through the eating of his flesh.

This same notion is developed more elaborately in the parable of the vine (15:4-7). There the branch is urged to remain in the vine. If it does, the believer will remain in Jesus (15:4 [twice], 5, 6, 7), and Jesus will remain in the believer (15:4, 5). If the branch does not remain in the vine, it will be cast out and wither. The relationship being emphasized is that between Jesus and the believer rather than that between Jesus and the Father. But while the notion here could refer to a unity based on conviction, in the light of 6:56 and the notion of "withering," it may well refer to the ontological reality of life itself.

In 14:23, the expression *monēn poiein* appears for the only time in the Gospel. Although it is not precisely the same expression as before, it has the same function and emphasizes the unity of the believer with the Father and Jesus.

Finally, the Paraclete is said to remain "among" you and be "in" you (14:17). This unique expression affirms that the Spirit too forms one aspect of such a relationship. In the third edition, he will be a continuing presence among the disciples. It is not insignificant that it is the Paraclete (and not simply the Spirit) who is said to remain within the believer since the Paraclete is precisely the Spirit of Truth as defined by the author.

In the third edition, the notion of being "in" the other continues to appear

Section 2. The Criteria Used for the Third Edition

(as it did in the second edition), but, as we saw above in the discussion of "oneness," the notion of the Father being in the Son and vice versa is now used to express the relation of the believer to Jesus (14:20; 17:22) and to both the Father and Jesus (17:21). It is the relation among believers that is the primary focus, and the relation of the Father and Son is used as the model of this.

Consequently, it is evident that the notion of immanence functions in different ways in the third edition from that of the second.

3E-43. In the third edition, there are four references to Jesus "choosing" the disciples. This contrasts with the second edition, where there is frequent mention of the Father "giving" believers/disciples to Jesus.

The notion of "giving" is a common one in the Gospel and is used in a considerable number of theologically significant ways. In one of these there is a pattern of (1) the Father (2) giving believers (3) to Jesus. This appears in the second edition (6:37; 10:29) and is taken over by the third author (17:9, 24) in Jesus' prayer to the Father (cf. also 6:39). However, in four texts (6:70; 13:18; 15:16, 19) Jesus is said to "choose" those who believe in him. These always appear in material identified as coming from the third edition and stress the initiative of Jesus alongside that of the Father.[220]

3E-44. In the third edition, there are repeated statements expressing the need, and the hope, for unity among believers. This does not appear in the other editions.

In 10:16, Jesus expresses the hope that there will be one flock and one shepherd. In 11:52-53, the narrator expresses the conviction that the death of Jesus will help bring "into one" the children of God scattered about. In 17:11, Jesus prays that the disciples "may be one as we are." In 17:21, he prays for the same unity among those of the next generation of believers who will believe through the word of the disciples. In 17:22, this same petition is made, and in 17:23, he prays that "they may be brought to perfect unity" as a sign of the unity between Jesus and the Father.

3E-45. In the third edition, the basis for belief continues to be the "witnesses" to Jesus as it was in the second edition(cf. 2E-14). However, in the third edition, the

---

220. This feature does not have a correlate in the second edition since the expression introduced by the second author also appears in the work of the third author, as I have indicated.

The Third Edition of the Gospel

list of witnesses is extended from four to six. In the first edition, the basis of belief had been only the "signs" performed by Jesus (1E-18).

In the first edition, the author had portrayed belief as the proper response to the signs of Jesus. In the second edition, the basis for belief was expanded to include the witness of John the Baptist, the words of Jesus, and the witness of Scripture. In the third edition, the basis for belief continues to be the witnesses that had been put forth in the second edition, but the third author now expands this list to include those witnesses that will be proper to the time after the resurrection of Jesus: the witness of the Paraclete and the witness of the disciples.

This appears in only one text (15:26-27), but that appearance is very significant and not only expands the number of witnesses from four to six, but the author does so in such a way that these witnesses will refute the views of his opponents.

5. Some Theological Features Introduced in the Second Edition and Taken Over by the Author of the Third

It will be recalled that in the discussion of the theology of the second edition certain features were listed that were introduced by the author of the second edition. These features contrasted sharply with the theology of the first edition but were taken over by the author of the third edition and so could not be said to be exclusive to the second edition. For the sake of completeness, those features are again listed here but designated as "3E-X."

3E-46X. In the third edition, the author continues the use of the title "Father" for God as it was introduced by the author of the second edition (2E-26). However, the material in which it appears is marked by other features distinctive of the third edition. As we have seen, the title does not appear in the first edition.

In the second edition, the title "Father" for God appeared sixty-one times. In the third edition it appears another forty-four times (1:14, 18; 3:35; 6:27, 57, 65; 8:28, 38; 10:15 [twice], 17, 18; 11:49, 50; 12:26, 49, 50; 14:2, 6, 13, 16, 21, 23, 24, 26, 28, 31 [twice]; 15:9, 10, 14, 15, 26 [twice]; 16:10, 15, 23, 26, 27 [twice]; 17:5, 11; 20:17 [twice]). In all these cases it appears in material identified on other grounds as coming from the third edition. However, because of the large number of instances, we will not treat the texts individually. It should be said that the third author does not modify the notion itself when he takes it over into his own composition, but rather uses it within a theological complex that is distinctive.

Section 2. The Criteria Used for the Third Edition

3E-47X. **The notion of Jesus as "Son" is introduced by the author of the second edition (2E-27X) and is taken over by the author of the third.**

The notion of Jesus as "Son" is central to both the second and third editions of the Gospel. This is the unqualified use of the term (excluding "Son of God," "Son of Man," and other uses not referring to Jesus or referring to his human sonship). In this sense it is useful primarily as a contrast with the material of the first edition. However, as we have seen (3E-26), the author of the third edition understands the sonship of Jesus differently from the author of the second edition by at times making explicit that Jesus was "unique." In fact, the first three times "Son" appears in the third edition, it is specified by this adjective (cf. 1:18; 3:16, 17) as if to establish firmly this attribute of the Son. The other times "Son" appears in the third edition (3:35, 36; 5:23 [twice], 26; 8:36; 14:13), it occurs with features that identify the material with the third edition. This will be demonstrated in the Commentary.

3E-48X. **The notion of Jesus as "sent" by the Father, which was introduced into the Gospel by the author of the second edition (2E-28X), is taken over by the author of the third.**

Within the third edition, *pempō* (in the nominal and adjectival forms) appears six times (8:29; 9:4; 12:49; 13:20; 14:24; 15:21). *Apostellō* appears twice (6:57; 20:21). It also appears in 13:20, but the identity of this verse cannot be determined. As was the case with the title "Father," the third author does not seem to have changed the concept itself, but has used it within his own distinctive theological context.

3E-49X. **The author of the third edition takes over the conception of eternal life of the second edition, where it was first introduced, but in the third edition this conception is qualified by conditions or requirements that are not evident in the texts of the second edition and which are elements in the author's response to the opponents at the time of 1 John.**

In the second edition, eternal life was presented in a "simple" framework. Although it was said that belief in (acceptance of) Jesus was necessary to obtain eternal life, it was the fact of this belief that was affirmed. However, in the third edition not only is the importance of belief in Jesus reaffirmed, but specific features of Jesus are pointed out as necessary to proper belief: that he is the "unique" Son of God; that he is "I AM"; that he is the *only* means of access to the

The Third Edition of the Gospel

Father; that he is "Jesus Christ." It is also dependent upon belief in the Resurrection, upon reception of the sacramental flesh and blood of Jesus. It is associated with "commandment" and other themes. These are listed below and discussed briefly. Further detail may be had in the Commentary.

In the third edition, *zōē* appears sixteen times (1:4; 3:15, 16, 36; 5:26, 29; 6:27, 51, 53, 54, 68; 11:25; 12:25, 50; 14:6; 17:3), and the verb *zaō* (apart from those instances where it refers to normal physical life) appears eight times (6:51 [twice], 57 [three times], 58; 11:25, 27).

In 1:4, *zōē* appears in the original material of the Prologue, which, as is described in detail in the Commentary, comes from a hymn in use within the community. In 3:15-16, eternal life is conditioned upon belief in Jesus as the *unique* Son of God (a confessional formula characteristic of the third edition). In 3:36, the author affirms that belief in, and obedience to, the Son is necessary for life. Again the context indicates that this is meant to address the issues of the community at the time of 1 John. In 5:26, Jesus' unique mode of possession of life is described (i.e., having life "in himself"). In 5:27, life is associated with bodily resurrection. Again, the topics are related to the crisis of 1 John.

In 6:27, it is the bread of life that the Son of Man will give. Not only is the bread here given by Jesus rather than being he, but Jesus is described in terms characteristic of the third edition (Son of Man). In 6:51, 53, 54, 57, 58, it is the living bread, and the bread is his flesh given for the life of the world. Thus, there is the sacramental interest and the notion of death as sacrificial typical of the third edition. John 6:68 is more difficult to determine, but given the character of the surrounding verses, it is reasonably certain that it comes from the third edition here.

In 8:12, Jesus declares that he is the "light of life." This terminology, together with imagery of light/darkness, is typical of the third edition. In 11:25-26, Jesus is inextricably associated with both the giving of life and the Resurrection. The saying in 12:25 is one of three that are incorporated together because of their similarity to sayings in the Synoptic tradition and because they show that the believer must be willing to accept the importance of death and suffering in imitation of Jesus. The saying in 12:25 explains the paradox of losing one's life and gaining eternal life. It comes from the third edition. In 12:50, life is associated with the term "commandment," a feature of the third edition. In 14:6, Jesus explains that he is the sole source of life and of access to the Father. This is intended to refute the view of the opponents of 1 John.

In 17:3, in the final occurrence of the term in the Gospel, we are told that eternal life is inextricably associated with both the Father and with Jesus, identified in terms typical of the third edition: "Jesus Christ."

Section 2. The Criteria Used for the Third Edition

"Living and Not Dying"

Also related to this concept are the texts that state that a person will not die (forever). In the second edition, this appears only in 6:50, 8:21, and 10:28. In the third edition, it appears three times (8:24, 51-52; 11:25-26). Although the references to "not dying" are generally added simply to emphasize the importance of the gift of life (e.g., 6:50; 10:28), in the second edition this is in accord with the "simple" conception of life typical of that edition. The contrast between the usage in the second and third editions is particularly noticeable in chapter 8. In 8:21 (from the second edition), dying in their sins is related to his going away before they turn to belief. This is a theme of the second edition, but in 8:24 (from the third edition) living and not dying requires belief that Jesus is "I AM." In 8:51-52, this living and not dying is related to keeping the word of Jesus. In 11:25-26, it is related to belief in Jesus as the Resurrection and the Life. All of the statements from the third edition require actions that are appropriate to the believer in 1 John.

3E-50X. **Among the words of the second edition taken over by the third author are "glory/glorify" and "witness." Although the terms are taken over from the second edition, they have different meanings when used by the author of the third.**

Glory/Glorify

As was the case in the second edition, "glory/glorify" refers to the true identity of a person as revealed by words and actions. The noun and verb (in boldface) appear fourteen times in the third edition (1:14; 8:50; 11:40; 12:**23**, 41; 13:**31** [twice], **32** [twice]; 14:13; 16:14; 17:4, **5**; 21:19). Although the third author continues to use it in the same sense in which it was found in the second edition, he also uses it with new connotations and applies it to new concepts. Thus the third author attempts to show that the true glory of Jesus involves certain elements that the opponents of 1 John would deny or ignore. For example, in 1:14, the nature of the "glory" that is perceived is specified as that of a "unique" son. In 11:40, Jesus uses the phrase "glory of God" in a unique way to refer to the raising of Lazarus. In 17:5, the glory of Jesus is said to include preexistence.

Witness

"Witness" continues to be used in the third edition. However, the number and type of witnesses are different. This is most apparent in 15:26-27, where the

The Third Edition of the Gospel

Paraclete is listed as a witness along with the human witnesses in the form of the disciples. This is a curious development, which contrasts with the conviction of the second edition that the (human) witness of John the Baptist is of minimal significance.

6. Features of the Third Edition That Become Apparent Once the Analysis Is Complete

Up to this point I have spoken of "characteristics" of the third edition. I have reserved this term for those elements of the third edition which can be used as criteria in identifying the material of the third edition.

However, there are other elements of the third edition which cannot be used properly as criteria but nevertheless emerge as consistent "features" of the edition. The consistency of these elements does not emerge until the analysis of the Gospel is completed. However, once the material has been identified as belonging to a given edition on the basis of other criteria, these features emerge as consistent within that edition. At the same time, once the consistency of their occurrence is noted, they become another source of confirmation that the analysis is indeed correct. These will be noted here and discussed briefly where appropriate. They will be discussed in greater detail in the appropriate places in the Commentary in Volume 2.

3E-51F. One of the most widespread features of the second and third editions is the type of formula used to introduce quotations from, and references to, Scripture. In the third edition, quotations and references are introduced by the formula "in order that the Scripture may be fulfilled . . ." *(hina plērōthē hē graphē . . .)* or some variation of it. In the second edition, quotations and references are introduced by the formula "as it is written . . ." *(kathōs estin gegrammenon . . .)* or a minor variation of it (2E-32F).

These are discussed in detail in the Volume 3, Appendix 1 (Quotations of the Old Testament), and that discussion will not be repeated here. The introductory formula typical of the third edition ("in order that the Scripture may be fulfilled . . ." *[hina plērōthē hē graphē . . .]*) occurs six times (13:18; 19:24, 28, 36, 37; 17:12). Two other times the third author appends a quotation to one from the second edition, and in those instances he uses a shorter form involving the verb "says" *(eipen)* (12:40; 19:37).

Section 2. The Criteria Used for the Third Edition

3E-52F. In the second edition, there is frequent mention of "the world" in both a positive and a negative sense. The same is true of the third edition. The precise meaning of this term is difficult to determine in all cases. However, one particular formulation using this term, namely, the expression "of this world," used as an indication of allegiance and identity, is dualistic and appears only in the third edition and in 1 John.

The first reflection of this dualistic conception of the world appears in 1 John 2:16. There the author explains that "everything in the world ... is not 'from the Father' but is 'from the world.'" Unless one understands this statement to be a dualistic one, it is meaningless.[221] That the things "in the world" are "from the world" would be so redundant as to be meaningless unless "the world" in the second phrase was understood to be a "source" or "origin" in such a way that it could be contrasted with the possibility of their being "from the Father." It can only be intended to express the two possible sources of the desires in the world (i.e., desire of the flesh, desire of the eyes, and arrogance regarding life). Such desires and attitudes are said to be typical "of the world."

This same dualistic framework is expressed again in 4:3-6. 4:1-6 as a whole contains one of the clearest dualistic paradigms of the Letter.[222] In it, the Spirit of God is contrasted with the spirit of the Antichrist. These two opposed spirits are manifest in two opposed groups on earth: those who confess Jesus Christ come in the flesh and those who "do away with" Jesus. The author concludes his chiastic discussion of the two spirits in v. 3c with the statement that the Antichrist "is now already in the world." Although this last phrase could indicate simply the fact that the Antichrist has already appeared, the subsequent context makes it clear that being "in the world" is intended to mean that the Antichrist is the spirit which determines the character of "the world." This is evident from vv. 5-6, where the false prophets and those who do not confess Jesus properly are said to be "of the world" and to be contrasted with the author and his followers, who are "of God."

The author then says that those who are "of the world" speak "out of the world." That is, they act according to their orientation, and others who are "of the world" listen to them. In contrast, those who are "of God" hear the author and his followers — and the one who is not "of God" does not hear them. Clearly the usage is dualistic.

The first instance of this dualistic usage in the Gospel appears in John

---

221. That the things "in the world" are "from the world" would be so redundant as to be meaningless unless "the world" in the second phrase was understood to be a "source" or "origin" in such a way that it could be contrasted with the possibility of their being "of the Father."

222. For further details regarding this passage, see the Commentary on 1 John.

The Third Edition of the Gospel

8:23, where Jesus proclaims that "you are of this world; I am not of this world." While this statement reflects the dualistic use of the term, the paradigmatic presentation of the term appears in John 15:19. Speaking to the disciples, Jesus says: "If you were of the world, the world would love its own, but because you are not of the world, but I chose you out of the world." Here there are two opposed groups: the world and those chosen by Jesus. "The world" loves its own but does not love the disciples.

In 17:6, Jesus addresses the Father and says that he has given the disciples to Jesus "out of the world" *(ek tou kosmou)*. That is, as Jesus says in 17:14: They are not "of the world," just as I am not "of the world."[223] Then, in 17:15, Jesus prays, not that the Father may take them out "of the world," but that he may protect them from the Evil One. Thus, those who are "of the world" belong to "the Evil One" and are loved by "the world." However, the disciples are not "of the world," and the world does not love them. Rather, they belong to the Father, and the Father has given them to Jesus. This is another of the ways the third author expresses his apocalyptic dualism in which persons belong either to one or the other of two opposed groups.

As is typical in such paradigmatic expressions, there is little discussion of movement from one group to the other.[224] Thus, in 17:9, Jesus does not pray for "the world" but only on behalf of those whom the Father has given to Jesus.

Two other instances of the phrase appear in the Gospel. The first appears in 13:1c ("having loved his own in the world, he loved them to the end"). While this statement is too brief to enable us to be certain of the worldview from which it is spoken, two factors suggest that it is intended to reflect the apocalyptic worldview. First, the theme of "loving his own in the world" echoes the dualistic paradigm described above in that here we read of Jesus loving his own as opposed to the world loving its own in 15:19 ("If you were of the world, the world would love its own; but because you are not of the world, but I chose you out of the world; for this reason the world hates you").

Secondly, the fact that 13:1c is identified as from the third edition by other features further suggests that the expression "of the world" here is also typical of that edition.

The case of 18:36 is more difficult. When Jesus speaks to Pilate, he says that his kingship is "not of this world." The phrase here is not precisely the same as in the other instances. The contrast here is not between what is "of God" and what is "of the world." Rather, the contrast is between this world and another world. At the same time, toward the end of this exchange with Pilate (v. 37), Jesus uses language that is clearly dualistic when he speaks of those who are "of

---

223. See also the nearly identical statement in 17:16.
224. But see 17:6, where Jesus chooses his own out of the world.

Section 2. The Criteria Used for the Third Edition

the truth" hearing his voice. Thus, it may be that the author intended the use of "world" in the dualistic sense here also even though he expressed it somewhat differently. It will be grouped with the dualistic sense in this Commentary.

3E-53F. In the third edition, the verbs "descend" *(katabainō)* and "ascend" *(anabainō)* have a theological meaning not found in the other editions of the Gospel.

Anabainō appears fifteen times in the gospel (1:51; 2:13; 3:13; 5:1; 6:62; 7:8 [twice], 10, 14; 10:1; 11:55; 12:20; 20:17 [twice]; 21:11). Of these, seven (2:13; 5:1; 7:10, 14; 11:55; 12:20; 21:11) refer to "going up" to Jerusalem or to a feast or, in the case of 21:11, going up on shore from the Sea of Galilee. Another instance (10:1) speaks of a thief "going up" into the sheepfold. None of these is relevant to the present inquiry.

The seven remaining instances have a theological or quasi-theological meaning. In 1:51 we read of angels "going up" and "coming down" on the Son of Man.[225] Two instances speak of the Son of Man "going up" (3:13; 6:62). Two (20:17 [twice]) speak of Jesus "going up." Finally, the two instances in 7:8 are meant to be ambiguous. They appear at first to refer to Jesus' going up to the feast. However, the precise wording is that he does not go up "at" this feast. This is a reference to his Passion.

From this analysis, it is apparent that the term, when used in a theological sense, is a quasi-technical term for Jesus' going to the Father through his Passion and Resurrection. Moreover, 6:63 is important as expressing a belief in the preexistence of Jesus (i.e., he will go up "to where he was before"). The consistency of usage and its identification with the third edition in 1:51; 3:13; 6:62; 7:8 (twice) enable us to use this as a criterion in the identification of 20:17 also coming from the third edition.

Katabainō appears seventeen times (1:32, 33, 51; 2:12; 3:13; 4:47, 49, 51; 5:7; 6:16, 33, 38, 41, 42, 50, 51, 58). Of these, two refer to the Holy Spirit (1:32, 33) and six refer to ordinary geographical movement (2:12; 4:47, 49, 51; 5:7; 6:16). These are not relevant to this inquiry. The remaining nine (1:51; 3:13; 6:33, 38, 41, 42, 50, 51, 58) refer to, or are associated with, the Son of Man (in chaps. 1 and 3) or the Bread from Heaven (the remaining instances).

Of particular importance is the instance in 3:13, where it is said that no one has ascended into heaven except the one who descended from heaven, the Son of Man. This expresses the full paradigm regarding the Son of Man: he has descended from heaven and will ascend there again. In this statement there is a

---

225. The meaning here would appear to be somewhat different. See the Note on 1:51.

The Third Edition of the Gospel

clear conviction of the preexistence of the Son of Man insofar as the Son of Man has "descended." Preexistence is also associated with the ascent of the Son of Man in 6:63, where it is said that the listeners may be scandalized if they see the Son of Man ascend *to where he was before.* This is true "parabola Christology."

The instances in chapter 6 constitute a particular problem and are discussed at length in the Addendum following the analysis of 6:30-50. That discussion is summarized here.

When we examine the instances in chapter 6, we find a usage which is at times ambiguous. We may note first that in the discourse of 6:30-58, there are statements which clearly indicate a belief in preexistence while there are others that almost surely do not. For example, the initial reference to the bread "from heaven" *(ek tou ouranou)* occurs in the quotation from Scripture (v. 31), and no preexistence is implied there. The same is true of its use in the reinterpretation of Scripture and its application to Jesus (v. 32). However, v. 46, where Jesus says: "Not that anyone has seen the Father except the one who is from the Father — this one has seen the Father," is a clear statement of preexistence.

When we turn to the verses (vv. 33, 41, 42, 50, 51) where the words "from heaven" appear with "come down" *(katabainō),* the meaning becomes more ambiguous. In the discussion of the Composition of v. 33, I argue that that verse would seem not to refer to preexistence but simply be an alternate way of expressing the idea contained in the original quotation and reinterpretation. Verse 41 is ambiguous. It certainly could be (and probably was) interpreted as referring to preexistence in the final edition of the Gospel. Yet it is possible that it originally came from the second edition and is simply intended to indicate that Jesus was sent by God.[226]

Verse 42 is an instance of misunderstanding and is also ambiguous, although I am inclined to think that, as originally composed, it was not intended to refer to preexistence. But the evidence is hardly clear. Nevertheless, the verse is susceptible to being understood as referring to preexistence in the context of the third edition. Verses 50-51 contain almost identical formulations of the expression regarding bread come down from heaven. The first comes from the second edition, and the following one comes from the third edition. In the statements themselves there is no unique formulation which would prove an intention to speak of preexistence.

Finally, for the reasons given in the Addendum to 6:25-50, I would judge v. 38 (as well as v. 46) to come from the third author.[227]

---

226. See the Note on v. 41 in the Commentary.
227. This is my own best judgment on the use of *katabainō* in chapter 6. It must be said, however, that if it could be proved that one or the other instance was the work of the third author, the overall interpretation of the chapter would not be changed.

Section 2. The Criteria Used for the Third Edition

3E-54F. In the third edition, the verb *hypsoō* ("to lift up") is used to refer to the Crucifixion of Jesus. This does not appear in the other editions.

The verb *hypsoō* appears five times in the gospel (3:14 [twice]; 8:28; 12:32, 34). In every case it appears in material of the third edition and is associated with the figure of the Son of Man. It is closely related to the use of *anabainō*. However, the meaning of *hypsoō* is more specific and refers to the Crucifixion itself rather than to the more comprehensive action of Jesus' "ascent," which includes the whole series of actions leading to his return to the Father.

3E-55F. In the third edition, it is said that Jesus has "seen" God and tells of what he has "seen." This is not present in earlier editions of the Gospel.

In the second edition of the Gospel, there are repeated references to the fact that Jesus speaks the word of the Father that he has *heard* (e.g., 5:30; 8:26, 40; 15:15; cf. also 12:50). However, in the third edition, Jesus is said to have both heard (8:40; 12:50; 15:15) and seen (1:18; 3:11, 32; 5:19c, 20; 6:46; 8:38, 57) the Father. Is this change accidental? It would seem not.

In 1:18, the third author glosses the hymn that prefaces the Gospel by adding that "No one has ever seen God; the unique Son, the one at the bosom of the Father, made him known." This verse makes it clear that Jesus was present with the Father and so "saw" what no human ever saw.

In 3:11, the third author describes Jesus as witnessing to what he has "seen." Following this (in v. 13), the third author makes it clear that the Son of Man is the only one who can speak of what he has seen because no one has ascended into heaven, and only the Son of Man has descended. The basis of Jesus' having seen the Father is made quite clear. No one else has *ascended* to heaven, and Jesus has *descended*. The third author repeats this almost verbatim in 3:31-32: "The one who comes from heaven [is above all]. What he has seen and heard, he bears witness to. . . ." It is quite clear in 6:62 (another Son of Man statement) that Jesus will "ascend," but it will be an ascent *to where he was before*. In this view, Jesus first descended and only later ascended. His prior presence with God is the basis for his seeing.

In 8:38, Jesus again says that he speaks what he has *seen* with the Father. And when he contrasts this with the experience of his listeners, he says that they do what they have *heard* from their father (the devil). If the choice of verbs was simply casual here, we would expect him to keep the parallelism with the previous clause by saying that the listeners do what they have *seen* with their father. But he does not. He does not claim that they have seen the devil, but only that by doing his will they are doing what they have *heard* from him. A final in-

The Third Edition of the Gospel

stance of what Jesus has "seen" is in 8:57, where it is said that he also saw Abraham. This instance appears in material that is identified on other grounds as coming from the third edition. At the same time, it is evident that this statement also presumes the preexistence of Jesus.

But now we need to return to 5:19-20. In both verses, there are references to Jesus seeing what the Father has done. In v. 19, we read that Jesus does what he *sees* the Father doing, and in v. 20, we read that the Father *shows* the Son all things which he himself does and that he will *show* him greater works than these. The references to the fact that the Father "shows" Jesus *all things which he himself does* is typical of third-edition material elsewhere and reflects the third author's attempts to articulate the equality between the Father and the Son. The fact that Jesus is said to do what he *sees* is consistent with the view of the third author elsewhere and so indicates that the instances of vv. 19-20 also come from the third edition.[228]

Finally, we examine 6:46. As was the case with 5:19-20, there is no major interruption of the text that would clearly indicate that v. 46 is an addition by the third author. However, when viewed in the context of the distinction between who has "seen" God and who has only been able to "hear" his word, the conclusion is unavoidable that the verse is an attempt to clarify the meaning of the previous verse. In v. 45 (2E), Jesus had explained that those listening to the Father would come to him (Jesus). But immediately v. 46 clarifies v. 45 by pointing out that no one has seen the Father except the one who is from the Father! The abruptness of this statement as well as its evident purpose of clarifying the previous statement can only mean that it is the work of the third author: only Jesus had seen the Father!

In addition, as has been pointed out above, all references to having "seen" the Father necessarily imply the preexistence of Jesus. It is only because Jesus was preexistent that he had seen the Father. Thus, again, we find a consistency with the theology of the third edition in a topic that distinguishes the third edition's Christology from that of the prior editions.

That the third author would have chosen to make such a distinction could not be predicted. It is a feature that emerges only from a review of the material already identified by the more formal criteria. Nevertheless, when viewed in this perspective, its appearance in the third edition is so consistent that it may be used in an auxiliary way to help in the identification of material.

---

228. It is the consistency of usage elsewhere (in both the second and the third editions) that leads to the conclusion that these instances also come from the third edition. See also the discussion of the Composition of 5:19-20 in the Commentary.

Section 2. The Criteria Used for the Third Edition

3E-56F. In the third edition, a number of passages and terms have been introduced into the Gospel because of their similarity to the Synoptic accounts. This does not appear in the other editions.

While there is material in the first and second editions that is similar in general content to the Synoptics (e.g., the multiplication of the loaves in the first edition; the cleansing of the Temple in the second edition), there is other material in the Gospel that gives the impression that it has been inserted into the Gospel *precisely for the purpose* of having a particular feature of the Synoptic Gospels reflected within the Johannine Gospel. Some of these features are quite brief; some are substantial. This material has certain distinctive features that identify it as an addition by the third author.

First, there are larger passages or comments that are similar to the Synoptics but whose chief characteristic is that, although it bears considerable similarity to the Synoptics, it has been incorporated into the Gospel only poorly and sometimes results in confusion. There are three striking instances of this.

The first appears in 4:44, which speaks of a prophet being without honor in his own country. As will be evident in the Commentary, there are insurmountable problems in correlating this verse with its literary context, and it can be correlated to the Gospel as a whole only in the most general way.

The second occurs in 12:1-8, which contains the account of the anointing of Jesus' feet by Mary at Bethany. As is discussed in detail in the Commentary, this passage contains elements from both the Marcan (Matthean) and the Lucan accounts of the anointing but combines them in a way that shows that the author did not fully understand the meaning of the Synoptic accounts. In addition, the passage as a whole is related more to the Synoptic context in which the anointing of the body of Jesus was to be done by women on the morning of the first day of the week rather than by Joseph of Arimathea and Nicodemus on the afternoon of the burial itself.

The third instance occurs in 19:23-24, where the author quotes Ps 22:19 regarding the dividing of garments and the casting of lots for the clothing of Jesus. Although the Psalm itself is written in poetic (synonymous) parallelism and describes only one action, the author of the Johannine account understands the verse to describe two distinct actions, thus manifesting a failure to recognize this feature of Hebrew poetry. Again, the details of this passage are discussed in the Commentary on the verses.

Thus, it would seem that not only was the third author intent on imitating the Synoptics, but at times he did so without fully understanding what he was duplicating.

Second, there are other insertions that bear a striking resemblance to the Synoptics but are much more brief. An example of this would be the insertion

The Third Edition of the Gospel

of "baptize in the Holy Spirit" (1:34). This term is found only here in the Gospel of John, yet it appears prominently in the Synoptics. Another example is the term "Kingdom of God" in 3:3 and 3:5. This term, which is so distinctive of the apocalyptic worldview of the Synoptics and so pervasive within the Synoptic Gospels, appears only in these two instances in the entire Gospel of John. Not only does the term appear only here, but it is not developed at all. While these might appear to be instances of "relics" of the first edition rather than insertions by the third author, there is a major difference. The features that Dodd called "undigested scraps" and which come from the first edition are elements that pertain primarily to narrative and do not continue to function in the narrative of the Gospel; moreover, they have little or no theological content. These are to be distinguished from such terms as "Kingdom of God." Although these could be seen as "relics" also, their function is markedly different. While they do not function within the overriding theology of the Gospel, they reflect a distinct theological view (i.e., that of the Synoptics and that of the apocalyptic viewpoint generally), and so they have a role within the Gospel. Moreover, while a given instance may not be developed, the presence of these features is consistent with the introduction of similar elements elsewhere in the Gospel. This is an entirely different situation from that accompanying the "relics" of the first edition.

In addition to these types of material with Synoptic affinities, there are other features which have as their purpose the correlation of the Johannine account with the Synoptic chronology. An example of this appears in 3:24. Without preparation, the text suddenly comments that "John had not yet been put in prison." There is no reason for this comment other than to attempt (an awkward) correlation of the Johannine account with the Synoptic one in which Jesus' ministry did not begin until after the arrest of John (cf. Mark 1:14). Other examples appear in 4:2 and 4:48.

In 4:2, we see one of the most awkward insertions in the Gospel. After three texts that indicate that Jesus had a baptizing ministry (3:22, 26; 4:1), we find the statement that Jesus himself was not baptizing but only his disciples (4:2). Most commentators note the awkwardness of this statement and suggest that the statement is intended to negate the "original" Johannine text and to correlate the account with that of the Synoptics.[229]

In 4:48, the term *sēmeia kai terata* appears in a verse that is generally recognized to be an editorial addition. The fact that the other editions had such distinctive terminology for miracles suggests that the use of the term here by

---

229. For example, Bernard, *Gospel* 1:133-34; Bultmann, *Gospel* 175; R. E. Brown, *Gospel* 1:164; Schnackenburg, *Gospel* 1:422; Moloney, *Gospel* 119. A particularly helpful discussion of the verse can be found in Meier, *Marginal* 1:195 n. 74.

Section 2. The Criteria Used for the Third Edition

the third author was intended to reflect one of the Synoptic terms for miracle (cf. Mark 13:22; Matt 24:24).

3E-57F. In the third edition, the author frequently makes brief modifications to the text by "bundling" (grouping) his additions together into a relatively brief context and then addressing the issue seldom or not at all again. This is not evident in the other editions.

Often the author of the third edition inserts the same comment or term several times in close succession, often in groups of two, three, or four. It is sometimes the case that this grouping will be the only reference to a particular point. Evidently he used such repetition as a means of establishing and emphasizing the presence of a particular concept. This feature, which appears only when the analysis is complete, occurs in connection with five sets of texts.

The Kingdom of God

It is well known that in the Gospel of John, the term "Kingdom of God" appears only in chapter 3. There it appears twice, once as the object of "seeing" (v. 3) and once as the object of the verb "entering" (v. 5), and it is awkward both times. What is awkward here is the fact that the term is so characteristic of the apocalyptic view of the Synoptics and appears so frequently there, but in John only here, in a context that is otherwise devoid of apocalyptic. It would seem that the author simply wanted his readers to know that the discussion of eternal life, which the second author presented in chapter 3, was to be understood in connection with this conception of the Kingdom.

"Unique Son"

This distinctive term appears twice in the Prologue (1:14, 18) and twice in chapter three (3:16, 18). In both instances the texts are in close proximity to one another but appear nowhere else in the Gospel. Yet the term has a clear polemical purpose for the third author and serves to distinguish the sonship of Jesus from the sonship of the believer.[230]

---

230. These texts are discussed in more detail in the Notes to these verses in the Commentary.

The Third Edition of the Gospel

"And I Will Raise the Person Up on the Last Day"

In 5:28, we find the most developed statement about bodily resurrection in the Gospel ("an hour is coming in which all those in the tombs will hear his voice and will come forth, those who have done good to a resurrection of life, those who have practiced evil to a resurrection of judgment"). As is shown in the Analysis, the belief in bodily resurrection is characteristic of the third edition. Apart from this statement, the only other time there is a reference to bodily resurrection is in chapter 6. There, in the Bread-of-Life discourse (6:30-58), the statement "and I will raise the person up on the last day" appears (with slight variations) four times: vv. 39c, 40c, 44c, and 54b. In each case the statement is awkward in its context and seems to be almost an afterthought. Again the repetition seems intended to emphasize the importance of the notion even though it will not appear elsewhere in the Gospel.

"The Twelve"

The use of this term to refer to the disciples appears three times in close succession (6:60, 70, 71) and elsewhere only at 20:24.

Liar/Lying

In 8:44, there is another instance of three references to "liar" and "lying." All appear in a single verse, but they develop clearly the image of the devil as Liar and the essential opponent of truth. Yet the term appears only one other place in the Gospel (8:55), and there it is not used in the "personalized" sense that appears in 8:44.

Judgment

In chapter 8, there are three comments on judging (vv. 15b-16, 26b, 50). While these are not the only instances of this term in the Gospel, their grouping in chapter 8 seems to be another example of this technique. What makes it particularly clear that these references have been inserted here is the fact that each is so awkward in its context. This will be detailed in the discussion of the Composition of those verses.

"I AM"

The divine title "I AM" is appropriated by Jesus three times in chapter 8 (vv. 24, 28, 58), once in chapter 13 (v. 19), and again in chapter 18 (v. 6). Although this cannot be called "bundling" in the strict sense since the title also appears in chapters 13 and 18, the grouping in chapter 8 is distinctive, given the fact that this is the first time the title is used in the Gospel.[231]

Petitionary Prayer

The third author has grouped the various sayings on the value of petitionary prayer (as well as the promises of such prayer being answered) within the Farewell Discourses, but he does not address the topic elsewhere. There are five such texts: 14:13-14; 15:7, 16; 16:23c-24, 26.

"The Paraclete"/"Spirit of Truth"

These terms appear only five times in the Gospel (14:15-17, 26; 15:26-27; 16:7-11, 12-15), all of which are grouped together in the Farewell Discourses. This grouping is perhaps the most striking and easily recognized by the average reader of the Gospel since each passage contains not only the distinctive term "Paraclete" but also refers to the Spirit as "the Spirit of Truth."

SECTION 3. SYNTHESIS OF THE THIRD EDITION

1. The Structure of the Third Edition

The author of the final edition incorporated his changes into the Gospel in two ways. First, he gave the Gospel a third overarching structure that complemented the first two without disturbing them. Second, besides providing the additions that develop the overarching thematic structure, he made numerous annotations, sometimes short, sometimes at greater length throughout the Gospel.

a. The Overarching Structure of the Third Edition

In the discussion of 1 John, I proposed (following insights by both Feuillet[232] and R. E. Brown[233]) that the structure of that Letter consisted of a Prologue, two major sections, and an Epilogue. Feuillet and Brown pointed out that there

---

231. As was discussed in connection with 3E-29 above, the instances in 4:26 and 6:20 are not those of this divine title but simple statements of self-identification.
232. Feuillet, "Structure."
233. Brown, *Epistles* 116-29, esp. 123-29.

The Third Edition of the Gospel

were numerous similarities between this view of the structure of 1 John and the structure of the Gospel. They argued that the author of 1 John had achieved this by imitating the structure of the Gospel.

While recognizing the similarities that Feuillet and Brown spoke of, I would take this analysis forward in two ways. First, the material to which Feuillet and Brown point comes from the third edition of the Gospel, and so this structure, while clearly present in the Gospel in its present form, is not that of the Gospel as a whole but was added only at the time of the final edition of the Gospel and overlays the structure of the earlier editions. Second, it is evident from a comparison of the material of the third edition with that of 1 John that 1 John was written before the final edition of the Gospel.

Based on the features of the third edition as revealed by literary analysis, I would propose that the structure of the Gospel at the time of the third edition is as follows:

(1) Prologue (1:1-18)
(2) Jesus as the Light of the World (1:19–12:50)
(3) Jesus as the Embodiment of Love (13:1–20:31)
(4) Epilogue (21:1-25)

The evidence for this view of the structure of the Gospel in its final form becomes clear when this material is looked at in more detail, as can be seen in the following.[234]

(1) The Prologue (1:1-18)

In the Prologue,[235] the coming of Jesus was presented as "light shining in the darkness" (1:5, 9). John was not the true light himself but witnessed to the light (1:7-8). Thus, the essential theme of the entire ministry is that of light shining in darkness without being overcome by the darkness.

(2) Jesus as the Light of the World (1:19–12:50)

Throughout his presentation of the public ministry, the third author develops a distinctive use of the theme of light and darkness to describe and frame the ministry.

---

234. In all cases, the material comes from the third edition, as identified by the characteristics identified earlier in this Introduction to the Third Edition. It is evident that while the third author allowed the overarching division of the second edition as two forms of glorification to stand, he overlaid his own conceptualization in terms of light and love.

235. Here I speak only of themes, and not of the issue of the prehistory of the hymnic material in the Prologue, nor its editing.

Section 3. Synthesis of the Third Edition

In 3:19-21, he explained again that the light had come into the world but most people preferred the darkness because their deeds were evil and did not want to come to the light lest they be shown to be evil, while everyone doing the truth comes to the light.

At the beginning of the discourse of 8:12, Jesus proclaims himself "the light of the world" and promises that the one who follows him will have the "light of life."

At the beginning of the complex of material containing the healing of the blind man, we read (9:5) for the first time that the theme of "light" is subsumed into the larger thematic framework of "day" and "night." Jesus explains that the night is coming when he will not work, but while he is in the world, he is "the light of the world."

Next, in 11:9-10, near the beginning of the Lazarus episode, and in response to the disciples' expression of fear of danger if they go to Judea to visit Lazarus, Jesus again explains that there are twelve hours in the day, and if a person walks during the day, "the person does not stumble because the light of this world is shining." He then goes on to explain that "if the person walks during the night, the person falls because the light is not in him."

In 12:35-36, near the end of his public ministry, Jesus explains that the light is among them for only a short time and that they should walk while they have the light lest they be overtaken by the darkness: "And the one who walks about in the darkness does not know where he is going. While you have the Light, believe in the Light, so that you may become sons of Light."

One other time, in the last words of his public ministry (12:46), Jesus explains: "I have come as light into the world, so that everyone believing in me may not remain in darkness." And he exhorts his listeners one final time to listen to and obey his words.

Then at the end of Jesus' final supper with his disciples (13:31), when Judas had taken the food given him by Jesus and so revealed himself as the one who was to betray him, the author states: "It was night."

Thus, the third edition has carefully structured the entire public ministry around the theme of Jesus as "light" come into the world for a set period of time and the appeal to believe in him while it is "day." But eventually the night comes, and the darkness descends, and Jesus' public ministry is over. And so the author turns to the Passion, where the theme of love will predominate.

(3) Jesus as the Embodiment of Love (13:1–20:31)

From the end of the Last Supper to the Resurrection, Jesus' ministry is a private one to his disciples who had believed in him. Although it is the "night," the Gospel will now demonstrate the love that Jesus has for his own.

The Third Edition of the Gospel

Up to chapter 13, love had not been a major theme but it does occur, just as references to love appear in the first "part" of 1 John. The most prominent example is in 10:15b-18, where (in an addition by the third author) the shepherd is said to lay down his life for his sheep. Even before the fall of the "night," Jesus' loving and humble service had been evident in his washing of the feet of the disciples (13:1-20). However, beginning with the general statement in 13:1de ("having loved his own in the world, he loved them to the end"), the theme of love assumes a major role. Not only is the love of Jesus and the Father for one another a repeated theme, but also the love of Jesus and the disciples for one another, as well as the need for love of the disciples for one another. Jesus loves the Father (14:31), and the Father also loves Jesus (10:17; 15:9; 17:24fg, 26cd). Above all, Jesus loves his own (13:1de; 15:9, 13).

Moreover, Jesus commands his disciples to love one another as he has loved them (13:34-35; 15:12, 13, 17). He urges them to keep his commandments and says that this is evidence that the person loves Jesus and will be loved by both the Father and by Jesus (14:21; 15:10; 17:26cd). They are also to keep his word, and this will be evidence that they love Jesus and the Father will love the person (14:23-24).

Also related to the theme of "love" is the theme of "hate," which is how the world responds to the disciples. The world hates them because it hated Jesus before them (15:18-21).

Thus, throughout the Farewell Discourses, Jesus explains the meaning of what is to come and does so repeatedly in terms of the totally reciprocal love among Jesus, the Father, and the disciple. But it is done entirely in the material of the third edition.

(4) Epilogue (21:1-25)

In the Gospel, the Epilogue is marked by a number of features as a final addition to the Gospel. First, it is evident from the way it follows the so-called "first conclusion." Second, it is evident in the way that it deals primarily with theological issues relevant to the later history of the community. Although it begins as a third appearance of Jesus to the disciples and yet another instance of the superiority of the BD to Peter, it goes on to deal with two issues important to the later period of the community: the person of the overall authority and leader of the community vis-à-vis the founder of the Johannine community and then finally the death of the BD.

Section 3. Synthesis of the Third Edition

b. Other Elements of the Structure of the Third Edition

(1) "Glossing"

Beyond this overarching framework within which the author casts the ministry, the final author works within the structure of the previous editions, appending and inserting comments (sometimes lengthy ones) in order to clarify, at appropriate points, his interpretation of various theological issues, particularly those disputed by the opponents within the community. But the third author also addresses other issues not related to the crisis of 1 John, issues such as bodily resurrection and leadership of the community.[236] However, because so much of this aspect of the third author's work is done by annotating (or "glossing"), it is difficult to show this aspect of his work in outline form.

(2) Addition by Grouping/Bundling

There is a pattern in the Gospel in which the author of the third edition often adds the same comment or terminology in groups of two, three, or four. It would seem that this was some sort of technique employed by the third author as a way of establishing by means of repetition the presence of a particular concept. These were described in 3E-57F above, and that discussion will not be repeated here.

2. The Literary Genre of the Material of the Third Edition

As was mentioned above and as can be seen from the discussion in the Commentary, the author of the third edition did not attempt to modify the overall structure of the Gospel as it had been conceived by the author of the second edition. Rather, the third author has attempted to view the ministry from another, overarching symbolic perspective, which transcended without disturbing the earlier structure. Beyond this structural overlay, the author of the third edition proceeds mainly by means of a series of shorter and longer additions that might properly be referred to as "glosses."

Finally, the third author also incorporates one of the community's hymns at the beginning of the Gospel. This hymn (now modified by the author as he incorporates it) was seen to provide in poetic format an overview of some of the main theological convictions of the community at the time of the third edition.

---

236. These will be discussed below (see "Elements of the Theology Not Related to the Community Crisis nor to 1 John").

In all of this, it is evident that the third author's interest, like that of the second author, is not narratological but theological. The most that can be said about the genre is that it is similar to that of "glossing."

3. The Theology of the Third Edition

As we shall see below,[237] there are substantial reasons for concluding that 1 John was written prior to the third edition of the Gospel. Consequently, when we discuss the theology of the third edition, it is important to keep in mind that this edition is concerned to incorporate into the Gospel insights and modifications that represent a stage of development beyond that of 1 John. Not only does the third author incorporate, within the Gospel, material that clarifies the tradition over against the views of the opponents but he also takes pains to address a number of issues distinctive of a fourth period in the community's history.

In order to fully understand the theology of the third edition and the purpose the author had in making his additions, it is necessary to understand the nature of the crisis that divided the community and precipitated the writing of 1 John. Consequently, it could be helpful for the reader to pause and to read the overview of the crisis and the response to it as composed by the author of 1 John. This overview is given in the introduction to 1 John, and the crisis is discussed in detail in Volume 3, Appendix 4.

At the same time, from a comparison between the thought of 1 John and that of the third edition of the Gospel, it is evident that the third edition addresses several issues that are not directly associated with the controversy of 1 John. An examination of these issues also is important for a proper understanding of the third edition.

In what follows, we will take an approach similar to that taken in the overview of the theology of the second edition, that is, we will attempt to provide a brief overview of the main lines of the theology. This overview will proceed by means of a series of numbered topics corresponding to the series as presented in the overview of the second edition. However, here we will provide the viewpoint of the author of the third edition on these matters, making a comparison with the views of the author of 1 John where appropriate.[238] After this, we will briefly comment on the topics introduced by the third author that go beyond those connected to the crisis of 1 John.

---

237. See the discussion of the dating of the third edition relative to the date of 1 John, under "Dating" below.

238. That elements of the Gospel address the same issues as 1 John has also been suggested by, among others, Segovia, "Theology" 115-28; Grayston, *Epistles* 10; Painter, "Tradition" 63-64; Talbert, *Gospel* 4, also 166.

Section 3. Synthesis of the Third Edition

In the discussion of the crisis that divided the Johannine community at the time of 1 John, it was pointed out that our understanding of the crisis is helped considerably by the literary analysis, which enables us to identify the Gospel in its second edition. For it is the similarity between the crisis and this stage of the tradition that enables us to see that the crisis was one of interpretation of the tradition at its second written stage. The purpose and meaning of some of the most striking features of the second edition were not fully understandable until they were viewed through the prism of 1 John.

The same thing is true for our understanding of the third edition of the Gospel. While the analysis of the third edition is done on the basis of features in the third edition itself, the meaning of some of these features becomes clearer in the light of the discussion in 1 John. The reason for this is that the additions of the third author within the narrative context of the Gospel are sometimes so subtle that, taken alone in their Gospel context, their larger purpose is unclear. However, within 1 John, which is a more analytical discussion of the differences between the two groups, many of the issues are presented more clearly and the contrast is more explicit.

For example, we saw in our analysis of 1 John that the author affirmed that the words of Jesus had a permanent validity and that ethical directives were important for the community. In the light of this perspective, we are able to see why the author of the third edition would call attention to "keeping the word" of Jesus as a commandment and why, in his presentation of the Spirit-Paraclete, he would explicitly state that the Paraclete "will not speak on his own." At the same time, the various literary indications that the passages in the Gospel dealing with the love commandment are later additions is confirmed by the knowledge of the crisis as it was viewed in 1 John.

Consequently, we see that 1 John continues to play a pivotal role in understanding the theology of both the second and the third editions. By using 1 John as a "handbook" to the crisis, it becomes possible not only to understand the purpose of the individual additions but to realize also that there was a unified and coherent complex of issues that gave rise to the need for the final editing of the Gospel.

a. Elements of Theology Related to the Crisis at the Time of 1 John

(1) Christology

As the author of the second edition had done, the author of the third edition regularly referred to Jesus as the "Son" "sent" by the "Father." But as the author of 1 John did before him, the author of the third edition emphasized the unique status of Jesus' sonship by making explicit a Christology that was even higher than that of the second edition. Like the author of 1 John, he referred to Jesus as the "unique" *(monogenēs)* Son of God and affirmed his preexistence. In his own distinctive way, he reflects the total equality of the Son with the Father in his presentation of Jesus claiming the "I AM" title of God. By incorporating a community hymn as the Prologue of the Gospel, he also affirmed the conviction that Jesus was the "Word" of God, that he was with God in the beginning, and that he *was* God. Further, he affirmed Jesus' presence and agency in creation. In keeping with his apocalyptic perspective, Jesus also performs the functions of the Son of Man.

Moreover, he states that Jesus possessed the Spirit "without measure," thus demonstrating that Jesus possessed the Spirit in a way different from that of the believer, who, according to the author of 1 John, had received "of the Spirit."

(2) Belief

While the author of the second edition had stressed the various types of evidence for believing in Jesus, the author of the third edition is not concerned with unbelief versus belief but rather with correct belief versus incorrect belief. Thus, *proper* confession of Jesus is important. Both groups have claimed to believe in Jesus, but the belief of the opponents is faulty. For example, the opponents do not understand Jesus properly; they do not recognize the need for ethical direction; and they do not understand the role of the Spirit and the role of the words of Jesus properly. Thus belief in the third edition seeks to reflect correct belief in such a way as to refute the views of the opponents.

(3) Pneumatology

The author of the third edition takes over from the second edition the notion that Jesus had brought about the outpouring of the Spirit; but, like the author of 1 John, the author of the third edition describes the Spirit as "the Spirit of Truth." But he takes this beyond the development of 1 John by, among other things, applying the title of Paraclete to the Spirit and by presenting the Spirit more as a person than a force. Moreover, he describes the function of the Spirit in much greater detail than previously.

(4) Eternal Life

While the author of the third edition takes over belief in eternal life from the second edition, like the author of 1 John he makes the essential and permanent role of Jesus in relation to eternal life much clearer. He also modifies the earlier understanding in other ways, as will be evident in the points that follow.

Section 3. Synthesis of the Third Edition

(5) Eschatology

Like the author of the second edition and the author of 1 John, the author of the third edition affirms the present reality of eternal life, but like the author of 1 John he views life from the perspective of apocalyptic and holds to a conviction that eternal life will have a new dimension "on the last day." Thus, he combined belief in present eschatology with belief in a future dimension of that life.

In keeping with his apocalyptic perspective, the author of the third edition affirms the reality of Jesus as the Son of Man who will exercise judgment on the last day.

(6) Knowledge of God

The author of the third edition continues to see the value of the "witnesses" to Jesus and so implicitly affirms the belief held by the authors of both the second edition and 1 John that the believer has no need of teachers. The disciples, nevertheless, are given the commandment to "keep the word" of Jesus, that is, to have the words of Jesus as their guide. This commandment is directly related to the commandment given to Jesus by the Father to speak the word of the Father. Even the Paraclete will not speak on his own but will remind them of what Jesus said and will explain his words to the disciples.

(7) Soteriology

Like the author of 1 John, the author of the third edition makes clear that Jesus' death was an atoning one that was for the life of the world and that took away the sin of the world. He is properly called "Savior of the world."

(8) Ethics

The author of the third edition makes no mention of perfectionism as such, but, by incorporating the commandment of mutual love, he makes clear the need for proper conduct toward other community members. He also makes other references to the importance of one's individual actions.

(9) Anthropology

The author's view of anthropology in the third edition continues in the same direction as that espoused by the author of 1 John. That is, without denying the exalted status of the believer, who is given the life of God and becomes a child of God through rebirth, the third author makes clear that the status of the believer cannot be confused with the status of Jesus Christ. He does this first by his view of Jesus as a "unique" son, by his attribution of preexistence to Jesus, and by his conviction that the Spirit was given to Jesus "without measure," whereas the author of 1 John had stressed that the believer was given "of" the Spirit.

(10) Ecclesiology

It is difficult to know whether the statements regarding ecclesiology in the third edition are intended to deal with issues of community as these were understood at the time of 1 John. Rather, it is more likely that the references in the third edition have yet other ecclesiological concerns in mind, as we shall see immediately below.

(11) Religious Significance of Material Reality

The author of the third edition, more than that of any stage of the tradition before him, asserts the importance of the material. Not only does he affirm the importance of the physical elements of reality in general (i.e., as they pertain to his becoming flesh, to the historical words of Jesus and his physical death on the cross, and to the pouring out of his blood) but he also affirms the importance of ritual actions. His clearest statements concern the Eucharist, but he also makes subtle reference to Baptism as well as to a ritual for the forgiveness of sin.

b. Elements of the Theology of the Third Edition Not Paralleled in 1 John

(1) Ecclesiology

The third edition demonstrates a special concern with ecclesiology — the role of human leadership among the followers of Jesus. This is a topic not evident earlier, either in the Gospel or in 1 John. This ecclesiological concern has two aspects to it.

First, it is clear from the Beloved Disciple passages that, at the time of third edition, the role of Peter was being discussed in a way that it was not before. In these passages, Peter always appears in a context in which the relative merits of both Peter and the BD are in question. This would indicate that by this time Peter had been given an importance that was not evident earlier, and the community needed to deal with it.

The community's answer to this situation is that the BD was far superior to Peter in matters of spiritual insight and in closeness to Jesus. However, as is

Section 3. Synthesis of the Third Edition

apparent from chapter 21, the author of the third edition also recognizes that the leadership of the community has been given to Peter, and he acknowledges the validity of that role.

Second, the third edition makes explicit the importance of and concern for unity among Christian communities. This is evident both in 10:16 and 11:52, two passages that concern not a mission to Gentiles but unity among those who are already "children of God" but who are "scattered about" and need to be brought "into one."[239]

(2) Ritual Concerns

The second type of "additional" material addresses other aspects of the author's (and the author of 1 John's) belief in the importance of the physical/corporeal dimension of human life.

(3) Bodily Resurrection

One of the most striking ways in which the author of the third edition goes beyond the thought of 1 John is in his explicit convictions in *bodily* resurrection on the last day. This is evident most clearly in John 5:27-29, but also in the various references to the believer being "raised up on the last day" (6:39c, 40c, 44c, 54). This agrees with the thought of 1 John in its emphasis on the role of the material, physical elements of creation, yet 1 John nowhere gives any indication of a bodily resurrection as a belief of the community in spite of the author's repeated emphasis on the role of the material and physical.

(4) Correlation with the Synoptic Gospels

In the third edition, there are a number of additions that address the relation between the Johannine and Synoptic traditions. These are discussed in greater detail in the section below entitled "The Relation of Material in the Third Edition to the Synoptics" and will not be discussed here.

(5) The Role of the Beloved Disciple

The BD appears only in the third edition, and his presence is universally recognized as one of the distinctive features of the Gospel as a whole. His function is twofold and relates to elements both internal and external to the community.

---

239. While it is possible that this could refer to unity within the Johannine satellite communities themselves (cf. the problems evident in 3 John), in the light of the remainder of the orientation of the third edition, it is more likely that the unity referred to is unity with the Great Church.

The Third Edition of the Gospel

With regard to elements internal to the community, the BD anchors the community's tradition in the historical experience of Jesus. Some within the community have understood the outpouring of the Spirit in a way that attributes all necessary knowledge and understanding to the Spirit. The later tradition (1 John and the third edition of the Gospel) attempts to clarify this in a variety of ways. One of the major techniques is to emphasize that the tradition being passed on to them is that of an eyewitness: the Beloved Disciple. What they are receiving is a historically based witness, not one that is the result primarily of prophetic, Spirit-inspired utterances.

The BD also has an important function in relation to the external situation of the community at the time of the third edition. Although the BD is shown to be superior to Peter throughout the Gospel, the final role of the BD is to accept and affirm the authority of the Petrine churches in relation to Johannine Christianity. Thus, there can be no doubt to any reader that the Johannine community is in unity with the remainder of early Christianity.

4. The Theology of the Third Edition and That of 1 John

For a number of years, scholars have noticed similarities between elements of the Gospel of John and 1 John. This has led to various theories. The most common is that the author of 1 John is also the final redactor of the Gospel. Yet it seems impossible to conclude that the author of the third edition is also the author of 1 John because the author of the third edition speaks of the founding witness of the tradition as "the Beloved Disciple." It is difficult to imagine that the person referred to by this title would have given it to himself. The title is so exalted that it can only be understood as an honorific title bestowed on the founding witness to the tradition by the author of the third edition. At the same time, as will be seen below, there is evidence that suggests that the author of 1 John is the same individual that is referred to as "the Beloved Disciple" in the third edition.[240]

Finally, there are differences in terminology between 1 John and the third edition. While this should not be confused with "style," such differences would seem to indicate that the authors of the two works are not the same. In order to put this in proper perspective, we will first examine some significant elements of the third edition that are not in 1 John and then point to some elements of 1 John that are not in the third edition.

---

240. See Vol. 3, Appendix 9 (The Beloved Disciple).

Section 3. Synthesis of the Third Edition

a. Similarities between the Third Edition and 1 John

As could be expected, the similarities between the third edition and 1 John are considerable. It would serve little to attempt to list them all. However, some similarities are of such importance that they deserve mention here.

(1) The Worldview of the Third Edition and That of 1 John

It is perhaps important to recall at this point that both the third edition and 1 John share an apocalyptic worldview. This is significant in light of the fact that prior to 1 John there is no evidence of this worldview in the Johannine tradition. As we have seen, particularly in the discussion of the worldview of the third edition above, the worldview of 1 John and of the third edition bears a particular closeness to the type of apocalypticism present in the SDQ and in the *T12P*. Some of the language and the concepts of 1 John and the third edition are found nowhere else in the extant literature except in the SDQ and the *T12P*.

(2) The Structure of 1 John and That of the Third Edition

In the Commentary on 1 John, it is proposed that 1 John begins with a Prologue and ends with an Epilogue and the remainder is structured around the two themes of "light" (which dominates the first half of the Letter) and "love" (which dominates the second half).

Above (Section 3.i.a), it was also argued that the third edition of the Gospel has a similar structure of Prologue, Epilogue, and the remainder structured around the themes of light and love. I argued above that this similarity is not accidental. In fact, it is a major similarity between the two works.

(3) Similarities in Terminology

Among the more important examples of terminology taken over from 1 John (and in some cases from the second edition of the Gospel) are the use of "witness" (found also in the second edition) and the practice of addressing believers as "brothers" and "little children."

b. Terminology in 1 John but Not in the Third Edition

The term "word of life" appears in 1 John (1:1), but it does not appear in the third edition of the Gospel, even though there are concepts that are quite similar (e.g., Jesus is life; my words are Spirit and life). In 1 John alone we hear of "fellowship" *(koinōnia)* (1:3, 6, 7). The First Letter of John refers to the figure of the Antichrist, a figure not present in Gospel of John (although the Gospel of John has "ruler of this world," an apocalyptic term). There are a number of other terms found in 1 John but not in the Gospel, for example, *anomia* (lawlessness), *bios* (life), *dokimazein* (to test), *hilasmos* (expiation), *pseudoprophētēs* (false prophet), *chrisma* (anointing), *parousia* (coming).[241]

Consequently, it seems appropriate to conclude that the author of 1 John and the author of the third edition share the same theological viewpoint and are confronting the same theological crisis within the community but that they are not the same individual.

c. Terminology in the Third Edition but Not in 1 John

The author of the third edition also has several instances of terminology unique to the third edition. For example, the "Word" in the Gospel Prologue is Jesus; in 1 John, it is the message of Jesus. In the Gospel Prologue, "beginning" is the beginning of time; in 1 John, "beginning" is the beginning of Jesus' ministry. In the third edition, Jesus is the light; in 1 John, God is the light. In the third edition, the commandments are "of God," while in the third edition they are "of Jesus." In the third edition, moreover, there is mention of commandments *given to Jesus,* while this notion does not appear in 1 John.

In the third edition, the term "Paraclete" is used of the Spirit; in 1 John it is not. The third edition refers to Jesus as *"the Lamb of God"* (1:29, 34), but this title does not appear in 1 John (although the concept of Jesus as a propitiatory sacrifice is present, as can be seen in 1 John 1:7, 9; 3:5; 4:10). There are references to Jesus as "Lord" *(kyrios)* in the third edition but not in 1 John. There are references to Jesus as *Son of Man* in the third edition but not in 1 John. There are references to the "Ruler of this world" in the third edition but not in 1 John (but see "Antichrist" and "the Evil One"). The notion of "day of judgment" *(hēmera*

---

241. For a complete listing, see Morgenthaler, *Statistik.* As early as 1882, Holtzmann wrote a series of articles comparing the language and thought of 1 John with that of the Gospel. In a chart, he listed fifty-one expressions he found to have parallels in the Gospel. (The tables referred to here are from the second of the articles ["Das Problem"].) This list was taken over by Brooke, *Epistles* i-iv. While Holtzmann and Brooke were interested in the similarities between the First Epistle and the Gospel as a whole, Holtzmann/Brooke list fifty-one features of the First Epistle that have parallels in sixty-eight instances in the Gospel. When Holtzmann and Brooke discussed these features, they treated them as matters of personal style indicative of authorship. In fact, almost all of these features are more properly to be attributed to similarity of worldview. But the lists of Holtzmann and Brooke are useful as unconscious confirmations of the presence of apocalyptic language in both works but also of the fact that, in the Gospel, this language occurs so consistently in material identified here as from the third edition.

tēs kriseōs) appears in the third edition, while "Second Coming" *(parousia)* appears in 1 John.

In one of the more surprising features, the author of the third edition makes repeated references to "glory" and "glorify," terms that were prominent in the second edition although neither term appears in 1 John. Although the particle *oun* appears 195 times in the Gospel (in all editions), it does not appear in 1 John.

5. The Identity and Social Location of the Community at the Time of the Third Edition

By the time of the third edition, the community is no longer part of a synagogue community but is now an independent community of persons who believe in Jesus. The tension with Judaism and with the synagogue, which so dominated the second edition, is now absent.

By this time, the community has also undergone a second crisis, this time an internal one caused by two interpretations of the Johannine tradition. This second crisis impinges on the circumstances of the third edition. As a result, the third edition addresses many of these issues by incorporating statements that affirm them as part of their Gospel tradition and as part of the witness of the BD that had been handed down to them.

The second, and new, factor in the community's circumstances is an evident desire to address issues that connect the Johannine tradition with the Great Church. This is evident in the various statements (discussed below) that deal with the relation of the Johannine tradition to the Synoptics as well as those topics that address larger issues of church unity and of Petrine authority. At this stage of its existence, the gaze is not toward the synagogue, nor toward the identity of the community, but toward the relation of the community with the Great Church.

In the third edition of the Gospel, there was a sudden change to the worldview of apocalyptic. This will be discussed in the section that follows, and we will see that the particular type of apocalypticism adopted by the community may well reveal more about the social location of this community at the time of 1 John and the third edition.

6. Background of the Material in the Third Edition

The background and worldview of the third edition have been discussed in detail in connection with the identification of ideological features of that edition.

The Third Edition of the Gospel

Consequently, there is no need for more than a brief reminder here that the background of the third edition is that of the modified dualism of Jewish apocalyptic. It can be further defined as being that of apocalyptic Judaism particularly as evidenced in the SDQ (Sectarian Documents from Qumran) and in the T12P.

What is not clear, however, is the reason for this considerable change of worldview. The worldview of the second edition was Jewish, but it was a non-apocalyptic Judaism. It has often been said that apocalyptic was not the worldview of the authoritative circles within first-century Judaism. It was primarily the worldview of sectarian groups, groups that were either reformist or in some other way associated with the fringes of society rather than the center of it. Had the change of worldview been a cause of the rift between the community and the synagogue? Or was it simply that after the expulsion from the synagogue, the community was attracted to this more dualistic worldview?

From its beginnings in the first edition, the community had been closely associated with the baptist movement of John. According to the first edition, Jesus himself had exercised a baptizing ministry. Although the baptizing ministry of John is viewed in apocalyptic terms within the Synoptic Gospels, the first edition of John gives evidence that his ministry could be interpreted in a non-apocalyptic way. Consequently, it probably is wrong to see the catalyst for the shift to an apocalyptic viewpoint in the contact with John.

On the other hand, the specific modes of expression used in the third edition bear a remarkable resemblance to the particular forms of apocalyptic dualism found at Qumran. This similarity need not mean that the community had contact with the community at Qumran; the contact could have been with another Essene community such as that residing in Jerusalem. We do have ample evidence that the Johannine community was familiar with Judea and Jerusalem.

It is also possible that the community adopted an apocalyptic viewpoint in order to manifest a greater similarity to the other forms of early Christianity evident both in the Pauline and in the Synoptic traditions. However, although it is not possible to examine this in detail here, it would seem that the type of apocalyptic dualism found in the Synoptics is somewhat different from that of the SDQ and from the apocalypticism of 1 John. Thus, in spite of changes that *de facto* bring the Johannine tradition closer to that of the Great Church, the community continues to go its own way.

Wisdom Motifs in the Third Edition

It is clear, nevertheless, that the third edition introduces Wisdom motifs in addition to those of the second edition. Two of the more obvious elements are:

Section 3. Synthesis of the Third Edition

(1) the notion of preexistence, which was not evident in the second edition, and (2) the Wisdom motifs in the Prologue.[242]

7. The Historical Value of Material Found in the Third Edition

The question of the historicity of the material of the third edition is a difficult one." There is little narrative, and the remainder of the additions by the third author are theological in nature. Because the author sought to correlate aspects of the Johannine tradition with the Synoptic tradition, the issue is less the historicity of the third author's material than it is the historicity of the Synoptic material. The third author seems more intent on harmony than on historicity.

In the third edition, the only material we have identified as narrative is the miraculous catch of fish in 21:1-14. In earlier discussions of historicity we turned to the analysis of Meier for help. However, here Meier, who sees 21:1-14 as an example of a post-Resurrection appearance, argues that such material is, within the canons of historical inquiry, unanalyzable — since historical inquiry is limited to "the empirically verifiable life of Jesus up until his death."[243] While this conclusion seems at first frustrating, closer inspection suggests that Meier is correct. Beyond this, it would seem that the issue of historicity is not a relevant one for the material of the third edition.

8. The Relation of Material in the Third Edition to the Synoptics[244]

The question of the relation of the Gospel of John to the Synoptics has been long debated, without any definitive conclusions. It is hoped that the analysis conducted here may contribute to the resolution of this problem.

The question of the relation between John and the Synoptics has traditionally been couched in two distinct questions: did John *know* the Synoptics? did John *use* the Synoptics?

---

242. There is also some influence of Wisdom on the Christology of the third edition. See Part 4, Section 1.5.

243. Meier, *Marginal* 2:904. In his analysis of this miracle (2:896-904), Meier asks two questions: (1) Is the Johannine account a variant of the narrative in Luke 5:1-11; (2) if so, which writer preserves the original setting for the miracle? Meier argues that they are both variants of the same account and that, on general grounds, the Johannine account probably preserves the original setting. It is then that he invokes the limitations of empirical historical inquiry and declines to be able to judge the matter further.

244. Scholarship in the twentieth century is surveyed and evaluated by D. M. Smith, *Among* (with complete bibliography). Among those that have appeared since Smith's volume, see Dunderberg, *Johannes*.

The Third Edition of the Gospel

We have already seen that in the first edition, while some material had parallels to the Synoptics, the Gospel preserved an independent view of the chronology and the content of Jesus' ministry. There was no attempt either to echo or to complement the Synoptic accounts. In the second edition, the issue of chronological sequence was of no significance to the author, and at times he even obscured the previous chronology (by reversing chapters 5 and 6) and ignored the Synoptic chronology (if indeed he knew it) by placing the account of the temple cleansing where he did. Nor was there sufficient material with parallels in the Synoptics to suggest either knowledge or use of them.

However, in the third edition, things are different. In the third edition, there are a number of features that bear a close similarity to the Synoptics. In fact, their appearance within the Gospel is often so awkward as to suggest that one of the third author's intentions was precisely to incorporate various elements of the Synoptic tradition into the Johannine Gospel. At the same time, it would seem that the author of the third edition did not feel constrained to do so by means of precise quotations but simply by the incorporation of the substance of a given tradition or viewpoint.

The following passages from the third edition provide some examples of material which seems to have been composed in the light of Synoptic concerns. They regularly exhibit five features: (1) the individual passages do not relate well with the surrounding context in the Gospel; (2) their relevance for the theology of the Gospel as a whole is not always evident; (3) their intrinsic importance is not always clear. Yet (4) they have in common the fact that they are remarkably similar to passages in the Synoptic tradition. Finally, (5) when they are viewed in context within the Synoptics, their meaning and relevance are evident.

In 1:33, we read that Jesus will "baptize in the Holy Spirit." This baptism is contrasted with that of John. While this expression appears only once in the Gospel, it also appears in the triple tradition within the Synoptics (Matt 3:11; Mark 1:8; Luke 3:16) and elsewhere (e.g., Acts 1:5; 11:16). In John, the promise that Jesus will baptize with the Holy Spirit is awkward standing alongside the repeated statements (3:22; 4:1) that Jesus was baptizing during his ministry.[245] Surely this was not "baptizing with the Holy Spirit." At the same time, in John, Jesus repeatedly offers the Spirit to those who believe in him, but this is never referred to as a "baptism." In the Synoptics, while there is also only one reference to Jesus baptizing with the Holy Spirit, there is no mention of Jesus himself baptizing during his ministry. Thus, it is likely that within the Gospel of John,

---

245. The awkwardness is indicated by an editor's attempt in 4:2 to deny the plain sense of 3:22; 4:1.

Section 3. Synthesis of the Third Edition

the reference to baptizing with the Holy Spirit is secondary and intended to echo the Synoptics.[246]

It has long been recognized that the term "kingdom of God" is central to the message of the Synoptic Jesus.[247] More than any other term, it is used to describe that which Jesus seeks to accomplish by his ministry. Yet in the Gospel of John it appears only twice, both in close succession in chapter 3 (vv. 3, 5). In the light of the theological consistency of the second edition throughout the Gospel, the presence of the term in chapter 3 becomes all the more curious. However, in the light of the widespread tendency elsewhere in the third edition to incorporate various types of Synoptic-like material in the Gospel, it is reasonable to conclude that the terms have been introduced here by the author of the third edition as a kind of "token" appearance precisely in order to have the terms represented within the Gospel.

In 3:24, we read the statement "John had not yet been put in prison." When viewed only within the context of the Johannine Gospel, this statement is entirely unexpected and unmotivated by anything in the context. There is no other mention of either the imprisonment or the ultimate death of John the Baptist in the Gospel. However, when the statement is viewed within the context of the Synoptics, we notice that Mark 1:14 (par. Matt 4:12) and Luke 3:20 make a point of locating the beginning of Jesus' ministry *after* John's arrest. What is the purpose of the Johannine statement? At the very least it attempts to show awareness of the Synoptic chronology and to correlate the baptizing activity of Jesus with it — and perhaps to explain that this baptizing activity took place before the beginning of the ministry as described in the Synoptics.[248]

In 4:2, we find one of the most awkward statements in the present Gospel. After stating twice (3:22; 4:1) that Jesus has been baptizing, and after a discussion between the disciples of John and John himself about the fact that this baptizing was more successful than John's (3:25-26), we read that Jesus himself was not baptizing but only his disciples. These references to a baptizing ministry by

---

246. Just what the baptism in the Holy Spirit was is not fully understood. For example, in Acts 11:16 the descent of the Spirit is described as a "baptism" although no rite is mentioned. In Acts 19:5-6, the converts who knew only the baptism of John are baptized "in the name of the Lord Jesus," and then Paul lays his hands upon them "and the Holy Spirit came upon them."

247. Two aspects of this are important. First, the term is central to the Synoptics. It appears in thirteen sayings in Mark, thirteen sayings in Q, twenty-five sayings in the material peculiar to Matthew, and six sayings peculiar to Luke. Second, the term is not at all central to the preaching of Paul (appearing in only seven passages in the undisputed Letters). (Statistics are taken from Meier, *Marginal* 2:238.)

248. Bauckham ("John" 147-61) proposes a much more elaborate explanation of the relationship between John and Mark based on this verse. However, Bauckham considers the Gospel to be the work of a single individual, and so he argues that the author of John's Gospel attempted to correlate his own account with that of the Synoptics.

The Third Edition of the Gospel

Jesus were awkward for the third author, almost certainly because the Synoptic tradition had no account of such activity and the final editor found it awkward and so tried to correct "the facts."

In 4:44, the statement that a prophet does not have honor in his own country is difficult to interpret within its Johannine context and at the same time contains indications of being an editorial addition. But within the context of the Synoptics, the saying (cf. Mark 6:1-6; Matt 13:54-58; Luke 4:16-30) portrays Galilee as Jesus' native place and a place not only of acceptance but also of rejection.

In 6:17d, the statement "and Jesus had not yet come to them" is unexpected and the reason for the comment is unclear. It is possible that it was intended to recall the similar Synoptic account where it is stated more plainly that Jesus intended to come to them over the sea and to calm the waters of the storm.

In the additions of the third author in 6:62, 66-71, we have what appears to be a Johannine version of the misunderstanding by the disciples in Mark 8:27-31. As is explained in detail in the Commentary, the incidents appear at the end of the Galilean ministries in each Gospel. Both contain predictions of suffering, and both contain confessions of faith by Peter. In Mark, the scandal is Jesus' prediction of his suffering. In John, a similar scandal is created by the third author's introduction of the death ("return") of the Son of Man. In the Synoptics, the prediction of suffering is met with incomprehension; in the third edition of John, many of the disciples simply do not continue to walk with him.

John 12:3-8 describes the anointing of Jesus' feet by Mary. The awkwardness of this episode has already been indicated by the statement in 11:2, where, when Mary is first identified, she is identified as "the one who had anointed the Lord with oil and had dried his feet with her hair." This proleptic reference is itself quite awkward and presumes the reader's prior knowledge of the event. The verse is probably intended to create the impression that 12:3-8 was an original part of the Gospel.

The episode itself is even more awkward. As is explained in more detail in the Commentary on the passage, its author confuses the actions of anointing with oil (which is done to the head) and the washing of feet (where the water is wiped off). This confusion seems to indicate that the author was less concerned with the intrinsic meaning of the passage than with simply having the passage represented. The fact that the hair is used for drying (rather than a towel!) is also a clear echo of the Synoptic accounts. Yet, within the Marcan context, the prefigurement of anointing for death is intended to be fulfilled in the actions of the women who came to the tomb on the morning of the first day of the week to complete the anointing of the body of Jesus that had been started on the day of death. Yet in the Johannine Gospel, the anointing of the body in preparation for burial is completed by Joseph of Arimathea and Nicodemus immediately fol-

Section 3. Synthesis of the Third Edition

lowing the death of Jesus. Consequently, there is no need for further anointing. All of this suggests that the incorporation of the passage is intended to echo the Synoptic portrayal. The fact that both the Synoptic event and the Johannine account occur in Bethany aids in the account although, in the Synoptics, the anointing takes place at the house of Simon the Leper rather than at the house of Lazarus. Both events occur soon before the Passover. However, just why the episode was thought to be so important is not at all clear.

John 12:24-26 awkwardly incorporates three independent sayings into a context that is more coherent if 12:23 leads directly to 12:27. The first saying (v. 24) has its closest parallel not in the Synoptics but in 1 Cor 15:36-37. The second (v. 25) is a variant of sayings that are found in Mark 8:35; Matt 10:39; 16:25; Luke 9:24; 17:33.[249] Verse 26 is paralleled in the Synoptics by Mark 8:34. So the last two sayings are joined in both Mark and in John but in reverse order. As they appeared in the context of the first prediction of Jesus' Passion in Mark, so they appear in John in the prelude to the Passion, when the Greeks come seeking Jesus and Jesus interprets this as the arrival of the "hour" for the Son of Man. Again similarity to the Synoptics accounts for all but v. 24.

John 13:20 ("Amen, amen, I say to you, the one who accepts the one I send accepts me; the one accepting me accepts the one sending me") is quite awkward and unexpected in its context and on these grounds seems to be an addition. On the other hand, it has prominent Synoptic parallels (Mark 9:37; Matt 18:5; Luke 9:48). And while the Johannine saying is not identical to any of the Synoptic counterparts, it has the same intention and the same three-step parallelism between the human person, Jesus, and the Father.

In 18:16, the fact that the gatekeeper is identified as a young maiden is historically implausible. It would be unlikely that a woman would stand such guard duty. The text is almost certainly to be explained as a conflation of the Synoptic "young woman" who was a servant of the high priest with the gatekeeper.[250]

The third edition introduces the term "the Twelve" four times: 6:60, 70, 71; 20:24. This term is common in the Synoptics but out of place in the Johannine literature, where the normal term is simply "disciple(s)" (used almost 80 times). In 6:70, Jesus asks: "Did I not choose you to be the Twelve . . . ?" Yet nowhere in John is there a mention of such a selection of the Twelve nor even the names of the Twelve. The evident purpose is to relate the Johannine text to the Synoptic accounts.

One might also ask whether the entire apocalyptic framework of the third

---

249. But the verse has been reformulated in Johannine terms by the addition of *zōē aiōnios*. See the particularly strong case made by Ashton, *Understanding* 215, and earlier by Dodd, *Interpretation* 146.

250. See the discussion of the Composition of 18:12-27 in the Commentary proper.

The Third Edition of the Gospel

edition is due to the author's desire to incorporate the worldview of the Synoptics into the Johannine Gospel. Was the introduction of apocalyptic with the references to Jesus as Son of Man, to a bodily resurrection, final judgment, and so on, intended to show that the Johannine tradition recognized this worldview as an appropriate framework for the interpretation of the events that had taken place with and through Jesus? We cannot be sure, but we can point to the fact of its presence and acknowledge that in fact this does bring some aspects of the Johannine theology much closer to that of the Synoptics (and much of the remainder of the New Testament!).

However, as clear as it may be that the third author was aware of the Synoptics, we cannot say that the author sought congruence only with the Synoptics. Many of the elements (particularly theological elements) the editor incorporates are known from sources beyond the Synoptics. For example, the concern to relate the authority behind the Johannine tradition to the larger tradition that recognized Peter as the "rock" upon which the church was built is certainly consistent with the emphasis in the Synoptics on the leadership of Peter, but it is also known from other sectors of the New Testament. The emphasis on the atoning death of Jesus is found in the Synoptics but even more so in Paul. The introduction of the apocalyptic worldview is typical of the Synoptics but also of Pauline Christianity.[251]

Relation of These Additions to the Third Edition

In the comments on the BD above, concern was expressed whether the BD passages were linked sufficiently with other material of the third edition to identify them as coming from the third edition. While the evidence was not overwhelming, it seemed best to conclude that they were.

However, in the case of these Synoptic-like insertions, the case is even more complicated. It could be argued that the third edition shows a number of theological affinities to the Synoptics (apocalyptic background, primacy of Peter as leader, interest in sacramental ritual). Consequently, it is possible that these sayings have been added by the author of the third edition.

9. The Author of the Third Edition

In our quest for the identity of the author of the third edition it may be helpful to make clear, first, who the author *is not*.

---

251. J. A. T. Robinson (*Priority* 10-12) has a discussion with some examples of isolated sayings that are parallel.

Section 3. Synthesis of the Third Edition

a. Is the Author of the Third Edition the Author of 1 John?

As we have seen above, the similarities in overall theological outlook, worldview, language, and historical situation are sufficient to indicate quite strongly that the author of the last edition of the Gospel and the author of 1 John shared a common viewpoint and a common purpose.

However, in spite of the similarities between 1 John and the third edition, it is unlikely that the final edition of the Gospel was written by the author of 1 John.[252] The thought and theology of 1 John, while in many ways extremely close to that of the Gospel, exhibits a number of substantial differences from the third edition that make it highly unlikely that the final editor of the Gospel is the author of 1 John.

b. Is the Author of the Third Edition the Beloved Disciple?

It is clear from the third edition that when that edition was written, the BD had already died. John 21:20-24, which comes from the third edition, attempts to deal with this fact. It is very unlikely that the title "Beloved Disciple" would have been a self-designation. Not only the title but also the description of this person are too exalted for them to be the work of the person himself. This was an honorific title given to the individual who was the foundational eyewitness of the tradition.

c. Who, Then, Is the Author of the Third Edition?

The most that can be said regarding the author of the third edition is that he is a representative of the Johannine community, writing after the death of the Elder. The author of the third edition shares the views of the Elder and was a member of the group who remained in fellowship with the Elder and his part of the community. By his frequent use of "we" it seems clear that he understands himself as part of an authoritative group responsible for the tradition. He (and the group he is a part of) was not someone who simply incorporated the insights of the Elder into the Gospel. It is clear that, when he wrote, a number of new circumstances had arisen that led him to go beyond the concerns of the Elder and

---

252. Among those who have proposed this are Boismard, "Évolution" 114-18; Thyen, "Johannes 13" 343-56; and Schnackenburg, *Gospel* 2:116-17. One of the most prominent proponents of this view is Richter, who has argued this position in "Fußwaschung, 23; idem, *Fußwaschung* 309-13; idem, "Deutung" 35-36. See also the authors listed by R. E. Brown (*Epistles* 108). But there are some variations within this group; in other words, some would hold that it is the same person in each case, some would not necessarily hold that it is the author of the *First* Epistle, etc.

The Third Edition of the Gospel

to address aspects of the community's theology not discussed in 1 John and so to have the community's Gospel reflect its agreement with other segments of early Christianity represented by the Great Church.

We may also gain another glimpse of the character of the author from a few hints in the third edition itself. Several times we see evidence that the author of the third edition did not fully understand the background of what he was writing. One of the clearest examples is his version of the anointing of the feet of Jesus by Mary at the home of Lazarus (12:3-8). When he recorded this story, it would seem that he did not understand the full import of such anointing and this led him to confuse the anointing (of the head) with oil and the washing (of the feet) with water. Uncertainty about the original meaning of a Synoptic saying about a prophet being without honor in his own country may also account for the confusing reference in 4:44, although this is less certain.

A clearer instance of failure to fully understand what he was including is evident in 19:23-24. Here the third author describes the dividing the garments of the crucified Jesus among the soldiers. The Scripture is written in poetic (synonymous) parallelism and is intended to refer to the single action of dividing up the garments. However, the third author misunderstands the parallelism and interprets it as two separate actions and so distinguishes the dividing of the outer garment from that of the inner garments.

If this would suggest that the third author did not know the techniques of Jewish poetry, it seems clear that the third author was able to recognize the homiletic format in chapter 6 and was able to develop it in 6:51-58. He was also thoroughly familiar with the categories and worldview of Jewish apocalyptic of the type that is reflected in the SDQ and the *T12P.*

These features would seem to indicate that, while the third author was almost certainly Jewish, he was not so familiar with all aspects of the tradition that he was incapable of errors. Further, it would seem that the author was much more familiar with his own, than he was with the Synoptic, tradition.

10. The Date of the Third Edition

a. Dating Relative to the Composition of 1 John

Although we are not able to assign a specific date to the composition of the third edition, there is a considerable amount of evidence that the third edition of the Gospel was composed *after* the writing of the First Epistle.[253] This posi-

---

253. There are significant problems associated with a theory that 1 John was composed *after* the Gospel as a whole. R. E. Brown (*Epistles* 33-34) lists four factors that would suggest that

Section 3. Synthesis of the Third Edition

tion is not adopted without considerable forethought. There is inevitably an enormous weight of opinion in favor of the traditional view of the sequence of composition. However, there is, in my opinion, just too much evidence in favor of this alternate view to be able to ignore it.

There are eight significant factors that indicate that the First Letter was written prior to the final edition of the Gospel.[254] First, in John 14:16, Jesus says to his disciples that he will send them "another" Paraclete. This is the first time that the Spirit, identified as "the Paraclete," has been mentioned in the Gospel, and nowhere in the Gospel is there a reference to anyone else being called "Paraclete." However, when we turn to 1 John 2:1, the Elder refers to Jesus as "a Paraclete before the Father." This epistolary statement stands on its own, without presuming any references to the Spirit as a Paraclete also. On the other hand, the statement in John 14:16 can only be fully understood once one reads 1 John to discover that the community also looked upon Jesus as a Paraclete.

---

1 John was earlier: (1) no passage in the Letters is a certain quotation of the Gospel; (2) some epistolary passages are more primitive than comparable passages in the Gospel; (3) the theology of 1 John is seen as less developed (in respect to the emphasis on the atoning death of Jesus and on future eschatology); (4) terminology is seen as being more apocalyptic and therefore earlier. As Brown says, whatever one's theory, one must account for these features. See also the remarks of Houlden, *Epistles* 14.

This has led a number of scholars to propose that 1 John was written before the Gospel (cf. recently Grayston, *Epistles* 12-14; Schnelle, *Antidocetic* 70, 232). However, these scholars argue that 1 John was written before *any part* of the Gospel was written. But, Talbert (*Gospel* 4-7) suggests that the final form of the gospel is produced either at the same time as 1 John or shortly after.

The view that I propose here accounts in a more nuanced way for both the "early" and the "late" elements of 1 John and of the Gospel in a way that simple theories of "before" or "after" the Gospel do not. To my knowledge, the only scholar to adopt precisely the position that I propose here is Hengel (*Question* 72-73), although without the detailed argumentation: ". . . we also have a fair number of references to the crisis in the school in the Gospel, which was completed some years after the Letters and edited after the death of the elder. . . ."

254. Arguments that 1 John is later than the Gospel generally include reference to the fact that the names of community members in the Letters are consistently Greek, suggesting a period later than that associated with the synagogue; that 1 John is later because it reflects an internal struggle while the Gospel reflects an external struggle; that if there were a problem of extreme Christology at the time of the Gospel, the author would not have held up the BD as more spiritually insightful than even Peter. Scholars such as Houlden (*Epistles* 67) point to 1 John 2:7 as "one of the clearest indications" that the Gospel was written before the Epistle.

Arguments for the priority of the Gospel (which are summarized by R. E. Brown, *Epistles* 32-35) are not impressive. The presence of Greek names is striking and may well mean that the community has incorporated Gentiles, but it should be remembered that two of the earliest disciples of Jesus who came from Bethsaida (Andrew and Philip) had Greek names. Other arguments are weakened or negated when one nuances the question by asking about earlier or later than *a specific stratum* of the Gospel rather than about the Gospel as a whole.

The Third Edition of the Gospel

Thus, while 1 John 2:1 does not need John 14:16 in order to be understood, John 14:16 presumes the existence of the material in 1 John 2:1 for full intelligibility. This would indicate that 1 John was already in existence and was known to the author of John 14:16. Thus, the priority of 1 John.[255]

A second aspect of this is the fact that in 1 John, only Jesus is called Paraclete; there is no reference to the Spirit by this title. Consequently, in this respect the third edition of the Gospel exhibits a development over 1 John by now referring to the Spirit as a Paraclete similar to Jesus. Suggesting that the order of composition is the traditional one makes it difficult to explain the relationship between these concepts.[256]

Second, much the same can be said of the designation of the Paraclete as "Spirit of Truth." While this term appears three times in the Gospel (14:17; 15:26; 16:13), its full significance and the worldview within which it is conceptualized are not fully evident until one reads 1 John 4:1-6, where the term appears with its correlative, the "Spirit of Deception." When both terms are seen together, it becomes clear that the author conceives of a *duality* of spirits such as is found in apocalyptic literature. Without mention of the correlative, there is no indication anywhere in the Gospel that the author is thinking of the Spirit in such a dualistic framework. Yet such a contrast is explicit in the First Epistle and indicates again that the author of the final edition was aware of 1 John and presumed the distinction and knowledge of the distinction expressed there.[257]

Third, in the third edition of the Gospel the commandment of mutual love is described as a "new" commandment. This is said only once (13:34), and no explanation is given why it should be called "new." However, in 1 John 2:8, there is a discussion of the notions of "new" and "old" as they apply to the commandments. In fact, this is the only other discussion of "new" and "old" in the Johannine literature. The author's discussion in 1 John 2:8 concerns the commandment to keep the word of God, but the discussion of "new" and "old" is pertinent for John 13:34. In 1 John 2:8, the author argues that the commandment

---

255. One could argue that Jesus was known as Paraclete in the oral tradition at the time of the Gospel even though it is not written. While this is possible, the fact that the written tradition takes the form it does is striking, and while it alone does not prove that 1 John is prior to the Gospel's Paraclete material, such a conclusion is not as speculative as one based on proposed oral tradition. When viewed alongside the other factors, the argument for the priority of 1 John becomes much more plausible.

256. So Strecker (*Epistles* 38), who comments: "1 John 2:1 reflects the older Johannine tradition that was also taken up . . . , creatively expanded and thus established as an important foundation pillar for Johannine pneumatology."

257. Once again, I do not mean to claim that this alone proved beyond a doubt that 1 John is prior to the third-edition material, but, as was the case in the prior instance, this is the most likely conclusion and with other elements provides a consistency of explanation superior to other theories.

Section 3. Synthesis of the Third Edition

is not a "new" commandment, but an "old" one. But then he goes on to say that in some respects it is a "new" one. The author's comments here are closely linked to his purpose in refuting the views of the opponents. The author argues that the commandment he gives them is not a "new" one but an "old" one that they have had from the beginning. Thus, he emphasizes that the commandment is one that has been handed down from the beginning of the tradition (in the ministry of Jesus) and not a new one in the sense that it derives from their inspiration by the Spirit, which leads them to "be progressive and not remain in the teaching of the Christ." But then he goes on to say that in another sense it can be said to be "new" inasmuch as this commandment of the word is being realized in Jesus and in the lives of believers. One might say that more specifically the commandment is not new but the actualization of it is new.

For our present purposes it is important to see that the statement of the third edition regarding the "new" commandment of love presumes the sort of explanation given heretofore only in 1 John and makes sense only if one is aware of that text. Thus we see another indication of the priority of 1 John.

Fourth, there is the peculiar shift in the source of the witness to the flow of blood and water from 1 John to the Gospel. In John 19:33-34, when the soldiers pierce the side of Jesus, blood and water pour out from Jesus' side. In v. 35, the author explains that the one who saw this bears witness, and his witness is true, and he knows he speaks the truth.

In 1 John 5:6-9, we read that Jesus has come "through water and blood." Later in the verse we read that it is the Spirit that witnesses to this. If both the Spirit and the disciples are valid witnesses, why is it that the author of 1 John calls upon the Spirit as witness and the author of the third edition calls upon the BD as the appropriate witness? Certainly the author of 1 John (the Elder) knows of the concept of humans as witnesses and uses it himself repeatedly (e.g., 1:2; 4:14). Why not here?

I would suggest that it is because the author of 1 John *is* the BD and does not want to attribute any special attention or validity to his own witness. It will be recalled that in the Gospel the flow of water and blood was something that only the BD (from among all the disciples) witnessed. If then the writer of 1 John calls upon the Spirit as witness, it is likely to be because he does not want to set himself forward as in any sense a unique, preeminent "authority." However, at the time of the final edition of the Gospel, the later author (who is not the BD himself) has no hesitation appealing to the stature of the BD, who possessed spiritual insight greater than even Peter, as the witness who confirmed the flow.[258] Once again this requires that 1 John be written prior to the material of the Gospel.

---

258. It will be noted below that at the time of 1 John there is no evidence of a concern about an authoritative figure who functions as leader/shepherd. This is congruent with the fact

The Third Edition of the Gospel

We now turn to another aspect of 19:34 that requires that it was written *after* the similar passage in 1 John 5:6-7. In 1 John 5:6-7, the author says that Jesus has come in water and in blood, *not in water only*. From this it is clear that there are some who claim that Jesus came in water only. These are the opponents of the author of 1 John. As R. E. Brown and others have rightly observed, the only other instance where water and blood are mentioned together is in John 19:34. However, if the author of 1 John was referring to that text, there would be no explanation of or even reference to the possibility of coming "in water only."

If, on the other hand, 1 John 5:6-7 is the earlier text, then we would look for a text in the second edition of the Gospel that proposed Jesus came in water (without mention of coming in blood). In the second edition, there are repeated offers of "living water" to the believer (e.g., John 4:10-15; 7:37-39). That "living water" is a reference to the giving of the Spirit is clear from 7:37-39, where it is said that rivers of living water will flow from the belly of Jesus at the time of his glorification. Immediately this is explained to refer to "the Spirit that those who believed in him were to receive. For the Spirit was not yet because Jesus was not yet glorified."

Thus, in keeping with their view that the sole purpose of the ministry of Jesus was to make available the eschatological outpouring of the Spirit, the opponents claim that Jesus came "in water alone." But the author of 1 John rejects this view and argues that he also came in blood, that is, to give his life as an atoning sacrifice (see 1 John 1:7).

But the best explanation of 19:34 is that it is later than 1 John 5:6-7 since the author of 1 John could not be referring to the text of 19:34 as the explanation of "coming in water."[259] Rather, 19:34 is included by the author of the third edition as an affirmation *within the narrative of the Gospel* of what was expressed theologically in 1 John. What happened historically (his death was actual, and serum and blood came from the wound) also happened theologically (he both gave the Spirit and died a sacrificial death).

Fifth, we have alluded above to the fact that in the Gospel there is a clear interest in the authoritative office given to Peter. This is evident from the portrayal of the BD as superior to Peter spiritually yet cognizant of the authority given Peter.

---

that in the Letter there is no mention of the BD nor any attempt on the part of the author to put himself forward as anyone other than a witness among those who have seen and heard and touched "from the beginning." Yet, in the third edition, when the issue of the authoritative figure of Peter as shepherd for all the sheep appears, it is at the same time and in the same passages where the importance and significance of the BD for the Johannine community appears.

259. In a remarkable departure from his reticence about the nature of the editing process in the Johannine tradition, R. E. Brown (*Epistles* 596 n. 11) suggests that 19:35 may have been added later than 1 John. He also is forced to conclude that chapter 21 is an addition.

Section 3. Synthesis of the Third Edition

However, in 1 John there is no indication of the existence of an authoritative office or interest in one. R. E. Brown points to this fact as one of the arguments against the position that the final edition of the Gospel was produced by the author of 1 John.[260] I would agree. In 1 John there is no evidence of authority beyond that of witness. The inspiration of the Spirit and the witness of the disciples to "what was from the beginning" remain the norm for identifying the truth. And this is the case during a crisis in which an appeal to authority would have been most helpful! This would indicate that at the time of the First Epistle, the issue of ecclesiastical authority and the community's relation to the Petrine churches was not yet a reality.

Even more importantly, it is difficult, if not impossible, to conceive of a movement from acceptance of an authoritative figure to a context without such a figure. This is also confirmed from the evidence of New Testament Christianity in general, where the movement is from a less to a more authoritative structure. Thus, the only viable explanation is that the third edition was written after 1 John.[261]

Sixth, the literary analysis has shown that in the Gospel there is a contrast between texts expressing a future eschatology (5:27-29) and those expressing a realized eschatology (5:24-26). Both 1 John and the third edition of the Gospel present a view of eschatology that involves both present and future elements, most notably a final universal judgment.

However, in the third edition of the Gospel, future eschatology involves bodily resurrection (5:28-29; 6:36, 40d, 44c, 54b). In 1 John, there is no indication of belief in, nor controversy regarding, bodily resurrection. Given the explicitness of the Gospel texts in this regard, it is clear that bodily resurrection was an important theological issue for the author of the third edition. If it had been an issue at the time of 1 John, we would expect to find, if not explicit discussion, at least some reference to it. Given the lack of reference in 1 John, we must conclude that the need to affirm a belief in bodily resurrection arose *after* the composition of 1 John. This in turn would confirm that the third edition of the Gospel was written after 1 John.

Seventh, it is regularly said that 1 John exhibits a less developed theology than that of the Gospel.[262] This is a complicated issue, and a full discussion is not possible here. But if the question is rephrased so as to ask whether the theology of 1 John is superior or inferior *to the theology of the second edition* and

---

260. Brown, *Epistles* 110.
261. It may also be that in 3 John 9 we have a scenario in which we are able to see the first inklings of a personal authority asserting itself. There a member of the community, Diotrephes ("who likes to be first among them"), is setting himself up as an authority figure and preventing the acceptance of the emissaries from the author's community.
262. For example, R. E. Brown, *Epistles* 33-35, 97-100; Kysar, *Gospel* 16, 31.

whether it is superior or inferior *to the theology of the third edition*, a radically new perspective is achieved.

In Part 4 of this volume, I will examine eleven major elements of Johannine theology, sketching the development of these concepts throughout the history of the tradition. *In every case where there are differences, 1 John shows development over the second edition and the third edition shows development over 1 John.* This properly nuances the view that 1 John has a less sophisticated theology than that of the Gospel. More properly it should be said that 1 John exhibits a theology that is more sophisticated than that of the second edition, but less sophisticated than that of the third edition. The features most commonly said to be more developed in the Gospel (pneumatology, Christology) exhibit that superior development precisely in passages that come from the third edition.

For example, if we contrast the unqualified use of the Spirit in the second edition of the Gospel with the Spirit passages in 1 John, we find a development in terms of the dualistic conception of opposed Spirits of Truth and Deception. Yet the most developed pneumatology is found in the Spirit-as-Paraclete passages that come from the third edition.[263] *Although the framework for the portrayal of the Spirit is dualistic both in 1 John and the third edition, the Spirit as Paraclete in the third edition is portrayed as possessing features that are more personal than those of either the second edition or 1 John.*

Although the Christology of the second edition is consistently "high," affirming the divinity of Jesus, there is no attribution of preexistence to Jesus in that edition. And although 1 John begins to speak of the preexistence of Jesus when it speaks of his being "revealed" (1 John 1:2a, 2g) and as having been "eternal" and "in the presence of the Father" (1 John 1:2ef), the highest and most unequivocal Christology is found in the third edition texts that contain the explicit affirmation of the preexistence of Jesus from the beginning of time and as an agent of creation and *Egō Eimi* statements (8:24, 28, 58; 13:19), the claim that Jesus has "life in himself" (John 5:26),[264] and the description of Jesus as "My Lord and my God (20:28)."

This is consistent with what is known of christological development throughout the New Testament. Such development moves in the direction of applying to *Jesus* attributes that had previously been reserved for God. We have seen this in the case of "Son of God," where the meaning attached to the title

---

263. R. E. Brown, *Epistles* 26, comments: "1 John offers much less specific reference to the Spirit than does GJohn." But Hengel (*Question* 180, n. 24) counters by pointing out that in 1 John the Spirit is mentioned seven times plus three instances of *chrisma*. On this basis, one would expect perhaps forty-nine references to the Spirit in the Gospel since it is seven times as long as 1 John. However, in the Gospel, "Spirit" appears nineteen times and there are four Paraclete passages.

264. On the significance of this expression, see the Note on John 5:26 in the Commentary.

Section 3. Synthesis of the Third Edition

moves from a traditional one to one affirming divinity in some sense, to the affirmation of a *unique* sonship.

While the Prologue of the Gospel and the Prologue of 1 John contain several similar ideas and expressions, the Prologue of the Gospel reflects a more developed state of several ideas found in the "Prologue" of 1 John. For example, the notion of the "word of life" in 1 John 1:1 is more metaphorical in its expression than is the Logos of the Gospel, and it could be better seen as a catalyst for the development of the Logos doctrine of the Gospel than the reverse.[265] The conviction of preexistence of the "word of life" in 1 John is less clearly articulated than it is in the Gospel.

Other instances have to do with the symbols of "light" and "darkness" and "commandments." It is commonly pointed out that in 1 John there are references to God as the light, and as the source of the commandments given to the disciples, while in the Gospel Jesus is said to be the light and the commandments are said to be from Jesus.[266] Moreover, in 1 John the Spirit is said to be "the Spirit of God" (4:2), while in the Gospel the Spirit is not so specified.

The literary analysis has shown that, within the Gospel, the notions of "light" and of "commandments" appear only in the third edition.[267] The traditional view of this is that what was first predicated of Jesus in the Gospel is later predicated of God in the Letters. This would be a curious "development." It is almost inconceivable that the community would shape its conception of God in the light of its conception of Jesus. Rather, the explanation for this difference is not to be found in terms of more or less developed theology but in the light of the nature of the crisis. We hear repeatedly in 1 John that the opponents claim to accept God but do away with Jesus. By speaking of the commandments as coming from God in 1 John, the author was simply seeking a "common ground" and formulating his argument on a level that the opponents would be bound to accept since they held to a belief in God the Father.

It is also true that the importance of ritual actions is clearer in the third edition than it is in 1 John. There are references in the third edition to human intermediaries in the forgiveness of sin (John 20:23). Whatever the precise meaning of "confessing" one's sins in 1 John 1:9, it is not so ritualized as is the process described in the Gospel.[268] The explicit affirmation of the importance of the Eucharist in John 6:51-58 has no parallel in the earlier 1 John.

---

265. R. E. Brown (*Epistles* 26) comments: "I John stresses aspects of a lower Christology in instances where GJohn stresses a higher Christology. The 'word' in the Prologue to I John seems to refer to the Gospel-message about life, whereas in the GJohn Prologue it is personified."

266. See particularly R. E. Brown, *Epistles* 26.

267. This is shown in the discussion of the Composition of the various texts.

268. See also the recognition of this in Schnackenburg, *Epistles* 82-83. R. E. Brown (*Epistles* 208) would disagree with Schnackenburg and argues that all instances involving "confess" in

The Third Edition of the Gospel

The question of a baptismal ritual is more difficult to decide. A number of scholars detect hints of an initiation rite in passages such as 1 John 1:5–2:2.[269] I am impressed with the parallels between the initiation ceremony at Qumran and the language of 1 John 1:5–2:2, but while at Qumran a ceremony is in view, in 1 John it is the conceptual framework, not a ritual, that is in view and being discussed.[270]

At the same time, it must be said that there is not extensive reference to Baptism in the third edition of the Gospel. As I have argued, I would hold that the reference to water has been added by the author of the third edition to the statement in John 3:5 (from the second edition) that one must be born of the Spirit.[271] It is also clear from a review of the second edition that the focus there is much more on giving the Spirit than on ritual actions. As a result, contrary to Bultmann's often quoted opinion, it is most likely that the mention of water is what is added, not the mention of the Spirit. If this is the case, then the mention of water is surely a reference to a baptismal rite (although it is also a model of brevity in doing so!).

Eighth, and finally, other aspects of the Gospel make more sense if they are seen to be developments subsequent to the writing of 1 John. For example, in the fourth of the Gospel's Paraclete sayings (16:7-11), the third author speaks of the Paraclete proving the world wrong about righteousness. This is the only use of the term "righteousness" *(dikaiosynē)* in the Gospel. Yet the way it is used in 16:8, 10 would seem to presuppose that it was familiar to the community. However, the term appears several times in 1 John, and Jesus himself is specifically said to be "righteous" *(dikaios)*. Moreover, righteousness is said to be a feature indicating that one belongs to God (3:10). The relationship between these texts becomes more intelligible if we see the texts in 1 John as the foundational development upon which the brief reference in John 16:8, 10 is based.[272]

The same relationship is also apparent with respect to the topic of petitionary prayer. In 1 John 5:13-17, it is explained in some detail that the possibility of direct petition to God is based on correct belief (i.e., belief in the name

---

the Gospel and the Letters involve some sort of *public* statement (although the others involve faith). He also points to 1 John 5:16 as an indication of a public concern for sin. But 5:16 refers to observing public sin, not public concern for sin. Brown also suggests that the community would have related this to the words of Jesus in 20:23. I find this unlikely since there is no mention at all in 1 John of any human intermediary in the process of confession as there is in John 20:23, nor is there any indication of the possibility of sin not being forgiven because of the decision of the intermediary (as there is in John 20:23).

269. R. E. Brown (*Epistles* 242-45) is a major proponent of this view.
270. See the further discussion in the Commentary on 1 John 1:5–2:2.
271. See the Commentary on John 3:5.
272. A detailed discussion is given in the Commentary on John 16:7-11.

Section 3. Synthesis of the Third Edition

of Jesus — v. 13) and that this belief leads to confidence that "if we ask for anything according to his [i.e., God's] will, he hears us" (v. 14). This is then repeated rhetorically in v. 15, and finally applied concretely to the fellow community member who is sinning a sin not unto death (vv. 16-17). The believer will ask, and God will give that person life. It is then on the basis of this development in 1 John that the brief references in John 16:23b-24, 26-28 (from the third edition) are incorporated into the Gospel. The relation between the two sets of references is more intelligible if those in 1 John are understood to be the foundational statement and the references in the third edition are understood to presume the understanding presented there.

We have now reviewed eight factors (one of which contained five additional elements) that suggest that the First Letter was written prior to the final edition of the Gospel. Together these features demonstrate how difficult it is to explain 1 John as following upon the completion of the Gospel. Rather, in all cases, the third edition either presumes the existence of the First Epistle or receives full intelligibility only in the light of it. Taken together, this is very strong evidence that the third edition of the Gospel was composed *after* the First Epistle.[273]

b. Assigning a Specific Date to the Third Edition

The date of the third edition, like that of the other editions, can only be determined approximately. Because with the completion of the third edition the Gospel reaches its final form, data regarding dating the Gospel as a whole become significant. This evidence is of two types, internal and external.

(1) External Evidence

On external grounds, we are able to put some general parameters to the date of the third edition on the basis of the earliest manuscript of the Gospel as well as the earliest citation of the Gospel.

(a) THE EARLIEST MANUSCRIPT EVIDENCE P[52] (the Rylands Fragment), the earliest fragment of any work of the New Testament, includes part of John 18:31-33 on the recto (front side) and parts of 18:37-38 on the verso. Applying

---

273. It is difficult to date the writing of 2, 3 John. At least it can be said that they are *theologically* dependent upon 1 John; that is, they would not be fully intelligible *to us* without the greater explanation found in 1 John. This tends to confirm the traditional sequence of writing and dating, which I find no reason to reject. More will be said of this in the Commentary on the Letters.

The Third Edition of the Gospel

the analysis performed in this book to the fragment, we see that the verses on the recto contain material from both the first and second editions: 18:31-32 come from the second edition, and v. 33 comes from the first. The verses on the verso come from the second and third editions: 18:37a comes from the second edition, 18:37b-38a comes from the third edition, and 18:38b comes from the second edition.

Thus, as small as the Rylands Fragment is (a single piece of papyrus measuring approximately 3½ inches high by 2 inches wide), it contains bits of all three editions and so indicates that the fragment was part of the Gospel in its final form.

P^{52} comes from Egypt and is generally dated to about A.D. 125.[274] On the basis of this evidence, we are able to determine that the final edition of the Gospel was produced before A.D. 125. How long it took to "migrate" to Egypt is unknown. From Ignatius, we can tell that the Gospel was known in Antioch perhaps ten years earlier (ca. 115). Consequently, it is reasonable to conclude on the basis of the external evidence that the Gospel reached its final version *before* A.D. 115. This tells us only that the final edition "had" to be in existence by that date; it could have been completed substantially earlier.[275] The manuscript evidence cannot tell us how much earlier.

(b) THE EARLIEST CITATION   There is considerable controversy about what constitutes the earliest citation of the Gospel of John by later writers. Boismard argued for references to the Gospel as early as Clement of Rome (around A.D. 96), but this has not gained much support.[276]

More widely accepted (but still a minority view) is the possibility of refer-

---

274. This dating is generally accepted and has been upheld by K. and B. Aland, *Text* 57. But also see Schmidt ("Anmerkungen" 11-12), who argues for a date about A.D. 170.

275. Boismard-Lamouille (*Pré-Johannique*, Vol. 1: *Jean 1,1-2,12* [published in two parts]; Vol. 2: *Jean 2,13-4,54*) have reconstructed what they consider to be an earlier version of the Gospel of John from the quotations in the homilies of Chrysostom. As J. K. Elliott in his review of the project (*NovT* 38 [1996] 90) comments, it is dangerous to presuppose that the fathers will have quoted the text exactly in all cases. In some cases they may have abstracted them within the homily proper. In any event, the existence of an earlier version, as remarkable as that would be as an independent document, would not affect the conclusion here since the manuscript evidence for a complete copy would remain even if Chrysostom, 225 years later, used another.

Comfort *(Quest)* has recently argued that P^5 (a third-century manuscript that ends with 20:25) and P^{75} (also third century; it ends at 15:8) came from versions of the Gospel that did not have chapter 21. Comfort calculates that to have the proper number of leaves for twenty-one chapters, the codex would have had two blank leaves at the beginning. Again, these codices are considerably later than P^{52}, which contains evidence of all three versions as defined in this Commentary.

276. Boismard, "Clément."

Section 3. Synthesis of the Third Edition

ences to the Gospel in Ignatius of Antioch, around A.D. 110-117.[277] Recently, Hengel,[278] Nagel,[279] and C. E. Hill[280] have argued that Ignatius of Antioch knew the Gospel, although he did not quote it word-for-word. The similarities are striking and are to material unique to John. Among the most striking are *Ephesians* 7:1 (// John 12:3, 13:31);[281] *Magnesians* 7:1 (// John 5:19 and 10:30);[282] *Magnesians* 8:2 (// John 1:1; 8:29; 7:28);[283] *Philadelphians* 7:1 (// John 3:8).[284]

The solution of this problem is largely dependent upon what is considered sufficient proof of a "citation." If we demand unassailable certainty and verbatim quotations as the only proper criterion, then we are probably right in looking, with Barrett and others,[285] to the period of about A.D. 170. The earliest citations generally recognized as certain appear in Tatian's *Diatesseron*,[286] in Melito of Sardis,[287] and in Irenaeus's *Adversus Haereses*,[288] all of which come from that period.

However, the criterion of verbatim quotation seems to be unnecessarily strict. Grant showed some years ago that Ignatius of Antioch could recount

---

277. F. M. Braun, *Jean* 1:262-82; Maurer, *Ignatius von Antiochien* 1-43, esp. 43; Grant, "Scripture" 322-35, see esp. 327; Bardsley, "Testimony" 207-20; Bauckham "Study" 369-403; Burghardt, "St. Ignatius" 1-26; Hoffman, "Authority" 71-79; Schoedel, *Ignatius* 1-7.

278. Hengel, *Question*, esp. 1-23.

279. Nagel, *Rezeption*.

280. C. E. Hill, *Corpus* 421-42.

281. In *Ephesians* 7:1, Ignatius speaks of Jesus receiving an anointment on his head *(myron elaben epi tēs kephalēs)*, an echo of John 12:3. In the same passage, he makes reference to the "ruler of this age" *(archōn tou aiōniou toutou)*, a phrase quite close to the Johannine "ruler of this world" *(archōn tou kosmou toutou)* (John 12:31; 14:30; 16:11).

282. In *Magnesians* 7:1, Ignatius states that Jesus "united with the Father, did nothing without the Father" *(aneu tou patros ouden epoiēsen, hēmenos ōn)*. This is a close parallel to John 5:19 ("the Son is not able to do anything of himself, except what he sees the Father doing") and 8:28 ("I do nothing of myself"), although neither is a verbatim quote.

283. In *Magnesians* 8:2, Jesus is described as "his son, who is his Word coming forth from silence, pleasing to the one sending him." This is an unmistakable reference to Jesus as the "Word" (John 1:1), although the notion of "coming forth from silence" is not Johannine. But later the description of Jesus as "pleasing to the Father" is also Johannine (cf. 8:29) and the reference to the Father as "the one sending him" is common in the Gospel (e.g., 4:34, etc.).

284. In *Philadelphians* 7:1, Ignatius states that the Spirit knows "whence it comes and whither it goes" *(oiden gar, pothen erchetai kai pou hypagei)*. This is an unmistakable reference to John 3:8, although the Johannine text speaks of persons as *not* knowing where the wind/Spirit comes from and where it goes.

285. See Barrett (*Gospel* 110-14) and R. E. Brown (*Epistles* 57).

286. Tatian makes the Johannine chronology the basis of the chronology of his *Diatesseron*.

287. Melito of Sardis, *Peri Pascha*, lines 552, 656. Melito makes undeniable reference to the Johannine episode of the raising of Lazarus.

288. Irenaeus, *Adversus Haereses* 2.22.5; 3.3.4.

The Third Edition of the Gospel

Scripture without actually quoting it.[289] For example, when Ignatius used the Old Testament, he did not always do so in the same way. Twice Ignatius quotes Proverbs (3:34; 18:17) with verbal accuracy. At the same time, it is certain that he knew and used the deuterocanonical 4 Maccabees, though he never actually names the document as such.[290]

It is indisputable, as Grant points out, that Ignatius used 1 Corinthians; yet at times he simply alluded to it while at other times he quoted it exactly.[291] Thus, it is certain that *some* of Ignatius's "free" allusions were to documents he was familiar with but which he simply chose not to quote verbatim. Consequently, it seems reasonable to conclude that the considerable number of parallels to distinctive elements of Johannine thought and language in Ignatius's writings can fairly be understood as indicating knowledge of the Gospel itself. A stricter standard is not necessary.[292]

If we reject the need for verbatim quotations, the first indication of the existence of the Gospel of John can be said to be in Ignatius, in the period of A.D. 110-117. Moreover, since one of the certain allusions is to material of the third edition, we are able to conclude that he knew the Gospel in its final form.[293] On this basis, we can put the certain *terminus ante quem* at A.D. 117.[294]

---

289. Grant, "Scripture."

290. It would seem that the book was particularly meaningful because it dealt with martyrdom, a fate that Ignatius himself faced. This is pointed out by Perler, "Vierte" 47-72.

291. Grant ("Scripture" 323) finds forty-six references, ranging from near quotes to allusions.

292. Within the last two decades, the first to argue this view extensively is Hengel *(Question)*, who set the agenda for more recent scholars. More recently, two monographs have dealt with this issue extensively. Nagel *(Rezeption)* deals only with the period up to A.D. 170, the period when the first verbatim references appear. C. E. Hill *(Corpus)* treats references up to the beginning of the third century. Both have for their purpose various aspects of the relation between the Johannine literature and Gnosticism. Both are also convinced that literature as early as Ignatius of Antioch testifies to the "orthodox" use of the Gospel. Hill specifically argues that the popular view (that the Gospel of John was not quoted before A.D. 170 because it was so gnostic in its tendencies and because it was used so frequently by the gnostics) cannot be substantiated by the evidence. He finds no indication in the pre-170 literature that the authors referring to the Johannine literature gave any indication that some apology need be made for its use. Nagel concludes that the Gospel was popular among gnostics, but that it was not gnostic in origin. While the purpose of both Nagel's and Hill's work is to address the issue of the reception of the Johannine literature, it is significant that they both independently agree that one need not be restricted to verbatim quotations in determining the earliest references to the Gospel and Letters.

293. For example, the reference in *Magnesians* 8:2 to the "Word" reflects knowledge of the Prologue, which comes from the third edition. Echoes of the second edition appear in (among other places) *Magnesians* 7:1; 8:2 and *Philadelphians* 7:1.

294. As is explained in the discussion of the date of 1 John, it is known that Ignatius died during the reign of Trajan (98-117). It is claimed in the *Chronicon* of Eusebius that Ignatius died in A.D. 108, but there is some discussion of the reliability of this date.

Section 3. Synthesis of the Third Edition

But this date is probably unnecessarily late. As I argue regarding the date of 1 John, if Ignatius died toward the middle of Trajan's reign and if the final edition was composed at or near Ephesus, then a date of composition near A.D. 100 is not unreasonable. Of course, it could have been composed substantially earlier.[295]

(2) Internal Evidence

Internal evidence is of some help in limiting the range of possibilities. The first type of evidence deals with the discussion in chapter 21 of the deaths of Peter and of the BD. A second type of evidence comes from a dating of the third edition relative to 1 John.

One firm point of reference is that the third edition was completed *after* the death of the BD. In 21:20-23, the narrator tells us that the report circulated among the "brothers" that the BD would not die. This report is corrected by explaining that Jesus had not said that the BD would not die but only "If I wish him to remain. . . ." Such a comment would be meaningful only if the BD had in fact died. Consequently, we may assume with certainty that the BD had died before the writing of the third edition but recently enough that his death was still a problem for the community.

When did the BD die? The reference to Peter's death as a martyr in 21:18-19 presumes that Peter's death has already taken place. Peter's death is generally considered to have occurred during the persecution of Nero (A.D. 64-66). Therefore, we can date the death of the BD to sometime *after* A.D. 64. But it almost surely took place some considerable amount of time later.

A first step toward determining how much later the BD died is to recall that the BD claimed to be an eyewitness to the ministry of Jesus. There are three elements of the presentation of the BD, all of which point to this conclusion. First, it is stated so often that the BD is a truthful witness and one who has *seen* and *heard* that for the facts to have been otherwise could only have been seen to be deceitful and would have undermined the integrity of the founding witness of the community's tradition. Second, throughout the third edition, each time the BD appears he is compared with Peter either implicitly or explicitly. In this case, the time of their deaths is contrasted. Peter died early, and the BD lived so long that some thought he would be alive at the return of Jesus.

If the BD could refer to himself as "the Elder" in 2 John and 3 John, it

---

295. Ignatius also shows substantial signs of confronting a group of dissidents who hold views similar to, but more advanced than, those of the opponents in 1 John. This would suggest that the Gospel was completed some time before A.D. 107. See Vol. 3, Appendix 4 (The Crisis That Divided the Johannine Community), Section J.2.

The Third Edition of the Gospel

would mean that his age was notably advanced. Presumably, an age of 70 would not be considered greatly advanced. Papias himself lived to that age and referred to a disciple of Jesus still alive as "John, the Elder." Therefore, the BD must have been significantly older than 70 when he died. A reasonable estimate would seem to be that this disciple died at about the age of 85 or 90. Thus he could have been an eyewitness, but not one of the Twelve, and of sufficiently advanced age that he would refer to himself as the Elder and could have spoken with Papias, who was born about the year 60. These factors point to a death in or near the last decade of the first century.

We might speculate that he wrote 2 and 3 John perhaps five years before his death. That would put their composition at about the year 80.

Some have argued that the concern for the authority and hierarchy evident in the report of the appointment of Peter as shepherd in chapter 21 indicates a development typical of the later first century. This would also be consistent with a date of about 90 for the composition of the final edition of the Gospel.

For a community such as this to articulate its role vis-à-vis Peter means that it is dealing with an issue that the Gospel of Mark dealt with by the year A.D. 70 and that Matthew and Luke dealt with in the 80's. This picture is also compatible with the view expressed in the third edition that the Johannine community sought unity with other sectors of early Christianity and that it was doing so somewhat belatedly.

c. Conclusions regarding the Dating of the Third Edition

In the light of the discussion above, we can say that on the basis of external evidence, it can be established with some certainty that the third edition of the Gospel was completed perhaps by A.D. 85-90, and certainly before A.D. 100.

In the light of the internal evidence, there is reason to move from these later dates to one that is substantially earlier. I have argued above that the internal evidence would suggest a date of the death of the Elder/BD between A.D. 85 and 90 and a date of A.D. 88-92 for the third edition. That would be a reasonable estimate for the date of the completion of the Gospel, although completion a decade earlier or later is not out of the question.

11. The Place of Composition

The place where the third edition was composed cannot be determined with certitude. However, a number of indications both external and internal suggest that the Gospel may have reached its final form in Ephesus.

Section 3. Synthesis of the Third Edition

a. External Evidence

It is noteworthy that Ephesus is the traditional location for the origin of the Gospel.[296] Of course, this can hardly be construed as "evidence," given the lack of accuracy such identifications often entail. Nevertheless, it is useful as a preliminary pointer.

From Acts 18:24–19:7, we hear of the existence of disciples of John the Baptist at Ephesus.[297] An Alexandrian Jew named Apollos was evidently one such disciple. His conversion was brought about by Priscilla and Aquila (Acts 18:24-26). When Paul came to Ephesus, he found a group of twelve who also had received only the baptism of John (Acts 19:1-7). In their later encounter with Paul, these disciples revealed that they were not aware of the Holy Spirit (which presumably means they did not know of the eschatological outpouring of the Spirit).[298] The prominence of a group of disciples of John the Baptist there is consonant with the emphasis on John the Baptist and the disciples of John in the Gospel from its earliest traditions.

It is significant that the earliest reference to the Johannine Letters appears in the letter of Polycarp of Smyrna, *To the Philippians*. (Smyrna was about twenty miles northwest of Ephesus.)[299] More importantly, in his letter *To the Philippians*, Polycarp identifies a heresy active at Philippi with the heresy countered by 1 John.[300] The heresy, we recall, was one that arose from a dispute precisely about the meaning of the Johannine tradition. Thus, we know that in that area there was evidence either of the actual Johannine heresy or one like it. Finally, Polycarp is said to have known John (the Elder).[301] All of this points to the area around Smyrna as one with close ties to the Johannine tradition.

---

296. Ephesus was the chief city (although Pergamum was the actual capital) of the Roman province of Asia. Along with Alexandria, Antioch, and Rome, it was one of the major cities of the empire. Its population is estimated at about 250,000 persons in NT times.

297. The other major source of information about followers of John the Baptist is the Pseudo-Clementine *Recognitions*. See the discussion in R. E. Brown, *Gospel* 1:lxvii-lxviii, 47.

298. It is difficult to make complete sense of this account. Just how "instruction in the Way of the Lord" led Apollos to know the facts of Jesus' life and the Scriptures without knowing about the outpouring of the Holy Spirit is not clear. Curiously, this preaching of Apollos bears some resemblance to the content of the first edition of the Gospel (as we have it). The first edition speaks of the baptism of John and of a group of his disciples who pointed to Jesus as being the one for whom John prepared. At the same time, it contains the "facts" about Jesus but does not mention the Spirit.

299. In 7.1, Polycarp combines 1 John 4:2-3 with 2 John 7 when he says: "For everyone who does not confess Jesus Christ to have come in flesh is an Antichrist."

300. For a discussion of this heresy, see Vol. 3, Appendix 4, Section E.

301. In Ignatius' letter to Florintinus, now extant only in a quote in Eusebius, *Hist.* (3.39.1), he says that Polycarp knew "John." Scholars regularly conclude that this was John the Elder, the author of 1 John.

The Third Edition of the Gospel

This view coincides with that of Schnackenburg, who has shown that, early in the history of the Christian community at Ephesus, the traditions were associated primarily with Paul, while, in later years, they were primarily associated with John.[302]

b. Internal Evidence

There are a number of similarities between the deutero-Pauline Letter to the Ephesians and John. This was noticed some time ago by Barrett, who proposed that "Ephesians, though in form entirely different, reveals a number of points of contact with John."[303] Barrett called attention to themes such as the unity of the church (Eph 1:10; 2:13-22), Christ as ascending and descending (Eph 4:8-10), the Holy Spirit as revealing the truth (1:17; 3:5); and the use in both of terminology such as "truth," "glory," "convict," "fruit," "darkness," and "light." It also speaks of "children of light" (Eph 5:8), an expression almost identical to the Johannine "sons of light" (12:36).

Some of these parallels in theology are also quite striking. For example, in Eph 5:6-13 we read of "the wrath of God upon the sons of disobedience" (disobedience and the wrath of God are associated apocalyptically in John 3:36); the contrast of light and darkness (cf. John 3:19-21); and "all those things shown to be wrong *(elenchomena)* by the light will be manifest" (cf. John 3:21).

As R. E. Brown points out, the image of "shepherding" seems to appear with greater frequency in Ephesus (cf. Acts 20:17) and Asia Minor (1 Pet 5:2).[304] This is reminiscent of the appointment of Peter as shepherd in the third edition.

It is sometimes pointed out that all of the names mentioned in 3 John (Gaius, Diotrephes, Demetrius) are Greco-Roman.[305] While this fact is hardly proof of a Gentile community (it will be recalled that both Andrew and Philip, two of the earliest disciples of Jesus who were from Bethsaida, also had Greco-Roman names), when joined with other elements, this does suggest a community with a substantial Gentile population.

From 2 and 3 John, we know that the Johannine community was composed of a number of smaller communities at some distance from that of the author. In the book of Revelation, a book that may have some distant relationship to the Johannine corpus, we see evidence of a group of communities that

---

302. Schnackenburg, "Ephesus" 41-64.
303. Barrett, *Gospel* 62-63.
304. R. E. Brown, *Epistles* 110 n. 255.
305. R. E. Brown, *Epistles* 34.

Section 3. Synthesis of the Third Edition

fits the general description of the satellite Johannine communities.[306] In this light, it is perhaps significant that the first of these to be mentioned is Ephesus.

While none of this proves a link between the Johannine community and Ephesus, together these features provide more links with Ephesus than with other areas.[307]

---

306. Rev 1:11; 2:1–3:22.

307. For another view, see Wengst (*Gemeinde* 157-79), who proposes that the Johannine community was located in Transjordan, the region governed by Agrippa II. But see the review by J. Becker *TRu* 51 (1986) 51-54.

PART 4

A History of the Development of Johannine Theology

The following discussion is devoted to a description of the development of selected topics in Johannine theology in the four stages of its development evident in the Gospel and the Letters. The reader will notice that the topic of each of these essays corresponds to eleven of the more significant features of the theology as it emerges throughout the four editions. It was also these eleven topics that structured the Overview of the Theology of each edition in the Analysis of the three editions above. The theology of 1 John and of the third edition of the Gospel was articulated, to a large extent, in dialogue with the convictions of the second edition. While the second edition took over elements of the first edition and was later expanded and modified by the author of the third edition, the theology of the second edition arguably represents the dominant and most substantial creative contribution within the tradition.

Discussions of the theology have appeared at various places in this volume. One appeared first in the discussion of the distinctive theological features in the listing of the criteria for the various editions (Section 1 of the Analysis of each edition). A brief summary of the discussion appeared in the Overview of the Theology of each edition (Section 2 of the Analysis of each edition). However, the discussion here represents the most detailed presentation and attempts not only to discuss each topic as completely as possible but, in addition, to do so in relation to both its role in the growth of the tradition and the particular worldview that informs it.

Although the arrangement of the following survey corresponds to the eleven convictions first set out in the Overview of the Theology of the second edition, the topics here are identified by their more common terms within the study of theology: Christology, belief, pneumatology, eternal life, eschatology, knowledge of God, soteriology, ethics, anthropology, ecclesiology, but the more general description of the last ("The Religious Significance of Material Reality") has been retained because the issues involved there are broader than those communicated by the term "ritual."

It is perhaps useful to recall once again the pivotal role of 1 John in understanding fully the range of the theology in the second edition as well as the nature and purpose of many of the additions in the third edition. But the relationship between these two editions of the Gospel and 1 John is reciprocal, for it is also when 1 John is viewed in the context of the second and third editions of the Gospel that the origin of many of the disagreements becomes clear.

In order to appreciate something of the background against which the Johannine traditions were understood at each of their four stages of development, I will also provide at times a brief sketch of the background of these ideas and modes of expression in both the Old Testament and in certain strains of late apocalyptic Judaism.[1] In some cases these are true parallels, but in other instances the various communities, while starting from similar worldviews, have developed distinctive theologies.

Such parallels can be quite helpful in corroborating a theory that would appear tenuous without such parallels. For example, if one is skeptical that the pneumatology of the second edition could be seen as the source of so many claims and prerogatives of the opponents in 1 John, the fact that this conception is also present throughout the Old Testament gives additional proof of the proposal advanced here. Likewise, the fact that the viewpoint of the author of 1 John and of the author of the third edition is paralleled often in the SDQ and the *T12P* gives additional proof that his worldview could be at home in at least one Jewish community of the first century.

Yet discussing such parallels entails risks and methodological restraints. These groups of documents do not contain a single monolithic conception of a given feature. Yet it is not possible to present all the varieties and nuances of expression in these documents in the present context. At most, some examples can be presented as a way of demonstrating the existence of the particular feature in the documents and in the hope that they will point the way to additional study. At the same time, this is, as far as the author is aware, the first attempt to write a history of the development of Johannine theology.[2]

---

1. References to the "Old Testament" throughout will be to the documents found in the Septuagint canon. This canon was that most frequently used by early Christians. References to the Hebrew canon will be noted as such.

2. De Boer (*Perspectives*) sees four distinct views of the death of Jesus in the Gospel and attempts to relate them to a series of historical periods within the community. However, de Boer does not see this as a "development" but a response to differing situations.

Section 1. The Development of Johannine Theology: Christology

SECTION 1. THE DEVELOPMENT OF JOHANNINE THEOLOGY: CHRISTOLOGY

While it is possible to detect clear emphases within the Christological views of the second and third editions, it is unrealistic to expect that every text associated with the Christology of a given edition can be identified with certainty.[3] This is true for a number of reasons.

First, the Christology of the third edition will overlap considerably with the material of the second edition. The third author agreed with much of the theology of the second edition. Consequently, he repeats and affirms much of the viewpoint of that earlier edition. Even though the third edition is his work, some aspects of this material will be quite similar, if not identical, with concepts from the second edition.

---

3. Scholars who approach the Christology of the Gospel without any interest in editorial history nevertheless comment on the problems involved in understanding the Gospel's Christology. For example, de Jonge (*Envoy* 120) comments: "On closer inspection, Johannine Christology is not as uniform and consistent as it sometimes looks; there are also considerable differences between the Gospel and the First Epistle in this respect.... Do those aspects of Johannine Christology that — in our view — can only with difficulty be combined with its central core represent traditional elements that are regarded as indispensable, but are not (yet) fully integrated, or are they relics not (yet) discarded, but without any function?"

Bühner *(Gesandte)* holds that there are two christological strains in the Gospel that should not and cannot be harmonized with one another. The first (in Bühner's view) is a Christology that develops against the background of apocalyptic. Later, this Christology develops into a view of Jesus portrayed against the (Jewish) background of the prophet/angel of Yahweh. Although Bühner does not attempt to assign these conceptions to distinct literary stages, it should be obvious that the two strains that Bühner has recognized as distinct conceptions correspond in considerable detail to the christologies of the second and third edition as presented here. However, I believe that there is convincing evidence that of the two strains, the apocalyptic is the later one. Anderson *(Christology)* discusses the Christology of the Gospel within the microcosm of John 6, points to a variety of views within that chapter, and concludes that the tensions are due in part to editorial history (with a Moses Christology at the earliest level) and in part to a dialectic (that relates later developments to the earlier views).

Boismard *(Moses or Jesus)* presents a proposal for the development of Johannine Christology based on his view of the origin of the Gospel. While I would agree that there is a clear emphasis on aspects of a Moses Christology in the first edition, I do not think that the author of that edition accepts "Prophet like Moses" as an appropriate title but presents "Christ" and "Son of God" as the most satisfactory titles, although his understanding of those titles differs from that of the later authors. To say that the titles "Christ" and "Son of God" are "satisfactory" is meant to indicate that they were the most widely accepted titles within the Johannine community and in other early Christian communities. However, the Johannine community employed many more specific and more descriptive titles. Yet these were ultimately understood to be aspects of Jesus' identity as "Christ" and "Son of God," and these latter titles remained appropriate *confessional* titles.

Second, while some editorial seams within discourse material can be identified quite clearly, at the same time it can be more difficult to identify editing in discourse material since not all editing is abrupt and awkward; some changes are quite subtle, and consequently the literary seams are difficult to detect. Not all editing leaves aporias in the text!

Third, it is sometimes impossible to be sure how a particular statement was intended to be understood due to inherent ambiguities. For example, one could argue that the statements about the subordination of Jesus to the Father are from a different author than those that speak of the Son's equality with the Father. Alternatively, one could argue that the two types of statements are simply aspects of a single perspective. An example of this is evident in Ashton's treatment[4] when he suggests that, if christological statements are understood against the background of a king and his emissary, then "*(i)n fact* the king is greater than his emissary; *in law* the emissary is the king's equal." This complicates the analysis, for we cannot always be certain precisely how each statement of the Gospel was understood by the community.

Fourth, our attempts are also complicated by such issues as how literally to understand various statements that by their very nature struggle to express conceptions that were not only new to the community but that by their very nature tend to strain the limits of human language. For example, Schnackenburg cautions that we should not read the affirmations regarding the unity of the Father and Son relationship as being concerned chiefly with metaphysical statements.[5] They are remarkable statements but nevertheless were still some of the first attempts made to articulate a series of relationships for which the community had no previous model.

There are also difficulties connected with reconstructing the Christology of the opponents in 1 John with the degree of specificity that we would like. Again, this should not be surprising. We know the opinions of the opponents only through the words of the author. The author of 1 John in turn does not provide a fully systematic exposition of either his or his opponents' position. Consequently, there are some elements that we must infer, given the lack of explicit evidence.

At the same time, the amount of uncertainty and ambiguity should not be exaggerated. It should be apparent throughout that when 1 John is coordinated with the second and third editions, the three bodies of material help illumine one another to a considerable extent. We will point to this again and again. However, in order to avoid duplication, the discussion here will presume details from the extended discussion of the nature of the crisis in Volume 3, Appendix 4.

---

4. Ashton, *Understanding* 316.
5. Schnackenburg, *Gospel* 2:185.

Section 1. *The Development of Johannine Theology: Christology*

1. The Christology of the First Edition

a. A Low Christology in the Affirmations about Jesus

In the first edition, the Christology is "traditional." Nowhere does the Christology speak of Jesus as divine. What confirms this view is the fact that not only are the titles and other affirmations about Jesus consistent with the traditional expectations of the Jews about the one-who-was-to-come but also *the charges* against Jesus by the religious authorities are formulated on this level.[6] Among the questions discussed in the first edition is whether he is the "Messiah" (1:41; 4:29; 7:26-27, 31, 41-42); whether he is "the one of whom Moses and the prophets spoke" (1:45); "the Son of God" (1:49); or "the King of Israel" (1:49). People speculate whether Jesus is "a" prophet (4:19; 9:16) or whether he is "the" Prophet (like Moses) (6:14; 7:40, 52). The authorities ask whether God is with Jesus (3:2); whether or not Jesus is from God (9:16, 29, 30); or whether God has spoken to him (9:29). All of these titles are intelligible against the background of, and within the ambit of, the traditional expectations of the Jews about the promised future deliverance of the nation.

The Titles "Messiah" and "Son of God"

Although it will not be fully evident until after the discussion of the later stages of the community's writings, the titles "Messiah" and "Son of God" retain an ambiguity throughout the Gospel. These titles, which are the most widely used titles for Jesus in the New Testament, are used in *all* literary strata of the Johannine tradition. Yet it is evident that, in the various strata, the titles took on a meaning that was distinct for each. Within the first edition there is no evidence that these titles were understood in any way other than the traditional.[7]

b. Low Christology in Accusations Brought against Jesus by the Jewish Authorities

In 4:1-4, the hostility of the authorities is first evident. But in these verses, the issue is the baptizing of Jesus and no titles are in dispute. In 7:48-49, we see the

---

6. As we will see in the discussion of the Christology of the second edition, the claims of Jesus as well as the titles and the charges against Jesus are all on the level of high Christology (i.e., dealing with claims to equality with God the Father).

7. Ashton ("Identity" 61) speaks of the discussion of Christology in 9:17 as "a relatively modest claim, one that had been made for Jesus from a very early stage," and of the discussion at the end of chapter 7 as "conducted on a relatively low level, arising out of claims already made for Jesus in the signs source" (ibid.).

authorities asserting that Jesus is not worthy of belief. He cannot be the Mosaic prophet because he comes from Galilee.[8] In the debate with the man born blind, the issue is whether Jesus is "from God";[9] his crime is that he violates the Sabbath and that God has not spoken to him (9:29). When the Sanhedrin condemns Jesus, it argues that if it allows him to continue, the Romans will come and take away its independence and destroy the Temple (11:48).

c. A Moses Christology

The presence of a "Mosaic" Christology in the Fourth Gospel is widely recognized.[10] This is, for example, the only Gospel to even mention the title "the Prophet" (like Moses). It is the only Gospel in which the narrator speaks the miracles of Jesus as his "signs." And it is the only Gospel in which the "signs" lead to belief rather than presume it. These are all major elements of the Gospel — and they are all found consistently and exclusively within the material of the first edition.[11]

This indicates that a major element of the portrayal of Jesus in the first edition is against the background of both his similarity and his superiority to the figure of Moses. Like the signs of Moses in the Exodus,[12] the signs of Jesus are meant to inspire belief. And the belief they are meant to inspire is precisely the fact that Moses/Jesus is "from God." When we look at the material of the first edition we see that it is precisely these issues that are discussed in connection with the signs of Jesus.

In addition to this portrayal of the miracles against the background of the Mosaic signs, the Gospel also makes explicit comparisons between Jesus and

---

8. For evidence that it is the Mosaic prophet that is spoken of here, see the Note on 7:52.

9. It will also be noted that the question whether Jesus is "from God," as it is expressed in the first edition, addresses the question of a prophetic sending and nowhere implies a descent "from above."

10. See, for example, Teeple, *Mosaic;* Glasson, *Moses.* More recently, see Boismard, *Moses;* von Wahlde, *Earliest* 164-66. Richter, a strong proponent of a Moses Christology in the first edition of the Gospel, claims that this understanding of Jesus as the prophet like Moses involved not only a traditional Christology but also one in which Jesus was "nur ein Mensch" ("Vater" 267-68). Richter proposes that the Resurrection of Jesus was then understood in the tradition of the assumption of Moses.

11. This is not to say that there is no interest in the figure of Moses in the later editions. For example, the superiority of Jesus to Moses again becomes an issue in the second edition in 6:30-50. However, in the second edition, this superiority to Moses is not a focus in itself but one of a series on major figures of Israel to whom Jesus is superior (i.e., "Are you greater than our father Jacob?" [4:12]; "Are you greater than our father Abraham . . . ?" [8:53]).

12. See, for example, Exod 4:1-9; Num 14:11-22.

Section 1. The Development of Johannine Theology: Christology

Moses. For example, in 9:28-29 the Pharisees tell the man born blind that they are "disciples of Moses" while he is a disciple of "that fellow." In the next verse the comparison continues: "We know that God has spoken to Moses, but we do not know where this one is from." The man responds in terms of low Christology: "We know that God does not hear sinners; but if a person is God-fearing and does his will, he listens to the person."

d. Other Elements of the Christology of the First Edition

However, the Moses Christology does not exhaust the christological perspective of the first edition, for Jesus is also identified positively by a variety of other titles. In chapter 1 he is identified by the disciples as "Rabbi" (1:38); "Messiah" (1:41); "the one that Moses (in the Law) and the Prophets wrote about" (1:45); "Son of God" and "King of Israel" (1:49). Elsewhere others give him various titles: "Messiah" (4:25; 7:26b-27, 31, 41-42); "a prophet" (9:17); "Rabbouni" (20:16). In the end, in the concluding formula of belief, Jesus is identified as "the Christ," "the Son of God."

"Rabbi" and its diminutive form "Rabbouni" should be considered part of "Christology" in an extended sense. They are titles that could be applied to any revered person who functions as teacher. The people proclaim Jesus "the Prophet" in 6:14. The Jerusalem crowds speculate about him in these terms in 7:40.

However, the Samaritan woman in an ambiguous statement essentially affirms Jesus as the Messiah (4:25); the crowd does so also in 7:26-27, 41.[13] "King of Israel" also appears in 1:49. It does not seem to have a significant role other than to support the view that Jesus was the fulfillment of a variety (or all!) of Israel's hopes.[14] "Son of God" appears, but only in the statement by Nathanael (1:49) and then in the final statement by the narrator of the first edition (20:30-31).

---

13. As can be seen, there is a curious parallel between the discussion of "the Prophet" and "the Christ" in these instances. Moreover, signs are associated with the Prophet in 6:14; they are associated with the Messiah in 7:31. The crowds speculate that Jesus may be the Prophet (7:40) and then immediately that he may be the Christ (7:41). Some have proposed yet additional parallels. If the article is read before "prophet" (see the Note to 7:52 in the Commentary), there is a clear parallel between the way the crowds say that the Christ does not come from Galilee in 7:41 and the way the Pharisees say that the Prophet does not come from Galilee in 7:52. In 1:41, Andrew says, "We have found the Messiah"; in 1:45 Philip says, "We have found the one that Moses wrote about in the Law — and the prophets." If we take the awkwardness of the phraseology to mean "We have found the one Moses wrote about in the Law . . . ," the phrase could well be intended to refer to "the Prophet." Both of these are suggested by Boismard, *Moses or Jesus* 28-30. As tantalizing as these parallels are, they may be too strained.

14. It appears again in 12:13 as an appendage to Ps 118, in material from the second edition.

In sum, it must be said that, judging from the text that remains, there is some tension within the Christology of the first edition. The Christology is Jewish and is traditional. There is no hint of attributing divinity to Jesus. But how the use of titles is to be reconciled with the "functional" Christology is not completely clear. Certainly the dominant functional Christology compares Jesus with Moses. This occurs not just by title but by terminology, theology, and deliberate comparison. Yet Jesus is also identified with a variety of other titles, and from among these, if we judge by the response of the narrator, Jesus is best seen to be "Messiah" and "Son of God." Because the text of the first edition is almost certainly incomplete, it seems best to note these features of the Christology but not to attempt to force them into a unity and coherence that is greater than is warranted by the text before us.[15]

As we will see in the discussion of the second and third editions, the titles "Christ" and "Son of God" will continue to be important in the later editions. But at the same time it will be clear that the subsequent editions will imbue these titles with new meaning and a higher Christology.

2. The Christology of the Second Edition

The second edition introduces a radical new Christology. It is the Christology that is generally thought to be most characteristic of the Gospel, although in fact it will be modified significantly by the authors of 1 John and of the third edition.

a. Jesus' Exalted Claims

(1) Jesus as the "Son" in Relation to "the Father"

In the second edition, there is a massive interest in Christology. The primary reason for this is that unless a person accepts the claims of Jesus and believes "in his name," the individual will not receive the Spirit that Jesus offers. However, at the time the second edition was written, there was considerable conflict between the Johannine community and the synagogue precisely regarding the identity of Jesus and the claims he made for himself.

---

15. Some have suggested that the title of the Prophet and the Christ were associated with one another in first-century Judaism and that this may explain the emphasis given to these titles in the Gospel of John (cf. Jeremias, "*Mōysēs*," in *TDNT* 4:859-64, followed by Glasson, *Moses* 20-26; Boismard, *Moses or Jesus* 25-30). But such an identification is not clear within the first edition as we now have it.

Section 1. The Development of Johannine Theology: Christology

In this edition, the dominant understanding of Jesus is as Son sent by the Father. This complex of ideas is introduced at the time of the second edition, but is also taken over in 1 John and in the third edition, although the ideas are modified, nuanced and clarified in these later stages of the tradition.

(2) Jesus as "Son"

The use of "Son" in the absolute sense[16] is introduced by the author of the second edition and is, as Schnackenburg says, "the privileged Christological title and Jesus' own preferred way of referring to himself."[17] When Jesus speaks of himself as "the Son," it is always (either implicitly or explicitly) in relation to God as "the Father": 5:19 (twice), 20, 21, 22, 23 (twice); 6:40; 14:13; 17:1 (twice). While the number of instances of the term "son" in this sense is relatively small, this is not surprising since, in most instances, it is Jesus who is speaking, and therefore he refers to himself as "I" or "me" rather than as "the son."

As can be seen from 5:17-18, these references to "Son" are essentially connected with the conception of God as "Father" in a literal way that far exceeds the traditional understanding of "son," and so elicits the charge of blasphemy from "the Jews."

(3) God as "Father"

"Father" is by far the most common designation of God by Jesus, occurring 110 times in the Gospel. It is introduced by the author of the second edition and is used twenty-four times in passages in the public ministry in which the authori-

---

16. By employing the adjective "absolute," I distinguish this use from uses (a) that occur in the title "Son of God," (b) that occur in the title "Son of Man," (c) that occur in the expression "unique son," (d) that do not refer to Jesus in a religious sense (i.e., Jesus as son of Joseph, 6:42), (e) that are the simple secular use referring to "sons" of various parents (1:42, 45; 4:5, 12, 46, 47, 50, 53; 9:19, 20), and (f) that otherwise do not refer to Jesus ("sons of light," 12:36; "son of destruction," 17:12; "son" referring to the BD, 19:26). The absolute use occurs in the second edition eleven times (5:19 [twice], 20, 21, 22, 23 [twice]; 6:40; 8:35; 17:1 [twice]).

In the first edition, "son" is used only in the title "Son of God" (1:49; 20:31). In the second edition, "son" is used in the absolute sense (see above) and in "Son of God" (1:34; 5:25; 10:36; 11:4; 19:7). In the third edition, the term is used in the absolute sense (3:17, 35, 36 [twice]; 5:26; 8:36; 14:13), in the title "Son of God" (3:18; 11:27), in the title "Son of Man" (1:51; 3:13, 14; 5:27; 6:27, 53, 62; 8:28; 9:35; 12:23, 34, 34; 13:31), and in the expression "unique Son" (1:18; 3:16, 18).

17. Schnackenburg (*Gospel* 2:102). It is important to study the Father-Son relationship apart from the title "Son of God." Each has a distinct genesis. Most importantly, the title "Son of God" has a long history of usage within Judaism while the absolute use of "S/son" does not. Moreover, within the early Christian community and particularly within the Johannine community, "Son of God" functioned as a confessional formula while the "Son" title does not. See also the helpful discussion in Moloney, *Son of Man*, esp. 208-9.

ties are identified as "the Jews."[18] It appears another forty times in passages that do not contain the term "the Jews" but that are identified as coming from the second edition on other grounds.[19]

It is almost always associated with the discourse and dialogue material of the Gospel. It appears primarily on the lips of Jesus, but at times it is also found on the lips of others who talk with Jesus. It is also used by the narrator. What is of greatest significance is that, in all of these instances, the term "Father" is used in a restricted sense to indicate the divinity of Jesus.

Yet at this stage of the tradition there is no full articulation of Jesus' relation to God. In spite of his exalted status as Son, he can also say that all he has and does is from the Father (5:19, 20b, 30). He seeks only the will of the Father (4:34; 5:30); he does nothing on his own (5:30, 36). He speaks the words given him by the Father (5:37; 8:26). He seeks only the glory of the Father (5:41-47).

(4) Jesus as "Sent" by the Father

The second edition introduces the notion of the Son as "sent" by the Father.[20] This notion of sending is communicated by the use of two Greek verbs: *pempō* and *apostellō*. However, there is no evident distinction in meaning between the two words, and it seems that the choice of one or the other is dictated primarily by the fact that the authors found some grammatical forms more convenient than others.[21] The designation "the one who sent me" appears *as a modifier of* "the Father" often: with *pempō* (5:23, 37; 6:44; 8:16, 18; **12:49;**[22] **14:24, 26**); with *apostellō* (5:36; **6:57**; 10:36; 11:42; 17:8, 18, 21, 23, 25; **20:21**).[23] At other times "the

---

18. 2:16; 5:17, 18; 6:32, 37, 44, 45, 46 [twice]; 8:26 [twice], 27 [twice], 29, 30, 32, 36, 37, 38 [twice]; 15:1, 8, 23, 24.

19. 5:19, 20, 21, 22, 23 [twice], 26, 36 [twice], 37, 43, 45; 8:16, 18, 19 [twice]; 11:41; 12:27, 28; 13:1, 3; 14:7, 8, 9, 10 [twice], 11, 12, 20; 16:3, 17, 25, 28 [twice], 32; 17:1, 24, 25; 18:11; 20:2.

20. Among the more important studies of the sending motif in the Gospel are Bühner, *Gesandte*; Miranda, *Sendung*; and idem, *Vater*. It will be noticed that, in the first edition, the recurring question was whether Jesus was "from God" and whether God was "with him." While the notion of sending as used in the second edition can theoretically be related to this use, the meaning is much more focused and is used with "Son" and "Father" in a way that is completely distinct from any usage in the first edition.

21. Only *pempō* appears in the participial phrase "the one who sent me"; and when it is used of Jesus, it always appears in such a participial phrase. *Apostellō* regularly appears in a *hoti* clause indicating a desired object of belief (e.g., "in order that they may believe that you sent me") (5:36, 38; 6:29; 11:42; 17:3, 8, 21, 23, 25), but *pempō* does not. Furthermore, "God" and "that one" (as a designation of God) are used as subjects of *apostellō* but not of *pempō*.

22. Boldface represents the usage in the third edition.

23. In addition to the use of *apostellō* with "Father," the verb also appears with *theos* ("God") as subject (3:17, 34; 17:3) and with *ekeinos* ("that one") as subject (5:38; 6:29; 7:29; 8:42). (*Pempō* does not appear in these combinations.)

Section 1. The Development of Johannine Theology: Christology

one who sent me" appears *alone* (with the verb *pempō*): 4:34; 5:24, 30; 6:38, 39; 7:16, 18, 28, 33; 8:26, **29**; **9:4**; 12:44, 45; **13:20**;[24] **15:21**; 16:5.[25] As can be seen from the list above, the term appears mainly in the second edition (twenty-six times in the second edition versus nine times in the third edition).

From these patterns within the Gospel, it is evident that this "sending" is conceived of as an important part of the larger relation of Father to Son. Although it is part of that overall conception, it has the specific function of pointing to the fact that the Son is the one sent. The effect of the phrase "the one who sent me" is to emphasize this aspect of the relationship and to show that Jesus regularly views the Father as his "Sender," that is, in relation to his function as the one who invests the Son with his mission.

The correlative of this notion of sending is that of "coming" (e.g., 16:27, 28, 30), although it does not have the restricted use that "sending" does in relation to Jesus.[26] This notion should not be distinguished theologically from that of being sent.

It should also be noted that of itself this notion of being sent is not the same as the notion of the descent and ascent of the Son of Man. While the notion of being sent is compatible with a belief in the descent of a preexisting Son, there are no texts that express this *in the second edition*. However, as we shall see, in the third edition the Son (of Man) is both preexistent and has descended and will return to where he was before (e.g., 6:62).

(5) The Son Does the Same Work as the Father

In the second edition, Jesus assumes to himself the prerogatives allowed only to God. When asked a justification for his work on the Sabbath (5:16-18), he appeals to the rabbinic conviction that God was allowed to work on the Sabbath and claims the same privilege for himself.

Moreover, he claims for himself the fundamental powers of God — to give life and to judge (5:19, 21b, 24-25, 30). These two powers are given to Jesus by the Father. Those who accept life through belief in Jesus will cross from spiritual death to spiritual life and will not come into judgment (5:24-25). His goal of giving life is expressed clearly in 10:10 ("I came so they might have life, and have it abundantly").

---

24. As will be seen in the Commentary, this verse may represent a true interpolation, that is, not coming from any of the three authors involved in the composition of the Gospel.

25. The participial use of *apostellō* with a relative pronoun as subject does not appear in the Gospel.

26. "Coming" is not a term restricted to Jesus, however. John the Baptist is said to "come" (1:31), the disciples are invited to "come" (1:39), Philip invites Nathanael to "come" (1:46; cf. v. 47).

The descriptive statements of the purpose of Jesus' coming highlight one or other aspect of this sending/coming. For example, it is described in general terms as (1) "doing the work(s) of the Father" (5:36; 7:21; 10:25, 31, 37, 38), as (2) "bringing the work of the Father to completion" (4:34; 5:17, 36; 9:3; 17:4; cf. 14:12), and as (3) "doing the will of the Father" (4:34; 6:38, 40). But these are related to the denotative purpose: to give life. This is evident from 5:40, where it is said that it is the will of the Father that everyone who sees the Son and believes in him should have eternal life. In addition, Jesus has been given authority over all flesh so that he might give eternal life to those who believe (17:2).

Although there was an Old Testament background for the understanding of someone as "son" of God (e.g., the king of Israel) and of someone as being "sent" (e.g., the Prophet) and of God as "Father," the claims made by Jesus go beyond — and are understood by his listeners to go beyond — this traditional understanding. He claims prerogatives that can only be said to be divine. It is these claims to divinity that set the community at odds with the synagogue.

b. Jesus' Dependency on, and Orientation toward, the Father

(1) The Priority of the Father

In spite of the repeated and varied assertions of the unity and identity of Father and Son, in the second edition the Father is superior to the Son.[27] It is the Father who has "consecrated" the Son (10:36) and who "witnesses" to the Son (5:37; 8:16). It is the Father who has given him the power to give life and to judge (5:19a-c, e, 20b, 24-25, 30). The Son does the will of the Father (6:38). The Son does nothing of himself but only what he sees the Father doing (5:19). In this sense the Son is totally empty of self-will or claims to self-importance; it is the Father to whom all glory is due.

(2) Jesus Does Only What He Hears from the Father

Jesus does not seek his own will (4:34; 5:30; 6:38, 40). He speaks what he has heard from the Father (8:26). His teaching is not his own (7:16-17). This dependence upon the Father is also communicated by Jesus' statements that he does nothing "of himself" (5:19, 30; 7:28; 8:28; 14:10).[28] But when the Son asks for something, the Father hears the Son (11:41).

---

27. The precise nature of the "equality" between the Son and the Father is difficult to determine. This will be discussed again after the treatment of the Christology of the third edition.

28. This is carried over into the third edition (e.g., 8:28; 12:49).

Section 1. The Development of Johannine Theology: Christology

(3) Jesus Seeks the Glory of the Father

Perhaps the most dramatic expression of Jesus' self-emptying is found in his comments about "glory." In 5:41-47, after making his most arrogant claims and giving the types of witness that testify to those claims, Jesus then proceeds to give all glory to the Father for what he possesses. He has not come in order to gain praise or estimation for himself. Rather, he has come "in the name of the Father" and so seeks only that people see what he does and then give glory to the Father because of it. Thus, the Jesus of the second edition claims no "glory" for himself but only for the Father.

In 7:18, Jesus has finished explaining that his teaching is not his own and that those who speak on their own seek their own glory but that he simply seeks the glory of the one who sent him. This notion is so foreign to his listeners that they cannot accept it. They are used to looking for and accepting only the glory that claims that their accomplishments are due to their own resources.

Jesus does not come in his own name (5:43); he does not work in his own name (10:25). Related to this is Jesus' assertion that the one who believes in Jesus believes, not in him, but in the one who sent him (12:44).

(4) Jesus' Success and His Glory as Given to Him by the Father

The success of Jesus' ministry is also due to the Father. It is not Jesus' own independent work. John the Baptist recognizes this and states that "a person cannot gain anything unless it is 'given' from heaven" (3:27). Jesus himself recognizes this fact and states it repeatedly. It is the Father who "gives" the believer to Jesus (6:37). No one "given" by the Father will be lost (6:39); no one can come unless the Father "draws" the person (6:44). Jesus repeats this for the disciples in 6:65. In his high-priestly prayer, Jesus again affirms that believers are "given" to him (17:2, 24).

Jesus does have a glory, but it is not one that he claims for himself. Rather, it is given to him by the Father (8:54; 17:22). The Father glorifies the Son during his ministry and during the Passion (12:28; 17:5).

(5) Jesus' Relationship with the Father

Jesus' intimacy and oneness of heart with the Father are expressed by the biblical notion of "knowing" the Father (8:55 [twice]; 10:15; 17:25). Moreover, the Father knows the Son (10:15). This aspect of his identity is contrasted with the frequent references to unbelievers as not knowing either Jesus or the Father (17:25).

Jesus also possesses a oneness with the Father. This is expressed in various

A History of the Development of Johannine Theology

ways. It is said once that "the Father and I are one" (10:30).²⁹ Jesus also says: "But the Father abiding in me *(en emoi menōn)* performs his works" (14:10). Five times the expression to be "in" is used to describe the relationship between Jesus and the Father (10:38; 14:10, 11, 20; 17:21). It always expresses both a unity and an intimacy and implies the constancy of this relationship. Jesus urges his listeners to come to realize "that the Father is in me, and I am in the Father" (10:38). Jesus also speaks of his "not being alone." In the discourse of chapter 8, it appears twice: "I am not alone, but I am together with the Father who sent me" (8:16). He also says: "[T]he one who sent me is with me. He did not leave me alone because I always do that which is pleasing to him" (8:29). In the Passion, the disciples will leave Jesus, but he will not be truly alone because the Father is with him (16:32). Although no one has seen the Father except Jesus, to see Jesus is to see the Father (14:9). To know Jesus is to know the Father (8:19; 14:7; 16:3).³⁰

In the Gospel, there are some texts that would suggest that Jesus was neither fully divine nor equal with the Father. The clearest of these is John 14:28 ("The Father is greater than I"). It would appear that this text is from the second edition. While it is difficult to know precisely how this statement was intended in the second edition, it seems clear that it represents a stage of christological reflection that is less fully developed than that of the third edition.³¹

c. Jesus as Preexistent in the Second Edition?

I have argued, and will argue below, that in the second edition there were no explicit statements about the preexistence of Jesus. However, it could well be said that several of the statements made about and by Jesus in the second edition seem to indicate such a belief.

In the first edition, there was a repeated question whether Jesus was "from God." It was overwhelmingly clear that in the first edition, this phrase simply meant: "Is this man sent by God?" It would be the kind of question that would be put to any prophet. Had he come from God? In this context, Jesus' "coming into the world" could well refer only to his ministry. This is the same meaning that is associated with the notion of Jesus being "sent" in the second edition. He is sent

---

29. It is difficult to know precisely what is intended by this statement. It certainly can be understood to express the degree of unity that is typical of the third edition, but it is also possible that, in the context of 10:22-39, it was simply intended to express a moral unanimity. See also the Interpretation of 10:22-39 in the Commentary.

30. This is carried over into the third edition, where it is made clear that all are to "honor the Son as they honor the Father. The one who does not honor the Son does not honor the Father who sent him" (5:23).

31. Some of the possible meanings of this text are discussed in greater detail in the Interpretation of the verse in the Commentary.

Section 1. The Development of Johannine Theology: Christology

by God, but this does not imply preexistence or divinity of itself. One could debate whether Jesus was sent by God or not, but this was a separate issue from the more challenging assertion that Jesus was "Son" and God was his "Father" in a way that surpassed all claims to God as Father in the history of Israel.

Another possible indication of Jesus' preexistence could perhaps be found in his statements saying that he spoke what he heard from the Father (e.g., 5:30; 8:26). These refer to special experiences, but they need not refer to preexistence but simply to special revelatory experiences such as were often thought to have been given to select figures throughout Jewish history. The theology of the second edition takes up this kind of experience and joins it with another set of convictions about the relation of the Father and Son that also had a background in Jewish thought, thus resulting in an understanding of Jesus that was Jewish but would also be unique in its combination.

As we look at the background of the Christology of the second edition, we find that the closest parallels suggested by scholars are all derived from human situations. These are human models that are thought to be adapted to the relationship of Jesus to the Father. In all of these instances, we see models and concepts that stretch the limits of previous categories and affirm the divinity of Jesus, but at the same time there are no statements in the second edition that can be said to rival those of 1 John — or those of the third edition — for clarity and explicitness about the equality of Jesus with God the Father.

d. Traditional Titles in the Second Edition

In addition to the massive concentration on the identification of Jesus as "Son" in relation to God as "Father," the second author continues to recognize the importance of traditional titles for Jesus. Prominent among these are "Son of God," "Christ," and "king."

(1) Son of God

The second author uses the title "Son of God" for Jesus in 1:34; 5:25; 10:36; 11:4; 19:7; (20:31?). In all instances, this term, which had also appeared in the first edition (and which will appear in 1 John and in the third edition) is understood in terms of the overarching Christology of "Son" and "Father."

(2) Christ

This title, which had also appeared in the first edition, and which will also appear in 1 John and in the third edition, appears in the second edition five times.

However, three of these are in discussions about whether John the Baptist is the Christ (1:20, 25; 3:28). Only in 9:22 and 10:24 does the second author apply the title to Jesus. Yet in 1 John the title becomes a major focus of Christology, and in the third edition it will continue to play a substantial role.

(3) King

While the title of "king" had been applied to Jesus (apparently approvingly) by the author of the first edition, it is rejected as a title by the author of the second edition. It appears in two contexts, first at what could well be called the end of the Galilean ministry (6:15) and then at the end of the Judean ministry (12:13, 15). In 6:15, the author explains that "Jesus, knowing that they were about to come and to take him by force so they might make him king, again went up the mountain alone, by himself."[32] In 12:13, after quoting Ps 117(118):26, the second author appends an explanatory phrase "and the King of Israel" in order to explain the meaning of the crowd's exclamation. However, Jesus corrects their understanding by entering the city seated on a donkey, an action that is explained in turn by Zech 9:9, which contrasts the horse as symbol of military might with the donkey as symbol of humble, domestic activity. In both instances the material is that of the second author, and in both instances the author rejects the application of the title to Jesus, at least as it is understood by the crowd.

e. Conclusions

This brief discussion of the second edition's Christology cannot claim to be complete. Nevertheless, the summary presented should be sufficient to demonstrate how radically different it is from the view presented in the first edition.

The picture of the Son and the Father and their relationship is uniquely profound and presents the remarkable paradox between the exalted claims of Jesus' equality with the Father and at the same time his recognition of total selflessness, dependency on, and subordination to, the Father. As such it is one of the most profound of the New Testament. At the same time, the second author continues to accept traditional titles for Jesus, although they do not play the same role for him as does his own more developed and more sophisticated understanding of sonship.

---

32. Meeks (*Prophet-King*) argues that this passage reflects a tradition of Moses as king as well as provider of food in the desert. If this is the background, it is clear that Jesus rejects it as it is understood by the crowd.

Section 1. The Development of Johannine Theology: Christology

3. The Background of the Christology of the Second Edition

The background of the second edition's Christology is complex. It continues to portray Jesus in the light of traditional categories by comparing him with Abraham, with Jacob, and with Moses and by associating his work with the most important Jewish feasts (Passover, Tabernacles, Dedication) and institutions (the Sabbath, temple worship).

But beyond this, there seem to be two conceptual complexes against which the second edition's Christology is portrayed: the Jewish understanding of revealed Wisdom and the Jewish understanding of such relationships as those of Authority/Emissary, Father/Son, and Master/Apprentice.

Ashton has recently called attention to the study of various aspects of the background of Johannine Christology within Judaism, aspects that go far toward explaining the particular features of this relationship as expressed within the Johannine Gospel. He addresses in turn the notions of mission, agency, and sonship.[33] I would agree that these conceptions play a major part in the background of the Gospel's Christology, but at the same time I would point out that these concepts *do not pervade the Gospel as a whole but are found first and most clearly in the second edition of the Gospel.* They are not found in the earliest stratum of material in the Gospel, and where they are found in the third, they are modified so as to address issues created by the crisis in the community at the time of 1 John. In other words, it is specifically in relation to the Christology of the second edition that these conceptions are formulated.

a. Sending

The first of these is most commonly associated with the role of the prophet who is sent by God. This is at times associated with a kind of "ascent" (see Jer 23:18, where the prophet, when speaking of false prophets, asks: "Who from among them has stood in the council of Yahweh to know and hear his word?"). In Jer 23:21, Yahweh declares: "I did not send the prophets . . . ; I did not speak to them, yet they prophesied. If they had stood in my council, they would have proclaimed my word." In these passages, being "in the (heavenly) council," being "sent," and "speaking the words of God" are all closely associated, as they are in the description of the Johannine Jesus. In the prophetic mission, there was a sense that the prophet did not possess his task or his powers on his own but was to refer them all to God.

---

33. Ashton, *Understanding* 308-29. The notion of agency is also taken up now by Witherington, *Gospel* 140-41.

b. Apprenticeship

Some years ago Dodd and Gächter argued that behind the statement of 5:19 ("The Son is not able to do anything of himself, but only what he sees the Father doing") is a parable that expresses the principle that an apprentice follows closely the work of the master.[34] Dodd cited several examples of variations of this parable from the Oxyrhynchus papyri. Although these examples are not specifically Jewish as are the prior parallels, the possibility of such a parable lying behind the formulation of 5:19 has been widely accepted.[35] Yet even so, as Ashton points out, this parable deals with *skill*, whereas the primary element of 5:19-25 is the transfer of *authority*. In the Johannine account, the emphasis is on authority.

c. Agency

P. Borgen has called attention to halakhic principles of agency in the rabbinic writings.[36] The principle is stated succinctly as "the agent is like the one who sent him."[37] This principle finds close parallels in John 12:44 ("The one who believes in me does not believe in me but in the one who sent me"). Borgen also points to similarities with John 5:23; 12:45; 13:20; 14:9; 15:23. In Jewish thought the relationship is juridical, but Borgen points out that, in some instances, there is a kind of mystical union between the sender and the one sent. For example, *Qiddushin* 43a states: "The agent ranks as his master's own person." This has parallels in the various statements of "immanence" in the second edition. Moreover, it will be recalled that the notion of immanence in the second edition was focused precisely on establishing the union of Son with Father.

Nevertheless, it was recognized (*Genesis Rabbah* 78) that "the sender is greater than the sent." This is echoed in John 13:16 ("The slave is not greater than his master, nor is the 'one sent' greater than the one sending him").[38] It was

---

34. This notion was developed by Dodd ("Parable" 30-40) and Gächter ("Form" 65-68). It has been widely accepted by commentators.

35. But see Beasley-Murray (*Gospel* 75), who, perhaps rightly, recognizes that the relationship of dependence is too widespread to be based simply on such a parable. Beasley-Murray finds the basis "in a deep consciousness of the unique relation of the Son to the Father," but this goes too far in the other direction. The most helpful proposal is that of Ashton, who suggests that the relation between Father and Son is expressed in terms of the legal relationships evident in Jewish law. As Ashton (*Understanding* 325) says, ". . . the fourth evangelist . . . has seized upon a conceptual system he found ready to hand in order to put the ineffable into words."

36. Borgen, "God's Agent" 137-48.

37. See Borgen, "God's Agent" 138 n. 2, for texts.

38. This appears in the third edition but was undoubtedly that author's acceptance of the Christological formulation of the second author.

Section 1. The Development of Johannine Theology: Christology

the legal expectation that the agent is to carry out the wishes of the sender obediently.[39] When the agent's mission is complete, he is to report to the sender. Borgen would see an echo of this report in the word of Jesus in John 17:4 ("I glorified you on earth, having brought to completion the work that you have given me to perform").[40]

Borgen goes on to suggest that the association of such notions of agency with heavenly beings can be found in merkabah mysticism.[41] While he would see a connection between the early stages of merkabah mysticism and the Johannine Christology, I do not find this aspect of his argument convincing.[42]

d. The Figure of Wisdom

Scholars have long called attention to a number of parallels between the description of the figure of Wisdom in the Wisdom literature and the presentation of Jesus in the Gospel of John.[43] Throughout the Wisdom literature, Wisdom is presented as personified (Prov 1:20-33; 8:1–9:6; Sir 1:1-18, 24:1-31; Wis 7–9; Bar 3:9-28, etc.). And, although this was simply a poetic description of Wisdom, it came to be applied to Jesus in a literal sense.

In the Gospel as a whole, many of the traits of Wisdom are associated with Jesus.[44] Wisdom typically speaks in long discourses, as does the Johannine Jesus. Wisdom teaches humanity things that are too profound to be known through ordinary means (Job 11:6-7; Wis 9:16-18); she speaks the truth (Prov 8:7; Wis 6:22); she gives instructions about the divine will (Wis 8:4; 9:9-10).[45]

---

39. See *'Erubin* 31b-32a; *Qiddushin* 2:4; *Terumot* 4:4. Compare, for example, John 6:38; 8:29, etc.

40. See *b. Ḥagigah* 76d, *Mekilta on Exodus* 12:1.

41. On the background of the notions of agency and sending, see also Bühner, *Gesandte* 181-267.

42. Both Borgen and Bühner would join the "sending" of the Son with the concept of the Son of Man. Moloney (*Son of Man* 237-44, esp. 241-43) would argue against this on grounds of theology. I would agree but add that the literary analysis of the materials prior to a discussion of theology indicates that the titles originate in different strata of the Gospel.

43. Most scholars find parallels primarily in Wisdom, Sirach, Proverbs, Job, and *1 Enoch*. Those parts of the wisdom literature with greatest relevance describe Wisdom herself rather than the characteristics of the life lived according to Wisdom. One of the first to call attention to this feature of Johannine Christology in a systematic way was R. E. Brown in his commentary. He also revisited the subject in an appendix to his book on NT Christology. I will refer to that treatment. Witherington in two books (*Sage* and *Gospel*) has also been a major proponent of the influence of Wisdom on John. See also Willet, *Wisdom*; Scott, *Sophia*.

44. Scholars find the most concentrated presentation of Jesus in terms of Wisdom in the Prologue of the Gospel. We will see this in the discussion of the third edition below.

45. This section is summarized from R. E. Brown's treatment in *Christology* 209.

A History of the Development of Johannine Theology

Wisdom leads people to life (Prov 4:13; 8:32-35; Sir 4:12; Bar 4:1; Wis 3:1-4; 6:18-19). Particularly appropriate are Prov 8:35 ("The one who finds me finds life") and Bar 4:1 ("All who hold fast to her [Wisdom] will live.").[46] Just as this life is conceived of as immortality in Wis 3:1-4; 6:18-19, so we find texts in John that speak of eternal life in terms of immortality (e.g., John 5:24-25).

The view of salvation in John is close to that given by Wisdom. Wisdom comes from the gift of God's Holy Spirit, and "the paths of those on earth were set right, and people were taught what pleases you, and were saved by wisdom" (Wis 9:17-18). This reflects the primary view of the Johannine Gospel, in which salvation is not from the atoning death of Jesus but from the gift of eternal life through the Spirit.[47]

Like Wisdom (Sir 24:17, 18), Jesus compares himself with the vine (15:1-5) and with water (4:10-15; 7:37-39). According to Bar 3:36, Wisdom is a fountain; in John Jesus is "living water" (4:10-15; 7:37-39). Like Wisdom, Jesus speaks in "I am" statements. According to R. E. Brown, the followers of Wisdom are her "children" (Prov 8:32-33; Sir 4:11; 6:18); Jesus refers to his followers as "little children" (John 13:33).[48] Just as Wisdom is *monogenēs* (Wis 7:22), so is the Johannine Jesus (1:18; 3:16, 18).[49]

In addition to more general thematic similarities, some interpreters find similarities in the portrayal of individual texts. For example, Witherington sees the notion of being "born from above" (John 3:3) as an echo of Wis 7:14, where it is said that Wisdom "comes down from above, passes into human souls, renewing all things, and [making] them friends of God and even prophets."[50] Witherington, following Dodd, also proposes Wis 16:6 with its reference to the serpent as a "symbol of salvation" as a background for John 3:14.[51]

The discourse of chapter 6 is recognized by many to have a sapiential background. It is said of Wisdom that, "those who eat of me will hunger for more, and those who drink of me will thirst for more" (Wis 24:21). In a way parallel, but superior, to Wisdom, those who come to Jesus will eat and drink and be satisfied (John 6:35).[52] In Prov 9:5, Wisdom invites people to "eat of my bread, and drink of the wine I have mixed." Jesus' claim to be the "bread of life"

---

46. See Boismard, *Victory* 114; R. E. Brown, *Christology* 208.

47. Witherington, *Gospel* 25.

48. R. E. Brown, *Christology* 209. While this is factually true, the use of "children" in the Gospel and Letters does not seem to be due to the Wisdom tradition but to the conviction that eternal life is a result of a birth that therefore entitles the believer to be called a child of God.

49. R. E. Brown, *Christology* 208.

50. Witherington, *Gospel* 25.

51. Witherington, *Gospel* 25; Dodd, *Interpretation* 306.

52. Boismard (*Victory* 114). Boismard also understands Wisdom as the "tree of life" (Prov 3:18) and sees this as the background of John's conception of the bread of life.

Section 1. The Development of Johannine Theology: Christology

(6:35) is understood to be an identification of himself with Wisdom come into the world.[53]

Wisdom parallels are also proposed for elements of chapters 7 and 8. Cory sees the notion of Wisdom "seeking and finding" as a major framing element of chapters 7 and 8.[54] For example, in John 7:34 we read: "You will seek me but not find me" (also John 7:36; 8:21; cf. 7:12-13, 13:33).[55] Cory and others point to Prov 1:28 (LXX) ("Then they call me, but I do not answer; the evil seek me, but do not find me"); (cf. also Prov 14:6, 8) as a close parallel. In addition, as R. E. Brown has pointed out, like Wisdom (Prov 1:20-21; 8:1-4), Jesus is said to regularly "cry out" to the people (7:28, 37; 12:44).[56]

Witherington suggests that the Farewell Discourses "characterized Jesus as a sage or as Wisdom conveying his legacy of wisdom to his 'learners' in private...."[57] Individual elements of the Farewell Discourses are said to have echoes of Sir 4:11-13:

(1) Wisdom teaches (Heb.)/exalts (Gk.) her children and gives help to those who seek her (//John 14–16).
(2) Whoever loves her loves life (//John 14:16ff.), and those who seek her from early morning are filled with joy (//John 15:11).
(3) Whoever holds her fast inherits glory (//John 17:22), and the Lord blesses the place she enters ... the Lord loves those who love her (//John 17:26).[58]

Witherington sees the references to "keeping the commandments" (John 14:15) as echoes of texts such as Wis 6:18.[59]

As this review indicates, there are a considerable number of parallels between the presentation of Jesus and that of Wisdom. However, this review also reveals that not all parallels are equally convincing. Some seem purely acciden-

---

53. Boismard, *Victory* 115.
54. Cory, "Rescue" 101.
55. Certainly not all instances of "seeking" *(zētein)* or "finding" *(heurein)* can be said to have this connotation. Yet several instances, particularly of *zēteō*, may echo the use in Wisdom literature (e.g., 4:23; 5:44; 6:26). It should also be noted that sometimes it is Wisdom who does the seeking (Wis 6:16).
56. R. E. Brown, *Christology* 209.
57. Witherington, *Gospel* 26. However, the Farewell Discourses are better understood against the background of the Farewell Discourse genre than that of a Wisdom speech.
58. While these parallels are compatible with Wisdom thought, they are so general, so few, and so scattered that it is difficult to think that they indicate any sort of attempt to model the Johannine text on Wisdom.
59. Again, the Johannine texts are compatible with Wisdom thought but echo Deuteronomic thought more closely. (For details of the Deuteronomic background, see von Wahlde, *Commandments* 227-29.)

tal. For example, the references to "children" of Wisdom and to Wisdom being "unique" *(monogenēs)* have no real similarity to references to the disciples as "children" or to Jesus as the "unique" son. While there is a verbal similarity, the similarity is purely accidental.

At other times, proposed parallels have other explanations. For example, while some references to "seeking and finding" may be patterned after the activity of Wisdom, others have purely mundane explanations. (The analysis of the editions presented here is helpful inasmuch as those references that most seem to echo the presentation of Wisdom occur in dialogue and refer not to some specific situation but to a more general activity. The majority, if not all, of these occur in the second edition.) Nevertheless, in spite of the need to treat proposed parallels critically, the portrayal of Jesus and his ministry in terms evocative of the Wisdom tradition cannot be denied and represent an important part of the background of the Gospel.

Finally, there are several observations that are important for properly understanding the presentation of Johannine Wisdom. First, it is important to recognize that, while all Israelite Wisdom was understood as a gift from God, Wisdom of Solomon links Wisdom specifically *with the gift of the Spirit* (Wis 9:17).[60] The primary gift of Jesus in the second edition of the Gospel is the gift of the Spirit. Thus, it is understandable that Jesus who possesses the Spirit could be presented in terms reminiscent of Wisdom itself.[61] Yet it is also important to realize that, although Jesus is presented in terms evocative of the portrayal of Wisdom, he does not *give* wisdom. He gives the Spirit. The second edition is clear on this. The gift of Jesus is eternal life, which comes through the Spirit. In fact, the word "wisdom" *(sophia)* does not appear at all in the Johannine corpus.[62]

Second, there is a major difference between the overall content of the Gospel of John and that of the traditional Wisdom literature. Traditional wisdom literature focused on the giving of a wide variety of practical advice, but we find none of this in John. Just the opposite. It is widely recognized that there is a remarkable lack of specific teaching in the Gospel and that in the Gospel

---

60. While relatively little attention is given to the link between the Spirit of God and Wisdom, even in the Wisdom of Solomon, this is understandable since the primary focus of the Wisdom literature is to speak to specific forms of behavior that should be informed by Wisdom. In spite of the fact that the connection between the Spirit and Wisdom is clear, Witherington overstates the issue when he says that the Wisdom of Solomon "equated Wisdom with God's Spirit" (*Gospel* 26).

61. In spite of the number of echoes of the Wisdom literature in the Gospel of John, there is no hint that the Gospel thinks of the ministry of Jesus itself in terms of giving Wisdom. The term *sophia* does not appear anywhere in the Johannine literature.

62. John Collins (*Jewish Wisdom* 1) treats the appearance of this term as the primary criterion by which he identifies the books that constitute the Wisdom tradition.

Section 1. The Development of Johannine Theology: Christology

the focus is almost exclusively on the person of Jesus. Thus, even if Jesus is presented as embodying many of the features of Wisdom, he does not engage in specific Wisdom teaching. Acceptance of Jesus was what was essential in the eyes of the Johannine community. If one accepted Jesus, the person would receive the Spirit and, in the understanding of the community at the time of the second edition, the Spirit would teach them all things. There would be no need for the specific instruction recorded in their Gospel.

Third, there are two elements of this Wisdom background that do not fit the Christology of the second edition. First, it is evident that one of the greatest concentrations of Wisdom motifs appears in the Prologue of the Gospel. But this Prologue comes from the third edition of the Gospel. Secondly, (and related to the first), in the second edition there is no belief in preexistence. Texts that speak of this come from the third edition. While Jesus was presented as one who taught wisdom at the time of the second edition, there was no attempt to take the poetic description of Wisdom as existing from the time of creation and apply it literally to Jesus. Part of the reason was undoubtedly that the primary focus in the second edition was on Jesus' own reception of the Spirit (1:32) and his giving of the Spirit (4:10-15; 7:37-39; 20:22). It was not until the third edition that the community came to articulate the full implications of the reality of Jesus, including his preexistence.

As we will see below, although the primary presentation of Jesus in terms of Wisdom occurs in the second edition, the third author was aware of this orientation and took it over and added to it. Even though the Wisdom tradition had been formed in the traditional (nonapocalyptic) worldview of the majority of the Old Testament, it is clear from the SDQ that Wisdom was capable of being incorporated into the worldview of apocalyptic at Qumran. It is in this form that it comes into the third edition of the Gospel. This mixture of Wisdom motifs together with an apocalyptic viewpoint is most evident in the Prologue that the third author has added to the Gospel. As we will see below, it is also the third author who introduces the notion of preexistence into the Gospel. It is more difficult to prove that the notion of preexistence *necessarily* derives from the (poetic) presentation of Wisdom, but it is a reasonable supposition. More will be said of this below.

e. Jesus as Possessing the Life of the Father

There is an aspect of the Johannine Christology that is not accounted for by this survey of the Jewish parallels: how one "whose father and mother we know" could be such a figure. The Johannine Jesus lives with divine life. He is Son in an ontological, not just a juridical, sense. This can only be because he lives with the life of God. In the discussion of pneumatology, I survey the Old Testament convictions about the effect of the final bestowal of the Spirit. Jesus himself lives with the life of God (which the Spirit bestows), and he himself exhibits all of the prerogatives of the Spirit: he is (the) "Christ"; he is (the) "son" of God; he knows the Father; he does his will; he is sinless; he lives forever; he will not die.

It would then seem that it is Jesus' possession of eternal life that becomes the basis for the ontological reality of sonship that is then developed and presented within categories (now transformed) taken from the world of legal and religious relationships of the time. This is the Christology that forms the basis of the second edition of the Gospel. It is the Christology that, although modified and nuanced, will be the foundation of both 1 John and of the third edition of the Gospel.

f. Conclusion

The discussion above has pointed out parallels to several aspects of the second edition's Christology. These have helped to shed light on the background out of which the second edition developed. In all cases, these parallels are clearly Jewish. But, while these parallels illumine aspects of the Christology, none is sufficiently similar to be called fully satisfactory. We have touched upon elements with clear parallels: the notions of agency, of sonship, and of wisdom. If some elements of the figure of the legal agent or messenger underlie the Christology of the second edition, these need to be combined with the notion of sonship as well as with the notion of the Son as one sent to bring to completion the Father's work of creation by giving new life.

It may well be that the further exploration of the juridical elements of the second edition in relation to the juridical aspects of the notion of agency will help tie together in a more complete way not only the understanding of the second author's Christology but also the relation between it and this other prominent aspect of the second edition. Much remains to be done in this regard, and it is hoped that the understanding of the literary development of the Gospel presented here will help achieve greater precision with respect to the understanding of this period in the growth of the tradition's Christology. But it would seem that in the last analysis the Christology of the second edition is in fact the author's own unique and creative combination as he struggled to articulate the reality of Jesus' relationship with the Father.[63]

63. Ashton (*Understanding* 315-16) perceptively calls attention to the fact that the Gospel itself is less focused on ontology than was the church of two hundred years later. Reading many of the Gospel's statements in the light of the Jewish background of agency rather than in the light of later interests could well lead us to a quite different understanding of a number of Johannine texts.

Section 1. The Development of Johannine Theology: Christology

4. The Christology of 1 John

Here we will discuss briefly the Christology of the opponents as it appears in 1 John; then we will discuss the Christology of the author of 1 John.[64]

a. The View of the Opponents

In 1 John, there is an atmosphere of debate. Lines are drawn and distinctions made between the views of the author and those who have seceded from the community. There can be no doubt that, since they had been members of the community and had departed from it (1 John 2:19), the opponents had been believers in Jesus. They had come to believe in Jesus, but now their belief differed from that of the others primarily in denying any permanent role for him in salvation. As a result, the Christology of 1 John is less detailed in its description of the identity of Jesus and more focused on affirming that a proper understanding of Jesus is essential to proper belief: the opponents deny the Son!

Who was Jesus for the opponents? They believed that Jesus was divine and was the son of God and that he possessed the Spirit and eternal life, that he was sent by God and was going to God. All of this had been presented in the second edition, and because the opponents had been members of the community they would have accepted this belief along with the others. While agreeing with the exalted view of Jesus in the second edition, the opponents believed that the sonship of Jesus was something that was able to be achieved by the believer also, through the reception of the Spirit by which they too would begin to live with the life of God (eternal life). (1) As Jesus had the Spirit (1:32), so they as believers would receive the Spirit (3:5-6; 4:10-15; 4:19-24; 7:38-39; 20:22). (2) As Jesus had eternal life (5:21; 6:33, 48, 50), so the believer will have eternal life (5:24-25; 6:40, 47). (3) As Jesus is a "son" of God, so the believer is born of God (3:3-6) and therefore implicitly a "child" (son/daughter) of God.[65] (4) The believer was said to have an anointing (1 John 2:20) just as Jesus did (cf. the numerous references to "Christ").

They did not deny that Jesus was the Christ (2:22); otherwise they would not have become believers in the first place. Rather, they denied that he was "the" Christ in a unique and exclusive sense. So also, although they confessed

---

64. In the analysis of 1 John, I will also call upon the material of 2 and 3 John where relevant since the three documents deal with the same general situation and share a common theological perspective.

65. The notion of being a "child" of God does not appear in the Gospel until the third edition, where it is affirmed of the believer by the author. Thus, in spite of the fact that the issue was disputed, the author of 1 John (and the author of the third edition) continue to affirm it.

that Jesus was "son," they did not confess him as Son (2:23) in the sense that his sonship was in any way unique or special. For them, Christology was blurred by anthropology.

There was also a second way in which the role of Jesus was not a permanent one: Jesus did not *do* anything by which it could be said that he himself achieved salvation for humanity. He announced the imminent gift of the Spirit and belief in him was necessary in order to receive the Spirit, but it was the reception of the Spirit that would give them eternal life, not anything Jesus himself did (i.e., laying down his life for his own). The words of Jesus were not of unique significance because the eschatological outpouring of the Spirit would lead the believer to direct and full knowledge of what God wanted. Nor was the death of Jesus significant other than as the prerequisite for the sending of the Spirit.

Thus, for the opponents, God the Father, in whom all Jews believed, was essential and the Spirit that he sent in the name of Jesus was the principle of the promised eternal life and so was essential. But Jesus was not. His role in "salvation" was temporary. He was divine and embodied the promised gifts of the Spirit. His mission was to announce the gift of the Spirit to those who believed in him. But it was the Spirit who gave life. He announced the gift of the Spirit and had a role in the giving of the Spirit, but his actions did not effect salvation. That role belonged to the Father and the Spirit.

b. The View of the Author of 1 John

In the face of what he saw as a distortion of the true identity of Jesus, the primary focus of the author of the First Letter was to affirm the continuing significance of Jesus and to clarify both the ways in which his identity was distinct from that of the believer and what his role in salvation was.

(1) The Unique Identity of Jesus

The author makes his case in a number of ways. He does it first by repeatedly affirming that the Son is of permanent significance for the believer. Not only is the Son essential, but one cannot truly believe in God the Father unless one believes in Jesus. Unless one has the Son, one cannot have the Father (1:3; 2:23); unless one has the Son, one cannot have life (5:12). The believer is to "remain" in Jesus (2:27; 3:6); and the one who believes is "in" the Son (2:24, 27, 28).

But what is one to confess about Jesus? First, the author regularly identifies Jesus as "the Son" in relation to the Father (eleven times: 1:3, 7; 2:22, 23; 4:9, 10, 14; 5:9, 10, 11, 12). This is strong evidence of how the author continues to af-

Section 1. The Development of Johannine Theology: Christology

firm the fundamental outlook of the second edition. Second, the believer is to confess that Jesus is the "Son of God" (4:15; 5:5, 10, 13) and that Jesus is "the Christ" (2:22, 23; 5:1, 5).

In addition to these instances where the titles are used in a context of confession or belief, the author himself uses the title "Son of God" three other times (3:8; 5:12, 20) and the title "Christ" once more (2 John 9). These continue to be important titles and continue the usage begun in the first edition.

Nevertheless, a significant change occurs in the use of titles. In 1 and 2 John, Jesus is also identified as "Jesus Christ" eight times (1:3; 2:13; 3:23; 4:15; 5:6, 20; 2 John 3, 7). This is a title that does not appear at all in either the first or second editions of the Gospel. Thus, the association of "Christ" with Jesus is closer and more immediate than ever.

Just as there is continuity and difference in the titles used for Jesus, so there is continuity and difference in the presentation of the identity of Jesus and the believer. As in the second edition, the believer continues to be a child of God, to possess the Spirit, and to possess eternal life. These will be detailed in the discussion of anthropology below. However, the author introduces two distinctions between Jesus and the believer that are not evident in the second edition. In both instances, these distinctions serve to increase the distance between Jesus and the believer so as to prevent a simple equation of the prerogatives of the two. First, the author affirms that the sonship of Jesus is not the same as that of the believer. Rather, the sonship of Jesus is unique (*monogenēs*; 4:9). Second, the Son is said to be preexistent. The author affirms this several ways. Jesus is never said to be "born." His ministry is a matter of his being "revealed" (1:2 [twice]; 3:5, 8). It is also said that the Son had been "in the presence of the Father" (1:2). Thus, the preexistence of Jesus is affirmed, but it is done in a way different from that which will appear in the third edition. It is fair to say that in 1 John these expressions are less polished and explicit than they are in the third edition of the Gospel. Jesus is also unique because of his unique soteriological function, as we shall see in below in Section 7.

(2) The Abiding Importance of Jesus

In contrast to the opponents, the author of 1 John proposes that the word of God spoken through Jesus has a unique and permanent importance and serves as an external guide by which to judge the "words" given by the Spirit. This is expressed through the terminology of the "commandments" God had given to the believer.[66] Those who claimed to "know" God but who did not keep his

---

66. The notion of "commandment" in 1 John is discussed more fully in Vol. 3, Appendix 5 (The Johannine Commandments).

(God's) commandments were liars, and the truth was not in those persons (2:4). But the one who "keeps his [God's] word" (2:5) is the one who truly loves God. But the word is not simply a "word" that is claimed through inspiration but is the word that they have heard "from the beginning" (1:1-3; 2:24). Because Jesus did not speak on his own or of himself, this can truly be said to be the word of God. But this word is an external word, received through the senses, "that which we have heard, which we have looked at with our eyes, which we have seen and our hands have touched..." (1:1). Thus, the word can be said to be the word of tradition rather than the word of spontaneous inspiration (cf. 2 John 9).

Finally, the Son has an essential and permanent role in soteriology. The First Letter of John repeatedly and by a wide variety of expressions affirms that the death of Jesus is what takes away sin. No such conviction is expressed in the second edition, and in fact, where the removal of sin is discussed, it is associated with the bestowal of the Holy Spirit rather than with the death of Jesus. While we will discuss this in greater detail in the sections on pneumatology and soteriology, it is important to emphasize here that the portrayal of Jesus' death as one that takes away sin also constitutes a significant aspect of the Christology of the First Letter.

5. The Christology of the Third Edition

The third edition of the Gospel affirms the basic Christology of 1 John and incorporates it into the text of the community's Gospel. But it does so with its own nuances, which are in harmony with 1 John but at the same time distinct from them. However, one of the major differences of the third edition is that, in contrast to the earlier editions of the Gospel, the Christology of the third edition is cast within the worldview of apocalyptic.[67]

Although the Christology of the second edition had been "high" and had been one of the chief sources of conflict with the synagogue, as this Christology was reflected on within the Johannine community, it came to be articulated in a way that made it even "higher." In doing so, the third author clarifies further the identity of Jesus in relation to the believer but also in relation to the Father. The third author expresses his Christology in various ways.[68]

---

67. See Bühner *(Gesandte)* for many helpful insights into the apocalyptic Christology of the Gospel. It will be recalled that Bühner proposed that the Gospel reflects two distinct strains of Christology, one of which is built on an apocalyptic model and the other of which is built on a prophetic/angelic model (see the discussion of the Christology of the second edition above). This agrees with the observations of Coppens ("Fils de l'homme"), who argued that the Son of Man passages came from a distinct literary level. On this, see above, 3E-14.

68. At the beginning of this overall discussion of Christology of the second and third edi-

Section 1. The Development of Johannine Theology: Christology

a. Jesus as Son

In the third edition, Jesus continues to be referred to as "Son" (in the absolute sense, without a qualifier) in 3:17, 35, 36 (twice); 5:26; 14:13. In this way, the third edition is in continuity with the Christology of the second edition and of 1 John. But, like the author of 1 John, the third author is concerned to distinguish Jesus' sonship from that of the believer, and so the author continues to affirm the uniqueness of Jesus' sonship by the term *monogenēs* ("unique") in 1:18; 3:16, 18.

b. Jesus' Possession of the Spirit

Not only is the sonship of Jesus unique, but the author of the third edition, while affirming that Jesus possessed the Spirit, affirms that Jesus' possession is different from that of the believer, for Jesus is given the Spirit without measure *(ou gar ek metrou)* (3:34). This statement (which appears only once in the Gospel) is not particularly striking in its context. However, as we shall see below, this is an important correlative of the statement in 1 John 4:13 that affirms that God has given the believer "of his Spirit" *(ek tou pneumatos autou dedōken hēmin)*. The use of the partitive genitive in this expression makes it clear that God has given the believer *a share* in his Spirit rather than an absolute and perfect possession of it. Consequently, the limitation of the believer's possession of the Spirit described in 1 John is now, in the third edition of the Gospel, explicitly said not to be true of Jesus: he possesses the Spirit *without measure*.

c. Jesus as Preexistent

The belief in the preexistence of Christ is clear in the third edition. It is affirmed first of all in the Prologue, where the Word is said to have existed "in the beginning" (1:1) and to have been with God "in the beginning" (1:2). He was

---

tion, a caution was expressed about the difficulty of assigning with complete precision all of the material to a given edition. But it was also stated that certain directions in the modification of the third edition are clear. In what follows, we will discuss the features that are more obvious and that reveal the orientation of the third edition. The varying degrees of certainty regarding the attribution of individual passages will be evident.

I would not be able to agree with Anderson (*Christology* 262-63) that the the subordinationist and egalitarian aspects of the Son are simply the "two sides of the same coin." Rather, the "egalitarian" (a term I am somewhat uncomfortable with as a description of any aspect of Johannine Christology) form of Johannine Christology is a result of a further level of reflection and involves a series of titles and descriptive discussions, as will be apparent in what follows.

present at creation, and an active intermediary in creation (1:3-4). We have pointed out that the origin of the Prologue is difficult to determine with precision. It was probably a community hymn taken over by the author of the third edition, edited by him, and affixed to the Gospel. Given the prominence of light and darkness imagery, it would seem to have been composed at a time after the composition of the second edition. At any rate, the most important factor in this is that its presence in the Gospel is due to the third author. In the body of the Gospel, preexistence is clear both in general descriptive statements (6:62; 17:5, 24)[69] and in the "divine" I AM statements (8:24, 28, 58; 13:19; 18:6, 8). In 6:62, Jesus speaks of returning "to where I was before." In 17:5, Jesus speaks of "the glory that I had with you [the Father] before the world existed." In 17:24, he speaks of the fact that "you loved me before the beginning of the world."

For the third author the theological significance of Jesus' preexistence is complex. It has its own intrinsic importance; but, in relation to the second edition, it clarifies the sonship of Jesus by extending it to a point beyond any sonship in human time. Thus, Jesus is not a son "born of the Spirit" in time as the believer is. He is distanced from the believer both by his divine qualities and by the fact of his existence with God from the beginning.

d. Jesus as Son of Man

In keeping with his apocalyptic viewpoint, the third author now refers to Jesus as the "Son of Man." This Son of Man is introduced in the enigmatic 1:51, where the Son of Man is the access point to heaven and the one upon whom the angels ascend and descend. Furthermore, it is he who has come down from heaven (thus indicating his preexistence) (3:13). In 3:14, we hear that the Son of Man must be lifted up. This is repeated in 6:62, where it is also said that he will ascend to where he was before but in doing so will cause scandal through his death on the cross. This is referred to again in 8:28, where Jesus is also identified as "I AM," one of the most unmistakable claims to identity with the Father. At the end of his public ministry, Jesus identifies himself again as the Son of Man about to be glorified (12:23) and "lifted up" (12:32-34). In 13:31, the glorification of the Son of Man within the public ministry comes to an end. Thus, it is

---

69. It has been proposed that other texts also express or presume preexistence. R. E. Brown would include 3:13; 5:19; 16:28; Schnackenburg would include 6:33, 50-51, 58; 7:28-29. These are more difficult to evaluate primarily because of the criteria involved; for example, do all "descent" passages necessarily imply a theology of preexistence? While such passages may be *compatible* with preexistence, they do not require it. In Chapter 6, for example, it would seem that the descent is metaphorical. Nevertheless, the unambiguous statements of preexistence all appear in the third edition.

Section 1. The Development of Johannine Theology: Christology

in connection with the Son of Man that the true "descent/ascent" motif is introduced and developed within the Gospel.[70]

In keeping with his apocalyptic nature, the Son of Man is judge (5:27). It is he who gives (6:27) and is (6:53) the bread that is the Eucharist. In 9:35, in keeping with his divinity, the Son of Man is the object of belief and the proper object of worship.

As a result, we see that the title is used in ways that are consistent with the apocalyptic background of the Son of Man, but we also see that, in the Johannine usage, this title is closely linked to preexistence and equality with God, issues central to the third edition.[71]

e. The Relationship between Jesus and the Father in the Third Edition

The third edition presents a view of Jesus in which he is ever more closely and intimately related to God the Father. At the same time, a clear distinction is preserved between them and their prerogatives. There are several elements to this presentation.

(1) Jesus as Egō Eimi

There are several texts in the third edition where the divine "I AM" appears (8:24, 28, 58; 13:19; 18:6, 8). It is these texts in which Jesus appropriates the designation for Yahweh in the LXX.[72] This appropriation of the divine name is one of the distinct characteristics of the Fourth Gospel, and there is no title for Jesus that could more definitely attribute divinity in its fullest extent to Jesus. Yet for Jesus to appropriate the title "I AM" is not to claim identity with God the Father. Jesus remains the Son but so completely reveals the Father that to see Jesus is to see "I AM."

The fact that these appear in the third edition is an indication of the third

---

70. Moloney (*Son of Man* 241-42) is correct in noticing also that the notion of being "sent" that is so typical of the Christology surrounding the use of "Son" in the absolute way, is never found in connection with the figure of the Son of Man. This is another indication of the independence of the two concepts.

71. Moloney (*Son of Man* 214) comments: "Almost every [Son of Man] saying is a concluding statement, on the lips of Jesus, resolving a series of questions or insufficient confessions about the nature of Jesus." This statement, with which I would largely agree, takes on new meaning in the light of the fact that it appears only in the last edition of the Gospel and in fact does serve to highlight issues that are unique to that edition.

72. For a discussion of the various uses of "I am" in the Gospel, see Vol. 3, Appendix 2 (The "I Am" Statements).

author's intention to make clear for his readers the full extent of Jesus' oneness with the Father. The author focuses his attention on the notion of "I AM" in chapter 8.

The statement of 8:24 is striking in its simplicity: "... if you do not believe that 'I AM,' you will die in your sins...." In 8:28, the third author combines the title "I AM" with that of "Son of Man" and, at the same time, continues to affirm Jesus' dependence upon the Father: "When you lift up the Son of Man, then you will know that I AM, and I do nothing of myself, but I speak these things just as the Father taught me." As divine as Jesus is, his divinity is not independent of the Father. In 8:58, the author combines it with the notion of preexistence: "... before Abraham was, I AM." Then in 13:19, Jesus informs the disciples that his ability to foretell events happening to him will be evidence that "I AM." Finally, in the act of being arrested (18:6, 8), Jesus identifies himself as "I AM," and the power inherent in the title causes the arresting party to fall to the ground.

(2) Jesus Is to Be Honored Just as the Father Is

In 5:22-23, Jesus claims that all are to "honor the Son, just as they honor the Father. The one who does not honor the Son does not honor the Father who sent him." In these verses that come from the author of the third edition, the essential equality of the Son and the Father is clearly stated.

Related to this conception is the conviction that Jesus is to be "worshiped" as the Father is worshiped. That God is to be worshiped is clear from 4:19-24 and 12:20; but in 9:38, in an addition by the third author, once the man born blind recognizes Jesus as the Son of Man, he falls down and worships him, thus giving to Jesus the honor that is also due to the Father.

(3) Jesus Is Addressed as "My Lord and My God"

One of the most universally recognized statements of "high" Christology in the New Testament is that of Thomas to Jesus in John 20:28. Here, in material of the third edition, after seeing the wounds of Jesus, Thomas declares: "My Lord and my God!" The words of Thomas are simply unambiguous. He and the Johannine community patently apply titles otherwise reserved for God the Father to Jesus. This happens nowhere else in the Gospels with such clarity.

*(4) Jesus' Continuing Dependence upon,
and Subordination to, the Father*

In spite of the increasingly unambiguous affirmation of the equality of Jesus with the Father, it cannot be denied that an integral part of the Christology of

Section 1. The Development of Johannine Theology: Christology

the third edition continues to be the dependence of the Son on the Father (8:42; 12:49). The third author affirms this in various ways.

First, he repeats expressions already found in the second edition. For example, Jesus does the will of his Father (6:39). Jesus speaks only what he has "seen" (8:38); he speaks only what he has "heard" (12:50; 15:15) from the Father; his word is not his own but the word of the Father (14:24). As the second author states that the Father has consecrated the Son (10:36), so the third author states that the Father has sealed the Son (6:27).

Second, in addition to these, the third author introduces new expressions of this reality: "The Son lives because of the Father" (6:57); "the Son is 'taught' by the Father" (8:28). Jesus can still refer to the Father as "his God" (cf. 20:17).

Third, one of the most striking and fully developed expressions of Jesus as dependent upon and subordinate to the Father is found in the conception of the commandments given to Jesus by the Father. These are discussed in detail in Volume 3, Appendix 5, and here we need only recall that Jesus is given a commandment as to what to "say" (12:49) and what to "do" (i.e., "to lay down his life for his own"; 10:17-18). The Son obeys these commandments and therefore remains in the Father's love (15:10).

This mention of "love" recalls that in the third edition there is an emphasis on love as the basis of the relationship between the Father and the Son: 3:35; 5:20; 10:17; 14:21, 31; 15:9; 17:23, 24, 26. It is noteworthy that all of these appear in the material of the third edition. Thus, it can be seen that just as the love of Jesus for the disciples is evident in his laying down his life for them, so the love between the Father and the Son is a model for the love between the disciples. In short, in the third edition, love plays a much greater role than in the earlier editions.

(5) The Abiding Importance of Jesus

As was the case with 1 John, the third author affirms the abiding importance of the words of Jesus as well as the fact that his death is not simply a departure to the Father, but a death that takes away sin.

In the third edition of the Gospel, the permanent importance of Jesus' word(s) is even more clearly articulated than in 1 John. In the Gospel, the theology of commandment is more developed. First, Jesus is given two commandments by the Father: to speak what he has heard (cf. 12:49) and to give his life out of love for his own (10:15b-18). Jesus in turn gives two commandments to his disciples: to keep his word (14:21, 23-24) and to love one another (15:10-15). Thus, in the third edition we see for the first time that two sets of commandments are given, one set to Jesus and one set to the disciples. These two sets are correlated with one another. Finally, the commandments given to the disciples are now specified as commandments of "Jesus" rather than of "God."[73] But in the Gospel the essential fact remains the same: the words of Jesus have a unique role and are not to be simply paralleled to the knowledge that is claimed to be from the (s)pirit.

Also as in 1 John, the third author introduces scattered references to the conviction that Jesus' death was destined to take away sin. The most notable examples are in 1:29, where John the Baptist identifies Jesus as "the Lamb of God who takes away the sin of the world," 1:34, where he is referred to briefly as "the Lamb of God," and 4:42, where he is identified as "the Savior of the world." In the third edition, Jesus is the good shepherd who lays down his life for his sheep (10:11-14, 15b).

(6) Jesus Has Been Given What He Has by the Father

The third author takes over from the second edition the conviction that what the Son possesses is given him by the Father. Yet, if the Father shares his powers with the Son, it seems that in the third edition the identity and sharing is even more complete. There is a sense of completeness and totality in statements such as "the Father . . . has given all things into his hands" (3:35).[74] Although it was the conviction of the second edition that Jesus possesses life, in the third edition Jesus is said to possess it "in himself" as God does (5:26). This notion was in direct opposition to the Jewish understanding of the status of the human person, for whom life was said to be "lent." Moreover, the third author affirms that "Everything the Father has is mine" (16:15).

(7) Conclusion

Thus, we see that, in the third edition, the Christology takes yet another major step forward. Yet this development is consistent with the development that the community had experienced previously. This development not only provides the final stage in the clarification of the identity of Jesus; it also clarifies much more the relation of Jesus to the status of the believer but also in relation to God the Father. It is here that the Johannine understanding of Christology reaches its zenith.

---

73. As we have seen, this is not a contradiction but simply the result of 1 John's emphasis on the roots of salvation in God the Father, the one who is the "common ground," the one the opponents claim to possess and whose role is not disputed.

74. Although verbally similar, 13:3 has a considerably different meaning.

Section 1. The Development of Johannine Theology: Christology

6. The Background of the Christology in the Third Edition

a. The Apocalyptic Son of Man

Scholarly discussion of the Son-of-Man figure has ranged between extremes in the past century, and a more moderate view is now appearing.[75] While the titular use is now recognized not to be as widespread as once thought, J. J. Collins has reaffirmed that there was a titular use and that such use is typical of apocalyptic.[76] Its use is particularly clear in Daniel 7; *1 Enoch* 46:1; 47:3; 70–71, and *4 Ezra* 13. In these latter works, Collins concludes (1) that the figure refers to an individual; (2) that the figure is identified with the "messiah"; (3) that he is preexistent; and (4) that he takes an active role in the destruction of the wicked. All of these features find some resonance in the usage in the third edition of the Gospel.

b. Wisdom Motifs

We have seen above that the figure of Wisdom in Jewish literature has contributed to the background of the Christology of the second edition. In the third edition, Wisdom motifs continue. In some cases these motifs are simply a repetition of those found in the second edition. But there are a number of important developments. The first development occurs in the Prologue of the Gospel, which is generally recognized to contain more allusions to Wisdom motifs than any other section of the Gospel.[77] Like the Logos in the Prologue, Wisdom was present at creation (Wis 7:22; 9:9-10; Prov 8:27-30); Wisdom came forth from the mouth of God (Sir 24:3); Wisdom sought a dwelling place but was rejected (Sir 24:8; *1 Enoch* 42:2; cf. Bar 3:37). At the same time, in the third edition this Wisdom orientation is joined to an apocalyptic worldview, much as Wisdom motifs were introduced into the apocalyptic worldview of the *Hodayot* from Qumran (1QH). Although this depiction of Wisdom as a (female) person and as "preexistent" was never intended (or apparently taken) literally among the Jews, it is argued that this portrayal of Wisdom facilitated the depiction of Jesus as preexistent.[78]

---

75. For a recent sketch of scholarship, see J. J. Collins, "Son of Man" 448-50. Further discussion and bibliography are given in the discussion of 3E-12.

76. See J. J. Collins, *Apocalyptic* 81-83, 142-53, 157-58, 165-66, 209-10, and his "Son of Man" (passim).

77. See, for example, Ashton, "Transformation"; R. E. Brown, *Christology* 205-10. While recognizing the popular attention to Wisdom in the Prologue, Witherington (*Gospel* 19-27) cautions against a failure to see its influence elsewhere.

78. While this is indeed possible, it should also be recognized that to suggest this as a pri-

Finally, also related to the notion of the preexistence of Wisdom is the description of Wisdom as "ascending and descending." This motif, which necessarily involves some belief in the preexistence of Jesus, also reflects the depiction of Wisdom as coming down from heaven and dwelling among humanity and then returning to God (cf. Proverbs 8 and Sirach 24). However, for the third author, although the motif of descent and ascent is present, it is *the Son of Man* that is said to do it rather than Wisdom.

Thus, we see that the third author recognized and adopted the presentation of Jesus in terms that are also reminiscent of Wisdom but, at the same time, modified and integrated this view with his own apocalyptic worldview.

c. The Son with the Full Authority of the Father

The notion of "sending" and its religious and legal background played an important role in the Christology of the second edition. However, in the third edition, it seems that this notion was developed in a direction that went beyond that of the second edition. Awareness of this view is due to the work of several scholars who argued that the notion of agency did not fully explain the role of Jesus in relation to the Father. As Ashton has pointed out: "... sons ... are rarely sent."[79] That is, the connection between sonship and mission is not an obvious one. However, Ashton finds a preliminary explanation in the background presupposed by the parable of the wicked tenants in Mark 12:1-11.[80] As Derrett explains in conjunction with that parable, the protest of the owner to the tenants could not be made through an agent but only through one who actually possessed the authority to expel the tenants. As a result, the son had to be sent, since he was the only one who actually possessed the authority of the owner.[81]

Bühner proposes that the juridical concept of "son of the house" as it developed in rabbinic thought can be seen as an element in Johannine por-

---

mary factor in attributing preexistence to Jesus would seem to neglect the considerable number of other factors that could have accounted for this major step in christological growth. As was indicated above, the apocalyptic Son of Man could also be thought of in these same terms. Consequently, while I recognize the compatibility of Wisdom motifs with the notion of preexistence and the possibility that this contributes to the early Christian recognition of Jesus himself as preexistent, I would be reluctant to see this as a major factor.

79. Ashton, *Understanding* 317-29, esp. 318. The discussion throughout this section is indebted to Ashton's perceptive analysis.

80. Ashton, *Understanding* 319-20.

81. Derrett, "Parable" 302-3. In relation to the Marcan parable, this shows that the figure of the Son need not be a Christian addition but was called forth by the Jewish legal principle itself. See the discussion in Ashton, *Understanding* 320-21.

Section 2. The Development of Johannine Theology: Belief

trayal.[82] According to *m. Shebuot* 7:8, as interpreted by the Babylonian Talmud (*Shebuot* 48b), the "son of the house" has complete authority granted him by the "lord of the house" over all of the lord's affairs. In most cases, this "son of the house" was the natural son, but the title "son of the house" was an official declaration by the father of the authority granted to the son. Bühner also points to *Exodus Rabbah* 15.30 on Exod 12:12, which speaks of the father giving "all" to the son when the son reached manhood.[83] One of the echoes of this legal relationship between father and son is found in the Johannine expression *didonai en tē cheiri* (literally, "to give into the hand," i.e., "to entrust to") (3:35; 13:3; cf. 17:2).[84]

The common element in these parallels is the notion that the son actually possesses all of the authority of the father. In the Gospel of John, the passages illumined by this notion all appear in the third edition. Thus, it would seem that the third author also possessed detailed knowledge of Jewish legal principles and could use them to illuminate his understanding of Christology.

SECTION 2. THE DEVELOPMENT OF JOHANNINE THEOLOGY: BELIEF

1. Belief in the First Edition

a. Belief Based on Signs

As far as can be discerned from the present state of the text, in the first edition of the Gospel belief is focused on a response to the signs of Jesus. This belief has several distinctive characteristics.[85] For example, this belief is (in contrast to belief in the Synoptic Gospels) a response to the signs and something that occurs *after* the miracle rather than before it. This is in keeping with the theological view of the signs of Moses that were given by God to confirm that God was with him.

In the first edition, belief is presented as something that was readily achieved by large numbers of people. These people came from a variety of geographical places (the disciples in Cana [2:11]; the people in Jerusalem at the Passover [2:23]; the Samaritan woman and many of the people of Sychar [4:29-30, 39]; the Galileans [4:45]; the official and his household [4:53]; the people following Jesus through Galilee [6:2]; the people who witnessed the multiplication

---

82. Bühner, *Gesandte* 181-206.
83. Bühner, *Gesandte* 197 n. 17.
84. Ashton, *Understanding* 321 n. 72.
85. These were discussed in detail in Part 1, Section 3.2.c. Here we will provide a summary.

A History of the Development of Johannine Theology

of the loaves [6:14]; the people at Tabernacles [7:31-32]; those who encountered him beyond the Jordan [10:41-42]; the Judeans who witnessed the raising of Lazarus [11:45]; and those who heard about the miracle and came from Jerusalem to see him [12:9-11; cf. 12:18-19]). The stereotyped form in which this belief is expressed reinforces this conviction from a literary point of view. It was only the religious authorities who failed to believe properly, and it was they who eventually had him put to death.

b. The Content of Belief

The content of belief in the first edition as it is evident to us is simple and straightforward. Understanding and acceptance of the signs of Jesus would lead one to believe that he was "from God." The first edition made his identity more concrete by portraying him in terms of a variety of Israel's hopes and heroes, as we saw in the discussion of the first edition's Christology. Ultimately this was to lead to the conviction that he was "the Christ and the Son of God" (20:30-31).

By portraying Jesus' ministry against the background of the signs of Moses, the community demonstrated that they understood belief in a way that was completely consistent with the Jewish background of the community. However, from the point of view of the later editions, this understanding of belief is quite simple and uncritical.

2. Belief in the Second Edition

a. Response to the Four Witnesses

In the second edition of the Gospel, the notion of belief undergoes a radical shift. No longer is belief seen simply as a response to the miracles of Jesus. Although such belief continues to be seen as valid, the author of the second edition puts it within the larger, more complex, and more sophisticated theological perspective of the "witnesses" to Jesus.

In the second edition, belief is warranted by four types of "witnesses": (1) the witness of John the Baptist (although this was a human witness and not essential); (2) the witness of Jesus' works; (3) the witness of Jesus' word, which was the word of the Father; and (4) the witness of the Scriptures. Their paradigmatic portrayal is found in 5:31-40.

Within the second edition as a whole, the author uses the presentation of these witnesses as a major structuring element. In 1:19–2:22 the author portrays the disciples as responding positively to all four witnesses. Moreover, the three

Section 2. The Development of Johannine Theology: Belief

essential witnesses (excluding that of John the Baptist) are made the basis of the theological argument and the literary organization of the narrative and discourse extending from 6:1–10:42.[86] Finally, in a brief statement within the Farewell Discourses (15:22-25), Jesus reminds the disciples of his appeal to "the Jews" through his words and his works and shows that their ultimate rejection of him was itself a demonstration of the witness of Scripture in his regard. Thus, in the eyes of the second author, belief is a much more complex affair, and more than just miracles will lead to its realization.

b. The Second Edition and a Critique of Faith Based on Signs?

In one sense, the first edition could be said to have a quite uncritical, almost naive, view of faith. The ordinary people are presented as believing in great numbers and without any hesitation and almost exclusively on the basis of Jesus' signs.

However, in the Gospel in its present state, there are frequent comments that seem to critique miraculous faith. Such comments appear, for example, in 1:50, 51; 2:24-25; 4:48; 6:26, and so on. None of these comes from the author of the first edition, nor do all of them seem to come from any one author. Apparently both the second and the third authors possessed a more critical attitude toward miraculous faith — but each did so from a distinct perspective.

The second edition does not discount miraculous faith but only puts it in perspective alongside the other legitimate grounds for belief. In 2:24-25, perhaps the strongest of the comments, it is not so much faith based on miracles that is being criticized, but the *nature* of the response that does not lead to a deeper appreciation of the identity of Jesus and his relation to the Father. The same seems to be true of 6:15, where the author of the second edition rejects the *content* of the crowd's belief when it interprets the sign of the multiplication as authorizing a claim to political kingship on the part of Jesus.

c. The Object of Belief

Like the first edition, the theology of the second edition involves both acceptance of Jesus' claims regarding his own identity and trust in his promises rather than this or that aspect of his message. Yet the second edition also presents its own unique view of the content of belief.

---

86. For more detail on this, see the discussion of "The Structure of the Second Edition" in Part 2, Section 3.1. See also the Addendum to the discussion of 5:41-47 in the Commentary.

It seems that the Johannine community at the time of the second edition conceived of belief before the death of Jesus as different from belief after his death. The first belief was intended to lead one to accept what Jesus said about himself as one qualified to announce the advent of the eschaton and the gift of the Spirit. This belief prepared the believer for the gift of the Spirit, for the Spirit was to be given only to those who believed in Jesus. But the gift of the Spirit raised the believer to another form of life and a new level of existence. Belief at this level was of an entirely different sort.

Thus, the disciples believed in Jesus from the beginning, but their belief was still deficient until they received the Spirit. When they received the Spirit, they were able to believe with a greater depth and understanding. The Gospel, which was written for the later community, aims primarily at a presentation of the meaning of full and final belief and so focuses on this rather than on the preliminary belief.

At the time of the second edition, full belief entailed a response to the four witnesses to Jesus. This was belief in the full profundity of the identity of Jesus, that he is the Son in relation to the Father (5:17-19), sent by the Father to bring his work to completion (4:34), and the one to whom the Father has given his own powers (5:19-20). Believers are said to "know" Jesus and the Father; unbelievers are said not to "know" Jesus (8:19) or the Father (7:28; 8:19, 27, 55; cf. 10:38). Yet it is said of the disciples that they did not fully believe in the word of Jesus and in the Scripture as it applied to him until after his Resurrection (2:22). The same is true of their understanding of Jesus' entry into Jerusalem and the actions of the crowd toward him until after he was glorified (12:16).

d. Belief, Eternal Life, and the Reception of the Spirit

Closely related to these two "phases" of belief is the question of when the believer receives eternal life. Scholars often understand the Gospel to say that the one who believes receives eternal life in the very act of believing. This is, I think, a misreading. But the problem is caused by the fact that the Gospel speaks sometimes from the perspective of the historical ministry and sometimes from the point of view of the later community, and the shift from one perspective to the other is not always clear.

As we have already seen, Jesus expected belief during his ministry. This belief was a prerequisite for receiving the Spirit. Yet 7:37-39 makes it clear that during the public ministry, the "Spirit was not yet because Jesus was not yet glorified." Therefore, until one had the Spirit, one could not be said to have eternal life. Therefore, within the public ministry, it was not yet possible for the be-

Section 2. The Development of Johannine Theology: Belief

liever to possess eternal life. It is only with the bestowal of the Spirit in 20:22 that eternal life is conferred upon the disciples.

Within this perspective, the words about rebirth, about the offer of living water, about worship in Spirit and truth, about the living bread, and so on necessarily contain an ambiguity in their very presentation. While on the narrative level they are addressed to persons within the historical ministry, the understanding that they intend and the *mis*understanding that they evoke are experiences that are actualized most fully only in the later Johannine community.

The author of the second edition has collapsed the experience and possibilities of the later community into the historical ministry. The result is a portrayal with immense relevance to the later Johannine community — but also some inevitable ambiguity because of the limitations of such a narrative presentation.

e. The Content of Belief

R. Bultmann described the Jesus of the Gospel of John as a "revealer without a revelation." While this is recognized by many to be an overstatement, it is important in that it calls attention to the almost exclusive focus on Christology in the Gospel. In fact, very little space is given to the "content" of belief. We can now understand the reason for this. In the light of the community's concentration on belief as acceptance of Jesus' claims and because of the conviction that the Spirit would teach them all things and give them direct knowledge of God and make ethics unnecessary, the community would see no need to focus on the historical words of Jesus as had other sectors of early Christianity.[87] At the same time, the object of belief (i.e., Christology) was all-important. One had to accept the claims of Jesus in order to receive the Spirit.

f. Belief and Being "Given" by the Father

One final aspect of the conception of belief in the second edition calls for brief mention. Several times, particularly in the discourses with "the Jews," Jesus explains "the Jews'" unbelief using a variety of expressions that have occasioned much debate among scholars and led some to conclude that the Johannine community held to a kind of determinism.

In 6:37, Jesus says that only those whom the Father "gives" will come to Jesus (cf. 6:65; 10:29; 17:2). In 6:44, he speaks of believers being "drawn" by the Father. In 10:26-30, Jesus explains that "the Jews" are not "of his sheep" and that no

---

87. For further detail, see the discussion of "Knowing God" below in Section 6.

one is able to take anyone "from the hand of the Father," once that person has been given.

While some would see in these expressions the possibility of a determinism, the context in every case is precisely Jesus' self-offering as the object of belief. It is only when he is rejected that the author (in keeping with the common Jewish belief) expressed his conviction that even such unbelief could not be a contravention of the plans of God but something foreseen and somehow even caused by him.

It has often been said that the great sin of the Gospel of John is unbelief.[88] This statement is strikingly put and captures one perspective of the Gospel, but it is not completely correct. To be more precise, the one sin that is discussed *as sin* in the second edition is failure to believe. Now it is clear why this is so: to reject belief in Jesus means that one will not receive the Spirit that is the principle of eternal life.[89]

As we shall see, in 1 John and in the third edition, there is explicit concern for proper behavior and sin is understood as ethical transgression. Yet even then all ethical obligation on the human level is summed up in the need to love one's brother.

3. The Background of Belief in the Second Edition

The background of belief in the second edition would seem to be that of normative Judaism without any distinctive coloration.

4. Belief in 1 John

a. The View of the Opponents

Our access to the opponents' understanding of belief is only through the words of the author of 1 John. However, we are able to determine the main lines of their position from various remarks of the author of 1 John.

We know from the fact that the opponents were for a time members of

---

88. This view is probably most associated with R. E. Brown. See, for example, Brown, *Community* 124-26; *Epistles* 81.

89. It should be said that, with his typical care, R. E. Brown does point to passages that have ethical significance. Yet he aptly characterizes the main view of the Gospel as being concerned with unbelief. This thrust is better explained by the fact that it was the second edition of the Gospel that contained this view, while it was the third edition that introduced the focus on the necessity of proper conduct.

Section 2. The Development of Johannine Theology: Belief

the community that the opponents considered themselves to have accepted the claims of Jesus.[90] Therefore, they were among those who had accepted the (four) "witnesses" to Jesus. They believed themselves to be recipients of the eschatological Spirit, and they relied upon the Spirit's inspiration for their "revelation." Thus, at the time of 1 John, the problem faced by the author is *not belief versus unbelief, but rather a problem of correct versus incorrect belief.* But what is "correct" belief?

b. The View of the Author

(1) The Abiding Importance of the Words of Jesus

In 1 John, there is a decided shift regarding the community's conception of the content of belief. While in the second edition there was no interest in the content of Jesus' teaching other than that which pertained to the person of Jesus and the outpouring of the Spirit, in 1 John there is a clear and consistent (but nevertheless general) focus on recalling the historical words of Jesus: "that which we have heard, which we have looked at with our eyes, which we have seen and our hands have touched," "which was from the beginning." It is in 2 John 9 that we get the clearest description of the position of the opponents. There the author describes the opponents as those "who are 'progressive' and who do not remain in the teaching of the Christ." The issue is clearly that something leads them to a "teaching" that is different from the teaching of (the historical) Jesus.

The nature of these opposing views is confirmed by numerous other statements. The author of 1 John is quite clear about what constitutes correct belief. At the very beginning of his "Letter," the author emphasizes the necessity of holding to what was "from the beginning" (1:1-3, 5), and he returns to this theme later in his work. For example, in 2:24 he reasserts: ". . . let what you heard from the beginning abide in you. If it abides in you (what you heard from the beginning), you abide in the Son and in the Father" (cf. also 2:13, 14). Thus, in the author's view, the opponents do not hold on to what the author considered to be the "tradition" (a word that he does not use).

The commandments play an especially important role in this dispute. When the author first discusses commandments, his emphasis on "old" versus "new" is carried over into his discussion of the commandments (2:7-8). It is not

---

90. In 2:19, the author says that "they were not of us," but this must be understood in a rhetorical sense to mean that they were not truly members of the community. He has already indicated in the same verse that they had been members of the community and that they "went out from us."

a "new" commandment that he speaks of but an old one that they have heard "from the beginning." Thus the commandment itself is part of the tradition.

Secondly, the importance of the received word is made clear precisely by the fact that keeping the word of God spoken through Jesus is identified as a "commandment" from God (2:5-7). If the second edition spoke of the importance of the "word" as a witness, 1 John (and later the third edition) speaks of the *permanent* importance of that word.

However, the author's refutation of the opponents was all the more difficult because, in spite of the fact that he and his community rejected the unrestrained response to the Spirit characteristic of the opponents, he and the community did hold to a belief in the importance of guidance by the Spirit. In spite of how easy it would have been to omit the topic altogether, and in spite of the fact that the author wants to affirm the importance of the historical word, he argues (2:27) that his followers have an anointing, and this "anointing teaches you about all things." But for the author of 1 John this has a special nuance, for he goes on to add, "and just as it taught you, you abide in him [Jesus]." Thus, for the author of 1 John, the Spirit teaches believers to retain their essential relation to the person and word of Jesus.

As we shall see shortly, this view of the opponents' position is confirmed by, and becomes even clearer in, the third edition, where the author will again emphasize the importance of the historical words of Jesus. Moreover, he will introduce the notion of the Spirit as "another" Paraclete and repeatedly assert his conviction that the Spirit *will not speak on its own.*

(2) The Correct Understanding of Jesus

As was the case in the second edition, a major focus of the author in 1 John remains centered on Christology — but it is the Christology that they have had "from the beginning." The author insists that the opponents have distorted the understanding of Jesus and his role in gaining eternal life. As we saw in the discussion of Christology, the believer is to confess that Jesus is the Son of God; that he is the Christ; that he has come in the flesh. This is a traditional understanding but one that it is necessary to reestablish. "Everyone denying the Son does not have the Father" (1 John 2:23); ". . . every spirit that does away with Jesus is not of God" (1 John 4:3). This is expressed in the first of the commandments variously as "keeping the word of God," "believing in the name of Jesus," and "walking in the truth."

But beyond the various affirmations about Jesus, we also see an emphasis on the necessity of "love," expressed in the second of the Johannine commandments (cf. 2:9-11). Moreover, there are repeated references to the need to "act justly." We will see this in greater detail below, in the discussion of ethics.

Section 2. The Development of Johannine Theology: Belief

Yet in spite of the general insistence on the importance of the historical words of Jesus, the author provides relatively little direct knowledge of the content of this "word." Apart from such topics as the reality of eternal life, pneumatology, ecclesiology, soteriology, and ritual, there remains something of a doctrinal vacuum. This is also true about the exact form of the Johannine ethics; their precise formulation remains tantalizingly general.

5. Belief in the Third Edition

The author of the third edition continues much of the theological program of 1 John by incorporating it into the Gospel tradition. However, in the process, his work is not simple imitation, for he introduces nuances and perspectives not fully evident previously.

a. The Further Witnesses to Jesus

In the second edition, the response to the witnesses to Jesus had been a major theological and literary tool in the presentation of the ministry of Jesus. It is clear that the author of the third edition recognizes and reconfirms the importance of the three essential witnesses to Jesus. Yet, in the Farewell Discourses, in the context of his private instruction to the disciples (15:22-25) as Jesus speaks of the witnesses for the last time, the third author makes a significant modification in the listing of witnesses. The third author now extends this list of witnesses to a total of five by affirming that both the Paraclete and the disciples will also serve as "witnesses," that they will assume the same importance as the original three, and that they are to be understood as being equally important (15:26-27).

While this inclusion of the Paraclete and the disciples as witnesses to Jesus has a certain general importance within the Gospel tradition, the fact that they are seen as *witnesses* is particularly significant for the refutation of the opponents. The Paraclete, who is identified as "the Spirit of Truth" (and therefore opposed to "the Spirit of Deception" of 1 John 4:1-6), is said to witness precisely *to Jesus*. It is not a general witness to the truth but a witness to the truth as found in Jesus. Likewise, the disciples will witness *to Jesus*. And the validity of their witness will be predicated precisely on the fact that they have been with Jesus "from the beginning" (John 15:27b) — thus not only the Paraclete but also the disciples will serve as anchors to the words of Jesus from the beginning, the same basis that was asserted in 1 John as the basis of true belief.

b. The Content of True Belief

As was the case with 1 John, the third edition focuses on Christology but modifies the expression of that Christology so as to make clear the interpretation of the community against the interpretation of the opponents. We have seen this in detail in the previous section.

Like 1 John, the third edition affirms a view of pneumatology, eschatology, ecclesiology, ethics, and the like that is different from that expressed in the second edition of the Gospel and from that of the opponents at the time of 1 John. But as with 1 John, although the third author asserts the importance of keeping the word of Jesus and of loving one another by speaking of them as the object of "commandments," he does not go significantly beyond the declaration of these as universal injunctions so as to provide a teaching that is as specific as the Synoptics.

c. The Permanent Importance of the Word of Jesus

We have seen that the author of the third edition continues to affirm the importance of the historical words of Jesus. We have also seen that he has done that by his recognition that the disciples are able to witness to what was "from the beginning." It is also evident in the third author's incorporation of the tradition of Jesus' commandment to the disciples to "keep his word." But here there is also a nuance not found in 1 John. As the commandment in 1 John was said to be *from God* (cf. 2:3-7), in the Gospel the mediation of this commandment through the word of Jesus is made explicit by the explanation that God gave a commandment to Jesus about *what to say* and Jesus in turn gives the disciples the commandment *to keep his word* (John 14:23-26). Thus, by keeping the word of Jesus, the disciples are still (ultimately) keeping the word of God. But the expression in the Gospel is altered to bring the primary focus on the role of Jesus.

d. The Spirit-Paraclete and the Words of Jesus

We will examine the Spirit-Paraclete passages in more detail below as part of the discussion of pneumatology. But it is important here to call attention to the way in which the Spirit (and only in the passages where he is identified as the Spirit-Paraclete) is said to be related to the words of Jesus. In the second of the Paraclete passages (14:25-26), Jesus asserts first that the Spirit "will teach you all things," thus confirming the role of the Spirit as a source of knowledge. This is a

Section 2. The Development of Johannine Theology: Belief

conviction that both the author and his opponents would have held.[91] However, Jesus goes on to say that the Spirit-Paraclete "will remind you of all things that I have told you." Thus, the teaching role of the Paraclete is defined in terms of clarifying precisely the teaching *of Jesus*.

In the final Paraclete passages (16:12-15) the role of the Paraclete is addressed in more detail with the focus entirely on the relationship between the Paraclete and the words of Jesus. Here the possibility of any Spirit-inspired revelation different from what Jesus had said is explicitly excluded since the Spirit "will not speak on his own, but will speak whatever he hears" (16:14). The words of the Spirit will be linked to those of Jesus, for Jesus goes on to say that the Spirit "will glorify me because he will take from what is mine and will proclaim it to you." The role of the Spirit is once again explicitly linked to the words of Jesus. Thus we see that, while the third author's theological program is the same as that of the author of 1 John, the third author's understanding and expression are his own.

e. Critique of Miracle-Faith

In the third edition, some comments that seem to be critiques of "miracle-faith" in fact have other purposes. For example, 4:40-42 has two purposes, to ground the faith of the people not just on hearsay but on experience of the word of Jesus itself and to present, on the lips of the Samaritans, the belief that Jesus was Savior of the world. This title stressed two elements: first, Jesus' active role in the achievement of salvation (a topic important for the author's refutation of his opponents) and the affirmation that his mission was a universal one.

In 4:44, the author of the third edition critiques "signs faith" by incorporating a Synoptic-like saying about the rejection of the prophet in his own country. Here the intention seems precisely to incorporate such Synoptic-like material.

At other times "belief material" from the first edition is amplified by the authors of both subsequent editions. In 1:50-51, the author of the second edition stresses the "greater things" that the disciples will see. This theme of "greater things" is typical of his theological orientation and points to their later experience of Jesus' ability to give life and judge. In 1:51, the third author takes the implications of the scene one step further by introducing Jesus as the Son of Man

---

91. It is evident that the author of 1 John holds views that are in many ways very close to those of the opponents. However, while affirming those views, he also affirms that those views need to be understood in a particular sense. Thus, throughout his work the author holds what I have called a "both-and" position. That is, true belief entails "both" what the opponents (and the second edition) had affirmed "and" requires further nuance.

here at the beginning of his ministry and identifying him as the contact point between heaven and earth.

6. The Background of Belief in 1 John and in the Third Edition

There is no distinctive background of the presentation of belief in 1 John and in the third edition of the Gospel that requires comment.

SECTION 3. THE DEVELOPMENT OF JOHANNINE THEOLOGY: PNEUMATOLOGY

Considerable attention has been given to the presentation of the Spirit within the Johannine tradition. It is not uncommon, even among scholars unconcerned with matters of editing, to notice a difference between the view of the Spirit presented in the Farewell Discourses (i.e., the Paraclete passages) and the view earlier in the Gospel. For example, Dodd described the conception of the Spirit elsewhere than the Farewell Discourses as occurring in the "neuter and impersonal sense that is most common in the Old Testament, and that was general in the early Church. . . ."[92] It is also common for scholars to consider the presentation of the Spirit in 1 John less developed or less personal than that in the Gospel.[93]

Within the context of the development of the tradition as it now appears, these anomalies can be understood in a new and clearer light. Here it will be noticed that the references to the Spirit in the second edition consist of those that Dodd and others referred to as "neuter and impersonal." These are the instances that most resemble the impersonal use in the Old Testament. In 1 John, the Spirit is conceptualized for the first time within an apocalyptic viewpoint, and the Spirit of Truth (i.e., the Spirit of God) is contrasted with the Spirit of Deceit and the Spirit of the Antichrist. At the same time, the author speaks of the Spirit in a more developed way, recognizing a variety of the Spirit's functions, some of which can clearly be seen to be personal. Yet the conception of the Spirit in 1 John does not fully rise to that of a personal being.

In the third edition, when the Spirit is put alongside Jesus as Paraclete for the believer, the full personal qualities of the Spirit become apparent. It is the purpose of this section to detail this development.

---

92. Dodd, "First Epistle" 146-48.
93. For example, R. E. Brown, *Epistles* 27.

Section 3. The Development of Johannine Theology: Pneumatology

It should be said that the background of the conception of the Spirit is particularly complex. While studies have been done of the understanding of the Spirit in the Jewish Scriptures, less has been done on Jewish expectations regarding the eschatological Spirit. Moreover, the use of spirit(s)/Spirit in the SDQ is in itself quite complex. Although an attempt is made to summarize this background, the presentation here is hardly comprehensive.

1. The Spirit in the First Edition

In what is left of the first edition in the present Gospel, there is no discussion of the Spirit. At first glance, this is a remarkable observation. It hardly seems possible to believe that a Gospel narrative, especially one adopted or created by the Johannine community, could have no reference at all to the (Holy) Spirit.[94] Yet while that fact is by itself striking, we need to remember that we do not have the first edition in its entirety. It could well be the case that the first edition did mention the Spirit, but that the references were removed. All we can do is observe that no references to the Spirit remain in what we have of the first edition and then refrain from drawing unwarranted conclusions for which we have no evidence.

2. The Spirit in the Second Edition

a. The Central Role of Pneumatology in the Second Edition

A proper understanding of the pneumatology of the second edition is essential to any correct understanding of the overall theology of that edition. According to the second edition, during his ministry Jesus proclaimed that, after his glorification and departure to the Father, he would bestow the Spirit on all those

---

94. It is dangerous to presuppose what the editing process *could not* do. Smalley (*John* 108) takes this approach when he says: "It is unlikely that a Gospel . . . ever existed in a form which contained narrative accounts, but little if any teaching of Jesus. . . ." By this method it would also be difficult to believe that a Gospel existed without mention of the Spirit. But it is necessary to remember that analysis of editing and composition must rely on the linguistic, ideological, and theological characteristics revealed by the text rather than on presuppositions about what it "must" be. If we went by presuppositions, it would be difficult to imagine a Gospel with as little mention of ethics or of church organization or of ritual as the Gospel of John. Yet one does exist!

Moreover, we cannot be sure that any of the editions prior to the third did not originally have material dealing with a given topic. All we can say is that *in the present state of the Gospel*, there is no evidence of such material. It could well have been excised by a later editor.

who had come to believe in him. This is the central promise of Jesus to and for the believer.[95]

There are two major aspects to the understanding of the role of the Spirit in the second edition. First, it is important to recognize the relation between the giving of the Spirit in the second edition and the Old Testament promises of the eschatological outpouring of Yahweh's Spirit. That is, the background of the presentation of the Spirit in the second edition is that of the canonical Jewish Scriptures.

Second, it is important to recognize the similarity between the benefits of the eschatological outpouring of the Spirit precisely as described in the Old Testament and many of the characteristic elements of the second edition's theology. As a result, the pneumatology of the second edition determines the particular form of many other of the community's convictions. Thus, all of the aspects of the community's theology that are discussed in the following sections (i.e., Sections 4 through 11) of Part 4 are ultimately conditioned by the community's convictions about the effects of the eschatological Spirit. For example, according to the Old Testament, it is one's spirit that is the principle of life and so it is the Spirit *of God* that becomes the means by which one receives *eternal* life (i.e., the life of God). It is the possession of the eschatological Spirit that enables one to come to truly "know" God by means of an internal knowledge that makes any other teacher than the Spirit unnecessary. It is precisely the conviction that the eschatological Spirit makes correct conduct spontaneous that accounts for the lack of attention to ethical conduct in the Gospel. It is this transformation by the Spirit that explains the "realized" (present) eschatology that makes a final judgment unnecessary.

All of these features that are so distinctive of the second edition are illuminated individually and as a group by the realization that these are all prerogatives of the eschatological outpouring of the Spirit. In order to do justice to the centrality of the Spirit in the second edition as well as to the relation between the Spirit and other characteristic aspects of Johannine theology, we will divide the treatment. In this section we will treat the general aspects of the Gospel's pneumatology and show its relation to Old Testament expectations regarding the eschatological outpouring of the Spirit. In the following sections, we will

---

95. It is common to speak of Christology as the central focus of the Gospel. This is true, but in ways and for reasons that are not always understood. This certainly was true of the Gospel in its second edition, but Christology was for the purposes of establishing the identity of Jesus as proof that he had the authority to bestow the eschatological Spirit. One needed to believe in Jesus in order to receive the Spirit. However, at the time of the internal crisis, when the role of the Spirit was seen to dominate and diminish the role of Jesus, the author of the third edition again turned to Christology and developed it even more in order to clarify the identity and the role of Jesus vis-à-vis that of the Spirit. The result is the massive focus on Christology in the present Gospel.

Section 3. The Development of Johannine Theology: Pneumatology

view the other distinctive elements of the second edition's theology and show in detail how they are related to this Old Testament understanding of the final outpouring of the Spirit.[96] In all cases we will distinguish the views of the second and third editions of the Gospel as well as that of 1 John and his opponents. We will also discuss the background of each of these as they are understood in the Old Testament and in the dualistic literature of late Second Temple Judaism.

* * *

As was shown in the Introduction to the second edition, it is in the second edition that we find the first references to the Spirit. Of all the references to "spirit" in the Gospel, all but 1:33; 3:34; and those instances in the Farewell Discourses come from the author of the second edition (i.e., 1:32; 3:5, 6, 8 [twice]; 4:23, 24; 6:63 [twice]; 7:39 [twice]; 11:33; 14; 19:30; 20:22).[97] It is important to notice also that all of the references to the Spirit in the second edition are to "the Spirit" in the unqualified sense rather than to "the Spirit of Truth" or "the Holy Spirit," conceptions that, as we shall see below, appear in the third edition and are presented within the framework of dualism and with decidedly "personal" qualities.[98]

Since other features of Johannine theology are heavily influenced by his theology of the Spirit, those elements will be postponed to the following sections and the presentation here will be limited to the most basic features.

b. The Spirit and Jesus

In the second edition, we learn first that Jesus himself possesses the Spirit. In 1:32, John the Baptist witnesses to the descent of the Spirit upon Jesus. It is difficult to know how this was interpreted by the community at the time of the second edition. If the Spirit descends upon Jesus when Jesus is with John, then what was the status of Jesus before the descent of the Spirit? Burge comments:

> ... this event [the meeting with John] hallmarked the anointing of Christ and inaugurated the indwelling and union of the Spirit in Jesus. Despite his Logos Proem, John cannot jettison the traditional foundation. It was the event of the Jordan that inaugurated Christ's ministry and empowered his

---

96. For the association of such qualities with the eschatological outpouring of the Spirit, see, for example, Sekki, *Ruaḥ* 87-88.

97. The instance in 11:33 does not refer to the Spirit of God and is not discussed here.

98. The instance in 20:22 may be an exception to this. See the discussion in the Commentary.

work. Even for John, Jesus is consistently presented as related to the Spirit of God in a remarkable, unique fashion.[99]

It is important to remember that at the time of the second edition there was no articulation of a belief in the preexistence of Jesus. In a Gospel tradition that did not yet articulate a belief in Jesus' preexistence, it would be possible to understand this scene as effecting a change in the status of Jesus.

c. The Spirit and the Believer

The primary emphasis in the Gospel is on the importance of the Spirit for the believer. In his ministry, Jesus offers the believer the Spirit (3:3-10; 4:10-15,[100] 35-38; 7:37-39; 20:22) and eternal life (5:21, 24-25, 40; 17:2) through the possession of the Spirit (3:3-10; 6:63-65; 7:37-39). In the Gospel, this is done both explicitly (6:63; 7:39; 20:22) and through images such as those of rebirth (3:3-10) and of receiving living water (4:10-15; 7:37-39). The actual giving of the Spirit will take place after the glorification of Jesus (7:37-39; 20:22).

Jesus insists that being reborn of the Spirit is necessary for all believers (3:3) and that being born of the Spirit raises one to a new level of life beyond that of the flesh (3:6; cf. 6:63). But this life of the Spirit is mysterious because no one knows where the wind/Spirit comes from and where it goes, and this is the way it is with one born of the Spirit (3:8).[101] In 4:10-15, Jesus offers the Samaritan woman "living water." Although not immediately identified as the Spirit in this passage, living water is explicitly identified with the Spirit in 7:37-39. In addition to the importance of the Spirit in these verses, we also see the link between the Spirit and life in the designation of this water as "living water." In 4:19-24, the Jesus of the second edition relativizes worship both on Gerizim and in Jerusalem by pointing out that the time is "now" when the true worshiper will worship "in Spirit, that is, in truth."[102] Worship in a material form is about to pass away; the Spirit is what is central, and it is the gift that Jesus brings.

In 6:63, a life that does not rise to the level of the Spirit is said to be "flesh": "The flesh is useless; that which gives life is the Spirit." Not only is the Spirit again said to be what is crucial, but again it is said that the Spirit is what gives

---

99. Burge, *Anointed* 50.

100. See also 4:19-24, where he speaks about the necessity of worshiping in the Spirit.

101. One difference between the Johannine presentation of his theology of the Spirit and life and that of the Jewish Scriptures is that the Johannine tradition conceived of this reception of life through the Spirit as a "rebirth" (John 3:3-8; 1 John 2:29; 3:9 [twice]; 4:7; 5:1 [three times], 4, 18 [twice]). This image is not used in the Jewish Scriptures.

102. For the use of hendiadys here, see the Note on 4:24.

Section 3. The Development of Johannine Theology: Pneumatology

life. In 7:37-39, Jesus invites all to come to him and to believe and then promises that they will receive "living water" from his side. This time we are told explicitly that Jesus is referring to the Spirit that those who believed in him were to receive. But we are now told also that one cannot receive the Spirit until after the glorification of Jesus.

The next time we hear of the Spirit is at the moment of Jesus' death, when it is said that Jesus "gave over the spirit" (19:30). "Giving over the spirit" can be understood simply as a reference to dying since one's spirit was thought to depart at the time of death. However, it is more likely that the appearance of such a phrase at the moment of death in this Gospel that is so marked by a theology of the Spirit is intended to refer to the giving forth or "release" (although not yet the bestowal) of the Spirit.[103]

Finally, according to 20:22, on Easter Sunday night the disciples are gathered in the upper room, and Jesus appears to them and, "breathing upon them" (the same action of "breathing" is associated with the giving of the natural spirit to Adam in Gen 2:7), says: "Receive the Holy Spirit."[104] The Spirit is bestowed upon the disciples. Here we witness the Johannine Pentecost, the fulfillment of the promises made throughout the Gospel — in the second edition.[105]

Within this framework, there is a complete and coherent presentation of the Spirit as the principle of eternal life and the gift of Jesus promised to all those who believe in him.

d. Is the Spirit Presented as a Personal Being in the Second Edition?

As was noted at the beginning of this section, there has been considerable discussion as to whether the presentation of the Spirit within the Johannine tradition is consistent and homogeneous. Once we are able to identify with some certainty the material of the second edition, we are able to see that Dodd's description of the Spirit in many passages as occurring in the "neuter and impersonal sense that is most common in the Old Testament, and that was general in the early Church" is correct — for the second edition. These are the instances that most resemble the impersonal use in the Old Testament. Thus, on the one hand, we are able to say that the presentation of the Spirit in the second edition is true to the Old Tes-

---

103. See Ashton (*Understanding* 424-25) for a particularly good discussion of this scene.

104. It should be noted that Spirit here is modified by "holy." Whether this designation was intended to portray the Spirit within a dualistic framework is unclear. See the discussion *ad locum* in the Commentary.

105. Thus, in the second edition, the Spirit is bestowed on the disciples on the evening of the first day. In the third edition, there is no specific mention of the actual bestowal, but (in the Paraclete passages) it is said to take place after Jesus has returned to the Father.

tament tradition. On the other hand, we are able to say that the presentation of the Spirit in the later edition demonstrates a modification of this conception.

3. The Background of the Presentation of the Spirit in the Second Edition

There can be no doubt that the background of the Johannine conception of the Spirit is to be found in Judaism, given the widespread attestation in Judaism of the belief in a definitive outpouring of the Spirit in the end times. This view is found in the Old Testament, in various documents from intertestamental literature, and in the SDQ.[106] The picture of the final giving of the Spirit is consistent, although not always fully developed, in a given document. This outpouring had three essential elements to it. We will look at these individually.

The first is the fact that there will be a final, definitive outpouring of the Holy Spirit in the last days. Within the Old Testament, we see this in Isa 32:14-15; 44:3; Ezek 11:17-19; 36:26-27; 39:29; Joel 2:28-29 (LXX 3:1-2).[107]

The second feature is that, while previously the Holy Spirit had been given only to the king and to the prophet, in the end times the Spirit was to be poured out on all the people of Israel.[108] For its bestowal on the king, see, for example, 1 Sam 11:6; 16:13. For the priest as anointed, see Lev 4:3, 5, 16; 6:15 (LXX). For its bestowal on the prophet, see, for example, 1 Sam 10:9-14. That the Spirit will be given to all people is implicit in the texts cited above; it is explicit in some, as can be seen from Joel 2:28-29 (LXX 3:1-2).

The third feature is that this giving of the Spirit was described as an "anointing" (Gk. *chrisma*). The person receiving the Spirit would then be said to be "anointed" *(christos)*. The classical text for this in the Old Testament is Isa 61:1. This Isaiah text was widely used by New Testament authors to describe the status of Jesus as the Christ (cf. Matt 11:5; Luke 4:18; 7:22; Acts 4:27; 10:38). This also lies at the heart of the conviction evident in 1 John 2:20, 27 that the believer also has an anointing.

---

106. Sekki (*Ruaḥ* 223) comments: "The evidence, then, points to Qumran as an eschatologically oriented community that saw itself as the heir of God's eschatological Spirit and regarded this Spirit as the basis and source of its spirituality." Sekki also sees the basic pneumatology of the sectarian Qumran documents as having its origin in the Old Testament, "especially in eschatological passages such as Ezek 36–37" (*Ruaḥ* 223). He would exclude 1QS 3:13–4:26; 1QH 15; 4Q186 as not being part of the "basic" pneumatology of the community.

107. This is also the basis of the universal conviction within early Christianity that the believer received the Spirit. The most obvious example is the outpouring of the Spirit described in Acts 2.

108. The conviction that this took place as a result of the ministry of Jesus is attested throughout the NT.

Section 3. The Development of Johannine Theology: Pneumatology

4. The Spirit in 1 John

In 1 John, references to the Spirit appear twelve times (3:24; 4:1 [twice], 2 [twice], 3, 6 [twice], 13; 5:6 [twice], 8). The Spirit continues to play an important role; yet at the same time, the presentation differs in several ways from that of the second edition.[109] In our discussion, we will present the opponents' view and then that of the author.

a. The View of the Opponents

It is clear from the arguments of the author of 1 John that his opponents claimed to have the Spirit.[110] The evidence for this is presented in detail in the Appendix in Volume 3 on the Crisis of 1 John.[111] The position of the opponents is particularly evident in 4:1-6, where the author implies that the opponents have a spirit, but that it is not the Spirit of Truth, but rather the Spirit of Deceit. That is, they also believe that the eschatological outpouring of the Spirit has taken place and that they are recipients of that Spirit. It was this conviction that led them to be members of the Johannine community. But the author argues that although they have a Spirit, it does not lead to correct belief or to correct action and therefore cannot be the Spirit of Truth.

The second major way in which the opponents claim to have the Spirit is that in all of the other points of conflict between the author and his opponents the issues are prerogatives of those who have the eschatological Spirit. We will see this in detail in the sections that follow.

b. The View of the Author

There can be no doubt that the author of 1 John also affirms that the members of the community have received and now possess the eschatological Spirit. This is clear from 2:20, 27; 3:24; 4:1-6; 5:6, 8. At the same time, the author clarifies the pneumatology of the community in several important ways.

---

109. For detailed discussions, see R. E. Brown, *Epistles* 26; Burge, *Anointed*, esp. 170-75, 219-20; Hengel, *Question* 55; Schnackenburg, *Epistles* 162-69.

110. That competing understandings of the role of the Spirit were at the heart of the crisis has been suggested by a number of scholars. See, for example, R. E. Brown, *Community* 138-44; Culpepper, *Gospel-Letters* 267-69; Grayston, *Epistles* 18-20, 22-27, 78-79, 118-211; Smith, "Learned" 217-235, 226.

111. See Vol. 3, Appendix 4, esp. Section D.2 (How the Two Groups Understood the Spirit) and Chart E-2.

First, the author of 1 John, when speaking of God's gift of the Spirit to the believer, makes it clear that the believer's possession of the Spirit is not comprehensive. Twice the author says that God has given the believer "of" his Spirit *(hoti ek tou pneumatos autou dedōken hēmin)* (3:24; 4:13). The use of the partitive genitive in this expression makes it clear that God has given the believer *a share* in his Spirit rather than a complete and perfect possession of it.[112] In the second edition of the Gospel, there had been no such qualification about the gift of the Spirit. The third author will also reflect this refinement of the manner in which the Spirit is possessed by the believer and by Jesus when he (the author) says that Jesus has been given the Spirit "without measure" (John 3:34). Thus, the third edition provides a needed nuance to the understanding of Jesus' own possession of the Spirit and so completes the nuancing of the possession of the Spirit distinctive of each.

Secondly, the author introduces the notion of the "Spirit of Truth" as a more precise description of the Spirit. Moreover, the author of 1 John contrasts this Spirit of Truth with the "Spirit of Deception" (4:1-6). Thus, he conceives of reality as containing a plurality of spirits, something typical of the modified dualism of apocalyptic. Although he does this, he continues to use "Spirit" in its unqualified sense to refer to the Spirit of God.

As a result of this notion of a plurality of spirits, it becomes necessary for the believer to discern between these spirits. And the author would claim that the opponents, who (as we saw above) claim to have the Spirit, do in fact have a spirit, but it is the Spirit of Deception. So they are not freed from sin, do not possess the truth, and so on. No element of this dualistic conception of spirits was present in either the first or the second edition of the Gospel.

While in the second edition of the Gospel the question was *whether or not* one had the Spirit (and this Spirit was contrasted with the "flesh"), in 1 John the essential question posed to the believer is *which* spirit the person possessed (the Spirit of Truth or the Spirit of Deception).

Third, in 1 John, the Spirit is nowhere explicitly linked with the giving of

---

112. See Schnackenburg (*Epistles* 191), who comments: "One should also note the unique formulation in 1 John 4:13, that God has given us 'of *(ek)* his Spirit.' Virtually synonymous is the saying that refers back to initiation in Heb. 6:4, that the Christians 'have shared in the Holy Spirit' (cf. also the Pauline metaphor of the 'first installment' of the Spirit that God has given to us, 2 Cor. 1:22; 5:5; Eph. 1:14)." Klauck (*Erste Johannesbrief* 256) notices the partitive genitive and calls attention to the difference between this expression and John 3:34. On the other hand, R. E. Brown (*Epistles* 466) does not notice the difference between John 3:34 and John 4:13. He also speaks of the Spirit as the direct object after John 14:16 and seeks to harmonize the three texts. However, the texts should not be harmonized but should be understood in the light of the theological and literary development described here, a development that takes proper account of the nuances of the texts in question.

Section 3. The Development of Johannine Theology: Pneumatology

life. Given the numerous times that Spirit and life are associated with one another in the second edition,[113] this absence is remarkable. At the same time, other prerogatives of the Spirit such as the Spirit's relation to the truth remain evident. Thus, the Spirit continues to be spoken of as a source of correct knowledge (4:6) and of testimony (3:24; 4:13; 5:6-7), but the explicit statements of 1 John relate life to Jesus (see 1:2; 4:9; 5:11-12, 13, 20).[114]

Fourth, in 1 John, some of the functions of the Spirit are described obliquely. The believer is said to have "an anointing from the Holy One" (2:20) that is the source of his or her ability to "know all." Thus, the author of 1 John continues to affirm that direct knowledge of God comes from this anointing, as it was said to come from the outpouring of the Spirit in the Old Testament and in the second edition, but the actual term "Spirit" does not appear.

Later the author says, "[T]he anointing that you received from him abides in you, and you do not have need that anyone teach you; but as his anointing teaches you about all things, and it is true and not false . . ." (2:27). Again the reference is clearly to the Spirit as it is described in Jer 31:33-34, but there is no explicit mention of the Spirit. Why the author speaks so obliquely about the Spirit is not certain, but one may suspect that he wishes to focus on the role of the Son and the Father and so, even when he is speaking of the Spirit, seeks to put the emphasis on the source of the Spirit rather than on the Spirit itself.

Thus, although the author reaffirms the essential aspects of the teaching about the Spirit from the second edition, he modifies the teaching in several respects and focuses more on the role of the Father and Son in relation to the Spirit. In so doing he preserves the teaching but corrects the opponents.

c. Is the Conception of the Spirit in 1 John Less Developed?

It is often said that 1 John exhibits a conception of the Spirit that is less developed than that in the Gospel.[115] It would be easy to conclude that, if one were to compare 1 John *with all of the Gospel*. However, if we compare the conception in 1 John with that of the second edition, it becomes clear that in fact the conception of the Spirit in 1 John is more developed and nuanced than it is in the second edition. In the second edition, the Spirit is described in terms that are impersonal. However, in 1 John we hear of the Spirit as a Spirit of Truth, as a

---

113. Within the second edition, Spirit and life are associated in 3:3-10; 4:10-15; 6:63-65; 7:37-39. This association is explicit and also made through images such as those of rebirth (3:3-10) and living water (4:10-15; 7:37-39). The association of Spirit and life is also evident from the way both the Spirit and life are described as that which is to be given to the believer by Jesus.

114. See also the discussion of eternal life in 1 John below.

115. Dodd, "First Epistle" 146-48; R. E. Brown, *Epistles* 26-27.

witness (a quality associated with "persons"), as a teacher (again a personal quality), and as one leading to proper confession of Jesus. Moreover, we find a nuance in the way the author describes the believer's possession of the Spirit. Yet if we compare the conception of the Spirit in 1 John with that in the third edition (as we shall shortly see), it becomes clear that only there does the understanding of the Spirit reach its full development.[116]

5. The Spirit in the Third Edition

When we turn to the portrayal of the Spirit in the third edition, we find that it is similar to that of 1 John in many respects, but at the same time the third author develops his own distinctive understanding of its identity and role. Like the author of 1 John, the author of the third edition continues to refer to the Spirit in absolute terms simply as "Spirit" but also introduces a dualistic conception where such a distinction is important.

One of the first changes the third author makes is to clarify that Jesus' possession of the Spirit is unique. Specifically in 3:34 the Spirit is said to be given to Jesus "without measure." We had seen in 1 John that the author made it clear that the disciples were given "of the Spirit" (i.e., a *share* in the Spirit; cf. 3:24; 4:13). In the third edition, the author complements that notion from the second edition by affirming that *Jesus'* possession was "without measure." When the two conceptions are viewed in relation to one another, it becomes clear that the authors have intended to distinguish Jesus' possession of the Spirit from that of the disciples.

The third author also distinguishes between Jesus' possession of the Spirit and that of the believer in another more subtle but equally important way — by the use of the theologically important term "remain" *(menein)*. It will be noted that in 1:33 the Spirit is described as descending and "remaining" upon Jesus *(menōn ep' auton)*. Yet, when Jesus describes the presence of the Paraclete among the disciples in 14:17, he says that the Paraclete "remains among you, and will be in you" *(par' hymin menei kai en hymin estai)*.[117] In both instances two verbs are employed ("descend" and "remain"; "remain" and "be in"). While of itself the use of two verbs to describe the coming of the Spirit is not remarkable, it later becomes clear that the distinction is significant. Not only does the Spirit descend upon Jesus, but it remains upon him. The presence of the Spirit with the community will be permanent, but it does not "remain" upon the individual

---

116. The background of this conception of the Spirit will be discussed after the discussion of the Spirit in the third edition of the Gospel.

117. This distinction in usage here is pointed out by Vellanickal, *Sonship* 271.

Section 3. The Development of Johannine Theology: Pneumatology

as it does on Jesus. Thus, the disciples' possession of the Spirit is less permanent and is capable of being lost through sin, as happened in the case of the opponents.

Like the author of 1 John, the third author makes it explicit at times that he holds a dualistic perspective in which the Spirit is in fact the Spirit "of Truth." The reader is thus to understand that the "Spirit of Truth" of the third edition is opposed to "the Spirit of Deception" (which had appeared in 1 John and which was the other dualistic spirit).[118]

In addition to describing the Spirit as the Spirit of Truth, it may also be that the author of the third edition is the one to introduce the references to the Spirit as the "holy" spirit. That title appears only three times (1:33; 14:26; and 20:22). In the first two instances other features indicate that the surrounding material is from the third edition; in 20:22 the case is less clear, although it is not impossible that the third author has made a slight modification in that verse also.[119]

The author of the third edition also describes the Spirit (as Paraclete) in such a way that the Spirit begins to be spoken of as having personal characteristics, something not present earlier in the tradition, where it functioned more as a "force" than as a "person."[120]

---

118. Smalley ("Paraclete" 290) proposes that the the references to the Spirit deal with the life of the individual believer and that the Paraclete passages deal with the life of the community. This assumes a dichotomy between the individual and the community that is not evident in the Gospel. The "you" who receive the Spirit in 20:22 are no different from the "you" of the Paraclete passages. Furthermore, passages such as 14:26 are as much directed at individuals as at the community as a whole.

119. If the title is introduced by the third author, the purpose is still not absolutely clear. It may be that its use in the Synoptics and in other sectors of early Christianity made its introduction into the Gospel attractive. It could also be that the author introduced it specifically because it too reflected the apocalyptic worldview by including the possibility of "unclean" (or "unholy") spirits. Thus, it would parallel the use of the term "Spirit of Truth," an apocalyptic term that is intended as one element of a contrasting pair, as is evident from the explicit contrast with "Spirit of Deception" in 1 John 4:1-6.

120. R. E. Brown (*Christology* 193 n. 287) makes reference to the problem of "when the NT authors began to think of the Spirit ... as a personal agent." If one supposes that 1 John was written after the Gospel (or after the third edition), the Johannine Gospel has no helpful answer to this problem. The present analysis sheds light on the problem insofar as it recognizes that the Spirit-Paraclete passages represent a *final* stage of theological development (rather than one prior to the development in 1 John). Thus, not only do we see a more even progression in the community's understanding of the Spirit, but also one in which the awareness of the Spirit as a personal agent takes place in the final stage of development (at the time of the third edition of the Gospel).

A History of the Development of Johannine Theology

a. The Spirit as Paraclete

Yet another way in which the third author's portrayal of the Spirit is distinctive is that he applies the title "Paraclete" to the Spirit whereas the author of 1 John had used it only of Jesus.

While the Paraclete passages are compatible with the Old Testament understanding of the Spirit and indeed take up a number of features of this understanding, the functions that are most distinctive of the Paraclete are precisely qualifications of the more traditional understanding. We can see this best by a brief review of the five Paraclete sayings outlining the function of the Paraclete in each.

The purpose of the first saying (14:15-17) is to introduce the title, associate it with the dualistic title "Spirit of Truth," and affirm that it is a spirit that the world does not have but which will remain in the disciples. In all of this the Paraclete's function is compatible with the Old Testament conception except that it is presented in a dualistic framework.

The second saying (14:25-26) identifies the Paraclete with the "Holy Spirit" and is linked to the Old Testament conception of enlightening its recipients. But the saying makes it clear that the knowledge imparted will be a recollection of what Jesus himself has said — it will not be an independent illumination. Thus, it both affirms ("will teach you all things") and qualifies ("and will remind you of all things that I have told you") the understanding of the Spirit in the second edition by linking his activity to the words of Jesus in the second edition. It is also more explicit in this regard than the discussion of the Spirit in 1 John.

The third saying (15:26) affirms again that the Paraclete is the "Spirit of Truth" and that it will have a role in the post-ministry period that is parallel to the role of the words, works, and Scripture as witnesses during the ministry. But like the three essential witnesses of the second edition, the Paraclete will witness (as will the disciples themselves) *to Jesus*.[121] This is a function that is spe-

---

121. It is often pointed out that the Spirit functions much in the same way as Jesus and that the Spirit is intended to extend the presence of Jesus into the post-ascension period. Thus, both Jesus (6:57) and the Paraclete (15:26) come forth from the Father. Jesus (3:17) and the Paraclete (16:7) are sent. Jesus is the truth (14:6); the Paraclete is the Spirit of Truth (14:17). The Paraclete is the Holy Spirit (14:26); Jesus is the Holy One (6:69). The Paraclete will remind the disciples of all that Jesus said (14:26).

However, it is essential to note that in all these cases, it is precisely the figure described as the *Paraclete* that has these functions, and not "the Spirit." In other words, the Paraclete's linkage to Jesus is not accidental, nor is there any such linkage to Jesus in passages where the figure is described as "the spirit." See, for example, Barrett, "Holy Spirit" 1-19; R. E. Brown, *Gospel* 2:1135-44); Burge, *Anointed* 35; Smalley, "Paraclete" 291; Kammler, "Jesus Christus" 87-190.

Section 3. The Development of Johannine Theology: Pneumatology

cifically Johannine in function and formulation and one that would be incompatible with the view held by the opponents.

The fourth saying (16:7-11) explains that the Paraclete will not come until Jesus departs.[122] But when it comes, it will show how the world was sinful because it did not believe that righteousness was accomplished through the departure of Jesus, which allowed for the coming of the Spirit, and it did not believe that the judgment of "the ruler of this world" (the dualistic title for Satan) took place through the Death and Resurrection of Jesus. Again, this is distinctively Johannine.

The fifth saying (16:12-15) explains that the Spirit of Truth will illumine the disciples and lead them "into all truth" (in keeping with the Old Testament conception), but it is explicitly said that "He will not speak on his own, but will speak whatever he hears, and will proclaim to you what is to come." Thus, the Paraclete is explicitly described, not as an independent source of illumination, but as one inextricably linked to the words of Jesus.[123] In v. 14, this is emphasized again when it is said that the Paraclete will specifically *glorify Jesus*. It will "take from what is mine and will proclaim it to you" (16:15). But then the reader is assured that neither is the revelation of Jesus independent of the Father, since "(e)verything the Father has is mine" (v. 15).

Thus we see that in the second, third, and fifth sayings there is an emphasis on the way the Spirit will relate to the person and words of Jesus. By this emphasis the author does away with any danger that the community will minimize the words of Jesus because they now possess the eschatological Spirit. In this respect, the third edition does not go beyond the thought of 1 John but makes its role much more explicit.

b. The Holy Spirit in 1:33

In the light of the above analysis, what can be said about the description of Jesus as "baptizing in the Holy Spirit" in 1:33b? Three observations seem pertinent and may help to explain the function of the verse. First, within the Gospel of

---

122. This may be intended to refer to its function in the period after the departure of Jesus. In the second edition, the giving of the Spirit is said to occur after the glorification of Jesus (cf. 7:37-39). This is accomplished in the giving of the Spirit by Jesus at the time of his first appearance to them after his rising from the dead (20:22).

123. This is not an undue restriction in the eyes of the Johannine community because it is the same Spirit that had been given to Jesus and that informed his words. However, the "restriction" gives an important emphasis to the words of Jesus and does not allow for any independent revelation that is not compatible with the revelation of Jesus. Thus, there is no justification for anyone being "progressive and not remaining in the teaching of the Christ" (2 John 9).

John the presence of such an expression causes particular problems because it is explicitly stated (3:26; 4:1) that Jesus conducts a baptizing ministry during his public life and prior to the bestowal of the Spirit in 20:22. How does baptism with the Holy Spirit relate to this other baptism of Jesus? This awkwardness is surely an indicator of the conflict of traditions. The references to Jesus baptizing with the Holy Spirit are found throughout the Synoptics, while references to a baptismal ministry within his public life are not. This would suggest that the reference to baptism with the Holy Spirit is a later addition.

Second, the phrase itself (including the use of "holy") is deeply rooted in the wider early tradition, as is evident from its parallels in the Synoptics and Acts (Mark 1:8b; Matt 3:11; Luke 3:16; Acts 1:5; 11:15).[124] This suggests that the presence of the expression here may be determined by the desire to imitate the wider tradition. As we have seen, several such statements, statements that are awkward in their Johannine context but which reflect Synoptic concerns and particularly those with an apocalyptic orientation, are the work of the third author. This suggests that the present verse is also an addition.[125]

Third, nowhere in the present Gospel does Jesus actually perform an action that can be said to be "baptizing in the Holy Spirit" with the possible exception of 20:22. There is no evidence within the Gospel for associating this bestowal of the Holy Spirit with an act of Baptism. Yet we may get an indication of how this phrase was understood in the wider tradition from its appearance in Acts. For, in the two cases where there is a reference to a realization of this baptism (Acts 1:5; 11:15), the fulfillment of the promise is also not associated with any act involving a ritual of baptism. Thus, although it was added at the time of the third edition, the author could well have seen its fulfillment in the scene from the second edition now in 20:22.

c. Conclusion

Thus we see that, although the conception of the Spirit in the third edition is the same as that in 1 John in many respects, the formulation and expression of that view are sufficiently different to suggest that they are the work of different stages of reflection on its reality and function.

---

124. Acts 1:5 and 11:16 make reference to the scene of Jesus' baptism and to the contrast of Spirit baptism with the water baptism of John. In Acts 1:5, Peter sees this fulfilled in the Pentecost experience of the disciples; in Acts 11:16, Peter sees it again fulfilled in the coming of the Spirit upon Cornelius and his household (cf. 10:44-48).

125. This is confirmed by an analysis of the verse in its surrounding context, as is described in the Commentary.

Section 3. The Development of Johannine Theology: Pneumatology

6. The Background of the Presentation of the Spirit in 1 John and in the Third Edition

The use of "spirit" *(ruaḥ)* in the SDQ is complicated by a number of factors.[126] Although there is a general recognition that the term refers at times to God's spirit, at times to man's spirit, and at still other times to an angelic being or spirit, there is still considerable disagreement about the meaning intended in particular texts.[127]

In addition, the SDQ themselves do not exhibit a unified, consistent concept of the Spirit. At one time many scholars interpreted all of Qumran pneumatology in the light of 1QS 3:14–4:26. However, scholars such as H. W. Kuhn[128] and von der Osten-Sacken[129] demonstrated that much of the Qumran pneumatology is consistent with, and undoubtedly derived from, the Old Testament usage while other elements are closer to the dualistic view expressed most clearly in 1QS 3:14–4:26.[130] While recognizing this tension, scholars have not reached agreement about how to resolve it.[131]

Yet another factor is the recognition that, within 1QS, 3:14–4:26 represents a secondary addition and presumably (since it is the later addition and since its presence near the beginning of the document is so prominent), it is almost surely intended to provide an interpretive framework for reading the remainder of the document.[132]

---

126. See the helpful survey of scholarship in Sekki, *Ruaḥ* 7-70. The most extensive study of the concept of spirit at Qumran is that of Sekki himself. However, Sekki's treatment has been critiqued on methodological grounds (see, e.g., reviews in *TLZ* [July 1991] 502-4 [S. Holm-Nielsen]; *CBQ* [July 1992] 544-46 [M. Horgan]; and *JSP* [October 1991] 117-118 [J. C. Reeves]). One of the chief problems is his decision to distinguish only biblical from nonbiblical documents. By doing so he fails to distinguish sufficiently among the various nonbiblical documents so as to isolate the distinctive sectarian writings of the community. Also, more attention to the distinct genres would seem to be called for. In addition, with the publication of other texts, the list of relevant material continues to grow. Nevertheless, Sekki's book contains many helpful insights. Two other relevant works to appear since Sekki's are those of Charlesworth, "Dead Sea Scrolls" in *Scrolls/Historical Jesus* 19-62 and Kvalvaag, "Spirit," in *Qumran* 159-80.

127. This same tension exists in the *T12P*, where at times these "spirits" seem to be dispositions within man and at other times they appear to be distinct entities, one of which is the Spirit of God.

128. Kuhn, *Enderwartung*.

129. Von der Osten-Sacken, *Gott und Belial*.

130. Other texts consistent with the view of 1QS 3-4 include 1QH 15 and 4Q186.

131. Recently J. J. Collins (*Apocalypticism* 117), speaking of various conceptions of life after death in the scrolls, has commented: "It is reasonable to assume that the various components of the scroll [1QS] were read in the light of each other in the community, even if they had been composed separately." This is an assumption that could perhaps be applied to the understanding of the Spirit texts in the SDQ also.

132. This tension is not unlike the tension that exists within the Johannine literature between the pneumatology of the second edition and the later (dualistic) pneumatology typical of

A History of the Development of Johannine Theology

While taking these cautions into account, our present task is made simpler by the fact that our purpose here is simply to show that the Qumran community recognized the importance of the eschatological Spirit and was convinced that they already possessed this Spirit through their life in the community. In addition, the community's conception of the Spirit was portrayed dualistically at times, and the author spoke not only of the Spirit of God but also of other spirits. In subsequent sections, we shall see that the Qumran community also understood themselves to possess various prerogatives of the eschatological Spirit.

The sectarian documents from Qumran are thoroughly eschatological. In 1QH, it is regularly said that God gives his Holy Spirit to the members of the community (4:26; 5:25; 6:25; 8:9, 11, 15; 12:31; 15:7; 17:32; 20:11-12). Another text that speaks of the eschatological bestowal of the Spirit is 4Q521 f2 ii 6, where the author describes the outpouring of God's Spirit ("And on the poor will rest his Spirit, and he will renew his faithful with his power"). The synonymous parallelism here shows the pouring out of the Spirit as part of the eschaton as well as expressing the effect of the Spirit. In 1QH 5:1-25, we see an extended discussion of man's inability to fathom the depths of God or to follow faithfully in his paths because he is a "man of flesh" (5:3, 19) and it is only because of the spirit given him (5: 25) that he can understand and live properly. There can be no doubt that the community spoke of their possession of the spirit as a present reality.

As in 1 John and the third edition, the Spirit in the SDQ is depicted at times in a dualistic mode and at times in an unqualified sense. The most famous of the dualistic texts is 1QS 3:14-4:23, where the Spirit of Truth and the Spirit of Deceit are contrasted. But in addition to these, there are other spirits allied to them (cf. 1QS 3:24). At times (e.g., 1QH 5:1-25), the "spirit" of God is spoken of alongside references to "the host of your spirits" (cf. 5:14). The plurality of evil spirits in league with Belial is evident in 4Q286 f7 col2 3-4, which utters a curse on "all the spir[its of] his [l]ot in their wicked plan, and may they be damned in their plans of [f]oul impurity. For they are the [l]ot of darkness..." (DSST).

Although the eschatological outpouring of the Spirit is not a major topic in the *T12P*, the outpouring of the Spirit is evident in *TJud* 24:2-4 and follows

---

the apocalyptic worldview and found in the third edition. For the Johannine community, there can be no doubt that the third author intended the other Spirit passages to be interpreted within the framework of his presentation. This is evident from the clear identification of the Paraclete, the Spirit of Truth, and the Holy Spirit with the Spirit in both the Gospel and 1 John. Because of the complexity in the presentation of the spirit in the SDQ, we can only hope to present a summary that will recognize some of this complexity while hoping to avoid some of the dangers of oversimplification.

Section 4. The Development of Johannine Theology: Eternal Life

the understanding in the Old Testament: "And the heavens will be opened upon him to pour out the Spirit as a blessing of the Holy Father. And he will pour out a spirit of grace upon you. And you shall be his sons in truth, and you will walk in his first and final decrees." Here the effusion of the Spirit also is the cause of "true" sonship and a faithfulness that would approach perfectionism, both eschatological benefits of the Spirit in the Old Testament.

Thus, as this brief review shows, the necessity of receiving an outpouring of God's Spirit and, in the case of the Essene community, the conviction that this had taken place are clearly in evidence both in the SDQ and in the *T12P*.

SECTION 4. THE DEVELOPMENT OF JOHANNINE THEOLOGY: ETERNAL LIFE

The notion of "(eternal) life" is central to the thought of the Gospel of John in its present form. Yet, as we shall see, its presence is not universal, nor is its meaning univocal. We will attempt to trace briefly the nature of eternal life as it was understood in the various editions of the Gospel and with reference to how it was understood in the Judaisms of the time.

1. Eternal Life in the First Edition

Although the role of the Spirit and life is central to the thought of the Gospel in its present form, in what is still extant from the first edition of the Gospel, there is no mention of eternal life.[133]

2. Eternal Life in the Second Edition

The notions of "life" *(zōē)* and "eternal life" *(zōē aiōnios)*[134] are introduced into the Gospel by the author of the second edition.[135] The understanding of life

---

133. Although "life" appears in 20:31 in close proximity to material from the first edition, the phrase in which it appears is almost surely from the second edition. See below and also the discussion of the Composition of 20:31 in the Commentary.

134. As van der Watt *("Aiōnios")* points out, there is no distinction between the terms "life" and "eternal life" as these are objects of an offer by Jesus; the one is simply a shortened form of the other. Consequently, both terms will be treated together in what follows.

135. *Zōē* appears thirty-three times in the Gospel: 1:4; 3:15, 16, 36; **4:14**, **36**; **5:24** [twice], 26, 29, **39**, **40**; 6:27, **33**, **35**, **40**, **47**, **48**, 51, 53, 54, **63**, 68; 8:12; **10:10**, 28; 11:25; 12:25, 50; 14:6; 17:2, 3; **20:31**. The verb *zaō* appears thirteen times (apart from those instances where it refers to normal

presumed in the second edition is that which is typical of the Old Testament and Jewish thought generally, namely, that "life" is due to the presence of a "spirit" placed within the person by God. In the second edition, however, the focus is on "eternal life." There Jesus promises that the eschatological Spirit of God will be poured out on those who believe in him and that as a result they will have "eternal life."[136] Thus, this eschatological Spirit will be a source of life for the believer. This "life" promised to the believer is the life that God himself possesses and which he has given to the Son. The Son in turn is able to give it to whomever he wishes (5:21).[137]

This eternal/divine life has several characteristics. From the point of view of existence before physical death, the reception of eternal life is equivalent to a new birth that transforms and "divinizes" the individual, making the person "a child of God." After physical death, the believer's existence will not end (because "death" is typical only of human life). Rather, because he/she lives with the life of God, the believer will continue to live forever. This promised life *(zōē aiōnios)* is not a *human* life that never ends, but the very life of God that by its nature is unending.

We meet the mention of "life" first in Jesus' offering of "living" water to the Samaritan woman. While this is not an explicit mention of "life," the passage is important in that the notion of "living water" here is a figurative allusion to the giving of the Spirit (cf. 7:37-39). Thus, Jesus offers the Spirit, which will be the source of (eternal) life. In 4:36, he speaks of the harvester who gathers up "fruit for eternal life." In 5:21, it is said that Jesus gives life to those he wishes. In 5:24a, Jesus says that the one who believes "has"[138] eternal life and has "crossed over from death to life." In 5:39-40, Jesus speaks of the Jewish hope to find eternal life in the Scriptures and of their failure to come to him, so they "may have life." In the Bread-of-Life discourse Jesus makes a series of statements identifying himself as the one who gives life to the world (6:33); he is the "bread of life" (6:35, 48); and the one who believes in the Son "will have eternal life" (6:40, 47).

---

physical life): **4:10, 11; 5:25;** 6:51 (twice), 57 (three times), 58; **7:38;** 11:25, 27; **14:19**. The cognate *zōopoieō* occurs in **5:21**. Also related to this concept are the texts that state a person will not die (forever): for example, 6:50; 8:21, 24, 52, 53; 11:25, 26. The texts in boldface occur in the second edition; the remainder occur in the third.

136. At times, it is expressed as an offer of the Spirit; at other times, it is expressed as an offer of (eternal) life.

137. Schnackenburg (*Epistles* 164) makes the entire process quite clear: "The believer becomes a child of God (cf. John 1:12) through an act of divine begetting, being born from above. In this act of God, the believer receives the divine Spirit as the principle of life." R. E. Brown (*Gospel* 1:140) makes the same point in his discussion of John 3:2-8: "If natural life is attributable to God's giving spirit to men, so eternal life begins when God gives His Holy Spirit to men."

138. On the temporal discrepancy in this statement, see the discussion in Part 2, Section 3 ("The Religious Significance of the Material Reality").

Section 4. The Development of Johannine Theology: Eternal Life

Most clearly he says in 6:63, "The Spirit is what gives life. . . . The words that I have spoken to you are Spirit and life."

In 10:10, Jesus says that he has come that his sheep may "have life, and have it abundantly." In 10:28, Jesus says that he gives his sheep "eternal life, and they are not lost for eternity." In 17:2, Jesus explains that the Father has given him authority to give eternal life to those whom the Father has given him.

Finally, there is one other appearance of the phrase "eternal life" that calls for our attention. That is in the conclusion to the first edition (20:31). Apart from the final phrase, "and that believing you may have life in his name," there is no reason to think that 20:30-31 come from the second edition or that the verses have been edited. At the same time, the term "life" is so intimately connected with the theology of the second (and third) editions, that it is difficult to believe that the phrase was originally part of v. 31. Consequently, it is concluded in the discussion of the Composition that it has been added to the verse but without any literary indication of editing. It was probably added by the author of the second edition, although it is possible that it is the work of the third.

All of the comments above have referred to the life that is promised to the believer. Only once in the second edition does the author speak of the life that Jesus has: in 14:19 he says simply, "I live, and you will live." As we shall see shortly, in the third edition there is more of a focus on the life that Jesus possesses, but here in the second edition his possession of life was not in focus, and as a result it was all but presumed.

a. The Present Possession of Eternal Life

It is commonly recognized by scholars that the dominant view of eternal life in the Gospel as a whole is what has come to be called "realized eschatology." That is, the believer possesses eternal life in the present rather than only at some future point at the end of time.

Although the second edition speaks simply and without qualification of the giving of the Spirit (and life) after the glorification of Jesus and therefore a giving in the "present," the clearest expression of this view of present eschatology is in 5:24-25. Here it is said that the believer "has" eternal life "and does not come into judgment but has crossed over from death to life." The "life" and "death" spoken of here are spiritual (not physical) life and death. That is, the believer will still die "physically," but he/she will continue in existence eternally because she/he lives with the life of God.

But what is meant by having eternal life "now"? When Jesus speaks of the believer "having" eternal life in the present, he is referring not to the "present" of the historical ministry but to the present of the post-Resurrection community. From the remainder of the second edition, especially from 7:37-39, it becomes evident that this life, which is possible only through the Spirit, will be made available only at the glorification of Jesus. Thus, from the perspective of the pre-Passion ministry, the believer did not (yet) have the Spirit. (The belief during the ministry was the belief necessary in order to receive the Spirit.) But, from the point of view of the Johannine community reading what is now chapter 5 of the Gospel, the believer had received the Spirit and did have life in the present.

b. Conclusion

Two final observations need to be made regarding eternal life in the second edition. First, it is important to realize that "eternal life" and "life," as used in the Gospel, refer to real entities that free the believer from death. For the Johannine believer "eternal life" was *not* something symbolic.[139] It was understood as a radical transformation resulting in a new level of existence that was literally a reception of the life of God himself. It was for this reason that believers could be called "children of God" and for this reason that the process of gaining eternal life can be called a "rebirth."[140] According to the theology of the second edition, this possession of eternal life began in the present (realized eschatology) and

---

139. It is remarkable how easily this is misunderstood. Even when discussing the gift of the Spirit in 7:37-39, Bultmann (*Gospel* 302-5) sees the "Spirit" and "life" simply as images for the undefined "gift" of the Revealer: "Without any doubt this [the water which quenches all thirst; cf. 7:37] refers to the gift that he brings as the Revealer no matter what images may be used to describe it on other occasions: it is the revelation, or better, Jesus himself. Admittedly in the Evangelist's note v. 39 the water that Jesus gives is interpreted in terms of the Spirit. . . . But this does not mean that the Evangelist has limited the gift to a specific object; for as we shall see from the Farewell Discourses, the Evangelist does not see the Spirit as a special gift that gives proof of its presence in the particular phenomena of the Christian life. Rather for him the *pneuma* is the *allos paraklētos* (14:16) who takes Jesus' place. . . ." Ashton (*Understanding* 217) also sees life merely as a symbol: ". . . once transferred to this world (and the present age) life has become a *symbol*, and if one insists on retaining the rendering 'eternal,' which is what *aiōnios* always means in secular Greek, then 'eternal life' can only be a *metaphor*. The new life enjoyed by the faithful is more than ordinary physical existence; it is the life of faith. Christians are no more immune from physical death than other folk. But the benefits that accrue to them from their acceptance of the message of Jesus are, for this evangelist, best symbolized by life." This is also the view of Kysar (*Gospel* 172), who comments: "Life [is to be] understood as a symbol for the benefits of the revelation."

140. It is true that the image of "(re)birth" is a metaphor insofar as "birth" always refers to a physical act and what is being spoken of is an act that is spiritual (cf. Schnackenburg, *Epistles* 164). But insofar as the term refers to an act of generation, it is not a metaphor. As John 3:6 says: "That which is born of the flesh is flesh, and that which is born of the Spirit is Spirit."

Section 4. The Development of Johannine Theology: Eternal Life

continued after physical death in a state that would be most precisely called spiritual immortality.[141]

Second, in the light of the realization that eternal life comes through one's possession of the eschatological Spirit, it is appropriate to clarify what it means to say that eternal life comes through faith in Jesus.[142] While the basic reality is that the one who believes in Jesus will receive the Spirit (which is the principle of life), the Jesus of the second edition expresses this elliptically at times. Thus, the expression "the one believing has eternal life," when stated more fully, would mean "the one believing will receive the Spirit, which is the principle of life." This is one of at least three such elliptical expressions. When Jesus says "I give them eternal life," he refers to the life that comes from the gift of the Spirit. When he explains that "my words are Spirit and life," he means that his words, if listened to and obeyed, will lead to the belief that prepares for the reception of the Spirit that gives life.

3. The Background of Eternal Life in the Second Edition

It is perhaps more appropriate to speak of a "foreshadowing" rather than a "background" of the notion of eternal life in Judaism, for the belief that the presence of God's Spirit within a person endows the person with eternal life is a correlate of the Jewish belief that the presence of a natural spirit was the principle of natural life.

a. Natural Life and Spirit

In the Old Testament, natural life is understood to be a result of a gift of "spirit" (*pneuma*; Heb. *ruaḥ*) from God.[143] This is evident in the description of creation

---

141. The conception of "immortality" did not involve a belief in a future existence of the physical body. This conception is found in the deuterocanonical Wisdom of Solomon, as will be seen in the treatment of the OT background below.

142. See, for example, Bultmann, *Gospel* 166-67. More recently Moloney (*Signs* 15) says, "Hearing the word of Jesus and having faith in the one who sent him produces eternal life (5:24)." As stated, this is incorrect. It is belief in Jesus that prepares for the gift of the Spirit, but it is the Spirit that gives life!

143. For a detailed discussion of this, see van Imschoot, "L'esprit." Within the OT, the *ruaḥ* of Yahweh is also used to refer not just to the principle of natural life but also to the Spirit of Yahweh himself. It is this Spirit that Yahweh sends upon the judges (on Othniel in Judg 3:10; on Samson in Judg 14:6). It brings about the power of prophecy in Balaam (Num 24:2), in Ezekiel (Ezek 11:5), and Hosea (Hos 9:7). That this is to be distinguished from the spirit as the principle of natural life is clear from the case of Saul. The *ruaḥ* of Yahweh was given to Saul (1 Sam 10:4) but

A History of the Development of Johannine Theology

of humanity in Gen 2:7, a text that has a particular relevance to the Johannine expression in John 20:22. In Gen 2:7, we read: "The LORD God formed man out of the earth, and breathed into his face the breath of life" *(enephysēsen eis to prosōpon autou pnoēn tēs zōēs)*. The similarity between this and John 20:22 ("He breathed on them, and said to them, 'Receive the Holy Spirit'") is apparent. As will be seen below in Isa 42:5, the terms *pnoē* and *pneuma* are synonymous. Second, the verb "breathed into" is the same verb that will be used by Ezekiel (see below) to describe the instilling of life into the bones.

This same conception lies behind Isa 42:5:

> "Thus says God, the LORD, who created the heavens and established them, who strengthened the earth and those things upon it, and who gave breath *(pnoēn)* to the people on it and spirit *(pneuma)* to those walking on it."[144]

According to the Psalmist, when God sends forth his spirit, he re-creates the face of the earth, and God's taking away his spirit results in death (Ps 103:29-30 LXX [104 Heb.]; 145:4 LXX [146 Heb.]). Job 34:14-15 says:

> "For if he [God] were to wish to withdraw and to withhold the spirit *(pneuma)* from it, all flesh would perish together."[145]

If the spirit is not present within a body, that body is not alive but simply a dead entity. It is this conception that lies behind the famous passage in Ezek 37:4-10.

> Then he said to me: "Prophesy over these bones, and say to them: Dry bones, hear the word of the LORD! And the LORD says these things to these bones: I am bringing the spirit of life *(pneuma tēs zōēs)* upon you, that you may come to life. I will put sinews upon you, and bring up flesh upon you, and cover you with skin, and I will give my[146] spirit to you, and you will live *(dōsō pneuma mou eis hymas kai zēsesthe)* and know that I am the LORD."

---

later it departed (1 Sam 16:14), yet the departure of this Spirit did not result in physical death but in a great change in the character of Saul. In the "last days" it was to be this Spirit that would be poured out on all people. See also the discussion of *ruaḥ* in Wolff, *Anthropology* 32-39.

144. In the Hebrew text the two terms here are *nĕshāmâ* and *ruaḥ*.

145. The Hebrew reads, "If he would take back his spirit *(ruaḥ)* and pull back to himself his breath *(nĕshāmâ)*."

146. The reference to this spirit as "my" spirit does not mean that it is anything other than a natural spirit that God gives to the bones. It is simply a spirit that has God as its source since God is the source of all life. Yet Gen 6:3 says: "My spirit will not remain in these people forever *(eis ton aiōna)* because they are flesh, their days will be one hundred and twenty years." See also Gen 6:17; 7:15.

Section 4. The Development of Johannine Theology: Eternal Life

I prophesied as I had been ordered, and even as I was prophesying, behold, a noise; it was a rattling as the bones came together as they should. I saw the sinews, and the flesh come upon them, and the skin came up upon them. But there was no spirit in them *(kai pneuma ouk ēn en autois)*. And he said to me: "Prophesy, son of man, prophesy to the spirit, and say to the spirit: The LORD says these things: From the four winds *(ek tōn tessarōn pneumatōn)* come, O Spirit, and breathe into *(emphysēson)* these dead, that they may come to life." I prophesied as he ordered me, and the spirit came into them; they came alive, and stood on their feet, a great gathering.[147]

So also Wis 15:11 reflects the same view in its description of God's action in creating human beings when it says that God ". . . inspired them with active souls, and breathed a living spirit into them." But the nature of this (natural) "spirit" God has given them is clear from v. 16, where this spirit is described as "borrowed."[148]

In a text from 2 Macc 7:22-23, which also is the first clear witness to a belief in bodily resurrection, we find the clear association of spirit and life in this present existence and also in the life to come. The mother whose seven sons are martyred speaks to them, saying:

". . . it was not I who gave you spirit and life *(pneuma kai zōēn)*. The Creator of the World will give you once again spirit and life *(pneuma kai zōēn).*" (LXX)

Here the association of spirit and life is really a case of hendiadys, that is, the spirit is the principle of life. So also in 2 Macc 14:46 God is referred to as Lord of life and spirit *(despozōn tēs zōēs kai tou pneumatos).*[149]

b. Eternal Life and the Spirit in the Old Testament

What makes this understanding of the relation between (natural) spirit and life so important is that the correlative of it was that in the last days, all people

---

147. That this text reflects the understanding of the composition of human life is also evident from the way this passage from Ezekiel becomes reinterpreted in 4Q385 2 and describes the bodily resurrection the faithful will experience on the last day. This will be discussed further below. See also Eccl 12:7, which explains that in normal human death "the dust returns to the earth as it was, and the spirit returns to God who bestowed it" (cf. Ps 145:4).

148. As is noted in the discussion of John 5:26, it is the fact that the (natural) spirit that human beings possess is "borrowed" that explains why a human cannot give life to another. On the other hand, Jesus is able to give life because he has life "in himself."

149. See also Wis 2:3.

would receive a new Spirit, not a natural one, but God's own Spirit. Therefore, with this reception of God's Spirit one would begin to live a new form of life. No longer would the individual live a "natural" life but would possess the same principle of life as God! Thus, they would live eternal life, the very life of God himself. In the most real of senses, the person would be "divinized."

Belief in life beyond death in Judaism developed only in the late Second Temple Period. Understandably then, within the canonical Hebrew Scriptures, we should not expect to find explicit testimony to the belief that possessing the Spirit of God brings about eternal life. However, this is not the whole story, for there are a number of features within the canonical and deuterocanonical Scriptures that speak of the Spirit in such a way as to indicate the development of such a belief. This belief becomes explicit in documents found at Qumran. There would seem to be four "currents" of thought leading to an explicit association of spirit and eternal life as it finds expression in the second edition of the Gospel and in documents from Qumran.

The first current would be the already present association of the possession of a natural spirit and the possession of natural life. This establishes the principle that is developed further with respect to eternal life.

The second current is the expressed relationship between "anointing," "spirit," and being a "son of God." This is evident in texts such as 2 Sam 7:14; Pss 2:7; 89:27, where the anointed king is declared to be a son of God. Although this does not speak of eternal life, it does imply some form of new relationship described as "sonship." In other texts such as 1 Sam 16:13 and Isa 61:1, such anointing is described as the vehicle of the Spirit. Yet these texts do not speak of the Spirit in terms of eternal life itself.

A third current leading to such belief is found in Wisdom of Solomon. Here there is a series of statements that indicate that, for the author, Wisdom is to be identified with the Spirit of God and is that which leads to eternal life. The possession of wisdom is considered to be a present possession by the author. Thus, he describes himself as born a mortal (7:1-6) but says that he prayed and that understanding and "the spirit of wisdom" were given him (7:7). This wisdom is described as a spirit (7:7, 22) and as "a breath of the power of God" (7:25), characteristics that are elsewhere attributed to the Spirit. In fact, in 9:17 Wisdom and Spirit are equated: "Who has learned your counsel unless you have bestowed Wisdom and have sent your holy Spirit from on high?"

In 7:22-23, Wisdom is described in ways that are similar to those in which the Spirit is said to function in the protocanonical Scriptures (e.g., a spirit that is intelligent, holy, unique, manifold, subtle . . . loving the good . . . beneficent . . .). Wisdom becomes the source of good deeds which lead to life beyond death (8:13), and the righteous who possess wisdom are called "children of God" (2:18). In chapter 15, the author explains why idols made by humans cannot have life but

Section 4. The Development of Johannine Theology: Eternal Life

are only dead things. His explanation is that they are made by humans "whose spirit is borrowed"; "people are mortal, and what they make with lawless hands is dead." This reflects the conviction that the source of life for humans is a "spirit" — but this spirit is borrowed, that is, given to them by God. But they cannot impart life to anything else because they do not have life "in themselves."[150]

Thus, there is some substantial similarity between the gift of the spirit of Wisdom and eternal life in Wisdom of Solomon. But there are differences also. While the possession of Wisdom is a present reality, there is no suggestion that the possession of eternal life is also a present reality. Nor is there direct evidence that the Spirit itself is the direct cause of eternal life, even though it would seem to be implied.

A fourth current appears in documents from Qumran, where there are statements that *explicitly* associate possession of the Spirit of God with eternal life. In 1QH 23 fragment 2:10-12, we read:

> ... and upon the dust you stretch out the spirit [...] in the mud [... the sons of] gods, to be in communion with the sons of heaven ... you have stretched out [your] holy [spirit] to cover the fault. *(DSST)*[151]

In 4Q385 2 fragment 5-8, we read:

> "Son of man, prophesy over the bones, and say: May a bone [connect] with its bone, and a joint [with its joint. And] s[o it happe]ned. And he said a second time: "Prophesy, and sinews will grow on them, and they will be covered with skin [all over." And so it happened.] ... and] a large crowd of men will r[i]se and bless YHWH Sebaoth wh[o caused them to live.] *(DSST)*

Thus, if the earlier currents point to a tendency to associate the spirit with eternal life, in the Qumran documents this association becomes explicit.

c. The Nature of Eternal Life in Pre-Christian Judaism

We now return to the Old Testament to outline briefly the views present there about the nature of life beyond death. A number of scholars have studied this field in detail, and here we point to some of their more general conclusions.[152]

---

150. See von Wahlde, "He Has Given."

151. The fragment was first identified and published by Puech. For his translation, see Puech, *Croyance* 402-3.

152. In order to clarify the conception of eternal life in the second edition, we need to ex-

Although throughout most of Israel's history there was no belief in life after death, in the Hebrew canon there are passages, primarily from the Psalms,[153] which speak in such a manner as to open the way for a belief in a life after death other than the shadowy existence of the soul in the netherworld. But what is envisioned is not clear. References to eternal life in these texts are judged, as do scholars such as J. J. Collins, as "ambiguous at best."[154]

By the late Second Temple period belief in the afterlife was becoming common. The Wisdom of Solomon witnesses to a state of "spiritual immortality," that is, a state in which the spirit continues in an unbroken state after death but without any corporeal form.[155] In the early chapters of Wisdom of Solomon, there are repeated references to the fact that unrighteousness leads to destruction and death (1:12, 16; 2:23-24; 5:14) and righteousness leads to life and immortality (3:1-4; 5:15-16; cf. 2:23-24).

In Dan 12:1-3, we find the first unambiguous reference to individual resurrection, but the exact nature of that resurrection as well as the state of the individual before that resurrection is unclear. This is best judged as a "resurrection of the spirit."[156] The first clear reference to *bodily* resurrection is in 2 Macc 7. The second of the seven brothers, when he was about to be put to death, says: "The king of the world will raise us, who die for his laws, up to live again forever" (7:9). The third son holds out his hands to have them cut off by his persecutors, and says, "It was from heaven that I received these; for the sake of his laws I disdain them; from him I hope to receive them again" (7:11). The fourth son speaks of the "hope God gives of being raised again by him. But for you there will be no resurrection to life *(soi men gar anastasis eis zōēn ouk estai)*!" (7:14). In these passages there are repeated assertions of a belief in everlasting life after a brief torture as well as resurrection involving the restoration of the mutilated body.

---

plain something of the alternate views held by Jews in the first century. This necessarily involves mention of bodily resurrection. However, the topic of bodily resurrection itself will be discussed in detail more in the following section, which deals with eschatology.

153. See for example, Pss 16:9-10; 21:4-5; 73:23.

154. J. J. Collins, *Apocalypticism* 111. For a complete listing of texts see Puech, *Croyance* 37-72. There are also a number of texts in the OT that speak of resurrection (e.g., Isa 26:29; Hos 6:2; Ezek 37:11), but their meaning is disputed. For example, Collins would see all as referring to the restoration of the Israelite nation, while scholars such as Nickelsburg (*Resurrection* 18) and Puech (*Croyance* 66-73) would see the text of Isa 26:29 as referring to individual resurrection.

155. So also J. J. Collins, *Apocalypticism* 113. It is perhaps significant that Collins (*Apocalypticism* 120-21) finds the closest parallel to the Wisdom of Solomon in John 5:24 (i.e., from the second edition). The Wisdom of Solomon is generally thought to have arisen under Hellenistic influence, but it also bears resemblances to elements of the SDQ. See also *Jos. Asen.* 8:5; 15:3-4.

156. J. J. Collins, *Apocalypticism* 112. Also Puech, *Croyance* 79-85. Collins would see this as present also in *1 Enoch* 22:9, as well as in chapters 91–105 and in *Jub.* 23:30-31.

Section 4. The Development of Johannine Theology: Eternal Life

Of these three forms of eternal life, it is eternal life in a spiritual state that is affirmed in the second edition of John. All discussion concerns a transformation into a spiritual state without a future aspect. Thus, the closest parallel is in the Wisdom of Solomon. But although this parallel is quite close, it is also clear that the second edition stresses that this life is something that begins in the present life and continues beyond death. In the Wisdom of Solomon there is no conviction that this eternal life had already begun in the present. Rather, it was something that began at death. Yet, as we shall see in the discussion of the background of eternal life in the SDQ, the community at Qumran held a belief that the messianic age had in some sense already begun and that they therefore already possessed this life in some respect.[157]

4. Eternal Life in 1 John

a. The View of the Opponents and the View of the Author of 1 John

In 1 John, the understanding of eternal life is essentially that of the second edition.[158] It is clear from 2:25 ("And this is the promise that he [Jesus] promised us: eternal life") that eternal life remains the central promise and hope of the community. In this sense, the author of 1 John is in complete agreement with his opponents. However, 1 John modifies considerably the context within which eternal life is understood and presented.

(1) The Role of Jesus in Relation to Eternal Life

Because of the opponents' challenge to the role of Jesus in salvation, the author of 1 John repeatedly emphasizes the role of Jesus in relation to eternal life. In fact, nowhere in 1 John is it said that the Spirit is the source of life! From the very beginning of his Letter, the author of 1 John identifies Jesus with life (1:2). Jesus is "the life that is eternal and that was in the presence of the Father." The Father "has sent his unique Son into the world so that we may live through him" (4:9). In 5:11-12, the author says: "And this is the witness, that God has

---

157. In the Wisdom of Solomon, eternal life was given to those who were "just." In the Johannine community, possession of eternal life was dependent upon a special gift of the Spirit. Yet in the third edition, the role of one's behavior again becomes important. Just how these two conceptions relate to one another is not altogether clear. It is perhaps possible that at the time of the second edition, belief in the promises of Jesus was the one "good deed" required. This would fit with the frequent observation that in the second edition the only "sin" is that of unbelief.

158. *Zōē* appears eleven times in the Letters, all in 1 John: 1:1, 2 (twice); 2:15, 25; 3:14, 15; 5:11, 12, 13, 16, 29. The verb *zaō* appears once: 1 John 4:9.

given us eternal life, and this life is in his Son. The one who has the Son has life; the one not having the Son of God does not have life." There is an emphasis and nuance here that were not present in the second edition of the Gospel. At the same time, the author could explain the purpose of writing 1 John as follows: so that the members of the community may "see that you have eternal life, believing in the name of the Son of God" (5:13). Finally, in his conclusion the author identifies the community as being "in the True One, in his Son, Jesus Christ. This one is the true God and eternal life" (5:20). Thus, he ends as he began, affirming the importance of having the Son as well as the Father in order to have eternal life.

(2) Eternal Life and Mutual Love

The second way that the author of 1 John modifies the overall theology of eternal life is by linking its possession with the performance of mutual love, the community's overall conception of ethical obligation. The believer has gone over from death to life, but this can be known from the fact that he/she loves his fellow community member (3:14; cf. 3:15). Thus, although in the Gospel (second edition) eternal life was dependent only upon belief, in 1 John it is dependent upon proper action as well as upon belief.

(3) The Future Dimension of Eternal Life

A third distinctive aspect of the author's treatment of eternal life is that it affirms both a present and a future dimension of that life. Perhaps the clearest statement of an expectation for the future by the author of 1 John appears in 2:17, where he says: "... the world is passing away along with its desire, but the one doing the will of God abides forever." But this future life also involves judgment. In a number of cases, his references are implicit. For example, he refers to "the last hour" (2:18 [twice]); he speaks of the future time when "[Jesus] is revealed" (2:28; 3:2); and he speaks of "his coming" (2:28). The fact that he speaks of the believer making the effort to make himself holy in anticipation of that day (3:3) implies judgment. There is also talk of the coming of the Antichrist (4:2), a figure associated with the end times. However, in 4:17, what had been implicit is made explicit in the reference to having courage "on the day of judgment."

At the same time, it would be wrong to conclude that the author of 1 John held to a belief in eternal life that had *only* a future dimension. That there is a realized element to his eschatology is clear from his comment in 3:14, where he sees brotherly love as being evidence that the believer has *already* passed from death to life.

Section 4. The Development of Johannine Theology: Eternal Life

(4) Eternal Life and Sin unto Death

In the closing verses of the Letter, the author speaks of yet another aspect of eternal life. In keeping with his conviction that God hears prayers, provided they are according to his will (5:14), the author urges the members of the community to ask God to give life to a brother "sinning a sin not unto death" (5:15). Just how the process was to take place is not clear, but it indicates a practice of prayer directed to the forgiveness of sin and the regaining of (eternal) life. Thus, although eternal life is "realized," it is not a once-and-for-all acquisition; it can be lost through sin.

These were all issues that were at stake between himself and his opponents.

(5) Bodily Resurrection in 1 John?

There are no explicit references to bodily resurrection in 1 John. And if the Letter was written after the Gospel, it is puzzling that there is no explicit mention of it as there is in the Gospel. Nevertheless, Schnackenburg finds an implicit reference in 3:2: "The Resurrection is obviously presumed here, for otherwise the word 'revealed' would be hardly intelligible. But either he [the author] has no interest in the resurrection of the body, or else he deliberately suppresses it. All he says is 'what we shall be.' Otherwise he is quite vague about it."[159] However, the statement "what we shall be" is simply an affirmation that there will be a future state of the individual that will be a completion and fulfillment of human existence; 3:2 says nothing about the nature of that future state.

R. E. Brown does not go as far as Schnackenburg but only comments that "the apocalyptic context favors" a belief in the resurrection.[160] It is true that bodily resurrection is often found in the context of an apocalyptic worldview, but, as was seen in our discussion of resurrection above, it is far from the case that *all* apocalyptic holds to such a view. Consequently, the mere presence of the apocalyptic genre cannot be an argument for seeing a reference to resurrection in 3:2.

If we read 1 John on its own terms and without reference to the Gospel, there would be no reason to think that the author held to a view of bodily resurrection, in 3:2 or elsewhere. The use of the verb "revealed" as applied to the believer does not imply resurrection; it simply implies the manifestation of a future status that will be different from the believer's present status. This is fully compatible with a view of spiritual immortality. Consequently, it must be said that there is no credible evidence of belief in bodily resurrection expressed in 1 John.[161]

---

159. Schnackenburg, *Epistles* 157.
160. R. E. Brown, *Epistles* 393.
161. This should not be interpreted as a denial of the Resurrection. We can say that bodily

In the light of the author's careful shaping of his argument throughout, it is significant that he makes no reference to bodily resurrection. Yet, as we shall see below, *at the time of the third edition, the author makes a special effort to link bodily resurrection with the future dimension of eternal life.* Evidently the question of a bodily dimension of this future life was not an issue at the time of 1 John. Consequently, it would seem that 1 John affirms neither simple spiritual immortality (since the Letter affirms a future judgment), nor a spiritual resurrection (since spiritual resurrection, which implies a break in existence, is precluded by the realized element of future life present in 1 John), nor bodily resurrection (as does the third edition of the Gospel).

Not only is this particular belief significant theologically, but it is another indication that 1 John represents a theological stage earlier than that of the third edition of the Gospel. It is highly unlikely that the community's belief would have changed *from* a bodily resurrection *to* a belief in the form of continuing spiritual existence subject to final judgment found in 1 John. Consequently, 1 John is almost certainly a witness to an earlier form of belief than that found in the third edition of the Gospel.

5. Eternal Life in the Third Edition

In the third edition, the basic understanding of eternal life and its offer by Jesus remains. However, some elements of its presentation undergo further change.

a. Jesus' Possession of Eternal Life

First is Jesus' own possession of eternal life. In 5:26a, we read the third author's most explicit statement about Jesus' own possession of life. The Father has given to the Son "to have life in himself." This expression emphasizes the fact that the Son has life *in the same way* as the Father does. Nowhere in the second edition or 1 John do we find anything that describes Jesus' possession of life in a way that identifies it so closely with the mode of the Father's possession of life!

b. Obedience and Eternal Life

Second, it is still the case that those who believe in Jesus will have eternal life (3:15, 16). But, as was the case in 1 John, the third author affirms that obedience

---

resurrection was not an issue about which the author of 1 John felt compelled to take a stand. Such was not the case at the time of the third edition.

Section 4. The Development of Johannine Theology: Eternal Life

is necessary for the believer to have eternal life: the one who does not obey the Son will not have life (3:36). Similarly, in 12:50 there is the statement in which Jesus proclaims that the commandment of the Father "is eternal life." This is another of the Gospel's elliptical statements whose full expression is that *obeying* the commandment of the Father *leads to* eternal life. While in 12:50 this is said of the commandment given *to Jesus,* it is undoubtedly intended to have implications for the believer also.

c. The Role of Jesus in the Bestowal of Eternal Life

Third, in the third edition, we notice an increased emphasis on Jesus as an essential element in the bestowal of life that serves as a balance over against the view of the Spirit as the principle of life. In the hymn of the Prologue, the Word is the agent of creation and it is stated that what came to be "in him [Jesus] was life" (1:4). In 8:12, there is a brief reference to Jesus as "the light of life," a phrase that echoes the symbolism and language of 1:4.[162]

This emphasis on the essential role of Jesus is also evident in 6:51-58. But there is a difference here. In the second edition, Jesus *was* the bread of life; in the third edition, Jesus is identified as *the Son of Man* and is said to *give* the bread of life that is the Eucharist. Thus, life is linked to Jesus. Also, in 14:6, Jesus proclaims that he is "the way, the truth, and the life." Throughout these additions of the third author, the focus is on the role of Jesus. Jesus is essential; one cannot have life only through the Spirit but must also have it through the Son (see 6:53, 54, 57).

d. Eternal Life and the Eucharist

A fourth difference from the earlier presentation of eternal life is that, in the third edition, possession of eternal life is also dependent upon participation in the community's ritual of the Eucharist. In 6:53, it is said that, unless you eat the flesh of the Son of Man and drink his blood, you do not have life in yourselves." This is repeated in v. 54: "The one feeding on my flesh and drinking my blood has eternal life. . . ." In 6:57, it is said that "the one feeding on me will live through me." This combines both the emphasis on the essential role of Jesus in

---

162. In 17:3, Jesus proclaims: "This is eternal life, that they know you, the only true God, and the one whom you have sent, Jesus Christ." Although phrased as an equation, the verse really describes one of the *effects* of having eternal life: that the believer will truly "know" God and Jesus.

eternal life and the necessity of participation in the ritual dimension of community life.

A fifth difference in the portrayal of life in the third edition is its explicit association with future bodily resurrection (5:29). For the author of the third edition eternal life is not only future spiritual existence beyond physical death but involves a future bodily resurrection. This is most explicitly affirmed in 5:28-29, where it is said that ". . . an hour is coming in which all those in the tombs will hear his voice and will come forth, those who have done good to a resurrection of life, those who have done evil to a resurrection of judgment." Here it appears as part of a complex of ideas affirming: (1) a future time of reckoning in which there will be (2) a general bodily resurrection, (3) a resurrection to life and one of judgment. It is the way in which this complex contrasts so sharply with the complex of ideas in vv. 24-25[163] that makes their distinctions so clear. This emphasis on bodily resurrection is also continued in the multiple statements that Jesus will "raise [the believer] up on the last day" (6:39, 40, 44, 54). In 11:25, in an example of synecdoche, Jesus affirms the central importance of the resurrection by proclaiming himself "the Resurrection and the Life" in the sense that he is the firstfruits of each and belief in him gives access to both.

6. The Background of the Presentation of Eternal Life in 1 John and in the Third Edition

The notion of life, both natural and eternal, in apocalyptic Judaism has much in common with more mainstream forms of Judaism but also has its own distinctive traits, as we shall see. The literature is considerable and so we will only be able to give a brief survey of some representative documents.

a. The Spirit and Natural Life

Evidence of the connection of spirit and life is not frequent in these writings, but it is certainly presumed, as can be judged from the contexts where it does appear. For example, in *TReu* 2:4 there is mention of "the spirit of life by which

---

163. In fact, it is precisely the contrast set up in these two sets of verses that makes it clear that the first complex was understood by the community (1) to refer first to a present spiritual life rather than a future one; (2) to make no reference to a concern for future physical life; (3) to assert that the future would involve nothing other than a continuation of the spiritual life begun before physical death; (4) and to warn those who did not have eternal life before death there would be no possibility of future events of any sort (resurrection of life or a resurrection of judgment) since without spiritual life, physical death was the final end of all existence.

Section 4. The Development of Johannine Theology: Eternal Life

the individual is brought into existence" *(prōton pneuma zōēs meth' hēs hē systasis ktizetai).*[164]

The spirit as the principle of life seems intended in 1QH 9:15, where, after speaking of the creation of the earth and the seas, he gives dominion "to the spirit of man which Thou hast formed in the world." Regularly humanity is described as "shaped from dust" (1QH 11:21; 12:29) and as having a corrupt spirit (1QH 11:21), which is purified by God (1QH 11:21) and by his holy spirit (1QH 8:21; 12:31). In the *T12P*, we also read (*TNaph* 2:2, 4): ". . . the Lord forms the body in correspondence to the spirit, and instills the spirit corresponding to the power of the body. . . . And just as the potter knows the use of each vessel and to what it is guided, so also the Lord knows to what extent the body will persist in goodness, and when it will be dominated by evil."

b. The Spirit and Eternal Life

In the SDQ, there are repeated references to various effects of the Spirit. Yet God is almost always presented as the effective agent who lifts up the community member to be with the angels or the "stars." The Spirit is the instrumental agent of God.[165] Nevertheless, there are two texts that speak of the role of the Spirit in eternal life.

The first text, 1QH 23 fragment 2 10-12, is partly corrupted but certainly speaks of eternal life as a result of the gift of the Spirit. The text, to which we have referred above, reads: ". . . and thou hast shed [Thy Holy] Spirit over dust . . . [to bring him into the company] of the 'gods' and unite them with the Sons of Heaven. . . . Thou hast shed Thy [Ho]ly [Spirit] to atone for guilt" *(CDSSE).* There is a parallelism in the two parts of the text. In each the Holy Spirit is granted to the individual, and in each a benefit of that reception of the Holy Spirit is described. In the first, the one made of dust (a common expression for humanity in 1QH) is given the Spirit and is then raised into the heavenly company, that is, eternal life. In the second, the giving of the Holy Spirit is said to atone for guilt for sin.

The second text (4Q385 2 5-8) is perhaps the clearest. This text is a reworking of Ezek 37:4-10, which had spoken of the process of instilling natural life into dead bones. However, in the present text, the same knitting together of

---

164. Although this is listed as the first of seven "spirits" that are generally thought to refer to dispositions within persons, this first spirit is of a different order.

165. The human is capable of little without the gift of the Spirit. In 1QH 18:6-7, the author admits his lack of strength and that he cannot be faithful without the spirit "that you have formed for me." It is also clear that the members of the Qumran community saw themselves as having already received the Holy Spirit in some form (1QH 4:26; 5:25; 15:7).

bones and sinews and the blowing in of the Spirit are used to describe the coming to life at the final resurrection.

In the *T12P* there is no explicit discussion of the Spirit as the principle of eternal life (nor is there an attribution of it to anything other than God). There is the almost constant affirmation of the presence of the Spirit of God (as opposed to the spirit of Beliar) and of this spirit as the influence of God upon the individual's life. There is a clear conviction of future eternal life in which the good will be "raised" (e.g., *TBenj* 10:7), but there is no discussion of the deeper principle of this life.

c. The Present Possession of Eternal Life in the Sectarian Documents of Qumran and the Testaments of the Twelve Patriarchs

In the SDQ and the *T12P*, we find close parallels to both the notion of an eternal life that has already begun and also to a notion of eternal life that will not be complete until some time in the future.[166]

The Qumran community believed that it lived in the last days, that eternal life was their present possession, and that it was to be continued in the future beyond death. This is evident in 1QS 4:6-8, 1QS 11:5-8, and 1QH 11:19-23. But this is a hope in eternal life without reference to bodily resurrection. J. J. Collins comments: "The glory that the elect hope to enjoy is a continuation of something that they already experience. This may explain why passages like the Instruction on the Two Spirits do not use the language of resurrection, and why death does not appear as a problem in these texts."[167]

d. "Having Life in Oneself"

The background of this notion is to be found in Wis 15:16-17.[168] There the author scolds those persons who make idols and worship them. He explains that a human being cannot make a real person because the person's spirit (his life) has been "lent" to him: "For a human made them, and one whose spirit had been lent to him made them. For no person is able to make a God like himself. For being mortal, he makes only a dead person with his lawless hands." Since they

---

166. Among the texts most commonly discussed in relation to the issue of future life are: 1QH 4:26, 32; 7:27-30; 9:20f.; 11:20-37; 12:22-23; 14:32-33, 37-38; 16:32; 18:5-7; 19:6-17, 27f.; 20:27-29; 21:14-16, 27-31, 34-38; 22:36-38; 23:23ff.; 25:3-16.

167. J. J. Collins, *Apocalypticism* 118. However, Puech (*Croyance* 425) would disagree and would argue that, in this text, eternal life is only anticipated, not already enjoyed.

168. See von Wahlde, "He Has Given."

Section 4. The Development of Johannine Theology: Eternal Life

are mortal, all humans can do is make "dead" gods. Thus, like God the Father, Jesus is said to have life "in himself," and so he can give life to others. This, then, is a claim to the very powers of the Father.

e. Eternal Life with Future Bodily Resurrection in the Sectarian Documents of Qumran and the Testaments *of the Twelve Patriarchs*

While there is disagreement about some individual texts, it is fair to say that there is general agreement among scholars that some texts in the SDQ and the T12P speak of eternal life as a present possession of the believer, a possession that will extend beyond death in a spiritual state. But with respect to the topic of bodily resurrection, the issue is more difficult and the disagreement more extensive.[169] Puech's *Croyance* is the most complete study of resurrection and eternal life at Qumran. In his two volumes, Puech has not only studied the antecedents of the concept as it is found at Qumran but has addressed all of the texts, both sectarian and other, which possibly provide evidence regarding the community's views of future life as well as the (contradictory) references to Essene beliefs in Josephus and Hippolytus and the evidence provided by the geographical orientation of the graves at Qumran. In spite of Puech's remarkable study, the discussion cannot be said to be settled.

In Puech's view, there are a number of texts from Qumran that speak of resurrection. These texts are both sectarian[170] and nonsectarian.[171] Recently, the matter has been reviewed by J. J. Collins, who disagrees with Puech regard-

---

169. Beyond the distinction between immortality and bodily resurrection, there are a variety of nuances. For example, not all texts speaking of resurrection seem to speak of bodily resurrection, nor do all texts referring to bodily resurrection necessarily refer to universal bodily resurrection (i.e., some seem to imply that only the good will be raised). Such distinctions are evident in the contrast between the way 1 John and the third edition portray eternal life in the future. While both affirm a future dimension different from that in the present, their understanding of the nature of that state is not the same. See the discussion below. For further details, see Nickelsburg, *Resurrection*.

170. Among the sectarian texts that refer to resurrection, Puech would include 1QH 5:29 (formerly 13:12) (*Croyance* 408-15); 1QH 14:32-33, 37-38 (= 6:32-33, 37-38) (*Croyance* 348-63); 1QH 19:10-14 (= 11:10-14) (*Croyance* 375-81). He would see some of the pre-Essene texts also as expressing a hope in resurrection (4QTest Qah 1 ii 3-8 and 4QVis^{c}Amr^f 1 ii). More importantly, he would also see a reference to resurrection in 4Q521 f2 ii 12; 4Q521 ff5+7 ii 6 (Puech, *Croyance* 684-92). Puech himself was responsible for the reconstruction and publication of the text of 4Q521 (DJD XXV, 1-38, pls. I-III) and would argue that it was probably a sectarian text and that it constitutes one of the oldest irrefutable texts of belief in the resurrection (*Croyance* 780).

171. Among the nonsectarian texts seen by Puech to contain references to resurrection is 4Q385 2 (Deutero-Ezekiel) (*Croyance* 605-16).

477

ing a number of texts.[172] Collins's own conclusion is that only one sectarian text can be determined with certainty to refer to bodily resurrection.[173] Two other texts that refer to bodily resurrection cannot be certainly identified as sectarian documents.[174] Thus, the disagreement between Puech and Collins is considerable.[175] Yet, in spite of this disagreement, these studies of the Qumran texts prove to be helpful for our present discussion.

If he resists seeing bodily resurrection as typical of the Qumran community, Collins would nevertheless recognize that "traditions about resurrection were clearly known at Qumran."[176] If there is ambiguity in the SDQ themselves about bodily resurrection, it is certain that the library of the community contained documents proposing such belief and that the community had not rejected them. Thus, at the very least, the scrolls from Qumran witness to something of a fluidity regarding the issue — with both views represented.

Collins sums up the views of the community in a paragraph that deserves to be quoted in full:

> The more distinctive sectarian idea does not entail resurrection, although it places great emphasis on eternal life. In the major sectarian rulebooks, eternal reward and punishment seem to follow directly on the life of the individual. Hence the need for a general resurrection seems to be obviated. It is possible that the sect still believed in a general, eschatological resurrection. Such an idea was familiar from the apocalypses and is nowhere denied. But the lack of clear references to resurrection in the major sectarian writings makes this belief purely hypothetical. The "messianic apocalypse" of 4Q521 seems to reflect at most a minority belief in the sect.[177]

---

172. J. J. Collins, *Apocalypticism* 110-29.

173. J. J. Collins here considers 4Q521 as likely to be sectarian (*Apocalypticism* 128).

174. J. J. Collins, *Apocalypticism* 126-28.

175. Puech attempts to take into account the way a given text relates to other biblical and nonbiblical texts (and even traditions) that reflect resurrection. Thus, he works within a different horizon than Collins, who focuses more on the specific wording of individual texts. The approaches are different; both are valuable. But the difference in approach does seem to account at least in part for the difference in results.

176. J. J. Collins, *Apocalypticism* 124. It could be argued that the preservation of documents such as *Deutero-Ezekiel* and the *Messianic Apocalypse* would indicate that their views were part of the range of ideas acceptable to the community. It is perhaps also true that theological unanimity should not be expected of those documents any more than it is of the NT.

Significant also in this regard is *Jub.* 23:30-31, which speaks of resurrection of the Spirit although the bones remain peacefully in the ground. Although *Jubilees* was known at Qumran, it was not written there.

177. J. J. Collins, *Apocalypticism* 129. Thus, in spite of his prior skepticism as to whether 4Q521 is a sectarian writing, Collins seems inclined to say it is.

Section 4. The Development of Johannine Theology: Eternal Life

This appears to be a fair assessment of the situation at Qumran. What is striking is that it may well also reflect something of the situation of the Johannine community during the periods represented by the second edition and 1 John! In the second edition of the Johannine Gospel, "eternal reward and punishment... follow directly on the life of the individual," a view that Collins predicates of the Qumran group. It has been noted above that in 1 John, although the apocalyptic worldview had been introduced and made the dominant worldview of the community — and although future judgment, which is the most common matrix for discussion of resurrection, is a major part of the belief of the Johannine community at the time, there is no clear reference in 1 John to belief in bodily resurrection. However, it would seem that, in the Johannine community, by the time of the third edition, this ambiguity was no longer acceptable and was resolved in favor of a view of eternal life that necessarily involved a bodily resurrection on the last day.

When we turn to the *T12P* we find a situation that is in some ways quite similar to that of the SDQ. In the *T12P* there are also a number of texts that refer to eternal life and that are thought by some to refer to bodily resurrection. *TAsh* 5:2 says: "Just deeds lead to life since eternal life puts off death" *(hypo zōēn [eisin] ta dikaia dio kai ton thanaton hē aiōnios zōē anamenei)*. Here there is no mention of resurrection but only of the life beyond death that awaits the just.

In *TAsh* 6:4, we read:

> For the final end of persons shows forth their righteousness making known the angels of the Lord and of Satan. For when the evil soul departs, it will be tormented by the evil spirit which he had served with its desires and evil deeds. But if quietly in joy, he will know the angel of peace who calls him to life.

This would seem to speak of future life without bodily resurrection.[178]

In *TSim* 6:7b[179] the patriarch is said to arise *(anastēsomai)* after the final judgment of evil. The notice is brief and ambiguous. *TJud* 25:1-5 speaks of the resurrection of Abraham, Isaac, and Jacob as well as of Judah and his brothers. There is also mention of judgment on Beliar. In *TZeb* 10:1-3 the patriarch makes a brief reference to the fact that he will rise again after a final judgment.[180]

TBenj 10:5-10 speaks of the future raising of Enoch, Seth, Abraham, Isaac, and Jacob and then the patriarchs "over their tribes." Then there will be a judg-

---

178. See also *TAsh* 7:3.
179. The two occurrences of the phrase "as a man" (in vv. 5 and 7c) are thought to be Christian interpolations and are not included. See Puech, *Croyance* 122.
180. Both of these scenarios reflect Dan 12:13.

ment over good and evil, first for Israel and then for all nations. Of all the descriptions of resurrection (and final judgment), this is the most detailed. Because this is the last of the *Testaments* and because of the parallels in expression to earlier statements (e.g., "being raised over the tribes"), it may be that this is the schema presumed in the earlier texts. But it is more difficult to know whether this is also true of the *Testament of Asher*, where the torment is not in punishment by God but by the evil spirit and the reward is made known by the angel of peace. It would seem likely that these are simply descriptions of other aspects of final judgment. However, the description of the future life bears close similarity to spiritual existence also in the terminology used. In short, the *T12P* do not present a unified, nor a clear, view of the future life.[181]

We have thus seen that there are relatively few texts in both the SDQ and the *T12P* that speak of bodily resurrection and that there continues to be ambiguity regarding other texts. Consequently, it would seem that the issue of bodily resurrection was not seen as central to the belief of the communities represented by these documents. It is likely that bodily resurrection was seen as one way of envisioning something that was considered much more central: their belief in life after death.

If we anticipate some of the conclusions from the discussion of eschatology (Section 5 below), we see that the issue of a future judgment involving reward for the good and punishment for the unjust is very well attested in the SDQ and the *T12P*, and is indeed central to the thought of the community at Qumran. This is evident from the numerous texts that describe it but also in the way scholars agree about its presence in the documents. Thus, the community's belief in final judgment is considerably clearer than that in bodily resurrection.

I have argued that the community at the time of the second edition of the Johannine Gospel held a view of eternal life that involved neither bodily resurrection nor final universal judgment. However, it is also clear from the pages of 1 John that while the community holds a belief in future universal judgment to be essential, the issue of bodily resurrection is not addressed. If the author considered the issue of bodily resurrection to be an essential belief of the community in his dispute with the opponents, one would expect it to be addressed in some way or at least alluded to; but it is not. The primary issue at the time of 1 John is future judgment and its implications for one's possession of eternal life, not the issue of bodily resurrection. Nevertheless, when we turn to the final edition of the Gospel, belief in future judgment leading to reward and punishment continues to be evident but this is unambiguously associated with bodily resurrection. Thus, it would seem that it was between the time of 1 John and the

---

181. Puech (*Croyance* 122-24) concludes that there is no clear belief in the resurrection in the *T12P*.

Section 4. The Development of Johannine Theology: Eternal Life

final edition of the Gospel that the issue of bodily resurrection had come into focus as a significant dimension of the community's belief.

If this reading is correct, the pages of 1 John would comprise the stage of development reflected in the SDQ, while the final edition of the Gospel would reflect a further stage in which bodily resurrection had become important enough to be expressed explicitly within the tradition. This is not to say that the Johannine tradition borrowed from or was dependent upon Qumran thought but simply that it reflects a similar development.[182]

f. Disputes over Immortality/Resurrection Elsewhere in Early Christianity

As a final note, it may be useful to point out that the conflict that arose within the Johannine tradition about the nature of eternal life was not unique to that tradition. There is evidence of considerable discussion in early Christianity whether, after death, the believer's life continued only in spiritual form or involved a final bodily resurrection.

One of the earliest disputes regarding the Resurrection is evident in 1 Cor 15:1-58. This may represent the earliest stage in the development of such conflict. The notion that there was no bodily resurrection is also evident in 2 Tim 2:18, where it is said that there are some "claiming that the resurrection has already taken place *(legontes [tēn] anastasin ēdē gegonenai).*" This is understood to refer to a spiritual "resurrection," which takes place in the gaining of new life. It is another way of expressing a belief in realized eschatology to the exclusion of a future physical existence. In his comments on the passage above, Conzelmann points to similar concerns in the *Acts of Paul* 14 ("that [the resurrection] has already occurred in the children we have").[183] The conflict is even clearer in the second century in the writings of Justin, who refers to opponents "who also say that there is no resurrection of the dead but at the time of their death, their souls are taken up into heaven" (*Dialogue with Trypho* 80.4).

---

182. Boismard *(Victory)* studies the notion of eternal life with and without bodily resurrection in the NT (and other texts). In his conclusion, Boismard makes the following comment: "Therefore, we are faced with the following fact. Biblical revelation teaches us with certainty the *fact* of our victory over death. But it is divided on the *how* of this victory.... We may conclude that the manner of our victory over death is not an object of revelation but remains an open question" (135). While Boismard addresses this to the modern Christian reader, it would seem that for the Johannine community, this would be far from true. By the time of the third edition, the tradition seems to affirm that the material aspect of life after death (i.e., bodily resurrection) is crucial and is essential to affirm.

183. Conzelmann, *Pastoral Epistles* 112.

A History of the Development of Johannine Theology

Clearly the problems of the Johannine community in this regard are not unique but are one instance of a set of questions being addressed by both Judaism and Christianity at the time. The issues are not the same in all cases, but the existence of a variety of views regarding the nature of life after death is clear.

SECTION 5. THE DEVELOPMENT OF JOHANNINE THEOLOGY: ESCHATOLOGY

Eschatology is used here to describe "last" events either of one's life or the time span of the world. Although the term was used originally to refer only to events thought to occur at the end of time, it is given a broader application since, in Johannine theology, some of those events are thought to occur at a decisive moment before the end of the world. As it applies to the Gospel of John, eschatology is concerned with three elements: (1) when does eternal life begin, now ("realized eschatology") or at some point in the future ("future eschatology"); (2) does the eschaton involve spiritual immortality or bodily resurrection; (3) does the eschaton involve a judgment that occurs in the present or does it refer to a future judgment at the end of time ("on the last day")? Of these elements of eschatology, the first and the third will be treated here. The nature of the life that continues after death (immortality or physical resurrection) was treated in the previous section, in connection with the understanding of the nature of eternal life. The second topic will be treated in Section 11 below.

The views of each edition of the Gospel are sketched out briefly below, together with some basic elements of the background of each.

1. Eschatology in the First Edition

In the material of the first edition as it remains within the present Gospel, there is no evidence of the author's belief regarding either the nature of eternal life, judgment, or the bodily resurrection of the faithful. But we are able to say something about the author's understanding of the Resurrection of Jesus.

In the present Gospel, there is only one post-Resurrection account stemming from the first edition (20:1, 11b-16). This is the account of Mary of Magdala discovering the empty tomb and then meeting Jesus in the garden. Mary does not recognize Jesus at first, but upon hearing his voice she realizes who it is. Although we could hope for more, we can at least say that there is no doubt that the first edition included an account of the appearance of the crucified Jesus. The account is simple and straightforward and reflects none of the issues that will become significant for the later editions.

Section 5. The Development of Johannine Theology: Eschatology

2. Eschatology in the Second Edition

When we turn to the second edition, we find considerable concern for eschatology. In this edition, we read that one's possession of eternal life begins with the believer's reception of the Spirit. In this view, the believer is said to have "crossed over from death to life" and will not come into judgment (5:24). Within the Johannine tradition, "judgment" carries the negative connotation of "declaring guilty," and so, in this view, the one who does not believe does not receive life and so is declared guilty and does not pass over from death to life.

For those who do not believe, there is judgment and no eternal life. This life to which the believer has passed over is, as we have seen in the previous section, eternal life — the life of God. It is a life that begins in the present age and continues beyond physical death. This eschatology is often called "realized" or "present" eschatology.

The second edition's presentation of this conception of eschatology is done in a "positive" way and not in such a way as to explicitly exclude other views of the nature of life after death.[184] If we were to read only the material of the second edition dealing with eschatology, it would be difficult to know whether this view of eternal life deliberately excluded any notion of a future bodily resurrection. However, when the material of the second edition dealing with eschatology is placed alongside that of 1 John and the additions of the third author, the extensive contrasts make clear how this view of eschatology was in fact understood. And it becomes clear that this understanding of eternal life was considered insufficient by the author of 1 John and by the author of the third edition. As we shall see in detail below, the author of 1 John introduces an emphasis on future eschatology, which carried with it the conviction of a future judgment (in the neutral sense) to which all are subject.[185]

It would be wrong, however, to polarize these views of eschatology excessively. It is *not* simply a case of a conviction regarding realized eschatology in the second edition and one of future eschatology in 1 John. Rather, the second

---

184. The author of the third edition was able to say in 3:18 that "the one who does not believe has already been judged" and, for him, this does not exclude the fact of another condemnation ("judgment") at the end of time.

185. It is curious that R. E. Brown (*Epistles* 669), in his discussion of 2 John 7, makes the observation that ". . . the adversaries may be denying the parousia, an error that has no exact parallel in GJohn and I John, although there are strains in the former work and in secessionist thought that would deemphasize the parousia." The notion of the parousia is necessarily connected with an apocalyptic view of the world, as Brown himself recognizes (*Epistles* 381), and is incompatible with the view of realized eschatology espoused by the opponents. This difference is also apparent in the contrast between texts such as John 5:24-26 (2E) (which speak of no future judgment) and John 5:28-29 (3E) (which refer to a future judgment of all at the end of time). Such a judgment necessarily involves the parousia of Christ.

edition *introduces* a view of realized eschatology into the Gospel, and the third edition *introduces* the notion of a future eschatology. The First Letter of John *does not deny* realized eschatology but only *supplements* it.[186] This is evident both from an analysis of the text of 1 John, which itself contains references to both realized and future dimensions of eschatology, but also from the third edition, which contains references to both realized and future eschatology. We will see more of this below.

a. Eternal Life in the Present

One of the major aspects of realized eschatology is its conviction of the present possession of eternal life. This was treated in the discussion of eternal life and will not be repeated here. Within the second edition, the emphasis is on the present as the decisive moment; no significance is given to the future other than to the conviction that the life that begins now extends beyond (physical) death and continues without end. In 4:23, Jesus states: "But an hour is coming and is now here...." In 5:24, we read that the believer "has crossed over from death to life." In 5:25, we have a clear expression of present actuality of that transformation: "... an hour is coming, and is now present, when the dead will hear the voice of the Son of God, and those hearing it will live." In v. 25, the emphasis on the present is so great as to be almost a denial of a future eschatology.

In the second edition, this eternal life is understood in terms of continued existence of one's spirit beyond physical death and there are no references to bodily resurrection for the believer.

b. References to Judgment

It is striking at first that, within the second edition, there are only three references to judgment (5:24, 30 [twice]).[187] In 5:24, Jesus affirms that the one who believes does not come into judgment. There is, then, only one other reference

---

186. I would hold this to be true from a theological point of view. However, the literary interweaving of these viewpoints, particularly in 5:24-25 and 26-29, is difficult. For example, the author of the second edition says that the one who believes "does not come into judgment" (5:24). This is true in one sense; but, from the point of view of the third author and of 1 John, it is possible for the person who was at one time a believer to sin and so rise on the last day to a resurrection of judgment (5:29) because the criterion for a resurrection of life and a resurrection of judgment according to the third author is whether the person has "done good" or "done evil" (5:29), not just whether the person has believed or not.

187. For the listing of all occurrences of *krinō* and *krisis* in the Gospel, see 3E-17.

to judgment in the second edition (5:30), and this statement, while affirming that Jesus judges, is not particularly helpful in determining the particulars of the second edition's view toward judgment. Consequently, although the notion of judgment inevitably played a role in the theology of the second edition, we can say little about it.[188]

3. The Background of the Eschatology in the Second Edition

Our attempt to determine the background of the eschatology of the second edition involves both parallels to the conception of a life beyond death as well as the notion of judgment. We have seen the background for the understanding of eternal life above. Here we will focus on the parallels to the notion of judgment associated with the second edition.

In the Old Testament, the notion of eschatology is present although it does not receive the the same attention and is not as developed as it is in later Jewish literature, especially apocalyptic. In the Old Testament, eschatology is related to the conviction that God is judge (e.g., Gen 18:25; Ps 9:7-8). This judgment is to reward the righteous (e.g., Pss 1:5-6; 72:2-4; 96:13) but also to punish those who are evil (e.g., Amos 5:18-20; Isa 2:12; Zeph 1:14-18). A common term used by the prophets to speak of the time of judgment was "the day of the Lord" (e.g., Amos 5:18-20; Zeph 1:14-18), "on that day" (e.g., Isa 24:21), and "the days are coming" (Jer 9:25-26). In Isa 2:1 (cf. 2:12) and Mic 4:1 there are references to "the days to come" in which the mountain of the Lord will be exalted above other mountains. This judgment occurs entirely within history. However, in the later books of the Old Testament, there are some indications of judgment beyond history, especially Dan 12:3, although Daniel is properly classed as an apocalyptic work.

For the first time in the deuterocanonical Wisdom of Solomon, there is clear evidence of belief in the reward of eternal life beyond physical death. God has created humanity for immortality (1:12-15; 2:21-24; 3:1-9; 5:15). The righteous, although they suffer in this life, are rewarded in future life (3:13b-15; 4:7). The wicked doubt this and bring death on themselves by their actions (1:16) They are punished (3:10) and will be brought to account on the day of judgment

---

188. Judgment is mentioned again in 8:15, but there the term does not seem to refer to "judgment" in the sense of adjudication of right and wrong but simply to the formation of an opinion. If it were not for 5:30, the question would present itself whether "judgment" in the sense of adjudication actually played a role in the second edition. The major emphasis on Jesus as judge in the third edition would also seem to suggest that there had been no emphasis on Jesus as judge in the second edition but only as the giver of the Spirit and therefore the giver of life.

(3:18; 4:20). Thus, there is a clear affirmation of both eternal life (without bodily resurrection) and of a future day of judgment. The possession of eternal life in Wisdom appears to be a present possession immediately after death. However, the relation between this and the day of judgment is not clear. Moreover, there is no evidence that this immortality is thought to begin before the moment of death as it does in the second edition.

A hint of a similar view is also evident in 2 Maccabees, a book that also betrays Hellenistic influence. Earlier we have seen passages that speak of resurrection; here we call attention to allusions to a future judgment of the unrighteous. Because of the narrative character of the book, there is little specific discussion of future judgment in spite of the fact that there are several references to future life. However, in 2 Macc 7, the seven brothers remind the king that he will have no resurrection of life (7:14). This is contrasted with the hope of resurrected life that inspires the brothers and is meant to contrast with it. Thus, it seems best to say that the background for the conception of eschatology in the second edition is found only imperfectly in either the Hebrew or Greek canons of the First Testament.

4. Eschatology in 1 John

a. The View of the Opponents

The author of 1 John does not explicitly confront the eschatological views of his opponents. Nor does he explicitly contrast his views with theirs. Rather, he speaks so clearly of his own views and their implications that it becomes clear that the opponents do not believe in a future eschatology of any sort.

b. The View of the Author

The author of 1 John held a view of eschatology that was *both* realized *and* future.[189] Future eschatology refers to the conviction that there will be events dealing with salvation or judgment at some future time and involving the return of Jesus. Thus, a reference to "the last day" may point to a future eschatology even if it does not speak specifically of the events to take place on that day (e.g., physical resurrection and/or judgment). References either to physical resurrection or final judgment also indicate a future eschatology even without mention of "the last day." The author of 1 John clearly believes in future eschatology.

---

189. On this, see also R. E. Brown, *Epistles* 26, 110.

Section 5. The Development of Johannine Theology: Eschatology

(1) The "Last Day" or the "Last Hour"

One of the most frequent indications of future eschatology in 1 John is the belief in an end of history. However, the author of 1 John is not concerned to write a theoretical treatise on eschatology but to address the crisis of the community. Within his horizon, rather than thinking of the "last day" (as the author of the third edition will be), the author speaks of the "last hour." The nature and extent of the crisis the community is facing indicates to him that *this* is the "last hour" (2:18 [twice]) and that the Antichrist has *already* appeared (4:3).

(2) A Future Coming of Jesus

The author also believes in a Second Coming of Jesus. In 2:28, the author explains that "When he is revealed," the believer is to "have confidence and not shrink from him at his coming."[190] The notion of "confidence" implies the reality of judgment or of reward and the hope with which the believer should approach it. This is even clearer in 4:17, where the author again speaks of having confidence on "the day of judgment."

(3) A Final Judgment

In 4:17, as we have just seen, the author of 1 John makes his only explicit reference to the "day of judgment." But although he does not use the term "judgment" elsewhere, he uses functional equivalents. For example, in 2:28 (discussed above) he refers to the believer having confidence and not shrinking from Jesus at his coming. This indicates that there will be an act of judgment at that coming. In both 2:28 and in 4:17, it is a matter of having confidence on that day, an even clearer indication that a day of judgment is referred to in both instances.

(4) A Future State of Eternal Life Different from the Present

The author of 1 John teaches that the believer has eternal life in the present. Yet the fact that all believers can undergo a future judgment indicates that, for the author of 1 John, the believer does not yet exist in a state of eternal life that makes sin impossible.

---

190. The author also proclaims that "the world is passing away along with its desire." Whether this is meant to echo the imminence of the end of the world is not certain. It certainly is compatible with a belief that the final appearance of Jesus is to take place within their lifetime.

In 3:2, the author makes clear that there is a difference between the present state of the believer and his future state: ". . . now we are children of God, and it has not yet been revealed what we will be. We know that when he [Jesus] is revealed, we will be like him. . . ." Thus, the author thinks of the time between the present and the future revelation of Jesus as a time in which the believer is to work at becoming more like Christ, and this will be the basis for confidence — and reward. As 3:3 says: "Everyone having this hope in him makes himself holy, as that one is holy."

In 4:12, the author asserts that "[i]f we love one another, . . . [God's] love is brought to perfection in us." This again recognizes a process by which one must strive to become perfect and reflects a view that is different from the perfectionism proclaimed by the opponents. This is even clearer in 4:17, where the author again speaks of having confidence on "the day of judgment (because, just as that one [Jesus] is, so are we, in this world)." Thus, the believer has come to imitate the life and holiness of "that one" [Jesus] and so has confidence. Yet, in spite of the present possession of eternal life, sin is still possible. This, then, clearly implies the distinction between the inchoative possession of eternal life now and the full possession of it after the final judgment.

So we see that the eschatology of 1 John differs greatly from that of the second edition. It does not deny the earlier view but complements it with belief in a future dimension of life and of judgment. Yet, as we shall see below, this conception of future eschatology is not precisely the same as that held by the author of the third edition.

5. The Background of Eschatology in 1 John[191]

In our discussion of the eschatology of 1 John, we spoke of the specific understanding of eternal life, of judgment, and of bodily resurrection found there. In the section on eternal life above, we saw that the SDQ held to a view that combined the present possession of eternal life with a consummation of that life in the future. Here we will indicate the views of the SDQ and the *T12P* on future judgment.[192]

According to J. J. Collins, the notion of a future judgment beyond history is typical of all apocalyptic and is a feature that distinguishes apocalyptic from the earlier biblical tradition. As Nickelsburg has shown, the first references to

---

191. In the matter of eschatology, the discussion of the background of 1 John is separated from that of the background for the third edition. The reason for this will be apparent below.

192. See also the overview of eschatology in the Hebrew Bible in J. J. Collins, *Expectation* 74-90.

Section 5. The Development of Johannine Theology: Eschatology

future judgment appear in contexts where they functioned to bring justice to those who had led a good life but died because of persecution — without reward from God in this life.[193] However, in later texts, the conception of a future judgment was not connected with issues of unjust persecution and death but simply in a context where a final judgment was meted out on the basis of one's behavior in this life, that is, on the basis of one's good or evil actions. It is this latter stage that is closest to the view in 1 John (and in the third edition) since the issue there is recompense for one's behavior.

a. In the Sectarian Documents of Qumran

The SDQ also hold to a notion of future judgment. The SDQ sometimes use the term "judgment," but they also regularly describe it as "visitation." One of the most well-known examples is that of 1QS 4:8-14, which describes in detail the "visitation" of those who walk in each spirit. For those who walk in the Spirit of Truth it will be "eternal joy in life without end," but for the others it will be "everlasting damnation by the avenging wrath of the fury of God." Two verses later 1QS 4:16 sums up the two alternatives at the final judgment: "And the whole reward for their deeds shall be, for everlasting ages, according to whether each man's portion in their [the two spirits] two divisions is great or small" *(CDSSE)*. It will be noticed that here the recompense is based on deeds rather than cast within the realm of unjust persecution and death.

Such judgment at Qumran also was expressed in a suprapersonal sense in 1QM, which speaks of the ultimate defeat of the forces of evil in the great war to come between the sons of light and the sons of darkness.[194] For example, 1QM 1:5: "[. . . There] will follow a time of salvation for the people of God and a period of rule for all the men of his lot, and of everlasting destruction for all the lot of Belial."

b. In the Testaments of the Twelve Patriarchs

In the *T12P,* both the concept of a final judgment and of the "last days" in which it takes place are similar to those of the rest of apocalyptic and in the material of

---

193. J. J. Collins (*Apocalypticism* 110) comments: "The belief in the judgment of individuals after death is one of the crucial elements that distinguish apocalyptic writings from earlier biblical tradition." Also: "All the apocalypses . . . involve a transcendent eschatology that looks for retribution beyond the bounds of history" (*Imagination* 9). Nickelsburg, *Resurrection* 19-140.

194. See J. J. Collins, *Imagination* 133-41.

the Johannine third edition. The notion of "judgment" is established in *TLev.* *TLev* 1:1; 3:3 speak of "the day of judgment" *(hēmera kriseōs)*; 4:1 says that "you know that the Lord will pass judgment" *(poiēsei . . . krisin)*; 18:2 says: "and he [the Lord] will pass a judgment of truth on the earth in the fullness of days."

Other Testaments also reflect this notion in their repeated references to the events at the end of time. *TBenj* 10:6-11 gives a detailed description of the "raising up" (resurrection) of the patriarchs and then the sons of the patriarchs, and their exaltation as heads of the tribes. "Then all will be changed, some for glory, others for dishonor. The Lord will judge all Israel and then the nations."

Repeated references to "the last days" and related concepts also appear in other texts in the *T12P*, emphasizing this future eschatology. *TJud* 18:1; *TZeb* 8:2; 9:5 speak of events "in the last days" *(en tais eschatais hemerais)*. Others of the Testaments have similar expressions. *TIss* 6:1 refers to events "in the last times" *(en eschatois kairois)*. *TReu* 6:8 mentions "the consummation of times" *(teleiōsis chronōn)*.

c. Elsewhere in Apocalyptic Judaism

During the second century before the time of Christ, passages such as Dan 7:26-27 and 12:1-3 speak of a judgment that is conducted beyond history and which leads to everlasting life and to punishment. In *1 Enoch,* there is a long description (chapters 51–54) of the preparations for judgment especially in 54:7 ("And in those days, the punishment of the Lord of the Spirits shall be carried out . . .") *(OTP)*. The same appears in 4 Ezra 14:35 ("For after death the judgment will come, when we shall live again; and then the names of the righteous will become manifest, and the deeds of the ungodly will be disclosed") *(OTP)*.[195]

6. Eschatology in the Third Edition

In the third edition of the Gospel, as in 1 John, the author asserts that the decisive moment for the believer is not just in the present. Rather, eternal life, which the believer receives with the gift of the Spirit, begins in the present but is not perfected until the future. Thus, there will be a future time in which

---

195. See also 2 *Bar.* 24:1: "For behold, the days are coming, and the books will be opened in which are written the sins of all those who have sinned, and moreover, also the treasuries in which are brought together the righteousness of all those who have proven themselves to be righteous" *(OTP)*.

Section 5. The Development of Johannine Theology: Eschatology

there is both a bodily resurrection and a final action of Jesus leading to reward or condemnation.[196]

a. Passages with a Present Eschatology

As we have seen in the essay on eternal life in the third edition, the third author affirms the present reality of eternal life. Within the third edition the author also speaks (3:17, 18, 19) of judgment in the present. As was indicated above, it is not a matter of the author disagreeing with realized eschatology but rather of complementing it with a future dimension. Although this may be surprising at first, it is clear from 1 John that the issue for the community was not "either" realized "or" future judgment but a matter of "both/and."[197] In addition, the notion of realized judgment in the third edition (i.e., 3:16-21) is not precisely the same as that of the second edition, because this judgment involves evaluation of behavior as well as of belief. As we shall see in more detail below, in the second edition the only "sin" is unbelief. However, in 1 John and in the third edition, the ethical dimension of life (sin) also involves the believer's behavior. Thus, in the third edition, the author speaks of those who love the darkness more than the light because "their works were sinful" (3:19). Their behavior orients them to unbelief. It is evident again in 3:21, where it is said that "the one who does the truth comes to the light so that his works may be manifest, that they have been done in God." These works are elements of the judgment, not just whether one believes in Jesus or not.

---

196. It should not be surprising that there was a disagreement within the Johannine community over the nature of judgment and of eternal life since there is evidence of such disputes elsewhere in early Christianity. One example can be found in Polycarp's *Letter to the Philippians* 7:1, where he says: "And whoever twists the sayings of the Lord to their own desires and says that there is no resurrection nor judgment, this one is the first born of Satan."

197. Consequently, we cannot say that the presence of realized eschatology is evidence of the second edition. The presence of realized eschatology does indicate that the material is not from the first edition, but we need to look to other factors to determine whether passages involving realized eschatology come from the second or third edition. Another way of saying this is that the second author *introduces* realized eschatology while the third author *takes over* this realized eschatology and *introduces* future eschatology.

Boismard ("L'Évolution" 507-24) argues that the realized and future eschatology came from different literary strata in the Gospel. However, the situation is more complex. Boismard-Lamouille cite 1 John as an example of future eschatology, but there is also realized eschatology in 1 John. Both in 1 John and in the third edition of the Gospel it is a matter of the authors complementing the view of realized eschatology with that of a future dimension.

b. Passages with a Future Eschatology

In the third edition, the author speaks of the coming of an "hour" (5:28-29), as did the author of the second edition. However, in the third edition, this "hour" is a reference to the last day, as is clear from that fact that it is coupled with the mention of final bodily resurrection. In addition to this, there are several other explicit references to "the last day" (6:39, 40c, 44c, 54b). These are concentrated in chapter 6 and are associated with bodily resurrection. The "last day" is also associated with judgment in 5:29, where those who emerge from the tombs will be subject to judgment. In keeping with this apocalyptic worldview, Jesus (identified as Son of Man) will be the judge.[198]

In chapter 12 (12:47 [twice], 48 [twice]), the third author again speaks of judgment in the future ("on the last day"). Here also there is no doubt that the comments about judgment are in an apocalyptic context and are surrounded by features that are associated with the third edition. The theology of this passage addresses concerns of the third edition. Jesus did not come to judge; his first intention was to save, not to judge. But that does not mean that he will not judge at all. Jesus explains that his word will be the judge. This is elliptical. His word will not do the judging, but the fact that he had spoken and they had heard it but not heeded it will be the cause of their judgment. Jesus then explains that the importance of his word is in the fact that it is really the word of the Father. And the Father had given Jesus a commandment about what to say. Thus, judgment will be related to the failure of the listener to take sufficiently seriously the historical words of Jesus.

c. Passages of the Third Edition Where the Time Aspect of Judgment Is Less Clear

In chapter 8, judgment appears three times, all of which are in the third edition. The fact that the references to judgment are added to an earlier text is evident from the awkward way each relates to its context. For example, it is evident that 8:14c-16a interrupts the original sequence of 8:14b-16b. In the original sequence of the second edition the issue was the validity of the *witness* of Jesus. It was explained that the witness of Jesus was valid because Jesus was not alone and the witness of two persons was valid. However, 8:14c-16a now interrupts that sequence and the relation of Son to Father is made the basis for

---

198. In Dan 7:14, the office of judge is reserved for the Ancient of Days, but it is attributed to the Son of Man in *1 Enoch* (cf. 49:4; 61:9; 62:2; 63:11; 69:27). See the discussion in Schnackenburg, *Gospel* 2:107.

Section 5. The Development of Johannine Theology: Eschatology

judgment. Thus, the unity of Father and Son is stressed as a basis for both judgment and for witness.

The appearance of the theme of judging in 8:26 is also awkward. Apart from the phrase "and to judge regarding you," the topic of 8:26 is the importance of the word of Jesus.[199] In this context, the words about judgment are an intrusion. Not only do they interrupt the surrounding sequence, but they are not developed in what follows. This is a clear indication of a gloss by the third author. But again the fact of judgment is what is stressed rather than an explicit distinction between realized and future, although it may be that a future judgment is implied by the fact that Jesus himself will do the judging.

The final reference to judgment in the chapter appears in 8:50. Again the mention of judgment is brief and awkward. Although v. 47 had clearly been speaking about the words of Jesus and although v. 51 clearly returns to (continues) that theme, vv. 48-50 do not relate to this. Those verses speak of demon possession and Jesus' refutation of the charge that he is possessed. It is in this context that the brief mention of the Father's judging appears. Although the brief statement may be an "appendage," it seems more likely that vv. 48-50 are a reworking of other material.

To this point we have spoken of the judgment that affects humanity. We have seen that this judgment has two "moments" to it. The first is an affirmation by the third author of the reality of judgment in the present (thus also affirming the view of the second author) (3:19). Also in keeping with his apocalyptic viewpoint, the third author affirms a moment of judgment of the individual at the end of time. But the author speaks of yet another moment in which the death of Jesus breaks the hold of Satan on the world. Jesus describes this as the "judgment of this world" — the moment when the "ruler of this world" is thrown out (12:31; cf. 14:30; 16:11). This is a judgment of a different type, one in which the power of Satan in the world is broken.

7. The Background of Eschatology in the Third Edition

We have seen above (in connection with the eschatology of 1 John) that the third author's conception of future judgment has parallels in the SDQ and the T12P. Consequently, there is no need to discuss that background further here. However, it may be helpful to recall that the conception of eschatology in the third edition is not identical with that of 1 John.

Like the author of 1 John, the author of the third edition focuses on future

---

199. It will be recalled that this is the overriding theme of 8:12-59 in the second edition. The theme is preserved and expanded in the third edition.

judgment in relation to one's behavior. Good and evil behavior will be brought to account in a future judgment. However, the third author differs from the author of 1 John in that he makes it clear that this future judgment will involve a bodily resurrection. As we have seen, in 1 John there is no mention of bodily resurrection. However, by the time of the Gospel's third edition, bodily resurrection had become a significant point of the community's belief. We have seen previously that disputes over both judgment and resurrection are attested elsewhere in early Christianity, both inside and outside the canonical writings. The Johannine tradition would seem to be another witness to such a dispute.

SECTION 6. THE DEVELOPMENT OF JOHANNINE THEOLOGY: KNOWING GOD

The verb "to know" *(ginōskein)* appears over 130 times in the Gospel and over forty times in the Letters and is one of the most distinctive terms of Johannine vocabulary. Not all instances are theologically significant, but even when these are excluded, the number is remarkable. The fact that the concept appears so often in the Gospel is one of the primary factors leading many scholars in the past to speak of the Gospel as somehow related to Gnosticism.

1. Knowing God in the First Edition

In spite of the importance of the term "know" in the Gospel as a whole, there is no theologically significant discussion of knowing God in the first edition. The verb appears in a nontheological sense, but those texts are not of importance for our study. In addition, there are a few scattered references to knowing whether Jesus is "from God" (e.g., 3:2; 7:27; 9:29-30), but their use in these instances is hardly the same as that sense of "knowing" that becomes so important in the later editions of the Gospel.[200]

2. Knowing God in the Second Edition

The author of the second edition introduces the theological sense of "knowing" and makes it a central category for his assessment of persons. The paradigm for

---

200. In 3:2, Nicodemus says to Jesus: "We know that you have come as a teacher from God." This claim to knowledge does not have the same connotation as the use in the second edition. The use in 3:2 is essentially the same as that in 7:27 and 9:29-30.

Section 6. The Development of Johannine Theology: Knowing God

true knowing is the mutual relationship of the Father and the Son. The Father knows Jesus (10:15), and Jesus knows the Father (7:29; 8:55 [twice]; 10:15; 17:25). Moreover, Jesus knows "his own" (10:14).[201] Those whom Jesus meets are expected to "know" (7:17; 10:38 [twice]), and in fact his own do know Jesus (10:4, 5, 14, 27; also implicit in 1:11;[202] and the instances associated with the disciples below). But knowing Jesus in this sense is not a human accomplishment. John the Baptist admits that he did not know Jesus (1:31, 33) and says that those who were listening did not know Jesus (1:26).

In the second edition, not knowing is consistently looked upon as culpable. For example, such seems to be the case with the Samaritan woman who does not know (4:10). But by far it is "the Jews" who do not know. They do not know (1) the Father (7:28; 8:19, 27, 55; 16:3; 17:25); (2) Jesus (8:19; 16:3); (3) "these things" (3:10); (4) or the parable about the sheep and the shepherd (10:6). At the same time "the Jews" say they know the father and mother of Jesus (6:42). They also claim to know Jesus, but actually they do not (7:28); and they claim to know where Jesus is from, but actually they do not (7:28). In addition to "the Jews," the world (1) is supposed to know that the Father has sent Jesus (17:23), (2) but in fact it did not know the Father (17:25).

It is only the disciples (who are probably to be considered identical with "his own") who truly know, but even they do not do so fully until after the Resurrection. It is noteworthy that it is almost entirely within the Farewell Discourses that the Gospel speaks of the disciples as "knowing." What they know is expressed with some variety but is focused on their knowing the Father (14:7, 7) and knowing Jesus (14:7). They will know that Jesus is in the Father, and the Father in him (14:20); they know the way Jesus is going (14:4). They know that the Father sent Jesus (17:25), that Jesus has come forth from the Father (17:8), and that all Jesus has the Father has given him (17:7). Yet in spite of this the disciples' knowing is still incomplete before Jesus' glorification (12:16; 13:7 [twice]; 14:9; 16:18, 30).

As can be seen from this review, "knowing" and "not knowing" truly are central concepts in the second edition.[203] Yet when this concept is placed within the larger context of the Gospel, several other related features increase the utter distinctiveness of the presentation. We will look briefly at four of these.

---

201. Jesus also knows what is going to happen (2:24, 25; 5:6, 42; 6:6, 15, 61, 64; 13:1, 3, 11; 16:19; 18:4; 19:28). Although these are features of the second edition, I do not think that their function is the same as the instances now being studied. There is no evidence of a claim on the part of community members or opponents of an ability to know future events as Jesus did.

202. In 1:10-11, the response of "the world" (v. 10) is contrasted with that of Jesus' "own" (v. 11). The world is said not to "know" Jesus, and his own are said to accept him. In this context it is evident that his own "know" him.

203. The failure to understand, which is presented as repeated "misunderstandings" of the message of Jesus, is due to the absence of the Spirit. See Leroy, *Rätsel* 188-91.

A History of the Development of Johannine Theology

a. Knowing Persons, Not Doctrine

In the second edition, the primary focus of knowing is on God the Father and on Jesus. Associated with this is knowing where Jesus is from. Ultimately this knowing should result in belief in Jesus. But it is not a matter of knowing "things" or doctrine; it is a matter of truly recognizing who Jesus is, his true identity, which includes his relation to the Father as well as his origin in the Father.

b. Teacher and Teaching

In the second edition, only Jesus and the Father are said to teach.[204] Jesus is said by the narrator (7:14, 28) and by Jesus himself (8:20; cf. 7:17) to teach. In 8:28, Jesus explains that he was taught by the Father (cf. also 7:16).[205] There is no hint of the disciples teaching during the ministry or in the future. Even in the third edition, the office attributed to the disciples is one of "witness" (15:27). This contrasts with the presentation of the disciples in the Synoptics, where they are said to teach during the ministry (Mark 6:30) and to be commissioned to teach in the future (Matt 28:20).

c. The Language of the Gospel

It can also be observed how different and distinctive is the language of the Gospel of John. It is regularly remarked that the diction of Jesus here is considerably different from his diction in the Synoptics. This is generally explained by attributing the actual formulation of the words on the lips of Jesus to the prophetic function of the Spirit within the community.[206]

d. Direct Knowledge of God and "Tradition"

In the second edition, there is a notable lack of attention to the content of the teaching of Jesus except insofar as it bears on the person of Jesus himself and insofar as it relates to the promise of the Holy Spirit. One of the more famous

---

204. The notion appears in all three editions. As a title, the notion of Jesus as "teacher" comes primarily from the first edition (1:38; 3:2; 11:28; 20:16). In the trial before the high priests, his message is referred to as his teaching by the narrator (18:19) and by Jesus himself (18:20). In the third edition, Jesus acknowledges the title as applied to him by the disciples (13:13, 14).

205. It will be noticed that in the third edition, the author attributes the role of teacher to Jesus (6:59) but also to the Spirit (14:26), although the Spirit is also referred to as witnessing (15:26).

206. On this see, for example, Smith, *Theology* 79. See also Smith, *John* 39.

Section 6. The Development of Johannine Theology: Knowing God

comments of Bultmann about the Johannine Jesus was that he was "a revealer without a revelation."[207] Although this has been hotly disputed, there is much truth in the statement, particularly when all "revelation" dealing with the identity of Jesus' own character is excluded.[208] It is true (and essential) to point out that among the revelations of Jesus in the Gospel is his promise that, when he goes to the Father, he will send the Spirit to those who believe in him. Yet beyond this, the primary focus is on the identity of Jesus himself.

However, if, in accord with Old Testament thinking, the community conceives of itself as having received the eschatological Spirit, then it will be the Spirit within them who will "reveal" what is to be known, and there will be no need for a historical record of the words of Jesus. While the conviction that the Spirit was the source of knowing is confirmed by Old Testament texts and by the lack of focus on the content of revelation in the Gospel, this is even more clearly brought into focus by the way the role of the Spirit is reformulated in 1 John and in the third edition. In both the third edition and in 1 John there is a clear emphasis on the importance of the historical words of Jesus and the necessity of remaining faithful to them. Thus, just as is the case with a number of other theological concepts introduced in the second edition, it is not until we read 1 John that we are able to understand how this concept was being interpreted within the community and to confirm that this understanding became a point of contention and formed part of the crisis between the author of 1 John and his opponents. As we will see below in the discussion of knowledge in 1 John and in the third edition, even though the actual amount of specific, concrete teaching of Jesus remains minimal, what changes is the general attitude toward the abiding importance of the "words of Jesus."

3. The Background of the Concept of Knowing God in the Second Edition

In the Old Testament, "knowing" Yahweh is a complex term referring both to actual knowledge and to the action which follows from that knowledge. It is a repeated lament of the prophets that in the past the people of Israel did not know Yahweh. For example, Isa 1:2-4 says: "The ox knows its owner, and the donkey its master's crib; but Israel does not know, my people do not understand" (NRSV). Jeremiah's lament is even stronger (9:2-3): "For they are all

---

207. Bultmann, *Theology* 2:66. This view is also taken up by Smith, *Johannine Christianity* 178: "Aside from his discourses and disputes about himself and his own role, Jesus utters no teaching whatever during his public ministry."

208. See, for example, R. E. Brown, *Epistles* 80 and the article by Brown referred to there.

adulterers, a band of traitors. They bend their tongues like bows; they have grown strong in the land for falsehood, and not for truth; for they proceed from evil to evil, and they do not know me, says the LORD" (NRSV).

But at the time of the New Covenant, this will all be changed and the people will truly "know" Yahweh. In Jer 24:7 we read: "I will give them a heart to know that I am the LORD; and they shall be my people and I will be their God, for they shall return to me with their whole heart" (NRSV).

The clearest statement of this is in Jer 31:33-34:

> But this is the covenant that I will make with the house of Israel after those days, says the Lord: I will put my law within them, and I will write it on their hearts; and I will be their God, and they shall be my people. No longer shall they teach one another, or say to each other, "Know the Lord," for they shall all know me, from the least of them to the greatest, says the LORD. (NRSV)

Such knowledge is similar in several respects to the Johannine understanding of the term. The first is that true knowledge of Yahweh is an eschatological gift; it is not something that the people have achieved. Second, this knowledge of God will be direct. That is, the people will not be dependent upon any intermediaries for attaining this knowledge. They will not need teachers (Jer 31:34). Third, this knowledge is not only intellectual comprehension but a comprehension that is directly linked to correct action (Jer 24:7).[209]

Within the second edition itself, the similarities to this conception of eschatological "knowledge" are considerable but implicit. It is evident in the massive focus on "knowing" in that edition, but it is also implicit in the fact that there is no body of doctrine being proposed other than that which pertains to the identity of Jesus himself. However, by the time of 1 John the connection of such knowledge with these Jewish hopes is explicit. Even at a time when he is arguing that the community must "keep the word" of Jesus, the author (in another of his "both/and" statements) also affirms that "you know all" (2:20) and "(y)ou have no need for anyone to teach you" (2:27).[210]

---

209. The fact that Jeremiah says "they will return to me" implies the action consequent upon this knowledge. See also the discussion of "The Spirit and Enthusiasm" in Dunn, *Unity* 174-202.

210. It is argued here that the notion of knowledge in the second edition is correctly understood against the background of OT thought about the prerogatives of the outpouring of the eschatological Spirit. Yet it would seem that in the later Johannine tradition (i.e., the second edition, the Letters, and the third edition) the conviction that such full knowledge of God was possible led to a focus on it and on the language about it in such a way that it was easy to isolate "knowing" from that OT background. Such isolation can be seen in the way the author

Section 6. The Development of Johannine Theology: Knowing God

4. Knowing God in 1 John

a. The View of the Opponents and the View of the Author of 1 John

In 1 John, both the author and his opponents claim a special ability to "know." In this respect, both are in continuity with the thought of the second edition. As we shall see, this involves a claim to a remarkable and radical ability. The author does not deny the possibility of knowing God, but rather he argues that true knowing can be identified and that the opponents do not truly know.

b. The Opponents Do Not "Know"

In the view of the author, the opponents (also identified as "the world") do not "know." They do not know the believers: 3:1 ("the world does not know us"). They do not know God: 3:1 (". . . it [the world] did not know him [the Father]"). And they do not know Jesus: 3:6 (". . . everyone sinning has not known him [Jesus]").

c. The Believer "Knows"

The author of 1 John makes it quite clear that the believer does have a special "knowing." In 2:20-21, he puts notable emphasis on this: "And you have an anointing from the Holy One, and you know all. I did not write to you that you do not know the truth but that you know it") (cf. also 2:27 below). He describes the "fathers" of the community as having "known" God from the beginning (2:13a, 14b).

d. The Expressions Used by the Author

The verb "to know" is used in two primary ways in 1 John. First, it is used with persons: to know God, Jesus, etc. In this way it is very similar to the dominant

---

of 1 John speaks of the claims of the opponents — "I have come to know him" (1 John 2:3, 4) — and elsewhere.

When this isolation took place, it provided a language and a concept that were attractive to movements whose fundamental orientation was different from the OT background against which the Gospel had been written. Undoubtedly, this explains the fondness of gnostics and others for this Gospel.

use of the second edition. Second, it is used to indicate the object that is known.[211] It would seem that this first sense is the primary one in the Letters, although there are grounds for seeing the second use as also important. Since this second use is less clearly derived from the community's understanding of eschatological knowledge, it will be treated later.

The notion of knowing God directly is expressed in two ways in 1 John. First, it is expressed by the verb "to know" as it was in the Gospel. But it is also expressed negatively by such statements such as "you have no need for anyone to teach you" (2:27).

e. The Believer Knows Persons

First and foremost the author explains that the believer "knows" God. For example, in 2:3 ("We are certain that we know him if we keep his commandments"); 2:4 ("the one . . . claiming to know him [God] but not keeping his commandments); 2:13 ("Fathers . . . you have known him from the beginning"); 2:14 ("Children . . . you have known the Father"); 2:14 ("Fathers . . . that you have known the one from the beginning"); 4:6 ("The one knowing God hears us; the one who is not of God does not hear us"); 4:7 (". . . everyone loving has been born of God and knows God"); 4:8 ("The one not loving did not know God because God is love"); 5:20 (". . . so that we know the true one").

Secondly, the believer knows the Spirit: 4:2 (". . . in this you know the Spirit of God: every Spirit that confesses Jesus Christ come in the flesh is of God"); 4:6 ("From this we know the Spirit of Truth and the Spirit . . .").[212]

f. The Nature of This Knowing and Its Source

This knowing does not come from being taught by another; it is direct and immediate: ". . . the anointing that you received from him abides in you, and you do not have need that anyone teach you; but as his [God's] anointing teaches you about all things . . ." (2:27). Not only is the knowledge direct, but it is also in some sense universal. As we have just read: "(Y)ou know *all*"

---

211. For example, 1 John 3:20 ("God is greater than our heart and knows all things"); 4:16 ("And we have known and have believed the love that God has for us").

212. In the Letters, the believer is never said to "know" *Jesus*; it is God the Father who is appropriately the object of "knowing." Rather, Jesus was heard, looked at, seen, touched, witnessed to (1:1-3), and also confessed (1 John 2:23; 4:2, 3, 15; 2 John 7).

Section 6. The Development of Johannine Theology: Knowing God

(2:20).[213] This same verse (2:20) tells us that the source of this knowledge is the Spirit.[214]

g. Tests for Determining True Knowing

The author believes that the opponents do not truly know but acknowledges their claim to do so. He proposes a number of ways that one can tell if a person truly "knows." For example, if a person truly knows, that person will keep the commandments (2:3-4).[215] If a person truly knows, that person will not keep on sinning (3:6). If a person truly knows, that person will not hate his brother (2:11). Thus, their actions will demonstrate whether their claims are correct.

(1) "Knowing" and the First Johannine Commandment

In addition to tests for true knowing, the First Letter of John begins to indicate that there are certain restraints on "knowing." At the time of 1 John, the author introduced the notion of "commandment" into Johannine theology and began to speak of two commandments "of God." These were not the Decalogue but commandments specific to the circumstances of the Johannine community.

The first of these commandments appears in various forms three times in 1 and 2 John (1 John 2:3-11; 3:23; 2 John 4-6) and is a commandment to "keep the word of God." This commandment is discussed in detail in Appendix 5 in Vol-

---

213. It may be that this "knowing all" would be seen as the basis for a number of other statements about knowing in the Letters. These instances do not represent the basic meaning but are characterized by knowledge of a thing rather than of a person, that is, "know that...": 2:5 ("the one who keeps his word.... By this, we know *that* we are 'in him [God]'"); 2:18 ("from this we know *that* it is the Last Hour"); 2:29 ("If you know *that* he [the Father] is just..."); 3:2 ("We know *that* when he [Jesus] is revealed, we will be like him..."); 3:5 ("And we know *that* that one was revealed to take away sins"); 3:14 ("... we know *that* we have gone over from death into life because we love the brothers"); 3:15 ("... you know *that* every murderer does not have eternal life abiding in himself"); 3:19 ("And in this we shall know *that* we are of the truth..."); 3:24 ("And in this we know *that* he [God] remains in us, from the Spirit that he [God] gave us..."); 5:2 ("In this we know *that* we love the children of God, whenever we love God..."); 5:13 ("I wrote these things to you in order that you might know *that* you have eternal life"); 5:15 (two times) ("And if we know *that* he hears us whatever we ask for, we know *that* we have the requests that we have requested from him"); 5:18 ("We know *that* everyone born of God does not sin..."); 5:19 ("We know *that* we are of God..."); 5:20 ("We know *that* the Son of God is coming...").

214. In some sense, it can also be said that this knowledge (insight) comes from Jesus (probably as the one who sends the Spirit or perhaps through his teaching about himself): "We know that... [the Son of God] has given us insight..." (5:20).

215. This is not the Decalogue but the commandments as conceived of by the Johannine community and articulated by the author.

ume 3. Here we will point out that even though the author and his followers hold to a theory of direct knowledge of God that comes from their possession of the Spirit, they are also convinced that they are to remember and obey the words of Jesus as they were delivered in the ministry.

(2) Stress on What Was "from the Beginning"

The second restraint on direct, internal knowledge was the repeated stress by the author of 1 John on the importance of what was "from the beginning." He makes this point in a way that is similar to his emphasis on the importance of the words of Jesus, that is, he asks his reader to recall what might be called the "sensory" Jesus — "that which was from the beginning, which we have heard, ... looked at with our eyes, ... seen and our hands have touched" (1:1); "we have seen ..." (1:2); "whatever we have seen and ... heard" (1:3). When he speaks about the "first" commandment, he reminds his readers that it is not "new" but "an old one that we have had from the beginning" (2:7). In 2:24, he again hopes: "[L]et what you heard from the beginning abide in you. If it abides in you (what you heard from the beginning), you abide in the Son and the Father." In 3:11, he reminds them of the proclamation that they heard "from the beginning."

(3) "Progressives" and the Teaching of the Christ

In 2 John 9, the author makes one of his clearest statements on the matter of correct belief and true knowing. In v. 8, the author warns his reader not to lose what they have worked for. In v. 9, he goes on to indicate that correct belief entails "remaining in the teaching of the Christ" rather than being "progressive" (i.e., literally, being "one who goes beyond" [Gk. *proagōn*]). Thus, even though one may claim to truly know, if that knowing goes beyond the inherited word of Jesus, then such knowing cannot be true. The author thereby indicates that there is a fixed content to the faith (the "word," the "teaching") that is to be adhered to, and any knowing that is not in accord with this cannot be true.

(4) Conclusions

Thus, with respect to "knowing" we see another of the author's "both/and" positions. He *both* affirms that the Spirit gives the believer the ability to "know all" *and* he makes it clear that there are tests for determining whether one truly knows. These tests include one's actions and also the content of what one claims to know. And so the tradition makes clear that any claim to a purely unfettered Spirit is not in keeping with the understanding of those who had witnessed

Section 6. The Development of Johannine Theology: Knowing God

from the beginning. This orientation will continue and become even clearer in the third edition of the Gospel.

5. Knowing God in the Third Edition

The third edition also exhibits a developed theology of "knowing." While it affirms dimensions of the earlier notions, it goes its own way both in relation to the second edition and in relation to 1 John. We will begin by examining the use of the verb "to know."

As in the earlier editions, "knowing" focuses primarily on knowing persons rather than things: "This is eternal life, that they know you, the only true God, and the one whom you have sent, Jesus Christ" (17:3). In the third edition, Jesus knows the Father (8:55); he knows that the Father's commandment is eternal life (12:50). He knows where he is from and where he is going (8:14); he also knows whom he has chosen (13:18). In fact, Jesus is said to know "all" (21:17), a statement that is almost identical to 1 John 2:20, where knowing "all" is predicated of the believer.

The disciples know that Jesus is the Holy One of God (6:69). They are asked if they know what Jesus has done for them (13:12). They know the Paraclete (14:17). As was the case in the second edition, the disciples do not fully "know" until after the Resurrection (20:9). Yet they are not kept in ignorance. Jesus explains that the slave does not know what the master is doing (15:20). Nevertheless, they did not recognize Jesus on the shore (21:4), and when they did, they were afraid to confirm it (21:12).

"The Jews" (as was the case in the second edition and in 1 John) do not know Jesus' word (8:43) and do not know the one who sent Jesus (15:21). Jesus argues, however, that one day they will know that Jesus is I AM (8:28). Yet if they remain in his word, they will know the truth (8:32).

If "the Jews" are unbelieving, so is "the world." As was the case both in the second edition and in 1 John, the world did not know Jesus (1:10) either. Nor will it know the Paraclete (14:7). But Jesus goes to his death so that the world may know that Jesus loves the Father (14:31).

The third edition also contains examples of knowing accompanied by "that" clauses: the most significant one is that the Samaritans know that Jesus is the Savior of the world (4:42).[216] But beyond the actual use of the verb "to know," the third author provides a number of other dimensions to his understanding of the ability to know which come from the eschatological outpouring of the Spirit.

---

216. While this could be an example of truly "knowing," the primary focus of the statement is to affirm a saving role for Jesus, in accord with the soteriology of the third edition.

A History of the Development of Johannine Theology

a. The First Commandment in the Third Edition

The author of 1 John had introduced the commandment tradition. The third author then develops this further in the third edition and makes two significant changes. First, he speaks of two commandments given to Jesus, and, second, when he speaks of the two commandments given to the disciples, they are said to be given by Jesus and are correlated with those given to Jesus by the Father.[217]

In the third edition, we meet, for the first time, the notion of commandments given to Jesus by the Father. He is ordered to speak what the Father has told him and to lay down his life out of love. This is a new concept, which stands alongside the concept (introduced by the second author) of the ministry as a "work" given by the Father to complete. Moreover, when the author speaks of the commandments given to the disciples, he identifies them as given by Jesus (rather than by God as in 1 John). Within the third edition, the author makes more explicit the role of Jesus in the giving of the commandments. Here we focus only on the first of the commandments. In 12:44-50 (esp. v. 49), Jesus indicates that belief in him is meant to be "passed on" to the Father and that belief in Jesus is really belief in the Father. Then in v. 49 he explains that he does not speak on his own authority, but the Father has commanded him "what to say and to speak." Thus, the message of Jesus is the message of the Father, and belief in Jesus should be belief in the Father.

But then in 14:21-24, the third author explains the first of the commandments given to the disciples. He does so by means of a chaining of ideas. First, Jesus explains that the one who keeps his commandments is the one who loves him (v. 21). Second, he explains that the one who loves him will keep his words (v. 23). Third, he speaks of the one who does not keep his words and says that that person does not love Jesus (v. 24a). Then he reminds the reader that "the word that you hear is not mine but of the Father who sent me" (v. 24). Thus, there is a clear identification between keeping the word of Jesus and keeping his commandment.

In this way the historical word of Jesus is identified as being central to belief in Jesus. It is no longer an unrestrained and unbridled Spirit that speaks to the believer. The believer must keep the words of Jesus.

b. The Additional Witnesses

Another of the indirect ways in which the "knowing" of the believer is channeled and restrained is through the two additional witnesses to Jesus intro-

---

217. This is also discussed in von Wahlde, *Commandments* 11-38, esp. 11-21.

Section 6. The Development of Johannine Theology: Knowing God

duced by the author of the third edition. This author, who was aware of the schema of the witnesses to Jesus in the second edition, extends this list of witnesses from the original three to include two additional witnesses: the Paraclete and the disciples (15:26-27).[218]

The Paraclete, who is identified as "the Spirit of Truth," will witness *about Jesus* (15:26). Thus, the third author indicates that the Spirit will not exclude the permanent role of Jesus but will in fact focus on him. Secondly, the disciples will also be witnesses to Jesus because they have been with him "from the beginning" (15:27). It is this notion of having been with Jesus "from the beginning" that founds the witness of the community of 1 John, for the author proclaims what was "from the beginning" (cf. 1 John 1:1-3; 2:13, 24; 3:11).

c. The Paraclete and the Words of Jesus

If the first Johannine commandment and the witness of both the Paraclete and the disciples pose an *implicit* restraint upon what believers could claim to come from the Spirit, two of the Paraclete passages do this *explicitly*. These passages make it patently clear that there can be no inspiration that claims to be from the Spirit that is not expressed in, or linked to, the words of Jesus. In 14:26 (the second of the Paraclete sayings), Jesus explains that the Paraclete "will teach you all things and will remind you of all things that I have told you." Thus, the author affirms the traditional (i.e., found in the second edition and in 1 John) conviction that the Spirit will help the believer to know all. But then, through the process of hendiadys, the author explains that "all things" are contained in all things *that I have told you*. Thus, the action of the Spirit is linked to the words of Jesus.

In 16:12-15 (the fifth of the Paraclete sayings), the author again begins by affirming the traditional belief: "He will lead you in all truth." He is the Spirit of Truth (v. 13) and will lead into truth. But then this "truth" is more clearly defined: "He will not speak on his own, but will speak whatever he hears, and will proclaim to you what is to come." The key words here are: "He will not speak on his own." Then, lest this be misinterpreted, Jesus says: "That one will glorify me because he will take from what is mine and will proclaim it to you." Thus, the words of the Spirit are inextricably linked to the words of Jesus and there can be no possibility of an unfettered inspiration. The words of Jesus have a unique and permanent status that cannot be done away with by claims to inspiration by the Spirit.

---

218. It will be recalled that the fourth witness, that of John the Baptist, was not an essential witness.

d. Direct Knowledge in the Third Edition

We have seen a number of ways in which the author of the third edition stresses the importance of the historical words of Jesus. His position in this respect is quite clear and explicit. At the same time, it should be pointed out that there are no statements in the third edition which *explicitly* affirm direct knowledge of God without an intermediary. With the continued emphasis on "knowing," such a belief must have certainly continued to be part of the belief of the community at the time of the third edition, but evidently the author does not feel the need to make the roots of this explicit as had the author of 1 John before him.

6. The Background of the Concept of "Knowing" God in 1 John and in the Third Edition

In our search for parallels to the position of 1 John, we find what really could be said to be more than we might expect. It will be recalled that the author of 1 John explicitly held to a "both/and" position, involving both direct knowledge given by God and a need to remain faithful to the "tradition."

In the SDQ, we find a parallel to *both* of these aspects of the thought of 1 John. We see clear parallels to the belief that the eschatological Spirit will teach all. For example, 1QH 14:12-13 speaks of teaching and knowledge of God being direct, without the need for a teacher: "You have brought [your truth and your] glory . . . without there being a mediator between the intelligent and your holy ones" (*DSST*).[219] In 1QH 20:12 we read: "I, the Instructor, have known you, my God, through the spirit that you gave me, and I have listened loyally to your wonderful secret through your holy spirit" (*DSST*). We also see repeated references to a distinction between a Spirit of Truth and a Spirit of Falsehood. This distinction would serve potentially to distinguish between a correct and an incorrect understanding of their community's beliefs and did in fact operate in this way, as we shall soon see.

More importantly, we see something parallel in content and function (but not in form) to the Johannine commandments within the scrolls. Within 1QS,

---

219. The full meaning of the text is obscured by a gap in the manuscript, but the directness of the experience of God is clear. See also 1QH 6:13; 11:12; 12:11-12; 13:24-25; 14:12-13, 25; 20:21-24. Nickelsburg (*Resurrection* 155) also recognizes that "insight into the mysteries of God" is already the present possession of the believer at Qumran. Kvalvaag ("Spirit" 159-80, quote on 173) comments: "By the gift of the spirit the sectarian has received knowledge of God and is able to seek God. According to this text, it is impossible for any human to understand the divine secrets and be purified except by God's Holy Spirit."

Section 6. The Development of Johannine Theology: Knowing God

there are repeated discussions (1QS 5:20-24; 6:13-23) of a "double scrutiny" that the members of the community had to undergo.[220] This double scrutiny concerned the member's "understanding and his deeds." This parallels closely the two Johannine commandments that concerned "belief" and "love expressed in action." This double scrutiny is variously identified as concerning "his understanding and practice of the Law" (1QS 5:21); "their understanding and their deeds" (1QS 5:23); "their spirit and deeds" (1QS 5:24); "his understanding and perfection of way" (1QS 5:24); "his understanding and his deeds" (1QS 6:14); "his spirit and his deeds" (1QS 6:17); "his understanding and observance of the Law" (1QS 6:18).

What is particularly striking is that the testing about understanding is sometimes described as a testing about his "spirit" (cf. 1QS 5:24; 6:17). In 1QS 5:20-21, we find a close parallel to 1 John 4:1-6: "They shall test their spirits in the Community (discriminating) between a man and his fellow, in respect of his insight and of his deeds in law. . . ." Thus, there is not only a general recognition of a difference in spirits but also these different spirits are manifest in the person's understanding and deeds in accordance with the Law.

Thus, in the SDQ we see both a parallel to the Johannine conviction of direct knowledge of God given through the Spirit and a parallel to the Johannine concern to have such knowledge be in accord with a particular "tradition" (expressed in the SDQ as proper "understanding").

7. Conclusion

In a discussion of Johannine ecclesiology, R. E. Brown comments on the effect created by the conviction that, imbued with the eschatological Spirit, each individual had within the power to know the truth. His comment is quite pertinent to our discussion of how one "knows" in the Johannine tradition:

> Perhaps the most serious weakness in Johannine ecclesiology, and the one most apparent in the Epistles, centers on the role of the Paraclete. The thought that there is a living, divine teacher in the heart of each believer — a teacher who is the ongoing presence of Jesus, preserving what he taught but interpreting it anew in each generation — is surely one of the greatest contributions made to Christianity by the Fourth Gospel. But the Jesus who sent the Paraclete never tells his followers what is to happen when believers who possess the Paraclete disagree with each other. The Johannine Letters tell us

---

220. For further discussion of this double scrutiny, see von Wahlde, *Commandments* 245-54.

what frequently happens: they break their *koinōnia* or communion with each other.... In my judgment there is no way to control such a division in a Paraclete-guided community of people.... Johannine ecclesiology is the most attractive and exciting in the NT. Alas, it is also one of the least stable.[221]

This expresses well the dilemma. Although Brown does not make reference to it, the author of 1 John, and the author of the third edition after him, sought to correct this weakness by stressing the importance of "what was from the beginning," of "keeping the word" of Jesus, and of rejecting those who were "progressive and not remaining in the teaching of the Christ." Nevertheless, even in 1 John and in the third edition of the Gospel, this exhortation remained quite general and scarcely moved to specifics.

SECTION 7. THE DEVELOPMENT OF JOHANNINE THEOLOGY: SOTERIOLOGY

As the term "soteriology" is commonly used, it refers to the view of the particular means by which sin is taken away and salvation is achieved. Although the word *sōtēria* (salvation) does not appear in the Johannine writings in connection with Jesus[222] and the personal form *sōtēr* appears only once in the Gospel (4:42) (3E) and once in 1 John 4:14, the concept of salvation in its broader meaning is clearly present.

1. Soteriology in the First Edition

As with many of the concepts discussed here, there is no evidence of soteriology within the material of the first edition. Whether there was a view and it was excised by later editors or whether there was no reference to it cannot be determined.

2. Soteriology in the Second Edition

In the second edition of the Gospel, soteriology assumes a central role and is almost entirely positive, focusing, not on removing sins, but on attaining eternal life, which is the life of God, the life that transforms one from the realm of the

---

221. R. E. Brown, *Churches* 121-23.
222. Its only appearance is in John 4:22 ("Salvation is from the Jews").

Section 7. The Development of Johannine Theology: Soteriology

flesh to the realm of the Spirit and from death to life. Soteriology in this sense is thus defined as gaining eternal life. We have examined the notion of eternal life above. Here we will call attention only to the fact that the Johannine Jesus offers eternal life and the possession of eternal life is the hope of all Johannine believers. This life, as we have seen, comes through the reception of the Spirit of God.

But what of the forgiveness of sin? In the majority of the New Testament, the notion of soteriology has an essentially negative orientation: the taking away of sins. The removal of sins is generally explained as taking place through the "expiatory" or "atoning" death of Jesus on the cross.[223] However, in the Gospel of John, even in its final form, there are relatively few references to the death of Jesus as expiatory or atoning. When we restrict our survey to the material of the second edition, we find that there are no such references. Instead, we find that Jesus speaks of his death as a departure to the Father.[224] Jesus speaks in terms of where he has come from and where he is going. These two types of statements form the dominant theme of the second author's material in 7:28-29; 7:33-36. The "whence and whither" motif is further developed in the second edition in the many references to Jesus' being "sent" by the Father. The departure motif is developed further in texts such as 13:33bcd, 36; 14:5.

How do we account for this strange lack of attention to any role for Jesus in the forgiveness of sin? In the material of the second edition itself, there is little positive evidence to determine this one way or the other. This is, indeed, another of the topics about which there is a "strange silence." But, as we shall see immediately below, there was repeated reference in the Old Testament (and in other Jewish literature) that the Spirit, poured out by God, would cleanse people from their sins.[225] Although there are no explicit statements of this in the

---

223. See, for example, Rom 5:6-11; 1 Cor 15:3; Gal 1:4; 2:20; Heb 10:12.

224. This is developed well by Forestell, *Word*, and by Nicholson, *Death* (see 161-68, esp. 167). See also Bultmann's statement that the death of Jesus does not have any real and independent significance (*Theology* 2:54). R. E. Brown understands the role of the secessionists in John in a way that overlaps this view considerably. For example, Brown (*Epistles* 73-79) comments: "... the real purpose of Jesus' earthly life was simply to reveal God's glory in human terms..., but not to do anything new that changed the relationship between God and human beings" (p. 75).

I would agree that the secessionists' understanding (which was based on the Gospel as it was formulated at the time of the second edition) of Jesus was that he was the exemplar of the one who possessed eternal life from the Father and that he announced (and offered from the Father) the outpouring of the Spirit in its eschatological fullness. Thus, in a very real sense, his *life* (and death) did not do anything new that in itself changed the relationship between God and human beings. It was the Spirit that would cleanse them from sin.

225. On this, see also von Wahlde, *Commandments* 138-98. De Boer, apparently without knowledge of my earlier proposal, made a similar proposal six years after mine but in connection with 1 John 5:6-7 (*Perspectives* 260-64).

second edition (one could well imagine that such references were excised by the later author), there are two passages that seem to hint at such a view. When this is coupled with the very clear views of 1 John regarding soteriology, it becomes certain that such was the view of the author of the second edition but that it was corrected by the author of 1 John and by the author of the third edition.

The first passage that suggests a cleansing from sin through the Holy Spirit is the scene of the footwashing (13:1-20). It will be recalled that there are two interpretations of the footwashing. One is from the second edition (13:8-10), and the other is from the third (13:12-18). Of these two, the second is clear: it is meant as a symbol of loving service to one another. But the first is more enigmatic. As I will argue in the Commentary, it is very likely that this scene refers to the washing of the disciples that will take place through the Holy Spirit. Regularly, the author of the second edition has spoken of the giving of the Spirit under the image of living water. Here he speaks of cleansing the feet of the disciples with water and its being symbolic of something they cannot yet understand. The time for the giving of the Spirit was at the glorification of Jesus, and so the disciples could not be expected to know. But at the same time, as we shall see below, there was considerable evidence in the Old Testament, in the SDQ, and elsewhere that the giving of the Spirit would result in a cleansing from sin. In the present state of the text, the cleansing is a two-stage process. However, as is argued in the Commentary on the verses, the material dealing with the "second" washing is an addition by the third author and refers, not to the bestowal of the Spirit, but to the secondary forgiveness of sin necessary for the disciples since, even though they are cleansed from sin by the Spirit and made inchoately "perfect," they are still capable of sin and so will require additional "washings."

The second passage that indicates a relationship between the reception of the Spirit and the forgiveness of sin is 20:23. Although this verse comes from the third edition, one could well ask why it is placed in its present location. Its intent is to give to the disciples the power to bind and to loose sin. This human mediation of the divine power is distinctive of the third edition and certainly would represent a departure from the thought of the second edition, where the need for human mediation of any sort was rejected. But why was it placed here? It is likely that the author of the third edition was aware of the opponents' connection of the reception of the Spirit with the forgiveness of sin and so thought of this as the appropriate place to speak of his own views on forgiveness of sin.[226]

When this ambiguous evidence is placed alongside the clear evidence of an Old Testament background for cleansing from sin by the Spirit and alongside the extraordinary emphasis, in both 1 John and in the third edition of the Gospel, on the conviction that it was Jesus who took away sin by his blood and that

---

226. De Boer (*Perspectives* 262) also recognizes the intimate relation of the two verses.

Section 7. The Development of Johannine Theology: Soteriology

his death was an atonement, there is little room for doubt that in the second edition forgiveness was seen to take place through the Spirit and not through Jesus.

3. The Background of Soteriology in the Second Edition

a. In the Old Testament

In the Old Testament, the eschatological outpouring of the Spirit will cleanse one from all past sin.[227] This is evident from a number of texts. In Jer 31:31-34, in addition to other transformations associated with the last days (direct knowledge of God, no need of teachers), there is also the promise that Yahweh will forgive their sins:

> All, from the least to greatest, shall know me, says the LORD, for I will forgive their evildoing and remember their sin no more. (NRSV)

Ezek 36:25-28 says:

> I will sprinkle clean water upon you, and you shall be clean from all your uncleannesses, and from all your idols I will cleanse you. A new heart I will give you, and a new spirit I will put within you; and I will remove from your body the heart of stone and give you a heart of flesh. I will put my Spirit within you, and make you follow my statutes and be careful to observe my ordinances. (NRSV)[228]

b. In the Sectarian Documents of Qumran

Although the SDQ are often couched in a dualistic worldview, the matter of forgiveness (or "purification," as the documents more often describe it) is dealt with repeatedly and is attributed to God, who cleanses sin through his holy spirit.[229] In this respect, it is similar to the view presented in the Old Testament.

---

227. On the association of the outpouring of the Spirit with the forgiveness of sins in the OT and in the Gospel see also Schnackenburg, *Gospel* 3:325.

228. See also Ezek 11:19; Zech 12:10; 13:1.

229. See particularly the discussion in Puech, *Croyance* 417. Unfortunately, Garnet's book, *Salvation*, is not helpful in this regard in spite of its title. However, the book is useful in showing that the notion of "atonement" (i.e., as understood and emphasized by the author of 1 John and the author of the third edition) is not an operative concept within the SDQ (*Salvation* 118-20).

The use of "spirit" in the Qumran documents is complex. In some instances it refers to

At times God's purification of the community member from sin is simply affirmed (e.g., 1QH 9:32; 11:21; 14:6, 8; 19:10; 1QS 11:14-15). At other times, it is specifically indicated that the agent of this purification is God's holy Spirit.[230] In 1QS 4:18-23 we read that God will "cleanse him with the spirit of holiness from every irreverent deed." God will pour the Spirit of Truth over the individual to cleanse the person from all iniquity. That this is an eschatological cleansing is clear, as is the association of Spirit, water, and cleansing from sin.[231]

In 1QH 8:19-20 we read:

> I have appeased your face by the spirit which you have given me, to lavish your favor on your servant for[ever], to purify me with your holy spirit, to approach your will according to the extent of your kindnesses.[232]

c. Elsewhere in Apocalyptic Judaism

This same conception is also evident elsewhere in apocalyptic Judaism. For example, *Jub.* 1:23 states: ". . . and I shall create for them a holy spirit, and I shall purify them so that they will not turn away from following me from that day and forever" *(OTP).*[233]

Thus, we see that this notion of cleansing through the power of God's Spirit was common in both the Old Testament and in the texts of various apocalyptic groups within Judaism.[234] That a group such as the Johannine commu-

---

God's spirit, at other times to dispositions within humanity, at still other times to angelic or demonic beings. Sekki *(Ruaḥ)* has as his primary goal to distinguish these various meanings within the documents. With regard to the present passage, Sekki would see the second reference in the passage as referring to God's Spirit, while the first and third refer to human dispositions (81-82). In any event, the human dispositions are reflections of the influence of God's Spirit and the spirit of Belial (Satan).

230. This is regularly recognized by scholars. As Puech says: "Sans doute, il [l'homme] rest faible, pécheur, mais Dieu l'a purifié et le purifiera par son esprit saint" *(Croyance* 417). So also Kvalvaag, "Spirit," in *Qumran* 159-80, here 171-72.

231. Sekki *(Ruaḥ* 208) argues that only the second use of "spirit" here (i.e., "spirit of holiness") refers to God's Spirit. The others describe an aspect of man's spirit. However, Sekki sees *ruaḥ* in 4:18ff. as "an eschatological gift of God which is to cleanse him from all evil deeds and to effect a radical change in his inherited spiritual nature."

232. According to Sekki *(Ruaḥ* 78-80, 230) both instances of "spirit" refer to God's spirit. See also 1QH 8:15; 11:21; 15:7; 1QS 3:6-9.

233. See also *4 Ezra* 6:26.

234. Although the *T12P* is oriented toward moral instruction and exhortation and although there are repeated references to a final judgment, there is no significant discussion of the forgiveness of sin or how purification from sin takes (or will take) place.

Section 7. The Development of Johannine Theology: Soteriology

nity who focused so intensely on the prerogatives of the outpouring of the eschatological Spirit would adopt such a view of the forgiveness of sin is fully understandable. This community then interpreted the death of Jesus as the necessary prerequisite for the bestowal of the Spirit but not as having an intrinsic soteriological function such as an atoning death.

4. Soteriology in 1 John

a. The View of the Opponents

Although the author of 1 John is primarily intent on presenting his own view of soteriology, he does make one clear reference to the view of the opponents. In 1 John 5:6, the author makes reference to the opponents' view by means of a symbolic reference when he says that: "(t)his is the one coming through water and blood, Jesus Christ. Not in water only but in the water and the blood." Thus, he argues that it is not just through the (living) water of the Spirit that sin is taken away but through the (atoning) blood of Jesus. This verse, which has been a perennial puzzle for scholars, takes on a new meaning when viewed within the context of the community crisis we have described here. The evidence for this view is addressed in detail in the Commentary on 1 John 5:6-7.

b. The View of the Author

As we have seen immediately above, for the author of 1 John Jesus was more than one who embodied and announced the eschatological giving of the Spirit. His death itself was a central element in the procurement of these eschatological benefits. It was an atonement or expiation, making amends through suffering for the sinful deeds of humanity. This understanding is expressed by a variety of closely related ideas.

(1) Jesus' Death Was a Death for His Own

In this understanding, the death of Jesus was intended as a benefit for the believer, but the benefit is not stated. In 1 John, this is evident in 3:16, which says, "[T]hat one [Jesus] has laid down his life for us *(hyper hēmōn)*" (see also 1 John 1:7 and 5:6 below).[235] Related to these are expressions that speak of Jesus "saving" (the world, us, etc.) and that attribute an efficacy to the actions of Jesus in

---

235. See, for example, Schnackenburg, *Epistles* 182.

themselves (as opposed to actions that prepare for the giving of the Spirit). Although these do not refer explicitly to the death of Jesus, they focus on the actions of Jesus as being themselves salvific, and so they also should be considered here. In 1 John this concept is less frequent, but in 1 John 4:14 we find that "the Father has sent the Son as Savior of the world."

(2) The Death of Jesus Takes Away Sin

There are two types of formulations that speak of the believer's sins being taken away by Jesus. The first set of statements is specific and identifies the death of Jesus as the means by which sin is taken away. For example, 1 John 2:2 states: "he [Jesus] is an atonement for our sins, and not only for ours but also for those of the entire world." In 4:10, we read: "he [God] sent his Son as an atonement for our sins." In 3:8, we read: "For this the Son of God was revealed, that he might do away with the works of the devil." Although the death of Jesus is not mentioned in the last, the formula is so similar to the prior one that there can be no doubt that the atoning death is referred to.[236]

The second set contains more general formulations and simply affirms the fact of the role of Jesus in the forgiveness of sins. Thus, 1 John 2:2 ("... if someone sins, we have a Paraclete before the Father, Jesus Christ, the Just One, and he is an atonement for our sins"); 2:12 ("... your sins are forgiven through his name"); 3:5 ("... that one [Jesus] was revealed to take away sins").

(3) The Death of Jesus Involved the Giving of His "Flesh" and "Blood," "for the Life of the World"

This language is the most specific and is also linked with the sacrificial interpretation of the death. In 1 John 1:7, we read: "The blood of Jesus his Son cleanses us from all sin." In 5:6, the author speaks of Jesus as "the one coming through ... blood."[237] Similar to these is 4:2, which speaks of Jesus "coming in the flesh." This expression probably refers also to Jesus' death as sacrificial.[238]

---

236. De Boer ("Death" 330) proposes that the view of the death of Jesus in 1 John is not that it is "a unique and inimitable act of atonement ... but this death [is] a *concrete* ("fleshly") and *imitable* (exemplary) act of love...." I am uncomfortable with this articulation of the matter. For the author of 1 John, the role of Jesus in salvation is essential and unique. His death is an expiatory one for the sins of the world. As an act of love, Jesus' death can be seen as an exemplary act that the disciples should imitate. As expiation, it is inimitable.

237. This is commonly accepted as reflecting the notion of atonement. See de Boer, "Death" 337. I would, however, not agree with de Boer that the reference to "coming in water" refers to the baptizing ministry of Jesus.

238. See the discussion in de Boer, "Death," referred to above. R. E. Brown (*Epistles* 505)

Section 7. The Development of Johannine Theology: Soteriology

With six different expressions, the author affirms that Jesus has died for our sins: (1) Jesus' blood cleanses us from sin (1:7); (2) he is an atonement for our sins, and not only for ours but also for those of the whole world (2:2; 3:5); (3) he does away with the works of the devil (3:8); (4) he laid down his life for us (3:16); (5) he is Savior of the world (4:14); (6) he came through water and blood (5:6-8). In all of these instances, the death of Jesus is seen (either explicitly or implicitly) to be the action that achieves salvific effects for the believer. This view is distinct from that, in the second edition, of his death as "departure."[239]

Thus, while the author of the third edition does not deny that the Spirit is the principle of life, there can be no doubt about the role of Jesus in the taking away of sin. Particularly instructive in this regard is the passage 4:9-10. Verse 9 says: "He has sent his unique Son into the world so that we may live through him." Here the gift of life is said to come through Jesus. Verse 10 constitutes an almost exact parallel[240] to this except that, rather than speaking of the gift of life, it speaks of the removal of sin. For the author of 1 John, Jesus has an essential role in both. Not only are both aspects predicated of Jesus but they are both articulated in parallel sentences immediately following one another and so showing their relationship to one another.

5. Soteriology in the Third Edition

Here we focus on texts of the third edition that speak of the meaning of Jesus' death. For the author of the third edition (as had been the case with the author of 1 John before him) Jesus was more than one who (embodied and) announced the eschatological giving of the Spirit. His death itself was a central element in the procurement of its benefits. It was an atonement or expiation, making amends through suffering for the sinful deeds of humanity.

As is often the case with such features, this view is pervasive in 1 John but is much less so within the Gospel. Nevertheless, there are a number of passages within the third edition which either presuppose or explicitly state this understanding of Jesus' death.[241] This understanding is expressed through a variety

---

and Schnackenburg (*Epistles* 201) both argue that the verse is intended to attribute a salvific, sacrificial meaning to the death of Jesus.

239. There are other passages that may hint at an understanding of the death as atonement, but they are not so clear. For example, 3:14 says: "The Son of Man must be lifted up so that everyone believing in him may have everlasting life." This statement occurs in material that is associated with the third edition. In addition, a very similar expression occurs in 1 John 4:9 ("He has sent his unique Son into the world so that we may live through him").

240. For further context, see the Interpretation of 1 John 4:7-12 in the Commentary.

241. Smalley (*1, 2, 3 John* xxvii) lists the following as texts in the Gospel of John speaking

of closely related concepts, all of which emphasize that his death was an act which took away sin; was done out of love; was done for humanity (the "world," "his own"); and was done "for the life of the world."²⁴²

a. Jesus' Death as a Death for His Own

The freeing from sin, as we have seen, is accomplished through the death of Jesus. The expressions just treated spoke of what was accomplished. Other passages speak of those for whom it is done. The expressions that speak of his death "for" *(hyper)* (his own, his sheep, us, etc.) are simply another way of expressing this.²⁴³ De Boer objects that this cannot be the case and proposes 13:37-38 as an example of a text where such a meaning would be senseless. He is certainly correct that this text (which speaks of Peter's willingness to die "for" Jesus) does not imply that Peter is willing to atone for Jesus.²⁴⁴ However, in a context where the death of Jesus is being spoken about, the use of *hyper* is a reliable indication that a substitutionary, vicarious death intended to make things right with God is intended. The expression is elliptical and, because of this, all elements that would indicate that the death is an atoning one cannot be expected to be present.

This is common elsewhere in the New Testament, for example, in Mark

---

of a sacrificial death of Jesus: 1:29, 36; 3:14-16; 10:14-18; 11:50-52. I find the reference in 3:14-16 to be ambiguous and do not include it in my list.

242. It should be noted, however, that the third edition does not make specific reference to "blood" in the passages dealing with the atoning death of Jesus as does 1 John, except in 19:34 where it would appear that the author is taking over the terminology from 1 John 5:6-8. Elsewhere in the third edition, where blood is mentioned in connection with the atoning death of Jesus (6:53-56), the reference is to the blood of Jesus in its sacramental form.

243. Barrett (*Gospel* 375) lists 6:51; 10:11, 15; 11:50-52; 18:14 as examples of the use of *hyper* in this sense, and comments, "The word, however, though certainly suggesting a sacrificial (in no technical sense) death for the benefit of others, conveys no more precise shade of meaning." Thompson (*Humanity* 92) comments: "When used with any verb meaning 'to die,' *hyper* suggests that such a death is 'for the benefit of others.'" Nicholson (*Death* 2) speaks of these *"hyper"* sayings as expressing the notion of sacrifice and atonement. The most detailed explanation of the background of this notion is by de Jonge, "Death" 147-49; *Envoy* 23-29.

For a contrary view, see Forestell, *Word* 74-76, and de Boer, *Perspectives* 232-35. Forestell argues that 10:11-13 speak only of the shepherd's devotion to the sheep and has no religious, sacrificial, or expiatory value. To say this is to forget that the image in chapter 10 is *a parable* (cf. *paroimia* in v. 6). Ordinarily shepherds do not die trying to kill a wolf. The passage cannot be understood except as a reference to the death of Jesus on behalf of his own. At the same time, there is no possibility of a specific reference to atonement in such circumstances precisely because it is a parable.

244. De Boer, *Perspectives* 232-34.

Section 7. The Development of Johannine Theology: Soteriology

14:24 ("This is my blood... poured out for many"); Rom 8:32 ("He who did not withhold his own Son but gave him up for all of us"); 1 Cor 15:3 ("Christ died for our sins"); and 2 Cor 5:21 ("For us, he made him sin who did not know sin in order that we might know justification").[245]

In the Gospel of John, the expression has the same meaning. Examples include 10:15b ("I lay down my life for the sheep [*hyper tōn probatōn*]");[246] 11:51 ("Jesus was about to die for the nation [*hyper tou ethnous*]").[247] I would also be inclined to think that 15:13 ("No one has greater love than this, that a person lay down his life for his friends [*hyper tōn philōn*]"), while not in itself a reference to an expiatory death, when applied to Jesus (as this text is) was intended to refer to his death as expiatory.[248]

b. The Death of Jesus Takes Away Sin

In the Gospel, there are no statements precisely like those of 1 John which affirm that Jesus died to take away sin. However, the idea is clearly present. First, as we have seen, there are clear statements that Jesus died for his own. Secondly, there are specific declarations that Jesus took away the sin of the world. In these declarations, Jesus is described as the "Lamb of God" (1:29, 36), a figure associated with the Passover Lamb that was killed and whose blood signaled freedom from death for the Israelites. This Lamb of God is also said explicitly to take away the sin of the world (1:29). This is fulfilled in 19:32-37, where Jesus' death is shown to be similar to that of the Passover lamb both as to the time of his death (while the lambs are being sacrificed for Passover) and to the fact that his legs were not broken (which is probably intended to indicate the fulfillment of Exod 12:10, 46; Num 9:12).[249] Thus, the conception of the death of Jesus as one that took away the sin of the world is present in the third edition.

---

245. See also additional examples in Luke 22:19-20; Rom 5:6-11; 14:15; 1 Cor 1:13; 11:24; Gal 1:4; 2:20; 3:13; Heb 2:9; 10:12.

246. See also 10:11b, where the similar expression appears in the parable itself. On this as referring to Jesus' sacrificial death, see Barrett, *Gospel* 376; Beasley-Murray, *Gospel* 171; R. E. Brown, *Gospel* 395; Bultmann, *Gospel* 384; Ridderbos, *Gospel* 362.

247. The essential elements here are that it is through the death of Jesus that this saving event takes place and that the death itself results in a benefit for others. So also, for example, Barrett, *Gospel* 406; Bultmann, *Gospel* 411-12; Dodd, *Interpretation* 233; Moloney, *Signs* 175.

248. Although 17:19 is a verbal parallel to the above expressions, the meaning is different. 18:14 is a repetition of 11:50 and probably did not have the sacrificial meaning, which was introduced only in the reinterpretation of those verses in 11:51-52. For further detail, see the analysis of the Composition of those verses.

249. It is possible, although less likely, that the verse alludes to Ps 33:21 (LXX). See the discussion in Grigsby, "Cross" 84-85. For a contrary interpretation of this title, see de Boer, *Perspectives* 277-80.

A History of the Development of Johannine Theology

c. The Death of Jesus Involved the Giving of His "Flesh" and "Blood," "for the Life of the World"

In the Gospel, 6:51 states: "The bread that I will give is my flesh for the life of the world" *(hē sarx mou estin hyper tēs tou kosmou zōēs).*[250] Here the preposition *hyper* is often used not only by John but elsewhere in early Christian literature to speak of the death of Jesus as having salvific importance, particularly when it is connected with the verb *(para)didomai.*[251]

Even though the references to the "blood" of Jesus in 6:53-56 should be understood in this context as a sacramental reference, the importance of the sacrament is linked to the understanding of his death as being "for the life of the world."[252] In 19:34, the author observes that the piercing of the side of Jesus brings forth "blood and water," a comment intended to refer to the importance of *both* the Spirit (living water) and the death (blood) of Jesus.[253]

d. The Death of Jesus Interpreted against the Model of Abraham's Sacrifice of Isaac

Another possible expression of this conviction can be found in John 3:16. As was pointed out above,[254] some scholars have proposed that in the Akedah tradition, Isaac was seen as the prime example of sacrifice, "one who willingly gave himself in death as a burnt offering." These scholars see a parallel between this tradition and John 3:16, where God is said to give his unique Son in order that the world might be saved through him. While this may indeed be part of the background against which the death of Jesus is portrayed, it is not as clear. This model for the death of Jesus does not have a parallel in the Letters.

---

250. Dodd (*Interpretation* 360) speaks of the "hint" of his death as violent and vicarious.

251. Menken ("John 6,51c-58" 1-26; see p. 10, nn. 26, 27) lists John 10:11, 15; 11:50-52; 15:13; 17:19; 18:14 as examples of this usage. He sees the expression elsewhere in Mark 14:24 and parallels; Rom 5:6-8; 1 Cor 5:14-15; 11:24; 15:3; Heb 6:20; 1 Pet 2:21; 1 John 3:16. With *didomai*, the expression occurs in Luke 22:19; Gal 1:4; 2:20; Eph 5:2, 25; 1 Tim 2:6; Tit 2:14. De Jonge ("Death" 142-51, esp. 145) also lists a number of these so-called "surrender" texts.

252. This is the understanding of the verse by Barrett, R. E. Brown, and Schnackenburg. See the discussion of the Composition of 6:51.

253. See the Note on 19:35 in the Commentary.

254. See the discussion in Part 3, Section 2, 3E-33.

Section 7. The Development of Johannine Theology: Soteriology

e. Jesus as "Saving" and as "Savior"

Finally, expressions that speak of Jesus "saving" (the world, us, etc.) attribute an efficacy to the actions of Jesus in themselves (as opposed to actions that prepare for the giving of the Spirit). Although these do not refer explicitly to the death of Jesus, they focus on the actions of Jesus as being themselves salvific and so they also should be considered here. In 1 John this concept is less frequent, but in 1 John 4:14 we find that "the Father has sent the Son as Savior of the world."

In the Gospel, this view is expressed in various ways and represents a development of the use of "saving" language. For example, we see: "God did not send his Son . . . to judge, but so that the world might be saved through him" (3:17); ". . . We know that this is truly the Savior of the world" (4:42); "If someone enters through me, he will be saved . . ." (10:9); and ". . . I did not come to judge the world but to save the world" (12:47).[255] In each of the cases above, as can be seen from the analysis of the Composition, the terminology appears in material of the third edition.

Thus, in all of these instances, the death of Jesus is seen (either explicitly or implicitly) to be the action that achieves salvific effects for the believer. It is a view that is distinct from the view, in the second edition, of his death as "departure."[256]

6. The Background of Soteriology in 1 John and in the Third Edition

We have already examined passages from the SDQ that speak of forgiveness of, and purification from, sin. As was apparent, the conception of this being accomplished through the Spirit of God was no different from that of the canonical Scriptures. The only difference was that the SDQ place this within an apocalyptic worldview.

---

255. This includes all religious uses of the verb, the abstract noun ("salvation"), and the personal noun ("Savior"). Three other instances (5:34; 11:12; 12:27) do not refer to the same sort of activity as is intended in the other passages. Of these, only 5:34 requires some comment. As is explained in more detail in the Commentary proper, the exact meaning of "save" in this verse is not clear. However, it is clear (1) that it does not refer to the saving act of the death of Jesus, and (2) that the witness of John is not considered a true source of salvation in any sense comparable to that of Jesus. Therefore it is unlikely that the verb should be taken in the sense intended in the third edition and equally unlikely that it comes from the third edition.

256. There are other passages that may hint at an understanding of the death as atonement, but they are not so clear. For example, 3:14 says: "The Son of Man must be lifted up so that everyone believing in him may have everlasting life." This expression occurs in material that is associated otherwise with the third edition. In addition, a very similar expression occurs in 1 John 4:9 ("He has sent his unique Son into the world so that we may live through him").

A History of the Development of Johannine Theology

a. The Concept of Vicarious Atonement in Judaism

As numerous studies have shown, the notion of atonement was known in Judaism.[257] Among the examples of atonement are the figures of the Suffering Servant of Isaiah 52:13–53:12 and the Akedah tradition dealing with Isaac, both of which were referred to above. De Jonge also calls attention to various Old Testament texts that speak of atonement by Moses (Exod 32:30-34; Ps 106:16-23) and Phinehas (Num 25; Ps 106:28-31; Sir 45:23).[258] We cannot enter into a detailed discussion of these texts. However, in none of them is there the figure who by his suffering averts the just anger of God or obtains forgiveness. For example, while the action of Phinehas in slaying the Israelite who is lying with a Midianite woman averts the anger of God, it is not through Phinehas's suffering but rather his zeal to punish the sins of others that this is accomplished.

Another approach would be to examine the Old Testament language associated with blood sacrifice. In Lev 17:11, we find evidence that could provide a background for understanding the death of Jesus as sacrificial and atoning: "For the life of all flesh is its blood, and I have given it to you to make atonement on the altar for your lives, for its blood will atone for life."[259] This is reflected in Heb 9:22, which connects such atonement with the forgiveness of sins: "According to the Law, almost everything is cleansed in blood, and without the shedding of blood there is no forgiveness."[260]

M. de Jonge, in the article referred to above, also proposes that the deaths of the seven brothers and their mother were spoken of in a way that indicates that their death was thought of as having the effect of atoning for the wrongs of the nation and of turning away the just anger of God from the nation (2 Macc 7:1-42; 4 Macc 5-7; 8-18). 2 Macc 7:38 (where the youngest son says, "I beg our God, ... through me and my brothers, to bring an end to the wrath of the Almighty that has justly fallen on our whole nation") seems to reflect the notion that a person's suffering and death could atone for the wrongdoing of others and for the entire nation. An equally clear instance of such thinking is evident in 4 Macc 6:28-29 ("... let our punishment be sufficient [for your people]. Make my blood their purification, and accept my life in exchange for theirs"). Yet this is not precisely what is spoken of in the third edition.

---

257. See, for example, Hengel, *Atonement*.
258. De Jonge, *Death* 147-49.
259. See, for example, the discussion in Dodd, *"Hilaskesthai"* 352-60; Tuckett, "Atonement in the NT," *ABD* 1, 518-22; de Boer, *Perspectives* 272-76.
260. See also Exod 30:10, where Aaron is told to make atonement with blood on the altar once a year. In 4 Macc 6:28-29 (referred to above) Eleazar hopes that his own blood will act to cleanse the people as a whole. Rom 3:21-26 connects the death of Jesus with the rite of Yom Kippur in the Holy of Holies, where the mercy of God was manifested.

Section 7. The Development of Johannine Theology: Soteriology

b. The Absence of an Atoning Eschatological Figure in Judaism

While it may be fairly said that the notion of atonement can be found in the Jewish tradition prior to Jesus, *the notion of the death of an eschatological figure as an atoning sacrifice is not a component of any strand of Jewish eschatological hopes.*[261] It would have been even more difficult for Jews to have conceived of a crucified individual as being an eschatological figure, let alone an atoning one, since a crucified person was looked upon as cursed by God (Deut 21:23).

c. The Concept of Vicarious Atonement Elsewhere in Early Christianity

In spite of the fact that there was no Jewish model for an atoning eschatological figure, it is obvious that the notion of the death of Jesus and his blood as an atonement for sin is regularly found elsewhere in the New Testament and is a central element of New Testament theology. Among the more prominent New Testament texts outside the Johannine literature are: Acts 20:28; Rom 3:25; 5:9; Eph 1:7; 2:13; Col 1:20; 1 Pet 1:2, 19; Rev 1:5; 5:9; 7:14. In addition, there are other texts that reflect the notion of dying "for our sins," for example, 1 Cor 15:3. Consequently, although the background of the concept of atonement is found in the Old Testament, its association with an eschatological figure can be said to be uniquely Christian.[262] What happened to Jesus was not expected to happen to the hoped-for eschatological figure of Judaism.

Thus, we may see that for a Jewish community interpreting the death of Jesus and the outpouring of the Spirit within the context of Jewish eschatological hopes, the primary expectation would be that the forgiveness of sin would come through the Spirit. This was, of course, the view of the community at the time of the second edition. It was a view that was supplemented and corrected both by the author of 1 John and by the author of the third edition.

---

261. R. E. Brown (*Christology* 160) concludes: "Thus far [in scholarship] we have no clear evidence of a pre-Christian description of a suffering Messiah." There were suffering figures, but there was no direct relationship to eschatological hopes. De Jonge ("Death" 142-43; *Christology* 173-88) provides a brief but helpful survey of the various attempts to understand the death of Jesus soteriologically and comes to the same conclusion. See also Hengel, *Atonement* 42, 70-74; Gubler, *Deutungen*, and Friedrich, *Verkündigung*

262. To explore the background of these concepts would take us too far afield from our present interests. However, as Hengel (*Atonement* 1-32) and others have shown, these conceptions have parallels within Greek and Roman religion, and it may be under the influence of Hellenization of Judaism that such concepts were used to interpret the death of Jesus.

A History of the Development of Johannine Theology

SECTION 8. THE DEVELOPMENT OF JOHANNINE THEOLOGY: ETHICS

Ethics is concerned with the prescriptions of conduct appropriate for the believer. Ethical perfectionism, in turn, holds that the individual is radically transformed so that proper conduct is inevitably achieved. The person's actions are spontaneously directed toward proper conduct, and so the individual is not in need of specific ethical directives.[263] Such a belief was evident in Jewish thought about the eschaton, and so it is not surprising that a community of believers, thoroughly steeped in Jewish thought, who believed that the eschatological age had dawned, might consider such to be a reality.[264]

1. Ethics in the First Edition

As is the case with a number of aspects of the community's thought, there is no evidence of a discussion of ethics in what remains of the first edition. The Pharisees accuse the man born blind (9:16, 24, 25, 31, 34) of being sinful, thus the reality of sin is acknowledged but no attitude toward it on the part of the author is evident.

2. Ethics in the Second Edition

When we turn to the second edition, it is important to recognize that the second edition does not address the topic of perfectionism directly. Rather, we encounter a striking *absence* of ethical directives. This lack of attention to ethical matters is regularly noticed by scholars. For example, R. E. Brown speaks of "the ethical silence of GJohn." He goes on to say: "No specific sins of behavior are mentioned in GJohn, only the great sin, which is to refuse to believe in Jesus (8:24; 9:41)."[265] Smith comments: "Only after he has withdrawn with his disci-

---

263. Bogart (*Perfectionism* 7) comments: "'Perfectionism' is the term generally applied to the view that man is capable of achieving sinlessness in his present existence." This definition primarily concerns the ethical aspect of perfection, that is, the achievement of ethical or moral purity; it may, however, be expanded to include spiritual perfection also, that is, the union with God or the beatific vision. Bogart himself chooses to include both aspects in his inquiry. Our focus here will be on the first of these aspects. Perfectionism is also called "impeccability" by some.

264. This perfectionism is only a future perfectionism and does not deal with the issue of past sins. The author of 1 John makes it quite clear that the believer has sinned in the past and that these sins have been taken away by Jesus' death (e.g., 1:7).

265. Brown, *Epistles* 80-81.

ples, his own, does Jesus offer instruction regarding the conduct of life. Even then his instructions lack specificity."[266] Meeks states bluntly, "[The Gospel] offers no explicit moral instruction.... The maxims (gnomes) that are so characteristic of Jesus' sayings in the Q, Synoptic, and Thomas traditions ... are missing altogether from John."[267]

Within the second edition, the major sin (and the only one to which any attention is given) is that of unbelief. Bultmann points out, regarding the Gospel as a whole: "Sin ... is not primarily immoral behaviour; it does not consist in any particular action, but is unbelief, and it will be defined as such explicitly in 16:8."[268] Brown echoes this, as we noted above.

Although 8:21 is not completely clear about what constitutes sin, given the overall context of the discussion, which concerns acceptance of the claims of Jesus, it would seem that the sin here also is unbelief. In 8:34, the context is also unclear but, likewise, probably refers to unbelief. In 15:22, 24, the context makes it clear that unbelief is the topic. In 19:11, the "sin" referred to is the betrayal of Jesus. While this could be looked on as "ethical failure," it is also the ultimate act of unbelief.

Thus, sin, conceived of as unbelief, is radical in that it rejects the claim that the eschatological outpouring of the Spirit has even taken place (or is about to) in and through the ministry of Jesus. This is an entirely different matter; but there remains the absence of genuine ethical directives — an absence that is glaring and without explanation within the second edition. Yet three factors converge to make the reason for this absence clear. First, as we have alluded to above, it was common to believe that in the eschatological age it would not be necessary to teach one another. Not only that, but ethics in particular would not be necessary. Second, the pages of 1 John make it clear that perfectionism was both a problem and a conviction. Both the author and his opponents believed that the community was "perfect" but disagreed about what this meant. Third, and finally, we see in the third edition of the Gospel a clear emphasis on ethics in the form of the love commandment.

The Importance of 1 John for Recognizing the Ethical Perfectionism of the Second Edition

If it were not for 1 John, we would be much less certain about the presence and nature of, and the reason for, the "perfectionism" in the theology of the second edi-

---

266. Smith, "Presentation," in *Johannine* 175-89, quotation on 178.
267. Meeks, "Ethics," 317-26, quote on 318. The most extensive treatment of Johannine morality (Lazure, *Valeurs*) even reflects the lack of specific ethical instruction by its title.
268. Bultmann, *Gospel* 551.

tion. From the second edition by itself, we notice only the lack of attention to specific ethical directives. Without 1 John, it would perhaps be possible to argue that the community at the time of the second edition had ethical directives but that for some reason they were simply not included in the written text of the Gospel. In the light of 1 John, this sort of explanation is not tenable. In 1 John, we see that this lack of attention to ethics is due to the fact that the community held to a theory of ethical perfectionism in which no ethics were thought to be necessary.[269]

But it is also clear from the pages of 1 John that it was not just the opponents who held to a theory of ethical perfectionism; both the author *and* his opponents held to variants of such a theory. The only debate was about the correct *understanding* of perfectionism. That debate takes place in the pages of 1 John.

3. The Background of Ethical Perfectionism in the Second Edition

When we seek a unifying factor in the various aspects of this topic, we find it precisely where we should expect it: in the Old Testament understanding of the prerogatives accompanying the eschatological outpouring of the Spirit.[270]

Perfectionism is evident in the Old Testament in two ways. First, those Old Testament texts that speak of full, direct knowledge of God link proper behavior to such knowledge. Such knowledge makes doing the right thing "spontaneous." Thus, it can be said to grant a state of sinlessness and perfectionism. Second, such a conviction is explicit and directly linked to the possession of the eschatological Spirit in Ezek 36:25-28,[271] where the opposite of forgiving sins is "making" one obey the Law. The gift of unerring faithfulness in an eschatological context is also evident in Jer 31:33-34.[272] Thus, the prerogatives spoken of in the Gospel match those of the promised Spirit in the Old Testament. As Vellanickal writes, "Impeccability through knowledge of God and Life by means of the active presence of the Spirit and Truth (Wisdom) and the Law in the hearts of men, was an eschatological theme both in biblical and Judaic tradition."[273] This perfectionism was based on the conviction that not only does the reception of God's

---

269. So also, for example, Bogart, *Perfectionism* 25-50; Grayston, *Epistles* 22-27, 138.

270. See esp. Bogart, *Perfectionism* 93-122; de la Potterie, "L'impeccabilité" 194-220; Schnackenburg, *Gospel* 1:370-71; Vellanickal, *Sonship* 269-70; von Wahlde, *Commandments* 164.

271. "I will pour clean water upon you, and you shall be cleansed from all your uncleanness, and from all your idols I will purify you. A new heart I will give you, and I will put a new spirit within you; and I will remove the heart of stone from your body and give you a heart of flesh. I will put my Spirit within you, and make you follow my commandments and be careful to observe my ordinances" (NRSV).

272. "I will place my law within them, and I will write it on their hearts. . . ."

273. Vellanickal, *Sonship* 267.

Section 8. The Development of Johannine Theology: Ethics

Spirit cleanse one from past sin, but possession of the Holy Spirit in its eschatological fullness will make one sinless for the future, thus providing a basis for "perfectionism."

4. Ethics in 1 John

When we turn to 1 John, we find that the issue of ethical perfectionism is hotly disputed within the community.[274] But it is equally clear that the dispute is not whether or not there is a perfectionism but regarding the proper understanding of perfectionism.

a. The View of the Opponents

First, we have seen that the opponents believed that the giving of the Spirit in its eschatological fullness resulted in a cleansing from sin, in a rebirth to the life of God, and in a rebirth to a state of truly knowing (and therefore living out) the will of God; all of this meant that the believer was transformed to a state of perfection in which there would be no future sin. In this ideal state, there would be no need for ethics.

Second, I have noted above the regular observation of scholars that the Gospel as a whole has little reference to ethics. All ethical directives are presented in the summary commandment of mutual love. Apart from this commandment (which comes from the third edition) there are no ethical directives at all!

Third, there is the evidence of 1 John itself. In 2:4-9, we read what was surely a reasonable summary of many of the opponents' views: they claim to "know" God but do not keep the commandments (2:4); they do not keep his word (2:5); they do not walk as he (Jesus) walked (2:6); and they hate the brothers (3:15-17). In short, there is no evidence that the opponents consider ethical directives necessary at all.[275]

---

274. Van der Watt ("Ethics") approaches the concept of ethics in the Johannine literature from the point of view of metaphors of the family in the ancient world. Although he does not address the issue of editing, the fact that he finds the starting point in 1 John is perhaps significant.

275. A proper understanding of ethical perfectionism also seems to have been a problem in other sectors of early Christianity. In Gal 5:13-26, Paul speaks of the "freedom" that believers have in Christ and of the focus of all ethics in the love commandment of Lev 19:18. He then (as does the author of 1 John) speaks of the way true living by the Spirit is manifest and contrasts this with the way of living according to the flesh. Paul argues (as does the author of 1 John) that, even though a person has received the Spirit, that person is still able to live by the flesh and so must strive to live "by the Spirit" (Gal 5:16, 25).

b. The View of the Author

The author of 1 John argues that, while believers are in a real sense perfect, nevertheless this is not a once-and-for-all achievement. On the one hand, the author makes it clear that the believer is "perfect": 3:6-8 ("Everyone remaining in him [Jesus] does not sin. Everyone sinning has neither seen him [Jesus] nor known him [Jesus]. The one committing sin is of the devil . . ."); 9a ("Everyone begotten of God does not commit sin because his [God's] seed remains in him"); 9b ("and he [the believer] is not able to sin because he has been begotten of God").

On the other hand, the author makes it abundantly clear that the believer is capable of sin and of losing eternal life. First, there are the repeated general injunctions to keep the commandments (2:4, 7-8; 3:22-23), to walk as he walked (2:6), and to love one's brother (2:9-11; 3:10c, 11, 14-18; 4:7, 11-12, 20-21; 5:1-2). Second, 1 John regularly speaks of the need to work to become more like Jesus (3:2-3). The possibility of a future state of likeness to Jesus implies not only that "ethical behavior" is necessary but that the state of the believer is at first imperfect and needs improvement, but also that the future state will be a more complete form of life. In addition, this will give one confidence on the day of judgment (4:17-18). Thus, we have a definite conviction about a future dimension to life that will be different from that of the present.

The author of 1 John emphasizes the need for proper behavior by introducing the commandment of mutual love as the principle that is to underlie all ethical conduct. Although the believer is inchoatively perfect, the believer must nevertheless put forward the effort to achieve in reality what he/she has in "root" already. Moreover, the author considers this love to be so important that he describes it as one of only two commandments in the tradition as the community understands them.

In the light of the ethical vacuum of the second edition, this introduction of, and these repeated references to, mutual love in 1 John are remarkable. It appears as a topic sixteen times explicitly in 1 John (3:10, 11, 14 [twice], 18, 23; 4:7 [twice], 8, 11, 12, 20, 21; 5:1, 2). It appears also in 2 John 5. Further, it is present implicitly in 2 John 11 and in 3 John 5-8.

That all directives for proper conduct could be summarized in terms of love is evident in the Synoptic Gospels' reference to the Great Commandment as the summation of the whole law (cf. Mark 12:28-34; Matt 22:34-40; Luke 10:25-28). As the second of the Great Commandments summarizes all the obligations toward one's neighbor in terms of love, so also does the Johannine commandment of mutual love. That love of one's neighbor was considered a summation of such ethical responsibility is also evident from the Pauline tradition in passages such as Gal 5:13-14.

Section 8. The Development of Johannine Theology: Ethics

Yet the Johannine love commandment is expressed in terms of mutual love rather than as love of "neighbor" or "love of enemies." This formulation of the obligation to love is cast within the typically apocalyptic framework of mutual love. Thus, although the Johannine tradition held to a belief in the love of Jesus for all persons (cf. John 3:16, etc.), the community formulated its ethics within a dualism that indicated that to "love" those who were not of the community was to love those who were of the world. But the world was evil, and to love those who were "of the world" would be to take part in their evil deeds, just as was the case in the context of 2 John 11, where it is said that to offer hospitality to those who come to the community and do not bring the proper teaching would be to take part in their evil deeds. Thus, within the dualistic perspective of apocalyptic there appears to be no possibility of love being extended to them in such a way as to bring about a change in their hearts.

5. Ethics in the Third Edition

In the third edition of the Gospel, we may distinguish three types of the ethical references.

a. Ethics and References to Sinful Actions

First, we notice brief references to the sinful actions of people (3:19-20, 36a). These comments are made only in passing and are surprisingly brief given the attention that is directed to the love commandment in the Farewell Discourses.

b. Ethics and Final Judgment

Second, we see explicit references to eschatological judgment by the Son of Man. The clearest of these is in 5:27-29, where we hear that the Father has given Jesus the power to judge because he is the Son of Man. The passage goes on to explain that this judgment will take place at the time when all arise from the tombs, for a resurrection of life or a resurrection of judgment. The conviction of such a final judgment determines the importance of ethical action because it states that the correctness of one's actions will be the basis of the judgment: "All those in the tombs will hear his voice and will come forth, those who have done evil to a resurrection of judgment" (5:29). A similar passage occurs in 9:39, where again the Son of Man (9:35) says, "I came into this world for judgment. . . ."

c. The Love Commandment

Third, we find the references to the commandment to love one another (13:34-35; 15:12, 17). These constitute a clear statement of the community's overarching ethical imperative, an imperative that the third edition of the Gospel carries over from 1 John.

However, the author of the third edition presents a more fully developed notion of the love commandment than his predecessor. This presentation diverges from that in 1 John in three ways. First, in the third edition, the commandments are said to be commandments "of Jesus" rather than "of God," as they were in 1 John.[276]

Second, and most importantly, the third author speaks not only of commandments given to the disciples but also of commandments given to Jesus by the Father. For our purposes here, it is important to notice that the commandments given to the disciples are directly linked to those given to Jesus.[277] Thus, just as Jesus received a commandment (cf. 10:18) from the Father to lay down his life for his own out of love (10:11b-14a, 15b, 17-18), so Jesus gives the disciples the commandment to love one another. If the second edition showed Jesus as the one who "knew" his sheep and called them by name, the author of the third edition presented Jesus also as the shepherd who had cared for his sheep and would lay down his life for them.

The third original element in the third edition is that the author now provides a model for the fulfillment of the love commandment in the love of Jesus for his own: "A new commandment I give you, that, as I love you, you also should love one another" (13:34). Moreover, the third author provides a new interpretation to the scene of the footwashing in chapter 13 as an example of this service for one another. In his secondary interpretation, the third author sees Jesus as giving the disciples an example of loving service to one another in the act of footwashing (13:12-19): "So if I, the master and teacher, washed your feet, you also ought to wash the feet of one another" (13:14). Thus, not all loving service need be of the heroic kind, as would be evident in dying for one's brother. It extends also to *humble* service.

---

276. For the significance of the attribution of the commandments to God the Father in the Letters, see above in the discussion of "knowing" and its relation to the "first" commandment in 1 John.

277. For a more detailed discussion, see von Wahlde, *Commandments* 11-38, esp. 11-12. Since the composition of *Commandments*, I have become convinced that 1 John was written before the third edition of the Gospel. However, this does not affect the understanding of the commandments within the (third edition of the) Gospel.

Section 8. The Development of Johannine Theology: Ethics

d. Conclusion

It could well be argued that even in the final edition, the Gospel gives relatively little attention to the matter of ethics. It certainly is true that the only ethical directive is the love commandment. At the same time it is true that such a reduction of all ethical obligations to the obligation to love is not unique to the Johannine tradition. It is also found in the two Great Commandments of the Synoptic tradition.[278] There can be no doubt that not only the Johannine community but the remainder of early Christianity saw the love commandment as a proper summation of one's ethical obligations, even if other sectors of early Christianity chose to explicate the demands of love in more detail.[279]

6. The Background of the Attitude toward Ethics in 1 John and in the Third Edition

In addition to the Old Testament statements regarding freedom from sin in the eschatological age, we find extensive evidence of ethical perfectionism in the SDQ and in other Jewish apocalyptic literature. Bogart comments: "In Jewish apocalyptic literature, perfection is one of God's eschatological gifts to the elect."[280]

a. Ethical Perfectionism and Sin in the Sectarian Documents of Qumran and in the Testaments of the Twelve Patriarchs

For the community at Qumran, humanity in its "natural" state was looked upon as almost totally sinful and full of iniquity. The recurring phrase for this is that man has a "spirit of flesh" (1QH 4:25; 5:19; 12:30). One of the more extended discussions of the Qumran community's view of humanity and sin can be found in

---

278. I am not claiming that the two Johannine commandments are the Johannine equivalent of the "Two Great Commandments" of the Synoptic tradition. Yet there is a similarity between the second of the two great commandments and the Johannine love commandment. For a summary and discussion of other two-commandment traditions and the difference between these and the Johannine tradition, see von Wahlde, *Commandments* 233-44.

279. Recently, Nissen ("Community" 194-212) has sought to explain this by his proposal that such ethics are less concerned with the individual and more with the community. Nissen sees the ground of this view in the larger theological framework of the Gospel, arguing that the "who we are" of the community was seen in the light of the story of the Gospel and that this determined "how we should act."

280. Bogart, *Perfectionism* 105.

1QH 12:29-37. Man without the Spirit of God is described as "in sin from his maternal womb, and in guilty iniquity right to old age." The ways of man "are not secure except by the spirit that God creates for him to perfect the path of the sons of Adam so that all his creatures come to know the strength of his power . . ." (DSST).

The Spirit provides both purification of earlier sin (cf. the discussion of "soteriology" above) and strength for future conduct. This is evident in 1QH 15:6:

> I give you thanks, Lord, because you have sustained me with your strength, you have spread your holy spirit over me so that I will not stumble, you have fortified me against the wars of wickedness, and in all their calamities you have not discouraged me from your covenant. (DSST)

One of the clearest statements of future freedom from sin is in 1QH 4:22: ". . . you prevent [the one whom you choose] from sinning against you."

In spite of the conviction that they had received the Spirit and that this was the source of true holiness, there is no evidence at Qumran that the community considered the gift of the Spirit as so totally transforming that further sin was impossible. This is evident from 1QH 4:21-24:

> . . . I have understood that [you establish] the path of the one whom you choose and in the insight [of your wisdom] you prevent him from sinning against you, you restore his humility through your punishments, and by your ord[eals streng]then his heart. [You, Lord, prevent] your servant from sinning against you, from tripping over all the words of your will. Engrave your com[mandments in him,] so that he can hold himself up against [fiendish] spirits, so that he can walk in all that you love and loathe all that you hate, [so he can do] what is good in your eyes. (DSST)

This prayer is one of confidence but also one of hope for the continued assistance of God in avoiding sin. Thus, although they saw themselves as the beneficiaries of the Spirit, they were still capable of sin. The community itself recognized this and so conducted an annual evaluation of their belief and of their conduct.

In this respect, the community at Qumran was not unlike the Johannine community at the time of 1 John and the Gospel's third edition. Both saw the possibility of future sin. At the same time both were convinced of the special help of God's Spirit.[281]

---

281. Thus, I would agree with Bogart, who would see the perfectionism of Qumran as one of "constant striving" (*Perfectionism* 106-8).

Section 8. The Development of Johannine Theology: Ethics

Evidence of perfectionism is not as strong in the *T12P* as it is elsewhere in Jewish apocalyptic literature, but it is nevertheless present. The *T12P* express hopes for the future and describe life when the eschaton arrives. There is no conviction that the eschaton is already present as there is in the SDQ. Nevertheless, several texts make reference to it. *TLev* 18:9 states that such perfectionism will be part of the ideal world at the time of the eschaton. *TJud* 24:2-3 states that those upon whom the Spirit rests will "walk in his decrees." Finally, *TBenj* 8:2-3 describes the one upon whom the Spirit of God rests as "having no pollution in his heart."

b. Ethical Perfectionism and Sin Elsewhere in Jewish Apocalyptic

The ideal of eschatological perfectionism continues in other apocalyptic literature. Bogart points to *1 Enoch* 5:8-9, which, couched as it is in an eschatological context and describing the benefits of that period, speaks of something very close to perfectionism.[282] *Jubilees* 5:12 is a clear instance that speaks of not sinning forever. Two other texts are equally important. Both 4 Ezra 6:26 and *Jub.* 1:20-21, 23 attribute perfectionism to a "spirit" created for them by God.

Thus, it is well attested that there was a belief/hope for perfectionism in the eschatological age as a result of the imparting of the (a) Spirit by God. However, the perfectionism (and here I refer to the view of the author of 1 John) of the Johannine community is closest to that of the Qumran community in that both claim to be living within the eschatological age and to have the fruits of the eschaton at least to some degree as a present possession.[283] At the same time, both the author of 1 John and the SDQ speak of the need to work in order to achieve what is already seminally present. It is only in these two groups that the notion of completely realized perfectionism is tempered by a conviction that striving is still necessary!

Thus, once again, we see that the framework of Johannine thought bears considerable similarity to that of the SDQ in general orientation (i.e., God's outpouring of the Spirit has begun/taken place) even though the content of the conviction (Qumran beliefs and Johannine Christianity) are quite different.

---

282. This is argued by Bogart, *Perfectionism* 104-5.
283. That the community saw itself as living in the end of days is explicit in 4QMMT 107 ("And this is the end of days . . .") as well as in 1Q28a 1:1 ("and this is the rule of the congregation in the final days . . ."). See J. J. Collins, "Expectation" 79.

c. Sectarian Love in the Sectarian Documents of Qumran and in the Testaments of the Twelve Patriarchs

It was indicated above that for the author of 1 John and the author of the Gospel's third edition, ethical conduct was subsumed under the rubric of mutual love. Again we find extensive parallels to the Johannine conception of restricted mutual love in the SDQ and in the *T12P.* These parallels are discussed in detail in 3E-15, where their association with apocalyptic dualism is evident. That discussion need not be repeated here.

SECTION 9. THE DEVELOPMENT OF JOHANNINE THEOLOGY: ANTHROPOLOGY

1. Anthropology in the First Edition

There is no distinctive anthropology in the first edition.[284] The view of the human person is the one common to the Jewish Scriptures. There is no (remaining) discussion of how the believer is transformed by faith or by other aspects of religious experience.

2. Anthropology in the Second Edition

If the Johannine Gospel is marked by an unparalleled view of the exalted nature and function of Jesus as Son (Christology), it is also marked by a remarkably exalted view of the status of the believer (anthropology). That this was so was due to the fact that the community at the time of the second edition considered the believer to have received many, if not all, of the prerogatives that had been given to Jesus. In order to put this into proper perspective, it is important to remember that these claims were made for the person Jesus, who was understood to be human first and foremost "the son of Joseph, whose father and mother we know" (6:30) and who was not considered to be preexistently divine but rendered divine by the gift of the Spirit at his meeting with John the Baptist. Because similar prerogatives were thought to be given to the believer by the gift of

---

[284]. Recent discussions that deal specifically with elements of anthropology have not proved particularly helpful for the present study. The study by Schnelle *(Human)* understands anthropology in a significantly different sense and includes topics that I see as quite distinct. Urban *(Menschenbild)* does not treat the full Gospel and so is less useful. In addition, Urban does not distinguish among various perspectives within the literature.

Section 9. The Development of Johannine Theology: Anthropology

the eschatological Spirit, there was the potential for blurring the distinction between the status of Jesus and the status of the believer.

That the prerogatives of Jesus are understood to be given to the disciples should not be surprising. He stated this without equivocation with regard to his miracles. If Jesus worked the works given him by the Father (5:36; 9:4; 10:25, 32 [twice], 33, 37, 38), Jesus also promised the disciples that they would perform the same works he performed (14:12). The disciples would also have a number of his other prerogatives because they possessed the same Spirit Jesus did.

By taking the promises associated with the eschatological outpouring of the Spirit with utmost seriousness, the Johannine community developed an understanding of the status of the believer that was arguably the most exalted of the New Testament. Both Jesus and the believer possessed the Spirit. The Spirit was said to descend upon Jesus at his baptism; the Spirit was repeatedly promised by Jesus (e.g., 4:10; 7:37-39) and indeed bestowed upon the disciples on the night of the Resurrection (John 20:22). Because the status of the believer was understood to be so exalted, it became a challenge to the unique role of Jesus.[285]

All of the prerogatives of the Spirit elevated the believer to a new and divine status. In every way that the believer was transformed, he took on a prerogative that was associated with those attributed to Jesus. Thus, this life rendered the believer sinless, gave him/her knowledge, made judgment unnecessary, made ethics unnecessary, and so on. In all of these ways, the believer had become like Jesus.[286]

Just as Jesus was the "son" of God, so the believer was born of God and was called a "child" of God.[287] The implication drawn from this was that just as

---

285. It is important to remember that, while the Gospel in its final form contains clear distinctions between the (unique) role of Jesus and that of the believer, *within the material of the second edition* there is no evidence of such a distinction.

286. For a similar view, see de Boer, "Death" 326-46, esp. 328. Smalley (*1, 2, 3 John* 146) comments with regard to the statement in 1 John (3:2) that at the time of the parousia, "We will be like him": "The expression grazes the edge of deification, but stops short of it." In the present text of the Gospel, it is the third edition itself that introduces the notion of the believer as "child" of God but at the same time takes care to qualify this vis-à-vis the sonship of Jesus.

287. In the Gospel, Jesus explains that it is necessary to be reborn of the Spirit (3:3-8). The implication was that the believer was truly "reborn" and therefore could be called a "child of God."

The notion of the "sonship" of Christians was not unique to Johannine Christianity. Paul speaks of the same type of divine prerogative in his Letter to the Romans, in terms that are in some respects even more direct:

"All who are led by the Spirit of God are sons of God *(huioi theou)*. For you did not receive a spirit making you slaves of fear again, but you received a spirit of adoption *(huiothesias)* in which we cry out, 'Abba, Father.' The Spirit witnesses along with our spirit that we are children of God. But if children, then heirs. On the one hand, heirs of God and, on the other, coheirs with Jesus if we now co-suffer in order that we may be co-glorified" (Rom 8:14-17).

Here the Christian is specifically called a "son" of God along with the more general

Jesus was "Son of God," so the believer was raised to that same level of divine existence as Jesus.[288] When the opponents in 1 John refused to confess that Jesus was the Son of God, they refused to grant him a *unique* status as Son of God.

The community at the time of the second edition also spoke of believers having an "anointing." This is one of the implications of the second edition that is not evident in the Gospel itself, although the fact that it was so can be readily reconstructed, given the association of "anointing" with the giving of the Spirit. Moreover, in 1 John, we see positive evidence that this was precisely the case (cf. 1 John 2:20). If the believer can be said to have an anointing, the opponents would also argue that the status of the believer meant that Jesus did not have a unique role in this respect either.[289] That Jesus is "the Christ" is the second of the confessions that the opponents refuse to make.

Both Jesus and the believer possessed eternal life. We have seen a detailed description of this in the section on eternal life. However, here we need to recall that, in the second edition of the Gospel, this gift of life is understood to have been bestowed upon the believer fully in the present and in such a way that one was radically transformed. Once transformed, the believer lived a new life that was no longer simply natural life (the life of the flesh; cf. 3:6; 6:63) but the life of

---

"child"; the Christian is also paralleled with Christ as "co-heir." As Dunn remarks, "... the experience of the Spirit of the Son crying, 'Abba! Father!' ... reproduc[es] that most intimate experience of and relation which characterized Jesus' own life on earth" (*Unity* 194). Paul also saw the Spirit as a principle of eternal life making the believer a "son of God." But at the same time, Paul distinguishes between this sonship and that of Jesus by describing the sonship of the believer as one of "adoption." Schnackenburg comments (*Epistles* 156): "Nowhere in the Johannine writings — in contrast to Paul — are Christians designated 'sons of God.' This is not because 'child' implies a different relationship from 'son.' Rather, it seems that John has coined a new usage. Paul himself apparently assumed that there was a difference between our sonship by grace and the ontological sonship of Christ, as he shows by the absolute phrase 'the son' (of God)." On this, see also Fitzmyer, *Romans* 497-504. The closest the Gospel gets to referring to the believer as "son" is 8:35, where, in a contrast with "slave," Jesus says that "'the son' remains forever."

That the Johannine tradition deliberately used "child" to designate the status of the believer but "son" to refer to the status of Jesus is frequently noted. See, for example, de Jonge, *Envoy* 121 and n. 24 there.

288. The bringing of the believer too close to the status of Jesus is referred to by Kelber as "the charismatic collapsing of the hierarchical distance between Jesus and his followers" ("Metaphysics" 129-54, esp. p. 132). The relationship between Jesus and the Christian is explained and qualified by the third author and by 1 John in such a way as to distinguish the sonship of Jesus from that of the Christian, but it is important to recognize that the view of the second edition is a logical reading of the promises made in that edition.

289. Most scholars recognize this in relation to the position of the opponents in the Letters (see below), but because of the intermixing of literary strata within the Gospel it has been more difficult to do in relation to the Gospel.

Section 9. The Development of Johannine Theology: Anthropology

God, eternal life. Human death was of no significance since eternal life was guaranteed.

Thus, it would seem that in the light of the second edition, a segment of the community had come to a perspective that obscured how the identity of Jesus was to be distinguished from the identity of the believer.[290]

3. The Background of the Anthropology of the Second Edition

The anthropology of the second edition of the Gospel corresponds to a literal interpretation of the prerogatives of the eschatological outpouring of the Spirit as these were presented in the Old Testament. In Jewish thought, the eschatological age was, of its nature, something totally new and unprecedented. Yet, it is evident that the anthropology of the second edition was in total accord with the expectations presented in the canonical Jewish Scriptures.

4. Anthropology in 1 John

a. The View of the Opponents and That of the Author

As was the case with regard to so many of the issues the author disputes with his opponents, the author of 1 John agrees with the opponents in affirming that the believer is similar to Jesus in a variety of ways. The author speaks of the believer becoming like Jesus, for example, in 3:2c, d ("We know that when he [Jesus] is revealed, we will be like him [Jesus] . . .") and in 4:17 (". . . because, just as that one is, so are we"). Jesus is the model to be imitated.

b. Believers as "Children of God"

This is true also of the concepts of being children of God and of being born of God. Schnackenburg, in his commentary on 1 John, provides an excursus on the meaning of these terms that contains many valuable insights and a view that is close to that of R. E. Brown.[291] Schnackenburg makes it quite clear that the title "child" of God that is given to the believer is not merely a polite form of address

---

290. There will be no discussion of the background of the anthropology of the second edition since it is presumed by the other aspects of the edition's theology.

291. Schnackenburg, *Epistles* 162-69. See also the extended discussion of the background of "children of God" in Culpepper, "Pivot" 17-31.

but is meant to be taken literally. The relationship spoken of is ontological and not merely an analogy. "Being a child of God is more than a matter of moral behavior, while being a child of the devil is less than a biological relationship."[292] This indicates how the author of 1 John must once again walk a tightrope, for he agrees with much of what the opponents say but at the same time sees the need to modify and nuance their position. We can see this in the statements culled from 1 John and listed below. In each, we can notice how the author is convinced that the believer is in a real sense very much like Jesus in status and destiny through the gift of the Spirit, but at the same time is to be distinguished from him.

That the author of 1 John sees the believer as similar to and in some sense *the same* as Jesus is indicated, first, by the similar terms he applies to both. We have seen above that the author refers to the believer as born of God and a "child" of God, terms that are very similar to the title "Son of God" given to Jesus. At the same time he never says that the believer is a "son" of God, even though this would be naturally applicable to a male believer. Clearly a distinction is intended. Yet the author of 1 John does not hesitate to develop the imagery of the believer as "begotten" of God (and therefore a child [son/daughter] of God). In the second edition, it is said (3:3-8) that the believer is "born" (of the Spirit). In 1 John, the author emphasizes the role of God in this birth by saying that the believer is begotten "of God." However, in 1 John, this motif assumes a greater prominence than in the second edition, appearing ten times within five passages (2:29; 3:9 [twice]; 4:7; 5:1 [three times], 4, 18 [twice]). Although this continues to emphasize the identity of the believer as a "child" of God, it is likewise true that in 1 John it is never said that Jesus was "born." Rather, he is said to have been "revealed" (3:5, 8).

c. Believers as "Anointed"

But what of his status as "anointed"? In 1 John, the believer is also said to have a *chrisma* (2:20, 27). This is a special gift, conferring special prerogatives, among which is "knowing all" (2:20) and not having the need for anyone to teach them, for the anointing teaches them "about all" (2:27).[293] This *chrisma* is both etymologically and theologically close to *christos*, the other primary title given to Jesus.[294] Even at a time when there was confusion about the respective identities

---

292. Schnackenburg, *Epistles* 162.

293. This was not a prerogative restricted to the Johannine tradition. The Christian is also said to be "anointed" in 2 Cor 1:21.

294. Smalley (*1, 2, 3 John* 105) comments: "A play on words is apparent in this passage. Central to the apostolic preaching is the confession of Jesus as 'the Christ' (*christos*, 'the anointed one'). Those who deny this are his opponents (*antichristoi*, 'antichrists,' v. 18); whereas

Section 9. The Development of Johannine Theology: Anthropology

of Jesus and the believer, the author recognizes this basic similarity between the believer and Jesus and continues to use terms that could contribute to the confusion. But, at the same time, the author never calls the believer *christos*, a title he reserves for Jesus, just as he had reserved the title "son" for Jesus.

But if the believer is like Jesus in important ways, there are also important ways in which the believer is not like Jesus. For example, when the author speaks of the holiness of the believer in comparison with the holiness of Jesus, as in 3:3, he makes it clear that such holiness for the believer is not a once-and-for-all gift, but something to be striven for and attained: "And everyone having this hope in him [Jesus] makes himself holy, as that one [Jesus] is holy." This is a statement that means that the believer has not yet achieved the status that would make him "like" Jesus. Sin is still possible. It is possible to lose what the person has striven for.

But these are hardly the only ways in which the author distinguishes the believer from Jesus. He also clarifies the distinctions between the believer and Jesus by means of his Christology.[295] If the Christology of the second edition had been "high," the author of 1 John recognizes that it was not high enough. Thus, the author makes clear that Jesus was preexistent, that his ministry was one in which he is "revealed," not one in which he came into existence. If we are to understand "life" in 1:2 as personified (and I think we are), then it is also said in 1:2 that Jesus was "in the presence of God," another expression indicating preexistence. Moreover, his sonship was "unique" (4:9) and so simply not the same as that of the believer. He has had a unique and permanent role in salvation through the giving of his blood (1:7) in an atoning death for others (e.g., 2:2). This was not something the believer could do without or could imitate. His words were normative in a way that any inspiration given to the believer could not be (1:1-3; 2:24). Finally, the author of 1 John implicitly distinguishes between the possession of the Spirit by Jesus and by the believer. As the author says in 4:13, God has given the believer "of" his Spirit. Thus, the believer does not have the Spirit in a complete and perfect way. As a result, we see that in

---

the faithful have received a divine 'anointing' *(chrisma)*. . . . The verb which lies behind all these terms is *chriō* ('I anoint'). . . ."

Grayston (*Epistles* 18-19) says that, for the opponents, "It is inappropriate to call Jesus the Christ *the* Anointed One, as if he alone could provide access to the Father; for they themselves have an anointing by the Spirit which gives them unmediated access to God. 'We are Christians,' they might have said, 'not because Jesus was anointed, but because we all are.'"

Beutler (*Johannesbriefe* 23) says: "Verstehen sich de Gegner . . . as Pneumatiker . . . so leuchtet ein, das sie als die 'Gesalbten' keinen 'Gesalbten' im herausragenden und heilsvermittelnden Sinne, also keinen 'Christus' mehr brauchen. . . . Mit anderen Worten: Die Anthropologie liefert im 1 John den Schlüssel zur Christologie und nicht umgekehrt."

295. The reader is referred to the discussion of the Christology of 1 John in Section 1 above for full details.

1 John, the author clarifies anthropology by clarifying not only anthropology itself but by nuancing other areas of theology that impact anthropology.

5. Anthropology in the Third Edition

In the view of the third author, the believer has been born anew and raised to a new form of life — the life of God. In these respects the third edition agrees with the second edition. However, the identities of both Jesus and the believer are clarified and specified in such a way that it is not possible to merge them. Thus, the author continues the track established by the author of 1 John. The believer continues to be identified as a "child" of God (1:12; 11:52). At the same time, in the third edition this is not as prominent a theme as it is in 1 John and there is no further reference to the believer as "born" ("of God" or "of the Spirit"). As was the case in 1 John, the believer is capable of sin and in need of the commandment of mutual love. But now it is explicit that the believer will also rise on the last day to either a resurrection of life or a resurrection of judgment.

As was the case in 1 John, the author clarifies the respective identities of the believer and of Jesus by showing the fully exalted status of Jesus in a way that goes beyond that of the second edition and even beyond that of 1 John. We have discussed these elements of the third edition in Section 1 (Christology) above. Here we will refer only briefly to those aspects that help distinguish Jesus from the believer. For the third author, Jesus is *monogenēs*, as he was for the author of 1 John. As in 1 John, Jesus' soteriological role is unique and his words have a permanent value. In correlation with 1 John 4:12, where we read that the believer has received "of" the Spirit, now in the third edition (John 3:34) we read that Jesus possesses the Spirit "without measure." But it is for the author of the third edition to make the equality of Jesus with the Father most fully clear by his statements in which Jesus accepts the divine title of YHWH: "I AM."[296]

Thus, the author of the third edition clarifies the distinction between Jesus and the believer in two ways. First, his understanding of "perfectionism" diminishes the prerogative of the believer in this regard, and he qualifies the way in which the believer possesses the Spirit. Second, he exalts the understanding of Jesus, making his equality with God all the more clear.[297]

---

296. For the meaning of this expression as a title of God, see the Note on 8:24 in Volume 2.

297. There will be no discussion of the background of the anthropology of 1 John or of the third edition since they are unique to the Christian tradition. Nevertheless, it should be clear that this anthropology is ultimately built on conceptions common to both OT and apocalyptic Judaism.

Section 9. The Development of Johannine Theology: Anthropology

6. The Background of the Anthropology of 1 John and of the Third Edition

a. The Anthropology of 1 John and the Third Edition and That of Apocalyptic

When we look for the background of the anthropology of the author of 1 John and of the author of the third edition, we find that it is, (1) in general, an anthropology that is consistent with the apocalyptic worldview, and (2) in fact the kind of anthropology that is found in the SDQ and the *T12P*. That is to say that many of the aspects of this anthropology are dictated by the fact that the apocalyptic worldview as we see it in the SDQ and the *T12P* understood the present time to represent the initiation of the eschatological age, an age that would be brought to completion at the end of time. Thus, judgment at the end of time inevitably entailed the possibility of future sin. This also necessarily implied that the present possession of eternal life was not perfect, nor was one's "knowing" God. Because of the inchoative nature of the eschatological blessings, it was also evident that one's possession of the Spirit could not said to be final and complete.

At the same time as the understanding of the prerogatives of the eschatological outpouring of the Spirit was modified, there was a concomitant development of Christology which led to a shortening of the distance between Jesus and the Father.

b. Similarities between the Anthropology of 1 John and the Third Edition and That of the Sectarian Documents of Qumran

It was pointed out above that, given the general perspective of the apocalyptic worldview, it was inevitable that the completely realized eschatology of the canonical Jewish Scriptures would be modified in 1 John and in the third edition. In fact, we have evidence of an anthropology within the sectarian Jewish writings of Qumran that a very similar anthropology existed in the first century.

We have seen examples above of many of the facets of the theology of the SDQ that speak of such an apocalyptic anthropology. The members of the community at Qumran believed that they already lived, to some extent, in the eschatological age. They possessed the Spirit in a special way and so already participated in the eschatological blessings, including a life that was in some respects elevated to life among the angels. At the same time, they still believed that members were capable of sin and that they would experience a final judgment. While the views of the Qumran community were not, and could not be, identical with those of the Johannine community (because of its belief in the role of Jesus), they nevertheless present a credible parallel to many aspects of the anthropology of the Johannine community as understood by the author of 1 John and the author of the third edition.

c. Parallels to the Anthropology of 1 John and of the Third Author Elsewhere in Early Christianity

While space does not permit a detailed presentation of parallels to the anthropology of 1 John and the third edition elsewhere in early Christianity, it should be clear that the convictions typical of these later developments within the Johannine theology reflect many aspects of early Christianity quite closely, especially Pauline theology.

SECTION 10. THE DEVELOPMENT OF JOHANNINE THEOLOGY: ECCLESIOLOGY

Ecclesiology is the term commonly used to describe the patterns of, and attitudes toward, social organization of the believing community and its theological justification.[298] Ecclesiology asks about the type of leadership the community had as well as how the members thought of their relationship with one another.

1. Ecclesiology in the First Edition

Within the first edition of the Gospel (as we know it from what remains in the present Gospel), there is no clear evidence of ecclesiology. Although it is not precisely "ecclesiology," some would argue that the Johannine tradition showed an unusual degree of attention to the importance of the roles of women in earliest Christianity. Specifically, R. E. Brown has pointed to the portrayal of the Samaritan woman, of Martha and Mary, and of Mary Magdalene as evidence of this. As Brown points out, in the first two cases the women have substantial roles within the narrative and their belief and attitudes are equal to, or surpass-

---

[298]. For a helpful survey of attitudes toward institutionalization within early Christianity as a whole, see R. E. Brown, *Churches*; Dunn, *Unity and Diversity* 103-23. On Johannine ecclesiology in particular, see Donfried, "Authority" 325-33; Scholtissek, "Kinder" 184-211; Smalley, *John* 263-64; Käsemann, *Testament* 27-55.

Section 10. The Development of Johannine Theology: Ecclesiology

ing those of men.[299] Indeed, Mary Magdalene is presented as the first to see the risen Lord (in contrast to Peter in the Synoptic tradition). This does seem to reflect a particularly high estimation of the role of women. From the analysis of the composition, it becomes clear that all of these narratives stem from the earliest period of the community's history.[300] While this is not "ecclesiology" in the normal sense of the term, it does reflect something of the community relations that must have existed from the earliest period.

2. Ecclesiology in the Second Edition

The second edition of the Gospel evidences a lack of concern for any sense of community organization other than the individual believer's relation to God,[301] Jesus, and the Spirit.[302] This is different from the first edition, where there was no evidence of any attitude regarding organization. In the second edition, there *is* evidence *that there was no* organization. Features of several types point to this, and we will review them individually. As has been the case before, the second edition manifests certain traits, but it is not until we see other attitudes contrasted with these that we are able to realize fully the implications of this. Some of those features are listed here.

First, as we have seen in the discussion of "knowing" God, the theology of the second edition mirrored closely the radicality of Jeremiah's words (31:34): "No longer shall they teach one another. . . ." The Father was a teacher, and so were Jesus and the Holy Spirit, but no one within the community was ever identified as a teacher. The individual believer is said to "know" God — and "the Jews" are said not to "know" him. But this knowledge is direct and unmediated by anyone except Jesus and the Spirit. The function of the believer was that of "witness."

---

299. R. E. Brown, *Churches* 94-95.

300. In the third edition, the role of Mary Magdalene in chapter 20 is subordinated somewhat to those of Peter and the BD by the fact that the narrative of their encounter with the tomb is inserted prior to the account of her meeting with Jesus in the garden. But I would judge the issue here to be not one of gender but of establishing the authenticity of the insight of the community's founder, for even though he is not the first to see the risen Lord, the BD is the first to come to belief, even before Peter.

301. With reference to the Gospel as a whole, R. E. Brown (*Churches* 85) speaks of "an unparalleled concentration on the relation of the individual believer to Jesus." Yet he does argue also for a "collectivity" in Johannine thinking evident in the symbolism of the vine and the branches and of the sheep and the shepherd even though the focus is on the relation of the branch to the vine and of the individual sheep ("he calls his own sheep by name") to the shepherd.

302. See also Smith (*Johannine* 212) for a similar view, although Smith speaks with respect to the entire Gospel in its present form.

A History of the Development of Johannine Theology

Second, as we shall see below, the community at the time showed no evidence of practicing any ritual and in fact seems to have been opposed to it. The absence of ritual is significant for the understanding of ecclesiology because the purpose of ritual is to reenact sacred moments in a social way. Thus, the absence of ritual indicates not only a disparagement of the realm of the physical and the material but also the apparent absence of social organization involving these moments.[303]

Third, even the eschatology of the second edition is individualistic, portraying as it does the consequences of belief and unbelief as pertinent to the members of the community as individuals rather than as a group. Although the parable of the shepherd speaks of the sheep following the shepherd, there is no mention of the relation of the sheep with one another.

Fourth, and finally, there is no hint of any authoritative structure or person in the second edition. Certainly we must consider the possibility that this could be just a failure to mention such a structure, but this likelihood is diminished by the fact that the third edition makes emphatic a comparison of the BD and Peter and provides a detailed account of a scene in which Peter is made the shepherd over the sheep.

If there is any hint of a common identity of the community at the time of the second edition, it would be that they saw themselves now as persons with a common experience. Not only did they share a belief in Jesus but also the experience of being excluded from the synagogue. Thus, they were a community that saw those who followed the views of "the Jews" as a group distinct from themselves, as representatives of "the world" that rejected all belief in Jesus.

3. A Background for the View of Ecclesiology in the Second Edition?

This individualistic approach to religious experience is grounded, as we have seen above, in the conviction derived from the Old Testament that in the eschatological age the Spirit would illumine each individual and teach each person individually.[304] There is no need to repeat that discussion here. The Old Testament conception of that relationship was couched within a strong, overriding sense of membership within the corporate whole of Israel. In the Old Testament that is taken for granted, even though it is not addressed directly by the

---

303. R. E. Brown (*Churches* 87-88) also points out that other NT documents not only have sacramental references but have commissioning statements for the performance of them (e.g., Matt 28:19: "Go forth . . . baptizing them . . ."; Luke 22:19; 1 Cor 11:25: "Do this in memory of me" in relation to the Eucharist).

304. See Part 4, Section 6 ("Knowing God").

eschatological texts. As a result, it would seem that there is little precedent for this view of "ecclesiology" in the Jewish tradition.

4. Ecclesiology in 1 John — and in 3 John

As in the other areas of Johannine theology surveyed here, attitudes toward ecclesiology changed over the course of history of the community. However, ecclesiology does not seem to have been the object of controversy with the opponents, as was the case with the other topics treated in this survey. Undoubtedly, the opponents continued to espouse views similar to those in the second edition, but their views are not evident in the pages of 1 John. As a result, I will not contrast the views of the author of 1 John with those of his opponents but simply describe the changes evident in the author's community as found in the Letters themselves.

a. Ecclesiology in 1 John

When we turn to 1 John, we see a significantly different orientation toward matters of ecclesiology from that of the second edition.[305] The First Letter of John represents a middle stage in the development of community structure between the second and third editions of the Gospel. It seems fair to say that in 1 John the notion of community is in its formative stages. But the evidence of a shift from the attitude of the second edition is unmistakable.

One of the obvious indications of a growing social sense is that the author refers four times to the community as recognizing the notion of fellowship *(koinōnia)* (1:3 [twice], 6, 7).[306] This is the first time we read of an awareness of group interrelatedness. The author makes this reference at the beginning of his Letter as if to set the tone for his Letter — that it was centrally involved with issues that affected membership in a community. Although the Johannine group had had a communal dimension in their presence within the synagogue and their subsequent expulsion from it, this is a substantial change from the second edition.

In addition to the mention of *koinōnia* itself, the author uses the notion of "remaining" or "abiding" *(menein)* to describe the desired relationship to the community. Proper membership involved a dimension of permanency.

---

305. On this, see esp. R. E. Brown, *Epistles* 110.
306. The term *ekklēsia*, the most common NT term for the community, does not appear in the Johannine literature until 3 John 6, 9, 10.

There is also a social dimension in the author's description of the love commandment. The love commandment is expressed as the need to "love one another" (3:11, 23; 4:7, 11, 12), to "love one's brother" (2:10; 3:10, 14; 4:20, 21), and to "love the children of God" (5:1, 2). The members of the community are called "brothers" (1 John 2:9, 10, 11; 3:10, 13, 14, 15, 16, 17; 4:20, 21; 5:16; 3 John 3, 5, 10), indicating a social dimension modeled on the family. 1 John 3:16 speaks of the believers' obligation to "lay down [their] lives for the brothers." Chapter 3:17 speaks of the evil involved when a believer "sees his brother in need and closes his heart from him." Clearly there is a strong sense of community within 1 John.

But there is no sense of an appointed leader. Even the author of 1 John, who does not identify himself, does not speak on his own authority as someone superior to others, but only as one of those who has witnessed "from the beginning." The author "proclaims" (1:2, 3, 5; 3:11). But this is a proclamation of that "which we have heard from him," and so it is not "teaching." His ability to speak to the community as "Children, Young People, and Fathers" (2:12-14) can only be based on a kind of dignity given him by the community. He certainly claims no special status.

There is also a sense that one can be a member of this community or not and that one can have been a member and have chosen to depart. This is evident from 2:19, where the opponents are described as departing from the author's group.[307] A good part of the author's effort is intended to exhort those to whom he writes to continue in fellowship with him.

The members of the community are to remain in the word of Jesus. There is to be no other teacher. That role is reserved, even in the midst of the crisis, for the Spirit. This is nowhere clearer that in 2:27 (". . . the anointing that you received from him [God] remains in you, and you do not have need that anyone teach you; but as his anointing teaches you about all things, and it is true and not false . . .").[308]

This is one of the remarkable aspects of the author's approach. In spite of the fact that he is confronting the dangers of an unbridled appeal to the inspiration of the Spirit and the consequent failure to remain in the word of Jesus (cf. 2 John 9), the author continues to affirm the importance of the inspiration of the Spirit and to hold this in tension with the affirmation of the importance of the historical word of Jesus in which they are to "remain."

---

307. Because of their departure, the author argues that, from his theological perspective, the opponents never were "of" us (2:19), but this is a theological, rather than a social, judgment.

308. R. E. Brown (*Epistles* 96) comments: "Their authority [i.e., of the Johannine school] is not as teachers but as witnesses who are vehicles of the Paraclete, the only teacher."

Section 10. The Development of Johannine Theology: Ecclesiology

b. Ecclesiology in 3 John

However, by the time we get to 3 John, we meet an individual who is exercising some form of leadership. The author warns the community about Diotrephes, "the one who loves to act as the preeminent one" *(philoprōteuōn)*. Just what is meant by the author's description here is not entirely clear. The etymology indicates that it is a matter of "loving" to act as the "leader." Diotrephes is said to prevent the emissaries of the author from entering the community. At the same time, the Elder rejects the actions of Diotrephes. This episode seems to mark the beginning of a trajectory that involves the recognition (and rejection) of humans who act as leaders. Is this to be seen as a variant of the form of leadership that the third edition attributes to Peter? I am inclined to think not. As we shall see below, Peter is appointed by Jesus and, although human, is recognized as the one to whom Jesus gave the care of his sheep. This role is much greater than that of leader in a local community. Nevertheless, whatever the role of Diotrephes as a leader, the possibility of there being a human leader is now being discussed![309]

5. Ecclesiology in the Third Edition

From the material of the third edition, we see that the process begun in 1 John has continued and that many of the attitudes evident in 1 John are incorporated into the Gospel — with some changes and additions.

The social dimension evident in 1 John continues. There are the several references to "we" in places that do not correspond to a plural in the narrative. These undoubtedly reflect the conviction of the shared witness of those who follow the witness of the Elder.[310]

There is mention of loving one another (13:34; 15:12, 17), but the other expressions found in 1 John (loving the brothers, loving the children of God) do not appear in the third edition. The term *koinōnia*, which we saw in 1 John, does not appear. The scene of the footwashing, which was narrated in the second edition, is now reinterpreted as a scene of humble mutual service within the community.[311] Yet we see that the portrayal of the "office" of the disciples does not move beyond the notion of them as witnesses (15:27). But the third edition introduces the figure of the "disciple whom Jesus loved" (BD). This figure is, as his title indicates, the only one of whom it is said in the Gospel that Jesus loved

---

309. Thus, it is possible that the situation with Diotrephes reflects a situation that is chronologically beyond that of the appointment of Peter in the third edition of the Gospel.

310. See 3E-20 in Part 3 above.

311. See also Smith, *Johannine* 211-16.

him.³¹² He is portrayed first as the one on whom the witness of the community rests. He was an eyewitness, faithful even at the foot of the cross, and to him was given the special care of Jesus' mother. He is the witness par excellence.

Moreover, in these BD passages we see the repeated comparison of the BD with Peter — and the repeated evidence of his superiority to Peter. This contrast between Peter and the BD is generally recognized as a reflection of the relationship between the Petrine churches of the Great Tradition and the churches of the Johannine tradition. The superiority of the insight and faithfulness of the BD is an indication of the Johannine community's estimation of its founder and of the insight enshrined within its tradition.

Yet it is within this context that the third edition portrays the commissioning of Peter to be shepherd of the sheep rather than the BD — and the Johannine community's acceptance of Peter's authority. This is one of the clearest indications of the presence and acknowledgment of a hierarchical authority by the community.³¹³

Finally, there is another new dimension to the ecclesiology of the third edition: a concern for the gathering together of believers who belong to other, distant communities. This is evident in two passages (10:16; 11:52). In the first, Jesus speaks of the shepherd who has sheep "not of this fold" and of the need to gather all the sheep together so that "there will be one flock and one shepherd." This statement is not related to the original parable and represents a secondary interpretation of it. The sheep he speaks of are not of the original fold, yet he will bring them together and there will be one flock.³¹⁴ Clearly there was a desire for (and perhaps a need for) a greater unity among communities that this verse sought to address.

The second passage is also an insertion into its context and addresses the same issue. The narrator explains that one of the purposes of Jesus' death was "that he might lead together into one the children of God scattered about." Although this verse is often interpreted as reflecting a missionary interest, this misses the point. The persons that are of concern are already children of God

---

312. The situation of Lazarus is different, and the "love" there seems to be a love of friendship rather than a love based on a special faithfulness and insight.

313. Significantly, R. E. Brown, who in his later years almost totally rejected the possibility of determining the history of the composition of the text, repeatedly suggests (*Epistles* 110-12, 744) that the appointment of Peter as shepherd "represents the ultimate Johannine concession to the ecclesiology of the Great Church and its structure, a concession conceivably made after the Letters were written."

314. It is difficult to tell how significant the desire for "one shepherd" is intended to be. It is possible that this is meant to indicate that the investing of authority in Peter as shepherd was also meant to indicate that he was the *only* shepherd. But this is uncertain; a similar interest does not appear in 11:52.

Section 10. The Development of Johannine Theology: Ecclesiology

— they have already been born of God and are members of a community, but they are scattered about and it is the intention of Jesus as expressed through the narrator to bring this less than satisfactory situation to an end.

Thus, in the third edition we see the taking over of some concepts and the continued affirmation of the reality and importance of community life. At the same time, the concerns and interests of the third author move beyond those of the earlier period and address the community's recognition of Petrine authority and of the need for unity also among the diverse communities of believers under one shepherd.

6. A Background of the Ecclesiology of the Johannine Letters and the Third Edition

We have seen that there was a development regarding the organization and leadership of the Johannine community within the period represented by the letters and by the third edition. Consequently, we cannot speak of a "background" *common* to this period. However, we may ask about possible parallels in the SDQ and elsewhere in earliest Christianity.

a. In the Sectarian Documents of Qumran

In our discussion of other areas of the community's theology, we have found parallels with the community reflected in the SDQ, and so it is reasonable to ask if there are similarities between the structure of the Johannine community and that of the community at Qumran.[315] However, if we compare the Johannine community with the community at Qumran in terms of organization, we find considerable differences. The community at Qumran, although having an unnamed leader ("The Teacher of Righteousness") similar in some ways to the figure of the Beloved Disciple, had a carefully organized structure including the Council of the Community (1QS 6:8-9).[316] Every member of the community

---

315. The SDQ speak of two types of community structure among those who followed the rule of the Essenes. The first was a monastic community that lived at Qumran. This community is described in detail in 1QS. However, there was also another type of community that was not segregated from society but lived a modified version of the rule. This is described in CD. (See Vermes, *Scrolls* 86-105.) Here we are concerned only with the first of these groups.

316. For a general survey of the community's organization, see Vermes, *Scrolls*, chap. 4, "Life and Institutions of the Sect," 87-115. The scrolls speak of an "assembly of the congregation" that would appear to be an assembly of the entire community. In addition, it speaks of an "assembly of the elders."

had his own rank assigned within the community (1QS 6:22). Rules and offenses are spelled out in great detail. This is far from the picture we get of the Johannine community.

b. Elsewhere in Earliest Christianity

At the same time, in the period represented by the third edition, where there is acknowledgment of the unique leadership of Peter, we find considerable parallels elsewhere in the New Testament.[317] Even at the midpoint of the first century, Peter was generally acknowledged as having a unique role among the apostles and in the church as a whole. This is evident from an analysis of Paul's comments in Galatians about his dealings with Peter.[318]

However, the Gospels' portrayal of the role of Peter is much simpler, and one that may be, in some respect, a later one that has been retrojected upon the ministry itself. In all of the Gospels, Peter is singled out from the other apostles/disciples as making a special confession of Jesus (Mark 8:27-33; Matt 16:16b-19; Luke 9:18-22). However, in Matthew, the scene of this confession is elaborated to include Jesus' commissioning of Peter as the "rock" upon whom the church *(ekklēsia)* would be built. This is an explicit commissioning similar in function to that of John 21. In this sense, the scene in the Gospel of Matthew provides a description of function of Peter that is almost identical to that portrayed in the third edition of the Johannine Gospel.

SECTION 11. THE DEVELOPMENT OF JOHANNINE THEOLOGY: THE RELIGIOUS SIGNIFICANCE OF MATERIAL REALITY

The subject of this chapter is the view of the various authors toward the physical and the material aspects of reality insofar as they are significant religiously. While on one level such an issue would not seem to be a crucial one for theology, the reverse will become apparent. But before we begin the analysis of the attitudes toward the material and physical, three prefatory remarks are appropriate.

First, in the past, one might have expected a treatment of the role of sacraments in Johannine theology in a discussion such as this, *or* one might per-

---

317. For a balanced and very helpful study of the role of Peter, see R. E. Brown et al., *Peter*.
318. From his own letters, it is apparent that Paul's relationship with Peter was complex. On one hand, Paul recognized a special role for Peter, but, on the other, he emphasized the independence of his own belief and the understanding of the meaning of Jesus (Gal 1:18; 2:1-10, 11-13). (See R. E. Brown et al., *Peter* 23-38.)

Section 11. The Religious Significance of Material Reality

haps expect a discussion of such epistolary phrases as "come in the flesh," but one would not expect both. Yet such apparently distinct topics were closely related within the Johannine tradition because they were both aspects of a more fundamental issue for the community: the importance of the realm of the material and physical for religion.

Second, if we review the history of scholarship regarding the sacramental texts in the Johannine literature, we see that there have been a wide variety of views regarding the presence of sacramental theology in the Gospel and Letters.[319] One extreme is represented by Bultmann, who held that it was the word alone that was important and that the disciples, and believers generally, were called upon simply to respond to the word of Jesus.[320] The other extreme is represented by O. Cullmann, who saw the Gospel as thoroughly imbued with sacramental references.[321] Other scholars range between these extremes; but these extremes point out how prominent scholars, by focusing on one set of texts rather than another, can hold such divergent views of Johannine theology. Yet, as we shall see, there are texts that justify both of these positions. Further, it can be said that, when one views the Gospel in terms of the stages of its development, the extreme positions are more accurate than the more "moderate" views. It is the identification of distinct editions of the Gospel that demonstrates that both views were advocated in different editions of the Gospel and at different periods in the history of the community.

Third, one of the most widely held theories regarding the Gospel, as well as regarding the crisis that divided the community at the time of 1 John, is that the opponents held to a form of docetism. Some see the Gospel as naively docetic; some see it as antidocetic. Some see the opponents of 1 John as docetic and the author as antidocetic. Scholars working from the Gospel as a whole have rightly recognized that the Gospel contains various elements that would appear to be related to docetism. Further, they have seen correctly that the issue in docetism ultimately is the relation between the physical and the spiritual.

However, as has been pointed out repeatedly and as will be particularly apparent in the section that follows, to label this issue "docetism" does not de-

---

319. For a discussion of sacraments in the Johannine literature, see Barrett, *Gospel* 82-85; R. E. Brown, "Sacramentary," in *Essays* 77-107; idem, "Eucharist and Baptism," in *Essays* 108-31; Cullmann, *Early*; C. R. Koester, *Symbolism* 257-62; Käsemann, *Testament* 32-33; Leon-Dufour, *Sharing*; Lindars, "Word and Sacrament" 49-63; Schnelle, *Antidocetic* 176-210.

320. Bultmann, *Gospel* 470-73, esp. 471-72. A clear statement of his position is found in his discussion of the footwashing; and, although there he speaks specifically of Baptism, his words have implications for the remainder of the sacraments: ". . . the service Jesus performs, through the word and as the word, is considered to be fundamentally opposed to every form of sacramental purification, baptism included."

321. Cullmann, *Early* (passim).

fine the problem precisely enough. Docetism deals primarily with Christology. In John, the issue was broader and had a different origin. While the relation between the physical and the spiritual was important in both docetism and in the Johannine crisis, in the Johannine crisis the spiritual was important because the Spirit had been poured out. This outpouring was understood to transform all aspects of religion and life. Consequently, in the second edition, there was a view that, while correct in one sense, was understood, in another sense, to make all material aspects of religion insignificant. That this is the case should become apparent in what follows.

1. The Religious Significance of Material Reality in the First Edition

There is no evidence in what remains of the first edition of the community's convictions about ritual. In other matters, it would seem that the first edition had a generally positive attitude toward the material realm.

2. The Religious Significance of Material Reality in the Second Edition

In the second edition, there is a very clear indication that the author viewed material reality and the physical aspects of religion (including ritual) as having no religious significance. What could well be identified as the programmatic statement of this view is found in 6:63: "The Spirit is what gives life; the flesh is useless." Thus, the very dimension of the physical seems to have been denigrated. That this is the case is evident in several ways.

First, there are clear statements that deny any religious importance to the "flesh" and that put all emphasis on the "spirit." In his discussion with Nicodemus (3:3-10), after commenting on the necessity of being born again, Jesus explains: "That which is born of the flesh is flesh, and that which is born of the Spirit is Spirit."

Second, in 4:19-24, in the discussion of the proper place of worship, Jesus states that neither Jerusalem nor Gerizim will be the proper place but that God is Spirit and seeks those who will worship him "in Spirit and in truth." Thus, the role of external ritual is rejected.[322] It is not a matter of the proper location for worship; there is no longer *any* proper geographical place for worship: it is to be done "in Spirit and in truth."

Third, in the second edition there are a large number of instances in

---

[322]. It would be wrong to conclude that this refers only to a denial of a role for *Jewish* worship in the light of the repeated statements about the importance of the Spirit elsewhere in contrast to the flesh.

Section 11. The Religious Significance of Material Reality

which Jesus' interlocutors misunderstand his words and take them on a material level whereas they were intended on a spiritual level. This repeated contrast confirms again and again the lack of value of anything material and physical as well as the inability of his listeners to rise above the level of the material. Thus, we see the misunderstanding of "birth" (3:3-10) and the misunderstanding of "water" (4:10-15). Jesus has a "food" that is spiritual, not material (4:31-34). Throughout chapters 6, 7, and 8, there are repeated misunderstandings of the origin of Jesus (6:41-42; 7:28-29[323]); the origin of his teaching (7:14-18); and the place to which he is ultimately going (7:33-36; 8:21-23).

Fourth, the irrelevance of the physical is evident in the lack of mention of a future life that would involve bodily resurrection. While it is difficult to build an argument about this from the second edition itself, by the time of the third edition, belief in the resurrection of the body was an important part of the community's belief and the reference to it in 5:28-29 gives every indication of being a conscious attempt to stress this fact. This means that the omission of such a belief in the second edition is almost certainly not an accident or a misreading of the second edition.

Fifth, as will be argued in more detail in the discussion of John 20:17, there is significant evidence that the resurrection of Jesus was looked upon as less than fully physical and this was confronted by the third author, particularly by means of his addition in 20:24-29.

Sixth, this attitude is evident from the notable lack of attention to rituals such as initiation rites, worship, and ritual meals. The lack of an account of the institution of the Eucharist at the Last Supper is particularly striking. Schnackenburg explains the problem well: "The fact that the fourth evangelist . . . does not mention the institution of the Eucharist in his representation of the Last Supper constitutes an important problem, the full seriousness of which has only rarely been considered." Schnackenburg goes on to remind his readers that the Lord's Supper was celebrated from the earliest period of Christianity and rapidly became "the central act and the source of strength in the life of the community, [and] its most important celebration." If this is so, Schnackenburg goes on to say: "then it is both extremely surprising and very irritating that one evangelist should pass over in silence the institution" of this sacrament.[324]

---

323. Here the author of the second edition builds on a comment from the first edition about the origin of Jesus, but in so building, he raises the argument to another level.

324. Schnackenburg, *Gospel* 3:42. Schnackenburg goes on to summarize seven types of attempts to deal with the problem and then presents his own explanation for the omission. Schnackenburg argues that the Evangelist is not antisacramental but what he calls "critical" of the sacraments and intending to focus on the deeper meaning of them rather than on the rite itself (p. 46). Thus, he recognizes the tension created by the presence of texts that are obviously sacramental and an attitude that seems to neglect them in the light of spiritual realities.

Although it is always difficult to argue from silence in such matters, when we turn to the third edition, we again see a conscious effort to incorporate references to the Eucharist and its importance — even if this discussion is presented in a different part of the Gospel than at the Last Supper. From these features, we are able to tell that the apparent silence of the second edition is not accidental or simply a misreading of the evidence; it reflects a deliberate aversion for such external ritual.

If we ask about the possibility of references to Baptism, we have less certainty, but it would seem that the second edition had no interest in Baptism. The text that is most likely to contain a reference to Baptism is John 3:5, which speaks of the need of being "born of water and the Spirit."[325] There are no overt markers of editing in this passage. However, when one recognizes the pervasive rejection of the realm of the material elsewhere in the second edition, the insistence here on the need for water appears completely out of place. In the second edition, the only water that is important is the "living water" that is a symbol of the Spirit and not important in its own right.[326]

3. The Background of the Attitude toward Material Reality in the Second Edition

We will discuss the background of the second edition's attitude toward the material after we have discussed the attitude of 1 John and the third edition to the same issue.

4. The Religious Significance of Material Reality in 1 John

a. The View of the Opponents

The opponents' views regarding the relative merits of the material and the spiritual world become apparent in two ways. In a few instances, the author of

---

325. It is often suggested that 13:1-20 contains references to the ritual of Baptism. This possibility is discussed in an Addendum to that passage in the Commentary. For the reasons given there, the possibility is rejected.

326. There is no evidence of Jewish thought that denigrates the realm of the physical, and so this must be looked upon as a uniquely Johannine development, understood to be a characteristic of the eschatological age. Nevertheless, it does seem fair to say that such a lack of attention to the realm of the material could be seen as consistent with the expectation that in the eschatological age there would be no need for human teachers or specific ethical directives. At the same time, such a denigration (at the time of the second edition) and the ambivalence (still evident in the final form of the Gospel) would have made the Gospel attractive to gnostic groups.

Section 11. The Religious Significance of Material Reality

1 John directly refutes the views of the opponents. However, at other times, the author so emphasizes elements of the tradition that attribute importance to the physical experiences of the believer that it becomes evident that this must have been a disputed point. These elements will be evident in the author's positive exposition and need not be repeated here.

b. The View of the Author

The author of 1 John presents a considerably different view from that of the second edition. Although the author continues to affirm the importance of the Spirit for the community, he also affirms the importance of the historical ministry of Jesus. The author recalls the permanent importance of what they had learned through their *sensory experience* of the ministry of Jesus through hearing, seeing, and touching (1:1, 3). Their teaching was not to come just through the Spirit. The historical events that they witnessed had a permanent value. In addition, but related to this, the author introduces the notion of a "commandment" to keep the word of Jesus. That is, Jesus' words also had permanent value, and the community was to remain faithful to them.

Moreover, the actions of Jesus himself had intrinsic soteriological value. He has "come in the flesh" (1 John 4:2; cf. 2 John 7). Jesus' death was of salvific significance by being an atonement for sin (2:2; 4:10). His blood cleanses us from sin (1:7). As the author says in 5:6-7, Jesus "came in blood."

But it may well be that at the same time the community began to see other aspects of material (physical) existence as also having an importance for one's relation with God. This second possibility would support the views of those scholars who find evidence of sacramental actions in 1 John.

Because most scholars view 1 John as written after the Gospel, it is perhaps easier to expect sacramental references in 1 John since (as we shall see) there are clear references to sacramental actions in the Gospel (i.e., the third edition). However, if 1 John was written after the second edition (which devalued the "flesh" so much) and before the third edition of the Gospel (where there are such clear references to sacramental rituals), we gain a new framework for evaluating this aspect of the First Letter.

In the Commentary, I have discussed those texts in 1 John that are most frequently thought to have sacramental references in them (1:5–2:2 [Confession of Sin, Baptism]; 2:20-23 [Anointing]; 5:6-8 [Baptism, Eucharist, Anointing]).[327] Although a number of scholars would see a reference to some sort of public confession of sin in the first of these passages, there is considerable un-

---

327. See the Addenda to each of the passages listed.

certainty about the nature of that confession. My own view is that, when the passage is examined within the context of the Letter as a whole, there is strong evidence for seeing the passage as referring to a confession of belief regarding the possibility and actuality of personal sin rather than referring to a sacramental ritual. In 2:20-23, the possibility of a reference to a rite of anointing is also rejected by most scholars. In the case of 5:6-8, there is little support for seeing Baptism and Eucharist as being referred to; there is no support for seeing a reference to anointing in 5:8.

The results of the analysis in each case suggest that the evidence is at best uncertain. Theories that see "allusions" of rites in the language of 1 John have not provided sufficient positive evidence to indicate that the language is intended to refer to ritual actions of any sort. Nor is there the scholarly agreement about these texts that there is about similar texts in the (third edition of the) Gospel. It is important, in this regard, to recall that it is not sufficient to argue that a given text *could* refer to sacraments, but rather that there is *some positive evidence* that this was the author's intention. While R. E. Brown proposes that the language of initiation lies behind the wording of various parts of 1 John, Brown himself refused to speculate what element of the overall initiation process it would pertain to.[328] In his excursus on "being born" of God, Schnackenburg observes that the author takes for granted that the believer is "born of God" and is a "child of God," but nowhere makes reference to the fact that such birth involves the Spirit nor does he make reference to the ritual by which this takes place. The author focuses on the reality rather than on the means by which this occurs.[329] For these reasons and those given in the individual discussions within the Commentary, I am of the opinion that there is no clear evidence of a ritual of Baptism, Anointing, Forgiveness of Sin, or Eucharist in 1 John. But even if there is no evidence of sacraments, it remains true that, within the Johannine Letters, there is a major shift in attitude toward the material aspects of reality.

---

328. Brown, *Epistles* 242 n. 44.

329. Schnackenburg, *Epistles* 162-63. Schnackenburg goes on to comment that the situation in the Gospel "is quite different. In the dialogue with Nicodemus, . . . the reply of Jesus leaves no doubt for a Christian audience that this takes place in baptism (3:5). The Holy Spirit is the decisive factor in this supernatural event (3:6). Therefore we must conclude that in 1 John baptism is tacitly presumed to be the place where we are born of God." But this is just that, a tacit presumption, and could be presumed only if there were a known history of ritual initiation into the community. However, the only known history of such ritual comes from a later period in the community's history.

Section 11. *The Religious Significance of Material Reality*

5. The Religious Significance of Material Reality in the Third Edition

When we come to the third edition of the Gospel, we notice a considerable advance along the trajectory established by 1 John with respect to the role of material reality in religion. The attitudes of the author of the third edition can be grouped into three categories. The first has to do with the importance of bodily reality, both with respect to Jesus and to the believer. The second has to do with the importance of ritual actions that mediate the spiritual reality. The third has to do with the role of human mediators in general.

a. The Importance of Material Reality in General

The author of the third edition continues to emphasize the importance of the fleshly existence of Jesus. This is evident in the hymn which he incorporates as the Prologue of the Gospel, where it is said that "the Word became flesh" (1:14). While not specifying the function of this "fleshness," its importance is evident.

The material dimension of reality is also of crucial significance with regard to the death of Jesus. It is his death that takes away the sin of the world (1:29), and he lays down his life for his sheep (10:11, 15). At his death, both blood and water came forth from his side (19:34).

We have also seen above, in the discussion of eschatology, that in the third edition there is an emphasis on the reality of the bodily resurrection of Jesus. That this could have been an issue is suggested by the statement of Jesus to Mary in the second edition that she should not "touch" him. This, together with the fact that he is described as passing through closed doors, indicates that the second edition may have thought of the status of Jesus after the Resurrection as less than totally corporeal. At the same time, in the third edition there is an evident emphasis on the corporeal reality of the risen Jesus in the way that Thomas is called upon to put his hands in the wounds of Jesus and to recognize that his body was truly the same physical body that suffered.

The affirmation of the religious importance of physical reality is also evident in the emphasis in the third edition on the reality of the believer's bodily resurrection. Again we have treated this in detail as part of the discussion of eschatology, but the emphasis on the value of the physicality of the believer's resurrection also confirms the overall orientation of the third edition in this respect.

b. The Importance of Ritual Actions

The second group of concerns has to do with what are often referred to as sacramental actions. In 3:5, the author has inserted the words "water and" to make reference to the initiation rite (Baptism) of the community. As was said above, these words have no other function in the context of 3:5, which elsewhere speaks exclusively of the role of the Spirit. At the same time, the reference to water here carries none of the symbolic meaning elsewhere associated with the figurative use of "living water." As a result, in spite of the fact that there are no overt markers of editing, it is almost certain that these words have been added to make reference to the importance of Baptism ('Unless a person is born of water . . . , that person is not able. . . .'")

The second instance of sacramental addition to the third edition is 6:51-58. Here the original discourse from the second edition is extended by means of a discussion of the Eucharist. This is the longest discussion of any of the sacraments, and the fact that it is intended as a discussion of the Eucharist is, in my view, certain. We have seen that there are changes of language and worldview that identify this material with the third edition. We have also seen that new vocabulary is introduced for the same actions *(phagein — trōgein)*. And the identification of the bread with Jesus' flesh — and the unwarranted introduction of references to Jesus' "blood" and the insistence that the believer is to "eat the flesh of the Son of Man and drink his blood." The insistence on this is unmistakable: "My flesh is true food, and my blood is true drink." This is necessary for the believer to have life. Clearly the author of the third edition is responsible for the verses and intends a sacramental reinterpretation of the final words of the Scripture which formed the basis for the synagogue homily.

A third instance of a sacramental action described by the third author is the forgiveness of sins in 20:23. Because the primary emphasis here is on the role of the disciples in this forgiveness, it will be treated immediately below.

c. The Role of Human Mediators

The first example of the importance now assigned to human mediators is the role of the disciples in the forgiveness of sin. In 20:23, we find the surprisingly abrupt introduction of the topic of forgiveness of sin. This is the only discussion of the forgiveness of sin in the Gospel — and it is done through the work of human mediators. The disciples are given the authority to decide what should and should not be loosed. While there is no doubt about the role of the disciples here, what is noteworthy is the way this contrasts with the attitude to the forgiveness of sin in 1 John.

In 1 John 5:14-17, the author introduced the topic of prayer of petition, that is, prayer that requests that God grant what the petitioner asks for. The author gave assurance that God will grant these petitions if they are made according to God's will. Then the author applied this to requests made by believers for the forgiveness of sin. After explaining that he is not talking about "sin-unto-death," the author explained that "he [the believer] will ask, and he [God] will give life to him [the sinner]...." Yet it is curious that there is no mention of human intermediaries in a text where their role would surely be mentioned if it was a part of the community's practice. Thus, we can be sure that the role of the disciples in the forgiveness of sin is something that was introduced after the time of 1 John.

The second example of the importance now assigned to human mediators is the recognition of the role assigned to Peter. In 21:15-17, we see a passage that acknowledges that Jesus had entrusted authority over the "sheep" to Peter. There are two important elements in the passage: first, that there is a source of human authority beyond that of the Spirit; second, that the bearer of this authority is not the Beloved Disciple.

If we concentrate only on the first of these issues here, we see yet another indication of the expanding awareness of the importance of "material reality" — here, as was the case with the forgiveness of sins — through the role of Peter as the human, "fleshly" intermediary of authority.[330]

d. Bodily Resurrection

The other major aspect of the importance of physical reality — and one that is unique to the third edition of the Gospel — is the explicit affirmation of bodily resurrection. The fullest expression of this appears in 5:28-29 and could not be more explicit: "... an hour is coming in which all those in the tombs will hear his voice and will come forth...." Moreover, there are a number of brief references to bodily resurrection in chapter 6. In addition to the reference in v. 39, there are three additional references added awkwardly to the end of 6:40, 44, and 54, all affirming that the believer will be raised up on the last day. Again in 11:24, Martha affirms belief in future resurrection and Jesus responds by stating that he is the source of such resurrection and life.[331] All of these references make it clear that existence after death will have a physical dimension.

---

330. Another implication of this scene is that it indicates that the Johannine community is in line with the tradition represented by the Synoptics in the matter of leadership. By acknowledging the one, the Johannine community acknowledged the other.

331. Although I have chosen to treat bodily resurrection as an aspect of the eschatology of the third edition, it is also significant as an indication of the third author's emphasis on the role of the material dimension of reality that the believer's *body* will be raised.

Wright (*Resurrection* 442) sees the texts dealing with resurrection and eternal life to be "effortlessly and seamlessly combined," although "some scholars have tried to prise [them] apart" (442). What Wright says of the passages dealing with eschatology, eternal life, and resur-

e. The Resurrection of Jesus

In the discussion of the second author's attitude to the Resurrection of Jesus, we have already seen a brief indication of the attitude of the third author. We now need to fill out that picture.

In the second post-Resurrection appearance (the core of which comes from the second edition), the third author has introduced the Risen Jesus, who has shown the disciples his hands and his feet. We are told that the disciples recognized Jesus and rejoiced to see him risen. We are then introduced to a third appearance, in 20:24-29, in which Jesus appears again to the disciples, among whom is Thomas who was absent the first time.

As is pointed out in the Commentary, there are three important aspects to this passage: (1) the emphasis on the physicality of the body of Jesus, (2) the remarkable confession of faith uttered by Thomas, and (3) the words of Jesus about those who believe without seeing. For the present only the emphasis on the physicality of Jesus and the identity of the risen Jesus with the Jesus who suffered is in view.

Scholars have long debated whether this passage was intended to counter a docetic view of Jesus within the community. Certainly docetists took over the high Christology of the Gospel and made it serve their purposes. But I do not find evidence of this as a problem for the Johannine community itself. Rather, in keeping with the orientation of the remainder of the third edition and with the fact that the opponents had rejected the value of the material, physical element of life, the third author has gone out of his way to affirm the physicality, not only of the resurrected believer, but also of the resurrected Jesus.

f. A Final Observation on the Significance of the Physical and Material in the Third Edition

In this analysis, we have singled out the "physical and material" as a topic regarding which the authors of the second and third editions disagreed. However, by now it may perhaps be apparent that, from another perspective, the relationship between the spiritual and the material was an issue that cut across a number of the categories of their theology. In the matter of knowledge, it was an issue of whether this knowledge came directly through the Spirit, or whether the historical (sensory) words and actions of Jesus were of essential importance. In

---

rection is, from the point of view of the Gospel as a finished product, understandable; but they do not reflect the complexity of the texts, which were, in fact, anything but "effortless and seamless."

soteriology, it was an issue of whether salvation came simply through the Spirit or through the physical, atoning death of Jesus in blood. In eschatology, it was an issue of whether eternal life consisted simply of spiritual existence beyond death or whether it also involved the resurrection of the body. In the issue of sacraments, it was a matter of whether the saving realities came directly through the Spirit or whether they were mediated through material rituals. In the matter of ecclesiology, it was an issue of whether authority came directly from the Spirit or whether it was to be mediated through human authority, either in the governing of the community (Peter) or in the forgiveness of sins. In short, although the issue of the relation between the this-worldly and the spiritual could be seen as one issue among many, in reality it seems that it was an issue that underlay many of the issues the community was confronting.

6. The Background of These Various Attitudes toward the Religious Significance of Material Reality

a. In the Old Testament

After the discussion of the rejection of the role of material reality in the second edition, we did not discuss the background for such a conception. This was due to the fact that we should not expect the Old Testament to address this issue since the eschatological age had not yet arrived. At the same time, it could be said that it could be implied from various texts in the Old Testament that elements of material reality would lose their importance in the end times. For example, if there was no clear conviction of bodily resurrection even with a view of eternal life, it would be possible to conclude that the bodily dimension was not of permanent importance. If one could know God directly, the community would have no need of anyone to teach them. Again, the role of human intermediaries (and therefore the material dimension) would no longer be important. These and other elements of what might be called orthodox Old Testament thinking regarding the eschatological age might well lead to a devaluing of the religious significance of everything material. But we can only speculate in this regard.

b. In the Sectarian Documents of Qumran

However, at Qumran we have an example of an eschatological community that held ritual actions in very high regard. According to Josephus, members of the community were to undergo ritual washing at least two times a day. Extensive archaeological evidence of ritual bath installations confirms this practice. While the members of the community believed in inner cleansing by the Spirit, they also practiced external bodily cleansing.

The communal meal of the community was also understood to have a religious function. Admittance and exclusion from the meal were indications of one's status within the community (e.g., 1QS 6:19; 8:22; 1Q28a 2:17-22). At Qumran, there was also a council that served as a judge in matters of religious importance (see 1QS 5:7) and that administered a code of conduct (1QS passim) much more detailed than that of the Johannine community even at the time of the third edition.

Thus it seems fair to say that in these ways they were completely at odds with the attitude of the Johannine community at the time of the second edition and considerably different from the Johannine community at the time of the third edition in terms of degree and detail of observance.[332]

---

332. There is no significant evidence of ritual or of definite convictions of the role of the physical dimension of reality in the *T12P.* This is understandable, given the nature of the documents.

PART 5

Reference

The Text of the Gospel

1:1-18   The Prologue to the Gospel

1 IN THE BEGINNING WAS THE WORD,
   AND THE WORD WAS WITH GOD, AND THE WORD WAS GOD.
2 THIS ONE WAS WITH GOD IN THE BEGINNING.

3 ALL THINGS CAME TO BE THROUGH HIM,
   AND WITHOUT HIM CAME TO BE NOT ONE THING THAT HAS COME TO BE.

4 IN HIM [JESUS] WAS LIFE
   AND THE LIFE WAS THE LIGHT OF ALL PEOPLE.

5 AND THE LIGHT SHINES IN THE DARKNESS,
   AND THE DARKNESS DID NOT OVERCOME IT.

6 A man came to be, sent from God. His name was John. 7 This man came as a witness, to witness about the light, in order that all might believe

---

In order to facilitate consulting the text of the Gospel and Letters while reading the Commentary, the text of the Gospel and Letters is reprinted here.

The material of the first edition is indicated by regular typeface. The material of the second edition is indicated by *italic* typeface. The material of the third edition is indicated by **bold** typeface. In the Prologue and in Chapter 21, the material from other sources is indicated by SMALL CAPITALS.

The Prologue and the prayer of Jesus in chapter 17 are printed in poetic format in order to recognize the special character of the material.

through him. 8 He was not the light but was intended to witness about the light. 9 The true light, which shines on every person, was coming into the world.

10 HE WAS IN THE WORLD, AND THE WORLD CAME TO BE THROUGH HIM;
AND THE WORLD DID NOT KNOW HIM.
11 HE CAME UNTO HIS OWN,
AND HIS OWN DID NOT ACCEPT HIM.

12 BUT TO AS MANY AS DID ACCEPT HIM
HE GAVE TO THEM POWER TO BECOME CHILDREN OF GOD,
TO THOSE BELIEVING IN HIS NAME,
13 who were born,
not from blood,
nor from the will of the flesh,
nor from the will of a man,
but from God.

14 AND THE WORD BECAME FLESH AND DWELLED WITH US,
AND WE SAW HIS GLORY, THE GLORY OF ONE UNIQUE
FROM THE FATHER, FULL OF GRACE AND TRUTH.

15 John witnesses about him and has cried out, saying, "This is the one about whom I said, 'The one coming after me existed before me because he ranks above me.'"

16 BECAUSE WE HAVE ALL RECEIVED FROM HIS FULLNESS,
INDEED GRACE UPON GRACE.

17 Because the Law was given through Moses; grace and truth came through Jesus Christ. 18 No one has ever seen God; the unique Son, the one at the bosom of the Father, made him known.

1:19-34 The First Witness to Jesus: John Witnesses about Himself and about Jesus

JOHN WITNESSES ABOUT HIMSELF

19 *And this is the witness of John,* when Judeans from Jerusalem sent [to him] priests and Levites to ask him, "Who are you?" 20 *And he confessed and did not deny; he confessed,* "I am not the Christ." 21 And they asked him, "What then? Are you Elijah?" And he said, "I am not." "Are you the Prophet?" And he responded, "No." 22 Then they said to him, "Who are you? so that we may give a response to those who sent us.

The Text of John 1:23-42

What do you say about yourself?" 23 He said, "I am a voice of one in the desert crying, 'Make straight the way for the Lord,' as Isaiah the prophet said." 24 And those sent were from among the Pharisees.

25 *And they asked him and said to him, "Why then do you baptize if you are neither the Christ nor Elijah nor the Prophet?"* 26 *John responded to them, saying, "I baptize in water. Among you stands one you do not know,* 27 *the one coming after me, the laces of whose sandals I am not worthy to untie."* 28 *These things took place in Bethany-beyond-the-Jordan where John was baptizing.*

John Witnesses about Jesus

29 *The next day he saw Jesus coming toward him and said,* **"Behold the Lamb of God, the one taking away the world's sin.** 30 **This is the one about whom I said, 'After me comes a man who existed before me because he ranks above me.'** 31 **And I did not know him, but in order that he might be revealed to Israel, I came baptizing in water."** 32 *And John witnessed, saying, "I have seen the Spirit coming down like a dove from the sky,* **and it remained upon him.** 33 **And I did not know him, but the one who sent me to baptize in water said to me, 'The one upon whom you see the Spirit descending and remaining is the one who baptizes in the Holy Spirit.'** 34 *And I have seen and I have witnessed that this is the Son of God."*

1:35-51   The Response of the First Disciples to the Witness of John

The Disciples of John Hear the Witness of John

35 *The next day* John was again standing, along with two of his disciples. 36 Seeing Jesus passing by, he said, **"Behold the Lamb of God."** 37 And his two disciples heard him say this, and they followed after Jesus. 38 Jesus, turning and seeing them following him, said to them, "What are you looking for?" They said to him, "Rabbi" (which, translated, means Teacher), "where do you stay?" 39 He said to them, "Come and see." So they went and saw where he stayed and remained with him that day. It was about the tenth hour.

The Disciples of Jesus

40 Andrew, the brother of Simon Peter, was one of the two hearing this from John and following Jesus. 41 He first found his own brother Simon and said to him, "We have found the Messiah" (which is translated Christ). 42 He led him to Jesus. Looking upon him, Jesus said, "You are Simon, the son of John. You will be called Cephas" (which, translated, means Peter).

43 *The next day, he decided to go to Galilee, and he found Philip. And Jesus said to him, "Follow me."* 44 *Philip was from Bethsaida, the hometown of Andrew and Peter.* 45 *Philip found Nathanael and said to him, "We have found the one that Moses (in the Law) and the Prophets wrote about: Jesus, the son of Joseph, from Nazareth."* 46 Nathanael said to him, "What good can come from Nazareth?" Philip said to him, "Come and see." 47 Jesus saw Nathanael coming toward him and said about him, "Look, truly this is an Israelite in whom there is no guile." 48 Nathanael said to him, "Whence do you know me?" Jesus responded and said to him, "Before Philip called you, I saw you under the fig tree." 49 Nathanael responded, "Rabbi, you are the Son of God; you are the King of Israel." 50 *Jesus responded and said to him, "Do you believe because I told you that I saw you under the fig tree? You will see greater things than these."* 51 **And he said to him, "Amen, amen, I say to you, (all of) you will see the sky opened up and the angels of God ascending and descending upon the Son of Man."**

2:1-12 The Second Witness to Jesus:
The Miracle at the Wedding Feast at Cana

1 *On the third day* there was a wedding in Cana of Galilee, and the mother of Jesus was there. 2 Both Jesus and his disciples were invited to the wedding. 3 When the wine ran out, Jesus' mother said to him, "They have no wine." 4 **[And] Jesus said to her, "Woman, how does this concern you and me? My hour has not yet arrived."**

5 His mother said to the servants, "Do whatever he tells you." 6 There were six stone jars lying there used for the purification ritual of the Jews, each holding two or three measures. 7 Jesus said to them, "Fill the jars with water." They filled them to the top. 8 And he said to them, "Draw some now, and bring it to the chief steward." They did so. 9 When the chief steward tasted the water become wine (he did not know where it was from, but the servants who had drawn the water knew), he called the bridegroom 10 and said to him, "Everyone puts out the good wine first, and when they are intoxicated, the wine of lesser quality. You have kept the good wine until now." 11 Jesus did this, the beginning of his signs, in Cana of Galilee, *and he revealed his glory*, and his disciples believed in him.

12 After this, he went down to Capernaum along with his mother and [his] brothers and his disciples, and stayed there a few days.

2:13-22 The Third and Fourth Witnesses:
Jesus and the Temple at Passover

13 The Passover of the Jews was near, and Jesus went up to Jerusalem.

The Text of John 2:14-3:10

14 And in the temple complex he found people selling oxen and sheep and doves, and money changers seated. 15 Making a rope whip, he expelled them all from the Temple, both the sheep and the oxen, and he dumped out the coins of the money changers and overturned their tables. 16 He said to those selling doves, "Take these things out of here. Stop making the house of my Father a house of commerce." 17 His disciples remembered that it was written, "Zeal for your house will consume me."

18 The Jews responded and said to him, "What sign do you show us to justify your doing this?" 19 Jesus responded and said to them, "Destroy this Sanctuary, and in three days I will raise it up." 20 Then the Jews said, "It took forty-six years to build this Sanctuary, and you will raise it up in three days?" 21 But he was speaking about the Sanctuary of his body.

22 When he was raised from the dead, his disciples remembered that he said this; and they believed the Scripture and the word that Jesus spoke.

2:23-3:10 The Spirit and Belief

23 When he was in Jerusalem at the Passover — at the feast — , many believed in his name, seeing his signs that he was performing. 24 But Jesus himself did not entrust himself to them because he knew all things, 25 and because he had no need of anyone to bear witness about human nature. For he himself knew human nature.

THE SIGNS AND BIRTH FROM THE SPIRIT

3:1 There was a Pharisee, Nicodemus by name, a ruler of the Jews. 2 This one came to him by night and said to him, "Rabbi, we know that you have come as a teacher from God. For no one is able to perform these signs that you perform unless God is with him."

3 Jesus responded and said to him, "Amen, amen, I say to you, unless a person is born again, that person is not able to see **the Kingdom of God**." 4 Nicodemus said to him, "How is one able to be born, once grown? Surely the person is not able to reenter the womb of his mother a second time and be born?" 5 Jesus responded, "Amen, amen, I say to you, unless a person is born of **water and** the Spirit, that person is not able to enter **the Kingdom of God**. 6 That which is born of the flesh is flesh, and that which is born of the Spirit is Spirit. 7 **Do not marvel that I said to you, 'It is necessary for (all of) you to be born again.'** 8 The wind blows where it wishes, and you hear its voice, but you do not know where it comes from and where it goes. Thus is everyone born of the Spirit."

9 Nicodemus responded and said to him, "How can these things happen?" 10 Jesus responded and said to him, "You are a teacher of Israel, and you do not know these things?"

3:11-21 The Son: Revelation, Life, and Judgment

THE SON OF MAN AND REVELATION

11 "Amen, amen, I say to you, we say what we know, and we bear witness to what we have seen, and (all of) you do not accept our witness. 12 If I have spoken to (all of) you about earthly realities and (all of) you do not believe, how will (all of) you believe if I speak to (all of) you about heavenly realities? 13 No one has ascended into heaven except the one come down from heaven, the Son of Man.

THE SON OF MAN AND LIFE

14 "Just as Moses lifted up the serpent in the desert, so the Son of Man must be lifted up, 15 so that everyone believing in him may have eternal life. 16 For God loved the world thus, that he gave his unique Son, so that whoever believes in him might not perish but might have eternal life.

THE SON NOT SENT FOR JUDGMENT

17 "For God did not send his Son into the world to judge the world, but so that the world might be saved through him. 18 The one who believes in him is not judged; the one who does not believe has already been judged because that person has not believed in the name of the unique Son of God.

19 "This is the judgment, that the light has come into the world, but people loved the darkness more than the light, for their works were evil. 20 Everyone doing wicked deeds hates the light and does not come to the light, lest his works be exposed. 21 But the one who does the truth comes to the light, so that his works may be manifest, that they have been done in God.

3:22-36 The Final Witness of John the Baptist

THE BAPTIZING MINISTRIES OF JOHN AND OF JESUS IN JUDEA

22 Later, Jesus and his disciples came into the Judean countryside. He stayed some time there with them and baptized. 23 John too was baptizing — in Aenon-near-Salim — because water was plentiful there. People were coming and being baptized. 24 **John had not yet been put in prison.**

The Text of John 3:25–4:12

JOHN THE BAPTIST EXPLAINS THE SUCCESS OF JESUS

25 Then a discussion arose between the disciples of John and a Judean about ritual cleansing. 26 They came to John and said to him, "Rabbi, the one who was with you across the Jordan, to whom you bore witness, look, he is baptizing and everyone is going to him." 27 *John responded and said, "A person cannot gain anything unless it is given from heaven.* 28 *You yourselves witness to me that I said [that] 'I am not the Christ, but I have been sent before him.'* 29 **The one with the bride is the bridegroom. But the friend of the bridegroom, the one standing and listening, rejoices when he hears the voice of the bridegroom. This is the joy that has been brought to fulfillment in me.** 30 He must increase; I must decrease.

31 "The one who comes from above is above all. The one who is of the earth is of the earth and speaks in an earthly way. The one who comes from heaven [is above all]. 32 What he has seen and heard he bears witness to, and no one accepts his witness. 33 The one who accepts his witness certifies that God is true. 34 For the one that God sent speaks the words of God, for he does not bestow the Spirit in a limited way. 35 The Father loves the Son and has given all things into his hands. 36 The one who believes in the Son has everlasting life. But the one who does not obey the Son will not see life; rather, the wrath of God awaits that person."

4:1-24 The Samaritan Woman and the Gift of the Spirit (Part 1)

1 **When therefore the Lord** learned that the Pharisees had heard that he was baptizing and making more disciples than John 2 — **actually Jesus himself was not baptizing but his disciples** — 3 he departed from Judean territory and returned again to Galilee.

4 He had to pass through Samaria. 5 So he came to the Samaritan town called Sychar, near the field that Jacob had given to his son Joseph. 6 Jacob's well was there. Jesus, tired from his traveling, sat down at the well. It was about the sixth hour.

7 A Samaritan woman came to draw water, and Jesus said to her, "Give me a drink." 8 His disciples had gone into the town to buy food. 9 The Samaritan woman said to him, "How is it that you, who are a Jew, ask for a drink from me, a Samaritan woman?" For Jews do not associate with Samaritans.

WATER: MATERIAL AND SPIRITUAL

10 *Jesus responded and said to her, "If you knew the gift of God and who it is that is saying to you, 'Give me a drink,' you would have asked him, and he would have given you living water."* 11 *[The woman] said to him, "Sir, you do not have a bucket and the well is deep, so how do you have living water?* 12 *Are you greater than our father Jacob,*

who gave us this well and who drank from it himself, along with his sons and his herds?" 13 Jesus responded and said to her, "Everyone who drinks this water will get thirsty again, 14 but whoever drinks the water that I will give will never get thirsty. Rather, the water that I will give will be a well within the person bubbling up to eternal life." 15 The woman said to him, "Sir, give me this water, so that I may not thirst nor come here to draw water."

16 He said to her, "Go, call your husband and come back."

17 The woman responded and said to him, "I do not have a husband." Jesus said to her, "You say well that you have no husband. 18 You have had five husbands, and the one you have now is not your husband. This you have said truthfully."

Worship: Material and Spiritual

19 The woman said to him, "Sir, I see that you are a prophet. 20 Our fathers worshiped on this mountain, and you say that the proper place for worship is in Jerusalem." 21 Jesus said to her, "Woman, believe me that an hour is coming when you will worship the Father neither on this mountain nor in Jerusalem. 22 You worship what you do not know; we worship what we know, because salvation is from the Jews. 23 But an hour is coming and is now here, when true worshipers will worship the Father in Spirit and truth. For the Father seeks out such people to worship him.

24 God is Spirit, and it is necessary that those who worship him do so in Spirit and truth."

4:25-42   The Samaritan Woman and the Gift of the Spirit (Part 2)

25 The woman said to him, "I know the Messiah is coming, the one called Christ. When he comes, he will announce all things to us." 26 Jesus said to her, "I am he, the one speaking to you."

27 At that moment, his disciples returned and marveled that he was talking with a woman. Nevertheless, no one said, "What are you inquiring about?" or "Why are you speaking with her?" 28 So the woman left her water jar and went into the town and said to the people, 29 "Come, see a person who told me everything I have done. This man isn't the Christ, is he?" 30 The people went out from the town and were coming to him.

Food and Harvest: Material and Spiritual

31 In the meantime, the disciples were inviting him, saying, "Rabbi, eat." 32 He said to them, "I have food to eat that you do not know about." 33 Then the disciples said to one another, "Someone else didn't bring him something to eat, did he?" 34 Jesus said to

them, *"My food is to do the will of the one who sent me and to bring his work to completion.* 35 **Do not you yourselves say, 'It is already the fourth month and the harvest is coming'? Behold, I say to you, lift up your eyes and look at the fields; they are white, ready for harvest. Already** 36 **the reaper is being paid and is gathering in fruit for everlasting life, with the result that the sower rejoices along with the reaper.** 37 **For, in this sense, the saying is true that the sower is one person and the reaper another.** 38 **I sent you to harvest what you have not labored for. Others have labored, and you have entered into their labor."**

39 From that town many of the Samaritans believed in him because of the word of the woman who witnessed, "He told me everything I have done."

40 When therefore the Samaritans came to him, they asked him to remain with them, and he remained there two days. 41 And many more believed because of his word. 42 They said to the woman, "No longer do we believe because of your report, for we ourselves have heard, and we know that this is truly the Savior of the world."

4:43-54 Arrival in Galilee and the Healing of an Official's Son

43 **After the two days**, he departed from there into Galilee. 44 **For Jesus himself bore witness that a prophet does not have honor in his own country.** 45 **When therefore he came into Galilee**, the Galileans welcomed him, having seen all that he had done in Jerusalem at the feast, for they too had come to the feast.

46 So he came again into Cana of Galilee where he had made water wine. And there was an official whose son was ill in Capernaum. 47 This man, hearing that Jesus had come from Judea into Galilee, came to him **and asked that he come down and heal his son, for he was at the point of death.** 48 **So Jesus said to him, "Unless you all see signs and wonders, you do not believe."** 49 The official said to him, "Sir, come down before my little boy dies." 50 Jesus said to him, "Depart. Your son lives." The man believed the word that Jesus spoke to him, and he departed.

51 While he was still on his journey down, his servants came to meet him, saying that his son was alive. 52 He found out from the servants the hour at which the son began to recover. They said to him, "Yesterday at the seventh hour the fever left him." 53 The father remembered that was the very hour when Jesus said, "Your son lives" — and he himself believed, and his entire household.

54 This was, again, the second sign that Jesus performed, coming from Judea to Galilee.

The Text of John 5:1-19

5:1-18 A Narrative of the Healing of the Paralytic at the Pool

THE HEALING OF A MAN PARALYZED FOR THIRTY-EIGHT YEARS

1 Later, there was a feast of the Jews, and Jesus went up to Jerusalem. 2 In Jerusalem, near the Sheep Gate, there is a pool (called, in Hebrew, Bethesda) that has five porticoes. 3 A crowd of sick, blind, lame, and paralyzed were lying in these porticoes. 5 There was a certain man there who had been sick for thirty-eight years. 6 Seeing this man lying there and knowing that he had been sick a long time, Jesus said to him, "Do you wish to be healed?" 7 The sick man answered him, "Sir, I do not have someone to put me in the pool when the water is stirred up. By the time I get there, another has entered before me." 8 Jesus said to him, "Get up, pick up your pallet, and walk." 9 And immediately the man was healed and took up his pallet and began to walk.

THE AFTERMATH OF THE HEALING

That day was a Sabbath. 10 *So the Jews said to the man who had been healed, "It is the Sabbath, and it is not permissible for you to pick up your pallet."* 11 *But he answered them, "The one who made me well, that one said to me, 'Pick up your pallet and walk.'"* 12 *They asked him, "Who is the man who said to you, 'Take it up and walk'?"* 13 *The man who had been healed did not know who it was, for Jesus slipped away because there was a crowd in the place.* 14 *Later, Jesus found him in the Temple and said to him, "You see that you have become well. Do not sin any more, lest something worse befall you."* 15 *The man went off and reported to the Jews that it was Jesus who made him well.* 16 *And so because of this the Jews were persecuting Jesus, because he was doing these things on the Sabbath.* 17 *But [Jesus] responded to them, "My Father works until now, and I work also."* 18 *Because of this the Jews sought all the more to kill him, because not only was he breaking the Sabbath but he was calling God his own father, making himself equal to God.*

5:19-30 A Discourse on the Relationship of the Son with the Father (Part 1): The Two Powers Given to Jesus

19 So Jesus responded and said to them, "Amen, amen, I say to you, the Son is not able to do anything of himself, **except what he sees the Father doing.** *For the things he does, the Son likewise does.*

The Text of John 5:20-35

The Power to Give Life and the Power to Judge

20 "For the Father loves the Son and shows him all things that he himself does, and he will show him *greater works than these in order that you may marvel.* 21 For just as the Father raises the dead and gives them life, so also the Son gives life to those he wishes. 22 The Father does not judge anyone but has given all judgment to the Son, 23 so that all may honor the Son, just as they honor the Father. The one who does not honor the Son does not honor the Father who sent him.

Life and Death: (Material and) Spiritual

24 *"Amen, amen, I say to you, the one who hears my word and believes in the one who sent me has eternal life, and does not come into judgment, but has crossed over from death to life.* 25 *Amen, amen, I say to you, an hour is coming, and is now present, when the dead will hear the voice of the Son of God, and those hearing it will live.* 26 For just as the Father has life in himself, so he has given life to the Son to have it in himself.

Judgment

27 "And he has given him the power to judge, because he is Son of Man. 28 Do not marvel at this, that an hour is coming in which all those in the tombs will hear his voice 29 and will come forth, those who have done good to a resurrection of life, those who have practiced evil to a resurrection of judgment.

30 *"I am not able to do anything of myself. As I hear, I judge; and my judgment is just, because I do not seek my own will but the will of the one who sent me.*

5:31-40 A Discourse on the Relationship of the Son with the Father (Part 2): The Four Witnesses to Jesus

31 *"If I witness about myself, my witness is not true.*

The Witness of John the Baptist

32 *"There is another who bears witness about me, and I know that the witness he bears about me is true.* 33 *You have sent people to John, and he has witnessed to the truth.* 34 *I do not accept human witness, but I say these things so that you may be saved.* 35 *He was the lamp, burning and shining. You wished to rejoice for a short time in his light.*

The Text of John 5:36–6:4

The Witness of the Works

36 "But I have a witness greater than that of John: the works that the Father has given me to bring to completion; the works themselves that I perform witness about me that the Father has sent me.

The Witness of the Word

37 "And the Father who sent me, he himself has witnessed about me. You have never heard his voice nor seen his form, 38 and you do not have his word remaining in you, because you do not believe the one whom he sent.

The Witness of the Scriptures

39 "You search the Scriptures because you think you have eternal life in them. And those also witness to me. 40 And you do not wish to come to me so that you may have life.

5:41-47 A Discourse on the Relationship of the Son with the Father (Part 3): The Glory That Jesus Does, and Does Not, Accept

41 "I do not accept glory from humans. 42 But I have known you — that you do not have the love of God in yourselves. 43 I have come in the name of my Father, and you do not accept me. If another comes in his own name, you accept that person. 44 How are you able to believe, accepting glory from one another — and you do not seek the glory from the only God? 45 Do not think that I will accuse you before the Father. The one accusing you is Moses, in whom you placed your hope. 46 For if you believed in Moses, you would believe in me, for he wrote about me. 47 If you do not believe in that one's writings, how will you believe in my words?"

6:1-21 A Narrative of a Miraculous Feeding by Jesus and an Appearance of Jesus Walking on the Sea

Later, Jesus departed to the other side of the Sea of Galilee, of Tiberias. 2 A large crowd was following him, because they had seen the signs that he was performing upon the sick. 3 Jesus went up the mountain and sat there with his disciples. 4 Passover, the feast of the Jews, was near.

The Text of John 6:5-24

A Miraculous Feeding of Five Thousand People

5 So Jesus, lifting up his eyes and seeing that a large crowd was coming toward him, said to Philip, "Where will we buy bread that these may eat?" 6 *He said this testing him, for he himself knew what he was about to do.* 7 Philip answered him, "Two hundred denarii worth of bread would not be sufficient for them so that each may have a small [amount]." 8 One of his disciples, Andrew the brother of Simon Peter, said to him, 9 "Here is a young boy who has five barley loaves and two fish. But what are these for so many?" 10 Jesus said, "Have the people recline." (There was considerable grass in the place.) The men then reclined, about five thousand in number. 11 Then Jesus took the loaves; and, having given thanks, he distributed them to those reclining; the same with the fish, as much as they wanted.

12 When they had enough, he said to his disciples, "Gather together the remaining pieces, so that nothing may be lost." 13 So they gathered them up, and they filled twelve baskets with fragments of the five barley loaves that were left over from those who had eaten. 14 The people, seeing the signs that he performed, said, "Truly this is the Prophet who is coming into the world." 15 *But Jesus, knowing that they were about to come and to take him by force so they might make him king, again went up the mountain alone, by himself.*

An Appearance of Jesus Walking on the Sea

16 When it was becoming evening, his disciples went down to the sea 17 and, embarking in a boat, started across the sea to Capernaum. It had already become dark **and Jesus had not yet come to them,** 18 and the sea was stirred up because a high wind was blowing. 19 Having rowed about three or three-and-a-half miles, they saw Jesus walking on the sea, coming near the boat; and they became afraid. 20 But he said to them, "It is I; do not be afraid." 21 They then wanted to take him into the boat, and immediately the boat arrived at the place where they were heading.

6:22-24 The Crowd Crosses to Capernaum

22 *The next day, the crowd, standing across the sea, saw* **that no other boat was there except one, and that Jesus did not enter the boat with his disciples, but that only his disciples went away.** 23 **But boats from Tiberias came near the place where they ate the bread after the Lord had given thanks.**
24 **When therefore the crowd saw** *that Jesus was not there nor his disciples, they themselves embarked in the boats and came to Capernaum seeking Jesus.*

The Text of John 6:25-50

6:25-50 A Discourse on the Witness of Scripture to Jesus as the True Bread

25 *And finding him across the sea, they said to him, "Rabbi, when did you get here?"* 26 Jesus responded and said to them, "Amen, amen, I say to you, you seek me not because you saw signs, but because you ate of the loaves and were filled. 27 Do not work for the bread that perishes, but for the bread that remains unto eternal life, which the Son of Man will give you. For this is the one on whom the Father, God, has put his seal of approval." 28 They said to him, "What should we do, to do the works of God?" 29 Jesus responded and said to them, "This is the work of God, that you believe in the one whom he sent."

30 *They said to him, "What sign do you perform, so that we may see and believe in you? What do you work? 31 Our fathers ate the manna in the desert, as it is written, 'He gave them bread from heaven to eat.'"* 32 So Jesus said to them, "Amen, amen, I say to you, it was not Moses who gave you the bread from heaven, but my Father gives you the true bread from heaven. 33 For the bread of God is that coming down from heaven and giving life to the world."

34 *Therefore, they said to him, "Sir, give us this bread always."* 35 Jesus said to them, *"I am the bread of life. The one who comes to me will not hunger, and the one believing in me will never thirst.* 36 But I said to you that you have seen [me] and you do not believe. 37 Everything the Father gives me comes to me, and that [one] coming to me I will not cast out, 38 **because I have come down from heaven not to do my will but the will of the one who sent me. 39 This is the will of the one who sent me, that I lose nothing of what he has given me, but that I raise it up on the last day.** 40 *For this is the will of my Father, that everyone who sees the Son and believes in him may have eternal life,* **and I myself will raise the person up on the last day."**

41 *So the Jews murmured about him because he said, "I am the bread come down from heaven," 42 and they said, "Is not this Jesus, the son of Joseph, whose father and mother we know? How does he say now, 'I have come down from heaven'?"* 43 Jesus responded and said to them, "Stop murmuring among yourselves. 44 No one is able to come to me unless the Father who sent me draws the person, **and I will raise that person up on the last day.** 45 *It is written in the prophets, 'And all will be taught by God.' Everyone listening to the Father and learning comes to me.* 46 **Not that anyone has seen the Father except the one who is from the Father — this one has seen the Father.** 47 *Amen, amen, I say to you, the one believing has eternal life. 48 I am the bread of life. 49 Your fathers ate the manna in the desert and died. 50 This is the bread come down from heaven, so that someone might eat of it and not die.*

6:51-59 The Eucharistic Bread of Life

51 "I am the living bread that has come down from heaven. If someone eats of this bread, that person will live forever. And the bread that I will give is my flesh for the life of the world." 52 The Jews then fought among themselves, saying, "How is this person able to give us [his] flesh to eat?" 53 So Jesus said to them, "Amen, amen, I say to you, unless you eat the flesh of the Son of Man and drink his blood, you do not have life in yourselves. 54 The one feeding on my flesh and drinking my blood has eternal life, and I will raise that person up on the last day. 55 For my flesh is true food and my blood is true drink. 56 The one who feeds on my flesh and drinks my blood remains in me, and I in that person. 57 Just as the living Father sent me, and I live because of the Father, so also the one feeding on me will live because of me. 58 This is the bread that has come down from heaven, not like the fathers ate and died. The one feeding on this bread will live forever." 59 *He said these things, teaching in the synagogue in Capernaum.*

6:60-71 The Unbelief of Some Disciples

60 *Therefore, many of his disciples, hearing him, said, "This word is offensive. Who is able to hear it?"* 61 *But Jesus, knowing in himself that his disciples were murmuring about this, said to them,* **"Does this cause you offense?** 62 **What if you see the Son of Man ascending to where he was before?** 63 *The Spirit is what gives life; the flesh is useless. The words that I have spoken to you are Spirit and life.* 64 *But there are some of you who do not believe." For Jesus knew from the beginning those not believing and who his betrayer was.* 65 *And he said, "Because of this I have said to you that no one is able to come to me unless it be given to him from the Father."* 66 So from that time on many of his disciples withdrew and no longer walked with him.

67 So Jesus said to the Twelve, "Do you too wish to depart?" 68 Simon Peter responded to him, "Master, to whom will we go? You have the words of eternal life, 69 and we have believed and have known that you are the Holy One of God." 70 Jesus responded to them, "Did I not choose you to be the Twelve, and one of you is a devil." 71 He was speaking about Judas, the son of Simon Iscariot. For this one, one of the Twelve, was going to hand him over.

7:1-13 A Narrative of Jesus at the Feast of Tabernacles (Part 1)

Jesus and His Brothers Discuss Going to Tabernacles

1 *And later Jesus moved about in Galilee. He did not want to move about in Judea because the Jews were seeking to kill him.* 2 *Tabernacles, the feast of the Jews, was near.*

3 So his brothers said to him, "Move on from here and go up to Judea so that your disciples may see your works that you are performing. 4 For no one works in secret and at the same time desires to be well known. If you are doing these things, make yourself known to the world." 5 For his brothers were not believing in him. 6 So Jesus said to them, "The time is not yet right for me, but the time is always right for you. 7 The world is not able to hate you, but it hates me because I bear witness about it that its works are evil. 8 You go up to the feast; I will not go up to this feast because the right time for me has not yet been fulfilled." 9 Having said these things, he remained in Galilee.

Jesus Goes to the Feast

10 But when his brothers went up to the feast, then he himself went up also — not openly but [as if] in secret. 11 *The Jews were seeking him at the feast and were saying, "Where is that man?" 12 And there was much murmuring about him among the common people. Some were saying, "He is a good man"; [but] others were saying, "No, he deceives the common people." 13 But no one spoke openly about him for fear of the Jews.*

7:14-30 A Narrative of Jesus at the Feast of Tabernacles (Part 2)

Where Jesus' Teaching Is From

14 *When the feast was already half over, Jesus went up to the Temple and taught. 15 The Jews marveled saying, "How does this man have learning since he has not been educated?" 16 Jesus responded and said to them, "My teaching is not mine but is from him who sent me. 17 If anyone wishes to do his will, that person will know within about my teaching, whether it is from God or whether I speak on my own. 18 Those who speak on their own seek their own glory. The one who seeks the glory of the one who sent him, this one is true and there is no injustice in him.*

19 "Has not Moses given you the Law? And not one of you obeys the Law. Why do you seek to kill me?" 20 The common people responded, "You are possessed. Who seeks to kill you?" 21 Jesus responded and said to them, "I have performed one work, and you all marvel. 22 For this reason Moses has given you circumcision — not that it is from Moses, but from the patriarchs — and you circumcise a person on the Sabbath. 23 If a person may receive circumcision on the Sabbath so that the Law of Moses not be broken, do you get angry at me because I made a person whole on the Sabbath? 24 **Stop judging superficially, but make your judgment just.**"

The Text of John 7:25-42

Where Jesus Is From

₂₅ **So some of the inhabitants of Jerusalem said, "Is not this the one they are seeking to kill? ₂₆ And, look, he speaks openly, and they say nothing to him.** Do you think the rulers truly know that this man is the Christ? ₂₇ But we know where this man is from. When the Christ comes, no one is to know his origin." ₂₈ *So Jesus, teaching in the Temple, cried out, saying, "And you know me, and you know where I am from. And I have not come of myself, but the one who sent me is true, and you do not know him. ₂₉ I know him, because I am from him, and he has sent me." ₃₀ Then they tried to seize him, and no one was able to lay a hand on him, because his hour had not yet come.*

7:31-52 A Narrative of Jesus at the Feast of Tabernacles (Part 3)

Where Jesus Is Going

₃₁ From among the common people, however, many believed in him; and they said, "When the Christ comes, will he perform more signs than this man?" ₃₂ The Pharisees heard the common people murmuring these things about him, and the chief priests and the Pharisees sent temple police to seize him. ₃₃ *So Jesus said, "I am with you for only a little time, and I go to the one who sent me. ₃₄ You will seek me, and you will not find [me]; and where I am, you are not able to come." ₃₅ Then the Jews said to one another, "Where is this man intending to go that we will not find him? He is not intending to go into the Greek Diaspora and to teach the Greeks, is he? ₃₆ What is this saying of his, 'You will seek me and you will not find [me], and where I am, you are not able to come?'"*

Jesus Promises Living Water

₃₇ *On the last and greatest day of the feast, Jesus stood forth and cried out, saying, "If anyone thirsts, let that person come to me and drink. ₃₈ The one who believes in me — as the Scripture says, 'Rivers of living water will flow* **from his belly.**'" ₃₉ *(He said this about the Spirit that those who believed in him were to receive. For the Spirit was not yet because Jesus was not yet glorified.)*

Where Jesus Is From (#2)

₄₀ Some of the common people, *hearing these words,* said, "This man is truly the Prophet." ₄₁ Others said, "This is the Christ," but they said, "But the Christ is not to come from Galilee, is he? ₄₂ Does the Scripture not say that the Christ comes 'from the seed of David' and 'from Bethlehem', the village where David was?" 43 Then a division arose in the common people because of him. 44 Some of them wanted to seize him, but no one laid hands on him.

45 So the temple police returned to the chief priests and Pharisees, and they said to the temple police, "Why have you not brought him in?" 46 The temple police responded, "No person ever spoke like this man before." 47 The Pharisees responded to them, "Are you too deceived? 48 Has any of the rulers or the Pharisees believed in him? 49 But the common people, who do not know the Law, are damned." 50 Nicodemus, the one who had come to him before and who was one of them, said to them, 51 "Our Law does not judge a person without first hearing from the person and knowing what the person has done, does it?" 52 They responded and said to him, "Are you too from Galilee? Search and see that the prophet does not come from Galilee."

8:12-30 A Discourse on the Witness of the Word of Jesus (Part 1)

THE PROPER FORM OF WITNESS

12 So again Jesus spoke to them, saying, "I am the light of the world. The one who follows me will not walk in darkness but will have the light of life." 13 So the Pharisees said to him, *"You bear witness to yourself. Your witness is not true."* 14 *Jesus answered and said to them, "Even if I bear witness to myself, my witness is true,* **because I know where I came from and where I am going. But you do not know where I come from nor where I am going.** 15 You judge according to the flesh; I do not judge anyone. 16 And, if I do judge, my judgment is true, *because I am not alone, but I am together with the Father who sent me. 17 And in your Law it is written that the witness of two persons is true. 18 I am one who bears witness about myself and the Father who sent me also bears witness about me."* 19 Then they said to him, "Where is your Father?" Jesus responded, "You know neither me nor my Father. If you knew me, you would also know my Father." 20 He spoke these words in the treasury, teaching in the Temple. And no one seized him because his hour had not yet come.

FAILURE TO RECOGNIZE JESUS AND HIS WORDS

Misunderstanding #1: Where Jesus Is From and Where He Is Going

21 So he said to them again, "I am going away, and you will seek me, and you will die in your sin. Where I am going, you are not able to come." 22 So the Jews said, "Is he going to kill himself since he says, 'Where I am going, you are not able to come'?" 23 And he said to them, "You are of the things below; I am of the things above. **You are**

of this world; I am not of this world. ₂₄So I said to you that you will die in your sins; for, if you do not believe that I AM, you will die in your sins." ₂₅*So they said to him, "Who are you?" Jesus said to them, "What I have been telling you from the beginning.* ₂₆*I have many things to say* **and to judge regarding you.** *But the one who sent me is true, and those things that I heard from him I speak to the world."* ₂₇*They did not know that he was talking to them about the Father.*

₂₈*So Jesus said [to them],* "When you lift up the Son of Man, then you will know that I AM, and *I do nothing of myself, but I speak these things just as the Father taught me.* ₂₉*And the one who sent me is with me. He did not leave me alone because I always do that which is pleasing to him."* ₃₀**When Jesus said these things, many believed in him.**

8:31-50   A Discourse on the Witness of the Word of Jesus (Part 2)

REMAINING IN THE WORD OF JESUS AND LISTENING
TO THE WORD OF THE DEVIL

Misunderstanding #2: Abraham and Freedom

₃₁So Jesus said to the Jews who believed in him, "If you remain in my word, you are truly my disciples; ₃₂and you will know the truth, *and the truth will make you free."* ₃₃*They responded to him, "We are seed of Abraham, and we have never been in slavery to anyone. How can you say, 'You will be free'?"* ₃₄*Jesus responded to them, "Amen, amen, I say to you, everyone who commits sin is a slave [of sin].* ₃₅*The slave does not remain in the house forever; the son remains forever.* ₃₆So if the Son frees you, you will be genuinely free. ₃₇*I know you are seed of Abraham, but you seek to kill me because my word does not dwell in you.*

Misunderstanding #3: Abraham and Sonship

₃₈"I speak what I have seen with my Father, and you do what you heard from your father." ₃₉They responded and said to him, "Our father is Abraham." Jesus said to them, "If you were children of Abraham, you would do the works of Abraham. ₄₀But now you seek to kill me, a person who has spoken the truth to you that I heard from God. Abraham did not do that. ₄₁You do the works of your father." [Therefore] they said to him, "We have not been born in adultery. We have one father, God." ₄₂Jesus said to them, "If God were your father, you would love me, for I came from God and am now present. I have not come on my own, but he sent me. ₄₃Why do you not know my message? Because you are not able to hear my word. ₄₄You are of your father the devil, and you want to do his wishes. He was a murderer from the beginning and has not stood with the truth because there is no truth in him. When he speaks a lie, he speaks from his own resources because he is a liar and the Father of Lying. 45 But because I speak the truth, you do not believe me. 46 Which of you convicts me of sin? If I speak the truth, why do you not believe me? 47 The one who is of God listens to the words of God. This is why you do not listen, because you are not of God." 48 The Jews responded and said to him, "Do we not correctly say that you are a Samaritan and that you are possessed?" 49 Jesus responded, "I am not possessed; but I honor my Father, and you dishonor me. 50 *I do not seek my glory; there is one who seeks it* and who judges.

8:51-59   A Discourse on the Witness of the Word of Jesus (Part 3)

KEEPING THE WORD OF JESUS AND JESUS' TRUE GLORY

Misunderstanding #4: Abraham and the Age of Jesus

51 "Amen, amen, I say to you, if a person keeps my word, that person will by no means see death forever." 52 [Therefore] the Jews said to him, "Now we know that you are possessed. Abraham died and also the prophets, and you say, 'If anyone keeps my word, that person will by no means taste death forever.' 53 *Are you greater than our father Abraham, who died? And the prophets died. Who do you make yourself to be?"* 54 *Jesus responded, "If I glorify myself, my glory is nothing. My Father is the one who glorifies me, the one whom you say is our God.* 55 *And you have not known him, but I know him. And if I were to say that I do not know him, I would be like you, a liar. But I do know him and I keep his word.* 56 Abraham your father rejoiced to see my day, and he did see it and rejoiced." 57 Then the Jews said to him, "You are not yet fifty years old, and you have seen Abraham?" 58 Jesus said to them, "Amen, amen, I say to you, before Abraham came to be, I AM." 59 *Then they picked up stones to cast at him. But Jesus hid himself and departed from the Temple.*

9:1-17   The Healing of a Man Born Blind

THE ENCOUNTER

1 And going farther along, he saw a person blind from birth. 2 And his disciples asked him, saying, "Rabbi, who sinned, this man or his parents, that he was born blind?" 3 Jesus responded, "Neither this man nor his parents sinned, but so that the works of God might be manifest in him. 4 **It is necessary for us to work the works of**

the One who sent me while it is day. Night is coming when no one is able to work. 5 While I am in the world, I am the light of the world."

THE HEALING

6 **Having said these things,** he spit on the ground and made mud from the spit and spread the mud on his eyes 7 and said to him, "Go and wash in the Pool of Siloam" (which is translated Sent). So he went off, and washed himself, and returned seeing. 8 The neighbors and those who had noticed that he was a beggar before said, "Is this man not the one who used to sit and beg?" 9 Others agreed that it was he. Others said, "No, but he looks like him." The man said, "I am he!" 10 So they said to him, "How [then] were your eyes opened?" 11 The man responded, "The man named Jesus made mud and covered my eyes and told me, 'Go to the Pool of Siloam and wash.'" So having gone off and washed, I could see." 12 And they said to him, "Where is that man?" He said, "I do not know."

THE FIRST INTERROGATION

13 They took the man who had been blind to the Pharisees. 14 For it was on a Sabbath that Jesus made mud and opened his eyes. 15 So the Pharisees interrogated him again, how it was that he gained his sight. But he said to them, "He put mud upon my eyes and I washed and I see." 16 Then some of the Pharisees said, "This man is not from God because he does not keep the Sabbath." [But] others said, "How is a sinful person able to perform such signs?" And there was a division among them. 17 Therefore, they said to the blind man again, "What do you say about him since he opened your eyes?" He said, "He is a prophet."

9:18-41 The Interrogation of the Man Born Blind

THE INTERROGATION OF THE PARENTS

18 But the Jews did not believe about the man that he was blind and regained his sight until they called the parents of the man who had regained his sight 19 and they asked them, saying, "Is this your son, whom you say was born blind? How therefore does he now see?" 20 So his parents responded and said, "We know that this is our son, and that he was born blind. 21 But how he now sees we do not know, nor do we know who opened his eyes. Ask him; he is of age. He will speak for himself." 22 His parents said these things because they were fearing the Jews, for the Jews had already agreed that if anyone confessed Jesus as the Christ, that person would be put out of the synagogue. 23 For this reason his parents said, "He is of age; ask him."

The Text of John 9:24–10:5

The Second Interrogation of the Man

24 So, for a second time, they called the man who had been blind and said to him, "Give glory to God. We know that this man is a sinner." 25 So the man answered, "Whether he is a sinner, I do not know. One thing I know: that I was blind and now I see." 26 So they said to him, "What did he do to you? How did he open your eyes?" 27 He said to them, "I told you already, and you did not listen. Why do you want to hear it again? Perhaps you too want to become his disciples?" 28 And they berated him and said, "You are a disciple of that fellow; we are disciples of Moses! 29 We know that God has spoken to Moses, but we do not know where this one is from." 30 The man responded and said to them, "This is what is surprising, that you do not know where he is from, and he opened my eyes. 31 We know that God does not hear sinners; but if a person is God-fearing and does his will, he listens to the person. 32 Never has it been heard that anyone has opened the eyes of a person born blind. 33 Unless this man was from God, he would not be able to do anything." 34 They responded and said to him, "You were born completely in sin and you teach us?" And they threw him out.

Jesus Meets the Man Again

35 Jesus heard that they had thrown the man out, and finding him, said [to him], "Do you believe in the Son of Man?" 36 The man responded and said, "And who is he, Sir, that I may believe in him?" 37 Jesus said to him, "You have seen him, and the one talking with you is he." 38 Then the man said, "I believe, Lord." And he worshiped him. 39 And Jesus said, "I came into this world for judgment so that those who do not see may see, and those who see may become blind." 40 Some of the Pharisees who were around him heard these things and said to him, "Are we blind also?" 41 Jesus said to them, "If you were blind, you would not be guilty of sin. But now you say, 'We see.' Your sin remains."

10:1-21 The Parable of the Shepherd and Its Explanation

The Parable

1 "Amen, amen, I say to you, the one not entering the sheepfold through the gate but entering another way is a thief and a bandit. 2 But the one entering through the gate is the shepherd of the sheep. 3 For this person, the gatekeeper opens the gate, and the sheep hear his voice, and he calls his own sheep by name and leads them out. 4 Whenever he takes out all his own, he goes before them; and the sheep follow because they know his voice. 5 They will by no means follow a stranger, but flee from such a person

because they do not know the voice of strangers." ₆Jesus told them this parable. But they did not understand what it was he was telling them.

#1: I Am the Gate

₇*So Jesus said again, "Amen, amen, I say to you,* **I am the gate for the sheep.** ₈*All who came [before me] were thieves and bandits, but the sheep did not listen to them.*
₉**"I am the gate. If someone enters through me, that person will be saved and will go in and come out and will find pasture.** ₁₀*The thief does not come except so that he may steal, slay, and destroy. I came so that they might have life, and have it abundantly.*

#2: I Am the Good Shepherd

₁₁*"I am the good shepherd.* **The good shepherd lays down his life for his sheep.** ₁₂Someone hired, who is not the shepherd, for whom the sheep are not his own, seeing the wolf coming, leaves the sheep and flees — and the wolf grabs them and scatters them — ₁₃because he is hired and he does not have a concern for the sheep.
₁₄**"I am the good shepherd,** *and I know mine and mine know me,* ₁₅*just as the Father knows me and I know the Father.* **And I lay down my life for the sheep.** ₁₆And I have other sheep that are not from this fold. It is necessary for me to lead them also, and they will listen to my voice, and there will be one flock, one shepherd. ₁₇For this reason the Father loves me, that I lay down my life so that I may take it up again. ₁₈No one takes it from me; rather, I lay it down of my own accord. I have the power to lay it down, and the power to take it up again. I received this commandment from my Father."

The Reaction

₁₉Again a division developed among the Judeans over these words. ₂₀Many of them said, "He is possessed and is raving. Why do you listen to him?" ₂₁Others were saying, "These are not the words of a possessed person. Do you think a demon would be able to open the eyes of the blind?"

10:22-42 The Discourse on Jesus' Works as Witness to Him and a Brief Reference to the Witness of John

The Discourse: At Dedication

22 Then Dedication took place in Jerusalem. It was winter, 23 and Jesus was walking in the Temple in the Portico of Solomon. 24 The Jews surrounded him and said to him, "How long will you keep us in suspense? If you are the Christ, tell us openly."

25 Jesus responded to them, "I told you, and you do not believe. The works that I do in my Father's name witness about me. 26 But you do not believe because you are not of my sheep. 27 My sheep hear my voice, and I know them, and they follow me; 28 and I give them eternal life, and they are not lost for eternity, and no one will snatch them from my hand. 29 What my Father has given me is greater than all else, and no one is able to steal from the hand of the Father. 30 The Father and I are one."

31 The Jews again took up stones to stone him. 32 Jesus responded to them, "I have shown you many good works from the Father. For what kind of work among them do you stone me?" 33 The Jews responded to him, "We do not stone you for a good work but for blasphemy, and because you who are a human make yourself God." 34 Jesus responded to them, "Is it not written in your Law, 'I said, you are gods'? 35 If it calls 'gods' those to whom the word of God came, and if Scripture cannot be contradicted, 36 can you say that I, the one whom the Father consecrated and sent into the world, blaspheme because I said: 'I am Son of God'? 37 If I do not do the works of my Father, do not believe me. 38 But if I do them, and if you do not believe me, believe the works, in order that you may come to know and abide in the knowledge that the Father is in me and I am in the Father." 39 [So] they sought again to seize him, and he escaped their grasp.

Beyond the Jordan

40 And he went off again beyond the Jordan to the place where John was first baptizing, and he remained there. 41 And many came to him and said, "On the one hand, John performed no sign; and, on the other, everything John said about this man was true." 42 And many believed in him there.

11:1-27 Life Is Restored to Lazarus (Part 1)

Jesus Hears of the Illness

1 There was a certain person who was ill, Lazarus of Bethany, from the village of Mary and Martha, her sister. 2 **Mary was the one who had anointed the Lord with**

oil and had dried his feet with her hair, whose brother Lazarus was ill. 3 So the sisters sent to him, saying, "Master, behold, the one you love is ill." 4 *When Jesus heard this, he said, "This disease will not end in death; it has occurred for the glory of God, so that the Son of God may be glorified through it."* 5 *Indeed, Jesus loved Martha and her sister and Lazarus.* 6 *When therefore he heard that he was sick,* then he remained two days in the place where he was. 7 *Thereupon, after this, he said to the disciples, "Let us go up to Judea again."* 8 *The disciples said to him, "Rabbi, just now the Jews were seeking to stone you, and you would go up there again?"* 9 **Jesus answered, "Are there not twelve hours in the day? If a person walks during the day, the person does not fall because he sees the light of this world.** 10 **But if a person walks during the night, the person falls because the light is not in him."** 11 **He said these things, and after this,** he said, "Lazarus our friend has fallen asleep, but I go to wake him up." 12 So the disciples said to him, "Master, if he is asleep, he will be saved." 13 Jesus was speaking about his death. But they thought that he was speaking about ordinary sleep. 14 Then Jesus said to them openly, "Lazarus has died. 15 *And for your sake I rejoice that I was not there, so that you may believe. So, let us go to him."* 16 *Then Thomas, called Didymus, said to his fellow disciples, "Let us go along too, so we may die with him."*

Jesus Arrives and Talks with Martha

17 So when Jesus arrived, he found him in the tomb for four days already. 18 Bethany was near Jerusalem, about fifteen stadia away. 19 So many Judeans had come to Martha and Mary to console them about their brother. 20 When Martha heard that Jesus was coming, she went to meet him. Mary was seated in the house. 21 Martha then said to Jesus, "Master, if you had been here, my brother would not have died. 22 [But] even now I know that whatever you ask God for, God will give to you." 23 **Jesus said to her, "Your brother will rise."** 24 Martha said to him, "I know that he will rise in the resurrection on the last day." 25 **Jesus said to her, "I am the Resurrection and the Life. The person who believes in me, even if the person dies, will live.** 26 **And every person who lives and believes in me will by no means die forever. Do you believe this?"** 27 She said to him, "Yes, Lord. I have believed that you are the Christ, the Son of God, the one who is coming into the world."

11:28-46   Life Is Restored to Lazarus (Part 2)

Martha Calls Mary

28 **And having said this,** she went off and called Mary her sister, saying secretly, "The teacher is present and is calling for you." 29 The sister, when she heard this, got

up quickly and went to him. 30 Jesus had not yet come into the village, but was still in the place where Martha had met him. 31 So the Judeans who were with her in the house and consoling her, seeing Mary get up quickly and depart, followed her, thinking that she was going to the tomb to weep there.

Jesus Talks with Mary

32 So Mary, when she came to the place where Jesus was, seeing him, fell at his feet, saying to him, "Master, if you had been here, my brother would not have died." 33 So, when he saw her weeping and the Judeans who accompanied her weeping, Jesus was deeply disturbed in spirit and was shaken, 34 and said, "Where have you laid him?" They said to him, "Master, come and see." 35 Jesus wept. 36 So the Judeans said, "Look how much he loved him." 37 But some of them said, "Was not this man, who opened the eyes of the blind man, able to prevent this man from dying?"

Lazarus Is Raised from the Dead

38 Jesus, once again deeply disturbed within, came to the tomb. It was a cave, and a stone lay in front of it. 39 Jesus said, "Take away the stone." Martha, the sister of the dead man, said to him, "Master, he is already giving off a stench, for it is the fourth day." 40 **Jesus said to her, "Did I not say to you that, if you would believe, you would see the glory of God?"** 41 So they removed the stone. *Jesus raised his eyes upward and said, "Father, I give thanks to you that you have heard me.* 42 *I knew that you always hear me, but for the sake of the crowd standing around I said this, so that they might believe that you have sent me."*

43 *And having said these things,* he cried out in a loud voice, "Lazarus, come forth!" 44 Then the dead man came out, bound hand and foot in burial wrappings, and his face was wrapped in a face cloth. Jesus said to them, "Unwrap him and let him go."

The Reaction of the People of Judea

45 So, many of the Judeans, those who had come to Mary and who had seen the things he had done, believed in him. 46 But some of them went off to the Pharisees and told them the things Jesus had done.

The Text of John 11:47–12:8

11:47-57 The Decision of the Sanhedrin to Kill Jesus

THE SANHEDRIN MEETS

47 So the chief priests and the Pharisees convened the Sanhedrin and said, "What are we to do because this man performs many signs? 48 If we allow him thus, everyone will believe in him, and the Romans will come and will destroy our Temple and our people." 49 One of them, Caiaphas, the chief priest that year, said to them, "You know nothing! 50 Nor do you realize that it is beneficial for us that one person die for the people lest the entire people be destroyed." **51 He did not say this on his own, but since he was chief priest that year, he prophesied that Jesus was about to die for the nation, 52 and not only for the nation but in order that he might lead together into one the children of God scattered about.**

53 So from that day, they took counsel to kill him. 54 So Jesus no longer moved openly among the Judeans, but departed from that place to the region near the desert, to a city by the name of Ephraim, and he remained there with his disciples.

THE PASSOVER PILGRIMS TALK ABOUT JESUS

55 The Passover of the Jews was near, and many from that region went up to Jerusalem before the Passover to purify themselves. 56 So they sought out Jesus and said to one another, standing in the Temple, "What do you think? He will not come to the feast, will he?" 57 The Pharisees and chief priests had given orders that, if anyone should know where he was, the person should provide information so they might seize him.

12:1-19 Jesus at Bethany and His Entry into Jerusalem

A DINNER FOR JESUS IN BETHANY

1 So six days before Passover, Jesus came to Bethany, where Lazarus resided, whom Jesus had raised from the dead. 2 They held a dinner for him there, **and Martha served,** and Lazarus was among those reclining with him. 3 **Mary, taking a litra of perfume of genuine, costly nard, anointed Jesus' feet and wiped his feet with her hair. The house was filled with the aroma of the nard.** 4 Judas Iscariot, one of his disciples, the one about to betray him, said, 5 "Why was this perfume not sold for three hundred denarii and given to the poor?" 6 But he said this not because he was concerned for the poor, but because he was a thief, and being in charge of the purse, he stole what was in it. 7 So Jesus said, "Let her be, so that she may keep it for the day of my burial. 8 For you always have the poor with you, but you do not always have me."

The Text of John 12:9-30

9 [The] large crowd of Judeans knew that he was there, and they came not only because of Jesus but so that they might see Lazarus, whom he raised from the dead. 10 The chief priests planned to kill Lazarus also, 11 since because of him many of the Judeans were going off and believing in Jesus.

Jesus Enters Jerusalem and Is Acclaimed by the Crowds

12 *The next day the large crowd, the one coming to the feast, having heard that Jesus was coming to Jerusalem,* 13 *took up palm fronds and went out to meet him and cried out, "Hosanna! Blessed is the one coming in the name of the Lord, [and] the King of Israel."* 14 *But Jesus, finding a donkey, sat upon it, as it is written:* 15 *"Do not fear, Daughter of Zion. Behold your king comes sitting on the foal of a donkey."* 16 *His disciples did not know these things at first; but after Jesus was glorified, then they remembered that these things were written about him, and that they did these things for him.*

17 So the crowd that was with him when he called Lazarus from the tomb and raised him from the dead was bearing witness. 18 Because of this [also] the crowd went out to receive him, because they heard that he had performed this sign. 19 So the Pharisees said to themselves, "You see that your efforts are useless. Behold, the world is going after him!"

12:20-36 The Judgment of Unbelief (Part 1)

The Coming of the Greeks and of the Hour

20 There were some Greeks among those going up to worship at the feast. 21 So these approached Philip, the one from Bethsaida in Galilee, and they were asking him, saying, "Sir, we wish to see Jesus." 22 Philip came and spoke to Andrew. Andrew and Philip came and spoke to Jesus.

23 **Jesus responded, saying to them, "The hour has come for the Son of Man to be glorified.** 24 **Amen, amen, I say to you, unless the grain of wheat, falling to the ground, dies, it remains solitary. But if it dies, it bears much fruit.** 25 **The one loving his life loses it, and the one hating his life in this world will protect it for eternal life.** 26 **If someone would serve me, let that person follow me, and where I am, there also my servant will be. If a person serves me, the Father will honor him."**

27 *"Now my soul is shaken. And what should I say: 'Father, save me from this hour?' But it was for this very reason that I came to this hour.* 28 *Father, glorify your name." Then a voice came from heaven, "I have already glorified it, and I will glorify it again."* 29 *Then the crowd standing near and hearing this said it was thunder. Others were saying, "An angel has spoken to him."* 30 *Jesus responded and said, "This voice did not speak for my sake but for yours."*

The Text of John 12:31–13:1

THE JUDGMENT

31 "Now is the judgment of this world; now the ruler of this world will be thrown out. 32 And, if I am lifted up from the earth, I will draw all to myself." 33 (He said this, indicating by what type of death he was about to die.) 34 Then the crowd answered him, "We heard in the Law that the Christ remains forever, and how do you say that it is necessary for the Son of Man to be lifted up? Who is this Son of Man?" 35 Then Jesus said to them, "Yet a brief time the light is among you. Walk about while you have the light, lest the darkness overtake you. And the one who walks about in the darkness does not know where he is going. 36 While you have the light, believe in the light, so that you may become sons of light." *Jesus said these things, and departing, he hid himself from them.*

12:37-50 The Judgment of Unbelief (Part 2)

37 But even though he did so many signs before them, they did not believe in him, 38 so that the word of Isaiah the prophet might be fulfilled that said, "Lord, who believed our report? And to whom was the arm of the Lord revealed?" 39 The reason they were not able to believe was that again Isaiah said, 40 "He blinded their eyes and hardened their hearts, lest they see with their eyes, and know in their hearts, and turn, and I will heal them." 41 Isaiah said these things because he saw his glory, and he spoke about him.

42 Nevertheless, indeed even many of the rulers believed in him, but because of the Pharisees *they did not confess it, lest they be put out of the synagogue.* 43 *For they loved glory among people rather than the glory of God.*

44 *Jesus cried out and said,* "The one who believes in me does not believe in me but in the one who sent me, 45 and the one seeing me sees the one who sent me. 46 I came as light into the world, so that everyone believing in me might not remain in the darkness. 47 And if anyone hears my words and does not keep them, I will not judge the person, for I did not come to judge the world but to save the world. 48 The one rejecting me and not accepting my words has a judge. The word that I spoke, that will judge the person on the last day, 49 because I do not speak of myself, but the Father who sent me has himself given me a commandment what to say and what to speak. 50 And I know that his commandment is eternal life. Therefore, those things that I say, I say just as the Father told me."

13:1-20 The Last Supper: The Washing of the Disciples' Feet

1 *Before the feast of the Passover, Jesus, knowing that his hour had come when he was to depart from this world to the Father,* **having loved his own in the world, he**

The Text of John 13:2-22

loved them to the end. 2 *And while the meal was in progress, the devil already having put it in the heart of Judas, the Iscariot, son of Simon, that he betray him,* 3 **knowing that the Father had put all things into his hands, and that he had come forth from God and that he was going to God,** 4 *he arose from the dinner and put aside his outer garment, and taking up an apron, he wrapped it around himself.* 5 *Then he poured water into a bowl and began to wash the feet of the disciples and to dry them with the apron with which he was wrapped.* 6 *So he came to Simon Peter. He said to him, "Master, you wash my feet?"* 7 *Jesus responded and said to him, "What I am doing you do not know now, but you will know later."*

INTERPRETATION #1: CLEANNESS

8 *Peter said to him, "You will not wash my feet ever." Jesus responded and said to him, "If I do not wash you, you have no heritage with me."* 9 *Simon Peter said to him, "Master, not only my feet but also my hands and my head."* 10 *Jesus said to him, "The one who has bathed has no need to wash,* **except for the feet,** *but is clean all over. You are clean, but not all of you."* 11 *(For he knew the one who would betray him. Because of this he said, "Not all of you are clean.")*

INTERPRETATION #2: HUMBLE SERVICE

12 *When therefore he washed their feet [and] took up his garments and reclined again, he said to them, "Do you know what I have done for you?* 13 *You call me 'the teacher' and 'the master,' and you are correct, for I am.* 14 *So if I, the master and the teacher, washed your feet, you also ought to wash the feet of one another.* 15 *For I have given you an example, so that, as I have done for you, so you might do also.* 16 *Amen, amen, I say to you, the slave is not greater than his master, nor is the messenger greater than the one sending him.* 17 *If you know these things, you are happy if you put them into practice.* 18 *I am not speaking about all of you. I know whom I have chosen. But so that the Scripture might be fulfilled, 'The one eating my bread raised his heel against me.'* 19 *From this point I will tell you before the event, so that when it takes place, you may believe that I AM.* 20 *Amen, amen, I say to you, the one who accepts the one I send accepts me; the one accepting me accepts the one sending me."*

13:21-30 The Last Supper: The Beloved Disciple and the Identification of the Betrayer

21 **Having said these things, Jesus was disturbed in spirit, and bore witness and said, "Amen, amen, I say to you, that one of you will betray me."** 22 *The disci-*

ples looked about at one another, uncertain about whom he was speaking. 23 One of his disciples, whom Jesus loved, was reclining at the breast of Jesus. 24 So Simon Peter nodded to him to find out whom he was talking about.

25 So, leaning back in this way at the chest of Jesus, he said to him, "Master, who is it?" 26 Jesus responded, "It is the one for whom I will dip a piece of food and give it to him." So having dipped the piece of food, [he took it and] gave it to Judas Iscariot, son of Simon. 27 And after the piece of food, Satan entered into him.

So Jesus said to him, "What you do, do quickly." 28 [But] none of those reclining knew why he said this to him. 29 For some thought that since Judas kept the purse, Jesus told him, "Purchase those things we need for the feast," or that he should give something to the poor. 30 So, taking the piece of food, Judas went out immediately. It was night.

13:31–14:14 The Farewell Discourses (Part 1a): The Departure of Jesus

31 When therefore he went out, Jesus said, "Now the Son of Man has been glorified, and God has been glorified in him. 32 [If God has been glorified in him], and God will glorify him in him, and he will glorify him immediately. 33 Little Children, *yet a little time I am with you. You will seek me, and as I told the Jews, 'Where I am going, you are not able to come,' I also tell you now.* 34 A new commandment I give you, that you love one another; as I loved you, you also should love one another. 35 By this all will know that you are my disciples, if you have love for one another."

36 *Simon Peter said to him, "Master, where are you going?" Jesus responded [to him],* "Where I am going, you are not able to follow me now, but you will follow later." 37 Peter said to him, "Master, why am I not able to follow you now? I will lay down my life for you." 38 Jesus responded, "Will you lay down your life for me? Amen, amen, I say to you, the rooster will not crow before you deny me three times.

14:1 *"Do not let your hearts be troubled. Believe in God and believe in me.* 2 In the house of my Father there are many rooms. If not, would I have told you that I go to prepare a place for you? 3 And if I go and prepare a place for you, I will come again and will take you up to myself, so that where I am, you also may be. 4 *And where I go, you know the way."*

5 *Thomas said to him, "Master, we do not know where you are going. How are we able to know the way?"* 6 And Jesus said to him, "I am the way, the truth, and the life. No one comes to the Father except through me. 7 *If you have known me, you will also know my Father. And from this moment you will know him and you have seen him."*

The Text of John 14:8-31

8 Philip said to him, "Master, show us the Father, and it is enough for us." 9 Jesus said to him, "I have been with you such a long time, and you have not known me, Philip? The one who has seen me has seen the Father. How do you say, 'Show us the Father'? 10 Do you not believe that I am in the Father and the Father is in me? The words I speak to you I do not speak of myself. But the Father abiding in me performs his works. 11 Believe me when I say that I am in the Father and the Father in me. If not, believe because of the works themselves. 12 Amen, amen, I say to you, the one believing in me will perform the works that I perform and will do greater than these, because I am going to the Father. 13 And whatever you ask for in my name, this I will do, so that the Father may be glorified in the Son. 14 If you ask me anything in my name, I will do it.

14:15-31 The Farewell Discourses (Part 1b): The Return of Jesus

15 "If you love me, you will keep my commandments. 16 And I will ask the Father, and he will give you another Paraclete to be with you forever, 17 the Spirit of Truth, whom the world is not able to accept because it does not see or know him. You know him because he remains among you, and will be in you. 18 I will not leave you orphans; I will come to you. 19 In just a little time the world will no longer see me, but you will see me because I live, and you will live. 20 On that day, you will know that I am in my Father, and you in me, and I in you. 21 The one possessing my commandments and keeping them is the one loving me. And the one loving me will be loved by my Father, and I will love him and will manifest myself to him."

22 Judas, not the Iscariot, said to him, "Master, what has happened that you are about to manifest yourself to us and not to the world?" 23 Jesus responded and said to him, "If a person loves me, the person will keep my word, and my Father will love the person, and we will come to the person and will make our abode with the person. 24 The one who does not love me does not keep my words. And the word that you hear is not mine, but of the Father who sent me. 25 I have said these things to you while I remain with you. 26 But the Paraclete, the Holy Spirit, whom the Father will send in my name, will teach you all things, and will remind you of all things that I have told you.

27 "I leave peace to you; my peace I give to you. Not as the world gives do I give to you. Do not let your hearts be troubled nor made fearful. 28 You have heard that I said to you, 'I depart, and I will come to you.' If you loved me, you would rejoice because I go to the Father, because the Father is greater than I. 29 And now I have told you before it takes place, so that when it happens, you may believe 30 No longer will I say many things with you, for the ruler of the world is coming, and he has nothing against me. 31 But in order that the world may know that I love the Father, I do just as the Father has commanded me. *Get up, let us leave.*"

The Text of John 15:1-17

15:1-17 The Farewell Discourses (Part 2a): The Parable of the Vine and an Exhortation to Mutual Love

The Vine, the Vinedresser, the Branches

1 *"I am the true vine, and my Father is the vine dresser.* 2*Every branch in me not bearing fruit, he removes;* **and everyone bearing fruit, he prunes/cleanses so that it can bear more fruit.** 3*Already you are clean because of the word that I spoke to you.*

Remaining in Jesus

4 "Remain in me, and I in you. As the branch is not able to bear fruit on its own unless it remains attached to the vine, so you also unless you remain in me. 5 I am the vine; you, the branches. The one remaining in me and I in that person, this is the one who bears much fruit, because without me you are not able to do anything. 6 Unless a person remains in me, that person is cast out like the branch and withers; and they gather them together and throw them into the fire, and they are burned. 7 If you remain in me and my words remain in you, ask for whatever you wish, and it will be granted to you. 8 *My Father is glorified in this, that you bear much fruit and become my disciples.*

Remaining in Love

9 "As the Father loved me, I also loved you. Remain in my love. 10 If you keep my commandments, you will remain in my love, just as I have kept the commandments of my Father and I remain in his love. 11 I have said these things to you in order that my joy may be in you, and your joy may be complete. 12 This is my commandment, that you love one another as I loved you. 13 No one has greater love than this, that a person lay down his life for his friends. 14 You are my friends if you do the things that I command you. 15 I no longer call you slaves, because the slave does not know what the master is doing. I have called you friends because I have made known to you all that I heard from my Father. 16 You did not choose me, but I chose you and have appointed you so that you might go and bear fruit, and that your fruit might remain, so that whatever you request from the Father in my name, he would give to you. 17 These things I command you: love one another.

15:18–16:4a The Farewell Discourses (Part 2b): The Hatred of the World

THE HATRED OF THE WORLD

18 "If the world hates you, know that it has hated me before you. 19 If you were of the world, the world would love its own; but because you are not of the world, but I chose you out of the world; for this reason the world hates you. 20 Remember the word that I spoke to you, 'The slave is not greater than the master.' If they persecuted me, they will persecute you also. If they kept my word, they will also keep yours. 21 But they will do all these things to you because of my name, because they do not know the one who sent me.

FAILURE TO RESPOND TO THE THREE ESSENTIAL WITNESSES

22 "If I had not come and spoken to them, they would have no guilt of sin. But now they have no excuse about their sin. 23 The one who hates me also hates my Father. 24 If I had not performed works among them that no one else performed, they would not be guilty of sin, but now they have seen and hated both me and my Father. 25 But in order that the word written in their Law might be fulfilled, 'They hated me without reason.'

THE TWO ADDITIONAL WITNESSES

26 "When the Paraclete comes, whom I will send to you from the Father, the Spirit of Truth that comes from the Father, he will witness about me. 27 And you bear witness because you are with me from the beginning.

PERSECUTION

16:1 "I have said these things to you so you will not be scandalized. 2 They will expel you from the synagogue. But an hour is coming in which those who kill you will think they are giving worship to God. 3 And they will do these things because they did not know the Father or me. 4a But I have said these things to you so that when their hour comes, you may remember that I said them to you.

16:4b-33 The Farewell Discourses (Part 3): The Paraclete, Departure, Return

THE DEPARTURE OF JESUS AND THE DISCIPLES' GRIEF

16:4b "I did not say these things to you from the beginning because I was with you. 5 But now I go to the one who sent me, and none of you asks me, 'Where are you going?' 6 But because I have said these things to you, pain has filled your hearts.

THE PARACLETE WILL ACCUSE THE WORLD AFTER THE DEPARTURE OF JESUS

7 "But I speak the truth to you; it is better for you that I depart. For if I do not depart, the Paraclete will not come to you. But if I leave, I will send him to you. 8 And when that one comes, he will show the world its error with regard to sin, to righteousness, and to judgment: 9 with regard to sin because they do not believe in me; 10 with regard to righteousness because I go to the Father and you will no longer see me; 11 and with regard to judgment because the ruler of this world has been judged.

THE PARACLETE WILL EXPLAIN THE WORDS OF JESUS AFTER HIS DEPARTURE

12 "I still have many things to say to you, but you are not able to bear them now. 13 But when that one comes, the Spirit of Truth, he will lead you in all truth. For he will not speak on his own, but will speak whatever he hears, and will proclaim to you what is to come. 14 That one will glorify me because he will take from what is mine and will proclaim it to you. 15 Everything the Father has is mine. Because of this I said that he takes from what is mine and will proclaim it to you.

IN A LITTLE WHILE JESUS WILL DIE, BUT A LITTLE WHILE LATER HE WILL RISE

16 "In a little time you will no longer see me, and again in a little time you will behold me." 17 Therefore, some of his disciples said to one another, "What is this he says to us, 'A little time and you will not see me, and again a little time and you will behold me'? and 'I go to the Father'?" 18 Then they said, "What is this 'a little time' he speaks about? We do not know what he is saying." 19 Jesus knew that they wished to ask him, and he said to them, "You inquire of one another about this, that I said, 'A little time and you will not see me, and again a little time and you will behold me'. 20 Amen,

amen, I say to you, that you will weep and lament, but the world will rejoice. You will weep, but your weeping will be turned into joy.

A Parable of Suffering

21 "A woman, when she gives birth, is sad because her hour comes; but when the child is born, she does not remember the suffering because of the joy that a person has been born into the world. 22 And so, now you are sad, but again I will see you, and your hearts will rejoice, and no one will take your joy from you. 23 And on that day you will not ask me anything.

Asking in Jesus' Name

"Amen, amen, I say to you, whatever you ask the Father in my name he will give to you. 24 Up to this point you have not asked for anything in my name. Ask and you will receive, in order that your joy may be fulfilled.

Speaking in Parables

25 "These things I have said to you in parables. The hour is coming when I will no longer speak to you in parables, but I will announce to you things about the Father openly.

Asking in Jesus' Name (#2)

26 "On that day you will ask in my name, and I do not say to you that I will ask the Father for you. 27 For the Father himself loves you because you have loved me and have believed that I came from God. 28 I came from the Father, and I have come into the world. Again I leave the world, and I go to the Father."

Speaking in Parables (#2)

29 His disciples said, "Behold, now you speak openly, and you use no parable. 30 Now we know that you know all things, and you have no need that anyone ask you. Because of this we believe that you have come from God." 31 Jesus responded to them, "Do you believe now? 32 Behold, an hour is coming, and has already come, in which each of you will be scattered to his own, and you will leave me alone. And I am not alone because the Father is with me. 33 I have said these things to you so that you might have peace in me. In the world you will have suffering but be of strong heart, I have conquered the world."

17:1-5 The Farewell Discourses (Part 4a): Jesus' Prayer for Himself

JESUS' PRAYER FOR HIMSELF

1 *Jesus said these things and,*
   having lifted up his eyes to heaven, said,

"Father, the hour has come.
Glorify your Son
   in order that the Son may glorify you,
      2 *just as you have given him authority over all flesh,*
         so that he might give eternal life to all that which you have given him.
            3 **And this is eternal life,**
               that they know you, the only true God, and the one
               whom you have sent, Jesus Christ.

4 *I glorified you on earth,*
   having brought to completion the work
      that you have given me to perform.

5 And now glorify me, Father, in your presence
   with the glory that I had with you before the world existed.

17:6-19 The Farewell Discourses (Part 4b): Jesus' Prayer for His Disciples

6 "I revealed your name to those
   whom you gave me out of the world.
      They were yours, and
      you have gave them to me, and
      they have kept your word.

7 *Now they have known*
   that all things you have given me are from you;
      8 *that the words that you gave to me*
         I gave to them,
and they accepted them,
and they knew truly
   that I came from you;
and they believed
   that you sent me.

The Text of John 17:9-17

9 *I pray on their behalf.*
I do not pray on behalf of the world but
> on behalf of those whom you have given to me,
>> because they are yours,
>>> 10 and all of mine are yours,
>>> and yours are mine,
>> and I have been glorified in them.

11 *And I am no longer in the world,*
and they are in the world,
and I come to you.

Holy Father,
> keep them in your name
>> which you have given me,
>>> so that they may be one as we are.

>>> 12 When I was with them,
I kept them in your name
which you have given me,
and I guarded them,
and none of them was destroyed
except the son of destruction
so that the Scripture might be fulfilled.

13 But now I come to you, and
I say these things in the world
> in order that they may have my joy brought to fulfillment in them.

14 I have given them your word, and
the world hated them
> because they are not of the world,
>> just as I am not of the world.

15 I do not pray
> that you take them
>> out of the world,
> but that you keep them
>> from the Evil One.
16 They are not of the world,
> just as I am not of the world.

17 Consecrate them
> in the truth.

Your word is truth.
18 As you sent me into the world,
   so I sent them into the world.

19 And I consecrate myself for their sake,
   so that they also may be consecrated in truth.

17:20-26 The Farewell Discourses (Part 4c): Jesus' Prayer for Those Who Will Also Believe

20 "I do not pray for these alone, but also
   for those believing in me through their word,
   21 so that all may be one,
   just as you, Father, are in me and
   I am in you,
      so that they also may be in us,
      so that the world may believe that you sent me.

22 "And I have given them the glory
   that you have given me,
      so that they may be one
         as we are one.
      23 I in them and you in me,
   so they may be brought to perfect unity,
   so that the world may know
      that you sent me and
      you loved them as you loved me.

24 "Father, about those whom you have given me:
   I wish
      that where I am
      those also may be with me,
         so they may see my glory,
            that you have given me,
               because you loved me before the foundation of the world.

25 "Righteous Father,
   the world did not know you,
   but I knew you, and
   these knew that you sent me. 26 And
   I made known to them your name, and
   I will continue to make it known,

> so that the love with which you loved me may be
> in them,
> and I in them."

18:1-11 The Passion (Part 1): The Arrest

Jesus Goes to the Garden

18:1 **Having said these things,** Jesus went out with his disciples across the winter-flowing Kidron, where there was a garden that Jesus and his disciples entered.

Judas and the Arrest

2 Judas, who handed him over, also knew the place because Jesus met there many times with his disciples. 3 So Judas, taking the cohort and the attendants of the Pharisees and chief priests, came there with lanterns, torches, and weapons. 4 So Jesus, *knowing all things that were to come upon him,* went out and said to them, "Whom do you seek?" 5 They answered him, "Jesus the Nazarene." He said, "I am he." Judas, the one who handed him over, was standing among them. 6 **When therefore he said to them, "I AM," they shrank back and fell to the ground.** 7 So again he asked them, "Whom do you seek?" They said, "Jesus the Nazarene." 8 Jesus answered, "I told you that I am he. If you seek me, let these go," 9 so that the word that he spoke, "Of those you have given me I did not lose any," might be fulfilled.

The Resistance of Peter

10 So Simon Peter, having a sword, drew it and struck the servant of the high priest, and cut off his right ear. The name of the servant was Malchus. 11 So Jesus said to Peter, "Put your sword into its sheath. The cup that the Father has given me, should I not drink it?"

18:12-27 The Passion (Part 2): The Hearings Before Annas and Caiaphas

12 So together the cohort and the tribune and the attendants of the Jews arrested Jesus, bound him, 13 and led him to Annas first. For he was the father-in-law of Caiaphas, who was the high priest that year. 14 It was Caiaphas who counselled the Jews that it was beneficial that one person die for the people.

The Text of John 18:15-28

Peter and Another Disciple in the Courtyard

15 Simon Peter and another disciple were following Jesus. That disciple was known to the high priest and entered the courtyard of the high priest along with Jesus. 16 Peter was standing outside by the gate. So the other disciple, the one known to the high priest, came out, spoke to the gatekeeper, and led Peter in. 17 So the young woman, the gatekeeper, said to Peter, "Are you not also one of the disciples of this person?" He said, "I am not." 18 The servants and the attendants were standing around — having made a charcoal fire because it was cool — and were warming themselves. Peter was standing among them and warming himself.

Jesus before Annas

19 So the high priest asked Jesus about his disciples and about his teaching. 20 Jesus answered him, "I have spoken openly to the world. I always taught in the synagogue and in the Temple, where all the Jews gather, and I have said nothing in secret. 21 Why do you ask me? Ask the listeners what I said to them. These certainly know what I said." 22 As Jesus was saying these things, one of the attendants standing nearby slapped Jesus, saying, "Do you answer the high priest in this way?" 23 Jesus answered him, "If I have spoken in an evil way, bear witness about the evil. If I have spoken properly, why do you strike me?"

Jesus before Caiaphas

24 So Annas sent him bound to Caiaphas, the high priest.

Peter's Second Denial

25 **Simon Peter was standing there and warming himself.** So they said to him, "Are not you also one of this man's disciples?" He denied it and said, "I am not." 26 One of the servants of the high priest, a relative of the one whose ear Peter cut off, said, "Did I not see you in the garden with him?" 27 Again Peter denied it. And right then a rooster crowed.

18:28-38a The Passion (Part 3): The Trial before Pilate

Jesus Is Accused

28 So they led Jesus from Caiaphas to the Praetorium. It was early in the morning, and they themselves did not go into the Praetorium so they would not be ritu-

ally defiled but might eat the Passover. 29 So Pilate came out to them and said, "What accusation do you bring against this man?"

30 They answered and said to him, "If this man were not doing evil, we would not have given him over to you." 31 Pilate then said to them, "You take him and judge him according to your Law." [Then] the Jews said to him, "We are not allowed to kill anyone," 32 so that the word of Jesus might be fulfilled which he uttered signifying how he was about to die.

Pilate Interrogates Jesus

33 So Pilate went back into the Praetorium again, and called Jesus, and said to him, "Are you the King of the Jews?" 34 Jesus answered, "Do you say this of yourself, or did others speak to you about me?" 35 Pilate answered, "Am I a Jew? Your people and the chief priests have handed you over to me. What did you do?"

36 Jesus answered, "My kingdom is not of this world. If my kingdom were of this world, my attendants would have put up a struggle so I would not be handed over to the Jews. But my kingdom is not from here." 37 Then Pilate said to him, "So then, you are a king?" Jesus answered, "You say that I am a king. I have been born for this, and for this I have come into the world, that I might bear witness to the truth. Everyone who is of the truth hears my voice." 38 Pilate said to him, "What is truth?"

18:38b-19:16a The Passion (Part 3b): The Trial Continues

The Release of Barabbas

And, having said this, *he again came out to the Jews and said to them,* "I find no guilt in him. 39 But you have a custom that I release one person to you at Passover. Do you want me to release the King of the Jews to you?" 40 They cried out again, saying, "Not this one, but Barabbas." Barabbas was a bandit.

The Scourging and Crowning

19:1 So then Pilate took Jesus and scourged him. 2 And the soldiers, weaving a crown out of thorns, put it on his head and wrapped him in a purple cloak, 3 and they kept coming up to him and saying, "Hail, King of the Jews," and slapping him. 4 And again Pilate came out and said to them, "See, I am leading him out to you, so that you may know that I find no guilt in him."

5 So Jesus came out, wearing the crown of thorns and the purple cloak. And he said to them, "Behold the man!" 6 When therefore the chief priests and the attendants saw him, they cried out, saying, "Crucify him! Crucify him!"

The Text of John 19:7-20

The Charge of Blasphemy

Pilate said to them, "Take him yourselves and crucify him, for I do not find guilt in him." 7 *The Jews answered him, "We have a law, and according to that law he ought to die because he made himself Son of God."* 8 *When therefore Pilate heard this statement, he feared more;* 9 *and he went back into the Praetorium again and said to Jesus, "Where are you from?" But Jesus did not give him an answer.* 10 *Pilate then said to him, "You do not speak to me? Do you not know that I have the power to free you and I have the power to crucify you?"* 11 *Jesus answered him, "You would have no power in my regard if it were not given to you from above. Because of this, the one betraying me to you has the greater sin."* 12 *From that point on, Pilate was looking for a way to free him. But the Jews cried out, saying, "If you free this man, you are not a friend of Caesar. Everyone who makes himself a king opposes Caesar."*

The Condemnation

13 So Pilate, having heard these words, led Jesus out and sat in the official's chair in the place called Lithostrotos (but in Hebrew, Gabbatha). 14 It was the preparation day for Passover, about the sixth hour. *And he said to the Jews, "Behold your king!"* 15 *So they cried out, "Take him away, take him away, crucify him!"* Pilate said to them, "Am I to crucify your king?" The chief priests answered, "We have no king but Caesar." 16 So he handed him over to them to be crucified.

19:16b-30 The Passion (Part 4): The Crucifixion, the Events at the Cross, and the Death of Jesus

The Crucifixion

19:16b So they took Jesus away. 17 And he went out, carrying his own cross, to what is called the Place of the Skull (which is called in Hebrew Golgotha), 18 where they crucified him, and with him two others, one on each side, with Jesus in the middle.

The Events at the Cross

#1: The Title on the Cross

19 Pilate wrote an inscription and placed it on the cross. It read, "Jesus the Nazarene, the King of the Jews." 20 Therefore, many of the people of Judea read this inscription because the place where Jesus was crucified was near the city. And it was

written in Hebrew, Latin, and Greek. 21 So the chief priests of the Jews said to Pilate, "Do not write, 'The King of the Jews,' but that he said, 'I am King of the Jews.'" 22 Pilate responded, "What I have written, I have written."

#2: The Division of Jesus' Garments

23 When the soldiers had crucified Jesus, they took his outer garment and divided it into four parts, with a part to each soldier, and likewise his tunic. But the tunic was seamless, woven from the top throughout. 24 So they said to one another, "Let us not divide it, but let us cast lots to see whose it will be" (so that the Scripture might be fulfilled that said, "They divided my outer garment among themselves, and for my clothing they cast lots"). This is what the soldiers did.

#3: The Mother of Jesus and the Beloved Disciple

25 But Jesus' mother, his mother's sister, Mary the wife of Clopas, and Mary from Magdala stood by Jesus' cross. 26 So Jesus, seeing his mother standing there and the disciple whom he loved, said to his mother, "Woman, behold your son." 27 Then he said to the disciple, "Behold your mother." And from that hour the disciple took her into his own home.

#4: The Offering of Sour Wine

28 *After this, Jesus,* knowing that already all things had been completed, said (so that the Scripture might be completed), "I thirst." 29 There was a jar lying there, full of sour wine. Putting a sponge full of sour wine on a sprig of hyssop, they brought it to his mouth.

THE DEATH OF JESUS

30 **When therefore he took the sour wine, Jesus** said, "It is completed." And inclining his head, he gave over the Spirit.

19:31-37 The Passion (Part 5): The Request to Remove the Body and the Piercing of the Side of Jesus

THE REQUEST TO REMOVE THE BODY OF JESUS

31 So the Judean bystanders, since it was Preparation Day, lest the bodies remain upon the cross on the Sabbath (for that Sabbath was a solemn day), asked Pilate **that their legs be broken and** they be taken away.

The Text of John 19:32-20:1

THE PIERCING OF THE SIDE OF JESUS AND THE FLOW
OF BLOOD AND WATER

32 So the soldiers came and broke the legs of the one and then of the other of those crucified with him. 33 But coming to Jesus, when they saw that he was already dead, they did not break his legs; 34 but one of the soldiers jabbed his side with a lance, and immediately blood and water came out. 35 And the one who saw has borne witness, and his witness is true, and that one knows that he speaks the truth, so that you also may believe. 36 For these things happened in order that the Scripture might be fulfilled, "No bone of his will be broken." 37 And again another passage of Scripture says, "They will look at the one they pierced."

19:38-42 The Passion (Part 6): The Removal of Jesus' Body and His Burial

THE REMOVAL OF JESUS' BODY

38 *But later, Joseph of Arimathea, one who was a disciple of Jesus secretly for fear of the Jews, asked Pilate for permission to take away the body of Jesus. And Pilate granted permission. So he came and took away his body.*

THE BURIAL

39 Nicodemus, who came to him first at night, came *also,* bringing a mixture of myrrh and aloes, weighing one hundred litras. 40 So *they* took the body of Jesus and bound it with burial cloths together with the spices, as is the burial custom of the Jews. 41 There was a garden in the place where Jesus was crucified, and in the garden was a new grave in which no one had yet been laid. 42 So, because it was the Preparation Day of the Jews and the tomb was nearby, *they* placed Jesus there.

20:1-18 The Empty Tomb, and the Belief of the Beloved Disciple and of Mary Magdalene

MARY ARRIVES AT THE TOMB

1 On the first day of the week, Mary from Magdala came to the tomb while it was still dark and saw that the stone had been taken away from the tomb.

The Text of John 20:2-22

Peter and the Beloved Disciple Come to the Tomb

2 So she ran and came to Simon Peter and the other disciple, whom Jesus loved, and said to them, "They have taken the master from the tomb, and we do not know where they put him." 3 So Peter and the other disciple left and came to the tomb. 4 The two ran together, and the other disciple ran faster than Peter and came to the tomb first. 5 And bending down, he saw the burial cloths lying there, but he did not go in. 6 So Simon Peter also arrived, following him, and went into the tomb. And he saw the burial cloths lying there, 7 and the face cloth that was on his head not lying with the burial cloths but apart and folded up. 8 Then the other disciple, the one who came first to the tomb, also entered, and he saw and believed. 9 For they had not yet understood the Scripture, that it was necessary that he rise from the dead. 10 So the disciples again went off by themselves. 11 But Mary was standing outside, in front of the tomb, weeping.

The Appearance of Jesus to Mary

When therefore she was weeping, she bent down into the tomb, 12 and she saw two angels clothed in white seated where the body of Jesus had lain, one at the head and one at the feet. 13 And they said to her, "Woman, why are you weeping?" She said to them, "They have taken my master, and I do not know where they have put him."

14 Having said these things, she turned around and saw Jesus standing there, and did not know that it was Jesus. 15 Jesus said to her, "Woman, why are you weeping? Whom do you seek?" Thinking that it was the gardener, she said to him, "Sir, if you took him, tell me where you have put him; and I will take him away." 16 Jesus said to her, "Mary." Turning around, she said to him in Hebrew, "Rabbouni" (which is translated Teacher). 17 *Jesus said to her, "Do not hold me, for I have not yet ascended to the Father.* **Go to my brothers and tell them, 'I ascend to my Father and to your Father, and my God and your God.'"** 18 Mary from Magdala went announcing to the disciples, "I have seen the Lord," and that he said these things to her.

20:19-23 Jesus Comes to the Disciples on the Evening of the First Day

19 *After dark, on that day, the first day of the week, with the doors closed where the disciples were, for fear of the Jews, Jesus came and stood among them and said to them, "Peace to you!"* 20 And having said this, he showed his hands and his side to them. So the disciples rejoiced at seeing the Lord. 21 So he said to them again, "Peace to you! As the Father has sent me I also send you." 22 *And having said this, he breathed on them and said to them, "Receive [the] Holy Spirit.* 23 **For those whose**

sins you dismiss, they are dismissed from them; for those whose sins you retain, they are retained."

20:24-29   The Appearance to Thomas

24 Thomas, one of the Twelve, the one called Didymus, was not with them when Jesus came. 25 So the other disciples said to him, "We have seen the Lord." But he said to them, "Unless I see the mark of the nails on his hands, and put my finger in the mark of the nails and put my hand in his side, I will not believe."
26 And eight days later, his disciples were again inside, and Thomas was with them. Jesus entered and stood in their midst although the doors were closed; and he said, "Peace to you!" 27 Then he said to Thomas, "Bring your finger here and behold my hands, and bring your hand and put it in my side, and be not unbelieving but believing." 28 Thomas responded and said to him, "My Lord and my God!" 29 Jesus said to him, "Because you have seen me you have believed? Happy are those not seeing and coming to belief."

20:30-31   The Conclusion of the First Edition

30 On the one hand, Jesus performed many and varied signs before [his] disciples that are not written in this book; 31 but, on the other, these have been written so that you may believe that Jesus is the Christ, the Son of God, *and that believing you may have life in his name.*

21:1-14   An Appearance at the Sea of Galilee

1 Later, Jesus manifested himself again to the disciples along the Sea of Tiberias. He manifested (himself) in this way. 2 SIMON PETER, AND THOMAS CALLED DIDYMUS, AND NATHANAEL, THE ONE FROM CANA IN GALILEE, AND THE SONS OF ZEBEDEE, AND TWO OTHERS OF HIS DISCIPLES WERE TOGETHER. 3 SIMON PETER SAID TO THEM, "I AM LEAVING TO GO FISHING." THEY SAID TO HIM, "WE ALSO WILL COME WITH YOU." THEY WENT OUT AND EMBARKED ON THE BOAT, AND DURING THAT NIGHT THEY CAUGHT NOTHING.
4 BUT WHEN IT HAD ALREADY BEGUN TO DAWN, JESUS STOOD ALONG THE SHORE. **But the disciples did not know that it was Jesus.** 5 SO JESUS SAID TO THEM, "YOUNG FELLOWS, YOU HAVEN'T HAD ANY SUCCESS, HAVE YOU?" THEY ANSWERED HIM, "NO." 6 HE SAID TO THEM, "CAST THE NET OFF THE RIGHT SIDE OF THE BOAT, AND YOU WILL FIND FISH." SO THEY CAST IT, AND WERE NOT

The Text of John 21:7-19

STRONG ENOUGH TO DRAW IT IN BECAUSE OF THE LARGE NUMBER OF FISH. 7 Then the disciple whom Jesus loved said to Peter, "It is the Lord." So Simon Peter, hearing that it was the Lord, tightened his outer garment around himself (for he was wearing only that) and threw himself into the sea. 8 THE other DISCIPLES CAME IN THE BOAT TOWING THE NET FULL OF FISH, FOR THEY WERE NOT FAR FROM LAND — ABOUT ONE HUNDRED YARDS.

9 WHEN THEREFORE THEY HAD DISEMBARKED ON LAND, THEY SAW A CHARCOAL FIRE, AND FISH LYING ON IT, AND BREAD. 10 JESUS SAID TO THEM, "BRING SOME OF THE FISH YOU JUST CAUGHT." 11 SO SIMON PETER WENT UP AND DRAGGED THE NET FILLED WITH ONE HUNDRED FIFTY-THREE LARGE FISH UP ON LAND. EVEN WITH SUCH GREAT FISH, THE NET DID NOT BREAK. 12 JESUS SAID TO THEM, "COME HERE, EAT SOME BREAKFAST." But none of the disciples was bold enough to ask him, "Who are you?" knowing that it was the Lord. 13 JESUS CAME AND TOOK THE BREAD AND GAVE IT TO THEM, AND THE FISH LIKEWISE. 14 This was already the third time Jesus manifested himself to the disciples after being raised from the dead.

21:15-25 The Commissioning of Peter, the Deaths of Peter and the Beloved Disciple, and the Second Conclusion of the Gospel

THE COMMISSIONING OF PETER

15 When therefore they had eaten breakfast, Jesus said to Simon Peter, "Simon, (son of) John, do you love me more than these?" He said to him, "Indeed, Lord, you know that I love you." He said to him, "Feed my lambs." 16 He said to him again a second time, "Simon, son of John, do you love me?" He said to him, "Indeed, Lord, you know that I love you." He said to him, "Shepherd my sheep." 17 He said to him a third time, "Simon, son of John, do you love me?" Peter became saddened that he said to him a third time, "Do you love me?" and said to him, "Lord, you know all things; you know that I love you." He said to him, "Feed my sheep."

THE DEATH OF PETER

18 "Amen, amen, I say to you, when you were younger, you used to fasten your own belt and go where you wanted. But when you grow old, you will hold out your hands, and another will put a belt around you and will carry you where you do not want to go." 19 (He said this signifying by what type of death he would glorify God.) And having said this, he said to him, "Follow me!"

The Text of John 21:20-25

THE DEATH OF THE BELOVED DISCIPLE

20 Peter, turning around, saw the disciple whom Jesus loved, following — the one who also had reclined at dinner at his breast and said, "Lord, who is the one who will betray you?" 21 So Peter, seeing this one, said to Jesus, "Lord, what about this one?" 22 Jesus said to him, "If I wish him to remain until I come, what would it be to you? You follow me." 23 Therefore, the word went out to the brothers that that disciple would not die. But Jesus did not say to him that he would not die; but, "If I wish him to remain until I come, [what would it be to you?]"

24 This is the disciple who bears witness about these things and who has written these things, and we know that his witness is true.

THE CONCLUSION IN THE THIRD EDITION

25 There are many other things that Jesus did, which, if they were all to be put in writing, I do not think the world would be able to hold the books which would be written.

The Text of the Johannine Letters

1 JOHN

1:1-4 Witness and Fellowship

1 That which was from the beginning,
    which we have heard,
    which we have looked at with our eyes,
    which we have seen and
        our hands have touched,
that which concerns the word of life —
2 and the life was revealed,
    and we have seen
    and we bear witness
    and we proclaim to you the life
        that is eternal and
        that was in the presence of the Father and
            was revealed to us! —

3 whatever we have seen
    and we have heard,

Throughout the Letters, I will arrange the text in sense lines in order to aid in noticing parallels and other features. Chiasms will be arranged in such a way that each element of the first half of the chiasm is indented further than the one before. The process will be reversed in the second half of the chiasm. Each element of the chiasm will also be identified by the presence of a "+" at the beginning of the element.

we proclaim to you also
so that you also may be in fellowship with us.

And our fellowship is
with the Father and
with his Son, Jesus Christ.

4 And we write these things so that our joy may be brought to fulfillment.

1:5–2:2   The Proclamation That God Is Light

5 And this is the proclamation
that we have heard from him [Jesus] and
that we proclaim to you,
that God is light and
there is not any darkness in him [God].

6 If we say that we have fellowship with him [God] and we walk in the darkness,
we lie and do not do the truth.
7 But if we walk in the light as he [God] is in the light,
we have fellowship with one another, and
the blood of Jesus his Son cleanses us from all sin.

8 If we say that we do not have sin,
we deceive ourselves, and
the truth is not in us.

9 But if we confess our sins,
he [God] is faithful and just, and so
forgives our sins and
cleanses us from all injustice.

10 If we say that we have not sinned,
we make him [God] a liar, and
his [God's] word is not in us.
2:1 (My Dear Children, I write these things to you so that you will not sin.)
But if someone sins,
we have a Paraclete before the Father, Jesus Christ, the Just One. 2 And
he [Jesus] is an atonement
for our sins, and
not only for ours but also for those of the entire world.

The Text of 1 John 2:3-13

2:3-11 The New Commandment: To Keep the Word

3 And by this we are certain that we have come to know him [God]:
   if we keep his [God's] commandments.
4 The one claiming, "I have come to know him [God]" but not keeping his [God's] commandments
   is a liar, and the truth is not present in him.

5 But the one who keeps his [God's] word —
   in this person the love of God has been truly brought to perfection.
   By this we know that we are "in him [God]."
6 The one claiming to abide "in him" [God]
   must himself also walk as that one [Jesus] walked.

7 Loved Ones, I am not writing to you about a "new" commandment,
   but an old one that you have had from the beginning.
      This "old" commandment is the word that you have heard.
   8 In another sense, I am writing to you about a new commandment.
      This is true in him [Jesus] and in you,
         that the darkness is being taken away and
         the true light is already shining.

9 The one claiming to be "in the light" and hating his brother
   is still in darkness.

10 The one loving his brother
   abides in the light, and
   there is no cause for stumbling in him.

11 But the one hating his brother
   is in the darkness and
   walks in the darkness and
   does not know where he is going
      because the darkness has blinded his eyes.

2:12-17 Exhortation to Children, Fathers, Young Men

12 I write to you, Dear Children,
   that your sins are forgiven through his [Jesus'] name.
13 I write to you, Fathers,
   that you have known the one [Jesus] from the beginning.

The Text of 1 John 2:14-22

I write to you, Young People,
  that you have conquered the Evil One.

14 I wrote to you, Dear Children,
  that you have known the Father.
I wrote to you, Fathers,
  that you have known the one [Jesus] from the beginning.
I wrote to you, Young People,
  that you are strong and
  the word of God abides in you, and
  you have conquered the Evil One.

15 Do not love the world, nor the things in the world.
  If a person loves the world,
  the love of the Father is not in that person,
      16 because everything in the world —
        the desire of the flesh, and
        the desire of the eyes, and
        the arrogance regarding life —
      is not from the Father but is from the world.
17 And the world is passing away along with its desire,
  but the one doing the will of God abides forever.

2:18-27 The Antichrists: Those Who Deny the Son

18 Dear Children,
  +it is the Last Hour,
    +and just as you heard that the Antichrist is coming,
    +and even now many Antichrists have come to be,
  +from this we know that it is the Last Hour.

+19 They went out from us, but they were not of us.
  +If they were of us, they would have abided among us —
+but that it might be made apparent that they are not of us.

+[A] 20 And you have an anointing from the Holy One,
  and you know all.

  +[B] 21 I did not write to you
    that you do not know the truth but that you know it, and
    that every lie is not of the truth.

      +[C] 22 Who is the Liar if not

>   the one denying that Jesus is the Christ?
> This is the Antichrist,
>   the one denying the Father and the Son.
>
>> +[D] 23 Everyone denying the Son does not have the Father.
>>   The one confessing the Son has the Father also.
>
> +[C'] 24 As for you —
>   +let what you heard from the beginning
>   +abide in you.
>   +If it abides in you
>   +(what you heard from the beginning),
>   +you abide in the Son and in the Father.
>
>   (25 And this is the promise that he [Jesus] promised us: eternal life.)
>
> +[B'] 26 I wrote these things to you about those deceiving you.

+[A'] +27 And as for you — the anointing that you received from him [God] abides in you,
   +and you do not have need that anyone teach you;
   +but as his [God's] anointing teaches you about all things, and it is true and not false,
   +and just as it taught you, you abide in him [Jesus].

2:28–3:10   Sin, the Children of God, and the Children of the Devil

>   28 And now, Dear Children, abide in him [Jesus],
>   so that when he [Jesus] is revealed,
>   we may have confidence and
>   not shrink from him [Jesus] at his coming.

29 If you know that he [the Father] is just,
you know that everyone acting justly has been begotten from him [the Father].

3:1 Behold how great a love the Father has given us,
   that we may be called children of God; and we are.
   Because of this the world does not know us —
   because it did not know him [the Father].
2 Beloved, now we are children of God,
   and it has not yet been revealed what we will be.
      We know
      that when he [Jesus] is revealed,

we will be like him [Jesus], and
that we will see him [Jesus] as he is.
3 And everyone having this hope in him [Jesus]
makes himself holy, as that one [Jesus] is holy.
4 Everyone committing sin
also commits lawlessness, and sin is lawlessness.
5 And we know that that one [Jesus] was revealed to take away sins,
and there is no sin in him [Jesus].

6 Everyone abiding in him [Jesus] does not sin.
Everyone sinning has neither seen him [Jesus] nor known him [Jesus].

7 Dear Children, let no one deceive you.
the one acting justly is just,
as that one [the Father] is just.
8 The one committing sin is of the devil,
because from the beginning the devil sins.
For this the Son of God was revealed,
that he might do away with the works of the devil.

9 +Everyone begotten of God
+does not commit sin
+because his [God's] seed abides in him [the believer],
+and he [the believer] is not able to sin
+because he has been begotten of God.

10 In this are the children of God
and the children of the devil made manifest:
Everyone not acting justly is not of God
— and the one not loving his brother.

3:11-18 The Proclamation to Love One Another

+11 Because this is the proclamation that you heard from the beginning, that we should love one another.
+12 Not as Cain, who was of the Evil One
+and slaughtered his brother.
+And why did he slaughter him?
+Because his works were evil, but those of his brother just.
+13 And, Brothers, do not be surprised if the world hates you.

14 We know that we have crossed over from death into life
   because we love the brothers.

The one not loving abides in death.
15 Everyone hating his brother is a murderer,
and you know that every murderer does not have
   eternal life abiding in himself.

16 In this we have known love,
   inasmuch as that one [Jesus] has laid down his life for us.
And we ought to lay down our lives for the brothers.

17 Whoever has the life of the world
   and sees his brother in need
   and closes his heart from him,
      how does the love of God abide in him?

18 Dear Children, let us not love
   in word nor with the tongue,
   but in work and truth.

3:19-24 The Commandment to Correct Belief
          and
          the Commandment to Mutual Love

19 And in this we shall know that we are of the truth,
and before him [God] we will convince our heart,
   20 with respect to what the heart accuses us of,
      that God is greater than our heart
      and knows all things.
21 Beloved, if the heart does not accuse us,
   we have confidence before God,

22 and whatever we may ask for, we receive it from him [God]
+because we keep his [God's] commandments and we do what is pleasing before him [God].
   +23 And this is his [God's] commandment,
      +that we believe in the name of his Son Jesus Christ and
      +that we love one another,
      +just as he [God] gave us commandment.
+24 And the one keeping his [God's] commandments abides in him [God], and he [God] in him.

The Text of 1 John 4:1-9

    And in this we know that he [God] abides in us,
       from the Spirit of which he [God] gave us.

4:1-6 The Spirit of Truth and the Spirit of Deception

1 Beloved, do not believe every spirit,
but test the spirits
   to see if they are from God,

+because many false prophets have gone out into the world.
   +2 In this you know the Spirit of God:
      +every spirit that confesses Jesus Christ come in the flesh is of God,
      +3 and every spirit that does away with Jesus is not of God.
   +And this is the (spirit) of the Antichrist, which you have heard is coming,
+and is now already in the world.

4 You are of God, Dear Children,
and you have conquered them,
   because he who is in you is greater than he who is in the world.

5 They are of the world;
   because of this they speak out of the world,
   and the world listens to them.

6 We are of God.
   The one knowing God hears us;
   the one who is not of God does not hear us.

From this we know the Spirit of Truth and the Spirit of Deception.

4:7-12 God's Love and Love of One Another

7 Beloved, let us love one another,
   +because love is of God
      +and everyone loving has been begotten of God and knows God.
      +8 The one not loving did not know God,
   +because God is love.

9 In this was the love of God revealed in us,
   that he has sent his unique Son into the world
      so that we may live through him.

10 In this is the love,
>   not that we have loved God,
>   but that he loved us and sent his Son
>   > as an atonement for our sins.

11 Beloved,
>   if God so loved us,
>   we too should love one another.

12 No one ever has seen God.
>   If we love one another,
>   > God abides in us
>   > and his love is brought to perfection in us.

4:13-19 The Spirit and Abiding

13 In this we know
>   that we abide in him [God]
>   and he [God] in us,
> because he [God] has given of his Spirit to us.

14 And we have seen and we witness
>   that the Father has sent the Son as Savior of the world.

15 Whoever confesses that Jesus is the Son of God,
>   God abides in that person,
>   and that person in God.

16 And we have known and have believed
>   the love that God has for us.
>   God is love,
>   > and the one abiding in love abides in God,
>   > and God abides in that person.

+17 In this love has been brought to perfection among us,
>   +that we have confidence on the day of judgment (because just as that one [Jesus] is so
>   are we in this world).
>   > +18 There is no fear
>   > > +in love,
>   > > > +but
>   > > +perfect love
>   > +casts out fear;

+because fear has punishment,
+and the one fearing has not been brought to perfection in love.

+19 Let us
  +love because
    +he [God]
    +first
  +loved
+us.

4:20–5:5 Loving God and Loving One Another
Loving God and Correct Belief

+20 If someone says,
  +"I love
    +God"
      +and
    +() his brother
  +(he hates),
+the person is a liar.

+For the one not loving
  +his brother, whom he has seen,
  +God, whom he has not seen,
+(he) is not able to love.

21 And we have this commandment from him [God],
  that the one loving God
  should also love his brother.

+5:1 Everyone believing that Jesus is the Christ
  +has been begotten of God, and everyone loving the begetter loves the one begotten of him. 2 In this we know that we love the children of God,
    +whenever we love God and obey his commandments.
      +3 For this is the love of God,
    +that we keep his commandments. And his commandments are not burdensome,
  +4 because everything begotten of God conquers the world. And this is the conquest that conquered the world — our faith. 5 Who is the one conquering the world if not
+the one believing that Jesus is the Son of God?

The Text of 1 John 5:6-14

5:6-12 Having the Son and Having Life

6 This is the one coming through water and blood, Jesus Christ.
    Not in the water only but
        in the water
        and the blood.

And the Spirit is the one bearing witness,
    because the Spirit is the Truth.

    7 Because there are three witnessing:
      8 the Spirit
      and the water
      and the blood,
        and these three are as one.

9 If we accept the witness of humans,
    the witness of God is greater,
        because this is the witness of God
            that he has witnessed about his Son.

10 The one believing in the Son of God has the witness in himself.
The one not believing God has made him [God] a liar
    because he has not believed in the witness
        that God has witnessed about his Son.

11 And this is the witness,
    that God gave us eternal life,
    and this life is in his Son.

12 The one who has the Son has life;
the one not having the Son of God does not have life.

5:13-21 Prayer for Sin and Conclusion

13 I wrote these things to you
    in order that you might know
        that you have eternal life,
        believing in the name of the Son of God.

14 And this is the confidence that we have before him [God],
    that if we ask for anything according to his [God's] will,
        he [God] hears us.

The Text of 1 John 5:15-21

15 And if we know
   that he [God] hears us regarding whatever we ask for,
we know
   that we have the requests
      that we have requested from him [God].

16 If anyone sees his brother
   +sinning a sin not unto death,
      +he [the believer] will ask,
         +and
      +he [God] will give life to him [the sinner],
   +to those [sinners] not sinning unto death.

There is a sin-unto-death.
   I do not say that a person should make a request about that.

+17 Every injustice
   +sin
      +(is),
         +and
      +there is
   +a sin
+not unto death.

18 We know
   that everyone begotten of God does not sin,
   but the one begotten of God protects himself,
   and the Evil One does not touch him.

19 We know
   that we are of God,
   and the whole world lies in the grasp of the Evil One.

20 We know
   that the Son of God has come,
   and he has given us insight
      so that we know the True One.
         And we are
            in the True One,
            in his Son, Jesus Christ.
            This is the True God
            and eternal life.

21 Dear Children, guard yourselves from idols.

The Text of 2 John 1-9

2 JOHN

1 The Elder to the Elect Lady and her children,
   whom I love in truth,
   and not I alone
      but all those who know the truth —
      2 through the truth abiding in us —
   and it will be with us forever.

3 May grace,
   mercy, and
   peace
      from God the Father and
      from Jesus Christ, the son of the Father,
         be with you,
            in truth and
            in love.

4 I rejoiced greatly to find
   +some of your children walking in truth,
      +just as we received a commandment from the Father. 5 And now I ask
      you, Lady, (not as one writing a new commandment to you but one
      that we have had
   from the beginning),
         +that we love one another.
        +6 And this is the love,
      +that you walk according to his commandments; this is the
      commandment, as you heard it from the beginning,
   +that we walk in it.

+7 Because many deceivers have gone out into the world,
   +persons not confessing Jesus Christ as coming in the flesh.
+This one is the Deceiver and the Antichrist.

8 Watch yourselves, in order that
   you not lose those things for which you have worked, but that
   you receive a full recompense.
9 Everyone
   who is "progressive" and
   who does not remain in the teaching of the Christ
      does not possess God;
the one
   who remains in the teaching has both the Father and the Son.

The Text of 2 John 10-13

10 If someone approaches you and does not bring this teaching,
   +do not receive
      +him
         +into your house and
         +greetings
      +to him
   +do not give.

11 For the one
   who gives him a greeting also
   takes part in his evil deeds.

12 Although I have many things to write to you,
   I did not want to,
      by paper and ink;
but I hope to be with you and
      to speak face to face,
         so that our joy may be the fullest.

13 The children of your elect sister greet you.

The Text of 3 John 1-10

3 JOHN

₁The Elder
  to Beloved Gaius,
    whom I love in truth.

₂Beloved, I pray that,
  +in all things,
    +you are doing well and
      +that you are in good health,
    +just as () is doing well
  +(your soul).

₃For I rejoiced greatly
  when the brothers came and bore witness to your truth,
    how you walk in truth.

₄I have no greater joy than this,
  that I hear my children
    are walking in the truth.

₅Beloved,
  +you (will) act faithfully in whatever you may do
    +for the brothers,
      +and this for strangers. (₆They witnessed to your love before the assembly!)
  +and you will act well, having sent them on in a way worthy of God.

+₇For, for the sake of the name, they went out,
  +accepting nothing
    +from the nations.
    +₈Therefore, we
  +ought to accept such as these,
+so that we may become co-workers for the truth.

₉I wrote something to the assembly.
  But Diotrephes, the one who loves to act as leader among them,
  does not receive us.

₁₀Because of this, if I come,
  I will bring up the things he is doing,
    bringing unjustified charges against us with evil words;
  and, not being satisfied with this, he does not receive the brothers himself,

and prevents those who wish to
and ejects them from the assembly.

11 Beloved,
 +do not imitate evil but
   +good.
  +The one doing good is of God.
 +The one doing evil has not seen God.

12 Demetrius has been
 witnessed to by all and
   by the truth itself.
 And we bear witness also, and
 you know that our witness is true.

13 I had many things to write to you, but
 I do not wish to write by ink and pen.
14 But I hope to see you very soon, and
 we will speak face to face.

15 Peace to you.
 The friends here greet you.
 Greet the friends there by name.

Bibliography

1. General Reference

Achtemeier, P. (ed.), *Herder's Dictionary of the Bible* (San Francisco: Harper and Row, 1985).

Aland, B. and K., *The Text of the New Testament* (ET; 2d ed.; Grand Rapids: Eerdmans, 1989).

Bauer, W., Danker, F., Arndt, W. F., and Gingrich, F. W., *A Greek-English Lexicon of the New Testament and Other Early Christian Literature* (3d ed.; Chicago: University of Chicago Press, 1999).

Dessau, H. (ed.), *Inscriptiones Latinae Selectae* (3 vols.; Berlin: Weidmann, 1892-1916) (Cited by inscription number.)

Kittel, G., and Friedrich, G. (eds.), *Theological Dictionary of the New Testament* (G. Bromiley, trans.; 10 vols. Grand Rapids: Eerdmans, 1964-76).

Metzger, B. M. (on behalf of and in cooperation with the Editorial Committee of the United Bible Societies' *Greek New Testament*), *A Textual Commentary on the Greek New Testament* (2d ed.; companion to the UBS 4th ed.; Stuttgart: Deutsche Bibelgesellschaft, 1994).

Rengstorf, K. H. (ed.), *A Complete Concordance to Flavius Josephus* (4 vols.; Leiden: E. J. Brill, 1973).

——— (ed.), *A Complete Concordance to Flavius Josephus,* Supplement I: *Namenwörterbuch zu Flavius Josephus* (by A. Schalit) (Leiden: E. J. Brill, 1968).

Zerwick, S.J., M., *Biblical Greek* (Eng. ed. adapted from 4th Latin ed.; Rome: Scripta Pontificii Instituti Biblici, 1963).

———, *A Grammatical Analysis of the Greek New Testament* (5th rev. ed.; Rome: Pontifical Biblical Institute, 1996).

2. Texts

The Apostolic Fathers: Greek Texts and English Translations of Their Writings (J. B. Lightfoot and J. R. Harmer, trans./eds.; rev. ed. M. W. Holmes; 2d ed.; Grand Rapids: Baker, 1992).

Commentaries on the Gospel of John

The Babylonian Talmud (I. Epstein, trans./ed.; London: Soncino, 1948).
Biblia Hebraica (R. Kittel, ed.; Stuttgart: Württembergische Bibelanstalt, 1949).
The Complete Dead Sea Scrolls in English (G. Vermes, trans.; Harmondsworth: Penguin, 1997).
The Dead Sea Scrolls: Hebrew, Aramaic, and Greek Texts with English Translations (J. H. Charlesworth, ed., with F. M. Cross, J. Milgrom, E. Qumron, L. H. Schiffman, L. T. Stuckenbruck, and R. E. Witaker; Tübingen: J. C. B. Mohr [Paul Siebeck]; Louisville: Westminster John Knox, 1994-). Vol. 1: *The Rule of the Community and Related Documents* (1994); vol. 2: *The Damascus Document, War Scroll, and Related Documents* (1994); vol. 4a: *Pseudepigraphic and Non-Masoretic Psalms and Prayers* (1997); vol. 4b: *Angelic Liturgy: Songs of the Sabbath Sacrifices* (1999).
The Dead Sea Scrolls Translated : The Qumran Texts in English (F. García-Martínez, trans.; 2d ed.; Grand Rapids: Eerdmans, 1996).
The Greek New Testament (B. Aland, K. Aland, J. Karavidopoulos, C. M. Martini, and B. M. Metzger, eds.; 4th ed. rev.; Stuttgart: Biblia-Druck, 1993).
Mekilta de Rabbi Ishmael: A Critical Edition on the Basis of the Manuscripts and Early Editions with an English Translation, Introduction and Notes (J. Z. Lauterbach, ed.; 3 vols.; Philadelphia: Jewish Publication Society, 1933-35).
The Mishnah (H. Danby, trans.; Oxford: Oxford University Press, 1933).
The Nag Hammadi Library in English (J. M. Robinson, ed.; New York: Harper and Row, 1977).
Novum Testamentum Graece (23d ed.; B. and K. Aland, J. Karavidopoulos, C. M. Martini, and B. M. Metzger, eds.; Stuttgart: Biblia-Druck, 1993).
The Old Testament Pseudepigrapha. Vol. 1: *Apocalyptic Literature and Testaments;* Vol. 2: *Expansions of the "Old Testament" and Legends, Wisdom and Philosophical Literature, Prayers, Psalms and Odes, Fragments of Lost Judeo-Hellenistic Works* (J. H. Charlesworth et al., eds.; Garden City, NY: Doubleday, 1983, 1985).
Oxyrhynchus Papyri (B. P. Grenfell and A. S. Hunt, eds.; multiple vols.; London: Egypt Exploration Fund, 1898-).
Papyrus Bodmer XVII [Text of P^{75}] (ed. R. Kasser; Cologny-Genève: Bibliotheca Bodmeriana, 1961).
Saint Justin Martyr (T. B. Falls, trans.; New York: Christian Heritage, 1948).
Septuaginta (A. Rahlfs, ed.; 2 vols.; Stuttgart: Württembergische Bibelanstalt, 1965).
The Testaments of the Twelve Patriarchs: A Critical Edition of the Greek Text (M. de Jonge, ed., in cooperation with H. W. Hollander, H. J. de Jonge, and T. Korteweg; Leiden: E. J. Brill, 1978).
Die Texte aus Qumran Hebräisch und Deutsch (E. Lohse, ed.; München: Kösel, 1971).
The Tosefta (J. Neusner, trans.; Peabody, MA: Hendrickson, 2002).

3. Commentaries on the Gospel of John[1]

Barrett, C. K., *The Gospel according to St. John* (2d ed.; Philadelphia: Westminster, 1978).

---

1. Commentaries on the Johannine Letters are in a separate bibliography. Commentaries on other books of the Bible are included in the bibliography of Articles and Monographs.

Bibliography

Bauer, W., *Das Johannesevangelium* (HNT 6; 3d ed.; Tübingen: Mohr-Siebeck, 1933).
Beasley-Murray, G. R., *John* (WBC 36; Waco, TX: Word, 1987).
Becker, J., *Das Evangelium nach Johannes* (Ökumenischer Taschenbuch-Kommentar zum Neuen Testament 4/1, 4/2; 2 vols.; Gütersloh: Gütersloher Verlagshaus Mohn; Würzburg: Echter-Verlag, 1979 (unrev. 2d ed. 1985).
Bernard, J. H., *A Critical and Exegetical Commentary on the Gospel of St. John* (ICC; 2 vols.; Edinburgh: T&T Clark, 1929).
Brodie, T. L., *The Gospel according to John* (New York: Oxford University Press, 1993).
Brown, R. E., *The Gospel according to John* (AB 29, 29a; Garden City, NY: Doubleday, 1966-70).
Bruce, F. F., *The Gospel of John* (Grand Rapids: Eerdmans, 1983).
Bultmann, R., *The Gospel of John: A Commentary* (Philadelphia: Westminster, 1970).
Busse, U., *Das Johannesevangelium* (BETL 162; Leuven: The University, 2002).
Carson, D. A., *The Gospel according to John* (Grand Rapids: Eerdmans, 1991).
Culpepper, R. A., *The Gospel and Letters of John* (Nashville: Abingdon, 1998).
Fenton, J. C., *The Gospel according to John* (NCBC; Oxford: Clarendon, 1970).
Haenchen, E., *The Gospel of John* (Hermeneia; 2 vols.; Philadelphia: Fortress, 1984).
Hoskyns, E. C., and Davey, F. N., *The Fourth Gospel* (2d ed.; London: Faber and Faber, 1947).
Keener, C., *The Gospel of John* (2 vols.; Peabody, MA: Hendrickson, 2003).
Kysar, R., *John* (ACNT: Minneapolis: Augsburg, 1986).
Lightfoot, R. H., *St. John's Gospel: A Commentary with the Revised Version Text* (C. F. Evans, ed.; Oxford: Oxford University Press, 1956).
Lindars, B., *The Gospel of John* (NCBC; London: Oliphants, 1972).
Malina, B., and Rohrbaugh, R. L., *Social-Science Commentary on the Gospel of John* (Minneapolis: Fortress, 1998).
Marsh, J., *Saint John* (Pelican New Testament Commentaries; Harmondsworth: Penguin, 1968).
Moloney, F. J., *John* (Sacra Pagina 4; Collegeville: Liturgical, 1998).
Morris, L., *The Gospel according to John: The English Text with Introduction, Exposition and Notes* (NICNT; rev. ed.; Grand Rapids: Eerdmans, 1995).
Ridderbos, H., *The Gospel of John: A Theological Commentary* (Grand Rapids: Eerdmans, 1997).
Sanders, J. N. (and B. A. Mastin), *A Commentary on the Gospel according to St. John* (London: A. & C. Black, 1968).
Schenke, L., *Johannes Kommentar* (Düsseldorf: Patmos, 1998).
Schnackenburg, R., *The Gospel according to St. John* (vol. 1; New York: Herder and Herder, 1966; vols. 2, 3; New York: Crossroad, 1980-82).
Schnelle, U., *Das Evangelium nach Johannes* (THKNT 4; Leipzig: Evangelische Verlagsanstalt, 1998).
Schultz, S., *Das Evangelium nach Johannes* (NTD 4; 12th ed.; Göttingen: Vandenhoeck & Ruprecht, 1972).
Smith, D. M., *John* (Abingdon New Testament Commentaries; Nashville: Abingdon, 1999).
Stibbe, M., *John* (Readings: A New Biblical Commentary; Sheffield: Journal for the Study of the New Testament, 1993).

Strathmann, H., *Das Evangelium nach Johannes* (Göttingen: Vandenhoeck & Ruprecht, 1963).
Talbert, C. H., *Reading John: A Literary and Theological Commentary on the Fourth Gospel and the Johannine Epistles* (New York: Crossroad, 1992).
Wellhausen, J., *Das Evangelium Johannis* (Berlin: Georg Reimer, 1908).
Wendt, H. H., *The Gospel According to St. John* (Edinburgh: T&T Clark, 1902).
Westcott, B. F., *The Gospel According to St. John* (reprint of 1881 original; Grand Rapids: Eerdmans, 1978).
Whitacre, R. A., *John* (IVP New Testament Commentary Series; Downers Grove, IL: InterVarsity, 1999).
Wilckens, U., *Das Evangelium nach Johannes* (NTD 4: Göttingen: Vandenhoeck & Ruprecht, 1997).
Witherington, B., *John's Wisdom: A Commentary on the Fourth Gospel* (Louisville: Westminster/John Knox, 1995).

4. Articles and Monographs on the Gospel of John

Achtemeier, P. J., "An Apocalyptic Shift in Early Christian Tradition: Reflections on Some Canonical Evidence," *CBQ* 45 (1984) 231-48.
Ackerman, J., "The Rabbinic Interpretation of Psalm 82 and the Gospel of John," *HTR* 59 (1966) 186-91.
Aland, K., "Eine Untersuchung zu Joh 1:3-4: Über die Bedeutung eines Punktes," *ZNW* 59 (1968) 174-209.
———, "Neue neutestamentliche Papyri III," *NTS* 20 (1974) 357-81.
Albright, W. F., "Some Observations Favoring the Palestinian Origin of the Gospel of John," *HTR* 17 (1924) 189-95.
———, "Recent Discoveries in Palestine," in *The Background of the New Testament: Festschrift C. H. Dodd* (Cambridge: Cambridge University Press, 1964) 153-71.
Alexander, P. S., "Rabbinic Judaism and the New Testament," *ZNW* 74 (1983) 237-46.
Alföldy, G., "Pontius Pilatus und das Tibereium von Caesarea Maritima," *Scripta Classica Israelitica* 18 (1999) 85-108.
Anderson, P. A., *The Christology of the Fourth Gospel: Its Unity and Disunity in the Light of John 6* (WUNT 2/78; Tübingen: J. C. B. Mohr [P. Siebeck], 1996).
———, "The Having-Sent-Me Father: Aspects of Agency, Encounter, and Irony in the Johannine Father-Son Relationship," in *God the Father in the Gospel of John*, A. Reinhartz, ed.; *Semeia* 85 (1999).
Appold, M. L., *The Oneness Motif in the Fourth Gospel* (WUNT 2/1; Tübingen: J. C. B. Mohr [P. Siebeck], 1976).
Arockiam, M., *The Concept of Joy in the Johannine Literature* (Delhi: ISPCK, 2002).
Ashton, J., *Understanding the Fourth Gospel* (Oxford: Clarendon, 1991).
———, *Studying John: Approaches to the Fourth Gospel* (Oxford: Clarendon, 1994).
———, "The Identity and Function of the *Ioudaioi* in the Fourth Gospel," *NTS* 21 (1985) 40-75.
———, "The Transformation of Wisdom: A Study of the Prologue of John's Gospel," *NTS* 32 (1986) 161-86.

Bibliography

Attridge, H. W., "Thematic Development and Source Elaboration in John 7:1-36," *CBQ* 42 (1980) 160-70.

———, "Genre Bending in the Fourth Gospel," *JBL* 121 (2002) 3-21.

Audet, J.-P., "Esquisse historique de genre littéraire de la 'Bénédiction' juive et de la 'Eucharistie' chrétienne," *RB* 65 (1958) 371-99.

———, "La soif, l'eau et la parole," *RB* (1959) 379-86.

Augenstein, J., *Das Liebesgebot im Johannesevangelium und in den Johannesbriefen* (BWANT Folge 7. Heft 14; Stuttgart: Kohlhammer, 1993).

———, "'Euer Gesetz': Ein Pronomen und die johanneische Haltung zum Gesetz," *ZNW* 88 (1997) 311-13.

Aune, D., *The Cultic Setting of Realized Eschatology in Early Christianity* (Leiden: E. J. Brill, 1972).

———, "Dualism in the Fourth Gospel and the Dead Sea Scrolls," in *Neotestamentica et Philonica* (D. Aune, T. Seland, and J. H. Ulrichsen, eds.; Leiden: E. J. Brill, 2003) 281-303.

Avigad, N., *Discovering Jerusalem* (Nashville: Nelson, 1983).

Bacon, B. W., "Immortality in the Fourth Gospel," in *Religion and the Future Life: The Development of the Belief in Life after Death* (E. H. Sneath, ed.; New York: F. H. Revell, 1922) 259-94.

Bahat, D., "Does the Holy Sepulchre Church Mark the Burial of Jesus?" *BAR* 12, 3 (May/June 1986) 26-45.

Bailey, J. A., *The Traditions Common to the Gospels of Luke and John* (NovTSup 7; Leiden: E. J. Brill, 1963).

Ball, D. M., *'I Am' in John's Gospel: Literary Function, Background and Theological Implications* (JSNTSup 124; Sheffield: Sheffield Academic Press, 1996).

Bammel, E., "*Philos tou Kaisaros*," *TLZ* 77 (1952) 205-10.

———, "'John Did No Miracle,'" in *Miracles: Cambridge Studies in Their Philosophy and History* (C. F. D. Moule, ed.; London: Mowbray; New York: Morehouse-Barlow, 1965) 181-202.

———, "The Baptist in Early Christian Tradition," *NTS* 18 (1971-72) 95-128.

Bampfylde, G., "More Light on John XII 34," *JSNT* 17 (1983) 87-89.

Barbet, P., *A Doctor at Calvary* (Garden City, NY: Doubleday, 1953).

Bardsley, J. J., "The Testimony of Ignatius and Polycarp to the Writings of St. John," *JTS* 14 (1913) 207-20.

Barosse, T., "The Seven Days of the New Creation in St. John's Gospel," *CBQ* 23 (1959) 507-16.

Barrett, C. K., *The Gospel of John and Judaism* (Philadelphia: Fortress, 1975).

———, *Essays on John* (London: SPCK; Philadelphia: Westminster, 1982).

———, "The Holy Spirit in the Gospel of John," *JTS* n.s. 1 (1950) 1-19.

———, "The Lamb of God," *NTS* 1 (1954-55) 210-18.

———, "The Theological Vocabulary of the Fourth Gospel," in *Current Issues in New Testament Interpretation: Essays in Honor of Otto A. Piper* (W. Klassen and G. F. Snyder, eds.; New York: Harper, 1962).

———, "'The Father Is Greater than I' (Jo 14,28): Subordinationist Christology in the New Testament," in *Neues Testament und Kirche: Für Rudolf Schnackenburg* (J. Gnilka, ed.;

Freiburg: Herder, 1974) 144-59; now in *Essays on John* (London: SPCK; Philadelphia: Westminster, 1982) 1-18.

Bassler, J. M., "The Galileans: A Neglected Factor in Johannine Community Research," *CBQ* 43 (1981) 243-57.

———, "Mixed Signals: Nicodemus in the Fourth Gospel," *JBL* 108 (1989) 635-46.

Bauckham, R. (ed.), *The Gospels for All Christians* (Grand Rapids: Eerdmans, 1998).

———, "The Study of Gospel Traditions outside the Canonical Gospels: Problems and Prospects," in *Gospel Perspectives: The Jesus Tradition outside the Gospels* (D. Wenham, ed.; Sheffield: JSOT, 1984) 369-403.

———, "The Parable of the Vine: Rediscovering a Lost Parable of Jesus," *NTS* 33 (1987) 84-101.

———, "The Martyrdom of Peter in the New Testament and Early Christian Literature," *ANRW* 2.26.1 (1992) 539-95.

———, "Mary of Clopas (John 19:25)," in *Women in the Biblical Tradition* (ed. G. J. Brooke; Lewiston, NY, 1992) 231-56.

———, "The Beloved Disciple as Ideal Author," *JSNT* 49 (1993) 21-44.

———, "Papias and Polycrates on the Origin of the Fourth Gospel," *JTS* 44 (1993) 24-69.

———, "Nicodemus and the Gurion Family," *JTS* n.s. 47 (1996) 1-37.

———, "For Whom Were the Gospels Written?" in *The Gospels for All Christians* (R. Bauckham, ed.; Grand Rapids: Eerdmans, 1998) 9-48.

———, "John for Readers of Mark," in *The Gospels for All Christians* (R. Bauckham, ed.; Grand Rapids: Eerdmans, 1998) 147-71.

———, "The Qumran Community and the Gospel of John," in *The Dead Sea Scrolls Fifty Years after Their Discovery* (L. H. Schiffman, E. Tov, and J. C. VanderKam, eds.; Jerusalem: Israel Exploration Society in cooperation with the Shrine of the Book, 2000) 105-15.

Baum-Bodenbender, R., *Hoheit in Niedrigkeit: Johanneische Christologie im Prozess Jesu vor Pilatus (Joh 18,28–19,16a)* (FB 49; Würzburg: Echter, 1984).

Beck, D. R., *The Discipleship Paradigm: Readers and Anonymous Characters in the Fourth Gospel* (Biblical Interpretation Series 27; Leiden: E. J. Brill, 1997).

Becker, H., *Die Reden des Johannesevangeliums und der Stil der gnostischen Offenbarungsreden* (FRLANT 50; Göttingen: Vandenhoeck & Ruprecht, 1956).

Becker, J., *Auferstehung der Toten im Urchristentum* (SBS 82; Stuttgart: Katholisches Bibelwerk, 1976).

———, "Aufbau, Schichtung und theologiegeschichtliche Stellung des Gebetes in Johannes 17," *ZNW* 60 (1969) 56-83.

———, "Wunder und Christologie: Zum literarkritischen und christologischen Problem der Wunder im Johannesevangelium," *NTS* 16 (1969-70) 130-48.

———, "Die Abschiedsreden Jesu im Johannesevangelium," *ZNW* 61 (1970) 215-46.

———, "Beobachtungen zum Dualismus in Johannesevangelium," *ZNW* 65 (1974) 71-87.

———, "Feindesliebe — Nächstenliebe — Bruderliebe: Exegetische Beobachtungen als Anfrage an ein ethisches Problemfeld," *ZEE* 25 (1981) 5-18.

———, "Ich bin die Auferstehung und das Leben: Eine Skizze der johanneischen Christologie," *TZ* 39 (1983) 138-51.

Bibliography

Becker, U., *Jesus und die Ehebrecherin: Untersuchungen zur Text- und Überlieferungsgeschichte von John 7,53–8,11* (BZNW 28; Berlin: Töpelmann, 1963).

Beker, J. C., *Paul the Apostle* (Philadelphia: Fortress, 1980).

Beneitez, M., "Notas sobre verbos 'sinonimos' en Jn," *Estudios Eclesiasticos* 49 (1974) 109-16.

Bennema, C., *The Power of Saving Wisdom: An Investigation of Spirit and Wisdom in Relation to the Soteriology of the Fourth Gospel* (WUNT 2 Reihe, Band 148; Tübingen: J. C. B. Mohr [P. Siebeck], 2002).

Benoit, P., "Praetorium, Lithostrotos, et Gabbatha," *RB* 59 (1952) 531-50.

———, "L'Antonia d'Hérode le Grand et le Forum Oriental d'Aelia Capitolina," *HTR* 64 (1971) 135-67.

———, "Le Prétoire de Pilate à l'époque byzantine," *RB* 91 (1984) 161-77.

Berger, K., *Im Anfang war Johannes: Datierung und Theologie des vierten Evangeliums* (Stuttgart: Quelle, 1997).

Bergmeier, R., "Zum Verfasserproblem des II. und III. Johannesbriefes," *ZNW* 57 (1966) 93-100.

———, "Glaube als Werk? Die 'Werke Gottes' in Damaskusschrift II, 14-15 und Johannes 6,28-29," *RevQ* 6 (1967) 253-60.

Bernard, J., "La guérison de Bethesda: Harmoniques judéo-hellénistiques d'un recit de miracle un jour de sabbat," *MScRel* 33 (1976) 13-34.

———, "Témoinage pour Jesus-Christ: Jean 5:31-47," *MScRel* 36 (1979) 3-55.

Bertram, G., *"Makarios,"* *TDNT* 4, 364-67.

Betz, O., *Offenbarung und Schriftforschung in der Qumransekte* (WUNT 6; Tübingen: J. C. B. Mohr [P. Siebeck], 1960).

———, *Der Paraklet: Fürsprecher im haretischen Spätjudentum, im Johannes-Evangelium und in neugefundenen gnostischen Schriften* (Institutum Iudaicum 2; Leiden: E. J. Brill, 1963).

———, "'To Worship God in Spirit and in Truth': Reflection on John 4:20-36," in *Standing before God. Studies on Prayer in Scriptures and in Tradition with Essays in Honor of John M. Oesterricher* (A. Finkel and L. Frizzell, eds.; New York: Ktav, 1981).

Beutler, J., *Martyria: Traditionsgeschichtliche Untersuchungen zum Zeugnis Thema bei Johannes* (Frankfurter theologische Studien 10; Frankfurt: Josef Knecht, 1972).

———, *Habt keine Angst* (SBS 116; Stuttgart: Katholisches Bibelwerk, 1984).

———, and R. Fortna (eds.), *The Shepherd Discourse of John 10 and Its Context* (Cambridge: Cambridge University Press, 1991).

———, "Die Heilsbedeutung des Todes Jesu im Johannesevangelium nach John 13,1-20," in *Der Tod Jesu* (K. Kertelge, ed.; QD 74; Freiburg: Herder, 1976) 188-204.

———, "Die 'Juden' und der Tod Jesu im Johannesevangelium," in *Exodus und Kreuz im ökumenischen Dialog zwischen Juden und Christen* (H. H. Henrix and M. Stöhr, eds.; Aachen: Einhard, 1978) 75-93.

———, "Litterarische Gattungen im Johannesevangelium: Ein Forschungsbericht 1919 bis 1980," *ANRW* 2.25.3 (1984) 2508-68.

———, "Das Hauptgebot im Johannesevangelium," in *Das Gesetz im Neuen Testament* (K. Kertelge, ed.; QD 108; Freiburg: Herder, 1986) 222-36.

———, "Der alttestamentlich-jüdische Hintergrund der Hirtenrede in Johannes 10," in

The Shepherd Discourse of John 10 and Its Context (J. Beutler and R. Fortna, eds.; Cambridge: Cambridge University Press, 1991) 18-32.

———, "Two Ways of Gathering: The Plot to Kill Jesus in John 11.47-53," *NTS* 40 (1994) 403-4.

———, "The Use of 'Scripture' in the Gospel of John," in *Exploring the Gospel of John* (R. Alan Culpepper and C. Clifton Black, eds.) 147-62.

Beyer, H. W., Review of *Festgabe für Adolf Jülicher* in *TLZ* 54 (1929) 606-17.

Bickermann, E. J., "The Warning Inscriptions from Herod's Temple," *JQR* 37 (1946-47) 387-405.

Bienaimé, G., *Moïse et la don de l'eau dans la tradition juive ancienne: Targum et Midrash* (AnBib 98; Rome: Pontifical Biblical Institute, 1984).

———, "L'annonce des fleuves d'eau vive en Jean 7,37-39," *RTL* 21 (1990) 281-310, 417-54.

Bieringer, R., Pollefeyt, D., and Vandecasteele-Vanneuville, F. (eds.), *Anti-Judaism and the Fourth Gospel: Papers from the Leuven Colloquium, 2000* (Jewish and Christian Heritage Series 1; Assen: Van Gorcum, 2001).

Birdsall, J. N., "John x.29," *JTS* 11 (1960) 342-44.

Bittner, W., *Jesu Zeichen im Johannesevangelium* (WUNT 2/26; Tübingen: J. C. B. Mohr [P. Siebeck], 1987).

Bjerklund, C. J., *Tauta Egeneto: Die Präzisierungssätze im Johannesevangelium* (Tübingen: J. C. B. Mohr [P. Siebeck], 1987).

Blank, J., *Krisis: Untersuchungen zur johanneischen Christologie und Eschatologie* (Freiburg: Lambertus, 1964).

———, "Frauen in der Jesusüberlieferung," in G. Dautzenberg, H. Merklein, and K. Müller (eds.), *Die Frau im Urchristentum* (QD 95; Freiburg: Herder, 1983) 9-91.

Bligh, J., "Jesus in Samaria," *HeyJ* 3 (1962) 329-46.

———, "The Man Born Blind," *HeyJ* 7 (1966) 129-44.

Blinzler, J., *The Trial of Jesus: The Jewish and Roman Proceedings against Jesus Christ Described and Assessed from the Oldest Accounts* (Westminster, MD: Newman, 1959).

———, "Eine Bemerkung zum Geschichtsrahmen des Johannesevangelium," *Bib* 36 (1955) 20-35.

Böcher, O., *Der johanneische Dualismus im Zusammenhang des nachbiblischen Judentums* (Gütersloh: Gerd Mohn, 1965).

Boers, H., *Neither on This Mountain nor in Jerusalem* (SBLMS 35; Atlanta: Scholars Press, 1988).

Bogart, J., *Orthodox and Heretical Perfectionism in the Johannine Community as Evident in the First Epistle of John* (SBLDS 33; Missoula: Scholars Press, 1977).

Boice, J. M., *Witness and Revelation in the Gospel of John* (Grand Rapids: Eerdmans, 1970).

Boismard, M.-É., *Du Baptême à Cana (Jean 1,19–2,11)* (Paris: Cerf, 1956).

——— (and A. Lamouille), *L'Évangile de Jean* (Synopse des quatre Évangiles, Vol. 3; Paris: Cerf, 1977).

——— (and A. Lamouille), *La vie des Évangiles: Initiation à la critique des textes* (Paris: Cerf, 1980).

———, *Moses or Jesus: An Essay in Johannine Christology* (Minneapolis: Fortress, 1993).

——— (and A. Lamouille), *Un Évangile Pré-Johannique*, vol. 1: *Jean 1,1–2,12* (published in two parts); vol. 2: *Jean 2,13-4,54* (published also in two parts) (Paris: Gabalda, 1993); vol. 3: *Jean 5,1-47* (Paris: Gabalda, 1996).

———, *Le martyre de Jean l'apôtre* (CahRB 35; Paris: Gabalda, 1996).

———, *Our Victory over Death: Resurrection?* (Collegeville, Minn.: Liturgical Press, 1999).

———, "Le chapitre xxi de saint Jean: Essai de critique littéraire," *RB* 54 (1947) 473-501.

———, "Clément de Rome et l'Évangile de Jean," *RB* 55 (1948) 376-87.

———, "Problèmes de critique textuelle concernant le quatrième évangile," *RB* 60 (1953) 347-71.

———, "Le caractère adventice de Jn 12,45-50," in *Sacra Pagina* (J. Coppens, ed.; Miscellanea Biblica: Congressus Internationalis Catholicus de Re Biblica; vol. 2; Gembloux: Duculot, 1959) 189-92.

———, "Les citations targumiques dans le quatrième évangile," *RB* 66 (1959) 374-78.

———, "L'évolution du thème eschatologique dans les traditions johanniques, *RB* 68 (1961) 507-24.

———, "Saint Luc et la rédaction du quatrième évangile," *RB* 69 (1962) 185-211.

———, "Les traditions johanniques concernant le baptiste," *RB* 70 (1963) 5-42.

———, "La royauté du Christ dans le quatrieme évangile," *LumVie* 57 (1963) 43-63.

———, "Le lavement des pieds (Jn. 13,1-17)," *RB* 71 (1964) 5-24.

———, "Aenon, près de Salem (Jean 3,23)," *RB* 24 (1973) 218-29.

———, "Un procédé rédactionnel dans le quatrième évangile: La *Wiederaufnahme*," in *L'Évangile de Jean: Sources, rédaction, théologie* (M. de Jonge, ed.; BETL 44; Gembloux: Duculot, 1977) 235-42.

———, "The First Epistle of John and the Writings of Qumran," in *John and the Dead Sea Scrolls* (J. H. Charlesworth, ed.; 2d ed.; New York: Crossroads, 1990) 156-65.

———, "Bethzatha ou Siloé," *RB* 106 (1999) 206-18.

Borgen, P., *Bread from Heaven: An Exegetical Study of the Conception of Manna in the Gospel of John and the Writings of Philo* (NovTSup 10; Leiden: E. J. Brill, 1965).

——— and Giversen, S. (eds.), *The New Testament and Hellenistic Judaism* (Peabody, MA: Hendrickson, 1997).

———, "The Unity of the Discourse in John 6," *ZNW* 50 (1959) 277-78.

———, "Observations on the Midrashic Character of John 6," *ZNW* 54 (1963) 232-40.

———, "God's Agent in the Fourth Gospel," in *Religions in Antiquity: Essays in Memory of Erwin Ramsdell Goodenough* (J. Neusner, ed.; Studies in the History of Religion 14; Leiden: E. J. Brill, 1968) 137-48.

———, "Observations on the Targumic Character of the Prologue of John," *NTS* 16 (1969-70) 288-95.

———, "Some Jewish Exegetical Traditions as Background for Son of Man Sayings in John's Gospel (Jn 3,13-14)," in *L'Évangile de Jean: Sources, Rédaction, Théologie* (M. de Jonge, ed.; BETL 44; Gembloux: Duculot, 1977) 243-58.

———, "John 6: Tradition, Interpretation and Composition," in *From Jesus to John: Essays on Jesus and New Testament Christology in Honour of Marinus de Jonge* (M. C. De Boer, ed.; JSNTSup 84; Sheffield: JSOT, 1993) 279-85.

Borig, R., *Der Wahre Weinstock: Untersuchungen zu Jo 15,1-10* (SANT 16; Munich: Kösel, 1967).

Articles and Monographs on the Gospel of John

Boring, M. E., "The Influence of Christian Prophecy on the Johannine Portrayal of the Paraclete and Jesus," NTS 25 (1978-79) 113-23.

Bornhauser, K., *Das Johannesevangelium, eine Missionsschrift für Israel* (Gütersloh: C. Bertelsmann, 1928).

Bornkamm, G., "Die Eucharistische Rede im Johannes-Evangelium," ZNW 47 (1956) 161-69.

Borsch, F. H., *The Son of Man in Myth and History* (London: SCM, 1967).

Botha, J. E., *Jesus and the Samaritan Woman: A Speech Act Reading of John 4:1-42* (NovTSup 65; Leiden: E. J. Brill, 1991).

Bovon, F., "Le privilège pascal de Marie-Madeleine," NTS 30 (1984) 50-62.

Bowker, J. W., "The Origin and Purpose of St. John's Gospel," NTS 11 (1964-65) 398-408.

Bowman, J., "Samaritan Studies I: The Fourth Gospel and the Samaritans," BJRL 40 (1958) 298-327.

Bratcher, R. J., "'The Jews' in the Gospel of John," BT (1975) 401-9.

Braun, F. M., *Jean le théologien et son évangile dans l'église ancienne* (2 vols.; Paris: Gabalda, 1959).

———, "L'arrière-fond judaïque du quatrième évangile et la communauté de l'alliance," RB 62 (1955) 5-44.

Braun, H., *Qumran und das Neue Testament* (2 vols.; Tübingen: J. C. B. Mohr [P. Siebeck], 1966).

———, "Literaranalyse und theologische Schichtung im Ersten Johannesbrief," ZTK 48 (1951) 262-92.

———, "Qumran und das Neue Testament," TRu 28 (1962) 193-234.

Bream, H. N., "No Need to Be Asked Questions: A Study of John 16:30," in *Search the Scriptures: New Testament Studies in Honor of Raymond T. Stamm* (J. M. Myers, O. Reimherr, and H. N. Bream, eds.; Gettysburg Theological Studies 3; Leiden: E. J. Brill, 1969) 49-74.

Breck, J., *Spirit of Truth: The Holy Spirit in Johannine Tradition* (2 vols.: Crestwood, NY: St. Vladimir's Seminary, 1991, 1997).

Brodie, T. L., *The Quest for the Origin of John's Gospel* (New York: Oxford University Press, 1993).

Broer, I., "Die Juden im Johannesevangelium: Ein beispielhafter und folgenreicher Konflikt," *Diakonia* 14 (1983).

———, "Die Juden im Urteil der Autoren des Neuen Testaments," TGl 82 (1992) 2-33.

———, "Knowledge of Palestine in the Fourth Gospel?" in *Jesus in the Johannine Tradition* (R. T. Fortna and T. Thatcher, eds.; Louisville: Westminster John Knox, 2001) 83-90.

Broshi, M., "Recent Excavations in the Church of the Holy Sepulchre," *Qadmoniot* 10 (1977) 30-32.

Brown, R. E. *New Testament Essays* (Garden City: Doubleday, 1965).

———. "The Qumran Scrolls and the Johannine Gospel and Epistles," in *New Testament Essays* (Garden City: Doubleday, 1965) 138-73.

——— (and Donfried, K. P., Reumann, J., eds.), *Peter in the New Testament* (New York: Paulist; Philadelphia: Fortress, 1973).

——— (and Donfried, K. P., Fitzmyer, J. A., Reumann, J., eds.), *Mary in the New Testament* (New York: Paulist; Philadelphia: Fortress, 1978).

———, *The Community of the Beloved Disciple* (New York: Paulist, 1979).

——— (and Meier, J. P.), *Antioch and Rome: New Testament Cradles of Catholic Christianity* (New York: Paulist, 1983).

———, *The Churches the Apostles Left Behind* (New York: Paulist, 1984).

———, *An Introduction to New Testament Christology* (New York/Mahwah: Paulist, 1994).

———, *The Death of the Messiah: A Commentary on the Passion Narratives in the Four Gospels* (2 vols.; New York: Doubleday, 1994).

———, *An Introduction to the Gospel of John* (F. J. Moloney, ed.; ABL; New York: Doubleday, 2003).

———, "The Paraclete in the Fourth Gospel," *NTS* 13 (1966-67) 113-32.

———, "Roles of Women in the Fourth Gospel," *TS* 36 (1975) 688-99.

———, "Johannine Ecclesiology: The Community's Origins," *Int* 31 (1977) 379-93.

———, "'The Mother of Jesus' in the Fourth Gospel," in *L'Évangile de Jean: Sources, Rédaction, Théologie* (M. de Jonge, ed.; BETL 44; Gembloux: Duculot, 1977) 307-10.

———, "'Other Sheep Not of This Fold': The Johannine Perspective on Christian Diversity in the Late First Century," *JBL* 97, 1 (1978) 5-22.

———, "The Narratives of Jesus' Passion and Anti-Judaism," *America* 172 (1995) 8-12.

Brown, S., "From Burney to Black: The Fourth Gospel and the Aramaic Question," *CBQ* 26 (1964) 323-39.

———, "John and the Resistant Reader: The Fourth Gospel after Nicea and the Holocaust," *Journal of Literary Studies* 5 (1989) 252-61.

Brown, T. G., *Spirit in the Writings of John* (JSNTSup 253; London: T&T Clark, 2003).

Brownlee, W. H., "Whence the Gospel according to John?" in *John and the Dead Sea Scrolls* (J. H. Charlesworth, ed.; 2d ed.; New York: Crossroads, 1990) 166-94.

Brumlick, M., "Johannes: Das judenfeindliche Evangelium," *Kirche und Israel* 4 (1989) 102-13 (reprinted in *Teufelskinder oder Heilsbringer — Die Juden im Johannes-Evangelium* [D. Neuhaus, ed.; 2d ed.; Frankfurt am Main: Haag und Herchen, 1993] 6-21).

Büchler, A., "The Levitical Impurity of the Gentile in Palestine before the Year 70," *JQR* 17 (1926-27) 1-81.

Bühler, P., "Ist Johannes ein Kreuzes theologe? Exegetisch-systematische Bemerkungen zu einer noch offenen Debatte," in *Johannes-Studien: Interdisziplinäre Zugänge zum Johannes-Evangelium* (Zürich: Theologischer Verlag, 1991) 191-207.

Bühner, J.-A., *Der Gesandte und sein Weg im 4. Evangelium: Die kultur- und religionsgeschichtlichen Grundlagen der johanneischen Sendungschristologie sowie ihre traditionsgeschichtliche Entwicklung* (WUNT 2/2; Tübingen: J. C. B. Mohr [P. Siebeck], 1977).

Bultmann, R., *Theology of the New Testament* (2 vols.; New York: Scribner's, 1955).

———, "Die Bedeutung der neuerschlossenen mandäischen und manichäischen Quellen für das Verständnis des Johannesevangeliums," *ZNW* 24 (1925) 100-146.

Burge, G. M., *The Anointed Community: The Holy Spirit in the Johannine Tradition* (Grand Rapids: Eerdmans, 1987).

Burghardt, W., "Did St. Ignatius of Antioch Know the Fourth Gospel?" *TS* 1 (1940) 1-26.

Articles and Monographs on the Gospel of John

Burke, D. G., "Translating *hoi Ioudaioi* in the New Testament," *Explorations* 9 (1995) 1-7.

Burkett, D., *The Son of Man in the Gospel of John* (JSNTSup 56; Sheffield: Sheffield Academic Press, 1991).

Burkitt, F. C., *The Gospel History and Its Transmission* (Edinburgh: T&T Clark, 1911).

Burney, C. F., *The Aramaic Origin of the Fourth Gospel* (Oxford: Clarendon, 1922).

Burridge, R., *What Are the Gospels?* (Cambridge: Cambridge University Press, 1991).

Busse, U. (and A. May), "Das Weinwunder von Kana (Joh 2,1-11): Erneute Analyse eines 'erratischen Blocks,'" *BN* 12 (1980) 35-61.

―――, "Open Questions on John 10," in *The Shepherd Discourse of John 10 and Its Context* (J. Beutler and R. Fortna, eds.; Cambridge: Cambridge University Press, 1991) 6-17.

―――, "The Beloved Disciple," *Skrif en Kerk* 15 (1994) 219-27.

―――, "Die Tempelmetaphorik als ein Beispiel von implizitem Rekurs auf die biblische Tradition im Johannesevangelium," in *The Scriptures in the Gospels* (C. M. Tuckett, ed.; Leuven: Leuven University Press, 1997) 395-428.

Buttrick, D. (ed.), *Jesus and Man's Hope* (Perspective Books 1; Pittsburgh: Pittsburgh Theological Seminary, 1970).

Byrne, B. J., *"Sons of God — Seed of Abraham": A Study of the Idea of Sonship of God of All Christians in Paul against the Jewish Background* (AnBib 83; Rome: Pontifical Biblical Institute, 1979).

―――, "The Faith of the Beloved Disciple and the Community in John 20," *JSNT* 23 (1985) 83-97, now reprinted in *The Johannine Writings* (S. E. Porter and C. R. Evans, eds.; Biblical Seminar 32; Sheffield: Sheffield University Press, 1995) 69-94.

Carmichael, C. M., *The Story of Creation: Its Origin and Its Interpretation in Philo and the Fourth Gospel* (Ithaca and London: Cornell University Press, 1996).

Carmignac, J., "Les dangers de l'eschatologie," *NTS* 17 (1970-71) 365-90.

Caron, G., *Qui Sont les Juifs de l'Évangile de Jean* (Recherches 35; Quebec: Bellarmin, 1997).

―――, "Exploring a Religious Dimension: The Johannine Jews," *Studies in Religion/Sciences Religieuses* 24 (1995) 159-71.

―――, "The Lifting Up of the Human One and the Johannine Jews," *Église et Théologie* 26 (1995) 319-29.

Carroll, K. L., "The Fourth Gospel and the Exclusion of Christians from the Synagogues," *BJRL* 40 (1957) 19-32.

Carson, D. A. (and Williamson, H. G. M., eds.), *It is Written: Scripture Citing Scripture: Essays in Honour of Barnabas Lindars, SSF* (Cambridge: Cambridge University Press, 1988).

―――, "Current Source Criticism of the Fourth Gospel: Some Methodological Questions," *JBL* 97 (1978) 411-29.

―――, "The Function of the Paraclete in John 16:7-11," *JBL* 98 (1979) 547-66.

―――, "Historical Tradition in the Fourth Gospel: After Dodd, What?" in *Gospel Perspectives*, vol. 2: *Studies of History and Tradition in the Four Gospels* (R. T. France and D. Wenham, eds.; Sheffield: JSOT Press, 1981) 83-145.

―――, "The Purpose of the Fourth Gospel: John 20:31 Reconsidered," *JBL* 106 (1987) 639-51.

―――, "John and the Johannine Epistles," in *It is Written: Scripture Citing Scripture": Es-

says in Honour of Barnabas Lindars, SSF (D. A. Carson and H. G. M. Williamson, eds.; Cambridge: Cambridge University Press, 1988) 245-64.

Casabo-Suque, J. M., "Los judíos en el evangélio de Juan y el antisemitismo," *RivB* 35 (1973) 115-29.

Casey, M., *Is John's Gospel True?* (London: Routledge, 1996).

———, "Idiom and Translation: Some Aspects of the Son of Man Problem," *NTS* 41 (1995) 164-82.

Cassidy, R. J., *John's Gospel in New Perspective: Christology and the Realities of Roman Power* (Maryknoll, NY: Orbis, 1992).

Cassien (Serge Besobrasoff), "La Pentecôte Johannique," *Études Théologiques et Religieuses* 13 (1938) 151-76, 254-77, 327-43; 14 (1939) 32-62, 98-106.

Cavallin, H. C. C., *Life after Death: Paul's Argument for the Resurrection of the Dead in 1 Cor 15, Part I: An Enquiry into the Jewish Background* (Lund: Gleerup, 1974).

Charlesworth, J. H., *The Odes of Solomon: The Syriac Texts* (SBLTT 13; Chico: Scholars Press, 1977).

———, *Jesus within Judaism* (New York: Doubleday, 1988).

——— (ed.), *John and the Dead Sea Scrolls* (2d ed.; New York: Crossroads, 1990).

——— (ed.), *Jesus and the Dead Sea Scrolls* (New York: Doubleday, 1992).

——— (and W. P. Weaver, eds.), *What Has Archaeology to Do with Faith?* (Philadelphia: Trinity Press International, 1992).

———, *The Beloved Disciple* (Valley Forge, PA; Trinity Press International, 1995).

——— (ed.), *Jesus and Archaeology* (Grand Rapids: Eerdmans, 2006).

———, and R. A. Culpepper, R. A. "The Odes of Solomon and the Gospel of John," *CBQ* 35 (1973) 298-322.

———, "Qumran, John, and the Odes of Solomon," in *John and the Dead Sea Scrolls* (J. H. Charlesworth, ed.; 2d ed.; New York: Crossroads, 1990) 107-36.

———, "A Critical Comparison of the Dualism in 1QS 3:13–4:26 and the 'Dualism' Contained in the Gospel of John," in *John and the Dead Sea Scrolls* 76-106.

———, "Archaeology, Jesus, and Christian Faith," in *What Has Archaeology to Do with Faith?* (J. H. Charlesworth and W. P. Weaver, eds.) 1-22.

———, "The Dead Sea Scrolls and the Historical Jesus," in *Jesus and the Dead Sea Scrolls* (J. H. Charlesworth, ed.) 19-62.

———, "The Dead Sea Scrolls and the Gospel according to John," in *Exploring the Gospel of John* (R. A. Culpepper and C. Black, eds.) 65-97.

Charlier, J.-P., "L'exégèse johannique d'un précepte legal: Jean 8,17," *RB* 67 (1960) 503-15.

Chavel, C. B., "The Releasing of a Prisoner on the Eve of Passover in Ancient Jerusalem," *JBL* 60 (1941) 273-78.

Chilton, B., "John xii 34 and Targum Isaiah lii 13," *NovT* 176-78.

Church, W., "The Dislocations in the Eighteenth Chapter of John," *JBL* 49 (1930) 375-83.

Clark-Soles, J., *Scripture Cannot Be Broken* (Leiden/New York: E. J. Brill, 2003).

Collins, J. J. (ed.), *Apocalypse: Toward a Morphology of a Genre* (Semeia 14; Missoula: Scholars Press, 1979).

———, *The Apocalyptic Imagination* (Philadelphia: Fortress, 1984).

———, *The Scepter and the Star: The Messiahs of the Dead Sea Scrolls and Other Ancient Literature* (New York: Doubleday, 1995).

Articles and Monographs on the Gospel of John

———, *Apocalypticism in the Dead Sea Scrolls* (New York: Routledge, 1997).
———, *Jewish Wisdom in the Hellenistic Age* (Edinburgh: T&T Clark, 1998).
———, "The Testamentary Literature in Recent Scholarship," in *Early Judaism and Its Modern Interpreters* (R. A. Kraft and G. W. E. Nickelsburg, eds.; The Bible and Its Modern Interpreters; Philadelphia/Atlanta: Fortress/Scholars Press, 1986) 268-78.
———, "The Son of Man in First-Century Judaism," *NTS* 38 (1992) 448-66.
———, "The Expectation of the End in the Dead Sea Scrolls," in *Eschatology, Messianism, and the Dead Sea Scrolls* (C. W. Evans and P. W. Flint, eds.; Grand Rapids: Eerdmans, 1997) 74-90.
———, "Apocalypticism and Literary Genre in the Dead Sea Scrolls," in *The Dead Sea Scrolls after Fifty Years* (P. W. Flint and J. C. VanderKam, eds.; Leiden: E. J. Brill, 1999).
———, "Qumran, Apocalypticism, and the New Testament," in *The Dead Sea Scrolls Fifty Years after Their Discovery* (J. H. Schiffman, E. Tov, and J. VanderKam, eds.; Jerusalem: Israel Exploration Society, 2000) 133-38.
Collins, R. F., *These Things Have Been Written* (Louvain Theological and Pastoral Monographs 2; Louvain/Grand Rapids: Peeters/Eerdmans, 1990).
———, "'A New Commandment I Give to You, That You Love One Another . . . ,'" in *These Things Have Been Written* 217-56.
Colpe, C., "New Testament and Gnostic Christology," in *Religions in Antiquity: Essays in Memory of Erwin Ramsdell Goodenough* (Studies in the History of Religions 14; Leiden: E. J. Brill, 1967) 227-43.
Colson, J., *L'énigme du disciple que Jésus aimait* (Théologie Historique 10; Paris: Beauchesne, 1969).
Comfort, P. W., *The Quest for the Original Text of the New Testament* (Grand Rapids: Baker, 1992).
———, "The Greek Text of the Gospel of John according to the Early Papyri," *NTS* 36 (1990) 625-29.
Cook, M. J., "The Gospel of John and the Jews," *RevExp* 84 (1987) 259-72.
———, "The New Testament: Confronting Its Impact on Jewish-Christian Relations," in *Introduction to Jewish-Christian Relations* (M. Shermis and A. E. Zannoni, eds.; New York/Mahwah, NJ: Paulist, 1991) 34-62.
Coppens, J., *La relève apocalyptique du messianisme royal*, vol. 3: *Le fils de l'homme neo-testamentaire* (BETL 55; Leuven: Peeters, 1981).
———, "Le fils de l'homme dans l'évangile johannique," *ETL* 52 (1976) 28-81.
———, "Le logia johannique du Fils de l'homme," in *L'Evangile de Jean: Source, Rédaction, Théologie* (M. de Jonge, ed.; BETL 44; Gembloux: Duculot, 1977) 311-15.
Cortés, E., "Los discursos de adiós de Gn 49 y Jn 13–17: Pistas para la historia de un género literario en la antiqua literatura judía (Colectánea San Paciano 23; Barcelona: Herder, 1976).
Cory, C., "Wisdom's Rescue: A New Reading of the Tabernacles Discourse (John 7:1–8:59)," *JBL* 116 (1997) 95-116.
Cross, Jr., F. M., *The Ancient Library of Qumran and Modern Biblical Studies* (2d ed.; Garden City, NY: Doubleday, 1961).
Cuadrado, J. F. T., *"El viniente": Estudio exegético y teológico del verbo ERCHESTHAI en la*

literatura joánica (Monografías de la Revista "Mayéutica" 1; Marcilla [Navarra]: Centro Filosófico-Teológico, 1993).

Cullmann, O., *Early Christian Worship* (A. S. Todd and J. B. Torrance, trans.; SBT 10; Chicago: Regnery, 1953).

―――, *The Christology of the New Testament* (ET; Philadelphia: Westminster, 1959).

―――, *Peter: Disciple, Apostle, Martyr* (2d ed.; Philadelphia: Westminster, 1962).

―――, *The Johannine Circle* (ET; Philadelphia: Westminster, 1976).

―――, "The Significance of the Qumran Texts for Research into the Beginnings of Christianity," in *The Scrolls and the New Testament* (K. Stendahl, ed.; New York: Harper & Brothers, 1957) 18-32.

Culpepper, R. A., *The Johannine School* (SBLDS 26; Missoula: Scholars Press, 1975).

―――, *The Anatomy of the Fourth Gospel* (Philadelphia: Fortress, 1983).

―――, and F. F. Segovia (eds.), *Semeia 53: The Fourth Gospel from a Literary Perspective* (Atlanta: Scholars Press, 1991).

―――, *John, the Son of Zebedee: The Life of a Legend* (Columbia: University of South Carolina Press, 1994).

―――, and C. C. Black (eds.), *Exploring the Gospel of John* (Louisville: Westminster/John Knox, 1996).

――― (ed.), *Critical Readings of John 6* (Biblical Interpretation Series 22; Leiden: E. J. Brill, 1997).

―――, "The Pivot of John's Prologue," *NTS* 27 (1981) 1-31.

―――, "The Gospel of John and the Jews," *RevExp* 84 (1987) 273-88.

―――, "The Johannine *hypodeigma*: A Reading of John 13:1-38," in *Semeia 53: The Fourth Gospel from a Literary Perspective* (R. A. Culpepper and F. F. Segovia, eds.) 133-52.

―――, "The Gospel of John as a Threat to Jewish-Christian Relations," in *Overcoming Fear between Jews and Christians* (J. H. Charlesworth, ed.; New York: Crossroad, 1993) 21-43.

―――, "The Plot of John's Story of Jesus," *Int* 49 (October 1995) 347-58.

―――, "Anti-Judaism in the Fourth Gospel as a Theological Problem for Christian Interpreters," in *Anti-Judaism and the Fourth Gospel: Papers from the Leuven Colloquium, 2000* (R. Bieringer, D. Pollefeyt, and F. Vandecasteele-Vanneuville, eds.; Jewish and Christian Heritage Series 1; Assen: Van Gorcum, 2001) 68-91.

Cuming, G. J., "The Jews in the Fourth Gospel," *ExpTim* 60 (1948-49) 290-92.

Cuvillier, É. "La Figure des Disciples en Jean 4," *NTS* 42 (1996) 245-59.

Dahl, N. A., "The Johannine Church and History," in *Current Issues in New Testament Interpretation* (W. Klassen and G. F. Snyder, eds.; London: SCM, 1962) 124-42.

―――, "Der Erstgeborene Satans und der Vater des Teufels (Polyk. 7.1 und Joh. 8.44)," in *Apophoreta* (W. Eltester, ed.; BZNW 30; Berlin: Töpelmann, 1964) 70-84.

Dahms, J. V., "The Johannine Use of *Monogenēs* Reconsidered," *NTS* 29 (1983) 222-32.

D'Angelo, M. R., "Intimating Deity in the Gospel of John: Theological Language and 'Father' in 'Prayers of Jesus,'" in *God the Father in the Gospel of John*, A. Reinhartz, ed.; *Semeia* 85 (1999).

Daniélou, J., "Les Quatre-Temps de Septembre et la fete des Tabernacles," *La Maison Dieu* 46 (1956) 114-36.

Articles and Monographs on the Gospel of John

———, "Le fils de perdition (Joh. 17,12)," in *Mélanges d'histoire des religions offerts à Henri-Charles Puech* (Paris: Presses Universitaires de France, 1974) 187-89.

Daube, D., *The New Testament and Rabbinic Judaism* (London: Athlone, 1956).

Dauer, A., *Die Passionsgeschichte im Johannesevangelium: Eine traditionsgeschichtliche und theologische Untersuchung zu John 18,1–19,30* (SANT; München: Kösel, 1972).

———, *Johannes und Lukas: Untersuchungen zu den johanneisch-lukanischen Parallelperikopen Joh 4,46-54/Luke 7,1-10 — Joh 12,1-8/Luke 7,36-50; 10,38-42 — Joh 20,19-29/Luke 24,36-49* (FB 50; Würzburg: Echter, 1984).

———, "Zur Herkunft der Tomas Perikope Joh 20, 24-29," in *Biblische Randbemerkungen: Schülerfestschrift für Rudolf Schnackenburg zum 60. Geburtstag* (H. Merklein and J. Lange, eds.; Würzburg: Echter Verlag, 1974) 56-76.

Davies, S., "Christology and Protology of the Gospel of John," *JBL* 111 (1992) 663-83.

Davis, J. A., *Wisdom and Spirit: An Investigation of 1 Corinthians 1.18–3.20 against the Background of Jewish Sapiential Traditions in the Greco-Roman Period* (Lanham, MD: University Press of America, 1984).

de Boer, M. C., *Johannine Perspectives on the Death of Jesus* (Contributions to Biblical Exegesis and Theology 17; Kampen: Kok Pharos, 1996).

———, "The Death of Jesus Christ and His Coming in the Flesh (1 John 4:2)," *NovT* 23, 4 (1991) 326-46.

———, "Narrative Criticism, Historical Criticism, and the Gospel of John," *JSNT* 47 (1992) 35-48.

de Jonge, M., *The Testaments of the Twelve Patriarchs: A Study of Their Text, Composition, and Origin* (Leiden: E. J. Brill, 1953).

——— (ed.), *Studies on the Testaments of the Twelve Patriarchs* (SVTP 3; Leiden: E. J. Brill, 1975).

——— (ed.), *L'Évangile de Jean: Sources, Rédaction, Théologie* (BETL 44; Gembloux: Duculot, 1977).

———, *Jesus: Stranger from Heaven and Son of God* (SBLSBS 11: Missoula: Scholars Press, 1977).

———, *The Testaments of the Twelve Patriarchs: A Commentary* (Leiden: E. J. Brill, 1985).

———, *Christology in Context* (Philadelphia: Westminster, 1988).

———, *Jewish Eschatology, Early Christian Christology and The Testaments of the Twelve Patriarchs* (Leiden: E. J. Brill, 1991).

———, *God's Final Envoy: Early Christology and Jesus' Own View of His Mission* (Grand Rapids: Eerdmans, 1998).

———, "The Use of the Word 'Anointed' in the Time of Jesus," *NovT* 8 (1966) 132-48.

——— and A. S. van der Woude, "11Q Melchizedek and the New Testament," *NTS* 12 (1966) 301-26.

———, "Nicodemus and Jesus: Some Observations on Misunderstanding and Understanding in the Fourth Gospel," *BJRL* 53 (1971) 337-59.

———, "The Interpretation of the *Testaments of the Twelve Patriarchs* in Recent Years," in *Studies on the Testaments of the Twelve Patriarchs* (SVTP 3; M. de Jonge, ed.; Leiden: E. J. Brill, 1975) 183-92.

———, "Christian Influence in the *Testaments of the Twelve Patriarchs*," in *Studies on the*

Testaments of the Twelve Patriarchs (SVTP 3; M. de Jonge, ed.; Leiden: E. J. Brill, 1975) 193-246.

———, "Signs and Works in the Fourth Gospel," in *Miscellanea Neotestamentica* (T. Baarda, A. F. J. Klijn, and W. C. van Unnik, eds.; Leiden: E. J. Brill, 1975) 107-25.

———, "The Beloved Disciple and the Date of the Gospel of John," in *Text and Interpretation: Festschrift für M. Black* (E. Best and R. McL. Wilson, eds.; Cambridge: Cambridge University Press, 1979) 99-114.

———, "The Main Issues in the Study of the *Testaments of the Twelve Patriarchs*," NTS 26 (1980) 508-24.

———, "Jesus's Death for Others and the Death of the Maccabean Martyrs," in *Text and Testimony: Festschrift A. F. J. Klijn* (T. Baarda et al., eds.; Kampen: Kok, 1988) 142-51.

———, "The Earliest Christian Use of *Christos*: Some Suggestions," in *Jewish Eschatology, Early Christian Christology and The Testaments of the Twelve Patriarchs* (Collected Essays) 102-24.

———, "The Role of Intermediaries in God's Final Intervention in the Future according to the Qumran Scrolls," in *Jewish Eschatology* 28-47.

———, "The Conflict between Jesus and the Jews and the Radical Christology of the Fourth Gospel," *Perspectives in Religious Studies* 20, 4 (1993) 341-55.

de la Potterie, I., *La vérité dans Saint Jean*, 2 vols. Vol. 1, *Le Christ et la vérité* (AnBib 73); vol. 2, *L'Esprit et la vérité* (AnBib 74; Rome: Pontifical Biblical Institute, 1977).

———, "Naître de l'eau et naître de l'esprit," *Sciences ecclésiastiques* 14 (1962) 417-43.

———, "L'impeccabilité," in *La vie selon l'esprit* (Paris: Gabalda, 1965) 194-204.

———, "Je suis la voie, la vérité, et la vie (Jn 14,6)," *NRTh* 88 (1966) 917-42.

———, "Ad Dialogum Jesu cum Nicodemo (Jo. 2,23–3,21)," *VD* 46 (1969) 141-50.

———, "Parole et Esprit dans S. Jean," in *L'Évangile de Jean* (M. de Jonge, ed.) 177-201.

———, "Genèse de la foi pascale d'après Jn. 20," *NTS* 30 (1983) 26-49.

———, "'Nous adorons ce que nous connaissons, car le salut vient des Juifs': Histoire de l'exégèse et interpretation de Jn. 4:22," *Bib* 64 (1983) 74-115.

Dekker, C., "Grundschrift und Redaktion im Johannesevangelium," *NTS* 13 (1966-67) 66-80.

Delff, H. K. H., *Die Geschichte des Rabbi Jesus von Nazareth* (Leipzig: W. Friedrich, 1889).

Denaux, A. (ed.), *John and the Synoptics* (BETL 44; Leuven: Leuven University Press, 1992).

Derrett, J. D. M., *Law in the New Testament* (London: Darton, Longman & Todd, 1970).

———, "Law in the New Testament: The Story of the Woman Taken in Adultery," *NTS* 10 (1963-64) 1-26.

———, "The Parable of the Wicked Vinedressers," in *Law in the New Testament* 286-312.

———, "Water into Wine," *BZ* n.f. 7 (1963) 80-97.

de Sion, A., *La Forteresse Antonia à Jérusalem et la question du prétoire* (Jerusalem: Franciscan Press, 1956).

Dettwiler, A., *Die Gegenwart des Erhöhten: Eine exegetische Studie zu den johanneischen Abschiedsreden (Joh 13,31–16,33) unter besonderer Berücksichtigung ihres Relecture-Charakters* (FRLANT 169; Göttingen: Vandenhoeck & Ruprecht, 1995).

DeVillers, L., "Les Trois Témoins: Une Structure pour le quatrième Évangile," *RB* 101 (1997) 40-87.

———, "La Lettre de Soumaïos et les *Ioudaioi* johanniques," *RB* 105 (1998) 556-81.

———, Une piscine peut en chacher une autre, propos de Jean 5,1-9a," *RB* 106 (1999) 175-205.

Dexinger, F., *Der Taheb: Ein "messianischer" Heilsbringer der Samaritaner* (Kairos, Religions-wissenschaftliche Studien 3; Saltzburg: O. Müller, 1986).

Dey, J., *ΠΑΛΙΝΓΕΝΕΣΙΑ: Ein Beitrag zur Klärung der religionsgeschichtlichen Bedeutung von Tit 3,5* (NTAbh 17, 5; Münster: Aschendorff, 1937).

Díaz, J. R., "Palestinian Targum and New Testament," *NovT* 6 (1963) 75-80.

Diebold-Scheuerman, C., *Jesus vor Pilatus: Eine exegetische Untersuchung zum Verhör durch Pilatus (John 18,28–19,16a)* (SBB 32; Stuttgart: Katholisches Bibelwerk, 1996).

Dietzfelbinger, C., *Der Abschied des Kommenden: Eine Auslegung der johanneischen Abschiedsreden* (WUNT 2/95; Tübingen: J. C. B. Mohr [P. Siebeck], 1997).

———, "Die Grossen Werke (John 14:12f.), *NTS* 35, 1 (1989) 24-47.

Dockx, S., *Chronologies néotestamentaires et vie de l'église primitive: Recherches exégétiques* (Paris/Gembloux: Duculot, 1976).

Dodd, C. H., *The Interpretation of the Fourth Gospel* (Cambridge: Cambridge University Press, 1953).

———, *Historical Tradition in the Fourth Gospel* (Cambridge: Cambridge University Press, 1965).

———, "Dialogue Form in the Gospels," *BJRL* 37 (1954-55) 54-67.

———, "Some Johannine 'Herrenworte' with Parallels in the Synoptic Gospels," *NTS* 2 (1955/1956) 75-86.

———, "Behind a Johannine Dialogue," Chapter 4 of *More New Testament Studies* (Grand Rapid: Eerdmans, 1968) 41-57 (originally published as "L'arrière-plan d'un dialogue johannique," *RHPR* 1 [1957] 5-17).

———, "The Prophecy of Caiaphas: John 11,47-53," in *More New Testament Studies* 58-68.

———, "A Hidden Parable in the Fourth Gospel," in *More New Testament Studies* 30-40.

Douglas, M., *Natural Symbols* (New York: Pantheon Books, 1982).

Dozeman, T. B., "*Sperma Abraam* in John 8 and Related Literature: Cosmology and Judgment," *CBQ* 42 (1980) 342-48.

Dreyfus, P., "Le thème de l'héritage dans l'Ancien Testament," *RSPT* 42 (1958) 3-49.

Dunderberg, I., *Johannes und die Synoptiker: Studien zu Joh 1–9* (Annales Academiae Scientiarum Fennicae; Dissertationes Humanarum Litterarum 69; Helsinki: Suomalainen Tiedeakatemia, 1994).

———, "John and Thomas in Conflict?" in *The Nag Hammadi Library after Fifty Years* (J. D. Turner and A. McGuire, eds.; Proceedings of the 1995 Society of Biblical Literature Commemoration; Leiden: E. J. Brill, 1997) 361-80.

Dunn, J. D. G., *Unity and Diversity in the New Testament* (2d ed.; London: SCM/Philadelphia: Trinity Press International, 1990).

———, *The Parting of the Ways* (Philadelphia: Trinity Press International, 1991).

——— (ed.), *Jews and Christians: The Parting of the Ways A.D. 70 to 135* (Wissenschaftliche Untersuchungen zum Neuen Testament 1; Reihe 66; Tübingen: J. C. B. Mohr [P. Siebeck], 1992).

———, *Jesus and the Spirit* (Grand Rapids: Eerdmans, 1997).

———, "John and the Oral Gospel Tradition," in *Jesus and the Oral Gospel Tradition* (H. Wansbrough, ed.; JSNTSup 64; Sheffield: JSOT, 1991) 351-79.

———, "The Question of Anti-Semitism in the New Testament," in *Jews and Christians: The Parting of the Ways A.D. 70 to 135* (WUNT 1; Reihe 66; Tübingen: J. C. B. Mohr [P. Siebeck], 1992) 177-211.

———, "The Embarrassment of History: Reflections on the Problem of 'Anti-Judaism' in the Fourth Gospel," in *Anti-Judaism and the Fourth Gospel* (R. Bieringer, D. Pollefeyt, and F. Vandecasteele-Vanneuville, eds.) 47-67.

Dupont, J., "'Béatitudes' égyptiennes," *Bib* 47 (1966) 185-222.

Duprez, A., *Jesus et les dieux guérisseurs* (CahRB 12; Paris: Gabalda, 1970).

———, "Probatique (Piscine)," *DBSup* 8, cols. 606-21.

Du Rand, J. A., "A Syntactical and Narratological Reading of John 10 in Coherence with Chapter 9," in *The Shepherd Discourse of John 10 and Its Context* (J. Beutler and R. Fortna, eds.; Cambridge: Cambridge University Press, 1991) 94-115.

Edwards, D. R., and McCulloch, C. T., *Archaeology and the Galilee: Texts and Contexts in the Graeco-Roman and Byzantine Periods* (South Florida Studies in Judaism, no. 143; Miami: University of Southern Florida Press, 1997).

Edwards, W. D., Gabel, W. J., and Hosmer, F. E., "On the Physical Death of Jesus Christ," *JAMA* 255 (1986) 1455-63.

Ehrmann, B. D., *The Orthodox Corruption of Scripture* (New York: Oxford University Press, 1993).

———, "Jesus and the Adulteress," *NTS* 34 (1988) 24-44.

Eisler, R., *Orpheus, The Fisher: Comparative Studies in Orphic and Early Christian Cult Symbolism* (London: J. M. Watkins, 1921).

Emerton, J. A., "Some New Testament Notes," *JTS* 11 (1960) 329-32.

———, "Binding and Loosing — Forgiving and Retaining," *JTS* 13 (1962) 325-31.

Ensor, P. W., *Jesus and His "Works": The Johannine Sayings in Historical Perspective* (WUNT 2/85; Tübingen: J. C. B. Mohr [P. Siebeck], 1996).

Eslinger, L., "The Wooing of the Woman at the Well: Jesus, the Reader and Reader-Response Criticism," *Literature and Theology* 1 (1987) 167-83.

Evans, C. A. (and Stinespring, W. F., eds.), *Early Jewish and Christian Exegesis: Studies in Memory of William Hugh Brownlee* (Atlanta: Scholars Press, 1987).

——— (and D. A. Hagner, eds.), *Faith and Polemic: Studies in Anti-Semitism and Early Christianity* (Minneapolis: Fortress, 1992).

———, "On the Quotation Formulas in the Fourth Gospel," *BZ* (n.f.) 26 (1982) 79-82.

———, "Obduracy and the Lord's Servant: Some Observations on the Use of the Old Testament in the Fourth Gospel," in *Early Jewish and Christian Exegesis* (C. A. Evans and W. F. Stinespring, eds.) 221-36.

———, "On the Prologue of John and the Trimorphic Protennoia," *NTS* 27, 3 (April 1981) 395-401.

Farmer, W. R. (ed.), *Anti-Judaism and the Gospels* (Harrisburg, PA: Trinity Press International, 1999).

———, "The Palm Branches in John 12,13," *JTS* 3 (1952) 62-66.

Faure, A., "Die alttestamentlichen Zitate im 4. Evangelium und die Quellenscheidungshypothese," *ZNW* 21 (1922) 99-121.

Articles and Monographs on the Gospel of John

Fee, G. D., "On the Text and Meaning of John 20:30-31," in *The Four Gospels 1992* (F. van Segbroeck et al., eds.) 2193-2205.

Fehribach, A., *The Women in the Life of the Bridegroom* (Collegeville, MN: Liturgical Press, 1998).

Felton, T., and Thatcher, T., "Stylometry and the Fourth Gospel," in *Jesus and the Johannine Tradition* (Fortna, R., and Thatcher, T., eds.; Louisville: Westminster John Knox, 2001) 209-18.

Fennema, D. A., "John 1:18: 'God the Only Son,'" *NTS* 31 (1985) 121-35.

Fensham, F. C., "Love in the Writings of Qumran and John," *Neotestamentica* 6 (1972) 67-77.

Feuillet, A., *Johannine Studies* (Staten Island: Alba House, 1965).

———, "La signification théologique du second miracle de Cana (Jo. IV.46-54)," *RSR* 48 (1960) 62-75.

———, "Les *ego eimi* christologiques du quatrième évangile," *RevScRel* 44 (1966) 5-22.

———, "The Structure of First John: Comparison with the Fourth Gospel," *BTB* 3 (1973) 194-216.

Finegan, J., *Handbook of Biblical Chronology* (Princeton: Princeton University Press, 1964).

Fisher, G., *Die himmlische Wohnungen: Untersuchungen zu John 14,2f* (Bern/Frankfurt: Lang, 1975).

Fitzmyer, J., *A Wandering Aramean: Collected Essays* (SBLMS 25; Missoula, MT: Scholars Press, 1979).

———, *The Gospel according to Luke* (AB 28, 28a; Garden City, NY: Doubleday, 1985).

———, *The Dead Sea Scrolls: Major Publications and Tools for Study* (2d ed.; Atlanta: Scholars Press, 1990).

———, *Romans* (AB 33; Garden City, NY: Doubleday, 1993).

———, *The Dead Sea Scrolls and Christian Origins* (Grand Rapids: Eerdmans, 2000).

———, "The Use of Explicit Old Testament Quotations in Qumran Literature and in the New Testament," *NTS* 7 (1960-61) 297-333.

———, "Crucifixion in Ancient Palestine, Qumran Literature, and the New Testament," *CBQ* 40 (1978) 493-513.

———, "The Aramaic 'Son of God' Text from Qumran Cave 4," in *Methods of Investigation of the Dead Sea Scrolls and the Khirbet Qumran Site* (M. W. Wise, ed.; New York: New York Academy of Sciences, 1994) 163-78.

———, "Qumran Messianism," Chapter 5 of *The Dead Sea Scrolls and Christian Origins* (Grand Rapids: Eerdmans, 2000) 73-110.

———, "A Palestinian Jewish Collection of Beatitudes," Chapter 6 of *The Dead Sea Scrolls and Christian Origins* 111-18.

Flusser, D., *Judaism and the Origins of Christianity* (Jerusalem: Magnes, 1988).

Forestell, T., *The Word of the Cross: Salvation as Revelation in the Fourth Gospel* (AnBib 57; Rome: Pontifical Biblical Institute, 1974).

Fortna, R. T., *The Gospel of Signs: A Reconstruction of the Narrative Source Underlying the Fourth Gospel* (SNTSMS 11; Cambridge: Cambridge University Press, 1970).

———, *The Fourth Gospel and Its Predecessor: From Narrative Source to Present Gospel* (Philadelphia: Fortress, 1988).

——— (and Gaventa, B., eds.), *The Conversation Continues: Studies in Paul and John in Honor of J. Louis Martyn* (Nashville: Abingdon, 1990).

——— (and Thatcher, T., eds.) *Jesus in the Johannine Tradition* (Louisville: Westminster/John Knox, 2001).

———, "Source and Redaction in the Fourth Gospel's Portrayal of Jesus' Signs," *JBL* 89 (1970) 151-66.

———, "From Christology to Soteriology: A Redaction-Critical Study of Salvation in the Fourth Gospel," *Int* 27 (1973) 31-47.

———, "The Theological Use of Locale in the Fourth Gospel," *AThRSup* 3 (1974) 58-94.

———, "Christology in the Fourth Gospel: Redaction-Critical Perspectives," *NTS* 21 (1974-75) 489-504.

———, "Jesus and Peter at the High Priest's House: A Test Case for the Relation between Mark's and John's Gospels," *NTS* 18 (1978-79) 371-83.

Fossum, J., *The Name of God and the Angel of the Lord: Samaritan and Jewish Concepts of Intermediation and the Origin of Gnosticism* (WUNT 36; Tübingen: J. C. B. Mohr [P. Siebeck], 1985).

Franke, A. H., *Das alte Testament bei Johannes: Ein Beitrag zur Erklärung und Beurteilung der johanneischen Schriften* (Göttingen: Vandenhoeck & Ruprecht, 1885).

Freed, E. D., *Old Testament Quotations in the Gospel of John* (NovTSup 11; Leiden, E. J. Brill, 1965).

———, "Variations in the Language and Thought of John," *ZNW* 55 (1965) 167-97.

———, "The Son of Man in the Fourth Gospel," *JBL* 86 (1967) 402-9.

———, "The Manner of Worship in John 4.23f.," in *Search the Scriptures: New Testament Studies in Honor of Raymond T. Stamm* (Gettysburg Theological Studies 3; Leiden: E. J. Brill, 1969) 33-48.

Frey, J., *Die johanneische Eschatologie*. Vol. 1: *Ihre Probleme im Spiegel der Forschung seit Reimarus*; vol. 2: *Das johanneische Zeitverständnis*; vol. 3: *Die eschatologische Verkündigung in den johanneischen Texten* (WUNT 96, 110, 117; Tübingen: J. C. B. Mohr [P. Siebeck], 1997, 1998, 1999).

———, and J. Schröter (eds.), *Deutungen des Todes Jesu im Neuen Testament* (WUNT 181; Tübingen: J. C. B. Mohr [P. Siebeck], 2005).

———, "Different Patterns of Dualistic Thought in the Qumran Library," in *Legal Texts and Legal Issues* (M. Bernstein, F. García-Martinez, and J. Kampen, eds.; STDJ XXIII; Leiden: E. J. Brill, 1995) 275-335.

Freyne, S., *Galilee from Alexander the Great to Hadrian, 323 B.C.E. to 135 C.E.* (Notre Dame: University of Notre Dame Press, 1980).

———, "Vilifying the Other and Defining the Self: Matthew's and John's Anti-Jewish Polemic in Focus," in *To See Ourselves as Others See Us: Christians, Jews, 'Others' in Late Antiquity* (J. Neusner and E. S. Frerichs, eds.; Chico: Scholars Press, 1985) 117-43.

———, "Archaeology and the Historical Jesus," in *Archaeology and Biblical Interpretation* (J. R. Bartlett, ed.; London: Routledge, 1997) 117-44.

Friedrich, G., *Die Verkündigung des Todes Jesu im Neuen Testament* (Biblisch-Theologische Studien 2; Neukirchen/Vluyn: Neukirchener, 1982).

Fuller, R. H., *The Foundations of New Testament Christology* (New York: Scribner's, 1965).

——— (ed.), *Essays on the Love Commandment* (Philadelphia: Fortress, 1978).
———, *The Formation of the Resurrection Narratives* (2d ed.; New York: Macmillan, 1980).
———, "The 'Jews' in the Fourth Gospel," *Dialog* 16 (1977) 31-37.
———, "John 20:19-23," *Int* 32 (1978) 180-84.
———, "Higher and Lower Christology in the Fourth Gospel," in *The Conversation Continues: Studies in Paul and John in Honor of J. Louis Martyn* (R. T. Fortna and B. R. Gaventa, eds.; Nashville: Abingdon, 1990) 357-65.
———, "Lord," *HDB*.
Funk, R. W., "Papyrus Bodmer II (P66) and John 8,25," *HTR* 51 (1958) 95-100.
Gächter, P., "Das dreifache 'Weide meine Lämmer,'" *ZKT* 69 (1947) 328-44.
———, "Zur Form von Joh 5,19-30," *Neutestamentliche Aufsätze: Festschrift für Prof. Josef Schmid zum 70. Geburtstag* (J. Blinzler, O. Kuss, and F. Mussner, eds.; Regensburg: Friedrich Pustet, 1963) 65-68.
Gardner-Smith, P., *Saint John and the Synoptic Gospels* (Cambridge: Cambridge University Press, 1938).
Garnet, P., *Salvation and Atonement in the Qumran Scrolls* (WUNT 2; Tübingen: Mohr, 1977).
Giblin, C. H., "Suggestion, Negative Response, and Positive Action in St. John's Gospel (John 2.1-11; 4.46-54; 7.2-14; 11.1-44)," *NTS* 26 (1979-80) 197-211.
———, "The Tripartite Narrative Structure of John's Gospel," *Bib* 71 (1990) 449-67.
Gibson, S., "The Pool of Bethesda in Jerusalem and Jewish Purification Practices of the Second Temple Period," *Proche-Orient Chrétien* 55 (2005) 270-93.
Glasson, T. F., *Moses in the Fourth Gospel* (SBT 40; London: SCM, 1963).
Goodman, P., *The Sukkot and Simhat Torah Anthology* (Philadelphia: Jewish Publication Society of America, 1973).
Gourbillon, J. G., "La parabole du serpent d'airain," *RB* 51 (1942) 213-26.
Gourgues, M., "Cinquante ans de recherche johannique," Chapter 7 of *Des Bien des Manières* (Lectio Divina 163; Montreal: Fides, 1995) 229-306.
Granskou, D., "Anti-Judaism in the Passion Accounts of the Fourth Gospel," in *Anti-Judaism in Early Christianity*, vol. 1: *Paul and the Gospels* (P. Richardson and D. Granskou, eds.; Studies in Christianity and Judaism 2; Waterloo: Wilfrid Laurier, 1986) 201-16.
Grant, R. M., "The Fourth Gospel and the Church," *HTR* 35 (1942) 95-116.
———, "One Hundred Fifty-Three Large Fish (John 21:11)," *HTR* 42 (1949) 273-76.
———, "Scripture and Tradition in St. Ignatius of Antioch," *CBQ* 25 (1963) 322-35.
Grässer, E., "Die antijudische Polemik im Johannesevangelium," *NTS* 10 (1964-65) 74-90.
———, "Die Juden als Teufelssöhne in Johannes 8,37-42," in *Antijudaïsmus im neuen Testament* (W. P. Eckert, N. P. Levinson, and M. Stohr, eds.; Münich: Kaiser, 1967) 157-70.
Greenhut, Z., "The 'Caiaphas' Tomb in North Talpiot, Jerusalem," *Atiqot* (English Series) 21 (1992) 63-71.
———, "Burial Cave of the Caiaphas Family," *BAR*, September/October 1992, 28-36, 76.
Grelot, P., *Les Juifs dans l'Évangile selon Jean: Enquête historique et réflexion théologique* (CahRB 34; Paris: Gabalda, 1995).

Bibliography

———, "L'interpretation pénitentielle du lavement des pieds," in *L'homme devant Dieu: Mélange H. de Lubach* (2 vols.; Paris: Aubier, 1963) 1, 75-91.

Grigsby, B., "The Cross as an Expiatory Sacrifice in the Fourth Gospel," *JSNT* 15 (1982) 51-80.

———, "Washing in the Pool of Siloam — A Thematic Anticipation of the Johannine Cross," *NovT* 27 (1985) 227-35.

Grossouw, W., "The Dead Sea Scrolls and the New Testament," *Studia Catholica* 26 (1951) 289-99 and 27 (1952) 1-9.

Gubler, M. L., *Die frühesten Deutungen des Todes Jesu* (Oriens Biblicus et Orientalis 15: Freiburg/Göttingen, 1977).

Guevara, H., *Ambiente político del pueblo judío en tiempos de Jesús* (Madrid: Chrístiandad, 1985).

Guilding, A., *The Fourth Gospel and Jewish Worship: A Study of the Relation of St. John's Gospel to the Ancient Jewish Lectionary System* (Oxford: Clarendon, 1960).

Gutbrod, W., "*Ioudaios, Israel, Hebraios* in the New Testament," *TDNT* 3, 375-91.

Haacker, K., "Gottesdienst ohne Gotteserkenntnis: Joh 4,22 vor dem Hintergrund des jüdisch-samaritanischen Auseinandersetzung," in *Wort und Wirklichkeit: Studien zur Afrikanistick und Orientalistik Eugen Ludwig Rapp zum 70. Geburtstag Herausgegeben* (B. Benzing, O. Böcher, and G. Mayer, eds.; Meisenheim: Hain, 1976) 110-26.

Haenchen, E., *Gott und Mensch: Gesammelte Aufsätze* (Tübingen: J. C. B. Mohr [P. Siebeck], 1965).

———, "Johanneische Probleme," *ZKT* 56 (1959) 19-54.

———, "'Der Vater der mich gesandt hat,'" *NTS* 9 (1962-63) 208-16.

———, "History and Interpretation in the Johannine Passion Narrative," *Int* 24 (1970) 198-219.

———, "Jesus vor Pilatus (Joh 18,28–19,15)," in *Gott und Mensch* 144-56.

Hahn, F., *The Titles of Jesus in Christology* (New York: World Publishing Company, 1969).

———, "Der Prozess Jesu nach dem Johannesevangelium," *EKKNT* Vorarbeiten 2 (Neukirchen-Vluyn: Neukirchener, 1970) 23-96.

———, "'Das Heil kommt von den Juden': Erwägungen zu John 4,22b," in *Wort und Wirklichkeit: Studien zur Afrikanistick und Orientalistik Eugen Ludwig Rapp zum 70. Geburtstag Herausgegeben* (B. Benzing, O. Böcher, and G. Mayer, eds.; Meisenheim: Hain, 1976) 110-26.

———, "'Die Juden' im Johannesevangelium," in *Kontinuität und Einheit: Für Franz Mussner* (P.-G. Müller and W. Stenger, eds.; Freiburg: Herder, 1981) 430-38.

Hall, B. W., *Samaritan Religion from John Hyrcanus to Baba Rabba: A Critical Examination of the Relevant Material in Contemporary Christian Literature, the Writings of Josephus, and the Mishnah* (Studies in Judaica 3; Sydney: Sydney University Press, 1987).

Hamerton-Kelly, R. G., *Pre-Existence, Wisdom and the Son of Man: A Study of the Idea of Pre-Existence in the New Testament* (SNTSMS 21; Cambridge: Cambridge University Press, 1973).

Hanson, A., "John's Citation of Psalm LXXXII Reconsidered," *NTS* 13 (1966-67) 363-67.

———, "The Old Testament Background to the Raising of Lazarus," in *SE VI* (E. A.

Livingstone, ed.; Texte und Untersuchungen zur Geschichte der altchristlichen Literatur 112; Berlin: Akademie, 1973) 252-55.
Harrington, D. J., *Wisdom Texts from Qumran* (London and New York: Routledge, 1996).
―――, "The Problem of 'the Jews' in John's Gospel," *Explorations* 8 (1994) 3-4.
Hartmann, G., "Die Vorlage der Osterberichte in Joh 20," *ZNW* (1964) 197-220.
Harvey, A. E., *Jesus on Trial: A Study in the Fourth Gospel* (London: SPCK, 1976).
Harvey, G., *The True Israel: Uses of the Names Jew, Hebrew and Israel in Ancient Jewish and Early Christian Literature* (AGJU 35; Leiden: E. J. Brill, 1996).
Hasitschka, M., "Die Parakletworte im Johannesevangelium: Versuch einer Auslegung in synchroner Testbetrachtung," *SUNT* 18 (1993) 97-112.
―――, "Die beiden 'Zeichen' am See von Tiberias: Interpretation von Joh 6 in Verbindung mit Joh 21,1-14," *Studien zum Neuen Testament und seiner Umwelt* 24 (1999) 85-102.
Hatina, T. R., "John 20,22 in Its Eschatological Context: Promise or Fulfillment?" *Bib* 74 (1993) 196-219.
Hauck, F., *"Makarios," TDNT* 4, 362-64.
Hauschild, W. D., *Gottes Geist und der Menschen: Studien zur frühchristlichen Pneumatologie* (BEvT 63: München: Kaiser, 1972).
Hawkin, D. J., *The Johannine World: Reflections on the Theology of the Fourth Gospel and Contemporary Society* (SUNY Series in Religious Studies; Albany: State University of New York, 1996).
Heekerens, H.-P., *Die Zeichen-Quelle der johanneischen Redaktion: Ein Beitrag zur Entstehungsgeschichte des vierten Evangeliums* (Stuttgart: Katholisches Bibelwerk, 1984).
Heil, J. P., *Blood and Water: The Death and Resurrection of Jesus in John 18–21* (CBQMS 27; Washington, DC: Catholic Biblical Association of America, 1995).
―――, "The Story of Jesus and the Adulteress (John 7,53–8,11) Reconsidered," *Bib* 72 (1991) 182-91.
―――, "A Rejoinder to 'Reconsidering "The Story of the Adulteress Reconsidered,"'" *Église et Théologie* 25 (1994) 361-66.
Heiligenthal, R., *Werke als Zeichen* (WUNT 2/9; Tübingen: J. C. B. Mohr [P. Siebeck], 1983).
Heise, J., *Bleiben: Menein in den johanneischen Schriften* (HUT 8; Tübingen: J. C. B. Mohr [P. Siebeck], 1967).
Hellig, J., "The Negative Image of the Jew and Its New Testament Roots," *JTSA* 64 (1988) 39-48.
Hengel, M., *Crucifixion* (Philadelphia: Fortress, 1977).
―――, *The Atonement* (Philadelphia: Fortress; London: SCM, 1981).
―――, *The Johannine Question* (Philadelphia/London: Trinity Press International/SCM, 1991).
―――, *Studies in Early Christology* (Edinburgh: T&T Clark, 1995).
―――, "The Kingdom of Christ in John," Chapter 6 of *Studies in Early Christology* (Edinburgh: T&T Clark, 1995) 333-57.
Herrojo, J., *Caná de Galilea y su localización: Un examen crítico de las fuentes* (Paris: J. Gabalda, 1999).
Hiebert, D. E., "An Exposition of 1 John 2:29–3:10," *BSac* 146 (1989) 198-216.

Bibliography

Hill, C. E., *The Johannine Corpus in the Early Church* (Oxford: Oxford University Press, 2004).

———, "What Papias Said about John (and Luke): A New 'Papian Fragment,'" *JTS* n.s. 49 (1998) 582-629.

Hill, R. A., *An Examination and Critique of the Understanding of the Relationship between Apocalypticism and Gnosticism in Johannine Studies* (Lewiston, NY: Mellen, 1997).

Himmelfarb, M., *Ascent to Heaven in Jewish and Christian Apocalypses* (Oxford: Oxford University Press, 1993).

Hirsch, E., *Studien zum vierten Evangelium* (BHT 11; Tübingen: J. C. B. Mohr [P. Siebeck], 1936).

———, *Das vierte Evangelium in seiner ursprünglichen Gestalt* (Tübingen: J. C. B. Mohr [P. Siebeck], 1936).

———, "Stilkritik und Literaranalyse im vierten Evangelium," *ZNW* 43 (1950-51) 128-43.

Hoegen-Rohls, C., *Der nachösterliche Johannes: Die Abschiedsreden als hermeneutischer Schlüssel zum vierten Evangelium* (WUNT 2/84; Tübingen: J. C. B. Mohr [P. Siebeck], 1996).

Hoffman, D., "The Authority of Scripture and Apostolic Doctrine in Ignatius of Antioch," *JETS* 28 (1985) 71-79.

Hofius, O. (and Kammler, H.-C., eds.), *Johannesstudien: Untersuchungen zur Theologie des vierten Evangeliums* (WUNT 2/88; Tübingen: J. C. B. Mohr [P. Siebeck], 1996).

———, "'Er gibt den Geist ohne Mass' Joh 3,34b," *ZNW* 90 (1999) 131-34.

Hofrichter, P. L., *Modell und Vorlage der Synoptiker: Das vorredaktionelle "Johannesevangelium"* (Theologische Texte und Studien 6; Hildesheim: Georg Olms, 1997).

Holwerda, D. L., *The Holy Spirit and Eschatology in the Gospel of St. John* (Kampen: Kok, 1959).

Holzmann, H. J., "Über das Problem des ersten johanneischen Briefes in seinem Verhältnis zum Evangelium," *Jahrbuch für Protestantische Theologie*, Art. I in 7 (1881) 690-712; Art. II in 8 (1882) 128-52; Art. III in 8 (1882) 316-42; Art. IV in 8 (1882) 460-85.

———, "Unordnungen und Ordnungen im vierten Evangelium," *ZNW* 3 (1902) 50-60.

Hooker, M., "The Johannine Prologue and the Messianic Secret," *NTS* 21 (1974/75) 40-58.

Horbury, W., "The Benediction of the *minim* and Early Jewish Christianity," *JTS* 33, 1 (1982) 19-61.

———, "The 'Caiaphas' Ossuaries and Joseph Caiaphas," *PEQ* 126 (1994) 32-48.

Horsley, G. H., *New Documents Illustrating Early Christianity* (New Ryde, N.S.W.: Macquarie University, 1981-86).

Horsley, R., "Popular Messianic Movements around the Time of Jesus," *CBQ* 46 (1984) 471-95.

———, "'Like One of the Prophets of Old': Two Types of Popular Prophets at the Time of Jesus," *CBQ* 47 (1985) 435-63.

Huber, K., "Theologie als Topologie: Bemerkungen zum Raumkonzept von Joh 1,43-51," *ZKT* 3 (1999) 300-310.

Hultgren, A., "The Johannine Footwashing (13, 1-11) as a Symbol of Eschatological Hospitality," *NTS* 28 (1982) 539-46.

Articles and Monographs on the Gospel of John

Ibuki, Y., "*kai tēn phōnēn autou akoueis:* Gedankenaufbau und Hintergrund des 3. Kapitels des Johannesevangelium," *Bulletin of Seikei University* 14 (1978) 9-33.

Jasper, A., *The Shining Garment of the Text: Gendered Readings of John's Prologue* (JSNTSup 165; Gender, Culture, Theory 6; Sheffield: Sheffield Academic Press, 1998).

Jaubert, A., *The Date of the Last Supper* (ET; Staten Island, NY: Alba House, 1965).

Jeremias, J., *The Rediscovery of Bethesda, John 5:2* (New Testament Archaeology Monographs 1; Louisville: Southern Baptist Theological Seminary, 1966).

———, *The Eucharistic Words of Jesus* (3d ed.; New York: Scribner's, 1966).

———, *Jerusalem in the Time of Jesus* (Philadelphia: Fortress, 1969).

———, "Zur Geschichtlichkeit des Verhörs Jesu vor dem hohen Rat," *ZNW* 43 (1950-51) 145-50.

Jocz, J., *The Jewish People and Jesus Christ* (London: SPCK, 1964).

———, "Die Juden im Johannesevangelium," *Judaica* 9 (1953) 129-42.

Johansson, N., *Paracletoi: Vorstellungen von Fürsprechern für die Menschen vor Gott in der alttestamentlichen Religion, im Spätjudentum und Urchristentum* (Lund: Gleerup, 1940).

Johnston, G., *The Spirit-Paraclete in the Gospel of John* (NTSMS 12; Cambridge: Cambridge University Press, 1970).

Johnson, L. T., "The New Testament's Anti-Jewish Slander and the Conventions of Ancient Polemic," *JBL* 108 (1989) 419-41.

Johnson, S., "Parallels between the Letters of Ignatius and the Johannine Epistles," in *Perspectives on Language and Text* (E. W. Conrad and E. G. Newing, eds.; Winona Lake: Eisenbrauns, 1987) 327-38.

Jones, L. P., *The Symbol of Water in the Gospel of John* (JSNTSup 145; Sheffield: Sheffield Academic Press, 1997).

Joulin, M., *La Passion selon saint Jean* (Paris: Desclée de Brouwer, 1997).

Käsemann, E., *The Testament of Jesus* (Philadelphia: Fortress, 1968).

Kammler, H.-C. (and Hofius, O., eds.), *Johannesstudien: Untersuchungen zur Theologie des vierten Evangeliums* (WUNT 2/88; Tübingen: J. C. B. Mohr [P. Siebeck], 1996).

———, "Jesus Christus und der Geistparaklet: Eine Studie zur johanneischen Verhältnis bestimmung von Pneumatologie und Christologie," in *Johannesstudien* 87-190.

Kaufman, P. S., *The Beloved Disciple: Witness against Anti-Semitism* (Collegeville, MN: Liturgical, 1991).

Keck, L., "Derivation as Destiny," in *Exploring the Gospel of John* (ed. R. A. Culpepper) 274-88.

Keener, C., *The Spirit in the Gospels and Acts: Divine Purity and Power* (Peabody, MA; Hendrickson, 1997).

Kelber, W. H., "Metaphysics and Marginality in John," in *What Is John? Readers and Readings of the Fourth Gospel* (F. F. Segovia, ed.; SBLSS 3; Atlanta: Scholars Press, 1996) 129-54.

Kieschke, H. G., *Rekonstruktion des Evangeliums nach St. Johannes: Ein Versuch zur Lösung des johanneischen Problems* (Frankfurt: R. G. Fischer, 1995).

Kimelman, R., "*Birkat Ha-Minim* and the Lack of Evidence for an Anti-Christian Jewish Prayer in Late Antiquity," in *Jewish and Christian Self-Definition*, vol. 2: *Aspects of*

Judaism in the Graeco-Roman Period (E. P. Sanders, ed., with A. I. Baumgarten and A. Mendelson; Philadelphia: Fortress, 1981) 226-44.

Kitzberger, I. R., "Mary of Bethany and Mary of Magdala — Two Female Characters in the Johannine Passion Narrative: A Feminist, Narrative-Critical, Reader-Response," *NTS* 41 (1995) 564-86.

Klaiber, W., "Der irdische und der himmlische Zeuge: Eine Auslegung von Joh 3.22-36," *NTS* 36 (1990) 23-34.

Klauck, H.-J., "Brudermord und Bruderliebe: Ethische Paradigmen in 1 Joh 3,11-17," in *Neues Testament und Ethik: Festschrift R. Schnackenburg* (H. Merklein, ed.; Freiburg: Herder, 1989) 151-69.

———, "Der Weggang Jesu: Neue Arbeiten zu Joh 13-17," *BZ* n.f. 40, 2 (1996) 236-50.

Klos, H., *Die Sacramente im Johannesevangelium* (SBS 46; Stuttgart: Katholisches Bibelwerk, 1970).

Knöppler, T., *Die Theologia Crucis des Johannesevangeliums: Das Verständnis des Todes Jesu im Rahmen der johanneischen Inkarnations- und Erhöhungschristologie* (WMANT 69; Neukirchen-Vluyn: Neukirchener, 1994).

Köstenberger, A. J., *The Missions of Jesus and the Disciples according to the Fourth Gospel: With Implications for the Fourth Gospel's Purpose and the Mission of the Contemporary Church* (Grand Rapids: Eerdmans, 1998).

Koester, C. R., *Symbolism in the Fourth Gospel* (Minneapolis: Fortress, 1995).

———, "The Savior of the World (John 4:42)," *JBL* 109 (1990) 665-80.

Koester, H., *Ancient Christian Gospels: Their History and Development* (Philadelphia: Trinity Press International, 1990).

———, and Robinson, J. M., *Trajectories through Early Christianity* (Philadelphia: Fortress, 1971).

———, "GNOMAI," in *Trajectories through Early Christianity* 114-57.

Koet, B. J., "'Today This Scripture Has Been Fulfilled in Your Ears': Jesus' Explanation of Scripture in Luke 4:16-30," *Bijdragen* 47 (1986) 368-94.

Kohler, H., *Kreuz und Menschwerdung im Johannesevangelium: Ein exegetisch-hermeneutischer Versuch zur johanneischen Kreuzestheologie* (ATANT 72; Zürich: Theologischer Verlag, 1987).

Konradt, M., "Menschen- oder Bruder liebe? Beobachtungen zum Liebesgebot in den Testamenten der Zwölf Patriarchen," *ZNW* 88 (1997) 296-310.

Kossen, H. B., "Who Were the Greeks of John XII 20?" in *Studies in John* (NovTSup 24; Leiden: E. J. Brill, 1970) 106-7.

Kovacs, J. L., "'Now Shall the Ruler of This World Be Driven Out': Jesus' Death as Cosmic Battle in John 12:20-36," *JBL* 114 (1995) 227-47.

Kowalski, B., *Die Hirtenrede (Joh 10,1-18) im Kontext des Johannesevangeliums* (SBB 31; Suttgart: Katholisches Bibelwerk, 1996).

Kraemer, R. S., "On the Meaning of the Term 'Jew' in Graeco-Roman Inscriptions," *HTR* 82 (1989) 35-53.

Kragerud, A., *Die Lieblingsjünger im Johannesevangelium* (Oslo: Osloer Universitätsverlag, 1959).

Kremer, J., "Jesu Verheissung des Geistes, Zur Verankerung der Aussage von Joh 16:13 im

Leben Jesu," in *Die Kirche des Anfangs* (R. Schnackenburg, J. Ernst, and J. Wanke, eds.; Erfurter Theologische Studien 38; Leipzig: St. Benno, 1977) 247-76.

Kügler, J., *Den Jünger, der Jesus Liebte: Literarische, theologische und historische Untersuchungen zu einer Schlüsselgestalt Johanneischer Theologie und Geschichte. Mit einem Excurs über die Brotrede in Joh 6* (SBB 16; Stuttgart: Katholisches Bibelwerk, 1988).

———, *Der andere König: Religionsgeschichtliche Perspektiven auf die Christologie des Johannesevangeliums* (SBS 178; Stuttgart: Katholisches Bibelwerk, 1999).

———, "In Tat und Wahrheit: Zur Problemlage des Ersten Johannesbriefes," *BN* 48 (1989) 61-88.

Kuhn, H.-J., *Christologie und Wunder: Untersuchungen zu Joh 1,35-51* (BU 18; Regensburg: Pustet, 1988).

Kuhn, H. W., *Enderwartung und gegenwärtiges Heil: Untersuchung zu den Gemeindeliedern von Qumran* (SUNT 4; Göttingen: Vandenhoeck & Ruprecht, 1966).

———, "Die in Palästina gefundenen hebräischen Texte und das Neue Testament," *ZTK* 47 (1950) 192-211.

Kuhn, K. G., "The Lord's Supper and the Communal Meal at Qumran," in *The Scrolls and the New Testament* (K. Stendahl, ed.; New York: Harper, 1957).

Kundsin, K., *Charakter und Ursprung der johanneischen Reden* (Acta Universitatis Latviensis 1; Riga: Latvijas Universitate, 1939).

———, *Topologische Überlieferungsstoffe in Johannes-Evangelium* (FRLANT 22; Göttingen: Vandenhoeck & Ruprecht, 1925).

Kurz, W. W., "Luke 22:14-38 and Greco-Roman and Biblical Farewell Addresses," *JBL* 104, 2 (1985) 251-68.

Kvalvaag, R. W., "The Spirit in Human Beings in Some Qumran Non-Biblical Texts," in *Qumran between the Old and New Testaments* (F. H. Cryer and T. L. Thompson, eds.; JSOTSup 290; Copenhagen International Seminar 6; Sheffield: Sheffield Academic Press, 1998) 159-80.

Kysar, R., *The Fourth Evangelist and His Gospel: An Examination of Contemporary Scholarship* (Minneapolis: Augsburg, 1975).

———, "The Source Analysis of the Fourth Gospel: A Growing Consensus?" *NovT* 15 (1973) 134-52.

———, "Community and Gospel: Vectors in Fourth Gospel Criticism," *Int* 31 (1977) 355-66.

———, "Anti-Semitism and the Gospel of John," in *Faith and Polemic: Studies in Anti-Semitism and Early Christianity* (C. A. Evans and D. A. Hagner, eds.) 113-27.

Labahn, M., *Jesus als Lebensspender: Untersuchungen zu einer Geschichte der johanneischen Tradition und ihrer Wundergeschichten* (BZNW 98; Berlin: de Gruyter, 1999).

Lagrange, M.-J., *Évangile selon Saint Jean* (EBib; Paris: Gabalda, 1964).

Landier, J., "Antijudaïsme de l'Évangile de Jean? Étude d'un parôle: 'Vous êtes de votre père, du diable!' Jn 8,44," *Christian Doctrine* 10 (1997) 113-28.

Langbrandtner, W., *Weltferner Gott oder Gott der Liebe: Der Ketzerstreit in der johanneischen Kirche* (BEvT 6; Frankfurt: P. Lang, 1977).

Lattke, M., *Einheit in Wort: Die spezifische Bedeutung von agapē, agapan und philein im Johannesevangelium* (SANT 41; München: Kösel, 1975).

Bibliography

———, "Joh 20,30f als Buchschluss," *ZNW* 78 (1987) 288-92.

———, "Die Messias-Stellen der Oden Salomos," in *Anfänge der Christologie: Festschrift F. Hahn* (C. Breytenbach and H. Paulsen, eds.; Göttingen: Vandenhoeck & Ruprecht, 1991).

Layton, B., "The Riddle of the Thunder," in *Nag Hammadi, Gnosticism and Early Christianity* (C. W. Hedrick and R. Godgson Jr., eds.; Peabody, MA: Hendrickson, 1986) 41-51.

Lazure, N., *Les Valeurs Morales de la théologie johannique: Évangile et Épîtres* (EBib; Paris: Gabalda, 1965).

———, "Le lavement des pieds," *AsSeign* 38 (1967) 40-51.

———, "La convoitise de la chair en I Jean II,16," *RB* 79 (1969) 161-205.

Leclercq, F., "Muratorianum," in *DACL*, vol. 12, pt. 1, cols. 543-46.

Lee, D., *The Symbolic Narratives of the Fourth Gospel: The Interplay of Form and Meaning* (JSNTSup 95; Sheffield: JSOT, 1994).

Leibig, J. E., "John and 'the Jews': Theological Antisemitism in the Fourth Gospel," *JES* 20 (1983) 209-34.

Leidig, E., *Jesu Gespräch mit der Samaritanerin und weitere Gespräche im Johannesevangelium* (Theologische Dissertationen 15; Basel: Friedrich Reinhardt, 1981).

Leistner, R., *Antijudaismus im Johannesevangelium?* (Theologie und Wirklichkeit 3; Bern/Frankfurt am Main: H. Lang, 1974).

Leivestad, R., "Der apokalyptische Menschensohn: Ein theologisches Phantom," in *Annual of the Swedish Theological Institute* VI (1960) 49-105.

———, "Exit the Apocalyptic Son of Man," *NTS* 18 (1971-72) 234-67.

Léon-Dufour, X. (ed.), *Les Miracles de Jésus selon le Nouveau Testament* (Parole de Dieu; Paris: Éditions du Seuil, 1977).

———, *Sharing the Eucharistic Bead* (Mahwah: Paulist, 1987).

———, "Trois chiasmes johanniques," *NTS* 7 (1960-61).

———, "Towards a Symbolic Reading of the Fourth Gospel," *NTS* 27 (1980) 439-56.

Leroy, H., *Rätsel und Mißverständnis: Ein Beitrag zur Formgeschichte des Johannesevangeliums* (Bonner biblische Beiträge 30; Bonn: Peter Hanstein, 1968).

Létourneau, P., *Jesus, Fils de l'homme et Fils de Dieu: Jean 2,23–3,36 et la double christologie johannique* (Recherches Nouvelles Série 27; Paris: Editions du Cerf, 1992).

Levine, L. I., *Judaism and Hellenism in Antiquity* (Peabody, MA: Hendrickson, 1998).

Levison, J. R., *The Spirit in First-Century Judaism* (Leiden: E. J. Brill, 1997).

Lewis, F. W., *Disarrangements in the Fourth Gospel* (Cambridge: Cambridge University Press, 1910).

Liebowitz, H., "Jewish Burial Practices in the Roman Period," *The Mankind Quarterly* 22 (1981-82) 107-17.

Lieu, J., *The Second and Third Epistles of John: History and Background* (Edinburgh: T&T Clark, 1986).

———, *The Theology of the Johannine Epistles* (Cambridge: Cambridge University Press, 1991).

———, *Image and Reality* (Edinburgh: T&T Clark: 1996).

———, *Neither Jew nor Greek? Constructing Early Christianity* (Edinburgh: T&T Clark, 2003).

———, "'Authority to Become Children of God': A Study of 1 John," *NovT* 23 (1981) 210-28.
———, "The Race of the God-fearers," *JTS* 46 (1995) 483-501.
———, "The Mother of the Son in the Fourth Gospel," *JBL* 117 (1998) 61-77.
———, "Temple and Synagogue in John," *NTS* 45 (1999) 51-69.
Lightfoot, J. B., *Biblical Essays* (London: Macmillan, 1893).
———, "The Fragments of Papias," in *The Apostolic Fathers* (J. B. Lightfoot and J. R. Harmer, trans./eds.; M. W. Holmes; 2d ed.; New York: Macmillan, 1893) 556-95.
———, "External Evidence for the Authenticity and Genuineness of St. John's Gospel," in *Biblical Essays* 1-44.
———, "Internal Evidence for the Authenticity and Genuineness of St. John's Gospel," in *Biblical Essays* 45-122.
———, "Additional Notes on the External Evidence for the Authenticity and Genuineness of St. John's Gospel," in *Biblical Essays* 194-98.
Lightfoot, R. H., *Locality and Doctrine in the Gospels* (London: Hodder & Stoughton, 1938).
Lincoln, A., "'I Am the Resurrection and the Life': The Resurrection Message of the Fourth Gospel," in *Life in the Face of Death: The Resurrection Message of the Fourth Gospel* (R. Longenecker, ed.; Grand Rapids: Eerdmans, 1998) 122-44.
Lindars, B., *New Testament Apologetic: The Doctrinal Significance of the Old Testament Quotations* (Philadelphia: Westminster, 1961).
———, *Behind the Fourth Gospel* (Studies in Creative Criticism 3; London: SPCK, 1971).
——— (and S. S. Smalley, eds.), *Christ and Spirit in the New Testament: Studies in Honour of Charles Francis Digby Moule* (Cambridge: Cambridge University Press, 1973).
———, "The Composition of John xx," *NTS* (1960/61) 142-47.
———, "The Son of Man in the Johannine Christology," in *Christ and Spirit* (B. Lindars and S. S. Smalley, eds.) 43-60.
———, "Re-enter the Apocalyptic Son of Man," *NTS* 22 (1975-76) 52-72.
———, "Word and Sacrament in the Fourth Gospel," *SJT* 29 (1976) 49-63.
———, "Traditions behind the Fourth Gospel," in *L'Évangile de Jean* (M. de Jonge, ed.) 107-24.
———, "The Son of Man in the Theology of John," in *Jesus, Son of Man* (London: SPCK, 1983) 145-57.
———, "Slave and Son in John 8:31-36," in *Essays in Honor of Bo Reicke* (W. C. Weinrich, ed.; Macon: Mercer University Press, 1984) 1, 270-86.
Little, E., *Echoes of the Old Testament in the Wine of Cana in Galilee (John 2:1-11) and the Multiplication of the Loaves and Fish (John 6:1-15): Towards an Appreciation* (CahRB 41; Paris: Gabalda, 1998).
Loader, W., *The Christology of the Fourth Gospel* (BBET 23; 2d ed.; Frankfurt: Peter Lang, 1992).
Locher, C., "Die Johannes-Christen und die Juden," *Orientierung* (Zürich) 48 (1984) 223-26.
Lohse, E., "Hosianna," *NovT* 6 (1963) 113-19.
Lopez, E., "Dos siglos de crítica literaria en torno al prólogo de San Juan," *Studium Ovetense* 1 (1973) 165-67, 178.

Lorenzen, T., *Die Lieblingjünger im Johannesevangelium: Eine redaktionsgeschichtliche Studie* (SBS 55; Stuttgart: Katholisches Bibelwerk, 1971).
Lowe, M., "Who Were the ΙΟΥΔΑΙΟΙ?" *NovT* 17 (1975) 101-30.
———, "ΙΟΥΔΑΙΟΙ of the Apocrypha," *NovT* 19 (1976) 51-90.
Lund, N., *Chiasmus in the New Testament* (Chapel Hill, NC: University of North Carolina Press, 1942).
———, "The Influence of Chiasmus upon the Structure of the Gospels," *AThR* 13 (1931) 42-46.
Lütgert, W., "Die Juden im Johannesevangelium," in *Neutestamentliche Studien für Georg Heinrici zu seinem 70. Geburtstag* (Leipzig: Hinrichs, 1914) 147-54.
Maccini, R. G., *Her Testimony Is True: Women as Witnesses according to John* (JSNTSup 125; Sheffield: Sheffield Academic Press, 1996).
MacDonald, John., *Theology of the Samaritans* (Philadelphia: Westminster, 1964).
MacGregor, G. H. C., "The Concept of the Wrath of God in the New Testament," *NTS* (1960/61) 101-9.
MacRae, G. W., "The Meaning and Evolution of the Feast of Tabernacles," *CBQ* 22 (1960) 251-76.
———, "Ego-Proclamation in Gnostic Sources," in *The Trial of Jesus: Cambridge Studies in Honour of C. F. D. Moule* (E. Bammel, ed.; SBT 2/13; London: SCM, 1970) 123-29.
———, "The Fourth Gospel and 'Religionsgeschichte,'" *CBQ* 32 (1970) 13-24.
———, "Theology and Irony in the Fourth Gospel," in *The Word in the World: Essays in Honor of Frederick L. Moriarty, S.J.* (R. J. Clifford and G. W. MacRae, eds.; Cambridge, MA: Weston College Press, 1973) 83-96.
———, "Nag Hammadi and the New Testament," in *Gnosis: Festschrift für H. Jonas* (B. Aland, ed.; Göttingen: Vandenhoeck & Ruprecht, 1978) 144-57.
Magen, Y., "Jerusalem as a Center of the Stone Vessel Industry during the Second Temple Period," in *Ancient Jerusalem Revealed* (H. Geva, ed.; Jerusalem: Israel Exploration Society, 1994) 244-56.
Malatesta, E., *Interiority and Covenant: A study of 'einai en' and 'menein en' in the First Letter of Saint John* (AnBib 69; Rome: Pontifical Biblical Institute, 1978).
———, "The Literary Structure of John 17," *Bib* 52 (1971) 190-214.
Malina, B. J., *The Palestinian Manna-Tradition* (Leiden: E. J. Brill, 1968).
———, *Christian Origins and Cultural Anthropology: Practical Models for Biblical Interpretation* (Atlanta: John Knox, 1986).
———, "The Social Sciences and Biblical Interpretation," *Int* 37 (1982) 229-42.
———, *The Gospel of John in Sociolinguistic Perspective* (H. C. Waetjen, ed.; Protocol of the Forty-Eighth Colloquy; Center for Hermeneutical Studies in Hellenistic and Modern Culture, 1984).
Manning Jr., G. T., *Echoes of a Prophet: The Use of Ezekiel in the Gospel of John and in Literature of the Second Temple Period* (JSNTSup 270; Sheffield: Sheffield Academic Press, 2005).
Manns, F., *"La Vérité vous fera libres": Étude exégétique de Jean 8/31-59* (Studium Biblicum Franciscanum, Analecta 11; Jerusalem: Franciscan, 1976).
———, *Le symbol eau-esprit dans le judaisme ancien* (Jerusalem: Fransciscan, 1983).
Manson, T. W., "The Pericope *de Adultera* (Joh 7,53-8,11)," *ZNW* 44 (1953) 255-56.

Marcus, J., "Rivers of Living Water from Jesus' Belly (John 7:38)," *JBL* 117 (1998) 328-30.
Marguerat, D., "La 'source des signes' existe-t-elle? Réception des récits de miracles dans l'évangile de Jean," in *La communauté johannique* (J.-D. Kaestli et al., eds., Genève: Labor et Fides, 1990) 69-93.
Marrow, S. B., *John 21: An Essay in Johannine Ecclesiology* (Unpublished dissertation; Rome: Gregorian University, 1968).
Marshall, I. H., "The Son of Man in Contemporary Debate," *EvQ* 42 (1970) 67-87.
———, "The Synoptic Son of Man Sayings in Recent Discussion," *NTS* 12 (1965-66) 327-51.
Martin, T., "Assessing the Johannine Epithet 'the Mother of Jesus,'" *CBQ* 60 (1998) 63-73.
Martin, V., *Papyrus Bodmer II: Évangile de Jean, 1-14* (Cologny/Geneva: Bibliotheca Bodmeriana, 1956).
———, *Papyrus Bodmer II: Supplement, Évangile de Jean, 14-21* (Cologny/Geneva: Bibliotheca Bodmeriana, 1958).
Martin, V., and Barns, J. W. B., *Papyrus Bodmer II: Supplement, Évangile de Jean, 14-21* (2d ed.; Cologny/Geneva: Bibliotheca Bodmeriana, 1962).
Martyn, J. L., *History and Theology in the Fourth Gospel* (2d ed.; Nashville: Abingdon, 1979).
———, *The Gospel of John in Christian History: Essays for Interpreters* (New York: Harper & Row, 1979).
———, "Source Criticism and Religionsgeschichte in the Fourth Gospel," *Jesus and Man's Hope* (vol. 1; Pittsburgh: Pittsburgh Theological Seminary, 1971) 247-73.
———, "Clementine Recognitions 1,33-71, Jewish Christianity, and the Fourth Gospel," in *God's Christ and His People: Festschrift für N. A. Dahl* (Oslo: Universitatsforlaget, 1976) 265-95.
———, "We Have Found Elijah," in *Jews, Greeks and Christians: Religious Cultures in Late Antiquity: Essays in Honor of William David Davies* (SJLA 21; Leiden: E. J. Brill, 1976) 180-219.
———, "Glimpses into the History of the Johannine Community: From Its Origin through the Period of Its Life in Which the Fourth Gospel Was Composed," in *L'Évangile de Jean* (M. de Jonge, ed.) 149-75.
Mastin, B. A., "The Imperial Cult and the Ascription of the Title *Theos* to Jesus (John 20,28)," *SE* 6 (1973) 352-65.
———, "A Neglected Feature of the Christology of the Fourth Gospel," *NTS* 22 (1975-76) 32-51.
Matera, F. J., "'On Behalf of Others,' 'Cleansing' and 'Return': Johannine Images for Jesus' Death," *LS* 13 (1988) 161-78.
———, "Jesus before Annas: John 18,13-14, 19-24," *ETL* 66 (1990) 38-55.
Mattill, A. J., "Johannine Communities behind the Fourth Gospel: Georg Richter's Analysis," *TS* 38 (1977) 294-315.
Mattila, S. L., "Two Contrasting Eschatologies at Qumran (4Q246 vs 1QM)," *Bib* 75 (1994) 519-38.
Maurer, C., *Ignatius von Antiochien und das Johannesevangelium* (ATANT 18; Zurich: Zwingli, 1949).
Maynard, A. H., "TI EMOI KAI SOI," *NTS* 31 (1985) 582-86.

Bibliography

McDonald, J. I. H., "The So-Called *Pericopa de Adultera*," *NTS* 41 (1995) 415-27.

McNeil, B., "The Quotation at John xii 34," *NovT* 19 (1973) 64-69.

Mealand, D. L., "The Language of Mystical Union in the Johannine Writings," *DRev* 95 (1977) 19-34.

Meeks, W., *The Prophet-King: Moses Traditions and the Johannine Christology* (NovTSup 14; Leiden: E. J. Brill, 1967).

———, "Galilee and Judaea in the Fourth Gospel," *JBL* 85 (1966) 159-69.

———, "Moses as God and King," in *Religions in Antiquity: Essays in Memory of Erwin Ramsdell Goodenough* (Studies in the History of Religions 13; Leiden: E. J. Brill, 1968) 354-71.

———, "The Man from Heaven in Johannine Sectarianism," *JBL* 91 (1972) 44-72.

———, "'Am I a Jew?' Johannine Christianity and Judaism," in *Christianity, Judaism, and Other Greco-Roman Cults: Studies for Morton Smith at Sixty* (SJLA 12; vol. 1; Leiden: E. J. Brill, 1975) 163-86.

———, "Breaking Away: Three New Testament Pictures of Christianity's Separation from Jewish Communities," in *To See Ourselves as Others See Us* (J. Neusner and E. S. Frerichs, eds.; Chico, CA: Scholars Press, 1985) 93-116.

———, "Equal to God," in *The Conversation Continues: Studies in Paul and John in Honor of J. Louis Martyn* (R. T. Fortna and B. R. Gaventa, eds.; Nashville: Abingdon, 1990) 308-21.

———, "The Ethics of the Fourth Evangelist," in *Exploring the Gospel of John* (R. A. Culpepper and C. C. Black, eds.; Louisville: Westminster, 1996) 317-26.

Mees, M., *Die frühe Rezeptionsgeschichte des Johannesevangeliums: Am Beispiel von Textüberlieferung und Väterexegese* (G. Scheuermann and A.-P. Alkofer, eds.; Forschung zur Bibel 72; Würzburg: Echter, 1994).

Mehlmann, J., "Propheta a Moyse Promissus in Jo 7,52 Citatus," *VD* 4 (1966) 79-88.

Meier, J. P., *A Marginal Jew: Rethinking the Historical Jesus*, vol. 1: *The Roots of the Problem and the Person*; vol. 2: *Mentor, Message, and Miracles*; vol. 3: *Companions and Competitors* (New York: Doubleday, 1991, 1994, 2001).

Mendner, S., "Johanneische Literarkritik," *TZ* 8 (1952) 418-32.

———, "Die Tempelreinigung," *ZNW* 47 (1956) 93-112.

———, "Nikodemus," *JBL* 77 (1958) 293-323.

Menken, M., *Old Testament Quotations in the Fourth Gospel: Studies in Textual Form* (Kampen: Kok Pharos, 1996).

———, "The Quotation from Isa. 40,3 in John 1,23," *Bib* 66 (1985) 190-205.

———, "The Provenance and Meaning of the Old Testament Quotation in John 6:31," *NovT* 30 (1988) 39-56.

———, "The Old Testament Quotation in John 6,45: Source and Redaction," *ETL* 64 (1988) 164-72.

———, "Die Form des Zitates aus Jes 6,10 in Joh 12,40: Ein Beitrag zum Schriftgebrauch des vierten Evangelisten," *BZ* n.f. 32 (1988) 189-209.

———, "Die Redaktion des Zitates aus Sach 9,9 in John 12,15," *ZNW* 80 (1989) 193-209.

———, "The Translation of Psalm 41.10 in John 13.18," *JSNT* 40 (1990) 61-79.

———, "The Old Testament Quotation in John 19,36: Sources, Redaction, Background," in *The Four Gospels 1992* (F. Van Segbroeck et al., eds.) 2101-18.

———, "John 6,51c-58: Eucharist or Christology," *Bib* 74, 1 (1993) 1-26.
———, "The Textual Form and the Meaning of the Quotation from Zechariah 12:10 in John 19:37," *CBQ* 55 (1993) 494-511.
———, "The Origin of the Old Testament Quotation in John 7:38," *NovT* 38 (1996) 160-75.
Metzger, B. M., "'Names for the Nameless' in the New Testament: A Study in the Growth of Christian Tradition," in *New Testament Studies: Philological, Versional, and Patristic* (Leiden: E. J. Brill, 1980) 23-45.
Meyer, R., *"Ochlos," TDNT* 5, 582-90.
Michaels, J. R., "Nathanael under the Fig Tree," *ET* 78 (1966) 182-83.
Michel, H.-J. *Die Abschiedsrede des Paulus an die Kirche Apg. 20.17-38* (SANT 35; Munich: Kösel, 1973).
Michel, O., "Der Menschensohn," *TZ* 27 (1971) 81-104.
Miguens, M., "Salió sangre y agua," *Studii Biblici Franciscani Liber Annuus* 14 (1963-64) 5-31.
Milik, J. T., *The Books of Enoch* (Oxford: Oxford University, 1976).
———, "Le rouleau de cuivre provenant de la Grotte 3Q (3Q15)," in *Les 'Petites Grottes' de Qumran* (M. Baillet, J. T. Milik, and R. de Vaux, eds.; DJD 3; Oxford: Clarendon, 1962).
———, "Turfan et Qumrân: Livre de Géants juif et manichéen," in *Tradition und Glaube: Das frühe Christentum in seiner Umwelt: Festgabe für Karl Georg Kuhn zum 65. Geburtstag* (Göttingen: Vandenhoeck & Ruprecht, 1971) 1117-27.
Minear, P., "The Beloved Disciple in the Gospel of John: Some Clues and Conjectures," *NovT* 19 (1977) 105-23.
Miranda, J. P., *Der Vater der mich gesandt hat: Religionsgeschichtliche Untersuchungen zu den johanneischen Sendungsformeln, zugleich ein Beitrag zur johanneischen Christologie und Ekklesiologie* (European University Papers 23, 7; Bern: Herbert Lang, 1972).
———, *Die Sendung Jesu im vierten Evangelium: Religion und theologiegeschichtliche Untersuchungen zu den Sendungsformeln* (SBS 98; Stuttgart: Katholisches Bibelwerk, 1977).
Mlakuzhyil, G., *The Christocentric Literary Structure of the Fourth Gospel* (Rome: Pontifical Biblical Institute, 1987).
Moeller, H. R., "Wisdom Motifs and John's Gospel," *BulETS* 6 (1963) 92-100.
Mollat, D., "Le chapitre VIe de Saint Jean," *LumVie* 31 (1957) 107-19.
———, "La guérison de l'aveugle-né," *BVC* 23 (1958) 22-31.
Moloney, F. J., *The Johannine Son of Man* (2d ed.; Biblioteca di Scienze Religiose 14; Roma: LAS, 1978).
———, *Mary: Woman and Mother* (Homebush: St. Paul Publications, 1988).
———, *Belief in the Word: Reading John 1–4* (Minneapolis: Fortress, 1993).
———, *Signs and Shadows: Reading John 5–12* (Minneapolis: Fortress, 1996).
———, *Glory, Not Dishonour: Reading John 13–21* (Minneapolis: Fortress, 1998).
——— (ed.), R. E. Brown, *An Introduction to the Gospel of John* (ABRL; New York: Doubleday, 2003).
———, "John 6 and the Celebration of the Eucharist," *DRev* 93 (1975) 243-51.
———, "The Johannine Son of God," *Salesianum* 38 (1976) 71-86.

———, "From Cana to Cana (Jn. 2:1-4:54) and the Fourth Evangelist's Concept of Correct and Incorrect Faith," *Salesianum* 40 (1978) 817-43.

———, "John 20: A Journey Completed," *Australasian Catholic Review* 59 (1982) 417-32.

———, "To Make God Known: A Reading of John 17:1-26," *Salesianum* 59 (1997) 463-89.

———, "The Fourth Gospel and the Jesus of History," *NTS* 46 (2000) 45-28.

———, "Can Everyone Be Wrong? A Reading of John 11.1-12.8," *NTS* 49 (2003) 505-27.

———, "The Gospel of John as Scripture," *CBQ* 67 (2005) 454-84.

Moody, D., "God's Only Son: The Translation of John 3:16 in the Revised Standard Version," *JBL* 72 (1953) 213-19.

Morgen, M., "Le Fils de l'homme élevé en vue de la vie éternelle (Jn 3,14-15 éclairé par diverses traditions juives)," *RevScRel* 68, 1 (1994) 5-17.

Morgenthaler, R., *Statistik des neutestamentlichen Wortschatzes* (3d ed.; Zürich: Gotthelf, 1982).

Morris, L., *Studies in the Fourth Gospel* (Exeter: Paternoster, 1969).

———, "The Meaning of HILASTERION in Romans III.25," *NTS* 11 (1965-66) 33-43.

Motyer, S., *Your Father the Devil? A New Approach to John and 'the Jews'* (Carlisle, U.K.: Paternoster, 1997).

———, "Is John's Gospel Anti-Semitic?" *Themelios* 23 (1998) 1-4.

Moule, C. F. D., "A Note on Didache IX 4," *JTS* 6 (1955) 240-43.

———, "Fulfillment Words in the New Testament: Use and Abuse," *NTS* 14 (1967-68) 293-320.

———, "A Neglected Factor in the Interpretation of Johannine Eschatology," in *Studies in John: Presented to Professor Dr. J. N. Sevenster on the Occasion of His Seventieth Birthday* (NovTSup 24 (Leiden: E. J. Brill, 1970) 155-66.

———, "'The Son of Man': Some of the Facts," *NTS* 41 (1995) 277-79.

Müller, M., "'Have You Faith in the Son of Man?'" *NTS* 37 (1991) 291-94.

Müller, U. B., *Messias und Menschensohn in jüdischen Apokalypsen und in der Offenbarung des Johannes* (StudNeot 6; Gütersloh: Gerd Mohn, 1972).

———, *Die Geschichte der Christologie in der johanneischen Gemeinde* (SBS 77; Stuttgart: Katholisches Bibelwerk, 1975).

———, "Die Parakletenvorstellung im Johannesevangelium," *ZTK* 71 (1974) 31-77.

———, "Die Bedeutung des Kreuzestodes Jesu im Johannesevangelium: Erwägungen zur Kreuzestheologie im Neuen Testament," *KD* 21 (1975) 49-51.

Munck, J., "Discours d'adieu dans le Nouveau Testament et dans la littérature biblique," in *Aux sources de la tradition chrétienne: Mélanges offerts à M. Maurice Goguel* (Bibliothèque théologique; Neuchâtel and Paris: Delachaux & Niestlé, 1950) 155-70.

Murphy, R., "Sahat in the Qumran Literature," *Bib* 39 (1958) 61-66.

Murphy-O'Connor, J., *The Holy Land* (Oxford Archaeological Guides; 4th ed.; Oxford: Oxford University Press, 1998).

———, "John the Baptist and Jesus: History and Hypotheses," *NTS* 36 (1990) 359-74.

———, "Jesus and the Money Changers (Mark 11:15-17; John 2:13-17)," *RB* 107 (2000) 42-55.

———, "Sites Associated with John the Baptist," *RB* 112 (2005) 253-66.

Nagel, T., *Die Rezeption des Johannesevangeliums im 2. Jahrhundert* (Arbeiten zur Bibel und ihrer Geschichte 2: Leipzig: Evangelische Verlagsanstalt, 2000).

Ndombi, J.-R., "Le langage des lieux dans L'Évangile de Jean," *Hekima Review* [Nairobi] 17 (1997) 53-65.
Neirynck, F., "The 'Other Disciple' in Jn. 18, 15-16," *ETL* 51 (1975) 113-41.
———, "L'Évangile de Jean: Examen critique du commentaire de M.-É. Boismard et A. Lamouille," *ETL* 53 (1977) 363-478.
———, "John and the Synoptics," in *L'Évangile de Jean* (M. de Jonge, ed.) 73-106.
———, "L'Epanalepsis et la critique littéraire: À propos de l'Évangile de Jean," *ETL* 56 (1980) 303-38.
———, "John and the Synoptics: The Empty Tomb Stories," *NTS* 30 (1984) 161-87.
———, "John and the Synoptics: 1975-1990," in *John and the Synoptics* (A. Denaux, ed.; BETL 101; Leuven: Leuven University Press, 1992) 3-63.
Neugebauer, J., *Die eschatologischen Aussagen in den johanneischen Abschiedsreden: Eine Untersuchung zu Johannes 13-17* (BWANT 140; Suttgart/Berlin/Cologne: W. Kohlhammer, 1995).
Neuhaus, D. (ed.), *Teufelskinder oder Heilsbringer — Die Juden im Johannes-Evangelium* (2d ed.; Frankfurt am Main: Haag & Herchen, 1993).
Neusner, J., "Money Changers in the Temple: The Mishnah's Explanation," *NTS* 35 (1989) 287-90.
Newsom, C. A., "Apocalyptic and the Discourse of the Qumran Community," *JNES* 49 (1990) 134-44.
———, "'Sectually Explicit' Literature from Qumran," in *the Hebrew Bible and Its Interpreters* (W. H. Propp, B. Halpern, and D. N. Freedman, eds.; Winona Lake, IN; Eisenbrauns, 1990) 167-87.
Neyrey, J., *An Ideology of Revolt: John's Christology in Social-Science Perspective* (Philadelphia: Fortress, 1988).
———, "Jacob Traditions and the Interpretation of John 4:10-26," *CBQ* 41 (1979) 419-37.
———, "John III — A Debate over Johannine Epistemology and Christology," *NovT* 23 (1981) 115-27.
———, "The Jacob Allusions in John 1:51," *CBQ* 44 (1982) 586-605.
———, "Jesus the Judge: Forensic Process in John 8,21-59," *Bib* 68 (1987) 509-41.
———, "I Said, 'You are Gods': Psalm 82:6 and John 10," *JBL* 108 (1989) 647-63.
———, and Rohrbaugh, R., "'He Must Increase, I Must Decrease' (John 3:30): A Cultural and Social Interpretation," *CBQ* 63 (July 2001) 464-83.
Nicholson, G. C., *Death as Departure* (SBLDS 63; Chico, CA: Scholars Press, 1983).
Nickelsburg, G. W. E., *Resurrection, Immortality, and Eternal Life in Inter-testamental Judaism* (HTS 26; Cambridge, MA: Harvard University Press, 1972).
———, "Revealed Wisdom as a Criterion for Inclusion and Exclusion: From Jewish Sectarianism to Early Christianity," in *To See Ourselves as Others See Us* (J. Neusner and E. S. Frerichs, eds.; Atlanta: Scholars Press, 1985) 73-91.
Nicol, W., *The Semeia in the Fourth Gospel* (NovTSup 32; Leiden: E. J. Brill, 1972).
Niederwimmer, K., "Zur Eschatologie im Corpus Johanneum," *NovT* 39 (1997) 105-16.
Nielsen, H. K., "John's Understanding of the Death of Jesus," in *New Readings in John: Literary and Theological Perspectives* (JSNTSup 182; Sheffield: Sheffield Academic Press, 1999) 232-54.
Niemand, C., *Die Fusswaschungserzählung des Johannesevangeliums: Untersuchungen zu*

ihrer Entstehung und Überlieferung im Urchristentum (SA 114; Rome: Pontificio Ateneo S. Anselmo, 1993).

Nissen, J., "The Distinctive Character of the New Testament Love Command in Relation to Hellenistic Judaism," in *The New Testament and Hellenistic Judaism* (P. Borgen and S. Giversen, eds.; Peabody, MA: Hendrickson, 1997) 123-50.

———, "Community and Ethics in the Gospel of John," in *New Readings in John: Literary and Theological Perspectives* (JSNTSup 182; Sheffield: Sheffield Academic Press, 1999) 194-212.

Noack, B., *Zur johanneischen Tradition: Beiträge zur Kritik an der literarkritischen Analyse des vierten Evangeliums* (Copenhagen: Rosenkilde, 1954).

Obermann, A., *Die christologische Erfüllung der Schrift im Johannesevangelium* (WUNT 2/83; Tübingen: J. C. B. Mohr [P. Siebeck], 1996).

O'Day, G. O., "'I Have Overcome the World' (John 16:33): Narrative Time in John 13–17," *Semeia* 53 (1991) 153-66.

———, "Show Us the Father, and We Will be Satisfied," *Semeia* 85 (1999) 11-17.

Odeberg, H., *The Fourth Gospel: Interpreted in Relation to Contemporaneous Religious Currents in Palestine and the Hellenistic-Oriental World* (Uppsala: Almqvist, 1929).

Okure, T., *The Johannine Approach to Mission* (WUNT 2/31; Tübingen: J. C. B. Mohr [P. Siebeck], 1988).

O'Neil, J. C., "John 13:10 Again," *RB* 101 (1994) 67-74.

———, "The Jews in the Fourth Gospel," *IBS* 18 (1996) 58-74.

Onuki, T., *Gemeinde und Welt im Johannesevangelium: Ein Beitrag zur Frage nach der theologischen und pragmatischen Funktion des johanneischen 'Dualismus'* (WMANT 56; Neukirchen-Vluyn: Neukirchener Verlag, 1984).

———, "Zur literatursoziologischen Analyse des Johannesevangeliums," *AJBI* 8 (1982) 162-216, esp. 179, 190-91.

Oppenheimer, A., *The 'Am ha-Aretz: A Study in the Social History of the Jewish People in the Hellenistic-Roman Period* (Leiden: Brill, 1977).

O'Rourke, J., "Asides in the Gospel of John," *NovT* 21 (1979) 210-19.

Osiek, C., *What Are They Saying about the Social Setting of the New Testament* (rev. ed; New York: Paulist, 1992).

Pagels, E. H., *The Johannine Gospel in Gnostic Exegesis: Heracleon's Commentary on John* (Nashville: Abingdon, 1973).

———, *The Gnostic Paul* (Philadelphia: Fortress, 1975).

———, "Conflicting Versions of Valentinian Eschatology: Irenaeus' Treatises vs. the Excerpts from Theodotus," *HTR* 67 (1974) 35-53.

Painter, J., *John: Witness and Theologian* (London: SPCK, 1975).

———, *The Quest for the Messiah* (2d ed.; Edinburgh: T&T Clark, 1993).

———, "John 9 and the Interpretation of the Fourth Gospel," *JSNT* 28 (1986) 31-61.

———, "The 'Opponents' in 1 John," *NTS* 32 (1986) 48-71.

———, "Tradition, History, and Interpretation in John 10," in *The Shepherd Discourse of John 10 and Its Context* (J. Beutler and R. Fortna, eds.; Cambridge: Cambridge University Press, 1991) 53-74.

Pamment, M., "The Son of Man in the Fourth Gospel," *JTS* n.s. 36 (1985) 56-66.

Pancaro, S., *The Law in the Fourth Gospel: The Torah. Moses and Jesus, Judaism and Christianity according to John* (NovTSup 42; Leiden: E. J. Brill, 1975).

———, "The Relationship of the Church to Israel in the Gospel of St. John," *NTS* 21 (1975-76) 396-405.

Panthapallil, M., *Mary, The Type of the Church in the Johannine Writings: A Biblico-Theological Analysis* (Oirsi Publications 182; Kottayam: Oriental Institute of Religious Studies India, 1996).

Parker, P., "Two Editions of John," *JBL* 55 (1956) 303-14.

———, "When Acts Sides with John," in *Understanding the Sacred Text: Essays in Honor of Morton S. Enslin on the Hebrew Bible and Christian Beginnings* (John Reumann, ed.; Valley Forge, PA: Judson, 1972) 201-15.

Pastorelli, D., *Le Paraclet dans le corpus johannique* (BZNW 142; Berlin: de Gruyter, 2006).

Paul, F. J., "On Two Dislocations in St. John's Gospel," *HibJ* (1908) 662-68.

Pedersen, S., "Anti-Judaism in John's Gospel: John 8," in *New Readings in John: Literary and Theological Perspectives* (JSNTSup 182; Sheffield: Sheffield Academic Press, 1999) 172-93.

Pendrick, G., *"MONOGENĒS,"* *NTS* 41 (1995) 587-600.

Perkins, P., *The Gnostic Dialogue: The Early Church and the Crisis of Gnosticism* (New York: Paulist, 1980).

———, *Love Commands in the New Testament* (New York: Paulist, 1982).

———, *Resurrection: New Testament Witness and Contemporary Reflection* (Garden City, NY: Doubleday, 1984).

———, *Gnosticism and the New Testament* (Minneapolis: Fortress, 1993).

———, "Gnostic Christologies and the New Testament," *CBQ* 43 (1981) 590-606.

Perler, O., "Das vierte Makkabäerbuch, Ignatius von Antiochen und die ältesten Martyrberichte," *Rivista di archeologia cristiana* 25 (1949) 47-72.

Perrin, N., *Rediscovering the Teaching of Jesus* (London: SCM Press, 1967).

Perry, J. M., "The Evolution of the Johannine Eucharist," *NTS* 39 (1993) 22-35.

Person, R. F., "A Reassessment of *Wiederaufnahme* from the Perspective of Conversation Analysis," *BZ* n.f. 43 (1999) 239-48.

Petersen, W. L., "*Oude egō se [kata] krinō*: John 8:11, the *Protoevangelium Iacobi*, and the History of the *Pericope Adulterae*," in *Sayings of Jesus: Canonical and Noncanonical* (W. L. Petersen, J. S. Vos, and H. J. de Jonge, eds.; NovTSup 89; Leiden: E. J. Brill, 1997) 191-221.

Peterson, N., *The Gospel of John and the Sociology of Light* (Valley Forge, PA: Trinity Press International, 1994).

Philonenko, M., *Les interpolations chrétiennes des Testaments des Douze Patriarches et les manuscrits de Qumran* (Cahiers de la RHPR 35; Paris: Presses universitaires de France, 1960).

Pierre, M.-J., and Rousée, J.-M., "Sainte-Marie de la Probatique, état et orientation de recherches," *Proche-Orient Chrétien* 31 (1981) 23-42.

Pilch, J. J., "Are There Jews and Christians in the Bible?" *Hervormde teologiese studies* 53 (1997) 119-25.

———, "No Jews or Christians in the Bible," *Explorations* 12, 2 (1998) 3.

Pilgaard, A., "The Qumran Scrolls and John's Gospel," in *New Readings in John: Literary and Theological Perspectives* (JSNTSup 182; Sheffield: Sheffield Academic Press, 1999) 126-44.

Poirier, J. C., "'Day and Night' and the Punctuation of John 9.3," *NTS* 42 (1996) 288-94.

Pollard, T. E., *Johannine Christology and the Early Church* (SNTSMS 13; Cambridge: Cambridge University Press, 1970).

———, "Jesus and the Samaritan Woman," *ExpTim* 92 (1980) 147-48.

———, "The Exegesis of John x.30 in the Early Trinitarian Controversies," *NTS* 3 (1956-57) 334-49.

Popkes, E. E., *Die Theologie der Liebe Gottes in den johanneischen Schriften* (Tübingen: J. C. B. Mohr [P. Siebeck], 2005).

Porsch, F., *Pneuma und Wort: Ein exegetischer Beitrag zur Pneumatologie des Johannesevangeliums* (Frankfurter Theologische Studien 16; Frankfurt: Josef Knecht, 1974).

———, "Ihr habt den Teufel zum Vater (Joh 8:44): Antijudaismus im Johannesevangelium?" *BK* 44 (1989) 50-57.

Porter, C., "Papyrus Bodmer XV [P75] and the Text of Codex Vaticanus," *JBL* 81 (1962) 363-76.

Prat, F., "Les places d'honneur chez les Juifs contemporains du Christ," *RSR* 15 (1925) 512-22.

Pratscher, W., "Die Juden im Johannesevangelium," *BLit* 59 (1986) 177-85.

Preisker, H., "Jüdische Apokalyptik und hellenistischer Synkretismus im Johannes-Evangelium, dargelegt an dem Begriff 'Licht,'" *TLZ* 77 (1952) 673-78.

Price, J., "Light from Qumran on Some Aspects of Johannine Theology," in *John and the Dead Sea Scrolls* (ed. J. Charlesworth) 9-37.

Pryor, J. W., *John: Evangelist of the Covenant People* (London: Darton, Longman & Todd, 1992).

———, "Jesus as Lord: A Neglected Factor in Johannine Christology," in *In the Fullness of Time: Festschrift D. W. B. Robinson* (D. Peterson and J. Pryor, eds.; Homebush West: Lancer, 1992).

Puech, É., *La croyance des Esséniens en la vie future: Immortalité, résurrection, vie éternelle? Histoire d'une croyance dans le judaïsme ancien* (2 vols.; Études bibliques n.s. 22; Paris: Gabalda, 1993).

———, "Les Esséniens et la Vie Future," *Le monde de la Bible* 4 (1978) 38-40.

———, "Une apocalypse messianique (4Q521)," *RQ* 15 (1991-92) 475-522.

———, "A-t-on redécouvert le tombeau du grand-prêtre Caiphe?" *Le monde de la Bible* 80 (1993) 42-47.

———, "Le diable, homicide, menteur et père du mensonge en Jean 8,44," *RB* 112 (2005) 215-52.

Quast, K., *Peter and the Beloved Disciple: Figures for a Community in Crisis* (JSNTSup 32; Sheffield: JSOT, 1989).

Reich, R., and Shukron, E., "The Pool of Siloam," *Qadmoniot* 39, December 2005, 91-96.

———, "Caiaphas's Name Inscribed on Bone Boxes," *BAR* 18, 5 (September/October 1992).

Reim, G., *Studien zum alttestamentlichen Hintergrund des Johannesevangeliums* (SNTSMS 22; Cambridge: Cambridge University Press, 1974).

———, "Joh 8.44 — Gotteskinder/Teufels kinder: Wie anti-Judaïstisch ist 'Die wohl antijudaïstischste Äusserung des NT?" *NTS* 30 (1984) 619-24.
Reinhartz, A. (ed.), *God the Father in the Gospel of John*, Semeia 85 (1999) (Atlanta: SBL, 1999).
———, *Befriending the Beloved Disciple* (New York: Continuum, 2001).
———, "A Nice Jewish Girl Reads the Gospel of John," *Semeia* 77 (1997) 177-93.
———, "The Johannine Community and Its Jewish Neighbors; A Reappraisal," in *What Is John?* vol. 2: *Literary and Social Readings of the Fourth Gospel* (F. F. Segovia, ed.) 111-38.
———, "Father as Metaphor in the Fourth Gospel," in *God the Father in the Gospel of John*, Semeia 85 (A. Reinhartz, ed.) 1-10.
———, "'And the Word Was Begotten': Divine Epigenesis in the Gospel of John," in *God the Father in the Gospel of John* (A. Reinhartz, ed.) 83-103.
Rengstorf, K. H., *"lēstēs," TDNT* 4, 257-62.
Rensberger, D., *Johannine Faith and Liberating Community* (Philadelphia: Westminster, 1988).
———, *Overcoming the World: Politics and Community in the Gospel of John* (London: SPCK, 1989).
———, "Anti-Judaism and the Gospel of John," in *Anti-Judaism and the Gospels* (William R. Farmer, ed.; Harrisburg, PA: Trinity Press International, 1999) 120-57.
Resseguie, J. L., "John 9: A Literary-Critical Analysis," in *Literary Interpretations of Biblical Narratives* (K. R. R. Gros Louis, ed.; vol. 2; Nashville: Abingdon, 1982) 295-303.
Rhea, R., *The Johannine Son of Man* (ATANT 76; Zürich: Theologischer Verlag, 1990).
Ricca, P., *Die Eschatologie des vierten Evangeliums* (Zurich: Gotthelf, 1966).
Richter, G., *Die Fußwaschung im Johannesevangelium* (BU 1; Regensburg: Pustet, 1967).
———, *Studien zum Johannesevangelium* (BU 13; Regensburg: Pustet, 1977).
———, "'Bist du Elias?' (Joh. 1,21)," in *Studien zum Johannesevangelium* 1-42 (original in *BZ* n.f. 6 [1962] 79-92, 238-56; 7 [1963] 63-80).
———, "Die Fußwaschung Joh 13,1-20," in *Studien zum Johannesevangelium* 42-57 (original in *MTZ* 16 [1965] 13-26).
———, "Die Deutung des Kreuzestodes Jesu in der Leidensgeschichte des Johannesevangeliums (Jo. 13–19)," in *Studien zum Johannesevangelium* 58-73 (original in *BibLeb* 9 [1968] 21-36).
———, "Zur Formgeschichte und literarischen Einheit von Joh 6,31-58," in *Studien zum Johannesevangelium* 88-119 (original in *ZNW* 60 [1969] 21-55).
———, "Blut und Wasser aus der durchbohrten Seite Jesu (Joh 19,34b)," in *Studien zum Johannesevangelium* 120-42.
———, "Die Fleischwerdung des Logos im Johannesevangelium," in *Studien zum Johannesevangelium* 149-98 (original in *NovT* 13 [1971] 81-126).
———, "Die alttestamentliche Zitate in der Rede vom Himmelsbrot, Joh. 6,26-51a," in *Studien zum Johannesevangelium* 199-265 (original in *Schriftauslegung* [J. Ernst, ed.; Münster in Westfallen: Schöninghaus, 1972] 193-279).
———, "Der Vater und Gott Jesu und seiner Brüder in Joh 20,17: Ein Beitrag zur Christologie des Johannesevangeliums," in *Studien zum Johannesevangelium* 266-80 (original in *MTZ* 24 [1973] 95-114; 25 [1974] 64-73).

———, "Zur sogenannten Semeia-Quelle des Johannesevangeliums," in *Studien zum Johannesevangelium* 281-87.

———, "Zu der Tauferzählung Mk 1,9-11 und Joh 1,32-34," in *Studien zum Johannesevangelium* 315-26 (original in *ZNW* 65 [1974] 43-56).

———, "Präsentische und futurische Eschatologie im 4. Evangelium," in *Studien zum Johannesevangelium* 346-82 (original in *Gegenwart und kommendes Reich: Schülergabe Anton Vögtle zum 65. Geburtstag* [P. Fiedler and D. Zeller, eds.; Stuttgart: Katholisches Bibelwerk, 1975] 117-52).

———, "Zum gemeindebildenden Element in den johanneischen Schriften," in *Studien zum Johannesevangelium* 383-414 (original in *Kirche im Werden: Studien zum Thema Amt und Gemeinde im Neuen Testament* [J. Hainz, ed.; München: Schöninghaus, 1976]).

Riesner, R., *Bethanien jenseits des Jordan: Topographie und Theologie im Johannes-Evangelium* (Studien zur biblischen Archäologie und Zeitgeschichte 12; Giessen: Brunnen, 2002).

———, "Bethany beyond the Jordan (John 1:28)," *Tyndale Bulletin* 38 (1987) 29-63.

———, "Bethany beyond the Jordan," *ABD* 1, 703-5.

Rigato, M.-L., "'L'apostolo ed evangelista Giovanni,' 'sacerdoto' levitico," *RevistB* 38 (1990) 451-83.

Rissi, M., "Die 'Juden' im Johannesevangelium," *ANRW* 2.26.3 (1996) 2099-41.

Ritt, H., *Das Gebet zum Vater: Zur Interpretation von John 17* (FB 36; Würzburg: Echter, 1979).

Roberge, M., "Notices de conclusion et rédaction du quatrième évangile," *LTP* 31 (1975) 49-53.

———, "Jean VI,22-24: Un problème de critique textuelle," *LTP* 34 (1978) 275-89.

———, "Jean VI,22-24: Un problème de critique littéraire," *LTP* 35 (1979) 139-51.

Roberts, C. H., *An Unpublished Fragment of the Fourth Gospel in the John Rylands Library* (Manchester: Manchester University Press, 1935).

Roberts, J. J. M., "The Old Testament's Contribution to Messianic Expectations," in *The Messiah: Developments in Earliest Judaism and Christianity* (J. H. Charlesworth, ed.; The First Princeton Symposium on Judaism and Christian Origins; Minneapolis: Fortress, 1992) 39-51.

Robinson, J. A. T., *Twelve New Testament Studies* (SBT 34; London: SCM, 1962).

———, *Redating the New Testament* (Philadelphia: Westminster, 1976).

———, *The Priority of John* (Oak Park, IL: Meyer Stone, 1985).

———, "The Parable of John 10:1-5," *ZNW* 46 (1955) 233-40, reprinted in *Twelve New Testament Studies* 67-75.

———, "The 'Others' of John 4,38," *SE* 1 (1959) 510-15.

Robinson, J. M. (and H. Koester), *Trajectories through Early Christianity* (Philadelphia: Fortress, 1971).

———, "The Miracles Source of John," *JAAR* 34 (1971) 339-48.

———, "Gnosticism and the New Testament," in *Gnosis: Festschrift für H. Jonas* (B. Aland, ed.) 125-43.

Rochais, G., "La Formation du Prologue [Jn 1:1-18]," *ScEs* 37 (1985) 5-44.

———, *Le récits de résurrection des morts dans le Nouveau Testament* (SNTSMS 40; Cambridge: Cambridge University Press, 1981).
Rowland, C. C., "John 1.51, Jewish Apocalyptic and Targumic Tradition," *NTS* 30 (1984) 498-507.
Ruck-Schröder, A., *Der Name Gottes und der Name Jesu* (WMANT 80; Neukirchen-Vluyn: Neukirchener, 1999).
Ruckstuhl, E., *Die literarische Einheit des Johannesevangeliums, der gegenwärtige Stand der einschlägigen Forschungen* (Studia Friburgensia n.f. 3; Freiburg: Ed. S. Paul, 1951).
———, "Literarkritik am Johannesevangelium und eucharistische Rede (Jo. 6,51c-58)," *Divus Thomas* 23 (1945) 153-90, 301-33.
———, "Johannine Language and Style: The Question of Their Unity," in *L'Évangile de Jean* (M. de Jonge, ed.) 125-48.
———, and Dschulnigg, P., *Stilkritik und Verfasserfrage im Johannesevangelium: Die johanneischen Sprachmerkmale auf dem Hintergrund des Neuen Testaments und des zeitgenössischen hellenistischen Schrifttums* (NTOA 17; Freiburg [Schweiz]: Universitätsverlag; Göttingen: Vandenhoeck & Ruprecht, 1991).
Russell, D. S., *The Method and Message of Jewish Apocalyptic* (London: SCM, 1964).
Sabbe, M., "The Arrest of Jesus in Jn 18,1-11 and Its Relation to the Synoptic Gospels," in *L'Évangile de Jean* (M. de Jonge, ed.) 203-34.
———, "The Footwashing in Jn 13 and Its Relation to the Synoptic Gospels," *ETL* 58 (1982) 279-308.
———, "John 10 and Its Relationship to the Synoptic Gospels," in *The Shepherd Discourse of John 10 and Its Context* (J. Beutler and R. Fortna, eds.; Cambridge: Cambridge University Press, 1991) 75-93.
Sanday, W., *The Criticism of the Fourth Gospel* (Oxford: Clarendon, 1905).
Sanders, E. P., Baumgarten, A. I., and Mendelson, A. (eds.), *Jewish and Christian Self-Definition*, 2: *Aspects of Judaism in the Graeco-Roman Period* (Philadelphia: Fortress, 1981).
———, *Jesus and Judaism* (Philadelphia: Fortress, 1985).
———, *Judaism: Practice and Belief 63 BCE–66 CE* (London: SCM; Philadelphia: Trinity Press International, 1992).
Sanders, J. N., *The Fourth Gospel in the Early Church* (Cambridge: Cambridge University Press, 1943).
———, "Who Was the Disciple Whom Jesus Loved?" in *Studies in the Fourth Gospel* (F. L. Cross and C. H. Dodd, eds.; London: A. R. Mowbray, 1957) 72-82.
Sava, A. F., "The Wound in the Side of Christ," *CBQ* 19 (1957) 343-46.
Schäfer, P., *Studien zur Geschichte und Theologie des rabbinischen Judentums* (Leiden: E. J. Brill, 1978).
———, "Die sogenannte Synode von Jabne: Zur Trennung von Juden und Christen im ersten/zweiten Jh. n. Chr.," in *Studien zur Geschichte und Theologie des rabbinischen Judentums* (Leiden: E. J. Brill, 1978) 45-55.
Schenk, W., *Kommentiertes Lexikon zum vierten Evangelium: Seine Textkonstituenten in ihren Syntagmen und Wortfeldern* (Text-Theoretical Studies of the New Testament 1; Lewiston, NY: Mellen, 1993).
Schenke, L. (with R. Feige and J. Neugebauer), *Johannesevangelium: Einführung, Text,*

dramatische Gestalt (Kohlhammer Urban-Taschenbücher; Bd. 446; Stuttgart: Kohlhammer, 1992).

———, "Die formale und gedankliche Struktur von Joh 6:26-58," *BZ* (n.s.) 24 (1980) 21-41.

———, "Die literarische Vorgeschichte von John 6,26-58," *BZ* (n.s.) 29 (1985) 65-89.

———, "Der 'Dialog mit den Juden' im Johannesevangelium: Ein Rekonstruktionsversuch," *NTS* 34 (1988) 573-603.

———, "Die literarische Entstehungsgeschichte von John 1,19-51," *BN* 46 (1989) 24-57.

———, "John 7-10: Eine dramatische Szene," *ZNW* 80 (1989) 172-92.

———, "Das johanneische Schisma und die 'Zwölf' (Johannes 6.60-71)," *NTS* 38 (1992) 105-21.

Schiffman, L. H., *Reclaiming the Dead Sea Scrolls* (Philadelphia: Jewish Publication Society, 1994).

———, "At the Crossroads: Tannaitic Perspectives on the Jewish-Christian Schism," in *Jewish and Christian Self-Definition*, II: *Aspects of Judaism in the Graeco-Roman Period* (E. P. Sanders et al., eds.; Philadelphia: Fortress, 1981) 115-56.

Schmidt, A., "Zwei Anmerkungen zu P.Ryl. III 457," *APF* 35 (1989) 11-12.

Schmithals, W., *Johannesevangelium und Johannesbriefe: Forschungsgeschichte und Analyse* (BZNW 64; Berlin/New York: de Gruyter, 1992).

Schnackenburg, R., "Logos-Hymnus und johanneischer Prolog," *BZ* 1 (1957) 69-109.

———, "Die situationsgelösten Redestücke in Joh 3," *ZNW* 49 (1958) 88-99.

———, "Die Erwartung des 'Propheten' nach dem Neuen Testament und den Qumran-Texten," in *SE* (Series 5, 18; Berlin: Akademie-Verlag, 1959) 622-39.

———, "Die Messiasfrage im Johannesevangelium," in *Neutestamentliche Aufsätze: Festschrift J. Schmid zum 70. Geburtstag* (J. Blinzler, O. Kuss, and F. Mussner, eds.; Regensburg: Pustet, 1963) 240-64.

———, "Zur Traditionsgeschichte von Joh 4,46-54," *BZ* n.s. 8 (1964) 58-88.

———, "Der Menschensohn im Johannesevangelium," *NTS* 11 (1964-65) 123-37.

———, "Das Johannesevangelium als hermeneutische Frage," *NTS* 13 (1966-67) 197-210.

———, "Zur Rede vom Brot aus dem Himmel: Eine Beobachtung zu Joh 6,52," *BZ* n.s. 12 (1968) 248-52.

———, "On the Origin of the Fourth Gospel," in *Jesus and Man's Hope* (D. Buttrick, ed.) 223-46.

———, "Entwicklung und Stand der johanneischen Forschung seit 1955," in *L'Évangile de Jean* (M. de Jonge, ed.) 19-44.

———, "Die johanneische Gemeinde und ihre Geisterfahrung," in *Die Kirche des Anfangs: Festschrift Heinrich Schürmann zum 65. Geburtstag* (R. Schnackenburg, J. Ernst, and J. Wanke, eds.; Leipzig: St. Benno-Verlag, 1977) 277-306.

———, "Die Hirtenrede John 10,1-18," in *Das Johannesevangelium*, IV: *Ergänzende Auslegungen und Exkurse* (Freiburg im Breisgau: Herder, 1984).

———, "Ephesus: Entwicklung einer Gemeinde von Paulus zu Johannes," *BZ* n.s. 15 (1991) 41-64.

Schneider, H., "'The Word Was Made Flesh': An Analysis of the Theology of Revelation in the Fourth Gospel," *CBQ* 31 (1969) 344-56.

Schneider, J., "Zur Komposition von Joh 10," *ConBNT* 11 (Lund: Gleerup, 1947) 220-25.

———, "Zur Komposition von Joh 7," *ZNW* 45 (1954) 108-19.

———, "Zur Komposition von Joh. 18,12-27," *ZNW* 49 (1958) 111-19.
———, "Die Abschiedsreden Jesu: Ein Beitrag zur Frage der Komposition von Johannes 13,31–17,26," in *Gott und Götter: Festschrift E. Fascher* (Berlin: Evangelischer Verlag, 1958) 103-12.
Schneiders, S., *The Revelatory Text* (San Francisco: Harper, 1991).
———, *Written That You May Believe: Encountering Jesus in the Fourth Gospel* (New York: Crossroad, 1999).
———, "The Face Veil: A Johannine Sign (Jn 20:1-10)," *BTB* 13 (1983) 94-97.
———, "A Case Study: A Feminist Interpretation of John 4:1-42," in *The Revelatory Text: Interpreting the New Testament as Sacred Scripture* (San Francisco: Harper, 1991) 180-91.
———, "John 20:11-18: The Encounter of the Easter Jesus with Mary Magdalene — A Transformative Feminist Reading," in *What Is John?* vol. 1 (F. F. Segovia, ed.) 154-68.
Schnelle U., *Antidocetic Christology in the Gospel of John* (Minneapolis: Fortress, 1992).
———, *The Human Condition: Anthropology in the Teachings of Jesus, Paul and John* (Minneapolis: Fortress, 1996).
———, "Die Tempelreinigung und die Christologie des Johannesevangeliums," *NTS* 42 (1996) 359-73.
———, "Die Juden im Johannesevangelium," in *Gedenkt an das Wort* (C. Kähler, M. Böhm, and C. Böttrich, eds.; Leipzig: Evangelische Verlagsanstalt, 1999) 217-30.
———, "Recent Views of John's Gospel," *Word & World* 21 (2001) 352-59.
Schoedel, W., *Ignatius of Antioch* (Hermeneia; Philadelphia: Fortress, 1985).
Scholem, G. G., *Major Trends in Jewish Mysticism* (London: Thames and Hudson, 1955).
———, *Gnosticism, Merkabah Mysticism and Talmudic Tradition* (2d ed.; New York: Jewish Theological Seminary, 1965).
Scholtissek, K., *In Ihm sein und bleiben: Die Sprache der Immanenz in den johanneischen Schriften* (Herders biblische Studien 21; Freiburg/Basel/Vienna: Herder, 2000).
———, "Kinder Gottes und Freunde Jesu," in *Ekklesiologie des Neuen Testaments* (Freiburg: Herder, 1996) 184-211.
———, "Antijudaismus im Johannesevangelium? Ein Gesprächsbeitrag," in *"Nun steht aber diese Sache im Evangelium . . .": Zur Frage nach den Anfängen des christlichen Antijudaismus* (R. Kampling, ed.; Zürich: Schöningh, 1999) 151-81.
Schottroff, L., *Der glaubende und die feindliche Welt: Beobachtungen zum gnostischen Dualismus und seiner Bedeutung für Paulus und das Johannesevangelium* (WMANT 47; Neukirchen-Vluyn: Neukirchener, 1970).
Schuchard, B., *Scripture within Scripture* (SBLDS 133; Atlanta: Scholars Press, 1992).
Schürer, E., *The History of the Jewish People in the Age of Jesus Christ* (revised by G. Vermes and F. Millar; 3 vols.; Edinburgh: T&T Clark, 1973).
Schultz, S., *Untersuchungen zur Menschensohn-Christologie im Johannesevangelium: Zugleich ein Beitrag zur Methodengeschichte der Auslegung des 4 Evangeliums* (Göttingen: Vandenhoeck & Ruprecht, 1957).
———, *Komposition und Herkunft der Johanneischen Reden* (Stuttgart: Kohlhammer, 1960).
Schwank, B., "Ortskenntnisse im Vierten Evangelium? Bericht über ein Seminar in Jerusalem," *ErbAuf* 57 (1981) 427-42.

Schwankl, O., *Licht und Finsternis: Ein metaphorisches Paradigma in den johanneischen Schriften* (Freiburg/New York: Herder, 1995).

Schwartz, E., "Aporien im vierten Evangelium," *Nachrichten von der königlichen Gesellschaft der Wissenschaften zu Göttingen* (1907) 342-72; (1908) 115-48, 149-88, 497-560.

Schweizer, E., *Ego Eimi . . . : Die Religionsgeschichtliche Herkunft und theologische Bedeutung der johanneischen Bildreden, zugleich en Beitrag zur Quellenfrage des vierten Evangeliums* (FRLANT 38; Göttingen: Vandenhoeck & Ruprecht, 1939).

———, *Neotestamentica: Deutsche und englische Aufsätze, 1951-1963* (Zürich: Zwingli, 1963).

———, "Das johanneische Zeugnis vom Herrenmahl," *Evangelische Theologie* 12 (1952/1953) 341-63.

———, "Der Menschensohn," *ZNW* 50 (1959) 185-209.

———, "Zum religionsgeschichtlichen Hintergrund der 'Sendungsformel' Gal 4,4f.; Röm 8,3f.; Joh 4,16f.; 1 Joh 4,9," *ZNW* 57 (1966) 199-210.

———, "Was meinen wir eigentlich wenn wir sagen 'Gott sandte seinen Sohn . . .'?" *NTS* 37 (1991) 204-24.

Scobie, C. H., "Johannine Geography," *SR* 11 (1982) 77-84.

Scott, M., *Sophia and the Johannine Jesus* (Sheffield: JSOT, 1992).

Segal, A., *Two Powers in Heaven: Early Rabbinic Reports about Christianity and Gnosticism* (SJLA 25; Leiden: E. J. Brill, 1977).

———, *Life after Death: A History of the Afterlife in the Religions of the West* (New York: Doubleday, 2004).

———, "Ruler of This World: Attitudes about Mediator Figures and the Importance of Sociology for Self-Definition," in *Jewish and Christian Self-Definition, 2: Aspects of Judaism in the Graeco-Roman Period* (E. P. Sanders, A. I. Baumgarten, and A. Mendelson, eds.; Philadelphia: Fortress, 1981) 245-68.

Segallo, G., "Un appello alla perseveranza nella fede in Gv 8,31-32?" *Bib* 62 (1981) 387-89.

———, *La preghiera di Gesù al Padre (Giov. 17): Un addio missionario* (Studi Biblici 16; Grescia: Paideia, 1983).

Segovia, F. F., *Love Relationships in the Johannine Tradition* (SBLDS 58; Missoula: Scholars Press, 1982).

———, *The Farewell of the Word: The Johannine Call to Abide* (Minneapolis: Fortress, 1991).

——— (ed.), *What is John?* vol. 1: *Readers and Readings of the Fourth Gospel* (SBLSS 3; Atlanta: Scholars, 1996).

——— (ed.), *What is John?* vol. 2: *Literary and Social Readings of the Fourth Gospel* (SBLSS 8; Atlanta: Scholars Press, 1998).

———, "The Love and Hatred of Jesus and Johannine Sectarianism," *CBQ* 43 (1981) 258-69.

———, "The Theology and Provenance of John 15:1-17," *JBL* 101 (1982) 115-28.

———, "John 13, 1-20: The Footwashing in the Johannine Tradition," *ZNW* 73 (1982) 31-51.

———, "John 15:18–16:4a: A First Addition to the Original Farewell Discourse?" *CBQ* 45 (1983) 219-30.

Sekki, A. E., *The Meaning of Ruaḥ at Qumran* (SBLDS 110; Atlanta: Scholars Press, 1989).

Senior, D., *The Passion of Jesus in the Gospel of John* (Collegeville, MN: Liturgical Press, 1991).
Setzer, C., *Jewish Responses to Early Christians* (Minneapolis: Fortress, 1994).
Shanks, H., "The Siloam Pool in Jesus' Time" *BAR* 31, 5 (September/October 2005) 16-23.
Sheehan, J. F. X., "Feed My Lambs," *Scripture* 16 (1964) 21-27.
Shein, B. E., *Following the Way: The Setting of John's Gospel* (Minneapolis: Augsburg Fortress, 1980).
Shepherd, Jr., M., "The Jews in the Fourth Gospel: Another Level of Meaning," *AThRSup* 3 (1974) 95-112.
Sherwin-White, A. N., *Roman Law and Roman Society in the New Testament* (Oxford: Clarendon, 1963; reprint Grand Rapids: Baker, 1981).
———, "The Trial of Jesus," in *Historicity and Chronology in the New Testament* (D. Nineham, ed.; Theological Collections 6; London: SPCK, 1965) 97-116.
Sidebottom, E. M., "The Ascent and Descent of the Son of Man in the Gospel of St. John," *AThR* 2 (1957) 115-22.
Siegert, F., *Der Erstentwurf des Johannes* (Münsteraner Judaistische Studien 16; Münster: Lit Verlag, 2004).
Simonis, A. J., *Die Hirtenrede im Johannes-Evangelium* (AnBib 29; Rome: Pontifical Biblical Institute, 1967).
Sjöberg, E., *Der verborgene Menschensohn in den Evangelien* (Lund: Gleerup, 1955).
———, "Wiedergeburt und Neuschöpfung im palästinischen Judentum," *ST* 4 (1950) 44-85.
———, "Neuschöpfung in den Toten-Meer-Rollen," *ST* 9 (1955) 131-36.
Ska, J.-L., "Jésus et la Samaritaine (Jn 4): Utilité de l'Ancien Testament," *NRTh* 118, 5 (1996) 641-52.
Skeat, T. C., *Oxyrhynchus Papyri L* (London: Egypt Exploration Fund, 1983).
Slater, T. B., "One Like a Son of Man in First-Century-C.E. Judaism," *NTS* 41 (1995) 183-98.
Sloyan, G. S., *What Are They Saying about John?* (Mahwah, NJ: Paulist, 1991).
Smalley, S. S., *John: Evangelist and Interpreter* (2d ed.; Downers Grove, IL: InterVarsity, 1998).
———, "'The Paraclete': Pneumatology in the Johannine Gospel and Apocalypse," in *Exploring the Gospel of John* (R. A. Culpepper and C. C. Black, eds.) 289-300.
Smallwood, E. M., *The Jews under Roman Rule* (SJLA 20; Leiden: E. J. Brill, 1976).
Smiga, G., *Pain and Polemic: Anti-Judaism in the Gospels* (Mahwah, NJ: Paulist, 1992).
Smith, D. M., *The Composition and Order of the Fourth Gospel: Bultmann's Literary Theory* (New Haven: Yale University Press, 1965).
———, *Johannine Christianity: Essays on Its Setting, Sources and Theology* (Columbia, SC: University of South Carolina, 1984).
———, *John among the Gospels* (Minneapolis: Fortress, 1992).
———, *The Theology of the Gospel of John* (J. D. G. Dunn, ed.; New Testament Theology; Cambridge: Cambridge University Press, 1995).
———, "The Milieu of the Johannine Miracle Source: A Proposal," in *Jews, Greeks and Christians: Religious Cultures in Late Antiquity: Essays in Honor of W. D. Davies* (R. Hamerton-Kelly and R. Scroggs, eds.; SJLA 21; Leiden: E. J. Brill, 1976) 164-80.

———, "The Setting and Shape of a Johannine Narrative Source," *JBL* 95 (1976) 231-41 (reprinted in *Johannine Christianity* 80-94).

———, "Johannine Christianity: Some Reflections on Its Character and Delineation," *NTS* 21 (1976) 222-48 (reprinted in *Johannine Christianity* 1-36).

———, "Judaism and the Gospel of John," in *Jews and Christians: Exploring the Past, Present and Future* (J. H. Charlesworth, ed.; New York: Crossroad, 1990) 76-99.

———, "What Have I Learned about the Gospel of John?" in *What is John?* vol. 1 (F. F. Segovia, ed.) 217-35.

———, "Johannine Studies since Bultmann," *Word & World* 21 (2001) 343-51.

Smothers, E. R., "Two Readings in Papyrus Bodmer II," *HTR* 51 (1958) 109-22.

Sneath, E. H. (ed.), *Religion and the Future Life: The Development of the Belief in Life after Death* (London: George Allen & Unwin, 1923).

Spicq, C., *Agapē in the New Testament* (3 vols.; St. Louis: Herder, 1966).

Spitta, F., *Das Johannes-Evangelium als Quelle der Geschichte Jesu* (Göttingen: Vandenhoeck & Ruprecht, 1910).

Sproston, W., "'The Scripture' in John 17:12," in *Scripture: Meaning and Method* (B. P. Thompson, ed.; Hull: Hull University Press, 1987) 24-36.

———, "Witnesses to What Was *ap' archēs*: 1 John's Contribution to Our Knowledge of Tradition in the Fourth Gospel," *JSNT* 48 (1992) 43-65.

Staley, J. L., *The Print's First Kiss: A Rhetorical Investigation of the Implied Reader in the Fourth Gospel* (Atlanta: Scholars Press, 1988).

———, "Disseminations: An Autobiographical Midrash on Fatherhood in John's Gospel," in *God the Father in the Gospel of John* (A. Reinhartz, ed.) 127-54.

Stauffer, E., *Jesus and His Story* (London: SCM, 1960).

———, "Abschiedsreden," *Reallexikon für Antike und Christentum* 1 (1950) 29-35.

Stegemann, H., "Die Bedeutung der Qumranfunde für die Erforschung der Apokalyptik," in *Apocalypticism in the Mediterranean World and the Near East* (D. Helholm, ed.; 2d ed.; Tübingen: J. C. B. Mohr [Paul Siebeck], 1989) 495-530.

Stemberger, G., *La symbolique du bien et du mal selon Saint Jean* (Paris: Seuil, 1970).

Stibbe, M., *John as Storyteller: Narrative Criticism and the Fourth Gospel* (SNTSMS 73; Cambridge: Cambridge University Press, 1992).

Stowasser, M., *Johannes der Täufer im vierten Evangelium* (Klosterneuberg: Österreichisches Katholisches Bibelwerk, 1992).

Strachan, R., "Is the Fourth Gospel a Literary Unity?" *ExpTim* 27 (1914-16) 22-26, 232-37, 280-82, 330-33.

Strange, J. F., "Some Implications of Archaeology for New Testament Studies" in *What Has Archaeology to Do with Faith?* (J. H. Charlesworth and W. P. Weaver, eds.) 23-59.

———, "First-Century Galilee from Archaeology and from the Texts," in *Archaeology and the Galilee: Texts and Contexts in the Graeco-Roman and Byzantine Periods* (D. R. Edwards and C. T. McCulloch, eds.; South Florida Studies in Judaism, no. 143; Miami: University of South Florida Press, 1997) 39-43.

Strayor, P. M., "Transpositions of Text in St. John's Gospel," *JTS* (1901-2) 137-40.

Strecker, G., "Juden und Christen — Kinder eines Vaters," in *Die Hebräische Bibel und ihre zweifache Nachgeschichte: Festschrift R. Rendtorff* (E. Blum et al., eds.; Neukirchen-Vluyn: Neukirchener, 1990) 689-705.

Stroud, W., *Treatise on the Physical Cause of the Death of Christ and Its Relation to the Principles and Practice of Christianity* (2d ed., London: Hamilton & Adams, 1971).

Swetnam, J., "The Meaning of πεπιστευκότας in John 8,31," *Bib* 61 (1980) 106-9.

———, "Bestowal of the Spirit in the Fourth Gospel," *Bib* 74 (1993) 556-76.

Sylva, D. B., "Nicodemus and His Spices (John 19,39)," *NTS* 34 (1988) 148-51.

Talbert, C. H., *What Is a Gospel: The Genre of the Canonical Gospels* (Philadelphia: Fortress, 1977).

———, "Artistry and Theology: An Analysis of the Architecture of John 1:19–5:47," *CBQ* 32 (1970) 341-66.

———, "The Myth of a Descending-Ascending Redeemer in Mediterranean Antiquity," *NTS* 22 (1975-76) 418-40.

Tanzer, S. J., "Salvation Is *for* the Jews: Secret Christian Jews in the Gospel of John," in *The Future of Early Christianity: Essays in Honor of Helmut Koester* (B. A. Pearson, ed.; Minneapolis: Fortress, 1993) 285-300.

Taylor, J., *Christians and the Holy Places: The Myth of Christian Origins* (Oxford: Clarendon, 1993).

———, "The Cave at Bethany," *RB* 94 (1987) 120-23.

———, "The Garden of Gethsemane, Not the Place of Jesus' Arrest," *BAR* 21 (July/August 1995) 26-35, 62.

———, "Golgotha: A Reconsideration of the Evidence for the Sites of Jesus' Crucifixion and Burial," *NTS* 44 (1998) 180-203.

Teeple, H. M., *The Mosaic Eschatological Prophet* (SBLMS 10; Philadelphia: SBL, 1957).

———, *The Literary Origin of the Gospel of John* (Evanston: Religion and Ethics Institute, 1974).

———, "Methodology in Source Analysis of the Fourth Gospel," *JBL* 81 (1962) 279-86.

Temple, S., *The Core of the Fourth Gospel* (London: Mowbrays, 1975).

———, "The Two Traditions of the Last Supper, Betrayal, and Arrest," *NTS* 7 (1960-61) 77-85.

———, "A Key to the Composition of the Fourth Gospel," *JBL* 80 (1961) 220-32.

———, "Two Signs in the Fourth Gospel," *JBL* 81 (1963) 169-74.

Tenney, M. C., "Literary Keys to the Fourth Gospel: The Old Testament and the Fourth Gospel," *BSac* 120 (1963) 300-308.

———, "Literary Keys to the Fourth Gospel: The Author's Testimony to Himself," *BSac* 129 (1972) 214-23.

Thatcher, T., "A New Look at Asides in the Fourth Gospel," *BSac* 151 (1994) 418-39.

Theobald, M., *Die Fleischwerdung des Logos: Studien zum Verhältnis des Johannesprologs zum Corpus des Evangeliums und zu 1 Joh* (NTAbh n.f. 20; Münster: Aschendorff, 1988).

Thomas, J. C., *Footwashing in John 13 and the Johannine Community* (JSNTSup 61; Sheffield: Sheffield Academic Press, 1991).

———, "The Fourth Gospel and Rabbinic Judaism," *ZNW* 82 (1991) 159-82.

Thompson, J. M., "Accidental Disarrangement in the Fourth Gospel," *ExpTim* 9 (1915) 421-37.

———, "Is John xxi. an Appendix?" *ExpTim* 10 (1915) 139-47.

———, "The Structure of the Fourth Gospel," *ExpTim* 10 (1915) 512-26.

———, "The Composition of the Fourth Gospel," *ExpTim* 11 (1916) 34-46.
———, "Some Editorial Elements in the Fourth Gospel," *ExpTim* 14 (1917) 214-31.
Thompson, M. M., *The Humanity of Jesus in the Fourth Gospel* (Philadelphia: Fortress, 1988).
———, "'God's Voice You Have Never Heard, God's Form You Have Never Seen': The Characterization of God in the Gospel of John," *Semeia* 63 (1993) 177-204.
———, "The Historical Jesus and the Johannine Christ," in *Exploring the Gospel of John* (R. A. Culpepper and C. C. Black, eds.) 21-42.
———, "The Living Father," in *God the Father in the Gospel of John* (A. Reinhartz, ed.) 19-31.
Thüsing, W., *Die Erhöhung und Verherrlichung Jesu im Johannesevangelium* (NTAbh 21; 2d ed.; Münster: Aschendorff, 1970).
———, *Herrlichkeit und Einheit: Eine Auslegung des Hohenpriesterlichen Gebetes Jesu (John 17)* (2d ed.; Münster: Aschendorff, 1975).
Thyen, H., *Studien zur Sündenvergebung im Neuen Testament und seinen alttestamentlichen und jüdischen Voraussetzungen* (FRLANT 96; Göttingen: Vandenhoeck & Ruprecht, 1970).
———, "Johannes 13 und die 'kirchliche Redaktion' des vierten Evangeliums," in *Tradition und Glaube: Das frühe Christentum in seiner Umwelt* (G. Jeremias, H. W. Kuhn, and H. Stegemann, eds.; Göttingen: Vandenhoeck & Ruprecht, 1971) 343-56.
———, "Aus der Literatur zum Johannesevangelium," *TRu* 39 (1974) 1-69, 222-52, 289-330; 42 (1977) 211-70; 43 (1978) 328-59; 44 (1979) 97-134.
———, "Entwicklungen innerhalb der johanneischen Theologie und Kirche im Spiegel von Joh 21 und der Lieblingsjüngertexte des Evangeliums," in *L'Évangile de Jean* (M. de Jonge, ed.) 259-99.
———, "'Niemand hat grossere Liebe als die, dass er sein Leben für seine Freunde hingibt' (Joh 15,13): Das johanneische Verständnis des Kreuzestodes Jesu," in *Theologia Crucis — Signum Crucis* (C. Andresen and G. Klein, eds.; Tübingen: J. C. B. Mohr [P. Siebeck], 1979) 467-81.
———, "Das Heil kommt von den Juden," in *Kirche: Festschrift G. Bornkamm* (Tübingen: J. C. B. Mohr [Paul Siebeck], 1980) 689-705.
———, "Johannesevangelium," in *Theologische Realenzyklopädie 17* (Berlin: W. de Gruyter, 1988) 200-225.
———, "Johannes und die Synoptiker — Auf der Suche nach einem neuen Paradigm zur Beschreibung ihrer Beziehungen anhand von Beobachtungen an Passions- und Ostererzählungen," in *John and the Synoptics* (A. Denaux, ed.; BETL 101; Leuven: Leuven University Press, 1992) 81-107.
———, "Johannes 10 im Kontext des vierten Evangeliums," in *The Shepherd Discourse of John 10 and Its Context* (J. Beutler and R. Fortna, eds.) 116-34.
———, "Ich bin das Licht der Welt: Das Ich- und Ich-Bin-Sagen Jesu im Johannesevangelium," *JAC* 35 (1992) 19-46.
Timmins, N. G., "Variation in Style in the Johannine Literature," *JSNT* 53 (1994) 47-64.
Tobin, T., "The Prologue of John and Hellenistic Jewish Speculation," *CBQ* 52 (1990) 252-69.
Tödt, H. E., *The Son of Man in the Synoptic Tradition* (London: SCM, 1965).

Tolmie, D. F., *Jesus' Farewell to the Disciples: John 13:1–17:26 in Narratological Perspective* (Biblical Interpretation 12; Leiden: E. J. Brill, 1995).

Tomson, P. J., "The Names 'Israel' and 'Jew' in Ancient Judaism and the New Testament," *Bijdragen, tijdschrift voor filosofie en theologie* 47 (1986) 120-40, 266-89.

———, "The New Testament Canon as the Embodiment of Evolving Christian Attitudes towards the Jews," in *Canonization and Decanonization* (A. van der Kooij and K. van der Toorn, eds.; Leiden: Brill, 1998) 107-31.

———, "'Jews'" in the Gospel of John as Compared with the Palestinian Talmud, the Synoptics and Some New Testament Apocrypha," in *Anti-Judaism and the Fourth Gospel* (R. Bieringer, D. Pollefeyt, and F. Vandecasteele-Vanneuville, eds.) 301-40.

Topel, L. J., "A Note on the Methodology of Structural Analysis in Jn. 2,23–3,21," *CBQ* 33 (1971) 211-20.

Torrey, C. C., "The Aramaic Origin of the Gospel of John," *HTR* 16 (1923) 305-34.

Tov, E., "Recensional Differences between the Masoretic Text and the Septuagint of Proverbs," in *Of Scribes and Scrolls* (H. W. Attridge et al., eds.; College Theology Society Resources in Religion 5; Lanham, MD: University Press of America, 1990) 43-56.

Tovey, D., *Narrative Art and Act in the Fourth Gospel* (JSNTSup 151; Sheffield: Sheffield Academic Press, 1997).

Tragan, P.-R., *La parabole du 'pasteur' et ses explications: La genèse, les milieux littéraires* (SA 67; Rome: Anselmiana, 1980).

Trilling, W., *Studien zur Jesusüberlieferung* (SBAB 1; Stuttgart: Katholisches Bibelwerk, 1988).

———, "Gegner Jesu — Widersacher der Gemeinde — Repräsentanten der 'Welt': Das Johannesevangelium und die Juden," in *Studien* 209-31.

Trumbower, J. A., *Born from Above* (HUT 29; Tübingen: J. C. B. Mohr [P. Siebeck], 1992).

Tuckett, C. M., "Atonement in the NT," *ABD* 1, 518-22.

Turner, J. D., "The History of Religions Background of John 10," in *The Shepherd Discourse of John 10 and Its Context* (J. Beutler and R. Fortna, eds.) 33-52.

Tzaferis, V., "Jewish Tombs at and near Giv'at ha-Mivtar," *IEJ* 20 (1971) 18-32.

Ulrichsen, J., *Die Grundschrift der Testamente der Zwölf Patriarchen* (Uppsala: Academiae Ubsaliensis, 1991).

Urban, C., *Das Menschenbild nach dem Johannesevangelium* (WUNT 2/137; Tübingen: J. C. B. Mohr [P. Siebeck], 2001).

van Belle, G., *The Signs Source in the Fourth Gospel* (BETL 96; Leuven: Leuven University Press, 1994).

———, "Les parenthèses johanniques," in *The Four Gospels 1992* (F. Van Segbroeck et al., eds.) 2101-18.

———, "The Faith of the Galileans: The Parenthesis in Jn 4,44," *ETL* 74 (1998) 27-44.

———, "Tradition, Exegetical Formation, and the Leuven Hypothesis," in *What We Have Heard from the Beginning* (T. Thatcher, ed.; Waco, TX: Baylor University Press, 2007) 325-37.

van den Broek, R., "The Present State of Gnostic Studies," *VigChr* 37 (1983) 41-71.

van den Hoek, A., "Techniques of Quotation in Clement of Alexandria: A View of Ancient Literary Working Methods," *VigChr* 50 (1996) 223-43.

VanderKam, J., *Textual and Historical Studies in the Book of Jubilees* (Atlanta: Scholars Press, 1977).
———, *The Dead Sea Scrolls Today* (Grand Rapids: Eerdmans, 1994).
———, *An Introduction to Early Judaism* (Grand Rapids: Eerdmans, 2001).
———, and Flint, P., *The Meaning of the Dead Sea Scrolls* (New York: HarperCollins, 2004).
van der Ploeg, J., and van der Woude, A., *Targum de Job de la grotte XI de Qumrâm* (Leiden: Brill, 1971).
van der Watt, J. G., "The Use of *aiōnios* in the Concept *zōē aiōnios* in John's Gospel," *NovT* 31 (1989) 217-28.
———, "Ethics in First John: A Literary and Socioscientific Perspective," *CBQ* 61 (1999) 491-511.
van der Woude, A. S., and de Jonge, M., "11Q Melchizedek and the New Testament," *NTS* 12 (1966) 301-26.
van Dyke Parunak, H., "Oral Typesetting: Some Uses of Biblical Structure," *Bib* 62 (1981) 153-68.
van Imschoot, P., "L'ésprit de Jahvé, source de vie dans l'Ancien Testament," *RB* 44 (1935) 481-501.
van Segbroeck, F., et al., eds., *The Four Gospels 1992: Festschrift F. Neirynck* (4 vols.; Leuven: Leuven University Press, 1992).
van Staden, P. J., "The Debate on the Structure of 1 John," *Hervormde teologiese Studies* 47, 2 (1991) 487-502.
van Tilborg, S., *Reading John in Ephesus* (NovTSup 83; Leiden: E. J. Brill, 1996).
van Unnik, W. C., "De Verbinding *tauta eipōn* in het Evangelie van Johannes," in *Ad Interim* (Kampen: J. J. Kok, n.d.) 61-73.
———, "The Quotation from the Old Testament in John 12:34," *NovT* 3 (1959) 174-79.
Vanhoye, A., "La composition de Jn. 5,18-30," in *Melanges Bibliques en hommage au R. P. Beda Rigaux* (A. Descamps and A. Halleux, eds.; Gembloux: Duculot, 1970) 259-74.
Vellanickal, M., *The Divine Sonship of Christians in the Johannine Writings* (AnBib 72; Rome: Pontifical Biblical Institute, 1977).
———, "'I AM' in the Fourth Gospel," *Biblebhashyam* 19 (1993) 47-58.
Venetz, H.-J., "'Durch Wasser und Blut gekommen': Exegetische Überlegungen zu 1 Joh 5,6," in *Mitte des Neuen Testaments: Festschrift für Eduard Schweizer* (U. Luz and H. Weder, eds.; Göttingen: Vandenhoeck & Ruprecht, 1983) 345-61.
Vermes, G., *The Dead Sea Scrolls: Qumran in Perspective* (Philadelphia: Fortress, 1977).
———, *Jesus the Jew: A Historian's Reading of the Gospels* (Philadelphia: Fortress, 1981).
———, "Qumran Forum Miscellanea I," *JJS* 43 (1992) 303-4.
Vielhauer, P., *Geschichte der urchristlichen Literatur: Einleitung in das Neue Testament, die Apokryphen und die Apostolischen Väter* (2d ed.; Berlin: de Gruyter, 1978).
Vincent, L.-H., "L'Antonia et le Prétoire," *RB* 42 (1933) 83-113.
———, "Lithostrotos évangelique," *RB* 59 (1952) 513-30.
———, "L'Antonia, palais primitif d'Herode," *RB* 61 (1954) 87-107.
Voigt, G., *Licht, Liebe, Leben* (Biblisch-theologische Schwerpunkte 6; Göttingen: Vandenhoeck & Ruprecht, 1995).
Von der Osten-Sacken, P., *Gott und Belial: Traditionsgeschichtliche Untersuchungen zum*

Dualismus in den Texten aus Qumran (SUNT 6; Göttingen: Vandenhoeck & Ruprecht, 1969).
von Dobschütz, E., "Johanneische Studien I," *ZNW* 8 (1907) 1-8.
von Schlatter, A., *Die Sprache und Heimat des vierten Evangelisten* (BCFT Jhrg. 6, Heft 4; Gütersloh: C. Bertelsmann, 1902).
———, *Der Evangelist Johannes* (Stuttgart: Calwer, 1948).
von Wahlde, U. C., *The Earliest Version of John's Gospel* (Wilmington, DE/Collegeville, MN: Michael Glazier/Liturgical Press, 1989).
———, "A Redactional Technique in the Fourth Gospel," *CBQ* 38 (1976) 520-33.
———, "The Terms for Religious Authorities in the Fourth Gospel: A Key to Literary Strata?" *JBL* 98 (1979) 231-53.
———, "Faith and Works in Jn vi 28-29: Exegesis or Eisegesis?" *NovT* 22 (1980) 304-15.
———, "The Witnesses to Jesus in John 5:31-40 and Belief in the Fourth Gospel," *CBQ* 43 (1981) 385-404.
———, "The Johannine 'Jews': A Critical Survey," *NTS* 28 (1982) 33-60.
———, "*Wiederaufnahme* as a Marker of Redaction in Jn 6,51-58," *Bib* 64 (1983) 542-49.
———, "Literary Structure and Theological Argument in Three Discourses with the Jews in the Fourth Gospel," *JBL* 103 (1984) 575-84.
———, "The Gospel of John and the Presentation of Jews and Judaism," in *Within Context* (L. Klenicki, D. Efroymson, and E. Fisher, eds.) 67-84.
———, "Community in Conflict: The History and Social Context of the Johannine Community," *Interpretation* 49 (1995) 379-89.
———, "The Relationships between Pharisees and Chief Priests: Some Observations on the Texts in Matthew, John, and Josephus," *NTS* 42 (1996) 506-22.
———, "'The Jews' in John's Gospel: Fifteen Years of Research (1983-1998)," *ETL* 76, 1 (2000) 30-55.
———, "'You Are of Your Father the Devil' in Its Context: Stereotyped Polemic in Jn 8:38-47," in *Anti-Judaism and the Fourth Gospel: Papers from the Leuven Colloquium, 2000* (R. Bieringer, D. Pollefeyt, and F. Vandecasteele-Vanneuville, eds.; Assen: Royal Van Gorcum, 2001) 418-44.
———, "The Samaritan Woman Episode, Synoptic Form-Criticism, and the Johannine Miracles: A Question of Criteria," in *Theology and Christology in the Fourth Gospel: Essays by the Members of the SNTS Johannine Writings Seminar* (BETL 184: Leuven: Peeters, 2004) 502-18.
———, "'He Has Given to the Son to Have Life in Himself' (John 5:26)," *Bib* 75 (2004) 409-12.
———, "The Gospel of John and Archaeology," in *Jesus and Archaeology* (J. Charlesworth, ed.; Grand Rapids: Eerdmans, 2006) 523-86.
———, "Judas, the Son of Perdition, and the Fulfillment of Scripture in John 17:12," in *The New Testament and Early Christian Literature in Greco-Roman Context: Studies in Honor of D. Aune* (J. Fotopoulos, ed.; Leiden: Brill, 2006) 167-82.
———, "The Interpretation of the Death of Jesus in John against the Background of First-Century Jewish Expectations" (BETL 200; Leuven: Peeters, 2007) 579-90.
Vouga, F., *Le cadre historique et l'intention théologique de Jean* (Paris: Beauchesne, 1977).
———, "Antijudaismus im Johannesevangelium?" *TGl* 83, 1 (1993) 81-89.

Bibliography

Waetjen, H. C. (ed.), *The Gospel of John in Sociolinguistic Perspective* (Protocol of the Forty-Eighth Colloquy; Berkeley: Center for Hermeneutical Studies in Hellenistic and Modern Culture, 1984).

———, *The Gospel of the Beloved Disciple* (Edinburgh: T&T Clark, 2005).

Walker, W. O., "The Origin of the Son of Man Concept as Applied to Jesus," *JBL* 91 (1972) 482-90.

———, "The Son of Man: Some Recent Developments," *CBQ* 45 (1983) 584-607.

Wallace, D. B., "Reconsidering 'The Story of Jesus and the Adulteress Reconsidered,'" *NTS* 39 (1993) 290-96.

Watson, W. G. E., "Antecedents of a NT Proverb," *VT* 20 (1970) 368-70.

Wead, D. W., *The Literary Devices in John's Gospel* (Theologische Dissertationen IV; Basel: F. Reinhart, 1970).

Wegner, U., *Der Hauptmann von Kafarnaum (Mt 7,28a; 8,5-10 par Luke 7,1-10): Ein Beitrag zur Q-Forschung* (WUNT 2/14; Tübingen: J. C. B. Mohr [P. Siebeck], 1985).

Weiss, H., "Footwashing in the Johannine Community," *NovT* 21 (1979) 298-325.

———, "The Sabbath in the Fourth Gospel," *JBL* 110 (1991) 311-21.

Welch, C., *Erzälte Zeichen: Die Wundergeschichten des Johannesevangelium literarisch untersucht; mit einem Ausblick auf Joh 21* (WUNT 2/69; Tübingen: J. C. B. Mohr [P. Siebeck], 1994).

Wellhausen, J., *Erweiterungen und Änderungen im vierten Evangelium* (Berlin: Reimer, 1907).

Wendt, H. H., *Die Schichten im vierten Evangelium* (Göttingen: Vandenhoeck & Ruprecht, 1911).

Wengst, K., *Bedrängte Gemeinde und verherrlichter Christus: Der historische Ort des Johannesevangeliums als Schlüssel zu seiner Interpretation* (2d ed.; BTS 3; Neukirchen-Vluyn: Neukirchener, 1983).

Westermann, C., *The Gospel of John in the Light of the Old Testament* (Peabody, MA: Hendrickson, 1998).

Whitacre, R. A., *Johannine Polemic* (SBLDS 67; Chico: Scholars Press, 1982).

White, M. C., *The Identity and Function of Jews and Related Terms in the Fourth Gospel* (Ph.D. dissertation; Ann Arbor: University Microfilms, 1972).

Widdicombe, P., "The Fathers on the Father in the Gospel of John," in *God the Father in the Gospel of John* (A. Reinhartz, ed.) 105-25.

Wilcox, M., "The Composition of John 13,21-30," in *Neotestamentica et Semitica* (Edinburgh: T&T Clark, 1969) 143-56.

———, "The 'Prayer' of Jesus in John XI.41b-42," *NTS* 24 (1977) 128-32.

Wilckens, U., *Der Sohn Gottes und seine Gemeinde: Studien zur Theologie der Johanneischen Schriften* (FRLANT 200; Göttingen: Vandenhoeck & Ruprecht, 2002).

Wilken, R. L. (ed.), *Aspects of Wisdom in Judaism and Early Christianity* (South Bend: University of Notre Dame Press, 1975).

Wilkens, W., *Die Entstehungsheschichte des vierten Evangeliums* (Zollikon-Zurich: Evangelischer, 1958).

———, *Zeichen und Werke: Ein Beitrag zur Theologie des 4. Evangeliums in Erzahlungs- und Redestoff* (Zurich: Zwingli, 1969).

———, "Die Erweckung des Lazarus," *TZ* 15 (1959) 22-39.

———, "Evangelist und Tradition im Johannesevangelium," *TZ* 16 (1960) 81-90.
Willemse, J., "La Patrie de Jésus selon Saint Jean, iv.44," *NTS* 11 (1964/65) 349-64.
Willett, M., *Wisdom Christology in the Fourth Gospel* (San Francisco: Mellen Research University Press, 1992).
Williams, C., *"I Am He"* (WUNT 2/113; Tübingen: J. C. B. Mohr [P. Siebeck], 2000).
Williams, R. H., "The Mother of Jesus at Cana: A Social-Science Interpretation of John 2:1-12," *CBQ* 59 (1997) 679-92.
Wilson, J., "The Integrity of John 3:22-36," *JSNT* 10 (1981) 34-41.
Wilson, R. McL., "Nag Hammadi and the New Testament," *NTS* 28 (1982) 289-302.
Wilson, S. G., *Related Strangers: Jews and Christians, 70-170 C.E.* (Minneapolis: Fortress, 1995).
Windisch, H., *The Spirit-Paraclete in the Fourth Gospel* (Facet Books; Biblical Series 20; Philadelphia: Fortress, 1968).
Winter, M., *Das Vermächtnis Jesu und die Abschiedsworte der Väter: Gattungsgeschichtliche Untersuchung der Vermächtnisrede im Blick auf Joh. 13–17* (FRLANT 161; Göttingen: Vandenhoeck & Ruprecht, 1994).
Winter, P., *On the Trial of Jesus* (Studia Judaica 1; Berlin: Walter de Gruyter, 1961).
Witherington, B., *Jesus the Sage and the Pilgrimage of Wisdom* (Minneapolis: Fortress, 1994).
Wojciechowski, M., "La source de Jean 13.1-20," *NTS* 34 (1988) 135-41.
Wolff, H. W., *The Anthropology of the Old Testament* (Philadelphia: Fortress, 1974).
Wöllmer, H., *Zeichenglaube und Zeichenbuch: Ein literarkritischer Beitrag zur Entstehungsgeschichte des Johannesevangeliums* (Dissertation; Leipzig, 1988).
Woll, D. B., *Johannine Christianity in Conflict: Authority, Rank, and Succession in the First Farewell Discourse* (SBLDS 60; Chico, CA: Scholars Press, 1981).
———, "The Departure of 'The Way': The First Farewell Discourse in the Gospel of John," *JBL* 99 (1980) 225-39.
Wright, N. T., *The Resurrection of the Son of God* (Minneapolis: Fortress, 2003).
Xavier, A., "Thomas in the Fourth Gospel," *IndTheolStud* 30, 1 (1993) 18-28.
Yadin, Y., *The Finds from the Bar-Kochba Period in the Cave of Letters* (Jerusalem: Israel Exploration Society, 1963).
Yamauchi, E., *Pre-Christian Gnosticism* (Grand Rapids: Eerdmans, 1973).
———, "Jewish Gnosticism? The Prologue of John, Mandaean Parallels, and the Trimorphic Protennoia," in *Studies in Gnosticism and Hellenistic Religions Presented to Gilles Quispel on the Occasion of His 65th Birthday* (R. van den Broeck and M. J. Vermaseren, eds.; EPRO 91; Leiden: E. J. Brill, 1981).
Zeiner, G., "Weisheitbuch und Johannesevangelium," *Bib* 38 (1957) 396-418; 39 (1958) 37-60.
Zeitlin, S., "The Names Hebrew, Jew and Israel," *JQR* 43 (1953) 365-79.
Zias, J., and Sekeles, E., "The Crucified Man from Giv'at ha-Mitvar: A Reappraisal," *IEJ* 35 (1985) 22-27.
Zimmermann, H., "Das absolute EGO EIMI als neutestamentliche Offenbarungsformel," *BZ* 4 (1960) 54-69, 266-76.
Zumstein, J., *Kreative Erinnerung* (ATANT 84; 2d ed.; Zürich: Theologischer Verlag, 2004).

Bibliography

―――, "L'Interprétation johannique de la mort du Christ," in *The Four Gospels 1992* (F. van Segbroeck et al., eds.) 2119-38.

5. Commentaries on the Johannine Letters

Balz, H. R., and Schrage, W., *Die katholischen Briefe* (4th ed.; Göttingen: Vandenhoeck & Ruprecht, 1993).

Beutler, J., *Die Johannesbriefe* (Regensburger Neues Testament; Regensburg: Pustet, 2000).

Bonnard, P., *Les Épitres Johanniques* (Commentaire du Nouveau Testament 23c; Genève: Labor et Fides, 1983).

Brooke, A. E., *A Critical and Exegetical Commentary on the Johannine Epistles* (ICC; Edinburgh: T&T Clark, 1912).

Brown, R. E., *The Epistles of John* (AB 30; Garden City, NY: Doubleday, 1982).

Bultmann, R., *The Johannine Epistles* (Hermeneia; Philadelphia: Fortress, 1973).

Culpepper, R. Alan, *The Gospel and Letters of John* (Nashville: Abingdon, 1998).

Dodd, C. H., *The Johannine Epistles* (MNTC; London: Hodder and Stoughton Limited, 1946).

de Jonge, M., *Brieven van Johannes* (Het Prediking van het Nieuwe Testament; 3d ed.; Nijkerk: Callenbach, 1978).

Edwards, R. B., *The Johannine Epistles* (New Testament Guides; Sheffield: Sheffield Academic Press, 1996).

Grayston, K., *The Johannine Epistles* (NCBC; London/Grand Rapids: Marshall, Morgan & Scott/Eerdmans, 1984).

Harnack, A., "Über den dritten Johannesbrief," *Texte und Untersuchungen* 15:3 (1897) 3-27.

Houlden, J. L., *A Commentary on the Johannine Epistles* (HNTC; New York: Harper and Row, 1973).

Johnson, T. L., *1, 2, and 3 John* (NIBC; Peabody, MA: Hendrickson, 1993).

Klauck, H.-J., *Der Erste Johannesbriefe* (EKKNT 23/1; Zurich: Benziger; Neukirchen-Vluyn: Neukirchener, 1991)

―――, *Der Zweite und Dritte Johannesbrief* (EKKNT 23/2; Zurich: Benziger; Neukirchen-Vluyn: Neukirchener, 1992).

Lieu, J., *The Second and Third Epistles of John* (Edinburgh: T&T Clark, 1986).

Loader, W. R. G., *The Johannine Epistles* (Epworth Commentaries; London: Epworth, 1992).

Painter, J., *1, 2, 3 John* (Sacra Pagina 18; Collegeville, MN: Liturgical Press, 2002).

Perkins, P., *The Johannine Epistles* (New Testament Message 21; Wilmington: Glazier, 1979).

Rensberger, D. K., *1 John, 2 John, 3 John* (Abingdon New Testament Commentaries; Nashville: Abingdon, 1997).

Schmithals, W., *Johannesevangelium und Johannesbriefe: Forschungsgeschichte und Analyse* (BZNW 64; Berlin/New York: de Gruyter, 1992).

Schnackenburg, R., *The Johannine Epistles* (ET of 7th Germ. ed. [1984]; New York: Crossroads, 1992).

Schunack, G., *Die Briefe des Johannes* (Zürcher Bibelkommentare; Zürich: Theologischer Verlag, 1982).

Smalley, S. S., *1, 2, 3 John* (WBC 51; Waco, TX: Word, 1984).
Smith, D. M., *First, Second, and Third John* (Interpretation; Louisville: John Knox, 1991).
Strecker, G., *The Johannine Epistles* (Hermeneia; Minneapolis: Fortress, 1989, ET 1996).
Thompson, M. M., *1-3 John* (The IVP New Testament Commentary Series; Downers Grove: InterVarsity, 1992).
Übele, W., *Viele Verführer sind in die Welt ausgegangen: Die Gegner in den Briefen des Ignatius von Antiochien und in den Johannesbriefen* (BWANT 8; Folge 11; Stuttgart: Kohlhammer, 2001).
Vogler, W., *Die Briefe des Johannes* (THKNT 17; Leipzig: Evangelische Verlagsanstalt, 1993).
Vouga, F., *Die Johannesbriefe* (HNT 15/III; Tübingen: J. C. B. Mohr [P. Siebeck], 1990).
Wengst, K., *Der erste, zweite und dritte Brief des Johannes* (Ökumenischer Taschenbuch-Kommentar zum Neuen Testament 16; Gütersloh: Gütersloher Verlagshaus Mohn; Würzburg: Echter-Verlag, 2d ed. 1990).
Windisch, H., *Die katholischen Briefe* (HNT 15; 3d ed.; Tübingen: Mohr-Siebeck, 1951) 168-71.

6. Articles and Monographs on the Johannine Letters

Bergmeier, R., "Zum Verfasserproblem des II. und III. Johannesbriefes," *ZNW* 57 (1966) 93-100.
Bogart, J., *Orthodox and Heretical Perfectionism in the Johannine Community as Evident in the First Epistle of John* (SBLDS 33; Missoula: Scholars Press, 1977).
Brooke, G. J., *Exegesis at Qumran: 4Q Florilegium in Its Jewish Context* (Sheffield: JSOT Press, 1985).
Bultmann, R., "Analyse des Ersten Johannesbriefes," in *Festgabe für A. Jülicher* (Tübingen: Mohr-Siebeck, 1927) 138-58.
———, "Die kirchliche Redaktion des I. Johannesbriefes," in *In Memoriam Ernst Lohmeyer* (W. Schmauch, ed.; Stuttgart: Evangelisches Verlagswerk, 1951) 189-201.
de Boer, M. C., *Johannine Perspectives on the Death of Jesus* (Contributions to Biblical Exegesis and Theology 17; Kampen: Kok Pharos, 1996).
———, "The Death of Jesus Christ and His Coming in the Flesh (1 John 4:2)," *NovT* 23, 4 (1991) 326-46.
de Jonge, M., "An Analysis of I John 1.1-4," *BT* (1978) 322-30.
———, "Jesus' Death for Others and the Death of the Maccabean Martyrs," in T. Baarda, et al. (eds.), *Text and Testimony* (Festschrift A. F. J. Klijn; Kampen: Kok, 1988) 142-51.
de la Potterie, I., "La notion de 'commencement' dans les écrits johanniques," in *Die Kirche des Anfangs* (R. Schnackenburg et al., eds.; Leipzig: St. Benno, 1977) 379-403.
Dodd, C. H., "*Hilaskesthai*, Its Cognates, Derivatives and Synonyms in the Septuagint," *JTS* 32 (1931) 352-60.
———, "The First Epistle of John and the Fourth Gospel," *BJRL* 21 (1937) 129-56.
———, *According to the Scriptures* (New York: Scribner's, 1953).
Donfried, K. P., "Ecclesiastical Authority in 2-3 John," in *L'Évangile de Jean: Sources, Redaction, Theologie* (M. de Jonge, ed.; BETL 44; Gembloux: Duculot, 1977) 325-33.

Bibliography

Ernst, J., *"Antichristos,"* in *Exegetisches Wörterbuch zum Neuen Testament* (H. Balz and G. Schneider, eds.; Stuttgart: Kohlhammer, 1978-83) 1, 265-67.

Exler, F. X. J., *The Form of the Ancient Letter: A Study in Greek Epistolography* (Washington, DC: The Catholic University of America, 1923).

Feuillet, A., "The Structure of First John: Comparison with the Fourth Gospel," *BTB* 3 (1973) 665-70.

Funk, R. W., "The Form and Structure of II John and III John," *JBL* 86 (1967) 424-30.

———, "The Apostolic Parousia," in *Christian History and Interpretation* (W. Farmer, ed.; Cambridge: Cambridge University Press, 1967) 249-68.

Giurisato, G., *Struttura e teologia della prima lettera di Giovanni: Analisi letteraria e retorica, contenuto, theologico* (AnBib 138; Rome: Pontificio Istituto Biblico, 1998).

Grayston, K., "'Logos' in I John 1,1," *ExpTim* 86 (1974-75) 279.

Griffith, T., *Keep Yourselves from Idols* (JSNTSup 233; Sheffield: Sheffield Academic Press, 2002).

Hanse, H., *"Gott Haben" in der antike und im frühen Christentum* (Religionsgeschichtliche Versuche und Vorarbeiten 27; Berlin: Töpelmann, 1939).

Harris, J. R., "A Study in Letter Writing," *ExpTim* 5, 8 (1898) 161-80.

Hiebert, D. E., "An Expositional Study of 1 John, Part 5 (of 10 parts): An Exposition of 1 John 2:29–3:12," *BSac* 146 (1989) 198-216.

Hills, J. V., "A Genre for First John," in *The Future of Early Christianity: Essays in Honor Helmut Koester* (B. A. Pearson, ed.; Minneapolis: Fortress, 1993).

Holtzmann, H. J., "Über das Problem des ersten johanneischen Briefes in seinem Verhältnis zum Evangelium," *Jahrbuch für Protestantische Theologie* 7 (1881) 690-712; 8 (1882) 128-52, 316-42, 460-85.

Käsemann, E., *Exegetische Versuche und Besinnungen I* (3d ed.; Göttingen: Vandenhoeck & Ruprecht, 1965).

———, "Ketzer und Zeuge," *ZTK* 48 (1951) 292-311.

Kim, C., *Form and Structure of the Familiar Letter of Recommendation* (SBLDS 4; Missoula: Scholars Press, 1972).

Kim, M.-G., *Zum Verhältnis des Johannesevangeliums zu den Johannesbriefen: zur Verfasserschaft der johanneischen Schriften in der Forschung* (Europäische Hochschulschriften, Reihe 23; Frankfurt am Main: Peter Lang, 2003).

Koskenniemi, H., *Studien zur Idee und Phraseologie des griechischen Briefes bis 400 n. Chr.* (Annales Academiae Scientiarum Fennicae; Series B; vol. 102, 2; Helsinki: n.p., 1956).

Kügler, J., "In Tat und Wahrheit: Zur Problemlage des Ersten Johannesbriefes," *BN* 48 (1989) 61-88.

Law, R., *The Tests of Life* (Edinburgh: T&T Clark, 1909).

Malherbe, A., "The Inhospitality of Diotrephes," in *God's Christ and His People* (J. Jervell and W. Meeks, eds.; Oslo: Universitetsforlaget, 1977) 222-32.

Malina, B. J., "The Received View and What It Cannot Do: III John and Hospitality," *Semeia* 35 (1986) 171-94.

Manns, J., "'Le péché, c'est Bélial': 1 Jn 3,4 à la lumière du Judaïsme," *RSR* 62 (1989) 1-9.

Mitchell, M., "'Diotrephes Does Not Receive Us': The Lexicographical and Social Context of 3 John 9-10," *JBL* 117 (1998) 299-320.

Articles and Monographs on the Johannine Letters

Mullins, T. Y., "Petition as a Literary Form," *NovT* 5 (1962) 46-54.

———, "Greeting as a New Testament Form," *JBL* 87, 4 (1968) 418-26.

Munck, J., "Presbyters and Disciples of the Lord in Papias," *HTR* 52 (1959) 223-43.

Nauck, W., *Die Tradition und der Charackter des ersten Johannesbriefes* (WUNT 3; Tübingen: Mohr, 1957).

Nida, E. et al., *Style and Discourse* (Cape Town: Bible Society, 1983).

Painter, J., *John, Witness and Theologian* (3d ed.; Melbourne: Beacon Hill, 1980) 115-25.

———, "The 'Opponents' in 1 John," *NTS* 32 (1986) 48-71.

Petrie, C. S., "The Authorship of 'The Gospel According to Matthew': A Reconsideration of the External Evidence," *NTS* 14 (1967-68) 15-32.

Piper, O. A., "1 John and the Didache of the Primitive Church," *JBL* 66 (1947) 437-51.

Roller, O., *Das Formular der paulinishcen Briefe* (Stuttgart: Kohlhammer, 1933).

Schenke, H. M., "Determination und Ethik im ersten Johannesbrief," *ZTK* 60 (1963) 203-15.

Schmid, H., *Gegner im 1. Johannesbrief?* (BWANT 159; Stuttgart: Kohlhammer, 2002).

———, "How to Read the First Epistle of John Non-Polemically," *Bib* 85 (2004) 24-41.

Schubert, P., *The Form and Function of the Pauline Thanksgivings* (BZNW 20; Berlin: A. Töpelmann, 1939).

Schweizer, E., *Church Order in the New Testament* (ET; SBT 32; Naperville, IL: A. R. Allenson, 1961).

Sproston, W., "Witnesses to What Was *ap' archēs*: 1 John's Contribution to Our Knowledge of Tradition in the Fourth Gospel," *JSNT* 48 (1992) 43-65.

Steen, H. A., "Les clichés épistolaires dans les lettres sur papyrus grecques," *Classica et Mediaevalia* 1 (1938) 119-76.

Thomas, J. C., "The Order of the Composition of the Johannine Epistles," *NovT* 37 (1995) 68-75.

Turner, N., *Syntax*. Vol. 3 of *A Grammar of New Testament Greek*, by J. H. Moulton (Edinburgh: T&T Clark, 1963).

———, *Style*. Vol. 4 of *A Grammar of New Testament Greek*, by J. H. Moulton (Edinburgh: T&T Clark, 1976).

van Staden, P. J., "The Debate on the Structure of 1 John," *HTR* 47 (1991) 487-502.

van Unnik, W. C., "The Quotation from the Old Testament in John 12:34," *NovT* 3, 3 (1959) 174-79.

———, "The Authority of the Presbyters in Irenaeus' Works," in *God's Christ and His People* (J. Jervell and W. Meeks, eds.; Oslo: Universitetsforlaget, 1977) 248-60.

von Wahlde, U. C., *The Johannine Commandments: 1 John and the Struggle for the Johannine Tradition* (New York: Paulist, 1990).

———, "The Theological Foundation of the Presbyter's Argument in 2 Jn (vv. 4-6)," *ZNW* 76, 3/4 (1985) 209-24.

———, "The Stereotyped Structure and the Puzzling Pronouns of 1 John 2:28–3:10," *CBQ* 64 (2002) 319-38.

———, "'You Are of Your Father the Devil' in Its Context: Stereotyped Polemic in Jn 8:38-47," in *Anti-Judaism and the Fourth Gospel: Papers from the Leuven Colloquium, 2000* (ed. R. Bieringer, D. Pollefeyt, and F. Vandecasteele-Vanneuville; Jewish and Christian Heritage Series 1; Assen: Van Gorcum, 2001) 418-44.

Bibliography

Weir, J. E., "The Identity of the Logos in the First Epistle of John," *ExpTim* 86 (1974-75) 118-20.

White, J. L., *The Form and Function of the Body of the Greek Letter* (SBLDS 2; Missoula: Scholars Press, 1972).

———, *The Form and Structure of the Official Petition* (SBLDS 5; Missoula, Mont.: Scholars Press, 1972).

———, *Light from Ancient Letters* (Philadelphia: Fortress, 1986).

———, "Introductory Formulae in the Body of the Pauline Letter," *JBL* 90, 1 (1971) 91-97.

———, "New Testament Epistolary Literature in the Framework of Ancient Epistolography," *ANRW* (1984) 2.1730-56.

Author Index

Aland, B. and K.: *Text,* 7, n.6, n.7, n.8; 8, n.9; 386, n.274; "Papyri III," 7, n.6
Anderson, P.: *Christology,* 397, n.3; 423, n.68
Arockiam, M.: *Joy,* 186, n.88
Ashton, J.: *Understanding,* 251, n.45; 253, n.51; 274, n.105; 373, n.249; 398, n.4; 411, n.33; 412, n.35; 418, n.63; 430, n.79, n.80, n.81; 431, n.84; 447, n.103; 462, n.139; "Identity," 64, n.2; 168, n.56; 399, n.7; "Transformation," 429, n.77
Audet, J.-P., "Esquisse," 334, n.214
Augenstein, J., *Liebesgebot,* 281, n.119
Aune, D., "Dualism," 256, n.58

Bacon, B. W., "Immortality," 325, n.197
Bardsley, J., "Testimony," 387, n.277
Barrett, C. K.: *Gospel,* 15, n.30; 70, n.18; 292, n.141; 294, n.144; 295, n.144; 296, n.149, n.151; 316, n.179, n.180, n.181, n.182; 387, n.285; 392, n.303; 516, n.243; 517, n.246, n.247; 549, n.319; "Holy Spirit," 454, n.121; "Lamb," 326, n.203
Bassler, J. M., "Galileans," 114, n.88
Bauckham, R.: "Beloved," 328, n.208; "For Whom," 116, n.90; 168, n.57; "John," 371, n.248; "Qumran," 256, n.58; 268, n.92; "Study," 387, n.277
Beasley-Murray, G. R., *Gospel,* 13; 15, n.30; 241, n.24; 270, n.96; 316, n.180, n.181; 412, n.35

Becker, J.: *Auferstehung,* 325, n.197; *Evangelium,* 13, n.16; 21, n.51; 64, n.2; 73, n. 29; 165, n.51; 237, n.8; 241, n.24; 252, n.46; 255, n.56; 256, n.57; 326; "Beobachtungen," 165, n.51; 252, n.46; (review: *TRu* 51), 393, n.307
Berger, K., *Im Anfang,* 133, n.134, n.135
Bergmeier, R., "Glaube," 243, n.30
Bernard, J. H.: "Guérison," 195, n.103; *Gospel,* 13; 74, n.31; 87, n.47; 240; 264, n.77, n.78; 295, n.148; 297, n.150; 350, n.229
Beutler, *Johannesbriefe,* 537, n.294
Böcher, O., *Dualismus,* 166, n.52; 245, n.33; 252, n.46; 268, n.89; 273, n.100, n.102
Bogart, J., *Perfectionism,* 315, n.177; 326, n.203; 522, n.263; 524, n.269, n.270; 529, n.280; 530, n.281; 531, n.282
Boismard, M.-É.: *Moses or Jesus,* 112, n.86; 397, n.3; 400, n.10; 401, n.13; 402, n.15; *Victory,* 414, n.46, n.52; 415, n.53; 481, n.182; "Clément," 386, n.276; "L'Évolution," 286, n.129; 375, n.252; 491, n.197; "Procédé," 19; 24, n.58; "Traditions," 79, n.37
with Lamouille, A.: *Jean,* 15, n.28; 18; 19, n.39; 21; 24, n.58; 64, n.2; 68, n.14; *Pré-Johannique,* 386, n.275; *Vie,* 19, n.39
Borgen, P.: *Bread,* 196, n.104; "God's Agent," 412, n.36, n.37; 413, n.42

Borig, R., *Weinstock*, 184, n.81
Boring, M. E., "Influence," 220, n.128
Botha, J. E., *Samaritan Woman*, 19, n.45
Braun, F. M.: *Jean*, 318, n.189; 387, n.277; "L'arrière-fond," 278, n.114; 281
Braun, H., *Qumran*, 252, n.46; 272, n.98;
Brooke, A. E., *Epistles*, 366, n.241
Brown, R. E.: *Christology*, 413, n.45; 414, n.46, n.49; 415, n.56; 429, n.77; 453, n.118; 521, n.261; *Churches*, 507; 508, n.221; 540, n.298; 541, n.299, n.301; 542, n.303; *Community*, 92, n.55; 326, n.203; 328, n.208; 436, n.88; 449, n.110; *Death*, 3, n.3; 118, n.91; 120, n.93; 122, n.100; 130, n.129, n.131; *Epistles*, 3, n.3, 184, n.81, n.83, n.84; 225; 229; 258; 265, n.80; 267; 297, n.154; 315, n.177; 326, n.203; 353, n.233; 375, n.252; 376, n.253; 380, n.259; 381, n.260, n.262; 382, n.263; 383, n.265, n.266, n.268; 384, n.269; 387, n.285; 392, n.304, n.305; 436, n.88; 442, n.93; 449, n.109; 450, n.112; 451, n.115; 471, n.160; 483, n.185; 486, n.189; 497, n.208; 509, n.224; 514, n.238; 522, n.265; 543, n.305; 544, n.308; 546, n.313; 554, n.328; *Essays*: "Eucharist and Baptism," 549, n.319; "The Johannine: Sacramentary," 549, n.319; "Scrolls," 252, n.46; 259, n.64; 278, n.114; 279, n.115; *Gospel*, 15, n.30, n.36; 22, n.54; 70, n.18; 71, n.23; 72, n.25; 79, n.37; 184, n.81; 238, n.11, n.12; 239, n.13, n.15; 240, n.18, n.23; 241; 264, n.76, n.77; 295, n.145, n.146, n.147; 296, n.149; 316, n.181; 350, n.229; 391, n.297; 424, n.69; 454, n.121; 460, n.137; 517, n.246; *Introduction/John*, 146, n.15; 149, n.23; *Peter*, 548, n.317, n.318
Bühner, J.-A., *Gesandte*, 397, n.3; 404, n.20; 413, n.41, n.42; 422, n.67; 431, n.82, n.83
Bultmann, R.: *Gospel*, 13; 14; 38; 39; 64, n.2; 77, n.35; 79, n.37; 105, n.72; 109, n.76; 169; 170, n.61; 238, n.11; 239, n.15; 240, n.17, n.18, n.19, n.21, n.22; 255, n.56; 270, n.96; 294, n.144; 296, n.151; 314, n.176; 316, n.180, n.181, n.182; 350, n.229; 462, n.139; 463, n.142; 517, n.247; 523, n.268; 549, n.320; *Theology*, 497, n.207; 509, n.224
Burge, G. M., *Anointed*, 446, n.99; 449, n.109; 454, n.121
Burghardt, W., "St. Ignatius," 387, n.277
Burkett, D., *Son of Man*, 274, n.105; 275, n.106

Carson, D. A., *Gospel*, 15, n.29, n.30; 19, n.45; 88, n.47; 194, n.99; "Source Criticism," 15, n.29
Charlesworth, J.: *Beloved*, 329, n.208; *Jesus within Judaism*, 125, n.109; "Critical," 252, n.46; 259, n.65; "Scrolls"/*Exploring*, 291, n.138; "Scrolls"/*Historical Jesus*, 457, n.126
Collins, J. J.: *Apocalyptic*, 429, n, 76; *Apocalypticism*, 251, n.45; 253, n.48, n.49; 457, n.131; 468, n.154, n.155, n.156; 476, n.167; 477; 478, n.172, n.173, n.174, n.176, n.177; 489, n.193; *Jewish Wisdom*, 416, n.62; *Morphology*, 251, n.45; "Expectation," 488, n.192; 531, n.283; "Son of Man," 274, n.105; 275, n.106; 276, n.109; 429, n.75; "Testamentary Literature," 254, n.53
Collins, R. F., "Commandment," 277, n.110; 278, n.114; 282, n.122
Comfort, P. W.: *Quest*, 386, n.275; "Greek Text," 8, n.9
Conzelmann, H., *Pastoral Epistles*, 481, n.183
Coppens, J.: "Fils de l'Homme," 274, n.105; 422, n.67; "Logia," 274, n.105
Cory, C., "Rescue," 415, n.54
Cross, F. M., *Ancient*, 51, n.45
Cullmann, O., *Early*, 549, n.319; 549, n.321
Culpepper, R.: *Anatomy*, 156, n.33; 169, n.60; 170, n.62, n.63; 171, n.64; *Gospel*, 71, n.22; 449, n.110; *Legend*, 3, n.3; 16; 329, n.209; "Pivot," 535, n.291

Dahms, J. V., "*Monogenes*," 309, n.166
Dauer, A., *Passionsgeschichte*, 90, n.50
de Boer, M. C., *Perspectives*, 309, n.167; 315, n.177; 396, n.2; 509, n.225; 514, n.236, n.237, n.238; 516, n.243, n.244; 517, n.249; 520, n.259

Author Index

de Jonge, M.: *Christology,* 521, n.261; *Envoy,* 397, n.3; 516, n.243; *Stranger,* 15, n.29; *Testaments,* 254, n.53; "Beloved," 328, n.208; 329, n.209; "Death," 516, n.243; 518, n.251; 520, n.258; 521, n.261; 533, n.286

de la Potterie, I.: *Vérité,* 266; 267, n.83, n.84, n.85; 270, n.96; 291, n.137, n.140; "L'impeccabilité," 524, n.270; "Parole," 273, n.100

Derrett, J., "Parable," 430, n.81

DeVillers, L., "Lettre," 91, n.54

Dodd, C. H.: *Epistles,* 315, n.177; *Interpretation,* 195, n.102; 316, n.182, n.184; 373, n.249; 517, n.247; 518, n.250; *Tradition,* 103; 120, n.93; 220, n.127; "First Epistle," 282, n. 123; 315, n.177; 442, n.92; 451, n.115; "Herrenworte," 220, n.127; "*Hilaskesthai,*" 520, n.259; "Holy Spirit," 332, n.211; "Parable," 412, n.34

Donfried, K. P., "Authority," 540, n.298

Dunderberg, I., *Johannes,* 369, n.244

Dunn, J. D. G., *Unity and Diversity,* 534, n.287; 540, n.298

Duprez, A., *Jesus,* 124, n.107

Elliott, J. K. (review: *NovT* 38), 386, n.274

Felton, T./Thatcher, T., "Stylometry," 21, n.49

Fensham, F. C., "Love," 277, n.110

Feuillet, A., "Structure," 258, 353, n.232

Fitzmyer, J.: *Luke,* 263, n.73, n.75; *Romans,* 534, n.287; *Wandering,* 241, n.24, n.25

Forestell, T., *Word,* 178, n.71; 315, n.177; 509, n.224; 516, n.243

Fortna, R.: *Predecessor,* 14, n. 26; 17; 38, n.85; 64, n.2; 75, n.32; 79, n.37, 294, n.144; *Signs,* 14; 15; 17, n.35; 18, n.38; 21; 24, n.58; "Locale," 84, n.44; 110, n.78; 114, n.88; 156, n.33; 162, n.44

Freyne, S., *Galilee,* 122, n.98

Friedrich, G., *Verkündigung,* 521, n.262

Fuller, R. H., *Essays,* 277, n.110

Gächter, P., "Form," 412, n.34

Garnet, P., *Salvation,* 511, n.229

Glasson, T. F., *Moses,* 112, n.86; 400, n.10; 402, n.15

Grant, R. M., "Scripture," 387, n.277; 388, n.289, n.291

Grayston, K., *Epistles,* 358, n.238; 377, n.253; 449, n.110; 524, n.269; 537, n.294

Grigsby, B., "Cross," 315, n.177, n.178; 318, n.189; 517, n.249

Grossouw, W., "Scrolls," 279, n.115

Gubler, M., *Deutungen,* 521, n.261

Haenchen, E., *Gospel,* 241, n.24; 316, n.180

Harvey, A. E., *Trial,* 215, n.122

Harvey, G., *True,* 72, n.25

Harvey, *Constraints,* 188, n.89

Heekerens, H.-P., *Zeichen-Quelle,* 19, n.45

Hengel, M.: *Atonement,* 315, n.177; 521, n.261; *Johannine Question,* 315, n.177; 377, n.253; 382, n.263; 387; 388, n.292; 449, n.109; 520, n.257

Hill, C. E., *Corpus,* 387, n.280; 388, n.292

Hirsch, E.: *Evangelium,* 14; *Studien,* 14, n.22; 64, n.2; "Stilkritik," 24, n.58

Hoffman, D., "Authority," 387, n.277

Holmes-Nielsen, S. (review: *TLZ,* July 1991), 457, n.126

Holtzmann, H., "Problem," 366, n.241

Horbury, W., "Benediction," 225, n.136

Houlden, *Epistles,* 377, n.253, n.254

Jeremias, J.: *Rediscovery,* 124, n.107; "Mouses," 402, n.15

Käsemann, E., *Testament,* 540, n.298; 549, n.319

Kammler, H.-C., "Jesus Christus," 454, n.121

Keck, "Derivation," 265, n.80

Kee, H. C., *Testaments* (OTP), 254, n.53; 255, n.54

Kelber, W. H., "Metaphysics," 534, n.288

Klauck, H.-J., *Erste Johannesbrief,* 450, n.112

Knöppler, T., *Theologia Crucis,* 315, n.177

Koester, H., *Symbolism,* 549, n.319

Author Index

Konradt, M., "Bruderliebe," 279, n.116; 280, n.118
Kovacs, J. L., "Ruler," 272, n.98
Kugler, J., *Jünger*, 328, n.208
Kuhn, H. W., *Enderwartung*, 457, n.128
Kvalvaag, R., "Spirit," 457, n.126; 506, n.219; 512, n.230
Kysar, R.: *Evangelist*, 13, n.18; 156, n.33; *Gospel*, 270, n. 96; 381, n.262; 462, n.139

Lazure, N., *Valeurs*, 523, n.267
Leon-Dufour, X.: *Sharing*, 549, n.319; "Miracles," 70, n.18
Leroy, H., *Rätsel*, 495, n.203
Levine, L. I.: *Judaism and Hellenism*, 76, n.34
Lieu, J., *Epistles*, 245, n.34
Lindars, B.: *Behind*, 13, n.18; 15, n.30; 96, n.59; *Gospel*, 264, n.77; 314, n.176; "Word and Sacrament," 549, n.319
Lorenzen, T., *Lieblingjünger*, 328, n.208; 329, n.209
Lowe, M., "*Ioudaioi*," 72, n.25

MacGregor, G. H. C., "Wrath," 292, n.141
Magen, Y., "Stone Vessel," 126, n.113
Malatesta, E., *Interiority*, 184, n.81
Malina, B./Rohrbaugh, R., *Social Science*, 72, n.25
Martin, V., and Barns, J. W. B., *Papyrus: Bodmer II, Supplement*, 7, n.6
Martyn, J. L., *Christian History*, 79, n.37; 127; 195, n.101
Maurer, C., *Ignatius von Antiochien*, 387, n.277
Mealand, D. L., "Language," 184, n.81
Meeks, W.: *Prophet-King*, 112, n.86, n.87; 223, n.132; 410, n.32; "Breaking," 114, n.88; "Ethics," 326; 523, n.267; "Galilee," 110, n.78; "Moses," 223, n.132
Meier, J. P.: *Marginal Vol. 1*, 38; 120, n.93; 121, n.95, n.96; 122, n.98, n.100; 188, n.89; 221, n.129; 289, n.134; 290, n. 135, n.136; 350, n.229; *Marginal Vol. 2*, 71, n.23; 72, n.25; 96, n.59; 105, n.72; 123, n.101, n.102, n.103, n.104; 124, n.108; 128, n.121, n.122, n.123, n.124; 216, n.123; 237, n.9; 288, n.133; 369, n.243; 371, n.247
Mendner, S., "Literarkritik," 13, n.18
Menken, M., "John 6,51C-58," 317, n.185; 518, n.251
Metzger, B., *Commentary*, 8, n.10; 296, n.150
Milik, J., *Books of Enoch*, 241, n.25
Miranda, J. P.: *Sendung*, 404, n.20; *Vater*, 404, n.20
Moloney, F. J.: *Belief*, 16, n.32; *Glory*, 16, n.32; *Gospel*, 5, n. 4; 16, n.32; 195, n.103; 316, n.180; 350, n.229; *Signs*, 316, n.182; 463, n.142; 517, n.247; *Son of Man*, 274, n.105; 403, n.17; 413, n.42; 425, n.70, n.71; "Jesus of History," 120, n.93
Moody, D., "Only Son," 308, n.165
Morgenthaler, R., *Statistik*, 366, n.241
Müller, U. B.: *Geschichte*, 315, n.177; "Bedeutung," 178, n.71

Nagel, T., *Rezeption*, 387; 388, n.292
Neirynck, F.: "Examen Critique," 19, n.45; "L'Epanalepsis," 24, n.58
Newsom, C.: "Apocalyptic," 253, n.49; "Sectually Explicit," 253, n.48
Nicholson, G., *Departure*, 178, n.71; 315, n.177; 316, n.179; 509, n.224; 516, n. 243
Nickelsburg, G., *Resurrection*, 251, n.45; 324, n.196; 325, n. 197; 468, n.154; 477, n.169; 506, n.219
Nicol, W., *Semeia*, 96, n.59
Nissen, J., "Community," 529, n.279

Oppenheimer, A., *'Am Ha'aretz*, 126, n.114

Painter, J.: *Quest*, 15, n.29; 68, n.12; 151, n.28; 236, n.7; 274, n.105; "Tradition," 358, n.238
Pancaro, S., *Law*, 112, n.86
Pendrick, G., "MONOGENES," 308, n.165
Perkins, P.: *Love*, 277, n.110; *Resurrection*, 324, n.196; 325, n.197
Perler, O., "Vierte," 388, n.290
Person, R. F., "Reassessment," 24, n.58
Philonenko, M., *Interpolations*, 254, n.53

Author Index

Pierre, M.-J./Rousée, J.-M., "Sainte-Marie," 124, n.107
Pilgaard, A., "Scrolls," 252, n.46
Porsch, F., "Teufel," 156, n.33
Price, "Light," 259, n.64
Puech, E., *Croyance*, 253, n.48; 324, n.196; 467, n.151; 468, n.154, n.156; 476, n.167; 477, n.170, n.171; 478, n.175; 479, n.179; 480, n.181; 511, n.229; 512, n.230

Reeves, J. (review: *JSP,* Oct. 1991), 457, n.126
Reich, R./Shuckron, E., "Pool," 125, n.108
Reim, G., *Hintergrund,* 264, n.76
Reinhartz, A., *Befriending,* 70, n.22
Rengstorf, Z., *Semeion,* 70, n.18
Rensberger, D., "Anti-Judaism," 70, n.22
Rhea, R., *Son of Man,* 274, n.105
Richter, G., 237, n.8; *Studien,* 14; "Deutung," 178, n.71; 375, n.252; "Fuwaschung," 375, n.252; "Sogenannten," 13, n.18; 105, n.72; "Vater und Gott," 105, n.72; 400, n.10
Ridderbos, H., *Gospel,* 316, n.181, n.182
Rissi, M., *Juden,* 12, n.25, n.26
Roberts, C. H., "Fragment," 7, n.6
Robinson, J. A. T., *Priority,* 133, n.134; 134, n.137; 374, n.251
Robinson, J. M./Koester, H., *Trajectories,* 18, n.38
Ruckstuhl, E.: *Einheit,* 12; 19; "Language," 19, n.42; and Dschulnigg, P., *Stilkritik,* 19, n.42, n.45

Sanders, E. P., *Judaism,* 126, n.115; 127, n.120; 129, n.125
Schenke, L., *Johannesevangelium,* 40, n.86
Schmidt, A., "Anmerkungen," 386, n.274
Schmithals, W., *Johannesevangelium,* 13, n. 18; 217, n.125
Schnackenburg, R.: *Epistles,* 184, n.81; 267; 278, n.114; 383, n.268; 449, n.109; 450, n.112; 460, n.137; 462, n.140; 471, n.159; 513, n.235; 515, n.238; 534, n.287; 535, n.291; 536, n.292; 554, n.329; *Gospel 1,* 70, n.18; 71, n.23; 241, n.24; 294, n.144; 296, n.149; 297, n.153; 350, n.229; 524, n.270; *Gospel 2,* 13, n.16; 190; 196, n.105; 246, n.37; 314, n.176; 334, n.215; 375, n.252; 398, n.5; 403, n.17; 424, n.69; *Gospel 3,* 328, n.208; 511, n.227; 551, n.324; "Ephesus," 392, n.302
Schneider, J., "Abschiedsreden," 270, n.96
Schneiders, S.: "A Case Study," 115, n.89
Schnelle, U.: *Antidocetic,* 68, n.14; 70, n.18; 377, n.253; 549, n.319; *Evangelium,* 15, n.30
Schoedel, W., *Ignatius,* 387, n.277
Scholtissek, K.: *In Ihm sein,* 184, n.81; "Kinder," 540, n.298
Schwartz, E., *Aporien,* 23, n.56
Schweizer, E., *Ego Eimi,* 19
Scobie, C. H., "Geography," 114, n.88
Scott, M., *Sophia,* 413, n.43
Segal, A.: *Life,* 325, n.197; "Ruler," 225, n.136; 272, n.100
Segovia, F.: *Relationships,* 277, n.110, n.112, n.113; "Theology," 358, n.238
Sekki, A. E., *Ruah,* 445, n.96; 448, n.106; 457, n.126; 512, n.231, n.232
Setzer, C., *Responses,* 225, n.136
Shanks, H., "Siloam," 125, n.108
Skeat, T. C., *Oxyrhyncus Papyri L,* 7, n.6
Slater, T. B., "One," 274, n.105
Sloyan, G. S., *Saying,* 13, n.18
Smalley, S.: *1, 2, 3 John,* 515, n.241; 533, n.286; 536, n.294; *John,* 443, n.94; 540, n.298; "Paraclete," 453, n.118; 454, n.121
Smith, D. M.: *Among,* 369, n.244; *Composition,* 13, n.15; 329, n.209; *Gospel,* 157, n.34; 162, n.44; *Johannine,* 13, n.18; 497, n.207; 522; 523, n.266; 541, n.302; *John,* 545, n.311; *Theology,* 496, n.206; "Learned," 223, n.133; 449, n.110
Spicq, C., *Agape,* 277, n.112
Spitta, F., *Johannes-Evangelium,* 63, n.2
Stegemann, H., "Bedeutung," 251, n.45
Stibbe, M., *John,* 16, n.32
Strecker, G., *Epistles,* 7, n.6; 184, n.81; 378, n.256

Talbert, C. H., *Gospel,* 16, n. 32; 199, n.111; 358, n.238; 377, n.253
Teeple, H. M.: *Mosaic,* 112, n.86; 400, n.10; *Origin,* 13, n. 18

Author Index

Thompson, M., *Humanity*, 316, n.179; 516, n.243
Thyen, H., 237, n.8; *Studien*, 178, n.71; "Entwicklungen," 249, n.42; 328, n.208; 329, n.209; "Johannes 13," 375, n.252; "Johannesevangelium," 133, n.134
Tomson, P. J.: "Jews," 127, n.119; "Names," 72, n.25
Trumbower, J. A., *Born*, 265, n.80
Tuckett, C., "Atonement in the NT," *ABD*, 520, n.259

Ulrichsen, *Grundschrift*, 254, n.53
Urban, C., *Menschenbild*, 532, n.284

van Belle, G., *Signs*, 13, n. 18; 21, n.50; 64, n.14; 105, n.72
VanderKam, J.: *Early Judaism*, 254, n.53; "Today," 256, n.58; 259, n.65
van der Osten-Sacken, P., *Gott und Belial*, 457, n.129
van der Ploeg and van der Woude, *Targum de Job*, 58; 241, n.25
van der Watt, J.: "Aionios," 459, n.134; "Ethics," 525, n.274
van Dyke Parunak, H., "Typesetting," 24, n.58
van Imschoot, P., "L'ésprit," 463, n.143
Vellanickal, M., *Sonship*, 524, n.270, n.273
Vermes, G.: *Jesus the Jew*, 241, n.24; *Perspective*, 259, n.65; *Scrolls*, 547, n.316
von Wahlde, U. C.: *Commandments*, 150, n.25; 155, n.31; 243, n.30; 248, n.39, n.40; 415, n.59; 504, n.217; 507, n.220; 509, n.225; 524, n.270; 528, n.277; 529, n.278; *Earliest Version*, 64, n.2; 68, n.12; 400, n.10; "Archaeology," 124, n.106; "Death," 179, n.75; "Faith," 243, n.30; "Fifteen," 71, n.22, n.23; 147, n.15; "He Has Given," 467, n.150; 476, n.168; "Jews," 37, n.80; 71, n.22, n.23; 72, n.25; "Relationships," 127, n.118; 148, n.20, n.21; "Technique," 19, n.40; 24, n.58; "Terms," 63, n.2; "Wiederaufnahme," 19, n.40; 24, n.58

Welch, C., *Zeichen*, 70, n.18; 151, n.28
Wellhausen, J.: *Erweiterungen*, 270, n.96; *Evangelium*, 14; 17; 18; 27, n.66; 28, n.67; 63, n.2
Wendt, H. H.: *Gospel*, 14; 17; 18; 28, n.67; 68, n.14; *Schichten*, 14, n. 21; 28, n.67; 68, n.14
Wengst, K., *Gemeinde*, 393, n.307
Westermann, C., *Gospel*, 22; 217, n.125
White, M. C., *Identity*, 63, n.2
Willet, M., *Wisdom*, 413, n.43
Wilson, S., *Strangers*, 225, n.136
Windisch, H., *Spirit-Paraclete*, 270, n.96
Witherington, B.: *Gospel*, 411, n.33; 413, n.43; 414, n.47, n.50, n.51; 415, n.57; 416, n.60; 429, n.77; *Sage*, 413, n.43
Wright, N. T., *Resurrection*, 324, n.196; 325, n.197; 557, n.331

Subject Index

Abiding: of believers with Father and Son, 335-337; of Son in the Father and Father in the Son, 151, 153, 184-187, 407-408, 494-495; with "in," 185; with *menein,* 185, 543; with "not being alone," 185-186

Accuracy: for historical ministry (*see also* First edition: historicity), 51, 102-103, 103, 120-129; for time of community, 193-195, 222-224 (*see also* Anachronisms)

Accusations against Jesus: blasphemy, 29, 51, 60, 87, 100, 101, 140, 146, 151, 153, 159-161, 175, 187, 189, 201, 403; "not from God," 29, 58, 61, 81, 85, 88, 99-100, 114, 116, 153, 178, 399-400, 408, 432, 494; success will cause Roman reaction, 85, 100, 112, 400; works on Sabbath, 81, 85, 112, 140, 143, 156, 175, 195-196, 223, 400, 405, 411

Agency, 412-413

Akedah: and death of Jesus, 317, 518

Ambiguity of features, 42, 98-101, 397-398, 399, 853

Anachronisms, 52, 85, 139, 172, 193-195, 212-213 (*see also* Accuracy)

Anointing (with the Spirit), 204, 206, 210, 366, 419, 438, 445, 448, 451, 466, 499, 500, 534, 536-538, 544, 554

Anthropology (*see* First edition, etc.: anthropology)

Apocalyptic (*see also* Dualism); general discussion of worldview, 115, 231-232, 250-255, 365

Aporias, 10-12, 12-16, 17, 23-25, 28, 30, 43, 65, 119, 196, 236, 270, 298, 398

Apprenticeship, 412

Ascent of Jesus (*see* Jesus: ascent of)

Atonement (*see* Jesus: death as atonement)

Authorship, 6-7; of First (Second, Third) edition (*see* First edition: author, etc.)

Baptism, 54, 128, 142, 216, 341-342, 362, 370, 384, 552, 554, 556

Beginning, how to read this commentary, 46-47

Beginning (of Jesus' ministry), 41, 301, 311, 323, 330, 379, 381, 422, 437-438, 440, 499, 500, 502, 505, 508, 544

Belief: as "easy," 97-98; based exclusively on miracles, 94-96; based on witnesses (*see* Witness); chain-reaction ("tandem"), 59, 79-80, 95, 109, 211; emphasis on variety of groups, 82-83; high Christology in second edition, 174-175; stereotyped formulas of, 76-79; traditional expectations, 98-101

Beloved Disciple (BD), 6-7, 54, 55, 193, 224, 234, 235, 237, 240, 244, 250, 297, 328-331, 356, 362-364, 365, 367, 374, 375, 379, 380, 389-390, 542, 545-547, 557

Subject Index

Birth: from above, 328; from God, 328; from Spirit, 328

Blasphemy: accusation of (*see* Accusations against Jesus)

Blood of Jesus (*see* Jesus: blood of)

Brother: developed first in 1 John, 305; religious sense, 31, 244, 249, 277, 278, 305, 326, 365, 389, 436, 470, 501, 525-527, 528, 544, 545; secular sense, 73, 80, 95, 103, 150, 152, 210, 279-282, 302, 303-304, 468, 479, 486, 520

"Bundling" in third edition, 351-353, 357

Child (*teknon*), 245-246; as developed first in 1 John (*see* 1 John: anthropology)

Christ: as confessional title (*see* Confessional titles)

Christology: First edition, etc. (*see* First edition, etc.: Christology); Mosaic motifs, 102, 400-401; traditional, 98-101, 114, 399-402

Chronology, of ministry, 61, 102, 109-110, 121-122, 128, 211, 218, 350, 370-374

Citation of Gospel, earliest, 386-389

Cleansing of the Temple, 125, 154, 162, 212, 221, 349

Commandments: as "new," 248, 301, 378, 437, 502

Commandments in 1 John, 248-249

Commandments given to disciples in the gospel: keep word of Jesus, 204, 247-248, 311-312, 340, 440-441, 501, 504, 505, 506-507, 544, 553; love one another, 35, 203, 209, 277-282, 506-507, 523, 527, 528, 543

Commandments given to Jesus in the gospel: what to say, 247-249; what to do, 246, 247

Community: at time of first edition, 50-51, 116-120; at time of second edition, 51-52, 214-217, 222-224; at time of third edition, 53-54, 367; overview of history of, 50-55

Composition of the Gospel; and coherence, 34-36; and imitation of style, 36; and interpretation, 2-5; circular argument, 42; criteria (general), 27-29; mixing of terms, 33-34; oral prehistory, 38-39; starting point of analysis, 27-28

Confessional titles, 101, 173-174, 215, 224, 240, 275, 307, 335, 340, 360, 372, 398, 399, 401, 402, 409, 420, 452, 548

Conquest/Conquer, 269, 272, 302-303, 304

Contextual approach, 46

Criteria: consistency of, 29-30, 67; types of, 25-27, 63, 144

Darkness: as opposed to light (*see* Dualism: light/darkness)

Day/Night: as conceptualization of ministry and passion, 305-306

Death of Jesus (*see* Jesus: death)

Demetrius, 594

Demonic possession (*see* Dualism: demonic possession)

Descent (*see* Jesus: descent of)

Dialogue in second edition (*see* Religious authorities: dialogue)

Diotrephes, 282, 304, 392, 545

"Doing the truth" (*see* Dualism: "doing the truth")

Doublets, 18

Dualism: being "of . . . ," 243, 262, 265-267, 304; demonic possession, 293, 298; "doing the truth," 291, 303, 355; Kingdom of God, 115, 232, 288-290, 350, 351, 371; "knowing the truth," 290-291; "the last day," 282-283, 487; light (vs. darkness), 54, 62, 166, 183, 192, 232, 243, 252-253, 256-260, 261-262, 263-265, 270, 278, 293, 299, 304, 305-306, 306-307, 318, 326-327, 340; love of one another (*see* Commandments); "sons of . . . ," 263-265; of Spirits, 168-169, 268-274, 302; "of the world," "not of the world," 343-345; "wrath of God" (*see* Wrath of God)

Ecclesiology (*see* First edition, etc.: ecclesiology); in 3 John, 543-545

Elder, 6, 53-54, 55, 224, 227, 235, 248, 281-282, 297, 304, 375, 377, 390, 391, 392, 545

Subject Index

Ephesus (*see* Third edition: place of composition)
Eschatology (*see* First edition, etc.: eschatology)
Eternal Life (*see* First edition, etc.: eternal life); as understood in context of 1 John, 339-340; possession of, future, 40, 133, 141, 207, 232-235, 283, 325, 361, 381, 470, 479, 480, 482, 486-488; possession of, present, 141, 181-182, 207, 324-326, 361, 444, 461-462, 465, 469, 470, 476, 483-484, 487-488, 491; sin unto death, and, 471; with resurrection of the body, 324-326; without resurrection of the body, 324-326
Ethics (*see* First edition, etc.: ethics; *see also* Commandments)
Eucharist (*see also* Flesh: eating flesh of Jesus as essential for life), 54, 142, 171, 235, 275, 298, 331-335, 362, 383, 425, 473-474, 553, 554, 556
Evil, 101, 142, 169, 176, 182, 251, 253, 256-260, 263-264, 267, 268, 269-272, 272-274, 277-282, 284, 285-286, 286-288, 288-290, 291, 303-304, 327, 344, 352, 356, 415, 458, 474, 481, 485, 493-494, 498, 511, 527, 543
Explanation of terms and customs: as "of the Jews," 91-92

Father: God as Father, in relation to Son, 189, 205, 246-249, 359-360, 402-406, 406-408, 417-418, 425-428, 435-436
Feast: unnamed, 221-222
First edition: Christology, 112-113, 114, 399-402; belief, 431-432; pneumatology, 443; eternal life, 459; eschatology, 482; knowing God, 494; soteriology, 508; ethics, 522; anthropology, 532; ecclesiology, 540-541; religious significance of material reality, 550; an independent tradition, 117-118; author, 131-132; chronology and geography, 109-110; date of composition, 133-134; geography, role of, 114-115, 135; historicity, 120-129; Mosaic Christology, 51, 112-113, 400-401;

narrative focus, 111-112; overview, 58-62; place of composition, 134-135; purpose, 109; relation to Synoptics, 117, 130-131, 133; ritual purity, references to, 117, 127; social location, 116-120; structure of, 105-108; worldview, 115
1 John: Christology, 419-422; belief, 436-439; pneumatology, 449-452; eternal Life, 469-472; eschatology, 486-490; knowing God, 499-502; soteriology, 508, 513-515; ethics, 525-527; anthropology, 535-538; ecclesiology, 543-545; religious significance of material reality, 552-554; and third edition, 47-48, 364-367; and structure of third edition (*see* Third edition: and structure of 1 John); written before third edition (*see* 1 John and third edition)
Flesh: contrasted with Spirit, 167-168, 177, 211, 218, 233-234, 235, 450, 509, 550-552; eating flesh of Jesus as essential for life, 171, 473-474; value (lack of), 4, 167-168, 177, 211, 218, 550-552; value of, 234-235, 316-317, 331-335, 340, 343, 553, 362, 555-557
Forgiveness/Cleansing of sin: by direct action of the Spirit, 142, 179-181, 208-209, 279-280, 509-511, 511, 512, 520, 554, 559-560; through human mediators, 54, 177, 292, 362, 383, 471, 556, 559; through Jesus (*see* under "Jesus")

Geographical terms: translation of, 73-75, 80, 92, 118; with unique and accurate details, 102-103, 103, 120-129
Geography: Second edition (*see* Second edition: geography)
Glory, Glorify: as introduced by second author, 97-98, 192; as used by third author, 341
Glossing: in third edition, 48, 233, 240, 289, 347, 357-358, 493
Great Church, 53, 54, 235, 367, 368, 376

Historical Accuracy: in first edition (*see* First edition: historicity; *see also* Accuracy)

Subject Index

Historical Jesus: in first edition, 120-129; in second edition, 218-222; words of, 219-220

Hour as segment of ministry or of day, 182-183; as time of Passion, 182-183; of Jesus, 182-183

Human mediators, 556-557

I AM (*see* Son: I AM); and "bundling" (*see* "Bundling")
Ignatius (of Antioch), 55
Immanence (*see* Abiding)
Indwelling (*see* Abiding)
Interpretation: first-century principles, 39-41

Jesus (*see also* Son): abiding importance of, 313, 421, 427-428; ascent of, 318-320, 345-346, 347, 405, 411, 425, 430; blood of, as salvific, 171, 179-181, 208, 235, 316, 317, 330, 334, 340, 362, 379, 380, 473, 510, 513, 514-515, 517, 518, 521, 537, 553, 556, 559; "choosing" the disciples, 337, 373; come "in water and blood," 180-181, 208, 317, 330, 334, 335, 379, 380, 513, 555; death as atonement, 141, 179, 181, 208-209, 315-318, 335, 361, 374, 380, 414, 509, 511, 513-515, 516, 520-521, 537, 553, 559; death as departure, 141, 177-179, 201, 234, 282-286, 315-318, 318, 332, 427, 443, 509, 515; death "for others, for his own," "for us," 178-179, 208, 316, 420, 426-427, 513-514, 515, 516-517, 528, 537; dependent on the Father, 406-408, 410, 426-427; descent of, 168, 178-179, 233, 244, 310, 318-320, 345-346, 347, 372, 405, 424, 430; eternal life and, 472, 473, 476-477; future coming (*see* 1 John and Third edition: eschatology; parousia); Lamb of God, 315, 366, 428, 517; life of the Father, possessing the, 417-418; preexistence, 99, 101, 133, 168, 178, 210, 233, 276, 307, 309-310, 318-320, 341, 345-348, 360, 362, 369, 382, 405, 408-409, 417, 421, 423-425, 426, 429-430, 446, 532, 537; role essential for salvation, 313-315; Savior of the World, 315-318, 361, 428, 441, 503, 514-515, 519;

"seeing" God, 347-348; supernatural knowledge: for benefit of reader, 163-164; supernatural knowledge: as miracle, 89-91

Jesus Christ: as title in third edition, 231, 241-242, 304, 340, 343, 362, 421, 470, 500, 503, 513, 514; title primarily in 1 John, 304-305

Jewish-Christian (*see* Community)

"Jews": as anachronistic, 193; as "Judeans," 70-73; as religious authorities (*see* Religious authorities: "the Jews"); in ethnic national sense, 71, 91-92; in Galilee, 213

Johannine tradition, complexity of, 1-2

John the Baptist: as "witness" to Jesus, 40, 52, 141, 152, 342, 432-433; followers of, 119-120, 216-217; in first edition, 58, 81, 83, 95, 105, 109, 112, 114, 117, 119-120, 123-124, 181; in second edition, 221, 198-203, 206, 211, 216-217, 221, 265-266, 407, 410, 428, 432-433, 445, 495, 532; in third edition, 310, 323, 330, 338, 371, 391

Joy: as irremovable, 186-187; eschatological, 322-324, 489

Judaism: specific accurate knowledge of, in first edition, 103; specific accurate knowledge of, in second edition, 193-195, 222-224

Judea: in first edition, 52, 114-115, 131-132, 134-135, 213

Judeans: not in dialogue with Jesus, 92-93

Judgment: in sense of condemnation, 181-182, 234, 286-288, 487, 491, 492; in neutral sense (*see* Universal accountability); and "bundling" (*see* "Bundling")

King: and reception of Spirit, 448; and title "Son of God," 466; as title, 95, 99-100, 101, 132, 163, 205, 223, 401, 410; "King of the Jews," 75, 92, 112

Kingdom of God (*see* Dualism: Kingdom of God); and "bundling" (*see* "Bundling")

Knowing the truth (*see* Dualism: "knowing the truth")

Subject Index

Knowing God (*see* First edition, etc.: knowing)

Lamb of God: Jesus as (*see* Jesus: Lamb of God)
Last Day (*see* Dualism: "the last day")
Liar/Lying, 248, 284, 303; and "bundling" (*see* "Bundling")
"Life in himself," 307-308
"Lifting up" of Jesus, 275, 347
Light: and structure of 1 John, 53, 365; and structure of third edition, 306-307, 354-355, 365; as opposed to darkness (*see* Dualism: light vs. darkness)
Literary Seams (*see* Aporias)
Lord: in religious sense, 237-241, 307, 426; in secular sense, 237-241
Love: and structure of 1 John, 353-356; and structure of third edition, 306-307, 353-356

Manuscripts of Gospel and Letters, 7-8 (*see also* Textual criticism)
Material Aspects of Reality (*see* First edition, etc.: religious importance of material reality)
Messiah: as (confessional) title (*see* Confessional titles); as title, 51, 58, 61, 74, 81, 86, 89, 90, 95, 98, 99, 114, 116, 132, 239, 322, 399, 401, 402, 409, 429; in SDQ and T12P, 255
Miracle: terms for (*see* Signs; Works)
Miracles: focus on greatness of, 96-97, 111; lack of focus on miracles, 140
Misunderstanding: as anachronistic, 194; in second edition, 169-172; in third edition, 169
Mixture: of features, 297-300; of terms for religious authorities, 300-301
Mosaic Christology (*see* First edition: Mosaic Christology)

Narrative foundation of Gospel, 102
Narrative orientation: first edition, 76-93, 105, 109-110, 111-112; second edition, 143, 165-172; third edition, 369
Narrative: chronology of, 102; relics of earlier, 103

Night/Day (*see* Day/Night)

Objectivity (in analysis), 26 n.1
Oneness: of believers (*see* Unity); of believers with Father and Son (*see* Abiding); of Father and Son (*see* Abiding)
Opponents, views of (*see* specific topic under 1 John)
Order of the editions, 37-38
Organization of the volume, 43-44, 57-58
Overview: of first edition, etc. (*see* First edition: overview, etc.); of Johannine community history, 50-55

Papias, 55
Paraclete: and "bundling" (*see* "Bundling"); general meaning, 216; Jesus as, 320-322, 377-378, 514; Spirit as, 4, 169, 173-174, 185, 224, 270-271, 288, 302, 320-322, 336, 338, 341-342, 353, 360, 366, 377-378, 382, 384, 438, 439, 452, 454-455, 503, 507-508; words of Jesus, and, 220, 311-313, 359, 361, 440-441, 505, 507-508
Parousia, 133, 264, 283-286, 366, 367, 442
Perfectionism, 142, 180, 203, 209, 234, 327, 361, 459, 488, 522-525, 525-527, 527-532
Peter, death of, 55
Petitionary prayer: and "bundling" (*see* "Bundling")
Plural of pronouns (unexpected), 294-297
Pneumatology (*see* First edition, etc.: pneumatology; *see also* Paraclete)
Polycarp, 55
Progressives, 378, 437, 502, 508
Prophet ("the"), 29, 58, 61, 84, 85, 87, 95, 99, 102, 401
Purity, ritual, 96, 103, 117, 118, 126, 127, 196, 458

Questions posed but not answered, 103-104, 196-197

Rabbi (Rabbouni), 401
Rabbinic: literature, 126; in second edition, 143, 146, 156, 195-196, 223-224

Subject Index

Raise up on the last day (*see* "Bundling"; *see also* Dualism: "the last day"; Resurrection)

Religious authorities: as criterion for composition, 27-28; concern for belief of masses, 85-86; dialogue with Jesus almost constant, 93, 139, 143, 164-165; dialogue with Jesus lacking, 192-93; division among, 83-84; division lacking among, 139, 162-163; fear by common people, 158-159; fear by common people lacking, 87-88; fear of common people, 88-89; hostility as constant, 156-158; hostility as increasing, 84-85; no concern for belief of masses, 161-162; "Pharisees," "chief priests," 63-68; "the Jews," 51-52, 139, 145-149, 214-216; reaction to miracles, 86-87; reaction to miracles lacking, 159-161

Religious terms: explanation of, 91-92; translation of, 73-75

Remaining (*see* Abiding)

Repetitive resumptive (*see* Wiederaufnahme)

Resurrection (*see also* Third edition: religious significance of material reality); bodily, 324-326, 363, 471-472, 557-558; disputes over, 481-482

Righteousness, 302

Ritual (*see* Third edition: religious significance of material reality)

Ritual purity (*see* Purity)

Rylands fragment, 385-386

Sacraments (*see* Third edition: religious significance of material reality; *see also* Baptism; Confession; Eucharist)

Scripture citations: introductory formula in second edition, 195; introductory formula in third edition, 342

Second edition: Christology, 205, 402-410; belief, 205-206, 432-436; pneumatology, 206, 434-435, 443-448; eternal life, 206-207, 458-469; eschatology, 207, 483-486; knowledge of God, 494-498; soteriology, 208-209, 508-513; ethics, 209, 522-525; anthropology, 209-210, 532-535; ecclesiology, 142, 210, 541-543; religious significance of material reality, 210-211, 550-552; anachronisms in, 193-195

Second edition: and historical Jesus (*see* Historical Jesus: and second edition); and Synoptics, 224; author, 224-225; date, 225-227; elements taken over by third edition, 187-192; genre, 211-214; geography, 213-214; narrative orientation, 139, 211-213; overview, 138-144; place of composition, 227; social location, 214-216; structure of, 197-203

Second John, 53, 204, 224, 235, 242, 245, 248, 249, 269, 277, 279, 284, 287, 290, 293, 303, 313, 323, 335, 389, 421, 422, 437, 501, 502, 526, 553

Sectarian Documents from Qumran (*see* individual topics in 1 John and in third edition)

Sign(s): pejorative sense, 153-155; as symbolic?, 113-114; emphasis on quantity and quantity, 80-82; term for miracle, 68-70

Sin: removal and ritual, 180; removal by blood of Jesus, 315-318; removal by death of Jesus, 315-318; removal by Spirit, 141, 179-181; unto death, 471 (*see also* Forgiveness)

Son: given all things by Father, 307-308, 428, 435-436; has everything the Father has, 307-308, 352-353, 430-431; I AM, 175, 221, 233, 275, 289, 307, 310, 327, 339, 425-426, 352-353, 360, 424, 425-426, 503, 538; in relation to Father, 189-190, 339, 402-403; preexistence of, 309-310; sent by the Father, 190-191, 339, 404-405, 411; to be honored just as Father, 307-308, 426; "unique," 4, 210, 233, 295, 307, 308-309, 318, 339, 340, 341, 347, 351-352, 360, 362, 383, 420-421, 423, 469, 515, 518, 533-534, 537 (*see also* Jesus)

Son of God: as confessional title (*see* Confessional titles); as title, 4, 61, 95, 98-101, 112, 116, 132, 205, 224, 239, 308-309, 313, 322, 339, 360, 382-383, 399, 401, 402, 409, 419, 421, 432, 438, 466, 470, 484, 514, 534, 536; in accusation of

Subject Index

blasphemy (*see* Accusations: in second edition)
Son of Man, 48, 115, 232, 251, 274-276, 284, 285, 287, 295, 298, 307-308, 310, 318, 339-340, 345-346, 347, 360, 361, 366, 372, 373-374, 405, 424-425, 426, 429-430, 441, 464, 473, 492, 527, 556
Soteriology (*see* First edition, etc.: soteriology)
"Spirit of Truth" (*see* Dualism: of Spirits); and anointing, 206; and "bundling" (*see* "Bundling"); and words of Jesus (*see* Paraclete: words of Jesus, and); contrasted with flesh, 167-168; contrasted with Spirit of Deceit, 168-169; does not speak on his own, 320-322, 440-441; eternal life, and, 475-476; Jesus' possession of, 307-308, 311, 423; natural life and, 474-475; nondualistic sense, 176-177
Spirit: personal being, 447-448 (*see* First edition, etc.: pneumatology; *see also* Paraclete)
Stereotyped formulas of belief (*see* Belief: stereotyped)
Style: as criterion, 19-21; imitation of, 36, 137; variations in, 36-37
Supernatural knowledge of Jesus: as miracle, 89-91; intended for reader, 163-164
Synagogue exclusion, 51, 52, 193-194, 214

Tauta eipon (and variants), 25
Teacher, 74, 361, 496, 498
Teknon, teknion (*see* Child)
Terms for miracle (*see* Signs; Works)
Testaments of the Twelve Patriarchs (*see* individual topics in 1 John and in third edition)
Textual criticism, 7-9
Theological characteristics: first edition, 93-101; second edition, 172-187; third edition, 305-353
Third edition and 1 John (*see* 1 John and third edition)
Third edition: Christology, 307-308, 359-360, 422-431; belief, 439-442; pneumatology, 360, 440-441, 452-459; eternal life, 360, 472-482; eschatology, 361, 491-494; knowledge of God, 361, 503-506; soteriology, 361, 515-521; ethics, 326-328, 361, 527-532; anthropology, 361-362, 538-540; ecclesiology, 362, 362, 545-548; religious significance of material reality, 331-335, 362, 363, 555-560; author, 374-376; date relative to 1 John, 376-385; genre, 357-358; historical value of, 369; overview, 231-236; place of composition, 390-393; social location, 367; structure of, 53-54, 353-357; structure of 1 John (relation to), 306-307; Synoptics (relation to), 349-351, 363, 369-374; worldview (*see also* Dualism), 53, 54, 250-255, 365, 367-368
3 John, 53, 224, 235, 244, 245, 281, 293, 303, 304, 322, 390, 392, 526, 543-545
Topics mentioned in the third edition: but developed in 1 John, 301-305
Topographical terms: accurate with "unique" details (*see also* Accuracy; Geographical terms; Geography), 102-103
Traditional "messianic" categories in accusations (*see* Accusations), 98-101, 399-400; in belief, 50-51, 98-101, 114, 399-400
Translation of religious and geographical terms, 73-75, 118-119 (*see also* Geographical terms; Geography)
Trial, Jesus' ministry as, 215-216
Twelve hours in day, and ministry of Jesus, 305-306
Twelve: and "bundling" (*see* "Bundling"); as designation of disciples, 249-250
Typefaces, use of to designate editions, 44-45, 561

Unique Son and "bundling" (*see* "Bundling")
Unity: among believers, 337 (*see also* Abiding)
Universal accountability, 181-182, 251, 282, 286-288, 325, 327, 381, 480

Water: in ritual (*see* Third edition:

religious significance of material reality)
Water: living, 141, 171, 191, 213, 317, 330, 332-335, 380, 414, 435, 446-447, 460, 510, 518, 552, 556
Wiederaufnahme, 18-19, 24-25, 49, 149
Wisdom, 218, 368-369, 411, 413-417, 429-430, 465-466, 469, 524, 530
Wisdom, as "unique," 416
Witness: as introduced by second author, 95-96, 141, 151, 173-174, 192, 432-433; as used by third author, 337-338, 341-342, 504-505
Words of Jesus: abiding importance, 204, 311-313, 437-438, 440, 497; keeping the, 204, 311-312, 544, 508, 553; permanent importance of, 311-312, 437-438, 497, 502
Work: as conception of the ministry of Jesus, 155-156
Works, to do the _____ of: as "to do the will of," 233, 242-243, 260-262; as term for miracle, 150-153
Worldview: first edition, 115; second edition, 165-168; third edition (*see* Apocalyptic)
Wrath of God, 232, 279, 291-292, 392, 489, 520

Index of Scripture and Other Ancient Literature

HEBREW BIBLE/ OLD TESTAMENT

Genesis
2:3	195
2:7	447, 464
6:3	464
6:17	464n.146
7:15	464n.146
18:25	485

Exodus
4:1-9	400n.12
12:10	315, 517
12:12	431
12:46	315, 517
16:4	320n.193
30:10	520n.260
32:30-34	520
34:10	151

Leviticus
4:3	448
4:5	448
4:16	448
6:15	448
17:11	520
19:18	525n.275

Numbers
9:12	517
14:11-22	400n.12
16:28	151
19:11-22	127n.120
24:2	463n.143
25	520

Deuteronomy
18:15-18	58, 99
21:23	521

Judges
3:10	463n.143
14:6	463n.143

1 Samuel
10:4	463n.143
10:9-14	448
11:6	448
16:3	448
16:13	466
16:14	464n.143

2 Samuel
7:14	466

2 Kings
4:25-37	115n.89
4:42-44	115n.89
14:25	129

Nehemiah
19:15	320n.193

Job
	241, 241n.25, 413n.43
11:6-7	413
34:14-15	464

Psalms
1:6	166
8:3	151
9:7-8	485
22:19	349
33:21	315n.178, 517n.249
51:11	271
77:24	320, 320n.193
95:9	292
103:29-30	464
104:40	320n.193
106:16-23	520
106:28-31	520
117:26	410
118	401n.14
145:4	464, 465n.147

Proverbs
1:20-21	415
1:20-33	413
1:28	415
3:18	414n.52
4:13	414

8:1-4	415	37:4-10	464, 475	**2 Maccabees**	
8:7	413	37:11	468n.154	7	468
8:27-30	429	39:29	448	7:1-42	520
8:32-35	414			7:14	486
8:35	414	**Daniel**		7:22-23	465
9:5	414	7	429	14:46	465
14:6	415	7:14	492n.198		
14:8	415	7:26-27	490	**4 Maccabees**	
30:1-4	275	12:1-3	468, 490	5-7	520
		12:3	485	6:28-29	520n.260
Ecclesiastes		12:13	479n.180	8-18	520
12:7	465n.147				
		Hosea		**Sirach**	
Isaiah		6:2	468n.154	1:1-18	413
1:2-4	497	9:7	463n.143	4:11	414
2:1	485			4:11-13	415
2:12	485	**Joel**		4:12	414
4:4	273	2:28-29	448	6:18	414
5:12-13	151	3:1-2	448	24:1-31	413
9:2	256			24:3	429
11:2	273	**Amos**		24:8	429
24:21	485	5:18	256n.58	24:17	414
26:29	468n.154	5:18-20	485	24:18	413
28:6	273			39:6	273
32:14-15	448	**Micah**		45:23	520
42:5	464	4:1	485		
42:6-7	166	7:8	166	**Tobit**	
44:3	448			5:14	291
61:1	448, 466	**Zephaniah**			
63:10	271	1:14-18	485	**Wisdom of Solomon**	
63:11	271			1:5	271
		Zechariah		2:3	465n.149
Jeremiah		9:9	409	3:1-4	414
9:2-3	497	12:10	511n.228	6:16	415n.55
9:25-26	485	13:1	511n.228	6:18	415
21:8	166			6:18-19	414
23:18	411			6:22	413
23:21	411			7-9	413
24:7	498			7:14	414
31:33-34	451, 498, 511, 524	**APOCRYPHA AND SEPTUAGINT**		7:22	414, 429
				8:4	413
Ezekiel				9:9-10	413, 429
11:5	463n.143	**Baruch**		9:16-18	413
11:17-19	448	3:9-28	413	9:17	271, 416
11:19	511n.228	3:36	414	9:17-18	414
36-37	448n.106	3:37	429	15:11	465
36:25-28	511, 524	4:1	414	15:16-17	476
36:26-27	448	24:1	490n.195	16:6	414

16:20	320n.193	Jubilees		20:1-5	273
24:21	414	1:20-21	531	22:2	285
		1:23	512, 531	24:2-4	458, 531
4 Ezra	275n.106	10:3	264	24:3	274
6:26	512n.233, 531	23:30-31	468n.156, 478n.176	25:1-5	479
13	429				
13:26	276	Testament of Asher		Testament of Levi	
14:35	490	4:5	280	1:1	490
		5:2	479	3:3	274, 490
		6:2	274	3:10	276n.108
OLD TESTAMENT PSEUDEPIGRAPHA		6:4	274, 479	8:15	285
		7:1-7	285	18:9	531
		7:3	479n.178	19:1	243, 259, 260, 261
2 Baruch		Testament of Benjamin		Testament of Naphtali	
24:1	490n.195	5:3	259	2:2	475
		6:1	274	2:4	475
1 Enoch		6:7	262n.71	2:6-7	256n.58
5:8-9	530	8:2-3	530	2:6-3:1	261
22:9	468n.156	8:3	274	2:9-3:1	260
42:2	429	9:1-2	290	2:10	243, 256n.58, 259
46:1	429	10:5-10	479		
47:3	429	10:6-11	490	Testament of Reuben	
48:3	276	10:7	476	1:3	245n.33, 274
49:4	492n.198			2:4	274
51-54	490	Testament of Dan		6:8	490
54:7	490	5:3	280		
61:9	492n.198	5:5	274	Testament of Simeon	
62:2	492n.198	5:6	274	2:7	274
63:11	492n.198	5:13-6:4	290	3:1	245n.33, 274
69:27	492n.198			4:4	273
70-71	429	Testament of Gad		6:1-7	285
70:1	276	4:1-6:1	280	6:5	285
95:2	267n.82	6:1	280	6:6-7	274
104:9	267n.82			6:7b	479
104:13	267n.82	Testament of Issachar			
105:2	267n.82	6:1	490	Testament of Zebulun	
106:7-13	291	7:6	280	5:1-8:6	280n.117
				8:2	490
		Testament of Joseph		8:5	245n.33
Jos. Asen.		2:5	276n.108	8:5-6	279
8:5	325n.197, 468n.155	20:2	259	9:5	490
15:3-4	468n.155			9:7	274
15:5	325n.197	Testament of Judah		9:8	259, 274
15:6	325n.197	18:1	490	10:1-3	479
16:16	325n.197	19:1-20:3	274n.103		
19:5	325n.197	19:4	274		

Index of Scripture and Other Ancient Literature

NEW TESTAMENT

Matthew
3:7	292
3:7-10	292
3:11	370, 456
4:12	371
6:13	256n.58
8:5-13	131
9:27-31	131
10:3	74n.30
10:39	373
11:5	448
13:54-58	372
15:21-28	131
16:16b-19	548
16:25	373
18:5	373
21:29-34	131
22:34-40	526
24:24	70n.20, 351
28:19	542n.303
28:20	496

Mark
1:8	370, 456
1:14	350, 371
3:18	74n.30
6:1-6	372
6:30	496
8:22-26	131
8:27-31	372, 548
8:34	373
8:35	373
9:37	373
10:46-52	131
12:1-11	430
12:28-34	526
13:22	70n.20, 350, 351
14:24	317n.185, 516-517, 518n.251

Luke
1:1-4	116n.90
3:7	292
3:16	370, 456
3:20	371
4:16-20	372
4:18	448
5:1	75n.33
5:1-11	369n.243
6:15	74n.30
7:1-10	131
7:22	448
9:18-22	548
9:24	373
9:48	373
10:25-28	526
12:3	256n.58
16:8	263, 263n.73, 263n.75
17:33	373
18:35-43	131
21:23	292
22:19	317n.185, 542n.303
22:19-20	517n.245, 518n.251

Acts
1:5	370, 456, 456n.124
2	448n.107
2:19	70n.20
2:22	70n.20
2:43	70n.20
4:27	448
4:30	70n.20
5:12	70n.20
6:8	70n.20
7:36	70n.20
7:58	157n.35
10:38	448
11:15	456
11:16	370, 371n.246, 456n.124
14:3	70n.20
15:12	70n.20
18:24-26	391
18:24-19:7	391
19:1-7	391
19:5-6	371n.246
20:17	392
20:28	521

Romans
1:18	292n.141
2:5	292, 292n.141
2:8	292
3:5	292, 292n.141
3:5-8	292
3:25	521
4:15	292n.141
5:6-8	317n.185, 518n.251
5:6-11	509n.223, 517n.245
5:9	292, 292n.141, 521
5:21-26	520n.260
8:14-17	533n.287
8:29	244n.31
8:32	516
9:22	292n.141
12:19	292n.141
15:19	70n.20

1 Corinthians
1:13	517n.245
1:22	116
5:14-16	317n.185, 518n.251
10:16	334
11:24	317n.185, 517n.245, 518n.251
11:25	542n.303
15:1-58	481
15:3	317n.185, 509n.223, 517, 518n.251, 521
15:36-37	373

2 Corinthians
1:21	536n.293
1:22	450n.112
4:4	273n.101
4:6	258n.63
5:5	450n.112
5:21	517
6:14	258n.63
6:15	259n.68
12:12	70n.20

Galatians
1:4	317n.185, 509n.223, 517n.245, 518n.251
1:18	548n.318
2:1-10	548n.318

2:11-13	548n.318	2:3	264	*Philadelphians*	
2:20	317n.185, 509n.223, 517n.245, 518n.251	2:9	70n.20	7:1	387, 387n.284
		1 Timothy		Justin	
3:13	517n.245	2:6	317n.185, 518n.251	*Dialogue*	
5:13-14	526			80:4	325n.198, 481
5:13-26	525n.275	2 Timothy			
5:16	525n.275	2:18	325n.198, 481	Eusebius	
5:25	525n.275			*History*	
		Titus		3.39.1	391n.301
Ephesians		2:14	317n.185, 518n.251		
1:7	521			Josephus	
1:10	392	Hebrews		*Antiquities*	
1:14	450n.112	2:4	70n.20	1:5	76n.34
2:3	292, 292n.141	2:9	517n.245	17.10.2	71n.24
2:3-6	292	2:9-10	244n.31		
2:13	521	3:8	292	*Jewish War*	
2:13-22	392	6:4	450n.112	2.12.3	91n.53
4:8-10	392	6:20	317n.185, 518n.251	2.16.2	91n.54
5:2	317n.185, 518n.251	9:22	520		
5:6	292, 292n.141	10:12	509n.223, 517n.245	*Life*	
5:6-14	292n.142, 392			23	145n.11
5:8	258n.63, 264, 392				
5:9	258n.63	1 Peter		Philo	
5:13	258n.63	1:2	521	*De Cherubim*	
5:25	317n.185, 518n.251	1:19	521	86–90	195
		2:9	256n.58		
Colossians		2:21	317n.185, 518n.251	*Legum Allegoriae*	
1:20	521	5:2	392	1.5-6	195
3:6	292n.141				
		Revelation			
1 Thessalonians		1:5	521		
1:10	292, 292n.141	1:11	393n.306	DEAD SEA SCROLLS	
2:14	145n.11	2:1–3:22	393n.306		
2:16	292, 292n.141	5:9	521	CD	243, 253, 547n.315
2:19	285	7:14	521	2:7	292
3:13	285			2:14-16	243, 260
4:14-17	284n.126			5:19	253
4:15	285			6:14	278
5:1-5	256n.58	OTHER LITERATURE		8:3	284
5:2	285n.127			8:15	292n.143
5:5	258n.63, 263	Ignatius of Antioch			
5:9	292, 292n.141	*Ephesians*		1Q28a	
5:23	285	7:1	387n.281	1:1	531n.283
				2:17-22	560
2 Thessalonians		*Magnesians*			
1:10	285n.127	7:1	387	1QH (Puech	
2:2	285n.127	8:2	387	numbering)	253n.48, 429

Index of Scripture and Other Ancient Literature

2:14	267n.83	14:32-33	476n.166, 477n.170	13:16	259, 263
4:21-24	530			14:1	292
4:22	530	14:37-38	476n.166, 477n.170	14:2-13	506
4:25	529			14:7	259n.66
4:26	458, 475n.165, 476n.166	15	448n.106, 457n.130	14:10	273
				14:16	263
4:32	476n.166	15:6	530	15:10	259n.66
5:1-25	458	15:7	458, 475n.165, 512n.232	15:14	273
5:19	529			16:10	259n.66, 263
5:25	458, 475n.165	15:26	291	17:8	267n.83
5:29	477n.170	16:32	476n.166		
6:12	291n.138	17:31	458	1QS	253, 259, 263, 267, 280, 289, 457n.131, 547n.315, 560
6:13	506n.219	17:35	291		
6:25	458	18:6-7	475n.165, 476n.166		
6:29	267n.83			1:1-4	278
7:27-30	476n.166	18:20	291	1:10	259, 263, 278
7:30	267n.83	18:29	291	2:14	267n.83
8:9	458	19:6-17	476n. 166	2:17	259n.67, 263n.74
8:11	458	19:9-10	291	2:19	289
8:15	458, 512n.232	19:10	512	2:24	267n.83
8:21	475	19:10-14	477n.170	2:25	264
9:15	475	20:11-12	458	2:26	267n.83
9:20-21	476n. 166	20:12	506	3-4	457n.130
9:32	512	20:21-24	506n.219	3:6-9	512n.232
9:35	267n.83, 291n.138	20:27-29	476n.166	3:13-4:26	106, 256n.58, 272n.100, 448n.457, 458
10:6	291	21:14-16	476n.166		
10:20	291n.138	21:27-31	476n.166		
10:27	267n.83	21:34-38	476n.166	3:14	263n.74
10:29	291n.138	22:36-38	476n.166	3:19	273
11:11	267n.83	23:23-24	476n.166	3:20	264
11:12	506n.219	25:3-16	476n.166	3:21	259, 265
11:19-23	476			3:22	264
11:20-37	476n.166	**1QH23 frag**		3:23	263n.74, 289
11:21	475, 512, 512n.232	2:10-12	467, 475	3:24	263n.74, 458
				3:25	259n.67, 264, 273
12:11-12	506n.219	**1QM**	253, 259	4:5	259n.67, 278
12:22-23	476n.166	1:1	263, 267n.83	4:5-6	267n.83
12:29	475	1:1-10	259	4:6	264
12:29-37	530	1:5	489	4:6-8	476
12:30	529	1:7	267n.83	4:7	264
12:31	458, 475	1:10	263	4:8-14	489
13:24-25	506n.219	1:13	263	4:11-12	292
14:6	512	12:8	289	4:16	489
14:8	512	12:19	289	4:18-23	512
14:12	291	13:6	259	4:21	264, 273
14:12-13	506n.219	13:11	273	4:22	264
14:25	506n.219	13:12	264	4:23	273
		13:12-13	273		

Index of Scripture and Other Ancient Literature

4:24	264	4Q286		RABBINIC WORKS	
5:7	560	f 7 col 2 3-4	458		
5:20-24	507			Mishnah	
5:21	507	4Q385		*m. Betzah*	
5:23	507	f 2	465n.147,	2:3	126n.113
5:24	507		477n.171	*m. Kelim*	
6:8-9	547	f 2, 5-8	467, 475	2:1	126n.113
6:13-23	507	f 5-8			
6:14	507			Talmud	
6:17	507	4Q403		*b. Erubin*	
6:18	507	1 i 28	241n.25	53a/b	126n.116
6:19	559				
6:22	548	4Q521	478,	*b. Hagigah*	
8:6	267n.83		478nn.173,177	24b	126n.116
8:19-20	512	f 2 ii 6	458, 477n.170	76d	413n.40
8:22	560	ff 5+7 ii 6	477n.170		
9:17	291			*b. Megillah*	
9:18	291	4QMMT		24b	126n.116
10:18	279	107	531n.283		
10:19-21	279			*b. Ta'anit*	
11:5-8	476	4QTest Qah		2a	195n.103
11:14-15	512	1 ii 3-8	477n.170		
				Tosefta	
4QEn^b		4QVis^{c}Amr		*t. Shabbat*	
1 iv 5	241, 241n.25	1 ii	477n.170	17:1	126n.113
				Mekilta Sabbata	
4Q186	448n.106,	11QMelch		2:25	195n.103
	457n.130	18		Genesis Rabbah	
				11:5	195n.103
4Q213	254n.53	11QPs^a		11:10	195n.103
		3.1.1	91n.53	11:12	195n.103
4Q215	254n.53	28:7-8	241n.25	78	412

www.ingramcontent.com/pod-product-compliance
Lightning Source LLC
Chambersburg PA
CBHW031537300426
44111CB00006BA/84